Vision Systems
Applications

Edited by
Goro Obinata and Ashish Dutta

Vision Systems - Applications

Edited by Goro Obinata and Ashish Dutta

Republished by InTech

Janeza Trdine 9, 51000 Rijeka, Croatia

Technical Editor Teodora Smiljanic

Cover Designer Dino Smrekar

Additional hard copies can be obtained from orders@intechopen.com

Vision Systems - Applications, Edited by Goro Obinata and Ashish Dutta
p. cm.
ISBN 978-3-902613-01-1

For EU product safety concerns:
IN TECH d.o.o., Prolaz Marije Krucifikse Kozulić 3, 51000 Rijeka, Croatia,
info@intechopen.com or visit our website at intechopen.com.

Preface

Computer Vision is the most important key in developing autonomous navigation systems for interaction with the environment. It also leads us to marvel at the functioning of our own vision system. In this book we have collected the latest applications of vision research from around the world. It contains both the conventional research areas like mobile robot navigation and map building, and more recent applications such as, micro vision, etc.
The fist seven chapters contain the newer applications of vision like micro vision, grasping using vision, behavior based perception, inspection of railways and humanitarian demining. The later chapters deal with applications of vision in mobile robot navigation, camera calibration, object detection in vision search, map building, etc.
We would like to thank all the authors for submitting the chapters and the anonymous reviewers for their excellent work.
Sincere thanks are also due to the editorial members of Advanced Robotic Systems publications for all the help during the various stages of review, correspondence with authors and publication.
We hope that you will enjoy reading this book and it will serve both as a reference and study material.

Editors

Goro Obinata
Centre for Cooperative Research in Advanced Science and Technology
Nagoya University, Japan

Ashish Dutta
Dept. of Mechanical Science and Engineering
Nagoya University, Japan

Contents

1

Micro Vision

Kohtaro Ohba and Kenichi Ohara
National Institute of Advanced Industrial Science and Technology (AIST)
Japan

1. Introduction

The observational and measurement system in the micro environments to manipulate objects in the micro world is becoming necessary in many fields, such as manufacturing; "Micro Factory (Fig.1)";one of the past Japanese national project, and medical usages; the micro surgery. Most of the past researches in the micro environments might be only focused on the micro manipulation but not on the micro observation and measurement, which might be very important to operate. Actually, the micro operation includes the scale factors; i.e. the van der Waals forces are larger than the Newton force in the micro environments. Furthermore the micro vision has the "optical scale factors" on this micro observation, i.e. the small depth of a focus on the microscope, which could not allow us to feel the micro environments, intuitively.
For example, if the focus is on some objects in the microscope, the actuator hands could not be observed in the same view at the same time with the microscope. On the other hand, if the focus is on the actuator hands, the object could not be observed. Figure 2 shows a simple 3D construction example constructing a micro scarecrow, 20um height, with 4 um six grass balls and one grass bar on the micro wafer. And Fig.3 show the two typical microscopic views putting the second glass ball onto the first glass ball. Left figure (a) in Fig.3 shows the first glass ball in focused, but the gripper is blurring at almost same position, because of the different depth. And right figure (b) shows the gripper in focused. Therefore, the operator has to change the focal distance with the microscope to observe while operating the micro-actuator, simultaneously.

Figure 1. Micro Factory

Figure 2. Micro Scarecrow

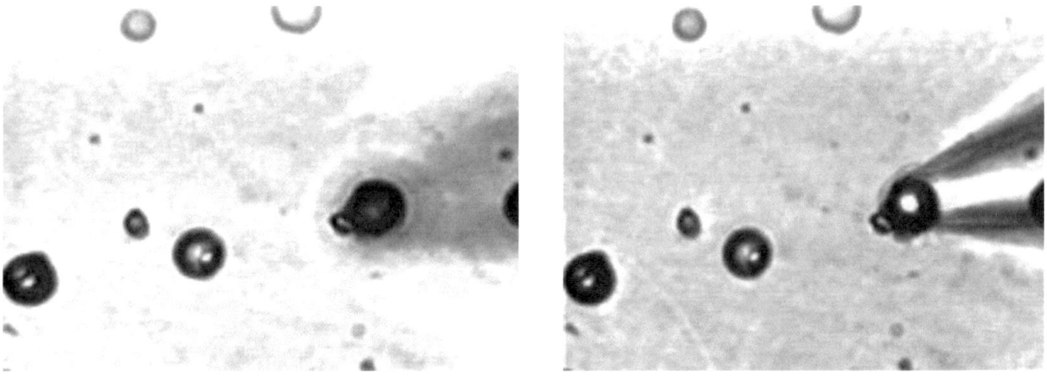

(a) (b)

Figure 3. Typical Microscopic Images with Micro Manipulation

Even though the big effort of the micro vision for the micro operation, there are few computer vision researches especially for the micro environments.

In the micro vision system, there could be categorized into two areas,

1. **The micro measurements techniques** to measure the micro object position for micro operation.
2. **The micro observation techniques** to show the 3D image only for human to know the interesting objects.

We will summarize these two areas into the following two sections.

2. Measurement Method for Micro Objects in Micro Environment

In the field of the computer vision, there are several 3D modelling criteria, so called "shape from X" problem. Most of these criteria are categorized as follows,

- the Shape from Triangular Surveying,
- the Shape from Coherence,
- the Shape from Time of Flight,
- the Shape from Diffraction,
- the Shape from Polarization.[1][2],
- And the shape from Focus/Defocus [3][4][5][6].

Each method has particular characteristics with algorithm, speed, range and resolution of measurements.

In the macro environments, the triangular surveying is mainly applied for the robotics, because of the simply to use. But it requires more than one set of two cameras or laser equipments to measure and soft/hard calibration, and big calculation cost in correlation with two images. Furthermore in the micro environments, because of the small depth of fields, the measurements range is quite limited in the cross in focus depth area of the two cameras.

Generally speaking, we have the "small depth of a focus" is one of the drawbacks for the micro operation with the microscope, as mentioned before. However, as the matter of fact, this small depth of a focus is one of the big benefits for the vision system to obtain the good resolution of the depth with the "shape from focus/defocus" criteria. In this section, the measurement method based on characteristics of the micro environment is mainly discussed. Secondly, the real-time micro VR camera system is reviewed with the two main factors.

2.1 Optics

The "depth from focus" criterion is based on the simple optical theory, which is focused on the depth of a focal range in the optical characteristic. Theoretically, the "depth of a focus" and the "depth of a photographic subject" are different as shown in Fig. 4. In this section, the optical criteria are briefly reviewed.

The optical fundamental equation:

$$\frac{1}{X}+\frac{1}{x}=\frac{1}{f}, \tag{1}$$

is well known as the Gaussian lens law. In this equation, X, x and f depict the object distance, the image distance and the focal distance of the lens, respectively.

Then, in the "depth of a focus", Δx is defined as the range of the distance of focal plane, which holds the image in focus on the focal plane, as shown in Fig. 4 (a).

$$\text{Infinity: } \Delta x = 2\delta\frac{f}{D} \tag{2}$$

$$\text{Finite: } \Delta x = 2\delta\frac{f}{D'} \tag{3}$$

where D and D' are the diameter of lens and the iris, respectively. The focus obviously depends on the radius of the circle of confusion delta, which caused by the resolution of the sensor device of camera.

The "depth of a photographic subject"; ΔX is defined as the range of the distance between object and lens as shown in Fig. 4 (b), which holds the sharpness on the focal plane;

$$\Delta X = \frac{2\delta XfD(X-f)}{f^2D^2 - \delta^2(X-f)^2} \tag{4}$$

In this equation, the depth of a photographic subject obviously depends on the distance of principle focus f and the distance between object and lens X.
Equation (2) or (3) decides the resolution of object distance with the depth of focus criteria. In the calibration process between the object distance and the image plane distance, the equation (4) is utilized.

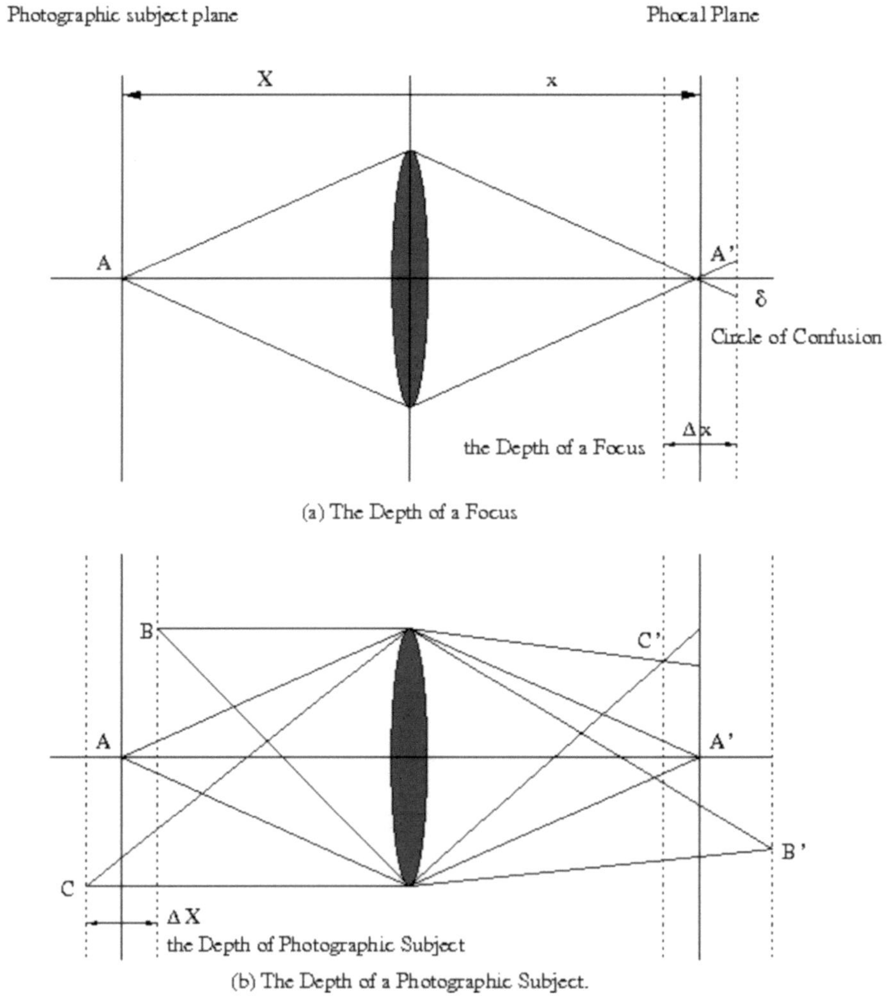

Figure 4. Depth of a focus and Depth of Photographic Subject

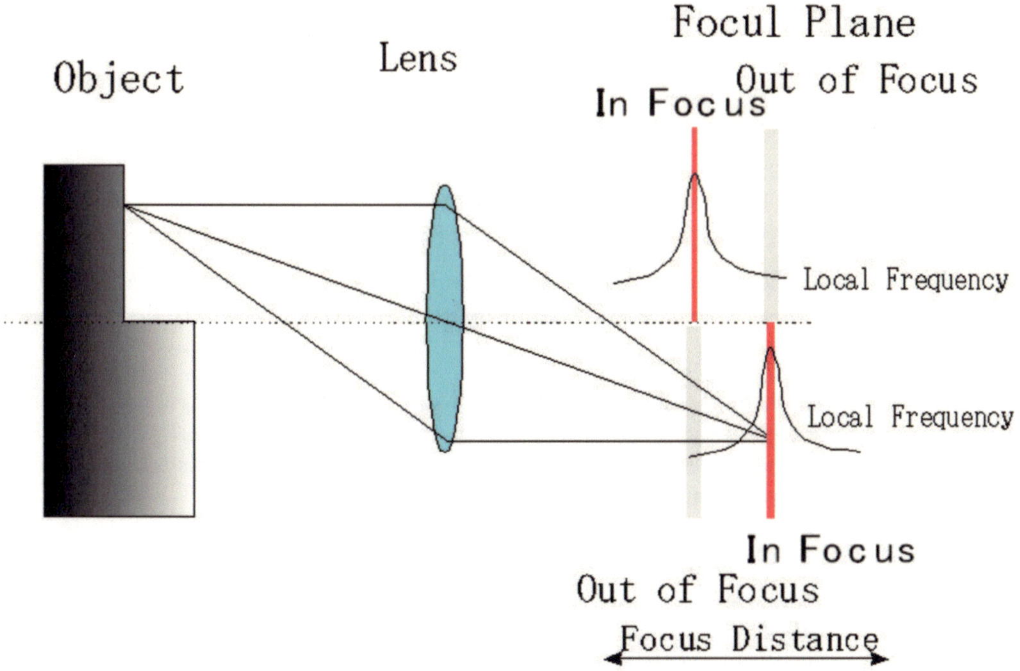

Figure 5. Concept Image of how to obtain the all-in-focus image

2.2 Depth from Focus Criteria

Figure.5 shows the concept of the "depth from focus" criteria based on the optics above. Each image points hold the optical equations (1). If several numbers of images are captured with the different image distances, then optimal in-focus point at each image points could be defined with the optical criteria. Then, the 3D object construction could be obtained with equation (1) of "image distance"; x or "focal distance"; f value at each pixel. Also, synthesized in-focus image could be obtained with mixing the in-focus image areas or points, which we call "all-in-focus image".

Actually, this criteria is quite simple but useful especially in the microscopic environments. However, the bad resolution with this criterion on the long distance, more than 2m, is well known because of the large "depth of a photographic subject" with the ordinal optical configuration on large objective distance.

Further more, the depth from defocus criteria is well known to estimate the 3D construction with several blurring images and optical model. It is not necessary to move the focal distance in the process of 3D reconstruction, but could not achieve the all-in-focus image, which might be important for the 3D virtual environments. In this section, "Depth from Focus Theory" is focused.

2.3 Image Quality Measurement

In the previous section, the optimal focal distance with particular objects could be obtained with the optical criteria. In this section, the criterion to decide the optimal focal distance with the image processing technique is reviewed.

To decide the optimal focal distance with images, the Image Quality Measure (IQM), which could detect the in-focus area in the image, is defined with the follow equation,

$$IQM = \frac{1}{|D|} \sum_{x=x_i}^{x_f} \sum_{y=y_i}^{y_f} \left(\sum_{p=-L_c}^{L_c} \sum_{q=-L_r}^{L_r} \left| I(x,y) - I(x+p, y+q) \right| \right) \quad (5)$$

where $(-L_c,-L_r)-(L_c,L_r)$ and $(x_i,y_i)-(x_f,y_f)$ are the area for the evaluation of frequency and the smoothing, respectively [7].And D is the total pixel number to make standard the image quality measure value with the number of pixels in the area $(-L_c,-L_r)-(L_c,L_r)$ and $(x_i,y_i)-(x_f,y_f)$.

With some variation of the focus values, once a peak of the IQM value at particular position of image pixel is detected, the optimal in-focus image point on each pixel points could be easily defined. Then the corresponding local intensity value and the focus value are finally the depth map and the all-in-focus image, respectively.

2.3 Real-time micro VR camera system

To realize the real-time micro VR camera system with the depth from focus criteria above, there are two big issues to be solved,

1. how to capture and process the high frame rate image sequences (vision part),
2. how to change the focal distance with high frequency and high accuracy(optical part).

Unfortunately, most of the vision system seems to be based on the video frame rate 30frame/sec. This video frame rate is good enough for human vision, but not good enough as a sensor system.

To realize a real-time micro VR camera with the depth from focus criteria mentioned before, a high-speed image capture and processing system is required. For example, if eight images are applied to obtain the depth map and the all-in-focus image with 30frame/sec, a 240 frame/sec image sequence is necessary to capture and process.

Furthermore, to change the focal distance with the microscope, motor control system could be used. But the range of frequency of the motor system is not enough frequency for the real-time micro VR camera system.

Next, section, we will show some of the proto type of the real-time micro VR camera systems, Finally product specification of Micro VR Camera System is shown.

2.3.1 First Prototype

At first, we developed the micro VR camera system shown in Fig.6 with a dynamic focusing lens[8] as shown in Fig. 7 and a smart sensor, an IVP C-MOS vision chip (MAPP2200) that has a resolution of 256*256pixel, a column parallel ADC architecture, and DSP processing.

A sample object in Fig. 8 and its sample images at four particular focal distances are shown in Fig. 9. The objects for demonstration were constructed in a four-step pyramidal shape: first stage, ϕ 10mm height 10mm; second, ϕ 7mm-10mm; third, ϕ 4mm-10mm; and top, ϕ 3mm-5mm. In real-usage cases, such as less than 1 mm size, the IQM value could be obtained with the original texture on the object without any artificial texture.

Figure 6. Micro VR Camera System

Figure 7. Dynamic Focusing Lens

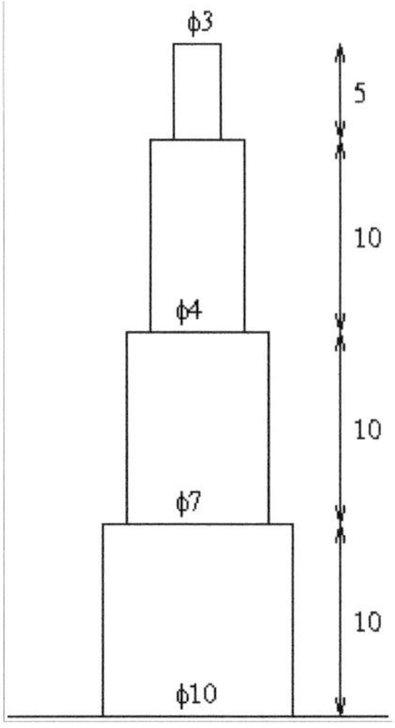

Figure 8. Sample Object for Evaluation of Micro VR Camera System

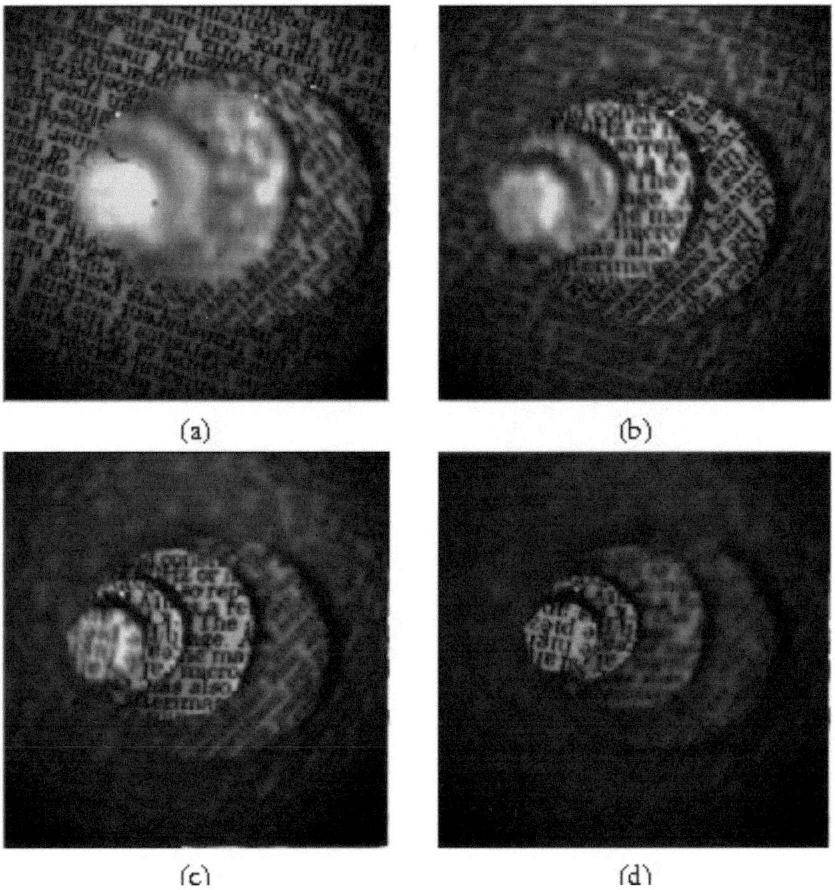

Figure 9. Sample of the Single Focus Image

The spatial resolution depends on the optical setting. For this demonstration, the view area is almost 16mm square with 256 pixels, and the spatial resolutions are 62.5um. The depth resolution is 1.67mm (21 frames with 35mm depth range, each 3V input voltage from -30V to +30V to charge the PZT), which directly depends on the number of input frames in the range of variable focusing. The "all-in-focus image" and the micro VR environments from one image sequence are shown in Fig. 10 and 11, respectively. The "all-in-focus image" gives a clear image to observe the whole object. However, the resolution of depth without any interpolation in Fig.11 does not seem enough. A simple way to increase the resolution of depth is to capture more images with other focal distances, which could also require a higher calculation cost.

(a) Processing Part

The processing time with an IVP chip is almost 2sec. for one final VR output. This is caused because the ADC/processing performance is not good enough for the gray level intensity on the vision chip MAPP2200. Actually, MAPP2200 has a good performance for binary images of more than 2000frame/sec.

(b) Optical Part

Changing the focus with usual optical configuration is quite difficult to actuate because of its dynamics. We had developed a compact and quick-response dynamic focusing lens, which is including the PZT bimorph actuator and the glass diaphragm shown in Fig. 7. This lens is capable to be a convex lens or concave lens with the voltage to drive the PZT bimorph, and was evaluated the robustness with more than 150Hz high frequency. See details in [10]. We applied this lens with the combination of the micro zoom lens.

Figure 10. Sample of All-in-Focus image

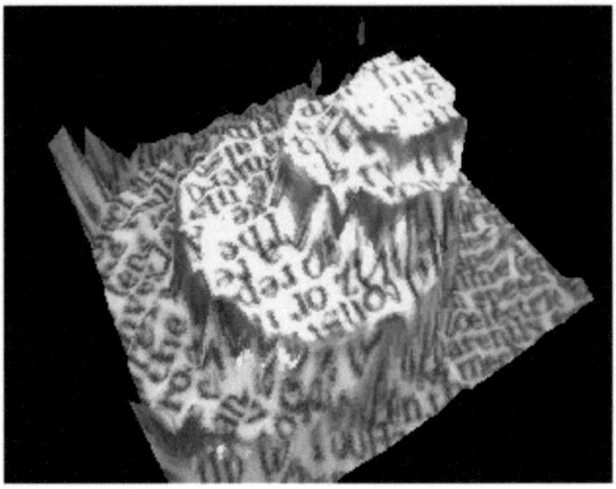

Figure 11. Sample of the Depth Image for Sample Object with Texture Based on All-in-Focus Image

2.3.2 Second Prototype

This paragraph shows the second prototype of the micro VR camera systems.

(a) Processing Part

Recently, the large-scale FPGA (Field Programmable Gate Array) has dramatically improved its performance and is being widely used because of its programmable capability. Then, in the second system shown in Fig.12, one FPGA (APEX EP20K600E, ALTERA) and SDRAM in the image-processing test board (iLS-BEV800, INNOTECH Co.) are used to calculate the IQM in equation (5) at each pixel all over image 512*480 pixel, 8bits with 240Hz, which has the TMDS (Transition Minimized Display Signaling) architecture interface to connect the sensor part and processing part as shown in Fig.13. Then, the image data 512*480 is captured with two parallel interfaces, and high-speed transmission 60Mbyte/sec (512*480*240Hz) from HSV to the dual-port SDRAM is realized. As a result, the performance of the FPGA is good enough to calculate the IQM value with 240Hz, and the total execution performance is less than 20% of the performance of FPGA.

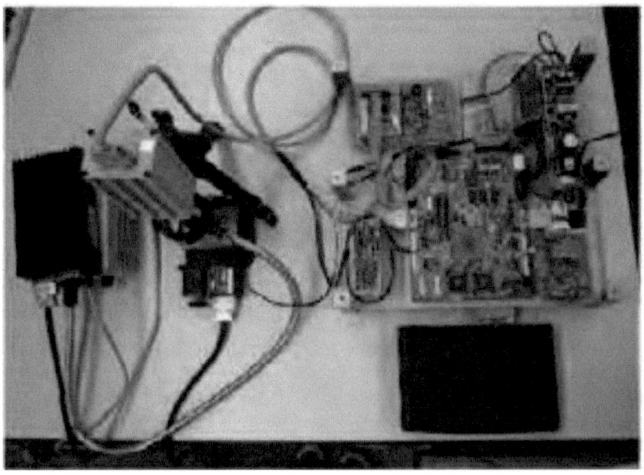

Figure 12. Sencond Prototype Systems

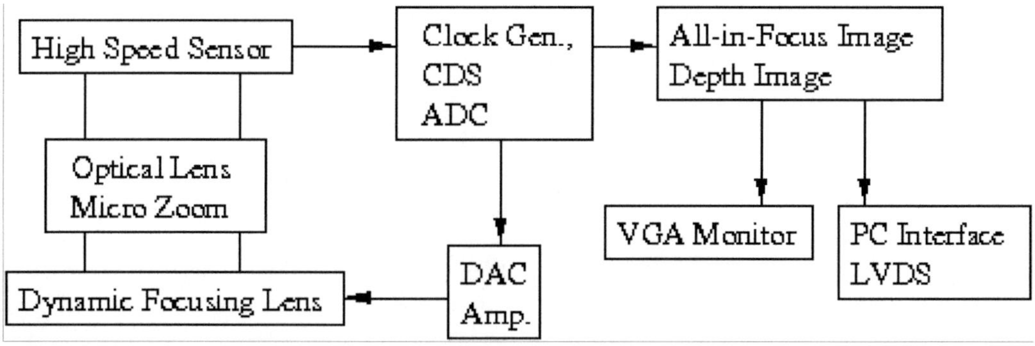

Figure 13. System Configuration

(b) Optical Part

A micro-zoom lens (Asahi Co. MZ-30, f=27.2-58.5mm, F7.5) with a dynamic focusing lens, the same as that used in our earlier system, is attached on the HSV. The dynamic focusing lens is controlled by FPGA through DA converter and Amplitude as mentioned in the first prototype. The relation between the input voltage to PZT and the objective distance is evaluated linearly in the range from 147mm to 180mm, corresponding to the input voltage from -30V to +30V in previous section. The resolution of the objective distance appears to increase with the objective distance. We apply 30Hz one-way ramp input to control the dynamic focusing lens, as shown in Fig.14, which may cause a hysteresis problem with round-trip input. However, a noisy image is observed in the first step because of the overshoot of the lens. To solve this problem, we planned to use seven images without the first image.

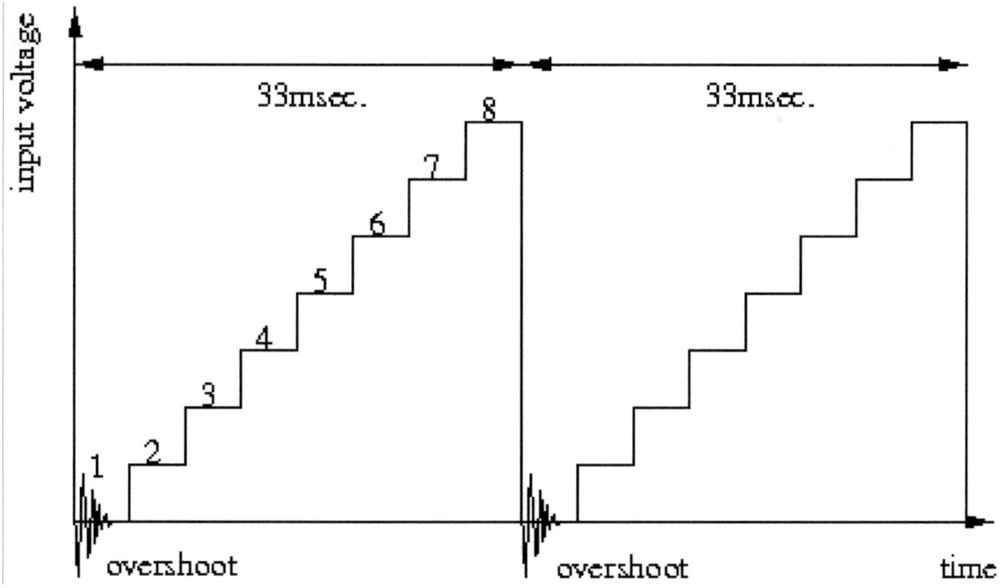

Figure 14. Ramp Input.

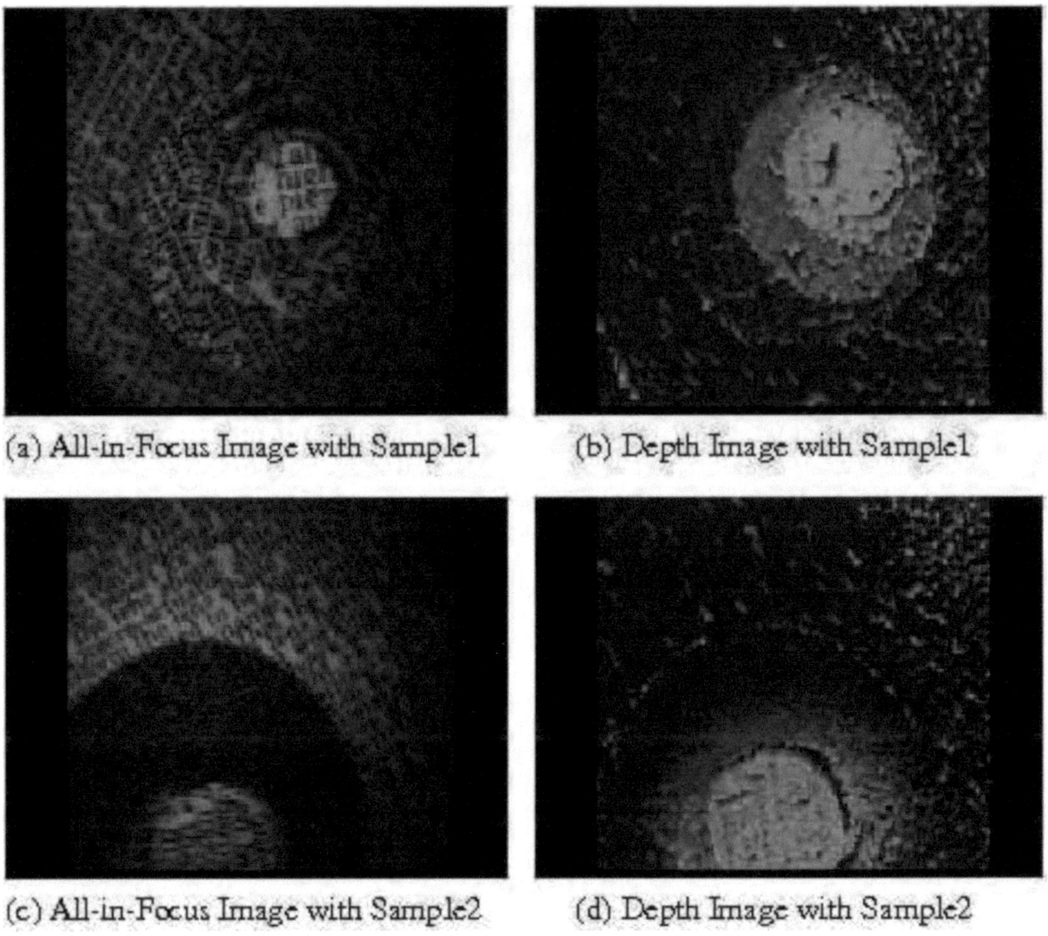

Figure 15. Sample Image of Second Prototype System

The spatial resolution in this system is 31.25mu, 16mm/512pixel. The depth resolution is 5.0mm (7 frames with 35mm depth), which can be improved with the input frame number. Up to now, the all-in-focus image and the depth image are stored in each memory space and could be separately observed with a VGA monitor through the analog RGB output. The VR display might be realized in a PC after the all-in-focus and depth images are transmitted into the PC directly.

2.3.3 Microscopic System

For real micro-applications, a microscopic system is developed with the processing part mentioned before, as shown in Fig.16. Instead of using a dynamic focusing lens, the PIFOC microscope objective nano-positioners and scanners P-721.20, PI-Polytec Co. are controlled by a high-speed nano-automation controller E-612.C0, PI-Polytec Co. and attached to a microscope, BX60, Olympus Co., to reduce the zoom factor with the dynamic focusing lens. The focus length is controlled to achieve a maximum of 0-100 um as the actuator input voltage 0-10V 30Hz ramp input from the FPGA. The real position could be observed with the sensor output from the controller. Actually, this system has no scaling factor on the images with different depth, because the image distance is changed with the scanner, besides the focal distance is changed in our earlier system with the variable focusing lens. You can observe two glass fabrics φ 4 um, each located in micro-3D environments with

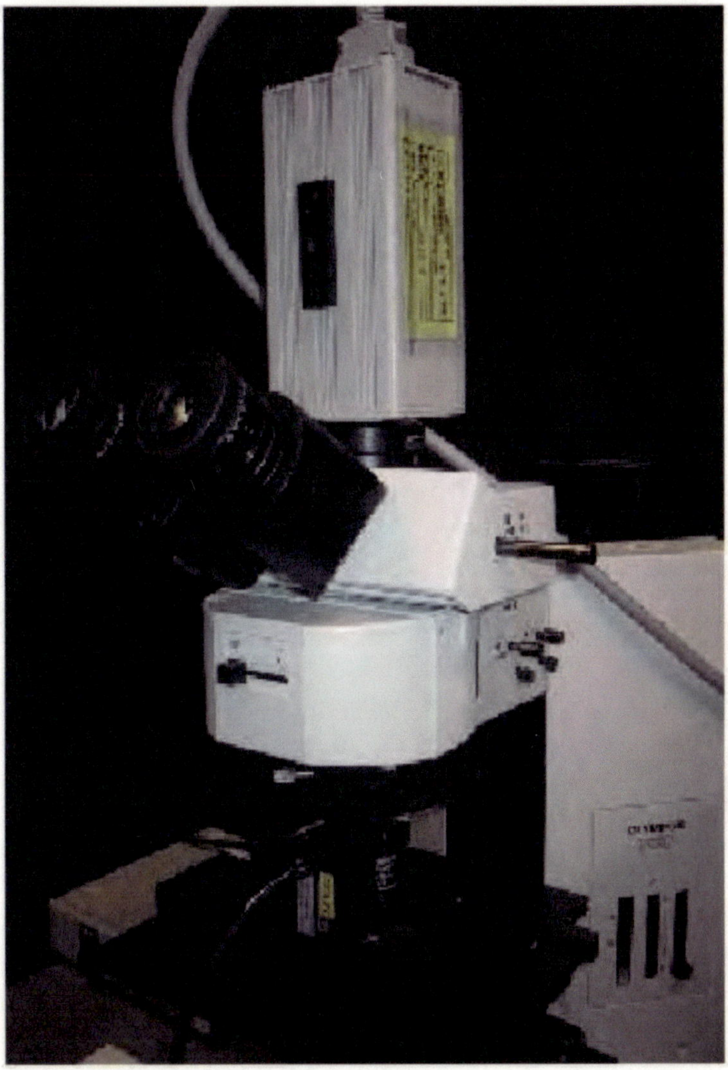

Figure 16. Micro Scopic System for Micro Application

optical magnitude 50X in the microscope. One fabric is located at a near distance, and the other is at a far distance. Figure 17 shows the usual focus images scanning the focus length from 0 um to 90 um. The near fabric is in focus in Figure 17(e), and the far fabric is in focus in Figure 17(h). The spatial resolution in this system is 0.195 um 100 um 512pixel. The maximum depth resolution is 0.781 um, 100 um128 bits. Figure 18 shows the all-in-focus image in the microscope. Compared with Fig.17, both fabrics can be seen in-focus in one view.

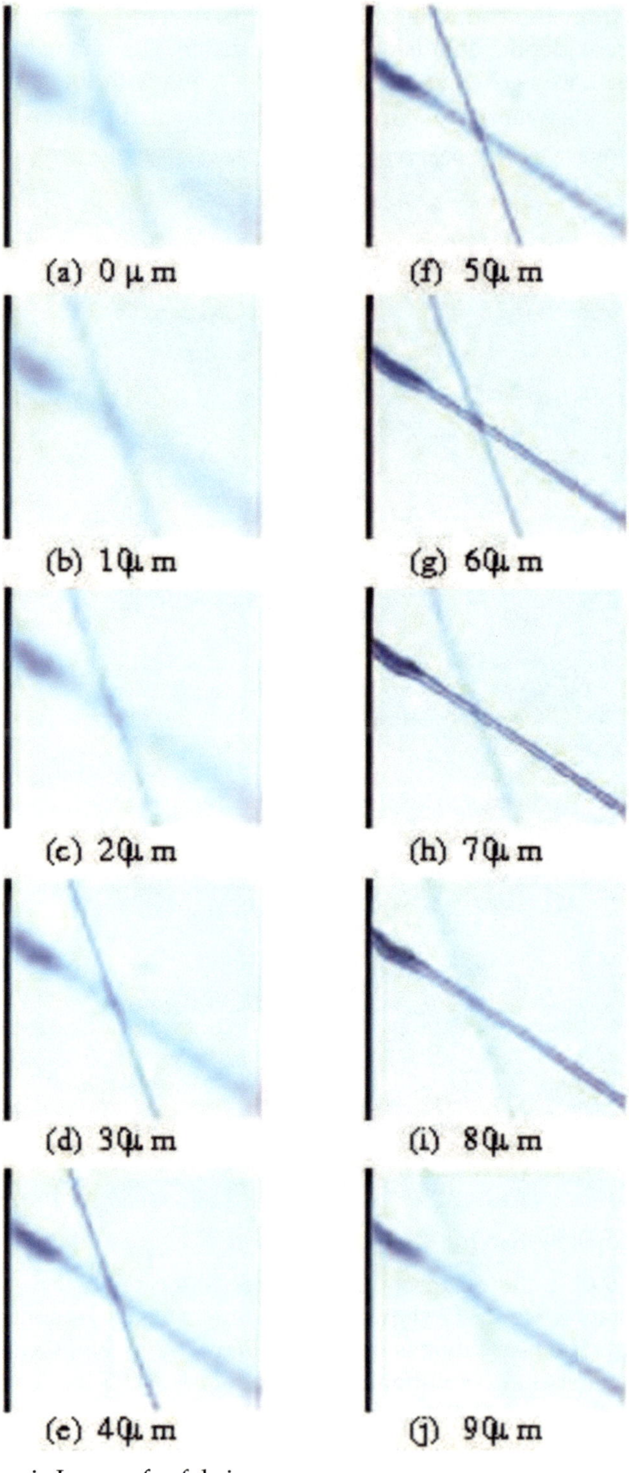

Figure 17. Microscopic Images for fabrics

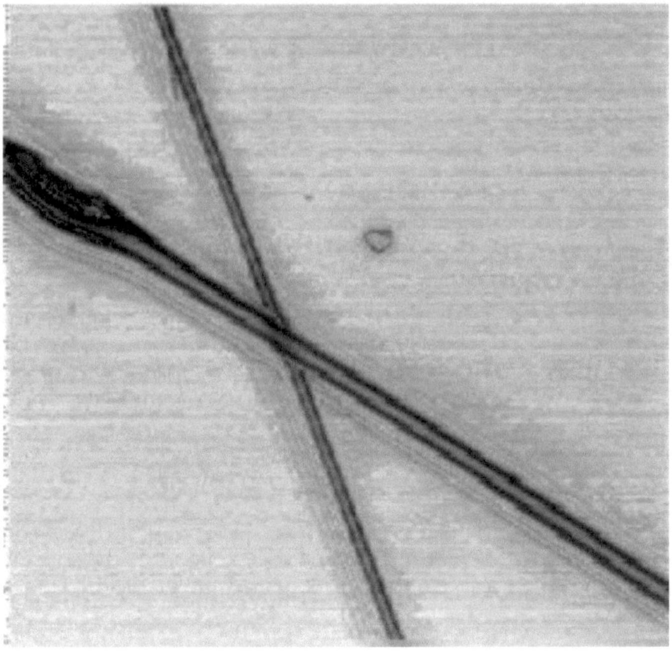

Figure 18. All-in-Focus Image with ghost

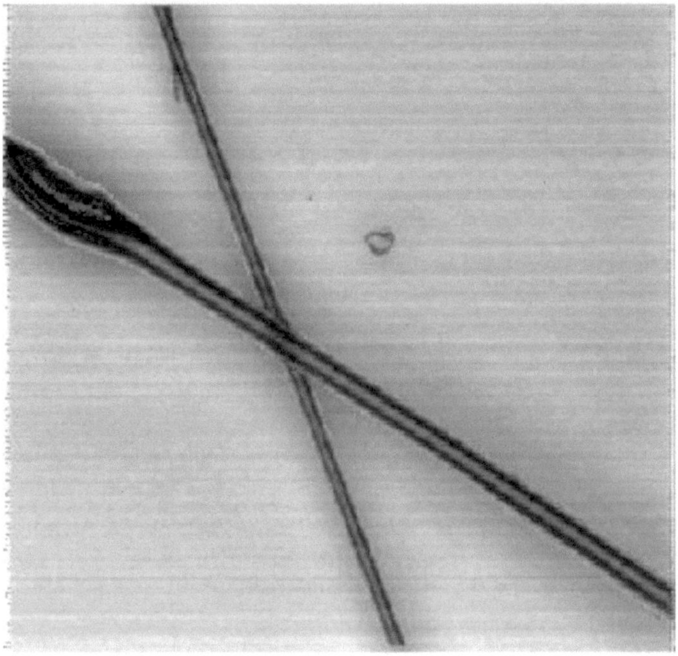

Figure 19. All-in-Focus Image without ghost

(a) without Ghost Filter (b) with Ghost Filter

Figure 20. A Comparison with Ghost-Filtering

A detail analysis indicated that several blurring edges could be observed just around the objects in Fig.18. This ghost is caused by several out-of-focus images. In the microscope, the out-of-focus image makes a large blurring region around the real object's location, as can be seen in Fig.18. This blurring region could cause miss-recognition of the all-in-focus area around the objects. To solve the ghost problem, the reliability of the IQM value should be evaluated to detect the real in-focus area. Then, the minimum IQM value; IQM_{min} is pre-defined, which could hold the in-focus clearly in the particular image sequences.

$$\text{In-focus-area: } IQM(x,y,f) \geq IQM_{\min} \tag{6}$$

$$\text{background: otherwize} \tag{7}$$

where IQM(x,y,f) is the image quality value at image location; (x,y) with the focus length; f. Figures 19 and 20 show the result obtained with this ghost-filtering technique.

2.3.4 Product System

Now, Micro VR Camera System is productization by Photron co.ltd in Japan [9], which is shown in Fig. 21. This system is more improved about resolution, which is 512 * 512 pixels per one the depth image and all-in-focus image. Moreover, this system can measure object depth in a step of about 3um, when the user use piezo actuator to be able to move 100 um. Figure 22 shows sample results of the all-in-focus and depth image with the latest system. Actually, this output result is real-time movie on this system. Even though the operator put the gripper in sight, the in-focus image could allow us to observe the object and the gripper simultaneously, although they are located at different depths.

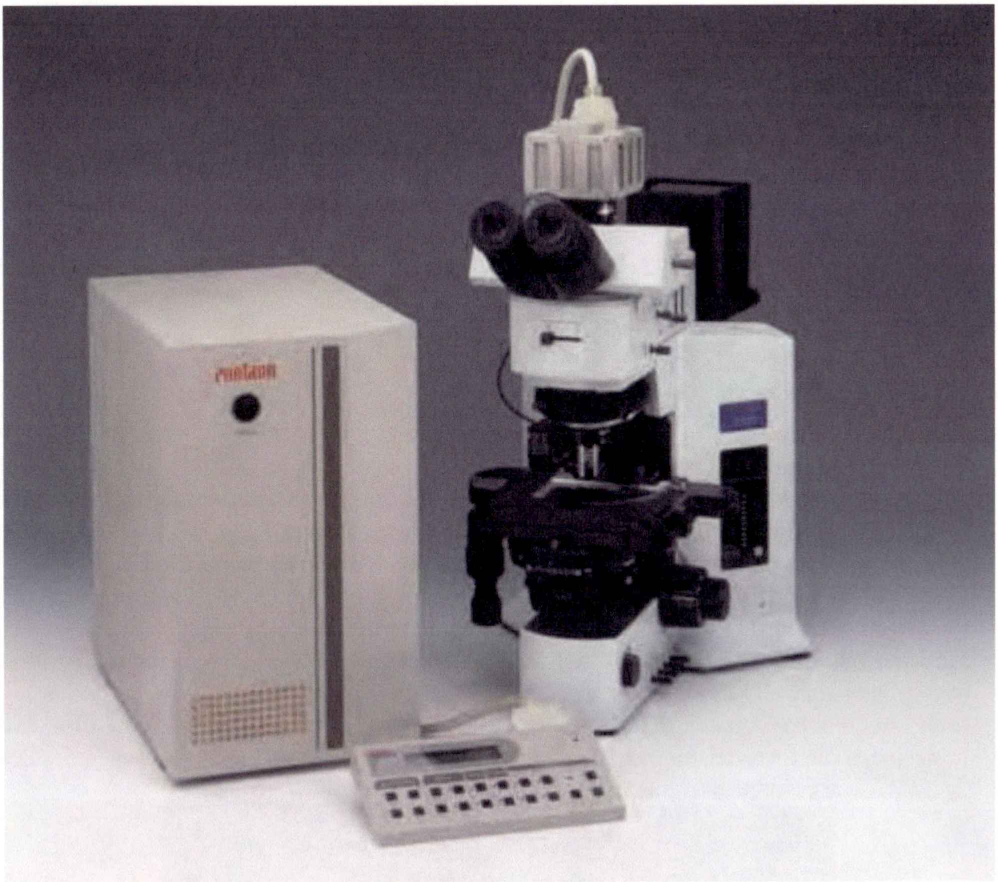

Figure 21. Product system for the Micro VR Camera

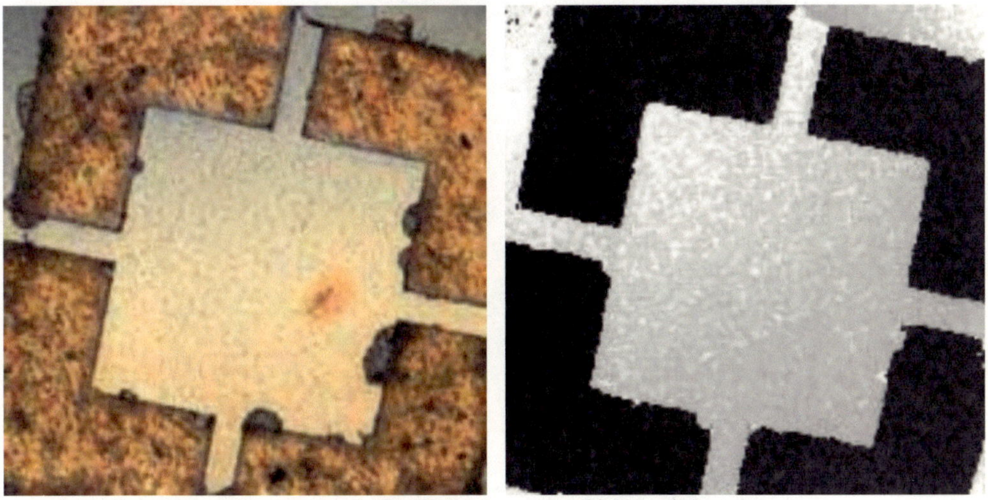

(a) All-in-Focus Image for MEMS device (b) Depth Image

Figure 22. Sample View of MEMS device with the product system

3. Micro Observation

In the previous section, micro measurement is describes. The micro observation system is introduced in this section.
Generally speaking, because the small depth of focus factor is quite strong, the microscopic view is quite different from the macroscopic images. Actually, to know the micro phenomena and micro object shape, operator should change the focal distance of the microscope very often. Then operator summarizes each image information in his brain.
If this summarize sequence could be obtained automatically, the operator could easily know the micro object phenomena and shape, intuitively.
This section mainly focuses on the algorithm to obtain the all-in-focus image in the micro VR Camera System, and the 3D voxel image, which has (R,G,B,alpha) parameter for each voxel, based on Micro VR Camera System.

3.1 All-in-Focus Image

In the previous section, overview about how to obtain depth image and all-in-focus image is described. In this subsection, detail algorithm is shown as follows;

1. Acquire a sequence of images while changing a focus distance using the PZT actuator.
2. Calculate the Image Quality Measurement (IQM) value (eq.(5)) at each pixel on all of the acquired images, which might be the index for in-focus or out-focus.
3. Find the maximum point on the IQM value considering the different focus distance at each pixel location; (x,y).
4. Integrate the in-focused pixel values at maximum IQM points into an all-in-focus image, and the focus distance information into the depth map.

Figure 23. Example of All-in-Focus Image about wire bounding

This system mainly applied to use the industrial usage as shown in Fig. 23. However, this algorithm has one big drawback in the case of the transparent object, such as crystal and cell in the biomedical usage, because there might be several possibilities of in-focused points on the transparent object as shown in Fig. 24. In other words, if we apply to use this system for the biomedical use, the depth information might be quite noisy; sometime the maximum IQM value is on the top surface of the object, but in other case, in-focused points is on the other back surface.

Figure 24. Example of the transparent object for micro application

3.2 Volume Rendering Method based on Image Quality Measurement

The micro VR camera system, mentioned before, could be mainly applied to use for industrial objects as shown in Fig. 23, not for the biomedical objects, such as transparent objects, which is targets.

Actually, in the algorithm of the all-in-focus image described in the previous section, the IQM value is calculated all over the image at each focus distance, but only one point of maximum IQM value at each pixel is selected for the all-in-focus image as shown in Fig. 5. In other words, most of the image information is trushed away to define the optimal focal distance.

By the way, in the field of computer graphics, the volume rendering technique is widely used. In the case of color objects, each 3D point; i.e. the volume cell (voxel) image, holds intensity and transparent data set: V[RGB|P], where R, G, and B depict color intensity values and P is the transparency data at each voxel (x,y,z), to visualize the transparent objects.

As the matter of fact in our previous researh, the image intensity data set could be already obtained while moving the focus distance in the micro VR camera system.
Then, a new volume rendering based method shown in Fig. 25, which reflects the IQM value as transparency parameter P with the Look Up Table (LUT) and visualizes 3D transparent object, is proposed in this section, because of the fact that the IQM value might be the index of in-focused area.
To realize the proposed method, the image intensity data and the IQM value at each focus distance with the previous micro VR camera system are stored in V[RGB|P] at each voxel (x,y,z) in the volume rendering system: VOLUME-PRO 500, and the volume rendering visualization could be obtained using the VGL library.
To show the validity of this proposed method, a φ4μm glass ball including one bubble inside is applied to use. Fig. 26 shows the microscopic view of the glass ball at several focus distances, which is acquired with the AIF system while moving the focus distance.
Then, the center view in Fig. 27 display a visualization results with the proposed method, and left side shows the slice view at any particular point. The shape of glass ball could be intuitively obtained in this figure, furthermore a bubble could be observed, even though any de-convolution technique is not utilized. The volume rendering tools "VGStudio MAX 1.1" is used in Fig. 27. In this viewer, we could chage the view angel, and change slice point for the slice view, as you want.

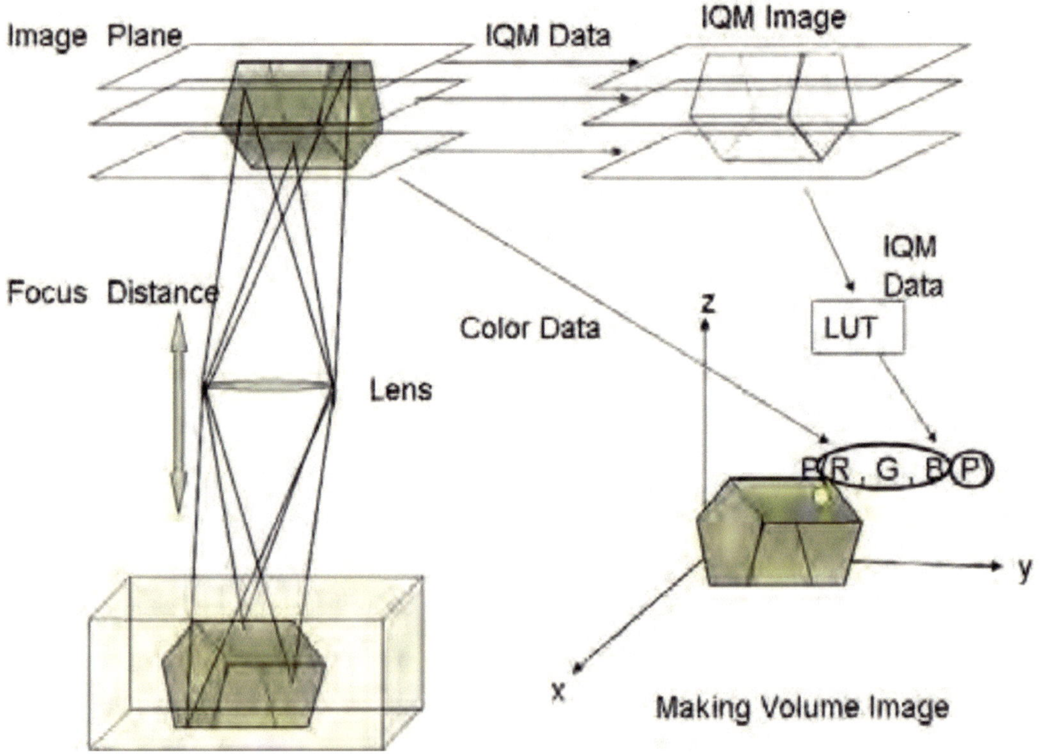

Figure 25. Volume Rendering Method based on Image Quality Measurement

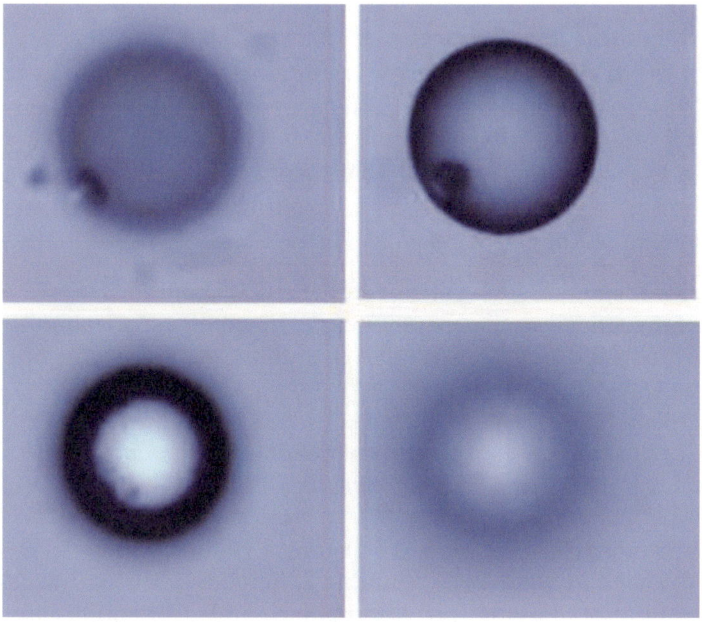

Figure 26. Several Focus Images of φ4um Grass Ball

Each of these two methods for visualization have each goodness and drawback. The all-in-focus image could show the intuitive object image, but most of the blurring images are trushed away. The volume rendaring technique could summarize the all images at each focal distance, but requires the volume rendaring viewers.

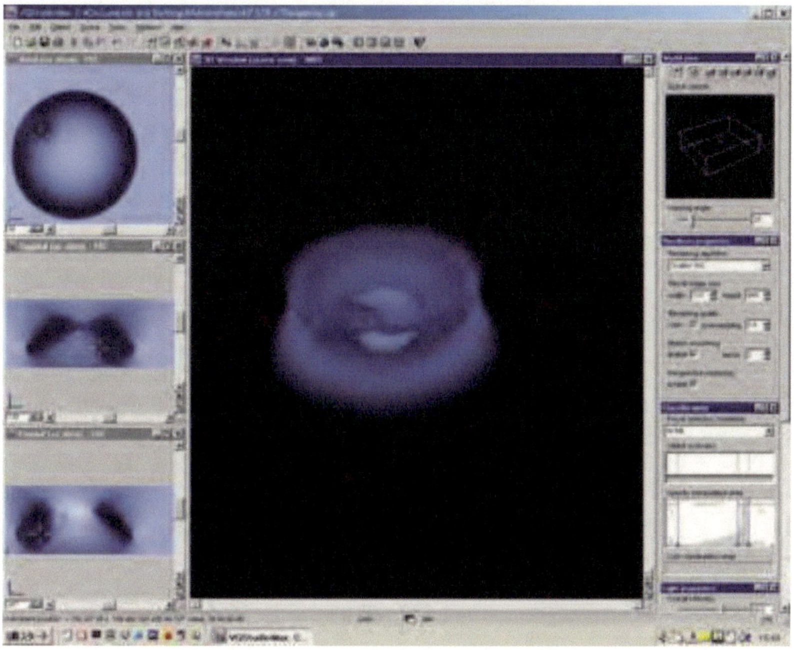

Figure 27. Voxel Image Based on Several Image of Grass Ball

4. Conclusion

In the field of the micro vision, there are few researches compared with macro environment. However, applying to the study result for macro computer vision technique, you can measure and observe the micro environment. Moreover, based on the effects of micro environment, it is possible to discovery the new theories and new techniques.

5. References

Daisuke Miyazaki, Megumi Saito, Yoichi Sato, and Katsushi Ikeuchi. (2002). Determining surface orientations of transparent objects based on polarization degrees in visible and infrared wavelengths. *Journal of Optical Society of America A (JOSA A)*. Vol. 19, No. 4, pp.687-694.

Megumi Saito, Yoichi Sato, Katsushi Ikeuchi, Hiroshi Kashiwagi. (1999). Measurement of surface orientations of transparent objects using polarization in highlight. *Proceedings of IEEE Conference on Computer Vision and Pattern Recognition (CVPR'99)*. pp. 381-386.

Kazuya Kodama, Kiyoharru Aizawa, and Mitsutoshi Hatori. (1999). Acquisition of an All-Focused Image by the Use of Multiple Differently Focused Images. The Trans. of the Institute of Electronics, Information and Communication Engineering Engineers. D-II, Vol.J80-D-II, No.9, pp.2298-2307.

Masahiro Watanabe and Shree K. Nayer. (1996). Minimal Operator Set for Passive Depth from Defocus. *CVPR'96*, pp.431-438.

Shree K. Nayer, Masahiro Watanabe, and Minoru Noguchi. (1995). Real-Time Focus Range Sensor. *ICCV'95*, pp.995-1001.

Shree K. Nayer, and Yasuo Nakagawa. (1994). Shape from Focus. *IEEE Trans. on PAMI.* Vol.16, No.8, pp.824-831.

Sridhar R. Kundur and Daniel Raviv. (1996). Novel Active-Vision-Based Visual-Threat-Cue for Autonomus Navigation Tasks. *Proc. CVPR'96*. pp.606-612.

Takashi Kaneko, Takahiro Ohmi, Nobuyuki Ohya, Nobuaki Kawahara, and Tadashi Hattori. (1997). A New, Compact and Quick-Response Dynamic Focusing Lens. *Transducers'97*.

Photron co.ltd. http://www.photron.com/

2

Active Vision based Regrasp Planning for Capture of a Deforming Object using Genetic Algorithms

Ashish Dutta, Goro Obinata and Shota Terachi
Nagoya University
Japan

1. Introduction

The ability to efficiently grasp an object is the basic need of any robotic system. This research aims to develop an active vision based regrasp planning algorithm for grasping a deforming 2D prismatic object using genetic algorithms (GA). The possible applications of the proposed method are in areas of grasping biological tissues or organs, partially occluded objects and objects whose boundaries change slowly. Most previous studies on robotic grasping mainly deal with formulating the necessary conditions for testing grasp points for static objects (Blake (1995), Chinellato et al. (2003), Galta et al. (2004), Mirtich et al. (1994)). Nguyen (1989) has suggested a strategy for constructing an optimal grasp using finger stiffness grasp potentials. A detailed review of multifinger grasping of rigid objects is presented in Bichi and Kumar (2000). There are few studies on grasping of deformable objects, such as Hirai et al. (2001) in which they present a control strategy for grasping and manipulation of a deformable object using a vision system. In this case the object deforms on application of fingertip forces, the deformation is recorded by a vision systems and based on the amount of deformation the object motion is controlled. Studies relating to searching and tracking of grasping configurations for deforming object are rare. Deforming objects are those that deform by themselves without application of external forces. Mishra et al. (2006) have proposed a method of finding the optimal grasp points for a slowly deforming object using a population based stochastic search strategy. Using this method it is possible to find the optimal grasp points satisfying force closure for 2D prismatic deforming objects. This method minimizes the distance between the intersection of fingertip normals and the object centre of gravity, and maximizes the area formed by the finger tip contact points. However their method fails in cases when the fingertip normals do not intersect at a point (as in case of a square object).

The problem of grasping deforming objects is a very challenging problem as the object shape changes with deformation. Hence the optimal grasp points have to be continuously found for each new shape. This process of recalculating the fingertip grasp points due to object shape change, slide or roll is called regrasping. The best method of determining the change in shape of an object is by using a vision system. A vision system not only captures the new shape but can also be used to track a moving object. The main objectives of this research are to use a vision system to capture the shape of a deforming object, divide the object boundary into a number of discrete points (pixels) and then find the optimal grasp points satisfying form closure. As the object changes shape the new shape is continuously updated by the vision system and the optimal grasp points are found. Once the solution for the first frame is obtained this solution is used as the initial guess in subsequent cases for finding the optimal grasp points. This enables faster solutions for later frames recording the deformation of the object. It is assumed that the object deforms slowly, the contact between the fingertip and the object is frictionless and the fingers do not cause deformation of the object. Hence four fingers are required to grasp a prismatic object in 2D. Simulations were carried out on 200 synthetic shapes that deformed slowly and the optimal grasp points found. An experiment was conducted in which a deforming object was simulated by a piece of black cloth that was held from below and deformed. The shape change of the cloth was captured by a camera and for each shape the optimum gasp points were obtained. Experimental results prove that the proposed method can be used in real time to find the optimal grasp points for a deforming object. In section 2 the algorithm used for determining the optimal grasp points is explained. The procedure for obtaining the regrasp solutions is discussed in section 3. Simulation results are explained in section 4, while the experimental setup is given in section 5. The experimental results are shown in section 6 and conclusions are drawn in section 7.

2. Determining optimal grasp points using GA

This section describes the concept of form closure using accessibility angle and the algorithm used to determine the optimal form closure grasp points. Form closure is a purely geometric constraint under which an object cannot escape in any direction after it is grasped by a number of frictionless fingertips. The mathematical conditions for obtaining form closure of an object by a multifinger hand are as given below (Yoshikawa, 1996):

$$T = \begin{bmatrix} a_1 \ldots\ldots\ldots a_n \\ p_1 \times a_1 \ldots p_n \times a_n \end{bmatrix} \alpha = D^T \alpha \tag{1}$$

Where T is the external forces and moment vector (total of six) acting at the centre of the object, a_i is the unit normal directed into the object at the fingertip contact points, p_i is the position vector of the fingertip contact points on the object, and $\alpha = [\alpha_1 \ldots\ldots \alpha_n]$ are the fingertip forces (n=total number of fingers). A necessary and sufficient condition for form closure are (i) rank D=6 and (ii) equation (1) has a solution such that $\alpha > 0$ (all forces are positive). Hence to obtain form closure in 3D we need seven contact points and in 2D we need four contact points. In this research we have proposed a geometrical method for finding the form closure grasps based on the concept of accessibility angle. The freedom angle (ϕ) of a two dimensional objects is defined as the angular region along which it can be translated away from the contact. The concept of freedom angle is as shown in Figure 1(a). It shows an object grasped with three contact points, for each individual contact point we define the direction (range) along which the object can move away from the contact points. The three freedom angles are as marked in the figure. Figure 1(b) show that after combining all the freedom angles there is still an angle left (escape angle) from where the object can escape. Hence it can be derived that the object is not in form closure. Figure 2(a) show the same object with four contact points and the corresponding freedom angles. In figure 2(b) it can be seen that all the total 360° are covered and hence the object is in form closure. If 'x' represents the position vector at a point on the object surface then the freedom angle " ϕ_i "at that point is computed as:

$$\phi_i = \{\angle(x_{i+1} - x_i), \angle(x_i - x_{i-1})\}$$

$$\psi = \{\phi_1 \cap \phi_2 \cap .....\phi_n\}$$

The accessibility angle is the common angle between all the freedom angles. The accessibility angle (ψ) (Sharma et al. (2006)) is calculated as shown in Figure 2(b). An object is in form closure if the accessibility angle is the null set (or escape angle is zero). This means that there is no way the object can move away (translate or rotate) from the gripper points.

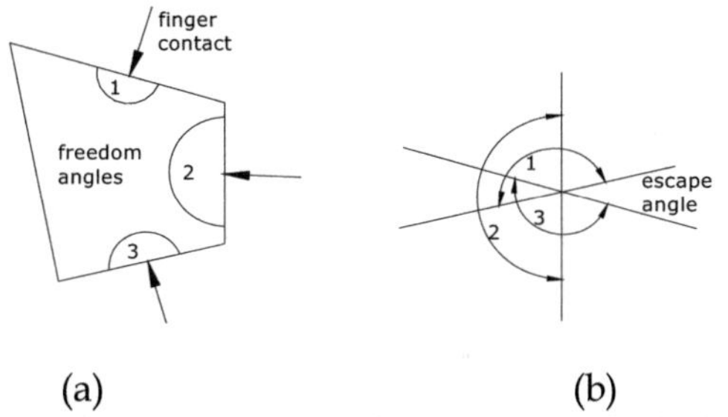

Figure 1. (a) The freedom angles showing the directions in which the object can move with respect to each individual finger contact, (b) direction in which the object is free to escape

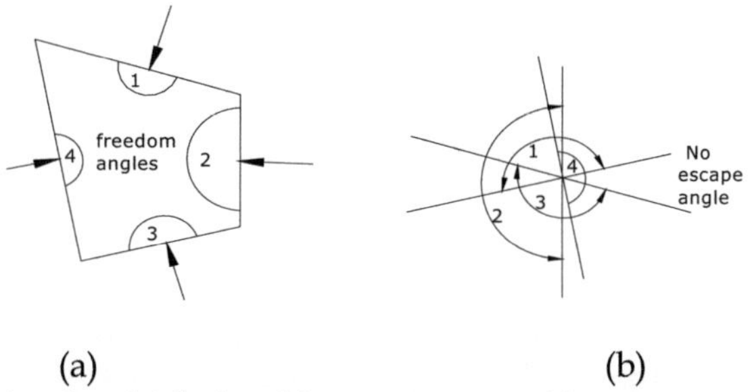

Figure 2. (a) The direction in which the object can move with respect to each finger contact, (b) the object cannot escape in any direction as there is no escape angle

Hence the method essentially searches for the best from closure grasp points by comparing all sets of four grasp points satisfying conditions of form closure. As the object boundary is made up of a very large number of points (pixels) and a good form closure grasp is desired this search is quite complex. Also as the search involves discrete points an efficient method to solve the problem is to use genetic algorithms.

GA is used to maximize an objective function subject to constraints. A traditional GA, like Gordy (1996), performs three operations on a population of genomes i.e. selection, crossover and mutation. The length of the binary string is equal to the number of discrete points on the object boundary. If a finger is present at a particular point then '1' is present or it is '0'. The binary string encoding the object boundary is as shown in Figure 3 .

010000000010000000000100..........0000001000000

Figure 3. Binary string (1 means finger present at that location, 0 means no finger present)

Selection is performed to choose better individuals for cross-over. In Gordy (1996), selection is performed using the roulette wheel procedure. If an individual has better fitness, its probability of getting selected is more. In this selection process, cumulative sum of the fitness of all individuals in the population is calculated and normalized by dividing it with the total sum of the fitness of individuals in the population. A random number between 0 and 1 is chosen. If that number lies within the span of normalized cumulative sum of any individual, that individual is selected. An individual can be selected multiple times based on how fit it is. Once the number of individuals equal to the original population size is selected into the mating pool, a single point crossover is performed. A split point is randomly generated and contents of the two individuals are swapped about this split point. Post crossover, mutation is performed with a very low probability. Each individual is scanned through and a gene is randomly mutated if the probability is lower than the mutation probability. Thus, a new population of vectors is obtained and individual fitness is computed. Finally, eliticism is invoked by replacing the worst individual of the new population with the best from the previous population.

The two conditions needed to be satisfied in order to get a good grasp are: a) the fingertips must be capable of resisting all the external forces and moment acting on the object and b) the placement of the fingers should be such that the moment applied is minimum. The proposed objective function maximizes the moment that the fingertips can resist, by considering different combination of fingertip positions taking four discrete points at a time. The constraint uses accessibility angle to ensure that all the feasible solutions satisfy form closure. If the accessibility angle is zero it means that the object is in form closure. In case the constraint is not met, a very high penalty is placed on the function value that eliminates the non-feasible solutions. The objective function used is given by:

$$f = \left(\frac{|M_{cw}| + |M_{ccw}|}{N_{cw} - N_{ccw} + \varepsilon} \right) + \sum_{i=1}^{4} U_i V_i^T \tag{2}$$

The first part of the right side of equation (2) is the objective function while the second part is the constraints. M_{cw} is the total clockwise moment and M_{ccw} is the total anticlockwise moment applied by the fingers. These two terms ensure that the individual moments are maximized in both the clockwise and anticlockwise directions. This indirectly leads to minimum normal forces at the contact. N_{cw} and N_{ccw} are the number of fingers applying clockwise and anticlockwise moment. This ensures that the fingers are placed all around the object and do not get concentrated at one location. A term 'ε' having a small value (0.01) has been added to ensure that the denominator does not become zero when both the anticlockwise and clockwise moments are equal. The constraints used are $U=[u_i]$ and $V=[v_i]$ which are given as :

1. u1=0 If total number of contact points is four , else u1=1;
2. u2=1 If area formed by contact points equals zero, else u2=0;
3. u3=0 If Both clockwise and anticlockwise moments exist, else u3=1;
4. u4=0 If object is in form closure, else u4=1;

'v_i' = - $1x10^{20}$ (i=1...4), hence if the constraints are not met the function takes a very high value and that particular solution is rejected. The normal function values for feasible grasp points are approximately $6.5x10^3$ and hence the large negative value of 'v_i' ensures that non-feasible solutions are rejected. In this way feasible solutions move towards feasible space and the non feasible solutions are eliminated.

3. Regrasp of deforming objects

This section describes how regrasp solutions are obtained as the object deforms. The optimal grasp points depend on the geometry of the object and the solution for the first frame is obtained using a random guess as the initial solution in the GA routine. Hence this solution takes the largest time for convergence. Once the initial solution is obtained, it is used as the initial guess in the next search. As the object deforms the vision system obtains the next shape of the object in terms of pixel boundary points. These discrete points form the new GA design variable and the earlier solution is used as an initial guess. The object deforms very slowly and hence the shape changes slowly. This property ensures that the new grasp points are in the neighborhood of the earlier optimal grasp points and are not random. Hence it was found that the time for finding an optimal solution rapidly decreases in subsequent searches once an initial solution is found.

4. Simulation

The proposed regrasp algorithm has been tested on 200 types of synthetic shapes that undergo slow deformation. Simulations were performed on a 1.86 GHz laptop computer with 512 RAM. We have assumed that the objects deforms slowly as the algorithm takes time (secs) to obtain a solution. An example of slow deformation is a rectangle that can slowly expands each side to become an octagon etc. However a rectangle cannot suddenly become a circle. This assumption is practical as an expanding object like a balloon does not change shape suddenly. The simulation was made in Matlab in which a closed object was constructed using straight lines segments. Each time a side of the object was expanded by dividing it into two or more segments and expanding it. In case of real objects the sides can be approximated by straight lines and hence this method can be used to approximately simulate deformable objects. A few sample cases of an object expanding are shown in Figure 4. As shown, an object (a) deforms to object (b), then (c) etc. by expanding one side at a time (all intermediate steps are not shown). The GA parameters used are:

1. Size of generation 60
2. Crossover 0.80
3. Mutation 0.12
4. Maximum number of iteration 5000
5. Maximum number of gains before stopping 1000

The time required to find the regrasp points was found in two ways for each object. In Case-I the time was found independently for each deforming object. There was no initial guess solution supplied to the algorithm. In Case II the time to get a solution was found by supplying the earlier solution as an initial guess to the algorithm. In both the cases for the same objects the four optimal finger positions were same but the time to get a solution was different, as shown in Table 1. It was seen that in Case II the time required to get each solution was very much less than in Case I. This can be explained by the fact that as the object deforms the optimal grasp points are not random but are related to the shape of the object.

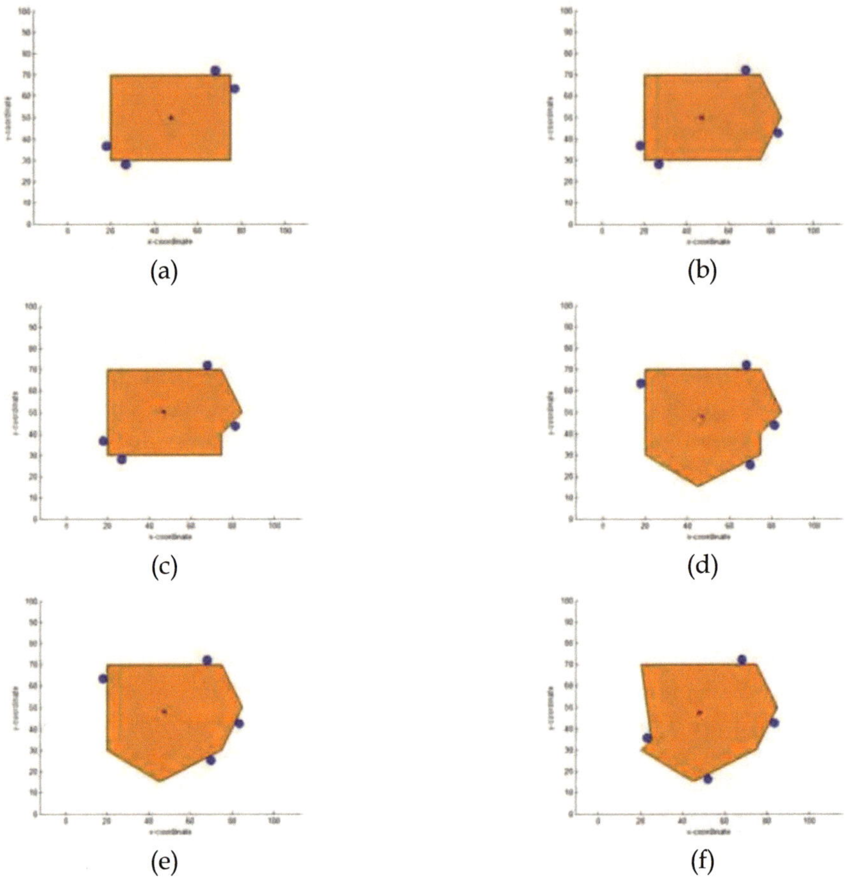

Figure.4. (a-f) Optimal grasp points for a slowly deforming object (the fingertip contact points are indicated by solid circles) x and y axis are in mm

Object No.	1	2	3	4	5	6
Case I Time(secs)	53	75	61	67	74	73
Case II Time (Sec)	53	37	23	31	21	24

Table 1. Comparison of time taken for calculating optimal grasp points for Case I and II

5. Experimental details

The experimental system (as shown in Fig 5) consists of a vision camera, a slowly deforming object, a PC with image processing software and a laptop PC on which the GA based algorithm runs. The deforming object was a piece of black cloth that was deformed by holding it from below and deforming it. The image was captured by a black and white CCD camera model 'SB-6B' manufactured by Wireless Tsukamoto Co., Japan. The camera can capture frames at a rate of 30 fps and each frame has a resolution of 100x100 pixels. The number of pixels determines the total number of discrete points on the object boundary that are considered by the binary string in the GA algorithm. Hence increasing the number of pixels in a frame increases the resolution of the picture but it also increases the time required for computation as the length of the binary string will be longer. It was found that using 100x100 pixels per frame gave satisfactory results and the image was captured at intervals of 10 seconds. The sequence of images captured of the deforming object is shown in Figure 6. Thresholding was used to segment each image into the foreground and background based on different pixel intensities. The input was a grey scale image and the output was a binary image representing segmentation. The boundary of the segmented image was obtained by using edge detection as shown in Figure 7. After the edge is detected the coordinate of all the pixels with reference to a reference coordinate frame was found. These coordinates of the object boundary pixels are then passed on to the GA based algorithm for calculating the best grasp points.

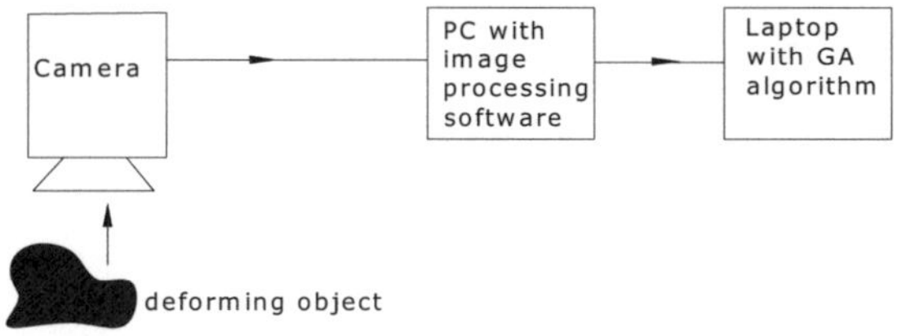

Figure 5. The experimental setup

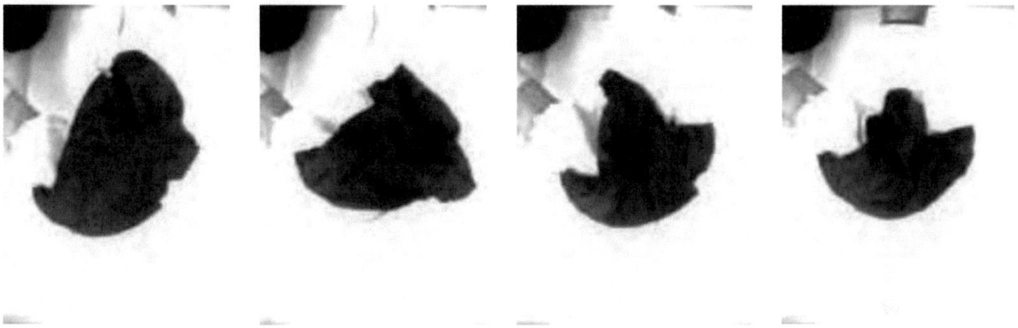

(a) (b) (c) (d)

Figure 6. (a-d) Image sequence of the deforming object

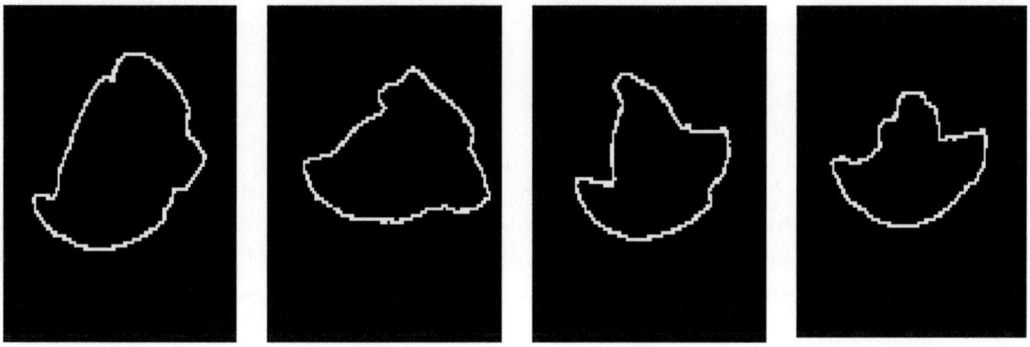

(a) (b) (c) (d)

Figure 7. (a-d) The edge of the deformed objects

6. Experimental results

The pixel coordinates of the boundary of the deforming object as obtained by the image processing software was input to the GA based grasping algorithm. Computations were performed on a 1.86 GHz laptop computer with 512 RAM. The results of the experiments are as shown in Figure 8. Each figure corresponds to the frame obtained by the vision camera in Figure 6. The GA parameters used in the algorithm are same as those used in the simulations. The optimal grasp points for the first frame were obtained by using a random initial guess solution in the GA algorithm. Subsequent solutions were obtained by using the previous solutions as the initial guess. Table 2 shows the time required to get each solution and it is again seen that the first frame required the most time.

Object No.	(a)	(b)	(c)	(d)
Time (secs)	46	22	27	25

Table 2. Time required for computing the grasp points

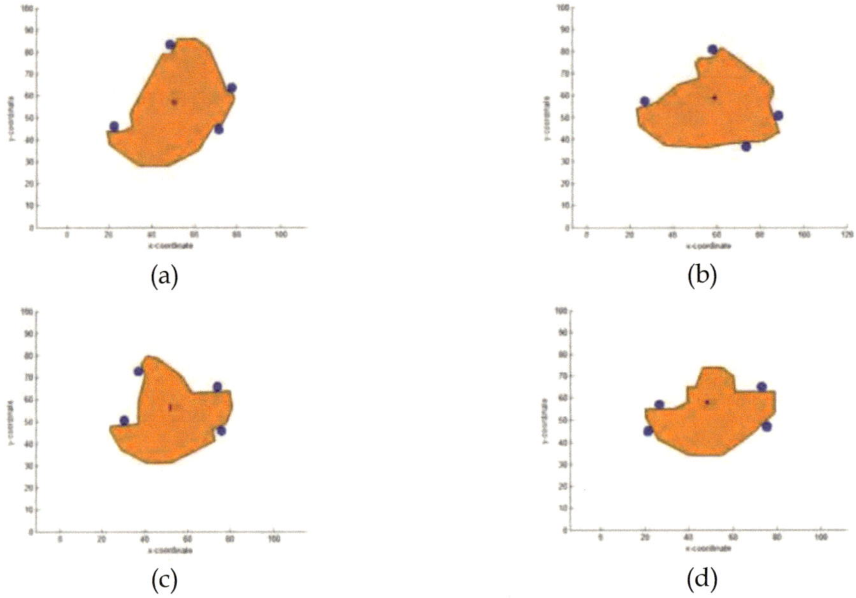

Figure 8. (a-d) The optimal grasp points for each of the deforming objects (x and y coordinates in mm)

6.1 Real time application

One of the potential uses of the proposed method is an application in which an autonomous multifinger robot with a vision camera has to capture a deforming object. In such applications the time from image capture to obtaining the optimal grasp points has be done in real time (in a few seconds). As shown earlier, the time required to get the first solution was the highest as it depended on parameters like, initial guess solution, total number of iterations and the total iterations before stopping if gains are not exceeded. Hence faster solutions can be obtained by dynamically tuning these parameters. Figure 9 shows two solutions for the same object obtained by varying the GA parameters. The final objective function values indicated that solution (a) with function value of 6.8x10³ (iteration 5000 and number of gains before stop 200) is better than solution (b) with function value 6.1x10³ (iteration 1000, number of gains before stop 100). The solutions were obtained in 6 seconds and 2 seconds respectively. Hence it is possible to obtain faster solutions in real time by dynamically tuning the GA parameters based on required function value or number of iterations, and also using a faster computer for running the algorithm. It is however not clear how the function value varies with different shapes and parameter values. In future, we hope to study how to adjust the GA parameters dynamically to obtain the fastest solutions in real time.

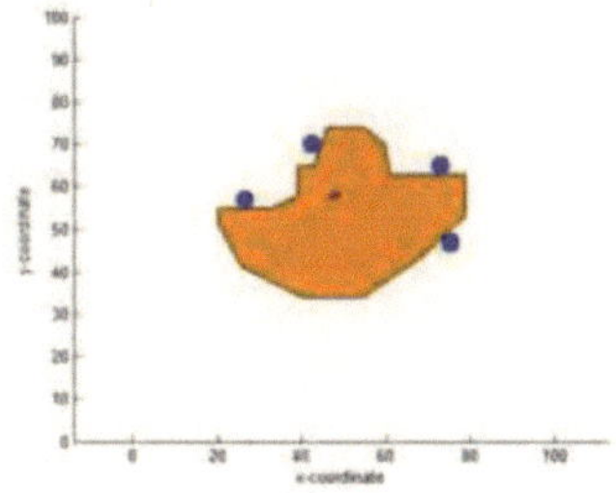
(a)

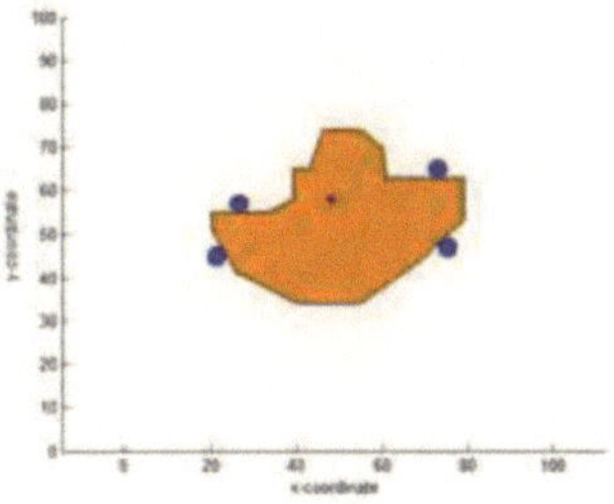
(b)

Figure 9. (a-b) Finger points for the same object for different functional values

7. Conclusion

The main contributions of this research are an effective vision based method to compute the optimal grasp points for a 2D prismatic object using GA has been proposed. The simulation and experimental results prove that it is possible to apply the algorithm in practical cases to find the optimal grasp points. In future we hope to integrate the method in a multifinger robotic hand to grasp different types of deforming objects autonomously.

8. References

Bicchi, A. & Kumar, V. (2000). Robot Grasping and Control: A review, *Proceedigns of the IEEE International Conference on Robotics and Automation,* pp. 348-353, ISSN 1050 4729.

Blake, A. (1995). A symmetric theory of planar grasp, *The International Journal of Robotics Research,* vol. 14, no. 5, pp. 425-444, ISSN 0278-3649.

Chinellato, E., Fisher, R.B., Morales, A. & del Pobil, A. P. (2003). Ranking planar grasp configurations for a three finger hand, *Proceedings of the IEEE International Conference on Robotics and Automation,* pp. 1133-1138, ISSN 1050 4729.

Gatla, C., Lumia, R., Wood, J. & Starr, G.(2004). An efficient method to compute three fingered planar object grasps using active contour models, *Proceedigns of the IEEE/RSJ International Conference on Intelligent Robots and Systems,* pp. 3674-3679, ISBN 07803-8463-6.

Gordy, M. (1996) A Matlab routine for function maximization using Genetic Algorithm. *Matlab Codes: GA.*

Hirai, S., Tsuboi, T. & Wada, T. (2001) Robust grasping manipulation of deformable objects, *Proceedings of the IEEE International Conference on Assembly and Task Planning,* pp. 411-416, ISBN 07803-7004.

Sharma, P., Saxena, A. & Dutta, A. (2006). Multi agent form closure capture of a generic 2D polygonal object based on projective path planning, *Proceedings of the ASME 2006 International Design Engineering Technical Conferences,* pp.1-8, ISBN 07918-3784.

Mishra T., Guha, P., Dutta, A. & Venkatesh K. S. (2006). Efficient continuous re-grasp planning for moving and deforming planar objects, *Proceedings of the IEEE International Conference on Robotics and Automation,* pp. 2472 - 2477, ISSN 1050 4729.

Mirtich, B. & Canny, J. (1994). Easily computable optimum grasps in 2D and 3D, *Proceedings of the IEEE International Conference on Robotics and Automation*, pp. 739-747.

Nguyen, V.D. (1989). Constructing stable force-closure grasps, *International Journal of Robotics Research*, vol. 8, no. 1, pp. 26-37, 0278-3649.

Yoshikawa, T. (1996). Passive and active closures by constraining mechanisms, *Proceedings of the IEEE International Conference on Robotics and Automation*, pp. 1477-1484, ISBN 07803-2988.

3

Multi-Focal Visual Servoing Strategies

Kolja Kühnlenz and Martin Buss
Institute of Automatic Control Engineering (LSR), Technische Universität München
Germany

1. Introduction

Multi-focal vision provides two or more vision devices with different fields of view and measurement accuracies. A main advantage of this concept is a flexible allocation of these sensor resources accounting for the current situational and task performance requirements. Particularly, vision devices with large fields of view and low accuracies can be used together. Thereby, a coarse overview of the scene is provided, e.g. in order to be able to perceive activities or structures of potential interest in the local surroundings. Selected smaller regions can be observed with high-accuracy vision devices in order to improve task performance, e.g. localization accuracy, or examine objects of interest. Potential target systems and applications cover the whole range of machine vision from visual perception over active vision and vision-based control to higher-level attention functions.

This chapter is concerned with multi-focal vision on the vision-based feedback control level. Novel vision-based control concepts for multi-focal active vision systems are presented. Of particular interest is the performance of multi-focal approaches in contrast to conventional approaches which is assessed in comparative studies on selected problems.

In vision-based feedback control of the active vision system pose, several options to make use of the individual vision devices of a multi-focal system exist: a) only one of the vision devices is used at a time by switching between the vision devices, b) two or more vision devices are used at the same time, or c) the latter option is combined with individual switching of one or several of the devices. Major benefit of these strategies is an improvement of the control quality, e.g. tracking performance, in contrast to conventional methods. A particular advantage of the switching strategies is the possible avoidance of singular configurations due to field of view limitations and an instantaneous improvement of measurement sensitivity which is beneficial near singular configurations of the visual controller and for increasing distances to observed objects. Another advantage is the possibility to dynamically switch to a different vision device, e.g. in case of sensor breakdown or if the one currently active is to be used otherwise.

The chapter is organized as follows: In Section 2 the general configuration, application areas, data fusion approaches, and measurement performance of multi-focal vision systems are discussed; the focus of Section 3 are vision-based strategies to control the pose of multi-focal active vision systems and comparative evaluation studies assessing their performance in contrast to conventional approaches; conclusions are given in Section 4.

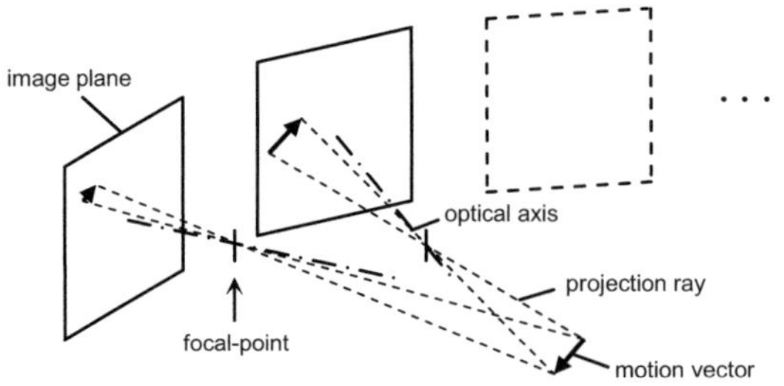

Figure 1. Schematical structure of a general multi-focal vision system consisting of several vision devices with different focal-lengths; projections of a Cartesian motion vector into the image planes of the individual vision devices

2. Multi-Focal Vision

2.1 General Vision System Structure

A multi-focal vision system comprises several vision devices with different fields of view and measurement accuracies. The field of view and accuracy of an individual vision device is mainly determined by the focal-length of the optics in good approximation and by the size and quantization (pixel sizes) of the sensor-chip. Neglecting the gathered quantity of light, choosing a finer quantization has approximately the same effect as choosing a larger focal-length. Therefore, sensor quantization is considered fixed and equal for all vision devices in this chapter. The projections of an environment point or motion vector on the image planes of the individual vision devices are scaled differently depending on the respective focal-lengths. Figure 1 schematically shows a general multi-focal vision system configuration and the projections of a motion vector.

2.2 Systems and Applications

Cameras consisting of a CCD- or CMOS-sensor and lens or mirror optics are the most common vision devices used in multi-focal vision. Typical embodiments of multi-focal vision systems are *foveated* (bi-focal) systems of humanoid robots with two different cameras combined in each eye which are aligned in parallel, e.g. (Brooks et al., 1999; Ude et al., 2006; Vijayakumar et al., 2004). Such systems are the most common types of multi-focal systems. Systems for ground vehicles, e.g. (Apostoloff & Zelinsky, 2002; Maurer et al., 1996) are another prominent class whereas the works of (Pellkofer & Dickmanns, 2000) covering situation-dependent coordination of the individual vision devices are probably the most advanced implementations known. An upcoming area are surveillance systems which strongly benefit from the combination of large scene overview and selective observation with high accuracy, e.g. (Bodor et al., 2004; Davis & Chen, 2003; Elder et al., 2004; Jankovic & Naish, 2005; Horaud et al., 2006).

An embodiment with independent motion control of three vision devices and a total of 6 degrees-of-freedom (DoF) is the camera head of the humanoid robot *LOLA* developed at our laboratory which is shown in Figure 2, cf. e.g. (Kühnlenz et al., 2006). It provides a flexible allocation of these vision devices and, due to directly driven gimbals, very fast camera saccades outperforming known systems.

Most known methods for active vision control in the field of multi-focal vision are concerned with decision-based mechanisms to coordinate the view direction of a telephoto vision device based on evaluations of visual data of a wide-angle device. For a survey on existing methods cf. (Kühnlenz, 2007).

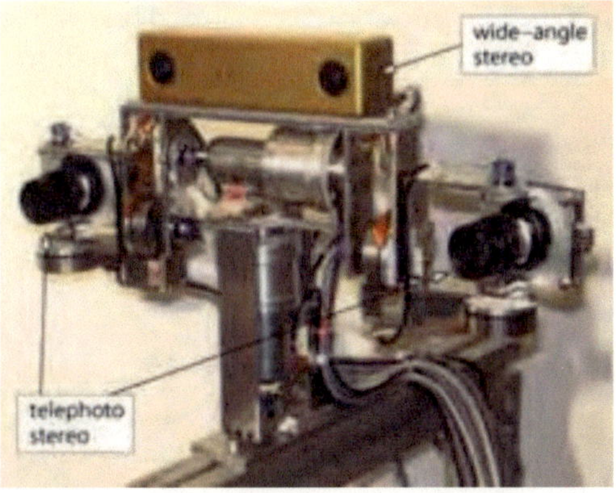

Figure 2. Multi-focal vision system of humanoid *LOLA* (Kühnlenz et al., 2006)

2.3 Fusion of Multi-Focal Visual Data

Several options exist in order to fuse the multi-resolution data of a multi-focal vision system: on pixel level, range-image or 3D representation level, and on higher abstraction levels, e.g. using prototypical environment representations. Each of these is covered by known literature and a variety of methods are known. However, most works do not explicitly account for multi-focal systems. The objective of the first two options is the 3D reconstruction of Cartesian structures whereas the third option may also cover higher-level information, e.g. photometric attributes, symbolic descriptors, etc.

The fusion of the visual data of the individual vision devices on pixel level leads to a common multiple view or multi-sensor data fusion problem for which a large body of literature exists, cf. e.g. (Hartley & Zisserman, 2000; Hall & Llinas, 2001). Common tools in this context are, e.g., projective factorization and bundle adjustment as well as multi-focal tensor methods (Hartley & Zisserman, 2000). Most methods allow for different sensor characteristics to be considered and the contribution of individual sensors can be weighted, e.g. accounting for their accuracy by evaluating measurement covariances (Hall & Llinas, 2001).

In multi-focal vision fusion of range-images requires a representation which covers multiple accuracies. Common methods for fusing range-images are surface models based on triangular meshes and volumetric models based on voxel data, cf. e.g. (Soucy & Laurendeau, 1992; Dorai et al., 1998; Sagawa et al., 2001). Fusion on raw range-point level is also common, however, suffers from several shortcomings which render such methods less suited for multi-focal vision, e.g. not accounting for different measurement accuracies. Several steps have to be accounted for: detection of overlapping regions of the images, establishment of correspondences in these regions between the images, integration of corresponding elements in order to obtain a seamless and nonredundant surface or volumetric model, and reconstruction of new patches in the overlapping areas. In order to optimally integrate corresponding elements, the different accuracies have to be considered (Soucy & Lauredau, 1995), e.g. evaluating measurement covariances (Morooka &

Nagahashi, 2006). The measurement performance of multi-focal vision systems has recently been investigated by (Kühnlenz, 2007).

2.4 Measurement Performance of Multi-Focal Vision Systems

The different focal-lengths of the individual vision devices result in different abilities (sensitivities) to resolve Cartesian information. The combination of several vision devices with different focal-lengths raises the question on the overall measurement performance of the total system. Evaluation studies for single- and multi-camera configurations with equal vision device characteristics have been conducted by (Nelson & Khosla, 1993) assessing the overall sensitivity of the vision system. Generalizing investigations considering multi-focal vision system configurations and first comparative studies have recently been conducted in our laboratory (Kühnlenz, 2007).

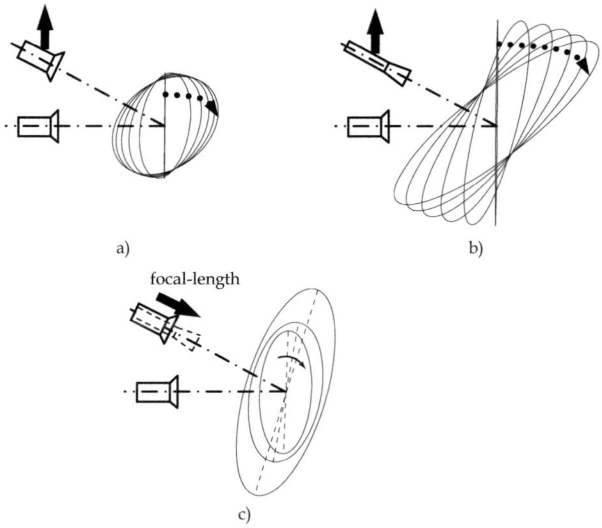

Figure 3. Qualitative change of approximated sensitivity ellipsoids of a two-camera system observing a Cartesian motion vector as measures to resolve Cartesian motion; a) two wide-angle cameras and b) a wide-angle and a telephoto camera with increasing stereo-base, c) two-camera system with fixed stereo-base and increasing focal-length of upper camera

The multi-focal image space can be considered composed of several subspaces corresponding to the image spaces of the individual vision devices. The sensitivity of the multi-focal mapping of Cartesian to image space coordinates can be approximated by an ellipsoid. Figure 3a and 3b qualitatively show the resulting sensitivity ellipsoids in Cartesian space for a conventional and a multi-focal two-camera system, respectively, with varied distances between the cameras. Two main results are pointed out: Increasing the focal-length of an individual vision device results in larger main axes of the sensitivity ellipsoid and, thus, in improved resolvability in Cartesian space. This improvement, however, is nonuniform in the individual Cartesian directions resulting in a weaker conditioned mapping of the multi-focal system. Another aspect shown in Figure 3c is an additional rotation of the ellipsoid with variation of the focal-length of an individual vision device. This effect can also be exploited in order to achieve a better sensitivity in a particular direction if the camera poses are not variable.

In summary, multi-focal vision provides a better measurement sensitivity and, thus, a higher accuracy, but a weaker condition than conventional vision. These findings are fundamental aspects to be considered in the design and application of multi-focal active vision systems.

3. Multi-Focal Active Vision Control

3.1 Vision-Based Control Strategies

Vision-based feedback control, also called visual servoing, refers to the use of visual data within a feedback loop in order to control a manipulating device. There is a large body of literature which is surveyed in a few comprehensive review articles, e.g. cf. (Chaumette et al., 2004; Corke, 1994; Hutchinson et al., 1996; Kragic & Christensen, 2002). Many applications are known covering, e.g., basic object tracking tasks, control of industrial robots, and guidance of ground and aerial vehicles.

Most approaches are based on geometrical control strategies using inverse kinematics of robot manipulator and vision device. Manipulator dynamics are rarely considered. A commanded torque is computed from the control error in image space projected into Cartesian space by the image Jacobian and a control gain.

Several works on visual servoing with more than one vision device allow for the use of several vision devices differing in measurement accuracy. These works include for instance the consideration of multiple view geometry, e.g. (Hollighurst & Cipolla, 1994; Nelson & Khosla, 1995; Cowan, 2002) and eye-in-hand/eye-to-hand cooperation strategies, e.g. (Flandin et al., 2000; Lipiello et al., 2005). A more general multi-camera approach is (Malis et al., 2000) introducing weighting coefficients of the individual sensors to be tuned according to the multiple sensor accuracies. However, no method to determine the coefficients is given. Control in invariance regions is known resulting in independence of intrinsic camera parameters and allowing for visual servoing over several different vision devices, e.g. (Hager, 1995; Malis, 2001). The use of zooming cameras for control is also known, e.g. (Hayman, 2000; Hosoda et al., 1995), which, however, cannot provide both, large field of view and high measurement accuracy, at the same time.

Multi-focal approaches to visual servoing have recently been proposed by our laboratory in order to overcome common drawbacks of conventional visual servoing (Kühnlenz & Buss, 2005; Kühnlenz & Buss, 2006; Kühnlenz, 2007). Main shortcomings of conventional approaches are dependency of control performance on distance between vision device and observed target and limitations of the field of view. This chapter discusses three control strategies making use of the individual vision devices of a multi-focal vision system in various ways. A switching strategy dynamically selects a particular vision device from a set in order to satisfy conditions on control performance and/or field of view, thereby, assuring a defined performance over the operating distance range. This sensor switching strategy also facilitates visual servoing if a particular vision device has to be used for other tasks or in case of sensor breakdown. A second strategy introduces vision devices with high accuracy observing selected partial target regions in addition to wide-angle devices observing the remaining scene. The advantages of both sensor types are combined: increase of sensitivity resulting in improved control performance and the observation of sufficient features in order to avoid singularities of the visual controller. A third strategy combines both strategies allowing independent switches of individual vision devices simultaneously observing the scene. These strategies are presented in the following sections.

3.2 Sensor Switching Control Strategy

A multi-focal active vision system provides two or more vision devices with different measurement accuracies and fields of view. Each of these vision devices can be used in a feedback control loop in order to control the pose of the active vision system evaluating visual information. A possible strategy is to switch between these vision devices accounting for requirements on control performance and field of view or other situation-dependent conditions. This strategy is discussed in the current section.

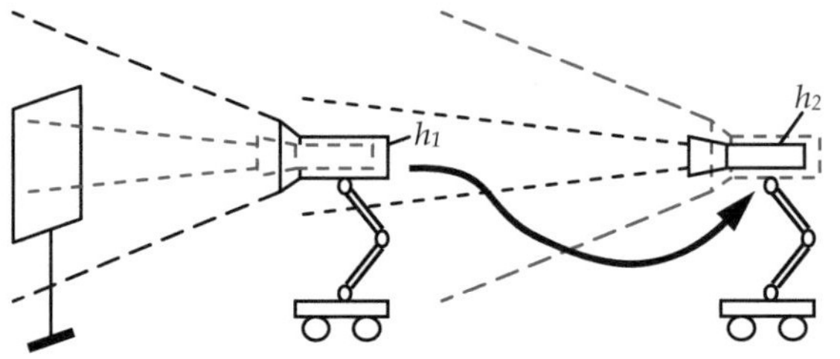

Figure 4. Visual servoing scenario with multi-focal active vision system consisting of a wide-angle camera (h_1) and a telephoto camera (h_2); two vision system poses with switch of active vision device

The proposed sensor switching control strategy is visualized in Figure 5. Assumed is a physical vision device mapping observed feature points concatenated in vector r to an image space vector ξ

$$\xi = h(r, x(q)), \tag{1}$$

at some Cartesian sensor pose x relative to the observed feature points which is dependent on the joint angle configuration q of the active vision device. Consider further a velocity relationship between image space coordinates ξ and joint space coordinates q

$$\dot{\xi}(q) = J(\xi(q), \dot{q})\dot{q}, \tag{2}$$

with differential kinematics $J=J_v R J_g$ corresponding to a particular combination of vision device and manipulator, visual Jacobian J_v, matrix $R=\text{diag}(R_c,\ldots,R_c)$ with rotation matrix R_c of camera frame with respect to robot frame, and the geometric Jacobian of the manipulator J_g, cf. (Kelly et al., 2000). A common approach to control the pose of an active vision system evaluating visual information is a basic resolved rate controller computing joint torques from a control error $\xi^d-\xi(t)$ in image space in combination with a joint-level controller

$$\tau = J^+ K_p(\xi^d - \xi) - K_v\dot{q} + g, \tag{3}$$

with positive semi-definite control gain matrices K_p and K_v, a desired feature point configuration ξ^d, joint angles q, gravitational torques g, and joint torques τ. The computed torques are fed into the dynamics of the active vision system which can be written

$$M(q)\ddot{q} + C(q, \dot{q})\dot{q} + g(q) = \tau, \tag{4}$$

with the inertia matrix M and C summarizing Coriolis and friction forces, gravitational torques g, joint angles q, and joint torques τ.

Now consider a set of n vision devices $\mathcal{H}=\{h_1,h_2,\ldots,h_n\}$ mounted on the same manipulator and the corresponding set of differential kinematics $J=\{J_1,J_2,\ldots,J_n\}$. An active vision controller is proposed which substitutes the conventional visual controller by a switching controller

$$\tau = J^{\eta^+} K_p(\xi^d - \xi) - K_v\dot{q} + g\,, \tag{5}$$

with a switched tuple of vision device h^η and corresponding differential kinematics J^η

$$< J^\eta \in J, h^\eta \in \mathcal{H} >,\quad \eta \in \{1,2,\ldots n\}\,, \tag{6}$$

selected from the sets J and $\mathcal{H}$.

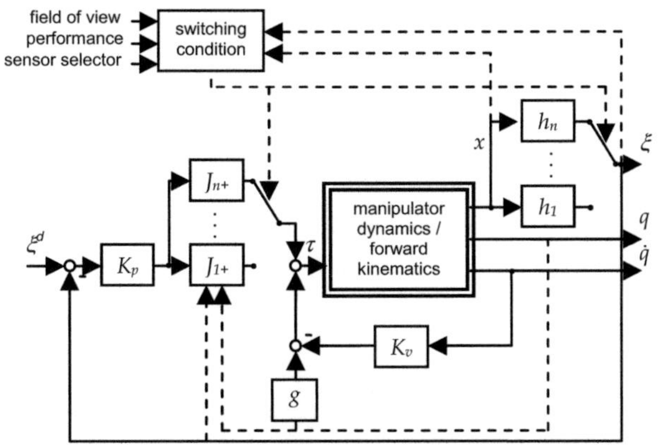

Figure 5. Block diagram of multi-focal switching visual servoing strategy; vision devices are switched directly or by conditions on field of view and/or control performance

This switching control strategy has been shown locally asymptotically stable by proving the existence of a common Lyapunov function under the assumption that no parameter perturbations exist (Kühnlenz, 2007). In case of parameter perturbations, e.g. focal-lengths or control gains are not known exactly, stability can be assured by, e.g., invoking multiple Lyapunov functions and the dwell-time approach (Kühnlenz, 2007).

A major benefit of the proposed control strategy is the possibility to dynamically switch between several vision devices if the control performance decreases. This is, e.g., the case at or near singular configurations of the visual controller. Most important cases are the exceedance of the image plane limits by observed feature points and large distances between vision device and observed environmental structure. In these cases a vision device with a larger field of view or a larger focal-length, respectively, can be selected.

Main conditions for switching of vision devices and visual controller may consider requirements on control performance and field of view. A straight forward formulation dynamically selects the vision device with the highest necessary sensitivity in order to provide a sufficient control performance, e.g. evaluating the pose error variance, in the current situation. As a side-condition field of view requirements can be considered, e.g. always selecting the vision device providing sufficient control performance with maximum field of view. Alternatively, if no measurements of the vision device pose are available the sensitivity or condition of the visual controller can be evaluated. A discussion of selected switching conditions is given in (Kühnlenz, 2007).

3.3 Comparative Evaluation Study of Sensor Switching Control Strategy

The impact of the proposed switching visual servoing strategy on control performance is evaluated in simulations using a standard trajectory following task along the optical axis. The manipulator dynamics are modeled as a simple decoupled mass-damper-system. Manipulator geometry is neglected. Joint and Cartesian spaces are, thus, equivalent. The manipulator inertia matrix is M=0.05diag(1kg, 1kg, 1kg, 1kgm^2, 1kgm^2, 1kgm^2) and matrices K_v+C=0.2diag(1kgs^{-1}, 1kgs^{-1}, 1kgs^{-1}, 1kgms^{-1}, 1kgms^{-1}, 1kgms^{-1}). The control gain K_p is set such that the system settles in 2s for a static ξ^d. A set of three sensors with different focal-lengths of $\mathcal{H}$={10mm, 20mm, 40mm} and a set of corresponding differential kinematics $\mathcal{J}$={J_1, J_2, J_3} based on the visual Jacobian are defined. The vision devices are assumed coincident. A feedback quantization of 0.00001m and a sensor noise power of 0.00001^{2}m^2 are assumed. A square object is observed with edge lengths of 0.5m at an initial distance of 1m from the vision system. The desired trajectory is

$$x^d(t) = \left[0 \quad 0 \quad \frac{7}{2}\sin\left(\frac{1}{5}t - \frac{\pi}{2}\right) - \frac{7}{2} \quad 0 \quad 0 \quad \frac{1}{5}t \right]^T, \tag{7}$$

with a sinusoidal translation along the optical axes and a uniform rotation around the optical axes. The corresponding desired feature point vector ξ^d is computed using a pinhole camera model.

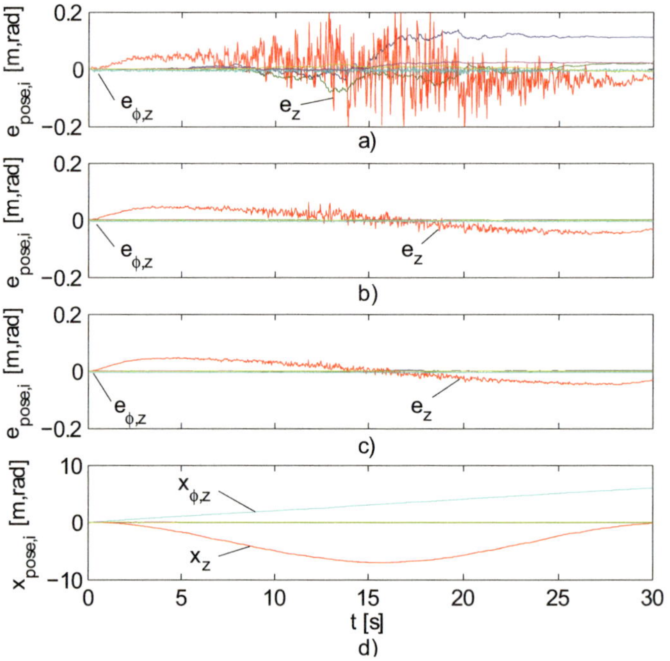

Figure 6. Tracking errors $e_{pose,i}$ and trajectory $x_{pose,i}$ of visual servoing trajectory following task; sinusoidal translation along optical (x_z-)axis with uniform rotation ($x_{\phi,z}$) ; focal-lengths a) 10mm, b) 20mm, c) 40mm

For comparison the task is performed with each of the vision devices independently and afterwards utilizing the proposed switching strategy. A switching condition is defined with a pose error variance band of σ^2=6.25 10^{-6}m^2 and a side-condition to provide a maximum field of view. Thus, whenever this variance band is exceeded the next vision device providing the maximum possible field of view is selected.

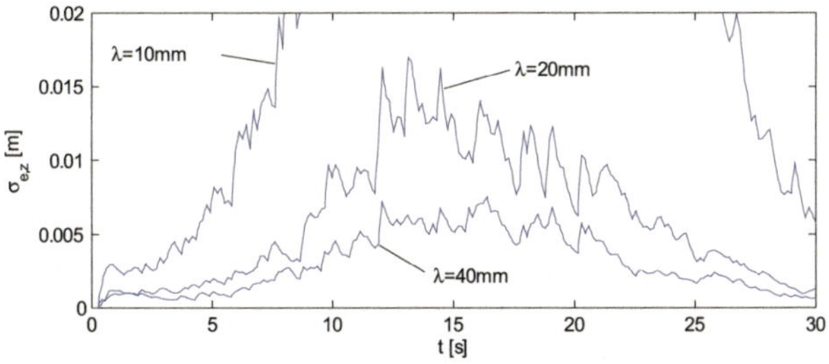

Figure 7. Corresponding tracking error standard deviation estimates for trajectory following tasks (Figure 6) with different cameras; three samples estimation window

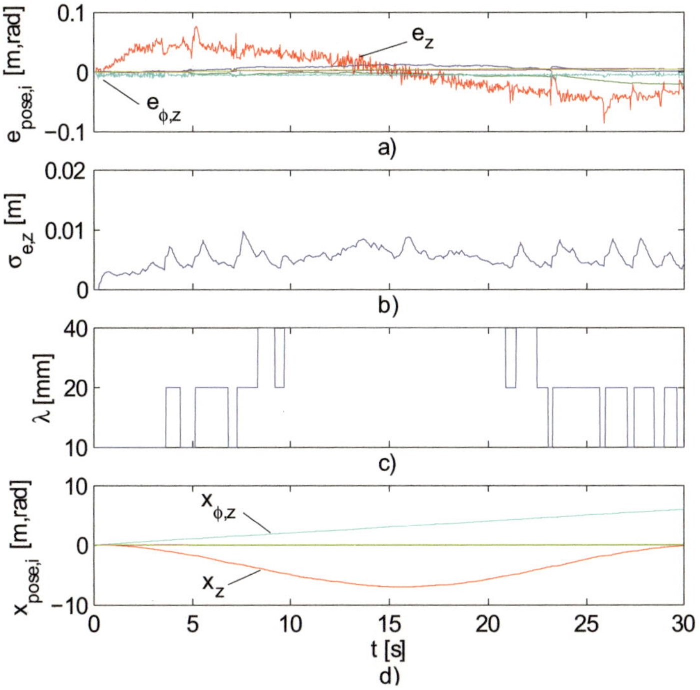

Figure 8. Results of sensor switching visual servoing strategy with multi-focal vision; sinusoidal translation along optical (x_z-)axis with uniform rotation ($x_{\phi,z}$); a) tracking errors, b) tracking error standard deviation estimates, c) current focal-length, d) pose trajectory

Figure 6 shows the resulting tracking errors for the trajectory following task for each of the individual vision devices. In spite of very low control error variances in image space of about 0.01 pixels^2 large pose error variances in Cartesian space can be noted which vary over the whole operating distance as shown in Figure 7. The distance dependent sensitivity of the visual controller and quantization effects result in varying pose error variances over the operating range caused by sensor noise. These effects remain a particular problem for wide range visual servoing rendering conventional visual servoing strategies unsuitable.

Figure 8 shows the results of the switching control strategy. The standard deviation (Figure 8b) is kept within a small band reaching from about 0.004m to 0.008m. The overall variability is significantly lower compared to the single-camera tasks (Figure 7). The spikes, which can be noted in the standard deviation diagram, are caused by the switches due to the delay of the feedback signal. After a switch the desired feature value changes with the sensor, but the current value is still taken from the previous sensor. Thus, the control error at this time instance jumps. This effect can be reduced by mapping the previous value of the feature vector to the image space of the new sensor or by definition of a narrower variance band as switching condition.
Figure 9 exemplarily illustrates the progression of the fields of view over time for a uniform single-camera translation task and the corresponding camera switching task. The field of view is defined by the visible part of the plane extending the surface of the observed object in x-direction. The variability achieved with the switching strategy is significantly lower.
The effectiveness of the proposed multi-focal switching strategy has been shown successfully. The contributions of this novel approach are a guaranteed control performance by means of a bounded pose error variance, a low variability of the performance over the whole operating range, and the consideration of situational side-conditions as, e.g., a maximum field of view.

3.4 Multi-Camera Control Strategy

If two or more vision devices of a multi-focal system are available simultaneously these devices can be used together in order to control the pose of the vision system. In this section a multi-focal multi-camera strategy is proposed in order to make use of several available vision devices with different fields of view and measurement accuracies. Major benefit is an improved control performance compared to single-camera strategies whereas only a partial observation of the reference object with high accuracy is necessary.

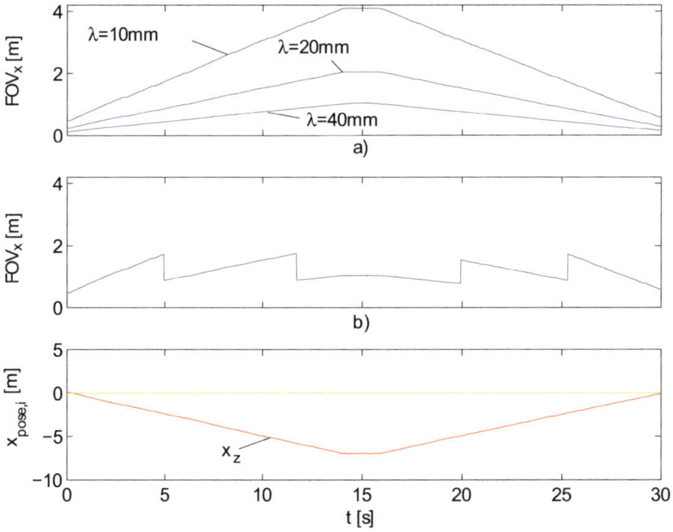

Figure 9. Progression of the extension of the field of view orthogonal to the optical axis of the observing vision device; uniform translation along optical (x_z-)axis; a) single-camera tasks, b) sensor switching strategy with multi-focal vision, c) pose trajectory

A vision-based controller computing joint torques from a control error in image space requires sufficient observed feature points to be mapped to the six Cartesian degrees of freedom. A minimum of three feature points composed of two elements in image space is needed in order to render the controller full rank. If the field of view of the observing vision device is too small to cover all feature points the controller becomes singular. However, high-sensitivity sensors needed in order to achieve high control performance only provide small fields of view.

A multi-camera strategy is proposed combining the advantages of vision devices with different characteristics. High-sensitivity devices are used for improving control performance and wide-field-of-view devices in order to observe the required number of remaining feature points to render the controller full rank.

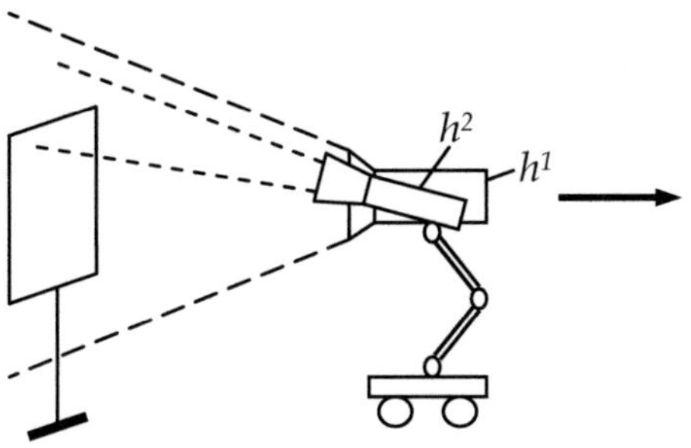

Figure 10. Visual servoing scenario with multi-focal active vision system consisting of a wide-angle camera (h^1) and a telephoto camera (h^2); both vision devices are observing different feature points of a reference object accounting for field of view constraints

The sensor equation (1) extends such that individual feature points are observed with different vision sensors

$$\begin{bmatrix}\xi_1^T & \cdots & \xi_i^T & \xi_j^T & \cdots\end{bmatrix}^T = \begin{bmatrix}h_1\left(\begin{bmatrix}r_1^T & \cdots & r_i^T\end{bmatrix}^T, x_1(q)\right) & h_2\left(\begin{bmatrix}r_j^T & \cdots\end{bmatrix}^T, x_2(q)\right) & \cdots\end{bmatrix}^T, \quad (8)$$

where a Cartesian point r_k is mapped to an image point ξ_l by vision device h_m. The proposed visual controller is given by

$$\tau = \begin{bmatrix}J_1^T & \cdots & J_1^T & J_2^T & \cdots\end{bmatrix}^{T+} K_p(\xi^d - \xi) - K_v\dot{q} + g, \quad (9)$$

with image feature vector $\xi = [\ \xi_1 \ldots \xi_i\ \xi_j \ldots]^T$ and differential kinematics J_m corresponding to vision device h_m.

Substituting the composition of individual differential kinematics J_m by a generalized differential kinematics J^* the proposed control strategy can be expressed by

$$\tau = J^{*+} K_p(\xi^d - \xi) - K_v\dot{q} + g, \quad (10)$$

which has been proven locally asymptotically stable (Kelly et al., 2000).

Utilizing the proposed multi-camera strategy an improved control performance is achieved even though only parts of the observed reference structure are visible for the high-sensitivity vision devices. This multi-camera strategy can be combined with the switching strategy discussed in Section 3.2 allowing switches of the individual vision devices of a multi-focal vision system. Such a multi-camera switching strategy is discussed in the following section.

3.5 Multi-Camera Switching Control Strategy

In the previous sections two concepts to make use of the individual vision devices of a multi-focal vision system have been presented: a sensor switching and a multi-camera vision-based control strategy. This section proposes the integration of both strategies, thus, allowing switches of one or more vision devices observing parts of a reference structure simultaneously. Thereby, the benefits of both strategies are combined.
The sensor equation (8) is extended writing

$$\begin{bmatrix} \xi_1^T & \cdots & \xi_i^T & \xi_j^T & \cdots \end{bmatrix}^T = \begin{bmatrix} h_1^{\eta}\left(\begin{bmatrix} r_1^T & \cdots & r_i^T \end{bmatrix}^T, x_1(q)\right) & h_2^{\eta}\left(\begin{bmatrix} r_j^T & \cdots \end{bmatrix}^T, x_2(q)\right) & \cdots \end{bmatrix}^T, \quad (11)$$

allowing the h_m^{η} of (8) to be selected dynamically from a set $\mathcal{H}=\{h_1,h_2,\ldots,h_n\}$. The visual controllers (5) and (10) are integrated writing

$$\tau = J^{\eta*+} K_p(\xi^d - \xi) - K_v\dot{q} + g, \quad (12)$$

where $J^{\eta*}$ is composed of individual differential kinematics J^m

$$J^{\eta*+} = \begin{bmatrix} J_1^{\eta T} & \cdots & J_1^{\eta T} & J_2^{\eta T} & \cdots \end{bmatrix}^T, \quad (13)$$

which are selected dynamically from a set $\mathcal{J}=\{J_1,J_2,\ldots,J_n\}$ of differential kinematics corresponding to the set $\mathcal{H}$ of available vision devices.
In the following section the proposed multi-camera strategies are exemplarily evaluated in a standard visual servoing scenario.

3.6 Comparative Evaluation Study of Multi-Camera Control Strategies

In this section a comparative evaluation study is conducted in order to demonstrate the benefits of the proposed multi-camera and multi-camera switching strategies. Considered is again a trajectory following task with a uniform translation along the optical axis of a main camera with a wide field of view (focal-length 5mm) as shown in Figure 10. A square reference object is observed initially located at a distance of 1m to the camera. A second camera observes only one feature point of the object. The characteristics of this camera are switchable. Either the same characteristics as of the wide-angle camera or telephoto characteristics (focal-length 40mm) are selectable. The inertia matrix is set to M=0.5diag(1kg, 1kg, 1kg, 1kgm^2, 1kgm^2, 1kgm^2) and matrices K_v+C=200diag(1kgs^{-1}, 1kgs^{-1}, 1kgs^{-1}, 1kgms^{-1}, 1kgms^{-1}, 1kgms^{-1}). The other simulation parameters are set equal to section 3.3.
Three simulation scenarios are compared: second camera with wide-angle characteristics, with telephoto characteristics, and switchable. Switches of the second camera are allowed after a time of 2s when a constant tracking error is achieved. A switch is performed when the tracking error standard deviation exceeds a threshold of 0.00004m.
Figure 11 shows the tracking error of the uniform trajectory following task with switched second camera which can be considered constant after about 2s. Figure 12 shows the resulting standard deviations of the tracking error for all three tasks. It can be noted that a

lower standard deviation is achieved by the multi-camera task (second camera with telephoto characteristics) compared to the wide-angle task. The multi-camera switching task additionally achieves a lower variability of the standard deviation of the tracking error.

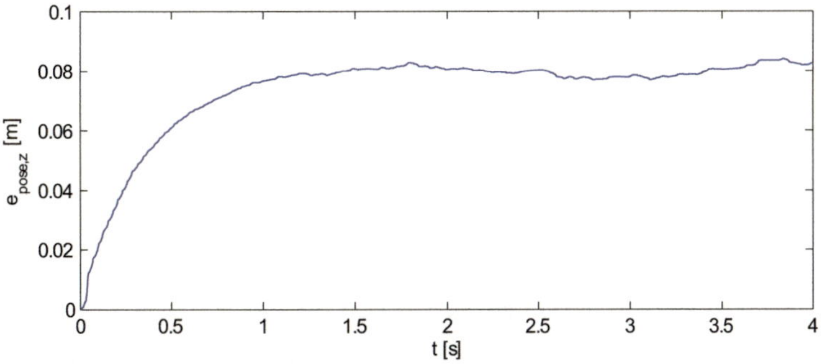

Figure 11. Tracking error of multi-focal two-camera visual servoing task with wide-angle and switchable wide-angle/telephoto camera; desired trajectory $x_z^d(t)$=-0.2ms^{-1}t-1m

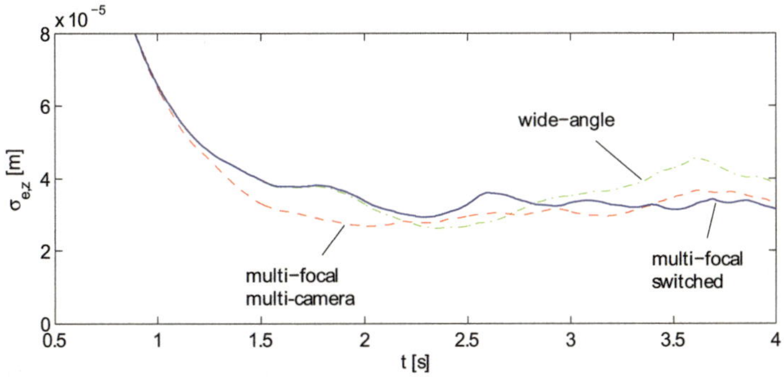

Figure 12. Standard deviation estimates of tracking error of unswitched single-camera task (wide-angle), of unswitched multi-focal multi-camera task with one feature point observed by additional telephoto camera, and of switched multi-focal multi-camera task with additional camera switching from wide-angle to telephoto characteristics at t=2.6s

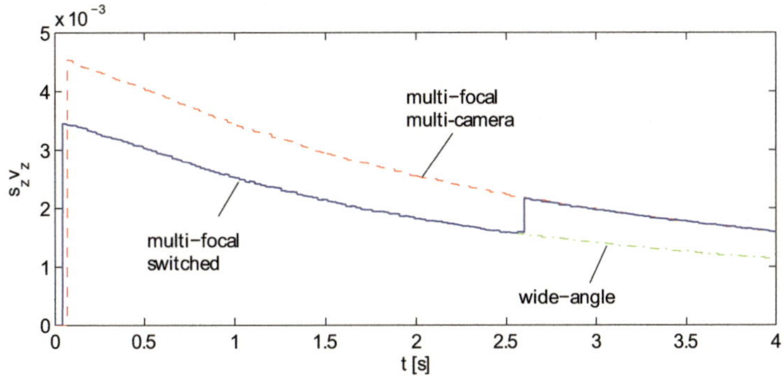

Figure 13. Sensitivities of the visual servoing controller along the optical axis of the central wide-angle camera corresponding to the tasks in Figure 12

Figure 13 shows the sensitivity ($s_z v_z$) of the visual controller for all three tasks along the optical axis of the wide-angle camera. It can be noted that the multi-camera strategies result in a better sensitivity of the controller compared to the wide-angle task.
Summarized, the simulations clearly show the benefits of the proposed multi-camera control strategies for multi-focal vision systems: an exploitation of the field of view and sensitivity characteristics in order to achieve improved control performance and a lower variability of the performance by switching of individual vision devices.

4. Conclusion

In this chapter novel visual servoing strategies have been proposed based on multi-focal active vision systems able to overcome common drawbacks of conventional approaches: a tradeoff between field of view and sensitivity of vision devices and a large variability of the control performance due to distance dependency and singular configurations of the visual controller. Several control approaches to exploit the benefits of multi-focal vision have been proposed and evaluated in simulations: Serial switching between vision devices with different characteristics based on performance- and field-of-view-dependent switching conditions, usage of several of these vision devices at the same time observing different parts of a reference structure, and individual switching of one or more of these simultaneously used sensors. Stability has been discussed utilizing common and multiple Lyapunov functions.
It has been shown that each of the proposed strategies significantly improves the visual servoing performance by reduction of the pose error variance. Depending on the application scenario several guidelines for using multi-focal vision can be given. If only one vision sensor at a time is selectable then a dynamical sensor selection satisfying desired performance constraints and side-conditions is proposed. If several vision sensors can be used simultaneously selected features of a reference object can be observed with high-sensitivity sensors while a large field of view sensor ensures observation of a sufficient number of features in order to render the visual controller full rank. The high-sensitivity sensors should preferably be focused on those feature points resulting in the highest sensitivity of the controller.

5. Acknowledgments

The authors like to gratefully thank Dr. Nicholas Gans and Prof. Seth Hutchinson for inspiring discussions and reference simulation code for performance comparison. This work has been supported in part by the German Research Foundation (DFG) grant BU-1043/5-1 and the DFG excellence initiative research cluster *Cognition for Technical Systems - CoTeSys,* see also *www.cotesys.org.*

6. References

Apostoloff, N. & Zelinsky, A. (2002). Vision in and out of vehicles: Integrated driver and road scene monitoring, *Proceedings of the 8th International Symposium on Experimental Robotics (ISER)*, 2002, Sant Angelo d'Iscia, Italy

Bodor, R.; Morlok, R. & Papanikolopoulos, N. (2004). Dual-camera system for multi-level activity recognition, *Proceedings of the 2004 IEEE/RSJ International Conference on Intelligent Robots and Systems (IROS)*, 2004, Sendai, Japan

Brooks, R. A.; Breazeal, C.; Marjanovic, M.; Scasselati, B. & Williamson, M. M. (1999). The Cog Project: Building a Humanoid Robot, In: *Computation for Methaphors, Analogy, and Agents*, C. Nehaniv, (Ed.), Springer, Germany

Chaumette, F.; Hashimoto, K.; Malis, E. & Martinet, P. (2004). TTP4: Tutorial on Advanced Visual Servoing, Tutorial Notes, IEEE/RSJ IROS, 2004

Corke, P. I. (1994). Visual Control of Robot Manipulators - A Review, In: *Visual Servoing*, K. Hashimoto, (Ed.), World Scientific, 1994

Cowan, N. (2002). Binocular visual servoing with a limited field of view, In: *Mathematical Theory of Networks and Systems*, Notre Dame, IN, USA, 2002

Dickmanns, E. D. (2003). An advanced vision system for ground vehicles, *Proceedings of the International Workshop on In-Vehicle Cognitive Computer Vision Systems (IVC2VS)*, 2003, Graz, Austria

Dorai, C.; Wang, G.; Jain, A. K. & Mercer, C. (1998). Registration and Integration of Multiple Object Views for 3D Model Construction, In: *IEEE Transactions on Pattern Analysis and Machine Intelligence*, Vol. 20, No. 1, 1998

Elder, J. H.; Dornaika, F.; Hou, B. & Goldstein, R. (2004). Attentive wide-field sensing for visual telepresence and surveillance, In: *Neurobiology of Attention*, L. Itti, G. Rees & J. Tsotsos, (Eds.), 2004, Academic Press, Elsevier

Flandin, G.; Chaumette, F. & Marchand, E. (2000). Eye-in-hand/eye-to-hand cooperation for visual servoing, *Proceedings of the IEEE/RSJ International Conference on Intelligent Robots and Systems (IROS)*, 2003

Hager, G. D. (1995). Calibration-free visual control using projective invariance, *Proceedings of the 5th International Conference on Computer Vision (ICCV)*, 1995

Hall, D. L. & Llinas, J. (2001). *Handbook of Multisensor Data Fusion*, CRC Press, 2001, Boca Raton, FL, USA

Hartley, R. I. & Zisserman, A. (2004). *Multiple View Geometry in Computer Vision*, Cambridge University Press, 2004, NY, USA

Hayman, E. (2000). *The use of zoom within active vision*, Ph.D. Thesis, University of Oxford, 2000, Oxford, UK

Hollighurst, N. & Cipolla, R. (1994). Uncalibrated stereo hand-eye coordination, In: *Image and Vision Computing*, Vol.12, No. 3, 1994

Horaud, R.; Knossow, D. & Michaelis, M. (2006). Camera cooperation for achieving visual attention, In: *Machine Vision and Applications*, Vol. 15, No. 6, 2006, pp. 331-342

Hosoda, K.; Moriyama, H. & Asada, M. (1995). Visual servoing utilizing zoom mechanism, *Proceedings of the IEEE International Conference on Robotics and Automation (ICRA)*, 1995

Hutchinson, S.; Hager, G. D. & Corke, P. I. (1996). A tutorial on visual servo control, In: *IEEE Transaction on Robotics and Automation*, Vol. 12, No. 5, 1996

Jankovic, N. D. & Naish, M. D. (2005). Developing a modular spherical vision system, *Proceedings of the 2005 IEEE International Conference on Robotics and Automation (ICRA)*, pp. 1246-1251, 2005, Barcelona, Spain

Kelly, R.; Carelli, R.; Nasisi, O.; Kuchen, B. & Reyes, F. (2000). Stable visual servoing of camera-in-hand robotic systems, In: *IEEE Transactions on Mechatronics*, Vol. 5, No. 1, 2000

Kragic, D. & Christensen, H. I. (2002). *Survey on Visual Servoing for Manipulation*, Technical Report, Stockholms Universitet, ISRN KTH/NA/P-02/01-SE, CVAP259, 2002

Kühnlenz, K. & Buss, M. (2005). Towards multi-focal visual servoing, *Proceedings of the IEEE/RSJ International Conference on Intelligent Robots and Systems (IROS)*, 2005

Kühnlenz, K. & Buss, M. (2006). A multi-camera view stabilization strategy, *Proceedings of the IEEE/RSJ International Conference on Intelligent Robots and Systems (IROS)*, 2006

Kühnlenz, K. (2007). *Aspects of multi-focal vision*, Ph.D. Thesis, Institute of Automatic Control Engineering, Technische Universität München, 2007, Munich, Germany

Kühnlenz, K.; Bachmayer, M. & Buss, M. (2006). A multi-focal high-performance vision system, *Proceedings of the 2006 IEEE International Conference on Robotics and Automation (ICRA)*, 2006, Orlando, FL, USA

Lipiello, V.; Siciliano, B. & Villani, L. (2005). Eye-in-hand/eye-to-hand multi-camera visual servoing, *Proceedings of the IEEE International Conference on Decision and Control (CDC)*, 2005

Malis, E. (2001). Visual servoing invariant to changes in camera intrinsic parameters, *Proceedings of the 8th International Conference on Computer Vision (ICCV)*, 2001

Malis, E.; Chaumette, F. & Boudet, S. (2000). Multi-cameras visual servoing, *Proceedings of the IEEE International Conference on Robotics and Automation (ICRA)*, 2000

Maurer, M.; Behringer, R.; Furst, S.; Thomanek, F. & Dickmanns, E. D. (1996). A compact vision system for road vehicle guidance, *Proceedings of the 13th International Conference on Pattern Recognition (ICPR)*, 1996

Morooka, K. & Nagahashi H. (2006). A Method for Integrating Range Images in Different Resolutions for 3-D Model Construction, *Proceedings of the IEEE International Conference on Robotics and Automation (ICRA)*, 2006

Nelson, B. & Khosla, P. (1993). *The resolvability ellipsoid for visually guided manipulation*, Technical Report, CMU-RI-TR-93-28, The Robotics Institute, Carnegie Mellon University, 1993, Pittsburgh, PA, USA

Nelson, B. & Khosla, P. (1995). An extendable framework for expectation-based visual servoing using environment models, *Proceedings of the IEEE International Conference on Robotics and Automation (ICRA)*, 1995

Pellkofer, M. & Dickmanns, E. D. (2000). EMS-Vision: Gaze control in Autonomous vehicles, *Proceedings of the IEEE Intelligent Vehicles Symposium*, 2000, Dearborn, MI, USA

Sagawa, R.; Nishino, K. & Ikeuchi, K. (2001). Robust and Adaptive Integration of Multiple Range Images with Photometric Attributes, *Proceedings of the IEEE International Conference on Computer Vision and Pattern Recognition (CVPR)*, 2001

Soucy, M. & Laurendeau, D. (1992). Multi-Resolution Surface Modelling from Multiple Range Views, *Proceedings of the IEEE International Conference on Computer Vision and Pattern Recognition (CVPR)*, 1992

Ude, A.; Gaskett, C. & Cheng, G. (2006). Foveated Vision Systems with Two Cameras Per Eye, *Proceedings of the 2006 IEEE International Conference on Robotics and Automation (ICRA)*, 2006, Orlando, FL, USA

Vijayakumar, S.; Inoue, M. & Souza, A. D. (2004). *Maveric – Oculomotor experimental vision head*, http://homepages.inf.ed.ac.uk/svijayak/projects/maveric/index.html, 2004

4

Grasping Points Determination Using Visual Features

Madjid Boudaba[1] , Alicia Casals[2] and Heinz Woern[3]
[1] *Design Center, TES Electronic Solutions GmbH, Stuttgart*
[2] *GRINS: Research Group On Intelligent Robots and Systems,Technical University of Catalonia, Barcelona*
[3] *Institute of Process Control and Robotics (IPR), University of Karlsruhe*
[1,3]*Germany,* [2]*Spain*

1. Introduction

This paper discusses some issues for generating point of contact using visual features. To address these issues, the paper is divided into two sections: visual features extraction and grasp planning. In order to provide a suitable description of object contour, a method for grouping visual features is proposed. A very important aspect of this method is the way knowledge about grasping regions are represented in the extraction process, which is used also as filtering process to exclude all undesirable grasping point (unstable points) and all line segments that do not fit to the fingertip position. Fingertips are modelled as point contact with friction using the theory of polyhedral convex cones. Our approach uses three-finger contact for grasping planar objects. Each set of three candidate of grasping points is formu- lated as linear constraints and solved using linear programming solvers. Finally, we briefly describe some experiments on a humanoid robot with a stereo camera head and an anthropomorphic robot hand within the "Centre of excellence on Humanoid Robots: Learning and co-operating Systems" at the University of Karlsruhe and Forchungszentrum Karlsruhe.

2. Related work

Grasping by multi-fingered robot hands has been an active research area in the last years. Several important studies including grasp planning, manipulation and stability analysis have been done. Most of these researches assume that the geometry of the object to be grasped is known, the fingertip touches the object in a point contact without rolling, and the position of the contact points are estimated based on the geometrical constraints of the 2 Madjid Boudaba, Alicia Casals and Heinz Woern grasping system. These assumptions reduce the complexity of the mathematical model of the grasp (see [Park and Starr, 1992], [Ferrari and Canny, 1992], [Ponce and Faverjon, 1995], [Bicchi and Kumar, 2000], [J. W. Li and Liu, 2003]). A few work, however has been done in integrating vision-sensors for grasping and manipulation tasks. To place our approach in perspective, we review existence methods for sensor based grasp planning. The existing literature can be broadly classified in two categories; vision based and tactile based. For both categories, the extracted image features are of concern which are vary from geometric primitives such as edges, lines, vertices, and circles to optical flow estimates. The first category uses visual features to estimate the robot's motion with respect to the object pose [Maekawa et al., 1995], [Smith and Papanikolopoulos, 1996], [Allen et al., 1999]. Once the robot hands is already aligned with object, then it needs only to know where the fingers are placed on the object. The second category of sensor uses tactile features to estimate the touch sensing area that in contact with the object [Berger and Khosla, 1991], [Chen et al., 1995], [Lee and Nicholls, 1999]. A practical drawback is that the grasp execution is hardly reactive to sensing errors such as finger positioning errors. A vision sensor, meanwhile, is unable to handle occlusions. Since an object is grasped according to its CAD model [Koller et al., 1993], [Wunsch et al., 1997], [Sanz et al., 1998], [N. Giordana and Spindler, 2000], [Kragic et al., 2001], an image also contains redundant information that could become a source of errors and ineffciency in the processing.

This paper is an extension of our previous works [Boudaba and Casals, 2005], [Boudaba et al., 2005], and [Boudaba and Casals, 2006] on grasp planning using visual features. In this work, we demonstrate its utility in the context of grasp (or fingers) positioning. Consider the problem of selecting and executing a grasp. In most tasks, one can expect various uncertainties. To grasp an object implies building a relationship between the robot hand and object model. The latter is often unavailable or poorly known. So selecting a grasp position from such model can be unprecise or unpracticable in real time applications. In our approach, we avoid to use any object model and instead it works directly from image features. In order to avoid fingers positioning error, a set of grasping regions is defined that represents the features of grasping contact point. This not only avoids detection/localization errors but also saves computations that could affect the reliability of the system. Our approach can play the critical role of forcing the fingers to a desired positions before the task of grasping is executed.

The proposed work can be highlighted in two major phases:

1. **Visual information phase**: In this phase, a set of visual features such as object size, center of mass, main axis for orientation, and object's boundary are extracted. For the purpose of grasping region determination, extracting straight segments are of concern using the basic results from contour based shape representation techniques. We will focus on the class techniques that attempt to represent object's contour into a model graph, which preserves the topological relationships between features.
2. **Grasp planning phase**: The grasping points are generated in the planning task taking as input these visual features extracted from the first phase. So a relationship between visual features and grasp planning is proposed. Then a set of geometrical functions is analysed to find a feasible solution for grasping. The result of grasp planning is a database contains a list of:
   - Valid grasps. all grasps that fulfill the condition of grasp.
   - Best Grasps. a criterion for measuring a grasp quality is used to evaluate the best grasps from a list of valid grasps.
   - Reject grasps. those grasps that do not fulfill the condition of grasp.

The remainder of this chapter is organized as follows: Section 3 gives some background for grasping in this direction. The friction cone modeling and condition of force-closure grasps are discussed. In section 4, a vision system framework is presented. The vision system is divided into two parts: the first part concerning to 2D grasping and the second part concerning 3D grasping. we first discuss the extracted visual information we have integrated in grasp planning, generation of grasping regions by using curves fitting and merging techniques, and discuss the method of selecting valid grasps using the condition of force-closure grasp. We then discuss the algorithm for computing feasible solutions for grasping in section 5. We verify our algorithm by presenting experimental results of 2D object grasping with three-fingers. Finally, we discuss the result of our approach, and future work in section 6.

3. Grasp Background

Our discussion is based on [Hirai, 2002]. Given a grasp which is characterized by a set of contact points and the associated contact models, determine if the grasp has a force-closure. For point contact, a commonly used model is point contact with friction (PCWF). In this model, fingers can exert any force pointing into friction cone at the edge of contacts (We use edge contact instead of point contact and can be described as the convex sum of proper point contacts). To fully analyze the grasp feasibility, we need to examine the full space of forces acting on the object. Forming the convex hull of this space is diffcult due to the nonlinear friction cone constraints imposed by the contact models. In this section, we only focus in precision grasps, where only the fingertips are in contact with the object. After discussing the friction cone modeling, a formalizme is used for analysing the force closure grasps using the theory of polyhedral convex cones.

3.1 Modeling the Point of Contact

A point of contact with friction (sometimes referred to as a hard-finger) im- poses non linear constraints on the force inside of its friction cones. For the analysis of the contact forces in planar grasps, we simplify the problem by modeling the friction cones as a convex polytopes using the theory of polyhedral convex cones attributed to [Goldman and Tucker, 1956]. In order to construct the convex polytope from the primitive contact forces, the following theorem states that a polyhedral convex cone (PCC) can be generated by a set of basic directional vectors.

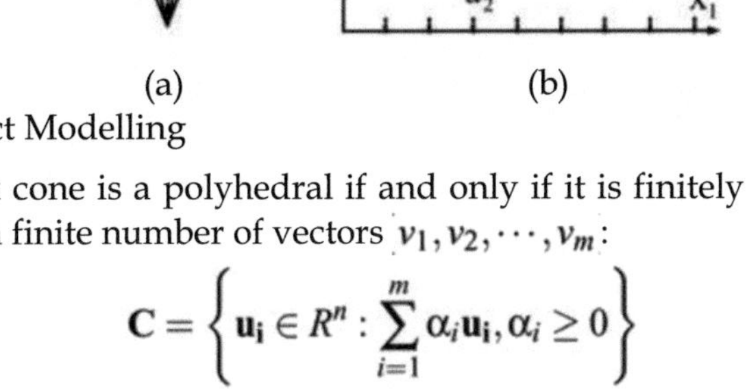

(a) (b)

Figure 1. Point Contact Modelling

Theorem 1. A convex cone is a polyhedral if and only if it is finitely generated, that is, the cone is generated by a finite number of vectors $v_1, v_2, \cdots, v_m$:

$$\mathbf{C} = \left\{ \mathbf{u_i} \in R^n : \sum_{i=1}^{m} \alpha_i \mathbf{u_i}, \alpha_i \geq 0 \right\} \tag{1}$$

where the coeffcients α_i are all non negative. Since vectors u_i through u_m span the cone, we write 1 simply by C=*span* $\{u_1, u_2, ..., u_m\}$. The cone spanned by a set of vectors is the set of all nonnegative linear combinations of its vectors. A proof of this theorem can be found in [Goldman and Tucker, 1956].
Given a polyhedral convex set C, let $vert(\mathbf{P})=\{u_1, u_2, ..., u_m\}$ stand for vertices of a polytope $\mathbf{P}$, while $face(\mathbf{P})=\{\mathbf{F}_1, ..., \mathbf{F}_M\}$ denotes its faces. In the plane, a cone has the appearance as shown in Figure 1(b). This means that we can reduce the number of cone sides, m = 6 to one face, C_i. Let's denote by $\mathbf{P}$, the convex polytopes of a modelled cone, and $\{u_1, u_2, u_3\}$ its three vertices. We can define such polytope as

$$\mathbf{P} = \left\{ \mathbf{x} \in R^n | x = \sum_{i=1}^{u_p} \delta_i \mathbf{u_i} : 0 \leq \delta_i \leq 1, \sum_{i=1}^{u_p} \delta_i = 1 \right\} \tag{2}$$

where u_i denotes the i-th vertex of $\mathbf{P}$, and up is the total number of vertices.
n=2 in the case of a 2D plane.

3.2 Force-Closure Grasps

The force-closure of a grasp is evaluated by analysing its convex cone. For a set of friction cone intersection, the full space can be defined by

$$\mathbf{C_1^k} = C(\mathbf{P_1}) \cap C(\mathbf{P_2}) \cap \cdots \cap C(\mathbf{P_k}) \tag{3}$$

where k is the number of grasping contacts. Note that the result of C_1^k is a set of polytopes intersections and produces either an empty set or a bounded convex polytopes. Therefore, the solution of (3) can be expressed in terms of its extreme vertices

$$\Omega_1^{v_p}(U) = \left\{ \sum_{i=1}^{v_p} \alpha_i u_{ci}, \quad \sum_{i=1}^{v_p} \alpha_i = 1, \quad \alpha_i \geq 0 \right\} \tag{4}$$

where v_p is the total number of extreme vertices.

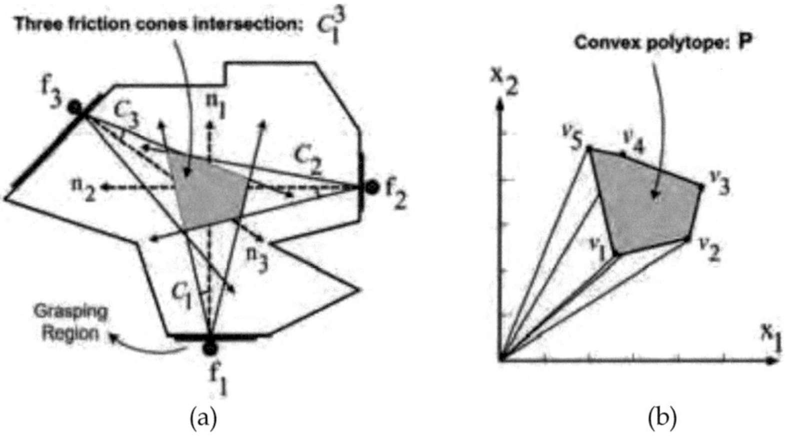

Figure 2. Feasible solution of a three-fingered grasp

Figure 2 illustrates an example of feasible solution of $\Omega_1^{v_p}(U)$ and its grasp space represented by its extreme vertices $P = \{v_1, v_2, \cdots, v_m\}$. From this figure, two observations can be

suggested: first, if the location of a fingertip is not a solution to the grasp, it is possible to move along its grasping region. Such displacement is defined by $u_i = u_{i0} + \beta_i t_i$ where β_i is constrained by $0 \leq \beta_i \leq l_i$ and u_i be a pointed vertex of C_i. Second, we define a ray passing through the pointed vertex u_i, by a function $v_{ci}^T X$ (i=1,...,k). The vector $v_{ci}=[v_{cix}, v_{ciy}] \in R^2$ varies from the lower to the upper side of the spanned cone C_i. This allows us to check whether the feasible solution remains for all v_{ci} in the cone spanned by u_2 and u_3 (see Figure 1(b)).
Testing the force-closure of a grasp now becomes the problem of finding the solutions to (4). In other words, finding the parameters of (3) that the (4) is a bounded convex polytopes.

4. System Description

We are currently developing a robotic system that can operate autonomously in an unknown environment. In this case, the main objective is the capability of the system to (1) locate and measure objects, (2) plan its own actions, and (3) self adaptable grasping execution. The architecture of the whole system is organized into several modules, which are embedded in a distributed object communication framework. There are mainly three modules which are concerned in this development: the extraction of visual information and its interpretation, grasp planning using the robot hand, the control and execution of grasps..

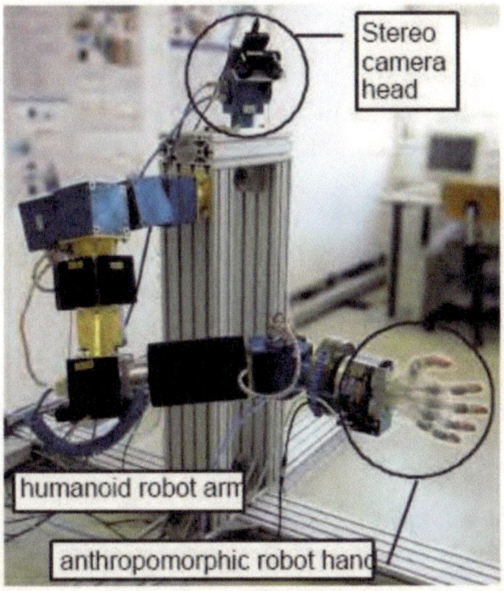

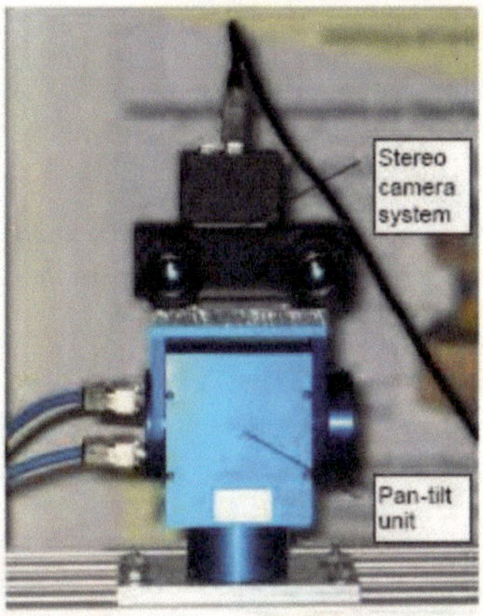

(a) Experimental setup (b) Stereo vision head

Figure 3. Robotic system framework. (a) An humanoid robot arm (7DOF) and an antropomorphic robot hand (10DOF). (b) Stereo vision system

4.1 The Robot Hand

The prototype of the anthropomorphic robot hands (see [Schulz et al. 2001]) has a 7 degrees of freedom (DOF) arm (see Fig. 3(a)). This first prototype is currently driven pneumatically and is able to control the 10 DOF separately, but the joints can only be fully opened or closed. The robot's task involve controlling the hand for collision-free grasping and manipulation of objects in the three dimensional space. The system is guided solely by visual information extracted by the vision system.

4.2 The Vision System

The vision system shown in Fig. 3(b) consists of a stereo camera (MEGA-D from Videre Design) mounted on pan-tilt heads equipped with a pair of 4.8 mm lenses and has a fixed baseline of about 9 cm. The pan-tilt head provides two additional degrees of freedom for the cameras, both of them rotational. The MEGA-D stereo head uses a IEEE 1394 firewire interface to connect to a workstation and has a SRI's Small Vision System (SVS) software for calibration and stereo correlation (see [Konolige, 1997]).
For its complexity, the flow diagram of visual information has been divided into two parts. The first part provides details of 2D visual features extraction. The second part is dedicated to 3D visual features retrieval. The image acquisition primarily aims at the conversion of visual information to electrical signals, suitable for computer interfacing. Then, the incoming image is subjected to processing having in mind two purposes: (1) removal of image noise via low-pass filtering by using Gaussian filters due to its computational simplicity and (2) extraction of prominent edges via high-pass filtering by using the Sobel operator. This information is finally used to group pixels into lines, or any other edge primitive (circles, contours, etc). This is the basis of the extensively used Canny's algorithm [Canny, 1986]. So, the basic step is to identify the main pixels that may preserve the object shape. As we are visually determining grasping points, the following sections provide some details of what we need for our approach.

Contour Based Shape Representation

Due to their semantically rich nature, contours are one of the most commonly used shape descriptors, and various methods for representing the contours of 2D objects have been proposed in the literature [Costa and Cesar, 2001]. Extracting meaningful features from digital curves, finding lines or segments in an image is highly significant in grasping application. Most of the available methods are variations of the dominant point detection algorithms [M. Marji, 2003]. The advantage of using dominant points is that both, high data compression and feature extraction can be achieve. Other works prefer the method of polygonal approximation using linking and merging algorithms [Rosin, 1997] and curvature scale space (CSS) [Mokhtarian and Mackworth, 1986].
A function regrouping parameters of visual features together can be defined by

$$B = \{vlist, slist, llist, com\} \tag{5}$$

where $vlist=\{v_1, v_2, \cdots, v_m\}$ is a list of consecutive contour's vertices with $v_i=(x_i, y_i)$ that represents the location of v_i relative to the center of mass of the object, $com=(x_c, y_c)$. $slist=\{s_1, s_2, \cdots, s_m\}$ is a list of consecutive contour's segments. Both lists $vlist$ and $slist$ are labelled counter-clockwise (ccw) order about the center of mass. During the processing, the boundary of the object, B is maintained as a doubly linked list of vertices and intervening segments as $v_1 s_1 v_2, \cdots, v_m s_m v_1$. The first segment s_1, connecting vertices v_1 and v_2, the last segment s_m, connecting vertices v_m and v_1. A vertex v_i is called reflex if the internal angle at v_i is greater than *180* degrees, and convex otherwise. *llist* is a list that contains the parameters of correspondent segments. Additional to the local features determined above, an algorithm for contour following is integrated. This algorithm follows the object's boundary from a starting point determined previously and goes counter-clockwise around the contour by ordering successively its vertices/edge points into a double linked list. The algorithm stops when the starting point is reached for the second time. The aim of this stage is to determine that all vertices/segments belong to the object's boundary which we will need further for the determination of the grasping points position.

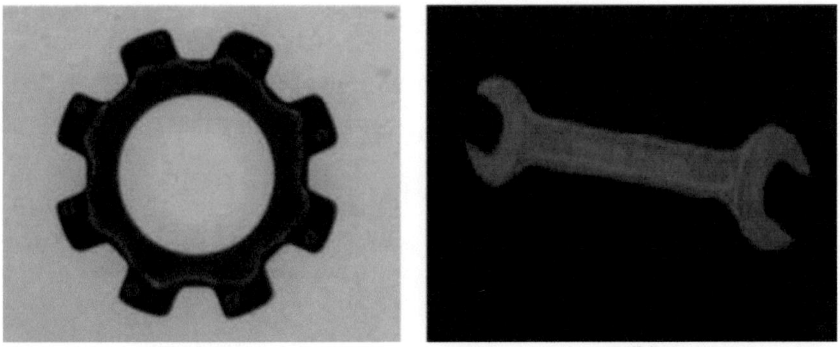

(a) (b)

(a) Binary object

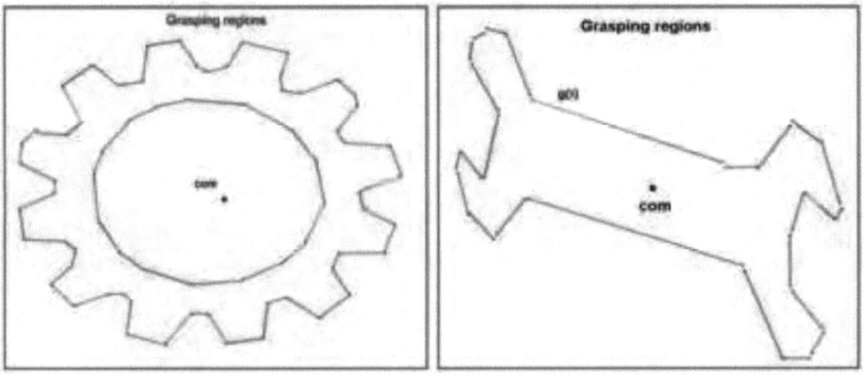

(a) (b)

(b) Visual features extraction

Figure 4. Object shape representation. (a) Images from original industrial objects
(b) Extraction of grasping regions

Extraction of Grasping Regions

Grasping regions are determined by grouping consecutive edge points from a binary edge image. This is usually a preliminary step before grasping takes place, and may not be as time critical as the task of grasping points determination. We deal with (5), the list $vlist=\{v_1, v_2, \cdots, v_m\}$ is the result that forms an ordered list of connected boundary vertices. We then need to store the parameters of these primitives instead of discrete points (or vertices) to fit a line segment to a set of vertices points that lie along a line segment. The aim of this step is to determine all salient segments that preserve the shape of the object contour. Figure 4(b) shows grasp regions on the object's contour. Afterwards, each grasping region is extracted as straight segment. The size of the grasping regions should be long enough for positioning the robot fingers. The curve fitting (as shown in Figure 5(a)) describes the process of finding a minimum set of curve segments to approximate the object's contour to a set of line segments with minimum distortion. Once the line segments have been approximated, the merging method (as shown in Figure 5(b)) is used to merge two lines segment that satisfied the merging threshold.

The final result of the algorithm is a list of consecutive line segments with a specified tolerance which preserve the object's contour. Briefly, merging methods, (1) use the first two vertices points to define a line segment (2) add a new vertex if it does not deviate too much from the current line segment (3) update the parameters of the line segment using least-squares measure (4) start a new line segment when edge points deviate too much from the line segment. The final result of the algorithm is a list of consecutive line segments with a specified tolerance which preserve the object's contour. We define such list by

$$slist = \{s_1, s_2, \cdots, s_m\} \tag{6}$$

where a segment s_i is defined by its ending vertices $v_i=(x_i, y_i)$ and $v_{i+1}=(x_{i+1}, y_{i+1})$ that represent the location of a segment in the plane. m is the number of segments containing the list *slist*.

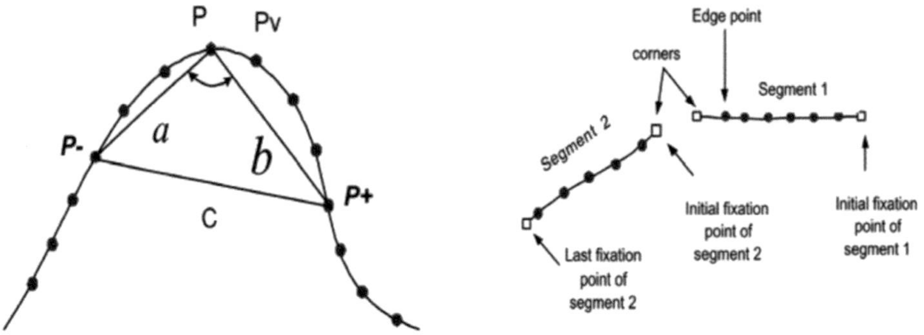

(a) Curve fitting (b) Segment merging

Figure 5. Curve fitting and merging methods. In each curve point p, a variable triangle (p^-, p, p^+) is defined. The admissible triangle is then checked by the following conditions: $d_{min} \leq |p - p^-|$, $d_{min} \leq |p - p^+|$, $\alpha \leq \alpha_{max}$, where $|p - p^-| = a$, $|p - p^+| = b$, and $\alpha = arccos\,(a^2 + b^2 - c^2)/2ab$ is the opening angle of the triangle

Critical Grasping Points

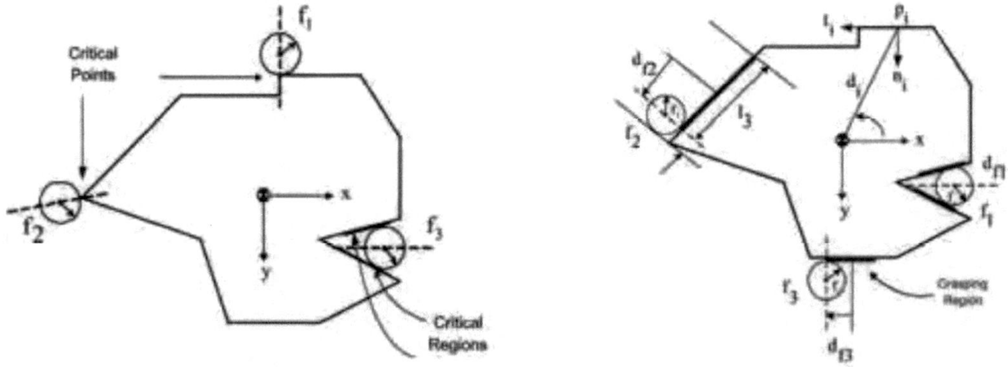

(a) Critical points (b) Finger displacement

Figure 6. (a) Critical grasping point. Possible displacement d_{fi} of a fingertip f_i on its corresponding grasping region (thicker region): Fingertip f_1 is placed at midpoint of its corresponding grasp region, d_{f1}=0. Fingertip f_2 is displaced at d_{f2} in positive direction from midpoint, and the fingertip f_3 is displaced at d_{f3} in negative direction from midpoint. We attach a left-handed frame (n_i, t_i) to each finger position p_i with a distance d_i to the center of mass. n_i and t_i) are normal and tangential direction of a finger f_i in the plane

To assure the robustness of contact placement, we make some assumptions in (6): **First assumption**, to avoid undesirable contacts at convex vertices and convex corners (see the position of finger f_1, f_2 in Figure 6(a)) which are not generally robust due to small uncertainty during the grasping phase. We also avoid the concave vertices having a size of concavity smaller than the size of the fingertip using the reachability conditions (see the position of finger f_3 in Figure 6(a)).
Second assumption, we estimate a fingertip as a sphere with radius f_r (see Figure 6). the grasping regions must be large enough for positioning the fingertip on it. Hence, a preprocessing (or prefiltering) is necessary in (6) to discard those segments with length less than the diameter of the sphere.
Based on both assumption, we define a small margin value at the endpoint of each segment by ε as shown in Figure 6 with $\varepsilon = f_r$. If a segment s_i contains all possible contact points from v_i to v_{i+1} then any grasping points must satisfy

$$\begin{cases} v_i + \varepsilon \leq s_i \leq v_{i+1} - \varepsilon \\ g_i = s_i - 2\varepsilon \\ g_i \geq 2f_r \end{cases} \tag{7}$$

Using the grasp criteria of (7) including the condition that the size of the grasp region must be large enough to place a finger on it, $g_i \leq 2f_r$ (see Figure 6). Equation (6) becomes

$$glist = \{g_1, g_2, \cdots, g_m\} \tag{8}$$

where *glist* is a linked list ordered in counterclockwise direction (see Figure 6(b)) and updated from the condition of (7).
Equation (8) is the result of a filtering test which excludes all grasping candidates that do not belong to the grasping regions and therefore reducing time consuming during grasp point generation.
Let

$$gparam_i = \{p_i, p_{i+1}, l_i, l_{gi}, d_i, \phi_i\} \tag{9}$$

be a function defining the parameter of a grasping region, g_i , where $p_i=(x_i,y_i)$ and $p_{i+1}=(x_{i+1},y_{i+1})$ represent its location in the plane, l_{gi} its length $\overline{p_i p_{i+1}}$, g_{ci} its center (midpoint), d_i is the perpendicular distance from $\overline{p_i p_{i+1}}$ to the object's center of mass, *com*. The relationship between the center of mass and grasping region is given in Figure 7(b). The sign of the area A defines the orientation of grasping region ϕ_i. The elements of (9) verify the following equations:

$$gparam_i : \begin{cases} l_i = \sqrt{(x_{i+1} - x_i)^2 + (y_{i+1} - y_i)^2} \\ l_{gi} = ((x_i + x_{i+1})/2, (x_i + x_{i+1})/2) \\ \phi_i = \arctan(y_{i+1} - y_i)/(x_{i+1} - x_i) \\ d_i = g_i / l_i, \quad g_i = a_i x + b_i y + c_i. \end{cases}$$

The last equation g_i is a linear equality constraint of a given grasping region in the plane (see Figure 7). An additional criteria should be added to avoid that two or three fingers are placed on the same contact point. In this paper we only assign one finger to each grasping region.

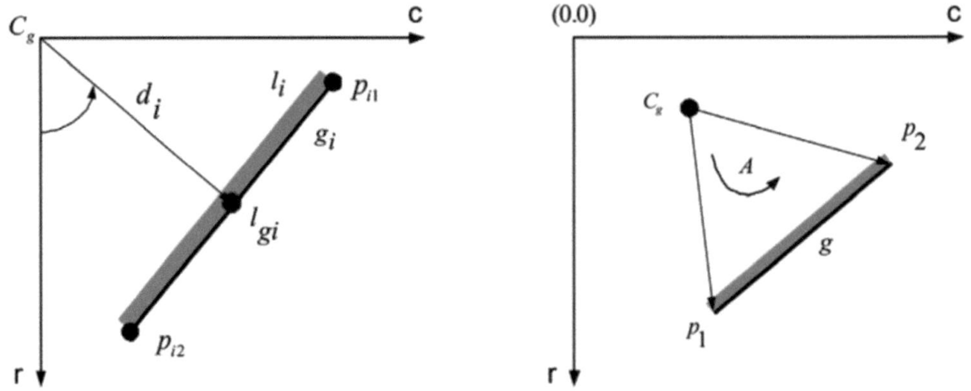

(a) (b)

Figure 7. Projection of grasping region g_i in the image plane (c, r)

5. Grasp Planning Algorithm

Grasp planning can be seen as constructing procedures for placing point contacts on the surface of a given object to achieve force-closure grasps. Taking as input the set of visual features extracted from the contour of the object, the output is a set of valid grasps. The relationship between visual features and grasp planning is given in next section.

5.1 Grasp Point Generation

Generating a number of valid grasps from a list of candidates and classifying the best among them is quite time consuming. Thus a preprocessing (or prefiltering) is necessary before the grasping points generation takes place. We first order the (8) in counterclockwise direction with a starting point from x-axis as shown in Figure 6(b). Second the initial contact of fingertips on grasping regions would be at the midpoint, which are considered as robust contacts and measured directly from the center of mass of the object. Then the displacement $\boldsymbol{d}_{fi}$ (see Figure 6(a)) of the fingertip on its corresponding grasping region (if necessary) should be first in the counterclockwise then in the clockwise direction.

The following equation describes the relationship between the visual features and grasp planning

$$G = f(glist, gparam, com) \tag{10}$$

where *glist*, *gparam* and *com* are the visual features observed on the image plane and G is a grasp map of outputs defined by the relationship between fingers and the location of contact points on its corresponding grasping regions. From the grasp map G three possible solutions are derived:

$$G: \begin{cases} G_s = \{G_{s_1}, G_{s_2}, \cdots, G_{s_{is}}\} \\ G_b = \{G_{b_1}, G_{b_2}, \cdots, G_{b_{ib}}\} \\ G_r = \{G_{r_1}, G_{r_2}, \cdots, G_{r_{ir}}\} \end{cases} \tag{11}$$

where G_s, G_b, and G_r are selected, best, and rejected grasp, respectively. The *is*, *ib*, and *ir* are the number of selected, best, and rejected grasps, respectively.

For a three-finger grasps, the selected grasps (G_s) is given in the following form:

$$G_s : \begin{cases} G_{s_1} = \{(f_1, g_1), (f_2, g_6), (f_3, g_9)\} \\ G_{s_2} = \{(f_1, g_2), (f_2, g_6), (f_3, g_{10})\} \\ \vdots \\ G_{s_{is}} = \{(f_1, g_1), (f_2, g_8), (f_3, g_{12})\} \end{cases}$$

A similar form can be given for representing the best grasps G_b and those rejected G_r.

5.2 The Algorithm

The algorithm is divided into three parts: Visual features part which are regrouped in (5) and (8); grasp planning part which is defined by (10) and (11); and Testing part that corresponds to (4). In the visual features part, the compact representation of the object's contour is obtained which includes the grasping regions and local parameters by using the standard image processing library. In the grasp planning, a relationship between visual features and the location of the contact points is obtained for selecting a valid grasp. In the testing part, the force-closure condition is based on determining the feasible solution of a grasps. We first model the friction cone as a convex polytopes. Then, we solve the problem of (3) and (4) for a given location of contact grasp using programming solvers as well as for computing the polytope convex cones, extreme vertices of polytopes, and calculating projections. One of the advantages of the proposed algorithm is that it does not require a geometrical model of the object and can grasp unknown objects.

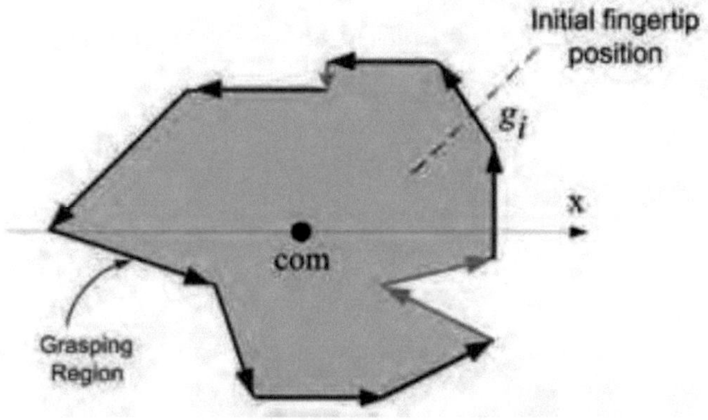

Figure 8. Grasp point generation. The fingertip range defined here is the range of its corresponding grasping regions and midpoint is its optimal contact positions, called initial pose

The whole algorithm is divided into several procedures and operates as follows:

1. *Visual features procedure*
   - *Function grouping visual features using (5)*
2. *Grasping point generation procedure*
   - *Pick three grasp regions from (8)*
   - *Determine the initial position of f_1, f_2 and f_3*
   - *Compute their friction cones using (2)*
   - *Compute the friction cones intersection of (3)*

3. *Grasping test procedure*
   - *Compute the feasible grasps using (4)*
   - *Check whether the polytopes given by (4) is bounded. If so, stop and save the selected grasps to G_s.*
   - *Else save the rejected grasps to G_r.*
4. *Quality test procedure*
   - *The last step of the algorithm consists of selecting the best grasps from a range of valid grasps from lower to upper acceptance measures by using the parameters measure given in table 1. Save to G_b.*

5.3 Implementation

We have implemented the visual features extraction and grasp planning algorithms in Matlab environment for computing feasible solution of a three-fingered grasp. We have experimented with two different kind of objects; a 3D object and a planar object. For both objects, the images extraction are saved in two jpeg files with a resolution of 320x240 and 160x220 pixels, respectively. Table 1 resumes the results of grasp planning algorithm. Three and four feasible grasp configurations have been selected from a total of 25 and 24 grasping regions generated on the object's boundary *obj*1 and *obj*2, respectively. d_1, d_2 and d_3 are distance measures of finger position f_1, f_2 and f_3 from the object's center of mass. x_1, x_2 are the coordinates of the focus point F in the plane. d is the measured distance between focus point and center of mass. R is the vector radius of the ball centered at F. The object's center of mass is located at *com* = 121.00098.000 and *com* = 115.00075.000, respectively. The angle of friction cone is fixed to α = 8.5 degrees for all grasp configurations. Figure 9 illustrates the grasp planing for object *obj*1. Three fingers are in contact with the object which is viewed from the top by the stereo vision head placed above the table. For the second object (*obj*2), the visual features are extracted from a single camera. The friction cone modelling and linear constraints programming have been implemented using [M. Kvasnica, 2005]. We further developed auxiliary function to compute various data such as extraction of visual features of the object, extraction of grasping regions, friction cone modelling, and grasp configurations.

6. Conclusions and Future Work

We have introduced an approach that combines vision and grasping. Based on the vision, visually determining grasping points is done by transforming the grasping regions into a geometrical optimization problem. The results shown in Figure 6 are obtained from applying the software packages in [20] to our Matlab 6.12 programming environment. In order to compute the feasible region of various grasps, we have integrated other linear programming solvers by providing a set of constraints for optimization procedure. Various grasps with three hard-fingers are tested on 2D original object and the feasible solution of grasps are determined by analysing the polytope region of grasps. The focus point inside the polytope convex and its distance from the object's center of mass are two measures used for selecting the best grasps.The most important aspects of our algorithm are how to select the grasping point set and to determine each one step of the grasping process. Three functions, pick(), insert(), and remove() are used. The initialization step picks a first grasping set. The while loop iterates by checking the feasible region of grasps and then by selecting a new candidate of grasp. A build library is used to store valid grasps by the insertion function

which inserts a valid candidate grasp into library, while the remove function deletes invalid grasp from the library. The results in this paper shows the potential to combine vision and grasping in a unified way to resemble the dexterity of human manipulation.
The second part of our visual processing: General flow diagram will be the future work for generating 3D grasps on unknown objects includes implementation on a humanoid robot with a stereo camera head and an anthropomorphic robot hand (as shown in Figure 3).

7. Acknowledgments

The authors would like to thank Prof. Dr. H. Woern and his co-workers from the IPR institute for their support in providing the facilities and the anthropomorphic robot hand for testing the proposed approach.

$\alpha = 8.5$ degrees for all configurations.					
obj	param.	d_1 d_2 d_3	$F(x_1,x_2)$	d	R
obj.1	GC.1	86.80 33.82 65.99	118.41 96.69	2.98	9.37
	GC.2	24.47 86.80 23.82	99.19 122.88	32.53	2.44
	GC.2	81.51 65.99 35.52	114.59 84.46	15.39	4.49
obj.2	GC.1	68.007 91.522 63.832	38.832 60.168	74.464	4.369
	GC.2	79.657 89.550 61.522	186.896 86.615	72.828	6.638
	GC.3	16.651 70.406 80.897	98.181 98.191	28.648	6.071
	GC.4	94.505 80.897 66.727	42.567 70.094	72.599	1.858

Table 1. Parameter measures of three fingered grasp configuration

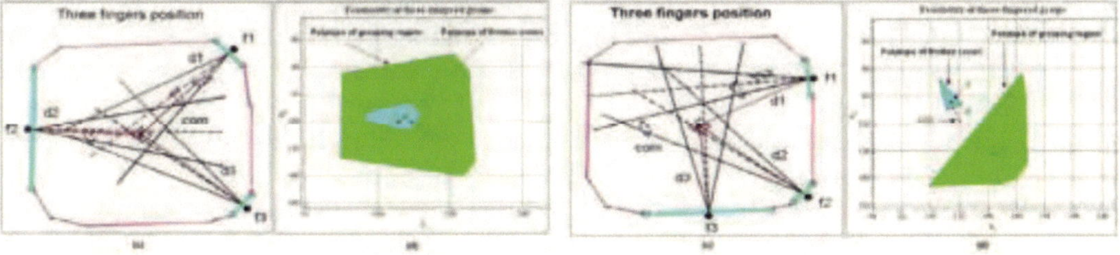

(a) Grasp configuration (**GC**): 1 (b) Grasp configuration (**GC**): 2-3
Figure 9. (a) Grasp planning setup. (b) Result of three fingered grasp configuration 1*to*3 for object *obj*1

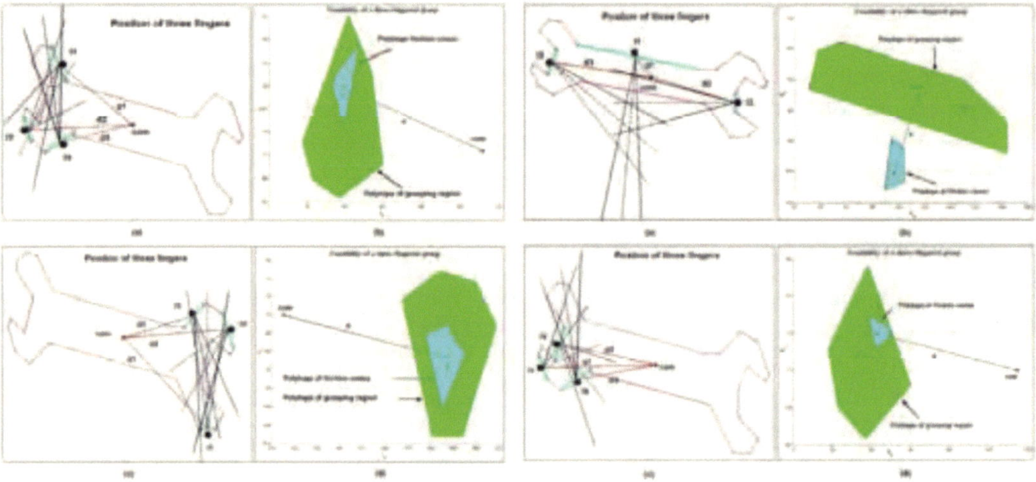

(a) Grasp configuration (**GC**): 1-2 (b) Grasp configuration (**GC**): 3-4

Figure 10. (a) Result of three fingered grasp configuration: 1–4 for object *obj*2

8. References

Allen, P., Miller, A., Oh, P., and Leibowitz, B. (1999). Integration vision, force and tactile sensing for grasping. Int. Journal of Intell. *Mechatronics*, 4(1):129–149. [Allen et al., 1999]

Berger, A. D. and Khosla, P. K. (1991). Using tactile data for real-time feedback. *Int. Journal of Robot. Res.* (IJR'91), 2(10):88–102. [Berger and Khosla, 1991]

Bicchi, A. and Kumar, V. (2000). Robotic grasping and contacts: A review. In *Proceedings of the IEEE International Conference on Robotics and Automation*, pages 348–353. [Bicchi and Kumar, 2000]

Boudaba, M. and Casals, A. (2005). Polyhedral convex cones for computing feasible grasping regions from vision. In *Proc. IEEE Symposium on Computational Intelligence in Robotics and Automation* (CIRA'05), pages 607–613, Helsinki, Finland. [Boudaba and Casals, 2005]

Boudaba, M. and Casals, A. (2006). Grasping of planar obbjects using visual perception. In *Proc. IEEE 6th International Conference on Humanoid Robots* (HUMANOIDS'06), pages 605–611, Genova, Italy. [Boudaba and Casals, 2006]

Boudaba, M., Casals, A., Osswald, D., andWoern, H. (2005). Vision-based grasping point determination on objects grasping by multifingered hands. In *Proc. IEEE 6th International Conference on Field and Service Robotics* (FRS'05), pages 261–272, Australia. [Boudaba et al., 2005]

Canny, J. (1986). A computational approach to edge detection. *IEEE Transaction on Pattern Analysis and Machine Intelligence*, 8(6):679–698. [Canny, 1986]

Chen, N., Rink, R. E., and Zhang, H. (1995). Edge tracking using tactile servo. In *Proc. IEEE/RSJ International Conference on Intelligent Robots and Systems* (IROS'95), pages 84–99. [Chen et al., 1995]

Costa, L. and Cesar, R. (2001). *Shape Analysis and Classification Theory and Practice*. CRC Press, Florida, USA, 1st edition. [Costa and Cesar, 2001]

Ferrari, C. and Canny, J. (1992). Planning optimal grasps. In *Proceedings of the IEEE International Conference on Robotics and Automation*, pages 2290–2295, Nice, France. [Ferrari and Canny, 1992]

Goldman, A. J. and Tucker, A. W. (1956). Polyhedral convex cones, in linear inequalities and related systems. *Annals of Mathematics Studies*, Princeton, 38:19–40. [Goldman and Tucker, 1956]

Hirai, S. (2002). Kinematics of manipulation using the theory of polyhedral convex cones and its application to grasping and assembly operations. *Trans. of the Society of Inst. and Control Eng.*, 2:10–17. [Hirai, 2002]

J. W. Li, M. H. J. and Liu, H. (2003). A new algorithm for three-finger force-closure grasp of polygonal objects. In *Proceedings of the IEEE International Conference on Robotics and Automation*, pages 1800–1804. [J. W. Li and Liu, 2003]

Koller, D., Danilidis, K., and Nagel, H. H. (1993). Model-based object tracking in monocular image sequences of road traffc scenes. *Int. Journal of Comp. Vision* IJCV'93, 3(10):257–281. [Koller et al., 1993]

Kragic, D., Miller, A., and Allen, P. (2001). Real-time tracking meets online grasp planning. In *Proc. IEEE International Conference on Robotics and Automatation* (ICRA'2001), pages 2460–2465, Seoul, Korea. [Kragic et al., 2001]

Lee, M. H. and Nicholls, H. R. (1999). Tactile sensing for mechatronics - a state of the art servey. *Mechatronics*, 9:1–31. [Lee and Nicholls, 1999]

M. Kvasnica, P. Grieder, M. B. F. J. C. (2005). *Multiparametric toolbox, user's guide.* [M. Kvasnica, 2005]

M. Marji, P. S. (2003). A new algorithm for dominant points detection and polygonization of digital curves. *Journal of the Pattern Recognition Society*, 36:2239–2251. [M. Marji, 2003]

Maekawa, H., Tanie, K., and Komoriya, K. (1995). Tactile sensor based manipulation of an unknown object by a multifingered hand with rolling contact. In *Proc. IEEE International Conference on Robotics and Automatation* (ICRA'95), pages 743–750. [Maekawa et al., 1995]

Mokhtarian, F. and Mackworth, A. (1986). Scale-based description and recognition of planar curves and two-dimensional shapes. *IEEE Trans. on Pattern Analysis and Machine Intelligence*, 8:34–43. [Mokhtarian and Mackworth, 1986]

N. Giordana, P. Bouthemy, F. C. and Spindler, F. (2000). Two-dimensional model-based tracking of complex shapes for visual servoing tasks. M. Vincze and G. Hager, editors, Robust vision for vision-based control of motion, pages 67–77. [N. Giordana and Spindler, 2000]

Park, Y. C. and Starr, J. P. (1992). Grasp synthesis of polygonal objects using a three-fingered robot hand. *IEEE International Journal of Robotics Research*, 11(3):163–184. [Park and Starr, 1992]

Ponce, J. and Faverjon, B. (1995). On computing three-finger force-closure grasps of polygonal objects. *Proceedings of the IEEE Transactions on Robotics and Automation*, 11(6):868–881. [Ponce and Faverjon, 1995]

Rosin, P. L. (1997). Techniques for assesing polygonal approximation of curves. *IEEE Trans. on Pattern Analysis and Machine Intell.*, 19:659–666. [Rosin, 1997]

Sanz, P., del Pobil, A., Iesta, J., and Recatal, G. (1998). Vision-guided grasping of unknown objects for service robots. In *Proc. IEEE International Conference on Robotics and Automatation* (ICRA'98), page 30183025, Leuven, Belgium. [Sanz et al., 1998]

Smith, C. and Papanikolopoulos (1996). Vision-guided robotic grasping: Issues and experiments. In *Proc. IEEE International Conference on Robotics and Automatation* (ICRA'96), pages 3203–3208. [Smith and Papanikolopoulos, 1996]

Wunsch, P., Winkler, S., and Hirzinger, G. (1997). Real-time pose estimation of 3d objects from camera images using neural networks. In *Proc. IEEE International Conference on Robotics and Automatation* (ICRA'97), pages 3232–3237. [Wunsch et al., 1997]

5

Behavior-Based Perception for Soccer Robots

Floris Mantz and Pieter Jonker
Delft University of Technology
The Netherlands

1. Introduction

The mission of this chapter is to show the possibility of boosting the performance of the vision system of autonomous perception-based robots, by implementing a behavior based software architecture with multiple independent sense-think-act loops. This research comes forth from a wider view of future robots having layered modular architectures, with higher layers controlling lower layers, in which all parts of the robots tasks (perception, behavior, motion) are behavior specific, and preferably all input-output mappings are learned. The work done in this chapter only focuses on improving the perception of robots. By implementing a behavior-based perception system of a goalie in a team of 4-legged soccer robots, we have increased its performance on localization and goal-clearing with more than 50 %. On top, we have significantly increased the performance of the image processing by making it entirely object specific, with a different color-table and set of grid-lines for each different object searched for. All improvements combined allow the robot to localize in various conditions where this was previously not possible.

2. Layered Modular Architectures

Soccer playing robots as can be found in the RoboCup (www.robocup.org), are the playground to gain experience with embodied intelligence. The software architectures of those robots - that can autonomously survive in a niche of the real physical world; with limited rules necessary to survive, limited physical circumstances to account for, and simple goals to achieve (Pfeifer & Scheier, 1999) - can very well serve as an example for more complex industrial machines such as photocopiers, wafer steppers, component placement machines, CT and MRI scanners. The architecture of those machines is usually built around a single "Sense-Think-Act" loop to allow the machine to perform its task in a physical world. It is quite common that several scientific / technical disciplines, each with its own expertise, cooperate in the design. As a consequence, the most obvious basic architecture is the one as presented in Figure 1, in which for instance an image processing group solves the sense task, the control theory group solves the act task, and an AI group solves the think task. Software engineers and mechanical engineers take the responsibility over the overall software and mechanical hardware design and maintainability, respectively.

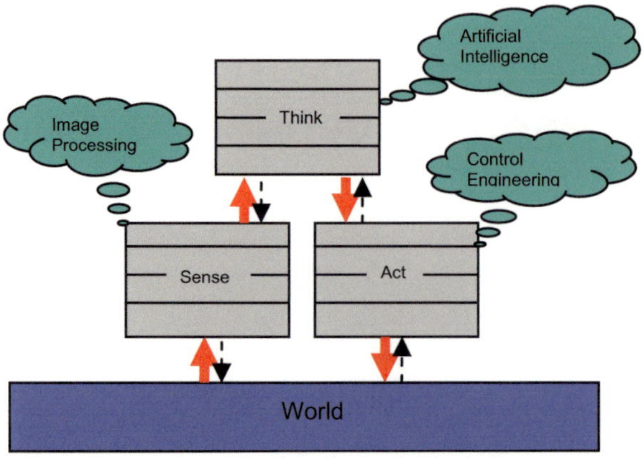

Figure 1. Architecture based on scientific / technical disciplines

Usually after an initial limited architecture phase, the interfaces are quickly established and all groups retract to their own lab to locally optimize their part of the problem, thereby often making assumptions what is c.q. should be done by the other group. In the end, the data is "thrown over the wall" to the other groups, who have to cope with it. As those embedded machines increase in complexity over the years, as well as the demands from the world they operate in, the software and hardware complexity grows, and all groups start to make their sub-system versatile, robust and optimal, and hence increasingly complex for the others to use.

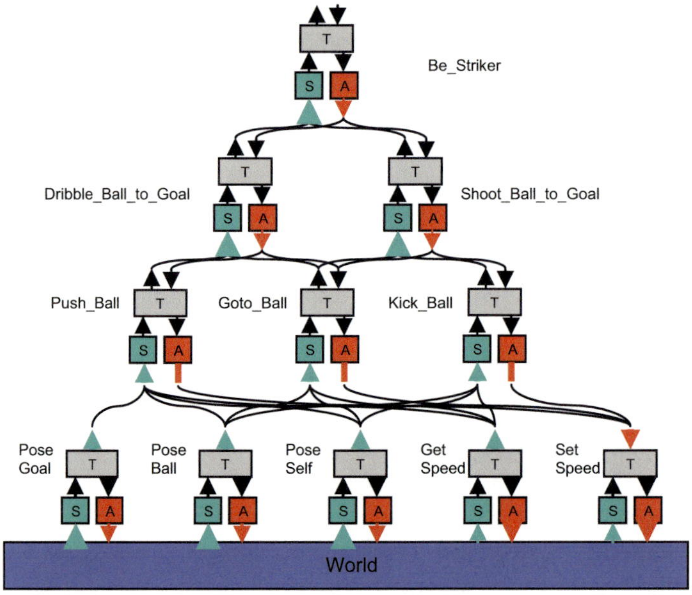

Figure 2. Layered architecture of Sense-Think-Act modules

From 1991 onward it was suggested (Brooks, 1991); (Arkin, 1998); (Parker, 1996) that a different architectural concept should be followed in the sense that a layered modular

architecture should be set-up in which higher layers control the lower layers, either by invocation actions from the lower layers or by promoting or suppressing behaviors from that lower layers. All modules run principally in parallel and on their turn invoke, promote or suppress actions of modules lower in the abstraction hierarchy.
Figure 2 shows the design for a soccer robot, detailed for its role of striker. Figures 3 and 4 show the same hierarchy of figure 2, but now in more detail. Moreover, Figure 3 shows more detail on the behavior (act) part of the hierarchy, whereas Figure 4 shows more detail on the perception (sense) part of the hierarchy.

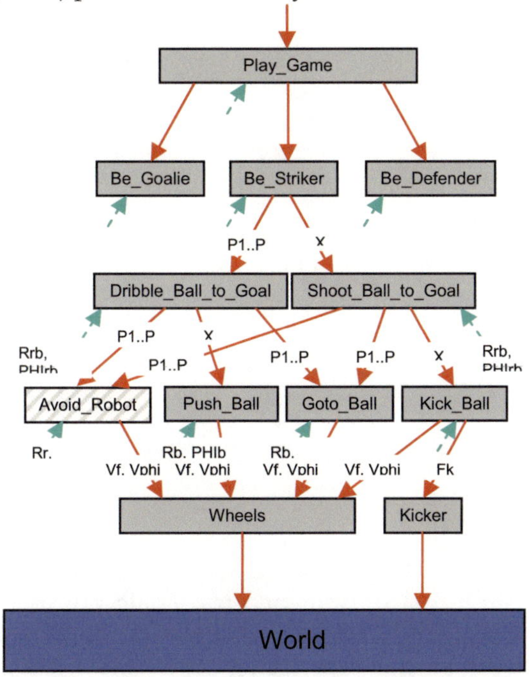

Figure 3. Soccer playing robot in the role of striker; behavior viewpoint

A striker can either dribble or shoot the ball to goal. The striker module decides on the best position (P1...P7) near the goal to dribble the ball to, from where it can successfully execute (X) a shoot to goal. Both for dribbling and shooting it needs to go to the best position behind the ball. For dribbling to goal it needs to push the ball without loosing it (avoiding others); for shooting to goal it needs to execute a kick.
To perform these three behaviors it needs to perceive the pose (position and orientation) of ball and goal with respect to itself, i.e. given by vectors (R, Ø) and to set and measure the forward and angular speed of the robot (Vf,Vø). For kicking one needs to specify the kicking force (F). The pose of ball, goal and itself are measured using the vision system and the odometry (RPM of the wheels for mobile robots or steps for walking robots). Figure 4 shows that all perception modules, e.g. as to mind ones own pose, can be split into a part to discover the pose when the pose is un-known and a module to track the pose when it is well-known.
To program behaviors of an autonomous system that needs to function under all circumstances in any environment, is often similar to maintaining a house of cards. Moreover, as one can not foresee as designer all possible states that the system encounter in

its life, learning the behaviors, e.g. based on reinforcement (Sutton & Barto, 1998); (Takahashi & Asada, 2004) is a valuable solution to overcome and learn from unknown situations. However, when the dimension of input-output / state-action space becomes too high (>8) learning becomes cumbersome (Jonker et al, 2004); (Dietterich, 2000). Hence, even / especially when reinforcement learning methods are used, one should aim for layered, modular "sense-think-act" architectures in which we can learn the basic behaviors and perhaps even the perceptions.

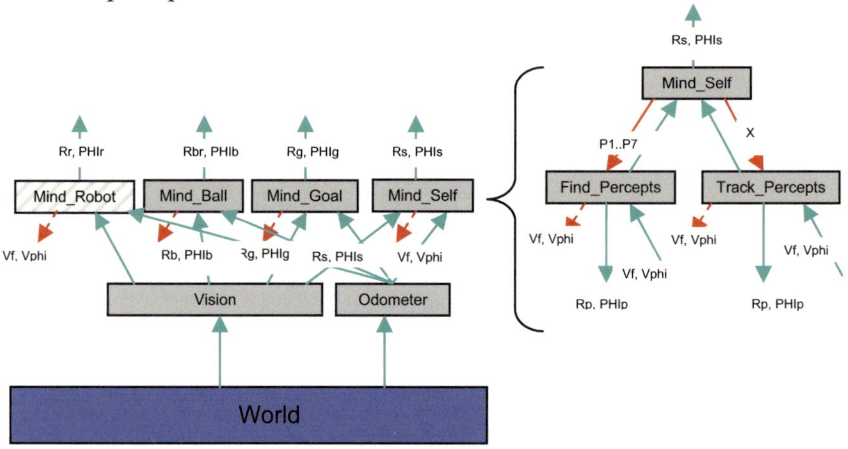

Figure 4. Soccer playing robot in the role of striker; perception viewpoint

3. Behavior Based Perception

In the previous chapter we argued that a layered modular architecture of sense-think-act modules is necessary to obtain robust software and we should prepare for systems that are able to learn their own behavior. In this chapter we will go one step further and argue that the perception modules should even be made specific for the behavior modules they serve. This notion of behavior specific perception modules was developed during a research project at Delft University of Technology (Mantz, 2004) and published before (Mantz et al, 2005).
The perception problem differs widely over different behaviors. At first this has to do with the location of robots. A robot guarding his own goal will mainly see the lines surrounding his penalty area, a couple of flags, and the opponent goal (far away). A striker will mainly see its opponent's goal (from not too far). At second, the perception problem is also greatly influenced by the kind of action the robot performs. When a robot is walking around, with its head at horizons' level, turning from left to right, it will likely perceive many objects and the quality of localization will be high. When the robot e.g. is handling a ball with its head (containing the camera), it will likely perceive neither goals nor flags for a longer period of time, and the quality of perception based localization will be very poor. One general vision system, serving all these behaviors, will be very complex and difficult to understand. It is difficult to oversee how changes, made to the system in order to improve performance in a certain behavior, will influence performance in other behaviors. Also in a general vision system, all algorithms will always be running. Even when not necessary in a specific behavior they will still use resources and limit the available resources for algorithms that do matter.

Because the perception problem can differ so widely over different behaviors, we have developed a software architecture for a team of soccer robots, with a behavior-based hierarchy of modules (Lenser et al, 2002) in which each module is treated and implemented as a separate sense-think-act loop. We will show that this architecture performs similar or better than an architecture based on monolithic discipline based modules, even when we omit learning.

With this new architecture we expect the following improvements:

1. That each (sense-think-act) module is simpler and hence can be better understood and used to design other behaviors (copy-past-modify) by other developers.
2. That effectively less and less complicated, code is running in the new situation then it was in the old situation. The crux in this is that in the old situation the code that was running not always contributed to the behavior, but was merely there for "general-purposeness".
3. That our goalkeeper performs better and more robust because it can use information on its location and behavior (action).

Location and behavior information (point 3) can be used either in improving the self localisation algorithms, which we call behavior specific self localisation or it can directly be used in optimizing the image processing algorithms, which we call behavior-specific image processing. Below we will discuss both options.

3.1 Behavior specific self localisation

With behavior specific self localisation, we make the self localisation algorithms specific for different behaviors. The first reason why behavior-specific self localisation can increase performance, is because it can use information on the kind of action the robot is performing. E.g. when particle filters are used for self localization, one always has to make a trade-off between robustness and speed. If the particles are updated slowly on new sensor inputs, the system is more robust against false sensor inputs. If the particles are updated fast, the system can be accurate despite unmodeled movements, such as uncertainty in odometry evaluation, collisions, or a pickup (kidnap) by the referee. With behavior-specific self localistation we can go for speed or robusness when required. When a robot is positioning (e.g. a goalie standing in the goal, or a field player walking around), the sensor input is qualitatively high and accurate localization is our aim; hence we use a fast update of the particles. When a robot is handling a ball, the sensor input has a low quality and the updating of the robot's pose is less urgent; hence we use a slow update of the particles.

Secondly, behavior-specific self localisation can increase performance by using the location information for a certain behavior. If a postion is already well known, the self locator could (partly) discard percepts indicating a totally different position. The self locator could also directly be told on which percepts it should put more or less emphasis on. E.g. For the goalie, the self localisation could always make less use of perceptions of its own goal. For a striker, the self localisation could put extra emphasis on detections of the opponent's goal.

In most situations, the best way to implement behavior-specific self localisation is to build one general self locator that takes paramters that can be set from the behaviors. These parameters could indicate the overall update rate of all particles, the rate of rejecting outlier measurments, and a weight for each possible detected object (blue goal, yellow goal, lines, blue flag… etc). If the situation or requirement in a certain behavior is really different from that in other behaviors, one could decide to implement an entire new self locator algorithm.

3.2 Behavior specific image processing

With behavior specific image processing, we optimize the image processing algorithms for different behaviors. What the robot can see, highly depends on the robot's location, which is strongly correlated with its behavior. There are several ways in which location information can lead to better localisation.

At first, unexpected objects can be discarded. The great advantage of discarding unexpected objects, is that they can not lead to false positives. We have experienced that many of the localisation problems are not due lack of good measuremenst, but because it thinks it sees objects where they are not (see Figure 5).

Figure 5. False positive. The robot not only detects the yellow goal, but also mistakes some blue in the playing field for a blue goal

Note that discarding unexpected objects could also be done in the self locator. The advantage of discarding them in an earlier stage, i.e. in the image processing stage is that the locator algorithms don't need to be executed, which saves CPU cycles.

Secondly, behavior specific image processing can be used to allow for different detection schemes for the same object, using e.g. distance information. A goalie for example, will see the opponent flag at far distance (fig 6a), while an attacker might come much closer to the same flag (fig 6b). Using different algorithms for the two situations could improve the performance of the detection.

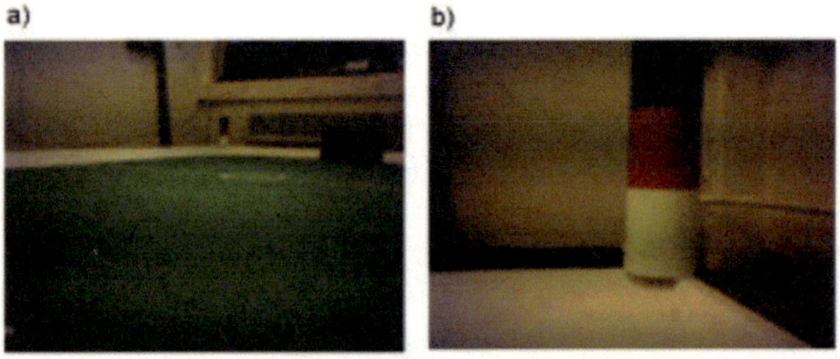

Figure 6. Images of a blue/pink flag; a) at 5 meter distance; b) at 30 cm distance

Finally, we could use image processing algorithms that are even more role c.q. behavior specific. E.g. a goalie could be localising mainly on the detection of the lines surrounding the penalty area. A defender could be localising mainly on the detection of the circle in the middle of the playing field.

The way we have implemented behavior-specific image processing, is by making the image processing completely modular. The detection of a goal, flag, lines or ball are all in separate modules and can be called independently. When an algorithm is called it takes a parameter, indicating e.g. the color of the object (blue/yellow), and the size (far/near). Every cycle, when the central image processing module is called, it will call a set of image processing algorithms, dependent on the behavior. In chapter 6 we will show the other advantages we found by making image processing completely modular.

3.3 Drawbacks of behavior based vision

There are limits and drawbacks to applying multiple sense-think-act loops to the vision system of robots.

The first thing to consider is that the use of location information in the image processing and self localization for discarding unexpected objects, gives rise to the chance of entering a local loop: when the robot would discard information based on a wrong assumption of its own position, it could happen the robot would not be able to retrieve its correct position. For avoiding local loops, periodic checking mechanisms on the own position are required (on a lower pace). Also one could restrict the runtime of behaviors in which much information is discarded and invoke some relocation behavior to be executed periodically.

The second drawback is, that due to less reusability, and more implementations of optimized code, the overall size of the system will grow. This influences the time it will take to port code to a new robot, or to build new robot-software from scratch.

The third drawback is that for every improvement of the system (for every sense-think-act loop), some knowledge is needed of the principles of image processing, mechanical engineering, control theory, AI and software engineering. Because of this, behavior-designers will probably reluctant to use the behavior-specific vision system. Note, however, that even if behavior designer are not using behavior-dependent vision, the vision system can still be implemented. In worst case a behavior designer can choose to select the general version of the vision system for all behaviors, and the performance will be the same as before.

4. Algorithms in old software

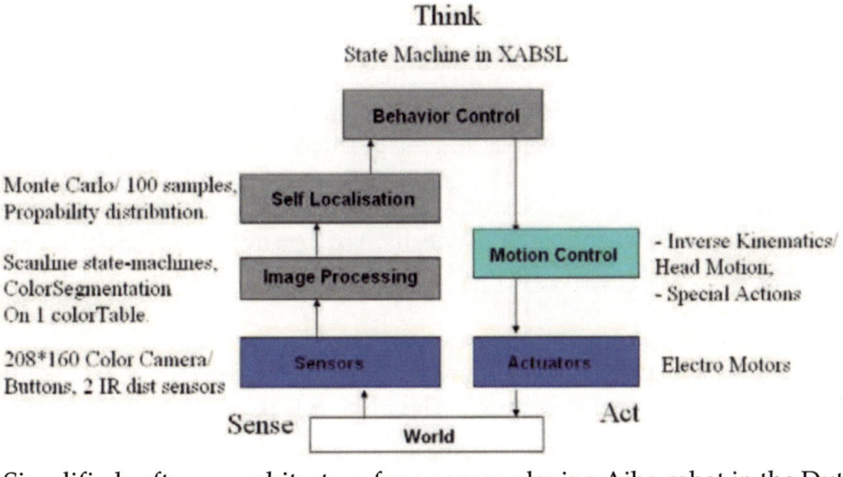

Figure 7. Simplified software architecture for a soccer-playing Aibo robot in the Dutch Aibo Team

In this paragraph, an overview will be given of the software architecture of soccer robots (Sony Aibo ERS-7) in the Dutch Aibo Team (Oomes et al, 2004), which was adapted in 2004 from the code of the German Team of 2003 (Rofer et al, 2003). This software was used as a starting point for implementing the behavior-based vision system as is described in the next paragraph. The DT2004 software was also used for testing the performance of new systems.
In Fig 7. A simplified overview of the DT2004 software architecture is depicted. The architecture can be seen as one big sense-think-act loop. Sensor measurements are processed by, Image Processing, Self Localisation, Behavior Control and Motion Control sequentially, in order to plan the motions of the actuators. Note that this simplified architecture only depicts the modules most essential to our research. Other modules, e.g. for detecting obstacles or other players, and modules for controlling LEDs and generating sounds, are omitted from the picture.

4.1 Image Processing

The image processing is the software that generates percepts (such as goals, flags, lines and the ball) from the sensor input (camera images). In the DT2004 software, the image processing uses a grid-based state machine (Bruce et al, 2000), with segmentation primarily done on color and secondarily by shapes of objects.

Using a color table

A camera image consists of 208*160 pixels. Each of these pixels has a three-dimensional value p(Y,U,V). Y represents the intensity; U and V contain color-information; each having an integer value between 0 and 254. In order to simplify the image processing problem, all these 254*254*254 possible pixel-values are mapped onto only 10 possible colors: white, black, yellow, blue, sky-blue, red, orange, green, grey and pink, the possible colors of objects in the playing field. This mapping makes use of a color-table, a big 3-dimensional matrix which stores which pixel-value corresponds to which color. This color-table is calibrated manually before a game of soccer.

Grid-based image processing

The image processing is grid-based. For every image, first the horizon is calculated from the known angles of the head of the robot. Then a number of scan-lines is calculated perpendicular to that horizon. Each scan-line then is then scanned for sequences of colored-pixels. When a certain sequence of pixels indicates a specific object, the pixel is added to a cluster for that possible object. Every cluster will be evaluated to finally determine whether or not an object was detected. This determination step uses shape information, such as the width and length of the detected cluster, and the position relative to the robot.
Grid-based image processing is useful not only because it processes only a limited number of pixels, saving CPU cycles, but also that each image is scanned relative to the horizon. Therefore processing is independent of the position of the robots' head (which varies widely for an Aibo Robot).

4.2 Self Localisation

The self localisation is the software that obtains the robot's pose (x,y, ø) from output of the image processing, i.e. the found percepts. The approach used in the Dutch Aibo Team is particle filtering, or Monte Carlo Localization, a probability-based method (Thrun, 2002); (Thrun et al, 2001); (Röfer & Jungel, 2003). The self locator keeps tracks of a number of particles, e.g. 50 or 100.

Each particle basically consists of a possible pose of the robot, and of a probability. Each processing cycle consists of two steps, updating the particles and re-sampling them. The updating step starts by moving all particles in the direction that the robot has moved (odometry), adding a random offset. Next, each particle updates its probability using information on percepts (flags, goals, lines) generated by the image processing. Also in this step the pose of the particles can be slightly updated, e.g. using the calculated distance to the nearest lines. In the second step, all particles are re-sampled. Particles with high probabilities are multiplied; particles with low probabilities are removed.
A representation of all 50 particles is depicted in figure 8.

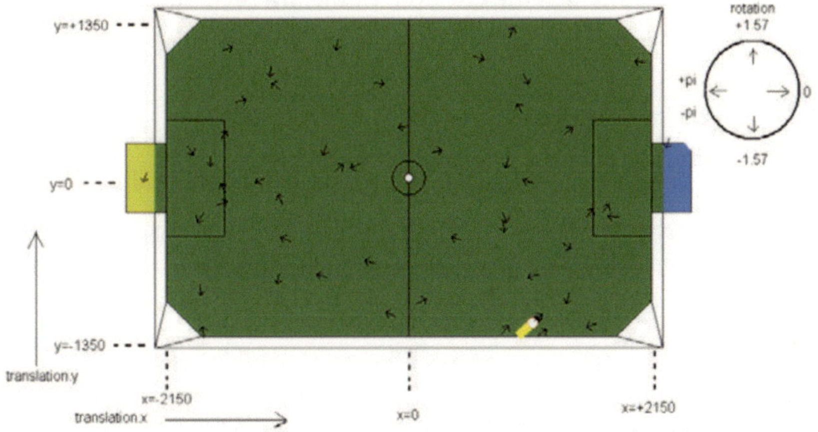

Figure 8. The self localization at initialization; 100 samples are randomly divided over the field. Each sample has a position x, y, and heading in absolute playing-field coordinates. The robot's pose (yellow robot) is evaluated by averaging over the largest cluster of samples.

4.3 Behavior Control

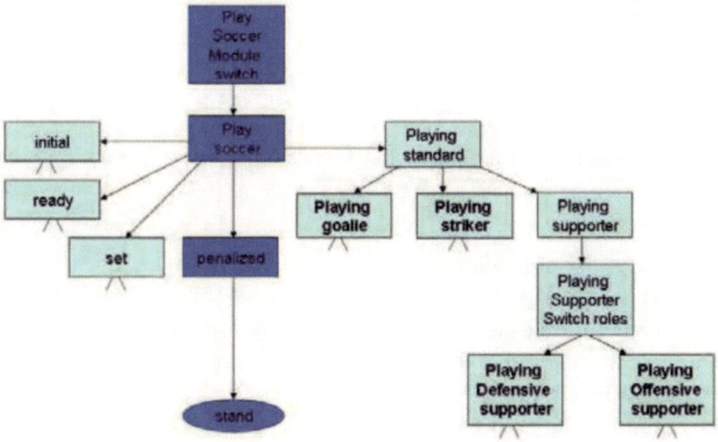

Figure 9. General simplified layout of the first layers of the behavior Architecture of the DT2004-soccer agent. The rectangular shapes indicate options; the circular shape indicates a basic behavior. When the robot is in penalized state and standing, all the dark-blue options are active

Behavior control can be seen as the upper command of the robot. As input, behavior control takes high level information about the world, such as the own pose, the position of the ball and of other players. Dependent on its state, behavior control will then give commands to motion control, such as walk with speed x, look to direction y, ... Behavior control in the DT2004 software is implemented as one gigantic state machine, written in XABSL (Lötzsch et al, 2004), an XML based behavior description language. The state machine distinguishes between options, states and basic behaviors. Each option is a separate XABSL file. Within one option, the behavior control can be in different states. E.g. in Figure 9, the robot is in the penalized state of the *play soccer* option, and therefore calls the penalized option. Basic behaviors are those behaviors that directly control the low level motion. The *stand* behavior in Figure 9 is an example of a basic behavior.

4.4 Motion control

Motion control is the part that calculates the joint-values of the robots joints. Three types of motion can be identified in the DT2004 software:

- Special actions

A special action is a predefined set of joint-values that is executed sequentially, controlling both leg and head joints. All kicking motions, get-up actions and other special movements are special actions.

- Walking engine

All walking motions make use of an inverse kinematics walking engine. The engine takes a large set of parameters (approx. 20) that result in walking motions. These parameters can be changed by the designer. The walking engine mainly controls the leg joints.

- Head motion

The head joints are controlled by head control, independently from the leg joints. The head motions are mainly (combinations of) predefined loops of head joint values. The active head motion can be controlled by behavior control.

5. Behavior-Based perception for a goalie

This paragraph describes our actual implementation of the behavior-based vision system for a goalie in the Dutch Aibo Team. It describes the different sense-think-act loops identified, and the changes made in the image processing and self localisation for each loop. All changes were implemented starting with the DT2004 algorithms, described in the previous paragraph.

5.1 Identified behaviors for a goalie.

For the goalkeeper role of the robot we have identified three different mayor behaviors, which each will be implemented as a separate sense-think-act loops. When the goalie is not in its goal (Figure 11a), it will return to its goal using the *return-to-goal* behavior. When there is no ball in the penalty area (Figure 11b) , the robot will position itself between the ball and the goal, or in the center of the goal when there is no ball in sight. For this the goalie will call the *position* behavior. When there is a ball in the penalty area (Figure 11c), the robot will call the *clear-ball* behavior to remove the ball from the penalty area. Figure 10 shows the software architecture for the goalie, in which different vision and localisation algorithms are called for the different behaviors. The 3 behaviors are controlled by a meta-behavior (Goalie in

Figure 10) that may invoke them. We will call this meta-behavior the goalie's governing behavior.

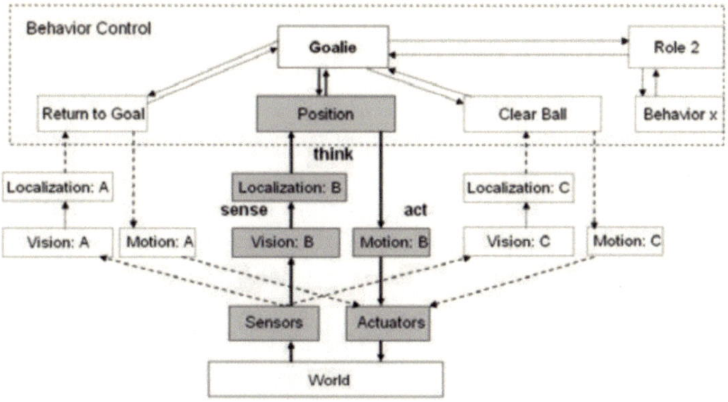

Figure 10. Cut-out of the hierarchy of behaviors of a soccer robot, with emphasis on the goalkeeper role. Each behavior (e.g. *position*) is an independently written sense-think-act loop

a) b) c)

Figure 11. Basic goalie behaviors: a) Goalie-return-to goal, b) Goalie-position, c) Goalie-clear ball. For each behavior a different vision system is used and a different particle filter setting

5.2 Specific perception used for each behavior.

For each of the 3 behaviors, identified in Figures 10 and 11, we have adapted both the image processing and self localization algorithms in order to improve localization performance.

- **Goalie-return-to-goal**. When the goalie is not in his goal area, he has to return to it. The goalie walks around scanning the horizon. When he has determined his own position on the field, the goalie tries to walk straight back to goal - avoiding obstacles - keeping an eye on his own goal. The perception algorithms greatly resemble the ones of the general image processor, with some minor adjustments.

Image-processing searches for the own goal, line-points, border-points and the two corner flags near the own goal. The opponent' goal and flags are ignored.

For localisation, an adjusted version of the old DT2004 particle filter is used, in which a detected own goal is used twice when updating the particles.

- **Goalie- position**. The goalie is in the centre of its goal when no ball is near. It sees the field-lines of the goal area often and at least one of the two nearest corner flags regularly. Localisation is mainly based of the detection of the goal-lines; the flags are used only to correct if the estimated orientation is off more than 45^0 off. This is necessary because the robot has no way (yet) to distinguish between the four lines surrounding the goal.

Image processing is used to detect the lines of the goal-area and for detecting the flags. The distance and angle to goal-lines are detected by applying a Hough transform on detected line-points.
For the detection of the own flags a normal flag detection algorithm is used, with the adjustment that too small flags are rejected, since the flags are expected relatively near.
For self localization, a special particle filter was used that localized only on the detected lines and flags. A background process verifies the "in goal" assumption on the average number of detected lines and flags.

- **Goalie-clear-ball**. If the ball enters the goal area, the goalie will clear the ball.

The image processing in this behavior is identical to that in the *goalie-position* behavior. The goalie searches for the angles and distances to the goal-lines, and detects the flags nearest to the own goal.
However, the self localization for the *clear_ball* behavior is different from that of the *position* behavior. When the goalie starts clearing the ball, the quality of the perception input will be very low. We have used this information, both for processing detected lines, and for processing detected flag.
For flags we have used a lower update rate: it will take longer before the detection of flags at a different orientation will result in the robot changing its pose. Lines detected at far off angles or distances, resulting in a far different robot-pose, are ignored. The reason for this mainly is that while clearing the ball, the goalie could come outside its' penalty area. In this case we don't want the robot to mistake a border line or the middle-line for a line belonging to the goal area.
When the goalie clears a ball, there is no checking mechanism to check the "in goal" assumption, as was in the *position* behavior. When the goalie has finished clearing the ball and has returned to the *position* behavior, this assumption will be checked again.

6. Object-Specific Image Processing

In other to enable behavior-dependent image processing, we have split up the vision system into a separate function per object to detect. We have distinguished between types of objects, (goals, flags), color of objects (blue/yellow goal), and take a parameter indicating the size of the objects (far/near flag). In stead of using one general grid and one color table for detecting all objects (Figure 12 left), we define a specific grid and specific color-table for each object (Figure 12 right).
For example, for detecting a yellow/pink flag (Figure 13b), the image is scanned only above the horizon, limiting the used processing power and reducing the chance on an error. For detecting the lines or the ball, we only can scan the image below the horizon (Figure 13a).
For each object we use a specific color-table (CT). In general, CTs have to be calibrated (Bruce at al, 2000). Here we only calibrated the CT for the 2 or 3 colors necessary for segmentation. This procedure greatly reduces the problem of overlapping colors. Especially in less well lighted conditions, some colors that are supposed to be different appear with identical Y,U,V values in the camera image. An example of this can be seen in Figures 14a-f.
When using object-specific color tables, we don't mind that parts of the "green" playing field have identical values as parts of the "blue" goal. When searching for lines, we define the whole of the playing field as green (Figure 14e). When searching for blue goals, we define the whole goal as blue (Figure 14c). A great extra advantage of having object-specific

color-tables is that it takes much less time to calibrate them. Making a color table as in Figure 14b, which has to work for all algorithms, can take a very long time.

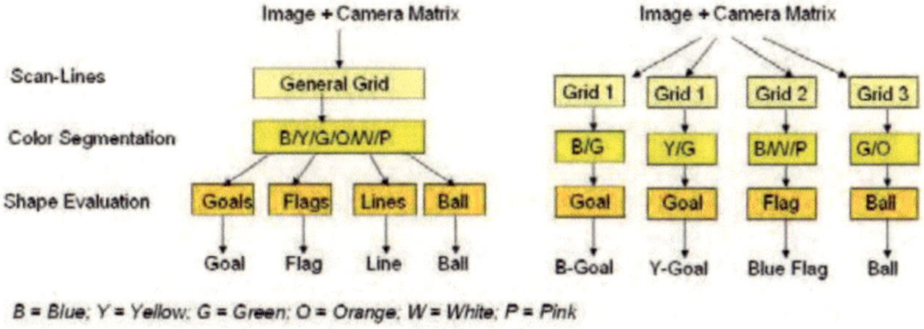

Figure 12. General versus object-specific image processing. Left one can see the general image processing. A single grid and color-table is used for detecting all candidates for all objects. In the modular image processing (right), the entire process of image processing is object specific

a) b) c)

Figure 13. Object-specific image processing: a) for line detection we scan the image below the horizon, using a green-white color table; b) for yellow flag detection we scan above the horizon using a yellow-white-pink color table; c) 2 lines and 1 flag detected in the image

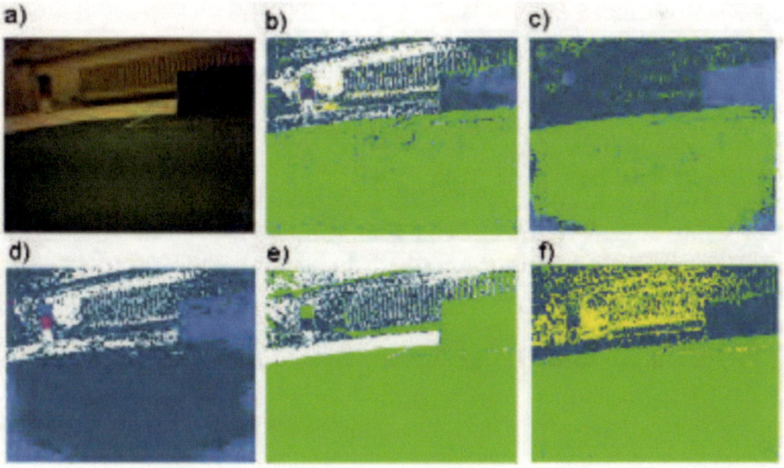

Figure 14. a) camera image; b) segmented with a general color-table; c) segmented with a blue/green color-table; d) segmented with a blue/white/pink color-table for the detection of a blue flag; e) segmented with a green/white color-table; f) segmented with a yellow/green color-table for the detection of the yellow goal

7. Performance Measurements

7.1 General setup of the measurements

In order to prove our hypothesis that a goalie with a behavior-based vision system is more robust, we have performed measurements on the behavior of our new goalie.

The localisation performance is commonly evaluated in terms of accuracy and/or reactiveness of localisation in test environments dealing with noisy (Gaussian) sensor-measurements (Röfer & Jungel, 2003). We, however, are interested mainly in terms of the system's reliability when dealing with more serious problems such as large amounts of false sensor data input, or limited amounts of correct sensor input.

The ultimate test is how much goals does the new goalie prevent under game conditions in comparison with the old goalie? Due to the hassle and chaotic play around the goal when there is an attack, the goalie easily loses track of where he is. So our ultimate test is now twofold:

1. How fast can the new goalie find back his position in the middle of the goal on a crowded field in comparison with the old goalie
2. How many goals can the new goalie prevent on a crowded field within a certain time slot in comparison with the old goalie

All algorithms for the new goalie are made object specific, as described in chapter 4. Since we also want to know the results of using behavior-based perception, results of all real-world scenarios are compared not only to results obtained with the DT2004 system, but also with a general vision system that does implement all object-specific algorithms.

The improvements due to object-specific algorithms are also tested offline on sets of images.

7.2 Influence of Object-Specific Image Processing

We have compared the original DT2004 image processing with a general version of our NEW image processing; meaning that the latter does not (yet) use behavior specific image processing nor self-localization. In contrast with the DT2004 code, the NEW approach does use object specific grids and color tables. Our tests consisted of, searching for the 2 goals, the 4 flags, and all possible line- and border-points. The images sequences were captured with the robot's camera, under a large variety of lighting conditions (Figure 15). A few images from all but one of these lighting condition sequences were used to calibrate the Color-Tables (CTs). For the original DT2004 code, a single general CT was calibrated for all colors that are meaningful in the scene, i.e.: blue, yellow, white, green, orange and pink. This calibration took three hours. For the NEW image processing code we calibrated five 3-color CTs (for the white-on-green lines, blue-goal, blue-flag, yellow-goal, and yellow-flag respectively). This took only one hour for all tables, so 30% of the original time.

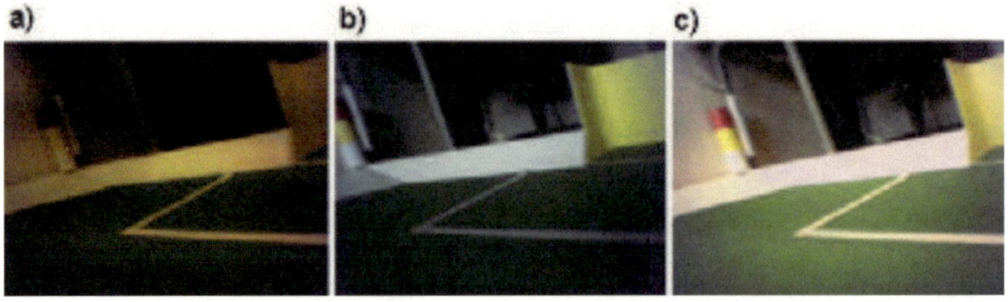

Figure 15. Images taken by the robots camera under different lighting conditions: a) Tube-light; b) Natural-light; c) Tube-light + 4 floodlights + natural light.

For all image sequences that we had acquired, we have counted the number of objects that were detected correctly (N true) and detected falsely (N false). We have calculated also the correctly accepted rate (CAR) being the number of objects that were correctly detected divided by the number of objects that were in principle visible. Table 1 shows the results on detecting flags and lines. The old DT2004 image processor uses a general grid and a single color table, the NEW modular image processor uses object-specific grids and color-tables per object. The calculation of the correctly accepted rate is based on 120 flags/goals that were in principle visible in the first 5 image sequences and 360 flags/goals in principle visible in the set where no calibration settings were made for. The image sequences for line detection each contained on average 31-33 line-points per frame.

Goals and flags	DT2004			NEW			DT2004	NEW
	N true	CAR (%)	N false	N true	CAR (%)	N false	Lines (%)	Lines (%)
1 flood light	23	19	0	65	54	0	18	94
Tube light	54	45	9	83	83	1	58	103
4 flood lights	86	72	0	99	99	0	42	97
Tube +flood lights	41	34	1	110	92	0	24	91
Tube,flood+natural	39	33	0	82	68	0	42	91
Natural light	47	39	0	68	57	0		
Non calibration set	131	44	28	218	73	16		

Table 1. The influence of object-specific algorithms for goal, flag and line detection

Table 1 shows that due to using object specific grids and color tables, the performance of the image processing largely increased. The correctly accepted rate (CAR) goes up from about 45 % to about 75%, while the number of false positives is reduced. Moreover, it takes less time to calibrate the color-tables. The correctly accepted rate of the line detection even goes up to over 90%, also when a very limited amount of light is available (1 Flood light).

7.4 Influence of behavior based perception

In the previous tests we have shown the improvement due to the use of object specific grids and color tables. Below we show the performance improvement due to behavior based switching of the image processing and the self localization algorithm (the particle filter). We used the following real-world scenarios.

- Localize in the penalty area. The robot is put into the penalty area and has to return to a predefined spot as many times as possible within 2 minutes.
- Return to goal. The robot is manually put onto a predefined spot outside the penalty area and has to return to the return-spot as often as possible within 3 minutes.
- Clear ball. The robot starts in the return spot; the ball is manually put in the penalty area every time the robot is in the return spot. It has to clear the ball as often as possible in 2 minutes.
- Clear ball with obstacles on the field. We have repeated the clear ball tests but then with many strange objects and robots placed in the playing field, to simulate a more natural playing environment.

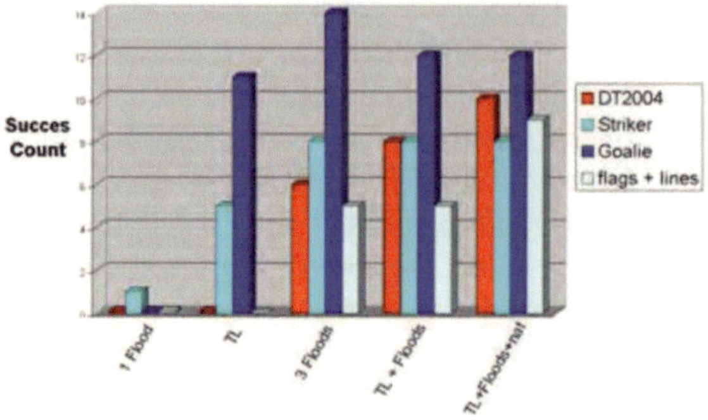

Figure 16. Results for localisation in the penalty area. The number of times the robot can re-localise in the penalty area within 2 minutes. The old DT2004 vision system cannot localise when there is little light (TL). The performance of the object specific image processing (without specific self localisation) is shown by the "flags and lines" bars. In contrast with the DT2004 code, the striker uses object specific image processing. The goalie uses object specific image processing, behavior based image processing and behavior based self localisation

In order to be able to distinguish between the performance increase due to object-specific grids and color-tables, and the performance increase due to behavior-dependent image processing and self localisation, we used 3 different configurations.

- DT2004: The old image processing code with the old general particle filter.
- Striker: The new object-specific image processing used in combination with the old general particle filter of which the settings are not altered during the test.
- Goalie: The new object-specific image processing used in combination with object-specific algorithms for detecting the field lines, and with a particle filter of which the settings are altered during the test, depending on the behavior that is executed (as described in chapter 5).

The results can be found in Figures 16-19.

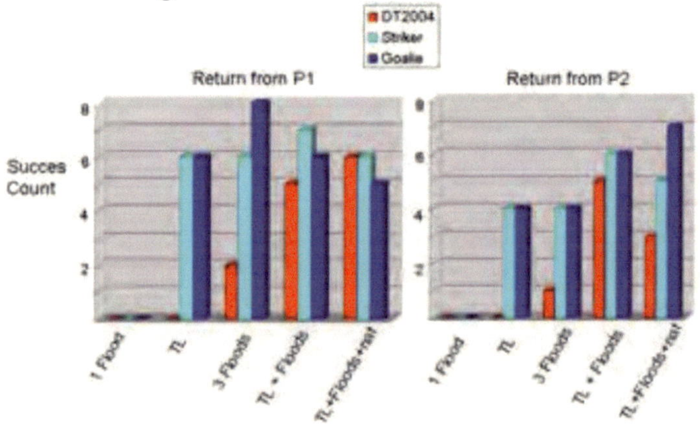

Figure 17. Results of the return to goal test. The robot has to return to its own goal as many times as possible within 3 minutes. The striker vision systems works significantly better than the DT2004 vision system. There is not a very significant difference in overall performance between the striker (no behavior-dependence) and the goalie (behavior dependence). This shows that the checking mechanism of the "in goal" assumption works correctly

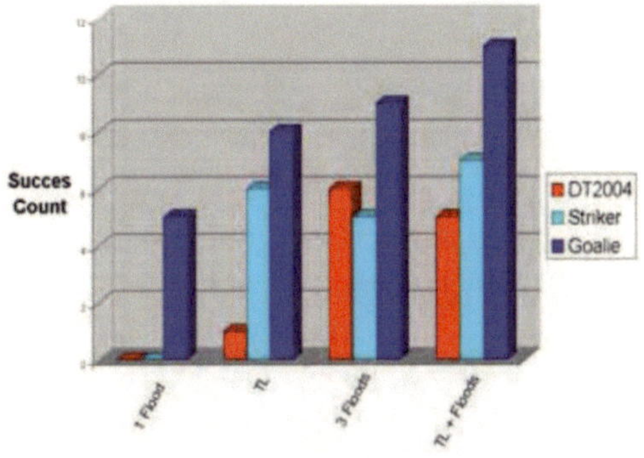

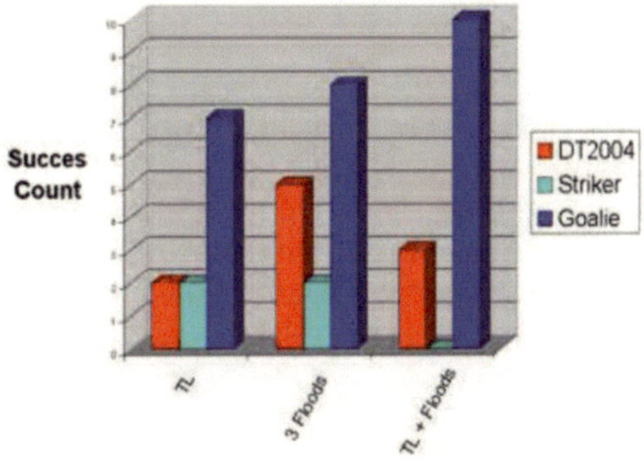

Figure 18. (left). Results of the clear ball test. The robot has to clear the ball from the goal area as often as he can in 2 minutes. Both the striker and the goalie vision systems are more robust in a larger variety of lighting conditions than the DT2004 vision system (that uses a single color table). The goalie's self-locator, using detected lines and the yellow flags, works up to 50 % better than the striker self-locator, which locates on all line-points, all flags and goals

Figure 18 (right). Results of the clear ball with obstacles on the field test. The goalie vision system, which uses location information to disregard blue flags/goals and only detects large yellow flags, is very robust when many unexpected obstacles are visible in or around the playing field.

8. Results

- The impact of behavior-based perception can be seen from the localization test in the penalty area (Figure 16) and from the clear-ball tests (Figure 18). The vision system of the *goalie*, with behavior based vision and self localisation, performs > 50 % better on the same task as a *striker* robot with a vision system without behavior-based perception.
- With object-specific grids and color-tables, the performance of the image processing (reliability) under variable lighting conditions has increased with 75-100% on sets of off-line images, while the color calibrating time was reduced to 30%.
- Behavior-based perception and object-specific image processing combined allows for localization in badly lighted conditions, e.g. with TL tube light only (Figure 16-18).
- The impact of discarding unexpected objects on the reliability of the system can most clearly be seen from the clear ball behavior test with obstacles on the field (Figure 18, right). With TL + Floods, the striker apparently sees unexpected objects and is unable to localize, whereas the goalie can localize in all situations.
- Using all object specific image processing algorithms at the same time requires the same CPU load as the old general DT2004 image processor. Searching for a limited number of objects in a specific behavior can therefore reduce the CPU load considerably.
- Due to the new architecture, the code is more clean and understandable; hence better maintainable and extendable. The main drawback is that one has to educate complete system engineers instead of sole image processing, software, AI, and mechanical experts.

9. References

Arkin, R.C. (1998). *Behavior based robotics*, MIT press, ISBN 0-262-01165-4

Brooks, R.A. (1991). Intelligence without Representation. *Artificial Intelligence*, Vol.47, 1991, pp.139-159.

Bruce, J.; Balch, T. & Veloso, M (2000). Fast and inexpensive color image segmentation for interactive robots. In *Proceedings of the 2000 IEEE/RSJ International Conference on Intelligent Robots and Systems (IROS '00)*, volume 3, pages 2061-2066.

Dietterich, T.G (2000). Hierarchical reinforcement learning with the MAXQ value function decomposition. *Journal of Artificial Intelligence Research*, 13:227-303, 2000

Jonker, P.P.; Terwijn, B; Kuznetsov, J & van Driel, B (2004). The Algorithmic foundation of the Clockwork Orange Robot Soccer Team, WAFR '04 (*Proc. 6th Int. Workshop on the Algorithmic Foundations of Robotics*, Zeist/Utrecht, July), 2004, 1-10.

Lenser, S; Bruce, J & Veloso (2002). M. A Modular Hierarchical Behavior-Based Architecture, in *RoboCup-2001*, Springer Verlag, Berlin, 2002.

Lötzsch, M.; Back, J.; Burkhard H-D & Jüngel, M (2004). Designing agent behavior with the extensible agent behavior specification language XABSL. In: *7th International Workshop on Robocup 2003* (Robot World Cup Soccer Games and Conferences in Artificial Intelligence, Padova, Italy, 2004.

Mantz, F. (2005). *A* behavior-based vision system on a legged robot. *MSc Thesis*, Delft University of Technology, Delft, the Netherlands.

Mantz, F; Jonker, P; Caarls W (2005); Behavior-based vision on a 4-Legged Soccer Robot. *Robocup 2005*, p. 480-487

Oomes, S; Jonker, P.P; Poel, M; Visser, A & Wiering, M (2004). The Dutch AIBO Team 2004, *Proc. Robocup 2004 Symposium* (July 4-5, Lisboa, Portugal, Instituto Superior Tecnico, 2004, 1-5. see also http://aibo.cs.uu.nl

Parker, L.E. (1996). On the design of behavior-based multi-robot teams. *Journal of Advanced Robotics*, 10(6).

Pfeifer, R & Scheier, C (1999). *Understanding Intelligence*. The MIT Press, Cambridge, Massechussets, ISBN 0-262-16181-8.

Röfer, T, von Stryk, O, Brunn, R; Kallnik, M and many other (2003). *German Team 2003. Technical report* (178 pages, only available online: http://www. Germanteam.org/GT2003.pdf)

Röfer, T. & Jungel, M. (2003). Vision-based fast and reactive monte-carlo localization. *In The IEEE International Conference on Robotics and Automation*, pages 856-861, 2003, Taipei, Taiwan.

Sutton, R.S & Barto, A.G (1998). *Reinforcement learning – an introduction.*, MIT press, 1998. ISBN 0-262-19398-1.

Takahashi, Y & Asada, M (2004). *Modular Learning Systems for Soccer Robot* (Takahashi04d.pdf). 2004, Osaka, Japan.

Thrun, S.; Fox, D.; Burgard, W & Dellaert (2001), F. Robust monte carlo localization for mobile robots. *Journal of Artificial Intelligence*, Vol. 128, nr 1-2, page 99-141, 2001, ISSN:0004-3702

Thrun, S. (2002). Particle filters in robotics. *In The 17th Annual Conference on Uncertainty in AI (UAI)*, 2002

6

A Real-Time Framework for the Vision Subsystem in Autonomous Mobile Robots

Paulo Pedreiras[1], Filipe Teixeira[2], Nelson Ferreira[2], Luís Almeida[1], Armando Pinho[1] and Frederico Santos[3]
[1]*LSE-IEETA/DETI, Universidade de Aveiro, Aveiro*
[2]*DETI, Universidade de Aveiro, Aveiro*
[3]*DEE, Instituto Politécnico de Coimbra, Coimbra*
Portugal

1. Introduction

Interest on using mobile autonomous agents has been growing (Weiss, G., 2000), (K. Kitano; Asada, M.; Kuniyoshi, Y.; Noda, I. & Osawa E., 1997) due to their capacity to gather information on their operating environment in diverse situations, from rescue to demining and security. In many of these applications, the environments are inherently unstructured and dynamic, and the agents depend mostly on visual information to perceive and interact with the environment. In this scope, computer vision in a broad sense can be considered as the key technology for deploying systems with an higher degree of autonomy, since it is the basis for activities like object recognition, navigation and object tracking.

Gathering information from such type of environments through visual perception is an extremely processor-demanding activity with hard to predict execution times (Davison, J., 2005). To further complicate the situation many of the activities carried out by the mobile agents are subject to real-time requirements with different levels of criticality, importance and dynamics. For instance, the capability to timely detect obstacles near the agent is a hard activity, since failures can result in injured people or damaged equipment, while activities like self-localization, although important for the agent performance, are inherently soft since extra delays in these activities simply cause performance degradation. Therefore, the capability to timely process the image at rates high enough to allow visual-guided control or decision-making, called real-time computer vision (RTCV) (Blake, A; Curwen, R. & Zisserman, A., 1993), plays a crucial role in the performance of mobile autonomous agents operating in open and dynamic environments.

This chapter describes a new architectural solution for the vision subsystem of mobile autonomous agents that substantially improves its reactivity by dynamically assigning computational resources to the most important tasks. The vision-processing activities are broken into separated elementary real-time tasks, which are then associated with adequate real-time properties (e.g. priority, activation rate, precedence constraints). This separation allows avoiding the blocking of higher priority tasks by lower priority ones as well as to set independent activation rates, related with the dynamics of the features or objects being processed, together with offsets that de-phase the activation instants of the tasks to further

reduce mutual interference. As a consequence it becomes possible to guarantee the execution of critical activities and privilege the execution of others that, despite not critical, have large impact on the robot performance.
The framework herein described is supported by three custom services:

- Shared Data Buffer (SDB), allowing different processes to process in parallel a set of image buffers;
- Process Manager (PMan), which carries out the activation of the vision-dependent real-time tasks;
- Quality of Service manager (QoS), which dynamically updates the real-time properties of the tasks.

The SDB service keeps track of the number of processes that are connected to each image buffer. Buffers may be updated only when there are no processes attached to them, thus ensuring that processes have consistent data independently of the time required to complete the image analysis.
The process activation is carried out by a PMan service that keeps, in a database, the process properties, e.g. priority, period and phase. For each new image frame, the process manager scans the database, identifies which processes should be activated and sends them wake-up signals. This framework allows reducing the image processing latency, since processes are activated immediately upon the arrival of new images. Standard OS services are used to implement preemption among tasks.
The QoS manager monitors continuously the input data and updates the real-time properties (e.g. the activation rate) of the real-time tasks. This service permits to adapt the computational resources granted to each task, assuring that in each instant the most important ones, i.e. the ones that have a greater value for the particular task being carried out, receive the best possible QoS.
The performance of the real-time framework herein described is assessed in the scope of the CAMBADA middle-size robotic soccer team, being developed at the University of Aveiro, Portugal, and its effectiveness is experimentally proven.

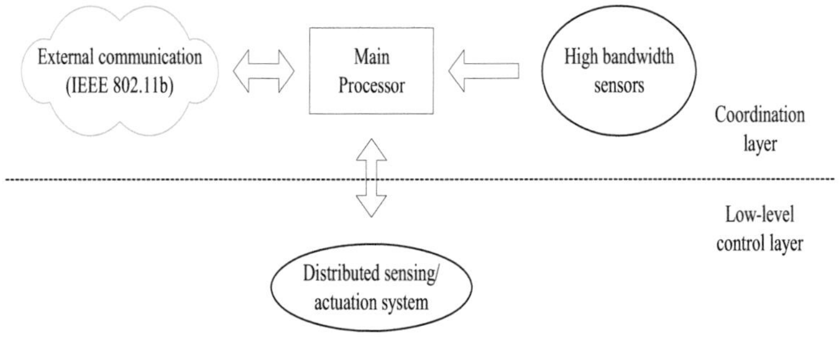

Figure 1. The biomorphic architecture of the CAMBADA robotic agents

The remainder of this chapter is structured as follows: Section 2 presents the generic computing architecture of the CAMBADA robots. Section 3 shortly describes the working-principles of the vision-based modules and their initial implementation in the CAMABADA robots. Section 4 describes the new modular architecture that has been devised to enhance the temporal behavior of the image-processing activities. Section 5 presents experimental results and assesses the benefits of the new architecture. Finally, Section 6 concludes the chapter.

2. The CAMBADA Computing Architecture

2.1 Background

Coordinating several autonomous mobile robotic agents in order to achieve a common goal is currently a topic of intense research (Weiss, G., 2000), (K. Kitano; Asada, M.; Kuniyoshi, Y.; Noda, I. & Osawa E., 1997). One initiative to promote research in this field is RoboCup (K. Kitano; Asada, M.; Kuniyoshi, Y.; Noda, I. & Osawa E., 1997), a competition where teams of autonomous robots have to play soccer matches.

As for many real-world applications, robotic soccer players are autonomous mobile agents that must be able to navigate in and interact with their environment, potentially cooperating with each other. The RoboCup soccer playfield resembles human soccer playfields, though with some (passive) elements specifically devoted to facilitate the robots navigation. In particular the goals have solid and distinct colors and color-keyed posts are placed in each field corner. This type of environment can be classified as a passive information space (Gibson, J., 1979). Within an environment exhibiting such characteristics, robotic agents are constrained to rely heavily on visual information to carry out most of the necessary activities, leading to a framework in which the vision subsystem becomes an integral part of the close-loop control. In these circumstances the temporal properties of the image-processing activities (e.g. period, jitter and latency) have a strong impact on the overall system performance.

2.2 The CAMBADA robots computing architecture

The computing architecture of the robotic agents follows the biomorphic paradigm (Assad, C.; Hartmann, M. & Lewis, M., 2001), being centered on a main processing unit (the brain) that is responsible for the higher-level behavior coordination (Figure 1). This main processing unit handles external communication with other agents and has high bandwidth sensors (the vision) directly attached to it. Finally, this unit receives low bandwidth sensing information and sends actuating commands to control the robot attitude by means of a distributed low-level sensing/actuating system (the nervous system).

The main processing unit is currently implemented on a PC-based computer that delivers enough raw computing power and offers standard interfaces to connect to other systems, namely USB. The PC runs the Linux operating system over the RTAI (Real-Time Applications Interface (RTAI, 2007)) kernel, which provides time-related services, namely periodic activation of processes, time-stamping and temporal synchronization.

The agents software architecture is developed around the concept of a real-time database (RTDB), i.e., a distributed entity that contains local images (with local access) of both local and remote time-sensitive objects with the associated temporal validity status. The local images of remote objects are automatically updated by an adaptive TDMA transmission control protocol (Santos, F.; Almeida, L.; Pedreiras, P.; Lopes, S. & Facchinnetti, T., 2004) based on IEEE 802.11b that reduces the probability of transmission collisions between team mates thus reducing the communication latency.

The low-level sensing/actuating system follows the fine-grain distributed model (Kopetz, H., 1997) where most of the elementary functions, e.g. basic reactive behaviors and closed-loop control of complex actuators, are encapsulated in small microcontroller-based nodes, interconnected by means of a network. This architecture, which is typical for example in the automotive industry, favors important properties such as scalability, to allow the future addition of nodes with new functionalities, composability, to allow building a complex system by putting together well defined subsystems, and dependability, by using nodes to ease the definition of error-containment regions. This architecture relies strongly on the network, which must support real-time communication. For this purpose, it uses the CAN (Controller Area Network) protocol (CAN, 1992), which has a deterministic medium access control, a good bandwidth efficiency with small packets and a high resilience to external interferences. Currently, the interconnection between CAN and the PC is carried out by means of a gateway, either through a serial port operating at 115Kbaud or through a serial-to-USB adapter.

3. The CAMBADA Vision Subsystem

The CAMBADA robots sense the world essentially using two low-cost webcam-type cameras, one facing forward, and the other pointing the floor, both equipped with wide-angular lenses (approximately 106 degrees) and installed at approximately 80cm above the floor. Both cameras are set to deliver 320x240 YUV images at a rate of 20 frames per second. They may also be configured to deliver higher resolution video frames (640x480), but at a slower rate (typically 10-15 fps). The possible combinations between resolution and frame-rate are restricted by the transfer rate allowed by the PC USB interface.

The camera that faces forward is used to track the ball at medium and far distances, as well as the goals, corner posts and obstacles (e.g. other robots). The other camera, which is pointing the floor, serves the purpose of local omni-directional vision and is used for mainly for detecting close obstacles, field lines and the ball when it is in the vicinity of the robot. Roughly, this omni-directional vision has a range of about one meter around the robot.

All the objects of interest are detected using simple color-based analysis, applied in a color space obtained from the YUV space by computing phases and modules in the UV plane. We call this color space the YMP space, where the Y component is the same as in YUV, the M component is the module and the P component is the phase in the UV plane. Each object (e.g., the ball, the blue goal, etc.) is searched independently of the other objects. If known, the last position of the object is used as the starting point for its search. If not known, the center of the frame is used. The objects are found using region-growing techniques. Basically, two queues of pixels are maintained, one used for candidate pixels, the other used for expanding the object. Several validations can be associated to each object, such as minimum and maximum sizes, surrounding colors, etc.

Two different Linux processes, Frontvision and Omnivision, handle the image frames associated with each camera. These processes are very similar except for the specific objects that are tracked. Figure 2 illustrates the actions carried out by the Frontvision process. Upon system start-up, the process reads the configuration files from disk to collect data regarding the camera configuration (e.g. white balance, frames-per-second, resolution) as well as object characterization (e.g. color, size, validation method). This information is then used to initialize the camera and other data structures, including buffer memory. Afterwards the process enters in the processing loop. Each new image is sequentially scanned for the presence of the ball, obstacles, goals and posts. At the end of the loop, information regarding the diverse objects is placed in a real-time database.

The keyboard, mouse and the video framebuffer are accessed via the Simple DirectMedia Layer library (SDL) (SDL, 2007). At the end of each loop the keyboard is pooled for the presence of events, which allows e.g. to quit or dynamically change some operational parameters

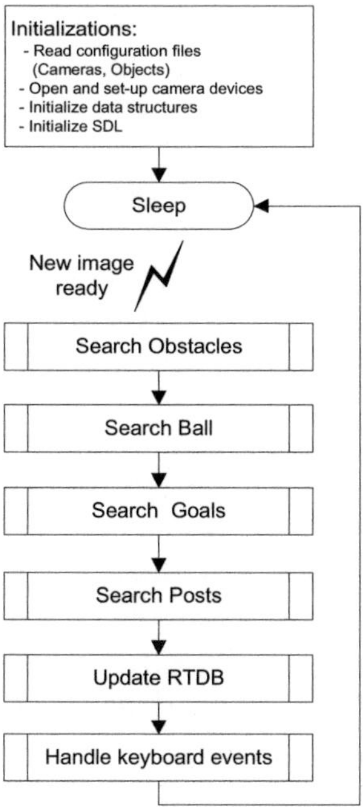

Figure 2. Flowchart of the Frontvision process

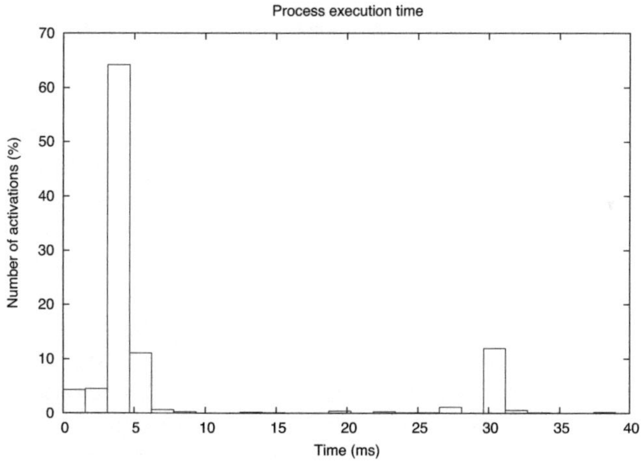

Figure 3. Ball tracking execution time histogram

4. A Modular Architecture for Image Processing: Why and How

As referred to in the previous sections, the CAMBADA robotic soccer players operate in a dynamic and passive information space, depending mostly on visual information to perceive and interact with the environment. However, gathering information from such type of environments is an extremely processing-demanding activity (DeSouza, G & Kak, A., 2004), with hard to predict execution times. Regarding the algorithms described in Section 3, it could be intuitively expected to observe a considerable variance in process execution times since in some cases the objects may be found almost immediately, when their position between successive images does not change significantly, or it may be necessary to explore the whole image and expand a substantial amount of regions of interest, e.g. when the object disappears from the robot field of vision (Davison, J., 2005). This expectation is in fact confirmed in reality, as depicted in Figure 3, which presents a histogram of the execution time of the ball tracking alone. Frequently the ball is located almost immediately, with 76.1% of the instances taking less than 5ms to complete. However, a significant amount of instances (13.9%) require between 25ms and 35ms to complete and the maximum observed execution time was 38,752 ms, which represents 77.5% of the inter-frame period just to process a single object.

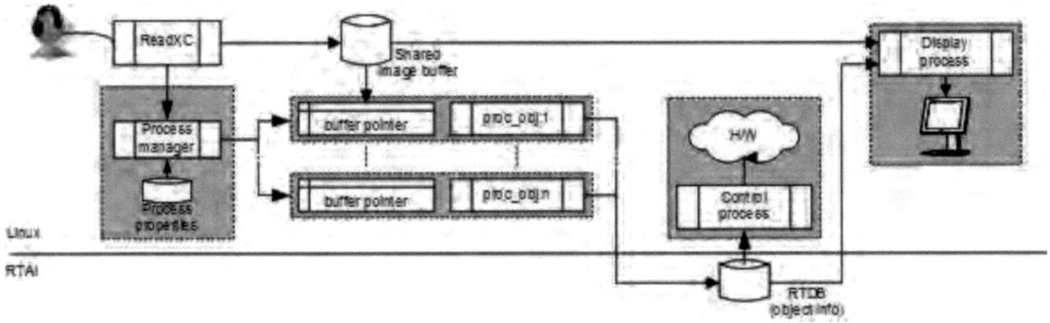

Figure 4. Modular software architecture for the CAMBADA vision subsystem

As described in Section 3, the CAMBADA vision subsystem architecture is monolithic with respect to each camera, with all the image-processing carried out within two processes designated Frontvision and Omnivision, associated with the frontal and omnidirectional cameras, respectively. Each of these processes tracks several objects sequentially. Thus, the following frame is acquired and analyzed only after tracking all objects in the previous one, which may take, in the worst case, hundreds of milliseconds, causing a certain number of consecutive frames to be skipped. These are vacant samples for the robot controllers that degrade the respective performance and, worse, correspond to black-out periods in which the robot does not react to the environment. Considering that, as discussed in Section 3, some activities may have hard deadlines, this situation becomes clearly unacceptable. Increasing the available processing power, either trough the use of more powerful CPUs or via specialized co-processor hardware could, to some extent, alleviate the situation (Hirai, S.; Zakouji, M & Tsuboi, T., 2003). However, the robots are autonomous and operate from batteries, and thus energy consumption aspects as well as efficiency in resource utilization render brut-force approaches undesirable.

4.1 Using Real-Time Techniques to Manage the Image Processing

As remarked in Section 1, some of the activities carried out by the robots exhibit real-time characteristics with different levels of criticality, importance and dynamics. For example, the latency of obstacle detection limits the robots maximum speed in order to avoid collisions with the playfield walls. Thus, the obstacle detection process should be executed as soon as possible, in every image frame, to allow the robot to move as fast as possible in a safe way. On the other hand, detecting the corner poles for localization is less demanding and can span across several frames because the robot velocity is limited and thus, if the localization process takes a couple of frames to execute its output is still meaningful. Furthermore prediction methods (Iannizzotto, G., La Rosa, F. & Lo Bello, L., 2004) combined with odometry data may also be effectively used to obtain estimates of object positions between updates. Another aspect to consider is that the pole localization activity should not block the more frequent obstacle detection. This set of requirements calls for the encapsulation of each object tracking activity in different processes as well as for the use of preemption and appropriate scheduling policies, giving higher priority to most stringent processes. These are basically the techniques that were applied to the CAMBADA vision subsystem as described in the following section.

4.2 A Modular Software Architecture

Figure 4 describes the software modular architecture adopted for the CAMBADA vision subsystem. Standard Linux services are used to implement priority scheduling, preemption and data sharing.

Associated to each camera there is one process (ReadXC) which transfers the image frame data to a shared memory region where the image frames are stored. The availability of a new image is fed to a process manager, which activates the object detection processes. Each object detection process (e.g. obstacle, ball), generically designated by proc_obj:x, x={1,2,...n} in Figure 4, is triggered according to the attributes (period, phase) stored in a process database. Once started, each process gets a link to the most recent image frame available and starts tracking the respective object. Once finished, the resulting information (e.g. object detected or not, position, degree of confidence, etc.) is placed in a real-time database (Almeida, L.; Santos, F.; Facchinetti; Pedreiras, P.; Silva, V. & Lopes, L., 2004), identified by the label "Object info", similarly located in a shared memory region. This database may be accessed by any other processes on the system, e.g. to carry out control actions. A display process may also be executed, which is useful mainly for debugging purposes.

4.2.1 Process Manager

For process management a custom library called PMan was developed. This library keeps a database where the relevant process properties are stored. For each new image frame, the process manager scans the database, identifies which processes should be activated and sends them pre-defined wake-up signals.

Table 1 shows the information about each process that is stored in the PMan database.

The process name and process pid fields allow a proper process identification, being used to associate each field with a process and to send OS signals to the processes, respectively. The period and phase fields are used to trigger the processes at adequate instants. The period is expressed in number of frames, allowing each process to be triggered every n frames. The phase field permits de-phasing the process activations in order to balance the CPU load over time, with potential benefits in terms of process jitter. The deadline field is optional and permits, when necessary, to carry out sanity checks regarding critical processes, e.g. if the high-priority obstacle detection does not finish within a given amount of time appropriate actions may be required to avoid jeopardizing the integrity of the robot. The following section of the PMan table is devoted to the recollection of statistical data, useful for profiling purposes. Finally, the status field keeps track of the instantaneous process state (idle, executing).

Process identification		
	PROC_name	Process ID string
	PROC_pid	Process id
Generic temporal properties		
	PROC_period	Period (frames)
	PROC_phase	Phase (frames)
	PROC_deadline	Deadline (μs)
QoS management		
	PROC_qosdata	QoS attributes
	PROC_qosupdateflag	QoS change flag
Statistical data		
	PROC_laststart	Activation instant of last instance
	PROC_lastfinish	Finish instant of last instance
	PROC_nact	Number of activations
	PROC_ndm	Number of deadline misses
Process status		
	PROC_status	Process status

Table 1. PMan process data summary

The PMan services are accessed by the following API:

- **PMAN_init**: allocates resources (shared memory, semaphores, etc) and initializes the PMan data structures;
- **PMAN_close**: releases resources used by PMan;
- **PMAN_procadd**: adds a given process to the PMan table;
- **PMAN_procdel**: removes one process from the PMan table;
- **PMAN_attach**: attaches the OS process id to an already registered process, completing the registration phase;
- **PMAN_deattach**: clears the process id field from a PMan entry;
- **PMAN_QoSupd**: changes the QoS attributes of a process already registered in the PMan table;
- **PMAN_TPupd**: changes the temporal properties (period, phase or deadline) of a process already registered in the PMan table;
- **PMAN_epilogue**: signals that a process has terminated the execution of one instance;
- **PMAN_query**: allows to retrieve statistical information about one process;
- **PMAN_tick**: called upon the availability of every new frame, triggering the activation of processes.

The PMan service should be initialized before use, via the **init** function. The service uses OS resources that require proper shutdown procedures, e.g. shared memory and semaphores, and the **close** function should be called before terminating the application. To register in the PMan table, a process should call the **add** function and afterwards the **attach** function. This separation permits a higher flexibility since it becomes possible to have each process registering itself completely or to have a third process managing the overall properties of the different processes. During runtime the QoS allocated to each process may be changed with an appropriate call to **QoSupd** function. Similarly, the temporal properties of one process can also be changed dynamically by means of the **TPupd** function. When a process terminates executing one instance it should report this event via the **epilogue** call. This action permits maintaining the statistical data associated with each process as well as becoming aware of deadline violations. The **query** call allows accessing the statistical data of each process registered in the database. This information can be used by the application for different purposes like profiling, load management, etc. Finally, the **tick** call is triggered by the process that interacts with the camera and signals that a new frame is ready for processing. As a consequence of this call the PMan database is scanned and the adequate processes activated.

4.2.2 Shared Data Buffers

As discussed previously, the robot application is composed by several processes which operate concurrently, each seeking for particular features in a given frame. The complexity of these activities is very dissimilar and consequently the distinct processes exhibit distinctive execution times. On the other hand the execution time of each process may also vary significantly from instance to instance, depending on the particular strategy followed, on the object dynamics, etc.. Consequently, the particular activation instants of the processes cannot be predicted beforehand. To facilitate the sharing of image buffers in this framework a mechanism called Shared Data Buffers (SDB) was implemented. This mechanism is similar to the Cyclic Asynchronous Buffers (Buttazzo, G.; Conticelli, F.; Lamastra, G. & Lipari, G., 1997), and permits an asynchronous non-blocking access to the image buffers. When the processes request access to an image buffer automatically receive a pointer to the most recent data. Associated to each buffer there is a link count which accounts for the number of processes that are attached to each buffer. This mechanism ensures that the buffers are only recycled when there are no processes attached to them, and so the processes have no practical limit to the time during which they can hold a buffer.
The access to the SDB library is made trough the following calls:

- **SDB_init**: reserves and initializes the diverse data structures (shared memory, semaphores, etc);
- **SDB_close**: releases resources associated with the SDB;
- **SDB_reserve**: returns a pointer to a free buffer;
- **SDB_update**: signals that a given buffer was updated with new data;
- **SDB_getbuf**: requests a buffer for reading;
- **SDB_unlink**: access to the buffer is no longer necessary.

The **init** function allocates the necessary resources (shared memory, semaphores) and initializes the internal data structures of the SDB service. The **close** function releases the resources allocated by the init call, and should be executed before terminating the application. When the camera process wants to publish a new image it should first request a pointer to a free buffer, via the **reserve** call, copy the data and then issue the **update** call to signal that a new frame is available. Reader processes should get a pointer to a buffer with fresh data via the **getbuf** call, which increments the link count, and signal that the buffer is no longer necessary via the **unlink** call, which decrements the buffer link count.

4.2.3 Dynamic QoS management

As in many other autonomous agent applications, the robotic soccer players have to deal with an open and dynamic environment that cannot be accurately characterized at pre-runtime. Coping efficiently with this kind of ambiance requires support for dynamic reconfiguration and on-line QoS management (Burns, A; Jeffay, K.; Jones, M. et al, 1996). These features are generally useful to increase the efficiency in the utilization of system resources (Buttazzo, G.; Lipari, G., Caccamo, M. & Abeni. L., 2002) since typically there is a direct relationship between resource utilization and delivered QoS. In several applications, assigning higher CPU to tasks increases the QoS delivered to the application. This is true, for example, in control applications (Buttazzo, G. & Abeni, L., 2000), at least within certain ranges (Marti, P., 2002), and in multimedia applications (Lee, C.; Rajkumar, R. & Mercer, C., 1996). Therefore, managing the resources assigned to tasks, e.g. by controlling their execution rate or priority, allows a dynamic control of the delivered QoS. Efficiency gains can be achieved in two situations: either maximizing the utilization of system resources to achieve a best possible QoS for different load scenarios or adjusting the resource utilization according to the application instantaneous QoS requirements, i.e. using only the resources required at each instant.

Process	Period (ms)	Priority	Offset (ms)	Purpose
Ball_Fr	50	35	0	Ball tracking (front camera)
BGoal / YGoal	200	25	50/150	Blue / Yellow Goal tracking
BPost / YPost	800	15	100/200	Blue / Yellow Post tracking
Avoid_Fr	50	45	0	Obstacle avoidance (front cam.)
Ball_Om	50	40	0	Ball tracking (omni camera)
Avoid_Om	50	45	0	Obstacle avoidance (omni camera)
Line	400	20	0	Line tracking and identification

Table 2. Process properties in the modular architecture

Both situations referred above require an adequate support from the computational infrastructure so that the relevant parameters of tasks can be dynamically adjusted. Two of the functions implemented by the PMAN library, namely **PMAN_TPupd** and **PMAN_QoSupd**, allow changing dynamically and without service disruption the temporal properties of each process (period, phase and deadline) and to manage additional custom QoS properties (the Linux real-time priority in this case), respectively. The robots decision level uses this interface to adjust the individual process attributes in order to control the average CPU load and to adapt the rates and priorities of the diverse processes according to the particular role that the robots are playing in each instant.

5. Experimental Results

In order to assess the performance of the modular approach and compare it with the initial monolithic one, several experiments were conducted, using a PC with an Intel Pentium III CPU, running at 550MHz, with 256MB of RAM. This PC has lower capacity than those typically used on the robots but allows a better illustration of the problem addressed in this chapter. The PC runs a Linux 2.4.27 kernel, patched with RTAI 3.0r4. The image-capture devices are Logitech Quickcams, with a Philips chipset. The cameras were set-up to produce 320*240 images at a rate of 20 frames-per-second (fps). The time instants were measured accessing the Pentium TSC. To allow a fair comparison all the tests have been executed over the same pre-recorded image sequence.

5.1 Monolithic Architecture assessment

The code of the Frontvision and Omnivision processes (Section 3) was instrumented to measure the start and finishing instants of each instance.

Process	Max. (ms)	Min. (ms)	Avg. (ms)	St.Dev. (ms)
FrontVision	143	29	58	24
OmniVision	197	17	69	31

Table 3. FrontVision and OmniVision inter-activation statistical figures

Figure 5 presents the histogram of the inter-activation intervals of both of these processes while Table 3 presents a summary of the relevant statistical figures.

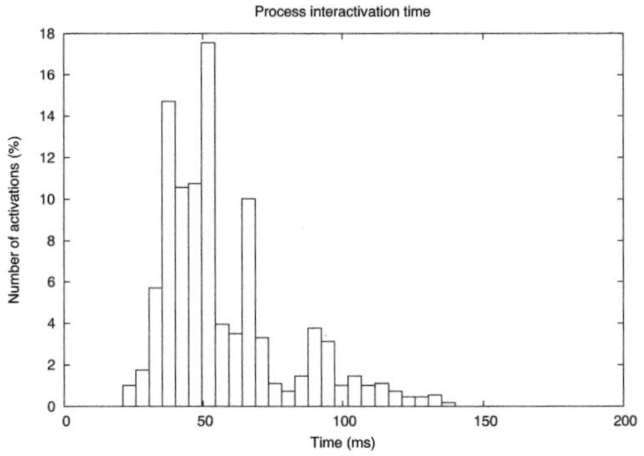

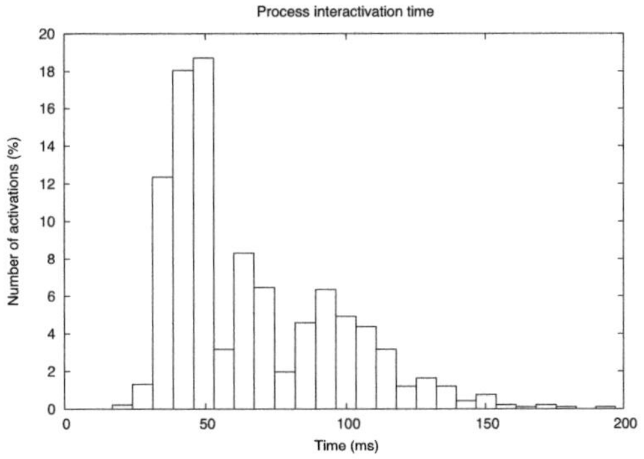

Figure 5. Histogram of the inter-activation time of the FrontVision (top) and OmniVision (bottom) processes

The response time of both processes exhibits a substantial variance, with inter-activation times ranging from 17ms to near 200ms and an average inter-activation time of 58ms and 69ms, respectively. Remembering that the image acquisition rate is 20 fps, corresponding to 50ms between frames, these figures indicate a poor performance. In fact the image processing is part of the control loop and so the high jitter leads to a poor control performance, a situation further aggravated by the significant amount of dropped frames, which correspond to time lapses during which the robot is completely non-responsive to the environment.

5.2 Modular Architecture

The different image-processing activities have been separated and wrapped in different Linux processes, as described in Section 4. Table 2 shows the periods, offsets and priorities assigned to each one of the processes.

The obstacle avoidance processes are the most critical ones since they are responsible for alerting the control software of the presence of any obstacles in the vicinity of the robot, allowing it to take appropriate measures when necessary, e.g. evasive maneuvers or immobilization.

Therefore these processes are triggered at a rate equal to the camera frame rate and receive the highest priority, ensuring a response-time as short as possible. It should be noted that these processes scan restricted image regions only, looking for specific features, thus their execution time is bounded and relatively short. In the experiments the measured execution time was bellow 5ms for each one of the processes, therefore this architecture allows ensuring that every frame will be scanned for the presence of obstacles.

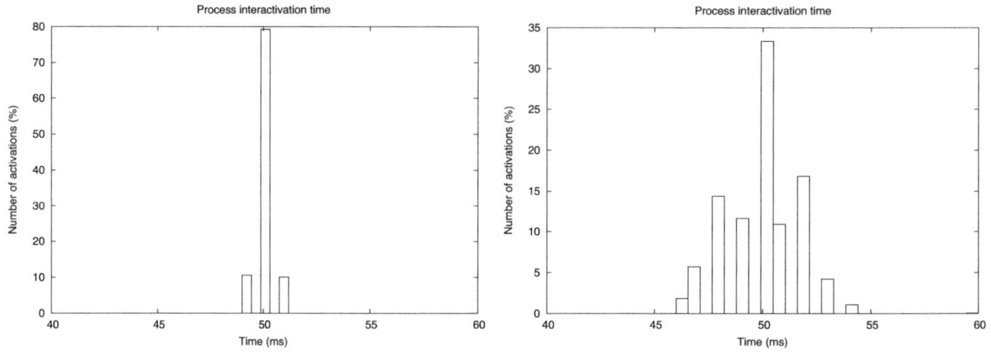

Figure 6. Front (left) and omni-directional (right) obstacle detection processes inter-activation intervals

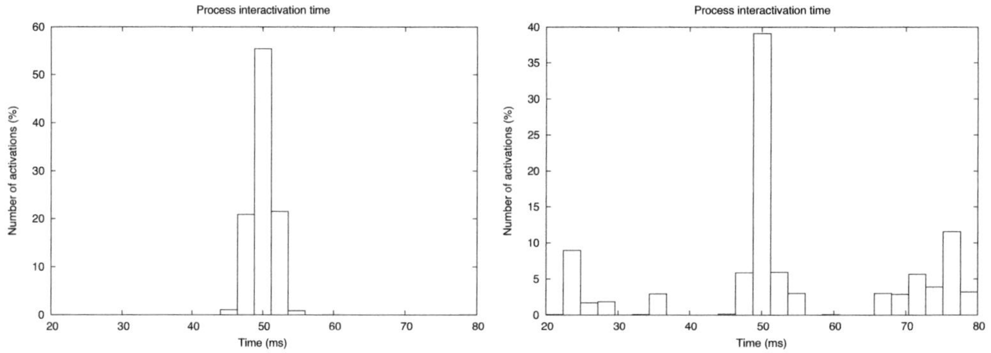

Figure 7. Omni-directional (left) and frontal (right) camera ball tracking processes inter-activation intervals

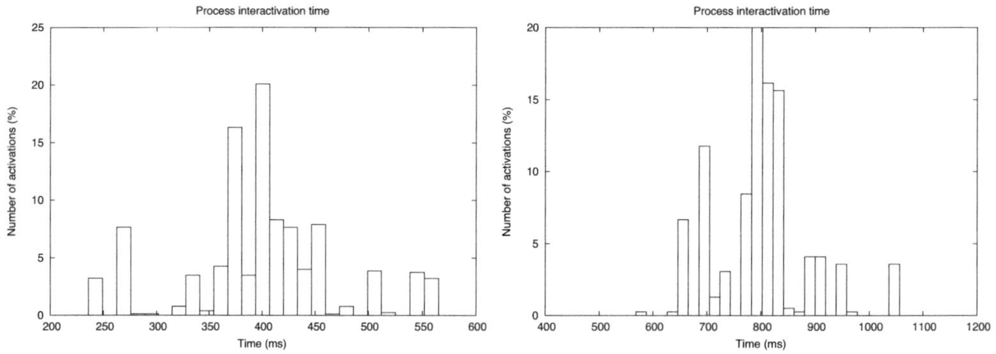

Figure 8. Line (left) and yellow post (right) tracking processes inter-activation intervals

The second level of priority is granted to the Ball_Om process, which tracks the ball in the omni-directional camera. This information is used when approaching, dribbling and kicking the ball, activities that require a low latency and high update rate for good performance.

Therefore this process should, if possible, be executed on every image frame, thus its period was also set to 50ms.
The third level of priority is assigned to the Ball_Fr process, responsible for locating the ball in the front camera. This information is used mainly to approach the ball when it is at medium to far distance from the robot. Being able to approach the ball quickly and smoothly is important for the robot performance but this process is more delay tolerant than the Ball_Om process, thus it is assigned a lower priority.

Process	Max. (ms)	Min. (ms)	Average (ms)	Standard deviation (ms)
Avoid_Fr	60.1	48.9	50.0	0.5
Avoid_Om	60.1	45.9	50.0	1.6
Ball_Om	60.1	46.0	50.0	1.6
Ball_Fr	80.0	19.9	50.0	2.1
Ygoal	362.2	61.1	207.9	58.3
BGoal	383.9	60.9	208.4	66.6
Line	564.7	235.6	399.9	71.9
BPost	1055.8	567.9	799.9	87.2
YPost	1156.4	454.4	799.6	114.3

Table 4. Modular architecture statistical data of inter-activation intervals

Some objects are stationary with respect to the play field. Furthermore, the robot localization includes an odometry subsystem that delivers accurate updates of the robot position during limited distances. This allows reducing the activation rate and priority of the processes related with the extraction of these features, without incurring in a relevant performance penalty. This is the case of BGoal and YGoal processes, which track the position of the blue and yellow goals, respectively, which were assigned a priority of 25 and a period of 200ms, i.e., every 4 frames.
The field line detection process (Line) detects and classifies the lines that delimit the play field, pointing specific places in it. This information is used only for calibration of the localization information and thus may be run sparsely (400ms). Post detection processes (BPost and YPost) have a similar purpose. However, since the information extracted from them is coarser than from the line detection, i.e., it is affected by a bigger uncertainty degree, it may be run at even a lower rate (800ms) without a relevant performance degradation.
The offsets of the different processes have been set-up to separate their activation as much as possible. With the offsets presented in Table 2, besides the obstacle and ball detection processes run every frame, no more than two other processes are triggered simultaneously. This allows minimizing mutual interference and thus reducing the response-time of lower priority processes.
Figure 6, Figure 7 and Figure 8 show the inter-activation intervals of selected processes, namely obstacle, ball, line and yellow post tracking, which clearly illustrate the differences between the modular and the monolithic architectures regarding the processes temporal behavior. The processes that receive higher priority (obstacle detection, Figure 6) exhibit a

narrow inter-activation variance, since they are not blocked and preempt other processes that may be running. Figure 7 shows the inter-activation intervals of the ball tracking processes. As stated above, the ball tracking process on the omni-directional camera has a higher priority since its data is used by more time sensitive activities. For this reason its inter-activation interval is narrower than the ball tracking process related to the front camera. As discussed in Section 4, the ball-tracking processes exhibit a significant execution time variance, since in some cases they are able to find the ball almost immediately while in other cases the whole image is scanned. For this reason the lower-priority ball-tracking process (frontal camera) exhibits a significantly higher inter-activation jitter than the higher-priority one. The same behavior is observed for the remaining processes, which see their inter-activation jitter increase as their relative priorities diminish.

Table 4 shows statistical data regarding the inter-activation intervals of these processes, which confirm, in a more rigorous way, the behavior observed above. The processes are sorted by decreasing priorities exhibiting, from top to bottom, a steady increase in the gap between maximum and minimum values observed as well as in the standard deviation. This is expected since higher priority processes, if necessary, preempt lower priority ones increasing their response-time.

Comparing the figures in Table 3 and Table 4, a major improvement can be observed with respect to the activation jitter of the most time-sensitive processes, which, for the most important tasks was reduced to 10ms (object avoidance and omni-directional ball tracking) and 30ms (frontal ball tracking). Furthermore, the standard deviation of the activation jitter of these processes is much lower (between 0.5ms and 2.1ms) and no frame drops have occurred, a situation that may have a significant impact on control performance.

During runtime higher priority processes preempt the lower priority ones, delaying its execution. This effect is clear in Table 4, with the goal, post and line processes exhibiting a much higher variability in their inter-activation times. Therefore, it can be concluded that the modular approach is effective, being able to privilege the execution of the processes that have higher impact on the global system performance.

5.3 Dynamic Qos adaptation

During runtime the robotic soccer players have to perform different roles, e.g., when a defender robot gets the ball possession and has a clear way in the direction of the opposite team goal it should assume an attacker role and some other team mate should take the defender role in its place. The relative importance of the image processing activities depends on the particular role that the robots are playing, e.g., in the situation described above the robot that is taking the defender role does not need to look for the ball in its vicinity, since this one is in the possession of a team mate, while it could benefit from a higher accuracy on the localization, achieved by tracking the field lines more often. Therefore, having the ability to change the image-processing attributes during runtime has the potential to increase the robot performance.

Another aspect that should not be neglected is that the environment strongly influences the image processing time since, depending on its *richness*, the algorithms may have to explore more or less regions of interest. As a result it is possible for the robotic players to perform differently in distinct environments or even in different times in the same environment, e.g., due to illumination variation. In these cases it may be interesting to manage the execution rates of the image-processing activities in order to take the best possible profit of the CPU but without incurring in overloads that penalize the control performance.

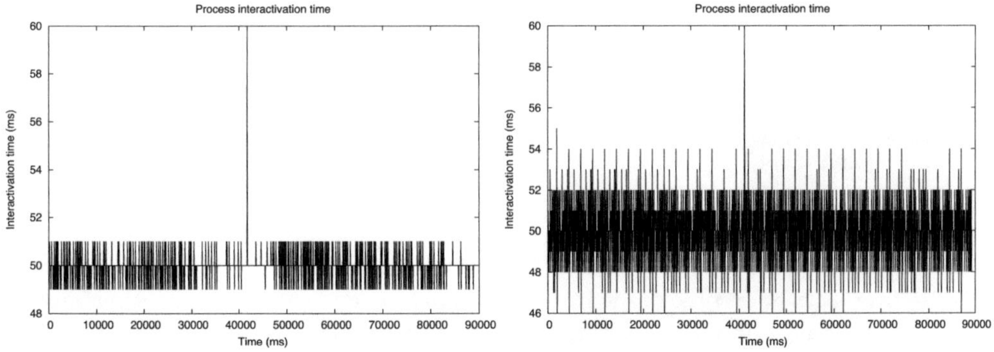

Figure 9. Inter-activation time of the high-priority frontal (left) and omnidirectional (right) avoid processes during a mode change affecting lower priority processes, only

As discussed in Section 4.2.1, the PMAN library permits to change the QoS properties of the processes, namely the period, phase, deadline and priority. To observe the impact of this service a situation was created in which the decision level requested a change in the role of a robot, from attacker to defender, as described before. Furthermore, a CPU overload was detected and thus the need to remove a lower importance process. The resulting actions were:

- to remove the ball tracking process in the omni-directional camera;
- to execute the front camera ball tracking process only once in each two frames;
- to execute the line tracking process for every frame;
- to raise its priority to 40, i.e., just below the obstacle avoidance processes.

Figure 9 and Figure 10 depict the inter-arrival time of the avoid, frontal camera ball-tracking and line tracking processes.

The first fact to be observed is that the higher priority processes are not affected, except for a small glitch on the instant of the QoS update, of similar magnitude as the jitter already observed (less than 10ms, see Table 4). This glitch may be explained by the need to access the PMAN table in exclusive mode and to call the Linux primitive sched_setscheduler()to change the priority of the line process. These operations are made within the PMAN_tick call, before the activation of the processes.

The second fact to be observed is that the line and frontal ball-tracking processes started to behave as expected immediately after the mode change, with periods of one and two frames, respectively.

The third fact to be observed is that the overload was controlled, and all the processes started to behave more regularly. This effect can be observed in medium priority processes (e.g. ball tracking) as well as in lower-priority processes (e.g. post seeking).

Therefore, it can be concluded that the PMAN services permit to change the process attributes at run-time, allowing both mode changes and CPU load management without disturbing the behavior of other processes not directly involved in the adaptation process and, consequently, it is possible to carry out the reconfiguration dynamically, since there is no service disruption.

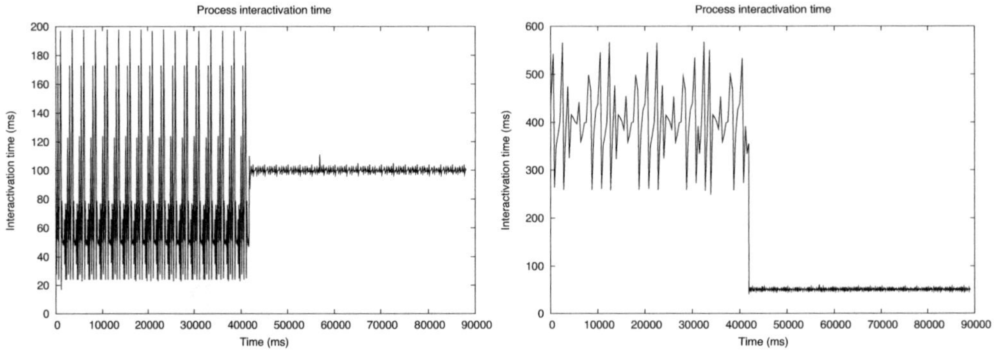

Figure 10. Inter-activation time of the frontal ball-tracking (left) and line (right) processes during a mode change in which the period of the former process was increased (50ms to 100ms) and the period of the latter was reduced (400ms to 50ms)

6. Conclusion

Computer vision applied to guidance of autonomous robots has been generating large interest in the research community as a natural and rich way to sense the environment and extract from it the necessary features. However, due to the robots motion, vision-based sensing becomes a real-time activity that must meet deadlines in order to support adequate control performance and avoid collisions. Unfortunately, most vision-based systems do not rely on real-time techniques and exhibit poor temporal behavior, with large variations in execution time that may lead to control performance degradation and even sensing black-out periods caused by skipped image frames.

In this chapter, the referred problem is identified in the scope of the CAMBADA middle-size robotic soccer team, being developed at the University of Aveiro, Portugal. Then, a new architectural solution for the vision subsystem is presented that substantially improves its reactivity, reducing jitter and frame skipping.

The proposed architecture separates the vision-based object-tracking activities in several independent processes. This separation allows, transparently and relying solely on operative system services, to avoid the blocking of higher priority processes by lower priority ones as well as to set independent activation rates, related with the dynamics of the objects being tracked and with its impact on the control performance, together with offsets that de-phase the activation instants of the processes to further reduce mutual interference.

As a consequence, it becomes possible to guarantee the execution of critical activities, e.g., obstacle avoidance and privilege the execution of others that, although not critical, have greater impact on the robot performance, e.g., ball tracking.

Finally, many robotic applications are deployed in open environments that are hard to characterize accurately at pre-runtime. The architecture herein proposed permits managing dynamically the resources assigned to tasks, e.g. by controlling their execution rate or priority, allowing a dynamic control of the delivered QoS. This approach permits either maximizing the utilization of system resources to achieve a best possible QoS for different load scenarios or adjusting the resource utilization according to the application instantaneous requirements, granting a higher QoS to the tasks that have higher impact on the global system performance.

The work described in this chapter is focused on robotic soccer robots but the results and approach are relevant for a wider class of robotic applications in which the vision subsystem is part of their control loop.

7. References

Almeida, L.; Santos, F.; Facchinetti; Pedreiras, P.; Silva, V. & Lopes, L. (2004). Coordinating distributed autonomous agents with a real-time database: The CAMBADA project. *Lecture Notes in Computer Science*, Volume 3280/2004, pp. 876-886, ISSN 0302-9743.

Assad, C.; Hartmann, M. & Lewis, M. (2001). Introduction to the Special Issue on Biomorphic Robotics. *Autonomous Robots*, Volume 11, pp. 195-200, ISSN 0929-5593.

Blake, A; Curwen, R. & Zisserman, A. (1993). A framework for spatio-temporal control in the tracking of visual contours. *International Journal of Computer Vision*, Vol. 11 No.2, pp. 127—145, ISSN0920-5691.

Burns, A; Jeffay, K.; Jones, M. et al (1996). Strategic directions in realtime and embedded systems. *ACM Computing Surveys*, Vol. 28, No. 4, pp. 751–763, ISSN 0360-0300.

Buttazzo, G.; Conticelli, F.; Lamastra, G. & Lipari, G. (1997). Robot control in hard real-time environment. *Proceedings of the 4th International Workshop on Real-Time Computing Systems and Applications*, pp. 152—159, ISBN 0-8186-8073-3, Taiwan, Oct. 1997, Taipei.

Buttazzo, G. & Abeni, L. (2000). Adaptive rate control through elastic scheduling. *Proceedings of the 39th IEEE Conference on Decision and Control*, pp. 4883-4888, ISBN 0-7803-6638-7, Dec. 2000, Sydney, Australia.

Buttazzo, G.; Lipari, G., Caccamo, M. & Abeni. L. (2002). Elastic scheduling for flexible workload management. *IEEE Transactions on Computers*, Vol. 51, No. 3, pp. 289–302, ISSN: 0018-9340.

CAN (1992). Controller Area Network - CAN2.0. *Technical Specification*, Robert Bosch, 1992.

Davison, J. (2005). Active search for real-time vision, *Proceedings of the 10th IEEE International Conference on Computer Vision*, Volume: 1, pp. 66- 73, ISBN 0-7695-2334-X.

De Souza, G. & Kak, A.(2004). A Subsumptive, Hierarchical, and Distributed Vision-Based Architecture for Smart Robotics. *IEEE Transactions on Systems, Man, and Cybernetics -- Part B: Cybernetics*, Vol. 34, pp. 1988-2002, ISSN 1083-4419.

Gibson, J. (1979). *The Ecological Approach to Visual Perception*, Lawrence Erlbaum Associates, Inc.,, ISBN 0-89859-959-8, Boston, MA.

Hirai, S.; Zakouji, M & Tsuboi, T. (2003). Implementing Image Processing Algorithms on FPGA-based Realtime Vision System, *Proceedings of the 11th Synthesis and System Integration of Mixed Information Technologies*, pp.378-385, March 2003, Hiroshima.

Iannizzotto, G., La Rosa, F. & Lo Bello, L. (2004). Real-time issues in vision-based Human-Computer Interaction. *Technical Report*, VisiLab, University of Messina , Italy.

Kitano, K.; Asada, M.; Kuniyoshi, Y.; Noda, I. & Osawa E. (1997). RoboCup: The Robot World Cup Initiative, *Proceedings of the First International Conference on Autonomous Agents* (Agents'97), W. Lewis Johnson and Barbara Hayes-Roth (Eds.), pp. 340—347, ISBN 0-89791-877-0, USA, Aug. 1997, ACM Press, N.Y.

Kopetz, H. (1997). *Real-Time Systems Design Principles for Distributed Embedded Applications*, Kluwer Academic Publishers, ISBN 0-7923-9894-7, Boston, MA.

Lee, C.; Rajkumar, R. & Mercer, C. (1996). Experiences with processor reservation and dynamic qos in real-time Mach. In *Multimedia Japan* 96, Japan, April 1996.

Marti, P. (2002). Analysis and Design of Real-Time Control Systems with Varying Control Timing Constraints. *PhD thesis*, Universitat Politecnica de Catalunya, Barcelona, Spain, July 2002.

RTAI (2007), RTAI for Linux, Available from http://www.aero.polimi.it/~rtai/, accessed: 2007-01-31.

Santos, F.; Almeida, L.; Pedreiras, P.; Lopes, S. & Facchinnetti, T. (2004). An Adaptive TDMA Protocol for Soft Real-Time Wireless Communication Among Mobile Computing Agents, *Proceedings of the Workshop on Architectures for Cooperative Embedded Real-Time Systems* (satellite of RTSS 2004). Lisboa, Portugal, Dec. 2004.

SDL (2007), Simple DirectMedia Layer, Available from http://www.libsdl.org/index.php, accessed: 2007-01-31.

Weiss, G. (2000). *Multiagent systems. A Modern Approach to Distributed Artificial Intelligence*, MIT Press, ISBN 0-262-23203-0, Cambridge, MA.

7

Extraction of Roads From Out Door Images

Alejandro Forero Guzmán M.Sc. and Carlos Parra Ph.D.
Departamento de Ingeniería Electrónica, Pontificia Universidad Javeriana, Bogotá Colombia

1. Introduction

The humanitarian demining process is very slow, expensive and most important, because it is done manually, it puts human lives at risk. Deminers are exposed to permanent danger and accidents. Even with the help of dogs, the demining process has not improved much during recent years (UNICEF, 2000).

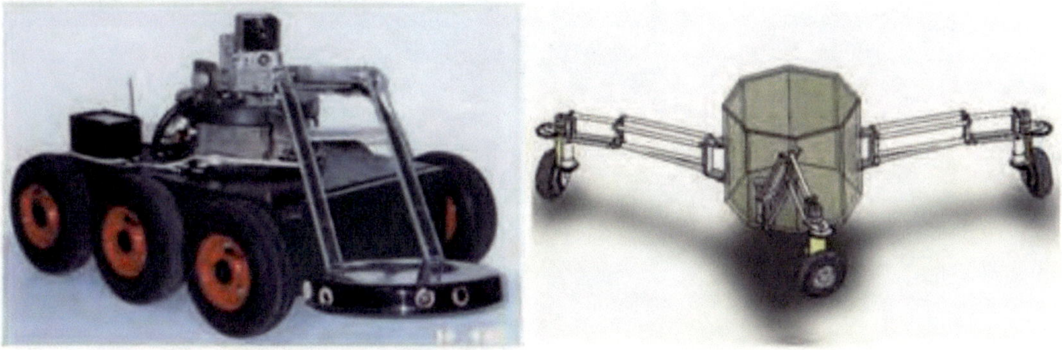

Figure 1. Left side: Ursula Robot. Right side Amaranta Robot Project

A few separate initiatives from the robotics community to design and prove a mechanical automated solution have taken place. Here at the Pontificia Universidad Javeriana, in Colombia, we are working in this problem: on a previous project the mobile robot Ursula was developed (Rizo et al., 2003); and now we are working in a new mobile robot called Amaranta (Figure1). One part of the humanitarian demining problem is the navigation, in the two projects the autonomous navigation task is executed based on a vision system that uses a camera mounted on the robot.
Landmines could be placed in any type of terrain: deserts, mountains, swamps, roads, forests, etc. This means that when trying to build a robot for demining operations, its workspace has to be previously defined and limited. In this work humanitarian demining, is limited to operate on places that have been modified by man and that represent great importance for a community, for example the roads or paths. Specifically, the systems have been designed for the Colombian territory (Rizo et al., 2003).

Figure 2. Typical images

This chapter presents two approximations made for the vision system in order to enable autonomous navigation in outdoor environments; both based on the road following principle.
Therefore, almost every vehicle facing the problem of autonomous navigation using vision systems solves this problem by following the track. How ever, this technique is widely implemented only over structured roads, because painted lines over the road are a reliable characteristic to exploit. When there are no painted roads to follow or simply no road at all, autonomous navigation based on visual systems, is usually reduced to avoid obstacles.
In the last two decades, autonomous navigations have been a goal sought by different authors (Turk et al., 1988) (Thorpe et al., 1988), yet today still an open area for research (Thrun et al.,2006).
Due to the danger involved in demining efforts, a cheap robot is required, equipped with an autonomous navigation system, in order to minimize the risk for the humanitarian demining team; and an architecture capable of supporting multiple sensors to acquire the most reliable information about the surrounding area. These limitations, along with the special terrain conditions of the Colombia topography guide the present research.
Bellow some concepts from the classic theory are presented and then the complete approach made by the authors is exposed, from the problem of navigation to the extraction of roads or paths in outdoor images as essential part of the autonomous navigation.

2. Important Concepts

2.1 Colour Spaces

In general, colour is the perceptual result of light in the visible region of the spectrum (Jain, 1989). There are many colour spaces reported in the literature, each one has its characteristics. For image processing, its is usually described by the distribution of the colour of the three components R (Red), G (Green) and B (Blue), moreover many other attributes can also be calculated from these components. The colour analysis is more difficult using the three components. In image processing of exterior scenes, the illumination is a very critical parameter. A first approach is to select a colour space expressed as two colour components and one intensity/luminance component (Ohta, HIS, LUV, L*a*b*) (Aviña-Cervantes, 2005)
For example, the CIE L*a*b* colour space was presented by the International Commission of Illumination. The model was based on two properties of an older colour space called CIE XYZ. The first of these properties is that the standard was created from the frequency response of several patients' eyes, making the system independent from electronic devices. The second property, taken from CIEXYZ, is that the mathematical representation of the space allows separating the luminance from the chrominance.
On the other hand, the originality of this colour space is that it introduces the concept of perceptual uniformity. It means that if two colours are similar to each other, in CIE L*a*b* they are close and this distance is measured by the Euclidean metric. In the CIE L*a*b* space L* represents the luminance, a* codifies the reddish and greenish sensation, while b* codifies the yellowish and bluish sensation.
The space transformation from RGB to L*a*b* has two steps. The first one is a linear transformation from RG to CIE XYZ (Eq. 1).

$$\begin{bmatrix} X \\ Y \\ Z \end{bmatrix} = \begin{bmatrix} 0.412453 & 0.357580 & 0.180423 \\ 0.212671 & 0.715160 & 0.072169 \\ 0.019334 & 0.119193 & 0.950227 \end{bmatrix} \begin{bmatrix} R \\ G \\ B \end{bmatrix} \quad (1)$$

The second transformation is a non-linear transformation from CIE XYZ to CIE L*a*b* (Eq. 2).

$$\begin{aligned} L^* &= \begin{cases} 116 \times (Y/Y_n)^{1/3} - 16 & \text{for } Y/Y_n > 0.008856 \\ 903.3 \times Y/Y_n & \text{for } Y/Y_n \leq 0.008856 \end{cases} \\ a^* &= 500 \times [f(X/X_n) - f(Y/Y_n)] \\ b^* &= 200 \times [f(Y/Y_n) - f(Z/Z_n)] \\ &\text{with} \\ f(t) &= t^{1/3} \qquad \text{for } t > 0.008856 \\ f(t) &= 7.787 \times t + \frac{16}{116} \qquad \text{for } t \leq 0.008856 \end{aligned} \quad (2)$$

The X_n, Y_n, Z_n values are the *tri stimuli* related with the white point. In some cases it can be measured, but there are also standards according to the light conditions. In this case, due to the weather conditions at the capturing moment, the CIE D65 (lightening day) (Eq.3), standard is normally selected (Broek & Rikxoort, 2004).

$$X_n = 0.9502 \quad Y_n = 1 \quad Z_n = 1.0884 \quad (3)$$

This method is not simple for computer implementation. The non-linear transformation takes important time of processing.

A second approach takes the relationship between the components of RGB. For example: R/G and B/G. This approach is also applied over the colour space YCbCr. The colour space YCbCr is used in video systems. Y is the brightness component and Cb and Cr are the blue and red chrominance components.

2.2 Semantic Model

This is an abstract representation; it gives a label, corresponding to a class, to each entity found in the scene (i.e. sky, road, tree, etc.) (Murrieta-Cid et al., 2002). In the semantic model, the classification is based on a priori knowledge given to the system (Fan et al., 2001).

This knowledge consists in:

A list of possible classes that the robot identifies in the environment.

Learning attributes for each class. The region characterization is developed by using several attributes computed from the colour information. Other attributes are texture and geometrical information.

The kind of environment to be analyzed; the nature of the region is obtained by comparing a vector of features with a database composed of different classed, issues of the learning process. The database is a function of the environment and problem restrictions.

3. General System

The approach used to solve the problem of navigation presented here is very similar to the one used with structured roads: find a path and then follow it (Bertozzi et al., 2002) (Aviña-Cervantes et al., 2003). Once the road or path has been identified, following it supposes a known problem in robotics. For this reason, the focus of this exposition is centered on the identification of the area that represents the path the robot will follow, and the extraction of some parameters necessary for the control stage.

Figure 2 shows the kind of images processed by the system. In all of these images there are certain characteristics in common: a set of pixels, mostly connected, represent the road; in a close range image (5 to 25 meters) it is highly probable to have only one road; a road that can be followed goes from the bottom of the picture till some point in the middle upper area of the picture.

Along with these ideas, other facts are implicit: the picture is taken horizontal to the ground, the sky is in the upper portion of the picture, there is sufficient light to distinguish the road or path, there are not objects obstructing the view of the road. All of these assumptions are easily fulfilled in real conditions. Every one of these characteristics is used as semantic information and helps to delimit the scope of the problem. The processing of the images is done to exploit all the semantic characteristics mentioned before. At the end, semantic rules are applied to extract the essential information in the image: the route over the navigable terrain.

Figure 3. Semantic characteristic in the image

3.1 Extraction of characteristics

Different approaches have been made to extract the path or road in outdoor images, colour segmentation is one of those, but this technique is very susceptible to changes in illumination, a big draw back in outdoor vision systems.

To overcome this difficulty many approximations have been presented by numerous authors (Turk et al., 1988) (Thorpe et al., 1988), but some times they are to complex to be implemented in a cheap system. Instead, we propose the use of semantic information, similar to the one we use as humans to follow a path, to reduce the complexity of the colour segmentation by using the possible meanings of the different characteristics found in the image and its relation with the context, hence reducing the universe of possibilities.

3.2 Semantic information

As the camera is upward and horizontal to the ground the representation of a typical image consists of the sky, above the horizon; and the segment below the horizon contains maximum two areas: path and not path regions. Figure 3 shows the typical target image and the principal semantic characteristic in it: sky, in the blue rectangle; horizon, the brown line; and road inside the red segment.

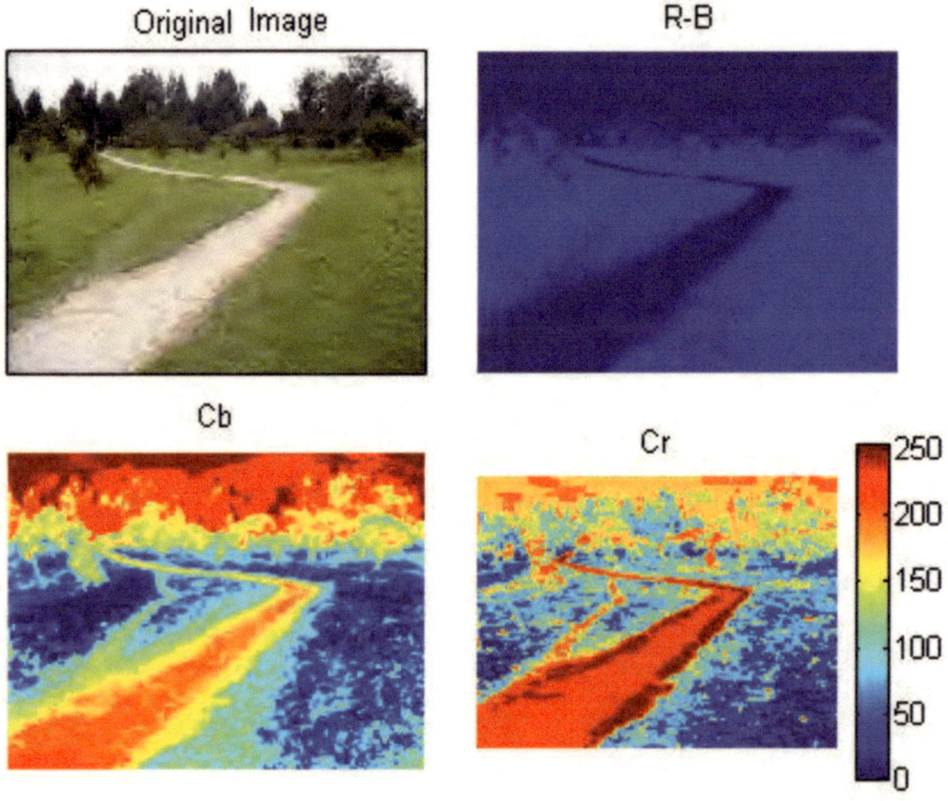

Figure 4. Examples of path visualization in differents color spaces

This simple representation reduces the complexity in the colour segmentation and enables the use of a wider space to separate the two regions below the horizon, what in time, reduces the negative effect of variable shadows and changes of illumination over the objective path.

In addition, the binary classes enable the use of techniques as simple as binarization to make the segmentation: only two classes below the horizon. Herewith the computation problem is reduced; as a result the computational resources can be reduced without increasing the time that the process consumes (Duda et al., 2001).

4. Algorithms

Two approximations were made to solve the problem; both of them use some colour segmentation along with semantic information. The first algorithm, which works in the RGB space, is the initial design (Forero & Parra, 2004). It was tested in Matlab® and designed to work along with the first implementation of the robot Ursula.
The second algorithm was conceived to work in an embedded system and it captures the image in the YCbCr colour space. In figure 4, for pictures show the image in different colour spaces. Next, both algorithms are explained in more detail.

Figure 5. From top to bottom, left to right: original image RGB, R-B plane, inverse R-B, image result from a median filter, image result from the first morphological filter, image thicken, image result from the second morphological filter, image segmented by connectivity, path selected

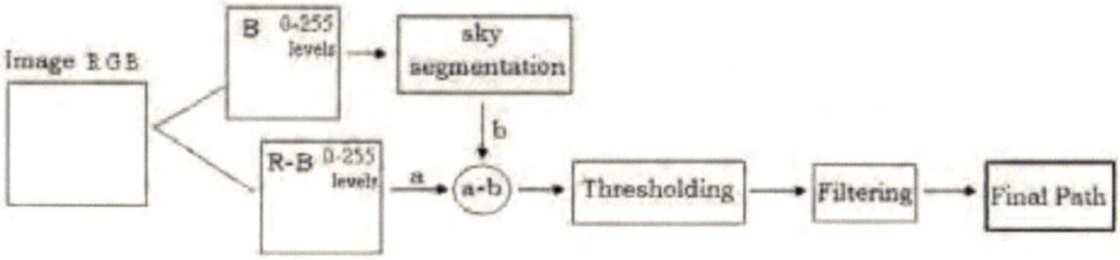

Figure 6. Flow diagram for the RGB implementation

4.1 RGB implementation

This algorithm works in 2 of the three components of the RGB space, the channels red and blue. Chanel blue is used to segment the sky and the projection R —B is used in the rest of the process. Channel green is not used because it has few or not information about the path. After the sky is identified, it is subtracted from the rest of the image, so the projection R —B does not contain the segment levelled as sky. This special projection $\alpha R - \beta B$, with constants α and β set to 0,5, is used because in it the *dirt* of the paths is enhanced and the effect of shadows is reduced (Turk et al., 1988).

The new image, the projection R —B, is subject to a threshold operation to obtain two classes in it; this is the first approximation to the road and not road classes. The threshold is selected using the Otsu Method (Otsu, 1979) so the separability of the two classes is maximized. Then, morphological filters are applied to reduce holes and increase the connectivity in the biggest region of this image.

After filtering, one of the biggest connected regions in the image should be the road. If more than one region has the characteristics the algorithm is looking for, the semantic rules should help to choose one: centroid, major axis length, minor axis length and orientation of the areas that contains each region are extracted and then the rules are applied to select one as the final path.

Figure 5 illustrates the different stages of the algorithm, and figure 6 illustrates the algorithm with a flow diagram.

4.2 YCbCr implementation

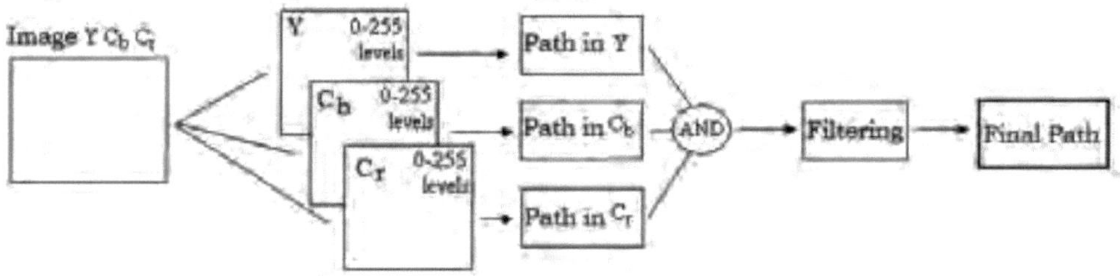

Figure 7. Flow diagram for the YCbCr implementation

This algorithm was developed after the RGB implementation (Maldonado et al., 2006), thinking of the online application; it takes the three channels of the space YCbCr, and uses each one as 256 level images. The dimension in all channels is reduced, so the portion of the sky is taken out. This reduction in the image is done by a geometric calculation, and if some pixels from the ground are also lost, they would be the far away pixels close to the horizon; this is not a problem because in future images the problem will be corrected, before the robot reaches that point.

Afterward, a threshold is applied to each channel, following the same idea used in the RGB implementation; then all the information in the three components its put together with an AND operator. This way the information is merging by adding the coincident pixels and extracting those who only represent a hit in one or two channels.

Finally, the result image is filtered to reduce the effect of noise and obtain a single path. A median filter with a 5 x 5 window is used for this purpose.

After one region is selected as the path, his centroid along with the direction of the path are extracted. This enables the control system to plan the path and overtake autonomous navigation. Figure 7 illustrates the algorithm with a flow diagram, and figure 8 illustrates the different stages of the algorithm.

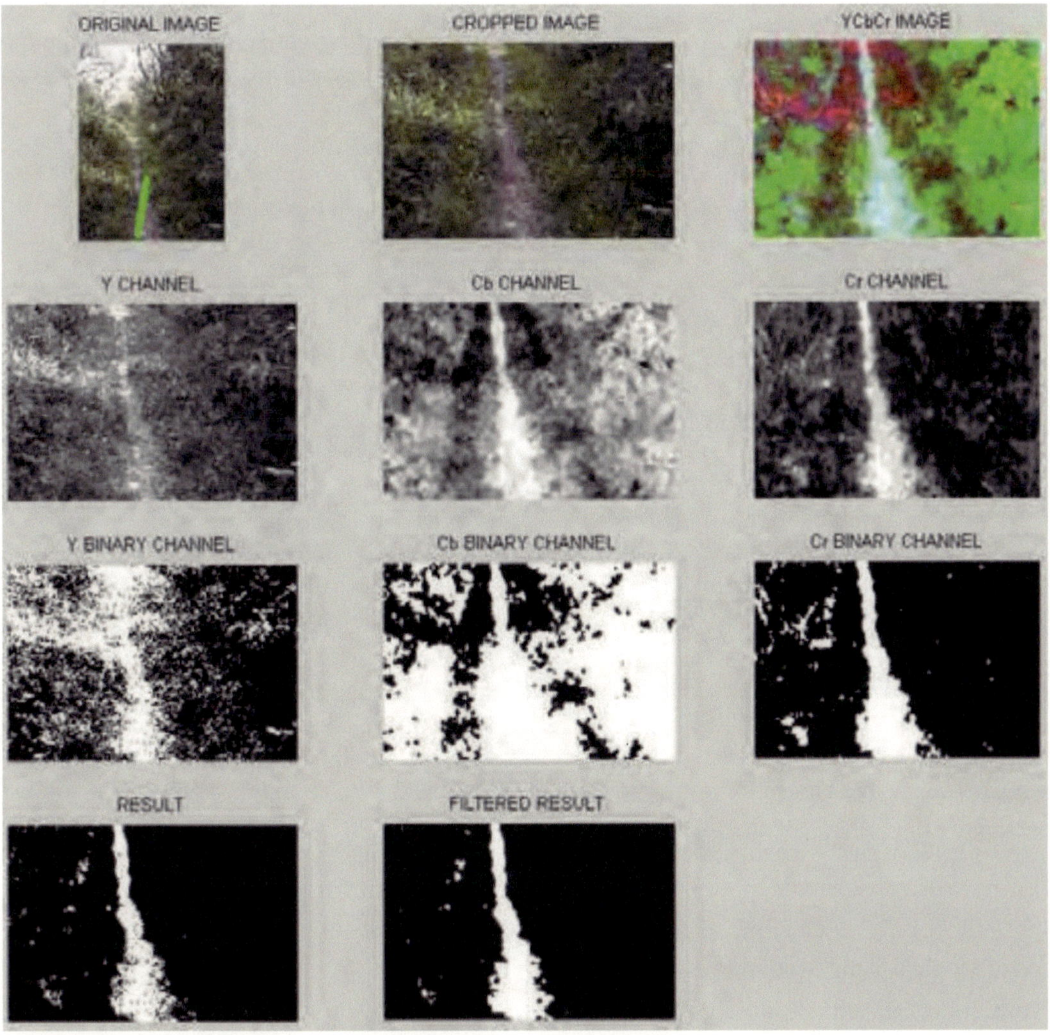

Figure 8. Real Time System Processing

5. Hardware realization

The algorithm was tested in Matlab®, and then implemented in a high-level language, C++ with the Intel's library OpenCV®. These steps were to help develop and analyse the algorithm. After concluding this stage, the complete process was implemented in embedded systems to achieve portability along with real time processing. Here after, the implementation in OpenCV® and the implementation in the Blackfin® Processors are explained with more detail.

5.1 OpenCV® implementation

The implementation in OpenCV® was done in a PC with Fedora Linux operative system, where the algorithm was programmed in C/C++. The Intel's compiler used came along with the OpenCV library. The final application takes as input an image in AVI (Audio Video Interleave) format and then executes the recognition algorithm, previously tested in Matlab®. The objective of using C++ to program the concluding version was to facilitate the migration of the application into the embedded version in the DSP EZKIT- LITE BF533 Blackfin®.

5.2 Blackfin® implementation

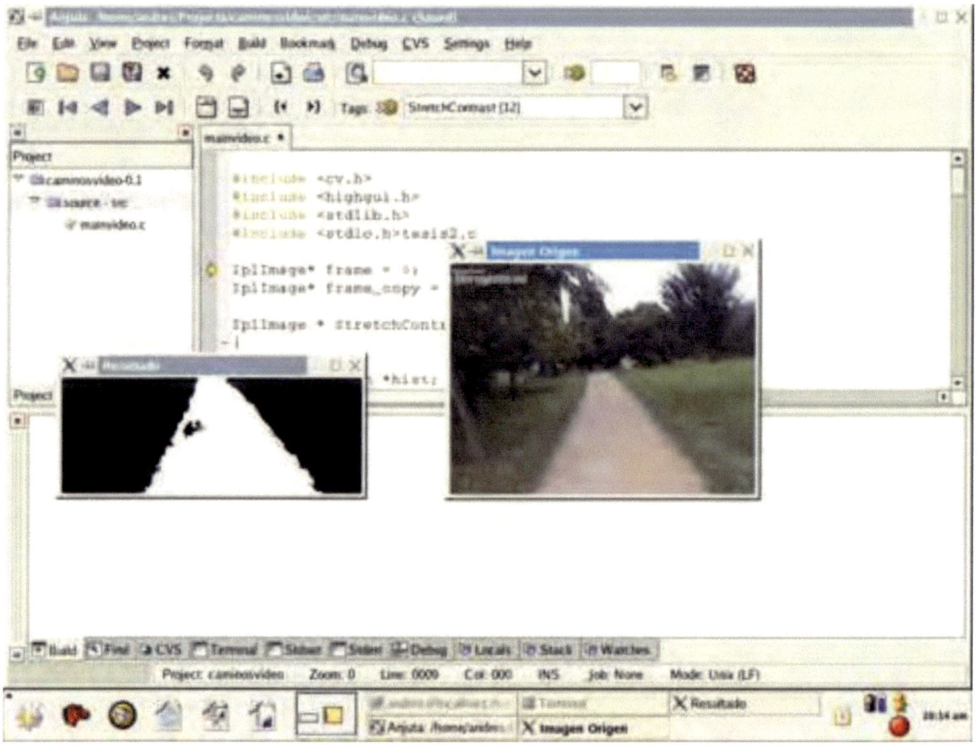

Figure 9. Real Time System Processing

To accomplish real time processing, as shown in figure 9, the DSP EZKIT- LITE BF533 Blackfin® was used. Three special functions were implemented to bring about the operation in the desire hardware:

Initialization, the Blackfin BF 533 processor and the developed card ADSP EZKIT - LITE BF533 are prepared to capture video and generate the interrupt and synchronism signals with the peripheries: a video decoder ADV7183 and a the embedded DMA. The first one transforms the analog video NTSC into digital video ITU-656, and the processor's DMA transfers the video information into the RAM memory in the developed card.

The processing stage starts with the extraction of each channel YCbCr from the image in memory. Them, it calls all procedures that execute the algorithm: Contrast estimation, histogram calculation, threshold calculation, and adding the three channels. Finally, it calculates the moments of the region of interest to extract the centroid and the orientation of the path.

In the last step, Transmission, the information concerning the path (centroid and the orientation) is transmitted by a RS-232 serial interface to a navigation module.

Besides these functions, other considerations had to be taken to run the algorithm in the embedded system:

New data types were created in C++ in order to be compatible with ADSP EZKIT- LITE BF533. These data structures manage the information in the image and handle all the parameters that the algorithm uses.

All the variables are defined according with the size and physical position that each one will take in the physical memory in the development kit. This execution allows a better use of the hardware resource and enables simultaneous processing of two images, one image is acquired by the DMA, and other is processed in the CPU.

Finally, The Blackfin's ALU only handles fixed-point values, so floating-point values have to be avoided in order to maintain the performance of the whole system.

6. Conclusion

Even when there has been an extensive development of works on road detection and road following during the last two decades, most of them are focused on well structured roads, making difficult its use for humanitarian demining activities. The present work shows a way to use the natural information in outdoor environment to extract the roads or paths characteristics, which can be used as landmarks for the navigation process.

Other important observation is that the information combines of two colors, (i.e. the projection R— B, Cb or Cr channels) hence reducing the harmful effect of the changing illumination in natural environment.

Good results were also achieved in the path planning process. The robot executes a 2½ D trajectory planning, which facilitates the work of the vision system because only the close range segmentation has to be correct to be successful in the path planning.

With regard to the semantic information, the results show how semantic characteristics make possible the use of low-level operations to extract the information required without spending too many time and hardware resources.

Finally, the system implemented is part of a visual exploration strategy which is being implemented in the robot Amaranta, and has other visual perception functions like the detection of buried objects by color and texture analysis. When the whole system will be functional it will integrate techniques of control visual navigation and would be a great tool to test how all the system can work together (Coronado et al., 2005).

7. References

Aviña-Cervantes, G. Navigation visuelle d'un robot mobile dans un environnement d'extérieur semi-structuré. *Ph.D. Thesis*. INP Toulouse. France. 2005.

Broek, E.L. van den; Rikxoort, E.M. van. Evaluation of color representation for texture analysis. *Proceedings of the 16th Belgium-Netherlands Conference on Artificial Intelligence*. University of Groningen. 21-22 October, 2004.

UNICEF- Colombia. *Sembrando Minas, Cosechando Muerte.* UNICEFBogotá. Colombia. September 2000.

Murrieta-Cid, R; Parra, C. & Devy M. Visual Navigation on Natural Environments. *Journal on Autonomous Robots*. Vol. 13. July 2002. pp 143-168. ISSN 0929-5593

Rizo, J.; Coronado, J.; Campo, C.; Forero A.; Otálora, C.; Devy, M. & Parra, C. URSULA : Robotic Demining System. *Proceedings of International Conference on Advanced Robotics ICAR*. ISBN: 9729688990. Coimbra. Portugal. 2003.

Jain, A. *Fundamental of Digital Image Processing*. Prentice-Hall International Editions. ISBN: 0-13-332578-4. United State of America. 1989.

Forero, A. & Parra C. Automatic Extraction of Semantic Characteristics from Outdoor Images for Visual Robot Navigation. *Proceedings of International Conference IEEE/ International Symposium on Robotics and Automation*. ISBN: 9709702009. Querétaro. Mexico. 2004.

Aviña-Cervantes, G.; Devy, M. & Marín, A. Lane Extraction and Tracking for Robot Navigation in Agricultural Applications. *Proceedings of International Conference on Advanced Robotics ICAR*. ISBN: 9729688990. Coimbra. Portugal. 2003.

Maldonado, A.; Forero A. & Parra, C. Real Time Navigation on Unstructured Roads. *Proceedings of Colombian Workshop on Robotics And Automation (CWRA/IEEE)*. Bogotá. Colombia. 2006.

Turk, M. A.; Morgenthaler, D. G.; Gremgan, K. D. & Marra, M. VITS- A vision system for autonomous land vehicle navigation. *IEEE Transactions on Pattern Analysis and Machine Intelligence*. Vol. 10. No. 3 May 1988. ISSN: 0162-8828.

Thorpe, C.; Hebert, M.; Kanade, T. & Shafer, S. Vision and navigation for the Carnegie-Mellon Navlab. *IEEE Transactions on Pattern Analysis and Machine Intelligence*. Vol. 10. No. 3 May 1988. ISSN: 0162-8828.

Fan, J.; Zhu, X. & Wu, L. Automatic model-based semantic object extraction algorithm. *IEEE Transactions on Circuits and Systems for Video Technology*. Vol. 11. No. 10. October 2001. ISSN: 1051-8215.

Duda, R.; Hart, P. & Stork, D. *Pattern Classification. Second Edition*. John Wiley & Sons, Inc. ISBN: 0-471-05669-3. Canada. 2001.

Berttozzi, M.; Broggi, A.; Cellario, M.; Fascioli, A.; Lombardi, P. & Porta, M. Artificial Vision on Roads Vehicles. *Proceedings of the IEEE*. Vol. 90. Issue 7. July 2002. ISSN: 0018-9219.

Otsu, N. A threshold selection method from grey-level histograms. *IEEE Transactions on System, Man and Cybernetics*. Vo. SMC. 9. No. 1. January 1979. ISSN: 1083-4427.

Thrun, S et al. Stanley: The Robot that Won the DARPA Grand Challenge. *Journal of Field Robotics*. Vo. 23 No.9. Published online on Wiley InterScience. 2006.

Coronado, J.; Aviña, G.; Devy, M. & Parra C. Towards landmine detection using artificial vision. *Proceedings of International Conference on Intelligent Robots and Systems. IROS/IEEE´05*. Edmonton. Canada. August 2005. ISBN: 0-7803-8913-1.

8. Acknowledgement

The present work was partially founded by Colciencias and Ecos-Nord Program.

8

ViSyR: a *Vi*sion *Sy*stem for *R*eal-Time Infrastructure Inspection

Francescomaria Marino[1] and Ettore Stella[2]
[1]*Dipartimento di Elettrotecnica ed Elettronica (DEE) Politecnico di Bari*
[2]*Istituto di Studi sui Sistemi Intelligenti per l'Automazione (ISSIA) CNR*
Italy

1. Introduction

The railway maintenance is a particular application context in which the periodical surface inspection of the rolling plane is required in order to prevent any dangerous situation. Usually, this task is performed by trained personnel that, periodically, walks along the railway network searching for visual anomalies. Actually, this manual inspection is slow, laborious and potentially hazardous, and the results are strictly dependent on the capability of the observer to detect possible anomalies and to recognize critical situations.

With the growing of the high-speed railway traffic, companies over the world are interested to develop automatic inspection systems which are able to detect rail defects, sleepers' anomalies, as well as missing fastening elements. These systems could increase the ability in the detection of defects and reduce the inspection time in order to guarantee more frequently the maintenance of the railway network.

This book chapter presents ViSyR: a patented fully automatic and configurable FPGA-based vision system for real-time infrastructure inspection, able to analyze defects of the rails and to detect the presence/absence of the fastening bolts that fix the rails to the sleepers.

Besides its accuracy, ViSyR achieves impressive performance in terms of inspection velocity. In fact, it is able to perform inspections approximately at velocities of 450 km/h (Jump search) and of 5 km/h (Exhaustive search), with a composite velocity higher than 160 km/h for typical video sequences. Jump and Exhaustive searches are two different modalities of inspection, which are performed in different situations. This computing power has been possible thanks to the implementation onto FPGAs. ViSyR is not only affordable, but even highly flexible and configurable, being based on classifiers that can be easily reconfigured in function of different type of rails.

More in detail, ViSyR's functionality can be described by three blocks: Rail Detection & Tracking Block (RDT&B), Bolts Detection Block (BDB) and Defects Analysis Block (DAB).

- RD&TB is devoted to detect and track the rail head in the acquired video. So doing it strongly reduces the windows to be effectively inspected by the other blocks. It is based on the Principal Component Analysis and the Single Value Decomposition. This technique allows the detection of the coordinates of the center of the rail analyzing a single row of the acquired video sequence (and not a rectangular window having more rows) in order to keep extremely low the time for I/O. Nevertheless, it allows an accuracy of 98.5%.

- BDB, thanks to the knowledge of the rail geometry, analyses only those windows candidate to contain the fastening elements. It classifies them in the sense of presence/absence of the bolts. This classification is performed combining in a logical AND two classifiers based on different preprocessing. This "cross validated" response avoids (practically-at-all) false positive, and reveals the presence/absence of the fastening bolts with an accuracy of 99.6% in detecting visible bolts and of 95% in detecting missing bolts. The cases of two different kinds of fastening elements (hook bolts and hexagonal bolts) have been implemented.
- DAB focuses its analysis on a particular class of surface defects of the rail: the so-called rail corrugation, that causes an undulated shape into the head of the rail. To detect (and replace) corrugated rails is a main topic in railways maintenance, since in high-speed train, they induce harmful vibrations on wheel and on its components, reducing their lifetime. DAB mainly realizes a texture analysis. In particular, it derives as significant attributes (features) mean and variance of four different Gabor Filter responses, and classifies them using a Support Vector Machine (SVM) getting 100% reliability in detecting corrugated rails, as measured in a very large validation set. The choice of Gabor Filter is derived from a comparative study about several approaches to texture feature extraction (Gabor Filters, Wavelet Transforms and Gabor Wavelet Transforms).

Details on the artificial vision techniques basing the employed algorithms, on the parallel architectures implementing RD&TB and BDB, as well as on the experiments and test performed in order to define and tune the design of ViSyR are presented in this chapter. Several Appendixes are finally enclosed, which shortly recall theoretical issues recalled during the chapter.

2. System Overview

ViSyR acquires images of the rail by means of a DALSA PIRANHA 2 line scan camera [Matrox] having 1024 pixels of resolution (maximum line rate of 67 kLine/s) and using the Cameralink protocol [MachineVision]. Furthermore, it is provided with a PC-CAMLINK frame grabber (Imaging Technology CORECO) [Coreco]. In order to reduce the effects of variable natural lighting conditions, an appropriate illumination setup equipped with six OSRAM 41850 FL light sources has been installed too. In this way the system is robust against changes in the natural illumination. Moreover, in order to synchronize data acquisition, the line scan camera is triggered by the wheel encoder. This trigger sets the resolution along y (main motion direction) at 3 mm, independently from the train velocity; the pixel resolution along the orthogonal direction x is 1 mm. The acquisition system is installed under a diagnostic train during its maintenance route. A top-level logical scheme of ViSyR is represented in Figure 1, while Figure 2 reports the hardware and a screenshot of ViSyR's monitor.

A long video sequence captured by the acquisition system is fed into Prediction Algorithm Block (PAB), which receives a feedback from BDB, as well as the coordinates of the railways geometry by RD&TB. PAB exploits this knowledge for extracting 24x100 pixel windows where the presence of a bolt is expected (some examples are shown in Figure 3).

These windows are provided to the 2-D DWT Preprocessing Block (DWTPB). DWTPB reduces these windows into two sets of 150 coefficients (i.e., $\boldsymbol{D\_LL_2}$ and $\boldsymbol{H\_LL_2}$), resulting respectively from a Daubechies DWT (DDWT) and a Haar DWT (HDWT). D_LL_2 and H_LL_2 are therefore provided respectively to the Daubechies Classifier (DC) and to the Haar Classifier (HC). The output from DC and HC are combined in a logical AND in order to produce the output of MLPN Classification Block (MLPNCB). MLPNC reveals the presence/absence of bolts and produces a Pass/Alarm signal that is online displayed (see the squares in Figure 2.b), and -in case of alarm, i.e. absence of the bolts- recorded with the position into a log file.

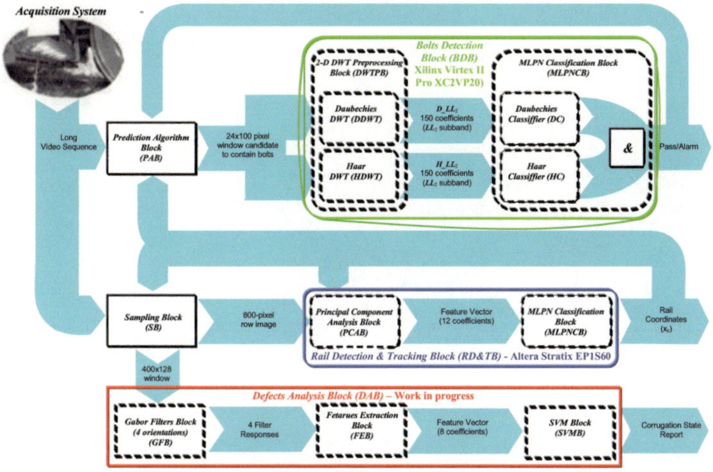

Figure 1. ViSyR's Functional diagram. Rounded blocks are implemented in a FPGA-based hardware, rectangular blocks are currently implemented in a software tool on a general purpose host

RD&TB employs PCA followed by a Multilayer Perceptron Network Classification Block (MLPNCB) for computing the coordinates of the center of the rail. More in detail, a Sampling Block (SB) extracts a row of 800 pixels from the acquired video sequence and provides it to the PCA Block (PCAB). Firstly, a vector of 400 pixels, extracted from the above row and centered on x_c (i.e., the coordinate of the last detected center of the rail head) is multiplied by 12 different eigenvectors. These products generate 12 coefficients, which are fed into MLPNCB, which reveals if the processed segment is centered on the rail head. In that case, the value of x_c is updated with the coordinate of the center of the processed 400-pixels vector and online displayed (see the cross in Figure 2.b). Else, MLPNCB sends a feedback to PCAB, which iterates the process on another 400-pixels vector further extracted from the 800-pixel row.

The detected values of x_c are also fed back to various modules of the system, such as SB, which uses them in order to extract from the video sequence some windows of 400x128 pixels centered on the rail to be inspected by the Defect Analysis Block (DAB): DAB convolves these windows by four Gabor filters at four different orientations (Gabor Filters Block). Afterwards, it determines mean and variance of the obtained filter responses and uses them as features input to the SVM Classifier Block which produces the final report about the status of the rail.

BDB and RD&TB are implemented in hardware on an a Xilinx Virtex IITM Pro XC2VP20 (embedded into a Dalsa Coreco Anaconda-CL_1 Board) and on an Altera StratixTM EP1S60 (embedded into an Altera PCI-High Speed Development Board - Stratix Professional

Edition) FPGAs, respectively. SB, PAB and DAB are software tools developed in MS Visual C++ 6.0 on a Work Station equipped with an AMD Opteron 250 CPU at 2.4 GHz and 4 GB RAM.

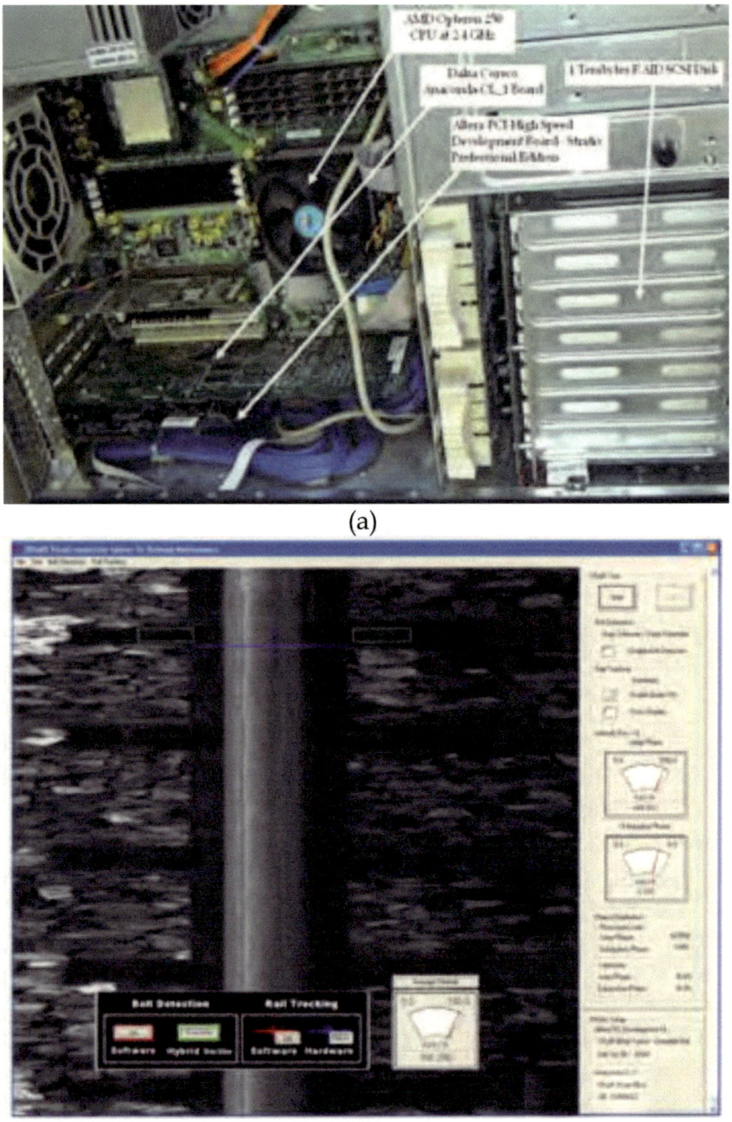

(a)

(b)

Figure 2. ViSyR: (a) hardware and (b) screenshot

Figure 3. Examples of 24x100 windows extracted from the video sequence containing hexagonal headed bolts. Resolutions along x and y are different because of the acquisition setup

3. Rail Detection & Tracking

RD&TB is a strategic core of ViSyR, since "to detect the coordinates of the rail" is fundamental in order to reduce the areas to be analyzed during the inspection. A rail tracking system should consider that:

- the rail may appear in different forms (UIC 50, UIC 60 and so on);
- the rail illumination might change;
- the defects of the rail surface might modify the rai geometry;
- in presence of switches, the system should correctly follow the principal rail.

In order to satisfy all of the above requirements, we have derived and tested different approaches, respectively based on Correlation, on Gradient based neural network, on Principal Component Analysis (PCA, see Appendix A) with threshold and a PCA with neural network classifier.

Briefly, these methods extract a window ("patch") from the video sequence and decide if it is centred or not on the rail head. In case the "patch" appears as "centred on the rail head", its median coordinate x is assigned to the coordinate of the centre of the rail x_c, otherwise, the processing is iterated on a new patch, which is obtained shifting along x the former "patch".

Even having a high computational cost, *PCA with neural network classifier* outperformed other methods in terms of reliability. It is worth to note that ViSyR's design, based on a FPGA implementation, makes affordable the computational cost required by this approach. Moreover, we have experienced that *PCA with neural network classifier* is the only method able to correctly perform its decision using as "patches" windows constituted by a single row of pixels. This circumstance is remarkable, since it makes the method strongly less dependent than the others from the I/O bandwidth. Consequently, we have embedded into ViSyR a rail tracking algorithm based on PCA with MLPN classifier. This algorithm consists of two steps:

- a data reduction phase based on PCA, in which the intensities are mapped into a reduced suitable space (Component Space);
- a neural network-based supervised classification phase, for detecting the rail in the Component Space.

3.1 Data Reduction Phase.

Due to the setup of ViSyR's acquisition, the linescan TV camera digitises lines of 1024 pixels. In order to detect the centre of the rail head, we discarded the border pixels, considering rows of only 800 pixels. In the set-up employed during our experiments, rail having widths up to 400 pixels have been encompassed.

Matrices **A** and **C** were derived according to equations (A.1) and (A.4) in Appendix A, using 450 examples of vectors. We have selected L=12 for our purposes, after having verified that a component space of 12 eigenvectors and eigenvalues was sufficient to represent the 91% of information content of the input data.

3.2 Classification Phase

The rail detection stage consists of classifying the vector $\mathbf{a}'$ -determined as shown in (A.8)- in order to discriminate if it derives from a vector $\mathbf{r}'$ centred or not on the rail head. We have implemented this classification step using a Multi Layer Perceptron Neural (MLPN) Network Classifier, since:

- neural network classifiers have a key advantage over geometry-based techniques because they do not require a geometric model for the object representation [A. Jain et al. (2000)];
- contrarily to the id-tree, neural networks have a topology very suitable for hardware implementation.

Inside neural classifiers, we have chosen the MLP, after having experimented that they are more precise than their counterpart RBF in the considered application, and we have adopted a 12:8:1 MLPN constituted by three layers of neurons (input, hidden and output layer), respectively with 12 neurons $n_{1,m}$ (m=0..11) corresponding to the coefficients of **a**′ derived by **r**′ according to (A.7); 8 neurons $n_{2,k}$ (k=0..7):

$$n_{2,k} = f\left(bias_{1,k} + \sum_{m=0}^{11} w_{1,m,k} n_{1,m} \right) \tag{1}$$

and a unique neuron $n_{3,0}$ at the output layer (indicating a measure of confidence on the fact that the analyzed vector **r**′ is centered or not on the rail head):

$$n_{3,0} = f\left(bias_{2,0} + \sum_{k=0}^{7} w_{2,k,0} n_{2,k} \right) \tag{2}$$

In (1) and (2), the adopted activation function $f(x)$, having range]0, 1[, has been:

$$f(x) = \frac{1}{1+e^{-x}} \tag{3}$$

while the weights $w_{1,m,k}$ and $w_{2,k,0}$ have been solved using the Error Back Propagation algorithm with an adaptive learning rate [Bishop. (1995)] and a training set of more than 800 samples (see Paragraph 7.3).

3.3 Rail Detection and Tracking Algorithm

The Rail Detection and Tracking Algorithm consists of determining which extracted vector **r**′ is centred on the rail.

Instead of setting the classifier using a high threshold at the last level and halting the research as soon as a vector is classified as centred on the rail ("rail vector"), we have verified that better precision can be reached using a different approach.

We have chosen a relatively low threshold (=0.7). This threshold classifies as "rail vector" a relatively wide set of vectors **r**′, even when these ones are not effectively centred on the rail (though they contain it). By this way, in this approach, we halt the process not as soon as the first "rail vector" has been detected, but when, after having detected a certain number of contiguous "rail vectors", the classification detects a "no rail". At this point we select as true "rail vector" the median of this contiguous set. In other words, we accept as "rail vector" a relatively wide interval of contiguous vectors, and then select as x_C the median of such interval.

In order to speed-up the search process, we analyse each row of the image, starting from a vector **r**′ centered on the last detected coordinate of the rail centre x_C. This analysis is performed moving on left and on right with respect to this origin and classifying the vectors, until the begin (x_B) and the end (x_E) of the "rail vectors" interval are detected. The algorithm is proposed in Figure 4.

```
xC = 512;    // presetting of the coordinate of the centre of the rail
do Start image sequence to End image sequence;
  set r' (400-pixel row) centered on xC;
  do:
    determine a' (12 coefficients) from r'
    input a' to the classifier and classify r'
    set the new r' shifting 1-pixel-left the previous r'
  while(r' is classified as rail)
// exit from do-while means you have got the begin of the "rail vectors" interval
  xB = median coordinate of r';
  r' (400-pixel row) centred on xC;
  do:
    determine a' (12 coefficients) from r'
    input a' to the classifier and classify r'
    set the new r' shifting 1-pixel-right the previous r'
  while(r' is classified as rail)
// exit from do-while means you have got the end of the "rail vectors" interval
  xE = median coordinate of r';
  output xC = (xB+xE)/2;
end do
```

Figure 4. Algorithm for searching the rail center coordinates

4. Bolts Detection

Usually two kinds of fastening elements are used to secure the rail to the sleepers: hexagonal-headed bolts and hook bolts. They essentially differ by shape: the first one has a regular hexagonal shape having random orientation, the second one has a more complex hook shape that can be found oriented only in one direction.

In this paragraph the case of hexagonal headed bolts is discussed.

It is worth to note that they present more difficulties than those of more complex shapes (e.g., hook bolts) because of the similarity of the hexagonal bolts with the shape of the stones that are on the background. Nevertheless, detection of hook bolts is demanded in Paragraph 7.6.

Even if some works have been performed, which deal with railway problems -such as track profile measurement (e.g., [Alippi *et al.* (2000)]), obstruction detection (e.g., [Sato *et al.* (1998)]), braking control (e.g., [Xishi *et al.* (1992)]), rail defect recognition (e.g., [Cybernetix Group], [Benntec Systemtechnik Gmbh]), ballast reconstruction (e.g., [Cybernetix Group]), switches status detection (e.g., [Rubaai (2003)]), control and activation of signals near stations (e.g., [Yinghua (1994)), etc.- at the best of our knowledge, in literature there are no references on the specific problem of fastening elements recognition. The only found approaches, are commercial vision systems [Cybernetix Group], which consider only fastening elements having regular geometrical shape (like hexagonal bolts) and use geometrical approaches to pattern recognition to resolve the problem. Moreover, these systems are strongly interactive. In fact, in order to reach the best performances, they

require a human operator for tuning any threshold. When a different fastening element is considered, the tuning phase has to be re-executed.
Contrariwise, ViSyR is completely automatic and needs no tuning phase. The human operator has only the task of selecting images of the fastening elements to manage. No assumption about the shape of the fastening elements is required, since the method is suitable for both geometric and generic shapes.

ViSyR's bolts detection is based on MLPNCs and consists of:

- a prediction phase for identifying the image areas (windows) candidate to contain the patterns to be detected;
- a data reduction phase based on DWT;
- a neural network-based supervised classification phase, which reveals the presence/absence of the bolts.

4.1 Prediction Phase

To predict the image areas that eventually may contain the bolts, ViSyR calculates the distance between two adjacent bolts and, basing to this information, predicts the position of the windows in which the presence of the bolt should be expected.
Because of the rail structure (see Figure 5), the distance *Dx* between rail and fastening bolts is constant -with a good approximation- and *a priori* known.
By this way, the RD&TB's task, i.e., the automatic railway detection and tracking is fundamental in determining the position of the bolts along the *x* direction. In the second instance PAB forecasts the position of the bolts along the *y* direction. To reach this goal, it uses two kinds of search:

- Exhaustive search;
- Jump search.

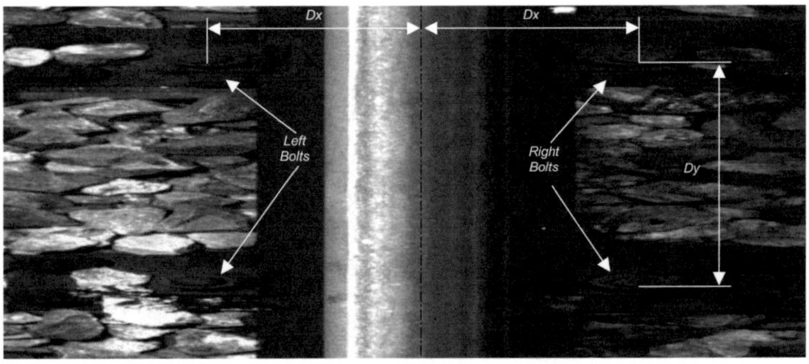

Figure 5. Geometry of a rail. A correct expectation for *Dx* and *Dy* notably reduces the computational load

In the first kind of search, a window exhaustively slides on the areas at a (well-known) distance *Dx* from the rail-head coordinate (as detected by RD&TB) until it finds contemporaneously (at the same *y*) the first occurrence of the left and of the right bolts. At this point, it determines and stores this position (*A*) and continues in this way until it finds the second occurrence of both the bolts (position *B*). Now, it calculates the distance along *y* between *B* and *A* (*Dy*) and the process switches on the Jump search. In fact, the distance along *y* between two adjacent sleepers is constant ad known. Therefore, the Jump search uses *Dy* to jump only in those areas candidate to enclose the windows containing the hexagonal-headed bolts, saving computational time and speeding-up the performance of the whole system. If, during the Jump search, ViSyR does not find the bolts in the position where it expects them, then it stores the position of fault (this is cause of alarm) in a log-file and restarts the Exhaustive search. A pseudo-code describing how Exhaustive search and Jump search commutate is shown in Figure 6.

```
do Start image sequence to End image sequence;
  repeat
    Exhaustive search;
    if found first left and right bolt store this position (A);
  until found second left and right bolt;
  store this position (B);
  determine the distance along y between B and A;
  repeat
    Jump search
  until the bolts are detected where they were expected;
end do
```

Figure 6. Pseudo code for the Exhaustive search - Jump search commutation

4.2 Data Reduction Phase

For reducing the input space size, ViSyR uses a features extraction algorithm that is able to preserve all the important information about input patterns in a small set of coefficients. This algorithm is based on 2-D DWTs [Daubechies (1988), Mallat (1989), Daubechies (1990 a), Antonini *et al.* (1992)], since DWT concentrates the significant variations of input patterns in a reduced number of coefficients. Specifically, both a compact wavelet introduced by Daubechies [Daubechies (1988)], and the Haar DWT (also known as Haar Transform [G. Strang, & T. Nuguyen (1996)]) are simultaneously used, since we have verified that, for our specific application, the logical AND of these two approaches avoids -almost completely- the false positive detection (see Paragraph 7.5).

In pattern recognition, input images are generally pre-processed in order to extract their intrinsic features. We have found [Stella *et al.* (2002), Mazzeo *et al.* (2004)] that orthonormal bases of compactly supported wavelets introduced by Daubechies [Daubechies (1988)] are an excellent tool for characterizing hexagonal-headed bolts by means of a small number of features[1] containing the most discriminating information, gaining in computational time. As an example, Figure 7 shows how two decomposition levels are applied on an image of a bolt.

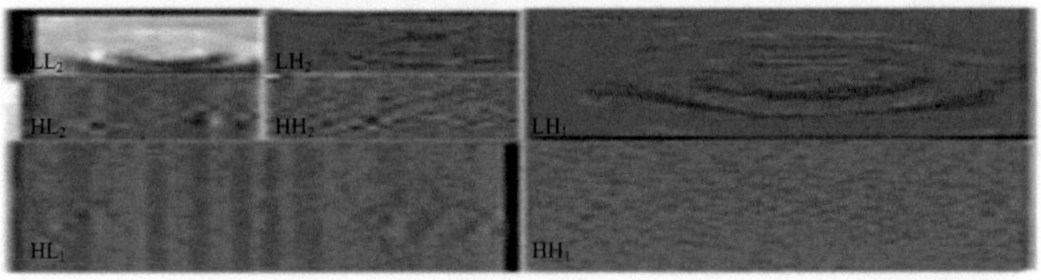

Figure 7. Application of two levels of 2-D DWT on a subimage containing an hexagonal-headed bolt

[1] These are the coefficients of the LL subband of a given decomposition level *l*; *l* depending on the image resolution and equal to 2 in the case of VISyR's set-up.

Due to the setup of ViSyR's acquisition, PAB provides DWTPB with windows of 24x100 pixels to be examined (Figure 3). Different DWTs have been experimented varying the number of decomposition levels, in order to reduce this number without losing in accuracy. The best compromise has been reached by the LL_2 subband consisting only of 6x25 coefficients. Therefore, BDB has been devoted to compute the LL2 subbands both of a Haar DWT [G. Strang, & T. Nuguyen (1996)] and of a Daubechies DWT, since we have found that the cross validation of two classifiers (processing respectively D_LL_2 and H_LL_2, i.e., the output of DDWT and HDWT, see Figure 1) practically avoids false positive detection (see Paragraph 7.5). BDB, using the classification strategy described in the following Paragraph, gets an accuracy of 99.9% in recognizing bolts in the primitive windows.

4.3 Classification Phase

ViSyR's BDB employs two MLPNCs (DC and HC in Figure 1), trained respectively for DDWT and HDWT. DC and HC have an identical three-layers topology 150:10:1 (they differ only for the values of the weights). In the following, DC is described; the functionalities of HC can be straightforwardly derived.
The input layer is composed by 150 neurons $D\_n'_m$ (m=0..149) corresponding to the coefficients $D\_LL_2(i, j)$ of the subband D_LL_2 according to:

$$D\_n'_m = \boldsymbol{D\_LL}_2(m/25, m \bmod 25) \tag{4}$$

The hidden layer of DC consists of 10 neurons $D\_n''_k$ (k=0..9); they derive from the propagation of the first layer according to:

$$D\_n''_k = f\left(D\_bias'_k + \sum_{m=0}^{149} D\_w'_{m,k} D\_n'_m\right) \tag{5}$$

whilst the unique neuron $D\_n'''_0$ at the output layer is given by:

$$D\_n'''_0 = f\left(D\_bias'' + \sum_{k=0}^{9} D\_w''_{k,0} D\_n''_k\right) \tag{6}$$

4where $D\_w'_{m,k}$ and $D\_w''_{k,0}$ are the weights respectively between first/second and second/third layers. The activation function $f(x)$ is the same as (3).
In this scenario, $D\_n'''_0$ ranges from 0 to 1 and indicates a measure of confidence on the presence of the object to detect in the current image window, according to DC.
The outputs from DC and HC ($D\_n'''_0$ and $H\_n'''_0$) are combined as follows:

$$\text{Presence} = (D\_n'''_0 > 0.9)\, AND\, (H\_n'''_0 > 0.9) \tag{7}$$

in order to produce the final output of the Classifier.
The *biases* and the weights were solved using the Error Back Propagation algorithm with an adaptive learning rate [Bishop (1995)] and a training set of more than 1,000 samples (see Paragraph 7.3).

5. Defects Analysis Block

The Defects Analysis Block, at the present, is able to detect a particular class of surface defects on the rail, the so-called rail corrugation. As it is shown in some examples of Figure 8.b, this kind of defect presents a textured surface.

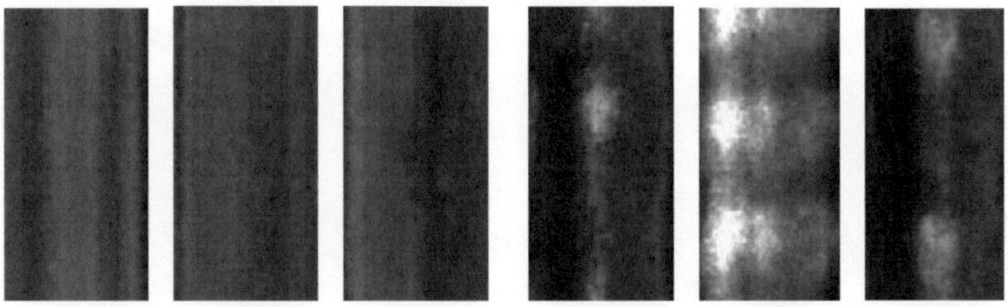

Figure 8. (a) Examples of rail head; (b) Examples of rail head affected by corrugation

A wide variety of texture analysis methods based on local spatial pattern of intensity have been proposed in literature [Bovik et al. (1990), Daubechies (1990 b)]. Most signal processing approaches submit textured image to a filter bank model followed by some energy measures. In this context, we have tested three filtering approaches to texture feature extraction that in artificial vision community have already provided excellent results [Gong *et al.* (2001), Jain *et al.* (2000)] (Gabor Filters, Wavelet Transform and Gabor Wavelet Transform), and classified the extracted features by means both of a k-nearest neighbor classifier and of a SVM, in order to detect the best combination "feature extractor"/"classifier".

DAB is currently a "work in progress". Further steps could deal with the analysis of other defects (e.g., cracking, welding, shelling ,blob, spot etc.). Study of these defects is already in progress, mainly exploiting the fact that some of them (as cracking, welding, shelling) present a privileged orientation. Final step will be the hardware implementation even of DAB onto FPGA.

5.1 Feature Extraction

For our experiments we have used a training set of 400 rail images of 400x128 pixels centered on the rail-head, containing both "corrugated" and "good" rails, and explored three different approaches, which are theoretically shortly recalled in Appendixes B, C and D.

Gabor Filters. In our applicative context, we have considered only circularly symmetric Gaussians (i.e., $\sigma_x = \sigma_y = \sigma$), adopting a scheme which is similar to the texture segmentation approach suggested in [Jain & Farrokhnia (1990)], approximating the characteristics of certain cells in the visual cortex of some mammals [Porat & Zeevi (1988)]. We have submitted the input image to a filter Gabor bank with orientation 0, $\pi/4$, $\pi/2$ and $3\pi/4$ (see Figure 9), σ=2 and radial discrete frequency F=$\sqrt{2}/2^3$ to each example of the training set. We have discarded other frequencies since they were found too low or too high for discriminating the texture of our applicative context.

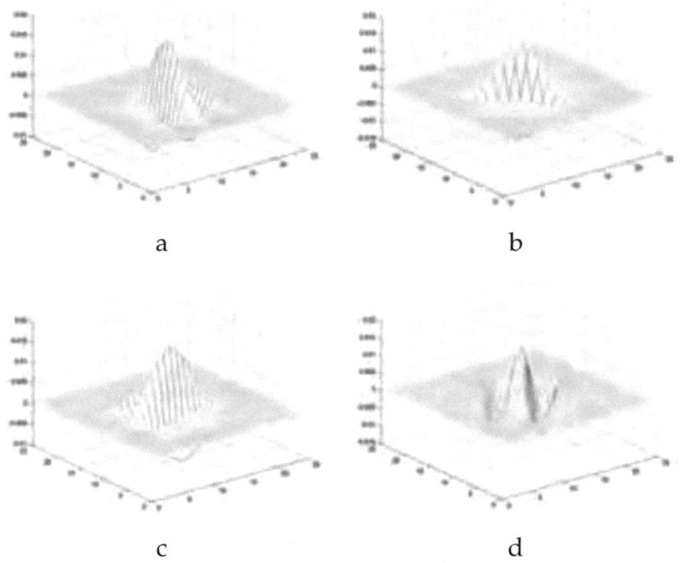

Figure 9. Gabor Filters at different orientations: (a) 0; (b) $\pi/4$; (c) $\pi/2$; (d) $3\pi/4$

The resulting images $i_\theta(x,y)$ (see Figure 10) represent the convolution of the input image $i(x,y)$ with the Gabor filters $h_\theta(x,y)$ where sub index θ indicates the orientation:

$$i_\theta(x,y)=h_\theta(x,y)*i(x,y) \tag{8}$$

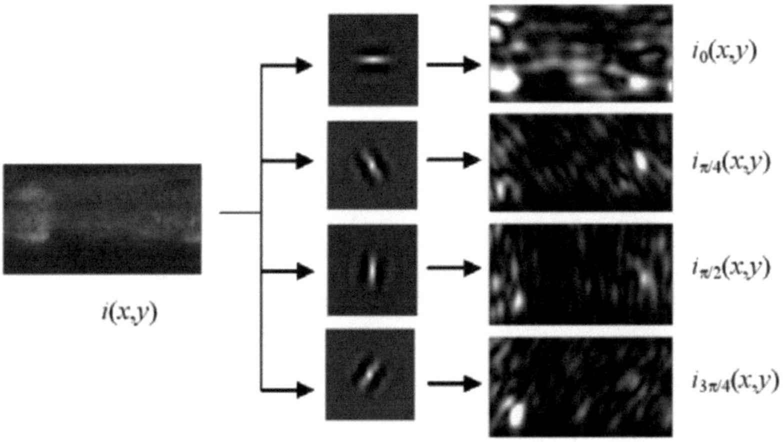

Figure 10. Examples of Gabor Filters ($F=\sqrt{2}/2^3$, σ=2) applied to a corrugated image

Wavelet Transform. We have applied a "Daubechies 1" or "haar" Discrete Wavelet transform to our data set, and we have verified that, for the employed resolution, more than three decomposition levels will have not provided additional discrimination.

Figure 11 shows how three decomposition levels are applied on an image of a corrugated rail.

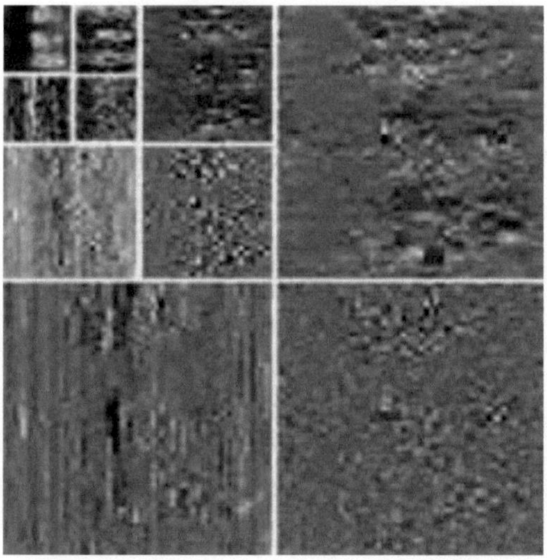

Figure 11. Example of "Daubechies 1" Discrete Wavelet transform (three decomposition levels) of the corrugated image

Gabor Wavelet Transform. A lot of evidence exists for the assumption that representation based on the outputs of families of Gabor filters at multiple spatial locations, play an important role in texture analysis. In [Ma & Manjunath (1995)] is evaluated the texture image annotation by comparison of various wavelet transform representation, including Gabor Wavelet Transform (GWT), and found out that, the last one provides the best match of the first stage of visual processing of humans. Therefore, we have evaluated Gabor Wavelet Transform also because it resumes the intrinsic characteristics both Gabor filters and Wavelet transform.

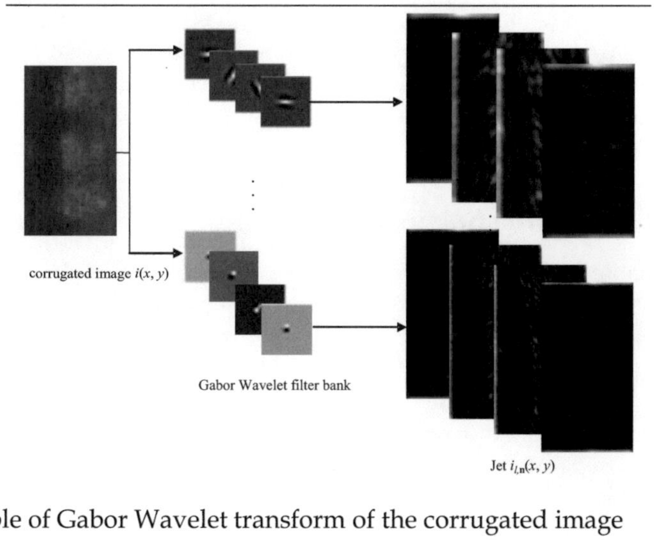

Figure 12. Example of Gabor Wavelet transform of the corrugated image

We have applied the GWT, combining the parameters applied to the Gabor Filter case and to the DWT case, i.e., applying three decomposition levels and four orientations (0, $\pi/2$, 3/4

π and π, with σ=2 and radial discrete frequency F=$\sqrt{2}/2^3$). Figure 12 shows a set of convolutions of an image affected by corrugation with wavelets based kernels. The set of filtered images obtained for one image is referred to as a "jet".
From each one of the above preprocessing techniques, we have derived 4 (one for each orientation of Gabor filter preprocessing), 9 (one for each subband HH, LH, HL of the three DWT decomposition levels) and 12 pre-processed images $i_p(x,y)$ (combining the 3 scales and 4 orientations of Gabor Wavelet Transform preprocessing). Mean and variance:

$$\mu_p = \iint |i_p(x,y)| dxdy \tag{9}$$

$$\sigma_p = \sqrt{\left(\iint |i_p(x,y)| - \mu_p\right)^2 dxdy} \tag{10}$$

of each pre-processed image $i_p(x,y)$ have been therefore used to build the feature vectors to be fed as input to the classification process.

5.2 Classification

We have classified the extracted features using two different classifiers as described in Paragraph 7.8. Considering the results obtained both by k-Nearest Neighbour and Support Vector Machine (see Appendix E), Gabor filters perform better compared to others features extractors. In this context, we have discarded Neural Networks in order to better control the internal dynamic.
Moreover, Gabor filter bank has been found to be preferred even considering the number of feature images extracted to form the feature vector for each filtering approach. In fact, the problem in using Wavelet and Gabor Wavelet texture analysis is that the number of feature images tends to become large. Feature vectors with dimension 8, 18, 24 for Gabor, Wavelet and Gabor Wavelet filters have been used, respectively. In addition, its simplicity, its optimum joint spatial/spatial-frequency localization and its ability to model the frequency and orientation sensitive typical of the HVS, has made the Gabor filter bank an excellent choice for our aim to detect the presence/absence of a particular class of surface defects as corrugation.

6. FPGA-Based Hardware Implementation

Today, programmable logics play a strategic role in many fields. In fact, in the last two decades, flexibility has been strongly required in order to meet the day-after-day shorter time-to-market. Moreover, FPGAs are generally the first devices to be implemented on the state-of-art silicon technology.
In order to allow ViSyR to get real time performance, we have directly implemented in hardware BDB and RD&TB. In a prototypal version of our system, we had adopted -for implementing and separately testing both the blocks- an Altera's PCI High-Speed Development Kit, Stratix™ Professional Edition embedding a Stratix™ EP1S60 FPGA. Successively, the availability in our Lab of a Dalsa Coreco Anaconda-CL_1 Board embedding a Virtex II™ Pro XC2VP20 has made possible the migration of BDB onto this second FPGA for a simultaneous use of both the blocks in hardware.

A top-level schematic of BDB and RDT&B are provided in Figure 13.a and 13.b respectively, while Figure 14 shows the FPGAs floorplans.

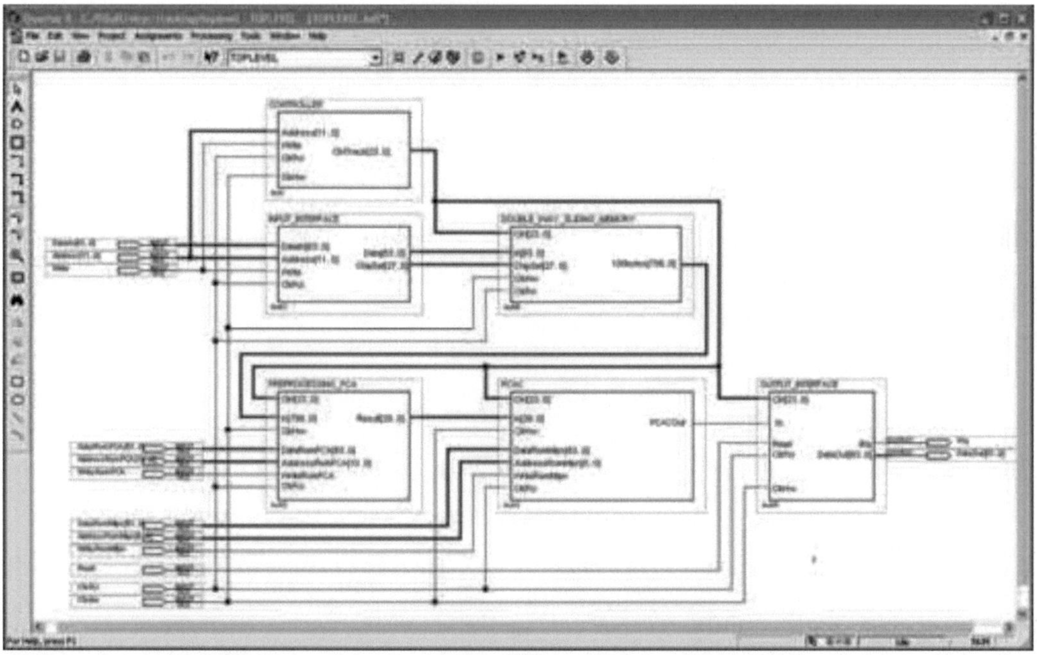

(a)

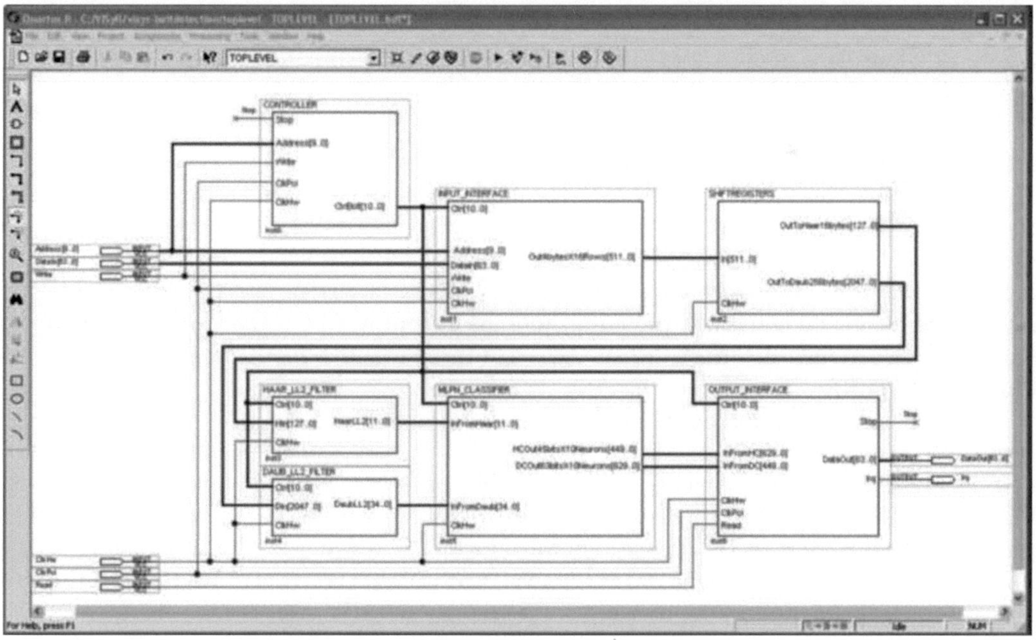

(b)

Figure 13. A top-level schematic of (a) RD&TB and (b) BDB, as they can be displayed on Altera's QuartusII™ CAD tool

Therefore, even if FPGAs were initially created for developing little glue-logic, they currently often represent the core of various systems in different fields.

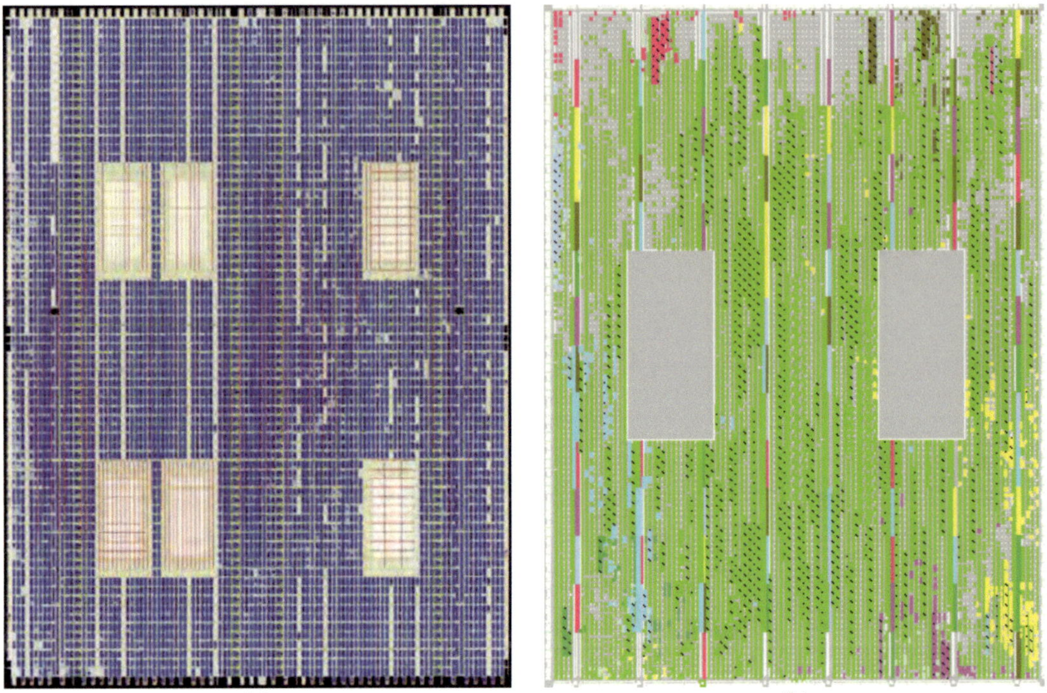

(a) (b)

Figure 14. Floorplans of (a) Altera Stratix™ EP1S60 and (b) Xilinx Virtex II™ Pro 20 after being configured

6.1 RD&TB: Modules Functionalities

The architecture can be interpreted as a memory: the task starts when the host "writes" a 800-pixel row to be analyzed. In this phase, the host addresses two shift registers inside the DOUBLE_WAY_SLIDING_MEMORY (pin address[12..0]) and sends the 800 bytes via the input line DataIn[31..0] in form of 200 words of 32 bits.

As soon as the machine has completed his job, the output line irq signals that the results are ready. At this point, the host "reads" them addressing the FIFO memories inside the OUTPUT_INTERFACE.

A more detailed description of the modules is provided in the follow.

Input Interface

The PCI Interface (not explicitly shown in Figure 13.a) sends the input data to the INPUT_INTERFACE block, through DataIn[63..0]. INPUT_INTERFACE separates the input phase from the processing phase, mainly in order to make the processing phase synchronous and independent from delays that might occur during the PCI input. Moreover, it allows of working at a higher frequency (clkHW signal) than the I/O (clkPCI signal).

Double Way Sliding Memory

As soon as the 800 pixel row is received by INPUT_INTERFACE, it is forwarded to the

DOUBLE_WAY_SLIDING_MEMORY, where it is duplicated into 2 shift registers. These shift registers slide in opposite way in order to detect both the end and the begin of the rail interval according to the search algorithm formalized in Figure 4.
For saving hardware resources and computing time, we have discarded the floating point processing mode and we have adopted fixed point precision (see Paragraph 7.7).
By this way, DOUBLE_WAY_SLIDING_MEMORY:

- extracts **r′** according the policy of Figure 4;
- partitions **r** in four segments of pixels and inputs them to PREPROCESSING_PCA in four trances via 100byte[799..0].

PCA Preprocessing

PREPROCESSING_PCA computes equation (A.7) in four steps. In order to do this, PREPROCESSING_PCA is provided with 100 multipliers, that in 12 clock cycles (ccs) multiply in parallel the 100 pixels (8 bits per pixel) of **r′** with 100 coefficients of $\mathbf{u}_m$(12 bits per coefficient, m=1..12). These products are combined order to determine the 12 coefficients a_l (having 30 bits because of the growing dynamic) which can be sent to PCAC via Result[29..0] at the rate of 1 coefficient per cc.
This parallelism is the highest achievable with the hardware resources of our FPGAs. Higher performance can be achieved with more performing devices.

Multi Layer Perceptron Neural Classifier

The results of PREPROCESSING_PCA has to be classified according to (1), (2) and (3) by a MLPN classifier (PCAC).
Because of the high hardware cost needed for arithmetically implementing the activation function $f(x)$ -i.e., (3)-, PCAC divides the computation of a neuron into two steps to be performed with different approaches, as represented in Figure 15.

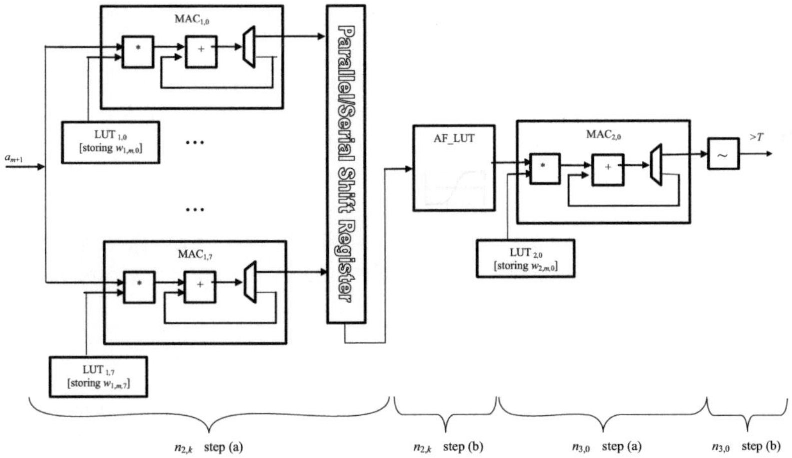

Figure 15. PCAC functionality

Specifically, step (a):

$$x = bias + \sum wn \tag{11}$$

is realized by means of Multiplier-and-ACcumulators (MACs), and step (b):

$$n = f(x) \tag{12}$$

is realized by means of a Look Up Table (for what concerns neurons $n_{2,k}$) and comparers (for what concerns neuron $n_{3,0}$). More in detail:

- neurons $n_{2,k}$, step (a): PCAC has been provided with 8 Multiplier-and-ACcumulators (MACs), i.e., $MAC_{1,k}$ (k=0..7), each one initialized with $bias_k$. As soon as a coefficient a_l (l=1..12) is produced by PREPROCESSING_PCA, the multipliers $MAC_{1,k}$ multiply it in parallel by $w_{1,m,k}$ (m=l+1, k=0..7). These weights have been preloaded in 8 LUTs during the setup, $LUT_{1,k}$ being related to $MAC_{1,k}$ and storing 12 weights. The accumulation takes 12 ccs, one cc for each coefficient a_l coming from PREPROCESSING_PCA; at the end of the computation, any $MAC_{1,k}$ will contain the value x_k.
- neurons $n_{2,k}$, step (b): The values x_k are provided as addresses to AF_LUT through a parallel input/serial output shift register. AF_LUT is a Look up Table which maps at any address x the value of the Activation Function $f(x)$. The adopted precision and sampling rate are discussed in Paragraph 7.4.
- neuron $n_{3,0}$, step (a): This step is similar to that of the previous layer, but it is performed using a unique $MAC_{2,0}$ which multiplies $n_{2,k}$ (k=0..7) by the corresponding $w_{2,k,0}$ at the rate of 1 data/cc.
- neuron $n_{3,0}$, step (b): Since our attention is captured not by the effective value of $n_{3,0}$, but by the circumstance that this might be greater than a given threshold T=0.7 (the result of this comparison constitutes the response of the classification process), we implement step (b) simply by comparing the value accumulated by $MAC_{2,0}$ with $f^{-1}(T)$.

Output Interface

Because of its latency, PCAC classifies each pattern 5 ccs after the last coefficient is provided by PREPROCESSING_PCA. At this point, the single bit output from the comparer is sent to OUTPUT_INTERFACE via PCACOut.

This bit is used as a stop signal for two counters. Specifically, as soon as a value "1" is gotten on PCACOut, a first counter C_B is halted and its value is used for determining which position of the shift of the DOUBLE_WAY_SLIDING_MEMORY is that one centered at the begin of the "rail vector" interval. Afterward, as soon as a value "0" is received from PCACOut, a second counter C_E is halted signaling the end of the "rail vector" interval. At this point, Irq signals that the results are ready, and the values of C_B and C_E packed in a 64 bits word are sent on DataOut[63..0]. Finally, the host can require and receive these results (signal read).

6.2 BDB: Modules Functionalities

Similarly to RD&TB, even BDB can be interpreted as a memory which starts its job when the host "writes" a 24x100 pixel window to be analysed. In this phase, the host addresses the dual port memories inside the INPUT_INTERFACE[2] (pins address[9..0]) and sends the 2400 bytes via the input line data[63..0] in form of 300 words of 64 bits. As soon as the machine has completed his job, the output line irq signals that the results are ready. At this point, the host "reads" them addressing the FIFO memories inside the OUTPUT_INTERFACE.

---

[2] In addition, INPUT_INTERFACE aims at the same goals of decoupling the input phase from the processing phase, as previously said in the case of RD&TB.

Daubechies DWT Preprocessing

Daubechies 2-D DWT preprocessing is performed by the cooperation of the SHIFTREGISTERS block with the DAUB_LL2_FILTER block.

Even in this case, we have discarded the floating point processing mode and we have adopted fixed point precision (see Paragraph 7.7). Moreover, since we are interested exclusively on the LL_2 subband, we have focused our attention only on that.

It can be shown that, for the 2-D DWT proposed by Daubechies in [Daubechies (1988)] having the 1-D L filter:

0,035226	-0,08544	-0,13501	0,45988	0,80689	0,33267

(13)

the LL_2 subband can be computed in only one bi-dimensional filtering step (instead of the classical twice-iterated two monodimensional steps shown in Figure 23 in Appendix C), followed by a decimation by 4 along both rows and columns. Figure 16 reports the applied symmetrical 16x16 kernel.

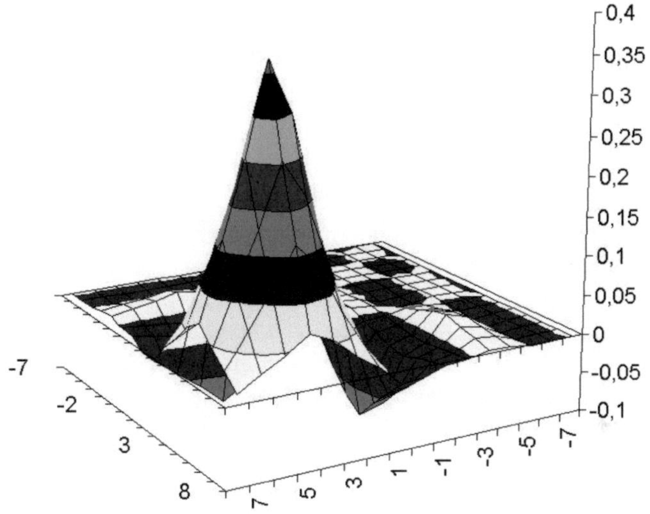

Figure 16. Symmetrical 16x16 kernel for directly computing in one 2-D step the LL_2 subband of the DWT based on the 1-D low-pass filter . The filtering has to be followed by decimation by 4 along both rows and columns

We decided of computing LL_2 directly in only one 2-D step, because:

- this requires a controller much simpler than the one used by the separable approach (Figure 23, in Appendix C);
- separable approach is greatly efficient in computing all the four subbands of each level. But ViSyR's classification process does not need other subbands than LL_2;
- when fixed point precision is employed, each step of the separable approach produces results with different dynamic, so doing, the hardware used at a certain step becomes unusable for implementing the further steps;
- the error (due to the fixed point precision) generated in a unique step does not propagate itself and can be easily controlled. Conversely, propagation occurs along four different steps when LL_2 is computed by means of separable approach.

In this scenario, SHIFTREGISTERS implements a 16x16 array which slides on the 24x100 input window shifting by 4 along columns at any clock cycle (cc). This shift along columns is realized by a routing among the cells as that one shown in Figure 17, that represents the jth row (j=0..15) of SHIFTREGISTERS.

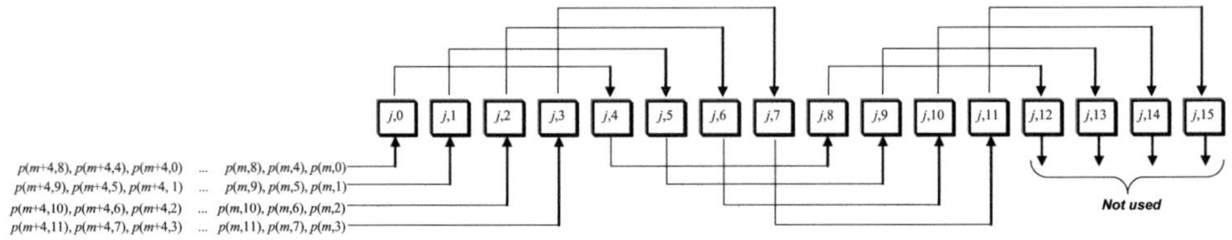

Figure 17. The jth row of the array of 16x16 shift registers in the SHIFTREGISTERS block. Each square represents an 8-bit register

The shift by 4 along the rows is performed by INPUT_INTERFACE which feeds into the jth row of the array only the pixels $p(m, n)$ of the 24x100 input window (m=0..23, n=0..99) where:

$$j \bmod 4 = m \bmod 4 \tag{14}$$

At any cc, sixteen contiguous rows of the input window are fed in parallel into SHIFTREGISTERS at the rate of 64 bytes/cc (4 bytes of each row for 16 rows) through IN[511..0]. Simultaneously, all the 256 bytes latched in the 16x16 array are inputted in parallel into DAUB_LL2_FILTER through OutToDaubLL256bytes[2047..0]. DAUB_LL2_FILTER exploits the symmetry of the kernel (see Figure 16), adding the pixels coming from the cells (j, l) to those ones coming from the cells (l, j) (j=0..15, l=0..15); afterwards, it computes the products of these sums and of the diagonal elements of the array by the related filter coefficients, and, finally, it accumulates these products.

As a result, DAUB_LL2_FILTER produces the $\boldsymbol{LL}_2$ coefficients after a latency of 11 ccs and at the rate of 1 coefficient/cc. These ones are now expressed in 35 bits, because of the growing of the dynamic, and are input into MLPN_CLASSIFIER via InFromDaub[34..0].

We are not interested in higher throughput, since -because of FPGA hardware resources- our neural classifier employs 10 multipliers and can manage 1 coefficient per cc.

Haar DWT Preprocessing

Computationally, Haar Transform is a very simple DWT since its 1-D filters are: L=[1/2, 1/2] and H=[1/2, -1/2]. Therefore, any coefficient $\boldsymbol{H\_LL}_2(i, j)$ can be computed in one step according to:

$$\boldsymbol{H\_LL}_2(i,j) = \frac{1}{16}\sum_{l=0}^{l=3}\sum_{k=0}^{k=3} p(4i+k, 4j+l) \tag{15}$$

In order to compute (15), we exploit the same SHIFTREGISTERS block used for performing Daubechies DWT and a HAAR_LL2_FILTER block. HAAR_LL2_FILTER trivially adds[3] the data coming from OutToHaar16bytes[255..0] which are the values of the pixels $p(m, n)$ of the 4x4 window centered on the 16x16 sliding array implemented by SHIFTREGISTERS.

By this way, after a latency of 2 cc, HAAR_LL2_FILTER produces 1 coefficient (expressed by 12 bits) per cc and provides it to MLPN_CLASSIFIER via HaarLL2[11..00]. Higher performance is unnecessary, since the data flow of this block is parallel at that of

[3] The scaling by 16 is simply performed by a shift left of the fixed point of 4 positions.

DAUB_LL2_FILTER.

Multi Layer Perceptron Neural Classifier

As we have seen in Paragraph 4, the MLPN_CLASSIFIER implements two classifiers (DC and HC, see Figure 1) . Their structure is similar to that already described in Figure 15. The logical AND of their output is sent to the OUTPUT_INTERFACE via DCOutXHCOut.

Output Interface

The result of the classification is extended in a word of 64 bits by and sent to the host DataOut[63..0].

7. Experimental Results and Performance

In order to design and test ViSyR's processing core, a benchmark video sequence of more than 3,000,000 lines, covering a rail network of about 9 km was acquired. These were used in order to conduct several experiments aiming firstly at defining some methodological strategies and then at designing and testing the resulting system. In the following, several of the above experiments are described.

7.1 Rail Detection Methodologies Definition

Firstly, the approach to be used for the rail head detection algorithm has been selected comparing different approaches. In order to do this, methods based on Correlation, on Gradient based neural network, on PCA with threshold, PCA with neural network classifier, were implemented in software. A subset of the benchmark video sequence was sampled at a rate of 1000 lines, taking care of including among them, several lines showing rail switches. The obtained vector, of more than 300 lines, was manually inspected, detecting the real value of x_c, to be used as reference in order to evaluate the precision reachable by the tested methods. Among those, PCA with neural network classifier resulted the most accurate.
In Figure 18 are reported the coordinates of x_c both real (i.e., manually extracted) and automatically estimated by the realized system. The average of the absolute error was 6.04 pixels. The only evident discontinuities occur in concomitance of three rail switches, resulting in the spikes of Figure 18.b which reports the magnified error. We would put in evidence that, five other switches have been correctly analyzed. Anyway, except in these cases, the errors are almost always less than 10 pixels, and never more than 20. This error makes the method fully efficient for our practical purpose.

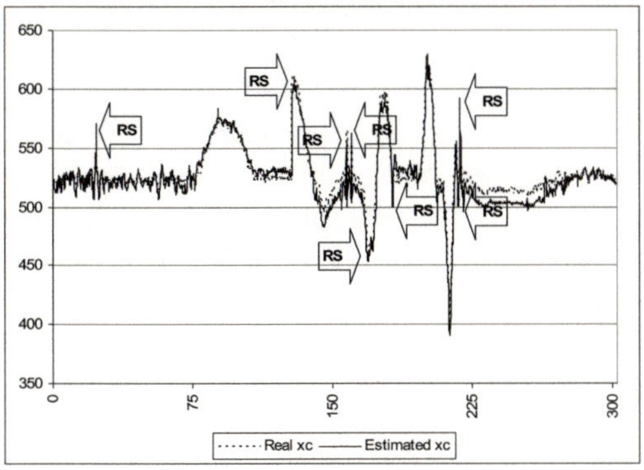

(a)

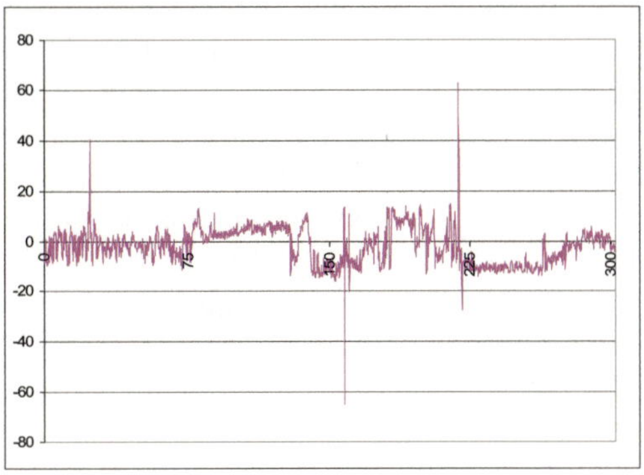

(b)

Figure 18. (a): Real and estimated coordinates of x_C . (b): error. RS denotes rail switch

7.2 Single Value Decomposition Matrices Construction Definition

Matrices **A** and **C** were derived according to (A.1) and (A.4) using 450 examples of vectors $\mathbf{r}_i$ extracted from the acquired video sequence. After having determined the eigenvectors $\mathbf{u}_j$ and their eigenvalues λ_j, we verified that 12 eigenvectors were enough to represent the 91% of the information content of input data.

7.3 MLPN Classifiers Training Value

Error Back Propagation algorithm with an adaptive learning rate [Bishop (1995)] was used to determine the biases and the weights of the PCAC classifier. The adopted training set contained 262 different 400-pixels vectors centered on the rail (positive examples) and 570 negative examples consisting of 400-pixels vectors extracted from the video sequence, for what concerned RD&TB, while, for BDB, 391 positive examples of hexagonal-headed bolts with different orientations, and 703 negative examples consisting of 24x100 pixels windows extracted from the video sequence were used.

7.4 Activation Function Design

The analytical hardware implementation of the activation function $f(x)$ -equation (3)- needs huge resources, as well as, introduces much latency. We have implemented it by a look up table AF_LUT, storing 4096 values $f(x')$ computed onto 4096 equidistant values in [-5, 5] and assuming:

$$f(x)=\begin{cases}\text{if} \quad x<-5 & : \; 0\\ \text{if} \quad -5\le x\le 5 & : \; \text{AF\_LUT}[x']\\ \text{if} \quad x>5 & : \; 1\end{cases} \qquad x' \;\text{ being the rounded value of } x \tag{16}$$

AF_LUT was filled using words of 5 bits, that was found the best compromise in terms of detection accuracy and hardware cost.

7.5 False Positive Elimination

In defining the preprocessing strategy, we observed that, though the classifier DC, based on Daubechies DWT, reached a very high detection rate (see Paragraph 7.9), it also produced a certain number of False Positives (FPs) during the Exhaustive search.

In order to reduce these errors, a "cross validation" strategy was introduced. Because of its very low computational overhead, Haar DWT was taken into account and tested. HC, a neural classifier working on the LL_2 subband of the Haar DWT, was designed and trained: HC reached the same detection rate of DC, though revealing much more FPs.

Nevertheless, the FPs resulting from HC were originated from different features (windows) than those causing the FPs output from DC. This phenomenon is put in evidence by Figure 19, where a spike denotes a detection (indifferently true and false positives) at a certain line of the video sequence revealed by DC (Figure 19.a) and by HC (Figure 19.b) while they analyzed in Exhaustive search (i.e., without jump between couple of bolts) 4,500 lines of video sequence. Figure 19.c shows the logical AND between the detections (both True and False Positive) of DC and HC. In other words, it shows the results of (7).

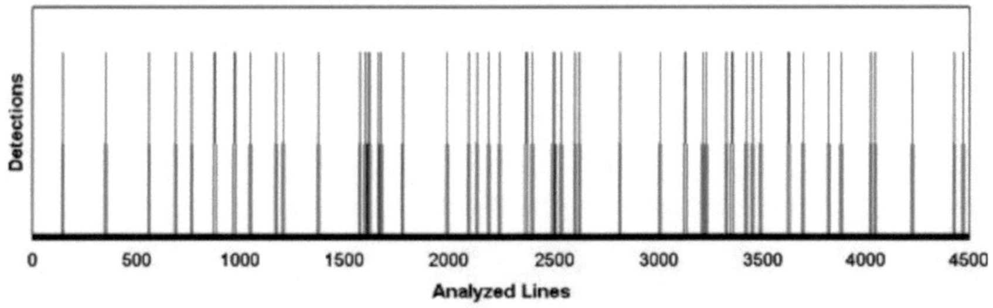

(a)

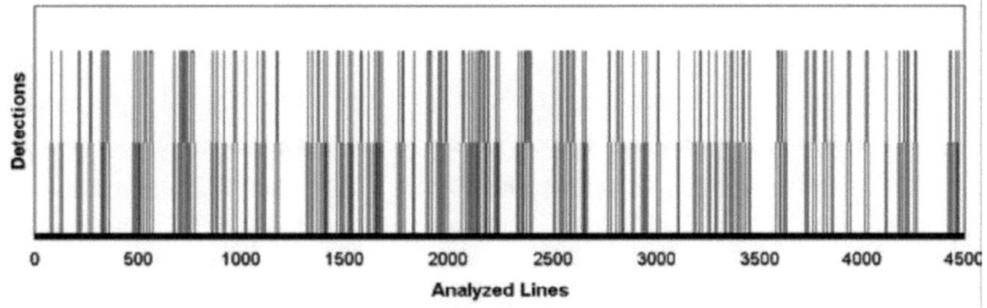

(b)

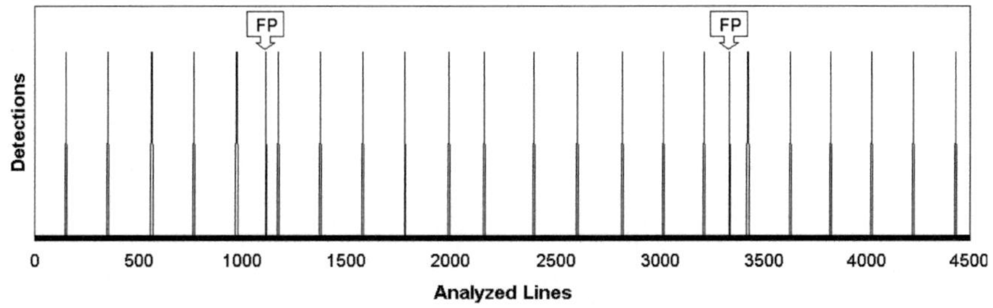

(c)

Figure 19. Detected couples of bolts vs video sequence, analyzed in Exhaustive search (i.e., without jump between couples of detected bolts). (a) Daubechies Classifier; (b) Haar Classifier; (c) Crossed validation

	True Positive (TP)	False Positive (FP)	FP/TP	FP/Analyzed Lines
Haar DWT	22 (100%)	90	409%	200.0‱
Daubechies DWT	22 (100%)	26	118%	57.8‱
AND (Daubechies, Haar)	22 (100%)	2	9%	4.4‱

Table 1. False Positive (Exhaustive Search)

As it is evidenced, only 2 FPs over 4,500 analyzed lines (90,000 processed features) are revealed by the crossed validation obtained by the logical AND of DC and HC. Numerical results are reported in Table 1.

It should be noted that the shown ratio FP/TP is related to the Exhaustive search, but it strongly decreases during the Jump search, which skips a large number of lines that of course do not contain bolts.

7.6 Hook Bolts Detection

In order to test the generality of our system in detecting other kinds of bolts, we have tested ViSyR even on the hook bolts. Firstly, a second rail network employing hook bolts (see Figure 20) and covering about 6 km was acquired.

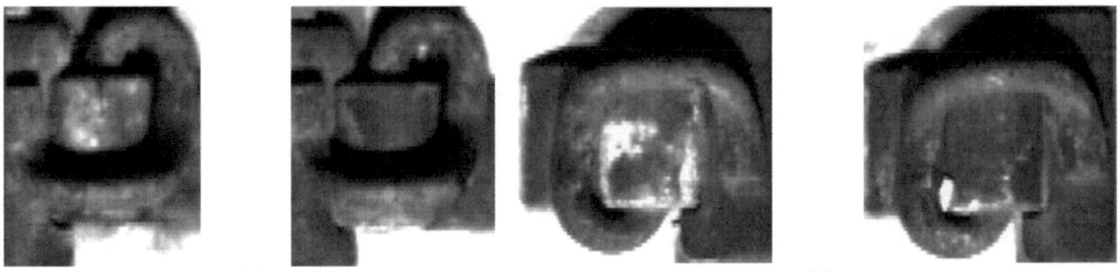

(a) (b)

Figure 20. Sample image patterns of the (a) right hook bolts and (b) left hook bolts

Two training sets TS1 and TS2 were extracted. They contained 421 negative examples, and respectively 172 positive examples of left hook bolts (TS1), and 172 examples of right hook bolts (TS2). Therefore, TS1 and TS2, were used for training the MLPN Classifiers devoted to inspect respectively the left and on the right side of the rail. Finally, the remaining video sequence was used to test the ability of ViSyR even in detecting hook bolts.

7.7 Hardware Design Definition

The report (file log) obtained from the above experiment was used as term of comparison for the reports of similar experiments aiming at defining the number of bits per words to be used in the hardware design. The fully-software prototype of ViSyR was modified changing the floating point operating mode into the fixed point mode. Different versions of ViSyR were compiled with different precisions (i.e., number of bits). For what concerned RD&TB, 12 bits for the eigenvectors coefficients and 28 bits for the weights of the classifier, allowed an accuracy only 0.6% lower than that one achievable using floating point precision while 23 bits for the filter coefficients and with 25 bits for the weights of both the classifiers led to detect visible bolts with accuracy only 0.3% lower than that obtained using floating point precision. These settings were considered acceptable, and the hardware design was developed using these specifications.

7.8 Rail Corrugation Analysis and Classification Strategy

As said in Paragraph 5, feature vectors have been respectively determined considering mean and variance of:

- each Gabor filter output image $i_\theta(x,y)$, one for orientation θ (0, π/2, π, ¾ π), getting a feature vector composed by 8 features;
- each HL, LH and HH subbands of each decomposition level, getting a feature vector composed by 18 features;
- each image of the jet (consisting of three decomposition levels -as in the wavelet transform case- per four orientations -as in the Gabor Filter case-), getting a feature vector composed by 24 features.

In order to test the performances of a k-Nearest Neighbor classifier, we have used a leave-one-out (LOO) procedure. Table 2 shows the number of misclassifications for different values of ***K***, for a training set of Gabor filtered images (GF), Wavelet filtered images (WF) and Gabor-Wavelet filtered images (GWF).

	K						
	3	5	7	9	11	13	15
GF	3	3	6	5	5	4	5
WF	3	4	10	13	14	14	16
GWF	3	5	4	5	5	4	5

Table 2. KNN Classifier: Number of misclassifications for different values of K

In order to make independent the results from the kind of classifier, we have performed a comparison with the SVM classifier. In a preliminary step, we have evaluated the optimal regularization parameter C and polynomial kernel K(x,y) in order to configure the SVM classifier and get the best performance in terms of accuracy for the whole system. The results, using the LOO procedure, are presented in Table 3 for a regularization parameter C=150 and a polynomial kernel $K(x,y)=[(xy)/k]$ where k is a normalization factor for the dot product.

	C=150, K(x,y)=[(xy)/k]
GF	0
WF	12
GWF	10

Table 3. SVM Classifier: Number of misclassifications for C=150 and K(x,y)=[(xy)/k]

7.9 Accuracy and Computing Performance

The accuracy of RD&TB was measured on a test set of more than 1,500 vectors (832 positives i.e., rails, 720 negatives i.e., non rails). 99.8% of positives and 98.2% of negatives were correctly detected. The accuracy in detecting the presence/absence of bolts was also measured. A fully-software prototype of ViSyR, employing floating point precision, was executed in "trace" modality in order to allow an observer to check the correctness of the automatic detections. This experiment was carried out over a sequence covering 3,350 bolts. ViSyR detected 99.9% of the visible bolts, 0.1% of the occluded bolts and 95% of the absences. These performances have been possible also thanks to the crossed classification strategy described in Paragraph 4.

Even more accurate was the recognition rate in case of hook bolts, since together with a 100% of detected absent and present bolts, the system also achieved an acceptable rate detection of partially occluded hook bolts (47% and 31% respectively for left and right), whereas, it was not so affordable in case of occluded hexagonal bolts. This circumstances is justified since the hexagonal shape could cause miss classification because its similarity with the stones on the background.

Moreover, a better behavior in terms of detection of occluded hook bolts even speeds up the velocity. In fact, though the velocities reached during the Jump and the Exhaustive search does not present significant differences with respect those obtained with the hexagonal bolts the system remains (in the case of hook bolts) for longer time intervals in the Jump search, because of the higher detection rate. This leads to a higher global velocity.

For what concerns DAB, the comparative study aiming at define the most accurate feature extractor-classifier paradigm, it was found that a SVM classifier with C=150 and

K(x,y)=[(xy)/k], cascaded to a Gabor Filter, as described in Paragraph 5 reached 100% of detection both of corrugated and non-corrugated rails.
Table 4 resumes ViSyR's accuracy.

		Detection Rate
RD&TB	rail vectors	99.8%
	non-rail vectors	98.2%
BDB	visible hexagonal bolts	99.6%
	occluded hexagonal bolts	0.1%
	absent hexagonal bolts	95%
	visible left hook bolts	100%
	occluded left hook bolts	47%
	absent left hook bolts	100%
	visible right hook bolts	100%
	occluded right hook bolts	31%
	absent right hook bolts	100%
DAB	corrugated rails	100%
	non-corrugated rails	100%

Table 4. Detection accuracy

Computing performance was measured too, for what concerns the functionality of RD&TB and BDB (i.e. the ViSyR's modules already implemented in hardware). In particular, over than 15,000 couples of bolts have been detected in more than 3,000,000 lines at the velocity of 166 km/h. This performance is given by the combination of the Jump search and of the Exhaustive search, being the velocities reached during these phases approximately of 4 km/h and 444 km/h, and obviously depends on the distribution of the two kinds of search for the inspected video sequence. For instance, Figure 21 shows how the two types of search commutate during the process, for the tested video sequence.

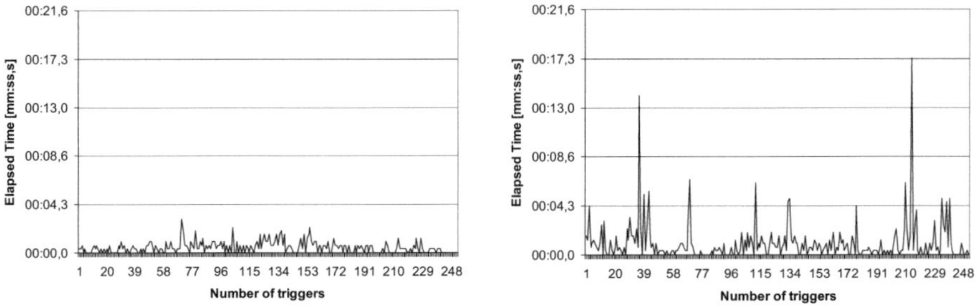

(a) (b)

Figure 21. The way in which the system commutates during (a) the Exhaustive search and (b) the Jump search

The maximum elapsed time in the Exhaustive search is less than 3". This means that the Exhaustive search finds a couple of bolts (left and right) after less than 3" in the worst cases. At this point the control switches on the Jump search that, because of its philosophy, is much faster. When activated, Jump search works uninterruptedly up to 17", for the analyzed sequence (Figure 21.b). Obviously, if the system remains in the Jump phase for a long time, performance can increase subsequently. Next work will be addressed in this direction, for example, automatically skipping those areas where the fastening elements are covered by asphalt (i.e., level crossing, where Exhaustive search is executed in continuous).

8. Conclusive Remarks

This paper has presented ViSyR, a visual system able to autonomously detect the bolts that secure the rail to the sleepers and to monitor the rail condition.
Thanks to a FPGA-based hardware implementation, it performs its inspection at velocities that can reach 460 km/h. In addition to this computing power ViSyR is also characterized by an impressive accuracy and is highly flexible and configurable, being the decision level of both RD&TB, BDB and DAB based on classifiers that can be easily reconfigured in function of different type of rails and bolts to be inspected and detected.
ViSyR constitutes a significant aid to the personnel in the railway safety issue because of its high reliability, robustness and accuracy. Moreover, its computing performance allows a more frequent maintenance of the entire railway network.
A demonstrative video of ViSyR is available at:
http://ftp-dee.poliba.it:8000/Marino/ViSyR_Demo.MOD

9. References

Alippi C., Casagrande E., Scotti F., & Piuri V. (2000) Composite Real-Time Image Processing for Railways Track Profile Measurement, *IEEE Trans. Instrumentation and Measurement*, vol. 49, N. 3, pp. 559-564 (June 2000).

Antonini M., Barlaud M., Mathieu P. & Daubechies I. (1992). Image Coding Using Wavelet Transform, *IEEE Trans. Image Processing*, Vol. 1, pp. 205-220. (1992).

Bahlmann C., Haasdonk B. & Burkhardt H. (2002). On-line Handwriting Recognition using Support Vector Machines - A kernel approach, *In Int. Workshop on Frontiers in Handwriting Recognition (IWFHR)* 2002, Niagara-on-the-Lake, Canada (August 2002).

Benntec Systemtechnik Gmbh, RAILCHECK: image processing for rail analysis, *internal documentation*, http://www.benntec.com

Bishop M. (1995). *Neural Networks for Pattern Recognition*, New York, Oxford, pp. 164-191.

Bovik AC, Clark M, Geisler WS (1990), Multichannel texture analysis Using Localized Spatial Filters. *IEEE Trans On PAMI* 12: 55-73

Coreco. http://www.coreco.com

Cybernetix Group (France), IVOIRE: a system for rail inspection, *internal documentation*, http://www.cybernetix.fr

Daubechies I. (1988). Orthonormal bases of compactly supported wavelets, *Comm. Pure & Appl. Math.*, vol. 41, pp. 909-996. (1988).

Daubechies I. (1990 a). The Wavelet Transform, Time Frequency, Localization and Signal Analysis, *IEEE Trans. on Information Theory*, vol. 36, n. 5, pp. 961-1005. (Sept. 1990).

Daubechies I (1990 b), *Ten Lectures on Wavelets. Capital City Press, Montpellier*, Vermont

Drucker H., Burges C., Kaufman L., Smola A., Vapnik V. (1997). "Support Vector Regression Machines," in: M. Mozer, M. Jordan, andT. Petsche (eds.), *Neural Information Processing Systems*, Vol. 9. MIT Press, Cambridge, MA.

Gong S. et al. (2001). *Dynamic Vision: From Images to Face Recognition*, Imperial College Press.

Jain A., Duin R., & Mao J. (2000). Statistical Pattern Recognition: A Review, *IEEE Transactions on Pattern Analysis and Machine Intelligenve,* vol. 22, no.1, pp.4-37, 2000.

Jain AK, Farrokhnia F (1990). *Unsupervised texture segmentation using Gabor filters. Pattern Recognition,* 24: 1167-1186

Lee T.S. (1996). Image Representation Using 2D Gabor Wavelets , *IEEE Trans. on PAMI* , Vol. 18 no. 10, 1996

Ma W. Y., Manjunath B.S. (1995) A comparison of wavelet transform features for texture image annotation, *Proc. Second International Conference on Image Processing (ICIP'95),* Washington, D.C., vol. 2, pp. 256-259. (Nov. 1995).

MachineVision. CAMERALINK: specification for camera link interface standard for digital cameras and frame grabbers, www.machinevisiononline.org

Mallat S.G. (1989). A theory for quadriresolution signal decomposition: the wavelet representation, *IEEE Trans on Pattern Analysis and Machine Intelligence,* vol. 2 pp.674-693 (1989).

Matrox. http://www.matrox.com/imaging/products/odyssey_xcl/home.cfm

Mazzeo P.L., Nitti M., Stella E. & Distante A. (2004). Visual recognition of fastening bolts for railroad maintenance, *Pattern Recognition Letters,* vol. 25 n. 6, pp. 669-677 (2004).

Osuna E., Freund R. & Girosi F. (1997) Training Support Vector Machines: an Application to Face Detection, *Proceedings of CVPR'97,* Puerto Rico. (1997).

Papageorgiou C. & Poggio T. (1999). A Pattern Classification Approach to Dynamical Object Detection, *Proceedings of ICCV,* pp. 1223-1228 (1999).

Porat M, Zeevi YY (1988), The generalized Gabor scheme of image representation in biological and machine vision, *IEEE Trans Pattern Anal Machine Intell* 10: 452-468

Rubaai A. (2003). A neural-net-based device for monitoring Amtrak railroad track system, *IEEE Transactions on Industry Applications,* vol. 39, N. 2 , pp. 374-381 (March-April 2003).

Sato K., Arai H., Shimuzu T., & Takada M. (1998). Obstruction Detector Using Ultrasonic Sensors for Upgrading the Safety of a Level Crossing, *Proceedings of the IEE International Conference on Developments in Mass Transit Systems,* pp. 190-195 (April 1998).

Stella E., Mazzeo P.L., Nitti M., Cicirelli G., Distante A. & D'Orazio T. (2002). Visual recognition of missing fastening elements for railroad maintenance, *IEEE-ITSC International Conference on Intelligent Transportation System,* pp. 94-99, Singapore (2002).

Strang G., & Nuguyen T. (1996). *Wavelet and Filter banks,* Wellesley College.

Vapnik N. (1998), *Statistical Learning Theory,* New York: John Wiley & Sons Inc. Pub.

Wen J, Zhisheng Y, Hui L (1994), Segment the Metallograph Images Using Gabor Filter, *International Symposium on Speech Image Processing and Neural Networks* pp 25-28, Hong Kong

Xishi W., Bin N., & Yinhang C. (1992). A new microprocessor based approach to an automatic control system for railway safety, *Proceedings of the IEEE International Symposium on Industrial Electronics,* vol. 2, pp. 842-843 (May 1992).

Yinghua M., Yutang Z., Zhongcheng L., & Cheng Ye Y. (1994). A fail-safe microprocessor-based system for interlocking on railways, *Proceedings of the Annual Symposium on Reliability and Maintainability,* pp. 415-420 (Jan. 1994).

Appendix A. Principal Component Analysis (PCA)

Let $\mathbf{i}_j$ row-images, each one having N pixels, object of the analysis.
Let R a set of P images $\mathbf{r}_k$ (k=1..P, $P \geq N$). Such images $\mathbf{r}_k$, having Q pixels with $Q < N$, have been extracted from the images $\mathbf{i}_j$, and chosen in order to select instances of the objects.

Figure 22. Rail head row image example

Let **A** the Q rows and P columns matrix:

$$\mathbf{A}=[\mathbf{h}_1 ,\ldots, \mathbf{h}_P] \tag{A.1}$$

with:

$$\mathbf{h}_k = \mathbf{r}_k - \boldsymbol{\mu} \tag{A.2}$$

where:

$$\boldsymbol{\mu}= [\mu_1,..,\mu_P]^T \tag{A.3}$$

with μ_k denoting the average of intensities in $\mathbf{r}_k$.
From **A**, the covariance matrix:

$$\mathbf{C}=\mathbf{A}\mathbf{A}^T \tag{A.4}$$

can be built. The QxQ matrix **C** contains information about mutual relationships among rail images $\mathbf{r}_k$.
In Principal Component Analysis [Gong *et al.* (2001), Jain *et al.* (2000).] the eigenvectors $\mathbf{u}_j$ (j=1..N) of **C** define a new reference space in which the variance among data is maximized. Moreover, an ordering relationship on $\mathbf{u}_j$ components can be induced sorting the eigenvectors $\mathbf{u}_j$ in such way that:

$$\lambda_q > \lambda_{q+1} \quad (q=1, .., Q-1) \tag{A.5}$$

where the eigenvalues λ_j of **C**, represent the variances of each one of $\mathbf{u}_j$. In other words, (A.5) means that the set of projections of the input data on $\mathbf{u}_q$ has variance higher than that one of the set of projections of the input data on $\mathbf{u}_{q+1}$.
By thresholding the eigenvalues λ_j it is possible to select the corresponding $L<Q$ eigenvectors sufficient enough to represent the biggest part of the informative content of the input data. Let λ_l (l=1..L, $L<Q$) the selected components, a generic vector $\mathbf{r}'$ can be expressed by:

$$\mathbf{r}' \approx \sum_{l=1}^{L} a_l \mathbf{u}_l + \boldsymbol{\mu}' \tag{A.6}$$

where $\boldsymbol{\mu}'$ is the average vector of $\mathbf{r}'$. From a computational point of view the eigenvectors and eigenvalues of **C** can be estimated by a Single Value Decomposition (SVD) of matrix **A** where the coefficients a_l are evaluated by the inner product:

$$a_l = (\mathbf{r}'-\boldsymbol{\mu}')\mathbf{u}_l^T \tag{A.7}$$

In this scenario, the vector

$$\mathbf{a}'=[a_1 ,\ldots, a_L]^T \tag{A.8}$$

can be considered a feature containing most of information content of $\mathbf{r}'$.

Appendix B. Gabor Filter

In the complex spatial 2D domain, Gabor filter is given by:

$$h(x,y)= g(x',y')\cdot e^{2\pi jFx'} \tag{B.1}$$

where

$$g(x,y)=\frac{1}{2\pi\sigma_x\sigma_y}\cdot e^{-\frac{1}{2}\left(\frac{x^2}{\sigma_x^2}+\frac{y^2}{\sigma_y^2}\right)} \tag{B.2}$$

and x' and y' are the rotated coordinates:

$$(x',y')=(x\cos\theta+y\sin\theta,-x\sin\theta+y\cos\theta) \tag{B.3}$$

σ_x and σ_y are the standard deviations of Gaussian envelope along the x and y directions, F frequency of sinusoidal plane and and θ is the orientation [Wen at al. (1994)].
Thus (B.1) is a complex sinusoidal grating modulated by a 2D gaussian function [25].
Gabor functions have been found useful because reach the lower bounds of the uncertainty inequalities $\Delta x\Delta u\geq 1/4\pi$ and $\Delta y\Delta v\geq 1/4\pi$ and achieve optimally joint resolution in space and spatial frequency [Bovik et al. (1990)].

Appendix C. Wavelet Transforms

The wavelet transform [Daubechies (1988), Mallat (1989), Daubechies (1990 a), Antonini *et al.* (1992)], is a mathematical technique that decomposes a signal in the time domain by using dilated/contracted and translated versions of a single finite duration basis function, called the prototype wavelet. This differs from traditional transforms (e.g., Fourier Transform, Cosine Transform, etc.), which use infinite duration basis functions. One-dimensional (1-D) continuous wavelet transform of a signal $x(t)$ is:

$$W(a,b)=\frac{1}{\sqrt{a}}\int x(t)\overline{\psi}\left(\frac{t-b}{a}\right)dt \tag{C.1}$$

where $\overline{\psi}\left(\frac{t-b}{a}\right)$ is the complex conjugate of the prototype wavelet, $\psi\left(\frac{t-b}{a}\right)$; a is a time dilation and b is a time translation.
Due to the discrete nature (both in time and amplitude) of most applications, different Discrete Wavelet Transforms (DWTs) have been proposed according to the nature of the signal, the time and the scaling parameters.
The two-dimensional (2-D) DWT works as a multi-level decomposition tool. A generic 2-D DWT decomposition level j is shown in Figure 23.

It can be seen as the further decomposition of a 2-D data set LL_{j-1} (LL_0 being the original input image) into four subbands LL_j, LH_j, HL_j and HH_j. The capital letters and their position are related respectively to the applied mono-dimensional filters (*L* for Low pass filter, *H* for High pass filter) and to the direction (first letter for horizontal, second letter for vertical). The band LL_j is a coarser approximation of LL_{j-1}. The bands LH_j and HL_j record the changes along horizontal and vertical directions of LL_{j-1}, respectively, whilst HH_j shows high frequency components. Because of the decimation occurring at each level along both the directions, any subband at the level *j* is composed by $N_j x M_j$ elements, where $N_j=N_0/2^j$ and $M_j=M_0/2^j$.

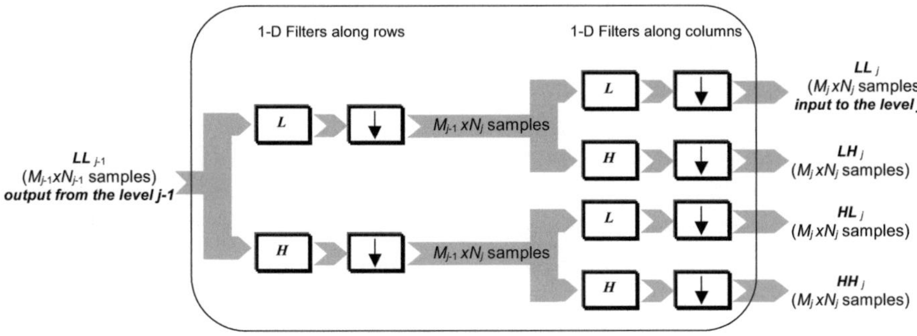

Figure 23. 2-D DWT: The jth level of subband decomposition. ↓ represents decimation by 2

Appendix D. Gabor Wavelet Transform

As seen in Appendix C, Wavelet transform can be chosen as mathematical model for its adaptability in resolution both in frequency and space domains relating to a scale parameter, while Gabor filters assure the lower limits of uncertainty inequalities (as described in Appendix B) in the space frequency domain. As consequence, Gabor functions can be considered as mother function of the Wavelet transform. On these bases, a set of 2D Gabor Wavelet filters can be defined through a projection of the signal into a family of *M* Gabor Wavelet functions $\Psi = \{\psi_{n_1}, \psi_{n_2}, \ldots, \psi_{n_M}\}$ derived from a process of contractions and dilations of a function, the so-called *mother Gabor-Wavelet*.
In two dimensions the Gabor Wavelet Functions [Lee (1996)] take the form:

$$\psi_{\mathbf{n}}(x,y) = \frac{s_x^{1/2}}{2\pi\sigma^2} e^{-\frac{1}{2\sigma^2}\left\{\left[s_x\left((x-c_x)\cos\theta+(y-c_y)\sin\theta\right)\right]^2+\left[s_y\left(-(x-c_x)\sin\theta+(y-c_y)\cos\theta\right)\right]^2\right\}} e^{2\pi j F s_x\left((x-c_x)\cos\theta+(y-c_y)\sin\theta\right)} \quad \text{(D.1)}$$

where $\mathbf{n}$ is a parametric vector $[c_x, c_y, \theta, s_x, s_y]$, with c_x and c_y representing the contractions of the GWT along *x* and *y* respectively, s_x and s_y represent the dilations along the two scales, and θ the orientation.
In addition, the dilations s_x and s_y can be selected as $s_x = s_y = 2^l$ for $l=0,\ldots, L-1$, with *L* is the number of decomposition levels, and $s_x\, c_x = s_y\, c_y = k$. As consequence, (D.1) can be written as:

$$\psi_{\mathbf{n}}(x,y) = \frac{s_x^{l/2}}{2\pi\sigma^2} e^{-\frac{1}{2\sigma^2}\left\{\left[2^l\left((x-k2^{-l})\cos\theta+(y-k2^{-l})\sin\theta\right)\right]^2+\left[2^l\left(-(x-k2^{-l})\sin\theta+(y-k2^{-l})\cos\theta\right)\right]^2\right\}} e^{2\pi j F 2^l\left[(x-k2^{-l})\cos\theta+(y-k2^{-l})\sin\theta\right]} \quad \text{(D.2)}$$

and the responses of Gabor-Wavelet filters $i_{l,\mathbf{n}}(x,y)$ can be defined as:

$$i_{l,\mathbf{n}}(x,y)=\psi_{\mathbf{n}}(x,y)*i(x,y) \tag{D.3}$$

where l is a certain level into pyramidal structure.

Appendix E. Support Vector Machine (SVM)

Support Vector Machine (SVM) [Vapnik (1998)] is based on the structural risk minimization principle from computational learning theory, or better on minimization of the misclassification probability of vectors with unknown distribution of data. With respect to the neural approach, SVM allows a better control of dynamics of the classifier. Examples of use of the SVM are given in [Bahlmann et al. (2002), Papageorgiou & Poggio. (1999) Drucker *et al.* (1997), Osuna *et al.* (1997)]. The basic idea of SVM consists of imagining some hyper-planes that divide the hyper-space containing the vectors **v** to be classified into two sub-hyper-spaces where positive examples of **v** (classified with +1) and negative examples of **v** (classified with -1) of the training set $S=\{\mathbf{v}_1,\mathbf{v}_2, ...,\mathbf{v}_N\}$ are respectively located.

There are many possible classifiers that can separate the data with hyper-planes $\mathbf{w}\cdot\mathbf{v}+b=0$, but there is only one that maximizes the distance between the closest vectors to the hyper-plane and the hyper-plane itself. SVM finds the optimal separating hyper-plane:

$$\mathbf{w}^*\cdot\mathbf{v}+b^*=0 \tag{E.1}$$

maximizing the margin and minimizing the number of misclassified patterns. In (E.1), the optimal weight vector is expressed as linear combination of the examples of the training set S:

$$\mathbf{w}^*=\sum_{i=1}^{N}\lambda_i^* y_i \mathbf{v}_i \tag{E.2}$$

where $y_i\in\{-1, 1\}$ is the label (or class) of the vector $\mathbf{v}_i$, and the optimum $\lambda^*=\{\lambda_1^*,\lambda_2^*, ...,\lambda_N^*,\}$ (where $\lambda_i^*\geq 0$) is a solution of a quadratic problem. The vectors $\mathbf{v}_i$ with $\lambda_i^*>0$ are said "support vectors". The classification of new vectors **v** involves the evaluation of the decision function $y=sign(f(\mathbf{v}))$ where:

$$f(\mathbf{v})=\mathbf{w}^*\cdot\mathbf{v}+b=\left(\sum_{i=1}^{N}\lambda_i^* y_i \mathbf{v}_i\right)\cdot\mathbf{v}+b^* \tag{E.3}$$

meaning that **v** can be classified by evaluating the dot product between **v** and some elements (support vectors) of the training set S.

9

Bearing-Only Vision SLAM with Distinguishable Image Features

Patric Jensfelt[1], Danica Kragic[1] and John Folkesson[2]
[1]*Centre for Autonomous Systems, Royal Institute of Technology*
[2] *Dept of Mechanical Engineering, Massachusetts Institute of Technology*
[1]*Sweden,* [2]*USA*

1. Introduction

One of the key competences for autonomous mobile robots is the ability to build a map of the environment using natural landmarks and to use it for localization (Thrun et al., 1998, Castellanos et al, 1999, Dissanayake et al, 2001, Tardos et al. 2002, Thrun et al., 2004). Most successful systems presented so far in the literature have relied on range sensors such as laser scanners and sonar sensors. For large scale, complex environments with natural landmarks the problem of SLAM is still an open research problem. Recently, the use of vision as the only exteroceptive sensor has become one of the most active areas of research in SLAM (Davison, 2003, Folkesson et al., 2005, Goncavles et al., 2005, Sim et al., 2005, Newman & Ho., 2005).

In this chapter, we present a SLAM system that builds maps with point landmarks using a single camera. We deal with a set of open research issues such as how to identify and extract stable and well-localized landmarks and how to match them robustly to perform accurate reconstruction and loop closing. All of these issues are central to success, especially when an estimator such as the Extended Kalman Filter (EKF) is used. Robust matching is required for most recursive formulations of SLAM where decisions are final. Even for methods that allow the data associations to change over time, e.g. (Folkesson & Christensen, 2004, Frese & Schröder 2006), reliable matching is very important.

One of the big disadvantages with the laser scanner is that it is a very expensive sensor. Cameras, on the other hand, are relatively cheap. Another aspect of using cameras for SLAM is the much greater richness of the sensor information as compared to that from, for example, a range sensor. Using a camera it is possible to recognize features based on their appearance. This provides the means for dealing with one of the most difficult problems in SLAM, namely data association.

The main contributions of this work are i) a method for the initialisation of visual landmarks for SLAM, ii) a robust and precise feature detector, iii) the management of the measurement to make on-line estimation possible, and iv) the demonstration of how this framework can facilitate real-time SLAM even with an EKF based implementation.

2. Related Work

Working with a single camera, the measurements will be of bearing only type. This means that a single observation of a landmark is not enough to estimate its full pose since the depth is unknown. This problem is typically addressed by combining the observations from multiple views as in the structure-from-motion (SFM) approaches in computer vision. The biggest difference between SLAM and SFM is that SFM considers mostly batch processing while SLAM typically requires on-line, real-time performance.

The fact that the full pose of a landmark cannot be estimated from a single observation leads to one of the most important problems that has to be addressed in bearing only SLAM; landmark initialisation. Several approaches have been presented in the literature. In (Davison, 2003) a particle filter was used to represent the unknown initial depth of features. The drawback of the approach is that the initial distribution of particles has to cover all possible depth values for a landmark, which makes it difficult to use when the number of detected features is large. A similar approach has been presented in (Dissanayake et al., 2005) where the initial state is approximated using a Gaussian Sum Filter for which the computational load grows exponentially with number of landmarks. The work in (Lemarie et al. 2005) proposes an approximation with additive growth. It uses a weighted Gaussian sum approximation for the depth estimate of uninitialised landmarks. Gaussians in the sum are deleted when they no longer are supported by subsequent observations. When a single Gaussian remains, the landmark is initialised given that a few other conditions are fulfilled.

Another, more practical problem associated with landmark initialisation comes from the limited field of view of a normal perspective camera in combination with the robot typically moving along the optical axis as pointed out in (Goncavles et al., 2005). To cope with the reconstruction problem, a stereo-based SLAM method was presented in (Sim et al., 2005) where Difference-of-Gaussians (DoG) is used to detect distinctive features which are then matched using SIFT descriptors. An important problem mentioned is that their particle filter based approach is inappropriate for large-scale and textured environments. One of the contributions of our work is that we deal with this problem by identifying only a few high quality features in the scene to perform SLAM.

Another problem mentioned in (Sim et al., 2005) is related to the time-consuming feature matching. We address this by using a KD-tree to make our matching process very fast. The visual feature detector used in our work is the Harris corner detector across different scales represented by a Laplacian pyramid, similar to what is suggested in (Mikolajczyk & Schmid 2003). For feature matching, we use a modified SIFT descriptor in combination with KD-trees.

Working in indoor environments means that the floor is typically flat and the SLAM problem can be simplified by assuming that the robot is constrained to a plane. However, there are many repetitive features stemming from, for example, right angle corners. A single SIFT descriptor is not discriminative enough in an image to solve the data association problem. To address this, ``chunks'' of SIFT points were used to represent landmarks in an outdoor environment in (Luke et al., 2005). This was motivated by the success that SIFT has had in recognition applications where the object/scene was represented as a set of SIFT points. In our approach, the position of a landmark is defined by a series of SIFT points representing different views of the landmark. Each such point is accompanied with a chunk of descriptors that make the matching/recognition of landmarks more robust. Our experimental evaluation shows also that our approach performs successful matching even with a narrow field of view, which was mentioned as a problem in (Goncavles et al., 2005, Sim et al., 2005).

Yet another problem in SLAM is loop closing, that is the ability to detect when the robot comes back to a position it has been to previously and thereby closing a loop. (Newman & Ho, 2005) argue for using laser for the geometric mapping but to rely on visual input to solve the loop-closing problem. The message is that robustness is best achieved if the same mechanism is not used for the mapping and the loop closing detection. In (Newman & Ho, 2005) visually salient, so called ``maximally stable extremal regions'' or MSERs, encoded using SIFT descriptors, are used to detect when the robot is revisiting an area. In (Gutmann & Konolige, 1999) scan matching is used to detect when loops are closed. We show in this chapter that our framework also can be used for loop closing detection.

In the remainder of this chapter we will make a distinction between recognition and location features. A single location feature will be associated with several recognition features. The recognition features' descriptors then give robustness to the match between the location features in the map and the features in the current image. The key idea is to use a few high quality features to define the location of landmarks and then use the other features for recognition. This contributes to a low complexity (few location features) while maintaining highly robust matching (many recognition features).

3. Feature Description

The SIFT descriptor (Lowe, 1999) has been used frequently in both computer vision and various robot vision applications. It has been shown in (Mikolajczyk & Schmid 2003) to be the most robust descriptor regarding scale and illumination changes. The original version of the SIFT descriptor uses feature points determined by the peaks of a series of Difference of Gaussians (DoG) on varying scales. In our system, peaks are found using Harris-Laplace features, (Mikolajczyk & Schmid 2001) since they respond to regions of high curvature, instead of blob-like image structures obtained by series of DoG. This leads to features accurately localized spatially, which is essential when features are used for reconstruction and localization, instead of just recognition.

In a sparse, indoor environment many of the detected features originate from corner features. The original SIFT descriptor assigns canonical orientation at the peak of smoothed gradient histograms. This means that similar corners but with a significant rotation difference can have similar descriptors. This may potentially lead to many false matches. For example, the four corners of the waste bin in Figure 2. may all match if rotated. Therefore, we use a rotationally 'variant' SIFT descriptor where we avoid the canonical orientation at the peak of smoothed gradient histogram and leave the gradient histogram as it is.

4. Landmark Selection and Initialisation

Landmark initialisation is a key issue in bearing only vision SLAM. To determine which image features that are worth turning into landmarks, we match the features across N frames. Features that are successfully matched over enough frames become candidates for landmarks in the map. Such a matching buffer also allows us to calculate an estimate of the 3D position of the corresponding landmark by multi view triangulation. The SLAM process is fed measurements from the output side of the frame buffer, which means that the measurements are delayed N frames with respect to the input side of the buffer. Figure 1. illustrates this idea.

Figure 1. A buffer of N image frames is used for matching, selection & triangulation

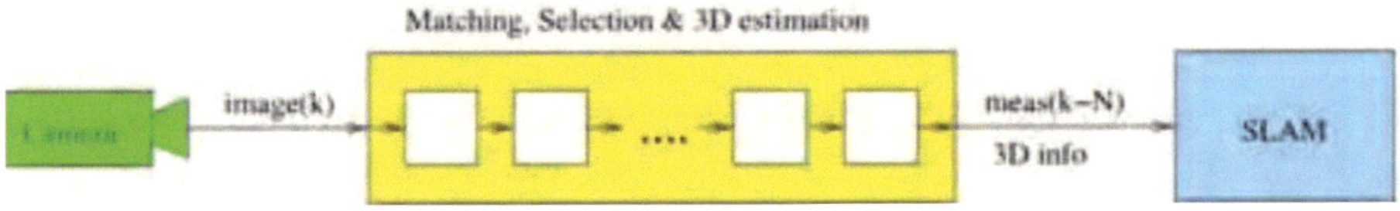

Figure 2. Many structures in indoor environments look similar even when rotated

The benefit of this is that the SLAM process can be fed with few and high quality landmarks. In addition, since an estimate of the 3D position of landmarks can be supplied with the first measurement of a landmark, the landmarks can immediately be fully initialised in the SLAM process. This allows immediate linearisation without the need to apply multiple hypotheses (Lemarie et al., 2005) or particle filtering (Davison, 2003) techniques to estimate the depth. It is important to point out that the approximate 3D position found from the buffer of frames is only used for initialising the point landmark at the correct depth with respect to the camera at the first observation. The uncertainty in depth is still assumed to be very high, as problems with incorporating information twice would otherwise occur. Comparing to a multiple hypothesis approach, it is like knowing which of the multiple hypotheses about the depth is correct right away which saves computations. Having the correct depth allows us, as said before, to reduce the linearisation errors that would results from having a completely wrong estimate of the depth.

Assuming that the delay caused by the length of the buffer is not too large, it is possible to make a quite accurate estimate of the current robot pose by using dead reckoning information to predict forward from the pose estimated by the SLAM process. For typical values of N, the addition to the robot position error caused by the dead reckoning is small and we believe that the benefits of being able to initialise landmarks using bearing-only information and perform feature quality checks are more significant. The predication forward in time is done in each iteration from the latest pose estimated by SLAM. This way there is no accumulation of dead reckoning errors other than over the short distances corresponding to the size of the buffer.

In addition to requiring that features can be tracked over more than a certain predefined number of frames, we require that the image positions of the feature allow good triangulation and that the resulting 3D point is stable over time in the image. Requiring that the feature can be tracked over several frames removes noise and moving targets that could otherwise severely damage the estimation process. Good triangulations rule out features that have a high triangulation uncertainty, typically because of small baseline or having bearings near the direction of motion. The third requirement removes features that lack sharp positions in all images due to parallax or a lack of a strong maximum in scale space. Difference in scales of the images can also cause apparent motion of features, such as for example a corner of a non-textured object.

We have used a fixed value for N, i.e. the length of the buffer, in our tests. The values between 10 and 50 have been tested. A buffer with all frames acquired from the same camera pose would be of little use for triangulation. Therefore, a new frame is added to the buffer when the camera has moved enough since the last added frame. This way, it is likely that there is enough baseline for estimating the location. The value of N depends very much on the motion of the robot/camera and the camera parameters. For a narrow field of view, camera mounted in the direction of motion of the robot as in our case the effective baseline will be quite small. An omnidirectional camera would offer one way to deal with the small field of view. Another idea is to actively control the direction of the camera as in (Vidal-Calleja et al., 2006).

5. Feature Tracking

The buffer with data from the past N frames does not contain the whole images, but rather the feature points that have been extracted in each frame. An even higher reduction of space could be achieved by using an indexing scheme as in (Nistér & Stewénius, 2006). The feature points are tracked over consecutive frames. To estimate if two feature points match, we use the distance between the descriptors, i.e. between the 128-dimensional vectors associated with the SIFT descriptors. On the left hand side of Figure 3. the organization of the frame memory is shown. Notice the lists that store the associations between the points for the different frames in the buffer. Ideally, each association list corresponds to one landmark in the world and denotes how the projection of this landmark moves in the image as the robot moves.

The SIFT descriptor is invariant to changes in scale and view angle but only up to a certain degree. The change between two consecutive observations in the buffer is however typically quite small and makes tracking possible. The different descriptors in the list correspond to different viewpoints of the same landmark.

As was previously described, the buffer is used to sort the good from the bad landmarks. The output from the frame memory is a small selection of all the features points in the oldest frame. These points are the ones that are judged to be the best with respect to the criteria mentioned earlier. Some of these points correspond to observations of already existing landmarks and some to the first observation of a new landmark. For each new landmark observation, an estimate of the 3D position is obtained by triangulating the points in the corresponding association list. The number of points that are used as observations in each frame is typically only a small fraction of all points in that frame. This helps reducing the complexity. The time to perform the tracking over frames has constant complexity assuming that the number of features in each frame is bounded.

Only using the similarity of the point descriptor for tracking has two problems. First, it requires that all points in the image are tested for similarity which is computationally expensive and second, it can lead to false matches in cases where there are similar structures in multiple places in the image. To address these issues we predict the approximate image location for the old point features in the new frame using odometry and optical flow estimates. The predicted image location allows us to narrow the search region for each feature match and thus increase efficiency. Notice that the buffer allows us to predict feature points observed not only in the very last frame but also further back. This increases the robustness in the tracking, as some feature points are not present in every frame.

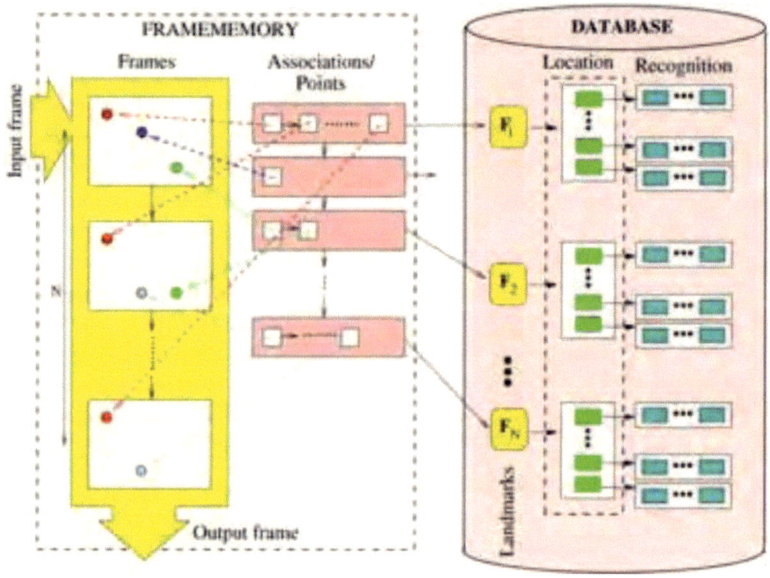

Figure 3. A schematic view of the frame memory and the database

Feature points in a new frame that do not match any of the old feature points with their predicted image locations are matched to a database of initialised landmarks. This allows the system to deal with loop closing situations, i.e. the case where the robot re-visits an area it has been to before. Landmarks are added to this database at the same time, as the first observation is output from the frame memory.

6. Landmark Re-Detection and Loop Closing

The database serves a purpose not only for true loop closing situations but also when the robot turns abruptly. Landmarks not in the field of view will eventually leave the frame memory. When the robot turns the camera back to this region it is important that new landmarks are not created but rather that matches are found to the already existing landmarks. As discussed in the previous section, landmarks appear different from different viewpoints. To handle this, the database stores a number of descriptors for each landmark, corresponding to its appearance from different viewpoints. The different descriptors for a

landmark in the database are provided by the frame memory. For every new observation of a landmark the descriptor is compared to the existing ones and used to augment the descriptor list if it is different enough.
The SIFT point descriptors are not globally unique (see Figure 2. again) and thus matching a single observation to a landmark is doomed to cause false matches in a realistic indoor environment. However, using large number of SIFT descriptors has proven to give robust matching results in object recognition applications. This is why we store, along with the landmark descriptor associated with the location of the landmark, the rest of the descriptors extracted from the same frame and use these for verification. We refer to the rest of the feature points in a frame as recognition features to distinguish them from the location feature associated with the location of the landmark.
The structure of the database is shown on the right hand side in Figure 3. Each landmark F_1,,F_2,...,F_N has a set of location descriptors shown in the dashed box. A KD-tree representation and a Best-Bin-First (Beis & Lowe, 1997) search allow for real-time matching between new image feature descriptors and those in the database. Each location descriptor has a set of recognition descriptors shown to the right.
When we match to the database, we first look for a match between a single descriptor in the new frame and the location descriptors of the landmarks (dashed box Figure 3.). As a second step, we match all descriptors in the new frame to the recognition descriptors associated with candidate location descriptors for verification. As a final test, we require that the displacement in image coordinates for the two location features (new frame and database) is consistent with the transformation between the two frames estimated from the matched recognition descriptors (new frame and database). This assures that it is not just two similar structures in the same scene but that they are at the same position as well. Currently, the calculation is simplified by checking the 2D image point displacement. This final confirmation eliminates matches that are close in the environment and thus share recognition descriptors such as would be the case with the glass windows in Figure 2.

7. SLAM

The previous sections have explained how we track features between frames to be able to determine which make good landmarks and how these are added to, represented in and matched to the database. In our current system, we use an EKF base implementation of SLAM. It is however important to point out that the output from the frame memory could be used as input to any number of different SLAM algorithms. It is possible to use normal EKF despite its limitation regarding complexity since most features extracted from the frames have been discarded by the matching and quality assessment process in the frame memory. Even though hundreds of features are extracted in each frame only a fraction of these are used for estimation. We are also able to supply the approximate 3D location of new landmark so that no special arrangement for this has to be added in the SLAM algorithm. This also makes the plug-n-play of SLAM algorithm easier.
We use the same implementation for SLAM that was used in (Folkesson et al, 2005). This is part of the freely available CURE/toolbox software package. In (Folkesson et al, 2005) it was used for vision SLAM with a camera pointing up in the ceiling.
To summarize, the division is such that the SLAM process is responsible for estimating the location of a landmark and the database for its appearance.

8. Experimental Evaluation

Figure 4. The PowerBot platform with the Canon VC-C4 camera

The camera used in the experimental evaluation is a Canon VC-C4 camera mounted in the front on a PowerBot platform from MobileRobotics Inc (see Figure 4.). The experimental robot platform has a differential drive base with two rear caster wheels. The camera was tilted upward slightly to reduce the amount of floor visible in the image. The field of view of the camera is about 45 degrees in the horizontal plane and 35 in the vertical plane. This is a relatively small field of view. In addition, the optical axis is aligned with the direction of motion of the platform so that it can be used for other navigation tasks. The combination of a small field of view and motion predominantly along the optical axis makes it hard to generate large baselines for triangulation.

The experimental evaluation will show how we are able to build a map of the environment with few but high quality landmarks and how detection of loop closing is performed.

The setting for the experiment is an area around an atrium that consists of loops of varying sizes. We let the robot drive 3 laps following approximately, but not exactly, the same path. Each lap is about 30m long. The trajectory along with the resulting map is shown in Figure 5. The landmarks are shown as small squares. Overlayed on the vision based map is a map built using a laser scanner (the lines). This second map is provided as a reference for the reader only. The laser scanner was not used at all in the vision experiments. Figure 6. shows the situation when the robot closes the loop for the first time. The lines protruding from the camera point out the points that are matched. Figure 7. shows one of the first acquired images along with the image in which the two matches shown in Figure 6. were found just as the loop is closed for the first time.

There are a number of important observations that can be made. First, there are much fewer landmarks than typically seen in maps built using point landmarks and vision, see e.g. (Sim et al., 2005, Se et al., 2002). We can also see that the landmarks are well localized as they fall closely to the walls. Notice that some of the landmarks are found on lamps hanging from the ceiling and that the area in the upper left corner of Figure 6. is quite cluttered. It is a student study area and it has structures at many different depths. A photo of this area is shown in

Figure 8. The line picked up by the laser scanner is the lower part of the bench where people sit and not the wall behind it. This explains why many of the points in this area do not fall on the laser-based line. Some of the spread of the point can also be explained by the small baseline. The depth error is inversely proportional to the baseline (Hartley & Zisserman, 2000).

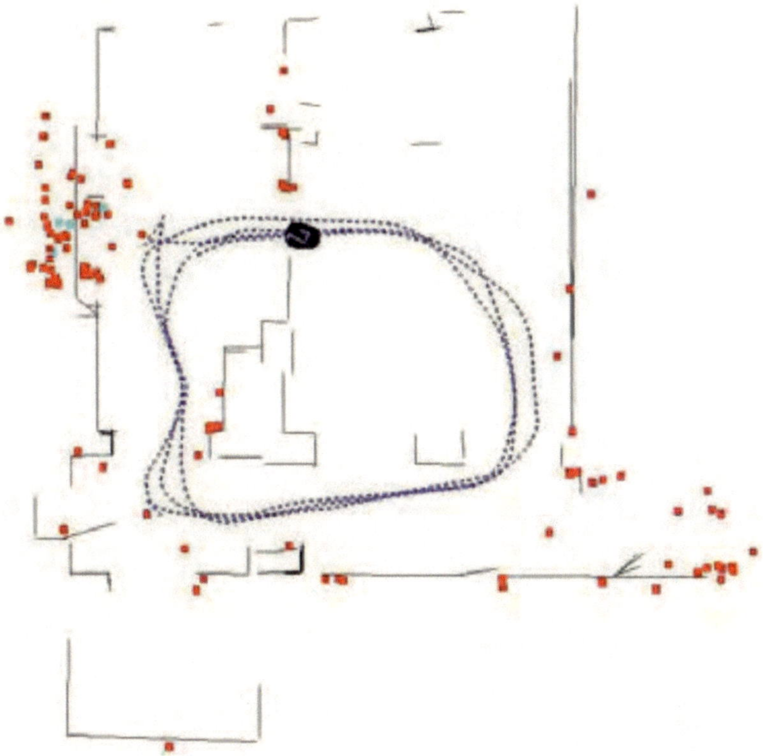

Figure 5. The landmark map with the trajectory and reference laser based map

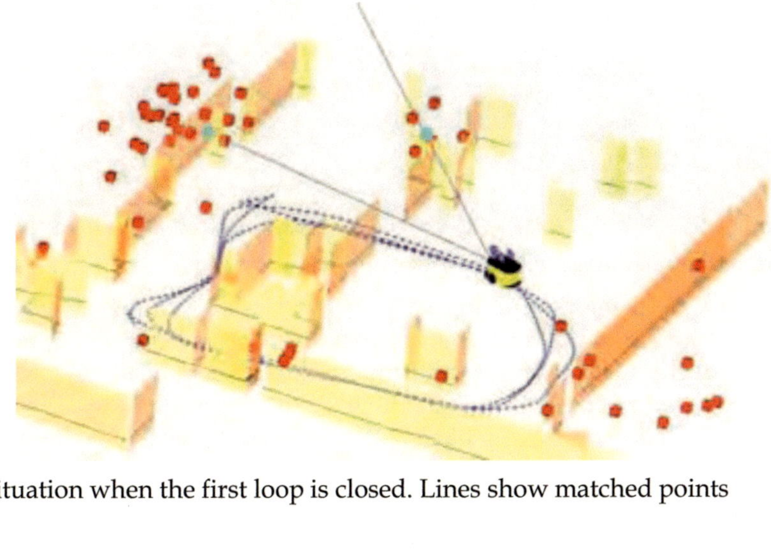

Figure 6. Situation when the first loop is closed. Lines show matched points

Another observation that can be made is that the final map contained 113 landmarks and that most of these were added to the map during the first loop (98). This indicates that landmarks were matched to the database rather than to be added to the map. Had this not been the case one would have expected to see roughly 3 times the number of landmarks.
As many as half of the features in each frame typically do not match any of the old features in the frame memory and are thus matched to the database. A typical landmark in the database has around 10 descriptors acquired from different viewing angles. The matching to the database uses the KD-tree in the first step that makes this first step fast. This often results only in a few possible matching candidates.

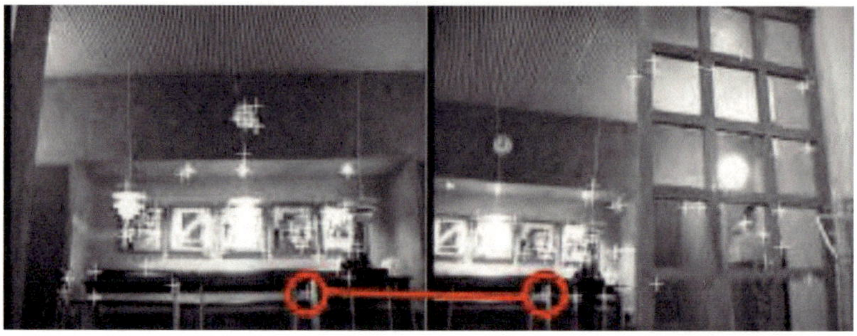

Figure 7. One of the matched points in the first loop detection (compare to Figure 6)

Figure 8. Cluttered area in upper right corner of Figure 5

In the experiments, an image resolution of 320x240 was used and images were grabbed at 10Hz. Images were added to the frame buffer when the camera had moved more than 3cm and/or turned 1 degree. The entire experimental sequence contained 2611 images, out of which roughly half were processed. The total time for the experiment was 8min 40s and the processing time was 7min and 7s on a 1.8GHz laptop. This shows that it can operate under real-time conditions

9. Conclusions and Future Work

For enabling the autonomy of robotic systems, we have to equip them with the ability to build a map of the environment using natural landmarks and to be able to use it for localization purposes. Most of the robotic systems capable of SLAM presented so far in the literature have relied on range sensors such as laser scanners and sonar sensors. For large scale, complex environments with natural landmarks the problem of SLAM is still an open research problem. More recently, the use of cameras and machine vision as the only exteroceptive sensor has become one of the most active areas of research in SLAM.

The main contributions presented in this chapter are the feature selection and matching mechanisms that allow for real-time performance even with an EKF implementation for SLAM. One of the key insights is to use few, well localized, high quality landmarks to acquire good 3D position estimates and then use the power of the many in the matching process by including all features in a frame for the verification. Another contribution is our use of a rotationally variant feature descriptor to better deal with the symmetries that are often present in indoor environments. An experimental evaluation was presented on data collected in a real indoor environment. Comparing the landmarks in the map built using vision with a map built using a laser scanner showed that the landmarks were accurately positioned.

As part of the future research we plan to investigate how the estimation process can be improved by using active control of the pan-tilt degrees of freedom of the camera on the robot. By such coupling, the baseline can actively be made larger to improve triangulation/estimation results. It would also allow the system to use good landmarks, otherwise not in the field of view, to improve the localization accuracy and thus the map quality.

10. References

Beis, J.S.; Lowe, D.G. (1997). Shape indexing using approximate nearest-neighbour search in high-dimensional spaces. *Proceedings of IEEE Conference on Computer Vision and Pattern Recognition (CVPR)*, pp.1000-1006.

Castellanos, J.A.; Tardós, J.D. (1999). *Mobile Robot Localization and Map Building: A Multisensor Fusion Approach*, Kluwer Academic Publishers.

Davison A.J. (2003). Real-time simultaneous localisation and mapping with a single camera. *Proceedings of the International Conference on Compupter vision (ICCV).*

Dissanayake, G.; Newman, P.; Clark, S.; Durrant-Whyte, H.F.; Corba, M. (2001). A solution to the slam building problem. *IEEE Transactions on Robotics and Automation*, 17, 3, 229-141

Folkesson, J.; Christensen, H.I. (2004). Graphical SLAM - A Self-Correcting Map, *Proceedings of the IEEE International Conference on Robotics and Automation (ICRA)*

Folkesson, J.; Jensfelt, P.; Christensen; H.I. (2005) Vision slam in the measurement subspace. *Proceedings of the IEEE International Conference on Robotics and Automation (ICRA).*

Frese, U.; Schröder, L. (2006) Closing a Million-Landmarks Loop, *Proceedings of the IEEE/RSJ International Conference on Intelligent Robots and Systems (IROS)*

Goncavles, L.; di Bernardo, E.; Benson, D.; Svedman, M.; Ostrovski, J.; Karlsson, N.; Pirjanian, P. (2005) A visual fron-end for simultaneous localization and mapping. *Proceedings of the IEEE International Conference on Robotics and Automation (ICRA)*.pp. 44–49.

Gutmann, J.; Konolige, K. (1999) Incremental mapping of large cyclic environments. *Proceedings of the IEEE International Symposium on Computational Intelligence in Robotics and Automation*, pp. 318-325

Hartley, R.; Zisserman, A. (2000). *Multiple View Geometry in Computer Vision,* Cambridge University Press, ISBN: 0521623049

Kwok, N.M.; Dissanayake, G.; Ha, Q.P. (2005) Bearing only SLAM using a SPRT based gaussian sum filter. *Proceedings of the IEEE International Conference on Robotics and Automation (ICRA).*

Lemaire, T.; Lacroix, S.; Sola, J. (2005) A practical 3D bearing-only SLAM algorithm, *Proceedings of the IEEE/RSJ International Conference on Intelligent Robots and Systems (IROS)*, pp 2757-2762

Lowe, D.G. (1999) Object recognition from local scale-invariant features. *Proceedings of the IEEE International Conference on Computer Vision (ICCV),* pp. 1150-57

Luke, R.H.; Keller, J.M.; Skubic, M.; Senger, S. (2005) Acquiring and maintaining abstract landmark chunks for cognitive robot navigation. *Proceedings of the IEEE/RSJ International Conference on Intelligent Robots and Systems (IROS)*

Mikolajczyk, K.; Schmid, C. (2001) Indexing based on scale invariant interest points. *Proceedings of the IEEE International Conference on Computer Vision (ICCV).* pp. 525-531

Mikolajczyk, K.; Schmid, C. (2003) A performance evaluation of local descriptors. *Proceedings of IEEE Conference on Computer Visiona and Pattern Recognition (CVPR),* pp. 257-263.

Newman, P.; Ho, K. (2005) SLAM-loop closing with visually salient features, *Proceedings of the IEEE International Conference on Robotics and Automation (ICRA). pp.* 644-651.

Nistér, D.; Stewénius, H. (2006) Scalable Recognition with a Vocabulary Tree, *Proceedings of the IEEE Conference on Computer Vision and Pattern Recognition (CVPR)*

Se, S.; Lowe, D.G.; Little, J. (2002) Mobile robot localization and mapping with uncertainty using scale-invariant visual landmarks. *Journal of Robotics Research*, 21, 8, 735-758

Sim, R.; Elinas, P.; Griffin, M.; Little, J. (2005) Vision-based slam using the rao-blackwellised particle filter, *Proceedings of the Workshop on Reasoning with Uncertainty in Robotics (IJCAI)*

Tardós, J.D.; Neira, J; Newman, P.M.; Leonard, J.J. (2002) Robust mapping and localization in indoor environments using sonar data, *Journal of Robotics Research, 4*

Thrun, S.; Fox, D.; Burgard, W. (1998) A probalistic approach to concurrent mapping and localization for mobile robots, *Autonomous Robots*, 5, 253-271

Thrun, S.; Liu, Y.; Koller, D.; Ng, A.; Ghahramani, Z.; Durrant-White, H. (2004) SLAM with sparse extended information filters, *Journal of Robotics Research, 23, 8,* 690–717

Vidall-Calleja, T.; Davison, A.J.; Andrade-Cetto, J.; Murray, D.W. (2006) Active Control for Single Camera SLAM, *Proceedings of the IEEE International Conference on Robotics and Automation (ICRA*), pp. 1930-36

10

An Effective 3D Target Recognition Imitating Robust Methods of the Human Visual System

Sungho Kim and In So Kweon
Korea Advanced Institute of Science and Technology
Korea

1. Introduction

Object recognition is an important research topic in computer vision. Not only it is the ultimate goal of computer vision, but is also useful to many applications, such as automatic target recognition (ATR), mobile robot localization, visual servoing, and guiding visually impaired people.
Great progress in this field has been made during the last 30 years. During 1970~1990, the research focused on the recognition of machine parts or polyhedral objects using edge or line information (Lowe, 2006, Faugeras & Hebert, 1986). A 2D invariant feature and hashing-based object recognition was popular during the 1990s (Mundy & Zisserman, 1992, Rothwell, 1993). Since the mid 1990s, view or appearance-based methods have become a popular approach in computer vision (Murase & Nayar, 1995). Current issues cover how to select a feature, handle occlusion, and cope with image variations in photometric and geometric distortions. Recently, object recognition methods based on a local visual patch showed successful performance in those environmental changes (Lowe, 2004, Rothganger et al., 2004, Fergus et al., 2003). But these approaches can work on textured complex object and do not provide 3D pose information of interesting objects.
The goal of our research is to get the identification and pose information of 3D objects or targets from either a visible or infrared band sensor in a cluttered environment. The conventional approaches as mentioned above do not provide satisfying results. To achieve this goal more effectively, we pay attention to the perception mechanism of the human visual system (HVS), which shows the best efficiency and robustness to the above mentioned problems. Especially, we focus on the components of HVS robustness.

2. Robust Properties of HVS

How have humans recognized objects robustly in a severe environment? What mechanisms cause a successful recognition of 3D objects? Based on these motivations, we researched various recent papers on psychophysical, physiological, and neuro-biological evidences and conclude the following facts:

2.1 Visual object representation in human brain

The HVS uses both view-based and model-based object representation (Peters, 2000). Initially, novel views of an object are memorized, and an object-centered model is generated through training many view-based representations. Another supporting evidence of this fact is that different visual tasks may require different types of representations. For identification, view-based representations are sufficient. 3D volume-based (or object centered) representations are especially useful for visual guidance of interactions with objects, like grasping them. In this paper, the goal is object identification and estimating the pose of objects for grabbing by a service robot. Therefore, both representations are suitable for our task.

2.2 Cooperative bottom-up and top-down information

Accordingly (Nichols & Newsome, 1999), not only the bottom-up process but also top-down information plays a crucial role in object recognition. Bottom-up process, called image-based, data-driven or discriminative process, begins with the visual information and analyses of smaller perception elements, then moves to higher levels. Top-down process is called knowledge-based perception, task dependent, or generative process. This process, such as high level context information (ex. place information) and expectation of the global shape, has an influence on object recognition (Siegel et al., 2000, Bar, 2004). So an image-based model is proper to the bottom-up and place context, and object-centered 3D model is suitable to top-down. The spatial attention is used to integrate separate feature maps in each process. From the detailed investigations in physiological and anatomical areas, many important functions of the bottom-up process were disclosed. Although the understanding of the neural mechanism of the top-down effects is still poor, it is certain that the object recognition is affected by both processes guided by the attention mechanism.

2.3 Robust visual feature extraction

(1) Hierarchical visual attention (Treisman, 1998): The HVS utilizes three kinds of hierarchical attention: spatial, feature and object. We utilize these attentions to the proposed system. Spatial attention is performed by a high curvature point like Harris corner, feature attention is made on local Zernike moments, and 3D object attention is done by the top-down process.

(2) Feature binding (Treisman, 1998): The binding problem concerns the way in which we select and integrate the separate features of objects in the correct combinations. Separate feature maps are bound by spatial visual attention. In the bottom-up process, we bind an edge map with a selected corner map and generate local structural parts. In the top-down process, we bind a gradient orientation map with gradient magnitude map focusing on a CAD model position.

(3) Contrast mechanism (VanRullen, 2003): Important information is not the amplitude of a visual signal, but is the contrast between this amplitude at a given point and at the surrounding location. This fact is true in the whole recognition process.

(4) Size-tuning process (Fiser et al., 2001): During object recognition, the visual system can tune in to an appropriate size sensitive to spatial extent, rather than to variations in spatial frequency. We use this concept for the automatic scale selection of the Harris corner.

(5) Part-based representation (Biederman, 1987): Visual perception can be done from part information supported by RBC (recognition by components) theory. It is related to the

properties of V4 receptive field, where the convex part is used to represent visual information (Pasupathy & Connor, 2001). A part-based representation is very robust to occlusion and background clutter. We represent visual appearance by a set of robust visual part.

Motivated by these facts, many computational models were proposed in computer vision. Researchers of model-based vision regarded bottom-up/top-down processes as hypothesis/verification paradigms (Kuno et al., 1988, Zhu et al., 2000). To reduce computational complexity, visual attention mechanism is used (Milanese et al. 1994). Top-down constraint is used to recognize face and pose (Kumar, 2002). Recently, an interesting computational model (HMAX) was proposed based on the tuning and max operation of a simple cell and a complex cell, respectively (Serre & Riesenhuber, 2004). In a computer vision society, Tu et al. proposed a method of unifying segmentation, detection and recognition using boosting and prior information by learning (Tu et al., 2005). Although these approaches have their own advantages, they modeled only on partial evidences of human visual perception, and did not pay attention to the robust properties of HVS more closely.

In this paper, we propose a computationally plausible model of 3D object recognition, imitating the above properties of the HVS. Bottom-up and top-down information is processed by a visual attention mechanism and integrated under a statistical framework.

3. Graphical Model of 3D Object Recognition

3.1 Problem definition

A UAV (unmanned aerial vehicle) system, such as a guided missile, has to recognize an object ID (identity) and its pose from a single visible or infrared band sensor. The goal of this paper is to recognize target ID and its pose in a UAV system, using a forward-looking visible or infrared camera. The object pose information is necessary for precise targeting.

We want to find the object name (θ_{ID}), the object pose ($\theta_C : \theta_{yaw}, \theta_{pitch}, \theta_{roll}$) relative to camera coordinates in a 3D world, the object position ($\theta_P : \theta_x, \theta_y$) and the object scale ($\theta_D$) in a 2D image. This information is useful in various applications. Similar processes exist in a primary visual cortex: ventral stream (what pathway) and dorsal stream (where pathway). The recognition problem can be formulated as the Bayesian inference by

$$\begin{aligned} P(\boldsymbol{\theta} \mid I) &= P(\boldsymbol{\theta} \mid Z_L, Z_C) \propto P(Z_L \mid \boldsymbol{\theta}, Z_C) P(\boldsymbol{\theta} \mid Z_C) \\ &= P(Z_L \mid \theta_{ID}, \theta_C, \theta_D, \theta_P, Z_C) P(\theta_{ID}, \theta_C, \theta_D, \theta_P \mid Z_C) \\ &\textit{where} \quad I = \{Z_L, Z_C\} \end{aligned} \tag{1}$$

where $\boldsymbol{\theta}$ means the parameter set as explained, I denotes input image, and it is composed of two sets: Z_L for object related local features Z_C for place or scene related contextual features. The likelihood of the equation (1), the first factor $P(Z_L \mid \boldsymbol{\theta}, Z_C)$ represents the posterior distribution of local features, such as local structural patch, edge information given parameters and contextual information. There is a lot of contextual information, but we restrict the information as place context and a 3D global shape for our final goal. This information alleviates the search space and provides accurate pose information. The second factor $P(\boldsymbol{\theta} \mid Z_C)$ provides context-based priors on object ID, pose which are related to the scene information by learning. This can be represented as a graphical model in a general form as Figure 1 (Borgelt et al., 2001). Scene context information can be estimated in a discriminative way using contextual features Z_C . Using the prior learning between scene and objects, initial object probabilities can be obtained from sensor observation. Initial pose information is also estimated in a discriminative way. Given those initial parameters, fine pose tuning is performed using a 3D global shape and sensor measurements, such as gradient magnitude and gradient orientation.

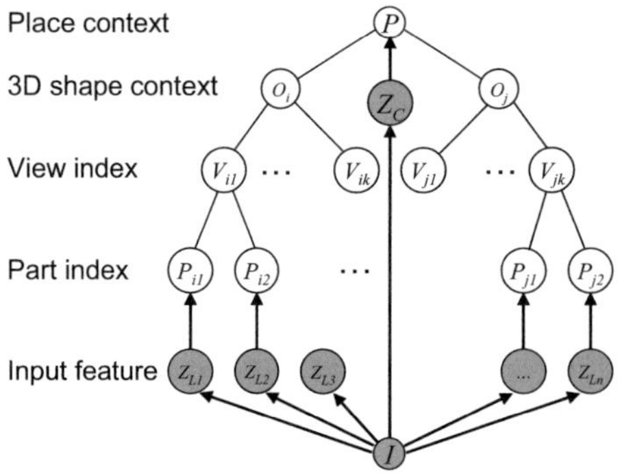

Figure 1. Graphical model of context-based object recognition: shaded circles mean observations and clear circles mean hidden variables

In the above graphical model, final parameters can be inferred from a discriminative method (bottom-up reasoning, such as directed arrows) and a generative method (top-down reasoning) with contextual information. To find an optimal solution from the equation (1), a MAP (maximum a posteriori) method is used generally. But it is difficult to obtain a correct posterior for a high dimensional parameter space (in our case 7 dimension). We bypass this problem by a statistical technique, drawing samples using a Markov Chain Monte Carlo (MCMC) technique (Green, 1996). The MCMC method is theoretically well-proved and a suitable global optimization tool for combining bottom-up and top-down information, which reveals superiority to genetic algorithm or simulated annealing although there are some analogies to the Monte Carlo method (Doucet et al., 2001). MCMC-like mechanism may not exist in the HVS, but it is a practically plausible inference technique in a high dimensional parameter space. Proposal samples generated from a bottom-up process achieve fast optimization or reduce burn-in time.

3.2 Basics of MCMC

A major problem of Bayesian inference is that obtaining the posterior distribution often requires the integration of high-dimensional functions. The Monte Carlo (or sampling) method approximates the posterior distribution as weighted particles or samples (Doucet et al., 2001, Ristic et al., 2004). The simplest kind is importance sampling, where random samples x are generated from $P(X)$, the prior distribution of hidden variables, and then weight the samples with their likelihood $P(y|x)$. A more efficient approach in high dimension is called the Markov Chain Monte Carlo (MCMC), a subset of particle filter. The Monte Carlo means samples and the Markov Chain means that the transition probability of samples depends only on a function of the most recent sample value. The theoretical advantage of the MCMC is that its samples are guaranteed to asymptotically approximate those which form the posterior. A particular implementation of the MCMC is the Metropolis-Hastings algorithm (Robert & Casella, 1999). The original algorithm is as follows:

Algorithm 1: Metropolis-Hastings algorithm

Draw an initial point θ_0 from a starting distribution $P(\theta)$.

For i=1..N

Draw candidate point θ_* from the jumping distribution $J_i(\theta_* \mid \theta_{i-1})$

Calculate the ratio

$$\alpha = \frac{f(\theta_*)J_i(\theta_{i-1} \mid \theta_*)}{f(\theta_{i-1})J_i(\theta_* \mid \theta_{i-1})}$$

Set $\theta_i = \theta_*$ with probability $\min(\alpha,1)$, otherwise $\theta_i = \theta_{i-1}$

End for

The key concept of the algorithm is that the next sample is accepted with a probability of α. The next sample is obtained from jumping distribution or state transition function. Through the iteration, a sub-optimal solution can be obtained. However, the main problems of the method are a large burn-in time (the number of iterations until the chain approaches stationary) and poor mixing (staying in small regions of the parameter space for a long time). This can be overcome using domain information by the bottom-up process. Therefore, the finally modified algorithm is composed of the initialization part, calculated by the bottom-up process, and the optimization part obtained by the top-down process (see the Algorithm 2).

3.3 Object recognition structure

Figure 2 shows the proposed computational model of object recognition reflecting the robust properties of the HVS, as explained in section 2. Globally, bottom-up and top-down information is integrated under the statistical framework, MCMC. The object is represented as appearance-based in bottom-up, and object-centered in top-down. Furthermore, these object models are related to the scene context. Spatial attention is used to combine low-level feature maps for both bottom-up (in a local structure feature extraction block) and top-down (in shape matching block) processes. Detail computational procedures of each block are explained in the next sections. (Alogrithm 2 will help you to understand the proposed method.)

From a computational viewpoint, the proposed MCMC consists of three components: initialization, MCMC sampling and optimization. The bottom-up process means accumulating evidence computed from local structures and discriminates scene identity. Based on the scene context and local structural information, initial parameters such as object ID, pose, position and scale are estimated. The initial parameters are used to activate the 3D shape context. The MCMC samples are generated by a jumping distribution, which represents state-transition probability. From this sample, a 3D shape model is rendered. The final decision of object recognition is made after iterative sample generation and global shape matching. The decision information is fed back to the bottom-up process for another object recognition in the same scene. Algorithm 2 summarizes the overall recognition steps.

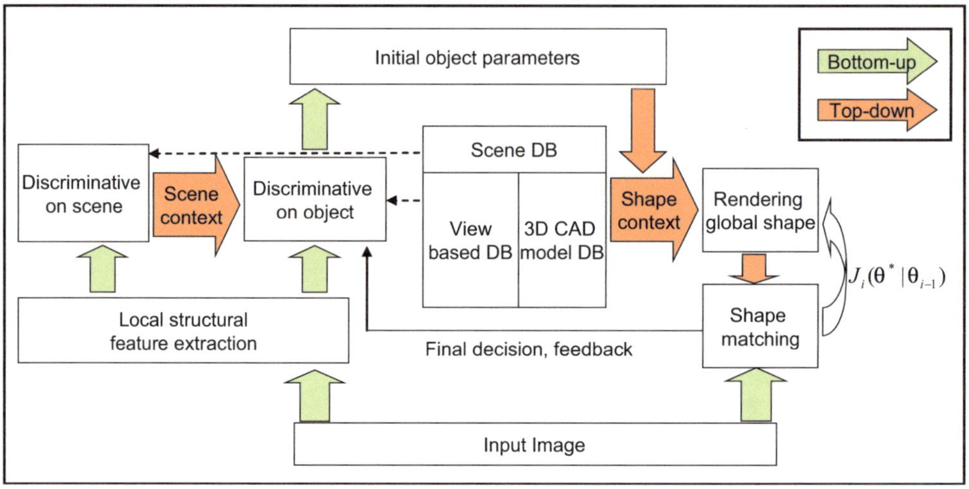

Figure 2. Overall functional model of the object recognition motivated by the robust properties of the HVS

Algorithm 2: Domain knowledge & context-based 3D object recognition algorithm

Stage I: Initialization by bottom-up process
- Step 1: Extract HCM, CEM in scale space
- Step 2: Find salient interesting points through scale space analysis.
- Step 3: Bind feature maps by relating salient HCM and the corresponding CEM
- Step 4: Extract local edge patches and calculate local Zernike moments
- Step 5: Discriminate scene ID through direct voting
- Step 6: Calculate the likelihood of object parameters from scene context and object discrimination by direct voting
- Step 6: Sort candidate parameters $\boldsymbol{\theta}_0 = \{\theta_{ID}{}^0, \theta_C{}^0, \theta_P{}^0, \theta_D{}^0\}$

Stage II: Optimization by top-down process
- Step 1: Extract GMM and GOM
- Step 2: Set initial point $\boldsymbol{\theta}_0 = \{\theta_{ID}{}^0, \theta_C{}^0, \theta_P{}^0, \theta_D{}^0\}$ from Stage I
- Step 3: Optimize parameters by MCMC sampling with feature map binding

For t = 0, …, T

Draw a candidate point $\boldsymbol{\theta}_*$ from the jumping distribution $J_t(\boldsymbol{\theta}_* | \boldsymbol{\theta}_{t-1})$

Render the 3D CAD model based on shape context and $\boldsymbol{\theta}_*$

Calculate the cost function $f(\boldsymbol{\theta}_*)$, by focusing on the rendered model and the integrated feature maps (GMM+GOM)

Calculate the ratio

$$r = \frac{f(\boldsymbol{\theta}_*) J_t(\boldsymbol{\theta}_{t-1} | \boldsymbol{\theta}_*)}{f(\boldsymbol{\theta}_{t-1}) J_t(\boldsymbol{\theta}_* | \boldsymbol{\theta}_{t-1})}$$

Accept $\boldsymbol{\theta}_t = \boldsymbol{\theta}_*$ with probability min(r, 1), or $\boldsymbol{\theta}_t = \boldsymbol{\theta}_{t-1}$

End for
Step 4: If $f(\boldsymbol{\theta}_T) < \varepsilon$, recognition finished and fed back to the step 6 in Stage I.
Else reject $\boldsymbol{\theta}_0$ and go to step 2 with the next candidate $\boldsymbol{\theta}_0$

4. Scene Context-based Database

Figure 3 shows the scene-context-based database which is composed of object-specific scenes, 3D object models and view-based visual parts and their corresponding graphical model. It is displayed on the left.

4.1 Scene database

Conventional object recognition methods usually tried to remove background information. However, the background information of a scene provides important cues to the existence of target objects which are static or immovable, such as buildings and bridges. We call this information scene context. Learning the scene context is simple. First, we store various scenes which contain an interesting object. Then local visual features are extracted and clustered. (Details are explained in the next section.) Finally, clustered features are labeled with a specific object name and stored in a database. This database is used to recognize scenes as in Figure 2.

4.2 Object-centered model representation

As we discussed in section 2, the HVS memorizes object models in an object-centered way through enormous training. A plausible computational model is a 3D CAD model constructed manually. In this paper, we use a simple wireframe model for global shape representation. This method is suitable for man-made rigid objects like buildings, bridges, and etc. A voxel-based 3D representation may be appropriate for a generally shaped 3D object. The global 3D shape model provides the information of shape context which is useful to get the pose information and decision of the existence in the top-down process as Figure 2.

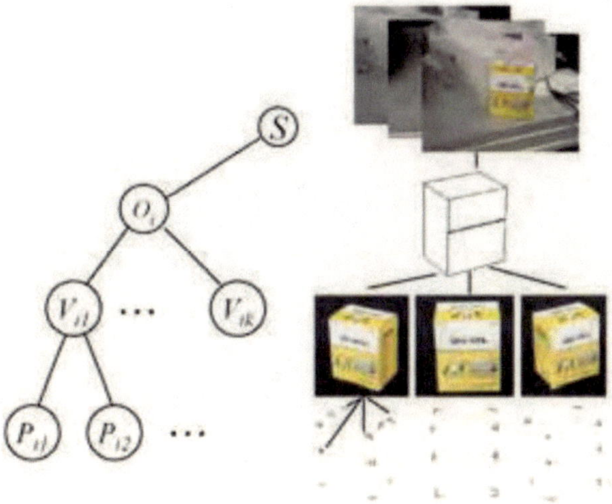

Figure 3. Configuration of the database: scene context + 3D CAD model + part-based view representation

4.3 View-based model representation

Basically, the HVS memorizes objects in an orientation dependent, view-based or appearance-based way (Edelman & Bülthoff, 1992). We quantize the view sphere by 30° and store each view as in Figure 3. Then, local visual parts for each view are extracted and represented using the proposed local feature. (Details will be explained in the next section).

5. Initialization by Bottom-up Process

A functional computational bottom-up process can be modeled as shown in Figure 2 (left half). Initial parameters are estimated through local feature extraction, discriminative method for scene recognition, and finally by discriminative process for object. Scene context provides prior information of a specific object ID which reduces the search space of the discriminative method for an object.

5.1 Local feature extraction

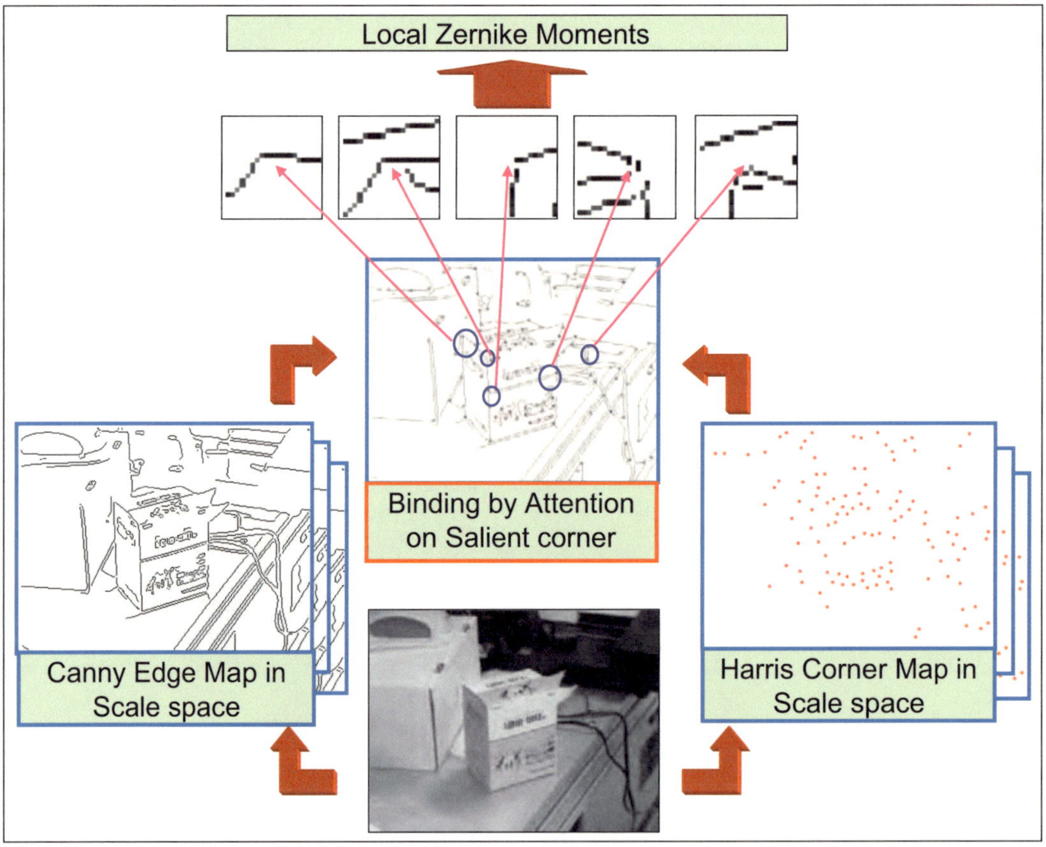

Figure 4. Block of local structural feature extraction: Canny Edge Map and Harris Corner Map are extracted in scale space which is bound by spatial attention on salient corners. Each local structural patch is represented using Zernike moments

Figure 4 shows the overall process for feature generation. We extract separate low-level feature maps such as Canny Edge Maps (called CEM) and Harris Corner Mapps (called HCM) in scale space. Then a perceptually salient corner and characteristic scale is calculated (Lindeberg, 1998). Locally structural visual parts are extracted by attending on CEM around salient corner points and scale tuned regions of HCM. The scale tuning process that exists is supported by the neuro-physiological evidence, as explained in section 2. Each patch whose size is normalized to 20×20 is represented by local Zernike moments introduced in (Kim & Kweon, 2005).

Step 1: Generation of separate feature maps

In the bottom-up process, we assume that an object is composed of local structures. According to (Parkhurst et al., 2002), Parkhurst et al. experimentally showed the fact that bottom-up saliency map-based attention of Itti's model is not suitable for learned object recognition. So, we adopt another spatial attention approach that the HVS usually attends on a high curvature point (Feldman & Singh, 2005). Although the HVS also attends on symmetrical points (Reisfeld et al., 1995), we only use the high curvature points for visual attention, since they are robust to a viewpoint and computationally easy to detect. We detect high curvature points directly from an intensity image using a scale-reflected Harris corner detector which shows highest repeatability in photometric, geometric distortions, and which contains enough information (Harris & Stephens, 1988, Schmid et al., 2000). A conventional Harris corner detector detects many clusters around a noisy and textured region. However, this doesn't matter, since the scale-reflected Harris detector extracts corners in noise removed images by Gaussian scale space. Furthermore, since salient corners are selected in scale space, corner clusters are rarely found, as in Figure 5. Canny edge detector is used to extract an edge map which reflects similar processing of a center-surround detection mechanism (Canny, 1986). The CEM is accurate and robust to noise. Both low level maps are extracted pre-attentively.

Step 2: Feature integration by attending on salient corners

Local visual parts are selected by giving spatial attention to a salient corner. We use the scale space maxima concept to detect salient corners. We define that a corner is salient if the measure of convexity (here, Laplacian) of corners in scale axis shows a local maxima. A computationally suitable algorithm is scale-adapted Harris-Laplace method which shows most robust to image variations (Schmid et al., 2000). Figure 5 shows the salient corner detection results. To detect a salient corner, first we make a corner scale space by changing the smoothing factor (σ). Then the convexity of corners are compared in scale axis.

Finally, salient corners are selected by selecting the maximum convexity measure in the tracked corners in scale space. As a by product, a scale tuned region can be obtained as Figure 5. This image patch corresponds to a local object structure.

Step 3: Local visual parts description by Zernike moments

The local visual parts are represented using modified Zernike moments introduced in (Kim & Kweon, 2005). The Zernike moments were used to represent characters because they are inherently rotation invariant, as well as possessing superior image representation properties, information redundancy, and noise characteristics. A normalized edge part is represented as 20 dimensional vectors where each element is the magnitude of a Zernike moment. Although we do not know how the HVS represents local visual image, we utilize the local Zernike moments, since this feature is robust to scale, rotation and illumination changes.

The performance is evaluated in terms of interest region selector and region descriptor using ROC curve (Mikolajczyk & Schmid, 2003). We used 20 object images as a reference, and made test images by changing the scale factor 0.8 times, planar rotation 45°, view-angle 25°, and illumination reduction by 0.7 time to the reference. For the comparison of the visual part detect, we used the same number of scale space, Zernike moment descriptor and image homography to check the correct matches. For the comparison of the descriptors, we use the same scale space, salient corner part detector and image homography for the same reason. Scale tuned region detector by the salient corner part detector almost outperform the SIFT (DoG-based) as in Figure 6 (a). In the descriptor comparison graph, SIFT and PCA show better performance than Zernike, as in Figure 6 (b). But this region of the low false positive rate is useless, because few features are found. In a noisy environment, our descriptor (Zernike) shows better performance. Figure 7 shows several matching examples using the salient corner with Zernike moments. Note the robust matching results in various environments.

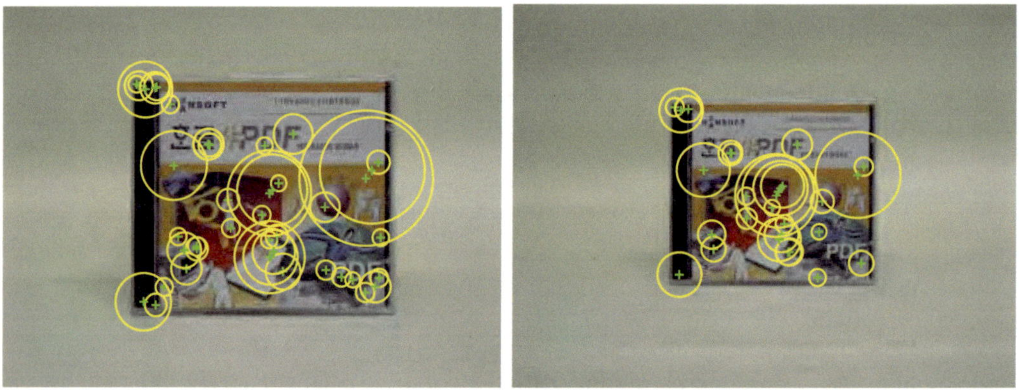

Figure 5. Examples of salient corners on a different scale

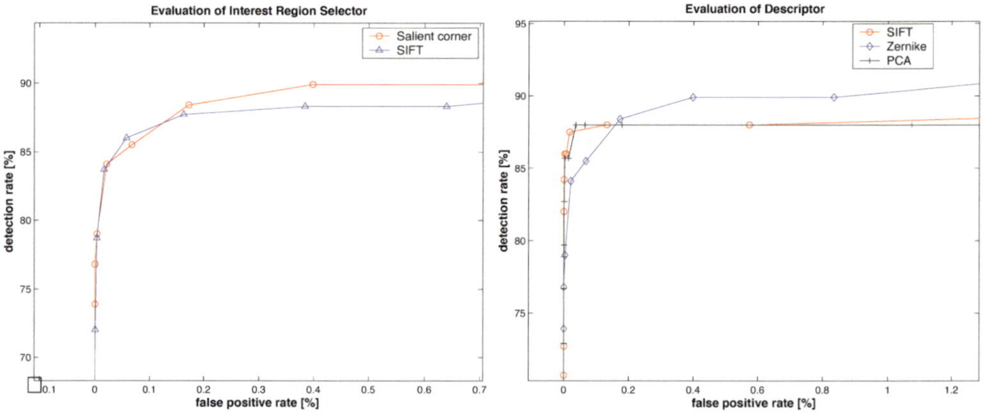

(a) (b)

Figure 6. (a) Performance comparison of interest part selector: Salient corner vs. SIFT, (b) performance comparison of local descriptor: SIFT, Zernike, and PCA

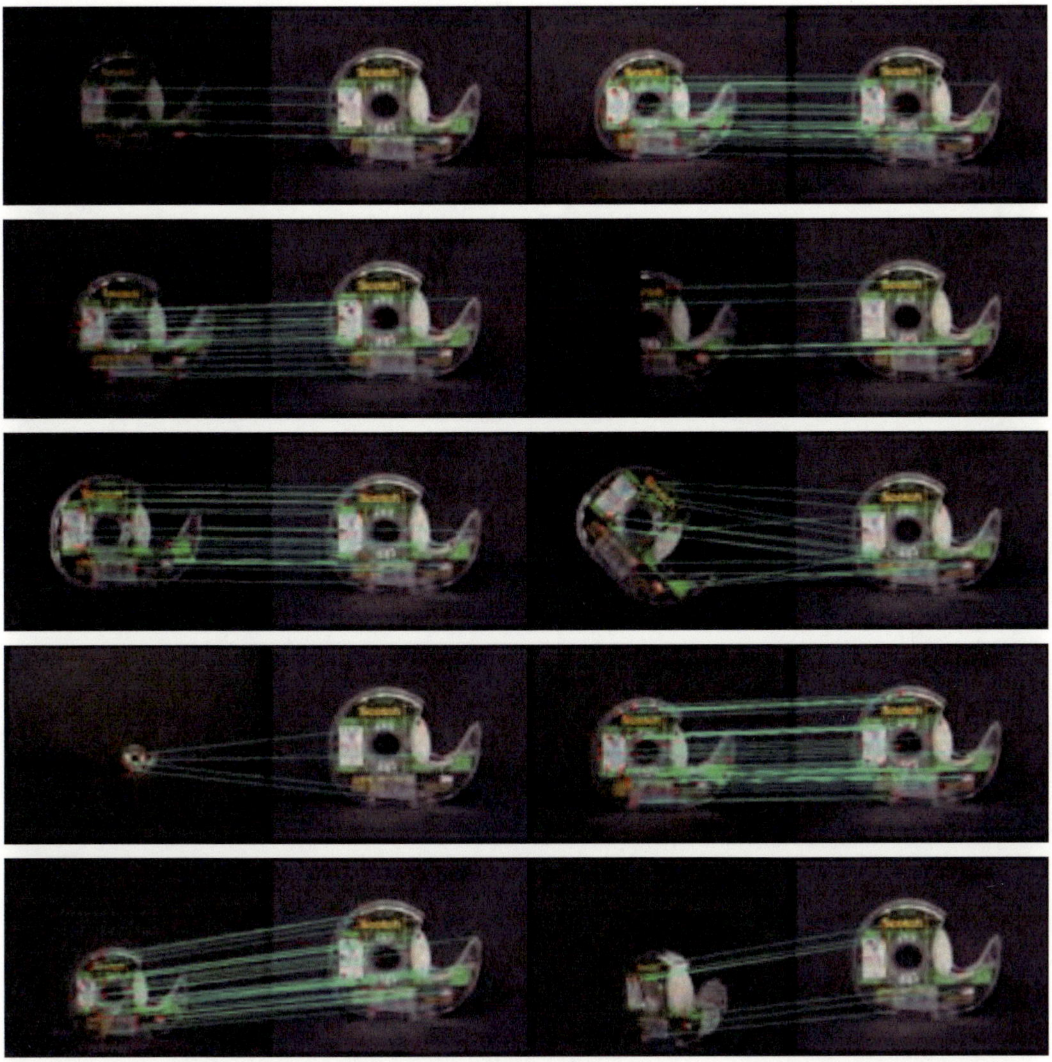

Figure 7. Examples of feature matching using a salient corner part detector and a Zernike moments descriptor in illumination, occlusion, rotation, scale and view angle changes

5.2 Initial parameter estimation by discriminative method

The initial parameters of an object are estimated using a discriminative method, 1-nearest neighbor based voting. In the first step, scene identity is found using direct voting. This scene context provides the information of probable object ID. In the next step, other initial pose, position, and scale parameters are estimated for the object, using the same voting method.

Step 1: Discriminative method on scene recognition,

In equation (1), the scene context term $P(\boldsymbol{\theta} \mid Z_C)$ provides object related priors especially object ID. If we assume one object per scene for simplification, then initial object ID can be estimated directly from the scene discrimination process as equation (2).

$$P(\theta_{ID} \mid Z_C) \approx P(s \mid Z_C) \tag{2}$$

The scene discrimination can be modeled as follows:

$$\theta_{ID} \sim S = \arg\max_{s} P(s \mid Z_C) \approx \arg\max_{l} \sum_{i=1}^{N_{Z_C}} P(s \mid Z_C^i) \tag{3}$$

where local feature Z_C^i belongs to scene feature set Z_C, which usually corresponds to background features. s is a scene label and N_{Z_C} is the number of input scene features. The posterior $P(s \mid Z_C)$ is approximated by the sum rule. We use the following binary probability model to design $P(s \mid Z_C^i)$:

$$P(s \mid Z_C^i) = \begin{cases} 1 & L(Z_C^i) \in s,\ K_E(Z_C^i, \hat{Z}^i) \geq \delta \\ 0 & otherwise \end{cases} \tag{4}$$

where $L(Z_C^i)$ denotes the label of feature Z_C^i searched by 1-nearest neighbor search and $K_E(Z_C^i, \hat{Z}^i)$ is Gaussian Kernel of Euclidean distance between input feature Z_C^i and corresponding scene DB feature $\hat{Z}^i$. The kernel threshold δ usually set to 0.7~0.8. The final scene discrimination result provides scene context, prior information of object ID.

Step 2: Discriminative method on initial object parameters

Initial object ID is directly estimated from the scene context as step 1. Other object-related parameters are estimated by the same voting on view-based object DB. In equation (1), the initial parameters used in $P(Z_L \mid \theta, Z_C)$ can be directly discriminated as step 1, the voting scheme. Since we already know the initial object ID, the search space of other parameters are reduced enormously. The only difference is that the voting spaces are dependent on the parameters. For example, if we want to estimate the initial pose θ_C, we vote the nearest match pairs to the corresponding pose space (azimuth, elevation) like equation (3), and select the max. Given the initial object ID and pose, the initial object scale θ_D, and position θ_P is estimated easily, since our part detectors extract characteristic part scale with its position in the image (see Figure 5). So, the initial scale is just the average of the characteristic scale ratio between scene and model image, and the initial object position is the mean of matching feature pairs (see Figure 5). Since object parameters are estimated based on salient feature and scene context which reduce the search space, there is no increase of estimation error. Figure 8 shows the sample scene database and scene discrimination result by direct voting for the test image. In this test, we used 20 scenes in canonical view points for database and the test image was captured on a different view point. The scene 16 is selected by max operation of the voting result. This scene contains the interesting object. So, we can initialize the object ID parameter from this scene context.

Figure 9 shows a bottom-up result, where the 3D CAD model is overlaid using the initial parameters. There are some pose, scale, location errors. In addition, we cannot trust the estimated object ID. These ambiguities are solved through a top-down process using 3D shape context information.

(a)

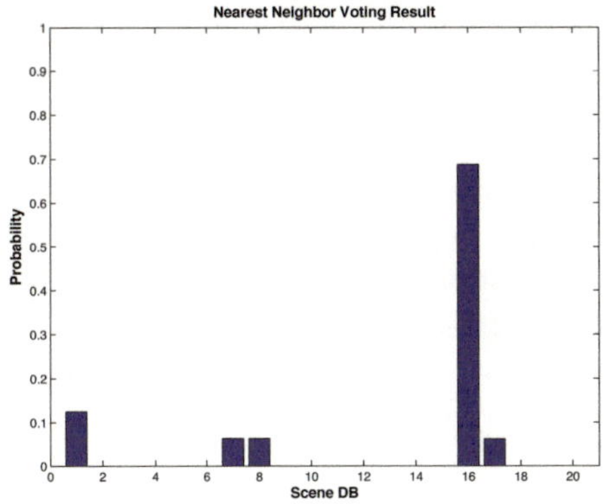

(b)

Figure 8. (a) Examples of scene DB and test image on the right, (b) Scene context: nearest neighbor-based direct voting

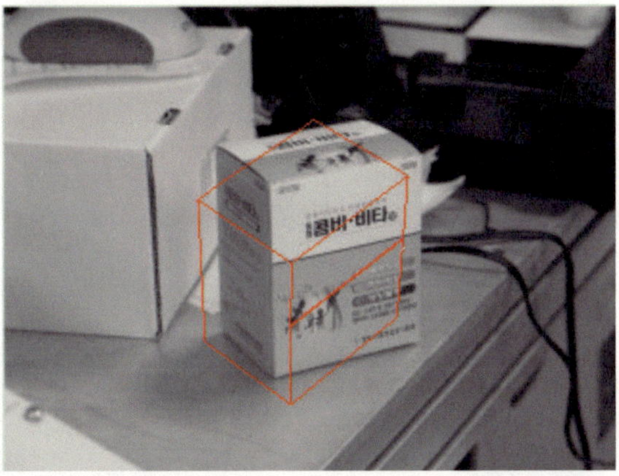

Figure 9. Initially estimated parameters by a bottom-up process

6. Optimization and Verification by Top-down Process

The Top-down process is crucial in the HVS. Although some top-down knowledge such as scene context information was already used for object discrimination, other context information like the expectation of a global 3D shape also has an important role in achieving more precise and accurate recognition. Figure 10 (or Figure 2: half right) shows the functional top-down procedures based on shape context initiated by a bottom-up process. Main components are model parameter prediction by jumping distribution and a global 2D shape matched by attending a shape model to combine gradient magnitude map (GMM) and gradient orientation map (GOM). The model parameter prediction and shape matching are processed iteratively for statistical optimization.

6.1 Generation of model parameters

A posteriori in equation (1) is approximated statistically by MCMC sampling. Based on the initial parameters obtained in bottom-up process, the next samples are generated based on the jumping distribution, $J_i(\theta_i \mid \theta_{i-1})$. It is referred to as proposal or candidate-generation function for its role. Generally, random samples are generated to prevent local maxima. However, we utilize the bottom-up information and top-down verification result for suitable sample generation. In this paper, we use three kinds of jumping types, i.e., object addition, deletion and refinement as Table 1.

The first type is to insert a new object and its parameters, depending on the result of a bottom-up process. The second is to remove a tested model and its parameters, determined by the result of top-down recognition. A jumping example of the third type is like equation (5). Next state depends on current state and random gain. This gain has uniform distribution (U) in the range of 30°, because the view sphere is quantized with this range. Here, θ_C^0 is initialized by the result of a bottom-up process.

$$\theta_C^t = \theta_C^{t-1} + \Delta\theta_C \tag{5}$$

$$\text{where } \theta_C = \begin{bmatrix}\theta_{yaw} & \theta_{pitch} & \theta_{roll}\end{bmatrix}^T, \Delta\theta_C \sim U(-15,15).$$

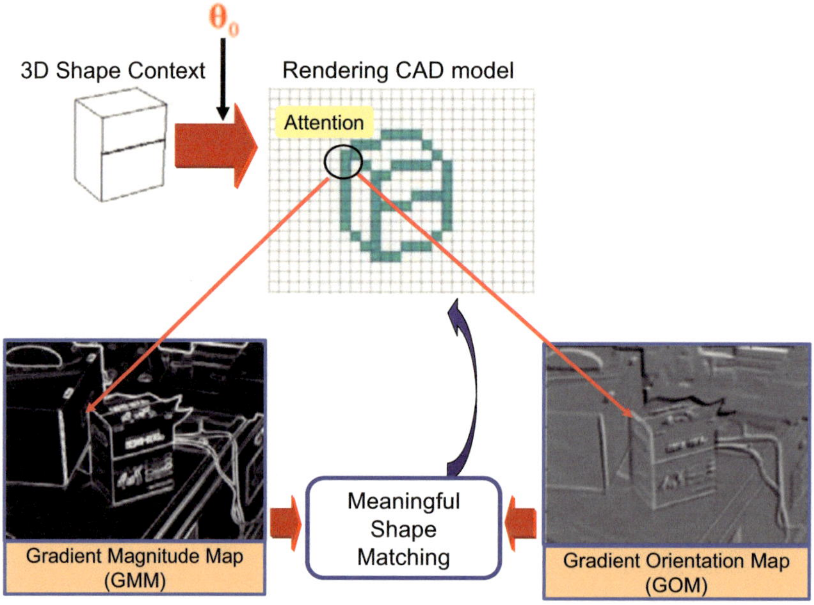

Figure 10. 3D shape context-based top-down shape matching using MCMC: the 3D CAD model is rendered using the initial object parameters, then meaningful shape matching is performed by attending on the rendered 2D shape location and GMM, GOM. Final decision is made based on the MCMC optimization value

Jump type	Function	Parameters	Jumping distribution
J1	Object addition	$\theta_{ID},\theta_C,\theta_D,\theta_P$,	Depend on bottom-up information
J2	Object deletion	$\theta_{ID},\theta_C,\theta_D,\theta_P$	Depend on top-down result
J3	Fine tuning of parameters	$d\theta_C,d\theta_D,d\theta_P$	$\theta_C=\{\theta_{yaw},\theta_{pitch},\theta_{roll}\}$ $d\theta_{yaw}\in U(-30,30)$ $d\theta_{pitch}\in U(-30,30)$ $d\theta_{roll}\in U(-10,10)$ $d\theta_D\in U(\theta_D-\theta_D/5,\theta_D+\theta_D/5)$ $\theta_P=\{\theta_x,\theta_y\}$ $d\theta_x=U\{-40,40\}$ $d\theta_y=U\{-40,40\}$

Table 1. Jumping types and corresponding distributions

6.2 Robust shape matching

A predicted 3D CAD model generated by jumping distribution is rendered on the GMM and GOM image. Attending on the shape model points, both map information is combined as Figure 10. The scoring function used in the MCMC algorithm is defined by the shape matching. The shape matching between the rendered 2D shape and both maps is based on the computational gestalt theory (Desolneux et al., 2004). We propose a novel ε-meaningful shape matching method motivated from this theory.

Two important concept of the theory is as follows:

- Helmholtz principle: This principle provides a suitable mathematical tool for modeling computational Gestalt. Basically, it assumes that an image has random distribution of pixel values or orientations. If some pixels break the randomness, then these pixels have a certain pattern, called gestalt.
- ε-meaningful event: A certain configuration is ε-meaningful if the expectation in an image of the number of occurrences of the event is less than ε.

ε-meaningful shape matching

Since we only deal with intensity image or infrared image, all the available local information is just these three.

- Pixel intensity: $u(x,y)$
- Gradient magnitude: $u'(x,y)=\left(\frac{\partial u}{\partial x},\ \frac{\partial u}{\partial y}\right)(x,y)$
- Gradient orientation: $\theta(x,y)=\frac{1}{\|Du(x,y)\|}\left(-\frac{\partial u}{\partial y},\ \frac{\partial u}{\partial x}\right)(x,y)$

The last two components are useful for shape matching, since they are robust to illumination and noise. If we assume the image is random, then we can measure the structural alignment to a certain pattern. We can think of a matching at x_i that satisfy both the image gradient and orientation. If the rendered shape model is compatible to the image gradient and orientation simultaneously, then this matching is meaningful.

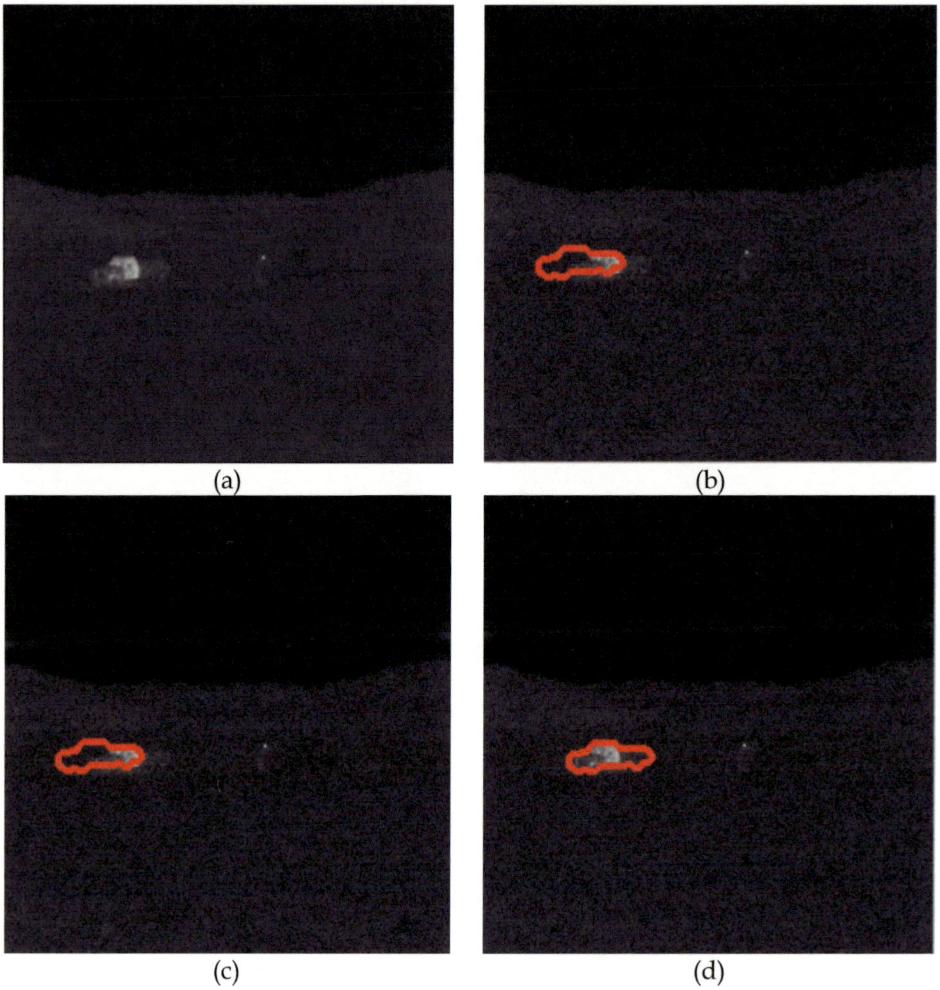

Figure 11. Shape matching examples on (http://www.cs.colostate.edu/~vision/ft_carson/): (a) original FLIR image, (b) GMM only, (c) GOM only, (d) proposed GMM+GOM

If the length of the rendered 2D shape is l, the probability of the event that gradient values ($C(\mathrm{x})$) are larger than a certain value, and orientation differences ($O(\mathrm{x})$) are within a precision along the shape model is defined in equation (6). The orientation precision is set to 8 directions.

$$P\left[C(\mathrm{x}_1) \geq \mu, O(\mathrm{x}_1) \leq \frac{\pi}{4}\right] \cdot P\left[C(\mathrm{x}_2) \geq \mu, O(\mathrm{x}_2) \leq \frac{\pi}{4}\right] \cdots P\left[C(\mathrm{x}_l) \geq \mu, O(\mathrm{x}_l) \leq \frac{\pi}{4}\right] = H(\mathrm{x}, \mu)^l \quad (6)$$

where, $H(\mathrm{x}, \mu) = \frac{1}{8} \cdot \frac{\text{num of } \{\mathrm{x} \mid C(\mathrm{x}) \geq \mu\}}{\text{total image size}}$,

$C(\mathrm{x}) = \left\| u'_I(\mathrm{x}) \right\|$, $O(\mathrm{x}) = \left| \theta_I(\mathrm{x}) - \theta_M(\mathrm{x}) \right|$, I for input, M for model, x:(x, y).

Definition: We call a matching between an image and a certain model is ε-meaningful shape matching if

$$f(\mathbf{\theta}) = N \times H(\mathrm{x}, \mu)^l \leq \varepsilon \tag{7}$$

where N is the number of the test. The smaller this value is, the better the shape matching is. We use this ε-meaningful shape matching as a scoring function for the MCMC optimization method because this function provides a measure of shape matching. The Scoring or cost function acts as a means of measuring the goodness of the proposed model parameters. Generated samples are accepted or rejected based on this function.
Figure11 shows the effectiveness of feature map binding in a top-down process. To show the power of feature map binding, we added Gaussian noise with a standard deviation 8. The binding GMM with GOM outperforms the single map based shape matching.

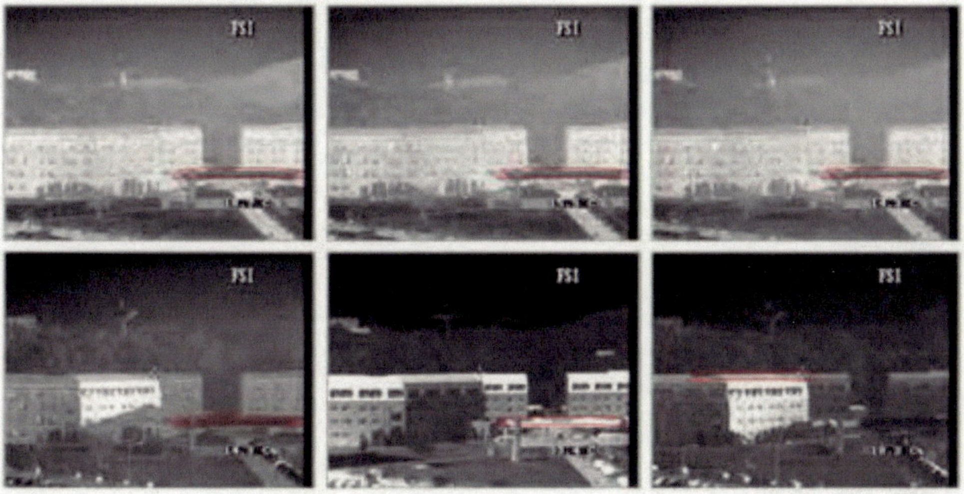

Figure 12. Shape matching results for temperature varying FLIR sequences. The proposed method is very robust to temperature changes. The last image shows a false matching result where the roof target hardly detectable by human eyes

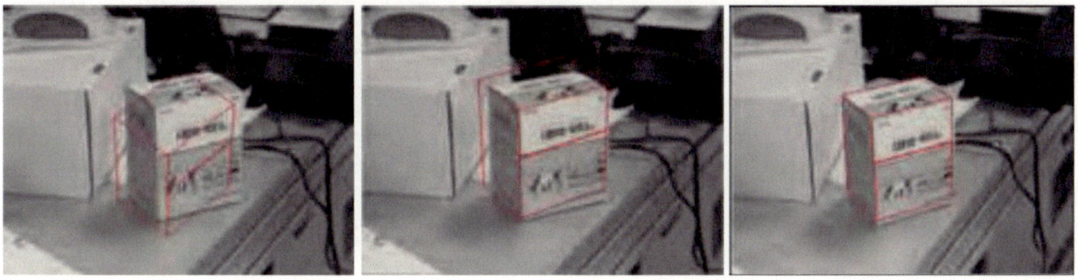

(a) (b) (c)

Figure 13. Parameter optimization by top-down process: (a) CAD model is overlaid with initial parameters, (b) after 10 iterations (c) after 40 iterations for the visible object

7. Experimental Results

In this paper, our main goal is to recognize man-made architectures such as building, bridge, container, and etc. using a FLIR camera. As an initial test, we experimented on a polyhedral object using a CCD camera. Then we evaluated the system on a FLIR dataset.
Figure 14 shows the overall interface of the target recognition system. This automatic target recognition system estimates the initial object parameters using scene and object DB. Then optimal parameter tuning is performed in top-down meaningful shape matching. From this result, the system makes a decision and feedbacks to the bottom-up process.

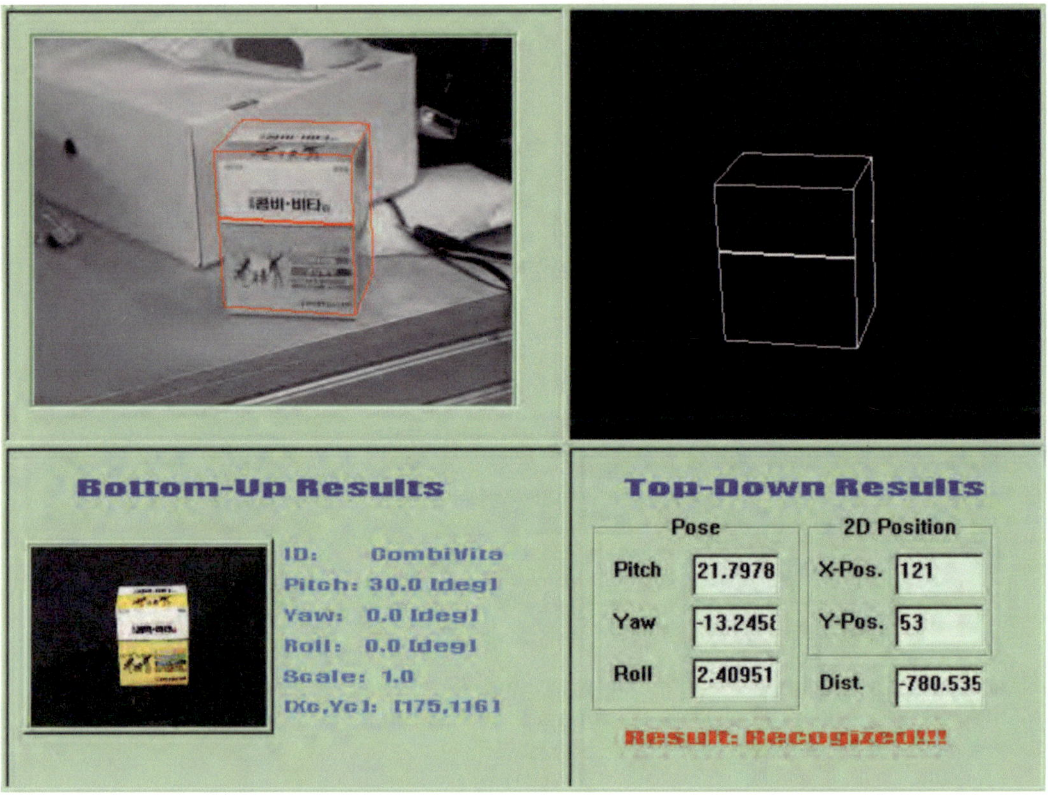

Figure 14. System interface-(upper left): input image with final result is overlaid, (upper right): rendered 3D CAD model generated from bottom-up and jump distribution, (lower left): bottom-up process result, (lower right): top-down process result which shows the optimal parameters

7.1 Test on visible database

First, we tested the algorithm for the objects captured using the CCD camera. We made a database for quantized views as explained. Figure 9 shows some results of the bottom-up process. We can get proper initial parameter values. Figure 13 shows the projection of a model with refined parameters by a top-down process for each object placed in the general environment. The overall computation time is 2 sec (0.5 sec for the bottom-up process) on the average under AMD 2400+.

7.2 Test on FLIR Database

The targets to recognize are shown in Figure 15. The sensor is FLIR Prism SP with resolution 320×240, NTSC interface. These models contain some background information which provide scene context. 3D CAD models are acquired by manual measurements.

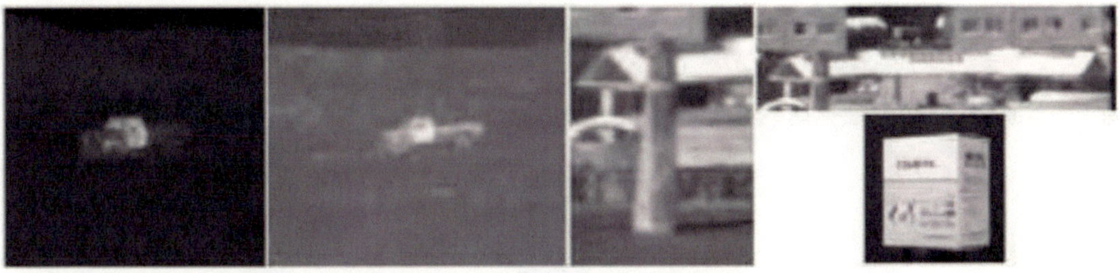

Figure 15. FLIR targets to recognize: cars, building, container, and tower

The test images are shown in Figure 16. They are composed of three types for the accurate performance evaluation for the practical use. The system has to recognize the targets in DB with high recognition rate and able to reject clutter objects or natural scenes.

Figure 16. The composition of test images: targets in DB, targets not in DB, and natural scenes

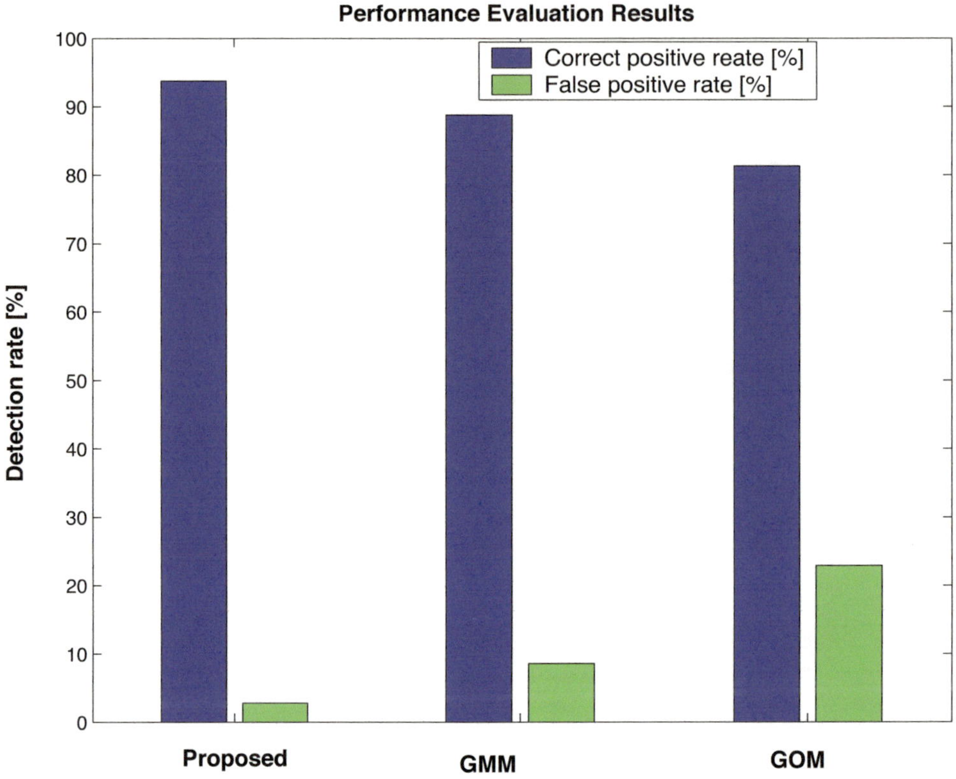

Figure 17. Evaluation of target recognition performance: the proposed method, GMM only, and GOM only

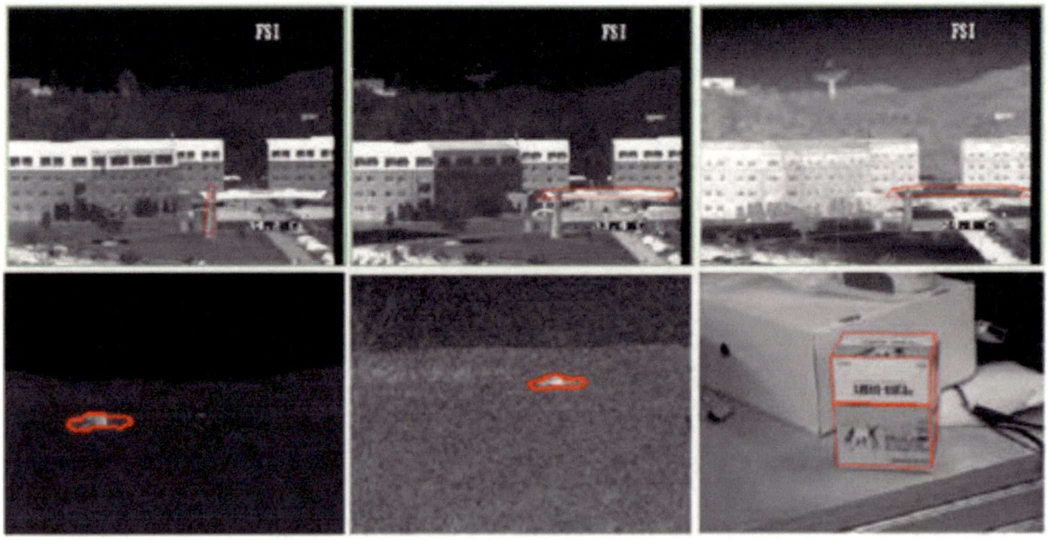

Figure 18. Successful recognition results

Figure 17 summarized our results compared with the methods of GMM only and GOM only. We used the performance measure as correct positive rate vs. false positive rate. In target recognition, the false positive rate is very important factor for practical system because false detections makes enormous damage. So, a good target recognition system has to high correct detection rate and very low false detection rate. During the performance comparison, we have the same bottom-up process with different top-down methods. We take all test images into consideration for the optimal parameter tuning. Our method outperforms the other two, with correct detection rate 93.75% and false detection rate only 2.85%. GOM-based method shows the worst performance. Figure 18 shows visual object recognition results for each object.

Figure 19 shows a typical failure case of the proposed system. The failures occurred from a bottom-up failure due to severe noise and a top-down failure due to low contrast.

Figure 19. Failure case due to top-down fails due to low contrast

8. Conclusions

We propose a new object recognition paradigm based on the robust properties of the HVS, especially in scene context and 3D shape context information in a bottom-up and a top-down process. Furthermore, we also propose the cooperative feature map binding by utilizing both bottom-up and top-down processes and validate the system performance with various experiments. The test results on several images demonstrate efficiency in optimal matching as well as feasibility of the proposed recognition paradigm. The same paradigm will be extended to the general object recognition problem by changing the model representation.

9. Acknowledgments

This work was supported in part by the Korea Science and Engineering Foundation (KOSEF) grant funded by the Korea government(MOST)(No. M1-0302-00-0064), by the MIC for the project, "Development of Cooperative Network-based Humanoids' Technology" of Korea.

10. References

Bar, M. (2004). Visual objects in context. *Nature Reviews: Neuroscience,* Vol. 5, 617-629.

Biederman, I. (1987). Recognition by Components: A Theory of Human Image Understanding. *Psychol. Review,* Vol. 94, No. 2, 115-147.

Borgelt, C. & Kruse, Z. (2001). *Graphical models: methods for data analysis and mining.* Wiley, New York, 1-12.

Canny, J. (1986). A computational approach to edge detection. *IEEE Transactions on Pattern Analysis and Machine Intelligence,* Vol. 8, No.6, 679-698.

Desolneux, A.; Moisan, L. & Morel, J.M. (2004). Gestalt theory and computer vision. In *Carsetti A. Seeing, Thinking and Knowing,* Kluwer Academic Publishers, New York, 71-101.

Doucet, A.; Freitas, N.D. & Gordon, N. (2001). *Sequential Monte Carlo methods in practice,* Springer, New York, 432-444, 3-13.

Edelman, S. & Bülthoff, H. (1992). Orientation dependence in the recognition of familiar and novel views of 3D objects. *Vision Research,* Vol. 32, 2385-2400.

Faugeras, O.D. & Hebert, M. (1986). The representation recognition, and locating of 3-D objects. *International Journal of Robotics Research,* Vol. 5, No. 3, 27–52.

Feldman, J. & Singh, M. (2005). Information along contours and object boundaries. *Psychological Review,* Vol. 112, No. 1, 243-252.

Fergus, R.; Perona, P. & Zisserman, A. (2003). Object class recognition by unsupervised scale-invariant learning. *Proceedings of the IEEE Conference on Computer Vision and Pattern Recognition,* 264-271, Madison, Wisconsin, June.

Fiser, J.; Subramaniam, S. & Biederman, I. (2001). Size Tuning in the absence of spatial frequency tuning in object recognition. *Vision Research,* Vol. 41, No. 15, 1931-1950.

Green, P. (1996). *Reversible jump Markov Chain Monte Carlo computation and Bayesian Model Determination,* Champman and Hall, London.

Harris, C.J. & Stephens, M. (1988). A combined corner and edge detector. In *Proceedings of 4th Alvey Vision Conference,* 147-151, Manchester.

Kim, S. & Kweon, I.S. (2005). Automatic model-based 3D object recognition by combining feature matching with tracking. *Machine Vision and Applications,* Vol. 16, No. 5, 267-272.

Kumar, V.P. (2002). Towards trainable man-machine interfaces: combining top-down constraints with bottom-up learning in facial analysis. *Ph.D Thesis,* MIT.

Kuno, Y.; Ikeuchi, K. & Kanade, T. (1988). Model-based vision by cooperative processing of evidence and hypotheses using configuration spaces. *SPIE Digital and Optical Shape Representation and Pattern Recognition,* Vol. 938, 444-453.

Lindeberg, T. (1998). Feature detection with automatic scale selection. *International Journal of Computer Vision,* Vol. 30, No. 2, 77-116.

Lowe, D.G. (1987). Three-dimensional object recognition from single two-dimensional images. *Artificial Intelligence*, Vol. 31, No. 3, 355-395.

Lowe, D.G. (2004). Distinctive image features from scale-invariant keypoints. *International Journal of Computer Vision*, Vol. 60, No. 2, 91-110.

Mikolajczyk, K. & Schmid, C. (2003). A performance evaluation of local descriptors. *Proceedings of the IEEE Conference on Computer Vision and Pattern Recognition*, 774-781, Madison, Wisconsin.

Milanese, R.; Wechsler H. & Gil, S. (1994). Integration of bottom-up and top-down for visual attention using non-linear relaxation. *Proceeding of IEEE Conference on Computer Vision and Pattern Recognition*, 781-785, Seattle, USA , June.

Mundy, J. & Zisserman, A. (1992). *Geometric invariance in computer vision*, 335-460, MIT Press, Cambridge, MA.

Murase, H. & Nayar, S. (1995). Visual learning and recognition of 3-D objects from appearance. *International Journal of Computer Vision*, Vol. 14, 5-24.

Nichols, M.J. & Newsome, W. T. (1999). The neurobiology of cognition. *Nature*, Vol. 402, No. 2, C35-C38.

Parkhurst, D.; Law, K. & Niebur, E. (2002). Modeling the role of salience in the allocation of overt visual attention. *Vision Research*, Vol. 42, 107-123.

Pasupathy, A. & Connor, C.E. (2001). Shape representation in area V4: position-specific tuning for boundary conformation. *Journal of Neurophysiology*, Vol. 86, No. 5, 2505-2519.

Peters, G. (2000). Theories of three-dimensional object perception - A Survey. In *Recent Research Developments in Pattern Recognition*, Transworld Research Network, Part-I, Vol. 1, 179-197.

Reisfeld, D.; Wolfson, H. & Yeshurun, Y. (1995). Context-free attentional Operators: the generalized symmetry transform. *International Journal of Computer Vision*, Vo. 14, No. 2, 119-130.

Ristic, B.; Arulampalam, S. & Gordon, N. (2004). *Beyond the Kalman filter: particle filters for tracking applications*, Artech House Publishers, London, 35-62.

Robert, C.P. & Casella, G. (1999). *Monte Carlo statistical methods*, Springer, New York.

Rothganger, F.; Lazebnik, S.; Schmid, C., & Ponce, J. (2004). Segmenting, modeling, and matching video clips containing multiple moving objects. *Proceedings of the IEEE Conference on Computer Vision and Pattern Recognition*, 914-921, Washington, DC, June.

Rothwell, C.A. (1993). Recognition using projective invariance, *Ph.D Thesis*, Oxford.

Schmid, C.; Mohr, R. & Bauckhage, C. (2000). Evaluation of interest point detectors. *International Journal of Computer Vision*, Vol. 37, No. 2, 151-172.

Serre, T. & Riesenhuber, M. (2004). Realistic modeling of simple and complex cell tuning in the HMX model, and implications for invariant object recognition in cortex. *AIM*, MIT.

Siegel, M.; Kording, K.P. & Konig, P. (2000). Integrating top-down and bottom-up sensory processing by somato-dendritic interactions. *Journal of Computational Neuroscience*, Vol. 8, 161-173.

Treisman, A. (1998). Feature binding, attention and object perception. *Philosophical Transactions: Biological Sciences* 29, Vol. 353, No. 1373. 1295-1306.

Tu, Z.; Chen, X.; Yuille, A. & Zhu, S.C. (2005). Image parsing: unifying segmentation, detection, and object recognition. (Marr Prize Issue, a short version appeared in ICCV 2003), *International Journal of Computer Vision*, Vol. 63, No. 2, 113-140.

VanRullen, R. (2003). Visual saliency and spike timing in the ventral visual pathway. *Journal of Physiology (Paris)* 97, 365-377.

Zhu, S.C.; Zhang, R. & Tu Z. (2000). Integrating bottom-up/top-down for object recognition by data driven Markov Chain Monte Carlo. *Proceedings of IEEE Conference on Computer Vision and Pattern Recognition*, 738-745, Hilton Head, SC, June.

11

3D Cameras: 3D Computer Vision of wide Scope

Stefan May, Kai Pervoelz and Hartmut Surmann
Fraunhofer Institute for Intelligent Analysis and Information Systems
Germany

1. Introduction

The human visual sense is the one among all other senses that gathers most information we receive. Evolution has optimized our visual system to negotiate one's way in three dimensions even through cluttered environments. For perceiving 3D information, the human brain uses three important principles: stereo vision, motion parallax and a-priori knowledge about the perspective appearance of objects in dependency of their distance. These tasks pose a challenge to computer vision since decades. Today the most common techniques for 3D sensing are CCD- or CMOS-camera, laser scanner or 3D time-of-flight camera based. Even though evolution has shown predominance for passive stereo vision systems, three additional problems are remaining for 3D perception compared with the two mentioned active vision systems above. First, the computation needs a great deal of performance, since the correlation of two images from a different point of view has to be found. Second, distances to structureless surfaces cannot be measured, if the perspective projection of the object is larger than the camera's field of view. This problem is often called aperture problem. Finally, a passive visual sensor has to cope with shadowing effects and changes in illumination over time.

That is why for mapping purposes mostly active vision systems like laser scanners are used , e.g. [Thrun et al., 2000], [Wulf & Wagner, 2003], [Surmann et al., 2003]. But these approaches are usually not applicable to tasks considering environment dynamics.

Due to this restriction, 3D cameras [CSEM SA, 2007], [PMDTec, 2007] have attracted attention since their invention nearly a decade ago. Distance measurements are also based on a time-of-flight principle but with an important difference. Instead of sampling laser beams serially to acquire distance data point-wise, the entire scene is measured in parallel with a modulated surface. This principle allows for higher frame rates and thus enables the consideration of environment dynamics.

The first part of this chapter discusses the physical principles of 3D sensors, which are commonly used in the robotics community for typical problems like mapping and navigation. The second part concentrates on 3D cameras, their assets, drawbacks and perspectives. Based on these examining parts, some solutions are discussed that handle common problems occurring in dynamic environments with changing lighting conditions. Finally, it is shown in the last part of this chapter how 3D cameras can be applied to mapping, object localization and feature tracking tasks.

2. Range Sensing

Before focusing on 3D cameras and their applications, a short comparison of range sensors and their underlying principles is given. Since there are many different types of sensors for range sensing, the section focuses on those that are most common in the domain of robotics, i.e. stereo vision systems, 3D laser scanners and of course 3D cameras. The section first introduces into underlying measurement principles before it describes real sensor systems in more detail.

2.1 Range Measurement Principles

Different types of sensors are based on different measurement principles. The two main principles for technical systems are triangulation and time-of-flight. Both principles can further be separated into two subcategories: active and passive triangulation or respectively pulsed and phase shifted time-of-flight.

2.1.1 Triangulation

This technique is called triangulation since the object whose distance should be measured forms a triangle with two parts of the sensor (cf. Figure 1). If the sensor consists of one receiver part and one active transmitter part, the measurement principle is called **active triangulation**. If it consists only of two passive receivers, it is called **passive triangulation**.

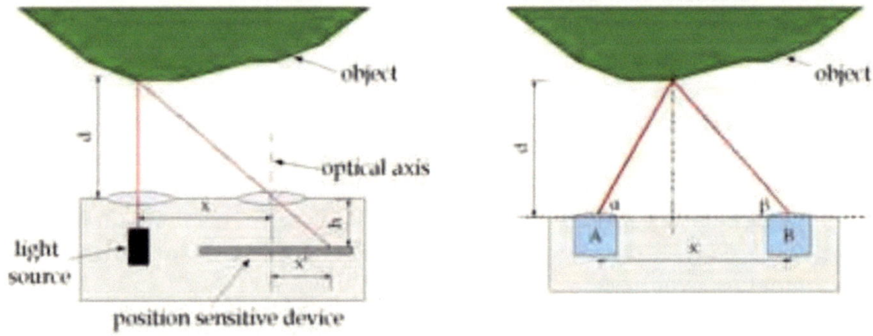

Figure 1. Left image: Working principle of active triangulation. Right image: Working principle of passive triangulation

Active triangulation. The configuration of a simple active triangulation sensor can be seen in figure 1. A light source projects a single point onto the object and the reflection of the light point is measured by the receiver part of the sensor. This receiver is a position sensitive device, which can determine the point where the light reflection has hit the receiver. By knowing the position of the sensor's optics, the distance between transmitter and receiver x, their distance to the optics h and the hitting point of the light reflection x', it is possible to calculate the distance d of the object by the formula:

$$d = h \cdot \frac{x}{x'} \tag{1}$$

Such a simple sensor configuration restricts the distance measurement capability to one single point. To determine the shape of an object, either the sensor or the object itself must be moved and several measurements have to be taken. Higher sophisticated triangulation sensor systems use two-dimensional light sources as well as two-dimensional receivers. They project a light pattern onto the object, which is received by, e.g. a 2D camera system. Such a system directly provides 3D shape information of the measured objects.

Passive triangulation. This principle is well known in nature and has been improved over millions of years since it is the basic principle of the human visual sense. Being more precise, it is the base of the human depth perception. It consists as well as a technical passive triangulation sensor of two receivers (the eyes or two cameras respectively) which are observing an overlapping area (cf. figure 1). If a specific point p is in the field of view of both receivers, it is possible to determine its distance d to the sensor. Therefore each receiver calculates the angle between the line from the sensor to point p and the optical axis of the receiver. In combination with the distance x between the two receivers the distance to the point p is calculated by

$$d = \frac{x}{\frac{1}{\tan\alpha} + \frac{1}{\tan\beta}}, \tag{2}$$

where α is the angle from receiver A to the point p and β is the angle from receiver B to the point p. This formula assumes that the optical axes of receiver A and B are parallel. The most important task here is to find distinctive points in the images and assign correspondences between the points in the two images. Each point in the image of receiver A has to be correctly identified in the image of receiver B. Wrong assignments will result in wrong distance measurements.

2.1.2 Time-of-Flight

As the name already implies, this principle utilizes the time a specific signal needs to travel from the sensor to the object and back. For calculating this time, different methods can be used. In the following, two of them will be described in more detail, namely the **impulse time-of-flight** method and the **phase difference** method.

Impulse Time-of-Flight. This method is the most obvious one, since a timer is started when a signal is sent to the object and stopped when its reflection is received. By knowing the speed of the signal, the distance to the object can be calculated directly. In practice most often a short laser impulse is sent out to the object and the time until it is detected by an optical receiver is measured.

From that travel time t, the distance d can be calculated by the formula

$$d = t \cdot c, \tag{3}$$

where c is the speed of light.

Phase difference. A more complex method is the calculation of the travel time by measuring the phase difference between the sent signal and its reflection from the object. In principle the modulation of light waves itself could be used but since their wavelengths are in the range of some nm it would be difficult to determine the phase difference. Therefore the light signal is modulated again with a much longer wavelength.

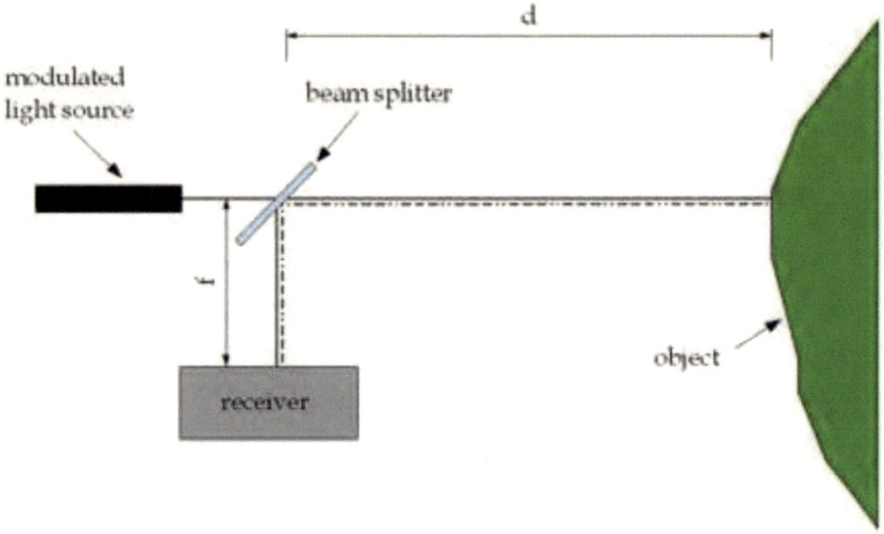

Figure 2. Drawing of the phase-difference time-of-flight measurement principle. A modulated light signal is split into a reference- and a measurement signal. The measured phase-difference gives the time-of-flight of the signal and thus the distance

As shown in figure 2 the modulated light signal is split into two signals by a semi permeable mirror, also called beam splitter. One of the signals, the reference signal, is sent directly to the internal receiver which has a distance f to the beam splitter. The other one, the measurement signal, is sent to the object which is located at a distance *d*. When the signal is reflected by the object and detected by the internal receiver of the range sensor, it has in total covered a distance *d'*, which is defined by

$$d' = f + (2 \cdot d)\,. \tag{4}$$

Since the second signal has traveled a longer distance than the reference signal, the phase of the incoming signal is different. With this measured phase difference ϕ and the wavelength of the signal modulation λ, the distance *d* of the object can be calculated by

$$d = \frac{\phi}{360} \cdot \frac{\lambda}{2}, \tag{5}$$

where λ is the wavelength of the signal modulation.
Since the phase of a modulated signal is periodic with a cycle of 360° or 2π respectively, it is not possible to determine in which cycle of the modulation the measured phase is located. This is essential for distance measurement and a real sensor needs to deal with this problem. How this can be done is explained in the section 2.2.2.

2.2. 3D Laser Scanners

Laser scanners are very common sensors for range measurement in many fields of application and belong to the group of sensors based on the time-of-flight principle. 2D laser scanners are being very common in robotic applications since a long period of time. They are based on a laser source, a rotating mirror and a photosensitive sensor, whereat the laser source and the photosensitive sensor are building a one dimensional time-of-flight range sensor. For reaching the second dimension, the mirror deflects the laser beam continuously while it is rotating. Such a scanner could scan a circumferential area, but normally it is reduced to a smaller angle, e.g., 240°. For many applications where three-dimensional objects act in or interact with a three-dimensional environment, a 2D range sensor is not sufficient and a 3D sensor is required.

A 3D laser scanner can be realized in different ways, either the laser signal is deflected in two directions by a mirror instead of only one, or one can use more than one laser source deflected by a mirror [Ibeo, 2007]. A third option for developing 3D laser scanner was used by several groups, e.g. [Fraunhofer IAIS, 2007], [RTS, 2007]. Here commercially available 2D laser scanners were pivot-mounted and rotated while they are scanning, which gives three-dimensional data. Two of them will be described in more detail in the following subsections.

2.2.1 3DLS – A 3D Laser Scanner

The 3DLS is based on a SICK 2D laser scanner which is pivot-mounted in the horizontal axis [Fraunhofer IAIS, 2007]. This axis is driven by a servo motor to extend the standard scanner to a 3D laser scanner. The underlying measurement principle is the *Impulse Time-of-Flight*. The laser source is an infrared laser with a wavelength of λ = 905nm. A maximum field of view of 180° horizontal and 124° vertical can be scanned with an angular resolution of 1/4th degree and a precision of ±15mm. Depending on the chosen resolution, the scan time for a full 3D scan can vary from 3.2s for a resolution of 1° to 26.64s for the maximum resolution of 0.25°. With a size of 284 x 286 x 166mm (width x height x depth) and a weight of 7.4kg the 3DLS can be used for medium-sized or large mobile robotic systems as well as for stationary applications.

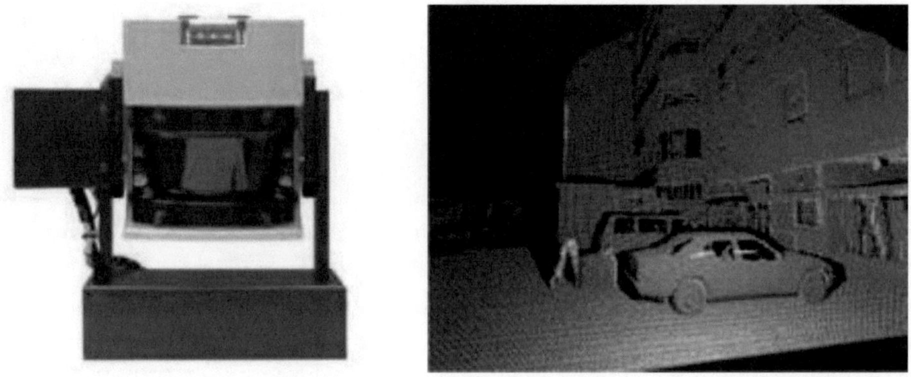

Figure 3. Left image: The 3D laser scanner system 3DLS with a SICK LMS291 laser scanner. Right image: 3D scan taken with the 3DLS

The 3DLS is available as indoor and outdoor version, which mainly differ in the operation temperature and the maximum range of the scanner. The maximum range is almost exclusively limited by the amount of light which is reflected by the measured object.

Theoretically, the maximum range of both versions is 80m but with an object reflectivity of only 10% (e.g. a black cardboard) the maximum range is specified with 10m for the indoor version and 30m for the outdoor version. Another property of the 3DLS which influences the quality of the resulting data is the diameter of the sent laser impulse, which signal increases over the traveled distance. For the 3DLS, the diameter of the laser impulse increased from around 1cm at the beginning to 15cm at a distance of 30m. This causes inaccuracies if the laser hits an edge and therefore is partially reflected from different distances.

The result of a 3D laser scan is a 3D point cloud, which can be seen in figure 3. The technical data of the 3DLS are summarized in the following table.

Resolution	721 x 517 scan points ($1/4^{th}$ °)
Field of view	180° x 124° (hor. x vert.)
Range	80m (30m with 10% reflectance)
Frame Rate	Up to 1 fps (reduced resolution)
Dimensions (mm)	284 (W) x 286 (H) x 166 (D)
Weight	7.4 kg
Power supply	24V dc

Table 1. Property table of the Fraunhofer IAIS 3DLS

2.2.2 A 3D laser scanner based on the Hokuyo URG

Figure 4. Left image: Hokuyo 3D Scanner. Right image: Scan taken with the Hokuyo 3D Scanner. Note that a field of view of 248° is reached by only one rotating servo

Similar to the 3DLS, this scanner is based on a 2D laser scanner, the Hokuyo URG-04LX [Kawata et al., 2005], [Hokuyo Automatic, 2007]. Since it is very small and light weighted it is directly mounted on a servo drive to get the additional rotation axis. By using a pan-tilt-head (cf. figure 4), different scanning setups are possible. In difference to the 3DLS, this scanner measures the range by using the *phase difference* principle. For generating the modulated light signal, an infrared laser diode with a wavelength of λ = 785nm is used. As described in chapter 2.1.2 it is not possible to detect if the measured phase difference is more than one cycle period and therefore out of the maximum measurement range. To handle

that problem, two laser signals with different modulation frequencies are emitted alternately. Both phase differences are measured separately and used for determining the real distance of the measured object.
The maximum apex angle of this 3D laser scanner is 270° horizontally and 248° vertically with a resolution of 0.36°. Depending on the measured distance, the precision is at least ±2% of the distance. A full resolution scan takes 50 seconds. The technical data are summarized in the following table.

Resolution	1000 x 667 scan points (0.36°)
Field of view	270° x 248° (hor. x vert.)
Range	4,095m
Frame Rate	0,02 fps (full resolution)
Dimensions (mm)	80 (W) x 120 (H) x 75 (D)
Weight	350 g
Modulation frequencies	46.55 MHz and 53.2 MHz

Table 2. Property table of the Hokuyo URG based 3D laser scanner

2.3. 3D Cameras
These devices belong to the group of time-of-flight sensors. They use the phase-shift principle to determine distances. While the environment is being illuminated with infrared flashes, the reflected light is measured by a CCD- or CMOS-sensor or a combined technology. Amplitude data is represented by the incoming wave's amplitude, intensity by its offset (i.e. the background light) and distance by its phase shift. For the experiments in section 4, we have used a SwissRanger SR-2 device that can be seen in figure 5.

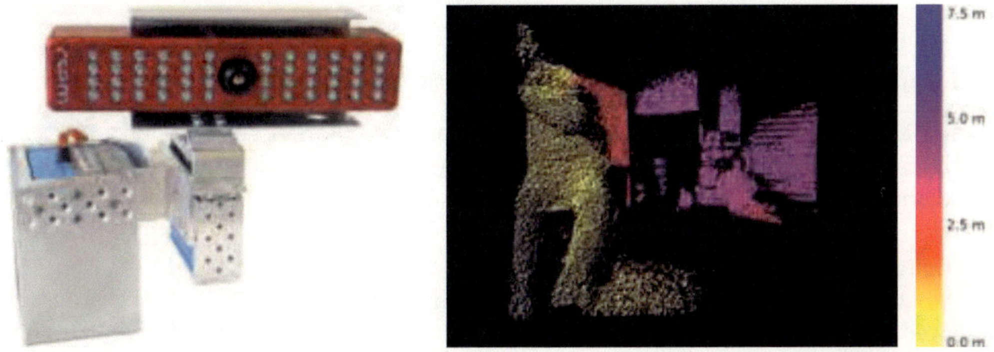

Figure 5. Left image: SwissRanger SR-2 device mounted on a pan-tilt unit. Right image: Sample image captured from a SwissRanger SR-2 device. The image is color coded (see color bar on the right side)

The SwissRanger SR-2 provides amplitude data, intensity data and distance data. All measurements are being organized by a FPGA, which provides an USB interface to access the data. The FPGA can be configured by setting one or more of its eleven registers. The most important register concerns the adjustment of the integration time, since the SR-2 does not provide an automatic integration time controller by itself (the follow-up model SR-3000 does). It ranges from 1 to 255, which are multiples of 255 μs. Finding the optimal value will be investigated in section 3.2.

Please pay some attention on table 3 and compare it with table 1. The comparison of the SwissRanger SR-2 and the Sick LMS device is important for the experiment in section 4.1.

Resolution	124 x 160
Field of view	43° x 46° (hor. x vert.)
Range	7.5 m
Frame Rate	Up to 30 fps
Dimensions (mm)	135 (W) x 45 (H) x 32 (D)
Weight	0.2 kg

Table 3. Property table of the SwissRanger SR-2 device

2.4. Stereo Cameras

Stereo vision is a mature technology in computer vision. Depth-measurements with stereo cameras have been investigated since decades, e.g. [Lucas & Kanade, 1981]. There are also lots of pre-calibrated systems available, but this technology still needs a great deal of performance since point correspondences from the left and the right image have to be found for enabling the calculation of depth information. For homogeneous regions it is difficult to find the correct correspondences. If these regions are bounded by unambiguous features, i.e. textured regions or edges and borders respectively an iteration scheme can be used to relax the correspondences of these features over the whole image. Otherwise there is no way to calculate any depth information. That is why related techniques have difficulties providing reliable navigation or mapping information for a mobile robot in real-time and like all passive visual sensors, they are difficult to handle in real world environments with changing light conditions. Due to this drawback, this chapter discusses not any passive visual sensor system any further.

3. 3D Cameras – A Step forward in Computer Vision

This section discusses the technology of 3D cameras more detailed since it has the application potential for tackling dynamics in the field of 3D computer vision. For the investigations following below the SwissRanger SR-2 was used.

3.1. Challenges and Limitations

The adjustment of 3D cameras to dynamic scenes is still a difficult task. The accuracy is influenced by a couple of parameters. Some of them are predefined by the design of hardware and cannot be influenced by the user. Anyway, these parameters should be mentioned in this section to facilitate the understanding for the presented effects in the remainder of this chapter.

First of all, the accuracy is proportional to the modulation frequency. Doubling the frequency doubles the accuracy. But the frequency also determines the unambiguous range, which can be seen in equation (6).

$$R = \frac{c}{2 \cdot f_m}, \tag{6}$$

where R is the unambiguity interval, c the speed of light and f_m the modulation frequency. A camera with a frequency of 20 MHz provides an unambiguous range of 7.5 m. A lower frequency provides a higher range but less accuracy. To satisfy both criteria multiple frequencies can be used. For instance, this technology is currently used by the PMD[vision]® A2 from PMDTec.

Since the principle is based on integrating discharged electrons from incoming light, the optical power also influences the reachable accuracy. These electrons are collected within a conversion capacity, which can result in oversaturation, if the integration time is too high [Lange, 2000]. Both mentioned manufacturers in this chapter use a burst mode to increase the power output for short intervals at the same energy level over time.

For an application, the best measurement capability has to be adjusted by the integration time. This value has to be high enough to provide a high signal level, but low enough to avoid oversaturation. Oversaturation is indicated by both, the intensity and the amplitude data. Theoretically the relation between intensity and amplitude is constant as shown in figure 6, but unfortunately it shows a small deviation due to a non-ideal sinusoidal wave emitted by the sensor's LEDs [Lange, 2000].

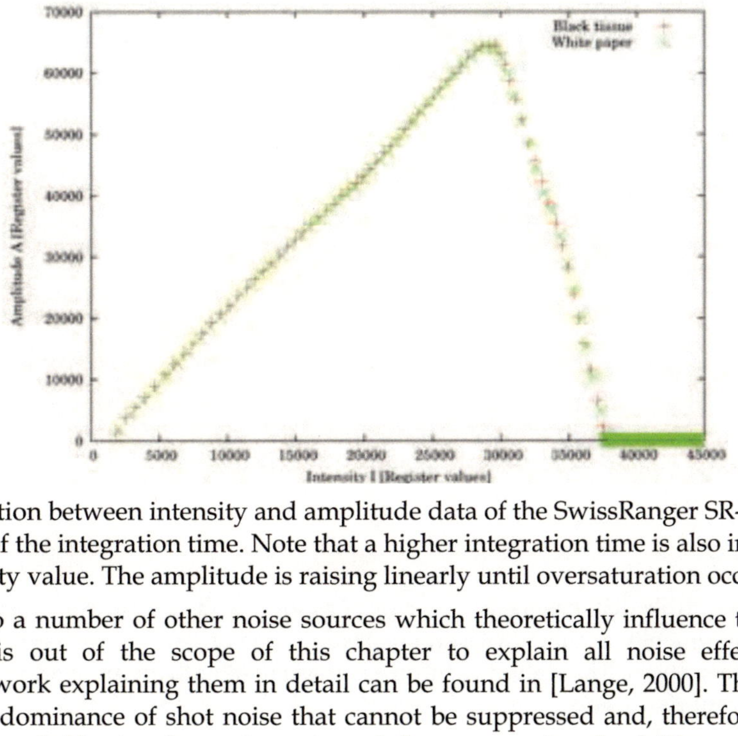

Figure 6. Relation between intensity and amplitude data of the SwissRanger SR-2 device in dependency of the integration time. Note that a higher integration time is also indicated by a higher intensity value. The amplitude is raising linearly until oversaturation occurs

There are also a number of other noise sources which theoretically influence the reachable accuracy. It is out of the scope of this chapter to explain all noise effects. A good theoretically work explaining them in detail can be found in [Lange, 2000]. This work also describes the dominance of shot noise that cannot be suppressed and, therefore, limits the theoretically reachable signal-to-noise ratio and the accuracy involved. Hence, the standard deviation ΔR is approximately given as:

$$\Delta R = \frac{c}{4 \cdot \pi \cdot f_m} \cdot \frac{\sqrt{I_l + I_b}}{\sqrt{2} \cdot A}, \quad (7)$$

where A is the amplitude and I the intensity. The intensity value is composed of the reflected constant component I_l of the LED illumination and the background illumination I_b.

As a rule, it can be said that the proper saturation of a pixel's capacitance provides its best accuracy. The emitted light is uniformly distributed (only approximately, see [Gut, 2004]) on a surface proportional to the quadratic distance. Therefore, the reflected intensity is also proportional to the quadratic distance, whereas the received background light (caused by sunlight) is independent of it [Schneider, 2003]. For both constituent parts the standard deviation yields a different dependency on the object's distance. If one of these components is dominant the standard deviation has the following characteristic[1]:

$$\Delta R \sim \begin{cases} r, if\ I_l >> I_b \\ r^2, if\ I_l << I_b \end{cases} \tag{8}$$

For indoor applications with less background illumination case one can be assumed. This relation will be relevant for the experiments mentioned below.

3.2. Tackling Environment Dynamics

Figure 7 shows the same scene taken twice with the SwissRanger SR-2 device at two different integration times. The integration time for the measurement shown in the left figure was not adjusted properly with respect to the near object. The bothered area of the hand indicates that effect. But this measurement might provide better values in the background area.

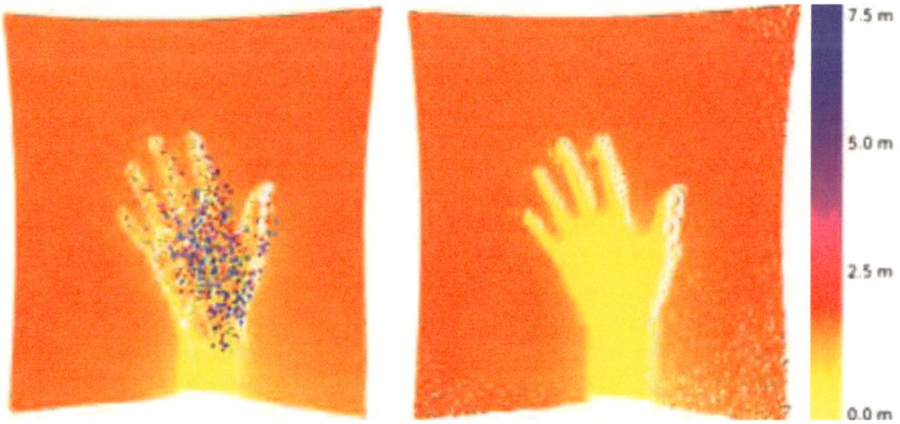

Figure 7. Two sample distance measurements of a close hand in false color representation. The left measurement was taken with an integration time of 15 ms, which is definitely too high for the near object. The right measurement was taken with an integration time of 4 ms and fits better for that scene

3.2.1 Setting up the integration time

The diffuse reflectivity of objects is an important parameter for precise measurements. Typically, a scene comprises objects with different reflectivity. It can vary from 2% for black rubber tire up to 100% for white paper at a wavelength of 900nm [Lange, 2000]. Let us assume scenarios containing only a small single object with high reflectance close to the sensor to explain the compromise that has to be met. Since the integration time can only be

[1] Note that also the amplitude has a quadratic dependency on the distance.

adjusted for all pixel elements together, one might guess that it is the best strategy to avoid each pixel from oversaturation. Focusing the small object will most likely decrease the accuracy for the remaining scene. This also means, that the signal level for objects with low diffuse reflectivity will be low if objects with high reflectivity are in the same range of vision during measurement.

One suitable method is to merge multiple captures at different integration times. It reduces the frame rate but increases the dynamic range.

In [May, 2006] we have presented an alternative integration time controller based on mean intensity measurements. This solution was empirically found and showed a suitable dynamic range for our experiments without affecting the frame rate. It also alleviates the effects of small bothering areas. The averaged amplitude in dependency of intensity can be seen in figure 8.

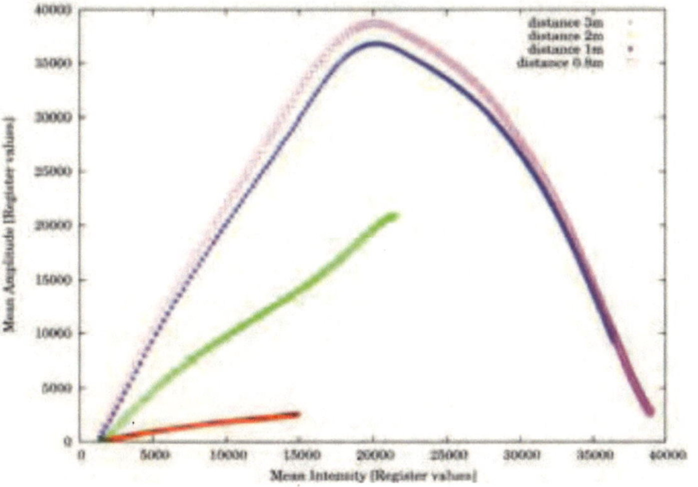

Figure 8. Relation between mean amplitude and mean intensity. Note that the characteristic is now a mixture of the characteristic of each single pixel (cf. figure 6)

We used a proportional closed-loop controller to adjust the integration time from one frame to the next as shown in the following itemization.

The control deviation variable I_a was assigned with a value of 15000 for the illustrations in this chapter. It has been chosen conservatively with respect to the characteristic shown in figure 8.

1. Calculate the mean intensity $\overline{I_t}$ from the intensity dataset I_t at time t.
2. Determine control deviation $D_t = \overline{I_t} - I_a$.
3. Update control variable $c_{t+1} = -V_p \cdot D_t + c_t$ for grabbing the next frame, where c_t and c_{t+1} are the integration times for two frames following one another, V_p the proportional closed loop deviation parameter and c_0 a suitable initial value.

Independent of the chosen control method, the integration time has always to be adjusted with respect to the application. A change of integration time causes an apparent motion considering the distance measurement values. Therefore, it is necessary for the application to take the presence of control deviation into account while using an automatic integration time controller.

The newest model from Mesa Imaging, the SwissRanger SR-3000 provides an automatic integration time exposure based on the amplitude values. For most scenes it works properly. In some cases of fast scene change it could occur that a proper integration time cannot be found. This is up to the missing intensity information due to the backlight suppression on chip. The amplitude diagram does not provide a non-ambiguous working point. A short discussion on the backlight suppression will be given in section 3.3.

3.2.2 Consideration of accuracy

It is not possible to guarantee certain accuracies for measurements of unknown scenes, since they are affected by the influences mentioned above. However, the possibility to evolve the accuracy information for each pixel eases that circumstance. In section 4 two examples using this information will be explained. For determining the accuracy equation (7) is used. Assuming that the parameters of the camera (in general this is the integration time for users) are optimally adjusted, the accuracy only depends on the object's distance and its reflectivity. For indoor applications with less background illumination, the accuracy is linearly decreasing (see equation (8)). Applying a simple threshold is one option for filtering out inaccurate parts of an image. Setting a suitable threshold primarily depends on the application. Lange stated with respect to the dependency between accuracy and distance [Lange, 2000]: "This is an important fact for navigation applications, where a high accuracy is often only needed close to the target". This statement does not hold for every other application like mapping, where unambiguousness is essential for registration. Unambiguous tokens are often distributed over the entire scene. Higher distances between these tokens provide geometrically higher accuracies for the alignment of two scans. After this consideration, increasing the threshold linearly with the distance for indoor applications suggests itself. This approach enlarges the information gain from the background and can be seen in figure 9.
A light source in the scene decreases the reachable accuracy. The influence of the accuracy threshold can be seen in figure 10. Bothered areas are reliably removed. The figure shows also that the small bothering area of the lamp does not much influence the integration time controller based on mean intensity values, even so that the surrounding area is determined precisely.

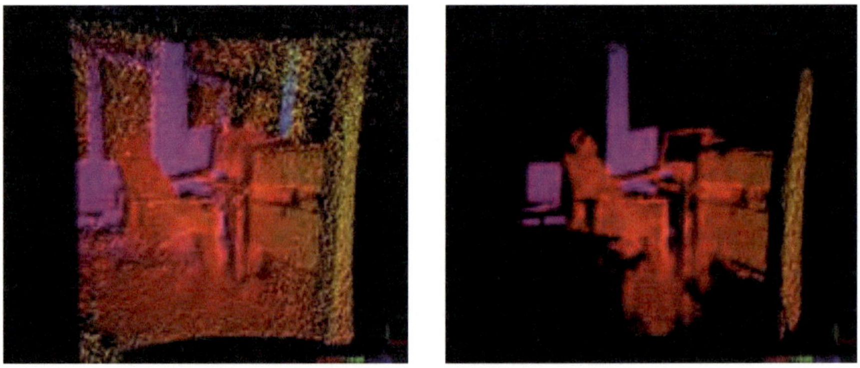

Figure 9. Two images taken with a SwissRanger SR-2 device of the same scene. Left image: without filtering. Right image: with accuracy filter. Only data points with an accuracy better than 50mm are remaining

Figure 10. Influence of light emitting sources. Top row: The light source is switched off. Lower Row: The light source is switched on. Note that the bothered area could reliably be detected

3.3. Latest Improvements and expected Innovations in Future

Considering equation (7) a large background illumination ($I_b >> I_l$) highly affects the sensor's accuracy by increasing the shot noise and lowering its dynamics. Some sensors nowadays are equipped with some background light suppression functionalities, e.g. spectral filters or circuits for constant component suppression, which are increasing the signal-to-noise ratio [Moeller et al., 2005], [Buettgen et al., 2006].

Suppressing the background signal has one drawback. The amplitude represents the infrared reflectivity and not the reflectivity we sense as human-beings. This might take effects on computer vision systems inspired by our human visual sense, e.g. [Frintrop, 2006]. Some works in the past had also proposed a circuit structure for a pixel-wise-integration capability [Schneider, 2003], [Lehmann, 2004]. Unfortunately, this technology did not become widely accepted due to a lower fill-factor. Lange explained the importance of the optical fill factor as follows [Lange, 2000]: "The optical power of the modulated illumination source is both expensive and limited by eye-safety regulations. This requires the best possible optical fill factor for an efficient use of the optical power and hence a high measurement resolution."

4. 3D Vision Applications

This section investigates the practical influence of upper mentioned thoughts by presenting some typical applications in the domain of autonomous robotics currently investigated by us. Since 3D cameras are comparatively new to other 3D sensors like laser scanners or stereo cameras, the porting of algorithms defines a novelty per se; e.g. one of the first 3D maps created with registration approaches mostly applied to laser scanner systems up to now was presented at the IEEE/RSJ International Conference on Intelligent Robots and Systems in 2006 [Ohno, 2006]. The difficulties to come across with these sensors are discussed in this section. Furthermore, a first examination on the capabilities for tackling environment dynamics will follow.

4.1. Registration of 3D Measurements

One suitable registration method for range data sets is called the Iterative Closest Points (ICP) algorithm and was introduced by Besl and McKay in 1992 [Besl & McKay, 1992]. For the readers convenience a brief description of this algorithm is repeated in this section. Given two independently acquired sets of 3D points, *M* (model set) and *D* (data set), which correspond to a single shape, we aim to find the transformation consisting of a rotation *R* and a translation *t* which minimizes the following cost function:

$$E(R,t) = \sum_{i=1}^{|M|} \sum_{j=i}^{|D|} \omega_{i,j} \left\| m_i - (Rd_j + t) \right\|^2 . \qquad (9)$$

$\omega_{i,j}$ is assigned *1* if the *i-th* point of *M* describes the same point in space as the *j-th* point of *D*. Otherwise $\omega_{i,j}$ is *0*. Two things have to be calculated: First, the corresponding points, and second, the transformation *(R,t)* that minimizes *E(R,t)* on the base of the corresponding points. The ICP algorithm calculates iteratively the point correspondences. In each iteration step, the algorithm selects the closest points as correspondences and calculates the transformation *(R,t)* for minimizing equation (9). The assumption is that in the last iteration step the point correspondences are correct. Besl and McKay prove that the method terminates in a minimum [Besl & McKay, 1992]. However, this theorem does not hold in our case, since we use a maximum tolerable distance d_{max} for associating the scan data. Such a threshold is required though, given that 3D scans overlap only partially. The distance and the degree of overlapping have a non-neglective influence of the registration accuracy.

4.2. 3D Mapping – Invading the Domain of Laser Scanners

The ICP approach is one upon the standard registration approaches used for data from 3D laser scanners. Since the degree of overlapping is important for the registration accuracy, the huge field of view and the high range of laser scanners are advantages over 3D cameras (compare table 1 with table 3). The following section describes our mapping experiments with the SwissRanger SR-2 device.

The image in figure 11 shows a single scan taken with the IAIS 3D laser scanner. The scan provides a 180 degree field of view. Getting the entire scene into range of vision can be done by taking only two scans in this example. Nevertheless, a sufficient overlap can be guaranteed to register both scans. Of course there are some uncovered areas due to shadowing effects, but that is not the important fact for comparing the quality of registration. A smaller field of view makes it necessary to take more scans for the coverage of the same area within the range of vision. The image in figure 12 shows an identical scene taken with a SwissRanger SR-2 device. There were 18 3D images necessary for a circumferential view with sufficient overlap. Each 3D image was registered with its previous 3D image using the ICP approach.

Figure 11. 3D scan taken with an IAIS 3D laser scanner

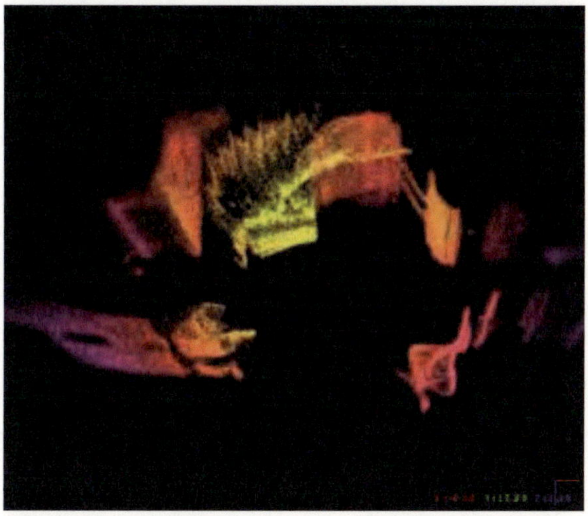

Figure 12. 3D map created from multiple SwissRanger SR-2 3D images. The map was registered with the ICP approach. Note the gap at the bottom of the image, that indicates the accumulating error

4.2.1. "Closing the Loop"

The registration of 3D image sequences causes a non-neglective accumulation error. This effect is represented by the large gap at the bottom of the image in figure 12. These effects have also been investigated in detail for large 3D maps taken with 3D laser scanners, e.g. in [Surmann et al., 2004], [Cole & Newman, 2006]. For a smaller field of view these effects occur faster, because of the smaller size of integration steps. Determining the closure of a loop can be used in these cases to expand the overall error on each 3D image. This implies that the present captured scene has to be recognized to be already one of the previous captured scenes.

4.2.2. "Bridging the Gap"

The second difficulty for the registration approach is that a limited field of view makes it more unlikely to measure enough unambiguous geometric tokens in the space of distance data or even sufficient structure in the space of grayscale data (i.e. amplitude or intensity). This issue is called the aperture problem in computer vision. It occurs for instance for images taken towards a huge homogeneous wall (see [Spies et al., 2002] for an illustration). In the image of figure 12 the largest errors occurred for the images taken along the corridor. Although points with a decreasing accuracy depending on the distance (see section 3.2.2) were considered, only the small areas at the left and the right border contained some fairly accurate points, which made it difficult to determine the precise pose. This inaccuracy is mostly indicated in this figure by the non-parallel arrangement of the corridor walls. The only feasible solution to this problem is a utilization of different perspectives.

4.3. 3D Object Localization

Object detection is a highly investigated field of research since a very long period of time. A very challenging task here is to determine the exact pose of the detected objects. Either this information is just implicitly available since the algorithm is not very stable against object transformations or the pose information is explicit but not very precise and therefore not very reliable. For reasoning about the environment it may be enough to know which objects are present and where they are located but especially for manipulation tasks it is essential to know the object pose as precise as possible. Examples for such applications are ranging from "pick and place" tasks of disordered components in industrial applications to handling task of household articles in service-robotic applications.

In comparison to color camera based systems the use of 3D range sensors for object localization provide much better results regarding the object pose. For example Nuechter et al. [Nuechter et al., 2005] presented a system for localizing objects in 3D laser scans. They used a 3D laser scanner for the detection and localization of objects in office environments. Depending on the application one drawback of this approach is the time consuming 3D laser scan which needs at least 3.2 seconds for a single scan (cf. table 1). Using a faster 3D range sensor would increase the timing performance of such a system essentially and thus open a much broader field of applications.

Therefore Fraunhofer IAIS is developing an object localization system which uses range data from a 3D camera. The development of this system is part of the DESIRE research project which is founded by the German Federal Ministry of Education and Research (BMBF) under grant no. 01IME01B. It will be integrated into a complex perception system of a mobile service-robot. In difference to the work of Nuechter et al. the object detection in the DESIRE perception system is mainly based on information from a stereo vision system since many objects are providing many distinguishable features in their texture. With the resulting hypothesis of the object and it's estimated pose a 3D image of the object is taken and together with the hypothesis it is used as input for the object localization.

The localization itself is based on an ICP based scan matching algorithm (cf. section 4.1). Therefore each object is registered in a database with a point cloud model. This model is used for matching with the real object data. For determining the pose, the model is moved into the estimated object pose and the ICP algorithm starts to match the object model and the object data. The real object pose is given by a homogeneous transformation. Using this object localization system in real world applications brings some challenges, which are discussed in the next subsection.

4.3.1 Challenges

The first challenge is the pose ambiguities of many objects. Figure 13 shows a typical object for a home service-robot application, a box of instant mashed potatoes. The cuboid shape of the box has three plains of symmetry which results in the ambiguities of the pose. Considering only the shape of the object, very often the result of the object localization is not a single pose but a set of possible poses, depending on the number of symmetry planes. For determining the real pose of an object other information than only range data are required, for example the texture. Most 3D cameras additionally providing gray scale images which give information about the texture but with the provided resolution of around 26.000 pixels and an aperture angle of around 45° the resolution is not sufficient enough for stable texture identification. Instead, e.g., a color camera system can be used to solve this ambiguity. This requires a close cooperation between the object localization system and another classification system which uses color camera images and a calibration between the two sensor systems. As soon as future 3D cameras are providing higher resolutions and maybe also color images, object identification and localization can be done by using only data from a 3D camera.

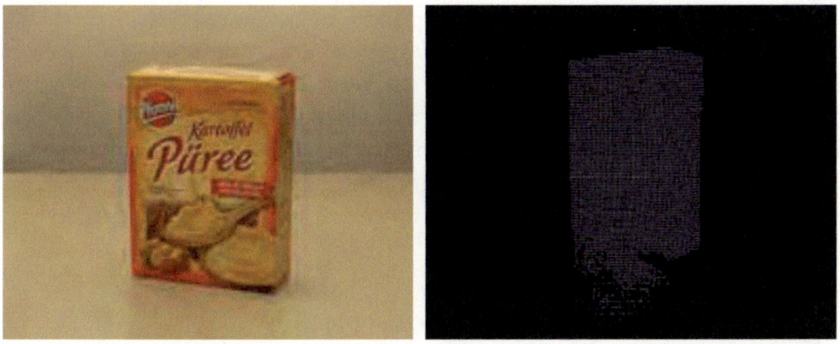

Figure 13. An instant mashed potatoes box. Because of the symmetry plains of the cuboid shape the pose determination gives a set of possible poses. Left: Colour image from a digital camera. Right: 3D range image from the Swissranger SR-2

Another challenge is close related to the properties of 3D cameras and the resulting ability to provide precise range images of the objects. It was shown that the ICP based scan matching algorithm is very reliable and precise with data from a 3D laser scanner, which are always providing a full point cloud of the scanned scene [Nuechter, 2006], [Mueller, 2006]. The accuracy is static or at least proportional to the distance. As described in section 3.2.2 the accuracy of 3D camera data is influenced by several factors. One of these factors for example is the reflectivity of the measured objects. The camera is designed for measuring diffuse light reflections but many objects are made of a mixture of specular and diffuse reflecting materials. Figure 14 shows color images from a digital camera and range images from the Swissrange SR-2 of a tin from different viewpoints. The front view gives reliable range data of the tin since the cover of the tin is made of paper which gives diffuse reflections. In the second image the cameras are located a little bit above and the paper cover as well as high reflecting metal top is visible in the color image. The range image does not show the top since the calculated accuracy of these data points is less than 30 mm. This is a loss of information which highly influences the result of the ICP matching algorithm.

Figure 14. Images of a tin from different view points. Depending on the reflectivity of the objects material the range data accuracy is different. In the range images all data points with a calculated accuracy less than 30mm are rejected. Left: The front view gives good 3D data since the tin cover reflects diffuse. Middle: From a view point above the tin, the cover as well as the metal top is visible. The high reflectivity of the top results in bad accuracy so that only the cover part is visible in the range image. Right: From this point of view, only the high metal top is visible. In the range image only some small parts of the tin are visible

4.4. 3D Feature Tracking

Using 3D cameras to full capacity necessitates taking advantage of their high frame rate. This enables the consideration of environment dynamics. In this subsection a feature tracking application is presented to give an example of applications that demand high frame rates. Most existing approaches are based on 2D grayscale images from 2D cameras since they were the only affordable sensor type with a high update rate and resolution in the past. An important assumption for the calculation of features in grayscale images is called intensity constancy assumption. Changes in intensity are therefore only caused by motion. The displacement of two images is also called optical flow. An extension to 3D can be found in [Vedula et al., 1999] and [Spies et al., 2002]. The intensity constancy assumption is being combined with a depth constancy assumption. The displacement of two images can be calculated more robustly. This section will not handle scene flow. However the depth value of features in the amplitude space should be examined so that the following two questions are answered:

- Is the resolution and quality of the amplitude images from 3D cameras good enough to apply feature tracking kernels?
- How stable is the depth value of features gathered in the amplitude space?

To answer these questions a Kanade-Lucas-Tomasi (KLT) feature tracker is applied [Shi, 1994]. This approach locates features considering the minimum eigenvalue of each 2x2 gradient matrix. Tracking features frame by frame is done by an extension of previous Newton-Raphson style search methods. The entire approach also considers multi-resolution to enlarge possible displacements between the two frames. Figure 15 shows the result of calculating features in two frames following one another. Features in the present frame (left feature) are connected with features from the previous frame (right feature) with a thin line. The images in figure 15 show that many edges in the depth space are associated with edges in the amplitude space. The experimental standard deviation for that scene was determined by taking the feature's mean depth value of 100 images. The standard deviation was then calculated from 100 images of the same scene. These experiments have been performed two times, first without a threshold and second with an accuracy threshold of 50mm (cf. formula 7). The results are shown in table 4 and 5.

Experimental standard deviation $\sigma = 0.053$m, Threshold $\Delta R = \infty$				
Feature #	Considered	Mean Dist [m]	Min Dev [m]	Max Dev [m]
1	Yes	-2.594	-0.112	0.068
2	Yes	-2.686	-0.027	0.028
3	Yes	-2.882	-0.029	0.030
4	Yes	-2.895	**-0.178**	**0.169**
5	Yes	-2.731	**-0.141**	**0.158**
6	Yes	-2.750	-0.037	0.037
7	Yes	-2.702	**-0.174**	**0.196**
8	Yes	-2.855	**-0.146**	**0.119**
9	Yes	-2.761	-0.018	0.018
10	Yes	-2.711	-0.021	0.025

Table 4. Distance values and deviation of the first ten features calculated from the scene shown in the left image of figure 15 with no threshold applied

Experimental standard deviation $\sigma = 0.017$m, Threshold $\Delta R = 50$mm				
Feature #	Considered	Mean Dist [m]	Min Dev [m]	Max Dev [m]
1	Yes	-2.592	-0.110	0.056
2	Yes	-2.684	-0.017	0.029
3	Yes	-2.881	-0.031	0.017
4	No	-2.901	**-0.158**	**0.125**
5	Yes	-2.733	**-0.176**	**0.118**
6	Yes	-2.751	-0.025	0.030
7	No	-2.863	**-0.185**	**0.146**
8	No	-2.697	**-0.169**	**0.134**
9	Yes	-2.760	-0.019	0.015
10	Yes	-2.711	-0.017	0.020

Table 5. Distance values and deviation of the first ten features calculated from the scene shown in the left image of figure 15 with a threshold of *50mm*

The reason for the high standard deviation is the noise criterion for edges. The signal reflected by an edge is a mixture of the background and object signal. A description of this effect is given in [Gut, 2004]. Applying an accuracy threshold alleviates this effect. The standard deviation is decreased significantly. This approach has to be balanced with the number of features found in an image. Applying a more restrictive threshold might decrease the number of features too much. For the example described in this section an accuracy threshold of ΔR = *10mm* decreases the number of features to *2* and the experimental standard deviation σ to *0.01m*.

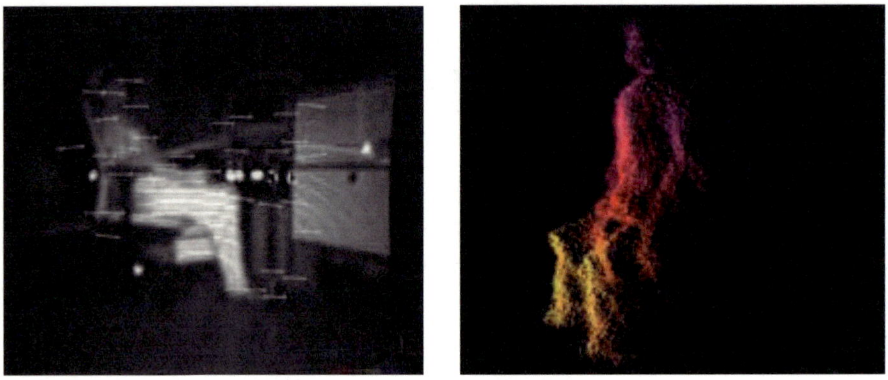

Figure 15. Left image: Amplitude image showing the tracking of KLT-features from two frames following one another. Right image: Side view of a 3D point cloud. Note the appearance of jump edges at the border area

5. Summary and Future work

First of all, a short comparison of range sensors and their underlying principles was given. The chapter further focused on 3D cameras. The latest innovations have given a significant improvement for the measurement accuracy, wherefore this technology has attracted attention in the robotics community. This was also the motivation for the examination in this chapter. On this account, several applications were presented, which represents common problems in the domain of autonomous robotics.

For the mapping example of static scenes, some difficulties have been shown. The low range, low apex angle and low dynamic range compared with 3D laser scanners, raised a lot of problems. Therefore, laser scanning is still the preferred technology for this use case.

Based on the first experiences with the Swissranger SR-2 and the ICP based object localization, we will further develop the system and concentrate on the reliability and the robustness against inaccuracies in the initial pose estimation. Important for the reliability is knowledge about the accuracy of the determined pose. Indicators for this accuracy are, e.g., the number of matched points of the object data or the mean distance between found model-scene point correspondences.

The feature tracking example highlights the potential for dynamic environments. Use cases with requirements of dynamic sensing are predestinated for 3D cameras. Whatever, these are the application areas 3D cameras were once developed.

Our ongoing research in this field will concentrate on dynamic sensing in future. We are looking forward to new sensor innovations!

6. References

Besl, P. & McKay, N. (1992). A Method for Registration of 3-D Shapes, *IEEE Transactions on Pattern Analysis and Machine Intelligence,* Vol. 14, No. 2, (February 1992) pp. 239-256, ISSN: 0162-8828

Buettgen, B.; Oggier, T.; Lehmann, M.; Kaufmann, R.; Neukom, S.; Richter, M.; Schweizer, M.; Beyeler, D.; Cook, R.; Gimkiewicz, C.; Urban, C.; Metzler, P.; Seitz, P.; Lustenberger, F. (2006). High-speed and high-sensitive demodulation pixel for 3D imaging, In: Three-Dimensional Image Capture and Applications VII. *Proceedings of SPIE,* Vol. 6056, (January 2006) pp. 22-33, DOI: 10.1117/12.642305

Cole, M. D. & Newman P. M. (2006). Using Laser Range Data for 3D SLAM in Outdoor Environments, In *Proceedings of the IEEE International Conference on Robotics and Automation (ICRA),* pp. 1556-1563, Orlando, Florida, USA, May 2006

CSEM SA (2007), *SwissRanger SR-3000 - miniature 3D time-of-flight range camera,* Retrieved January 31, 2007, from http://www.swissranger.ch

Frintrop, S. (2006). *A Visual Attention System for Object Detection and Goal-Directed Search,* Springer-Verlag, ISBN: 3540327592, Berlin/Heidelberg

Fraunhofer IAIS (2007). *3D-Laser-Scanner,* Fraunhofer Institute for Intelligent Analysis and Information Systems, Retrieved January 31, 2007, from http://www.3d-scanner.net

Gut, O. (2004). *Untersuchungen des 3D-Sensors SwissRanger,* Eidgenössische Technische Hochschule Zürich, Retrieved January 21, 2007, from http://www.geometh.ethz.ch/publicat/diploma/gut2004/Fehlereinfluesse/index_fe.html

Hokuyo Automatic (2007), *Scanning laser range finder for robotics URG-04LX,* Retrieved January 31, 2007, from http://www.hokuyo-aut.jp/products/urg/urg.htm

Ibeo Automobile Sensor GmbH (2007), *Ibeo ALASCA XT Educational System,* Retrieved January 31, 2007, from http://www.ibeo-as.com/deutsch/products_alascaxtsingle_educational.asp

Kawata, H.; Ohya, A.; Yuta, S.; Santosh, W. & Mori, T. (2005). Development of ultra-small lightweight optical range sensor system, *International Conference on Intelligent Robots and Systems* 2005, Edmonton, Alberta, Canada, August 2005.

Lange, R. (2000). 3D time-of-flight distance measurement with custom solid-state image sensors in CMOS/CCD-technology, *Dissertation,* University of Siegen, 2000

Lehmann, M.; Buettgen, B.; Kaufmann, R.; Oggier, T.; Stamm, M.; Richter, M.; Schweizer, M.; Metzler, P.; Lustenberger, F.; Blanc, N. (2004). *CSEM Scientific & technical Report* 2004, CSEM Centre Suisse d'Electronique et de Microtechnique SA, Retrieved January 20, 2007, from http://www.csem.ch/corporate/Report2004/pdf/SR04-photonics.pdf

Lowe, D. G. (2004). Distinctive Image Features from Scale-Invariant Keypoints, *International Journal of Computer Vision,* Vol. 60, No. 2, (November 2004) pp. 91-110, ISSN: 0920-5691

Lucas, B. D. & Kanade, T. (1981). An Interative Image Registration Technique with an Application to Stereo Vision, In *Proceedings of the 7th International Conference on Artificial Intelligence* (IJCAI), pp. 674-679, Vancouver, British Columbia, August 1981

May, S.; Werner, B.; Surmann, H.; Pervoelz, K. (2006). 3D time-of-flight cameras for mobile robotics, *In Proceedings of the IEEE/RSJ International Conference on Intelligent Robots and Systems* (IROS), pp. 790-795, Beijing, China, October 2006

Moeller, T.; Kraft H.; Frey, J.; Albrecht, M.; Lange, R. (2005). *Robust 3D Measurement with PMD Sensors*, PMDTechnologies GmbH. Retrieved January 20, 2007, from http://www.pmdtec.com/inhalt/download/documents/RIM2005-PMDTech-Robust3DMeasurements.pdf.

Mueller, M.; Surmann, H.; Pervoelz, K. & May, S. (2006). The Accuracy of 6D SLAM using the AIS 3D Laser Scanner, In *Proceedings of the IEEE International Conference on Multisensor Fusion and Integration for Intelligent Systems* (MFI), Heidelberg, Germany, September 3-6, 2006

Nuechter A., Lingemann K., Hertzberg J. & Surmann, H. (2005). Accurate Object Localization in 3D Laser Range Scans, In *Proceedings of the 12th International Conference on Advanced Robotics* (ICAR '05), ISBN 0-7803-9178-0, pages 665 - 672, Seattle, USA, July 2005.

Nuechter A. (2006). Semantische dreidimensionale Karten für autonome mobile Roboter, *Dissertation*, Akademische Verlagsgesellschaft Aka, ISBN: 3-89838-303-2, Berlin

Ohno, K.; Nomura, T.; Tadokoro, S. (2006). Real-Time Robot Trajectory Estimation and 3D Map Construction using 3D Camera, In *Proceedings of the IEEE/RSJ International Conference on Intelligent Robots and Systems* (IROS), pp. 5279-5285, Beijing, China, October 2006

PMD Technologies (2007), "*PMD Cameras*", Retrieved January 31, 2007, from http://www.pmdtec.com/e_inhalt/produkte/kamera.htm

RTS Echtzeitsysteme (2007), *Mobile Serviceroboter*, Retrieved January 31, 2007, from http://www.rts.uni-hannover.de/index.php/Mobile_Serviceroboter

Schneider, B. (2003). Der Photomischdetektor zur schnellen 3D-Vermessung für Sicherheitssysteme und zur Informationsübertragung im Automobil, *Dissertation*, University of Siegen, 2003

Shi, J. & Tomasi, C. (1994). Good Features to Track, In *Proceedings of the IEEE Conference on Computer Vision and Pattern Recognition* (CVPR), pp. 595-600, Seattle, June 1994

Spies, H.; Jaehne, B.; Barron, J. L. (2002). Range Flow Estimation, *Computer Vision Image Understanding* (CVIU2002) 85:3, pp.209-231, March, 2002

Surmann, H.; Nuechter, A.; Lingemann K. & Hertzberg, J. (2003). An autonomous mobile robot with a 3D laser range finder for 3D exploration and digitalization of indoor environments, *Robotics and Autonomous Systems*, 45, (December 2003) pp. 181-198

Surmann, H.; Nuechter, A.; Lingemann, K. & Hertzberg, J. (2004). 6D SLAM A Preliminary Report on Closing the Loop in Six Dimensions, In *Proceedings of the 5th IFAC Symposium on Intelligent Autonomous Vehicles* (IAV), Lisabon, Portugal, July 2004

Thrun, S.; Fox, D. & Burgard, W. (2000). A real-time algorithm for mobile robot mapping with application to multi robot and 3D mapping, In *Proceedings of the IEEE International Conference on Robotics and Automation* (ICRA), pp. 321-328, ISBN: 0-7803-5886-4, San Francisco, February 1992

Vedula, S.; Baker, S.; Rander, P.; Collins, R. & Kanade, T. (1999). Three-Dimensional Scene Flow, *In Proceedings of the 7th International Conference on Computer Vision* (ICCV), pp. 722-729, Corfu, Greece, September 1999

Wulf, O. & Wagner, B. (2003). Fast 3d-scanning methods for laser measurement systems, *In Proceedings of International Conference on Control Systems and Computer Science* (CSCS14), Bucharest, Romania, February 2003

12

A Visual Based Extended Monte Carlo Localization for Autonomous Mobile Robots

Wen Shang[1] and Dong Sun[2]
[1]*Suzhou Research Institute of City University of Hong Kong*
[2]*Department of Manufacturing Engineering and Engineering Management of City University of Hong Kong*
P.R. China

1. Introduction

Over the past decades, there are tremendous researches on mobile robots aiming at increasing autonomy of mobile robot systems. As a basic problem in mobile robots, self-localization plays a key role in various autonomous tasks (Kortenkamp et al., 1998). Considerable researches have been done on self-localization of mobile robots (Borenstein et al., 1996; Chenavier & Crowley, 1992; Jensfelt & Kristensen, 2001; Tardos et al., 2002), with the goal of estimating the robot's pose (position and orientation) by proprioceptive sensors and exteroceptive techniques. Since proprioceptive sensors (e.g., dead-reckoning) are generally not sufficient to locate a mobile robot, exteroceptive techniques have to be used to estimate the robot's configuration more accurately. Some range sensors such as sonar sensors (Drumheller, 1987; Tardos et al., 2002; Wijk & Christensen, 2000) and laser range finders (Castellanos & Tardos, 1996), can be employed for the robot localization. However, the data obtained from sonar sensors is usually noisy due to specular reflections, and the laser scanners are generally expensive. As a result, other sensory systems with more reliable sensing feedback and cheaper price, such as visual sensors (Chenavier & Crowley, 1992; Dellaert et al., 1999; Gaspar et al., 2000), are more demanded for mobile robot localization.
Probabilistic localization algorithm (Chenavier & Crowley, 1992; Fox et al., 1999b; Nourbakhsh et al., 1995) is a useful systematic method in sensor-based localizations, providing a good framework by iteratively updating the posterior distribution of the pose space. As a state estimation problem, pose estimation with linear Gaussian distribution (unimodal) can be done by Kalman filters for pose tracking (Chenavier & Crowley, 1992; Leonard & Durrant-White, 1991), which exhibits good performance under the condition that the initial robot pose is known. Nonlinear non-Gaussian distribution (multimodal) problem can be solved by multi-hypothesis Kalman filters (Jensfelt & Kristensen, 2001) or Markov methods (Fox et al., 1999b; Nourbakhsh et al., 1995) for global localization. The multi-hypothesis Kalman filters use mixtures of Gaussians and suffer from drawbacks inherent with Kalman filters. Markov methods employ piecewise constant functions (histograms) over the space of all possible poses, so the computation burden and localization precision depend on the discretization of pose space.

By representing probability densities with sets of samples and using the sequential Monte Carlo importance sampling, Monte Carlo localization (MCL) (Dellaert et al., 1999; Fox et al., 1999a) represents non-linear and non-Gaussian models with great robustness and can focus the computational resources on regions with high likelihood. Hence MCL has attracted considerable attention and has been applied in many robot systems. MCL shares the similar idea to that of particle filters (Doucet, 1998) and condensation algorithms (Isard & Blake, 1998) in computer vision.
As a sample based method with stochastic nature, MCL can suffer from the observation deviation or over-convergence problem when the sample size is smaller or encountering some poorly modeled events (to be discussed in detail in Section 2.2) (Carpenter et al., 1999; Thrun et al., 2001). Many approaches have been proposed to improve the efficiency of MCL algorithm. A method of adaptive sample size varying in terms of the uncertainty of sample distribution, was presented in (Fox, 2003). However, the sample size of this method must meet a condition of an error bound of the distribution, which becomes a bottleneck for a real global localization. A resampling process through introduction of a uniform distribution of samples was further applied for the case of non-modeled movements (Fox et al., 1999a). Likewise, a sensor resetting localization algorithm (Lenser & Veloso, 2000) was also implemented using a resampling process from visual feedback, based on an assumption that the visual features with range and bearing are distinguishable. Such a method may be applicable to RoboCup, but not to a general office environment. Several other visual based Monte Carlo methods (Kraetzschmar & Enderle, 2002; Rofer & Jungel, 2003) were implemented under the condition that the environment features must be unique. A mixture MCL (Thrun et al., 2001) and condensation with planned sampling (Jensfelt et al., 2000) incorporated the resampling process to MCL for efficiency improvement, which require fast sampling rate from sensors every cycle.
In order to achieve higher localization precision and improve efficiency of MCL, a new approach to extended Monte Carlo localization (EMCL) algorithm is presented here. The basic idea is to introduce two validation mechanisms to check the abnormity (e.g., observation deviation and over-convergence phenomenon) of the distribution of weight values of sample sets and then employ a resampling strategy to reduce their influences. According to the verification, the strategy of employing different resampling processes is employed, in which samples extracted either from importance resampling or from observation model form the true posterior distribution. This strategy can effectively prevent from the premature convergence and be realized with smaller sample size. A visual-based extended MCL is further implemented. The common polyhedron visual features in office environments are recognized by Bayesian network that combines perceptual organization and color model. This recognition is robust with respect to individual low-level features and can be conveniently transferred to similar environments. Resampling from observation model is achieved by the triangulation method in the pose constraint region.
The remainder of this chapter is organized as follows. Section 2 introduces conventional MCL algorithm and discusses the existing problems when applied to the real situations. Section 3 proposes the extended MCL (EMCL) with brief implementation explanations showing the difference from conventional MCL, which is followed by the implementation details of a visual-based EMCL application example in Section 4. Section 5 presents experiments conducted on a mobile robot system to verify the proposed approach. Finally, conclusions of this work are given in Section 6.

2. Conventional Monte Carlo Localization

2.1 Conventional MCL

Monte Carlo localization (MCL) (Dellaert et al., 1999; Fox et al., 1999a) is a recursive Bayesian filter that estimates the posterior distribution of robot poses conditioned on observation data, in a similar manner to Kalman filters (Chenavier & Crowley, 1992) and Markov methods (Fox et al., 1999b; Nourbakhsh et al., 1995). The robot's pose is specified by a 2D Cartesian position x_k and y_k, and a heading angle θ_k, where k denotes the index of time sequences. It is assumed that the environment is Markov when using Bayesian filters, that is, the past and the future data are (conditionally) independent if one knows the current state. The iterative Markov characteristic of Bayesian filters provides a well probabilistic update framework for all kinds of probability-based localization algorithms.

MCL is implemented based on SIR (Sampling/Importance Resampling) algorithm (Carpenter et al., 1999; Doucet, 1998) with a set of weighted samples. For the robot pose $X_k = [x_k \quad y_k \quad \theta_k]^T$, define the sample set as follows:

$$S_k = \{s_k^{(i)} = < X_k^{(i)}, w_k^{(i)} > | i = 1, \cdots, N_k\}$$

where the sample $s_k^{(i)}$ consists of the robot pose $X_k^{(i)}$ and the weight $w_k^{(i)}$ that represents the likelihood of $X_k^{(i)}$, i is the index of weighted samples, and N_k denotes the number of samples (or sample size). It is assumed that $\sum_{i=1}^{N_k} w_k^{(i)} = 1$, since the weights are interpreted as probabilities.

During the localization process, MCL is initialized with a set of samples reflecting initial knowledge of the robot's pose. It is usually assumed that the distribution is uniform for global localization when the initial pose is unknown, and a narrow Gaussian distribution when the initial pose is known. Then samples are recursively updated with the following three steps executed (see Table 1).

Step 1: Sample update with robot motion (prediction step)

The probabilistic proposal distribution of robot pose in the motion update is

$$q_k = p(X_k \mid X_{k-1}, u_{k-1}) \times Bel(X_{k-1}) \tag{1}$$

where $p(X_k \mid X_{k-1}, u_{k-1})$ denotes probabilistic density of the motion that takes into account the robot properties such as drift, translational and rotational errors, $u_{k-1} = [\Delta x_{k-1} \quad \Delta y_{k-1} \quad \Delta\theta_{k-1}]^T$ denotes variation of the robot pose at time k-1, and $Bel(X_{k-1})$ denotes posterior distribution of the robot pose X_{k-1}. Then, extract a new sample set S'_k with $<\overline{X}_k^{(i)}, \overline{w}_k^{(i)}>$ from the proposal distribution q_k, by applying the above motion update to the posterior distribution, where $\overline{X}_k^{(i)}$ and $\overline{w}_k^{(i)}$ denote the extracted pose and weight after motion update, respectively.

Step 2: Belief update with observations (sensor update step)

Robot's belief about its pose is updated with observations, mostly from range sensors. Introduce a probabilistic observation model $p(Z_k \mid X_k^{(i)})$, where Z_k denotes measurements from the sensor. Re-weight all samples of S'_k extracted from the prediction step, and we then have

Algorithm Conventional MCL

Prediction step:

for each $i = 1, \cdots, N_k$

Draw sample $\overline{X}_k^{(i)}$ from S_{k-1} according to (1)

$\overline{w}_k^{(i)} = 1 / N_k$

$< \overline{X}_k^{(i)}, \overline{w}_k^{(i)} > \rightarrow S'_k$

end for

Sensor update step:

for each $i = 1, \cdots, N_k$

$\hat{w}_k^{(i)} = \overline{w}_k^{(i)} \cdot p(Z_k \mid \overline{X}_k^{(i)})$

$\widetilde{w}_k^{(i)} = \dfrac{\hat{w}_k^{(i)}}{\sum_{j=1}^{N_k} \hat{w}_k^{(j)}}$

$< \overline{X}_k^{(i)}, \widetilde{w}_k^{(i)} > \rightarrow S''_k$

end for

Resampling step (importance resampling):

for each $\widetilde{s}_k^{(i)} =< \overline{X}_k^{(i)}, \widetilde{w}_k^{(i)} >$ in S''_k

$cw(\widetilde{s}_k^{(i)}) = \sum_{j=1}^{i} \widetilde{w}_k^{(j)}$ {Cumulative distribution}

end for

for each $i = 1, \cdots, N_k$

r=rand(0,1); {random number r}

j=1

while($\mathrm{j} \leq N_k$) do

if($cw(\widetilde{s}_k^{(j)}) > r$)

$X_k^{(i)} = \overline{X}_k^{(j)}$

$w_k^{(i)} = 1 / N_k$

$< X_k^{(i)}, w_k^{(i)} > \rightarrow S_k$, break

else j=j+1

end if

end while

end for

Table 1. Conventional MCL algorithm

$$\hat{w}_k^{(i)} = \overline{w}_k^{(i)} \cdot p(Z_k \mid \overline{X}_k^{(i)}) \tag{2}$$

where $\hat{w}_k^{(i)}$ denotes the non-normalized weight during the sensor update.

Normalize weights as follows to ensure that all beliefs sum up to 1:

$$\widetilde{w}_k^{(i)} = \frac{\hat{w}_k^{(i)}}{\sum_{j=1}^{N_k} \hat{w}_k^{(j)}} \tag{3}$$

Then, the sample set after sensor update, denoted by S_k'' with $<\overline{X}_k^{(i)}, \widetilde{w}_k^{(i)}>$, is obtained. The observation model $p(Z_k \mid X_k^{(i)})$ is also named as importance factor (Doucet, 1998), which reflects the mismatch between the probabilistic distribution q_k after the prediction step and the current observations from the sensor.

Step 3: Resampling step

The resampling step is to reduce the variance of the distribution of weight values of samples and focus computational resources on samples with high likelihood. A new sample set S_k is extracted with samples located nearby the robot true pose. This step is effective for localization by ignoring samples with lower weights and replicating those with higher weights. The step is to draw samples based on the importance factors, and is usually called importance resampling (Konolige, 2001). The implementation of such importance resampling is shown in Table 1.

2.2 Problems of Conventional MCL

When applied to the real situations, conventional MCL algorithm suffers from some shortcomings. The samples are actually extracted from a proposal distribution (here is the motion model). If the observation density deviates from the proposal distribution, the (non-normalized) weight values of most of the samples become small. This leads to poor or even erroneous localization result. Such phenomenon results from two possible reasons. One is that too small sample size is used, and the other is due to poorly modeled events such as kidnapped movement (Thrun et al., 2001). To solve the problem, either a large sample size is employed to represent the true posterior density to ensure stable and precise localization, or a new strategy is employed to address the poorly modeled events.

Another problem when using conventional MCL is that samples often converge too quickly to a single or a few high-likelihood poses (Luo & Hong, 2004), which is undesirable in the localization in symmetric environments, where multiple distinct hypotheses have to be tracked for periods of time. This over-convergence phenomenon is caused by the use of too small sample size, as well as smaller sensor noise level. The viewpoint that the smaller the sensor noise level is, the more likely over-convergence occurs, is a bit counter-intuitive, but it actually leads to poor performance. Due to negative influences of the smaller sample size and poorly modeled events, implementation of conventional MCL in real situations is not trivial.

Since sensing capabilities of most MCLs are achieved by sonar sensors or laser scanners, the third problem is how to effectively realize MCL with visual technology, which can more accurately reflect the true perceptual mode of the natural environments.

3. Extension of Monte Carlo Localization (EMCL)

In order to overcome limitations of conventional MCL when applied to real situations, a new approach to extended Monte Carlo localization (EMCL) methodology is proposed in this section.

In the proposed extended MCL algorithm, besides the prediction and sensor update steps that are the same as in the conventional MCL, two validation mechanisms in the resampling step are introduced for checking abnormity of the distribution of weight values of sample sets. According to the validation, different resampling processes are employed, where samples are extracted either from importance resampling or from observation model. Table 2 gives the procedures of the proposed extended MCL algorithm.

Algorithm Extended MCL

Prediction step:
Sensor update step:
Same as conventional MCL algorithm;
Resampling step: (different from conventional MCL)
Quantitatively describe the distribution of (normalized and non-normalized) weight values of sample set;
Two validation mechanisms:
if (over-convergence); **over-convergence validation**
sample size n_s resampling from observations
for each $i = 1, \cdots, N_k - n_s$
importance resampling $X_k^{(i)}$ from S_k''
$w_k^{(i)} = 1 / N_k$
$< X_k^{(i)}, w_k^{(i)} > \to S_k$
end for
for each $i = N_k - n_s + 1, \cdots, N_k$
sensor based resampling
$X_k^{(i)} \leftarrow p(X_k \mid Z_k)$
$w_k^{(i)} = 1 / N_k$
$< X_k^{(i)}, w_k^{(i)} > \to S_k$
end for
else if (sum of (non-normalized) weight $< W_{th}$); **uniformity validation**
resampling size $n_s = N_k$
sensor based resampling (same as the above)
else importance resampling
end if
end if

Table 2. Extended MCL algorithm

Two Validation Mechanisms
The two validation mechanisms are uniformity validation and over-convergence validation, respectively.
Uniformity validation utilizes the summation of all non-normalized weight values of sample set after sensor update to check the observation deviation phenomenon, in which the non-normalized weight values in the distribution are uniformly low, since the observation

density deviates from the proposal distribution due to some poorly modeled events.
Since the samples are uniformly distributed after the prediction step and re-weighted through the sensor update step, summation of non-normalized weight values of all samples W can be, according to (2), expressed as

$$W = \sum_{i=1}^{N_k} \hat{w}_k^{(i)} = \sum_{i=1}^{N_k} \overline{w}_k^{(i)} p(Z_k \mid \overline{X}_k^{(i)}) = \frac{1}{N_k} \sum_{i=1}^{N_k} p(Z_k \mid \overline{X}_k^{(i)}) \tag{4}$$

where, N_k denotes the sample size at time index k; $\overline{w}_k^{(i)}$ and $\hat{w}_k^{(i)}$ denote the weight values of sample $\overline{X}_k^{(i)}$ after motion update and after sensor update, respectively.

Define W_{th} as the given threshold corresponding to the summation of the weight values. If the summation W of all non-normalized weight values of samples is larger than the given threshold W_{th}, the observation can be considered to be consistent with the proposal distribution, and the importance resampling strategy is implemented. Otherwise, deviation of observations from the proposal distribution is serious, and the sensor-based resampling strategy is applied by considering the whole sample size at the moment as the new sample size. The given threshold should be appropriately selected based on the information of the observation model and the observed features.

Over-convergence validation is used to handle the over-convergence phenomenon, where samples converge quickly to a single or a few high-likelihood poses due to smaller sample size or lower sensor noise level. Over-convergence validation is employed based on the analysis of the distribution of normalized weight values of sample set, in which entropy and effective sample size are treated as measures for validation. When over-convergence phenomenon is affirmed, the strategy of both importance resampling and sensor-based resampling will be applied.

Entropy denotes the uncertainty of probabilistic events in the form of $H = -\sum p_i \log p_i$, where p_i is the probability of events. In MCL, the importance factors indicate the matching probabilities between observations and the current sample set. Therefore, we can represent the uncertainty of the distribution of weight values of sample set by entropy.

Effective sample size (ESS) of a weighted sample set is computed by (Liu, 2001):

$$ESS = \frac{N_k}{1 + cv^2} \tag{5}$$

where N_k denotes the sample size at time index k, and cv^2 denotes variation of the weight values of samples, derived by

$$cv^2 = \frac{\text{var}(w(i))}{E^2(w(i))} = \frac{1}{N_k} \sum_{1}^{N_k} (N_k \cdot w(i) - 1)^2 \tag{6}$$

in which $E(w(i))$ and $\text{var}(w(i))$ denote the mean and variance of the distribution of weight values of samples, respectively.

If the effective sample size is lower than a given threshold (percentage of the sample size), over-convergence phenomenon is confirmed. It is then necessary to introduce new samples, with the number of $n_s = c(N_k - ESS)$, where c is a constant. Otherwise, the difference of entropy of the distribution of weight values before and after sensor update is further examined to determine whether the over-convergence phenomenon happens, in the following way

$$\frac{H_c - H_p}{H_p} \geq \lambda \tag{7}$$

where, H_p and H_c denote the entropy of the distribution of weight values before and after sensor update, respectively; $\lambda \in (0,1)$ is a benchmark to check the relative change of entropy, which decreases as H_p increases. The larger the difference is, the more likely over-convergence occurs. When over-convergence is confirmed in this manner, the number of new samples to be introduced is $n_s = (1-\lambda)(N_k - ESS)$.

By the analysis of the distribution of weight values of sample set, the abnormity cases can be effectively checked through the two validation mechanisms, and thereby premature convergence and deviation problem caused by non-modeled events can be deliberately prevented. In addition, more real-time requirements can be satisfied with smaller sample size. Further, the strategy of employing different resampling processes is to construct the true posterior distribution by treating the observation model as part of the proposal distribution, which is guaranteed to be consistent with the observations even when using smaller sample size or more precise sensors.

4. An Implementation of Visual-Based Extended Monte Carlo Localization

In this section, an implementation of the proposed extended MCL algorithm with visual technology will be discussed. The observation model $p(Z_k \mid X_k^{(i)})$ is constructed based on visual polyhedron features that are recognized by Bayesian networks. The triangulation-based resampling is applied.

4.1 Sample Update

In the prediction process, samples are extracted from the motion equation

$$X_k = \mathrm{f}(X_{k-1}, u_{k-1}, v_{k-1})$$

where v_{k-1} denotes the sensor noise during the motion. Note that u_{k-1} consists of the translation Δs_{k-1} and the rotation $\Delta\theta_{k-1}$, which are independent between each other and can be modeled with the odometry model (Rekleitis, 2003b).

When the robot rotates by an angle of $\Delta\theta_{k-1}$, the noise caused by odometry error is modeled as a Gaussian with mean zero and sigma proportional to $\Delta\theta_{k-1}$. Therefore, the heading angle of the robot is updated by

$$\theta_k = \theta_{k-1} + \Delta\theta_{k-1} + \varepsilon_{\Delta\theta_{k-1}} \tag{8}$$

where $\varepsilon_{\Delta\theta_{k-1}}$ is a random noise derived from the heading error model $N(0,\sigma_{rot}\Delta\theta_{k-1})$, and σ_{rot} is a scale factor obtained experimentally (Rekleitis, 2003a). Likewise, there exists a translation error denoted by $\varepsilon_{\Delta s_{k-1}}$, which is related to the forward translation Δs_{k-1}. Furthermore, the change in orientation during the forward translation leads to the heading deviation. Then, the pose of samples can be updated by

$$X_k = \begin{bmatrix} x_k \\ y_k \\ \theta_k \end{bmatrix} = \mathrm{f}(X_{k-1}, u_{k-1}, v_{k-1}) = \begin{bmatrix} x_{k-1} + (\Delta s_{k-1} + \varepsilon_{\Delta s_{k-1}})\cos(\theta_k) \\ y_{k-1} + (\Delta s_{k-1} + \varepsilon_{\Delta s_{k-1}})\sin(\theta_k) \\ \theta_{k-1} + \Delta\theta_{k-1} + \varepsilon_{\Delta\theta_{k-1}} + \varepsilon_{\theta_1} \end{bmatrix} \quad (9)$$

where, $\varepsilon_{\Delta s_{k-1}}$ and ε_{θ_1} are random noises from the error models $N(0,\sigma_{trans}\Delta s_{k-1})$ and $N(0,\sigma_{drift}\Delta s_{k-1})$, σ_{trans} and σ_{drift} are scale factors experimentally obtained for the sigma of these Gaussian models (Rekleitis, 2003a); the sensor noise v_{k-1} includes random noise $\varepsilon_{\Delta\theta_{k-1}}$ estimated by the heading error model $N(0,\sigma_{rot}\Delta\theta_{k-1})$, as well as the translational error $\varepsilon_{\Delta s_{k-1}}$ with Gaussian model of $N(0,\sigma_{trans}\Delta s_{k-1})$ and the heading deviation ε_{θ_1} with zero mean, estimated by $N(0,\sigma_{drift}\Delta s_{k-1})$.

To generate samples, the robot heading angle is firstly calculated by (8), and then the robot pose by (9). Figure 1 illustrates a distribution of samples generated in travelling 3.5 m along a straight line, with a known initial pose (on the right end) and the two noise parameters $(\sigma_{trans}, \sigma_{drift})$, where only the two-dimensional pose in x and y directions are given. As shown in this figure, the sample distribution spreads more widely as the travelled distance increases (the solid line with an arrow depicts the odometry data).

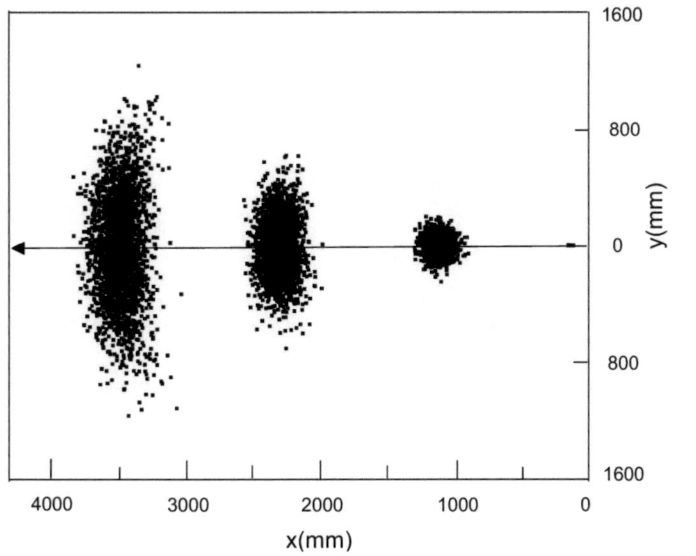

Figure 1. Sample distribution of straight line motion with error $\sigma_{trans} = 5$ and $\sigma_{drift} = 1$

4.2 Visual Sensor Update

Observations from exteroceptive sensors are used to re-weight the samples extracted from the proposal distribution. Observations are based on sensing of polyhedrons in indoor office environments. Using the observed features, an observation model can be constructed for samples re-weighting, and the triangulation-based resampling process can be applied.

Visual polyhedron features

Polyhedrons such as compartments, refrigerators and doors in office environments, are used as visual features in this application. These features are recognized by Bayesian network (Sarkar & Boyer, 1993) that combines perceptual organization and color model. Low-level geometrical features such as points and lines, are grouped by perceptual organization to form meaningful high-level features such as rectangular and tri-lines passing a common point. HIS (Hue, Intensity, Saturation) color model is employed to recognize color feature of polyhedrons. Figure 2 illustrates a model of compartment and the corresponding Bayesian network for recognition. More details about nodes in the Bayesian network can be found in the paper (Shang et al., 2004).

This recognition method is suitable for different environment conditions (e.g., different illuminations and occlusions) with different threshold settings. False-positives and false-negatives can also be reduced thanks to considering polyhedrons as features. Furthermore, there are many low-level features in a feature group belonging to the same polyhedron, which are helpful in matching between observations and environment model since the search area is constrained.

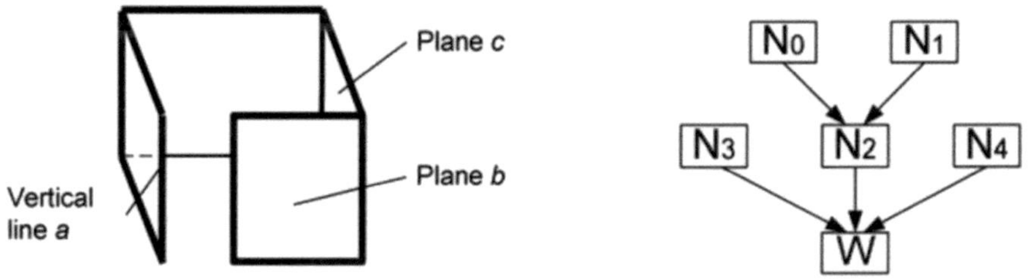

(a) (b)

Figure 2. Compartment model (a) and Bayesian network for compartment recognition (b)

Consider a set of visual features $Z_k = [z_k^1, z_k^2 \cdots, z_k^m]^T$ to be observed. The eigenvector of each visual feature *j*, denoted by $z_k^j = [t_k^j, \phi_k^j]^T$, is composed of the feature type t_k^j and the visual angle ϕ_k^j relative to the camera system, developed by

$$\phi_k^j = \arctan((width/2 - u_k^{cj}) \times \tan(\beta/2) / (width/2))$$

where $width$ is the image width, u_k^{cj} is the horizontal position of feature in the image, and β is half of the horizontal visual angle of the camera system.

Visual observation model

As described in Section 2, the sample weight is updated through an observation model $p(Z_k \mid X_k^{(i)})$. It is assumed that the features are detected solely depending on the robot's pose. Therefore, the observation model can be specified as:

$$p(Z_k \mid X_k^{(i)}) = p(z_k^1, \cdots, z_k^m \mid X_k^{(i)}) = p(z_k^1 \mid X_k^{(i)}) \times \cdots \times p(z_k^m \mid X_k^{(i)}) \tag{10}$$

The observation model for each specific feature j can be constructed based on matching of the feature type and the deviation of the visual angle, i.e.,

$$p(z_k^j \mid X_k^{(i)}) = \delta(t_k^j - t_k^{j0}) \cdot \frac{e^{-\frac{(\phi_k^j - \phi_k^{j0})^2}{2\sigma_\phi^2}}}{\sqrt{2\pi}\sigma_\phi} \tag{11}$$

where, t_k^j and t_k^{j0} are feature types of current and predictive observations, respectively, and $\delta(\cdot)$ is a Dirac function; ϕ_k^j and ϕ_k^{j0} are visual angles of current and predictive observations, and σ_ϕ is variance of ϕ. When $t_k^j = t_k^{j0}$, the observed feature type is the same as the predictive ones. When the number of the predictive features is more than that of the observed ones, only part of the predictive features with the same number of observed features are extracted after they are sorted by the visual angle, and then a maximum likelihood is applied.

4.3 Resampling Step

As discussed in Section 3, two validation mechanisms in the resampling step are firstly applied to check abnormity of the distribution of weight values of sample sets. Then according to the validation, the strategy of using different resampling processes is employed, where samples are extracted either from importance resampling or from observation model. Importance resampling has been illustrated in Section 2 (see Table 1). Here we will discuss the resampling method from the visual observation model.

As we have mentioned that the threshold W_{th} for uniformity validation should be appropriately selected. For our application example, the threshold W_{th} is determined as follows based on the observation model (11):

$$W_{th} = k_w \cdot \prod_{i=1}^{m} \frac{1}{\sqrt{2\pi}\sigma_\phi} \tag{12}$$

where k_w is a scale factor, and m is the number of current features.

Sensor-based Resampling

In the resampling from observations, $p(X_k \mid Z_k)$ is also treated as the proposal distribution, which can provide consistent samples with observations to form the true posterior distribution. According to the SIR algorithm, samples must be properly weighted in order to represent the probability distribution. Note that such sensor-based resampling is mainly applied in some abnormal cases (e.g., non-modeled events), which is not carried out in every iterative cycle. Furthermore, after completing the sensor-based resampling, all samples are supposed to be uniformly distributed and re-weighted by motion/sensor updates in the next cycle.

The triangulation method is utilized for resampling from visual features, where visual angles are served as the observation features in the application (Krotkov, 1989; Mufioz &

Gonzalez, 1998; Yuen & MacDonald, 2005). Ideally, the robot can be uniquely localized with at least three features, as shown in Figure 3 (a), where the number 1~3 denotes the index of features. In practice, however, there exists uncertainty in the pose estimation due to observation errors and image processing uncertainty. The pose constrained region C_0 shown in Figure 3 (b), illustrates the uncertain area of the robot pose with uncertain visual angle, where $\phi^- = \phi - \Delta\phi$, $\phi^+ = \phi + \Delta\phi$, ϕ and $\Delta\phi$ are visual angle and the uncertainty, respectively. The uncertain pose region just provides a space for resampling. The incorrect samples can be gradually excluded as the update process goes on.

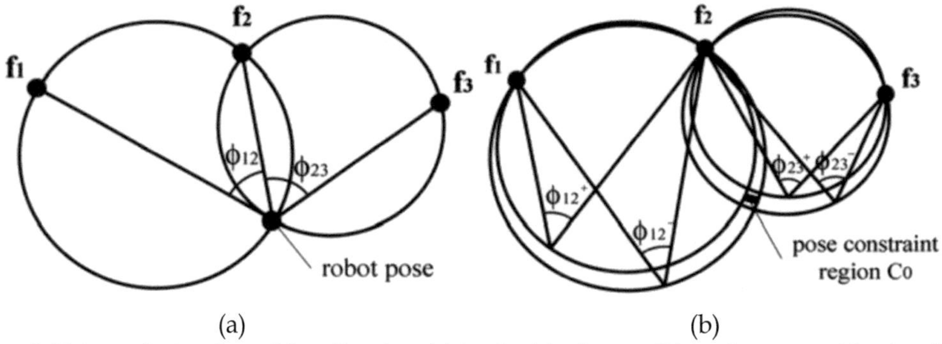

Figure 3. Triangulation-based localization (a) in the ideal case, (b) in the case with visual angle error

In the existing triangulation methods, visual features are usually limited to vertical edges (Mouaddib & Marhic, 2000), which are quite similar and have large numbers. While in our application, polyhedron features recognized by Bayesian networks combine perceptual organization and color model, and therefore reduce the number of features and simplify the search. In addition, the sub-features of polyhedrons such as vertical edges in recognized compartments, can also be used for triangulation.

In the process of searching features by interpretation tree (IT), the following optimizations can be applied:

1. Consider all polyhedrons as a whole, and the position of each polyhedron as the central position of each individual feature.
2. As visual angle of the camera system is limited, form the feature groups that consist of several adjacent features according to their space layout. The number of features in each feature group should be more than that of the observed features. The search area of the interpretation tree is within each feature group.
3. Search match in terms of the feature type, and then verify by triangulation method the features satisfying the type validation, to see whether the pose constraint regions each formed by visual angles of two features, are intersected as is shown by the pose constraint region C_0 in Figure 3 (b).

Then, the random samples $(x_k^{(i)}, y_k^{(i)})$ can be extracted from the pose constraint region. The orientations of the samples are given by

$$\theta_k^{(i)} = \frac{1}{m} \sum_{j=1}^{m} (\arctan((y_k^{(i)} - y_k^j)/(x_k^{(i)} - x_k^j)) - \phi_k^j) \tag{13}$$

where x_k^j, y_k^j, ϕ_k^j are position and visual angle of the feature *j*, respectively, and m is the number of observed features.

Figure 4 (a) illustrates the sample distribution after sampling from two observed features f_1 and f_2, for a robot pose (3800mm, 4500mm, -120°). The visual angle error is about five percent of the visual angle. There are about 1000 generated samples that are sparsely distributed in the intersection region formed by the observed features. Figure 4 (b) illustrates the sampling results from three features f_1, f_2 and f_3, for a robot pose (3000mm, 4200mm, -100°). It can be seen that all extracted samples locate in the pose constraint region and are close to the true robot pose.

5. Experiments

To verify the proposed extended MCL method, experiments were carried out on a pioneer 2/DX mobile robot with a color CCD camera and sixteen sonar sensors, as shown in Figure 5. The camera has a maximum view angle of 48.8 degrees, used for image acquisition and feature recognition. Sonar sensors are mainly for collision avoidance. Experiments were performed in a general indoor office environment as shown in Figure 6 (a). Features in this environment are compartments (diagonal shadow), refrigerators (crossed shadow) and door (short thick line below). Layout of features is shown in Figure 6 (b).

In the experiments, the sample size was set as a constant of 400. Parameters of the extended MCL are: the percentage threshold of effective sample size was 10%, the constant *c* was 0.8, λ was 0.15~0.25, and the scale factor k_w was 50%. Parameters for conventional MCL (with random resampling) were: percentage threshold of effective sample size is still 10%, *c*=0.3, λ =0.35, and k_w =30%.

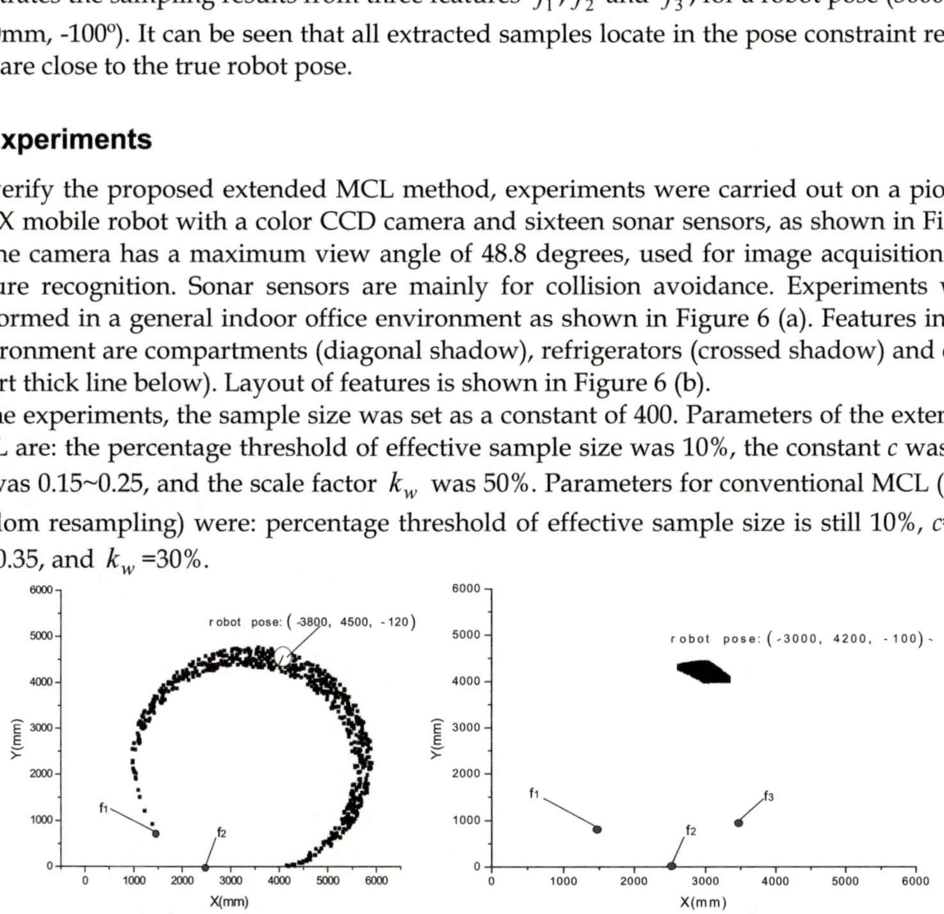

(a) two features observed (b) three features observed

Figure 4. Sampling from observations with two and three features respectively

Figure 5. Pioneer 2/DX mobile robot, equipped with a color CCD camera and sixteen sonar sensors around

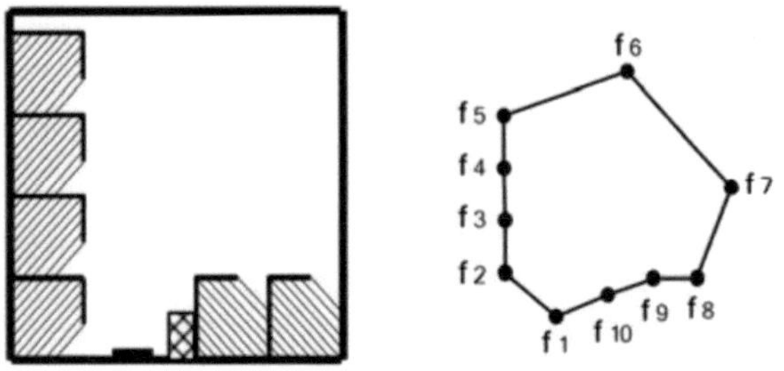

(a) (b)

Figure 6. (a) Experiment environmental model. (b) Layout of environmental features

5.1 Global Localization with Kidnapped Movement

First, the proposed extended MCL method was applied for global localization as well as an non-modeled movement (e.g., kidnapped problem), with time-variant sample distributions, entropy and effective sample size. Figure 7 illustrates the whole motion trajectory. It is seen that the robot started the motion from position *a* to position *b*, then was kidnapped to position *c*, and then continued to move to the end position *d*. Figures 8 and 9 illustrate results when the sample size was within 400. Figure 8 shows that the effective sample size and entropy are time varying. Sample distributions at different iterations are shown in Figure 9, where (a) ~ (f) corresponds to the initial, the 1st, the 8th, the 9th, the 17th, the 18th and the 26th iterations, respectively. As shown in Figure 9 (a), the initial distribution was uniform. At the first iteration, when two compartments f_4 and f_5 were observed, entropy after sensor update decreased, as shown in Figure 8 (b), and both importance resampling and triangulation-based resampling were applied. Due to existence of multi-matches, importance resampling was applied in all successive iterations, as multi-clusters shown in Figure 9 (b). At the 9th iteration, the feature of the door f_1 was observed, and a single sample cluster shown in Figure 9 (c) was obtained until reaching position *b*, where all samples were distributed nearby the true pose of the robot, as seen in Figure 9 (d). At the 18th iteration, the robot was kidnapped to the position *c* with a largely-changed heading angle. At this moment, the effective sample size and the entropy decreased greatly, as shown in Figure 8 (a) and (b). With observations of the features of the door f_1, the refrigerator f_{10}, and the compartment f_9, sample distribution was obtained as shown in Figure 9 (e), after applying importance resampling and triangulation-based resampling, until to the end position *d* where the sample distribution is shown in Figure 9 (f).

From the above localization process, it can be seen that the sensor-based resampling, after an effective examination of weight values of samples by over-convergence validation, can well solve the robot kidnapped problem. Due to too many similar features in the environment, there were still some samples with higher weights after the kidnapped motion, and therefore only over-convergence validation was executed without the uniformity validation. If the robot is kidnapped to a region without similar features, the uniformity validation can be executed.

5.2 Comparison of Localization Errors

Through applying the strategy of different resampling processes in the extended MCL, the localization error becomes smaller than that with the conventional MCL, especially in the non-modeled movements. Figure 10 illustrates a comparison of the localization errors between the extended MCL and the conventional MCL appended by random resampling, with the same observation model and the same sample size before and after the kidnapped motion. Suppose that the robot's pose obtained from odometry was accurate enough for a short moving distance on the smooth floor. As is seen from Figure 10, at the moment when localization error increases at the 5th iteration, robot was kidnapped. The localization error under the extended MCL (with triangulation-based resampling), is much smaller than that under conventional MCL (with random resampling). This is to verify the improved localization performance of the proposed extended MCL.

5.3 Time Performance

We further demonstrate that the computational resources of the extended MCL could be effectively utilized by appropriately using the sensor-based resampling. As seen from the previous experiments, the number of samples (sample size) with EMCL is only 400, while the number of sample size with conventional MCL is usually much higher than it to obtain good localization performance.

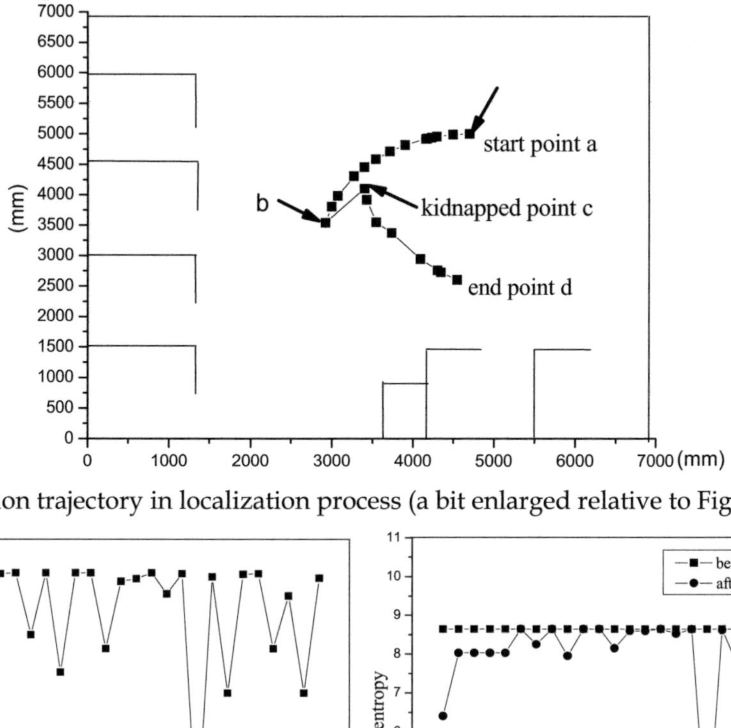

Figure 7. Motion trajectory in localization process (a bit enlarged relative to Figure 6 (a))

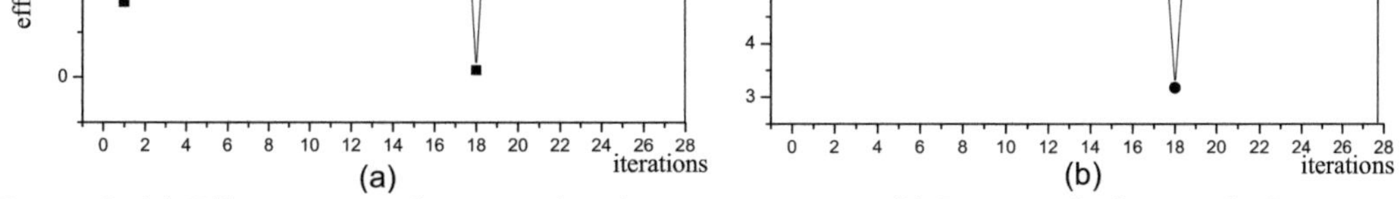

Figure 8. (a) Effective sample size in localization process. (b) Entropy before and after sensor update

Figure 11 (a) illustrates the total update time of the resampling process with respect to different numbers of samples. It can be seen when the sample size is less than 1500, the update time is lower and increases slowly as the sample size increases; when the sample size is more than 2000, the update time is higher and increases fast as the sample size increases. This indicates higher computational efficiency since high number of samples is not required, and thus the update time can be saved.

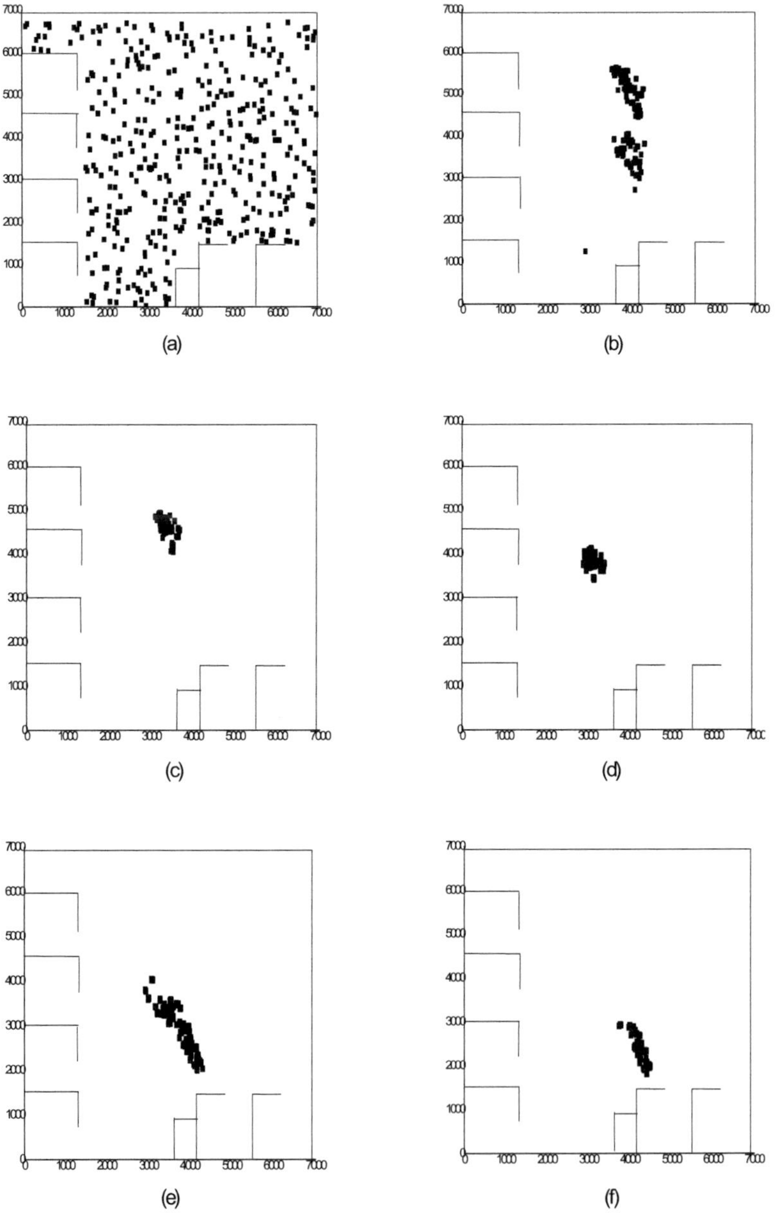

Figure 9. Sample distributions at different iterations (a) initial time and (b) ~ (f) 8th, 9th, 17th, 18th and 26th iterations

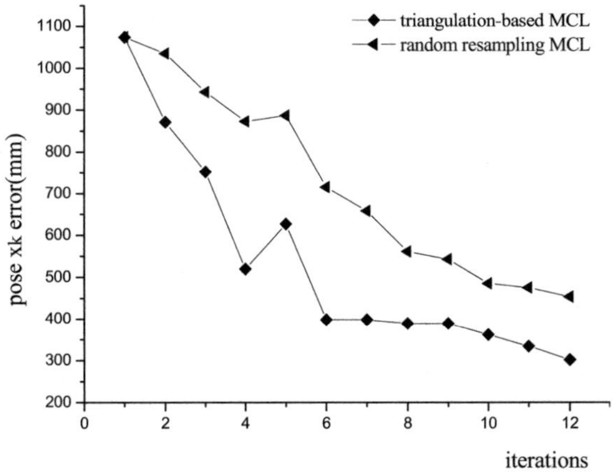

Figure 10. Localization error comparison between extended MCL and MC

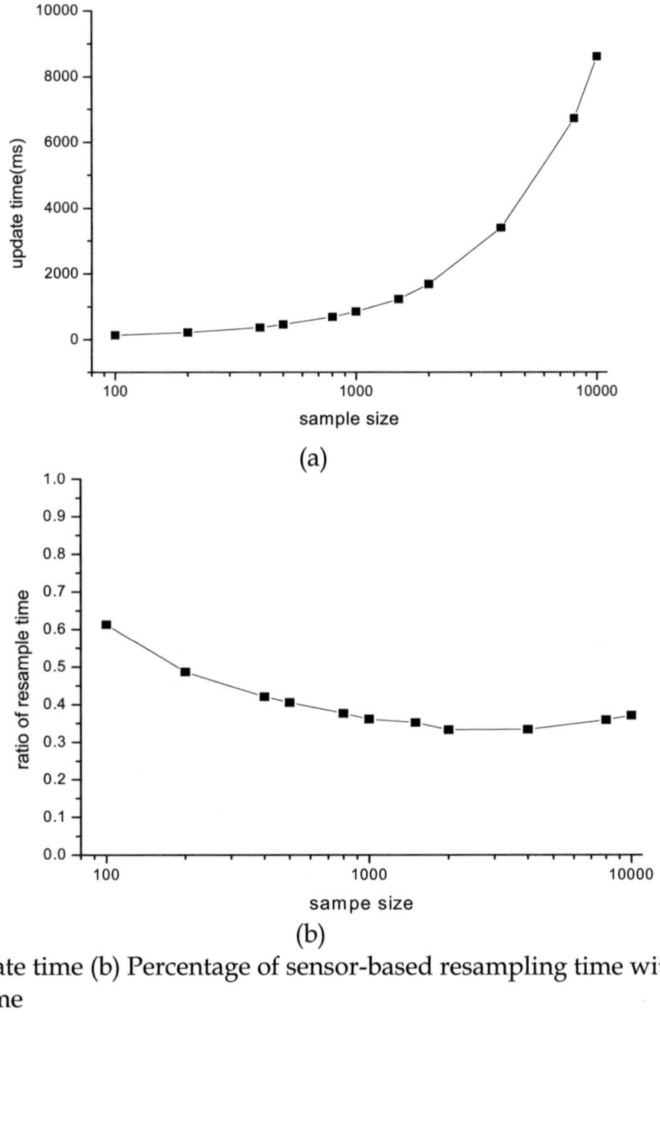

Figure 11. (a) Update time (b) Percentage of sensor-based resampling time with respect to the total update time

Figure 11 (b) further illustrates the percentage of the sensor-based resampling time with respect to the total update time versus different number of samples. The percentage of resampling time decreases as the sample size increases, i.e., from 48.6% with 200 samples to 35.9% with 8000 samples. Since many samples are not deleted in a large sample set, the sensor-based resampling is not necessarily performed, and the process without resampling dominates the whole process. When the sample size increases to a certain extent, the percentage of the resampling time does not change obviously. This implies that the extended MCL with smaller sample size has the similar localization performance to that with relative larger sample size. Although the percentage of the sensor-based resampling time in the whole update time with smaller sample size is higher than that with higher sample size, the total update time is reduced when using smaller sample size.

6. Conclusion

An extended Monte Carlo localization (EMCL) method is proposed in this book chapter by introducing two validation mechanisms to apply a resampling strategy to conventional MCL. Two validation mechanisms, uniformity validation and over-convergence validation, are effectively used to check abnormity of the distribution of weight values of sample set, e.g., observation deviation or over-convergence problem. The strategy of employing different resampling processes is proposed to construct more consistent posterior distribution with observations. This new approach is aimed to improve localization performance particularly with smaller sample size in the non-modeled robot movements, and thus achieve global localization more efficiently. A vision-based extended MCL is further implemented, utilizing triangulation-based resampling from visual features in a constraint region of the pose space. Experiments conducted on a mobile robot with a color CCD camera and sixteen sonar sensors verify efficiency of the extended MCL method.

7. Acknowledgement

This work was supported in part by a grant from Research Grants Council of the Hong Kong Special Administrative Region, China [Reference No. CityU 119705], and a grant from City University of Hong Kong (project no. 7002127).

8. References

Borenstein, J.; Everett, H. & Feng, L. (1996). Where am I? *Sensors and Methods for Autonomous Mobile Robot Positioning*. Wellesley. Mass.:AK Peters,

Carpenter, J.; Clifford, P. & Fearnhead, P. (1999). Improved particle filter for nonlinear problems, *IEE proceedings on Sonar and Navigation*, pp. 2-7.

Castellanos, J. & Tardos, J. (1996). Laser-based segmentation and localization for a mobile robot, *Proceedings of the 6th Symposium (ISRAM)*, pp. 101-108, ASME Press, New York, NY.

Chenavier, F. & Crowley, J. (1992). Position estimation for a mobile robot using vision and odometry, *Proceedings of the IEEE International Conference on Robotics and Automation*, pp. 2588-2593.

Dellaert, F.; Burgard, W. & Fox, D. (1999). Using the condensation algorithm for robust, vision-based mobile robot localization, *Proceedings of the IEEE International Conference on CVPR*, pp. 588-594.

Doucet, A. (1998). On sequential simulation-based methods for Bayesian filtering, Cambridge University, Department of Engineering, Cambridge, UK, *Technical Report*. CUED/FINFENG/ TR 310.

Drumheller, M. (1987). Mobile robot localization using sonar, *IEEE Transactions on Pattern Analysis and Machine Intelligence*, Vol.PAMI-9, No.2, 325–332.

Fox, D. (2003). Adapting the sample size in particle filter through KLD-Sampling, *International Journal of Robotics Research*.

Fox, D.; Burgard, W. & Dellaert, F. (1999a). Monte Carlo localization: efficient position estimation for mobile robots, *Proceedings of the AAAI-9*, pp. 343-3499, Orlando, Florida.

Fox, D.; Burgard, W. & Thrun, S. (1999b). Markov localization for mobile robots in dynamic environments, *Journal of Artificial Intelligence Research*, Vol. 11, 391-427.

Gaspar, J.; Winters, N. & Santos-Victor, J. (2000). Vision-based navigation and environmental representations with an omnidirectional camera, *IEEE Transactions on Robotics and Automation*, Vol. 16, No. 6, 890-898.

Luo, R. & Hong, B. (2004). Coevolution based adaptive Monte Carlo localization (CEAMCL), *International Journal of Advanced Robotic Systems*. Vol. 1, No. 3, 183-190.

Isard, M. & Blake, A. (1998). Condensation-conditional density propagation for visual tracking, *International Journal of Computer Vision*, Vol. 29, No. 1.

Jensfelt, P. & Kristensen, S. (2001). Active global localization for a mobile robot using multiple hypothesis tracking, *IEEE Transactions on Robotics and Automation*, Vol. 17, No. 5, 748-760.

Jensfelt, P.; Wijk, O.; Austin, D. & Anderson, M. (2000). Experiments on augmenting condensation for mobile robot localization, *Proceedings of the IEEE International Conference on Robotics and Automation*.

Konolige, K. (2001). Robot motion: probabilistic model; sampling and Gaussian implementations; Markov localization, AI Center, SRI International, *Technical Note*.

Kortenkamp, D.; Bonasso, R. & Murphy, R. (1998). (Eds.), *AI-based Mobile Robots: Case Studies of Successful Robot Systems*, MIT Press, Cambridge, MA.

Kraetzschmar, G. & Enderle, S. (2002). Self-localization using sporadic features, *Robotics and Autonomous Systems*, Vol. 40, 111-119.

Krotkov, E. (1989). Mobile robot localization using a single image, *Proceedings of the IEEE International Conference on Robotics and Automation*, pp. 978-983.

Lenser, S. & Veloso, M. (2000). Sensor resetting localization for poorly modeled mobile robots, *Proceedings of the IEEE International Conference on Robotics and Automation*, pp. 1225-1232.

Leonard, J. & Durrant-White, H. (1991). Mobile robot localization by tracking geometric beacons, *IEEE Transactions on Robotics and Automation*, Vol. 7, 89–97.

Liu, J.; Chen, R. & Logvinenko, T. (2001). A theoretical framework for sequential importance sampling and resampling, In *Sequential Monte Carlo in Practice*, Springer-Verlag, New York,.

Mouaddib, E. & Marhic, B. (2000). Geometrical matching for mobile robot localization, *IEEE Transactions on Robotics and Automation*, Vol. 16, No. 5, 542-552.

Mufioz, A. & Gonzalez, J. (1998). Two-dimensional landmark-based position estimation from a single image, *Proceedings of the IEEE International Conference on Robotics and Automation*, pp. 3709-3714.

Nourbakhsh, I.; Powers, R. & Birchfield, S. (1995). Dervish: An office-navigating robot, *AI Magazine*, Vol. 16, No. 2, 53-60.

Rekleitis, I. (2003a). Cooperative Localization and Multi-Robot Exploration, *PhD Thesis*, School of Computer Science, McGill Univ., Montreal, Quebec, Canada.

Rekleitis, I. (2003b). Probabilistic cooperative localization and mapping in practice, *Proceedings of the IEEE International Conference on Robotics and Automation*, pp. 1907-1912.

Rofer, T. & Jungel, M. (2003). Vision-based fast and reactive Monte-Carlo localization, *Proceedings of the IEEE International Conference on Robotics and Automation*, pp. 856-861.

Sarkar S. & Boyer, K. L. (1993). Integration, inference, and management of spatial information using Bayesian networks: perceptual organization, *IEEE Transactions on Pattern Analysis and Machine Intelligence*, Vol. 15, No. 3, 256-273.

Shang, W.; Ma, X. & Dai, X. (2004). 3D objects detection with Bayesian Networks for vision-guided mobile robot navigation, *Proceedings of the IEEE International Conference on Control, Automation, Robotics and Vision*, pp.1134-1139.

Tardos, J.; Neira, J.; Newman, P. & Leonard, J. (2002). Robust mapping and localization in indoor environments using sonar data, *International Journal of Robotics Research*, Vol. 21, No. 4, 311-330.

Thrun, S.; Fox, D.; Burgard, W. & Dellaert, F. (2001). Robust Monte Carlo localization for mobile robots, *Artificial Intelligence*, Vol. 128, 99-141.

Wijk, O. & Christensen, H. (2000). Triangulation based fusion of sonar data with application in robot pose tracking, *IEEE Transactions on Robotics and Automation*, Vol. 16, No. 6, 740-752.

Yuen, D. & MacDonald, B. (2005). Vision-based localization algorithm based on landmark matching, triangulation, reconstruction, and comparison, *IEEE Transactions on Robotics*, Vol. 21, No. 2, 217-226.

13

Optical Correlator based Optical Flow Processor for Real Time Visual Navigation

Valerij Tchernykh, Martin Beck, Klaus Janschek
Technische Universität Dresden
Germany

1. Introduction

Autonomous visual navigation, i.e. determination of position, attitude and velocity (ego motion) by processing of the images from onboard camera(s), is essential for mobile robots control even in the presence of GPS networks, as the accuracy of GPS data and/or the available map of surroundings can be insufficient. Besides, GPS signals reception can be unstable in many locations (inside buildings, tunnels, in narrow streets, canyons, under trees, etc).

Up to now most of the practical visual navigation solutions have been developed for ground robots moving in cooperative and/or well determined environment. However, future generations of mobile robots should be also capable of operating in complex and non-cooperative 3D environments. Visual navigation in such conditions is much more challenging, especially for flying robots, where full 6DOF pose/motion should be determined. Generally 3D environment perception is required in this case, i.e., determination of a local depth map for the visible scene.

3D scene information can be obtained by stereo imaging; however this solution has certain limitations. It requires at least two cameras, precisely mounted with a certain stereo base (can be critical for small vehicles). Due to fixed stereo base the range of the depth determination with stereo imaging is limited. A more universal solution with less hardware requirements can be achieved with optical flow processing of sequential images from a single onboard camera.

The ego motion of a camera rigidly mounted on a vehicle is mapped into the motion of image pixels in the camera focal plane. This image motion is commonly understood as image flow or optical flow (OF) (Horn & Schunck, 1981). This vector field of 2D image motion can be used efficiently for 3D environment perception (mapping) and vehicle pose/motion determination as well as for obstacle avoidance or visual servoing. The big challenge for using the optical flow in real applications is its computability in terms of its density (sparse vs. dense optical flow), accuracy, robustness to dark and noisy images and its real-time determination. The general problem of optical flow determination can be formulated as the extraction of the two-dimensional projection of the 3D relative motion into the image plane in form of a field of correspondences (motion vectors) between points in consecutive image frames.

This article addresses a real-time solution for high precision optical flow computation based on 2D correlation of image fragments on the basis of an optical correlator. It exploits the principle of Joint Transform Correlation (JTC) in an optoelectronic setup using the Optical Fourier Transform (Goodman, 1968). Based on the experience of the authors with different successful optical processor developments (Tchernykh et al., 2004, Janschek et al., 2004a, Tchernykh et al., 2000, Janschek et al., 2005a) a new optical processor design is presented, which makes use of advanced optoelectronic technology. The proposed optoelectronic optical flow processor (OE-OFP) shows to be very compact with low mass and low power consumption and provides the necessary high performance needed for navigation applications in the field of robotics (ground, aerial, marine) and space flight (satellites, landing vehicles). The paper recalls briefly the underlying principles of optical flow computation and optical correlation, it shows the system layout and the conceptual design for the optoelectronic optical flow processor and it gives preliminary performance results based on a high fidelity simulation of the complete optical processing chain.

2. Requirements to Optical Flow Processor

Considering a flying platform moving in a complex non-cooperative 3D environment (indoor or outdoor) as a target mission, the following requirements to the Optical Flow Processor (OFP) can be formulated.

1. *Image quality tolerance.* As various illumination conditions can be expected, the OFP should be able to process dark and noisy images with low texture contrast.
2. *Optical flow density.* The required resolution of the optical flow fields depends on scene complexity. On the authors' experience, the depth information should be obtained for at least 32x32 (better 64x64) locations for adequate perception of complex 3D environment (required for navigation). This means, that at least 32x32 (better 64x64) optical flow vectors should be determined for each frame.
3. *Frame rate.* Considering relatively high motion dynamics of the flying robot, processing of up to 10 frames per second is required for navigation purposes.
4. *Accuracy.* Considering a maximal acceptable error of 10 percent for local depth determination to get a reasonable 3D environment perception, the error of the OF vectors determination should be also within 10 percent. This means that OF vectors with magnitude of a few pixels should be determined with sub pixel accuracy (errors should be within a few tenths of a pixel).
5. *Size/mass/power consumption.* To allow installation onboard a flying platform these parameters should be minimized. Roughly the volume of the OFP should be within a few tens of cubic centimetres, mass - within a few tens of grams and power consumption - within a few watts.

3. Existing solutions (optical flow determination background)

The problem of the optical flow computation is being investigated for more then two decades. Many methods for the OF determination have been developed (Beauchemin & Barron, 1995, Bruhn et al., 2003, McCane et al, 1998, Liu et al., 1998). All these methods have in common, that rather dense and accurate OF needs low noise images and requires high computational power, which is hardly realizable with embedded processors (Liu et al., 1998). Existing pure digital high performance solutions based on conventional PC or FPGA technology (Bruhn et al., 2003, Bruhn et al., 2005, Diaz et al., 2006) additionally consume a lot of power, mass and volume which does not fit the requirements of mobile robotics, especially if application onboard a flying platform is considered. The recently developed and currently very popular SIFT approach (Lowe, 1999, Se et al., 2001) allows a computationally efficient determination of more or less sparse OF fields in well structured environments. Some specialized high speed OF sensors on hybrid analogue-digital technology (Barrows & Neely, 2000, Zufferey, 2005) provide even super real-time performances but are suffering from the required accuracy of the OF vectors for navigation purposes. A most robust approach is the area correlation, applied originally for image registration (Pratt, 1974). Area correlation uses the fundamental property of the cross-correlation function of two images, which gives the location of the correlation peak directly proportional to the displacement vector of the original image shift.

For each pair of sequential images the OF field is determined by subdividing both images into small fragments and 2D correlation of corresponding fragments. As a result of each correlation the local shift vector at the specific location is determined; a whole set of local shift vectors forms an optical flow matrix (Figure 1).

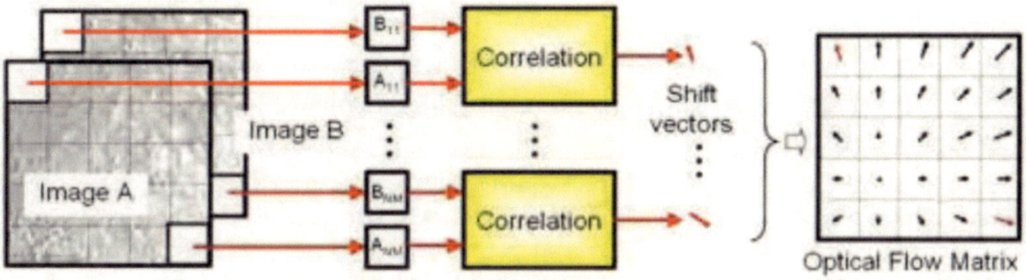

Figure 1. Principle of correlation based optical flow determination

The optical flow determination method, based on 2D correlation of the image fragments, offers a number of advantages:

- high sub pixel accuracy ;
- low dependency on image texture properties (no specific texture features required);
- high robustness to image noise (suitable for short exposures and/or poor illumination conditions)
- direct determination of multi-pixel shifts (suitable for fast image motion).

Simultaneously this method requires a very large amount of computations which prevents practically this method from a real time realization with conventional digital processors onboard a flying robot.

Generally, none of the existing OF determination techniques satisfies all of the requirements to the Optical Flow Processor, suitable for installation onboard a flying platform (listed in section 2). To reach the real time performance and to satisfy the strict size/mass/power limitations while keeping the accuracy and robustness of the 2D correlation based approach, we propose to perform the correlations with an onboard optical correlator.

4. Optical correlator technology

A very efficient method for 2D correlation requiring only double Fourier transform without phase information is given by the Joint Transform Correlation (JTC) principle (Jutamulia, 1992).

The two images $f_1(x,y)$ and $f_2(x,y)$ to be correlated are being combined to a joint image $I(x,y)$ (Figure 2). A first Fourier transform results in the joint power spectrum $S(u,v)=F\{I(x,y)\}$. Its magnitude contains the spectrum $F(u,v)$ of the common image contents augmented by some periodic components which are originating from the spatial shift $\vec{G}$ of f_1 and f_2 in the joint image I. A second Fourier transform of the squared joint spectrum $J(u,v)=S(u,v)^2$ results in four correlation functions. The centred correlation function $C_{ff}(x,y)$ represents the auto-correlation function of each input image, whereas the two spatially shifted correlation functions $C_{ff}(x \pm G_x, y \pm G_y)$ represent the cross-correlation functions of the input images. The shift vector $\vec{G}$ contains both the technological shift according to the construction of the joint image $I(x,y)$ and the shift of the image contents according to the image motion. If the two input images f_1 and f_2 contain identical (but shifted) image contents, the cross-correlation peaks will be present and their mutual spatial shift $\vec{\Delta}=\vec{G}-\left(-\vec{G}\right)$ allows determining the original image shift in a straightforward way.

This principle can be realized in hardware by a specific optoelectronic setup, named *Joint Transform Optical Correlator (JTOC)*. The required 2D Fourier transforms are performed by means of diffraction-based phenomena, incorporating a so called optical Fourier processor (Goodman, 1968). A laser diode (Figure 3) generates a diverging beam of coherent light which passes a single collimating lens focusing the light to infinity. The result is a beam of parallel light with plane wave fronts. The amplitude of the plane wave front is modulated by a transmissive or reflective spatial light modulator (SLM). The SLM actually works as a diffraction grid and the resulting diffraction pattern can be made visible in the focal plane of a second lens (Fourier lens). Under certain geometric conditions the energy distribution of this pattern is equal to the squared Fourier transform (power spectrum) of the modulated wave front. The power spectrum can be read by a CCD or CMOS image sensor located in the focal plane of the Fourier lens of the optical Fourier processor. The position of the correlation peaks in the second power spectrum (correlation image) and the associated shift value can be measured with sub-pixel accuracy using e.g. standard algorithms for centre of mass calculation.

Optical processing thus allows unique real time processing performances of high frame rate video streams.

This advanced technology and its applications have been studied during last years at the Institute of Automation of the Technische Universität Dresden (Tchernykh et al., 2004, Janschek et al., 2004a, Janschek et al., 2007). Different hardware models have been manufactured, e.g. under European Space Agency (ESA) contracts (Figure 4). Due to special design solutions owned by TU Dresden, the devices are robust to mechanical loads and deformations. (Tchernykh et al., 2000, Janschek et al., 2005a). One of the models has been successfully tested in an airborne test campaign, where very promising performances have been shown (Tchernykh et al., 2004).

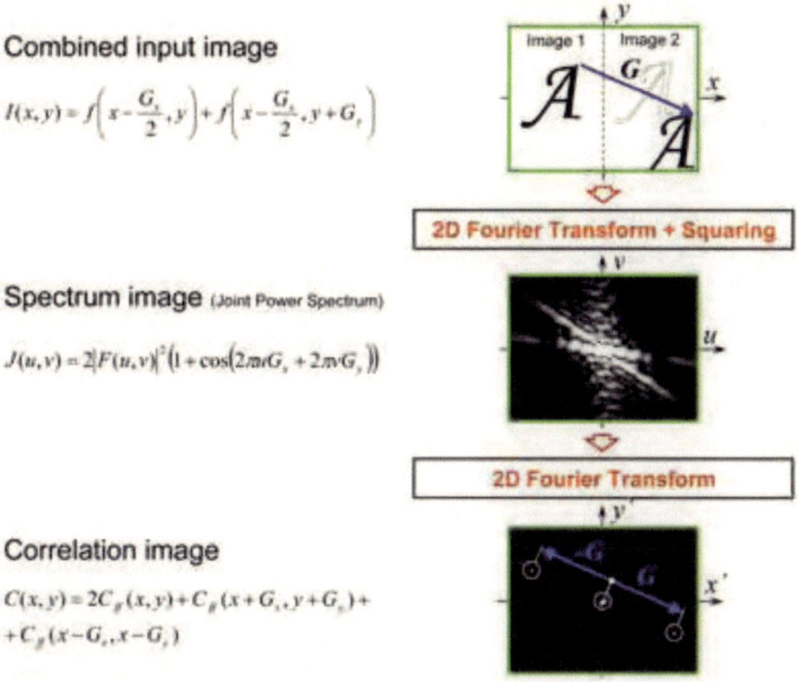

Figure 2. Principle of the joint transform correlation

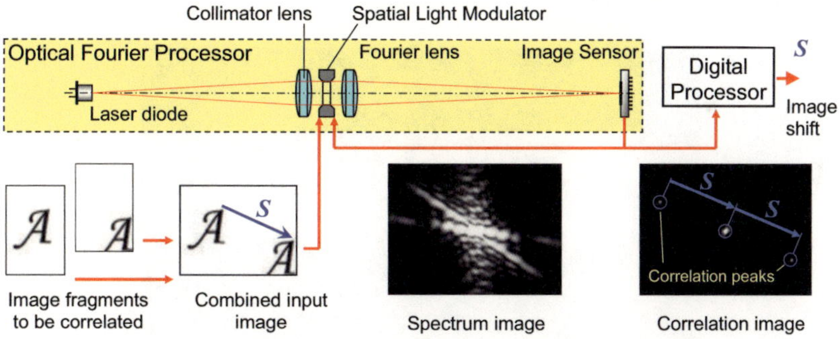

Figure 3. Principle of the Joint Transform Optical Correlator (JTOC)

Figure 4. Hardware model of an optical correlator

5. Determination of the optimal size of correlated fragments

5.1 Simulation experiment description

The dimensions of correlated fragments determine both the accuracy and reliability of the 2D correlation operation. Larger window size improves the reliability of the optical flow determination in poorly textured image areas and reduces the errors of the obtained OF vectors. At the same time, increasing the correlated fragments size smoothes the obtained OF field, it suppresses small details and produces additional errors in areas with large variations of local depth.

The goal of the simulation experiment was to estimate the optimal size of the correlated fragment, making the best compromise between the accuracy/reliability of correlation and preservation of small details of the underlying 3D scene.

The experiment has been performed with a high fidelity software model of the proposed optical flow processor. The model includes the detailed model of the complete processing chain of the optical correlator. Image processing algorithms simulate all relevant operations of the optoelectronic hardware realization of the optical correlator (optical diffraction effects, dynamic range limitation and squaring of the output images by image sensor, scaling of the output images according to focal length value, etc.).

The experiment has been performed using simulated images from synthetic 3D scenes of a planetary surface generated during an ESA (European Space Agency) study on the visual navigation of a planetary landing vehicle (Janschek et al., 2005b). The images contain parts of rich texture as well as flat low texture regions and dark shadows. The image sequence of an inclined landing trajectory (example image see Figure 5) has been generated on base of a 3D model of the landing site using standard ray tracing software considering the Modulation Transfer Function (MTF) of the camera as well as photonic and readout noise and pixel response non-uniformity.

Figure 5. Synthetic 3D scene for testing and performance evaluation

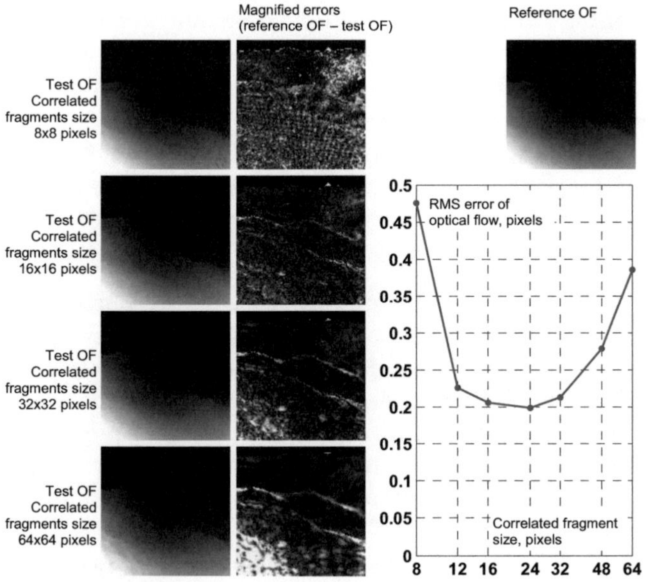

Figure 6. Results of the optical flow sensitivity with respect to correlation window size

5.2 Simulation experiment results

The OF fields have been determined with a correlated fragments size varying in the range from 8x8 to 64x64 pixels and they have been compared with a reference (ideal) OF field to determine the OF errors. The reference OF field has been produced directly from the reference trajectory data and the known 3D model of the landing site. Figure 6 shows the results of the optical flow accuracy sensitivity for different correlation window sizes. Images in the left column represent the 2D patterns of the OF vectors magnitudes (brighter pixels represent larger OF vectors), the middle row contains the error patterns, determined as the difference between the reference (ideal) and test OF fields. RMS error values are shown in the diagram at the bottom right corner.

According to this sensitivity analysis, minimal OF errors are expected for a window size of 24x24 pixels.

For the selected window size (24x24 pixels) the sensitivity to additive and multiplicative image noise on the OF error has been investigated. It has been found, that random noise with standard deviation within 8% of average image brightness (signal-to-noise ratio above 12 dB) has little influence on the OF field accuracy. Starting from $\sigma = 8\%$, however, the effect of image noise rapidly increases. According to these results, the limit of acceptable image noise for optical flow determination with fragments size 24x24 can be set to $\sigma = 8\%$ of average image brightness.

6. Optical flow processor concept

Based on the result of previous theoretical studies and experimental works (software simulations and hardware models testing) a detailed concept of a compact OptoElectronic Optical Flow Processor (OE-OFP), suitable for installation onboard a flying robot has been developed.

The main purpose of the OE-OFP is the real time determination of the optical flow field for the visible surrounding environment. Figure 7 shows the general data flow chart for the optical flow computation according to the Joint Transform Correlation (JTC) principle.

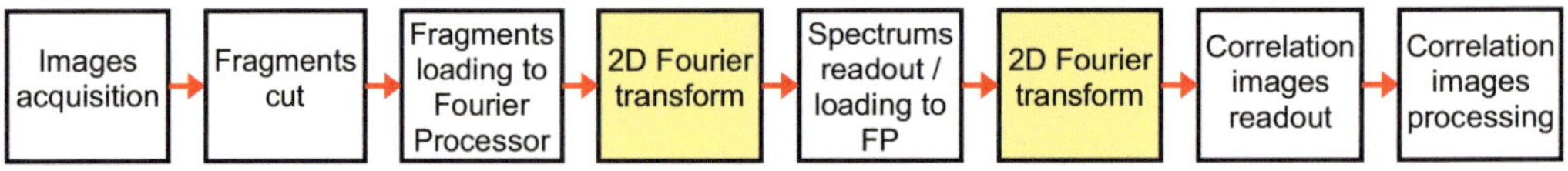

Figure 7. Main operations for optical flow determination according to JTC principle

The operations of 2D Fourier transform are most time and resource consuming for a digital realization of the OF processor. With optical realisation however, Fourier transform is practically performed instantly (with "speed of light") and requires power only for SLM illumination. In this case other operations in the data processing chain (images readout/loading, fragments cut and correlation images processing) are practically determining the limits of performance improvement and size/mass/power minimization. Therefore, optimization of these operations is particularly essential for optimal design of the optoelectronic OF processor.

The concept of the OE-OFP has been developed assuming a realization of the input/output and digital processing operations directly on the image sensors and SLM chips. This solution eliminates the need for a dedicated digital processing electronics and reduces dramatically the power consumption.

The unpackaged chips can be mounted close to each other on a single substrate (Chip-on-Board - COB mounting). A small distance between the dies (Figure 8) is offering direct chip-to-chip connections. This avoids the need for powerful buffers inside the processor and in consequence reduces further the OFP power consumption. As the processor outputs only the OF vectors coordinates, the output data rate and therefore the power consumption of the output buffers are also limited.

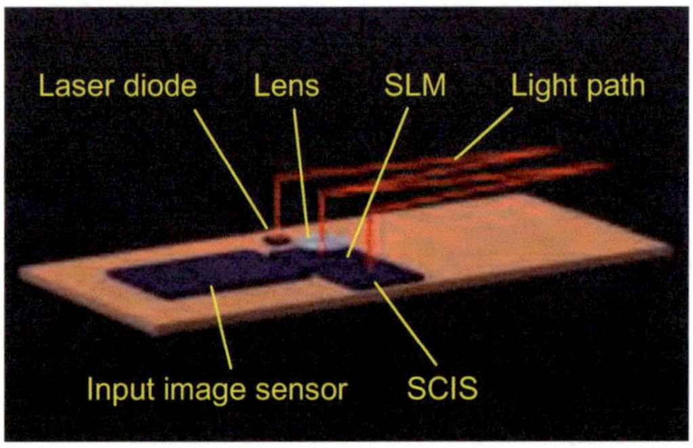

Figure 8. Realization concept of the OE-OFP

The optical system of the OF processor has been designed using a reflective SLM, which modulates the phase of the reflected wave front. To reduce the overall processor size and to increase the mechanical stability, a folded optical system design on the base of a small block of glass or optical plastic is currently considered. The small dimensions of the optical system allow a realization of the whole OF processor including an interface board and the lens in a compact housing, suitable for installation on a flying platform (Figure 9).

Figure 9. Possible OF processor housing configuration

The operation of the presented optoelectronic processor is briefly explained in the following. The lens forms an image of the surrounding environment on the input image sensor. After exposure, the image data are recorded in an on-chip memory within the image sensor. The fragments for correlation are cut from two sequential frames according to the pre-programmed pattern - this operation is also performed within the input image sensor. The fragments prepared for correlation are sent to the SLM. Coherent light, emitted by a laser diode, reflects from the aluminized side of a glass block and illuminates the SLM surface via the embedded lens (can be formed as a spherical bulb on the surface of the block). The phase of the wave front reflected from the SLM, is modulated by the input image. It is focused by the same lens and forms (after intermediate reflection) the amplitude image of the Fourier spectrum of the input image on the surface of the Spectrum/Correlation Image Sensor (SCIS). After a second optical Fourier transform, the correlation image is obtained. The optical flow vector (equal to the shift between the correlated fragments) is calculated from the correlation peaks positions within the correlation image. This operation is performed directly inside the SCIS chip. The coordinates of the OF vectors are sent to the output buffers, installed on a small printed board.

The expected performances of the OE-OFP (Table 1) have been estimated on the base of the conceptual design of the processor and the results of simulation experiments, taking into account also the test results of the existing hardware models of the optical correlator developed within previous projects (Tchernykh et al., 2004, Janschek et al., 2004a).

Input	3D scene
Output	optical-flow fields
Optical-flow resolution (max)	64x64=4096 vectors/field
Optical-flow resolution (min)	8x8=64 vectors/field
OF fields rate @ 4096 vectors/field	10 fields/s
OF fields rate @ 64 vectors/field	500 fields/s
Processing delay	One frame (0.002 … 0.1 s)
Inner correlations rate	50000 correlations/s
OF vectors determination errors	σ = 0.1 … 0.25 pixels
OF processor dimensions	50x20x8 mm (w/o lens)
OF processor mass	within 20g (w/o lens)
Power consumption	within 2 W

Table 1. Expected performances of the Optoelectronic Optical Flow Processor

Comparison of Table 1 with the requirements listed in section 2 shows that the proposed optoelectronic Optical Flow processor is expected to satisfy the requirements, listed in section 2. To compare the proposed processor with other currently available solutions for real time optical flow determination, it is however important to evaluate a performance measure related to mobility, which takes into account also the processor power consumption and volume related to the computing performance in terms of flow vectors per second and accuracy.
Figure 10 shows these performance-to-mobility measures taking into account also the power consumption and the volume of the optical-flow processor module. It follows that the proposed optoelectronic optical flow processor design (OE-OFP) shows unique performances in comparison with the fastest digital optical-flow computation solution currently available (Bruhn et al., 2005, Diaz et al., 2006).

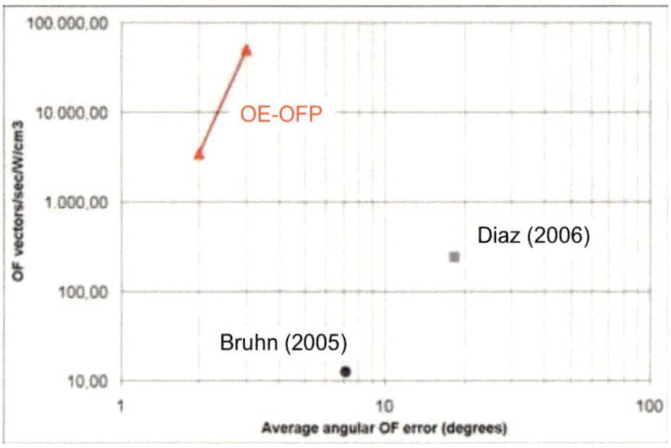

Figure 10. Performance-to-mobility comparison of optical flow processors

7. Application areas

The proposed optical flow processor is intended to be used mainly in the field of visual navigation of mobile robots (ground, aerial, marine) and space flight (satellites, landing vehicles). The small size, mass and power consumption makes the proposed OE-OFP particularly suitable for application onboard micro air vehicles (MAVs).
From the obtained optical flow, 3D information can be extracted and a 3D model of the visible environment can be produced. The considerable high resolution (up to 64x64 OF vectors) and very high accuracy (errors $\sigma \leq 0.25$ pixels) of the determined optical flow makes such 3D environment models detailed and accurate. These 3D environment models can be used for 3D navigation in complex environment (Janschek et al., 2004b) and also for 3D mapping, making the proposed OF processor ideally suited for 3D visual SLAM. The applicability of the optical flow data derived with the proposed principles (joint transform correlation) and technology (optical correlator) to real world navigation solutions even under unfavourable constraints (inclined trajectories with considerable large perspective distortions) has been proved by the authors in recent work (Janschek et al., 2005b, Tchernykh et al., 2006), some simulation results are also given in the next section.
The anticipated real time performance of the processor (up to 500 frames/s with reduced OF field resolution) provides a wide range of opportunities for using the obtained optical flow for many additional tasks beyond localization and mapping, e.g. vehicle stabilization, collision avoidance, visual odometry, landing and take-off control of MAVs.

8. Application example: visual navigation of the outdoor UAV

The concept of visual navigation for a flying robot, based on 3D environment models matching has been proposed by the authors (Janschek et al., 2005b, Tchernykh et al., 2006) as one of the most promising applications of high resolution real time optical flow. 3D models of the visible surface in the camera-fixed coordinate frame will be reconstructed from the OF fields. These models will be matched with the reference 3D model with known position/attitude (pose) in a surface-fixed coordinate frame. As a result of the matching, the reconstructed model pose in the surface-fixed frame will be determined. With position and attitude of the reconstructed model known in both camera-fixed and surface-fixed frames, the position and attitude of the camera can be calculated in the surface-fixed frame.

Matching of 3D models instead of 2D images is not sensitive to perspective distortions and is therefore especially suitable for low altitude trajectories. The method does not require any specific features/objects/landmarks on the terrain surface and it is not affected by illumination variations. The high redundancy of matching of the whole surface instead of individual reference points ensures a high matching reliability and a high accuracy of the obtained navigation data. Generally, the errors of vehicle position determination are expected to be a few times smaller than the resolution of the reference model.

To prove the feasibility of the proposed visual navigation concept and to estimate the expected navigation performances, a software model of the proposed visual navigation system has been developed and an open-loop simulation of navigation data determination has been performed.

A simulation environment has been produced using the landscape generation software (Vue 5 Infinity from e-on software) on the base of 3D relief, obtained by filtering of a random 2D pattern. Natural soil textures and vegetation have been simulated (with 2D patterns and 3D models of trees and grass), as well as natural illumination and atmospheric effects (Figure 11). A simulation reference mission scenario has been set up, which includes the flight along a predetermined trajectory (loop with the length of 38 m at a height about 10 m over the simulation terrain).

Figure 11. Simulation environment with UAV trajectory (side and top views)

Simulated navigation camera images (Figure 12) have been rendered for a single nadir-looking camera with a wide angle (fisheye) lens (field of view 220°), considering the simulated UAV trajectory.

A reference 3D model of the terrain has been produced in a form of Digital Elevation Model (DEM) by stereo processing of two high altitude images (simulating the standard aerial mapping). Such model can be represented by a 2D pseudo image with the brightness of each pixel corresponding to the local height over the base plane.
The optical flow determination has been performed with a detailed simulation model of the optical correlator. The correlator model produces the optical flow fields for each pair of simulated navigation camera images, simulating the operation of the real optical hardware. Figure 13 shows an example of the optical flow field. The 3D surface models have been first reconstructed as local distance maps in a camera-fixed coordinate frame (Figure 13), then converted into DEMs in a surface-fixed frame using the estimated position and attitude of the vehicle. Figure 14 shows an example of both the reconstructed and reference DEMs.

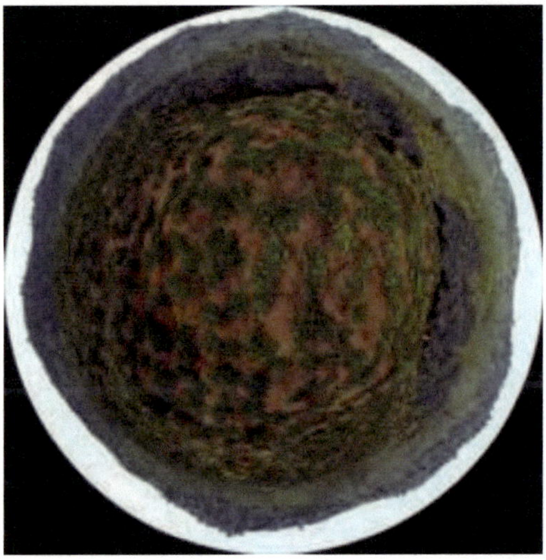

Figure 12. Example of simulated navigation camera image (fisheye lens)

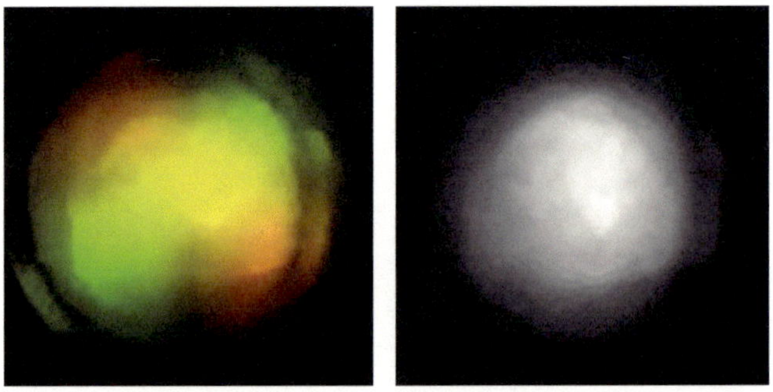

Optical flow field (magnitude of vectors coded by brightness, direction – by color)

Distance map (local distance coded by brightness)

Figure 13. Example of an optical flow field and corresponding distance map

Navigation data (position, attitude and velocity of the robot) have been extracted from the results of the matching of the reconstructed and reference models and compared with the reference trajectory data to estimate the navigation errors. As a result of the test, the RMS position error for the translation part of the trajectory was 0.20 m and the RMS attitude error was 0.45 degrees. These have been obtained by instantaneous processing of the optical flow data, i.e. without any time filtering, and without any additional navigation aids (except the DEM reference map). The navigation accuracy can be further improved by some filtering, and by using data from inertial measurement unit.

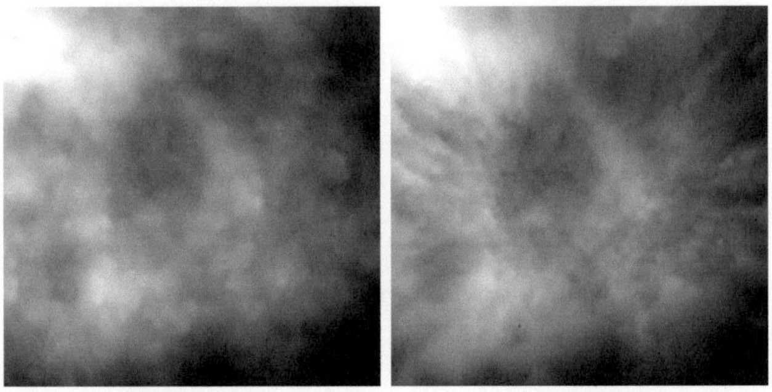

Figure 14. Reference and reconstructed DEMs

9. Summary and conclusions

The conceptual design of an advanced embedded optical flow processor has been presented. Preliminary performance evaluation based on a detailed simulation model of the complete optical processing chain shows unique performances in particular applicable for visual navigation tasks of mobile robots. The detailed optoelectronic design work is currently started.

10. References

Barrows, G. & Neely, C. (2000). Mixed-mode VLSI optic flow sensors for in-flight control of a micro air vehicle, *Proc. SPIE* Vol. 4109, *Critical Technologies for the Future of Computing*, pp. 52-63, 2000.

Beauchemin, S.S. & Barron, J.L. (1995). The computation of optical flow, *ACM Computing Surveys (CSUR)*, Vol. 27, no. 3, (September 1995), pp. 433 – 466.

Bruhn, A., Weickert, J., Feddern, C., Kohlberger, T. & Schnörr, C. (2003). Real-Time Optic Flow Computation with Variational Methods, *CAIP 2003*, LNCS, Vol. 2756, (2003), pp. 222-229.

Bruhn, A., Weickert, J., Feddern, C., Kohlberger, T. & Schnörr, C. (2005). Variational Optical Flow Computation in Real Time. *IEEE Transactions on Image Processing,* vol. 14, no. 5, (May 2005)

Díaz, J., Ros, E., Pelayo, F., Ortigosa, E.M. & Mota, S. (2006) FPGA-Based Real-Time Optical-Flow System, *IEEE Transactions on Circuits and Systems for Video Technology*, vol. 16, no. 2, (February 2006)

Goodman, J.W. (1968). *Introduction to Fourier optics*, McGraw-Hill, New York.

Horn, B.K.P. & Schunck, B.G. (1981). Determining Optical Flow, *Artificial Intelligence*, Vol. 17 (1981), pp. 185-203.

Janschek, K., Tchernykh, V. & Dyblenko, S. (2004a). Opto-Mechatronic Image Stabilization for a Compact Space Camera, *Preprints of the 3rd IFAC Conference on Mechatronic Systems - Mechatronics 2004*, pp.547-552, Sydney, Australia, 6-8 September 2004,. (Congress Best Paper Award).

Janschek, K., Tchernykh, V. & Beck, M. (2004b). Optical Flow based Navigation for Mobile Robots using an Embedded Optical Correlator, *Preprints of the 3rd IFAC Conference on Mechatronic Systems - Mechatronics 2004*, pp.793-798, Sydney, Australia, 6-8 September 2004.

Janschek, K., Tchernykh, V. & Dyblenko, S. (2005a) „Verfahren zur automatischen Korrektur von durch Verformungen hervorgerufenen Fehlern Optischer Korrelatoren und Selbstkorrigierender Optischer Korrelator vom Typ JTC", Deutsches Patent Nr. 100 47 504 B4, Erteilt: 03.03.2005.

Janschek, K., Tchernykh, V. & Beck, M. (2005b). An Optical Flow Approach for Precise Visual Navigation of a Planetary Lander, *Proceedings of the 6th International ESA Conference on Guidance, Navigation and Control Systems*, Loutraki, Greece, 17 - 20 October 2005.

Janschek, K., Tchernykh, V. & Dyblenko, S. (2007). Performance analysis of opto-mechatronic image stabilization for a compact space camera, *Control Engineering Practice*, Volume 15, Issue 3, March 2007, pages 333-347

Jutamulia, S. (1992). Joint transform correlators and their applications, *Proceedings SPIE*, 1812 (1992), pp. 233-243.

Liu, H., Hong, T.H., Herman, M., Camus, T. & Chellappa, R. (1998). Accuracy vs Efficiency Trade-offs in Optical Flow Algorithms, *Computer Vision and Image Understanding*, vol. 72, no. 3, (1998), pp. 271-286.

Lowe, D.G. (1999). Object recognition from local scale invariant features, *Proceedings of the Seventh International Conference on Computer Vision (ICCV'gg)*, pp. 1150-1157, Kerkyra, Greece, September 1999.

McCane, B., Galvin, B. & Novins, K. (1998) On the Evaluation of Optical Flow Algorithms, *Proceedings of 5th International Conference on Control, Automation, Robotics and Vision*, pp. 1563-1567, Singapur, 1998.

Pratt, W.K. (1974) Correlation techniques of image registration, *IEEE Transactions on Aerospace Electronic Systems*, vol. 10, (May 1974), pp. 353-358.

Se, S., Lowe, D.G. & Little, J. (2001) Vision-based mobile robot localization and mapping using scale-invariant features, *Proceedings 2001 ICRA - IEEE International Conference on Robotics and Automation*, vol. 2, pp. 2051 – 2058, 2001.

Tchernykh, V., Janschek, K. & Dyblenko, S. (2000). Space application of a self-calibrating optical processor or harsh mechanical environment, *Proceedings of 1st IFAC Conference on Mechatronic Systems - Mechatronics 2000*, Vol 3, pp.309-314, Darmstadt, Germany, September 18-20, 2000, Pergamon-Elsevier Science.

Tchernykh, V., Dyblenko, S., Janschek, K., Seifart, K. & Harnisch, B. (2004). Airborne test results for a smart pushbroom imaging system with optoelectronic image correction. *In: Sensors, Systems and Next-Generation Satellites VII, Proceedings of SPIE*, Vol. 5234 (2004), pp.550-559.

Tchernykh, V., Beck, M. & Janschek, K. (2006). Optical flow navigation for an outdoor UAV using a wide angle mono camera and DEM matching, *submitted to 4th IFAC Symposium on Mechatronic Systems – Mechatronics 2006*, Heidelberg, Germany.

Zufferey, J.C. (2005) Bio-inspired Vision-based Flying Robots, *Thèse n° 3194, Faculté Sciences et Techniques de l'Ingénieur*, EPFL, 2005.

14

Simulation of Visual Servoing Control and Performance Tests of 6R Robot Using Image-Based and Position-Based Approaches

M. H. Korayem and F. S. Heidari
Robotic Research Laboratory, College of Mechanical Engineering, Iran University of Science & Technology, Tehran
Iran

1. Introduction

Visual control of robots using vision system and cameras has appeared since 1980's. Visual (image based) features such as points, lines and regions can be used to, for example, enable the alignment of a manipulator / gripping mechanism with an object. Hence, vision is a part of a control system where it provides feedback about the state of the environment. In general, this method involves the vision system cameras snapping images of the target-object and the robotic end effector, analyzing and reporting a pose for the robot to achieve. Therefore, 'look and move' involves no real-time correction of robot path. This method is ideal for a wide array of applications that do not require real-time correction since it places much lighter demands on computational horsepower as well as communication bandwidth, thus having become feasible outside the laboratory. The obvious drawback is that if the part moves in between the look and move functions, the vision system will have no way of knowing this in reality this does not happen very often for fixture parts. Yet another drawback is lower accuracy; with the 'look and move' concept, the final accuracy of the calculated part pose is directly related to the accuracy of the 'hand-eye' calibration (offline calibration to relate camera space to robot space). If the calibration were erroneous so would be the calculation of the pose estimation part.

A closed-loop control of a robot system usually consists of two intertwined processes: tracking pictures and control the robot's end effector. Tracking pictures provides a continuous estimation and update of features during the robot or target-object motion. Based on this sensory input, a control sequence is generated.

Y. Shirai and H. Inoue first described a novel method for 'visual control' of a robotic manipulator using a vision feedback loop in their paper. Gilbert describes an automatic rocket-tracking camera that keeps the target centered in the camera's image plane by means of pan/tilt controls (Gilbert et al., 1983). Weiss proposed the use of adaptive control for the non-linear time varying relationship between robot pose and image features in image-based servoing. Detailed simulations of image-based visual servoing are described for a variety of manipulator structures of 3-DOF (Webber &.Hollis, 1988).

Mana Saedan and M. H. Ang worked on relative target-object (rigid body) pose estimation for vision-based control of industrial robots. They developed and implemented an estimation algorithm for closed form target pose (Saedan & Marcelo, 2001).
Image based visual controlling of robots have been considered by many researchers. They used a closed loop to control robot joints. Feddema uses an explicit feature-space trajectory generator and closed-loop joint control to overcome problems due to low visual sampling rate. Experimental work demonstrates image-based visual servoing for 4-DOF (Kelly & Shirkey, 2001). Rives et al. describe a similar approach using the task function method and show experimental results for robot positioning using a target with four circle features (Rives et al. 1991). Hashimoto et al. present simulations to compare position-based and image-based approaches (Hashimoto et al., 1991).
Korayem et al. designed and simulated vision based control and performance tests for a 3P robot by visual C++ software. They minimized error in positioning of end effector and they analyzed the error using ISO9283 and ANSI-RIAR15.05-2 standards and suggested methods to improve error (Korayem et al., 2005, 2006). A stationary camera was installed on the earth and the other one mounted on the end effector of robot to find a target. This vision system was designed using image-based-visual servoing. But the vision-based control in our work is implemented on 6R robot using both IBVS and PBVS methods. In case which cameras are mounted on the earth, i.e., the cameras observe the robot the system is called "out-hand" (the term "stand-alone" is generally used in the literature) and when one camera is installed on the end effector configuration is "in-hand". The closed-form target pose estimation is discussed and used in the position-based visual control. The advantage of this approach is that the servo control structure is independent from the target pose coordinates and to construct the pose of a target-object from two-dimension image plane, two cameras are used. This method has the ability to deal with real-time changes in the relative position of the target-object with respect to robot as well as greater accuracy.
Collision detection along with the related problem of determining minimum distance has a long history. It has been considered in both static and dynamic (moving objects) versions. Cameron in his work mentioned three different approaches for dynamic collision detection (Cameron, 1985, 1986). Some algorithms such as Boyse's and then Canny's solve the problem for computer animation (Boyse, 1979) and (Canny, 1986); while others do not easily produce the exact collision points and contact normal direction for collision response (Lin, 1993). For curved objects, Herzen etc have described a general algorithm based on time dependent parametric surfaces (Herzen et al. 1990). Gilbert et al. computed the minimum distance between two convex objects with an expected linear time algorithm and used it for collision detection (Gilbert & Foo, 1990). Collision detection along with the related problem of determining minimum distance has a long history. It has been considered in both static and dynamic (moving objects) versions. Cameron in his work mentioned three different approaches for dynamic collision detection. He mentioned three different approaches for dynamic collision detection. One of them is to perform static collision detection repetitively at each discrete time steps (Cameran & Culley, 1986).
Using linear-time preprocessing, Dobkin and Kirkpatrick were able to solve the collision detection problem as well as compute the separation between two convex polytopes in $O(\log|A|.\log|B|)$ where A and B are polyhedra and $|.|$ denotes the total number of faces (Canny, 1986). This approach uses a hierarchical description of the convex objects and

extension of their previous work (Lin, 1993). This is one of the best-known theoretical bounds.
Some algorithms such as Boyse's and then Canny's solve the problem for computer animation (Gilbert & Foo, 1990); while others do not easily produce the exact collision points and contact normal direction for collision response (ANSI/RIA R15.05-2, 2002). For curved objects, Herzen et al. have described a general algorithm based on time dependent parametric surfaces (ISO9283). Gilbert et al. computed the minimum distance between two convex objects with an expected linear time algorithm and used it for collision detection (Ponmagi et al.).
The technique used in our work is an efficient simple algorithm for collision detection between links of 6R robot undergoing rigid motion ,determines whether or not two objects intersect and checks if their centers distance is equal to zero or not.
Due to undefined geometric shape of the end effector of the robot we have explained and used a color based object recognition algorithm in simulation software to specify and recognize the end effector and the target-object in image planes of the two cameras. In addition, capability and performance of this algorithm to recognize the end effector and the target-object and to provide 3D pose information about them are shown.
In this chapter the 6R robot that is designed and constructed in IUST robotic research Lab, is modeled and simulated. Then direct and inverse kinematics equations of the robot are derived and simulated. After discussing simulation software of 6R robot, we simulated control and performance tests of robot and at last, the results of tests according to ISO9283 and ANSI-RIAR15.05-2 standards and MATLAB are analyzed.

2. The 6R robot and simulator environment

This 6 DOFs robot, has 3 DOF at waist, shoulder and hand and also 3 DOF in it's wrist that can do roll, pitch and yaw rotations (Figure 1). First link rotates around vertical axis in horizontal plane; second link rotates in a vertical plane orthogonal to first link's rotation plane. The third link rotates in a plane parallel to second link's rotation plane.
The 6R robot and its environment have been simulated in simulator software, by mounting two cameras in fixed distance on earth observing the robot. These two cameras capture images from robot and it's surrounding, after image processing and recognition of target-object and end effector, positions of them are estimated in image plane coordinate, then visual system leads the end effector toward target. However, to have the end effector and target-object positions in global reference coordinate, the mapping of coordinates from image plan to the reference coordinates is needed. However, this method needs camera calibration that is non-linear and complicated. In this simulating program, we have used a neural network instead of mapping. Performance tests of robot are also simulated by using these two fixed cameras.

3. Simulator software of the 6R robot

In this section, the simulation environment for the 6R robot is introduced and its capability and advantages with respect to previous versions are outlined. This simulator software is designed to increase the efficiency and performance of the robot and predict its limitation and deficiencies before experiments in laboratory. In these packages by using a designed interface board, rotation signals for joints to control the robot are sent to it.

To simulate control and test of 6R robot, the object oriented software Visual C++6 was used. This programming language is used to accomplish this plan because of its rapidity and easily changed for real situation in experiments. In this software, the picture is taken in bitmap format through two stationary cameras, which are mounted on the earth in the capture frame module, and the image is returned in form of array of pixels. Both of the two cameras after switching the view will take picture. After image processing, objects in pictures are saved separately, features are extracted and target-object and end effector will be recognized among them according to their features and characteristics. Then 3D position coordinates of target-object and end effector are estimated. After each motion of joints, new picture is taken from end effector and this procedure is repeated until end effector reach to target-object.

Figure 1. 6R robot configuration

With images from these two fixed cameras, positions of objects are estimated in image plane coordinate, usually, to transform from image plan coordinates to the reference coordinates system, mapping and calibrating will be used. In this program, using the mapping that is a non-linear formulation will be complicated and time consuming process so a neural network to transform these coordinates to global reference 3D coordinate has been designed and used. Mapping system needs extra work and is complicated compared to neural network. Neural networks are used as nonlinear estimating functions. To compute processing matrix, a set of points to train the neural system has been used. This collection of points are achieved by moving end effector of robot through different points which their coordinates in global reference system are known and their coordinates in image plane of the two cameras are computed in pixels by vision module in simulator software. The position of the end effector is recognized at any time by two cameras, which are stationary with a certain distance from each other. The camera No.1 determines the target coordinates in a 2-D image plan in pixels. The third coordinate of the object is also computed by the second camera.

A schematic view of simulator software and the 6R robot in its home position is depicted in Figure 2. In this figure, 6R robot is in homeposition and target-object is the red sphere. The aim of control process is guiding the end effector to reach the target-object within an acceptable accuracy.

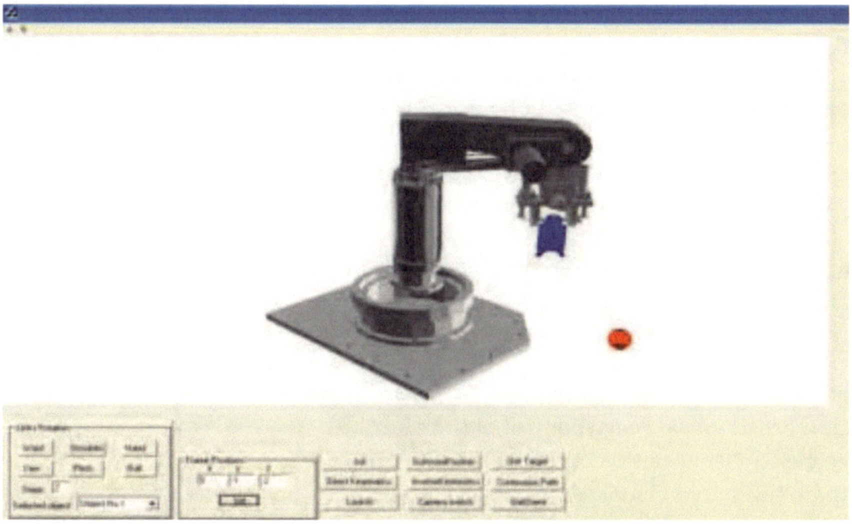

Figure 2. Schematic view of simulator software designed for 6R robot

In this software, not only controlling of the 6R robot is possible but also performance tests according to ISO and ANSI standards are accomplished and results could be depicted.

3.1 Capabilities of the simulator software

Different capabilities of simulator software are introduced. In Figure 3 push buttons in dialog box of simulator environment are shown. 'Link Rotation' static box (in left of Figure 3) is used for rotating each link of the 6R robot around its joint. Each of these rotations is performed in specified Steps; by adjusting amount of step, it is possible to place the end effector at desired pose in the robot's workspace. 'Frame positions' panel depicts 3D position of selected frame in 'Selected object' list box and also x, y, z coordinate of selected frame can be defined by user and placed in that coordinate by pushing 'Set' button.

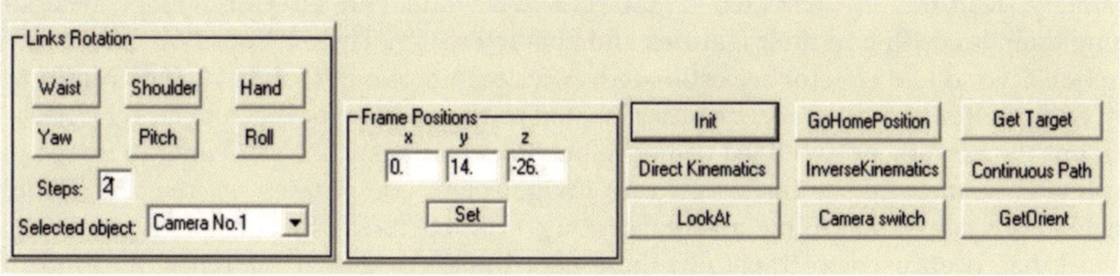

Figure 3. Control buttons in simulator software of the 6R robot

Init: At beginning of the program, this button is pushed to initialize variables in dialogue box.

GoHomePosition: Places frames and robot links in their homeposition and sets joint variables to their initial values.

Get Target: By pushing this button control process to guide end effector to reach the target is performed.
Direct Kinematics: Performance tests for direct kinematics are accomplished. Joint variables are determined in a text file by user.
Inverse kinematics: Inverse kinematics tests for the robot are done. Transformation matrix is defined by user in a text file. This file would be read and joint variables are determined to rotate joints to reach the end effector in desired pose.
Continuous Path: It guides the end effector during continuous paths such as circle, line or rectangle to simulate performance tests. Paths properties are defined in text file by user.
Look At: By pushing this button observer camera will look at robot at any pose.
Camera switch: change the view between two stationary camera's views. Switch from camera 1 to camera 2 or vice versa.
GetOrient: Changes the orientation of selected camera frame.

4. Visual servo control simulation

The goal of this section is to simulate:

- Position based visual servo control of the 6R robot
- Image based visual servo control of the 6R robot
- Compare these two visual servo control approaches

To attain these goals different theories of computer vision, image processing, feature extraction, robot kinematics, dynamics and control are used. By two stationary cameras observing the robot and workspace, images are taken, after image processing and feature extraction, target-object and the end effector are recognized, and their 3D pose coordinates are estimated by using a neural network. Then the end effector is controlled to reach the target. For simulating image based visual servo control of the 6R robot one of the cameras are mounted on the end effector of the robot and the other one is stationary on the earth.

4.1 Position based visual control simulation

In simulator software, function Capture Frame takes picture in bitmap format through two stationary cameras mounted on the earth and the images are returned in the form of array of pixels. Both of the two cameras after switching the view will take picture (to estimate 3D pose information of frames). After image processing, objects in pictures are saved separately, features are extracted and target-object and end effector will be recognized among them according to their features and characteristics. Then 3D position coordinates of target-object and end effector are estimated. After each motion of joints, new picture is taken from end effector and this procedure is repeated until end effector reach to target-object.
With images from these two fixed cameras, positions of objects are estimated in image plane coordinate, usually, to transform from image plan coordinates to the 3D reference coordinates system, mapping and calibrating will be used. In this program, a neural network has been used to transform these coordinates to global reference 3D coordinate. Mapping system needs extra work and is complicated compared to neural network. Neural networks are used as nonlinear estimating functions. A set of points has been used to train the neural system to compute processing matrix. Control procedure of robot to reach to target-object is briefly shown in Figs 4 and 5.

Figure 4. Robot at step 2 of control process in view of camera1 and camera2

Figure 5. Robot at step 2 of control process in view of camera1 and camera2

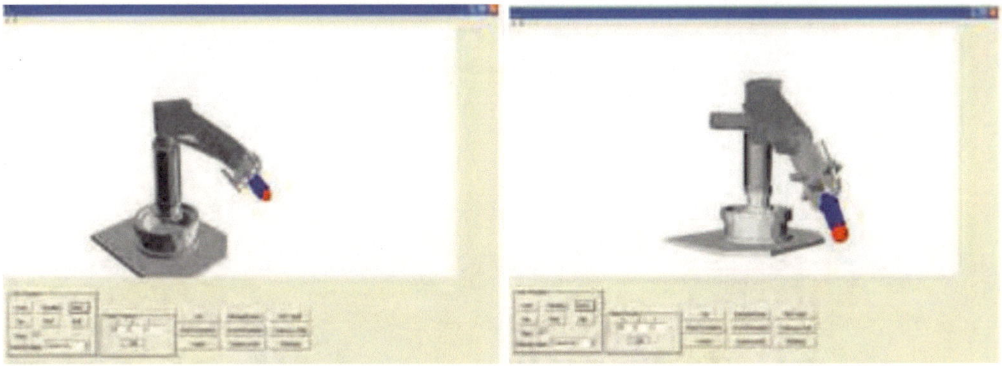

Figure 6. Robot at last step of control process reached to target-object in view of camera1 and camera2

Test steps:

1. Initialize the simulator environment by clicking Init button.
2. Select frame object No.1 from Selected object box.
3. Specify its 3D x, y, z position in Frame Position and click Set icon.
4. By Get Target icon, control process is accomplished.

Problems 1-2:

Set the target-object in four corners of a rectangle with coordinates as: (3,0,-2), (3,0, 2), (-3,0,-2), (-3,0, 2) and guide the end effector to attain the target-object.

For reaching end effector in (2,-1, 2) position, compute joint angles and compare them with actual joint angles at the end of the control process.

4.2 Mapping points in image plane to 3D system

As mentioned before a neural network has been used to transform 2D coordinates of image planes to global reference 3D coordinate. Collection of points to train the net are achieved by moving end effector of robot through different points that their coordinates in global reference system are known and their coordinates in image plane of the two cameras are computed in pixels by VisionAction module in simulator software. The position of the end effector is recognized at any time by two cameras, which are fixed with a certain distance from each other. The camera No.1 determines the target coordinates in a 2D image plan in pixels. The 3rd coordinate of the object is also computed by information from the second camera.

The used neural network is a back propagation perception kind network with 2 layers. In input layer (first layer) there are 4 node entrance including picture plan coordination pixels from two fixed cameras, to adapt a very fit nonlinear function 10 neurons in this layer with 'tan sigmoid' function have been used. In the second layer (output layer) there are 3 neurons with 30 input nodes and 3 output nodes which are 3D coordinates x, y and z of object in the earth reference system. The transfer function in this layer is linear.

This network can be used as a general function approximator. It can approximate 3D coordinates of any points in image plane of two cameras arbitrarily well, with given sufficient neurons in the hidden layer and tan sigmoid functions. As shown the training results in Figure 7 performance of trained net is 0.089374 in less than 40 iterations (epochs). This net approximates 3D coordinates of points well enough.

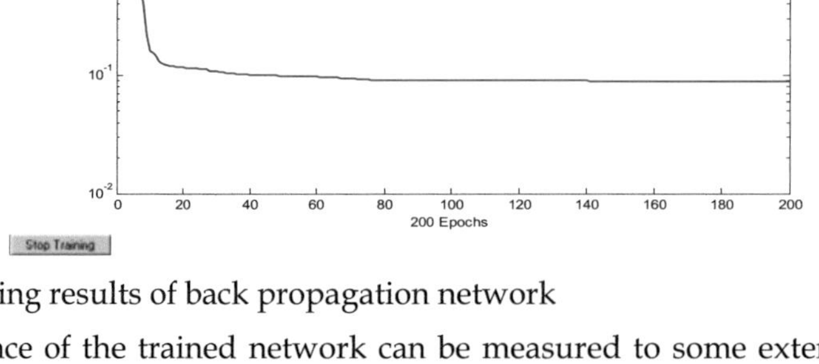

Figure 7. Training results of back propagation network

The performance of the trained network can be measured to some extent by the errors on the training, validation and test sets, but it is useful to investigate the network response in more detail. A regression analysis between the network response and the corresponding targets are performed. Network outputs are plotted versus the targets as open circles (Figure 8). The best linear fit is indicated by a dashed line. The perfect fit (output equal to targets) is indicated by the solid line. In this trained net, it is difficult to distinguish the best linear fit line from the perfect fit line, because the fit is so accurate. It is a measure of how well the variation in the output is explained by the targets and there is perfect correlation between targets and outputs. Results for x, y and z directions are shown in Figure 8.

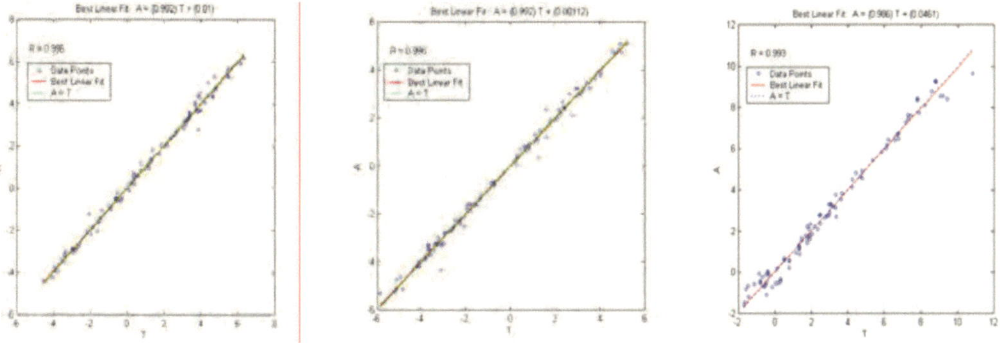

(a) (b) (c)

Figure 8. Regression between the network outputs coordinates in a) x, b) y, c) z direction and the corresponding targets

4.3 Image based visual servo control simulation

Image-based visual servo control uses the location of features on the image plane directly for feedback i.e. by moving the robot the camera's view (mounted on the end effector) changes from initial to final view. The features of images comprise coordinates of vertices, areas of the faces or any parameter and feature of the target-object that change by moving the end effector and so camera installed on it.

For a robot with a camera mounted on its end effector the viewpoint and hence the features of images are functions of the relative pose of the camera and the target-object. In general, this function is non-linear and cross-coupled such that motion of the end effector will result in the complex motion of many features. For example, camera rotation can cause features to translate horizontally and vertically on the image plane. This relationship may be linearized about the operating point to become more simple and easy.

In this version of simulator software the end effector is guided to reach the target-object, using feature based visual servo approach. In this approach global 3D position of target and the end effector are not estimated but features and properties of the target images from two cameras are used to guide the robot.

For image based visual servo control simulation of the 6R robot, two cameras are used. One is mounted on the end effector (eye in hand) and the other one is fixed on the earth observing the robot within its workspace (eye to hand). Obviously eye in hand scheme has a partial but precise sight of the scene whereas the eye to hand camera has a less precise but global sight of it. In this version of simulator software, the advantages of both, stand-alone and robot-mounted cameras have been used to control robot's motion precisely. Pictures are taken in bitmap format by both cameras through camera switch function then each image is returned in form of array of pixels.

System analysis is based on the stereovision theory and line-matching technology, using the two images captured by the two cameras. The vision procedure includes four stages, namely, calibration, sampling, image processing and calculating needed parameters.

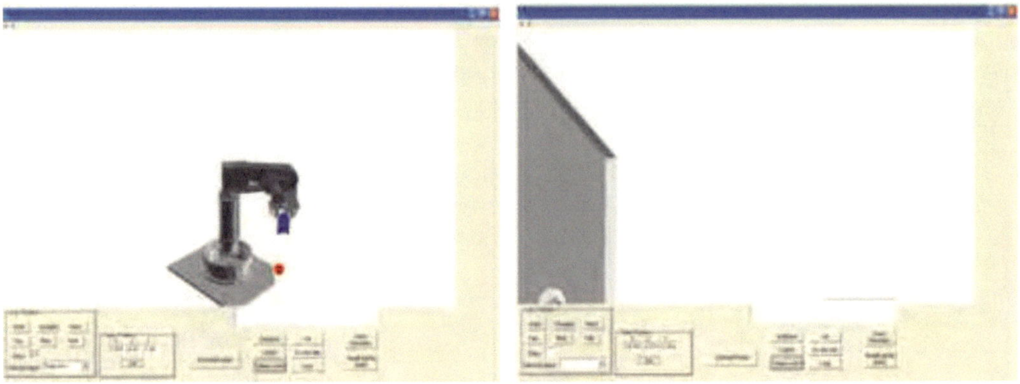

Figure 9. Robot in homeposition at beginning of control process in view of camera1 & camera2

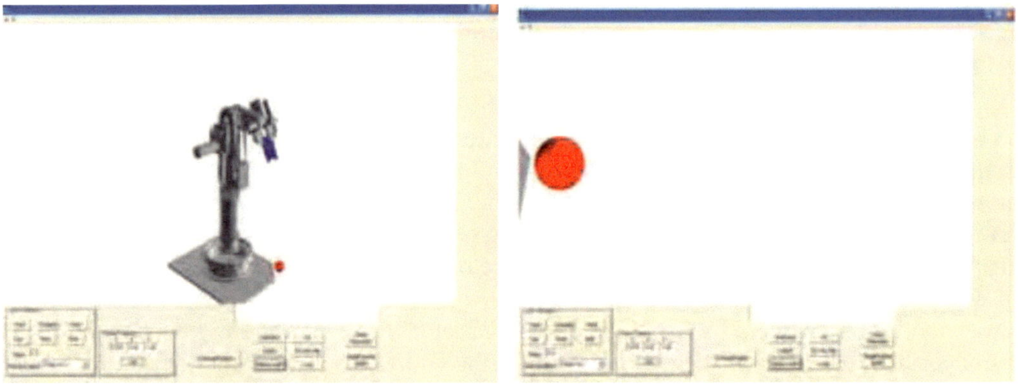

Figure 10. Robot at step 2 of control process in view of camera1 and camera2

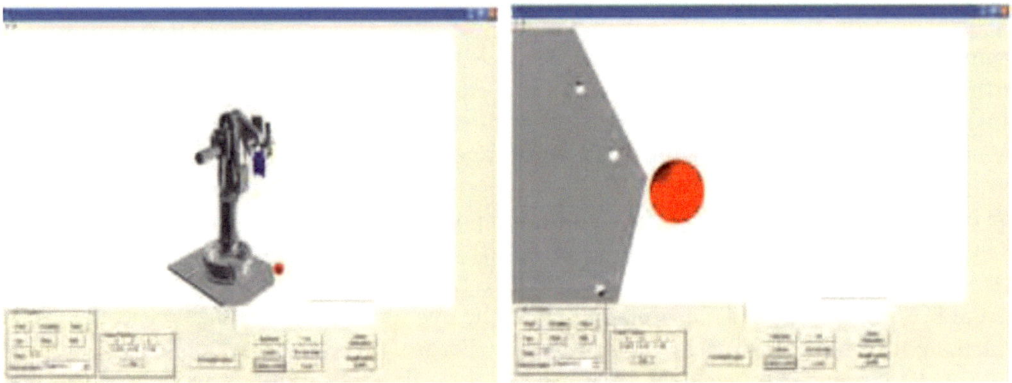

Figure 11. Robot at step 5 of control process in view of camera1 and camera2

First, the precision of this measuring system must be determined for simulator software. To maintain robot accuracy, calibration equipment is needed. In this simulator software, a self-calibrating measuring system based on a camera in the robot hand and a known reference object in the robot workspace is used. A collection of images of the reference target-object is obtained. From these the positions and orientations of the camera and the end effector, using image processing, image recognition and photogram metric techniques are estimated. The essential geometrical and optical camera parameters are derived from the redundancy in the measurements. By camera calibration, we can obtain the world coordinates of the start points of robots motion and the relation between images of the target-object and its relative distance to the end effector. So amount and direction of the end effector's motion is estimated and feedback for visual servo system will be obtained.

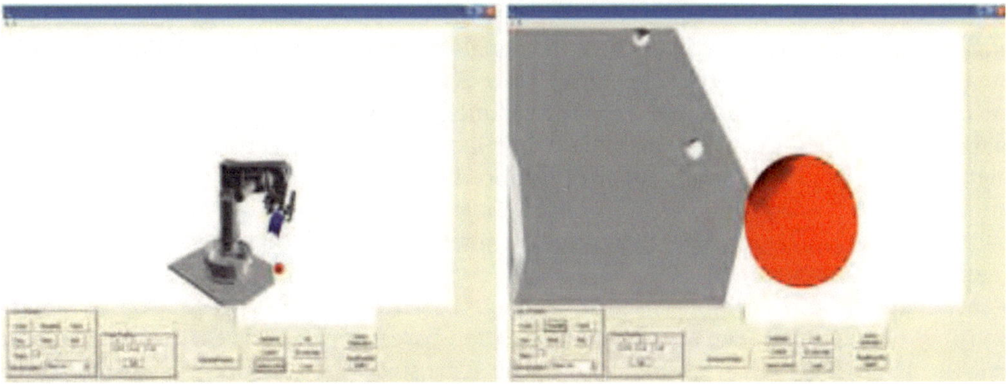

Figure 12. Robot at step 10 of control process in view of camera1 and camera2

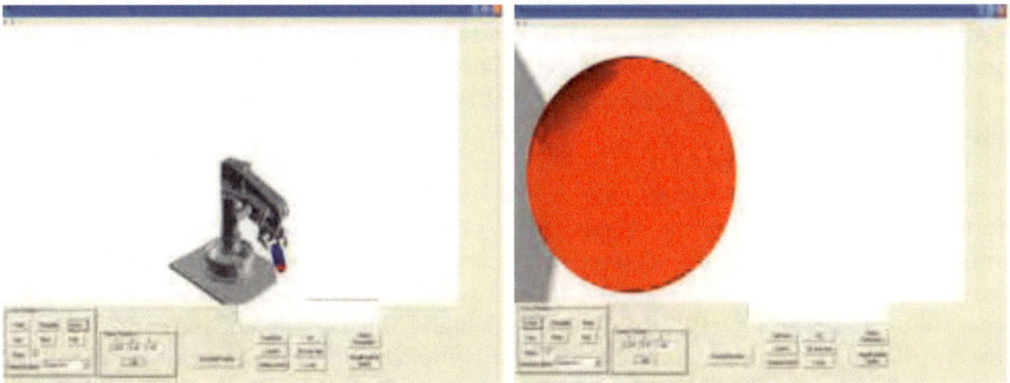

Figure 13. Robot at last step of control process reached to target-object in view of camera1 and camera2

At first control step as position of the target-object in 3D global reference system are not distinct, the end effector of the robot is moved to such a pose that target-object becomes visible in eye in hand camera view. It means that the end effector would find the target-object within robot's workspace. For this purpose, hand and wrist of the 6R robot rotate to reach the end effector to top point of workspace. By finding the target-object, the robot moves toward it to attain it. In each step, two cameras take picture from target and compare features in these images with reference image to assess required motion for each joints of the 6R robot. This procedure is repeated until the camera mounted on the end effector observes the target-object in middle of its image plane in desired size. Also in this algorithm, pictures taken by two cameras are saved in arrays of pixels and after threshold operations, segmentation, and labeling, the objects in the pictures will be extracted and each single frame is conserved separately with its number. Distance between end effector and target-object will be estimated, by using inverse kinematics equations of 6R robot, each joint angle will be computed then by revolution of joints end effector will approach to target. Control procedure of robot to reach to target-object is briefly shown in Figs 9 to 13.

4.4 Comparing IB and PB visual servoing approaches

Vision based control can be classified into two main categories. The first approach, feature based visual control, uses image features of a target object from image (sensor) space to compute error signals directly. The error signals are then used to compute the required actuation signals for the robot. The control law is also expressed in the image space. Many researchers in this approach use a mapping function (called the image Jacobian) from the image space to the Cartesian space. The image Jacobian, generally, is a function of the focal length of the lens of the camera, depth (distance between camera (sensor) frame and target features), and the image features. In contrast, the position based visual control constructs the spatial relationship, target pose, between the camera frame and the target-object frame from target image features.

In this chapter, both position based and image based approaches were used to simulate control of the 6R robot. The advantage of position-based approach is that the servo control structure is independent from the target pose reconstruction. Usually, the desired control values are specified in the Cartesian space, so they are easy to visualize. In position-based approach, target pose will be estimated. But in image based approach 3D pose of the target-object and end effector is not estimated directly but from some structural features extracted from image (e.g., an edge or color of pixels) defined when the camera and end effector reach the target as reference image features, the robot is guided and camera calibrating for visual system is necessary.

To construct the 3D pose of a target object from 2D image feature points, two cameras are needed. Image feature points in each of the two images have to be matched and 3D information of the coordinates of the target object and its feature points can then be computed by triangulation. The distance between the feature points in the target object, for example, can be used to help compute the 3D position and orientation of the target with respect to the camera. However, in systems with high DOF using image based approach and camera calibrating to guide the robot will be complicated, rather than in position-based approach we have used a trained neural net to transform coordinates. The image based approach may reduce computational delay eliminate the necessity for image interpretation and eliminate errors in sensor modeling and camera calibration. However, it does present a significant challenge to controller design since the process is non-linear and highly coupled.

In addition, in image-based approach, guiding the end effector to reach target will be completed in some steps but in position-based, the end effector is guided directly toward the target-object. The main advantage of position-based approach is that it directly controls the camera trajectory in Cartesian space. However, since there is no control in the image, the image features used in the pose estimation may leave the image (especially if the robot or the camera are coarsely calibrated), which thus leads to servoing failure. Also if the camera is coarse calibrated, or if errors exist in the 3D model of the target, the current and desired camera pose will not be accurately estimated. Nevertheless, image based visual servoing is

known to be robust not only with respect to camera but also to robot calibration errors. However, its convergence is theoretically ensured only in a region (quite difficult to determine analytically) around the desired position. Except in very simple cases, the analysis of the stability with respect to calibration errors seems to be impossible, since the system is coupled and non-linear.
In this simulator software control simulating of the 6R robot by using both position based and feature based approaches depicted that position based was faster but feature based more accurate. For industrial robots with high DOFs position based approach is used more, specially for performance testing of the robots we need to specify 3D pose of the end effector in each step so position based visual servo control is preferred.
Results for comparing two visual servo control process PBVS and IBVS are summarized in Table 1. These two approaches are used to guide the end effector of the robot to reach the target that is in a fixed distance from the end effector of the robot. Final pose of the wrist is determined and compared with target-object pose so the positioning error and accuracy is computed. However, the time duration for these processes is counted and control speed is compared in this way.

Visual Servoing Method	Control Accuracy (min error)	Performance Speed (process duration)	Computation delay	Controller design
PBVS Control	0.04 mm	20 sec	30 sec	simple
IBVS Control	0.01 mm	60 sec	10 sec	highly coupled

Table1. Results for comparing PBVS and IBVS approaches

5. The 6R robot performance tests simulation

In this version of software, performance tests of robot including direct kinematics, inverse kinematics and motion of end effector in continues paths like circle, rectangle and line is possible. In point to point moving of end effector, each joint angle is determined and robot will move with joints rotation. In inverse kinematics test, desired position and orientation of end effector is determined in transformation matrix T. amount of joint angles that satisfy inverse equations will be found and wrist will be in desired pose. Two observer cameras take pictures and pose of end effector will be estimated to determine positioning error of robot.
Then using ISO9283, ANSI-RIA standards, these errors will be analyzed and performance characters and accuracy of the robot will be determined. Results of these standard tests are used to compare different robots and their performance. In this chapter, we represent some of these tests by using camera and visual system according to the standards such as ISO-9283, and ANSI-RIA.

5.1 Performance test of 6R robot according to ISO9283 standard

a) Direct kinematics test of 6R robot (point-to-point motion)
In this part of test, position accuracy and repeatability of robot is determined. With rotation of joints, the end effector will move to desired pose. By taking pictures with two stationary cameras and trained neural network, we will have position of end effector in 3D global reference frame. To determine pose error these positions and ideal amounts will be compared. Positioning error in directions x, y, z for 10 series of direct kinematics tests is

depicted in Figure 14. Amount of joint angles θi are defined by user in a .txt file this file is read by software and through RotateJonint function, each joint rotates to its desired value.

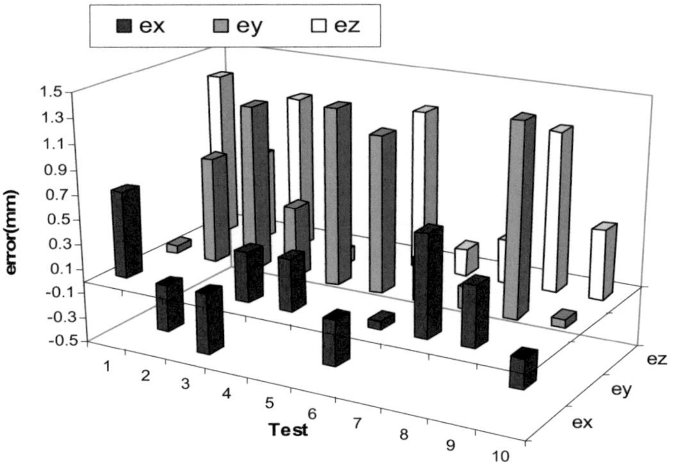

Figure 14. The error schematics in x, y, z directions for direct kinematics tests

b) Inverse kinematics test

In this stage, desired pose of the end effector is given to robot to go there. Transformation matrix containing position and orientation of the wrist frame is given by user in txt file. By computing joint angles from inverse kinematics equations and rotation of joints, end effector will go to desired pose. By taking pictures with two fixed cameras and trained neural network, we will have position coordinates of end effector in 3D global reference frame. By comparing the desired position and orientation of wrist frame with attained pose, the positioning error will be determined. Positioning error in directions x, y, z for 10 series of inverse kinematics tests is shown in Figure 15.

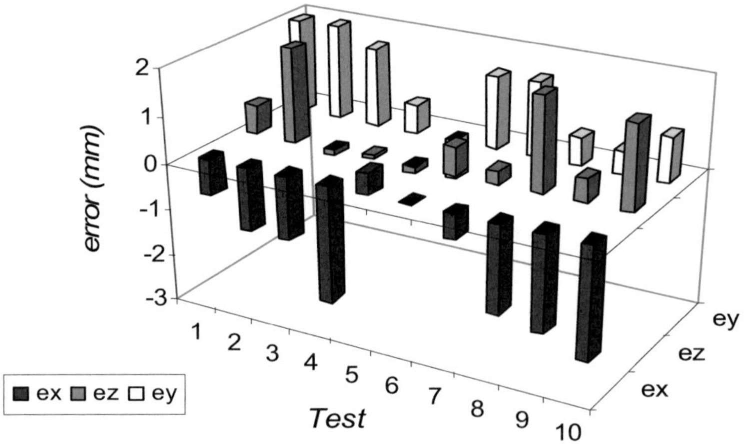

Figure 15. The error schematics in x, y, z directions for inverse kinematics tests

c) Continuous path test

To determine accuracy of robot in traversing continues paths wrist of robot is guided along different paths. In simulator software, three standard paths are tested (direct line, circular and rectangular paths). Results of moving the end effector along these continuous paths are depicted in Figure 16.

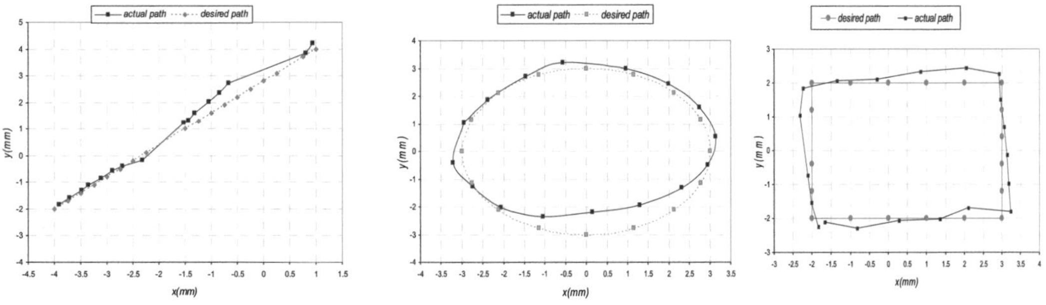

a): line paths b): circular path c): rectangular path

Figure 16. Continuous path test results for the 6R robot

5.2 Test steps

In this part, procedure to accomplish visual servo control and performance tests in simulator software for the 6R robot are prescribed. To control the robot by vision system, two camera frames have been installed on the earth watching the robot and its environment in front and right view. The camera one is lpCamera1 installed in point A(0,14,-26) and the other one is lpCamera2 installed in B(28,4,-1). Monitoring is possible through each of these cameras. Then images from these two cameras were saved in bmp format and used to train the neural network to find 3D positions of points in reference base coordinate. Position of two cameras can be changed through Frame position toolbox in simulator software. After image processing and recognition of the end effector, estimating its coordinate in image plane by neural network this coordinate are transformed to global reference coordinate. These steps are programed in simulator software and are done automatically. Performance tests of robot include direct kinematics, and motion of the end effector in continuous paths like circle, rectangle and line. In point to point moving of end effector, each joint angle is determined and robot will move with joints rotation. These joint angles are defined by user in a txt file. Two observer cameras take pictures and pose of end effector will be estimated to determine positioning error of robot. Standards such as ISO9283, ANSI-RIA are used to specify the robot error and path accuracy for continuous paths.

5.2.1 Direct kinematics test

Define amount of joint angles θi in angles.txt file in radian and save it. This file is read by software and through RotateJonint function, each joint rotates to its desired value.

When end effector stops two cameras take pictures from it and through VisionAction function and trained neural net x,y,z of center of the end effector in 3D Cartesian system is determined. It is saved in out_dirk1.txt file. Compute positioning error of robot during direct kinematics test.

Problem-3

In direct kinematics test, rotate joints in angles given in Table 2. Compute positioning error for each test in x, y, z directions and rotation of each joint and draw its graph.

test	1	2	3	4	5	6	7	8	9,10	
θ1	0.85	1.57	-3	-2	3.14	4.71	-1.2	0.8	1.8	-1
θ2	0	1	2	-1	-1	-0.5	1.57	0.75	-0.75	1.2
θ3	-0.25	2	2	2	3.14	1.57	-0.75	-0.5	1	-1.2
θ4	1	0	0.15	0.5	-0.5	0.75	0.5	-0.5	-0.5	0.5
θ5	0.5	0	0.5	-3	-1.57	-0.75	0.3	0.2	0.2	-1
θ6	1.1	0	-2	4	1	-1	0.5	-0.5	-0.5	1

Table 2. Joint angles for direct kinematics test

5.2.2 Inverse kinematics test

In this stage, desired pose of the end effector is given to robot to go there. Transformation matrix containing position and orientation of the wrist frame is given in txt file. Specify position and orientation of end effector in a transformation matrix of the wrist with respect to base T, in Tmatrix.txt file.

This matrix is used in InverseKinematics function to determine joint angles for desired pose of the end effector. By computing joint angles from inverse kinematics equations and rotation of joints, end effector will go to desired pose. By taking pictures with two fixed cameras and trained neural network, we will have position coordinates of end effector in 3D global reference frame.

Attained pose of end effector is saved in out_inv1.txt file. Positions and orientation error of this test are computed by data in this file.

By comparing the desired position and orientation of wrist frame with attained pose, the positioning error will be determined.

Problem-4

	desired position		
number	x	y	z
1	5.29	7.25	2.06
2	9.38	11.37	7.51
3	-12.08	-1.786	-0.22
4	-2.84	12.4	0.599
5	0.156	-13	1.09
6	10.5	1.53	0.12
7	3.34	3.57	-1.04
8	-1.165	6	1.707
9	-2.32	12	3.4
10	-3.48	8	5.1

Table 3. End effector positions for inverse kinematics test

In inverse kinematics test, define transformation matrix T with position of wrist according to Table 3. Orientation of the end effector can be defined by approach, normal and sliding vectors. Compute positioning error and accuracy of the robot in each test. Compare these errors with direct kinematics test results.

5.2.3 Continuous path test

To determine accuracy of robot in traversing continuous paths wrist of robot is guided along different paths. In simulator software, three standard paths are tested (direct line, circular and rectangular paths).

Specify type of path c for circular, r for rectangular and l for linear path and their specifications in path.txt file and save it. Each path must be entered in a distinguished line and its parameters in that line. For example:

Linear path: x1, y1, z1 is coordinates of start point of the linear path and x2, y2, z2 is for end point of the path.

l, x1, y1, z1, x2, y2, z2. (Fig. 17)

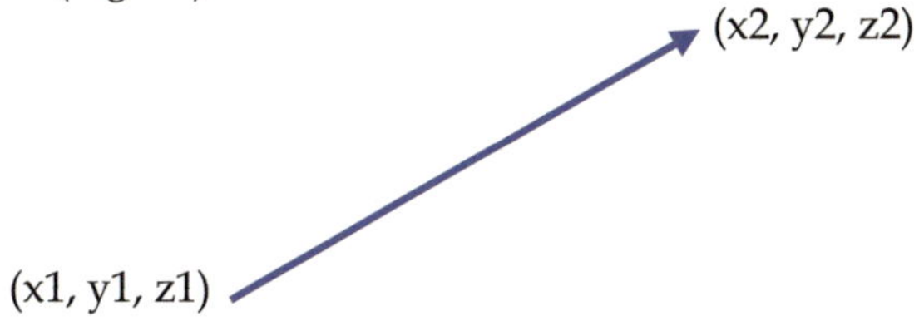

Figure 17. Coordinates specified for line path in performance tests of the robot

Rectangular path: x0, y0 determine coordinates of one corner of the rectangle and a, b are length and width of the rectangle.

r, x0, y0, a, b. (Fig. 18)

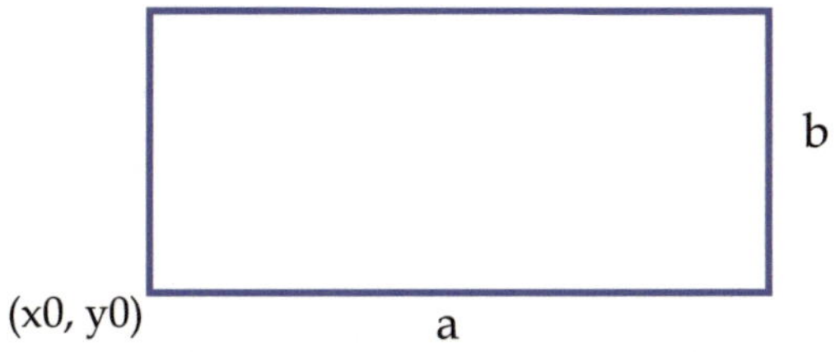

Figure 18. Coordinates specified for rectangular path in performance tests of the robot

For a circular path: x, y is coordinate of center of circular path and r is its radius.

c, x, y, r. (Figure 19-c)

Approach vector direction is normal to direction of paths i.e. wrist is always normal to its path. With pose of end effector and inverse kinematics equations of robot, joint angles will be computed. Joints rotate and end effector will be positioned along its path. Coordinates of end effector in global reference frame is determined by taking pictures with two fixed cameras and trained neural network.

Compute path accuracy and error of the robot by data saved in out_path.txt file.

Problem-5

Test motion of the end effector for given paths as following and draw the traversed paths by the end effector and desired path in one graph to compare them.

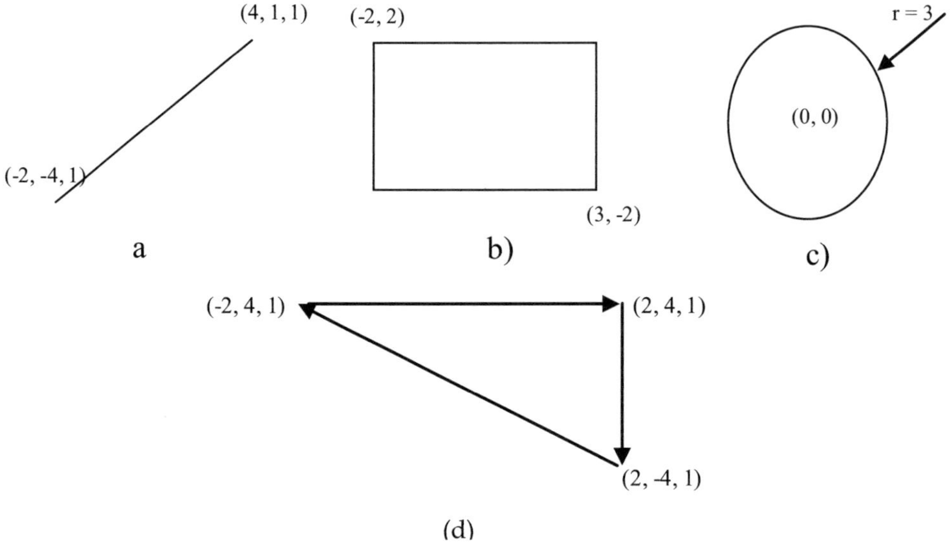

Figure 19. Continuous paths for performance tests of the robot

6. Error analysis of the 6R robot tests

Now we analyze results of previous tests according to different standards and we determine performance parameters and accuracy of 6R robot according to ISO9283 and ANSI/RIA.

6.1 Error analysis according to ISO9283

In this standard some performance parameters of robot to position and path traversing such as pose accuracy and distance accuracy are determined. For direct, inverse kinematics and continuous path tests of the 6R robot results are depicted in Figure 20.

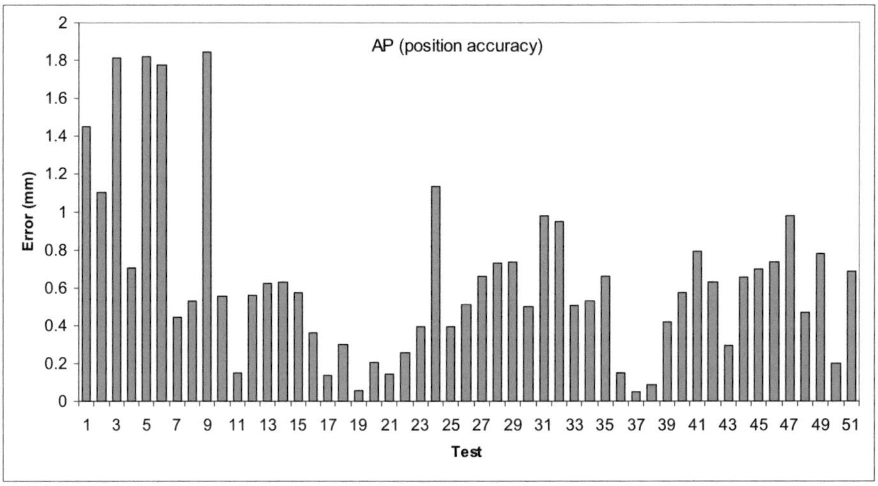

Figure 20. Position accuracy for the 6R robot in direct and inverse kinematics tests

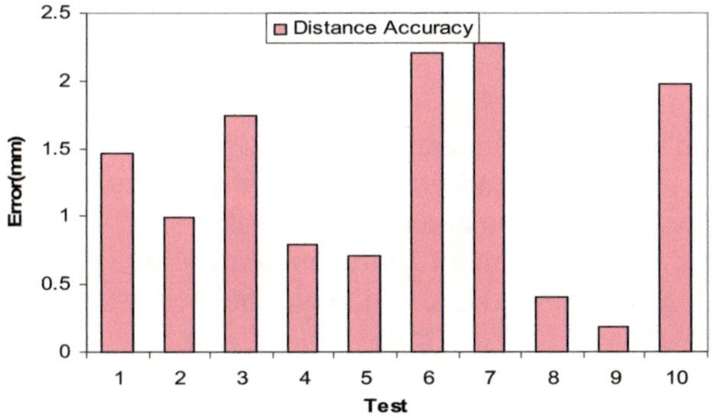

Figure 21. Distance accuracy investigated in positioning tests according to ISO9283

Traversing of the end effector in corners causes sharp changes in velocity so if these changes are high positioning and path accuracy of the robot must be controlled. For that, corners of paths are smoothed and curved to avoid sharp velocity changes. Error and accuracy of robot in traversing corners of paths are specified by cornering round off error (CR) and cornering overshoot parameters that are computed for the 6R robot during its motion in rectangular paths. These results are summarized in Figure 22.

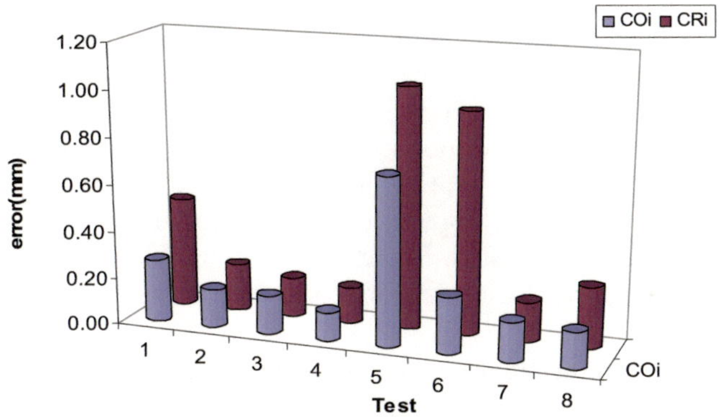

Figure 22. Cornering round off error and cornering overshoot in rectangular path tests according to ISO9283

6.2 Error analysis according to standard ANSI-RIA

Results of simulated tests in previous sections are analyzed with standard ANSI-RIA to compare with results of ISO9283.

TEST	AC	$\overline{AC}$	CR	CO
line	0.67	0.21	-	-
rectangle	0.47	0.09	0.47, 0.20, 0.17, 0.15	1.03, 0.95, 0.17, 0.26
circle	0.48	0.25	-	-

Table 4. Repeatability & cornering overshoot according to ANSI standard

Cornering round off error CR in this standard is defined as the minimum distance between the corner point and any point on the attained path. *Cornering overshoot* CO is defined as the largest deviation outside of the reference path after the robot has passed the corner. For rectangular path test of 6R robot the value of CR and CO are calculated. (Table 4) The tests were repeated 10 times (n = 10). Two cameras, observing the end effector at fixed distance in specified periods, take picture from end effector and its environment. Its coordinates are achieved from image plan with position based visual system.
To transform coordinates of wrist of robot to the reference frame as mentioned before, in this work we have used neural networks. Using neural networks we map coordinates from image plan into reference system, in order to have real distances. Maximum and mean path accuracy FOM and for rectangular path tests corner deviation error (CR) and cornering over shoot (CO) are listed in Table4.

7. Experimental results for performance tests of 6R robot

In this part, experimental results of the visual servo control and performance tests for the 6R robot are presented. To control the robot by vision system, two stationary webcams have been installed on the earth watching the robot and its environment in front and right view. Two webcams are installed in points A(0,-1,0) and B(1,0,0) as in Figure 23. Monitoring is possible through each of cameras. Then images from these two cameras were saved in bmp format and used to train the neural network to find 3D positions of points in reference base coordinate. After image processing and recognition of the end effector, estimating its coordinate in image plane by neural network this coordinate are transformed to global reference coordinate. These performance tests of robot include direct kinematics, and motion of the end effector in continuous paths like circle, rectangle and line. In point to point moving of end effector, each joint angle is determined and robot will move with joints rotation. Two observer cameras take pictures and pose of end effector will be estimated to determine positioning error of robot. Standards such as ISO9283, ANSI-RIA are used to specify the robot error and path accuracy for continuous paths.

7.1 Direct kinematics test of 6R robot (point-to-point motion)

In these tests, position accuracy and repeatability of robot is determined. Amount of rotation for each joint angle of the robot is specified in deg. With rotation of joints, the wrist will move to desired pose. By taking pictures with two stationary cameras and trained neural network, we will have position of end effector in 3D global reference frame. To determine pose error these positions and ideal amounts will be compared. Positioning error in directions x, y, z for 10 series of direct kinematics tests is depicted in Figure 24. Amount of joint angles θi (deg) are defined by user in running program of the robot written by Delphi software. In image processing and object recognition algorithm due to noises and ambient light, there were many noises and deviation from simulation results.

7.2 Continuous path test

Pictures taken by two cameras are saved in bmp format and they are processed through vision algorithm written in VC++. After image processing, objects in pictures are saved separately, features are extracted and target-object and end effector will be recognized among them according to their features and characteristics. Then 3D position coordinates of target-object and end effector are estimated. After each motion of joints, new picture is taken from end effector and this procedure is repeated until end of process. To determine accuracy of robot in traversing continuous paths wrist of robot is guided along different paths. In experimental tests, three standard paths are tested.

a) Direct line

To move end effector along a direct line its start and end must be determined. Approach vector direction is normal to direction of line path i.e. wrist is always normal to its path. With pose of end effector and inverse kinematics equations of robot, joint angles will be computed. Joints rotate and end effector will be positioned along its path. At each step, two stationary cameras take images from robot and its workspace. From these pictures and trained neural network coordinates of the wrist in global reference frame is determined. The positioning error is determined by comparing the ideal pose and actual one. Error of robot in traversing direct line path is shown in Figure 25-a.

b) Circular path

We investigate the accuracy, repeatability and error of robot on the circular continuous path traversing. Circle is in horizontal plane i.e. height of end effector is constant from earth level. Orientation of wrist is so that end effector is always in horizontal plane and normal to circular path and wrist slides along perimeter of circle. In this way sliding, approach and normal vectors are determined and inverse kinematics equations can be solved. During motion of wrist on the path, images have been taken from end effector using two webcams. In this way, end effector coordinates in image plan will be collected. Using neural network, image plan coordinates of points will be transformed to the reference frame. The desired path and actual path traversed by robot is shown in Figure 25-b.

Figure 23. Webcams positions in experimental tests of robot (front and right cameras)

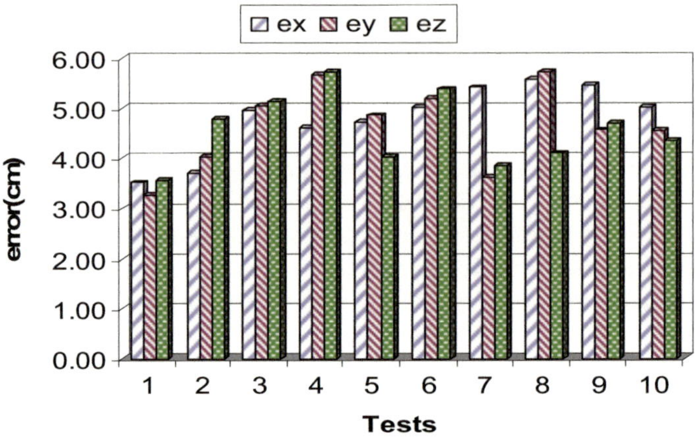

Figure 24. The error schematics in x, y, z directions for direct kinematics tests of the 6R robot

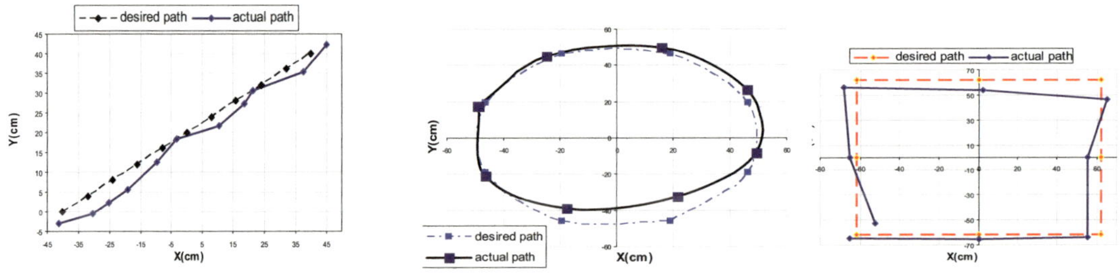

a): line paths b): circular path c): rectangular path

Figure 25. The error investigated in continuous path

c) Rectangular path

Path accuracy for movement of the end effector in rectangular path was also tested. Orientation of end effector is tangent to path. The desired path and actual path for rectangular path have been drawn in Figure 25-c.

8. Collision detection for the 6R robot using spheres

Collision detection or contact determination between two or more objects is important in robotics simulation and other computer simulated environments. Objects in simulated environments are stationary or dynamic. The previous works are mostly restricted to models in static environments. However, some of them concern the more sophisticated algorithms, such as BSP (one of the commonly used tree structure, binary space partitioning tree, to speed up intersection tests in CSG ,constructive solid geometry) (Lin, 1993) for dynamic simulation environments. We have used an efficient simple algorithm for collision detection and contact determination between links of 6R robot undergoing rigid motion. This technique however is a quite simple procedure but it is very useful also can be used for simulated environments with many dynamic objects moving with high speed. The main characteristic of this algorithm is its simplicity and efficiency. It has been implemented on simulation of control and performance tests of 6R robot to avoid contact of different parts of robot with each other and surrounding objects.

Main points in a simulation of collision among objects can be separated into three parts: collision detection, contact area determination, and collision response (Ponamgi et al). In this research, we have considered the first part to prevent penetration of links of the 6R robot in each other during their motion.
To determine whether or not two objects intersect, we must check if distance between their border edges is equal to zero or not. So lower bound for the distance between each pair of objects is equal to zero. In this paper the collision detection technique uses spheres attached to different parts of robot and moved as well as them. These spheres are arranged compactly enough to fit the robot shape so we have used a large number of spheres to do.
In an environment with D moving objects and S stationary objects, number of possible collision for each pair of the objects will be: $\binom{D}{2} + DS$ pairs at every time step. Which determining all of them would be time consuming as D and S are large. By considering the robot geometry and its joints rotations we can determine which pairs of spheres may contact and which pairs may not. So the total number of pairwise collisions will decrease and much time would be saved.
In Figure 26 schematic shape of 6R robot and bounding spheres on different parts of it are shown. Diameter of each sphere is determined according to size of object which is bounded by the sphere.

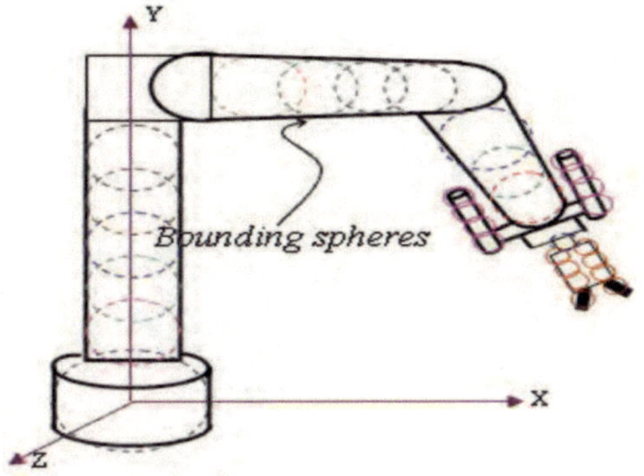

Figure 26. The 6R robot and bounding spheres

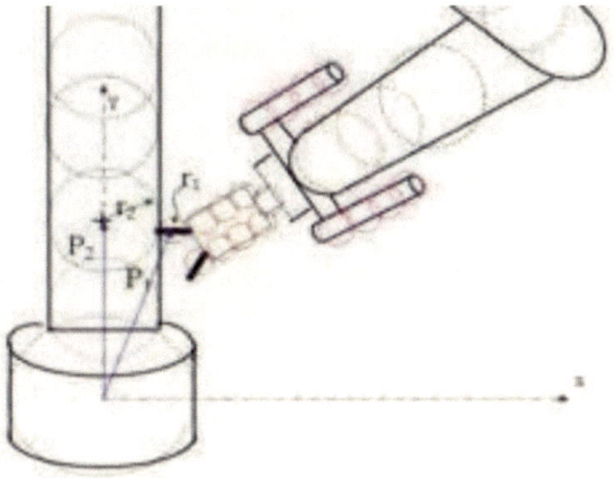

Figure 27. Collision between two spheres in the 6R robot

8.1 Colliding bounding spheres in the 6R robot

To avoid collision among different parts of the 6R robot, links and objects in simulated environment are bounded by small spheres (Figure 26). As joints of robot revolute, the links may collide and penetrate each other. We consider the situation when the tip of end effector collides to the waist of the robot (Figure 27) and find intersection point of two collided spheres. This procedure is the same for each pair of colliding spheres.

The simplest possible way to test collision between two bounding spheres is to measure the squared distance between their centers and to compare the result with the squared sum of their radii.

9. Object recognition algorithm

After taking pictures by two fixed cameras, these images must be processed to determine 3D information of the target-object and the end effector of robot and to estimate their pose in Cartesian global coordinate. So recognition of objects in the visual system is a key task. But the end effector of the 6R robot does not have any especial basic shape so we decided to use a definite color for it and it would be recognized according to its color. Upon this in simulation of the object recognition we used color based algorithm.

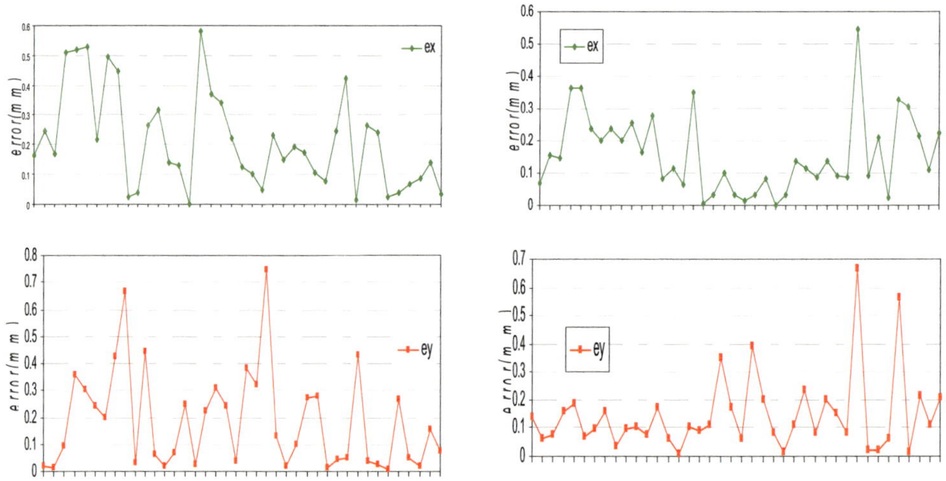

Figure 28. Performance of simulation color based object recognition algorithm to determine pose of (a) the end effector (b) target-object

Object recognition algorithm has two steps: first to assess objects of interest in pictures taken by two cameras and then to provide required information (e.g. pose) about these objects. To do the first step, the model or properties of objects of interest are provided for the vision system. As said before the end effector is not in basic geometric shape and also due to its roll and pitch rotations its dimensions and appearance are not the invariant in two cameras' view each time. So we can not use dimensions or distance set to recognize the end effector. We must identify the image features that are invariant with respect to image scaling, translation and rotation and partially invariant with respect to illumination changes. Also they are minimally affected by noise and small distortions. Lindeberg showed that under some rather general assumptions on scale invariance, the Gaussian kernel and its derivatives are the only possible smoothing kernels for scale space analysis (Low). To achieve rotation invariance and a high level of efficiency, we have defined two special RGB color for the target-object and the end effector of the 6R robot separately. By image processing RGB of each pixel in images are found and if they are the same as RGB of the object of interest, coordinate of those pixels will be saved and the center position of them in two image plane will be determined and then by using neural network we will have 3D coordinates of target-object and the end effector in global reference frame. The results obtained from simulation of color based object recognition algorithm for the end effector and target-object are presented in Figure 28. In these figures error of position estimation of the end effector and target-object in x, y and z directions are shown.

10. Conclusion

In this chapter, both position based and image based approaches were used to simulate control of the 6R robot. The IBVS control approach, uses image features of a target-object from image (sensor) space to compute error signals directly. The error signals are then used to compute the required actuation signals for the robot. The control law is also expressed in the image space. Many researchers in this approach use a mapping function (called the image Jacobian) from the image space to the Cartesian space. The image Jacobian, generally, is a function of the focal length of the lens of the camera, depth (distance between camera (sensor) frame and target features), and the image features. In contrast, the PBVS control constructs the spatial relationship, target pose, between the camera frame and the target-object frame from target image features. Many construction algorithms have been proposed. The advantage of position-based approach is that the servo control structure is independent from the target pose reconstruction. Usually, the desired control values are specified in the Cartesian space, so they are easy to visualize. In position-based approach, target pose will be estimated. But in image based approach 3D pose of the target-object and end effector is not estimated directly but from some structural features extracted from image (e.g., an edge or color of pixels) defined when the camera and end effector reach the target as reference image features, the robot is guided and camera calibrating for visual system is necessary. Test errors have been analyzed by using different standards and MATLAB to compute performance parameters of 6R robot such as accuracy, repeatability, and cornering overshoot. Performance parameters computed according to ANSI and ISO standards are fairly close to each other. Statistical quantities computed by MATLAB also certificate standards analysis. In simulator environment, we have determined collision between two parts of robot by using bounding-spheres algorithm. To improve the accuracy of the collision detection we have used very small bounding spheres, breaking links of robot into several parts and enclosing each of them in a bounding sphere of its own.
Finally simulation results of color based object recognition algorithm used to provide required information (e.g. pose) about target-object and the end effector were presented.

11. References

American National Standard for Industrial Robots and Robot Systems Path-Related and Dynamic Performance Characteristics Evaluation. ANSI/RIA R15.05-2. 2002.

Boyse, J. W. (1979) *Interference detection among solids and surfaces. ACM,* 22(1):3-9.

Cameron S.A. (1985) A study of the clash detection problem in robotics. *Proc. IEEE ICRA*, pages pp. 488-493.

Cameron, S.A. & Culley R. K. (1986) Determining the minimum translational distance between two convex polyhedra. *Proc. IEEE ICRA*, pages pp. 591-596.

Canny, J. (1986) Collision detection for moving polyhedra. *IEEE Trans. PAMI*, 8:pp. 200-209.

Gilbert E. & Foo C.P. (1990) Computing the distance between general convex objects in three dimensional space. *IEEE Trans. Robotics Aut.*, 6(1).

Gilbert, A. Giles, M. Flachs, G. Rogers, R. & Yee, H. (1983). A real time video tracking systems, *IEEE, Trans. Pattern Anal. Mech. Intell.* 2(1), pp. 47 - 56

Hashimoto, H. Kimoto, T. and Ebin, T. (1991). Manipulator control with image based visual servoing, *In Proc. IEEE, Conf. robotics and automation*, pp. 2267 - 2272.

Herzen, B. V. Barr A. H. & Zatz H. R. (1990) Geometric collisions for time dependent parametric surfaces. *ACM Computer Graphics*, 24(4), August. ISO9283, (1998) Manipulating industrial robots performance criteria & related test methods

Kelly, R. Shirkey, P. & Spong, M. (2001). *Fixed camera visual servo control for planar robots.*

Korayem, M. H. Khoshhal, K. and Aliakbarpour, H. (2005) Vision Based Robot Simulation and Experiment for Performance Tests of Robot", *International J. of AMT, Vol.25, No. 11-12*, pp. 1218-1231.

Korayem, M H. Shiehbeiki, N. & Khanali, T. (2006). Design, Manufacturing and Experimental Tests of Prismatic Robot for Assembly Line, *International J. of AMT, Vol.29, No. 3-4*, pp. 379-388.

Lin. M.C. (1993) Efficient Collision Detection for Animation and Robotics. *PhD thesis*, Department of Electrical Engineering and Computer Science, University of CB.

Ponamgi, M.K. Manocha D. and Lin. M.C. *Incremental algorithms for collision detection between solid models*, Department of Computer Science University of N. Carolina

Rives, P. Chaumette, F. & B. Espiau. (1991) Positioning of a robot with respect to an object, tracking it and estimating its velocity by visual servoing. In *Proc. IEEE Int. Conf. Robotics and Automation*, pp 2248-2253.

Saedan M. & Ang M Jr. (2001) 3D Vision-Based Control of an Industrial Robot, *Proceedings of the IASTED Int. Conf. on Robotics and Applications*, Florida, USA, pp. 152-157.

Webber, T & Hollis, R. (1988) *A vision based correlation to activity damp vibrations of a coarse fine manipulator*, Watson research center.

15

Image Magnification based on the Human Visual Processing

Sung-Kwan Je[1], Kwang-Baek Kim[2], Jae-Hyun Cho[3] and Doo-Heon Song[4]
[1]Dept. of Computer Science, Pusan National University
[2]Dept. of Computer Engineering, Silla University
[3]Dept. of Computer Engineering, Catholic University of Pusan
[4]Dept. of Computer Game and Information, Yong-in SongDam College
Korea

1. Introduction

Image magnification is among the basic image processing operations and has many applications in a various area. In recent, multimedia techniques have advanced to provide various multimedia data that were digital images and VOD. It has been rapidly growing into a digital multimedia contents market. In education, many researches have used e-learning techniques. Various equipments - image equipments, CCD camera, digital camera and cellular phone - are used in making multimedia contents. They are now widespread and as a result, computer users can buy them and acquire many digital images as desired. This is why the need to display and print them also increases (Battiato & Mancuso, 2001; Battiato et al., 2002).

However, such various images with optical industry lenses are used to get high-resolution. These lenses are not only expensive but also too big for us to carry. So, they are using the digital zooming method with the lenses to solve the problem. The digital zooming method generally uses the nearest neighbor interpolation method, which is simpler and faster than other methods. But it has drawbacks such as blocking phenomenon when an image is enlarged. Also, to improve the drawbacks, there exist bilinear interpolation method and the cubic convolution interpolation commercially used in the software market. The bilinear method uses the average of 4 neighborhood pixels. It can solve the blocking phenomenon but brings loss of the image like blurring phenomenon when the image is enlarged. Cubic convolution interpolation improved the loss of image like the nearest neighbor interpolation and bilinear interpolation. But it is slow as it uses the offset of 16 neighborhood pixels (Aoyama & Ishii, 1993; Candocia & Principe, 1999; Biancardi et al., 2002).

A number of methods for magnifying images have been proposed to solve such problems. However, proposed methods on magnifying images have the disadvantage that either the sharpness of the edges cannot be preserved or that some highly visible artifacts are produced in the magnified image. Although previous methods show a high performance in special environment, there are still the basic problems left behind. Recently, researches on Human vision processing have been in the rapid progress. In addition, a large number of models for modeling human vision system have been proposed to solve the drawbacks of

machine vision such as object recognition and object detection (Suyung, 2001). In the field of optical neural, many researches have been conducted in relation with physiology or biology to solve the problem of human information processing. Features of biological visual systems at the retinal level serve to motivate the design of electronic sensors. Although commercially available machine vision sensors begin to approach the photoreceptor densities found in primate retinas, they are still outperformed by biological visual systems in terms of dynamic range, and strategies of information processing employed at the sensor level (Shah & Levine, 1993). However, most of the retina models have focused only on the characteristic functions of retina by generalizing the mechanisms, or for researcher's convenience or even by one's intuition. Although such a system is efficient to achieve a specific goal in current environment, it is difficult to analyze and understand the visual scene of a human body. The current visual systems are used in very restricted ways due to the insufficiency of the performance of algorithms and hardware.
Recently, there are many active researches to maximize the performance of computer vision technology and to develop artificial vision through the modeling of human visual processing. Artificial vision is to develop information processing procedures of the human visual system based on the biological characteristics. Compared with the machine vision technology, it can be effectively applied to industry. By investing over 20 billion yen between 1997 and 2016, Japan is conducting research on the areas of machine intelligence, voice recognition and artificial vision based on the information processing mechanism of the brain. By the National Science Foundation (NSF) and the Application of Neural Networks for Industries in Europe (ANNIE), America and Europe are also conducting research on artificial vision, as well as artificial intelligence and voice recognition using the modeling of the brain's information processing (Dobelle, 2000).
This paper presents a method for magnifying images that produces high quality images based on human visual properties which have image reduction on retina cells and information magnification of input image on visual cortex. The rest of this paper is organized as follows. Section 2 presents the properties on human visual system and related works that have proposed for magnifying image. Section 3 presents our method that extracts the edge information using wavelet transform and uses the edge information base on the properties of human visual processing. Section 4 presents the results of the experiment and some concluding remarks are made in Section 5.

2. Related works and human visual processing

2.1 Related works

The simplest way to magnify images is the nearest neighbor interpolation by using the pixel replication and basically making the pixels bigger. It is defined by equation (1). However, the resulting magnified images have a blocking phenomenon (Gonzalez & Richard, 2001).

$$\begin{aligned} &Z(i,j) = I(k,l), \quad 0 \le i, j, \ integer \\ &k \equiv int\left[\frac{i}{2}\right], l = int\left[\frac{j}{2}\right], \ where\ Z(i,j)\, is\ a\ magnified\ image \end{aligned} \tag{1}$$

Other method is the bilinear interpolation, which determines the value of a new pixel based on a weighted average of the 4 pixels in the nearest 2×2 neighbourhood of the pixels in the original image (Gonzalez & Richard, 2001). Therefore this method produces relatively smooth edges with hardly any blocking and is better than the nearest neighbor but appears blurring phenomenon. It is defined as equation (2).

$$\begin{aligned} Z(i,2j) &= I(k,l), \quad Z(i,2j+1) = \tfrac{1}{2}[I(k,l), I(k,l+1)] \\ Z(2i,j) &= I_i(k,l), \quad Z(2i+1,j) = \tfrac{1}{2}[I_i(k,l), I_i(k+1,l)] \end{aligned} \tag{2}$$

More elaborating approach uses cubic convolution interpolation which is more sophisticated and produces smoother edges than the bilinear interpolation. Bicubic interpolation uses a bicubic function using 16 pixels in the nearest 4×4 neighborhood of the pixel in the original image and is defined by equation (3). This method is most commonly used by image editing software, printer drivers and many digital cameras for re-sampling images. Also, Adobe Photoshop offers two variants of the cubic convolution interpolation method: bicubic smoother and bicubic sharper. But this method raises another problem that the processing time is too long due to the computation for the offsets of 16 neighborhood pixels (Keys, 1981).

$$f(x) = \begin{Bmatrix} (a+2)|x|^3 - (a+3)|x|^2 + 1, 0 \le |x| < 1 \\ a|x|^3 - 5a|x|^2 + 8a|x| - 4a, 1 \le |x| < 2 \\ 0, \quad elsewhere \end{Bmatrix} \text{ where a=0, or -1} \tag{3}$$

Recently, research on interpolation images taking into account the edges has gained much attention. (Salisbury et al., 1996) proposed methods that search for edges in the input images and use them to assure that the interpolation does not cross them. The problem is how to define and find the important edged in the input image.

Other edge-adaptive methods have been proposed by (Li & Orchard, 2001). The commercial software Genuine Fractals also used an edge adaptive method to magnify images, but the details of the algorithm are not provided. Currently, the methods presented in (Muresan & Parks, 2004) are the most widely known edge-adaptive methods. They can well enough avid jagged edges, but have limitation that they sometimes introduce highly visible artifacts into the magnified images, especially in areas with small size repetitive patterns (Johan & Nishita, 2004).

In section 3, we will propose an efficient method by image reduction and edge enhancement based on the properties on human visual processing.

2.2 Human visual processing

In the field of computer vision, many researches have been conducted in relation with edge information to solve the problem of magnification. Image information received from retina in Human visual system is not directly transmitted to the cerebrum when we recognize it. This is why there are many cells playing in Human visual system (Bruce, 2002).

First, the visual process begins when visible light enters the eye and forms images on the retina, a thin layer of neurons lining the back of the eye. The retina consists of a number of different types of neurons, including the rod and cone receptors, which transform light energy into electrical energy, and fibers that transmit electrical energy out of the retina in the optic nerve. Second, The signals generated in the receptors trigger electrical signals in the next layer of the retina, the bipolar cells, and these signals are transmitted through the various neurons in the retina, until eventually they are transmitted out of the eye by ganglion cell fibers, These ganglion cell fibers flow out of the back of the eye and become fibers in the optic nerve. Ganglion cells can be mapped into P-cells and M-cells. P-cells contain major information of images on 'what', whereas M-cells contain edge information of images. That is, information related to perceiving 'What' is transmitted to P-cells; and P-cells comprise 80% of total ganglion cells and minimize the loss during transmission. Whereas, information related to 'Where' is sent to M-cells; and M-cells comprise 20% of total ganglion cells (Duncan, 1984)

The biological retina is more than just a simple video camera. It not only converts optical information to electrical signals but performs considerable processing on the visual signal itself before transmitting it to higher levels. Various local adaptation mechanisms extend the retina's dynamic range by several orders of magnitude. In order to meet the transmission bottleneck at the optic nerve, the retina extracts only those features required at later stages of visual information processing (suyung, 2001).

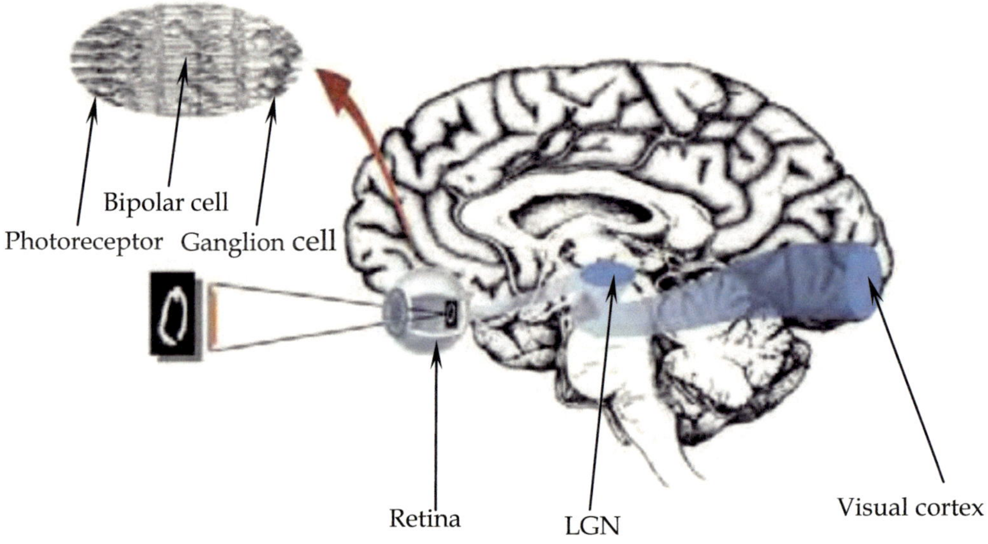

Figure 1. The processing steps of human vision system

Third, most of these optic nerve fibers reach the lateral geniculate nucleus (LGN), the first major way station on the way to the brain. The LGN is a bilateral nucleus, which means that there is an LGN on the left side of the brain, and also one on the right side. Finally, fibers transfer from the LGN to the primary visual receiving area, the striate cortex, or V1 in the occipital lobe. In conclusion, the main properties in human visual processing are as follows:

First, in retinal cells, the large difference between the number of receptors and the number of ganglion cells means that signals from many receptors converge onto each ganglion cell. Second, in visual cortex, this cell responds to the directions such as vertical, horizontal and orthogonal. Finally, the signal from ganglion cells coming from retina in fovea needs more space on the cortex than the signals from retina in periphery. The result is the cortical magnification factor (Bruce, 2002).

We propose the magnification method considering the properties of human visual processing in section 3.

3. Image magnification by the properties of human vision system

Based on the properties of human visual processing discussed in section 2, we now describe a magnification method for improving the performance of conventional image magnification methods.

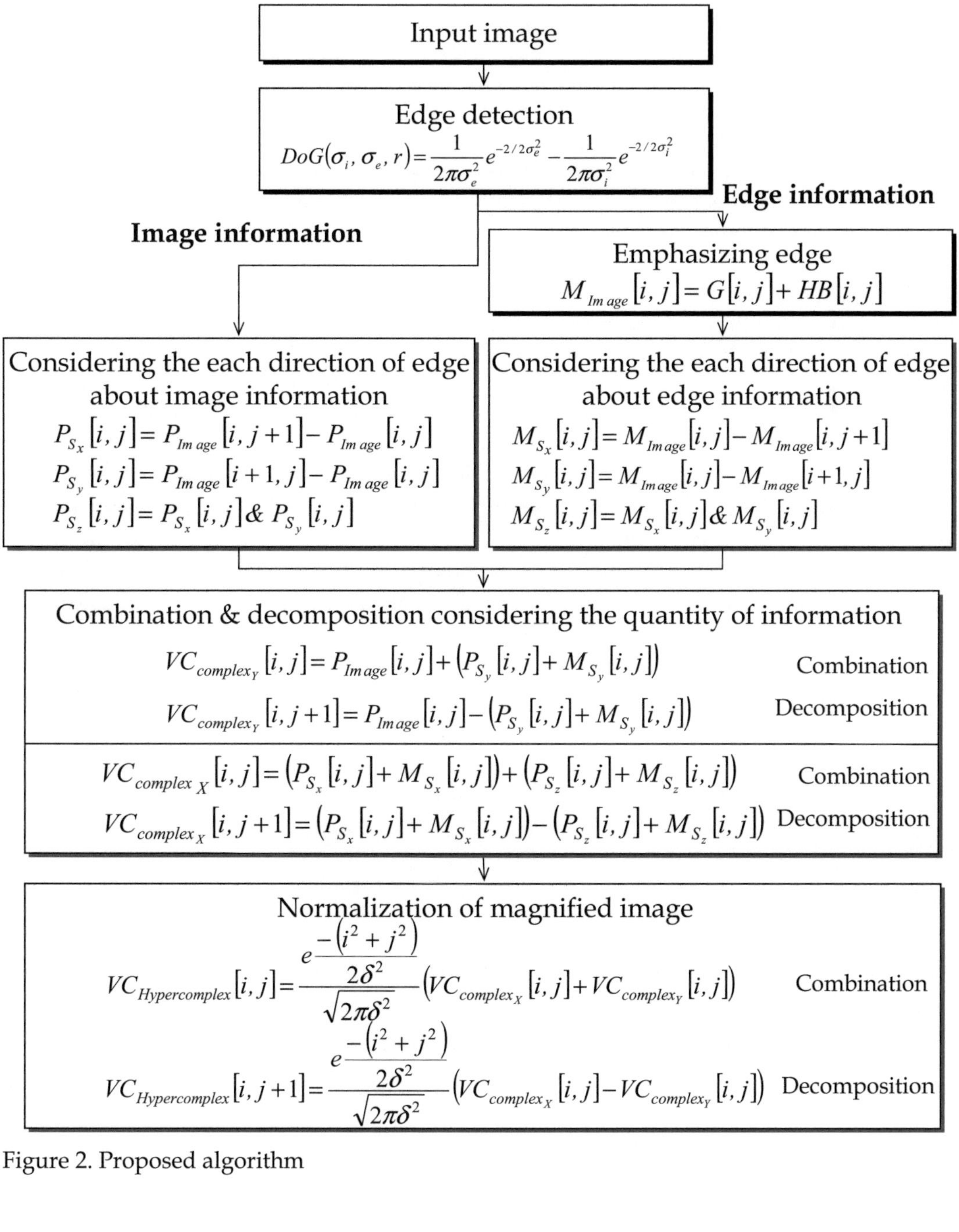

Figure 2. Proposed algorithm

Human vision system does not transfer image information from retina to visual cortex in the brain directly. By the properties of retinal cells, there is the reduction of information when vision information is transferred from receptors to ganglion cells. In addition, the reduced information from retina is transfer to the visual cortex with the magnified information. We proposed the magnification method with these properties. The proposed magnification uses edge information which is not used in interpolation based image processing. In image processing, the interpolated magnified image uses the average or offset of neighborhood pixels. It is not an ideal method since it only uses neighborhood pixels.
The edge information is important to distinguish the background and object. If a pixel were edge information, it wouldn't be able to distinguish the background and object using neighborhood pixels. It was insufficient to detect the edge information. In this paper, we calculated the edge information of a whole image. In order to solve the problem of magnification, the direction of the edge information will be considered. The schematic diagram of the method is shown as Fig. 2.

3.1 Edge Detection

First, we calculated the edge information from the input image. There are many methods in edge detection such as Laplacian operator, Sobel operator and Gaussian operator. In this paper, we calculated the edge information by using the DoG (Difference of two Gaussian) function, which is used in the human vision system. Wilson proposed the model that has been detected the edge information by the simulated results. It was simulated in the retina of the human vision system using the second derivative function $\nabla^2 G$ (LoG, Laplacian of a Gaussian). According to Marr and Hildreth, the DoG function has similar result to $\nabla^2 G$. And it is faster and more effective about the intensity change detection of the image than $\nabla^2 G$ (Dowling, 1987; suyung, 2001). In this paper, by setting the distance from the center as r, in equation (4), one obtains temporal change in the input image by the Gaussian filter.

$$G_e(\sigma_e, r) = \frac{1}{2\pi\sigma_e^2} e^{-r^2/2\sigma_e^2} \tag{4}$$

$$G_i(\sigma_i, r) = \frac{1}{2\pi\sigma_i^2} e^{-r^2/2\sigma_i^2} \tag{5}$$

$$DoG(\sigma_i, \sigma_e, r) = \frac{1}{2\pi\sigma_e^2} e^{-r^2/2\sigma_e^2} - \frac{1}{2\pi\sigma_i^2} e^{-r^2/2\sigma_i^2} \tag{6}$$

Consequently, by setting the excitatory synapsing standard deviation as σ_e, inhibitory synapsing standard deviation as σ_i, excitatory synapsing distribution as $G_e(\sigma_e, r)$, and inhibitory synapsing distribution as $G_i(\sigma_i, r)$, in equation (6), one obtains a symmetrical structure using the DoG function. It was optimal filter to the signal stimulated overlapping each other cells when the Gaussian function's standard deviation ratio is $\sigma_i / \sigma_e = 1.6$. The DoG function has similar result to the cell's reaction in the human vision.

However, it has less edge information than the other second derivative functions (Laplacian operator and Sobel operator) which are used mostly in image processing. In order to solve the problem, we propose an algorithm that emphasizes the image by using contrast regions. The Unsharp mask tool is used to emphasize an image in image processing. However, it causes a loss of the image and that adds the noise to the image and in result, it drastically reduces intensity gradient when the image is sharpened spatial edges, namely, emphasized contrast region. To solve the problem, we added the convoluted high-boost filter and edge information again.

$$M_{Image}[i,j] = G[i,j] + HB[i,j]$$

where,

$$HB = -\frac{\alpha}{9}\begin{bmatrix} 1 & 1 & 1 \\ 1 & w/\alpha & 1 \\ 1 & 1 & 1 \end{bmatrix} \qquad (7)$$

$$w = 9\alpha - 1$$

HB is a high-boost filter. It sharpened the image and added to $G[i,j]$. By setting $w = 9\alpha - 1$, in equation (7), one obtains the enhanced edge information $(M_{Image}[i,j])$. The proposed method improves sensitivity to detect the edge of an object.

3.2 Magnification using Combination & Decomposition

In the field of computer vision, many researches have been conducted in relation with edge information to solve the problem of magnification. The edge information was composed of through high frequencies. Accordingly, it is important to restore the high frequency in magnification to solve the problem like blurring phenomenon. In image processing, a possible solution is edge detection that uses the second derivation function. But, it causes a loss of image by the error of edge information. It is the zero crossing in edge detection that detects edge gradients (Schultz & Stevenson, 1994; Gonzalez & Richard, 2001). We proposed the magnification algorithm that considered the direction of edge. To solve the problem like the error of edge information, we calculated each direction (horizontal, vertical and diagonal) to the input image and calculated the edge information. We used the difference operation which is the simplest and fastest operation in edge detection using gradient function. In equation (8), we calculated the horizontal and vertical direction by using the difference operation that calculated the increment of the input image $(i+1)$. It is the difference in pixel brightness to the neighborhood pixel, namely, which calculated the gradient.

$$P_{S_y}[i,j] = P_{Image}[i+1,j] - P_{Image}[i,j] \qquad (8)$$

$$P_{S_x}[i,j] = P_{Image}[i,j+1] - P_{Image}[i,j] \qquad (9)$$

By setting the input image to P_{Image}, in equation (8), one obtains the vertical direction of input image P_{S_y}. In the same way, in equation (9), one obtains the horizontal direction of the input image P_{S_x} where i and j are the vertical and horizontal index of image.

The diagonal direction uses the vertical direction and horizontal direction. By setting the diagonal direction to P_{S_z}, in equation (10), one calculates the AND operation to the vertical direction and horizontal direction.

$$P_{S_z}[i,j] = P_{S_x}[i,j] \,\&\, P_{S_y}[i,j] \tag{10}$$

Information on the vertical, horizontal and diagonal direction of the input image was calculated through the use of equation (8), (9) and (10). In the same way, information on the vertical, horizontal and diagonal direction of the detected edge information was calculated by using equation (11).

$$\begin{aligned} M_{S_y}[i,j] &= M_{Image}[i,j] - M_{Image}[i+1,j] \\ M_{S_x}[i,j] &= M_{Image}[i,j] - M_{Image}[i,j+1] \\ M_{S_z}[i,j] &= M_{S_x}[i,j] \,\&\, M_{S_y}[i,j] \end{aligned} \tag{11}$$

In equation (11), M_{Image} is the detected edge information, M_{S_y} is the vertical direction in the detected edge information, M_{S_x} is the horizontal direction, and M_{S_z} is the diagonal direction.

Thus, we calculated 7 pieces of information collected from the input image. They were the detected edge information, vertical, horizontal, diagonal direction of input image and vertical, horizontal, diagonal direction of the detected edge information. They all have a position, direction and edge information. However, they have different quantities of information in regards to the edge. It holds different quantities of information for the vertical direction of the input image and detected edge information. The difference in the quantity of information in the vertical and horizontal direction is due to the edge. By equation (8), the detected edge information was an error on the left hand side of the ideal detecting edge information by the difference operation. In the same way, by equation (11), the detected edge information has an error on the right hand side of the ideal detecting edge information by the difference operation. To solve this problem, we calculated the ADD operation to the same direction of the detected edge information. And we processed the combination and decomposition considering the quantity of image information (pixel intensity) and edge information in each direction, the input image and 7 pieces of information. Therefore, most of the information contained is made up of the input image, the vertical direction of input image and the vertical direction of the detected edge information.

By setting, the larger quantity of image information and direction as $VC_{complex_y}$ and the smaller quantity of image information and direction as $VC_{complex_x}$, we can process the combination and decomposition in equation (12).

$$\begin{aligned} VC_{complex_y}[i,j] &= P_{Image}[i,j] + \left(P_{s_y}[i,j] + M_{s_y}[i,j]\right) \\ VC_{complex_y}[i,j+1] &= P_{Image}[i,j] - \left(P_{s_y}[i,j] + M_{s_y}[i,j]\right) \end{aligned} \tag{12}$$

By setting, the input image as P_{Image}, the vertical direction of the input image as P_{S_y}, and the vertical direction of the detected edge information as M_{S_y}, one obtains a large quantity of image information and direction. This is known as $VC_{complex_y}$. The $VC_{complex_y}$ is a combination of the input image and the vertical direction that is added to the vertical direction of the input image and the detected edge information. When the combination of the larger quantity of images is created, we process the ADD operation. In the same way, when there is a decomposition of the smaller quantity of images, we process the difference operation. Accordingly, we emphasized the edge information by using the ADD and difference operation for the combination and decomposition.

First, we calculated the ADD operation to the same direction of the input image and the calculated edge information. The $VC_{complex_x}$ was a combination of the larger quantity of images which was in the horizontal direction and this was added to the horizontal direction of the input image and the calculated edge information. When there is a combination of the larger quantity of images, we use the ADD operation.

$$\begin{aligned} VC_{complex_x}[i,j] &= \left(P_{s_x}[i,j] + M_{s_x}[i,j]\right) + \left(P_{s_z}[i,j] + M_{s_z}[i,j]\right) \\ VC_{complex_x}[i,j+1] &= \left(P_{s_x}[i,j] + M_{s_x}[i,j]\right) - \left(P_{s_z}[i,j] + M_{s_z}[i,j]\right) \end{aligned} \tag{13}$$

By setting, the horizontal direction of the input image as P_{S_x}, the diagonal direction of the input image as P_{S_z}, the horizontal direction of the detected edge information as M_{S_x} and the diagonal direction of the detected edge information as M_{S_z}, in equation (13), one obtains a smaller quantity of image information and its direction is $VC_{complex_x}$. The $VC_{complex_x}$ is a combination of the horizontal and diagonal direction that was added to the horizontal and diagonal direction of the input image and the detected edge information. In the same way as equation (12), when it is a decomposition of the smaller quantity of images, we process the difference operation. Likewise, we emphasized the edge information by using the ADD and difference operation for the combination and decomposition. We were able obtain the magnified image by using the combination and decomposition to solve the problem of loss of high frequencies. But the magnified image has too much information on high frequencies in the $VC_{complex_y}$ and $VC_{complex_x}$. To reduce the risk of error of edge information in high frequencies, we processed the normalizing operation by using the Gaussian operator. The Gaussian operator is usually used in analyzing brain waves in visual cortex. And once a suitable mask has been calculated, and then the Gaussian smoothing can be performed using standard convolution methods.

$$VC_{hpercomplex}[i,j]=\frac{e^{\frac{-(i^2+j^2)}{2\delta^2}}}{\sqrt{2\pi\delta^2}}\left(VC_{comptex_x}[i,j]+VC_{comptex_y}[i,j]\right)$$
$$VC_{hpercomplex}[i,j+1]=\frac{e^{\frac{-(i^2+j^2)}{2\delta^2}}}{\sqrt{2\pi\delta^2}}\left(VC_{comptex_x}[i,j]-VC_{comptex_y}[i,j]\right) \tag{14}$$

By setting, the average of input image as δ, the Gaussian operator as $\frac{e^{\frac{-(i^2+j^2)}{2\delta^2}}}{\sqrt{2\pi\delta^2}}$, thus one can obtain the magnified image $VC_{complex_x}$.

In summary, first, we calculated edge information by using the DoG function and emphasized the contrast region by using the enhanced Unsharp mask. We calculated each direction of the input image and edge information to reduce the risk of error in the edge information. To evaluate the performance of the proposed algorithm, we compared it with the previous algorithm that was nearest neighborhood interpolation, bilinear interpolation and cubic convolution interpolation.

4. Experimental results

We used the Matlab 6.5 in a Pentium 2.4GHz, with 512MB memory, in a Windows XP environment and simulated the computational retina model based on the human visual information processing that is proposed in this paper. We used the SIPI Image Database and HIPR packages which is used regularly in other papers on image processing. SIPI is an organized research unit within the School of Engineering founded in 1971 that serves as a focus for broad fundamental research in signal and image processing techniques at USC. It has studied in all aspects of signal and image processing and serviced to available SIPI Image Database, SIPI technical reports and various image processing services. The HIPR (Hypermedia Image Processing Reference) serviced a new source of on-line assistance for users of image processing. The HIPR package contains a large number of images which can be used as a general purpose image library for image processing experiments. It was developed at the Department of Artificial Intelligence in the University of Edinburgh in order to provide a set of computer-based tutorial materials for use in taught courses on image processing and machine vision. In this paper, we proposed the magnification by using edge information to solve the loss of image problem like the blocking and blurring phenomenon when the image is enlarged in image processing. In performance, the human vision decision is the best. However, it is subjective decision in evaluating the algorithm. We calculate the PSNR and correlation to be decided objectively between the original image and the magnified image compared with other algorithms.

First, we calculated the processing time taken for the 256×256 sized of the Lena image to become enlarged to a 512×512 size. In Fig. 3, the nearest neighborhood interpolation is very fast in processing time (0.145s), but it loses parts of the image due to the blocking phenomenon. The bilinear interpolation is relatively fast in the processing time (0.307s), but it also loses parts of the image due to the blurring phenomenon. The cubic convolution interpolation does not have any loss of image by the blocking and blurring phenomenon, but is too slow in the processing time (0.680) because it uses 16 neighborhood pixels. The proposed algorithm solved the problem of image loss and was faster than the cubic convolution interpolation in the processing time (0.436s).

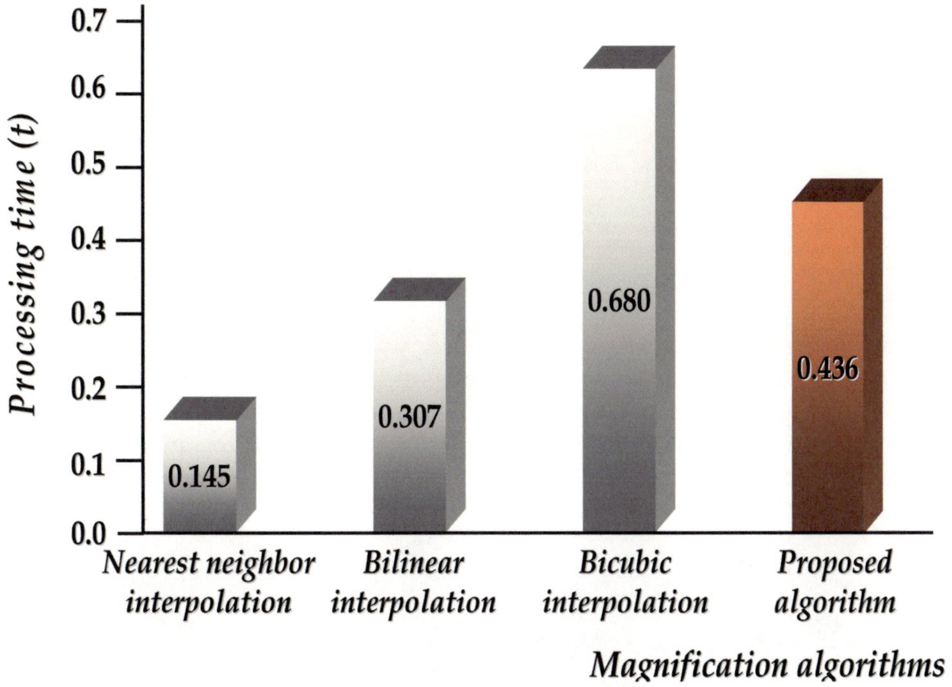

Figure 3. Comparison of the processing time of each algorithm

To evaluate the performance in human vision, Fig. 4, shows a reducion of 512×512 sized Lena image to a 256×256 sized by averaging 3×3 windows. This reduction is followed by an enlargement to the 512×512 sized image through the usage of each algorithm. We enlarged the central part of the image 8 times to evaluate vision performance. In Fig. 4, we can find the blocking phenomenon within vision in the nearest neighborhood interpolation (b). And we can also find the blurring phenomenon within vision in the bilinear interpolation(c). The proposed algorithm has a better resolution than the cubic convolution interpolation in Fig. 4(d, e).

We calculated the PSNR for objective decision. By setting the original image as X, and the magnified image as X^*, in equation (15), one obtains the PSNR.

$$PSNR = 20\,log_{10}\frac{255^2}{MSE}$$
$$MSE = \frac{1}{N}\frac{1}{M}\sum_{i=0}^{N-1}\sum_{j=0}^{M-1}\left(X(i,j) - X^*(i,j)\right)^2 \tag{15}$$

The MSE is a mean square error between the original image and the magnified image. Generally, the PSNR value is 20~40db, but the difference can not be found between the cubic convolution interpolation and the proposed algorithm in human vision. In table 1, there exist difference between two algorithms. The bilinear interpolation has a loss of image due to the blurring phenomenon, but the PSNR value is 29.92. This is better than the cubic convolution interpolation which has a value of 29.86. This is due to the reduction taken place by the averaging method which is similar to the bilinear interpolation. We can conclude from the table 1 that the proposed algorithm is better than any other algorithm as the PSNR value is 31.35.

$$X = X - Average(X)$$
$$X^* = X^* - Average(X^*) \tag{16}$$
$$Cross-correlation(X, X^*) = \frac{\sum_{i=0}^{n} X_i \sum_{i=0}^{n} X_i^*}{\sqrt{\sum_{i=0}^{n} X_i^2}\sqrt{\sum_{i=0}^{n} X_i^{*2}}}$$

To evaluate objectively in another performance, we calculated the cross-correlation in equation (16). In table 1, the bilinear interpolation is better than the cubic convolution interpolation in regards to the PSNR value. It also has similar results in cross-correlation. This is because we reduced it by using the averaging method and this method is similar to the bilinear interpolation. Thus we can conclude that the proposed algorithm is better than any other algorithm since the cross-correlation is 0.990109.

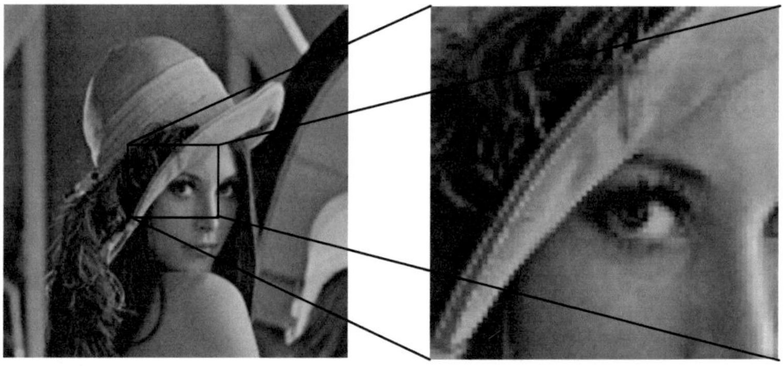

(a) 512×512 sized image (b) nearest neighborhood interpolation

(c) bilinear interpolation (d) cubic convolution interpolation (e) proposed algorithm

Figure 4. Comparison of human vision of each algorithm

Evaluation performance / Magnification method	PSNR(db)	Cross-correlation
Nearest neighborhood interpolation	19.54	0.978983
Bilinear interpolation	29.92	0.985436
Cubic convolution interpolation	29.86	0.985248
Proposed algorithm	31.35	0.990109

Table 1. Comparison of Evaluation performance of each algorithm by averaging 3×3 windows

Performance / Magnification method	PSNR(db)	Cross-correlation
Nearest neighbor interpolation	29.86	0.987359
Bilinear interpolation	30.72	0.989846
Cubic convolution interpolation	31.27	0.991336
Proposed algorithm	31.67	0.991363

Table 2. Comparison of Evaluation performance of each algorithm by the mean of a 3×3 window

Standard images / Magnification method	Baboon	Peppers	Aerial	Airplane	Boat
Nearest neighbor interpolation	20.38	26.79	22.62	32.55	25.50
Bilinear interpolation	23.00	31.10.	25.46	33.44	25.50
Cubic convolution interpolation	23.64	31.93	26.64	33.72	29.39
Proposed algorithm	23.81	32.04	27.65	34.52	30.27

Table 3. Comparison of the PSNR of our method and general methods in several images

In Table 2, we reduced the image by the mean of 3×3 windows to evaluate objectively in another performance. And then, we enlarged to a 512×512 sized image by using each algorithm. We calculated the PSNR and cross-correlation again. The bilinear interpolation's PSNR value is 30.72, and the cubic convolution interpolation's PSNR value is 31.27. Thus, the cubic convolution interpolation is better than the bilinear interpolation. The proposed algorithm is better than any other algorithm in that the PSNR and cross-correlation can be obtained by using reduction through averaging and reduction by the mean. The proposed algorithm uses edge information to solve the problem of image loss. In result, it is faster and has higher resolution than cubic convolution interpolation. Thus, we tested other images (Baboon, Pepper, Aerial, Airplane, and Barbara) by the cross-correlation and PSNR in Table 3 and 4. Table 3 and 4 show that the proposed algorithm is better than any other methods in PNSR and Correlation on other images.

Standard images / Magnification method	Baboon	Peppers	Aerial	Airplane	Boat
Nearest neighbor interpolation	0.834635	0.976500	0.885775	0.966545	0.857975
Bilinear interpolation	0.905645	0.991354	0.940814	0.973788	0.977980
Cubic convolution interpolation	0.918702	0.992803	0.954027	0.975561	0.982747
Proposed algorithm	0.921496	0.993167	0.963795	0.976768	0.986024

Table 4. Comparison of the correlation value of our method and general methods in several images

5. Conclusions

In image processing, the interpolated magnification method brings about the problem of image loss such as the blocking and blurring phenomenon when the image is enlarged. In this paper, we proposed the magnification method considering the properties of human visual processing to solve such problems. As a result, our method is faster than any other algorithm that is capable of removing the blocking and blurring phenomenon when the image is enlarged. The cubic convolution interpolation in image processing can obtain a high-resolution image when the image is enlarged. But the processing is too slow as it uses the average of 16 neighbor pixels. The proposed algorithm is better than the cubic convolution interpolation in the processing time and performance. In the future, to reduce the error ratio, we will enhance the normalization filter which has reduced the blurring phenomenon because the Gaussian filter is a low pass one.

6. References

Battiato, S. and Mancuso, M. (2001) An introduction to the digital still camera Technology, *ST Journal of System Research, Special Issue on Image Processing for Digital Still Camera*, Vol. 2, No.2

Battiato, S., Gallo, G. and Stanco, F. (2002) A Locally Adaptive Zooming Algorithm for Digital Images, *Image and Vision Computing*, Elsevier Science B.V., Vol. 20, pp. 805-812, 0262-8856

Aoyama, K. and Ishii, R. (1993) Image magnification by using Spectrum Extrapolation, *IEEE Proceedings of the IECON*, Vol. 3, pp. 2266 -2271, 0-7803-0891-3, Maui, HI, USA, Nov. 1993, IEEE

Candocia, F. M. and Principe, J. C. (1999) Superresolution of Images based on Local Correlations, *IEEE Transactions on Neural Networks*, Vol. 10, No. 2, pp. 372-380, 1045-9227

Biancardi, A., Cinque, L. and Lombardi, L. (2002) Improvements to Image Magnification, *Pattern Recognition*, Elsevier Science B.V., Vol. 35, No. 3, pp. 677-687, 0031-3203

Suyung, L. (2001) A study on Artificial vision and hearing based on brain information processing, *BSRC Research Report:* 98-J04-01-01-A-01, KAIST, Korea

Shah, S. and Levine, M. D. (1993) Visual Information Processing in Primate Retinal Cone Pathways: A Model, *IEEE Transactions on Systems, Man and Cybernetics*, Part B, Vol. 26, Issue. 2, pp. 259-274, 1083-4419

Shah, S. and Levine, M. D. (1993) Visual Information Processing in Primate Retina: Experiments and results, *IEEE Transactions on Systems, Man and Cybernetics*, Part B, Vol. 26, Issue. 2, pp. 275-289, 1083-4419

Dobelle, W. H. (2000) Artificial Vision for the Blind by Connecting a Television Camera to the Visual Cortex, *ASAIO journal*, Vol. 46, No. 1, pp. 3-9, 1058-2916

Gonzalez, R. C., and Richard E. W. (2001) *Digital Image Processing*, Second edition, Prentice Hall, 0201180758

Keys, R. G. (1981) Cubic Convolution Interpolation for Digital Image Processing, *IEEE Transaction on Acoustics, Speech, and Signal Processing*, Vol. 29, No. 6, pp. 1153-1160, 0096-3518

Salisbury, M., Anderson, C., Lischinski, D., and Salesin, D. H. (1996) Scale-dependent reproduction of pen-and ink illustration, In *Proceedings of SIFFRAPH 96*, pp. 461-468, 0-89791-746-4, ACM Press, New York, NY, USA

Li, X., and Orchard, M. T. (2001) New edge-directed interpolation, *IEEE Transactions on Image Processing*, Vol. 10, Issue. 10, pp. 1521-1527, 1057-7149

Muresan, D. D., and Parks, T. W. (2004) Adaptively quadratic image interpolation, *IEEE Transaction on Image Processing*, Vol. 13, Issue. 5, pp. 690-698, 1057-7149

Johan, H., and Nishita, T. (2004) A Progressive Refinement Approach for Image Magnification, In *Proceedings of the 12th Pacific Conference on Computer Graphics and Applications*, pp. 351-360, 1550-4085

Bruce, G. E. (2002) *Sensation and Perception, Sixth edition*, Wadsworth Pub Co., 0534639917

Duncan, J. (1975) Selective Attention and the Organization of Visual Information, *Journal of Experimental Psychology*: General, American Psychological Assn., Vol.113, pp. 501-517, 0096-3445

Bernardino, A. (2004) Binocular Head Control with Forveal Vision: Methods and Applications, *Ph.D in Robot Vision*, Dept. of Electrical and Computer Engineering, Instituto Superior Técnico, PORTUGAL

Dowling, J.E. (1987) *The Retina: An Approachable Part of the Brain*, Belknap Press of Harvard University Press, Cambridge, MA, 0-674-76680-6

Hildreth, E. C. (1980) A Theory of Edge Detection, *Technical Report:* AITR-579, Massachusetts Institute of Technology Cambridge, MA, USA

Schultz, R. R. and Stevenson, R. L. (1994) A Bayesian Approach to Image Expansion for Improved Definition, *IEEE Transaction of Image Processing*, Vol. 3, No. 3, pp. 233-242, 1057-7149

Shapiro, J. M. (1993) Embedded Image coding using zerotrees of wavelet coefficients, *IEEE Trans. on Signal Processing*, Vol. 41, No. 12, pp. 3445-3462, Dec., 3445-3462

The HIPR Image Library, http://homepages.inf.ed.ac.uk/rbf/HIPR2/

The USE-SIPI Image Database, http://sipi.usc.edu/services/database

16

Methods of the Definition Analysis of Fine Details of Images

S.V. Sai
Pacific national university
Russia

1. Introduction

Definition is one of the most important parameters of the color image quality and is determined by the resolution of channel brightness and chromaticity. System resolution is traditionally determined by a number of the television lines, calculated on the maximal spatial frequency value at which threshold contrast of the reproduced image is provided. Traditional methods of definition analysis are developed for standard analog color TV systems. Specific kind of distortions in digital vision systems is associated with the restrictions imposed by a particular compression algorithm, used for handling static and dynamic images.

Such distortions may lead to an inconsistency between a subjective estimate of the decoded image quality and the program estimate based on the standard calculation methods.

Till now, the most reliable way of image quality estimation is the method of subjective estimation which allows estimating serviceability of a vision system on the basis of visual perception of the decoded image. Procedures of subjective estimation demand great amount of tests and a lot of time. In practice, this method is quite laborious and restricts making control, tuning and optimization of the codec parameters.

The most frequently used root-mean-square criterion (RMS) for the analysis of static image quality does not always correspond to the subjective estimation of fine details definition, since a human vision system processes an image on local characteristic features, rather than averaging it elementwise. In particular, RMS criterion can give "good" quality estimations in vision systems even at disappearance of fine details in low contrast image after a digital compression.

A number of leading firms suggest hardware and software for the objective analysis of dynamic image quality of MPEG standard (Glasman, 2004). For example Tektronix PQA 300 analyzer; Snell & Wilcox Mosalina software; Pixelmetrix DVStation device. Principles of image quality estimation in these devices are various.

For example, PQA 300 analyzer measures image quality on algorithm of "Just Noticeable Difference - JND", developed by Sarnoff Corporation. PQA 300 analyzer carries out a series of measurements for each test sequence of images and forms common PQR estimation on the basis of JND measurements which is close to subjective estimations.

To make objective analysis of image quality Snell & Wilcox firm offers a PAR method – Picture Appraisal Rating. PAR technology systems control artifacts created by compression

under MPEG-2 standard. The Pixelmetrix analyzer estimates a series of images and determines definition and visibility errors of block structure and PSNR in brightness and chromaticity signals.
The review of objective methods of measurements shows that high contrast images are usually used in test tables, while distortions of fine details with low contrast, which are most common after a digital compression, are not taken into account.
Thus, nowadays there is no uniform and reliable technology of definition estimation of image fine details in digital vision systems.
In this chapter new methods of the definition analysis of image fine details are offered. Mathematical models and criteria of definition estimation in three-dimensional color space are given. The description of test tables for static and dynamic images is submitted. The influence of noise on the results of estimations is investigated. The investigation results and recommendations on high definition adjustment in vision systems using JPEG, JPEG-2000 and MPEG-4 algorithms are given.

2. Image Definition Estimation Criteria in Three-Dimensional Color Space

The main difficulty in the objective criterion development is in the fact that threshold vision contrast is represented as a function of many parameters (Pratt, 2001). In particular, while analyzing the determined image definition, threshold contrast of fine details distinctive with an eye is represented as a function of the following parameters:

$$K_{th} = F(\alpha, t, C_o, C_b, \overline{\sigma})$$

where α is the object angular size, t is the object presentation time, C_o is the object color coordinates; C_b is the background color coordinates, $\overline{\sigma}$ is the root-mean-square value of noise.
Solving the task it was necessary first to find such metric space where single changes of signals would correspond to thresholds of visual recognition throughout the whole color space, both for static, and for dynamic fine details.
One of the most widespread ways of color difference estimation of large details of static images is transformation of RGB space in equal contrast space where the area of dispersion of color coordinates transforms from ellipsoid to sphere with the fixed radius for the whole color space (Krivosheev & Kustarev, 1990).
In this case the threshold size is equal to minimum perceptible color difference (MPCD) and keeps constant value independently of the object color coordinates.
The color error in equal color space, for example, in ICI 1964 system (Wyszecki, 1975) is determined by the size of a radius - vector in coordinates system and is estimated by the number of MPCD

$$\varepsilon = 3\sqrt{(W_o^* - \widetilde{W}_o^*)^2 + (U_o^* - \widetilde{U}_o^*)^2 + (V_o^* - \widetilde{V}_o^*)^2} \quad (1)$$

where W_o^*, U_o^*, V_o^* is the color coordinates of a large object in a test image and $\widetilde{W}_o^*, \widetilde{U}_o^*, \widetilde{V}_o^*$ is the color coordinates in a decoded image; $W^* = 25\, Y^{1/3} - 17$ is the brightness index; $U^* = 13 W^* (u - u_o)$ and $V^* = 13 W^* (v - v_o)$ is the chromaticity indexes; u and v is the

chromaticity coordinates in D. Mac-Adam diagram (Mac Adam, 1974); u_o = 0,201 and v_o = 0,307 is the chromaticity coordinates of basic white color.
When comparing color fields located in "window" on a neutral background one can notice, that color differences (1) are invisible at $\varepsilon \leq 2...3$ (MPCD) for the whole color space which is explained by the properties of equal color spaces (Novakovsky, 1988).
Color difference thresholds will increase with the reduction of objects sizes and will depend on the observable color. That is explained by the properties of visual perception. That's why equal color spaces practically are not used for the analysis of color transfer distortions of fine details since the property of equal spaces is lost.
As a result of the researches, the author (Sai, 2002) offers and realizes a method of updating (normalization) of equal space systems which are aimed to be used both for the analysis of large details distortions and for estimation of transfer accuracy of fine color details. Equal color space normalization consists in the following.
Determine color difference between two details of the image in size of a radius - vector

$$\Delta E = 3\sqrt{(W_1^* - W_2^*)^2 + (V_1^* - V_2^*)^2 + (U_1^* - U_2^*)^2}\,, \tag{2}$$

where $W_1^* U_1^* V_1^*$ is the color coordinates of the 1-st object; $W_2^* U_2^* V_2^*$ is the color coordinates of the 2-nd object.
As against (1), equation (2) determines color difference between objects of one image, instead of between objects of images "before" and "after" digital processing.
If one of the objects is background, color contrast "object - background" is determined as follows:

$$\Delta E = 3\sqrt{(W_o^* - W_b^*)^2 + (V_o^* - V_b^*)^2 + (U_o^* - U_b^*)^2} \tag{3}$$

or in difference coordinates:

$$\Delta E = \sqrt{(\Delta W^*)^2 + (\Delta U^*)^2 + (\Delta V^*)^2}\,, \tag{4}$$

where $\Delta W^* = 3(W_o^* - W_b^*)$, $\Delta U^* = 3(U_o^* - U_b^*)$, $\Delta V^* = 3(V_o^* - V_b^*)$ is the difference values (MPCD) according to brightness and chromaticity indexes; $W_o^* U_o^* V_o^*$ is the object color coordinates; $W_b^* U_b^* V_b^*$ is the background color coordinates.
Assume, that the large detail of the image is recognized with an eye under the following condition:

$$\Delta E \geq \Delta E_{th}\,, \tag{5}$$

where ΔE_{th} = 2…3 (MPCD) is the threshold contrast which keeps constant value within the limits of the whole color space.
Further, we shall substitute (4) in (5) and convert to the following:

$$\sqrt{\left(\frac{\Delta W^*}{\Delta E_{th}}\right)^2 + \left(\frac{\Delta U^*}{\Delta E_{th}}\right)^2 + \left(\frac{\Delta V^*}{\Delta E_{th}}\right)^2} \geq 1 \tag{6}$$

The contrast sensitivity of human vision is reduced with the reduction of details sizes and threshold value (ΔE_{th}) becomes dependent on the object size (α), both in brightness, and chromaticity. Thus the criterion of fine details difference is defined as

$$\sqrt{\left(\frac{\Delta W^*}{\Delta W^*_{th}(\alpha)}\right)^2 + \left(\frac{\Delta U^*}{\Delta U^*_{th}(\alpha)}\right)^2 + \left(\frac{\Delta V^*}{\Delta V^*_{th}(\alpha)}\right)^2} \geq 1 \qquad (7)$$

where ΔW^*_{th}, ΔU^*_{th} and ΔV^*_{th} is the threshold values according to brightness and chromaticity indexes which usually depend on color background coordinates, time of object presentation and noise level.

Write (7) in the following way:

$$\sqrt{(\Delta \overline{W}^*)^2 + (\Delta \overline{U}^*)^2 + (\Delta \overline{V}^*)^2} \geq 1 \qquad (8)$$

where $\Delta \overline{W}^* = \Delta W^* / \Delta W^*_{th}$, $\Delta \overline{U}^* = \Delta U^* / \Delta U^*_{th}$ and $\Delta \overline{V}^* = \Delta V^* / \Delta V^*_{th}$ is the normalized values of object - background contrast. Provided condition (8) is true, color difference between object and background is visible with an eye, hence fine details are perceptible.

Thus, transition from equal space into normalized equal space allows on the basis of criterion (8) to estimate objectively color difference of both large and fine details under preset conditions of color image supervision.

In vision systems where the receiver of the decoded images is the automatic device, and vision properties are not taken into account, the criterion of fine details difference can be received directly in three-dimensional space of *RGB* signals:

$$\sqrt{(\Delta R)^2 + (\Delta G)^2 + (\Delta B)^2} \geq \Delta K_{th},$$

where ΔK_{th} is the threshold contrast value, which depends on device sensitivity and noise level at an output of a system.

In order to use criterion (8) in practice it is necessary to determine numerical values of fine details threshold contrast at which they are visible with an eye, depending on the size of details for the set of supervision conditions.

To solve this task it was required:

1. To develop a synthesis algorithm of the test image consisting of small static and dynamic objects with regulated contrast in MPCD values. 2. To develop a procedure of the experiment and on the basis of subjective estimations to determine threshold values of fine details contrast.

3. Test Image Synthesis

The author has developed a test image algorithm synthesis in equal color space, that allows to set initial contrast of object - background directly in color thresholds, that is basically different from the known ways of synthesis when the image contrast is set by the percentage of object brightness to background brightness.

The synthesis algorithm consists in the following.

At the first stage form, sizes, spatial position and color coordinates ($W^*U^*V^*$) of objects and background for the basic first frame of test sequence are set. The vectors of movement are set for the subsequent frames.

At the second stage the transformation $\{W^*_{m,i,j}\, U^*_{m,i,j}\, V^*_{m,i,j}\} \rightarrow \{R_{m,i,j}\, G_{m,i,j}\, B_{m,i,j}\}$ which is necessary for visualization of the initial sequence on the screen and for submission of digital *RGB* signals on the input of the system under research is carried out for each frame of test sequence on the basis of mathematical model which have been developed. Where *m* is the frame number; *i* and *j* is the pixels numbers in columns and lines of image.

At the third stage, cyclic regeneration of the *M* frames with the set frequency (f_{frame}) is carried out. When reproducing the test sequence, dynamic objects move on the set trajectory to the number of pixels having been determined by the motion vector.

On the basis of the above described algorithm the test table and video sequences are developed into which all the necessary elements for the quality analysis of fine details of static and dynamic images are included.

Let's consider the basic characteristics of the test table which is developed for the quality analysis of static images.

The table represents the image of CIF format (360×288), which is broken into 6 identical fragments (120×144). Each fragment of the table contains the following objects: a) horizontal, vertical and inclined lines with the stripes width of 1, 2, 3 or more 3 pixels; b) single small details of rectangular form. Objects of the image are located on a grey unpainted background.

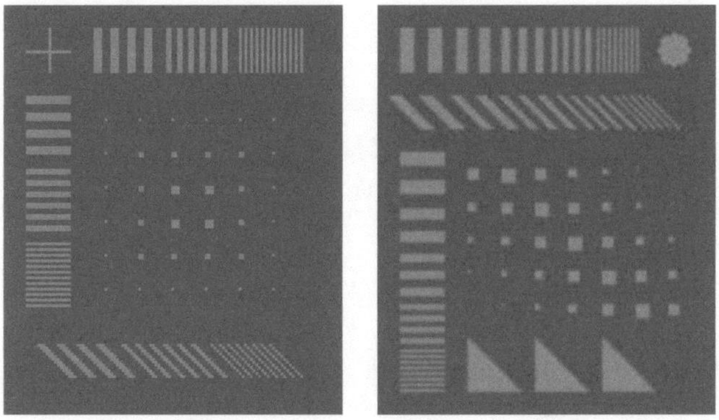

a) b)

Figure 1. A fragments of the test image: a) 1-st variant; a) 2-nd variant

The object - background brightness ΔW^* contrast is set by MPCD number for the 1-st and the 2-nd fragments

$$\Delta W^* = \pm 3(W^*_o - W^*_b),\ \text{at}\ \Delta U^* = 0\ \text{and}\ \Delta V^* = 0.$$

The object - background chromaticity ΔU^* contrast is set by MPCD number for the 3-rd and the 4-th fragments

$$\Delta U^* = \pm 3(U^*_o - U^*_b),\ \text{at}\ \Delta W^* = 0\ \text{and}\ \Delta V^* = 0.$$

The object - background chromaticity ΔV^* contrast is set by MPCD number for the 5-th and the 6-th fragments

$$\Delta V^* = \pm 3(V_o^* - V_b^*), \text{ at } \Delta W^* = 0 \text{ and } \Delta U^* = 0 .$$

As an example, fragments (120×144) of the test image on brightness for two variants of tables are shown on Figure 1.
Three types of test video sequences with formats 360×288, 720×576 and 1440×1152 pixels are developed for the quality analysis of dynamic images.
The table with a format 360×288 is used as the basis (I-frame) of test video sequence. The sequence consists of 12 frames cyclically repeated at a certain frequency f_{frame} = 30 Hz.
Spatial coordinates of the m - frame objects are displaced relatively the frame number m-1 on the value of motion vector. During the sequence regeneration all the details of the image of the test table become dynamic.
In test sequence with a format 720×576 every frame consists of 4 fragments of a format 360×288. And, at last, for sequence of a format 1440×1152 every frame contains 4 fragments of a format 720×576.

4. Experimental Estimation of Visual Thresholds

The test table and sequence with format 352×288 are synthesized to determine the threshold of visual perception of the image fine details.
The developed user program interface allows adjusting the following image parameters: background brightness, object contrast on brightness and chromaticity indexes.
Threshold values of contrast for static details on brightness and chromaticity indexes were received experimentally with the help of subjective estimations with the following technique.

1. The test image with adjustable values of color contrast on axis ΔW^* with step 1 MPCD and on axes ΔU^* and ΔV^* U with step 2 MPCD was offered to the observer.
2. During the experiment the observer changed the contrast value beginning with the minimal until the stripes became distinct.
3. As an estimation criterion of threshold contrast the following condition was set: the stripes should be distinguishable with an eye in comparison with the previous image i.e. at which contrast was one step lower.
4. Under condition (3) the observer fixed value of contrast at which, in his opinion, sufficient "perceptibility" of lines was provided.

Students and employees of Khabarovsk state technical university (Pacific National University) participated in the experiments.

δ	>3	3	2	1
ΔW_{th}^*	2	3	4	6
ΔU_{th}^*	26	34	48	72
ΔV_{th}^*	24	36	52	76

Table 1. Dependences of threshold contrast from the size of objects

Table 1. shows subjective average estimations of threshold contrast from the size (δ) of objects for background brightness is W_b^* = 80 MPCD, arithmetic-mean value being received by estimation results of 20 observers.

In the table the size of objects is set by pixels number, and the threshold value by the MPCD number. For example, at the minimal sizes of lines (δ =1) the average value of a visual threshold on brightness index is equal to 6 MPCD and on chromaticity index it is equal to 72 and 76 MPCD.

For example, at the minimal sizes of stripes the average value of a visual threshold on brightness index is equal to 6 MPCD and on chromaticity index it is equal to 72 and 76 MPCD.

The results of the experiments show, that values of threshold contrast on an unpainted background on axes ΔU^* and ΔV^* are approximately identical, and exceed values of thresholds on axis ΔW^* in 10 … 13 times. Change of background brightness from 70 up to 90 MPCD does not essentially influence the thresholds of fine details visual perception.

Experimental estimations of color thresholds in $L^*u^*v^*$ system show, that estimations on coordinates of chromaticity u^* and v^* 1.5 … 1.8 times differ. Therefore the use of $W^*U^*V^*$ system is more preferable.

The values of threshold contrast for mobile details of test sequence are received by experimentally with the help of subjective estimations by the following technique.

During the experiment the observer changed of contrast value, beginning with the minimal until the mobile objects became distinct.

The results of the experiments show that, at movement of objects, contrast threshold values in comparison with the data of Table 1, increase, depending on *t* according to function $f(t) = 1/(1 - e^{-t/\vartheta})$, where ϑ = 0,05 is the time of vision inertia; *t* is the time interval, during which the object moves on a certain number of pixels set by the vector.

In particular, at *t* = 0,033 (f_{frame} = 30 Hz) values of contrast threshold of fine details have increased approximately in 1,8 … 2 times.

Thus, the received experimental data allow using criterion (8) in practice as an objective estimation of transfer accuracy of both static and dynamic fine details of the test image.

5. Analysis of Definition and Distortions of Test Table Fine Details

The analysis of definition and distortions of test table fine details consists of the following stages.

At the first stage, the test sequence of 12 image frames in *RGB* signal space, where $W^*U^*V^*$ space is used as initial object color coordinates, is synthesized.

Contrast of stripes image and fine details two - three times exceeds the threshold values. Such choice of contrast is caused by the fact that in the majority of cases fine details with low contrast are more distorted during digital coding and images transfer.

At the second stage, digital *RGB* signals of test sequence move on an input of the test system and are processed using coding algorithm.

At the third stage after decoding, the test sequence is restored and $\widetilde{R}_{m,i,j}, \widetilde{G}_{m,i,j}, \widetilde{B}_{m,i,j}$ signals are transformed into $\widetilde{W}^*_{m,i,j}, \widetilde{U}^*_{m,i,j}, \widetilde{V}^*_{m,i,j}$ signals for each frame. All 12 frames of the restored sequence write in a RAM of the analyzer.

At the fourth stage, contrast and distortions of fine details are measured by the local fragments of the restored image, and definition estimation is obtained by the objective criteria.

Let's consider a measurement method of stripes contrast of the first image frame.

For an estimation of definition impairment it is necessary to measure contrast for each fragment of the decoded image of stripes with the fixed size and to compare the received value to threshold value. We assume that stripes are distinguished by the observer, if the condition is satisfied:

$$\Delta\overline{\widetilde{E}}(\delta,k)=\sqrt{\left(\frac{\Delta\overline{\widetilde{W}}^*(\delta,k)}{\Delta W^*_{th}(\delta)}\right)^2+\left(\frac{\Delta\overline{\widetilde{U}}^*(\delta,k)}{\Delta U^*_{th}(\delta)}\right)^2+\left(\frac{\Delta\overline{\widetilde{V}}^*(\delta,k)}{\Delta V^*_{th}(\delta)}\right)^2}\geq 1 \tag{9}$$

where $\Delta\overline{\widetilde{E}}(\delta,k)$ is the average normalized value of stripes contrast, average on the k "window" area of the image; $\Delta\overline{\widetilde{W}}^*$, $\Delta\overline{\widetilde{U}}^*$ and $\Delta\overline{\widetilde{V}}^*$ is the average values of contrast on brightness and chromaticity indexes; k — the parameter determining the type the "window" under analysis (k = 0 - vertical stripes, k = 1 - horizontal, k = 2 - sloping); $\Delta W^*_{th}(\delta)$, $\Delta U^*_{th}(\delta)$ and $\Delta V^*_{th}(\delta)$ is the contrast threshold values from Table 1.

Since the test image is divided into fragments on brightness and chromaticity indexes, the criteria of distinction of stripes on each coordinate are determined as follows:

$$\Delta\overline{\widetilde{E}}_{W^*}(\delta)=\frac{\Delta\overline{\widetilde{W}}^*(\delta)}{\Delta W^*_{th}(\delta)}\geq 1,\ \Delta\overline{\widetilde{E}}_{U^*}(\delta)=\frac{\Delta\overline{\widetilde{U}}^*(\delta)}{\Delta U^*_{th}(\delta)}\geq 1,\ \Delta\overline{\widetilde{E}}_{V^*}(\delta)=\frac{\Delta\overline{\widetilde{V}}^*(\delta)}{\Delta V^*_{th}(\delta)}\geq 1, \tag{10}$$

where making calculations the minimal value of contrast from the three (k) "windows" under analysis is chosen on each color coordinate, which allows taking into account the influence of spatial orientation of lines for decoding accuracy.

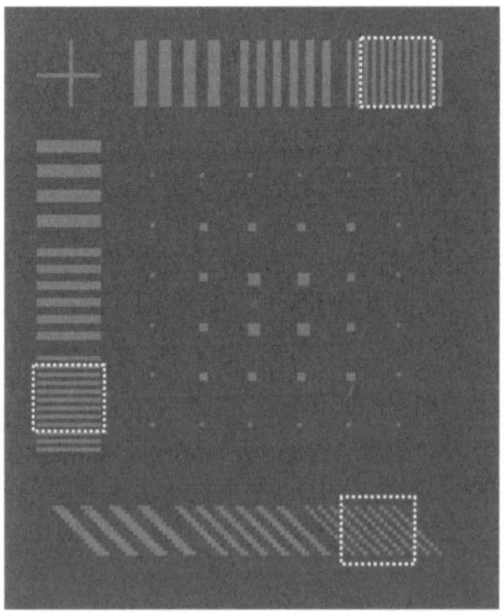

Figure 2. Image fragment "windows" under analysis

Figure 2 shows the example of spatial position of the image fragment "windows" under analysis on the brightness index with contrast ΔW_{th}^{*} = 18 MPCD which is three times higher than the threshold value for the finest details (δ = 1).
Average contrast values on brightness and chromaticity indexes are equal to the initial values if there are no distortions. In this case, contrast of all the "windows" of the test image under analysis three times exceeds threshold values and, hence, definition does not become worse.
Average contrast value of the "windows" of the test image under analysis decreases, if there are distortions. But, if the contrast on brightness or chromaticity index becomes less than threshold value, i.e. conditions (10) are not satisfied, the conclusion is made that the observer does not distinguish fine details.
Finally, minimal size of stripes with the contrast which satisfies criteria (10) makes it possible to determine maximum number of distinct elements of the image that constitutes the image definition estimation on brightness and chromaticity.
It is obvious, that the estimation by criteria (10) depends on the initial image contrast.
In particular the stripes contrast decrease on 1 … 2 thresholds gives "bad" results when using test image with low contrast. But when the initial contrast exceeds threshold values 10 times, definition impairment is not observed in such contrast decrease.
Thus, the criterion (8) gives an objective estimation of definition impairment of fine details of low contrast image.
To exclude initial contrast influence on indeterminacy of estimations, we should take the following equation for brightness index:

$$\varepsilon_{W^*}(\delta)=\frac{1}{\Delta W_{th}^{*}(\delta)\cdot N}\sum_{i=0}^{N-1}\left|\Delta W^{*}(\delta)-\Delta\widetilde{W}_i^{*}(\delta)\right|<Q_{W^*} \qquad (11)$$

where $\varepsilon_{W^*}(\delta)$ is the threshold- normalized deviation of contrast from the initial value; Q_{W^*} is the quality parameter determining admissible values of contrast decrease on brightness index; *N* is the pixels number in the "window" under analysis.
Calculations on chromaticity are made on analogy.
Calculations having been made, the program analyzer compares the results received with the quality rating in a ten-point scale and establishes estimation.
It is shown in (Sai, 2003) that high-quality reproduction of fine details with the rating not less than 6 … 7 points, is obtained under the following conditions: a) contrast reduction of stripes on brightness should be not more than 50 % of the threshold values for the stripes width of 1 pixel or more; b) contrast reduction of stripes on chromaticity should be not more than 75 % of the threshold values for the stripes width of 3 pixels or more, i.e.

$$\varepsilon_{W^*}(\delta\geq 1)<0{,}5;\ \varepsilon_{U^*,V^*}(\delta\geq 3)<0{,}75 \qquad (12)$$

The experimental results of the images quality analysis in different compression systems show that, when these criteria are met, the reduction of the visual sharpness of fine details is only barely visible or almost imperceptible.
The developed method differs from the known in the fact that contrast of fine details at the exit of a system is estimated by the threshold- normalized average value of the "window" area of the stripes image under analysis, but not by the amplitude value of the first harmonic of brightness and chromaticity signals.

Object - background initial contrast is also set not by the maximal value, but in two - three times exceeding threshold value that allows to estimate the effectiveness of coding system in up to threshold area where distortions are the most essential.
Thus, the offered method allows estimating objectively the reduction of the visual sharpness since it takes into account thresholds of visual perception of fine details and possible fluctuations of color coordinates caused by linear distortions of signals and noise presence in digital system.
In image coding digital systems using nonlinear transformations not only linear reduction of high-frequency component of decoded *RGB* signals is possible, but also nonlinear distortions may occur.
Therefore, in some cases, the estimation of contrast reduction by criteria (12) can lead to incorrect results.
To take into account the influence of nonlinear distortions on objectivity of estimations the following decision is offered.
In addition to estimations (12), the normalized average deviation of reproduced color coordinates relative to the initial ones in the image "window", for example, on brightness is offered to estimate:

$$\Delta_{W^*}(\delta)=\frac{1}{\Delta W^*_{th}(\delta)\cdot N}\sum_{i=0}^{N-1}\left|\tilde{W}^*_i(\delta)-W^*_i(\delta)\right| \tag{13}$$

It is shown in (Sai, 2003) that in order to provide high-quality reproduction of fine details with the rating not less than 6 … 7 points, it is necessary to satisfy the following conditions in addition to criteria (12): a) the root-mean-square deviation of brightness coordinates in all "windows" under analysis must be not more than 30 %; b) the root-mean-square deviation of chromaticity coordinates not more than 50 % for the details not less than three pixels in size.

$$\Delta_{W^*}(\delta\geq 1)< 0{,}3;\quad \Delta_{U^*,V^*}(\delta\geq 3)< 0{,}5 \tag{14}$$

Consider the method of distortions estimation of fine single details of a rectangular form.
For the test image fragment, for example on brightness, find the normalized average deviation of object contrast and initial value on the object area:

$$\eta_{W^*}(\delta)=\frac{1}{\Delta W^*_{th}(\delta)\cdot N}\sum_{i=0}^{N-1}\left|\Delta\tilde{W}^*_i(\delta)-\Delta W^*(\delta)\right| \tag{15}$$

As against (11), number *N* is determined by the image "window" with a single object being included into it. For example, at the analysis of distortions of point object the "window" size is 1×1 pixels. At the analysis of distortions of object 2×2 pixels in size, the "window" size is 2×2, etc.
It is obvious from the experiments, that in order to ensure high-quality reproduction of fine details with the rating not less than 6 … 7 points, it is necessary to satisfy the following conditions: a) the root-mean-square deviation on brightness must be not more than 1,5 for all the details; b) the root-mean-square deviation on chromaticity must be not more than 0,8 for the details 3 or more pixels in size.

$$\eta_{W^*}(\delta\geq 1)<1{,}0;\quad \eta_{U^*,V^*}(\delta\geq 3)<0{,}5 \tag{16}$$

Thus a program analyzer can estimate visual quality of reproduction of striped lines and fine details of the test image by criteria (12), (14) and (16).
Table 1 shows the experimental dependence of parameters (11), (13) and (15) from quality rating.
Results are received after JPEG compression of the image in Adobe Photoshop 5 using ten-point scale of quality. The results are received for the test image with fine details contrast exceeding threshold values two times. Thus according to Table 1., it is possible to estimate the quality rating for each of the six parameters.
The average quality rating of each frame of the test sequence is calculated as follows:

$$Q_m = \frac{1}{6}\sum_{i=1}^{6} Q_i \,.$$

Q	1	2	3	4	5	6	7	8	9	10	
	Low		Medium			High		Maximum			
ε_{W^*}	1,006	0,966	0,948	0,690	0,498	0,225	0,099	0,071	0,012	0,013	δ =1
Δ_{W^*}	0,690	0,700	0,686	0,627	0,519	0,338	0,240	0,145	0,083	0,015	
η_{W^*}	2,039	2,039	1,722	1,617	1,512	1,409	0,998	0,295	0,097	0,001	
ε_{U^*}	1,528	1,617	1,569	1,073	0,772	0,557	0,391	0,241	0,009	0,002	δ =3
Δ_{U^*}	0,960	0,955	0,917	0,688	0,505	0,432	0,331	0,238	0,143	0,053	
η_{U^*}	1,124	1,070	1,024	1,143	0,456	0,460	0,477	0,299	0,124	0,047	

Table 1. The experimental dependence of parameters from quality rating

Consider a measurement technique for mobile objects of the test sequence.
For an estimation of definition it is necessary to calculate average values of contrast deviation of stripes on brightness and chromaticity for every *m* of the frame of test sequence and to estimate average value for the set of 12 frames:

$$\varepsilon_{W^*}(\delta) = \frac{1}{M}\sum_{m=1}^{M}\left[\frac{1}{N}\sum_{i=0}^{N-1}\frac{\left|\Delta W^*(\delta) - \Delta \overline{W}_i^*(\delta,m)\right|}{\Delta W_{th}^*(\delta)\cdot f(t)}\right] \tag{17}$$

where M = 12 is the frames number; $f(t)$ is the function taking into account recession of contrast - sensitive vision characteristic depending on objects presentation time.
Reduction of stripes contrast on chromaticity is calculated similarly.
Calculations (17) having been made, conditions (12) are checked.
If (14) is satisfied on brightness and chromaticity, the decision is made, that the observer distinguishes fine mobile details and definition reduction is slightly visible.
For the estimation of parameters (13) and (15) average values on 12 frames of test sequence are calculated on analogy to the equation (17).

6. Noise Influence Analysis

The developed criteria of image quality estimation are received without taking into account noise in *RGB* signals. Hence the correctness of the results is true in the case when noise level in the received image is small enough.
The analysis of noise influence in a digital video system can be divided into two parts: analysis in up to threshold area and analysis in higher of threshold area.
In the up to threshold area the transfer quality of coded video data is high, and noise presence in the system results only in small fluctuations of *RGB* signals.
But, if the noise level and probability of mistakes exceed the threshold value, abrupt image quality impairment is observed because of possible changes of pixels spatial position and distortions of signal peak values.
In order to analysis noise influence on the image definition reduction in the up to threshold area take advantage of the following assumptions:

1. Interaction of signals and noise is additive.
2. Density distribution law of stationary noise probabilities is close to the normal law.
3. Noise in *RGB* signals of the decoded image is not correlative.

Noise in the system results in "diffusion" of both objects color coordinates and background in the decoded image. Thus a point in RGB space is transformed into ellipsoid with semi axis. Their values are proportional to root-mean-square noise levels.
Calculating the stripes contrast, make the following transformation:

$$\{R_{m,i,j}\, G_{m,i,j}\, B_{m,i,j}\} \rightarrow \{W^*_{m,i,j}\, U^*_{m,i,j}\, V^*_{m,i,j}\}.$$

Hence, values of equal coordinates become random variables with root-mean-square deviations: $\sigma_{W^*}, \sigma_{U^*}, \sigma_{V^*}$.

Dispersions of W^*, U^* and V^* coordinates are received with the help of a linearization method (Ventzel & Ovtharov, 2000) of the functions $W^* = 25\, Y^{1/3} - 17$, $U^* = 13\, W^*(u - u_0)$ and $V^* = 13\, W^*(v - v_0)$.

Define dispersion of brightness index $W^* = 25\, Y^{1/3} - 17$. Linearization of the functions $W^* = \varphi(Y^{1/3})$ is the approached representation of this function by first two members of Taylor series. In this case, the dispersion $\sigma^2_{W^*}$ can be found in the approximate way:

$$\sigma^2_{W^*} \approx \left(\frac{\partial W^*}{\partial Y}\right)^2 \cdot \sigma^2_Y = \left(\frac{25}{3 \cdot Y^{2/3}}\right)^2 \cdot \sigma^2_Y,$$

where, the brightness coordinate is determined by linear transformation: $Y = 0{,}299 L_R + 0{,}587 L_G + 0{,}114 L_B$.

Therefore

$$\sigma^2_Y = 0{,}299^2 \cdot \sigma^2_R + 0{,}587^2 \cdot \sigma^2_G + 0{,}114^2 \cdot \sigma^2_B.$$

Define dispersion of chromaticity index U^* with the help of a linearization method of the function $U^* = 13\,W^*(u-u_0)$

$$\sigma_{U^*}^2 \approx \left(\frac{\partial U^*}{\partial R}\right)^2 \cdot \sigma_R^2 + \left(\frac{\partial U^*}{\partial G}\right)^2 \cdot \sigma_G^2 + \left(\frac{\partial U^*}{\partial B}\right)^2 \cdot \sigma_B^2,$$

where derivatives are found in the following way:

$$\frac{dU^*}{dR} = 13\left(\frac{25a_4}{3Y^{2/3}}(u-u_0) + \frac{a_1T - b_1U}{T^2}W^*\right);$$

$$\frac{dU^*}{dG} = 13\left(\frac{25a_5}{3Y^{2/3}}(u-u_0) + \frac{a_2T - b_2U}{T^2}W^*\right);$$

$$\frac{dU^*}{dB} = 13\left(\frac{25a_6}{3Y^{2/3}}(u-u_0) + \frac{a_3T - b_3U}{T^2}W^*\right),$$

where $T = U + V + W$; $u = U/T$; $v = V/T$;
$U = a_1R + a_2G + a_3B$; $V = a_4R + a_5G + a_6B$; $W = a_7R + a_8G + a_9B$;
$a_1 \ldots a_9$ is the constants, and $b_1 = a_1 + a_4 + a_7$; $b_2 = a_2 + a_5 + a_8$; $b_3 = a_3 + a_6 + a_9$.

Dispersion of chromaticity index V^* is calculated similarly.

Estimate of noise influence on visual sharpness reduction of the test image (Figure 1).

As, the test image is divided into fragments on indexes of brightness and chromaticity, root-mean-square deviations of difference color coordinate for each fragment can be estimated of the following expressions:

$$\sigma_{\Delta W^*} \approx 3\sqrt{\sigma_{W_o^*}^2 + \sigma_{W_b^*}^2}\text{ , at } \Delta U^* = 0 \text{ and } \Delta V^* = 0;$$

$$\sigma_{\Delta U^*} \approx 3\sqrt{\sigma_{U_o^*}^2 + \sigma_{U_b^*}^2}\text{ , at } \Delta W^* = 0 \text{ and } \Delta V^* = 0;$$

$$\sigma_{\Delta V^*} \approx 3\sqrt{\sigma_{V_o^*}^2 + \sigma_{V_b^*}^2}\text{ , at } \Delta W^* = 0 \text{ and } \Delta U^* = 0.$$

Define criterion at which the observer distinguishes image stripes with noise.

The known « three sigma » rule is used to solve the task. This rule means that deviation probability of a random variable X from its mean value not less than three sigma, provided the law of distribution is close to normal, does not exceed 1/9.

Criteria, at which the observer distinguishes stripes in the test image with noise on brightness, are found in the following way:

$$\frac{\left|\Delta W^*(\delta)\right| - 3\sigma_{\Delta W^*} \cdot \varphi_{W^*}(\delta)}{\Delta W_{th}^*(\delta)} \geq 1 \tag{18}$$

where $\varphi(\delta)$ is the weight function.

Criteria of chromaticity indexes U^* and V^* is calculated similarly.

Introduction of weight function into (18) is caused by the fact that vision contrast sensitivity decreases with the reduction of the details sizes and hence the influence of noise on their perceptibility is greater.

Experimental research results have shown that the maximal value of weight function ($\varphi(\delta)=1$) corresponds to the minimal size ($\delta=1$) of stripes, and weight function values decrease with the increase of the stripes size. This is proportional to the reduction of threshold values (Table 1).

The numerical solution of the developed mathematical model allows estimating the influence of additive noise on definition reduction depending on root-mean-square values of noise in *RGB* signals on the system output.

Dependences of root-mean-square deviations of color coordinates on brightness and chromaticity from ($\sigma \approx \sigma_R \approx \sigma_G \approx \sigma_B$) are shown in Table 2, provided that noise levels in *R*, *G* and *B* signals are approximately identical.

Value (σ) is given in percentage ratio to maximal amplitude of *R*, *G* and *B* signals.

Objects color coordinates of the test image with the contrast equal to threshold value for the details with the minimal sizes are used in calculations, i.e., W_b^* = 80 MPCD, ΔW^* = 6 MPCD, ΔU^* = 72 MPCD and ΔV^* = 76 MPCD.

σ %	0.2	0.4	0.6	0.8	1.0	1.2	1.4	1.6	1.8	2.0
σ_{W^*}	0.31	0.61	0.92	1.22	1.53	1.84	2.14	2.45	2.76	3.06
σ_{U^*}	1.20	2.40	3.60	4.81	6.01	7.19	8.43	9.61	10.8	12.1
σ_{V^*}	2.10	4.20	6.30	8.41	10.5	12.6	14.8	16.8	18.9	21.0

Table 2. Dependences of root-mean-square deviations of W^*, U^* and V^* color coordinates

The results received allow to estimate the influence of noise in *RGB* signals on system output on threshold contrast increase (18) and, hence, on impairment of visual sharpness.

For example, to make finest details of the image distinguished by the observer at a relative noise level in *RGB* signals is $\sigma_R \approx \sigma_G \approx \sigma_B = \sigma = 2\%$ (Ψ = 34 dB) their contrast should be increased on 9 MPCD in brightness and on 36 MPCD and 63 MPCD in chromaticity.

Selective average dispersion values on indexes of brightness and chromaticity are used for the proof of a correctness of the developed mathematical model.

For example, for an brightness index

$$\overline{\sigma}^2_{W^*} \approx \frac{1}{N^2} \sum_{i=1}^{N} \sum_{j=1}^{N} (W^*_{i,j} - \overline{W}^*)^2 ,$$

where, $\overline{W}^*$ is the selective average value of W^* coordinate in a window with size $N \times N$ pixels. Comparison calculated both experimental data proves a correctness of the developed mathematical model of noise transformation. Insignificant deviations into comparison results do not exceed 3 … 5 % and explained of a linearization method errors.

7. Practical Results

The developed methods are used in practice for the analysis and adjustment of video systems parameters, to get high quality transfer and reproduction of images fine details.

The results of the analysis are given below and the recommendations on adjustment for high definition in vision systems using JPEG, JPEG-2000 and MPEG-4 algorithms are offered.

The experimental analysis of coding quality of static images is carried out by the following technique.
At the first stage the influence of the coder parameters on the decoded image quality of the test table is analyzed with the help of a computer analyzer.
The computer analyzer calculated the following dependences of image quality parameters on the coder adjustment parameters: a) reduction of stripes contrast (11) on brightness and chromaticity; b) average deviation (13) of stripes color coordinates; c) average deviation (15) of a single object contrast.
At the second stage the coder parameter at which the results of the analysis correspond to high quality rating of ($Q \geq 6$ ... 7) is selected.
At the third stage, the efficiency of digital compression of test images is estimated. Original test photo images containing 50 ... 70 percent of thin structural elements were used at the experiment.

Quality analysis of JPEG and JPEG2000 images

The results of quality analysis of JPEG and JPEG2000 images coded in Adobe Photoshop CS are given below. In Table 3 one can see reproduction quality parameters of stripes and fine details of the test image on brightness for low, average and high rating quality.
In column (Var) values of adjustment parameters of images quality, being used in Adobe Photoshop CS are shown.
Fragments of the test image with various quality rating are shown on Figure 3.

JPEG	ε_{W^*}	Δ_{W^*}	η_{W^*}	**Var**	**JPEG2000**	ε_{W^*}	Δ_{W^*}	η_{W^*}	**Var**
$Q = 2$	0,97	0,70	2,04	**4**	$Q = 2$	1,09	0,69	1,72	**25**
$Q = 4$	0,69	0,63	1,62	**7**	$Q = 4$	0,93	0,57	1,62	**30**
$Q = 7$	0,10	0,24	0,99	**9**	$Q = 7$	0,19	0,13	0,31	**65**

Table 3. Quality parameters JPEG and JPEG2000

The analysis of the results received shows that such adjustment parameters as: Var ≥ 9 at JPEG compression and Var ≥ 65 at JPEG2000 compression are to be established for providing high images definition in Adobe Photoshop CS.
The quality analysis of JPEG and JPEG2000 images coded in ACD See 8 is done in the similar way. The analysis of the results received shows that such adjustment parameters as: Var ≥ 80 at JPEG compression and Var = Compression ratio ≤ 30 at JPEG2000 compression are to be established for providing high images definition in ACD See 8.

	Adobe Photoshop CS		ACD See 8		
	JPEG (9)	JPEG2000 (65)	JPEG (80)	JPEG2000 (30)	
Cf	6,4	3,1	12	27	Lena
Cf	8,5	7,0	13	30	Barbara

Table 4. Test images compression factors

As an example of compression efficiency of test images of Lena and Barbara at the established parameters of JPEG and JPEG2000 codecs on high definition are shown in table 4, where Cf is the compression factor. The initial format of test images is equal 512×512×3 Bytes.

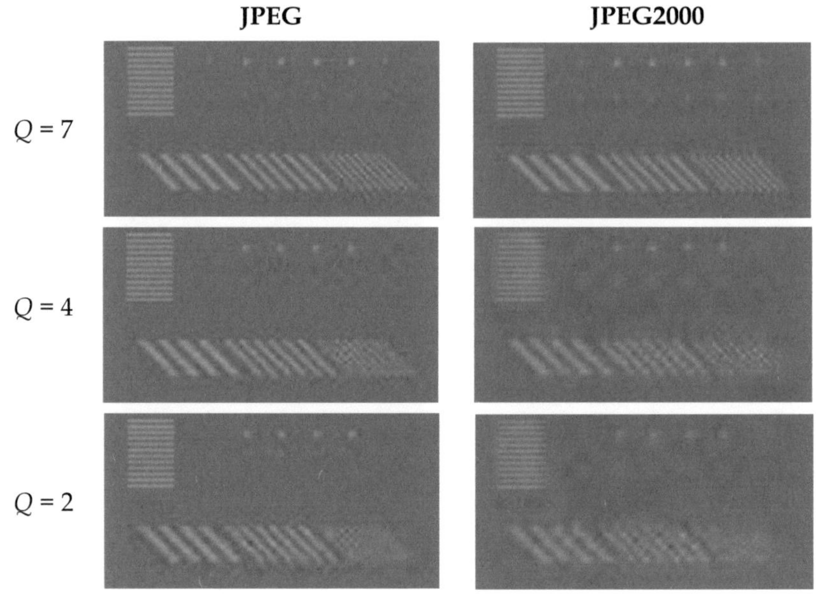

Figure 3. Fragments of the test image on brightness

The analysis of the received results allows making the following conclusion.

The JPEG and JPEG2000 codecs in ACDSee 8 provide higher compression factor of photo images in comparison with codecs of Adobe Photoshop CS at the established high quality reproduction of fine details.

Quality analysis of MPEG-4 video images

The experimental analysis of coding quality of dynamic images was carried out by the following technique (Sai, 2006).

At the first stage, test sequence of 12 frames (360×288) was transformed by means of Adobe Premiere 6.0 into a video clip without compression of video data with *.avi expansion.

At the second stage, the test video clip was compressed by the MPEG-4 Video compressor with the tuning dial ranging from 1 up to 100 % for quality adjustment of video clips.

At the third stage, each frame of the compressed video clip was transformed into BMP format and passed into the program analyzer.

At the fourth stage, the quality of the decoded frames sequence was rated.

Figure 4 shows test sequence fragments on brightness (contrast is increased) for 1 and 6 frames, MPEG-4 Video algorithm for parameters Var = 90 %, Var = 70 % and Var = 50 % having been executed.

Table 5 shows numerical results of quality rating estimation of the decoded sequence. Compression factors in relation to volume of the video data of the initial test sequence (14,2 Mb) are also shown here.

Figure 5 shows fragments of the video clip frame with the real image after compression in MPEG-4 Video with high and low quality rating.

Visual comparison of images speaks to the fact that distortions of fine details (thin lines on the sweater) with low contrasts are practically imperceptible for vision at high quality rating. Low quality rating compression results in disappearance of low contrasts fine details from the image

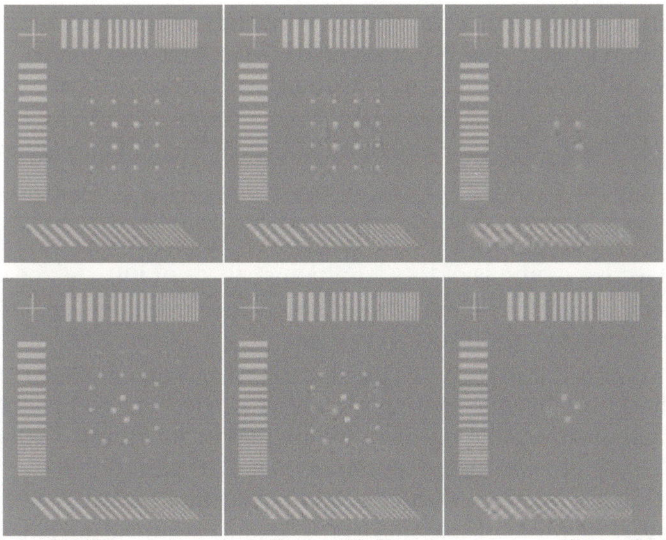

Var = 90 % Var = 70 % Var = 50 %

Figure 4. Test sequence fragments on brightness

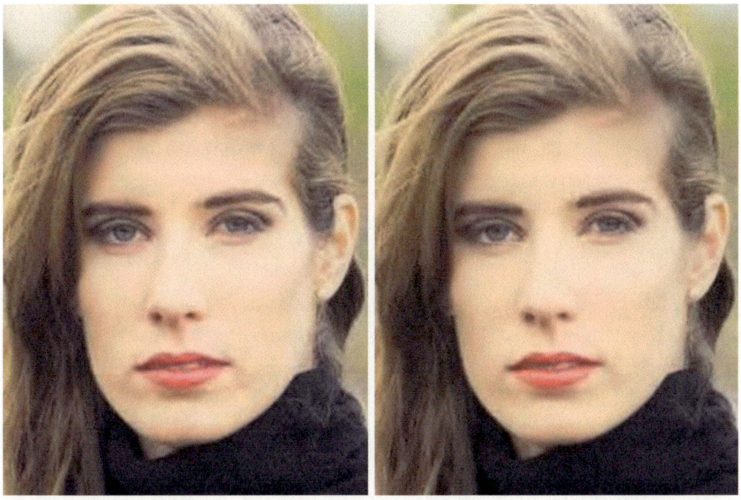

Q = High *Q* = Low

Figure 5. Fragments of the video clip frame

.Var	90%	70%	50%
Rating	High	Medium	Low
Q	6,8	4,3	2,7
Cf	29,6	62,6	123,5

Table 5. Quality rating MPEG-4

The received results lead to a conclusion that the adjustment scale should be established not less than 90 % when using MPEG-4 Video with high reproduction quality of images fine details.

Other types of MPEG-4 compressor are also investigated in this work.
In particular, it follows from the experimental results that the quality rating of the test sequence is 3,6 points for the DivX (Fast - Motion) compressor and 4,2 points for the DivX (Low - Motion). Thus, the use of these compressors results in average rating and does not allow receiving objectively high reproduction quality of video images fine details.

8. Conclusion

The developed objective methods of the definition analysis of images fine details practically prove to be effective and can be used for adjustment and optimization of codec parameters on high visual sharpness in various vision systems.
The main distinctive features of the developed methods should be noted in the summary.

1. The visual sharpness analysis is suggested to be carried out on the test image with low contrast, the initial contrast of fine details being set by a number of minimal color vision thresholds two - three times exceeding the average thresholds values.
2. Reduction in visual sharpness is suggested to be estimated by the normalized to vision thresholds, average value of test image fine details contrast deviation from the initial values of contrast in three-dimensional equal color space.
3. Image noise is suggested to be estimated by the root-mean-square values of color W^*, U^* and V^* coordinates deviations which are calculated by the quantity of minimal color vision thresholds.

To provide high quality reproduction of images fine details is the task of paramount importance at designing vision systems of various applications.
The author hopes that the methods offered in this work will help designers of vision systems to solve this task more effectively.

9. References

Glasman, K. (2004). MPEG-2 and Measurements. *625*, No. 1, pp. 34-46, ISNN 0869-7914

Krivosheev, M.I. & Kustarev, A.K. (1990). *Color Measurements*. Energoatom, Moscow, ISBN 5-283-00545-3.

Mac Adam, D.L. (1974). Uniform Color Scales. *JOSA*, Vol. 64, pp. 1691-1702.

Novakovsky, S.V. (1988). *Color in Color TV*. Radio and communication, Moscow, ISBN 5-256-00090-X.

Pratt, W.K. (2001) *Digital Image Processing*. Wiley, ISBN 0471374075.

Sai, S.V. (2002). Definition Analysis of Color Static Images in Equal Contrast Space. *Digital signals processing*, No. 1., pp. 6-9, ISNN 1684-2634.

Sai, S.V. (2003). *The Quality of Transmission and Reproduction of Fine Details in Color Television Images*. Dalnauka, Vladivostok, ISBN 5-8044-0345-1.

Sai, S.V. (2006). Quality Analysis of MPEG-4 Video Images. *Pattern Recognition and Image Analysis*, Vol. 16, No. 1, pp. 50-51, ISNN 1054-6618.

Ventzel, E.S. & Ovtharov, L.A. (2000). *Probability Theory and its Engineering Application*. Higher school, Moscow. ISBN 5-06-003830-0.

Wyszecki, G. (1975). Uniform Color Scales: CIE 1964 U*V*W* Conversion of OSA Committee Selection. *JOSA*, Vol. 65, pp. 456-460.

17

A Practical Toolbox for Calibrating Omnidirectional Cameras

Davide Scaramuzza and Roland Siegwart
Swiss Federal Institute of Technology, Zurich
Switzerland

1. Introduction

An omnidirectional camera is a vision system providing a 360° panoramic view of the scene. Such an enhanced field of view can be achieved by either using catadioptric systems, which opportunely combine mirrors and conventional cameras, or employing purely dioptric fish-eye lenses. Omnidirectional cameras can be classified into two classes, central and non-central, depending on whether they satisfy the single effective viewpoint property or not (Baker & Nayar, 1998). As noted in (Svoboda & T. Pajdla, 1997), it is highly desirable that such imaging systems have a single effective viewpoint. When this property is verified, there exists a single center of projection, that is, every pixel in the sensed images measures the irradiance of the light passing through the same viewpoint in one particular direction. The reason a single viewpoint is so desirable is that it allows the user to generate geometrically correct perspective images from the pictures captured by an omnidirectional camera. Moreover, it allows applying the known theory of epipolar geometry, which easily allows the user to perform ego-motion estimation and structure from motion from image correspondences only.

As shown in (Baker & Nayar, 1998), central catadioptric systems can be built by combining an orthographic camera with a parabolic mirror, or a perspective camera with a hyperbolic or elliptical mirror. Conversely, panoramic cameras using fish-eye lenses cannot in general be considered central systems, but the single viewpoint property holds approximately true for some camera models (Micusik & Pajdla, 2003).

In this chapter, we focus on calibration of central omnidirectional cameras, both dioptric and catadioptric. After outlining previous works on omnidirectional camera calibration, we describe our novel procedure and provide a practical Matlab Toolbox, which allows any inexpert user to easily calibrate his own camera.

Accurate calibration of a vision system is necessary for any computer vision task requiring extracting metric information of the environment from 2D images, like in ego-motion estimation and structure from motion. While a number of calibration methods has been developed for standard perspective cameras (Zhang, 2000), little work on omnidirectional cameras has been done. The first part of this chapter will present a short overview about previous methods for calibration of omnidirectional cameras. In particular, their limitations will be pointed out. The second part of this chapter will present our calibration technique whose performance is evaluated through calibration experiments. Then, we will present our

Matlab toolbox (that is freely available on-line), which implements the proposed calibration procedure. We will also describe features and use of our toolbox.

2. Related Work

Previous works on omnidirectional camera calibration can be classified into two different categories. The first one includes methods which exploit prior knowledge about the scene, such as the presence of calibration patterns (Cauchois et al., 2000; Bakstein & Pajdla, 2002) or plumb lines (Geyer & Daniilidis, 2002). The second group covers techniques that do not use this knowledge. The latter includes calibration methods from pure rotation or planar motion of the camera (Gluckman & Nayar, 1998), and self-calibration procedures, which are performed from point correspondences and epipolar constraint through minimizing an objective function (Kang, 2000; Micusik & Pajdla, 2003).

All mentioned techniques allow obtaining accurate calibration results, but primarily focus on particular sensor types (e.g. hyperbolic and parabolic mirrors or fish-eye lenses). Moreover, some of them require special setting of the scene and expensive equipment (Bakstein & Pajdla, 2002; Gluckman & Nayar, 1998). For instance, in (Bakstein & Pajdla, 2002), a fish-eye lens with a 183° field of view is used as an omnidirectional sensor. Then, the calibration is performed by using a half-cylindrical calibration pattern perpendicular to the camera sensor, which rotates on a turntable.

In (Geyer & Daniilidis, 2002; Kang, 2000), the authors treat the case of a parabolic mirror. In (Geyer & Daniilidis, 2002), it is shown that vanishing points lie on a conic section which encodes the entire calibration information. Thus, the projections of two sets of parallel lines suffice for the intrinsic camera calibration. However, this property does not apply to non-parabolic mirrors. Therefore, the proposed technique cannot be easily generalized to other kinds of sensors.

In contrast with the techniques mentioned so far, the methods described in (Kang, 2000; Micusik & Pajdla, 2003; Micusik et al., 2004) fall in the self-calibration category. These methods require no calibration pattern, nor a priori knowledge about the scene. The only assumption is the capability to automatically find point correspondences in a set of panoramic images of the same scene. Then, calibration is directly performed by epipolar geometry by minimizing an objective function. In (Kang, 2000), this is done by employing a parabolic mirror, while in (Micusik & Pajdla, 2003; Micusik et al., 2004) a fish-eye lens with a view angle greater than 180° is used. However, besides focusing on particular sensor types, the mentioned self-calibration techniques may suffer in case of tracking difficulties and of a small number of features points (Bougnoux, 1998).

The calibration methods described so far focus on particular sensor types, such as parabolic and hyperbolic mirrors or fish-eye lenses. In contrast with these methods, in the last years, novel calibration techniques have been developed, which apply to any central omnidirectional camera. For instance, in (Micusik & Pajdla, 2004), the authors extend the geometric distortion model and the self-calibration procedure described in (Micusik & Pajdla, 2003), including mirrors, fish-eye lenses, and non-central cameras. In (Ying & Hu, 2004; Barreto & Araujo, 2005), the authors describe a method for central catadioptric cameras using geometric invariants. They show that any central catadioptric system can be fully calibrated from an image of three or more lines.

The work described in this chapter also handles with calibration of any central omnidirectional camera but aims at providing a technique that is very easy to apply also for

the inexpert user. Indeed, our technique requires the use of a chessboard-like pattern that is shown by the user at a few different positions and orientations. Then, the user is only asked to click on the corner points of the images of the pattern.
The strong point of our technique resides in the use of a new camera model that adapts according to the appearance of the pattern in the omnidirectional images. The peculiarity of this model is that it can also handle the cases where the single effective viewpoint property is not perfectly satisfied. Indeed, although several omnidirectional cameras exist directly manufactured to have this property, for a catadioptric system this requires to accurately align the camera and the mirror axes. In addition, the focus point of the mirror has to coincide with the optical center of the camera. Since it is very difficult to avoid camera-mirror misalignments, an incorrectly aligned catadioptric sensor can lead to a quasi single viewpoint system (Swaminathan & Grossberg, 2001).
The method described in this chapter was first introduced in (Scaramuzza et al., 2006). In that work, we proposed a generalized parametric model of the sensor, which is suitable to different kinds of omnidirectional vision systems, both catadioptric and dioptric. In that model, we assume that the imaging function, which manages the projection of a 3D real point onto a pixel of the image plane, can be described by a Taylor series expansion whose coefficients are the parameters to be calibrated.
In this chapter, we will first summarize the generalized camera model (section 3) and the calibration method introduced in our previous work (section 4). Then, in section 5, we will introduce our Matlab Toolbox (named OcamCalib Toolbox). There, we will outline the features of the toolbox, with particular regard to the automatic detection of the center of the omnidirectional camera. Indeed, in previous works, the detection of the center is performed by exploiting the visibility of the circular external boundary of the mirror. In those works, the mirror boundary is first enhanced by using an edge detector, and then, a circle is fitted to the edge points to identify the location of the center. In our approach, we no longer need the visibility of the mirror boundary. The algorithm described in this chapter is based on an iterative procedure that uses only the points selected by the user.
In section 6, the performance of our toolbox will be evaluated through calibration experiments.

3. Omnidirectional Camera Model

In this section, we describe our omnidirectional camera model. In the general central camera model, we identify two distinct reference systems: the camera image plane (u',v') and the sensor plane (u'',v''). The camera image plane coincides with the camera CCD, where the points are expressed in pixel coordinates. The sensor plane is a hypothetical plane orthogonal to the mirror axis, with the origin located at the plane-axis intersection.
In figure 1, the two reference planes are shown for the case of a catadioptric system. In the dioptric case, the sign of u'' would be reversed because of the absence of a reflective surface. All coordinates will be expressed in the coordinate system placed in O, with the z-axis aligned with the sensor axis (see Figure 1.a).
Let $\boldsymbol{X}$ be a scene point. Then, assume $\boldsymbol{u''}=[u'',v'']^T$ be the projection of $\boldsymbol{X}$ onto the sensor plane, and $\boldsymbol{u'}=[u',v']^T$ its image in the camera plane (Figure 1.b and 1.c). As observed in (Micusik & Pajdla, 2003), the two systems are related by an affine transformation, which

incorporates the digitizing process and small axes misalignments; thus $\boldsymbol{u}''=\mathrm{A}\boldsymbol{u}'+\mathrm{t}$, where $\mathrm{A}\in\Re^{2x2}$ and $\mathrm{t}\in\Re^{2x1}$.

At this point, we can introduce the imaging function *g*, which captures the relationship between a point $\boldsymbol{u}''$, in the sensor plane, and the vector $\boldsymbol{p}$ emanating from the viewpoint *O* to a scene point $\boldsymbol{X}$ (see figure 1.a). By doing so, the relation between a pixel point $\boldsymbol{u}'$ and a scene point $\boldsymbol{X}$ is:

$$\lambda\cdot p=\lambda\cdot\boldsymbol{g}(\boldsymbol{u}'')=\lambda\cdot\boldsymbol{g}(\mathrm{A}\boldsymbol{u}'+\mathrm{t})=\mathrm{P}\boldsymbol{X},\quad \lambda>0, \tag{1}$$

where $\boldsymbol{X}\in\Re^4$ is expressed in homogeneous coordinates and $\mathrm{P}\in\Re^{3x4}$ is the perspective projection matrix. By calibration of the omnidirectional camera we mean the estimation of the matrices *A* and *t* and the non linear function *g*, so that all vectors $g(\mathrm{A}\boldsymbol{u}'+\mathrm{t})$ satisfy the projection equation (1). We assume for $\boldsymbol{g}$ the following expression

$$\boldsymbol{g}(u'',v'')=(u'',v'',f(u'',v''))^{\mathrm{T}} \tag{2}$$

Furthermore, we assume that function *f* depends on u'' and v'' only through $\rho''=\sqrt{u''^2+v''^2}$. This hypothesis corresponds to assume that function g is rotationally symmetric with respect to the sensor axis.

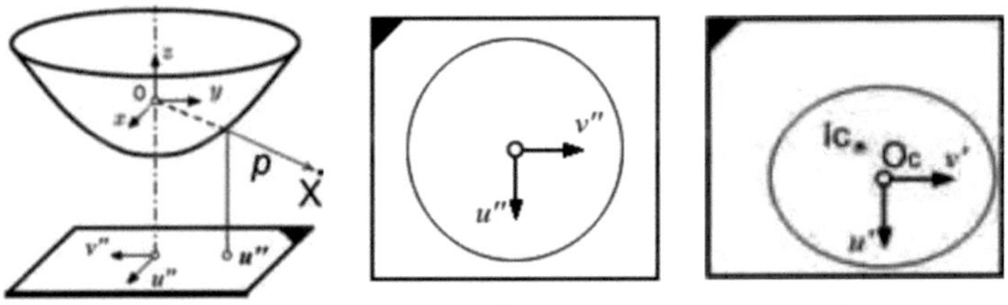

(a) (b) (c)

Figure 1. (a) Coordinate system in the catadioptric case. (b) Sensor plane, in metric coordinates. (c) Camera image plane, expressed in pixel coordinates. (b) and (c) are related by an affine transformation

Function f can have various forms depending on the mirror or the lens construction. These functions can be found in (Kumler & Bauer, 2000), (Micusik et al., 2004), and (Svoboda & Pajdla, 2002). Unlike using a specific model for the sensor in use, we choose to apply a generalized parametric model of f, which is suitable to different kinds of sensors. The reason for doing so, is that we want this model to compensate for any misalignment between the focus point of the mirror (or the fisheye lens) and the camera optical center. Furthermore, we desire our generalized function to approximately hold with those sensors where the single viewpoint property is not exactly verified (e.g. generic fisheye cameras). We propose the following polynomial form for f

$$f(u'',v'')=a_0+a_1\rho''+a_2\rho''^2+\ldots+a_N\rho''^N \tag{3}$$

where the coefficients a_i, $i=0,1,2,\ldots\mathrm{N}$ and the polynomial degree N are the calibration parameters that we want to determine. This polynomial description of f can be more simplified by considering that all previous definitions of *f* always satisfy the following:

$$\left.\frac{df}{d\rho}\right|_{\rho=0} = 0 \tag{4}$$

This property holds for hyperbolic and parabolic mirrors or fisheye cameras (see (Kumler & Bauer, 2000), (Micusik et al., 2004), and (Svoboda & Pajdla, 2002)).
This simplification allows us to assume $a_1 = 0$, and thus (3) can be rewritten as:

$$f(u'',v'') = a_0 + a_2\rho''^2 + ... + a_N\rho''^N \tag{5}$$

As a consequence, we reduced the number of parameters to be estimated.
To resume, equation (1) can be rewritten as

$$\lambda \cdot \begin{bmatrix} u'' \\ v'' \\ w'' \end{bmatrix} = \lambda \cdot \mathbf{g}(\mathrm{A}\boldsymbol{u}'+\mathrm{t}) = \lambda \cdot \begin{bmatrix} (\mathrm{A}\boldsymbol{u}'+\mathrm{t}) \\ f(u'',v'') \end{bmatrix} = \mathrm{P} \cdot \boldsymbol{X}, \qquad \lambda > 0 \tag{6}$$

4. Camera Calibration

4.1 Solving for intrinsic and extrinsic parameters

According to what we told so far, to calibrate an omnidirectional camera, we have to estimate the parameters *A*, *t*, $a_0, a_2, ...,$ and a_N.

In our approach, we decided to separate the estimation of these parameters into two stages. In one, we estimate the affine parameters *A* and *t*. In the other one, we estimate the coefficients $a_0, a_2, ...,$ and a_N.

The parameters *A* and *t* describe the affine transformation that relates the sensor plane to the camera plane (figures 1.b and 1.c). *A* is the stretch matrix and *t* is the translation vector $\overline{I_c O_c}$ (figure 1.c). To estimate *A* and *t* we introduce a method, which, unlike other previous works, does not require the visibility of the circular external boundary of the mirror (sketched by the ellipse in figure 1.c). This method is based on an iterative procedure, which starts by setting *A* to the identity matrix *Eye* and *t=0*. This assumption means that the camera plane and the sensor plane initially coincide. The correct elements of *A* will be estimated afterwards by non linear refinement, while *t* will be estimated by an iterative search algorithm. This approach will be detailed in section 4.3.
According to this, from now on we assume *A=Eye* and *t=0*, which means $\boldsymbol{u}'' = \boldsymbol{u}'$. Thus, by substituting this relation in (6) and using (5), we have the following projection equation

$$\lambda \cdot \begin{bmatrix} u'' \\ v'' \\ w'' \end{bmatrix} = \lambda \cdot \mathbf{g}(\boldsymbol{u}') = \lambda \cdot \begin{bmatrix} u' \\ v' \\ f(\rho') \end{bmatrix} = \lambda \cdot \begin{bmatrix} u' \\ v' \\ a_0 + a_2\rho'^2 + ... + a_N\rho'^N \end{bmatrix} = \mathrm{P} \cdot \boldsymbol{X}, \ \lambda > 0 \tag{7}$$

where now u' and v' are the pixel coordinates of an image point with respect to the image center, and ρ' is the Euclidean distance. Also, observe that now only *N* parameters ($a_0, a_2, ..., a_N$) need to be estimated. From now on, we will refer to these parameters as intrinsic parameters.

During the calibration procedure, a planar pattern of known geometry is shown at different unknown positions, which are related to the sensor coordinate system by a rotation matrix $R \in \Re^{3x3}$ and a translation $T \in \Re^{3x1}$. R and T will be referred to as extrinsic parameters. Let I^i be an observed image of the calibration pattern, $\boldsymbol{M}_{ij} = [X_{ij}, Y_{ij}, Z_{ij}]$ the 3D coordinates of its points in the pattern coordinate system, and $\boldsymbol{m}_{ij} = [u_{ij}, v_{ij}]^T$ the correspondent pixel coordinates in the image plane. Since we assumed the pattern to be planar, without loss of generality we have $Z_{ij} = 0$. Then, equation (7) becomes:

$$\lambda_{ij} \cdot \boldsymbol{p}_{ij} = \lambda_{ij} \cdot \begin{bmatrix} u_{ij} \\ v_{ij} \\ a_0 + a_2 \rho'^2 + ... + a_N \rho'^N \end{bmatrix} = \mathrm{P}^i \cdot \boldsymbol{X} = \begin{bmatrix} \boldsymbol{r}_1^i & \boldsymbol{r}_2^i & \boldsymbol{r}_3^i & T^i \end{bmatrix} \cdot \begin{bmatrix} X_{ij} \\ Y_{ij} \\ 0 \\ 1 \end{bmatrix} = \begin{bmatrix} \boldsymbol{r}_1^i & \boldsymbol{r}_2^i & T^i \end{bmatrix} \cdot \begin{bmatrix} X_{ij} \\ Y_{ij} \\ 1 \end{bmatrix} \quad (8)$$

where $\boldsymbol{r}_1, \boldsymbol{r}_2$ and $\boldsymbol{r}_3$ are the column vectors of R.

Therefore, in order to solve for camera calibration, the extrinsic parameters have also to be determined for each pose of the calibration pattern.

Observing equation (8), we can eliminate the dependence from the depth scale λ_{ij} by multiplying both sides of the equation vectorially by $\boldsymbol{p}_{ij}$. This implies that each point p_j contributes three homogeneous non linear equations

$$\begin{cases} v_j \cdot (r_{31} X_j + r_{32} Y_j + t_3) - f(\rho_j) \cdot (r_{21} X_j + r_{22} Y_j + t_2) = 0 & (9.1) \\ f(\rho_j) \cdot (r_{11} X_j + r_{12} Y_j + t_1) - u_j \cdot (r_{31} X_j + r_{32} Y_j + t_3) = 0 & (9.2) \\ u_j \cdot (r_{21} X_j + r_{22} Y_j + t_2) - v_j \cdot (r_{11} X_j + r_{12} Y_j + t_1) = 0 & (9.3) \end{cases}$$

where the sub-index i has been removed to lighten the notation, and t_1, t_2 and t_3 are the elements of T.

Observe that in (9), X_j, Y_j and Z_j are known, and so are u_j, v_j. Also, observe that only (9.3) is linear in the unknown $r_{11}, r_{12}, r_{21}, r_{22}, t_1, t_2$.

From now on, the details for the resolution of equation (9) can be found in (Scaramuzza et al., 2006). The principle of the technique consists first in solving for the parameters $r_{11}, r_{12}, r_{21}, r_{22}, t_1$, and t_2 by linearly solving equation (9.3). Next, we use the solution of (9.3) as input to (9.1) and (9.2), and solve for the remaining parameters $a_0, a_2, ..., a_N$ and t_3. In both steps, the solution is achieved by using linear least-square minimization.

Up to now, we didn't specify which polynomial degree N one should use. To compute the best N, we actually start from N=2. Then, we increase N by unitary steps and we compute the average value of the reprojection error of all calibration points. The procedure stops when a minimum error is found. Typical empirical values for N are usually N=3 or N=4.

4.2 Detection of the Image Center

As stated in sections 1 and 2, a peculiarity of our calibration toolbox is that it requires the minimum user interaction. One of the tools that accomplish this task is its capability of

identifying the center of the omnidirectional image O_c (figure 1.c) even when the external boundary of the sensor is not visible in the image.
At the beginning of section 4.1, we made the following assumptions for *A* and *t*, namely *A=Eye* and *t=0*. Then, we derived the equations for solving for the intrinsic and extrinsic parameters that are valid only under those assumptions.

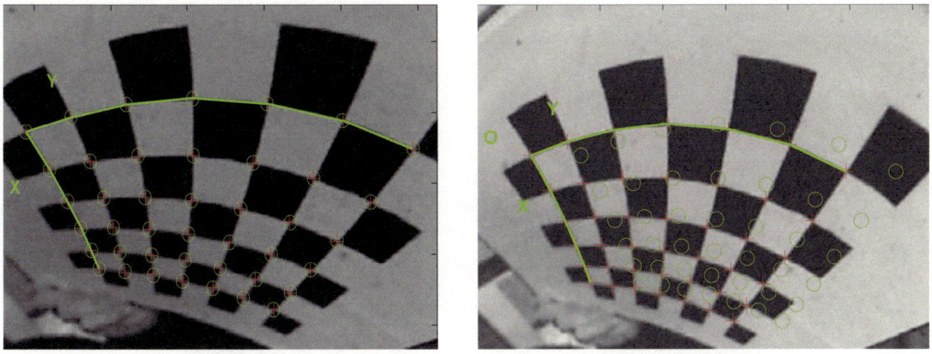

(a) (b)

Figure 2. When the position of the center is correct, the 3D points of the checker board do correctly project (green rounds) onto the calibration points (red crosses) (a). Conversely, when the position of the center is wrong, the points do not project onto the real calibration points (b)

In figure 2.a, the reader can see what happens when the position of the center is correct. The red crosses are the input calibration points selected by the user. The green rounds are the 3D points reprojected onto the images according to the intrinsic and extrinsic parameters estimated by the calibration. As the reader can see, the 3D points perfectly overlay the input points, meaning that the calibration worked properly. Figure 2.b shows the result when the input position of the center is wrong, that is, the reprojection error is large. Motivated by this observation, we performed many trials of our calibration procedure for different center locations, and, for each trial, we computed the Sum of Squared Reprojection Errors (SSRE). As a result, we verified that the SSRE always has a global minimum at the correct center location.
This result leads us to an exhaustive search of the center O_c, which stops when the difference between two potential center locations is smaller than a certain ε (we used ε=0.5 pixels). The algorithm is the following:

1. At each step of this iterative search, a fixed number of candidate center locations is uniformly selected from a given image region (see figure 3).
2. For each of these points, calibration is performed by using that point as a potential center location and SSRE is computed.
3. The point providing the minimum SSRE is taken as a potential center.
4. The search proceeds by selecting other candidate locations in the region around that point, and steps 1, 2 and 3 are repeated until the stop-condition is satisfied.

Observe that the computational cost of this iterative search is so low that it takes less than 3 seconds to stop.
At this point, the reader might be wondering how we do estimate the elements of matrix *A*. In fact, at the beginning we assumed *A=Eye*. The iterative algorithm mentioned above

exhaustively searches the location of the center (namely O_c) by leaving A unchanged. The reason for doing so is that the eccentricity of the external boundary of an omnidirectional image is usually close to zero, which means A~Eye. Therefore, we chose to estimate A in a second stage by using a non linear minimization method, which is described in section 4.3.

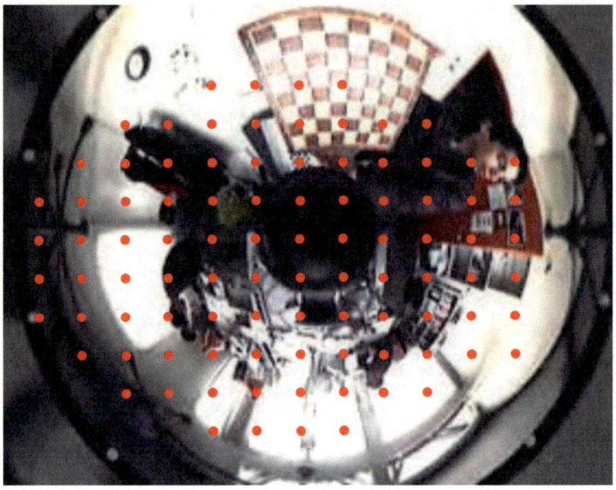

Figure 3. An omnidirectional image used for calibration with a chessboard used as a calibration pattern. The red points identify the candidate center locations taken during the first step of the algorithm. At each step, the candidate points occupy a smaller and smaller region around the final convergence point

4.3 Non Linear Refinement

The linear solution given in section 4.1 is obtained through minimizing an algebraic distance, which is not physically meaningful. To this end, we chose to refine the calibration parameters through maximum likelihood inference.

Let us assume that we are given K images of a model plane, each one containing L corner points. Next, let us assume that the image points are corrupted by independent and identically distributed noise. Then, the maximum likelihood estimate can be obtained by minimizing the following functional:

$$E = \sum_{i=1}^{K}\sum_{j=1}^{L}\left\| m_{ij} - \hat{m}\left(R_i, \boldsymbol{T}_i, A, O_c, a_0, a_2, ..., a_N, \boldsymbol{M}_j\right)\right\|^2 \tag{10}$$

where $\hat{m}\left(R_i, \boldsymbol{T}_i, A, O_c, a_0, a_2, ..., a_N, \boldsymbol{M}_j\right)$ is the reprojection of the point $\boldsymbol{M}_j$ of the plane i according to equation (1). R_i and T_i are the rotation and translation matrices of each plane pose. R_i is parameterized by a vector of 3 parameters related to R_i by the Rodrigues formula. Observe that now we incorporate into the functional both the stretch matrix A and the center of the omnidirectional image O_c.

By minimizing the functional defined in (10), we actually find the calibration parameters which minimize the reprojection error. In order to speed up the convergence, we decided to split the non linear minimization into two steps. The first one refines the extrinsic parameters, ignoring the intrinsic ones. Then, the second step uses the extrinsic parameters

just estimated, and refines the intrinsic ones. By performing many simulations, we found that this splitting does not affect the final result with respect to a global minimization.
To minimize (10), we used the Levenberg-Marquadt algorithm (Levenberg, 1944; Marquardt, 1963), as implemented in the Matlab function `lsqnonlin`. The algorithm requires an initial guess for the parameters. These initial parameters are the ones obtained using the linear technique described in section 4.1. As a first guess for A, we used the identity matrix, while for O_c we used the position estimated through the iterative procedure explained in subsection 4.2.

5. Introduction to the OcamCalib Toolbox for Matlab

The reason we implemented the OcamCalib Toolbox for Matlab is to allow any user to easily and quickly calibrate his own omnidirectional camera. The OcamCalib toolbox can be freely downloaded from the Internet (e.g. google for "ocamcalib"). The outstanding features of the toolbox are the following:

- Capability of calibrating different kinds of central omnidirectional cameras without any knowledge about the parameters of the camera or about the shape of the mirror.
- Automatic detection of the center.
- Visual feedback about the quality of the calibration result by reprojecting the 3D points onto the input images.
- Computer assisted selection of the input points. Indeed, the selection of the corner points on the calibration pattern is assisted by a corner detector.

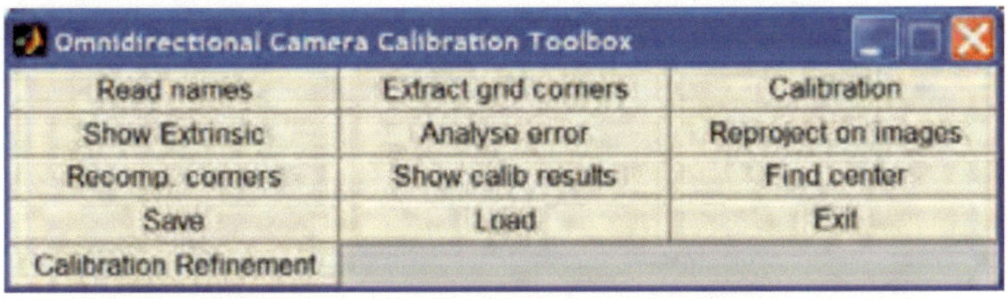

Figure 4. The graphical user interface of the OcamCalib Toolbox

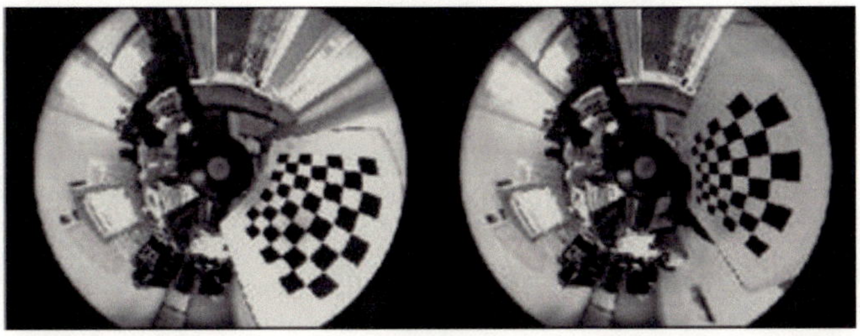

Figure 5. Some pictures with the checker board used as a calibration grid. In our experiments, we used at least 5 or more images with the grid shown all around the camera

The user interface of the toolbox is depicted in figure 4. After having collected a few pictures of a chessboard shown all around the omnidirectional camera (see figure 5), the images can be loaded for calibration (i.e. use "Read names"). In the second step, the user can start selecting the corner points of the pattern using the "Extracting grid corners" tool. By this tool, the user is asked to click on all the corner points by following the left-right order. To achieve high accuracy in the selection of the input points, the clicking is assisted by a Harris base corner detector (Harris & Stephens, 1988).

In the third step, the calibration can be done by means of two tools. The "Calibration" tool will ask the user to specify the position of the center in case he knows, if not, the user can directly use the "Find center" tool, which automatically applies the iterative search algorithm described in 4.2. In both cases, the calibration is performed by using the linear estimation technique mentioned in 4.1. The optimal calibration parameters in the maximum likelihood sense can be estimated by the "Calibration Refinement" tool, which implements the non linear minimization described in 4.3. After the previous steps, the user can choose among several tools:

- "Show Extrinsic" visualizes the reconstructed 3D poses of the grid in the camera reference frame (figure 6).
- "Analyze error" visualizes the reprojection error of each calibration point along the x-y-axes.
- "Reproject on images" reprojects all the 3D points onto the images according to the calibrated parameters.
- "Recompute corners" attempts to automatically recompute the position of every corner point hand selected by the user. This is done by using the reprojected 3D points as initial guess locations for the corners.

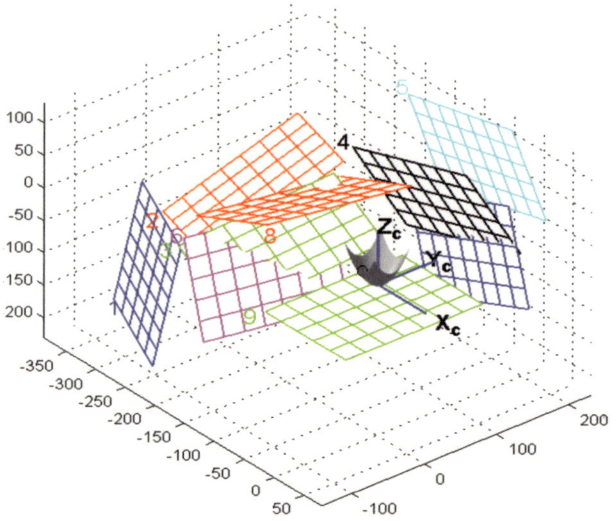

Figure 6. A picture of our simulator showing several calibration patterns and the virtual omnidirectional camera at the axis origin

After the calibration, all the parameter can be accessed through the structure "ocam_model". The calibrated camera model can then be used for other applications by means of the following two functions:

- **m = world2cam(M, ocam_model),** which reprojects a 3D point (`M`) onto the image and returns its pixel coordinates (`m`).
- **M = cam2world(m, ocam_model),** which, for every image point `m`, returns the 3D coordinates of the correspondent vector (`M`) emanating from the single effective viewpoint. This function is the inverse of the previous one.

6. Results

We evaluated the performance of our toolbox through calibration experiments both on synthetic and real images. In particular, we used synthetic images to study the robustness of our calibration technique in case of inaccuracy in detecting the calibration points. To this end, we generated several synthetic poses of a calibration pattern. Then, Gaussian noise with zero mean and standard deviation σ was added to the projected image points. We varied the noise level from σ=0.1 to σ=3.0 pixels, and, for each noise level, we performed 100 independent calibration trials and computed the mean reprojection error. Figure 7 shows the plot of the reprojection error as a function of σ. Observe that we separated the results obtained by using the linear minimization alone from the results of the non linear refinement. As the reader can see, in both cases the average error increases linearly with the noise level. Furthermore, the reprojection error of the non linear estimation keeps always smaller than the error computed by the linear method. Finally, notice that when σ=1.0, which is larger than the normal noise in practical situations, the average reprojection error of the non linear method is lower than 0.4 pixels.

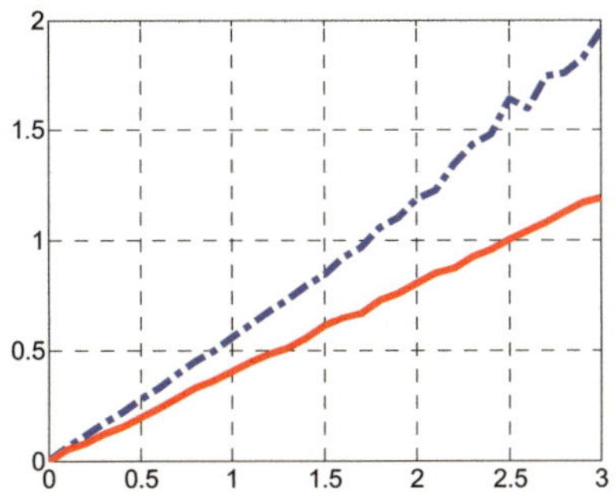

Figure 7. The reprojection error versus σ. The dashed line represents the results obtained by using the linear minimization alone. The solid line shows the results after the non linear refinement. Both units are considered in pixels

An indirect method to evaluate the quality of the calibration of a real camera consists in reconstructing the 3D structure of an object from its images and checking then the quality of the reconstruction. This problem is known by the computer vision community as structure from motion. The object we used in this experiment is a trihedron made up of three orthogonal chessboard-like patterns of known geometry (see figure 8.a). Our omnidirectional camera is KAIDAN 360° One VR with a hyperbolic mirror.

After having calibrated the camera, we took two images of the trihedron from two different unknown positions (see figure 8.b). Next, several point matches were hand selected from both views of the object and the Eight Point algorithm was applied (Longuet-Higgins, 1981). In order to obtain good reconstruction results, more than eight points (we used 135 points) were used. The method mentioned so far gives a first good 3D reconstruction of the points. A better estimation of the 3D structure can be obtained by densely using all the pixels of the images. To accomplish this task, we used the first estimation along with normalized cross correlation to automatically match all the points of the image pair. Finally, all matches were used to compute the structure. The results of the reconstruction are shown in figure 8.c.

As the reconstruction with one single camera can be done up to a scale factor, we recovered the scale factor by comparing the average size of a reconstructed checker with the real size on the trihedron. In the end, we computed the angles between the three planes fitting the reconstructed points and we found the following values: 94.6°, 86.8° and 85.3°. Moreover, the average distances of these points from the fitted planes were respectively 0.05 cm, 0.75 cm and 0.07 cm. Finally, being the size of each checker 6.0 cm x 6.0 cm, we also calculated the dimension of every reconstructed checker and we found an average error of 0.3 cm. These results comply with the expected orthogonality of the surfaces and the size of the checkers in the ground truth.

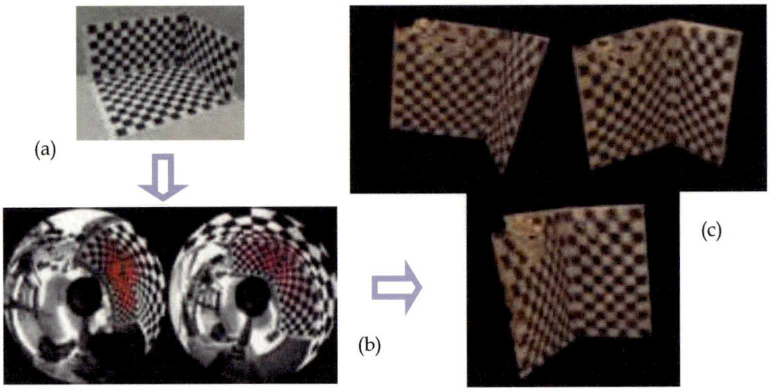

Figure 8. (a) The object to be reconstructed. (b) Two omnidirectional pictures of the object taken from two unknown positions. (c) Dense 3D reconstruction of the object. The reconstruction is very good, meaning that the model of the camera was well estimated

7. Conclusion

In this chapter, we presented a method for calibrating any central omnidirectional camera both dioptric or catadioptric. The method relies on a generalized parametric function that describes the relation between a given pixel point and the correspondent 3D vector emanating from the single effective view point of the camera. We describe this function by means of a polynomial expansion whose coefficients are the parameters to be calibrated.

Furthermore, we presented a toolbox for Matlab (named OcamCalib) that implements the mentioned calibration procedure. The toolbox is available on-line. We described the tools and the main features of our toolbox, one of which being the capability to automatically identify the center of the omnidirectional image. The toolbox relies on the use of a chessboard-like calibration pattern that is shown by the user at a few different positions and orientations. Then, the user is only asked to click on the corner points of the patterns. The performance of the toolbox was finally evaluated through experiments both on synthetic and real images. Because of its ease of use, the toolbox turns out to be very practical, and allows any inexpert user to calibrate his own omnidirectional camera.

8. Acknowledgements

This work was conducted within the EU Integrated Projects COGNIRON ("The Cognitive Robot Companion") and BACS ("Bayesian Approach to Cognitive Systems"). It was funded by the European Commission Division FP6-IST Future and Emerging Technologies under the contracts FP6-IST-002020 and FP6-IST-027140 respectively.

We want to thank Zoran Zivkovic and Olaf Booij, from the Intelligent Systems Laboratory of Amsterdam (University of Amsterdam), for providing the sample images included in our toolbox.
Furthermore, we want to thank Dr. Jean-Yves Bouguet, from Intel Corporation, for providing some functions used by our toolbox.

9. References

Baker, S. & Nayar, S.K. (1998). A theory of catadioptric image formation. *Proceedings of the 6th International Conference on Computer Vision*, pp. 35–42, ISBN 81-7319-221-9, India, January 1998, IEEE Computer Society, Bombay.

Svoboda, T., Pajdla T. & Hlavac, V. (1997). Central panoramic cameras: Geometry and design. *Research report K335/97/147*, Czech Technical University, Faculty of Electrical Engineering, Center for Machine Perception, Czech Republic, December 1997. Praha.

Micusik, B. & Pajdla, T. (2003). Estimation of omnidirectional camera model from epipolar geometry. *Proceedings of the International Conference on Computer Vision and Pattern Recognition*. ISBN 0-7695-1900-8, US, June 2003, IEEE Computer Society, Madison.

Zhang, Z (2000). A Flexible New Technique for Camera Calibration. *IEEE Transactions on Pattern Analysis and Machine Intelligence*. Volume 22, No. 11, November 2000, ISSN 0162-8828.

Kumler, J. & Bauer, M. (2000). Fisheye lens designs and their relative performance. *Proceedings of SPIE Conference*. Vol. 4093. pp. 360-369. 2000.

Micusik, B., Martinec, D. & Pajdla, T. (2004). 3D Metric Reconstruction from Uncalibrated Omnidirectional Images. *Proceedings of the Asian Conference on Computer Vision*. January 2004, Korea.

Svoboda, T. & Pajdla, T. (2001). Epipolar Geometry for Central Catadioptric Cameras. In. *Panoramic Vision: Sensors, Theory and Applications*, Benosman R. & Kang, S.B., pp. 85-114, Springer.

Cauchois, C., Brassart, E., Delahoche, L. & Delhommelle, T. (2000). Reconstruction with the calibrated SYCLOP sensor. *Proceedings of the IEEE International Conference on Intelligent Robots and Systems*, pp. 1493–1498, ISBN: 0-7803-6348-5, Japan, October 2000, IEEE Computer Society, Takamatsu.

Bakstein, H. & Pajdla, T. (2002). Panoramic mosaicing with a 180° field of view lens. *Proceedings of the IEEE Workshop on Omnidirectional Vision*, pp. 60–67, ISBN: 0-7695-1629-7, Denmark, June 2002, IEEE Computer Society, Copenhagen.

Geyer, C. & Daniilidis, K. (2002). Paracatadioptric camera calibration. *IEEE Transactions on Pattern Analysis and Machine Intelligence*, Vol. 24, No. 5, May 2002, pp. 687-695, ISSN 0162-8828.

Gluckman, J. & Nayar, S. K. (1998). Ego-motion and omnidirectional cameras. *Proceedings of the 6th International Conference on Computer Vision*, pp. 999-1005, ISBN 81-7319-221-9, India, January 1998, IEEE Computer Society, Bombay.

Kang. S.B. (2000). Catadioptric self-calibration. *Proceedings of the IEEE International Conference on Computer Vision and Pattern Recognition*, pp. 201-207, ISBN: 0-7695-0662-3, USA, June 2000, IEEE Computer Society, Hilton Head Island.

Micusik, B., & Pajdla, T. (2004). Para-catadioptric Camera Auto-calibration from Epipolar Geometry. *Proceedings of the Asian Conference on Computer Vision*. January 2004, Korea.

Micusik, B., D.Martinec & Pajdla, T. (2004). 3D Metric Reconstruction from Uncalibrated Omnidirectional Images. *Proceedings of the Asian Conference on Computer Vision*. January 2004, Korea.

Bougnoux, S. (1998). From projective to Euclidean space under any practical situation, a criticism of self-calibration, *Proceedings of the 6th International Conference on Computer Vision*, pp. 790–796, ISBN 81-7319-221-9, India, January 1998, IEEE Computer Society, Bombay.

Swaminathan, R., Grossberg, M.D. & Nayar. S. K. (2001). Caustics of catadioptric cameras". *Proceedings of the IEEE International Conference on Computer Vision*, pp. 2-9, ISBN: 0-7695-1143-0, Canada, July 2001, IEEE Computer Society, Vancouver.

Ying, X. & Hu, Z. (2004). Catadioptric Camera Calibration Using Geometric Invariants, *IEEE Transactions on Pattern Analysis and Machine Intelligence*, Vol. 26, No. 10, October 2004, pp. 1260-1271, ISSN: 0162-8828.

Ying, X. & Hu, Z. (2004). Can We Consider Central Catadioptric Cameras and Fisheye Cameras within a Unified Imaging Model?, *Proceedings of the European Conference on Computer Vision*, pp. 442-455, Czech Republic, Lecture Notes in Computer Science, May 2004, Prague,

Barreto, J. & Araujo, H. (2005). Geometric Properties of Central Catadioptric Line Images and their Application in Calibration, *IEEE Transactions on Pattern Analysis and Machine Intelligence*, Vol. 27, No. 8, pp. 1327-1333, August 2005.

Sturm, P. & Ramaligam, S. (2004). A Generic Concept for Camera Calibration, *Proceedings of the European Conference on Computer Vision*, pp. 1-13, Czech Republic, Lecture Notes in Computer Science, May 2004, Prague,

Scaramuzza, D., Martinelli, A. & Siegwart, R. (2006). A Toolbox for Easy calibrating Omnidirectional Cameras. *Proceedings of the IEEE International Conference on Intelligent Robots and Systems*, pp. 5695–5701, China, October 2006, Beijing.

Scaramuzza, D., Martinelli, A. & Siegwart, R. (2006). A Flexible Technique for Accurate Omnidirectional Camera Calibration and Structure from Motion, *Proceedings of IEEE International Conference on Computer Vision Systems*, USA, January 2006, New York.

Levenberg, K. (1944). A Method for the Solution of Certain Problems in Least Squares, *Quarterly of Applied Mathematics*, Vol. 2, No. 2, pp. 164-168, July 1944.

Marquardt, D. (1963). An Algorithm for Least-Squares Estimation of Nonlinear Parameters, *SIAM Journal on Applied Mathematics*. Vol. 11, No. 2, pp. 431-441, 1963.

Harris, C. & Stephens, M.J. (1988). A combined corner and edge detector, *Proceedings of The Fourth Alvey Vision Conference*, pp. 147-151, UK, 1988, Manchester.

Longuet-Higgins, H.C. (1981). A computer algorithm for reconstructing a scene from two projections. *Nature*, Vol. 293, Sept 1981, pp. 133–135.

18

Dynamic 3D-Vision

K.-D. Kuhnert , M. Langer, M. Stommel and A. Kolb
University Siegen
Germany

1. Introduction

Measuring and recognising the surfaces of the surrounding world forms a ubiquitous problem in automation and robotics. The knowledge of the environment allows a flexible and autonomous behaviour in different situations. Stereo vision belongs to the most popular techniques for gathering this information because it provides the dense depth information necessary for complex grasping tasks. Compared to laser scanners stereo cameras also have the advantage of higher framerates, so they are widely used for mobile robots. Porta (2005) e.g. uses the Small Vision stereo system (Konolige, 1997) to enhance localisation of a mobile robot: Features from depth maps are used additionally to appearance based intensity features. Other examples include Zhu et al. (2004) or Kang et al. (1995). However, the main problems of stereo vision remain speed and robustness. In order to accelerate the time-consuming registration of the stereo images and avoid specialised hardware, Sun (2002) employs an intelligent subregioning mechanism which reduces the search space of the correspondence analysis. Another approach builds upon the usage of modern SIMD processor instructions as documented by Sunyoto et al. (2004). Kim et al. (2005) on the other hand achieve real-time behaviour by segmenting foreground objects from the background. Depth information is then only updated for moving objects. Of course this approach is problematic for mobile robots. The lack of robustness of stereo analysis for particular scenes mainly arises from depth discontinuities and ambiguous surface texture. Kang et al. (1995) avoid these ambiguities by projecting textured light on the scene, but this is no general solution. Kim et al. (2005) made experiments with an adaptive matching window to increase the accuracy near edges. Zhao and Katupitiya (2006) examined the effect of occlusion and developed a method that detects occlusion areas and adapts a matching window appropriately. To evaluate and compare the robustness of different stereo algorithms, Scharstein et al. (2001) propose a taxonomy for different stereo algorithms and create a testbed including stereo images with groundtruth. Using this testbed we will document the results of the software system for the computation of dense disparity maps presented here. Our stereo system unites some of the speed optimisations mentioned above and hence achieves real-time behaviour. The calibration procedure and some comments on the brightness change constraint will be given. We will also present results for the distance measurements with a PMD camera ("Photonic Mixer Device", Schwarte (2001), Kraft et al. (2004)) which is a technique for measuring the distance of an object by the time of flight of an active infrared illumination. The calibration procedure and the specifics of the measurements will be described, especially for scenes with surfaces almost in parallel to the optical axis of the system. Finally the results on combining the stereo and PMD technique will be given, discussing the advantages and disadvantages.

2. Stereo

Depth measurement by stereo vision algorithm is done by computing a so called (sparse or dense) *disparity map*. Disparity maps encode the depth for each reference pixel in the stereo images. Using the well-known stereo geometry formula 12 and the disparity map, one can easily calculate the depth value of any given pixel. The calculation of disparity maps leads to the so called *stereo correspondence problem*.

The stereo correspondence problem can be formulated as the problem to efficiently traverse a two-dimensional search space consisting of any intensity value at any position in the stereo images. Algorithms finding corresponding pixel pairs in acceptable time will be presented later.

When one pixel of one stereo image is compared with one pixel of the other stereo image, the degree of correspondence between these pixels is calculated using a certain metric. Two of the most prominent metrics are the *sum of absolute differences (SAD)* and the *sum of squared differences (SSD)*. Both metrics have in common that they calculate the correspondence value over a certain block size. This block size is usually represented by a rectangular region pixel by pixel around the pixels that are to be matched. SAD sums up both rectangular regions and takes the absolute value of the difference of these sums, whereas SSD takes the squared value of the difference of these sums. Both functions can be efficiently computed using modern SIMD (Single Instruction, Multiple Data) processor instruction sets.

2.1 Review

In this part we review various stereo correspondence algorithms for the traversing of the two-dimensional search space mentioned earlier. First these algorithms are briefly described, then concrete implementations of these algorithms are discussed.

All of the reviewed algorithms belong to the class of *block-matching* methods along a *horizontal scanline*. Therefore, the images must be - at least approximately – rectified if the optical axes of the cameras are not adjusted in parallel. Due to the rectification and the epipolar constraint (see Faugeras, 1993), it can be presumed that corresponding pixels in stereo image pairs can be found on the same horizontal lines in both images. Then we define a three-dimensional correspondence candidate matrix (also called *cost matrix*) $C(x,y,d(x,y))$ holding all disparity value candidates d of a given reference pixel at position (x,y). After building this matrix, one needs to find efficient algorithms for reordering the optimal disparity value for any given reference pixel. Several geometric and object specific constraints reduce the search space and lead to an increase in both speed and quality of the results of the correspondence analysis. A set of the most important constraints is given in the following.

The so called *brightness change constraint* states that if a pixel in one of the stereo images has a corresponding pixel in the other image, the intensity values of these pixels need to be same. Fulfilling this requirement makes a reliable pixel matching even possible, because all of the later discussed algorithms work intensity based. This is actually one of the most important constraints concerning the quality of the correspondence analysis' results.

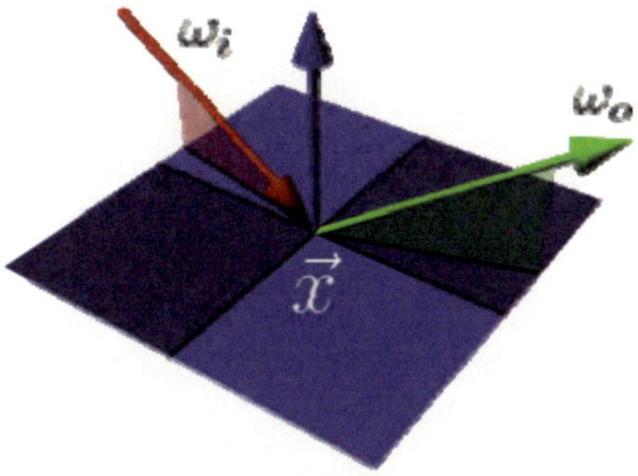

Figure 1. Incoming light ray (marked red) with angle $\mathbf{\omega}_i = (\theta_i, \varphi_i)$ and outgoing/reflected light ray (marked green) with angle $\mathbf{\omega}_o = (\theta_o, \varphi_o)$ at point $\mathbf{x}$

Object surfaces need to be *piecewise smooth*. This prerequisite ensures that corresponding pixel pairs in both images have almost the same disparity values. This enables a further reduction of the search space, because corresponding pixels can be found around a certain offset on a scanline in the analyzed image.

The object surfaces are highly *textured*. The more textured the surfaces are, the more reliably corresponding pixels can be found. If for instance an object surface has only one colour, it is almost impossible to distinguish corresponding pixels from non-corresponding pixels on these surfaces because they look identical.

The *monotony constraint* demands that, if the stereo images are rectified, corresponding pixel pairs are to be searched in the same direction on a scanline. That means fulfilling the monotony constraint, the pixel pairs' occurrence is ordered on the scanlines.

As a last important constraint the objects are supposed to be *equally visible* for both cameras of the stereo-system. That means, objects in a scene are not partially occluded. Partial occlusion leads to different projections of the same object onto the image planes of the stereo-cameras, because the cameras look at the objects from slightly different angles. The consequence of that effect is that the left and the right stereo image possess different, even mutually exclusive information of the object in the scene. Hence errors can be expected when trying to match pixels in one image along a scanline in the other image where the other image actually has no information about these pixels at all.

As being said, the brightness change constraint belongs to the most important constraints for the set of intensity based stereo matching algorithms. The majority of errors occurring in the matching process can be classified as violations of this constraint. The reason why this constraint is so easily violated is mainly due to the angle dependent *reflection properties* of an object as well as the problem of *subpixel edge shift*.

The reflection properties of an object mainly depend on the surface of the object as well as on the light reaching the object surface. These two factors determine the equation of the reflected light intensity

$$L_o(\mathbf{x}, \mathbf{\omega}_o) = \int_\Omega f(\mathbf{x}, \mathbf{\omega}_i \to \mathbf{\omega}_o) L_i(\mathbf{x}, \mathbf{\omega}_i) \cos\theta_i d\omega_i, \tag{1}$$

where $\omega_i = (\theta_i, \varphi_i)$ and $\omega_o = (\theta_o, \varphi_o)$ denote the solid angle of incoming and reflected light rays at point $\mathbf{x}$ as shown in Figure 1.
L1 and L2 denote the light intensities of the incoming and outgoing direction of the light rays. The term $f(\mathbf{x}, \omega_i \rightarrow \omega_o)$ represents the so called *bidirectional reflectance distribution function* (BRDF) measuring the physical reflectance behaviour of the surface material. For any light ray with given entry angle Ω hitting the object at point $\mathbf{x}$, the BRDF yields the quotient of irradiance and emittance of any reflected light ray. The model of the BRDF is based on the concept of so called *micro facets*. Micro facets are microscopically small mirrors randomly aligned and distributed all over the object's surface. The alignment of these mirrors is determined by the probability distribution of eq. 2:

$$f(\mathbf{x}, \omega_i \rightarrow \omega_o) = \frac{1}{\pi} \frac{F \cdot D \cdot G}{\langle \omega_o \circ \mathbf{n} \rangle \langle \omega_i \circ \mathbf{n} \rangle}, \qquad (2)$$

F denotes the *fresnel-factor* which models the fraction properties of the object material, D is the *probability distribution function* of the micro facets and G is the *geometry factor* modelling shading between the micro facets. An in-depth look into the complex mathematical deduction of these parameters can be found in related textbooks. To yield the overall light intensity reflected from a point $\mathbf{x}$, one has to integrate over the entire spatial angle Ω. This complex procedure requires extensive computation time.
The problem of subpixel edge shift results from to the inherently limited resolution of cameras. To measure the light intensity of a pixel of recorded scene, the camera has to integrate the light intensity over a certain area of the scene predetermined by the camera resolution. This causes problems on edges in the scene, because edges typically mark an abrupt change in light intensity values. So the integration process averages the light intensities in the given areas over the edges. Due to high angle dependency of the projection of edges (as described earlier) in such a subpixel integration area, the intensity values of corresponding pixels may differ significantly. This problem can be reduced just slightly by using high resolution cameras.
Hence, when performing intensity based stereo correspondence analysis, one always has to consider these inherent problems. There is no general solution to address these problems and the results need to be interpreted respectively. In the following sections some of the most popular approaches of stereo correspondence analysis are presented.

2.1.1 Winner Takes it All (WTA)

One of the simplest algorithms for searching in the matching matrix is the *Winner Takes it All* method. WTA works as follows: For a given reference pixel WTA walks through the cost matrix selecting that pixel which has the lowest difference to the reference pixel. This is a simple minimum search on a given set of numbers. It is also a local method, because the algorithm operates only on *one* vector of the matching matrix for each reference pixel.
The biggest advantage of such a primitive local method is the easy way of its implementation. Furthermore WTA can most easily be optimized. The disadvantages on the other hand are that local methods highly depend on the constraints discussed earlier. There is also the possibility that identical pixels of the cost matrix are assigned to reference pixels more than once.

2.1.2 Global Methods

In contrast to local methods, global methods perceive the stereo correspondence problems as the problem of minimizing a global energy function. The goal is to find a disparity function *d* which minimizes the global energy function

$$E(d) = E_d(d) + \lambda E_s(d), \qquad (3)$$

as it is described in (Scharstein & Szeliski, 2001). The term $E_d(d)$ measures how well the disparity function *d* matches the stereo pixel pair which is to be evaluated. This is done by eq. 4 which takes all possible corresponding pixel pairs into account. λ is a global constant denoting a weight for $E_s(d)$.

$$E_d(d) = \sum_{(x,y)} C(x, y, d(x, y)) \qquad (4)$$

$E_s(d)$ is responsible for introducing the *piecewise smoothness*-constraint.

After stating the global energy function to be optimized, we now show some popular algorithm for its optimization.

2.1.3 Dynamic Programming (DP) with Scanline Optimization (SO)

The optimization of regular functions $E_s(d)$ using naïve approaches is an NP complete problem. The use of a *dynamic programming* approach helps finding the global minimum of mutually independent scanlines in polynomial time.

DP was first introduced by Richard Bellman in 1953. It describes the process of solving complex problems where one has to find the best decisions to solve this problem one after another. The basic idea of DP is to break down the complex problem into smaller subproblems. After solving these subproblems optimally, the original problem can be solved. The subproblems themselves are broken down into smaller subproblems and so forth until the subproblems have a trivial solution. An important step in DP is memorising (also called *memoization*) the solutions of the already solved subproblems. Otherwise one would have to compute the solutions to the same subproblems over and over again as in the simple recursive approach of computing Fibonacci numbers. DP is especially well suited for finding shortest paths in matrices with associated cost values.

In our case the correspondence analysis is treated like an n-dimensional search problem. The matching costs (defined as the SAD or SSD values of the examined pixel pairs) of *every* point of a scanline assemble the search space. Hence this is a global method. In contrast to local methods (like WTA) not just certain pairs of pixels are taken into account, but a two-dimensional matrix of candidate pixels is considered. Such a matrix is constructed of all reference pixels versus their corresponding candidate pixels. To find the best corresponding pixel out of the candidates, one has to find the shortest path with lowest matching costs in the matrix.

We use *x-d-submatrices* of the whole cost matrix *C(x,y,d(x,y))* as subproblems that are to be optimized. Firstly a certain area in which the path will be searched is preselected. The preselection is done to save computing time and the width of that area may vary. Secondly for every pair of corresponding scanlines in the left and right stereo image, the shortest path through the matrix with least pairwise matching costs is selected.

An extension to the classical dynamic programming approach presented above, is the scanline optimization for which the same prerequisites as discussed above apply. An additional cost-constant is introduced distributing penalties to the candidate pixels, if the values of neighbouring pixels differ too much (like it is the case at object edges). Hence big jumps in disparities are highly penalized disqualifying themselves for the later path search. The decision when to penalize a disparity value is predefined.
Dynamic programming algorithms have the advantage of a higher robustness compared to local methods. This especially holds true if some of the constraints of section 2.1 are not fulfilled. The algorithms exploit the monotony and piecewise-smoothness constraint so that the search space for disparity values can be reduced to pixels located on object surfaces. So it is not possible to select a candidate pixel that is actually located far from the object surface but coincidentally possesses almost an identical intensity value to the reference pixel.
The disadvantage on the other hand is the problem of finding a suitable path in the search space concerning partially occluded pixels. Another drawback is the heavily increased computing time compared to simple local methods.

2.1.4 Simulated Annealing (SA)

Simulated annealing is a heuristically based method in computer science. It is used to solve optimization problems that have a high complexity, which makes going through all combinations to solve the problem computationally infeasible.
SA is inspired by natural annealing processes. For instance, the slow annealing of liquid metal provides enough time for the molecules inside the metal to align them in a way to build a stable crystal structure. That way a low energy state is achieved close to the optimum. Transferred to our optimization problem the temperature corresponds to an acceptance threshold. Below that threshold an intermediate result of the optimization process is still allowed to temporarily worsen.
There are two major algorithms in this field: the *metropolis algorithm* and the *hill climbing algorithm*. The hill climbing algorithm has the ability to leave a local optimum trying to find an even better one. Hence it is the more sophisticated algorithm. A more detailed description of these two algorithms can be found in (Metropolis; Rosenbluth & Teller, 1953).
Simulated annealing yields a very high confidence in the stereo correspondence analysis. Alas it has a very bad runtime due to the very high computational complexity. There can be no real-time behaviour expected from algorithms falling into this category.

2.2 Robustness

We compared various stereo correspondence algorithms with regard to the run-time behaviour and the quality of the computed (dense) disparity maps. We concentrated our work around the implementation of Scharstein/Szeliski (Scharstein & Szeliski, 2001) from the Middlebury University. We optimised their original algorithms with a series of steps like smoothing the images first and working on recursively down sampled sub-images to decrease overall computing time as proposed by Sun (2002). To further decrease the computation time, we also used the MMX processor extensions as proposed by Sunyoto et al. (2004). Using sample stereo-images and their corresponding *groundtruth* images from the Middlebury University we were able to calculate the quality of the resulting disparity map counting the incorrect disparity values (Figure 2). We used the following formula to calculate these values:

$$BP = \frac{1}{N} \sum_{(x,y)} (d_C(x,y) - d_T(x,y) > \delta_d) \quad (5)$$

The variable d_C denotes one element of the calculated disparity map, whereas d_T is an element of the groundtruth map at position *(x,y)*. δ_d is a fault tolerance value. We set it to 1.0.

Figure 2. Left image and groundtruth image of sample stereo image

Matcher	Method		Time [s]	Bad Pixels [%]
Schar/Szel	WTA	SAD	1.04	4.60
		SSD	1.12	4.85
	DP/SO	SAD	4.34	6.46
		SSD	4.35	6.63
	SA	SAD	158.28	4.35
		SSD	147.88	4.54
	building matching-matrix		0.95	N/A
optimized Schar/Szel	WTA	SAD	0.25	7.47
		SSD	0.27	6.14
	DP/SO	SAD	1.09	6.87
		SSD	1.05	6.96
	SA	SAD	39.09	5.74
		SSD	37.10	5.14
	building matching-matrix		0.23	N/A

Table 1. Performance and quality results of different matching algorithms measured on an AMD Athlon XP 1700+ system with 512MB RAM

The results of the different algorithms for the example pictures shown in Figure 2 are presented in table 1. We used a fixes block size of 16x16 pixels. In the top half of the table one can see the values obtained from the original version of the Scharstein/Szeliski implementation. The lower half shows the values achieved with the optimizations extending this implementation. The second column enlists the different matching algorithms used in conjunction with either SAD or SSD as correspondence measurement. The last two columns show the run-time behaviour as well as the quality (measured in the rate of falsely computed disparity values) of the implementation computing the disparity maps of the pictures like shown in Figure 2. The pictures are 32 Bit truecolour images with images sizes of 450 x 375 pixels. Figure 3 shows the corresponding disparity map and the difference image of the groundtruth image with the computed stereo image.

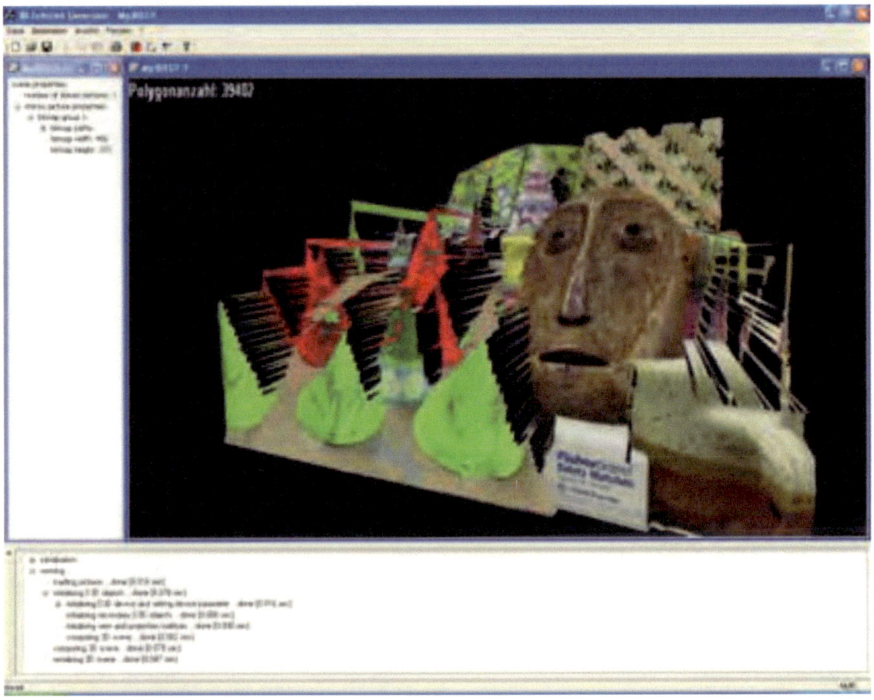

Figure 4. Reconstructed 2.5D-view of the sample scene

Figure 5. A left and a right image of a stereo camera

Table 1 clearly shows that the simple WTA method performs best (in the original *and* optimized version) with regard to run-time behaviour and is only slightly worse than SA with regard to the quality of the computed disparity values. SA on the other hand is about 150 times slower than the simple WTA algorithm and yields to an improvement of just 0.25% - 2.00% regarding disparity quality.

The difference picture of the calculated disparity maps (Figure 3 - right side) shows that errors mainly occur on edges due to partial occlusion. The brightness change constraint in this case is preserved hence leading to no additional errors. It can be expected that under normal conditions the brightness change constraint will be violated and DP/SO may yield better results than the simple WTA, because DP/SO is more robust in this case.

Figure 3. Computed disparity map (using WTA with SSD method) and difference map according to the groundtruth map

We also used other images mainly taken from the (Stereo Vision Research Page, 2007). The results of those pictures resemble the results presented in table 1.

In Figure 4 we present a reconstruction of the original scene using the stereo-images and their corresponding disparity map. This of course cannot be a full 3D-view of the scene because there is only one stereo image pair made from a certain angle. Hence we call this a 2.5D-view of the original scene. The viewer can clearly distinguish which objects were closer to the camera and which were lying in the background.

2.3 Variable Block Size and Interest Operators

Some cameras offer the possibility to automatically control the brightness of the image. Concerning single camera images this is often an improvement. However, for the matching of two images from different cameras this is a clear disadvantage. In a stereo setup the length of the baseline between the cameras causes deviations in the fields of view of the cameras, so only a part of the scene can be seen in both images. The rest of the images is different for the two cameras and influences the brightness control. As a result, also the common image parts have a different brightness. In that case we made good experiences by matching the derivation of the image instead of the pure image intensities.

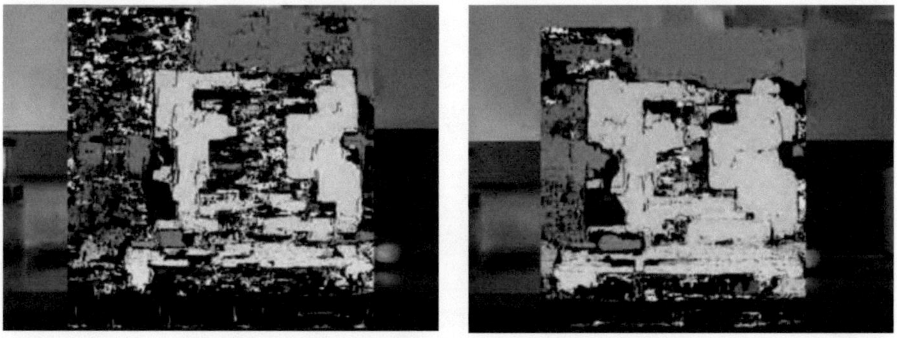

Figure 6. Disparities for a block size of 30x10 pixels and 60x20 pixels

The derivative can also be used as an interest operator, to accelerate matching and in particular to determine the size of the image regions being matched. The following explanations refer to a WTA block-matching algorithm with SSD as similarity measure. The algorithm finds matches by comparing a block from the left image to all positions on the corresponding epipolar line in the right image. Interest operators were introduced by Moravec (1977). Their purpose is to limit image processing operations to the relevant image area and save computational cost. A review on different methods can be found in Bähr and Vögtle (1991). We use the horizontal derivative to find textured image positions in the left image which can be matched robustly to the right image, and to find image positions in the right image which are candidates for a correspondence. Other positions in the right image are not compared, which heavily reduces the computational effort. Since the robustness of stereo analysis relies on texture, we examined the use of maxima of the derivative as positions for matching. The result is a comparatively sparse disparity map because for a given block in the left image there is only one matching position per edge in the right image. The number of positions depends also on the threshold for maxima detection and often a correct maximum is not recognized because the gradient falls below a given threshold. However, the results are quite robust. To increase the number of correspondences, we replaced the maxima detection by simple thresholds for the gradient magnitude. We use a higher threshold for the left image and a lower threshold for the right image, to make sure we obtain all corresponding positions in the right image despite the image noise. The results are both more dense and more robust.

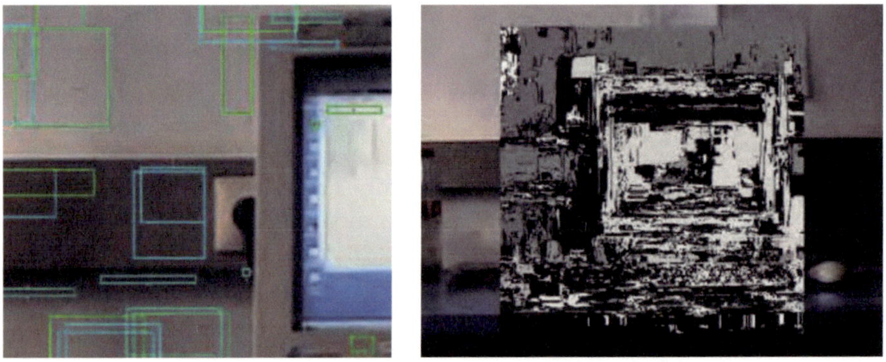

Figure 7. Adaptive block size for the cross method and resulting disparities

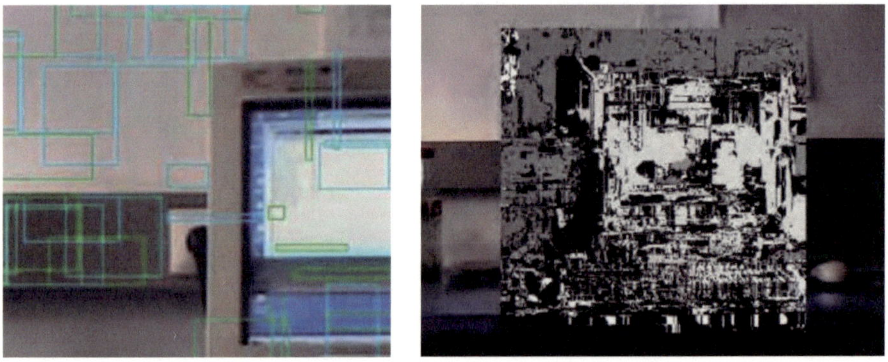

Figure 8. Adaptive block size for the region method and resulting disparities

The stability of the stereo analysis depends also on the chosen block size. Figure 6. shows the disparity maps for the stereo image pair from Figure 5 for different block sizes. Light values indicate a higher disparity, dark areas a lower disparity. Missing values are marked as black. They result from the plausibility test proposed by Faugeras (1993): The matching result in the right image is searched for in the left image. The resulting second match should be the original block in the left image. If this test fails, the disparity value is discarded. For a block size of 30x10 pixels 53 percent of all possible disparity values could be computed. For a block size of 60x20 pixels this value increases to 59 percent. As can be seen from the picture, this is an improvement especially for homogeneous regions. The drawbacks of an

increased block size are the additional computational effort and the lower accuracy, in particular near depth discontinuities.
To overcome these disadvantages, a locally adaptive block size is introduced. In homogeneous regions a higher block size is chosen than in textured regions to make matching more robust if there are few characteristic image features. To reduce the inaccurateness near depth discontinuities, bigger blocks are not allowed to cross sharp edges. For every image position the block size is determined by evaluating the gradient magnitude along the respective image row and column. Starting with an initially small block, the block size is increased horizontally and vertically until the borders of the block reach an edge in the row or column through the centre pixel. If there are no edges the block growth is stopped after a certain maximum size has been reached. The search along a cross was chosen because size determination can be performed very quickly. Figure 7 shows some of the blocks as rectangles. Little dots indicate the edges which stopped the block growth. The right part of Figure 7 shows the resulting disparity map for a maximum block size of 60x60 pixels. In comparison to the disparity map in Figure 6 the results for homogeneous regions have improved. On the other hand, some of the stable but inaccurate disparities near the edges of the monitor are missing now. This is a result of the smaller block size in textured image regions and absolutely correct taking into account the occlusion effects in that area. A drawback of this method is that only edges lying on a cross through the block center have an influence on the block size. The disparity values near the corners of the monitor hence are still inaccurate. To improve that, a second strategy for the size determination is examined. Starting from an initial block size the block is expanded alternating by one row or one column, respectively, if there is no edge in this new row or column. If the block growth is stopped in one dimension, it continues in the other dimension until also there an edge has been reached. The results can be seen in Figure 8. Concerning the corners of the monitor, the disparities are more accurate now, while the remaining values are similar to the results before. For both methods of size determination the gain in density and accurateness of the disparity maps has the disadvantage of a higher computational cost, which is primarily a result of the increased block size for homogeneous regions. The computation of the disparity map by the cross method took three times longer than for a fixed block size of 30x10 pixels. The method, which tested the whole area of a block for edges, was even four times slower. It should also be mentioned that the matching results for homogeneous regions are comparatively unstable even for large blocks. A soft edge at the border of a block caused by a depth change in the scene together with smoothing etc. can dominate the whole structure inside that block and thus influence the resulting disparity value.

2.4 Post Processing: Disparity Histogram and Subpixel Accurate Disparity

Ideally, disparity maps consist of big areas with steadily changing disparities for flat surfaces and abrupt changes for depth discontinuities. In homogeneous regions the results deviate strongly from this ideal. After removing most of these unstable disparities using a suitable interest operator, mid-size areas of homogeneous disparity remain. These areas are surrounded by areas without results. The remaining false matches appear as single disparities deviating much from their neighbourhood. These observations motivate the following assumptions: (a) A correct disparity value belongs to a certain homogeneous surface. It probably appears there multiple times. (b) Errors are rare. (c) Wrong disparities do not belong to a certain surface and hence take on arbitrary values. The same wrong value appears probably only a few times. That means in reverse: Frequent disparity values are usually right, while rare values are often wrong. For our experiments we computed the histogram of disparity values and used a threshold on the histogram to discard uncommon values. Our experiments lead to good results for thresholds in the range of a few tenth of a percent. With these thresholds sometimes up to 50 percent of the removed values were actually wrong disparities. Of course, the results depend also on the image contents and perhaps a comparison with neighbouring disparity values could lead to further improvements. In general this is a good supporting method if most of the unstable disparities are already filtered out by an interest operator. Then this method discards a high percentage of wrong values at almost no computational cost without removing too many disparity values.

For applications which require a high precision rather than high speed the disparity can be computed with subpixel accuracy. A robust way to determine the subpixel shift between two corresponding block is to minimise the square error

$$e = \sum_x (g(x+s) - f(x))^2 \tag{8}$$

between the pixel intensities g of the block in the left image and the intensities f of the corresponding block right image. The variable x denotes a pixel position inside the block and the variable s denotes a subpixel shift along the epipolar line. The intensity of a block with subpixel shift is linearly interpolated using the image derivative according to the formula

$$g(x+s) = g(x) + sg'(x)\,. \tag{9}$$

The subpixel shift is then obtained by finding the root of the derivation of the error, i.e. the value of s for which

$$e' = \sum (2sg^2 + 2gg' - 2g'f) = 0\,. \tag{10}$$

The subpixel shift results thus to

$$s = \frac{\sum 2g'f - \sum 2gg'}{\sum 2g^2}\,. \tag{11}$$

In practice, this method leads to smooth subpixel shifts in areas of uniform disparity. Outliers occur only where the disparity value already deviates from the neighbourhood for pixel accuracy. Since at wrong positions the subpixel shift often is greater than half a pixel, the subpixel shift is well suited to indicate wrong disparity values. Since such great values correspond to a neighbouring matching position with a lower subpixel shift, the disparity must already be wrong at pixel level and thus can be discarded.

2.5 Camera Calibration and Accuracy of the Distance Measurements

We use a stereo setup with two *DFK 21F04* cameras by *The Imaging Source* and Cosmicar/Pentax lenses to compute the accuracy of the distance measurements. These cameras provide images with a resolution of 640 x 480 pixels. They are mounted on separate 10mm aluminium plates which can be adjusted in yaw, pitch and roll angle. The baseline length of the camera setup is 20 cm. The lens aperture is set to 5.6, the focus to infinity. The lens of the right camera has a focal length of 8mm.

To save computation time during operation the stereo images are not rectified in software. Instead we rely on a careful manual adjustment of the camera orientation. By changing the zoom of the lens of the left camera, the image sizes are brought into accordance with pixel accuracy. Because the stereo algorithms we use belong to the category of scanline matching, the roll and pitch angles of the cameras are adjusted in a way that the line correspondence between the left and the right image is maximised. We obtain an error of less than 1/100 pixels for the roll angle and less than 1 pixel for the pitch angle. For reasons of simplicity, stereo systems are often built with parallel optical axes. But for a working distance of 1.5m-4m that was chosen with regard to a later data fusion with the PMD camera, the images had a common field of view too small for stereo analysis. Therefore, the optical axes are directed towards each other, so that both camera images centre an object at a distance of 4m.

Assuming a pinhole camera model, we can compute the distance z of a point in 3D-space by the well-known formula

$$z = \frac{b}{x_r / f - x_l / f}, \tag{12}$$

where f denotes the focal length of both cameras and x_r and x_l denote the horizontal coordinate of the corresponding position in the right and the left camera image. The variable b denotes the length of the baseline. For the proposed stereo setup the formula changes to

$$z = \frac{b}{\tan(\alpha + \tan^{-1}(-x_r u / f_1)) - \tan(\beta + \tan^{-1}(-x_l u / f_2))}. \tag{13}$$

Here, α and β denote the deviation of the yaw angles of the optical axes from a parallel setup. The values f_1 and f_2 are used because the focal length is not necessarily the same for both cameras. The variable u denotes the size of one pixel on the CCD-sensor. It is given by the Sony ICX098BQ data sheet as 5.6μm/pixel.

B	0.0024691
α	0.3045662
β	0.3041429
F_1	0.7583599
F_2	0.7580368

Table 2. Camera parameters obtained by the genetic algorithm

To find the parameters b, α, β, f_1 and f_2, a series of sample images of a flat, highly textured test surface is taken at known distances between 1.6m and 4m. For the stereo analysis we use the "Winner Takes It All" method with the SSD similarity measure based on the implementation by Scharstein et al. (2001). The resulting pixel accurate disparity values (x_r - x_l) are averaged over the test surface. Then a genetic algorithm was used to find a good parameter set that minimises the integrated squared error between the distance values obtained by the formula above and the measured distance. A standard deviation of 0.0077 was achieved for the distance values (in meter), when the algorithm was stopped after a sufficient number of cycles. The resulting parameter values are given by table 2. Averaging the disparity values in practice results in the loss of the absolute image position. For every averaged disparity value the absolute coordinates x_r and x_l can be computed by adding an arbitrary offset to the disparity, keeping in mind that the disparity is valid for a larger image region. Some optimisation methods do not take this into account and thus find parameter sets with a significantly lower standard deviation, but then the distance values are only plausible for the chosen offset.

3. PMD

The advent of the photonic mixer device (PMD) leads to new possibilities in real-time depth measurement. Compared to the use of stereo correspondence analysis, laser scanning or other depth information yielding technology, PMD-cameras have the advantage of recording a scene providing intensity images *and* depth images at once. No further time consuming computation needs to be done. PMD cameras integrate the sensor hardware plus the needed software for gathering the images in one device. Figure 9 shows a PMD camera.

Figure 9. Picture of a PMD camera

3.1 General Operation

The principle of a PMD camera will be briefly described. The camera emits an amplitude modulated light signal, which is reflected back onto the camera sensor array by the surface. The sensor is coupled with the modulation emitter and because of that capable of separating the electrons, which are generated by the reflected photons according to their distance. This process of comparing the optical signal with the electrical reference signal of the emitter is responsible for gathering three-dimensional information of the scene.
The scheme of depth measuring with PMD sensors is shown in Figure 10. The modulation source sends amplitude modulated light (usually at wavelengths of about 800nm) to the object surfaces. The modulation frequency is set to 20MHz, so that a full oscillation of the signal has a length of 15m. This also limits the band of unambiguously yielding depth information to 7.5m (half the oscillation length). Hence beyond 7.5m the camera yields false depth information and should only be used at ranges below that limit.
There are two light penetrable photo gates on the surface of the semiconductor elements, which are set to a voltage equivalent to the light modulation. The incoming photons release electrons in the underlying p-layer of the photo gate. Due to the voltage the semiconductor is set to, a potential gap is induced. This deflects the electrons to one of the reading diodes. Changing the polarity of the voltage the electrons are deflected to the other reading diode. That way we get two capacitors collecting electrons. Unmodulated background light is distributed equally to both capacitors thus eliminating its effect for detection. The modulated light on the other hand together with the push-pull voltage causes correlated

readout signals, which directly correspond to the phase difference. Hence the "mixing" is done by mixing electrons of the incoming signals with the signal of the push-pull voltage. The incoming signal is integrated over its amplitude and the measured result is put into its corresponding pot. The difference of the capacity of both pots is directly related to the phase difference which is linearly related to the distance of the camera to the recorded object.

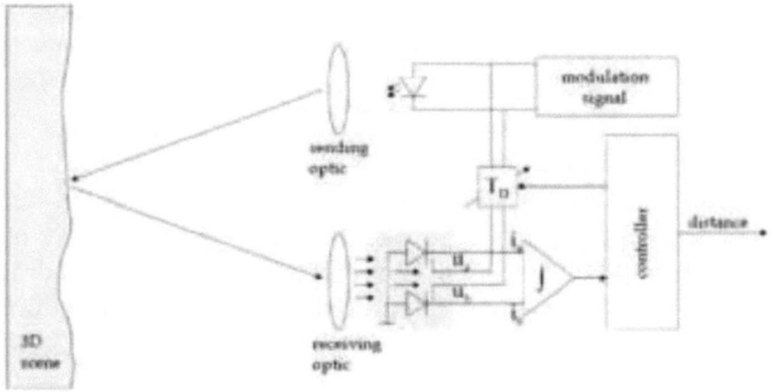

Figure 10. Scheme of a PMD measurement system

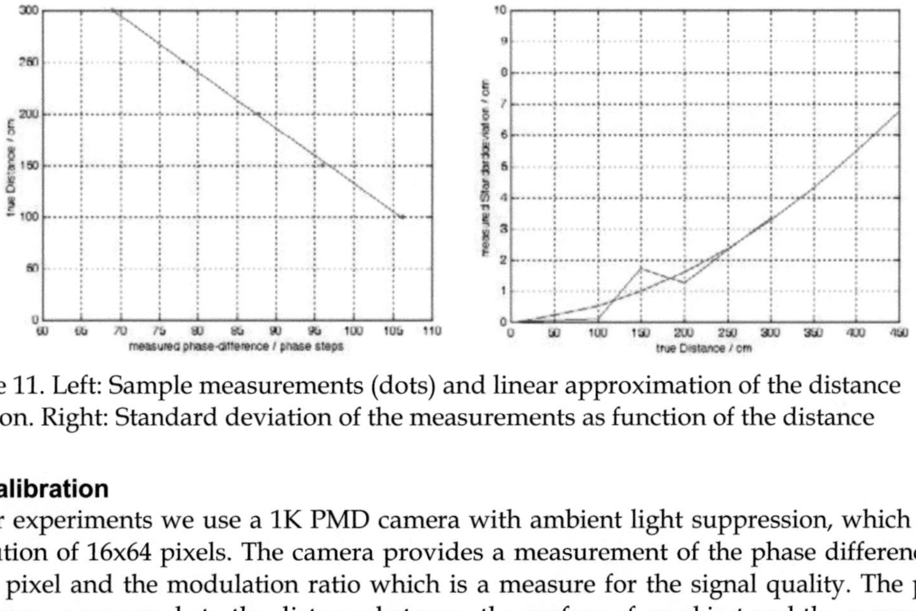

Figure 11. Left: Sample measurements (dots) and linear approximation of the distance function. Right: Standard deviation of the measurements as function of the distance

3.2 Calibration

In our experiments we use a 1K PMD camera with ambient light suppression, which has a resolution of 16x64 pixels. The camera provides a measurement of the phase difference for every pixel and the modulation ratio which is a measure for the signal quality. The phase difference corresponds to the distance between the surface of an object and the camera. For ease of use we transform the distance data to a representation in Cartesian coordinates. To this end the camera geometry is approximated by central projection and the illumination by a point source at the centre of projection. With these approximations we obtain directly distance measurements in polar coordinates: The angles of the coordinates are built between the rays from the centre of projection through the grid cells of the sensor array. The distance is given by the measurements themselves. This representation is then converted to Cartesian coordinates. A side effect of this procedure is that a slight increase of the lateral resolution towards the image borders is visible now. It is caused by the large aperture angle of 70.5 degree of the camera. To increase the accuracy of our approximations, lens distortion was corrected during the coordinate transformation. Besides that, the coordinate system was shifted by 1.3 pixels horizontally and 2.5 pixels vertically to account for an offset between the optical axis and the centre of the sensor chip.

To determine the relation between the phase difference and the distance, a flat surface with high reflectance was recorded for several distances. The phase difference was averaged over the middle 5 pixels of the array because there our approximations have the smallest error. The distance function $z(\varphi)$ was then approximated by the linear function

$$z(\varphi) = -5.4022\varphi + 672.5143 \tag{14}$$

with a remaining maximum error of about three percent (see Figure 11 left). Beside the distance function also the relation between distance and standard deviation is of major importance because the accuracy of the measurements depends heavily on the amount of light received by the camera. Since the illumination decreases quadratically with the distance, a second order polynomial was fitted to the data. The resulting function

$$\sigma(\varphi) = 2.734 * 10^{-5}\varphi^2 + 2.86723 * 10^{-3}\varphi - 4.229692 * 10^{-2}\,. \tag{15}$$

can be seen in Figure 11 right. Figure 12 shows a calibrated distance matrix of the test surface used for camera calibration as well as two nearer marker objects.

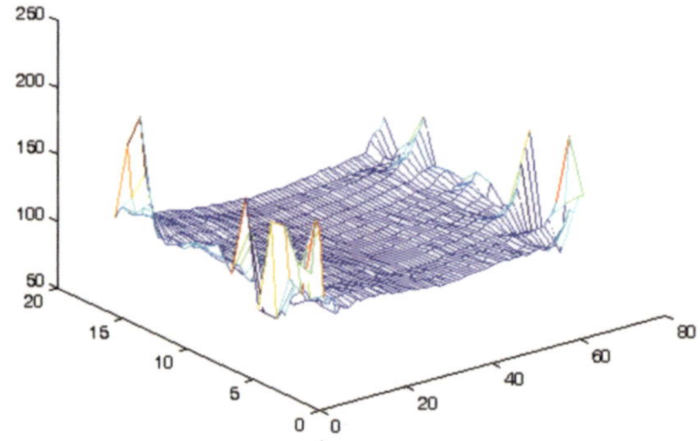

Figure 12. Distance matrix of a flat surface at 3m distance

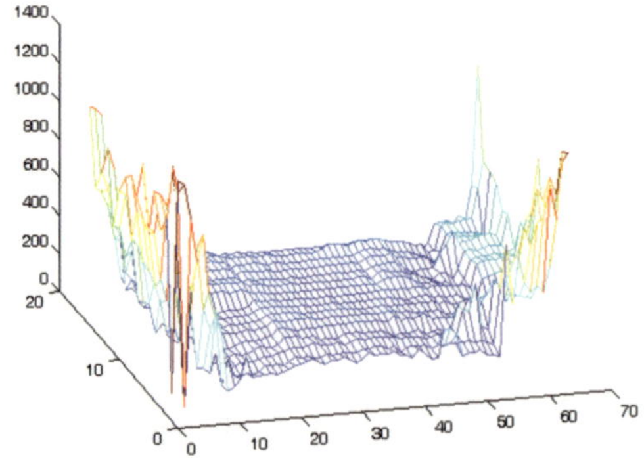

Figure 13. Calibrated distance measurements for a near flat surface (1m distance)

The remaining errors are mainly caused by model inaccuracy for small distances, by too low signal strength and by difficulties with the recorded scene. It turned out that for distances

smaller than 1.5 meters the camera model is not appropriate and the light source should better be modelled by a transmitter with finite area (see Figure 13). The problem of a too low signal occurs mainly at the borders of the sensor array and for very distant objects. But also the reflectance of the objects plays a role and the angle between the light source and the optical axis. Besides that, there is a nonlinear relation between the phase and the signal amplitude due to deviations from the ideal sinus wave shape. To account for these problems, a threshold for the modulation ratio which indicates the signal strength is introduced. Pixels with a modulation ratio below 30 percent are ignored. This procedure ensures that the measurements are in good accordance to function 15.
Beside the reflectance of the recorded objects also their geometry can cause inaccuracies. If the border of an object is mapped to one sensor element, the sensor receives a mixed signal from the object in the front and the background. Then the recorded signal is a linear combination of two sinus waves which are weighted by the reflectance and distance of both objects. It is also possible that the signal is composed of more sinus waves if there are more objects occluding each other. For these sensor elements the true distance cannot be computed. A reasonable assumption then is that the real distance is somewhere between the neighbouring distances. A simple way of handling this is to introduce a minimum and a maximum depth map. The minimum depth map is result of a 3x3 minimum operator on the distance matrix, the maximum map is the result of an analogue 3x3 maximum operator. This is a fast method and accounts for the distance dependency of the error.

3.3 Experimental Results

We present in this section some results from experiments that were conducted to find out more about the real world behaviour of the PMD camera. The goal of the experiments was to gain a calibrating function for any pixel yielding a mapping from a measured value to a standardised value. First we tried to do the calibration process in front of a white wall, but later a board was taken instead of the wall. The reason for that will be addressed later in this section.

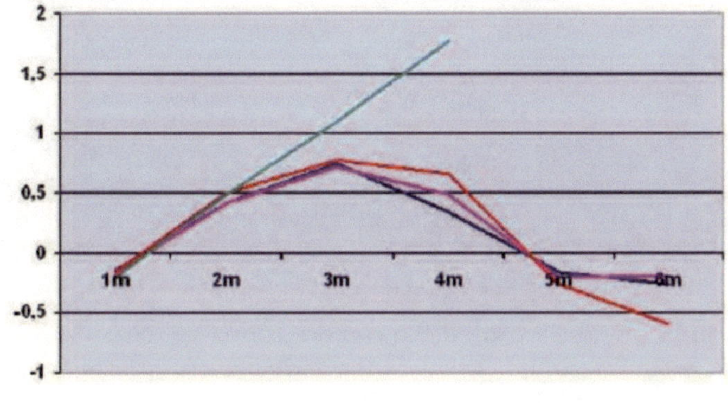

Figure 14. Phase differences of the "wall-scene" and the the "board-scene" (green line)

The camera was placed in front of the wall at distances of 1m to 6m with steps of 1m, which is in the range of 7.5m (see section 4.1). Each time a full measurement was taken by the camera. For all the experiments a tape measure was used instead of the internal alignment function of the camera to measure exactly the distance of the camera to the wall. To

suppress the effect of noise 2500 measurements were taken and every pixel was integrated over a 5x5 area at each distance step.
Up to a distance of 3m the phase difference values show expected linear behaviour. But at distances beyond 3m the values start decreasing again (see Figure 14). This might be due to the fact that the surface of the wall is too smooth so that the light is not reflected in a diffuse manner. Hence the modulated light might not find its way back to the PMD sensor. Further tests showed that this effect is almost independent to the exposure time of the camera.
As an alternative we chose a board with fine but coarse surface resulting in a better diffuse light reflection. With this, the camera showed the expected behaviour. The phase difference values are linearly increasing even beyond the point of 3m (green line). It has to be said that the calibration process could not measure distances of 5m and 6m, because above 4m the board was not big enough to cover the entire image plane of the camera.

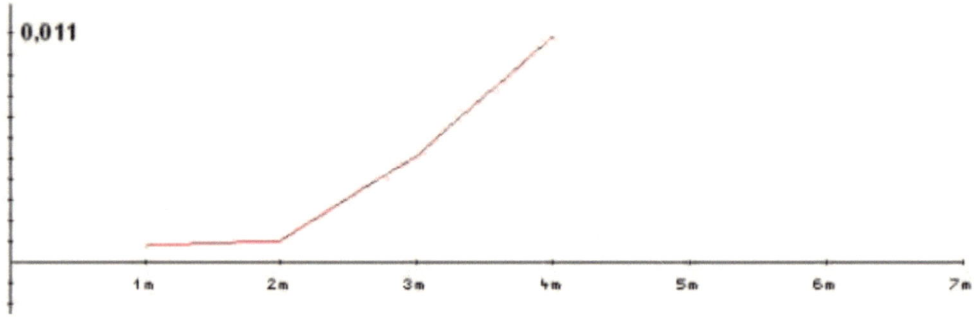

Figure 15. Standard deviations of measurements

We also compared the standard deviations of measurements. The results are presented in Figure 15. This clearly shows the influence of noise at higher distances. The higher noise ratio leads to the increase of the standard deviation.

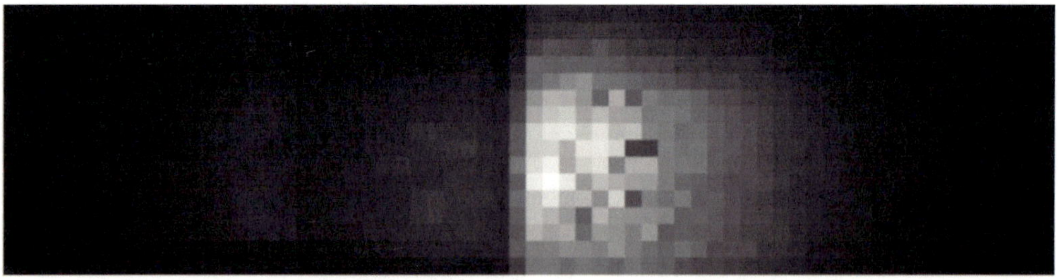

Figure 17. Modulation image of the edge scene

Beside the calibration process we used the camera trying to measure the depth of various scenes. One of the most interesting scenes is the "edge-scene" presented in Figure 16 a) and b). The goal of this experiment is to find out if the camera produces reliable results on object edges. The distance of the wall on the left is 150cm, the distance of the right wall is 80cm. For the scene in Figure 16 a) the depth measurement of the camera is quite accurate with 158cm for the far and 77cm for the near wall differing only 3%-5% from the exact depth values. Moving the camera slightly to the left (as shown in Figure 16 b) in contrast yields unreliable results. The camera looks on the edge at a very beaked angle filling almost a two pixel column. The modulation picture (Figure 17) shows that the degree of modulation decreases rapidly in the border area of the two walls not allowing any reliable measurements. The reason is the flat angle transporting the light away from the camera instead of reflecting it right back to the sensors. Hence for reliable results one has to make sure the camera is aligned orthogonally towards flat objects. The phase difference picture for Figure 16 a) is presented in fig 18.

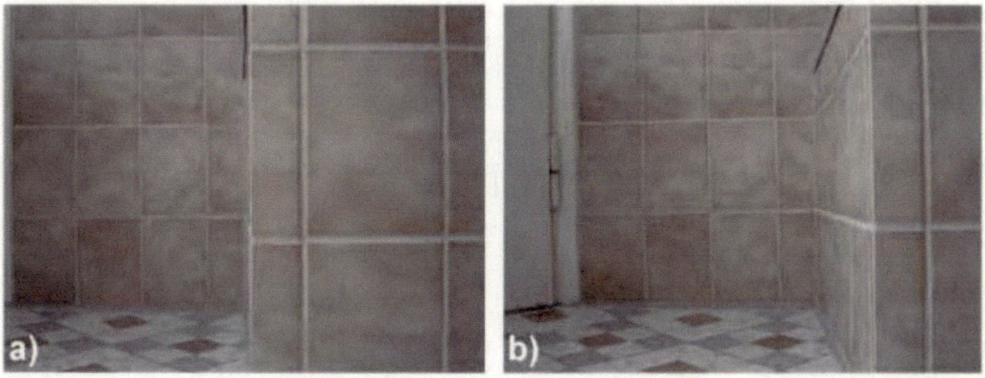

Figure 16. Edge scene – a) camera looking at edge of the wall orthogonally – b) camera looking at edge of the wall at a beaked angle

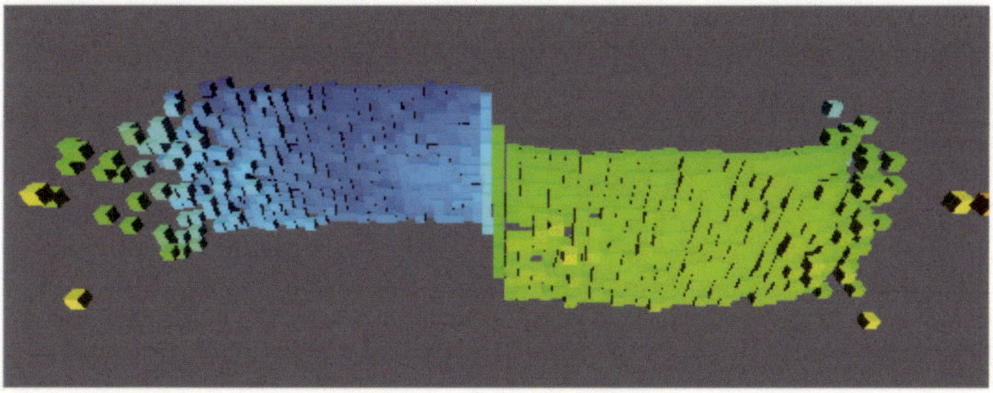

Figure 18. Phase differences for the "wall-scene" using a 3D-view

4. Fusion of PMD and Stereo Data

In comparing the stereo measurements and the results of the PMD camera, the stereo system has the advantage of a high precision with regard to the distance measurements as well as the lateral resolution. Unfortunately, the results depend heavily on the image contents and can be very unstable for ambiguous scenes. The PMD-camera on the other hand provides stable results independently of the surface texture. Here, the coarse resolution of the sensor is unfavourable. Also, the accuracy of the depth measurements is inferior to the results of the stereo camera. Therefore, we made experiments to fuse the results of both techniques in order to obtain depth measurements both robust and precise.

4.1 Fusion Mechanism

Our fusion method is based on the intersection of confidence intervals for the results of both camera types. A schematic of the fusion algorithm is given in Figure 19. The starting point for the computation of the confidence intervals are the depth maps of the camera systems. The depth maps consist of the image coordinates together with the corresponding depth values. Since the camera geometry is known for both systems from the calibration step, the depth values are stored as points in Cartesian coordinates with a metric coordinate system centred at the camera. During camera calibration also the standard deviation of the depth measurements is determined. For the stereo camera the confidence intervals are computed from a depth map by adding, respectively subtracting, twice the standard deviation of the depth values. This corresponds to a 95 percent interval around the mean of a normal distribution. The result is a minimum and a maximum depth map, respectively. For missing depth values, i.e. values recognised as unstable, a large depth interval of 10m is set.

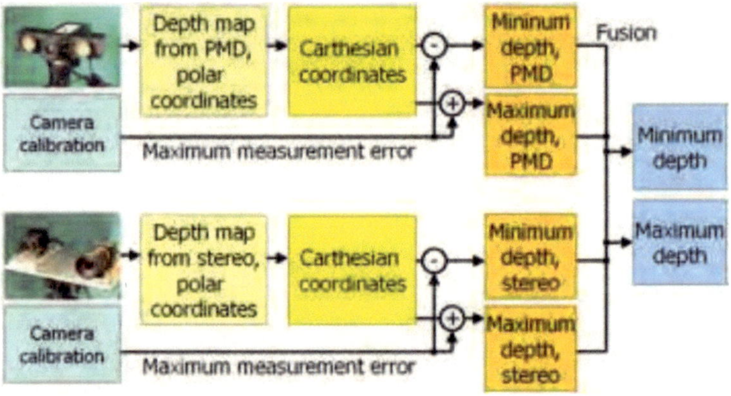

Figure 19. Fusion of the distance data

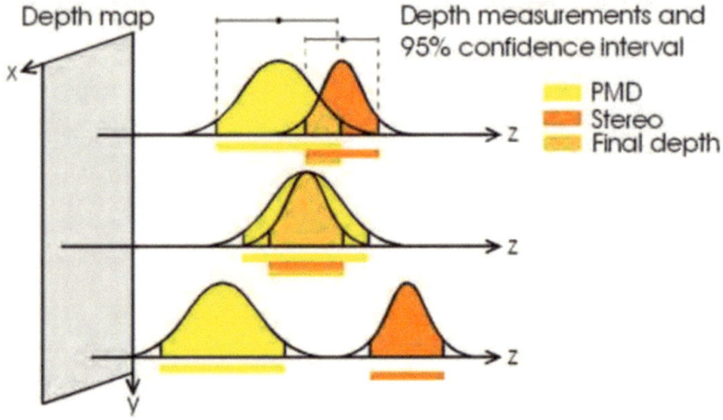

Figure 20. Intersecting the depth intervals of the stereo and the PMD camera

For the PMD-camera the minimum and maximum depth maps are computed by taking the minimum and maximum value of a 3x3 environment around every point in the depth image. This is because for occluding edges a mixed signal of the nearer and farther object surface is received. Then the depth maps are corrected by the measurement error. To compensate for different aperture angles of the camera systems and different lateral

resolutions the depth map of the PMD camera is scaled by appropriate factors in vertical and horizontal direction.
The depth maps now form arrays which give a depth interval for every x- and y-coordinate. Data fusion is then done by intersecting the intervals of the PMD-camera with the intervals of the stereo camera. Figure 20 illustrates three different cases. The first case is that the depth intervals partially overlap. The area marked as 'final depth' is the intersection of the two depth intervals. The second case shown is that one depth interval completely covers the other one. Here, both sensors deliver the same depth value, but with different measurement accuracy. The third case is that there is no overlap. In that case one sensor or both deliver wrong values. Without taking further assumptions, nothing more can be said here about the true depth value, so the final value is marked as missing.

4.2 Experimental Results

Figure 21 shows a scheme of the experimental setup and the recorded scene. The experiments were conducted in a corridor of the university. The only changes to the original scene are the person we asked to stand in the corridor and the low carton placed in the foreground. In particular, we did not facilitate the depth recognition by e.g. hanging up highly textured
posters. The environment can thus be considered as a natural indoor scene (for office buildings). The distance between the cameras and the objects of the scene was 3m to 4m. The stereo camera was placed behind the PMD camera because of the smaller aperture angle of 23 degree compared to the 70.5 degree of the PMD camera. It was also placed 30cm higher to avoid the PMD camera of being visible in the stereo images.
Figure 22 shows a pair of images from the stereo camera. These images are problematic for stereo analysis in many ways. First, there are big homogeneous regions, primarily the white walls and the white column. Scanline stereo or block matching fails in these regions due to the lack of characteristic image features. Secondly, the shirt of the person shows a repetitive pattern causing multiple solutions to the correspondence problem. In the remaining parts of the image stereo analysis is affected by occlusion. This concerns mainly the ceiling and the environment around the person. Figure 23 shows the resulting disparity and depth maps. Since most parts of the images lead to unstable results, a sobel operator was applied to the images to find areas where stable results can be expected. Disparity values in unstable regions are discarded. In the given depth map these areas are marked black. They are replaced by the mentioned 10m interval before fusion with the PMD camera.

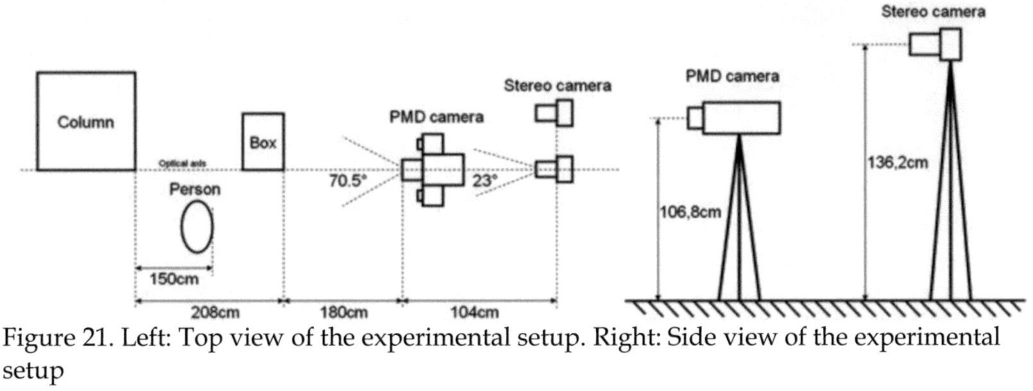

Figure 21. Left: Top view of the experimental setup. Right: Side view of the experimental setup

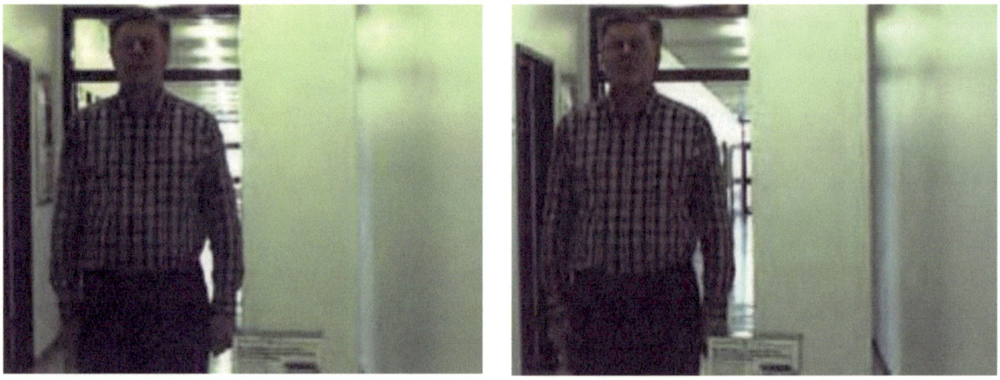

Figure 22. Left and right image of the stereo camera

Figure 23. Left: Disparity map. Right: Resulting depth map (in image coordinates)

Figure 24. Size of the overlapping depth intervals (left) and average depth (right)

The results of the sensor fusion can be seen in Figure 24. The left picture shows the size of the overlapping depth intervals, the right image shows the mean depth. The coarse block structure results from the low resolution of the PMD camera. Coordinates without overlapping depth intervals are marked as white. The bright blocks in the left figure indicate big depth intervals around the person, at the edges of the column and around the box. This inaccuracy results from depth discontinuities because there the PMD camera receives a signal both from the far and the near surface. By contrast, the stereo camera is quite accurate for these positions and delivers in general the distance to the nearer object. Although the depth map from the stereo analysis is relatively sparse, the result after sensor fusion is dense. Missing results from stereo are replaced by values from the PMD camera because the stereo system provides sufficient large depth intervals when a result is unknown. The few missing values in the fused depth map occur when both systems report a high accuracy for their results, although one of the depth values or the accuracy itself is wrong. Although the fusion mechanism itself is comparatively straight forward, it seems to preserve the advantages of both 3D sensors while avoiding their disadvantages

6. Conclusion

Common state of the art mechanisms for the measurement of the surrounding environment in real time usually pose a trade off between high speed, robustness and accuracy. With applications for mobile robots in mind, this work focuses on the faster methods stereo analysis and PMD camera. Our research aims at the computation of robust and dense depth maps in real time.

First, the performance of three standard stereo algorithms is examined with regard to two different measurements of similarity. The subsequent optimisation of the standard methods by using modern SIMD instructions and programming techniques like e.g. recursive subdivision leads to an increase of speed by a factor of four. As a result, for the Winner-Takes-It-All algorithm we achieve a computation time of 250ms (plus 230ms for building the cost matrix), which can be considered real time. The accuracy of our stereo setup is determined experimentally and a scene reconstructed from stereo data is shown.

To improve robustness and speed the image derivative is evaluated. In order to deal with poorly structured environments experiments with an adaptive block size are conducted. The resulting disparity maps are more dense but the resulting block sizes for homogeneous regions slow down the correspondence analysis. Hence, this approach is not suitable for real time. A fast post processing step dealing with a disparity histogram is introduced to discard wrong matches. The subpixel disparity is computed as a measure of plausibility.

As a comparatively new technique the PMD camera is used for distance measurement. The PMD camera provides directly the depth information for every pixel without the intensive computation that characterises stereo analysis. The camera was calibrated with an accuracy of 5 percent for distances over 1.5m. For smaller distances a more complex model than a pinhole camera with a point light source is needed. We observe that the measurement error increases quadratically with the distance, which is an effect of the reduced amount of light received from distant surfaces. Other inaccuracies result from the reflectance properties of the recorded surfaces or extreme geometric arrangements of the scene. A big advantage of the PMD camera is that it does not rely on the texture of a surface or the visibility of objects in a second camera like a stereo camera. With an (adjustable) integration time of 80ms per image it is also much faster. On the other hand, the stereo camera has a higher image resolution as well as higher depth accuracy. Especially the behaviour on and near edges is better. We thus made experiments combining both methods and they turn out to compensate the disadvantages of each other very well. As a result, we obtain robust and dense depth information in real time.

7. References

Bähr, H.-P. & Vögtle, T. (1991). *Digitale Bildverarbeitung. Anwendung in Photogrammetrie,* Kartographie und Fernerkundung, Wichmann, Karlsruhe, ISBN 3-87907-224-8

Faugeras, O. (1993). *Three-Dimensional Computer Vision - A Geometric Viewpoint,* MIT Press, Cambridge, Mass., ISBN 0-262-06158-9

Kang, S.; Webb, J.A.; Zitnick, C. & Kanade, T. (1995). A multibaseline stereo system with active illumination and real-time image acquisition, *Proceedings of the Fifth International Conference on Computer Vision (ICCV '95),* June 1995, pp. 88-93.

Kim, H.; Min, D.B. & Sohn, K. (2005). Real-Time Stereo Using Foreground Segmentation and Hierarchical Disparity Estimation, in *Ho, Y.S. & Kim, H.J. (Eds.): PCM 2005,* Part I, LNCS 3767, Springer-Verlag, Berlin, Heidelberg, pp. 384-395.

Konolige, K. (1997). Small Vision System: Hardware and Implementation, *In Proceedings of the 8th International Symposium on Robotics Research,* Japan.

Kraft, H.; Frey, J.; Moeller, T.; Albrecht, M.; Grothof, M.; Schink, B.; Hess, H. & Buxbaum, B. (2004). 3D-Camera of high 3D-frame rate, depth-resolution and background light elimination based on improved PMD (photonic mixer device)-technologies, OPTO, Nuernberg, May 2004.

Moravec, H.P. (1977). Towards automatic visual obstacle avoidance. *Proceedins of the Fifth International Joint Conference on Artificial Intelligence, IJCAI-77.*

Metropolis, N.; Rosenbluth, A.; Rosenbluth N.; Teller A. & Teller E. (1953). Equation of State Calculations by Fast Computing Machines, *Journal of Chemical Physics,* article 21, pages 1087-1159.

Porta, J.M.; Verbeek, J.J. & Kröse, B.J.A. (2005). Active appearance-based robot localization using stereo vision, *Autonomous Robots* 18(1), pages 59-80.

Scharstein, D.; Szeliski, R. & Zabih, R. (2001). A taxonomy and evaluation of dense two-frame stereo correspondence algorithms, *Proceedings of the IEEE Workshop on Stereo and Multi-Baseline Vision,* Kauai, HI, Dec. 2001.

Schwarte, R. (2001). *Dynamic 3D-Vision, IEEE Int. Symp. on Electron Devices for Microwave and Opto-electronic Applications,* EDMO 2001, Wien.

Stereo Vision Research Page (2007). http://cat.middlebury.edu/stereo/newdata.html, Middlebury University, 30.1.2007.

Sun, Ch. (2002). Fast Stereo Matching using Rectangular Subregioning and 3D Maximum Surface Techniques, *International Journal of Computer Vision,* 47(1/2/3), May 2002

Sunyoto, H.,; van der Mark, H. & Gavrila, D.M. (2004). A Comparative Study of Fast Dense Stereo Vision Algorithms, University of Parma, Italy - 2004 *IEEE Intelligent Vehicle Symposium.*

Zhao, J. & Katupitiya, J. (2006a). A Fast Stereo Vision Algorithm with Improved Performance at Object Borders, *IEEE/RSJ International Conference on Intelligent Robots and Systems (IROS'06),* Beijing, China, October 9-15, 2006.

Zhao, J. & Katupitiya, J. (2006b). A Dynamic Programming Approach Based Stereo Vision Algorithm Improving Object Border Performance, *IEEE/RSJ International Conference on Intelligent Robots and Systems (IROS'06),* Beijing, China, October 9-15, 2006.

Zhu, Z.; Karuppiah, D.R.; Riseman, E. & Hanson, A. (2004). Adaptive panoramic stereo vision for human tracking with cooperative mobile robots, *Robotics and Automation Magazine,* Special Issue on Panoramic Robots, 14 (10): pages 69-78.

19

Bearing-only Simultaneous Localization and Mapping for Vision-Based Mobile Robots

Henry Huang, Frederic Maire and Narongdech Keeratipranon
Faculty of Information Technology, Queensland University of Technology
Australia

1. Introduction

To navigate successfully, a mobile robot must be able to estimate the spatial relationships of the objects of interest accurately. A *SLAM* (Simultaneous Localization and Mapping) system employs its sensor data to build incrementally a map of an unknown environment and to localize itself in the map simultaneously. Thanks to recent advances in computer vision and cheaper cameras, vision sensors have become popular to solve SLAM problems (Bailey, 2003; Costa et al., 2004; Davison et al., 2004; Goncavles et al., 2005; Jensfelt et al., 2006; Mouragnon et al., 2006). The proposed bearing-only SLAM system requires only a single camera which is simple and affordable for the navigation of domestic robots such as autonomous lawn-mowers and vacuum cleaners.

Solutions to SLAM problems when the mobile robot is equipped with a sensor that provides both range and bearing measurements to landmarks are well developed (Leonard & Durrant-Whyte, 1991; Zunino & Christensen, 2001; Spero, 2005; Bailey & Durrant-Whyte, 2006). With a single camera, landmark bearings can be derived relatively easily from a grabbed image, however it is much more difficult to obtain accurate range estimates. Due to the low confidence in range estimates from vision data, it is desirable to solve SLAM problems with bearing only measurements.

One of the fundamental tasks of a SLAM system is the estimation of the landmark positions in an unknown environment. This task is called *Landmark Initialization.* A typical bearing-only SLAM system requires multiple observations for landmark initialization through triangulation. With only one observation, a stereo vision can provide range measurements because its multiple cameras grab images from slightly different viewpoints. However the reliable vision range in a stereo vision is limited due to the distance between the two cameras. Several observations at different locations are required to provide a robust range estimate.

Structure From Motion (SFM) is a process to construct the map of an environment with the video input from a moving camera. SFM allows a single camera to grab images at some vantage points for landmark initialization, such as a sufficient baseline and a straight movement. The requirement of SFM is well satisfied with a mobile robot, some recent works had utilized SFM to bearing-only SLAM (Goncavles et al., 2005; Jensfelt et al., 2006). Our method to bearing-only SLAM is inspired from the techniques used in both stereo vision and SFM.

Existing approaches to bearing-only SLAM require the readings from an odometer to estimate the robot locations prior to landmark initialization. It can be argued that such approaches are not strictly bearing-only SLAM as they rely on odometric information. This chapter presents a new 2-dimensional bearing-only SLAM system that relies only on the bearing measurements from a single camera. Our proposed system does not require any other sensors like range sensors or wheel encoders. The trade-off is that it requires the robot to be able to move in a straight line for a short while to initialize the landmarks. Once the landmark positions are estimated, localization becomes easy. The induced map created by our method is only determined up to a scale factor as only bearing information is used (no range or odometry information). All the object coordinates in the map multiplied by a scale factor would not change the bearing values.

The structure of this chapter is as follows. First, we introduce a direct localization method using only the bearings extracted from two panoramic views along a linear trajectory. We explain how to induce a Cartesian coordinate system with only two distinguishable landmarks. The method is then extended to landmark initialization with more landmarks in the environment.

In general, vision sensors are noisy. Dealing with sensory noise is essential. Two different methods are presented to compute the spatial uncertainty of the objects:

1. A geometric method which computes the uncertainty region of each landmark as the intersection of two vision cones rooted at the observation points.
2. A probabilistic method which computes the *PDFs* (Probability Density Functions) of the landmark positions. Formulas are derived for computing the PDFs when an initial observation is made.

The proposed SLAM system requires only a single camera, an interesting setup for domestic robots due to its low cost. It can be fitted to a wheeled robot as well as a legged robot.

2. Related work

The term *SLAM* was first introduced by Leonard and Durrant-Whyte (1991), it refers to Simultaneous Localization and Mapping. SLAM is one of the fundamental tasks in the navigation of an autonomous mobile robot. In robotic navigation, a *map* is a representation of the spatial relationship between the objects of interest in the environment. A map usually contains the positions of certain objects of interest, such as landmarks and obstacles. The process of a robot to determine its position in a map is called *localization*. *GPS* (Global Positioning System) is a popular localization system, in which the map is given for navigation. GPS is well suited for vehicles to navigate in a large scale outdoors environment, for instance, to navigate from city to city. For a domestic robot, however, a GPS is not accurate enough and does not work properly indoors and in some built-up areas. Further, the map of a particular environment may not be always available. A domestic robot cannot localize itself without a map. A SLAM system needs to build incrementally a map while it explores the environment and to determine its location in the map simultaneously.

For localization the robot needs to know where the landmarks are, whereas to estimate the landmark positions the robot needs to know its own position with respect to the map. The problem of SLAM is considered as a "chicken-and-egg" problem (Siegwart & Nourbaksh, 2004). To predict the position of the robot, conventional SLAM systems rely on odometry. Unfortunately, the accumulation of odometric errors (due mainly to wheel slippage) makes

the accuracy of the position estimates based only on odometry deteriorate rapidly. Updating the estimates with other sensory input is needed if the robot navigates for a long time.
Solutions to SLAM can be found if both range and bearing measurements to landmarks are obtained through sensors (Leonard & Durrant-Whyte, 1991; Zunino & Christensen, 2001; Spero, 2005; Bailey & Durrant-Whyte, 2006). Such a sensor reading refers to a *Full Observation*. A full observation can be achieved by either a single sensor (i.e., a laser range finder) or a combination of two sensors (i.e., a sonar senor and a camera). Range and bearing measurements constitute a full state of the environment. The sensors which observe the full state of the environment (i.e., both range and bearing) are called *range-bearing sensors*. A full observation is sufficient to form an estimate, such as an uncertainty region, of a landmark position. A typical uncertainty region is a Gaussian distribution over the possible positions of a landmark. Updating an estimate can be achieved by fusing the estimates from the subsequent observations. However, a range-bearing sensor is too expensive for a domestic robot. Solving the SLAM problems with a cheaper sensor is desirable.
A sensor reading with either range-only or bearing-only measurement to a landmark is called a *Partial Observation*. A partial observation is insufficient to completely determine a landmark position. A partial observation generates only a non-Gaussian distribution over an unbounded region for the landmark position (Bailey & Durrant-Whyte, 2006). Multiple observations from several vantage points are required to estimate the landmark position. A sensor reading obtained from a single camera constitutes only a partial observation because it provides bearing measurements but does not provide accurate range measurements. In general, a vision sensor is relatively cheaper than a range-bearing sensor. We wish to solve SLAM problems with bearing-only measurements. Next section reviews related work on vision based navigation for bearing-only SLAM.

2.1 Vision based navigation

Vision based navigation for a mobile robot had been investigated since early nineties of last century. Levitt and Lawton (1990) developed a Qualitative Navigator based on vision sensors. This navigator was able to explore the environment and to determine the relative positions of all the objects of interest. In general, an image contains very rich information for mapping the corresponding environment. A certain feature can be recognized through its specific color, shape and size. The frame rate up to 30 Hz from a video camera also enhances to SLAM, in particular to solve the data association problem.
Landmark bearings can be derived from a panoramic image taken by an omni-directional vision sensor (for example, a single camera aiming at a catadioptric mirror). A panoramic image offers a 360^0 view of the environment. Because of the robustness of bearing estimates and the complete view of the environment, previous works have utilized omni-directional vision sensors in robotic navigation (Rizzi & Cassinis, 2001; Usher et al., 2003; Menegatti et al., 2004; Huang et al., 2005b).
Stereo vision is another option used in robotic navigation. In addition to the bearing information, a stereo vision sensor can also measure the depth to a landmark (Murray & Jennings, 1998; Se et al., 2002; Sabe et al., 2004). A typical stereo vision sensor consists of two cameras, also known as a *Binocular Vision*. The disparity of the images taken from two slightly different viewpoints determines the landmark's range through triangulation. A *Baseline* in stereo vision is a line segment connecting the centres of two cameras' lens. Some stereo vision systems consist of three cameras, they are called *Trinocular Visions*. Common

configuration of a trinocular vision is to put three cameras on a right angle polygonal line. A trinocular vision can achieve better results than a binocular vision because the second pair of cameras can resolve situations that are ambiguous to the first pair of cameras (Se et al., 2002; Wooden, 2006).

The length of the baseline is essential in stereo vision, because it affects the precision of depth estimation and the exterior design of robotic hardware. QRIO (Sabe et al., 2004), a humanoid robot having a 5cm baseline in its binocular vision. The error of the depth measurement at a distance of 1.5m is over 80mm. The depth estimates of objects with the distances of 2m or more are omitted. LAGR (Wooden, 2006), an outdoor robot equipped with a trinocular vision of Point Grey Bumblebee. A maximum vision range of 6m was reported with a baseline of 12cm. To maximize the vision range of a stereo vision sensor, a longer baseline is required. Based on the mobility of a mobile robot, it is possible to extend the distance of any two viewpoints of a single camera (called a *Monocular Vision*). If a robot can move straight, the estimation of a landmark range from a monocular vision will be the same as the estimation in a stereo vision. Such approach was first proposed by Huang et al. (2005a). In this paper, a localization method with two observed bearings along a linear trajectory was presented. The method is particularly useful and accurate if the robot can move straight, i.e., the robot's yaw is toward to a specific landmark.

In computer vision, *Structure From Motion* (SFM) refers to the process of building a 3D map of a static environment from the video input from a moving camera. This is very similar to stereo vision where a 3D map is built from two simultaneous images of the same landmark. In both cases, the same landmark is taken into multiple images and the disparities of images are used to compute the landmark location. In stereo vision, the images are taken at different viewpoints simultaneously. In SFM, due to the robot's motion, the images are taken at different viewpoints at different time steps. Visual odometry (Nister et al., 2004) employs SFM to estimate the motion of a stereo head or a single moving camera based on video data. The front end of this system is a feature tracker. Point features are matched between pairs of frames and linked into image trajectories at video rate. SFM presents significant advantages compared with a stereo vision due to the low cost of a monocular vision and the flexible baseline. However, SFM can build a map with respect to a static environment only because of the images are obtained at different time steps.

Goncavles *et al.* (2005) presented a framework to bearing-only SLAM based on SFM from three observations. They utilized a wall corner as the landmark for guiding the robot to move straight. Three images were taken while the robot was moving toward the wall corner. Each image was taken when the robot had moved 20cm approximately. A similar work (Jensfelt et al., 2006) was using N images for landmark initialization, here N is a sufficient number to obtain an accurate estimation. To ensure a proper triangulation, the images were discarded if the robot had not moved more than 3cm (i.e., baseline under 3cm) or turned more than 1 degree (i.e., not a straight movement). Both of the approaches solve the bearing-only SLAM problem using a monocular vision. However, they require an odometer to determine robot's motion. Our method to bearing-only SLAM is similar to SFM with a monocular vision, but does not rely on odometric information.

2.2 Dealing with uncertainty

In general, vision sensors are noisy. Dealing with sensory noise is essential in robotic navigation. The uncertainty of an object location can be represented with a PDF (Probability Density Function). When a robot is initially placed in an unknown environment without any prior information, the PDF of the robot position is uniform over the whole environment. Once the robot starts to sense the environment, information gathered through the sensors is used to update the PDF. Smith and Cheeseman (1986) estimated the object locations by linking a series of observations through an *approximate transformation*. The transformation includes compounding and merging the uncertain spatial relationships from sensor readings. Stroupe et al. (2000) showed how to fuse a sequence of PDFs of 2-dimensional Gaussians estimated from noisy sensor readings.

Robustness to sensory noise can be achieved with probabilistic methods such as *Extended Kalman Filters* (EKF) or *Particle Filters* (PF). The PF follows the *Sampling Importance Resampling* (SIR) algorithm, also known as the *Monte Carlo Localization* (MCL) algorithm in robotics (Fox et al., 1999). In PF, the number of particles is an important factor to the computing complexity. Montemerlo et al. (2003) proposed an efficient algorithm called FastSLAM based on PF with a minimized number of particles. Davison (2003) used a separate PF to estimate the distance from the observation point to the landmark with a single camera. The estimated distance is not correlated with other observations due to the limitation of the field of view. The follow-up work (Davison et al., 2004) improved the SLAM results by applying a wide-angle camera. In (Menegatti et al., 2004), omnidirectional images were employed to the image-based localization combining with MCL technique. Sim et al. (2005) solved SLAM problem with PF using a stereo vision sensor.

EKF is computationally efficient for positional tracking. However, an initial estimate of Gaussian distribution over the landmark position is required. This estimate can be refined efficiently with the estimates from subsequent observations. It is important to have an initial estimate relatively close to the real solution. Many works have focused on the problem of landmark initialization. In (Bailey, 2003), previous poses of the robot were stacked in the memory to perform the landmark initialization. Once the landmarks were initialized, the batch of observations was used to refine the whole map. Costa et al. (2004) presented an iterative solution to the landmark initialization of bearing-only SLAM problem with unknown data association (i.e., all landmarks are visually identical). The authors estimated landmark positions through Gaussian PDFs that were refined as new observations arrived.

Bundle adjustment is a process which adjusts iteratively the robot's pose and the landmark positions in order to obtain the optimal least squares solution. Combining EKF with bundle adjustment ensures a robust estimate. Such an optimization is usually calculated off line due to expensive in computation. In (Mouragnon et al., 2006), landmark initialization was carried out with a bundle adjustment in an incremental way, in the order of video frames. An incremental method can improve the computing efficiency compared with the usual hierarchical method.

Landmark initialization based on memorizing previous measurements or iterative methods cause time delay for estimation. These methods belong to the delayed methods of landmark initialization (Sola et al., 2005). Some immediate initialization methods to bearing-only SLAM called *undelayed* methods of landmark initialization were introduced; Kwok and Dissanayake (2004) presented a multiple hypotheses approach to solve the problem in a computationally efficient manner. Each landmark was initialized in the form of multiple

hypotheses distributed along the direction of the bearing measurement. The validity of each hypothesis was then evaluated based on the *Sequential Probability Ratio Test* (SPRT). Sola et al. (2005) gave a new insight to the problem and presented a method by initializing the whole *vision cone* (see Figure 4(a)) that characterizes the direction of the landmark. This cone is covered by a sequence of ellipses that represent the likelihood of the landmark.
Undelayed method of landmark initialization is efficient to identify the directions of all landmarks when the first bearing measurements are made. It does not state explicitly the locations of the landmarks. Further observations are still required to initialize the landmark positions. Lemaire et al. (2005) applied an undelayed initialization method to a 3D bearing-only SLAM. The landmark initialization is similar to the method proposed in (Kwok & Dissanayake, 2004) by maintaining a mixture of Gaussians. The updating process was done by comparing the likelihoods of subsequent observations. If the likelihood falls below a certain threshold then the Gaussian is removed. Once only a single Gaussian is left in the cone, the landmark is initialized and added into the map for EKF-SLAM.

2.3 Our approaches

This chapter presents two methods to compute the spatial uncertainties of the objects based solely on bearing measurements only: namely a geometric method and a probabilistic method. These methods are similar to the approach of the undelayed method of landmark initialization. Since the estimate based on a partial observation (known bearing but unknown range) is insufficient to completely determine a landmark position, a second observation from a vantage position is required to generate an explicit estimate.
In the geometric method, we manipulate directly each vision cone as a polyhedron instead of a sequence of Gaussians. Each cone contains a landmark position. After a second observation in a linear trajectory, the *uncertainty region* (the set of possible landmark positions that are consistent with the first and second observations) of the landmark becomes the intersection of two cones rooted at the two observation points, see Figure 4(b). Depending on the difference of bearings, the intersection is either a quadrangle (four-side polygon) or an unbounded polyhedron. For each estimation, we change the bases from the local frame (the robot-based frame, denoted by F_R) into the global frame (the landmark-based frame, denoted by F_L). The uncertainties of all objects are re-computed with respect to F_L by the change of bases. A global map with the estimated positions of all objects and their associated uncertainties can be gradually built while the robot explores its environment.
In the probabilistic method, a landmark position is represented by a PDF $p(r,\alpha)$ in a polar coordinate where r and α are independent. Formulas are derived for computing the PDF of landmark position when an initial observation is made. The updating of the PDF with the subsequent observations can be done by direct computing from the formulas. We select a number of sample points in the uncertainty region (computed from the geometric method) by the rejection method (Leydold, 1998). These sample points are used to represent the PDF in F_R. By changing the bases from F_R to F_L, the PDFs of all object positions in the global frame F_L can also be computed.

Without range measurement, we assume the probability density of an object location is constant along the range. It is a more realistic assumption than the one made by other existing methods (Davison, 2003; Davison et al., 2004; Kwok & Dissanayake, 2004; Sola et al., 2005) which assume that the probability density of the object location is a Gaussian or a mixture of Gaussians. Indeed, if only bearing information is given, the probability that the landmark is between 4 and 5 metres should be the same as the probability that the landmark is between 5 and 6 metres. The representation with a Gaussian or a mixture of Gaussians fails in this constraint. With our PDF representation, the probability that the landmark is between 4 and 5 metres will be the same as the probability that the landmark is between 5 and 6 metres.

3. A direct localization method using only the bearings extracted from two panoramic views along a linear trajectory

In this section, we describe a direct method (in the sense it does not use an iterative search) based solely on vision for localizing a mobile robot in a 2-dimensional space. This method relies only on the bearings derived from two images taken along a linear trajectory. We only assume that the robot can visually identify landmarks and measure their bearings. This method does not require any other sensors (like range sensors or wheel encoders) or the prior knowledge of relative distances among the objects. This method can be adopted in a localization system which utilizes only a single camera as the sensor for navigation. Given its low cost, such a system is well suited for domestic robots such as autonomous lawn-mowers and vacuum cleaners.

3.1 Method description

In order to describe our method we need to introduce some notation. The robot position at i^{th} observation point is denoted by O_i. The position of jth landmark is denoted by L_j. The notation β_i^j denotes the bearing measurement at O_i with respect to L_j. The line going through two points x_1 and x_2 will be denoted by $\Gamma(x_1,x_2)$. This section shows how to compute the Cartesian coordinates of landmarks and the robot positions from the bearings measured at O_1 and O_2 relatively to L_1 and L_2. We consider two right-handed coordinate systems, the robot-based frame denoted by F_R, and the landmark-based frame denoted by F_L. In Figure 1(a), the coordinates of O_1 and O_2 in F_R are respectively $[0,0]'$ and $[1,0]'$. Similarly, in F_L (see Figure 1(b)), the coordinates of L_1 and L_2 are respectively $[0,0]'$ and $[1,0]'$. The frame F_L is a global frame since all the landmarks are assumed static in the environment. The distance $\| L_1 - L_2 \|$ is taken as the measurement unit for the localization system.

While the robot moves in a linear trajectory, two images are taken at O_1 and O_2 respectively. The landmark bearings are derived from these two images. The position L_j in F_R is computed as the intersection of two lines $\Gamma(O_1,L_j)$ and $\Gamma(O_2,L_j)$. The equations of this two lines can be obtained from the bearings β_1^j and β_2^j, and the coordinates of O_1 and O_2 in F_R. Once L_j is available in F_R, we can determine the affine transformation that relates the coordinates $X_L(x)$ and $X_R(x)$ of a point x in the two coordinate systems F_L and F_R. That is, an expression of the form $X_L(x) = a * X_R(x) + b$, here a is a matrix and b is a vector. The coordinates of O_1 and O_2 in F_L are then easily derived.

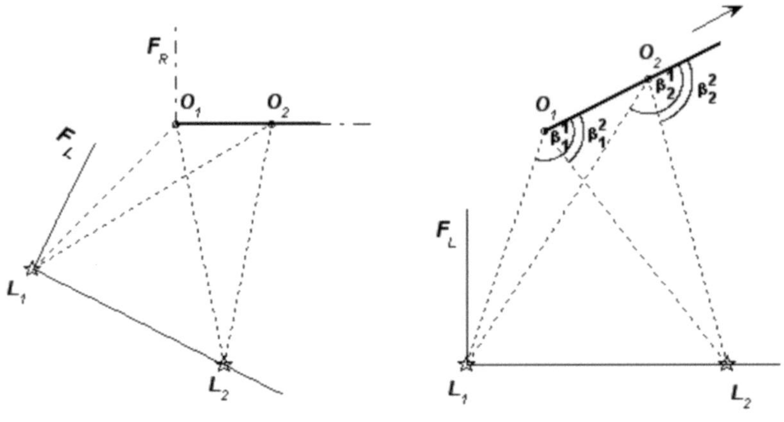

(a) Right handed coordinate systems (b) Landmark bearings

Figure 1. From two landmark bearings observed at points O_1 and O_2, the coordinates of L_1 and L_2 in F_R are computed. Then a simple change of bases gives the positions of O_1 and O_2 in the global frame F_L

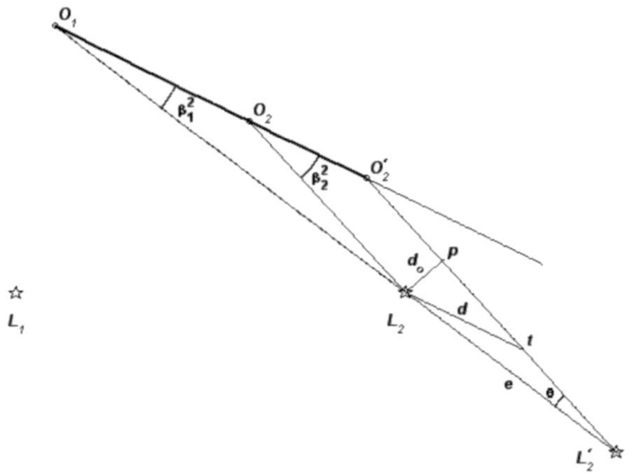

Figure 2. The estimated error e on L_2 depends on the relative difference in bearings

In order to determine the relative position of a landmark, this landmark should not be on the line $\Gamma(O_1,O_2)$. For example, if L_1, O_1 and O_2 are on the same line, then $\Gamma(O_1,L_1)\cap\Gamma(O_2,L_1)$ is not a single point but a whole line.

Experiments in simulation and on a real robot (see Section 3.2) indicate that the accuracy of this localization system is sensitive to the relative difference of bearings. Let e be the estimated error of landmark position. Figure 2 shows that $d_0 = d*\sin(\beta_2^2) = e*\sin(\theta)$, here $\theta = \beta_2^2 - \beta_1^2$, d_0 is the distance between L_2 and $\Gamma(O_2', L_2')$, and $d = \| O_2 - O_2' \|$. We have $e = \frac{d*\sin(\beta_2^2)}{\sin(\theta)}$. That is, e is proportional to the landmark range d and the inverse of the relative difference in bearings. Assume the landmark range is fixed and the bearings angles are small, the ratio $\frac{e}{d}$ will be approximately equal to $\frac{\beta_2^2}{\beta_2^2 - \beta_1^2}$. This result confirms our intuition that a large relative change in bearings should give a more accurate position estimate.

3.2 Empirical Evaluation

Our localization method was evaluated on a Khepera robot equipped with a color camera (176 x 255 resolution). The average error between the measured and actual bearings is about ± 2 degrees. In this experiment, the second landmark was placed 20 centimetres apart from the first landmark. Four different starting points were used, and 20 trials at each point were conducted. The moving distance in all cases was 30 centimetres. The moving directions were westwards parallel to the landmarks. The results are shown in Figure 3. In this figure, landmarks are denoted by stars, trajectories are shown as arrows, and the estimated positions by our localization method are displayed as scatter points.

The localization error, average distances between the estimated positions and the actual positions, at positions *a, b, c,* and *d* (in Figure 3) are respectively 0.6, 1.2, 2.2, and 2.8 centimetres. The errors are small compared to the diameter of the robot (6 centimetres). Other experimental results have confirmed that the error is inversely proportional to the relative difference in bearings.

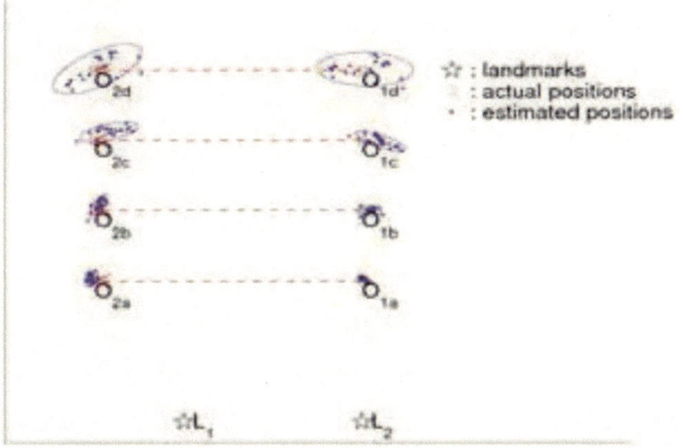

Figure 3. Estimated positions of the robot determined by the proposed localization method

When more than two landmarks are present, the localization accuracy can be further improved by fusing the estimated positions, giving more importance to the estimation returned by the pair of landmarks that has a larger relative difference in landmark bearings.

In summary, we have introduced a novel effective approach for robot self-localization using only the bearings of two landmarks. This technique can be viewed as a form of stereo-vision. The method we propose is well suited for real-time system as it requires very little computation.

When more than two landmarks exist in the environment, the robot can determine the relative positions of the landmarks provided some weak visibility constraints are satisfied. Indeed, suppose there are two pairs of landmarks $\{L_1, L_2\}$ and $\{L_3, L_4\}$ visible from a segment O_1O_2 (notice that $\{L_1, L_2\}$ and $\{L_3, L_4\}$ do not have to be in direct line of sight). Then using three different bases, the first one B_0 attached to O_1O_2, the second one $B_{1,2}$ attached to $\{L_1, L_2\}$, and the third one $B_{3,4}$ attached to $\{L_3, L_4\}$, we can determine the change of basis matrices $M_{B_0,B_{1,2}}$ and $M_{B_0,B_{3,4}}$. The matrix product $M^{-1}_{B_0,B_{1,2}} M_{B_0,B_{3,4}}$ allows us to compute the positions of the pairs of landmarks $\{L_1, L_2\}$ and $\{L_3, L_4\}$ relatively to each other.

This method enables a mobile robot to localize itself with only two observed bearings of two landmarks. Such a localization system will be invaluable to an indoor robot as well. As the bearings of the sides of a door frame can play the roles of the landmarks L_1 and L_2 and tell the robot exactly where it stands relative to the door. In next section, we employ this method to solve the landmark initialization problem in bearing-only SLAM.

4. Sensitivity Analysis to Landmark Initialization of Bearing-Only SLAM – A geometric approach

In this section, we propose a geometric method to solve the landmark initialization problem in bearing-only SLAM. The assumptions and the localization method are the same as in Section 3, with the exception that vision error is taken into consideration. The estimate of a landmark position becomes an uncertainty region instead of a single point. In particular, we show how the uncertainties of the measurements are affected by a change of frames. That is, we determine what can an observer attached to a landmark-based frame F_L deduced from the information transmitted by an observer attached to the robot-based frame F_R.

4.1 Method description

The notations in this section are the same as in Section 3.1. The uncertainty region of L_j is denoted by A_{L_j}. Assume that the error range for the bearing is $\pm\varepsilon$. In other words, at an observation point O_i, a landmark position L_j is contained in the *vision cone* which is formed by two rays rooted at O_i. The first ray is defined by O_i and the bearing $\beta_i^j + \varepsilon$; the second ray is defined by O_i and bearing $\beta_i^j - \varepsilon$. Figure 4(a) shows the vision cones in the robot-based frame F_R based on the reading of the landmark bearings from O_1.

After reading the bearing measurements from both O_1 and O_2, the uncertainty region A_{L_j} becomes the intersection of two cones rooted at O_1 and O_2 respectively. Figure 4(b) shows that a typical intersection is a 4-sided polygon. If the cones are almost parallel, their intersection can be an unbounded polyhedron.

The spatial relationships in Figure 4(b) are expressed in F_R. Since the robot is moving over time, the base of F_R changes too. Therefore, it is necessary to change coordinate systems to express all positions in the global frame F_L. Figure 5 illustrates the difficulty of expressing the robot centred information in the global frame F_L. The uncertainty on the landmarks prevents us from applying directly a change of bases. In next section, we will show how to solve this problem.

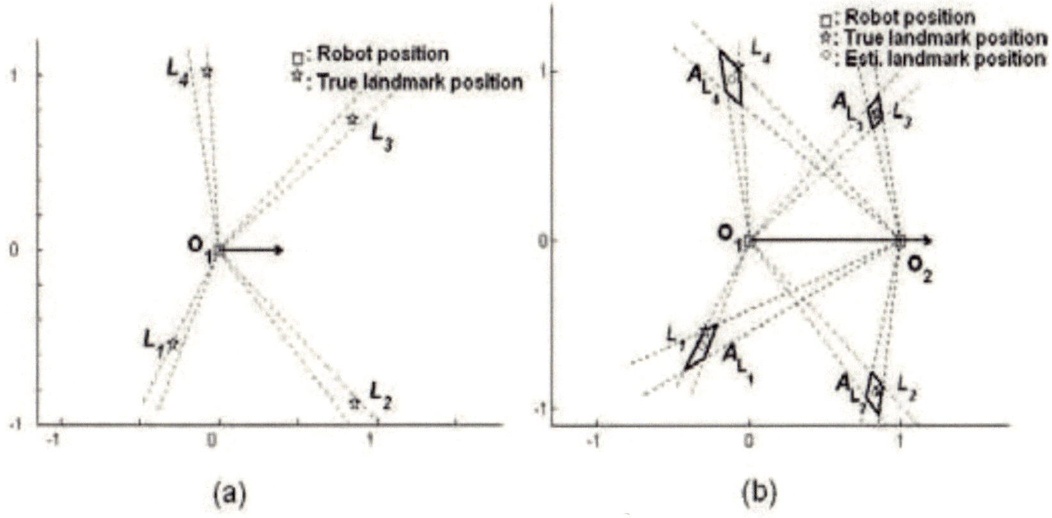

Figure 4. (a) The vision cones rooted at O_1 contain the landmarks. Each cone represents the unbounded uncertainty of the associated landmark. The diagram is drawn with respect to the robot-based frame F_R. (b) The intersections of the vision cones form the uncertainty region A_{L_j}

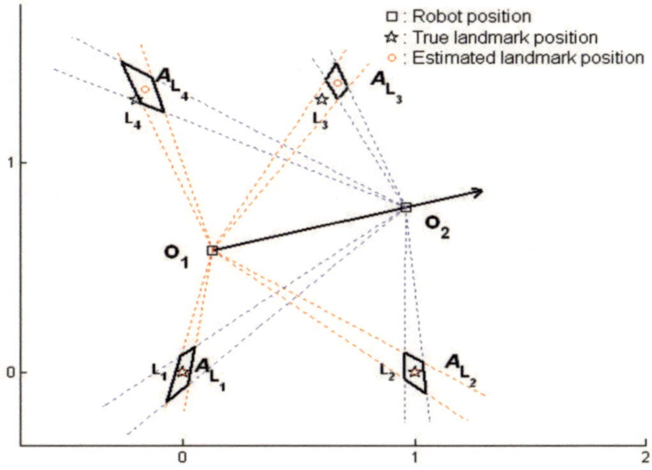

Figure 5. When L_1 and L_2 are not certain, a simple change of bases does not induce correct uncertainty regions of L_3 and L_4

4.2 Uncertainty and change of frames

From the uncertainties of landmark positions estimated in the robot-based frame F_R, we would like to derive the uncertainty regions of the observed objects with respect to the landmark-based frame F_L. Given a point x, if $X_R(x)$ and $X_L(x)$ denote the coordinate vector of x in frames F_R and F_L respectively.

Consider the simple case of Figure 6(a) which contains only two landmarks and two robot positions. Assume the robot (the observer) sees L_1 clearly from O_1 and O_2, but sees L_2 with some noise. The uncertainty region of L_1 in F_R is reduced to a single point (no ambiguity). Whereas, the uncertainty region of L_2 in F_R is a polyhedron.

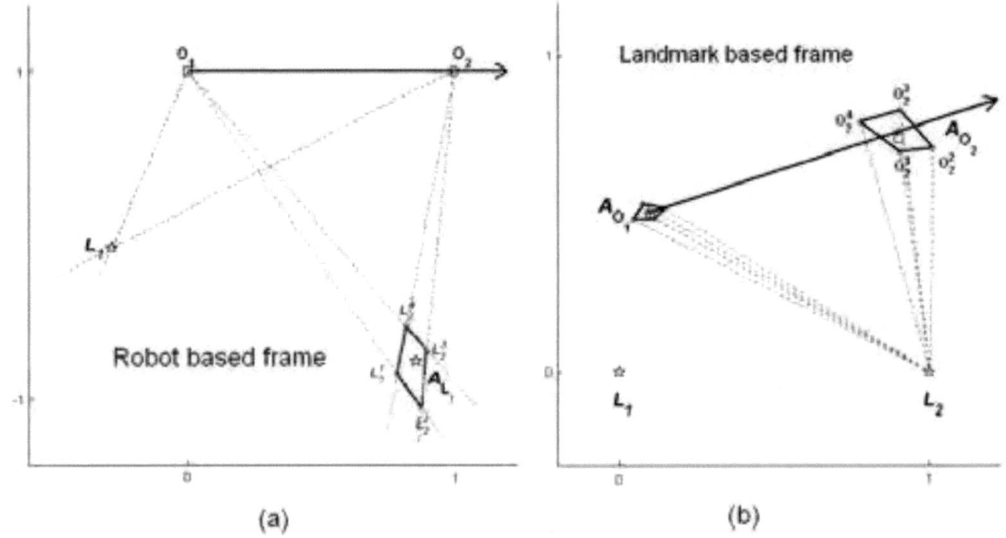

Figure 6. (a) A simple case in F_R, where we assume L_1 is clearly observed without ambiguity, the uncertainty region of L_2 is A_{L_2}. The four vertices of A_{L_2} are denoted by L_2^k, $k = 1...4$

(b) After the change of frames, the uncertainty regions of O_1 and O_2 are denoted by A_{O_1} and A_{O_2}. We obtain O_2^k from Equation (4) with respect to L_2^k, $k = 1...4$.

The uncertainty regions of O_1 and O_2 with respect to F_L can be obtained by considering all possible hypotheses for the location of L_2 consistent with the observations. That is, we consider the set of possible coordinate vectors $X_R(L_2)$ of L_2 in F_R. For each hypothesis $X_R(L_2) = h_2$, a standard change of bases returns the coordinates $X_L(O_1)$ and $X_L(O_2)$ of respectively O_1 and O_2 in F_L. Making h_2 range over the vertices of A_{L_2} in Figure 6(a), create the polyhedra A_{O_1} and A_{O_2} of uncertainty regions with respect to F_L (see Figure 6(b)).

In the general case, when uncertainty exists for both L_1 and L_2, to transfer the information from F_R to F_L, we consider simultaneously all the possible locations of L_1 and L_2 consistent with the observations. We hypothesize,

$$X_R(L_1) = h_1 \text{, and } X_R(L_2) = h_2 \tag{1}$$

Let τ_{h_1,h_2} be the affine transformation function for changing frames from F_R to F_L. That is,

$$X_L(L_1) = \tau_{h_1,h_2}(X_R(L_1)) = [0,0]' \tag{2}$$

$$X_L(L_2) = \tau_{h_1,h_2}(X_R(L_2)) = [1,0]' \tag{3}$$

The above constraints completely characterize τ_{h_1,h_2}. For any point x, the coordinates transfer between the two frames is done with Equation (4).

$$X_L(x) = \tau_{h_1,h_2}(X_R(x)) \tag{4}$$

In other words, the uncertainty region A_{O_i} of the robot position in F_L is

$$X_L(A_{O_i}) = \bigcup_{h_1 \in A_{L_1}, h_2 \in A_{L_2}} \tau_{h_1,h_2}(X_R(O_i)) \tag{5}$$

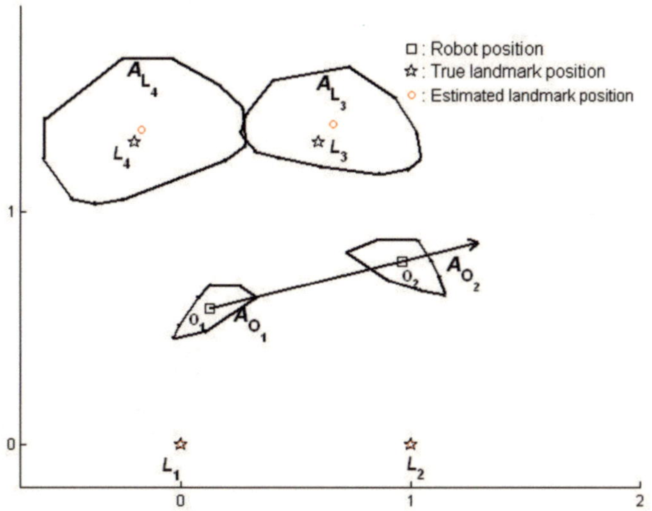

Figure 7. The uncertainty regions in F_L are derived from the uncertainty regions in F_R (see Figure 5). The centroids of the uncertainty regions are used to represent the estimated positions of different objects. The areas of the polyhedra quantify how uncertain the estimates are

The uncertainty regions A_{L_j} for L_3 and L_4 in F_L are computed similarly,

$$X_L(A_{L_j}) = \bigcup_{h_1 \in A_{L_1}, h_2 \in A_{L_2}} \tau_{h_1,h_2}(X_R(A_{L_j})) \qquad (6)$$

The computation in this example, we take the four vertices (the extreme points) L_1^k and L_2^k ($k=1...4$) from A_{L_1} and A_{L_2}. Figure 7 shows the estimated uncertainties of O_1, O_2 and L_3, L_4 in F_L. The polyhedron $X_L(A_{O_i})$ approximates the set of all consistent points for O_i and the polyhedron $X_L(A_{L_j})$ approximates the set of all consistent points for L_j. Although the uncertainty region $X_L(A_{L_j})$ is not a polyhedron, in practice it can be approximated by a polyhedron. We have tested the proposed method both in simulation and on a real robot. These results are presented in next section.

4.3 Simulation

We tested the proposed method in simulation in an environment with four landmarks (at unknown positions to the localization system). The robot moves in a polygonal line around the centre with some randomness. Since we focus on landmark initialization, Figure 8 shows only the estimated positions of the landmarks.

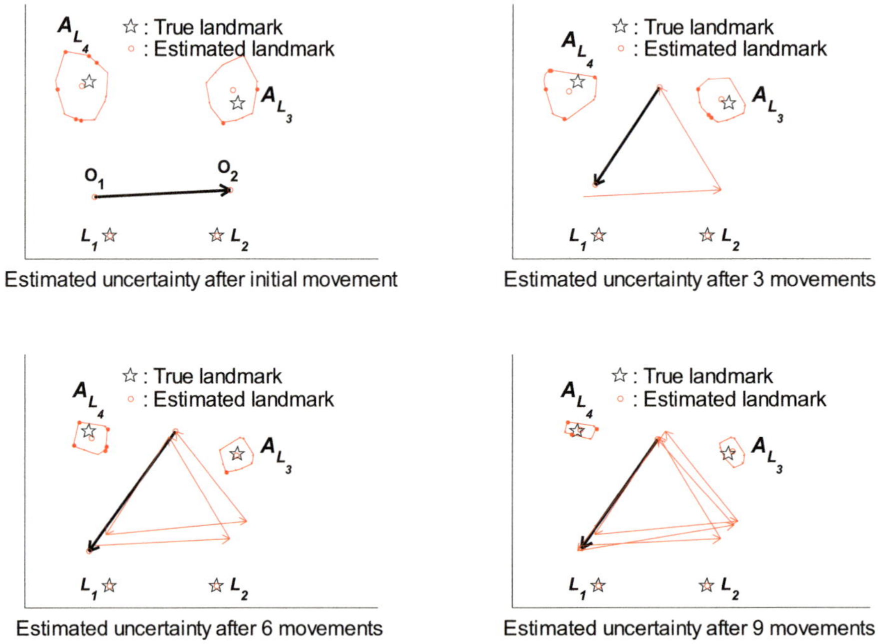

Estimated uncertainty after initial movement

Estimated uncertainty after 3 movements

Estimated uncertainty after 6 movements

Estimated uncertainty after 9 movements

Figure 8. The uncertainty regions A_{L_3} and A_{L_4} gradually shrink as the number of observations increases. The arrows represent the robot movements

Two landmarks are arbitrarily selected as L_1 and L_2. With the change of frames from F_R to F_L, the uncertainty regions A_{L_3} and A_{L_4} are computed. When another pair of observations is available after the robot has moved again, new A_{L_3} and A_{L_4} are obtained in the same manner. The estimated positions from all movements are unifiable since they are with respect to the same frame F_L. Figure 8 shows how the uncertainty regions are refined after several movements. The polyhedra A_{L_3} and A_{L_4} shrink gradually. A global map with the estimated positions and the corresponding uncertainties of all landmarks can be incrementally built.

4.4 Evaluation on a Real Robot

Our method was evaluated using a Khepera robot. The Khepera robot has a 6 centimetre diameter and is equipped with a color camera (176 x 255 resolution). A kheperaSot robot soccer playing field, 105 x 68 square centimetres, was used as the experimental arena (see Figure 15). There were four artificial landmarks in the playing field. Only one landmark was distinct from the others. The second landmark was placed 20 centimetres apart from the first landmark.

During the experiments, the robot moved in a polygonal line. Two panoramic images were taken in each straight motion. Landmark bearings were extracted from the panoramic images using a color thresholding technique. Bearings from each pair of observations were used to estimate the landmark positions. The vision error ε is limited to ±2 degrees.

Figure 9(a) shows the estimated uncertainties of landmark positions after 10 pairs of observations. The actual landmark positions are denoted by stars, the estimated landmark positions are shown as circles, and the areas of the polyhedra represent the uncertainties.

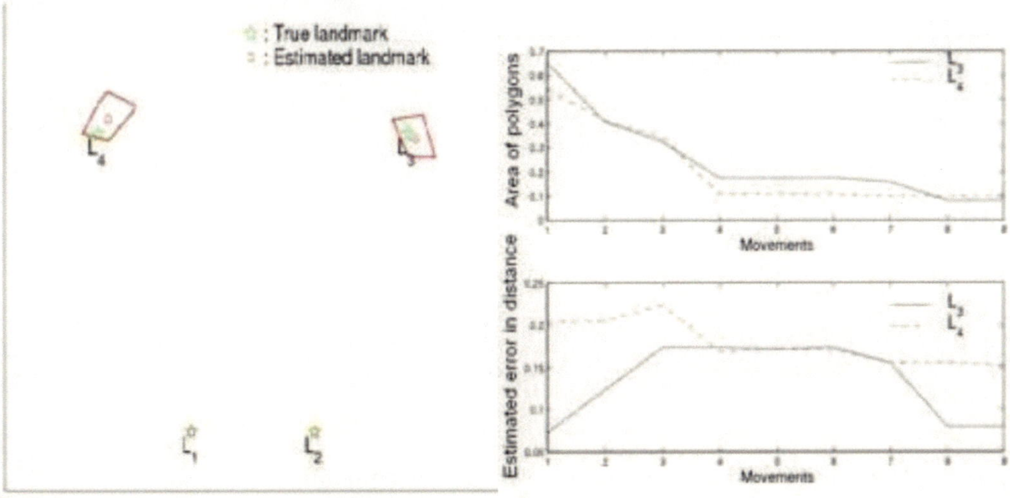

Figure 9. (a) Estimated landmark positions after 10 pairs of observations. (b) The uncertainties of the third and fourth landmarks

The uncertainties of L_3 and L_4 decrease rapidly in the first few observations and does not change much after the third observation as shown in the top chart of Figure 9(b). The bottom chart of Figure 9(b) displays the estimated errors of L_3 and L_4 are 2 centimetres and 3 centimetres respectively. The measurement unit in this chart equals to 20 centimetres.

We carried out another experiment to study the sensitivity of vision error ε. The top chart of Figure 10 shows the relationship between ε and the uncertainties of L_3. The amount of the vision error ε was varied from 2 to 7 degrees. The uncertainties are proportional to ε in a linear manner. The bottom chart of Figure 10 shows that the estimated error might not decrease monotonically. This is because we assign the centroid of the uncertainty region as the estimated landmark position.

In this section, we introduced a method for analyzing how uncertainty propagates when information is transferred from one observer attached to a robot-based frame to an observer attached to a landmark-based frame. The accuracy of this method was demonstrated both in simulation and on a real robot. In next section we will employ a probabilistic method to compute the uncertainties of object positions.

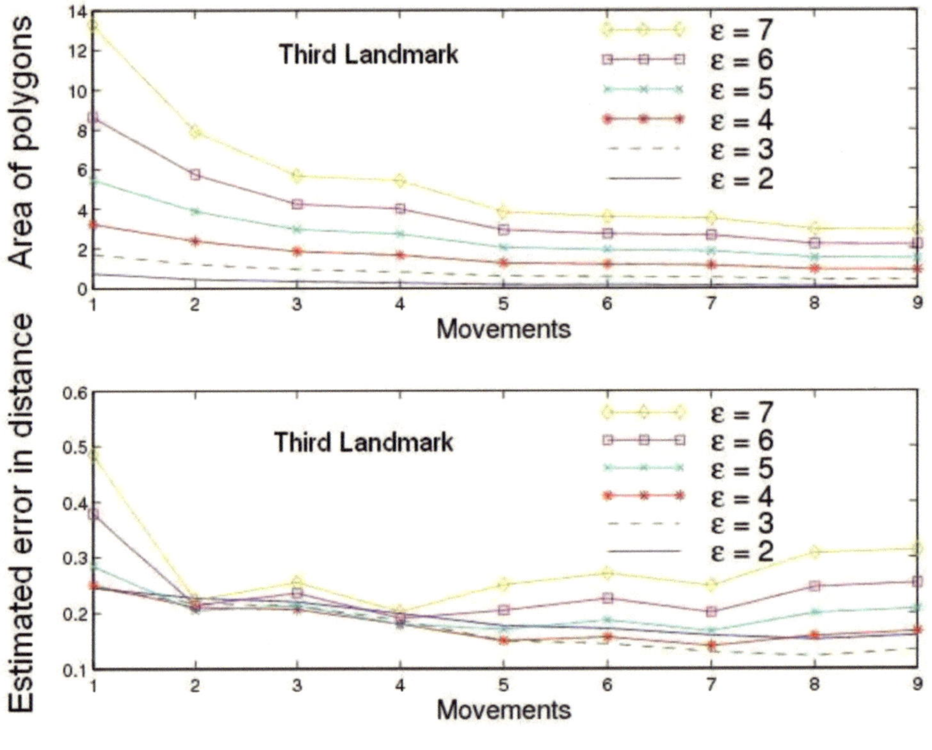

Figure 10. Uncertainties and estimated errors at different amounts of vision error ε in degrees

5. Sensitivity Analysis to Landmark Initialization of Bearing-Only SLAM – A probabilistic approach

In this Section, we describe a probabilistic method to solve the landmark initialization problem in bearing-only SLAM. The assumptions in this method are the same as Section 3. We characterize $p(r,\alpha)$ the PDF of landmark position expressed in polar coordinates when

r is independent on α. Formulas are derived for computing the *PDF* (Probability Density Function) when an initial observation is made. The updating of the PDF when further observations arrive is explained in Section 5.2.A.

5.1 Method description

Let $p(r,\alpha)$ be the PDF of the landmark position in polar coordinates when only one observation has been made. We characterize $p(r,\alpha)$ when r and α are independent. Let β denote the measured landmark bearing. Assume that the error range for the bearing is $\pm\varepsilon$. The landmark position is contained in the *vision cone* which is formed by two rays rooted at the observation point with respect to two bearings $\beta-\varepsilon$ and $\beta+\varepsilon$ (see Figure 11).

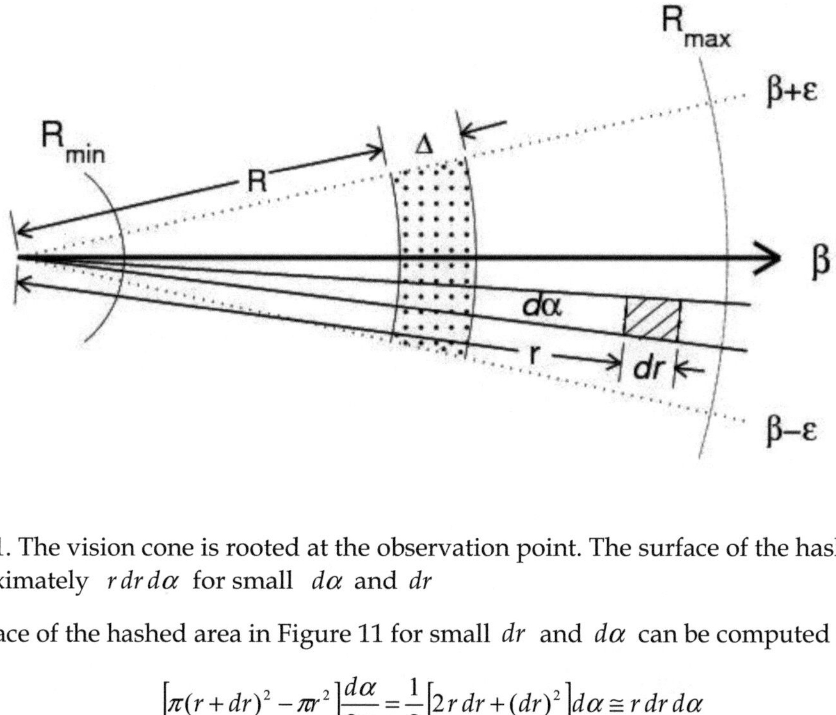

Figure 11. The vision cone is rooted at the observation point. The surface of the hashed area is approximately $r\,dr\,d\alpha$ for small $d\alpha$ and dr

The surface of the hashed area in Figure 11 for small dr and $d\alpha$ can be computed as

$$\left[\pi(r+dr)^2 - \pi r^2\right]\frac{d\alpha}{2\pi} = \frac{1}{2}\left[2r\,dr + (dr)^2\right]d\alpha \cong r\,dr\,d\alpha$$

Because the probability of the landmark being in the vision cone is 1, we have

$$\int_{\beta-\varepsilon}^{\beta+\varepsilon}\int_{R_{min}}^{R_{max}} p(r,\alpha)\,r\,dr\,d\alpha = 1 \tag{7}$$

In Equation (7), R_{max} and R_{min} are the bounds of the vision range interval. We define $F(R)$ as the probability of the landmark being in the area $\{(r,\alpha)\,|\,r\in[R_{min},R],\ \alpha\in[\beta-\varepsilon,\beta+\varepsilon]\}$, $F(R)$ can be represented as:

$$F(R) = \int_{\beta-\varepsilon}^{\beta+\varepsilon}\int_{R_{min}}^{R} p(r,\alpha)\,r\,dr\,d\alpha \tag{8}$$

We define $\Psi(R,\Delta)$ as the probability of the landmark being in the dotted area in Figure 11. Since $\Psi(R,\Delta) = F(R+\Delta) - F(R)$, we have

$$\Psi(R,\Delta) = \int_{\beta-\varepsilon}^{\beta+\varepsilon} \int_{R}^{R+\Delta} p(r,\alpha)\, r\, dr\, d\alpha \tag{9}$$

If the range r and the angle α are independent, then $\Psi(R,\Delta)$ is constant with respect to R. That is, $\dfrac{\partial \Psi(R,\Delta)}{\partial R} = 0$. From Equation (9), we derive

$$\frac{\partial F(R+\Delta)}{\partial R} = \frac{\partial F(R)}{\partial R} \tag{10}$$

Because of the independence of α and r, $p(r,\alpha)$ can be factored as

$$p(r,\alpha) = f(r)\, g(\alpha) \tag{11}$$

Without loss of generality, we impose that $\int g(\alpha)\, d\alpha = 1$. After factoring, Equation (8) becomes $F(R) = \int_{R_{\min}}^{R} f(r)\, r\, dr$. Because of the property of the integration, we have

$$\frac{\partial F(R)}{\partial R} = f(R) R \tag{12}$$

From Equations (10) and (12), we deduce that $f(R+\Delta)(R+\Delta) = f(R)R$. Therefore, $R\left[\dfrac{f(R+\Delta) - f(R)}{\Delta}\right] + f(R+\Delta) = 0$. By making Δ goes to zero, we obtain $R f'(R) + f(R) = 0$. The equality $f'(R)/f(R) = -1/R$ can be re-written as $[\log(f(R))]' = -[\log(R)]'$. After integrating both sides, we obtain

$$\log(f(R)) = -\log(R) + c = \log\left(\frac{1}{R}\right) + c = \log\left(\frac{e^c}{R}\right)$$

Where c is a constant, let $\xi = e^c$, we obtain $f(R) = \dfrac{\xi}{R}$

From Equations (7) and (11), ξ can be calculated and thus $\xi = \dfrac{1}{R_{\max} - R_{\min}}$

$$f(r) = \frac{1}{(R_{\max} - R_{\min})\, r}$$

Therefore, $p(r,\alpha)$ can be re-written as

$$p(r,\alpha) = \frac{1}{(R_{\max} - R_{\min})\, r} \times g(\alpha) \tag{13}$$

If we use a Gaussian function for $g(\alpha)$ with mean β and standard deviation σ, the PDF

$p(r,\alpha)$ can be re-written as Equation (14). Figure 12 shows the PDF of $p(r,\alpha)$

$$p(r,\alpha) = \frac{1}{(R_{\max} - R_{\min})\ r} \times \frac{\exp\left[-\frac{(\alpha-\beta)^2}{2\sigma^2}\right]}{\sqrt{2\pi}\ \sigma} \tag{14}$$

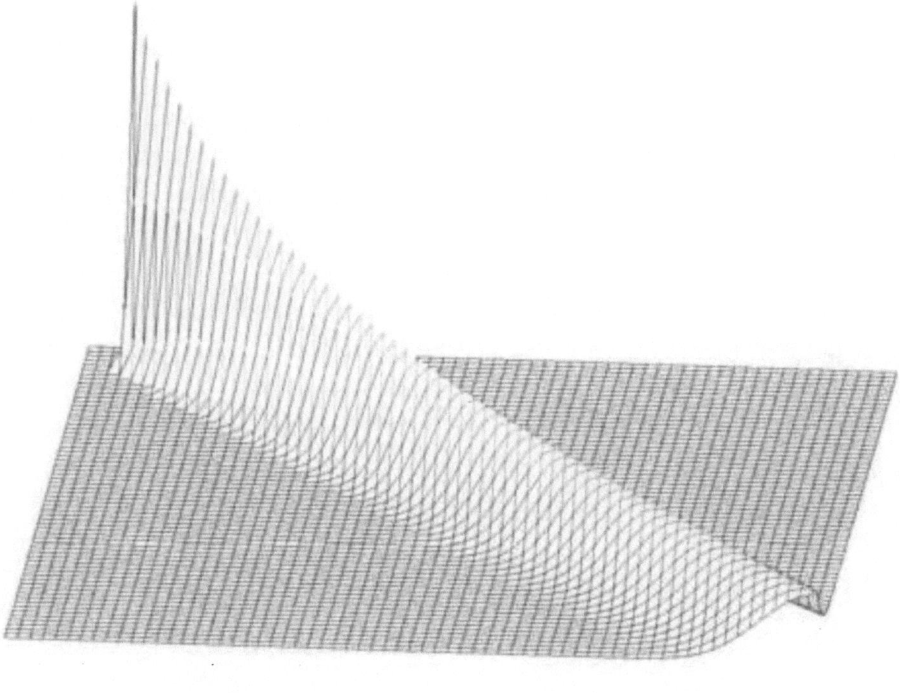

Figure 12. The PDF of the landmark position following Equation (14)

5.2 Utilization of the PDF for bearing-only SLAM

We illustrate the application of the PDF for our bearing-only SLAM system. Section 5.2-A describes how the PDF can be updated with a second observation. In Section 5.2-B, we present experimental results on a real robot.

A. Updating the PDF with a second observation

When a second observation is made after a linear motion, the landmark position falls in the uncertainty region which is the intersection of two vision cones rooted at the first and the second observation points O_1 and O_2. We denote with p_1 and p_2 the PDFs of the landmark positions computed from Equation (14) with respect to O_1 and O_2 respectively. Let p denote the PDF of the landmark position after fusing the sensory readings from O_1 and O_2. From the work of Stroupe et al. (2000), we have $p = p_1 p_2 / \int p_1 p_2$.

We want to approximate p with a Gaussian distribution q. To compute the parameters of q, we generate a set S according to the PDF p by the *Rejection Method* (Leydold, 1998). We determine the maximum probability density p_{max} of p by computing $p_1 p_2$ at the intersection of two bearings. The sampling process selects uniformly a sample point s and a random number $\{v \mid v \in |0,1|\}$. If $|p(s)/p_{max}| < v$, s is rejected, otherwise s is accepted and added to S. The sampling process is repeated until enough points are accepted. Figure 13 shows the generated samples in the uncertainty regions of four landmarks.

The mean $\bar{x}$ and the covariance matrix C of q are obtained by computing the mean and the covariance matrix of S as previously done by Smith & Cheeseman (1986) and Stroupe et al. (2000). In Figure 13, the contour plots present the PDFs of landmark positions.

The estimated PDFs in Figure 13 are expressed in the robot-based frame F_R. Since the robot is moving over time, its frame changes too. Therefore, it is necessary to change the coordinate systems to express all the estimations in the global frame F_L. We use the method introduced in Section 4 to transfer the samples in S from F_R to F_L. After the change of frames, the uncertainties of L_1 and L_2 are transferred to other objects. The samples of other objects are taken to approximate the PDFs of the object positions in F_L. Figure 14 shows the distribution of the samples after the change of frames. The contour plots present the PDFs of the object positions in the global frame F_L associated to the points (L_1, L_2).

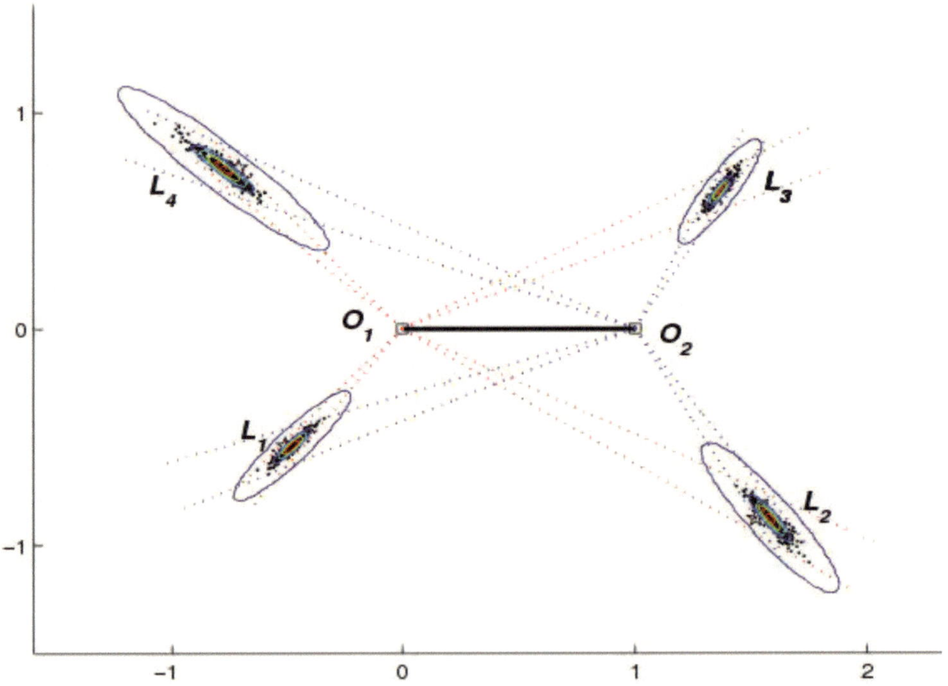

Figure 13. The PDFs and the contour plots of four landmarks in the robot-based frame F_R; in this example, the uncertainty region of each landmark is a bounded polygon. The generated samples are distributed in the uncertainty regions

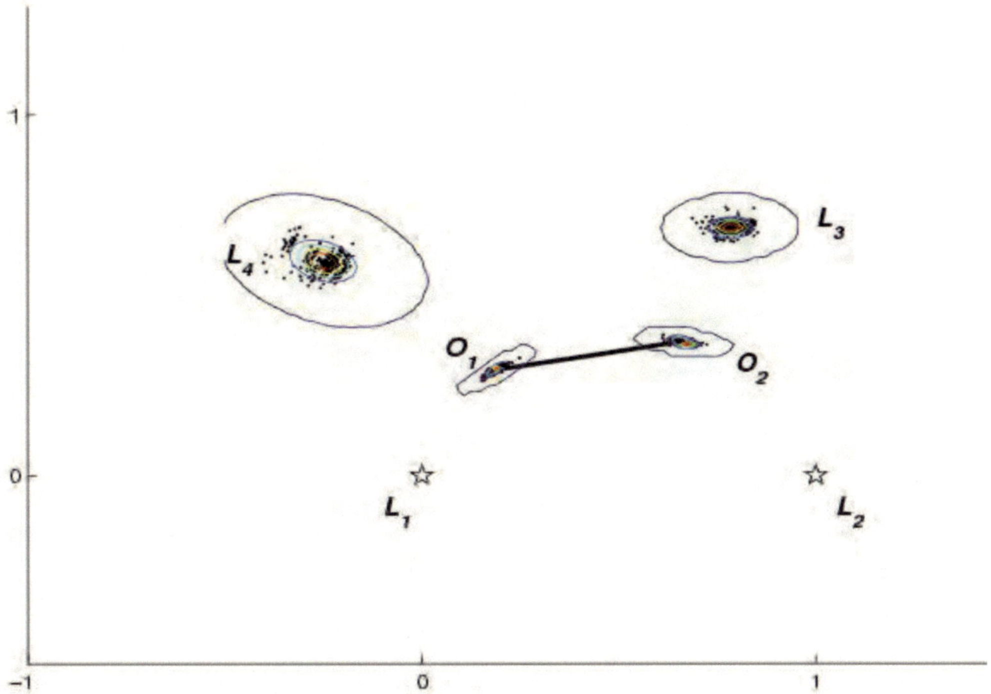

Figure 14. After the change of frames from F_R to F_L, the PDFs and the contour plots of O_1, O_2 and L_3, L_4 are presented in the global frame F_L

B. Experimental Results

Our method was evaluated using a Khepera robot equipped with a colour camera (176 x 255 resolution). The Khepera robot has a 6 centimetres diameter. A KheperaSot robot soccer playing field, 105 x 68 square centimetres, was used for the experiment arena (see Figure 15). There were four artificial landmarks in the playing field. The first and second landmarks were placed at the posts of a goal, 30 centimetres apart from each other.

The objective of the experiment is to evaluate the accuracy of the method by estimating the positions of the third and the fourth landmarks. At each iteration, the robot was randomly placed in the field. The robot took a panoramic image and then moved in a straight line and captured a second panoramic image. Landmark bearings were extracted from the panoramic images using colour thresholding.

A total of 40 random movements were performed in this experiment. $R_{\min}$ was set to 3 centimetres, $R_{\max}$ was set to 120 centimetres, and the vision error ε was ± 3 degrees. Figure 16(b) shows the errors of the estimated landmark positions. For L_3, the estimated error was reduced from approximately 9 centimetres at the first iteration to less than 1 centimetre at the last iteration. For L_4, the error was reduced from 14 centimetres to 2.77 centimetres. The experiment shows that the estimated error of landmark position is sensitive to the relative distance with respect to L_1 and L_2.

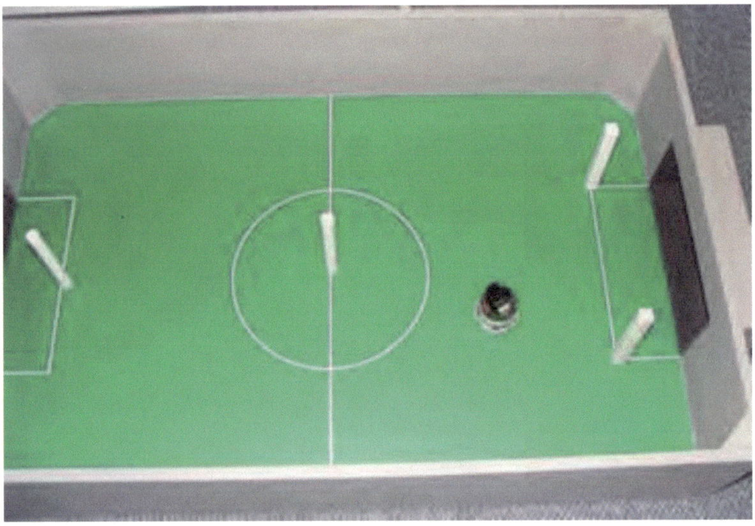

Figure 15. Experimental setup, the landmarks are the vertical tubes

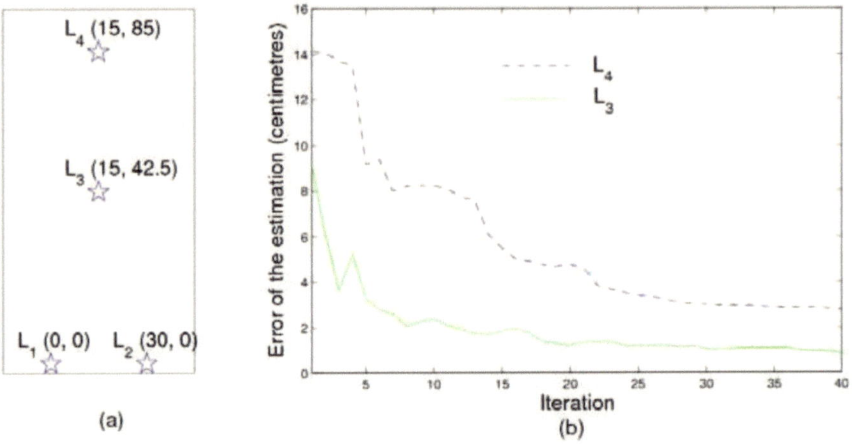

Figure 16. (a) Diagram of the experimental setup. (b) The errors of the estimated landmark positions

We made another experiment to test the sensitivity of the errors of the landmark positions with respect to the different directions of the robot's moving trajectories. We let the robot move in four different directions with respect to three landmarks. In Figure 17(a), stars denote the landmark positions and arrows denote the moving trajectories. The robot repeated 10 iterations for each trajectory.

The errors on L_3 in four trajectories after the tenth iteration were 2.12, 1.17, 1.51, and 13.99 centimetres respectively. The error of the fourth trajectory is large because the robot moves along a line that is close to L_3. Therefore, the vision cones at the first and the second observations are nearly identical.

The estimation of the landmark position is more accurate when the intersection of two vision cones is small. This is the case of the second trajectory where the intersection is the smallest among all trajectories.

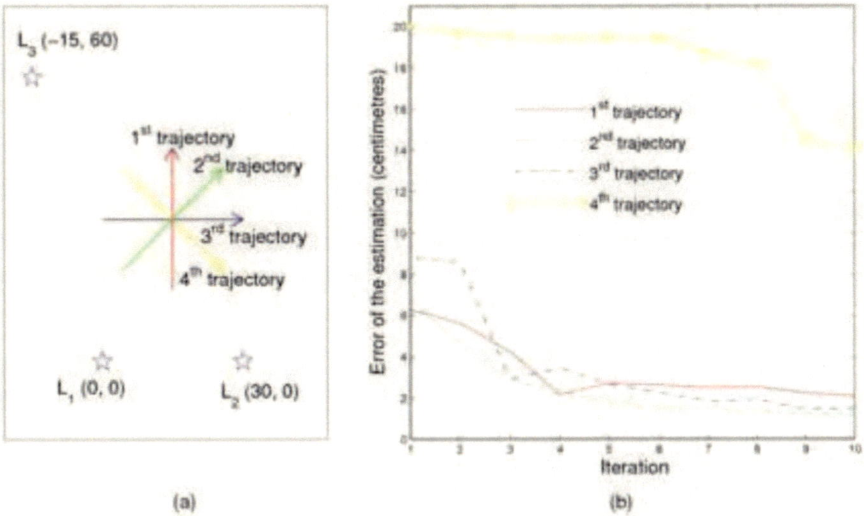

Figure 17. (a) Trajectories of the robot for the experiment to study the relationship between moving directions and estimated errors of landmark positions. (b) The errors on L_3 at each iteration

Although the intersecting area of L_3 for the first and the third trajectories are the same, the intersecting areas of L_1 and L_2 for the first trajectory are much bigger than the areas from the third trajectory. This is the reason why the estimated error from the third trajectory is smaller than the one for the first trajectory.

6. Conclusion

In this chapter, we proposed a vision-based approach to bearing-only SLAM in a 2-dimensional space. We assumed the environment contained several visually distinguishable landmarks. This approach is inspired from techniques used in stereo vision and Structure From Motion. Our landmark initialization method relies solely on the bearing measurements from a single camera. This method does not require information from an odometer or a range sensor. All the object positions can be estimated in a landmark-based frame. The trade-off is that this method requires the robot to be able to move in a straight line for a short while to initialize the landmarks. The proposed method is particularly accurate and useful when the robot can guide itself in a straight line by visually locking on static objects.

Since the method does not rely on odometry and range information, the induced map is up to a scale factor only. In our method, the distance $\| L_1 - L_2 \|$ of two landmarks is taken as the measurement unit of the map. The selection of L_1 and L_2 is critical for the accuracy of the map. In Section 3.1, the mathematical derivation shows that the estimated error of a landmark position is proportional to the range of the landmark and the inverse of the relative change in landmark bearings. Choosing L_1 and L_2 with larger change in bearings produces a more accurate mapping of the environment.

In the sensitivity analysis, we showed how the uncertainties of the objects' positions are affected by a change of frames. We determine how an observer attached to a landmark-based frame F_L can deduce the uncertainties in F_L from the uncertainties transmitted by an observer attached to the robot-based frame F_R. Each estimate of landmark uncertainties requires a pair of the observations in a straight movement. The simulation in Section 4.3 shows how the uncertainties of landmark positions are refined when the robot moves in a polygonal line.

With dead reckoning, the error of the estimated robot's location increases with time because of cumulated odometric errors. In our method, we set O_1 and O_2 (pair of observation points in a straight movement) at $[0,0]'$ and $[1,0]'$ in F_R. There is no dead reckoning error on O_1 and O_2 by construction. In practice, the robot's movement may not be perfectly straight. However, the non-straight nature of the trajectory can be compensated by increasing the size of the confidence interval of the bearing.

The induced map created by our method can be refined with EKF or PF algorithms. With EKF, the uncertainty region computed from the geometric method can be translated into a Gaussian PDF. With PF, the weights of the samples can be computed with the formulas derived in Section 5.1. Since the samples are drawn from the uncertainty region, the number of samples is minimized.

The accuracy of our method was evaluated with simulations and experiments on a real robot. Experimental results demonstrate the usefulness of this approach for a bearing-only SLAM system. We are currently working on the unknown data association when all landmarks are visually identical. In future work, we will deal with the problems of object occlusion and non-planar environments. That is, the system will be extended from a 2-dimensional to a 3-dimensional space.

7. References

Bailey, T. (2003). Constrained Initialisation for Bearing-Only SLAM, *Proceedings of IEEE International Conference on Robotics and Automation*, pp. 1966 - 1971, 1050-4729

Bailey, T. & Durrant-Whyte, H. (2006). Simultaneous Localization and Mapping (SLAM): Part II, *IEEE Robotics and Automation Magazine*, page numbers (108-117), 1070-9932

Costa, A.; Kantor, G. & Choset, H. (2004). Bearing-only Landmark Initialization with Unknown Data Association, *Proceedings of IEEE International Conference on Robotics and Automation*, pp. 1764 - 1770

Davison, A. (2003). Real-time simultaneous localization and mapping with a single camera, *Proceedings of International Conference on Computer Vision*, pp. 1403-1410, Nice, October

Davison, A.; Cid, Y. & Kita, N. (2004). Real-time 3D SLAM with wide-angle vision, *Proceedings of IAV2004 - 5th IFAC/EURON Symposium on Intelligent Autonomous Vehicles*, Lisboa, Portugal, July

Fox, D.; Burgard, F.; Dellaert, W. & Thrun, S. (1999). Monte Carlo localization: Efficient position estimation for mobile robot, *Proceedings of National Conference on Artificial Intelligence*, pp. 343-349

Goncavles, L.; Bernardo, E. d.; Benson, D.; Svedman, M.; Karlsson, N.; Ostrovski, J. & Pirjanian, P. (2005). A visual front-end for simultaneous localization and mapping, *Proceedings of IEEE International Conference on Robotics and Automation*, pp. 44-49

Huang, H.; Maire, F. & Keeratipranon, N. (2005a). A Direct Localization Method Using only the Bearings Extracted from Two Panoramic Views Along a Linear Trajectory, *Proceedings of Autonomous Minirobots for Research and Edutainment (AMiRE)*, pp. 201-206, Fukui, Japan

Huang, H.; Maire, F. & Keeratipranon, N. (2005b). Uncertainty Analysis of a Landmark Initialization Method for Simultaneous Localization and Mapping, *Proceedings of Australian Conference on Robotics and Automation*, Sydney, Australia

Jensfelt, P.; Kragic, D.; Folkesson, J. & Bjorkman, M. (2006). A Framework for Vision Based Bearing Only 3D SLAM, *Proceedings of IEEE International Conference on Robotics and Automation*, pp. 1944- 1950, 0-7803-9505-0, Orlando, FL

Kwok, N. M. & Dissanayake, G. (2004). An Efficient Multiple Hypothesis Filter for Bearing-Only SLAM, *Proceedings of IEEE International Conference on Intelligent Robots and Systems*, pp. 736- 741, 0-7803-8463-6

Lemaire, T.; Lacroix, S. & Sola, J. (2005). A practical 3D Bearing-Only SLAM algorithm, *Proceedings of IEEE International Conference on Intelligent Robots and Systems*, pp. 2757-2762

Leonard, J. J. & Durrant-Whyte, H. F. (1991). Simultaneous localization for an autonomous mobile robot, *Proceedings of IEEE Intelligent Robots and System*, pp. 1442-1447, Osaka, Japan

Levitt, T. S. & Lawton, D. M. (1990). Qualitative navigation for mobile robots, *Artificial Intelligence*, Vol. 44, No. 3, page numbers (305-360)

Leydold, J. (1998). A Rejection Technique for Sampling from log-Concave Multivariate Distributions, *Modelling and Computer Simulation*, Vol. 8, No. 3, page numbers (254-280)

Menegatti, E.; Zoccarato, M.; Pagello, E. & Ishiguro, H. (2004). Image-based Monte Carlo localisation with omnidirectional images, *Robotics and Autonomous Systems*, Vol. 48, No. 1, page numbers (17-30)

Montemerlo, M.; Thrun, S.; Koller, D. & Wegbreit, B. (2003). FastSLAM 2.0: An improved particle filtering algorithm for simultaneous localization and mapping that provably converges, *Proceedings of International Joint Conferences on Artificial Intelligence*, pp. 1151-1156, Morgan Kaufmann, IJCAI

Mouragnon, E.; Lhuillier, M.; Dhome, M.; Dekeyser, F. & Sayd, P. (2006). 3D Reconstruction of complex structures with bundle adjustment: an incremental approach, *Proceedings of IEEE International Conference on Robotics and Automation*, pp. 3055 - 3061, Orlando, USA

Murray, D. & Jennings, C. (1998). Stereo vision based mapping and navigation for mobile robots., *Proceedings of IEEE International Conference on Robotics and Automation*, pp. 1694 - 1699, New Mexico

Nister, D.; Naroditsky, O. & Bergen, J. (2004). Visual Odometry, *Proceedings of IEEE Computer Society Conference*, pp. I-652 - I-659, Princeton

Rizzi, A. & Cassinis, R. (2001). A robot self-localization system based on omnidirectional color images, *Robotics and Autonomous Systems,* Vol. 34, No. 1, page numbers (23-38)

Sabe, K.; Fukuchi, M.; Gutmann, J.-S.; Ohashi, T.; Kawamoto, K. & Yoshigahara, T. (2004). Obstacle Avoidance and Path Planning for Humanoid Robots using Stereo Vision, *Proceedings of International Conference on Robotics and Automation*, pp. 592 - 597, New Orleans

Se, S.; Lowe, D. & Little, J. J. (2002). Mobile Robot Localization and Mapping with Uncertainty Using Scale-Invariant Visual Landmarks, *International Journal of Robotics Research,* Vol. 21, No. 8, page numbers (735 - 758)

Siegwart, R. & Nourbaksh, I. R. (2004). *Introduction to Autonomous Mobile Robots*, The MIT Press, Cambridge, Massachusetts

Sim, R.; Elinas, P.; Griffin, M. & Little, J. J. (2005). Vision-based slam using the rao-blackwellised particle filter, *Proceedings of IJCAI Workshop on Reasoning with Uncertainty in Robotics*, Edinburgh, Scotland

Smith, R. & Cheeseman, P. (1986). On the Representation and Estimation of Spatial Uncertainty, *The International Journal of Robotics Research,* Vol. 5, No. 4, page numbers (56-68)

Sola, J.; Monin, A.; Devy, M. & Lemaire, T. (2005). Undelayed Initialization in Bearing Only SLAM, *Proceedings of IEEE/RSJ International Conference on Intelligent Robots and Systems (IROS)*, pp. 2751-2756

Spero, D. J. (2005). Simultaneous Localisation and Map Building: The Kidnapped Way, Intelligent Robotics Research Centre, Monash University, Melbourne, Australia.

Stroupe, A. W.; Martin, M. C. & Balch, T. (2000). Merging Probabilistic Observations for Mobile Distributed Sensing, Pittsburgh, Robotics Institute, Carnegie Mellon University.

Usher, K.; Ridley, P. & Corke, P. (2003). Visual Servoing of a Car-like Vehicle - An Application of Omnidirectional Vision, *Proceedings of IEEE International Conference on Robotics and Automation*, pp. 4288- 4293, 0-7803-7736-2

Wooden, D. (2006). A Guide to Vision-Based Map Building, *IEEE Robotics and Automation Magazine, June 2006*, page numbers (94-98)

Zunino, G. & Christensen, H. I. (2001). Simultaneous localization and mapping in domestic environments, *Proceedings of International Conference on Multisensor Fusion and Integration for Intelligent System*, pp. 67 - 72

20

Object Recognition for Obstacles-free Trajectories Applied to Navigation Control

W. Medina-Meléndez, L. Fermín, J. Cappelletto, P. Estévez, G. Fernández-López and J. C. Grieco
Universidad Simón Bolívar, Grupo de Mecatrónica, Valle de Sartenejas, Caracas Venezuela

1. Introduction

In this chapter applications of image and video processing to navigation of mobile robots are presented. During the last years some impressive real time applications have been showed to the world, such as the NASA missions to explore the surface of Mars with autonomous vehicles; in those missions, video and image processing played an important role to rule the vehicle.
Algorithms based on the processing of video or images provided by CCD sensors or video cameras have been used in the solution of the navigation problem of autonomous vehicles. In one of those approaches, a velocity field is designed in order to guide the orientation and motion of the autonomous vehicle. A particular approach to the solution of the navigation problem of an autonomous vehicle is presented here. In the first section of this introduction a state of the art review is presented, after it, the proposed algorithm is summarized; the following sections present the procedure. Finally, some experimental results are shown at the end of the chapter.

1.1 Review of Navigation of Autonomous Robots using Vision Techniques.

In the area of autonomous navigation using vision techniques, the previous works (Santos-Victor & Sandini,1997), and (Nasisi & Carelli, 2003) are corner stones. In the first mentioned study, robot control techniques are explored, using both cameras on board of the robots and external cameras. In that work it is shown that it is possible to accomplish effective control actions without doing a complete processing of the image captured or without the calibration of the camera. In the job of Nasisi & Carelli, a set of equations needed to establish relationships among a bidimensional image captured by a video camera and its corresponding tri-dimensional image is obtained, an equation set that is important when a single camera is being used. The jobs of S. Skaar et al., (who participated in the 2003 Mars Exploration Rover experiment of NASA), over the concept of Camera Space Manipulation (CSM) (Skaar et al., 1992) and the concept of Mobile Camera Space Manipulation (MCSM) (Seelinger et al., 2002), must be cited. The MCSM method consists of the estimation of the relationship among the characteristics position of the manipulator and its corresponding points in the image spaces of the two cameras mounted over the robot; the CSM concept is quite similar but with more restrictions. Both methods, the CSM and the MCSM require not

only the parameters of the cameras to be completely known, but also the kinematics model of the manipulator, even if they don't require the complete calibration of the camera and the manipulator. These methods require a set of cameras, while the methodology proposed in (Santos-Victor & Sandini,1997) and (Nasisi & Carelli, 2003) involves only one.
One vital characteristic of every navigation strategy is the way that the decisions are taken on it when the sensory system indicates the presence of obstacles on the robot trajectory. Different obstacle avoidance strategies have been presented; among those strategies the use of electrostatic fields - where the robot is modeled as a positive electric charge, as also the obstacles, and the objective of the trajectory is modeled as a negative charge - must be mentioned (Dudek & Jenkin, 2000) and (Khatib, 1985); the Coulomb law is applied to determine the trajectory of the mobile robot.
In 1995, Li and Horowitz presented the concept of velocity fields (Li & Horowitz, 1995); in such a case, a vector velocity is defined over the trajectory of the robot for each possible position coding a specific task. Using control schemes with the velocity field as the reference for the system, has allowed approaches to the problem employing different control schemes instead of the classic following trajectory problem. In this approach, the improvement of coordination and synchronization among the degrees of freedom of the robot are much more important than the time to execute a given task. In the Figure 1 an example of this strategy is presented.

Figure 1. Velocity Field for a manipulator in the plane

With the introduction of the concept of velocity fields, also emerged the strategy of Passive Velocity Field Control (PVFC). In this control strategy the tasks are coded using the velocity and energy that the system could transfer to the environment and that it is limited by a constant (Li & Horowitz, 1999). Li and Horowitz presented the properties of the PVFC strategy doing special emphasis on the contour following problem in (Li & Horowitz, 2001a) and (Li & Horowitz, 2001b).
In many research works related with velocity fields, the stability of the control schemes is pursued; Cervantes et al. (Cervantes et al., 2002) proposed a Proportional - Integral Controller based on compensation errors techniques where it is not necessary to have a deep knowledge of the robot dynamics, obtaining semi global asymptotically stable conditions on the following errors of the velocity fields. Moreno and Kelly, in (Moreno & Kelly, 2003a),

(Moreno & Kelly, 2003b) and (Moreno & Kelly, 2003c), proposed different control schemes using velocity fields focusing mainly on the asymptotically stable conditions.

Other investigations related to velocity fields have focused in other areas, such as adaptive control (Li, 1999). In that work, Li proposed an adaptive control scheme using velocity fields as references for robots with unknown inertia parameters. Also in (Dixon et al., 2005) an adaptive derivative control is presented in order to follow a velocity field. In almost all the previous cases, the works had as an objective the design of control schemes taking a velocity field as a time-invariant reference, obtained after a theoretical or analytical procedure. Only few works in the literature have considered the case when the field is time-dependent.

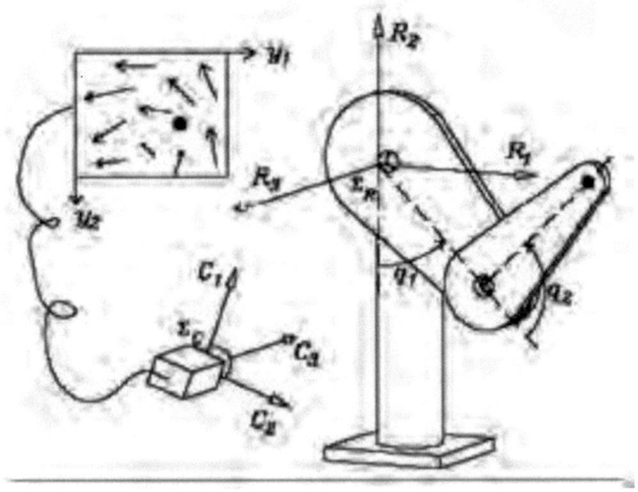

Figure 2. Robot system employed in (Kelly et al., 2004a)

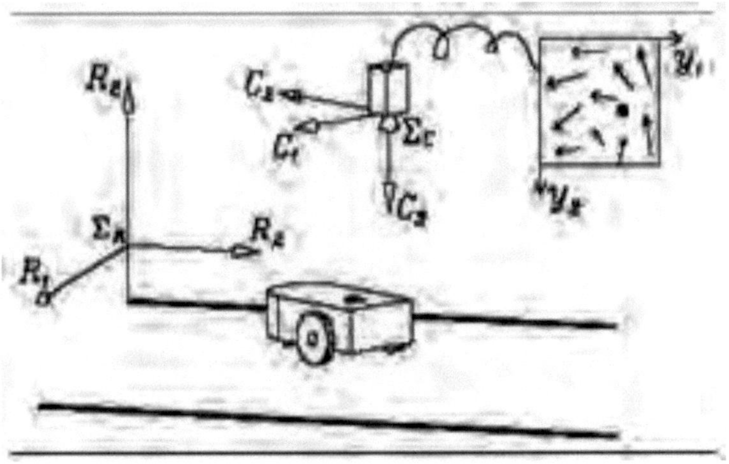

Figure 3. Robot system employed in (Kelly et al., 2004b)

Yamakita et al., in (Yamakita & Suh, 2000) and (Yamakita & Suh, 2001), applied PVFC to cooperative robots, obtaining field velocity generating algorithms for tasks where it is necessary to follow certain orders of a master robot. For this work the authors created an augmented dynamic system using an inertia flywheel, in order to avoid the problems of control following by velocity fields. Recently, Kelly and collaborators in (Kelly et al., 2004a) and (Kelly et al., 2004b), used a camera as a main sensor in a control scheme by velocity fields in order to control a mobile robot and a robot manipulator. Particularly in (Kelly et al., 2004a) is presented a controller by velocity fields for a manipulator of two degrees of freedom that incorporates an external camera to capture the manipulator movements and the work environment. On the captured image a theoretical velocity field that the manipulator is capable to follow is pre-defined. In the Figure 2 an example for this case is presented.

In (Kelly et al., 2004b), the control is applied to a wheeled mobile robot where the video camera is located over the robot. Like in the previous case, the camera is located in such a way that covers the environment and the robot itself. In the Figure 3 can be visualized the system under study.

1.2. The proposed approach

During last years, as it was mentioned, the use of artificial vision in robot tasks has been increasing. In many applications, such as rescue jobs, the use of vision to generate velocity fields is under study. The dynamic modification and generation of the velocity field itself, changing it with the environment modifications, is a new research area. If timing is not an issue in the control objectives, then velocity field control, where the speed can be adjusted as desired, is a potentially important technique. For instance, if the objective is to control a vehicle's trajectory at 80 Km/h, the velocity field can be adjusted to that speed and modified in order to avoid obstacles detected by a camera (either on board or external), while keeping close to the original trajectory in order to reach the final objective. This approach could be of crucial importance in rescue tasks where a flying machine could be "understanding" the environment, and changing the velocity field references for another robot on the ground. Another potential application is in automatic warehouses where changing the velocity field references could be assigned different and changing tasks to the manipulator. In the future, the dynamic velocity field generator that is presented in this work will be modified to in order to allow the generation of a 3-dimensional velocity field. Also, the algorithm is going to be used to coordinate the tasks of cooperative robots for Futbot, submarine vehicles coordination, cooperative multi-robot observation, etc.

In order to perform the tests, an experimental setup has been integrated. This experimental setup consists of:

1. A Hemisson differential mobile robot, created by the Swiss company "K-Team Corporation".
2. 2.4 GHz wireless video camera, model XC10A and its wireless receptor VR31A. This is the only sensor employed in the experiments in order to detect the robot and the obstacles. The camera has a resolution of 640 x 480 pixels and offers up to 30 frames per second (fps).
3. Image acquisition card model NI-PXI-1407 using the Standard RS-170 for monochromatic video signals. All the characteristics can be seen in Table 1.
4. A PXI module from National Instrument is employed to process the data. The module is the NI-PXI-1000B.

Description	Standard monochromatic
Bus	PXI/CompactPCI
Video Inputs	1
Spatial Resolution	640 × 480 RS-170
	768 × 576 CCIR
Píxel depth	8 bits
Video input Standard	RS-170, CCIR
Digital I/O	1

Table 1. Characteristics of the NI-PXI-1407

On the NI-PXI-1000B run all the LabView DLL's and Matlab applications.
The working environment consists of an area of approximately 6 square meters where the robot navigates. The wireless video camera was located 2.5 meters over this area. In Figure 4 is shown a sketch of the experimental arrangement.

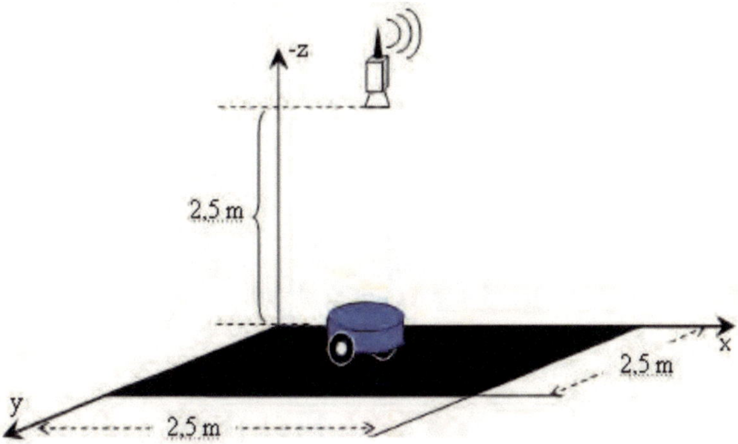

Figure 4. Environment employed for the experiments

The problem for the generation of a dynamic velocity field was divided in three different steps:

1. A generator of the initial velocity field.
2. The processing by the artificial vision system.
3. The generator of the evading velocity field.

1.3. Description of the generated system

Initially the user must define the task without taking into account the obstacles that might appear in the trajectory of the mobile robot. In order to indicate the trajectory a generator was developed for the initial velocity field. This generator is presented later in this chapter. In order to avoid the obstacles presented during the trajectory of the mobile robot, it is necessary to identify their existence, determining its location, size and orientation. In order to solve this problem the artificial vision system was. The information supplied by the artificial vision system is employed to modify the initial velocity field using the generator of the evading field. Once the desired task is well known and also the position and orientation of the obstacles the system creates the local velocity fields that surrounds each obstacle; the

final navigation field is obtained adding the initial field with the evading fields pondering each one properly.
In first place and before testing the system in the experimental setup, the results were validated using the Easy Java Simulations platform. The results are presented also in this chapter.

2. Vision System Implementation

This section describes two implementations of the vision system for the robot and obstacle identification process. In both cases the robot detection was made by using a pattern matching technique, and for the obstacle detection were employed two different approaches.
The first implementation is based on the hypothesis that any object present in the scene can be described as any of the following regular shapes: circle, square and rectangle. In this case it was utilized a classification strategy for its identification.
For the other system, the obstacle detection was made through a particle analysis, in order to cope with those problems arisen by using the previous approach in images containing obstacle with irregular shapes.

2.1. Robot identification by pattern matching

The pattern matching process consists of the fast detection into the image of those regions that have a high concordance with a previously known reference pattern. This reference pattern contains information related with edge and region pixels, thus allowing the deletion of redundant information contained into a regular shape.

2.1.1. Normalized Cross-Correlation

The correlation process based on the Euclidian distance, is described by the following equation:

$$d_{f,t}^{2}(u,v)=\sum_{x=0}^{L-1}\sum_{y=0}^{M=1}\left[f(x,y)-t(x-u,y-v)\right]^{2} \tag{1}$$

Where *f* is the input image of size *LxM*, and the sum is done over *(x, y)* in the window containing the sub-image *t* localized at *(u, v)*, of size *JxK*. By expanding d^2 we obtain:

$$d_{f,t}^{2}(u,v)=\sum_{x=0}^{L-1}\sum_{y=0}^{M-1}\left[f^{2}(x,y)-2\cdot f(x,y)\cdot t(x-u,y-v)+t^{2}(x-u,y-v)\right] \tag{2}$$

Where $\sum_{x=0}^{L-1}\sum_{y=0}^{M-1}t^{2}(x-u,y-v)$ is a constant. If $\sum_{x=0}^{L-1}\sum_{y=0}^{M-1}f^{2}(x,y)$ is almost constant, then the resulting term for the cross correlation is the measure of similitude or concordance between the image and the pattern. For this case u = 0, 1,…, *M*-1, and v = 0, 1,…, *L*-1, and *J*=*M* and *K*=*L*.

$$C(u,v)=\sum_{x=0}^{L-1}\sum_{y=0}^{M-1}f(x,y)\cdot t(x-u,y-v) \tag{3}$$

Figure 5 shows the correlation process assuming that the origin for *f* is placed in the upper left corner. Therefore, the correlation process consists on moving the template *t* through the area of the input image and to calculate the value for C. By this method, the maximum value for C points the position where is the highest similitude between *t* and *f*.

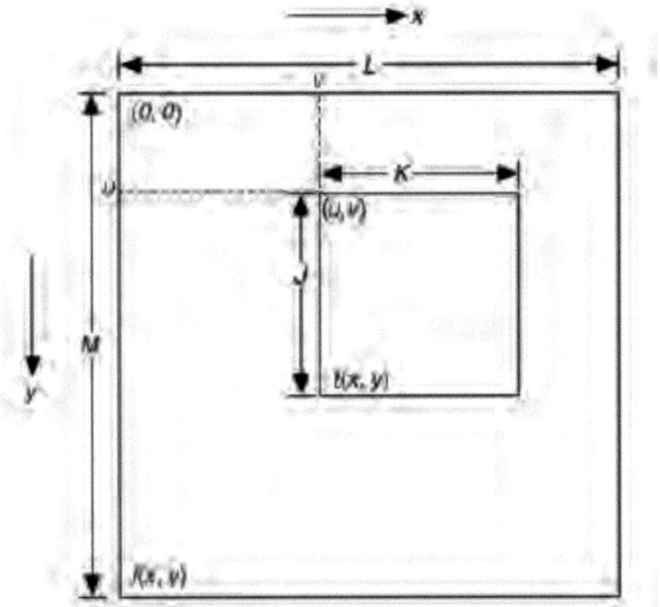

Figure 5. Window movement during the correlation process

Due to the dependence of the correlation values to intensity variation in the image, is required to compute the normalized version for the correlation given by (4):

$$R(u,v)=\frac{\sum_{x=0}^{L-1}\sum_{y=0}^{M-1}\left(f(x,y)-\bar{f}_{u,v}\right)\cdot\left(t(x-u,y-v)-\bar{t}\right)}{\left[\sum_{x=0}^{L-1}\sum_{y=0}^{M-1}\left(f(x,y)-\bar{f}_{u,v}\right)^2\cdot\sum_{x=0}^{L-1}\sum_{y=0}^{M-1}\left(t(x-u,y-v)-\bar{t}\right)^2\right]^{\frac{1}{2}}} \quad (4)$$

Where $\bar{t}$ is the average intensity value for the pixels in the image and $\bar{f}_{u,v}$ is the average of *f(x,y)* in the template. The obtained value for *R* is normalized between -1 and 1, and is independent to intensity of *f* and *t* images.

2.1.2. Pattern recognition process.

The detection pattern process is divided in to main subsystems: learning and recognition itself.

The learning phase analyzes the template image in order to extract features that can improve recognition process compared to standard approach.

The pattern learning algorithm can be described as follows (National, 2004):

- Pseudo-random Image sub-sampling: By this method, it can be obtained more uniformity on sampling distribution through the image, without using a predefined grid. With a uniform grid information like the presence of horizontal and vertical borders could be lost. In the other hand, completely random sampling can produce large areas with poor sampling or over-sampled areas.

- Stability analysis: The pixels sampled by pseudo-random algorithm are analyzed in order to verify stability (uniformity) on their vicinities. Based on this information, each pixel is classified according to its uniform vicinity size (i.e. 3x3, 5x5). By doing so, it is reduced the number of comparisons required for further matching process.
- Features identification: it is an edge detection process, which output is used to detailed adjustment for the placement of the recognized pattern.
- Rotation invariance analysis: is based on the identification of a circular intensity profile on the pattern image, that will be used later to localize rotated versions of the same pattern because those versions will have the same profile with an displacement factor proportional to its original rotation.

The learning phase is computationally complex. It can take several seconds to be completed. However, this process is done only once and its result can be stored for further applications. The pattern recognition algorithm consists on two processes:

- The utilization of a circular intensity profile obtained in the learning phase, in order to localize rotated and displaced versions of that profile through the image.
- The utilization of those pixels obtained in the pseudo-random sub-sampling, that are employed in a correlation process between the candidates previously identified, giving it a score that is used to determine if that candidate can be classified as a pattern match.

2.1.3. Pattern recognition subsystem – Implementation

As it was stated in the previous section, the pattern recognition subsystem is separated in to stages: learning and matching; each of them was implemented as an VI in LabVIEW v7.1®. The corresponding VI for the matching stage also contains the implementation for the obstacle detection. However, in this section it will be described only the pattern recognition system.

Pattern Learning

The learning stage starts by loading an image that contains the pattern to be recognized. For this implementation, the desired recognition target is a mobile robot model Hemisson. Then it is performed the pattern learning and the resulting information is stored in a PNG image file.

Figure 6 shows the block diagram for the pattern learning process, described with more details in further sections.

- Initialization: A blank image with 8 bits per pixel is created.
- Image file loading: Over the previously created image it is loaded the file image containing the desired pattern.
- Image conversion: The image is converted into a grayscale one, to be processed by the learning module.
- Learning module configuration: it is configured so it generates information for the pattern recognition rotation invariant.
- Storing: The information related to the pattern learning in a new PNG image file.

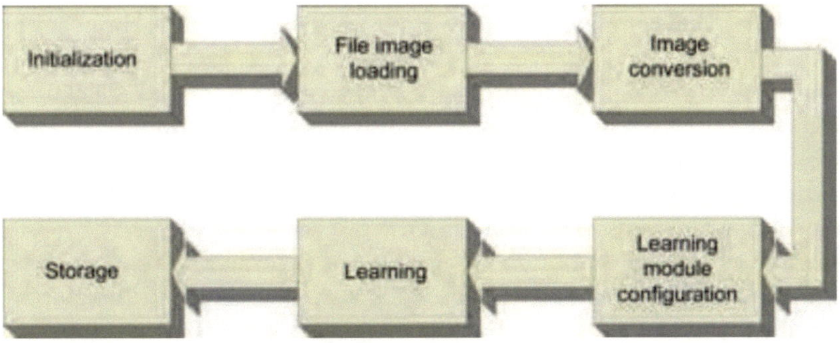

Figure 6. Block diagram of Pattern Learning Process

Figure 7 shows the VI created for this learning subsystem.

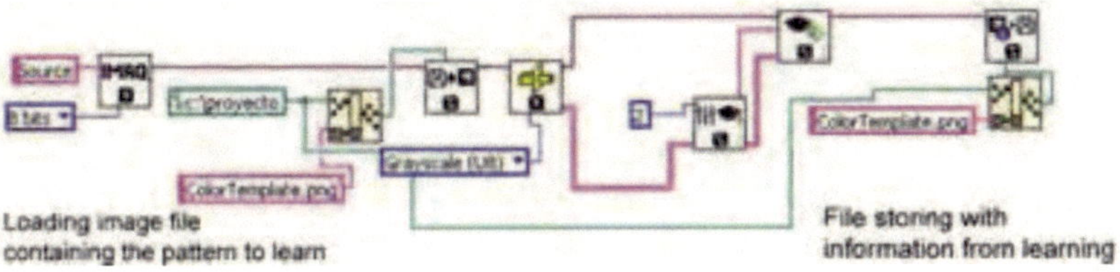

Figure 7. VI for the learning stage

This VI has neither explicit input nor output parameters, because it relays upon the loading of an image file for the learning process. After de VI construction, it is created a Dynamic Link Library (DLL) using the Math Interface Toolkit from LabVIEW®. This provides a DLL file with the subroutines so they can be called from Matlab®.

Pattern recognition

The recognition process consists in taking a snapshot from the workspace, loading the file containing the learning pattern previously obtained, and searching such pattern on the captured image. Later, it is determined the position and orientation of the pattern. The recognition process is described in Figure

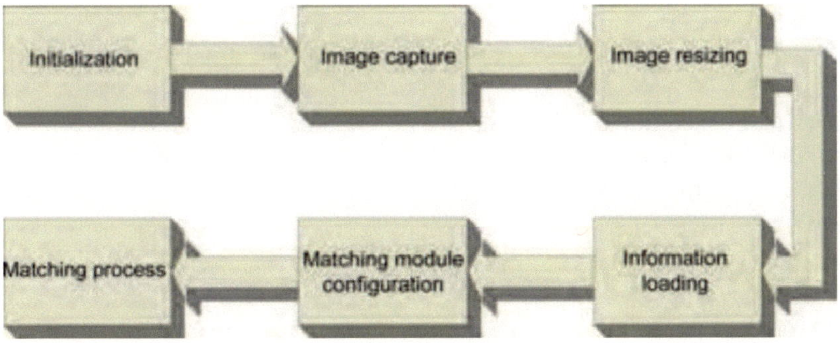

Figure 8. Block Diagram of the pattern matching process

- Initialization: two blank images with 8 bpp are generated. One image corresponds to the video capture and the other one is for the patter image loading. It is also started the video acquisition through the NI IMAQ 1407 module.

- Image Capture: It is acquired a real image from the workspace, the resulting image in grayscale.
- Image resizing: In order to improve position calculation and detection speed, the captured image is resized from 640 x 480 to 480 x 480 by cropping it. This image size corresponds to a physical working area of 4 m^2.
- Information loading: It is loaded the information related to the learning pattern contained in the PNG image file stored in the previous system.
- Matching module configuration so it performs the invariant rotation pattern search.
- Matching process: This process will be done with the acquired image and the image loaded with the learning information. In case of a successful detection of the desired pattern, it will be obtained the position of the coincidence in the working space and its rotation, as shown in Figure 4.7.

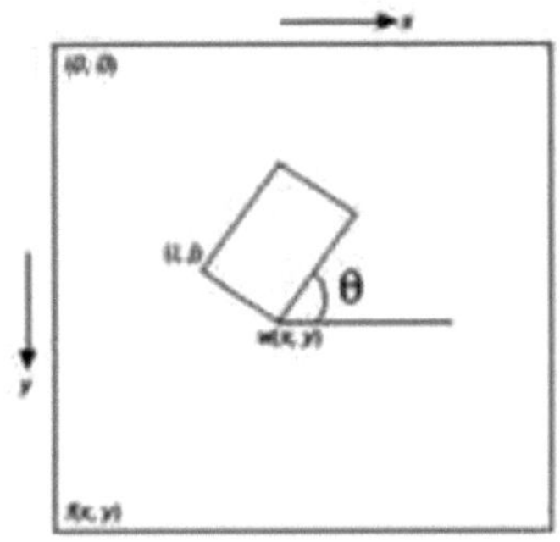

Figure 9. Representation of position and rotation convention

As it was done for the VI of the learning stage, it was created a DLL file from the pattern recognition VI, which we will identify as "detection engine". The matching process has no input parameters; it only loads the image containing the information in the learning process. The output parameters are the position and orientation for the detected pattern.

2.2. Obstacle Detection

2.2.1. Classification technique.

The obstacle detection is based on the classification of binary particles, in which an unknown particle is identified by comparison of their most relevant features against a set of characteristics that conceptually describes previously known classes samples.
The obstacle detection based on classification techniques has two main phases: the learning process, which was implemented utilizing the NI Vision Classification Training tool, and the classification process itself.

Learning Process

The training process consists in the recollection of a set of samples images that contains possible obstacles that can be found and detected by the camera. From these samples is obtained a set of features, known as characteristics vector that describe unequivocally each class of known sample. For example, it could be the object circularity or elongation. Once determined the characteristics vector and collected the samples, each object class is labeled.

Classification Process

The classification process involves the pre-processing of the input image, the features extraction and classification, as is shown in Figure 10.

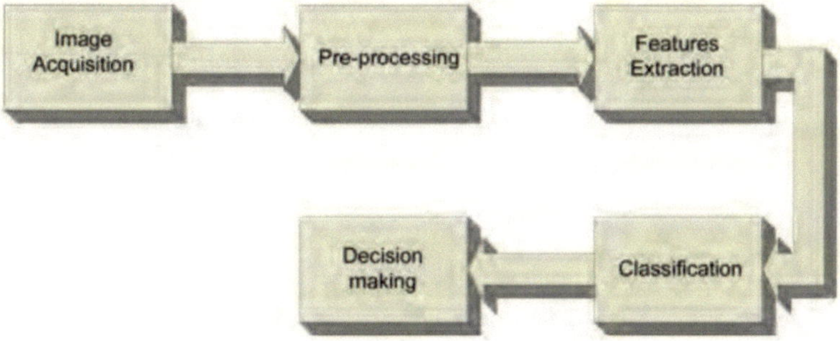

Figure 10. Steps for the Classification process

During the pre-processing stage, the image is prepared for the classification by adjusting the brightness to a level where the classifier can detect the object. This value depends of scene illumination at detection process. Other pre-processing operations are done, like thresholding and binary morphology: the input image in grayscale is converted into a binary image, and later an eroding process is applied to delete irrelevant particles.

Through feature extraction, the information contained in the image is reduced because only distinctive characteristics are retained to distinguish each class. Also, those features are scaling, rotation o symmetrical transformations invariant, while they still allows to do correct objects classification.

The final step is to classify the captured objects in the images by using the extracted features. The classificatory algorithm employed was Nearest Neighbor (*NN*), because it computational simplicity and effectiveness in low features situations. It was employed Manhattan metric.

Under this classification algorithm, the distance between a given feature input set X and an unknown class C_j is defined as the distance to the closest sample that represents such class:

$$D(X,C_j)=\min_i d(X,X_i^j) \tag{5}$$

Where $d(X, X_i^j)$ is the Manhattan distance between X and X_i^j.

Finally, applying the *NN* algorithm it is obtained the following rule:

$$X\in \text{class}\, C_j \text{ if } D(X,C_j)=\min_i D(X,C_i) \tag{6}$$

2.2.2. Implementation of the Obstacle Classification and Detection System.

As it was shown in section 2.2.1, the obstacle detection process by using the classification technique has two stages: learning and classification. The learning process is done through the Classification Training of NI Vision interface that generates a CLF file containing all the information related to the different obstacle classes. In the classification phase, it is loaded the information generated in the training interface and it is performed the specific classification of found objects.

Object Learning (Training interface):

As it was above mentioned, the learning process is done through NI Classification Training software. Figure 11 shows the sequence followed to create the classification file.

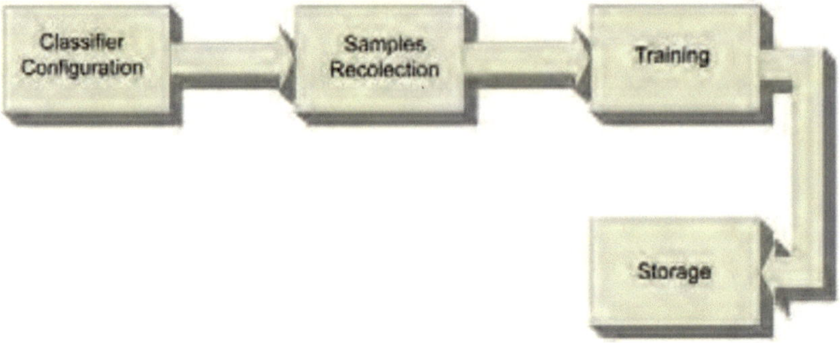

Figure 11. Block diagram of Object Learning phase

- Classifier configuration: features are selected according to specific requirements for the classifying process. It can be controlled the thresholding method called "clustering", that consists in sorting the image histogram into a discrete number of classes according the number of phases detected in the image.
- It is also configured so it can detect brilliant figures because many of the used objects have high white levels.
- In the engine options, it is selected the desired classification method (NN) and the distance metric (Manhattan).
- Sample recollection: are loaded files containing the pattern to be classified. If the image file contains more than one pattern, the desired one can be enclosed in a rectangle. Then, it is identified the class to where the object belongs, and a tag is added. Once the tag is specified one can proceed to add the sample.
- Training: once the sample has been added, it is performed the features vector of the sample that will identify in a unique way a class. This process must be repeated for each added class.
- Storing: at this stage, all the obtained data is saved into a file with information of each class.

Based on the file obtained on the previous section, is possible to create a classification session in a VI of LabVIEW that performs the object classification for the images acquired through the camera.

Objects detection and classification

As it was stated in section 2.1.3, this module is implemented with the pattern matching module in the same VI file, so the first three steps are almost the same; the only difference is that this specific module requires four white images.

This module has as inputs Brightness, Contrast and Gamma from the acquired image, which default values are 50, 45 and 1 respectively. According to the existing illumination in the scene, those values can be adjusted son the vision system can "see" the objects in the visual field. Usually is enough to increase the Brightness value.

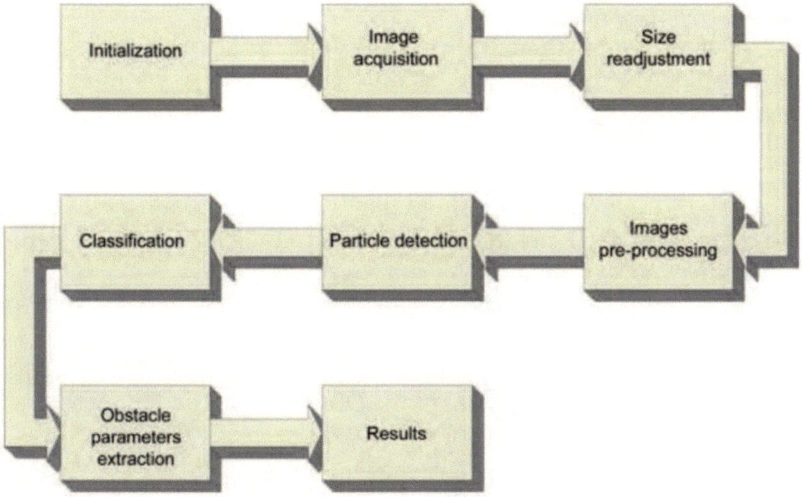

Figure 12. Block Diagram of the Object Detection and Classification Process

The detection and classification process is illustrated in Figure 12, and is implemented in the following way:

- Image pre-processing: a level inversion is applied to the grayscale image and a particle analysis is applied converting the grayscale into a binary image via thresholding. Then, the image is filtered through the morphological process of erosion in order to delete meaningless particles from the particle analysis.
- Particle detection: A classification particle analyzer is applied to the filtered image, which is similar to the simple particle analysis, but this one also provides the mass center of the particles, and the coordinates of the rectangle that enclose it.
- Classification: the particles in the binary images are classified with the particles positions and the classification sections created in the learning process.
- Obstacle parameters: once the object has been classified, it is calculated the diagonal of the smallest null-rotated rectangle that encloses the figure. For the cases of rectangle and square detection it is also extracted the object orientation, by using *Rotation Detect* from IMAQ Vision.

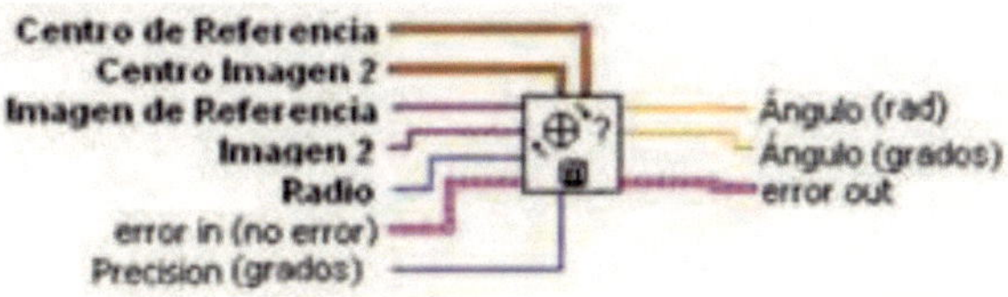

Figure 13. Function of NI-IMAQ package for detecting Object Rotation

- Results: the final outputs for the object detection and classification system are the positions of the detected figures on the original image, values obtained in the particle detection phase. Those values are sorted into an array for each corresponding figure, thus giving three different arrays for object positions. The rotation angles and diagonal lengths are also sorted according to the related figure, so it gives three more arrays for the angles y other three for the calculated diagonals.

4.2.3 Particle *Analysis Technique*

A particle is a group of pixel with non-zero values in an image, usually binary. The particles can be characterized by measurements related to its attributes as position, area, shape and others (National, 2004).

The particle detection consists in applying an erosion process to the original image so it can be removed small particles generated by noise present in the image acquisition. The resulting image is passed through a threshold filter in order to obtain a binary image.

The non-zero pixels and their neighbors with connectivity '8' create a particle with an arbitrary shape, but avoid the apparition of some holes.

The vision system here proposed takes the detected particles and for each one of them extracts the following parameters:

- DF: Maximum Feret's Diameter.
- F_{x1}: X coordinate for the starting point of the DF.
- F_{y1}: Y coordinate for the starting point of the DF.
- F_{x2}: X coordinate for the ending point of the DF.
- F_{y2}: Y coordinate for the ending point of the DF.
- Angle for DF: $\beta = \arctan\left(\frac{F_{y2} - F_{y1}}{F_{x2} - F_{x1}}\right)$
- Coordinates of the points that form the convex hull.

The Feret's Diameter (DF) is the straight line that connects the two most separated particles of a particle, and the convex hull is the convex polygon of minimum area that contains all the points of the particle.

With the coordinates of the convex hull, are found those points its points more separated at each side of the DF, which are used to define a perpendicular line to it. The combination of both straight lines defines the rectangle with lower area that contains the particle. By algebraic manipulation of this rectangle it is obtained the circumscribed ellipse. The Figure 14 shows this process:

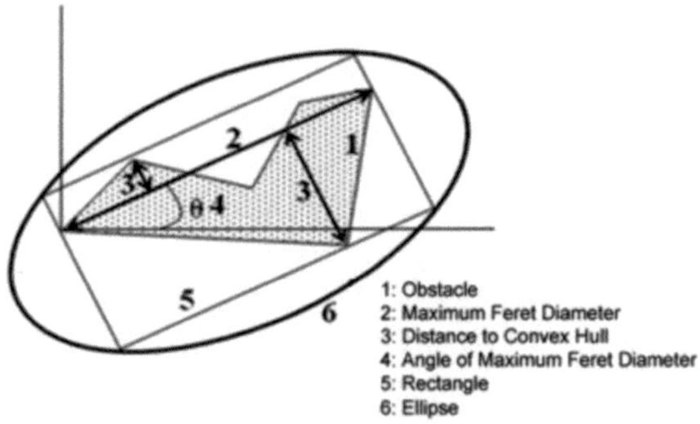

Figure 14. Parameter extraction process from particle analysis

3. Applications of the Vision System

3.1. Velocity Field Generation

As it was previously mentioned, expressing tasks or trajectories in terms of velocity is a research area very important today. It allows the use of velocity controllers, passive controllers, and help to improve the performance of the robot while it is doing its job.

Using the Vision System proposed consisting on a single camera watching the workspace of the robot is possible to detect the obstacles presented on the robot trajectory. The application of Velocity Field Generation based on Artificial Vision constitutes a valuable contribution to the state of the art.

In the following paragraphs a strategy to generate obstacles free velocity trajectories is presented. The problem was divided into two stages linked through the Vision System implementation. These stages are: the generation of an initial velocity field, and the generation of an evader velocity field for each object detected.

3.1.1. Initial velocity Field Generation

The system allows user defined trajectory to be followed by the robot. It can be a hand made one or a set of straight lines. The algorithm developed was tested for 41x41 velocity fields and can be described as follows.

The vision system takes a snapshot of the robot's workspace. This image is cropped to hold only the ROI which is subsampled to a 41x41 image (this resolution of the velocity field offers 1 vector each 5 cm, which is less that a half of the robot dimensions). Over it, the user traces the desired trajectory.

When the user finish defining the desired trajectory, coordinates of the pixels to be part of the trajectory are extracted by a thresholding process and stored in an N-size 1D array of (X,Y) coordinates pairs. N is the number of points or pixels of initial trajectory.

Trajectories can be open or closed. In both cases a sorting process is performed, establishing as sorting parameter the Euclidean distance from one point to another, organizing them from closers to more distant. When the trajectory is open, it is necessary knowing where it begins and where ends. Studying neighbors of each element of the sorted array, the start and end point are obtained.

Then an approximation vector field is defined. For that, it was considered a 2D array of 41x41 elements containing the coordinates (X,Y) of all pixels of a 41x41 image, i.e. element (i, j) have a value of (i,j). For each element of the 2D array, the closest element of the trajectory is searched based on the Euclidean distance from point (i, j) of the 2D array to each element of the 1D array containing the coordinates of trajectory. Each approximation vector is defined as the normalized one whose direction is obtained from the subtraction of the closest point of trajectory and the point of the 2D array being analyzed.

A tangent vector field is also defined. Each vector is obtained from the subtraction of the element $p + 1$ with element $p - 1$, where p is the index of the closest point of the trajectory to the point (i, j) being studied. When the closest point is the point where the trajectory starts, the subtraction is performed between elements $p + 2$ and p $(p = 0)$, whereas if it is the ending one, points subtracted are the p and $p - 2 (p = N - 1)$. With this assumption, tangent vectors will always have congruent senses. Tangent vectors are normalized too.

The "initial" velocity field is obtained performing a weighted sum, expressed in (7), between the approximation and tangent vector fields. The selection of weights depends directly of the distance between point (i, j) and the closest one of the trajectory. As a weight function a sigmoid was chosen. If point (i, j) is close to trajectory, the tangent vector will prevail over the approximation one and vice versa.

$$\vec{V}_{ij} = \vec{V}_{a_{ij}} \cdot f_1(d_{ij}) + \vec{V}_{t_{ij}} \cdot f_2(d_{ij}) \tag{7}$$

where $\vec{V}_{ij}$ is the vector of the final velocity field, $\vec{V}_{a_{ij}}$ and $\vec{V}_{t_{ij}}$ are the approximation and tangent vectors at *ij*, respectively. d_{ij} is the Euclidean distance from point *ij* to the desired trajectory, whereas $f_1(d_{ij})$ and $f_2(d_{ij})$ are defined by (8) y (9).

$$f_1(d_{ij}) = \frac{2}{1+e^{-0.4 \cdot d_{ij}}} - 1 \tag{8}$$

$$f_2(d_{ij}) = 1 - f_1(d_{ij}) \tag{9}$$

Figure 15 shows the effect of the weighting functions expressed in (8) y (9).
Parameter *a* was chosen to be 0.4 because this value allows an important attenuation of the tangent vectors when $d_{ij} > 6$ (3 times the dimensions of the robot). Figure 15 shows the effect of the weighting functions expressed in (8) y (9).

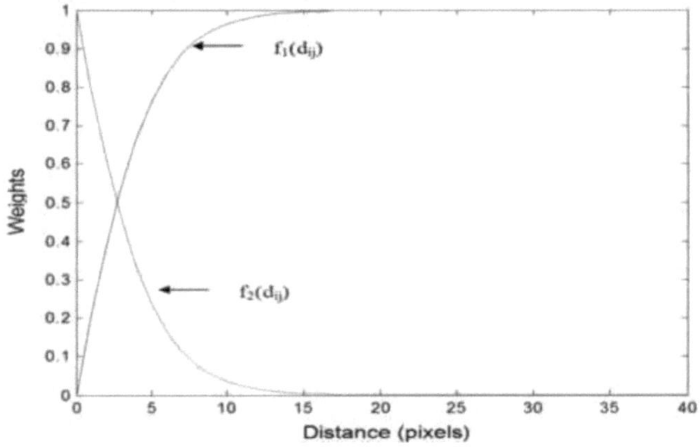

Figure 15. Weighting functions f_1 and f_2 effect. Note that for little distances the tangent vector is greater than the approximation one, and vice versa

3.1.2. Dynamic Velocity Field Modification

The "evader" velocity field generation module takes information provided by the vision system, parameterizes the correspond ellipse for each obstacles and create a velocity field that surrounds the object.
The proposed algorithm contemplates dividing the ellipse into four regions: one for entry, one for exit and two for transitions.
In the transition regions the velocity field is chosen to be parallel to the trajectory given by the ellipse contour, i.e. tangent to the ellipse. The general tangent line equation at any point (X_0, Y_0) is given by (10).

$$\frac{(X-P)\cdot(X_0-P)}{A^2} + \frac{(Y-Q)\cdot(Y_0-Q)}{B^2} = 1 \tag{10}$$

where (P, Q) are the coordinates of the location of the ellipse and A and B represent a half of the major and minor axes respectively. From (10), the unit tangent vector at any point (X_0, Y_0) can be deduced to be

$$\vec{V}_t(X_0,Y_0)=\left(V_{t_x},V_{t_y}\right) \tag{11}$$

$$V_{t_x}(X_0,Y_0)=\frac{A^2\cdot(Y_0-Q)}{\sqrt{A^4\cdot(Y_0-Q)^2+B^4\cdot(X_0-P)^2}} \tag{12}$$

$$V_{t_y}(X_0,Y_0)=\frac{-B^2\cdot(X_0-P)}{\sqrt{A^4\cdot(Y_0-Q)^2+B^4\cdot(X_0-P)^2}} \tag{13}$$

In the entry region the field is defined in the direction and sense toward the ellipse contour and is turned aside smoothly until it converges to the tangent vector as the point is closer to the transition region. This is achieved through a weighted sum of the approximation and tangent vectors to the ellipse, where the weights depends on the proximity to the distance from a given point to the edge between entry and transition regions.

Entry and exit regions are always of the same size. Transitions regions too. The size (angle) for each region is chosen such as they have an area equal to a quarter of the ellipse's area. To accomplish this requirement, the area of the entry (or exit) region is given by (14)

$$\int_{\theta-\alpha}^{\theta+\alpha}\int_0^{r(\gamma)}\rho d\rho d\gamma=\frac{1}{2}\cdot\int_{\theta-\alpha}^{\theta+\alpha}\rho^2 d\rho=\frac{\pi\cdot A\cdot B}{4} \tag{14}$$

Consider Figure 16 where angles related to an ellipse are defined. Based on it, is possible to obtain the relations shown in (15).

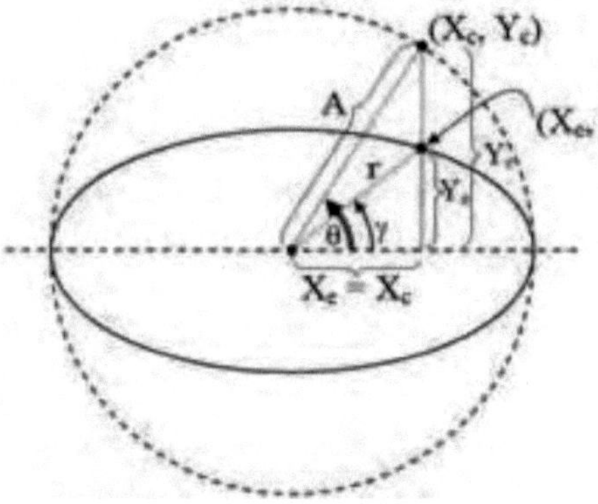

Figure 16. Definition of Angles and coordinates of the point belonging to the ellipse

$$Xc=A\cdot\cos(\theta) \qquad X_e=r\cdot\cos(\gamma)$$

$$Y_c=B\cdot\sin(\theta) \qquad Y_e=r\cdot\sin(\gamma) \qquad Y_e=B\cdot\sin(\theta) \tag{15}$$

r is defined by (16) in terms of θ, or, considering (17), it can be defined by (18) in terms of γ.

$$r(\theta)=\sqrt{A^2\cdot\cos^2(\theta)+B^2\cdot\sin^2(\theta)} \tag{16}$$

$$\tan(\theta)=\frac{A}{B}\cdot\tan(\gamma) \tag{17}$$

$$r(\gamma) = A \cdot \sqrt{\frac{1+\tan^2(\gamma)}{1+\left(\frac{A}{B}\right)^2 \cdot \tan^2(\gamma)}} \qquad (18)$$

Solving (14), the size (angle) of the entry and exit region is defined by (18).

$$2 \cdot \varphi = 2 \cdot \arctan\left(\sqrt{\frac{\left(\frac{B}{A}\right)^2 + \tan^2(\gamma)}{1+\left(\frac{B}{A}\right)^2 \cdot \tan^2(\gamma)}}\right) \qquad (19)$$

The orientation of regions is given by the angle of the original field at the point where the object is located. Regions must be rotated for achieving an entry region aligned with the original velocity field.

For the exit region the same approach used for the entry region is employed. However, in this case, the field is defined leaving the ellipse.

Approximation vectors a any point (X_0, Y_0) is given by (20)

$$\vec{V}_a(X_0, Y_0) = (V_{a_x}, V_{a_y}) \qquad (20)$$

$$V_{a_x}(X_0, Y_0) = \frac{B^2 \cdot (X_0 - P)}{\sqrt{A^4 \cdot (Y_0 - Q)^2 + B^4 \cdot (X_0 - P)^2}} \qquad (21)$$

$$V_{a_y}(X_0, Y_0) = \frac{A^2 \cdot (Y_0 - Q)}{\sqrt{A^4 \cdot (Y_0 - Q)^2 + B^4 \cdot (X_0 - P)^2}} \qquad (22)$$

The division proposed by using the defined regions wants to achieved an "evader" velocity field similar to the sketch shown in Figure 17.

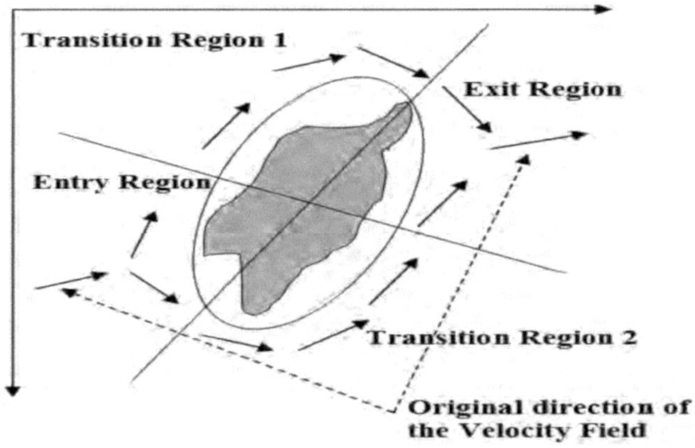

Figure 17. Sketch of "evader" field. Following the direction and sense of the initial field at the point where is located the obstacle, the different regions are defined. Note the deviations of field in the entry and exit regions

3.1.3. Results of the Vision-Based Velocity Field Generator

For testing the "initial" velocity field generator two hand made traces was introduced. Figure 18 shows the obtained velocity fields.

In case (a) the trajectory is open, has an 'Z' shape, and the field generated converged successfully to it; inclusive, the end point of the trajectory results to be a sink, as it was desired. Case (b) corresponds to the well known circular trajectory (Li & Horowitz, 1995) (Moreno & Kelly, 2003c), here hand-traced. It is observed that velocity field converged as expected. It is important to remark that while the distance to the desired trajectory is higher the approximation vector prevails over the tangent one, and when it is lower, the tangent one prevails.

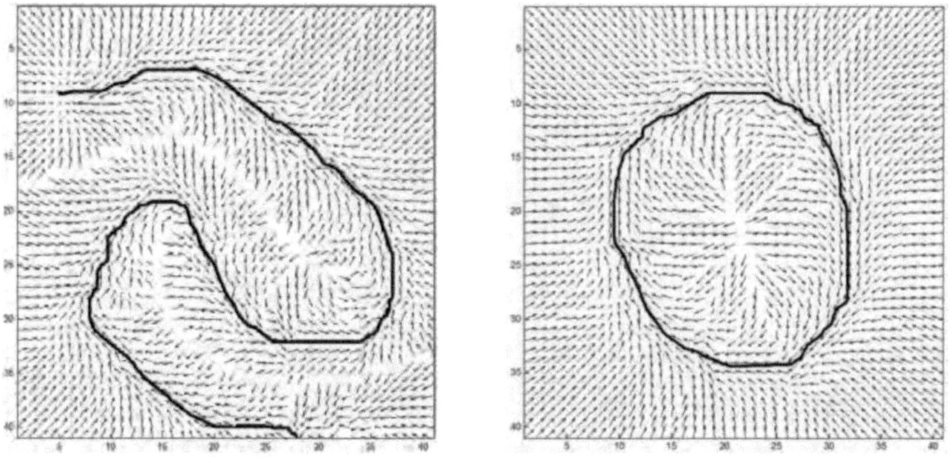

Figure 18.Velocity Field. Note the hand made desired trajectory remarked in black

The "evader" algorithm responds to an arbitrary object as shown in Figure 19.

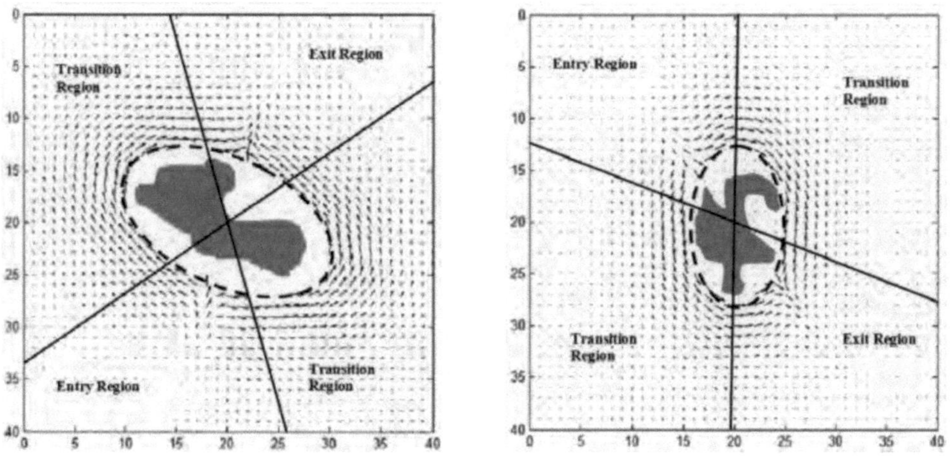

Figure 19. "Evader" velocity field for an arbitrary object. The four predefined regions are shown and the behavior of the algorithm can be observed

Figure 19.a shows an object located on a place where the original field has an orientation of −75° and the circumscribed ellipse has 25°. Figure 19.b presents the evader field for an object whose circumscribed ellipse has 90° and the original field at the point the object is placed has 55°. In both figures the exponential fading imposed is shown. This effect assures that the evader field only affects the neighborhood of the object.
Now it is presented a test of the system with the three modules combined. Figure 14 resumes the results obtained.

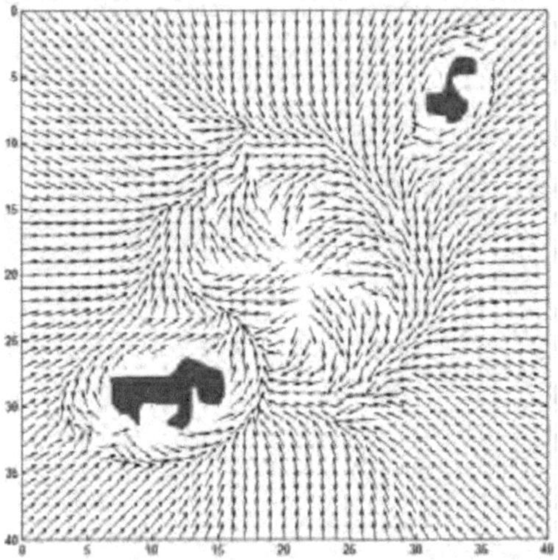

Figure 20. Modified velocity field for two obstacles detected

Inserting two arbitrary objects at two arbitrary positions for the circular velocity field shown in Figure 20, the final velocity field obtained offers a free-obstacles trajectory, however, at the edges between the influence "evader" field and the initial one, it is not enough smooth as desired.

3.2. Fuzzy Logic Controller and Velocity Field Control

The purpose of this system is to control the position of a small wheeled mobile platform on a two dimensional work space, using an overhead vision system. The main sensor used is a wireless camera placed at 2.7 m from the floor and able to observe all the workspace of the mobile platform. This camera can provide a maximum of 30 frames per second of 640x480 pixels, but the sample rate used is determined by the processing speed of the algorithm, since it works over a snapshot taken on each cycle and, usually, processing cycle is larger than the sampling rate. The image acquired is cropped in order to provide an image of 480x480 pixels, covering an area of 6.25 m^2.
For test purposes, a 2.4GHz Wireless Color Camera model XC10A was used, connecting it to the PC by a generic RCA to USB adapter. The robot employed was a differential drive Lynxmotion Carpet Rover The software was developed employing LabVIEW v7.1 with NI IMAQ Vision v7.1 and Matlab v7.1. All the experiments were done with RGB images, and the surface of the workspace was not altered to deal with the differences of luminosity and other typical issues associated with vision systems.

3.2.1. *Vision System Description*

The objective of this stage is to obtain the position (in pixels) and the angle (in degrees) of the mobile platform at any moment. This is achieved using a slight modification of the system proposed by (Bolaños et. al., 2006).

Mobile Robot Detection

The pattern matching algorithm (National, 2004) consists in the localization of regions that match with a known reference pattern on a RGB image. The reference pattern is also known as template, and contains information related to edge and region pixels, removing redundant information in a regular image. In this way, the matching process is done in a faster and more accurate manner. In the case where a pattern appearing rotated in the image is expected, it is possible to store pixels specially chosen, whose values reflect the pattern rotation.

The comparison between the template and different regions of the camera image in the pattern matching process is done using a correlation algorithm based in the calculus of the squared Euclidean distance:

$$d_{f,t}^2(u,v) = \sum_{x,y} [f(x,y) - t(x-u, y-v)]^2 \tag{23}$$

where *f* is the image. The sum is performed over *(x, y)*, in the window containing the sub-image *t* located at *(u, v)*. Expanding d^2, and making some considerations (Bolaños et. al, 2006), the remaining term of the cross correlation

$$C(u,v) = \sum_{x,y} f(x,y) \cdot t(x-u, y-v) \tag{24}$$

is the similarity or matching measure between image and template.

Process Description

The detailed description of the pattern matching algorithm implementation is as follows (Bolaños et al., 2006):

- Initialization: Two RGB blank images are generated.
- Image capture: A real RGB image from the workspace is captured.
- Cropping: The captured image is cropped to a 480x480 pixels (from 640x480 pixels). This image size allows the visualization of a workspace of 6.25 m^2.
- Information load: The information (related to pattern learning) contained in the PNG image stored in the learning process is loaded.
- Pattern matching module setup: The pattern matching module is set to rotation-invariant mode so it can detect the desired pattern regardless of its rotation.
- Matching: The matching process is done according to the configuration above described between the captured image and the loaded image (with the information from the learning process). If the desired pattern is located, the result will be its position within the image and its orientation.

3.2.2. Graphic Interface

The graphic interface was made in LabVIEW v7.1. First the user selects the template the software will try to find, in this case the mobile platform, with an angle of 0° (Figure 21.a).

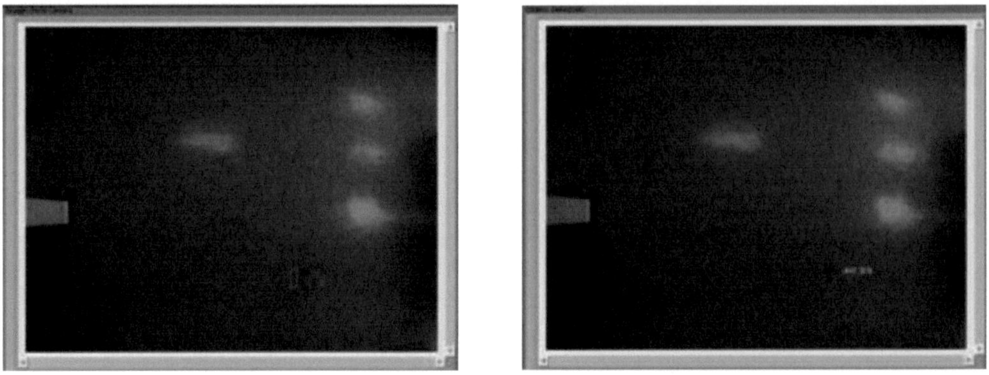

Figure 21. Template selection process and pattern matching illustration

Once the template is selected the software is able to find the best match and return the X and Y coordinates of its position in pixels (Figure 21.b).

In practice, there is a problem due the uncontrolled luminosity. Sometimes the algorithm gives false matches which affect the whole system. To deal with this problem, the developed program was allowed to give not only the match with the highest correlation but also others with a lower correlation. A discriminator then verifies which of the matches is inside the neighborhood of the last position. Besides, the algorithm gives a noisy estimation, which is reduced by filtering it.

With these considerations the response of the system is highly improved, obtaining an accurate position in most of the cases.

3.2.3. Controllers Implementation

In this case the task of the controller is to move the platform from one point to another regardless of the trajectory. The problem is that the system is highly non-linear and even if lineal controllers have shown good performance when non-linear systems are linearized, other controllers exhibit better performance. Neural and fuzzy controllers are among them.

The control technique was based in the idea of decoupling the locomotion system of the mobile platform. To achieve this, the error in X and Y coordinates (Cartesian mode) is transformed into magnitude and angle errors (Polar mode), then these errors are taken by the controller which gives a new references for linear and rotational velocity. Finally these references are transformed into references of right and left velocities (Dudek & Jenkin, 2000) by the equation (25).

$$\begin{aligned} v_{left} &= v_{linear} + w \cdot a \\ v_{right} &= v_{linear} - w \cdot a \end{aligned} \tag{25}$$

A. Linear Controller

This controller was a conventional PI where the error and the sum of previous errors are added to generate the control signal. The inputs of the control system are distance and angle errors and the outputs are references for right and left velocities directly. The control scheme employed is shown in Figure 22.

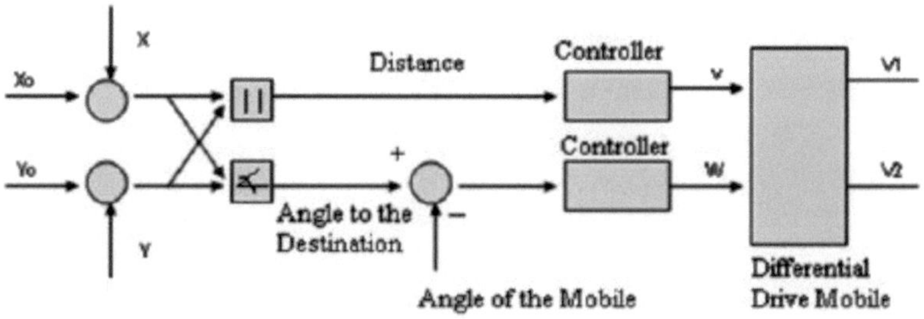

Figure 22. Linear control scheme

B. Fuzzy Logic Controller

As an option to the linear controller, a fuzzy logic one was designed to work on the same inputs and outputs as the linear controller. The FIS Editor of Matlab v7.1 was used for this purpose. Triangular membership functions were chosen because of their simplicity to implement in microcontrollers.

The range of each of these variables was divided in the following membership functions:

- Angle Error (Degrees): Small Positive (0. -90.), Big Positive (90. -180.), Small Negative (180. -270.) and Big Negative (270. -360.).
- Distance to the destination: Far (150 cm - 800 cm), close (20 cm -150 cm) and very close (0 cm - 40 cm).
- Velocities (Left and Right wheels): Fast (8.5cm/s), Medium (5 cm/s), slow(3.5cm/s) and very slow(0.8cm/s).

With these membership functions the system of fuzzy inference is based on the Mamdani's aggregation method (Ying, 2000), with 9 fuzzy rules, and defuzzyfication technique based on the gravity center.

The base of rules was formed like is shown in Table 2.

Distance	Angle Error	Left Velocity	Right Velocity
Very Close	X	Very Slow	Very Slow
Close	Small Positive	Slow	Very Slow
Close	Small Negative	Very Slow	Slow
Close	Big Positive	Medium	Very Slow
Close	Big Negative	Very Slow	Medium
Far	Small Positive	Fast	Medium
Far	Small Negative	Medium	Fast
Far	Big Positive	Fast	Slow
Far	Big Negative	Slow	Fast

Table 2. Fuzzy Rules Base

Proposed linear controller for this system is able to guide the robot towards the desired position, but presented some problems. Figure 23 shows the resulting trajectory when the proposed linear controller was used, and can be observed how the robot oscillates near the final position. Oscillations at the end point were very strong around it and impossible to eliminate, since controllers parameters that worked well far from the destination, did not give good results in its proximity. The controlled variables saturated in some circumstances, affecting the response of the controller. Also the tuning of the controller was very difficult due to the interdependence between v_{linear} and ω.

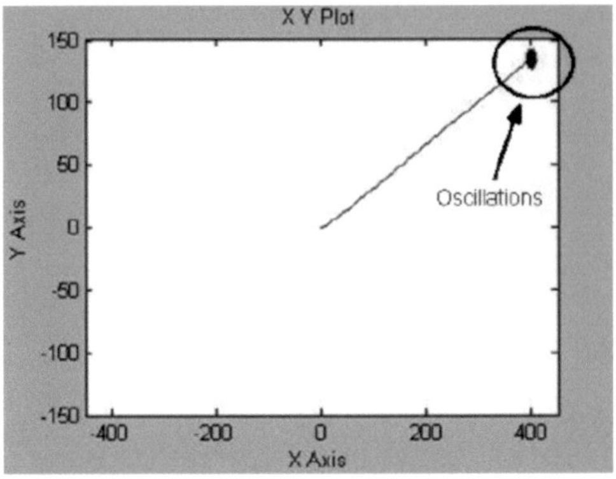

Figure 23. Resulting Trajectory with the linear controller

The Fuzzy controller response shown in Figure 24 was more reliable. The robot stops at destination showing a good behavior both far and in the proximity of the destination. Also, the characteristics of the membership functions ensure that the outputs won't saturate and its decoupling facilitates the design and tuning of the controller.

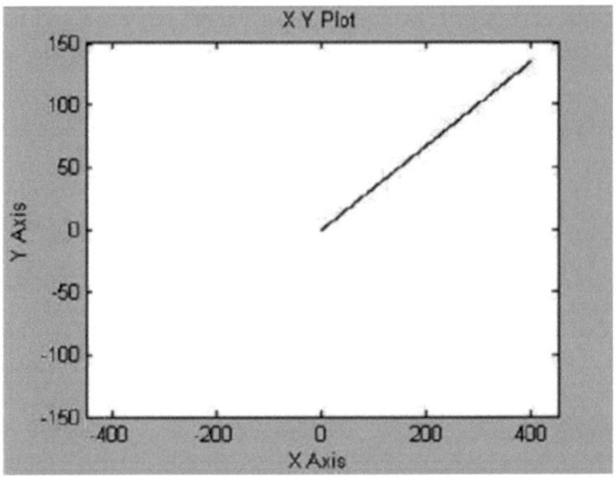

Figure 24. Resulting Trajectory with the fuzzy controller

The system was able to produce a reliable position measurement based only in the visual sensor and the related vision system, working in difficult situations of illumination and noise, thanks to the spatial continuity considerations taken into account.

The implemented controllers guided the robot towards the final destination, but the fuzzy system showed advantages over the linear controller both in the design and tests stages. The fuzzy logic controller has a better performance mainly because it is non-linear and is designed to deal with non-linear systems. Also it can absorb possible errors of the vision platform, by minimizing its effect in the controller. Additionally it is easier to tune than the linear one.

5. References

Bolaños, J. M.; Medina-Meléndez, W.; Fermín, L.; Cappelletto, J.; Fernández-López, G. & J. C. Grieco. (2006). Object recognition for obstacle avoidance in mobile robots. *Artificial Intelligence and Soft Computing, ICAISC 2006, Lecture Notes in Computer Science*, pp. 722–731, ISBN: 3-5403-5748-3, Zakopane, Poland, June 2006.

Cervantes I.; Kelly, R.; Alvarez, J. & Moreno J. (2002). A robust velocity field control. *IEEE Transactions on Control, Systems and Technologies*, Vol. 10, No. 6, (November 2002) 888–894, ISSN: 1063-6536.

Dixon, W. E.; Galluzo, T.; Hu, G. & Crane, C. (2005). Adaptive velocity field control of a wheeled mobile robot. *Proceedings of the 5th International Workshop on Robot Motion and Control, RoMoCo '05*, pp. 145–150, ISBN: 83-7143-266-6, Poznan, Poland, June 2005.

Dudek, G. & Jenkin M. (2000) *Computational Principles of Mobile Robotics*, Cambridge University Press, ISBN: 0-5215-6876-5, U.S.A.

Kelly, R.; Moreno, J. & Campa, R. (2004). Visual servoing of planar robots via velocity fields. *Proceedings of the IEEE 43rd Conference on Decision and Control*, pp. 4028–4033, ISBN: 0-7803-8682-5, Atlantis, Paradise Island, Bahamas, December 2004.

Kelly R.; Bugarín, E. & Campa, R. (2004). Application of velocity field control to visual navigation of mobile robots. *Proceedings of the 5th IFAC Symposium on Intelligent Autonomous Vehicles*, on CD, Lisbon, Portugal, June 2004.

Khatib, O. (1985). Real-time obstacle avoidance for manipulators and mobile robots, *Proceedings of the IEEE International Conference on Robotics and Automation*, pp. 500–505, St. Louis, U.S.A., March 1985.

Li, P. Y. & Horowitz, R. (1995). Passive velocity field control of mechanical manipulators. *Proceedings of the IEEE International Conference on Robotics and Automation ICRA'01*, pp 2764–2770, ISBN: 0-7803-1965-6, Nagoya, Japan, April 1995.

Li, P. Y. (1999). Adaptive passive velocity field control. *Proceedings of the 1999 American Control Conference*, Vol. 2, pp. 774–779, ISBN: 0-7803-4990-3, San Diego, U.S.A., June 1999.

Li, P. Y. & Horowitz R. (1999). Passive velocity field control of mechanical manipulators. *IEEE Transactions on Robotics and Automation*, Vol. 15, No. 4, (August 1999) 751–763, ISSN: 1042-296X.

Li, P. Y. & Horowitz R. (2001). Passive velocity field control (PVFC): Part I - Geometry and Robustness. *IEEE Transactions on Automatic Control*, Vol. 46, No. 9, (September 2001) 1346–1359, ISSN: 0018-9286.

Li, P. Y. & Horowitz R. (2001). Passive velocity field control (PVFC): Part II - application to contour following. *IEEE Transactions on Automatic Control*, Vol. 46, No. 9, (September 2001) 1360–1371, ISSN: 0018-9286.

Mitchell, T. (1997). *Machine Learning*, McGraw-Hill Science/Engineering/Math, ISBN: 0-0704-2807-7, U.S.A.

Moreno J. & Kelly R. (2003a). On manipulator control via velocity fields. *Proceedings of the 15th IFAC World Congress*, pp. 1420–1427, Barcelona, Spain, Julio 2003.

Moreno J. & Kelly R. (2003b). Velocity control of robot manipulator: Analysis and experiments. *International Journal on Control*, Vol. 76, No. 14, (September 2003) 1420–1427, ISSN: 0020-7179.

Moreno J. & Kelly R. (2003c). Hierarchical velocity field control for robot manipulators. *Proceedings of the IEEE International Conference on Robotics and Automation ICRA'03*, Vol. 3, pp. 4374–4379, ISBN: 0-7803-7736-2, Taipei, Taiwan, September 2003.

National Instruments (2004). *IMAQ Vision Concepts Manual*, National Instruments.

Santos-Victor, J. & Sandini G. (1997). Visual Behaviors for Docking. *Computer Vision and Image Understanding: CVIU*, Vol. 67, No. 3, (September 1997) 223–238, ISSN: 1077-3142.

Seelinger, M.; Yoder J-D.; Baumgartner, E. T. & Skaar, S. B. (2002). High-precision visual control of mobile manipulators. *IEEE Transactions on Robotics and Automation*, Vol. 18, No. 6, (December 2002) 957–965, ISSN: 1042-296X.

Skaar, S. B.; Yalda-Mooshabad I. & Brockman W. H. (1992). Nonholonomic camera-space manipulation. *IEEE Transactions on Robotics and Automation*, Vol. 8, No. 4, (August 1992) 464–478, ISSN: 1042-296X.

Yamakita, M. & Suh, J. H. (2000). Adaptive generation of desired velocity field for cooperative mobile robots with decentralized PVFC. *Proceedings of the IEEE/RSJ International Conference on Intelligent Robots and Systems IROS'00*, pp. 1841–1846, ISBN: 0-7803-6348-5, Takamatsu, Japan, Oct./Nov. 2000.

Yamakita, M. & Suh, J. H. (2001). Adaptive generation of desired velocity field for leader follower type mobile robots with decentralized PVFC. *Proceedings of the IEEE International Conference on Robotics and Automation ICRA'01*, pp. 3495–3501, ISBN: 0-7803-6576-3, Seoul, Korea, May 2001.

Ying, H. (2000). Fuzzy Control and Modeling: Analytical Foundations and Applications, IEEE Press Series on Biomedical Engineering, Wiley-IEEE Press, ISBN: 0-7803-3497-7, U.S.A.

21

Omnidirectional Vision-Based Control From Homography

Youcef Mezouar, Hicham Hadj Abdelkader and Philippe Martinet
LASMEA / Blaise Pascal University
France

1. Introduction

Vision-based servoing schemes are flexible and effective methods to control robot motions from cameras observations (Hutchinson et al 1996). They are traditionally classified into three groups, namely position-based, image-based and hybrid-based control (Espiau et al 1992), (Hutchinson et al 1996), (Malis et al 1999). These three schemes make assumptions on the link between the initial, current and desired images since they require correspondences between the visual features extracted from the initial image with those obtained from the desired one. These features are then tracked during the camera (and/or the object) motion. If these steps fail the visually based robotic task can not be achieved. Typical cases of failure arise when matching joint images features is impossible (for example when no joint features belongs to initial and desired images) or when some parts of the visual features get out of the field of view during the servoing. Some methods have been investigated to resolve this deficiency based on path planning (Mezouar et al 2002), switching control (Chesi et al 2003), zoom adjustment (Benhimane et al 2003). However, such strategies are sometimes delicate to adapt to generic setup.
Conventional cameras suffer thus from restricted field of view. There is significant motivation for increasing the field of view of the cameras. Many applications in vision-based robotics, such as mobile robot localization (Blaer et al 2002) and navigation (Winter et al 2000), can benefit from panoramic field of view provided by omnidirectional cameras. In the literature, there have been several methods proposed for increasing the field of view of cameras systems (Benosman et al 2000). One effective way is to combine mirrors with conventional imaging system. The obtained sensors are referred as catadioptric imaging systems. The resulting imaging systems have been termed central catadioptric when a single projection center describes the world-image mapping. From a theoretical and practical view point, a single center of projection is a desirable property for an imaging system (Baker et al 1999). Baker and Nayar in (Baker et al 1999) derive the entire class of catadioptric systems with a single viewpoint. Clearly, visual servoing applications can also benefit from such sensors since they naturally overcome the visibility constraint. Vision-based control of robotic arms, single mobile robot or formation of mobile robots appear thus in the literature with omnidirectional cameras (refer for example to (Barreto et al 2002), (Vidal et al 2003), (Mezouar et al 2004). Image-based visual servoing with central catadioptric cameras using

points has been studied by in (Barreto et al 2002). The use of straight lines has also been investigated in (Mezouar et al 2004).
This paper is concerned with homography-based visual servo control techniques with central catadioptric cameras. This framework (called 2 1/2 D visual servoing) has been first proposed by Malis and Chaumette in (Malis et al 1999). The 2 1/2 D visual servoing scheme exploits a combination of reconstructed Euclidean information and image-space information in the control design. The 3D informations are extracted from a homography matrix relating two views of a reference plane. As a consequence, the 2 1/2 D visual servoing scheme does not require any 3D model of the target. The resulting interaction matrix is triangular with interesting decoupling properties and it has no singularity in the whole task space. Unfortunately, in such approach the image of the target is not guaranteed to remain in the camera field of view. Motivated by the desire to overcome this deficiency, we extend in this paper homography-based visual servo control techniques to an entire class of omnidirectional cameras. We describe how to obtain a generic homography matrix related to a reference plane for central catadioptric cameras using imaged points or lines. Then the 3D informations obtained from the homography is used to develop 2 1/2 D visual servoing schemes based on points and lines features. Simulations as well as experimental results on a six degrees of freedom robotic arm illustrate the efficiency of omnidirectional vision-based control with homography.

2. Central catadioptric imaging model

The central catadioptric projection can be modelled by a central projection onto a virtual unitary sphere, followed by a perspective projection onto an image plane. This virtual unitary sphere is centered in the principal effective view point and the image plane is attached to the perspective camera. In this model, called unified model and proposed by Geyer and Daniilidis in (Geyer et al 2000), conventional perspective camera appears as a particular case.
In this chapter applications of image and video processing to navigation of mobile robots are presented. During the last years some impressive real time applications have been showed to the world, such as the NASA missions to explore the surface of Mars with autonomous vehicles; in those missions, video and image processing played an important role to rule the vehicle.
Algorithms based on the processing of video or images provided by CCD sensors or video cameras have been used in the solution of the navigation problem of autonomous vehicles. In one of those approaches, a velocity field is designed in order to guide the orientation and motion of the autonomous vehicle. A particular approach to the solution of the navigation problem of an autonomous vehicle is presented here. In the first section of this introduction a state of the art review is presented, after it, the proposed algorithm is summarized; the following sections present the procedure. Finally, some experimental results are shown at the end of the chapter.

2.1 Projection of point

Let F_c and F_m be the frames attached to the conventional camera and to the mirror respectively. In the sequel, we suppose that F_c and F_m are related by a simple translation along the Z-axis (F_c and F_m have the same orientation as depicted in Figure 1). The origins C

and M of F_c and F_m will be termed optical center and principal projection center respectively. The optical center C has coordinates $[0\ \ 0\ \ -\xi]^T$ with respect to F_m and the image plane $Z=f.(\varphi-2\xi)$ is orthogonal to the Z-axis where f is the focal length of the conventional camera and ξ and φ describe the type of sensor and the shape of the mirror, and are function of mirror shape parameters (refer to (Barreto et al 2002b)).
Consider the virtual unitary sphere centered in **M** as shown in Figure 1 and let **X** be a 3D point with coordinates $\mathbf{X}=[X\ Y\ \ Z]^T$ with respect to F_m . The world point **X** is projected in the image plane into the point of homogeneous coordinates $\mathbf{x_i} = [x_i\ \ y_i\ 1]^T$. The image formation process can be split in three steps as:

- **First step:** The 3D world point **X** is first projected on the unit sphere surface into a point of coordinates in F_m :

$$\mathbf{X_m} = \frac{1}{\|\mathbf{X}\|}\begin{bmatrix} X \\ Y \\ Z \end{bmatrix}$$

The projective ray $\mathbf{X_m}$ passes through the principal projection center **M** and the world point **X**.

- **Second step:** The point $\mathbf{X_m}$ lying on the unitary sphere is then perspectively projected on the normalized image plane $Z=1-\xi$. This projection is a point of homogeneous coordinates $\underline{\mathbf{x}} = \begin{bmatrix} \mathbf{x}^T & 1 \end{bmatrix}^T = \mathbf{f}(\mathbf{X})$ (where $\mathbf{x} = [x\ y]^T$):

$$\underline{\mathbf{x}} = f(\mathbf{X}) = \begin{bmatrix} \dfrac{X}{Z+\xi\|\mathbf{X}\|} & \dfrac{Y}{Z+\xi\|\mathbf{X}\|} & 1 \end{bmatrix}^T \qquad (1)$$

- **Third step:** Finally the point of homogeneous coordinates $\mathbf{x_i}$ in the image plane is obtained after a plane-to-plane collineation **K** of the 2D projective point **x**:

$$\underline{\mathbf{x}}_{\mathbf{i}} = \mathbf{K}\underline{\mathbf{x}}$$

The matrix **K** can be written as $\mathbf{K}=\mathbf{K_c}\,\mathbf{M}$ where the upper triangular matrix $\mathbf{K_c}$ contains the conventional camera intrinsic parameters, and the diagonal matrix **M** contains the mirror intrinsic parameters:

$$\mathbf{M} = \begin{bmatrix} \varphi-\xi & 0 & 0 \\ 0 & \varphi-\xi & 0 \\ 0 & 0 & 1 \end{bmatrix} \quad \text{and} \quad \mathbf{Kc} = \begin{bmatrix} \varphi-\xi & 0 & 0 \\ 0 & \varphi-\xi & 0 \\ 0 & 0 & 1 \end{bmatrix}$$

Note that, setting $\xi=0$, the general projection model becomes the well known perspective projection model.

In the sequel, we assume that $Z \neq 0$. Let us denote $\eta = s\|\mathbf{X}\|/|Z| = s\sqrt{1+X^2/Z^2+Y^2/Z^2}$, where s is the sign of Z. The coordinates of the image point can be rewritten as:

$$x=\frac{X/Z}{1+\xi\eta} \quad \text{and} \quad y=\frac{Y/Z}{1+\xi\eta}$$

By combining the two previous equations, it is easy to show that η is the solution of the following second order equation:

$$\eta^2-(x+y)^2(1+\xi\eta)-1=0$$

Noticing that the sign of η is equal to the sign of Z, it can be shown that the exact solution is:

$$\eta=\frac{-\gamma-\xi(x^2+y^2)}{\xi(x^2+y^2)-1} \tag{2}$$

where $\gamma=\sqrt{1+(1-\xi)(x^2+y^2)}$ Equation (2) shows that η can be computed as a function of image coordinates $\mathbf{x}$ and sensor parameter ξ. Noticing that:

$$\mathbf{X_m}=(\eta^{-1}+\xi)\bar{\mathbf{x}} \tag{3}$$

where $\bar{\mathbf{x}}=\begin{bmatrix}\mathbf{x}^T & \frac{1}{1+\xi\eta}\end{bmatrix}^T$, we deduce that $\mathbf{X_m}$ can also be computed as a function of image coordinates $\mathbf{x}$ and sensor parameter ξ.

2.2 Projection of lines

Let $\mathbf{L}$ be a 3D straight line in space lying on the interpretation plane which contains the principal projection center $\mathbf{M}$ (see Figure 1). The binormalized Euclidean Plücker coordinates (Andreff et al 2002) of the 3D line are defined as: $\mathbf{L}=\begin{bmatrix}\bar{\mathbf{h}}^T & \bar{\mathbf{u}}^T & \mathbf{h}\end{bmatrix}^T$. The unit vectors $\bar{\mathbf{h}}=(h_x \quad h_y \quad h_z)^T$ and $\bar{\mathbf{u}}=(u_x \quad u_y \quad u_z)^T$ are respectively the orthogonal vector to the interpretation plane and the orientation of the 3D line $\mathbf{L}$ and are expressed in the mirror frame F_m. h is the distance from $\mathbf{L}$ to the origin of the definition frame. The unit vectors $\bar{\mathbf{h}}$ and $\bar{\mathbf{u}}$ are orthogonal, thus verify $\bar{\mathbf{h}}^T\bar{\mathbf{u}}=0$. If the 3D line is imaged with a perspective camera then the unit vector $\bar{\mathbf{h}}$ contains the coefficient of the 2D line $\mathbf{l}$ in the image plane, i.e the homogeneous coordinates $\mathbf{x}$ of the perspective projection of any world point lying on $\mathbf{L}$ verifies:

$$(\mathbf{K}^{-T}\bar{\mathbf{h}})^T\mathbf{x}=\mathbf{l}^T\mathbf{x}=0 \tag{4}$$

If the line is imaged with a central catadioptric camera then the 3D points on the 3D line $\mathbf{L}$ are mapped into points $\mathbf{x}$ in the catadioptric image lying on a conic curve:

$$\mathbf{x}^T\mathbf{K}^{-T}\mathbf{\Omega}\mathbf{K}^{-1}\mathbf{x}=\mathbf{x}^T\mathbf{\Omega_i}\mathbf{x}=0 \tag{5}$$

Where $\mathbf{\Omega_i}=\mathbf{K}^{-T}\mathbf{\Omega}\mathbf{K}^{-1}$ and:

$$\mathbf{\Omega}\propto\begin{bmatrix} h_x^2-\xi(1-h_y^2) & h_xh_y(1-\xi^2) & h_xh_z \\ h_xh_y(1-\xi^2) & h_y^2-\xi(1-h_x^2) & h_yh_z \\ h_xh_z & h_yh_z & h_z^2 \end{bmatrix}$$

2.3 Polar lines

The quadratic equation (5) is defined by five coefficients. Nevertheless, the catadioptric image of a 3D line has only two degrees of freedom. In the sequel, we show how we can get a minimal representation using polar lines.

Let **Φ** and **A** be respectively a 2D conic curve and a point in the definition plane of **Φ**. The polar line **l** of **A** with respect to **Φ** is defined by **l** α **ΦA**. Now, consider the principal point $\mathbf{Oi} = [u_0\ v_0\ 1]^T = \mathbf{K}[0\ 0\ 1]^T$ and the polar line $\mathbf{l}_i$ of $\mathbf{O}_i$ with respect to $\mathbf{\Phi i}$: $\mathbf{l}_i$ α $\mathbf{\Phi i}\ \mathbf{O}_i$, then:

$$\begin{aligned} \mathbf{l_i} &\propto \mathbf{K}^{-T}\Omega\mathbf{K}^{-1}\mathbf{O_i} = \mathbf{K}^{-T}\Omega\mathbf{K}^{-1}\mathbf{K}\begin{bmatrix}0 & 0 & 1\end{bmatrix}^T \\ &\propto \mathbf{K}^{-T}\bar{\mathbf{h}} \end{aligned} \tag{6}$$

Moreover, equation (6) yields:

$$\bar{\mathbf{h}} = \frac{\mathbf{K}^T\mathbf{l_i}}{\left\|\mathbf{K}^T\mathbf{l_i}\right\|} \tag{7}$$

It is thus clear that the polar line $\mathbf{l}_i$ contains the coordinates of the projection of the 3D line **L** in an image plane of an equivalent (virtual) perspective camera defined by the frame Fv = Fm (see Figure 2) with internal parameters chosen equal to the internal parameters of the catadioptric camera (*i.e* $\mathbf{K}_v = \mathbf{K}_c\ \mathbf{M}$). This result is fundamental since it allows us to represent the physical projection of a 3D line in a catadioptric camera by a simple (polar) line in a virtual perspective camera rather than a conic. Knowing only the optical center $\mathbf{O}_i$, it is thus possible to use the linear pin-hole model for the projection of a 3D line instead of the non linear central catadioptric projection model.

3. Scaled Euclidean reconstruction

Several methods were proposed to obtain Euclidean reconstruction from two views (Faugeras et al 1988}. They are generally based on the estimation of the fundamental matrix (Faugeras et al 96) in pixel space or on the estimation of the essential matrix (Longuet and Higgins 1981} in normalized space. However, for control purposes, the methods based on the essential matrix are not well suited since degenerate configurations can occur (such as pure rotational motion). Homography matrix and Essential matrix based approaches do not share the same degenerate configurations, for example pure rotational motion is not a degenerate configuration when using homography-based method. The epipolar geometry of central catadioptric system has been more recently investigated (Geyer et al 2003, Svoboda et al 1998). The central catadioptric fundamental and essential matrices share similar degenerate configurations that those observed with conventional perspective cameras, it is why we will focus on homographic relationship. In the sequel, the collineation matrix **K** and the mirror parameter ξ are supposed known. To estimate these parameters the algorithm proposed in Barreto et al 2002 can be used. In the next section, we show how we can compute homographic relationships between two central catadioptric views of co-planar points and co-planar lines.

Let **R** and **t** be the rotation matrix and the translation vector between two positions F_m and F_m^* of the central catadioptric camera (see Figs. 1 and 2). Consider a 3D reference plane (π) given in F_m^* by the vector $\pi^T = [\mathbf{n}^* \ -d^*]$, where $\mathbf{n}^*$ is its unitary normal in F_m^* and d^* is the distance from (π) to the origin of F_m^*.

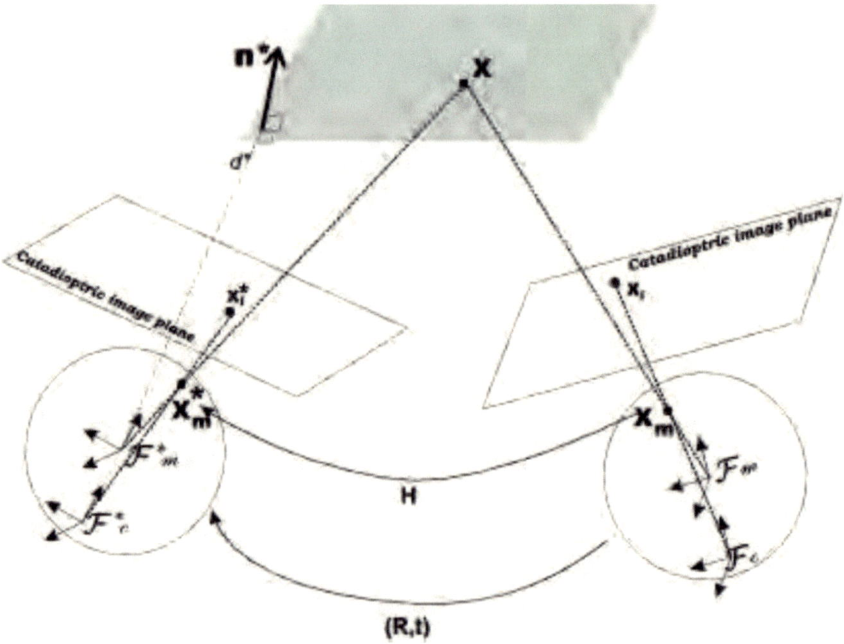

Figure 1. Geometry of two views, the case of points

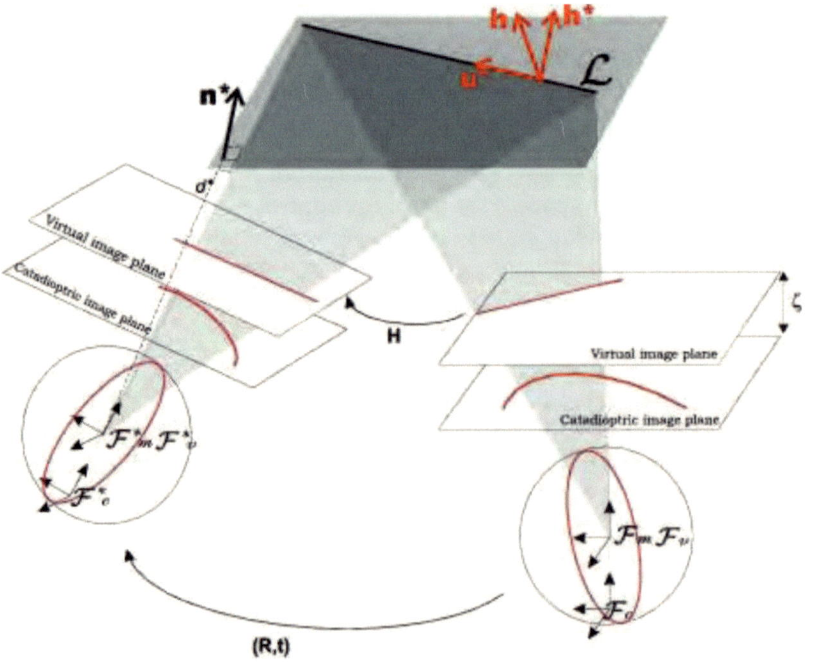

Figure 2. Geometry of two views, the case of lines

3.1 Homography matrix from points

Let **X** be a 3D point with coordinates **X** = [X Y Z]T with respect to Fm and with coordinates X = [X* Y* Z*]T with respect to $\overset{*}{F_m}$. Its projection in the unit sphere for the two camera positions is:

$$\mathbf{X}_m = (\eta^{-1}+\xi)\bar{\mathbf{x}} = \frac{1}{\rho}[X \quad Y \quad Z]^T \text{ and } \mathbf{X}_m^* = (\eta^{*-1}+\xi)\bar{\mathbf{x}}^* = \frac{1}{\rho}\left[X^* \quad Y^* \quad Z^*\right]^T$$

Using the homogenous coordinates $\underline{\mathbf{X}} = [X \quad Y \quad Z \quad H]^T$ and , we can write:

$$\rho(\eta^{-1}+\xi)\bar{\mathbf{x}} = [\mathbf{I}_3 \quad 0]\underline{\mathbf{X}} = [\mathbf{R} \quad \mathbf{t}]\underline{\mathbf{X}}^* \tag{8}$$

The distance d(**X**,π) from the world point X to the plane (π) is given by the scalar product $\pi^{*T}.\underline{\mathbf{X}}^*$ and:

$$d(\mathbf{X}^*,\pi^*) = \rho^*(\eta^{*-1}+\xi)\mathbf{n}^{*T}.\bar{\mathbf{x}}^* - d^*H^*$$

As a consequence, the unknown homogenous component H* is given by:

$$H^* = = \frac{\rho^*(\eta^{*-1}+\xi)}{d^*}\mathbf{n}^{*T}.\bar{\mathbf{x}}^* - \frac{d(\mathbf{X}^*,\pi^*)}{d^*} \tag{9}$$

The homogeneous coordinates of **X** with respect to $\overset{*}{F_m}$ can be rewritten as:

$$\underline{\mathbf{X}}^* = \rho^*(\varphi^{*-1}+\xi)\left[\ddot{I}_3 \quad 0\right]^T\bar{\mathbf{x}}^* + \left[0_{1x3} \quad H^*\right] \tag{10}$$

By combining the Equations (9) and (10), we obtain:

$$\underline{\mathbf{X}}^* = \rho^*(\eta^{*-1}+\xi)[\mathbf{I}_3 \quad 0]^T\mathbf{A}\bar{\mathbf{x}}^* + \mathbf{b}^* \tag{11}$$

Where

$$\mathbf{A}^* = \begin{bmatrix}\mathbf{I}_3 & \dfrac{\mathbf{n}^*}{d^*}\end{bmatrix}^T \text{ and } \mathbf{b}^* = \begin{bmatrix}\mathbf{0}_{1x3} & -\dfrac{d(\mathbf{X},\pi)}{d^*}\end{bmatrix}^T$$

According to (11), the expression (8) can be rewritten as:

$$\rho(\eta^{-1}+\xi)\bar{\mathbf{x}} = \rho^*(\eta^{*-1}+\xi)\mathbf{H}.\bar{\mathbf{x}}^* + \alpha\mathbf{t} \tag{12}$$

With $\mathbf{H} = \mathbf{R} + \frac{\mathbf{t}}{d^*}\mathbf{n}^{*T}$ and $\alpha = -\frac{d(\mathbf{X},\pi)}{d^*}$. **H** is the Euclidean homography matrix written as a function of the camera displacement and of the plane coordinates with respect to $\overset{*}{F_m}$. It has the same form as in the conventional perspective case (it is decomposed into a rotation matrix and a rank 1 matrix). If the world point **X** belongs to the reference plane (π) (*i.e* α = 0) then Equation (12) becomes:

$$\bar{\mathbf{x}} \propto \mathbf{H}\bar{\mathbf{x}}^* \quad (13)$$

Note that the Equation (13) can be turned into a linear homogeneous equation $\bar{\mathbf{x}} \times \mathbf{H}\bar{\mathbf{x}}^* = 0$ (where x denotes the cross-product). As usual, the homography matrix related to (π), can thus be estimated up to a scale factor, using four couples of coordinates $(\mathbf{x}_k;\ \mathbf{x}_k^*)$, k= 1 ... 4, corresponding to the projection in the image space of world points $\mathbf{X}_k$ belonging to (π). If only three points belonging to (π) are available then at least five supplementary points are necessary to estimate the homography matrix by using for example the linear algorithm proposed in (Malis et al 2000). From the estimated homography matrix, the camera motion parameters (that is the rotation **R** and the scaled translation $\mathbf{t}_{d^*} = \frac{\mathbf{t}}{d^*}$, and the structure of the observed scene (for example the vector **n***) can thus be determined (refer to (Faugeras et al 1988). It can also be shown that the ratio $\sigma = \frac{\rho}{\rho^*}$ can be estimated as follow:

$$\sigma = \frac{\rho}{\rho^*} = (1 + \mathbf{n}^{*T}\mathbf{R}\mathbf{t}_{d^*})\frac{(\eta^{*-1} + \xi)\mathbf{n}^{*T}\bar{\mathbf{x}}^*}{(\eta^{-1} + \xi)\mathbf{n}^{*T}\mathbf{R}^T\bar{\mathbf{x}}} \quad (14)$$

This parameter is used in our 2 1/2 D visual servoing control scheme from points.

3.2 Homography matrix from lines

Let **L** be a 3D straight line with binormalized Euclidean Plücker coordinates $\begin{bmatrix}\bar{\mathbf{h}}^T & \bar{\mathbf{u}}^T & h\end{bmatrix}^T$ with respect to F_m and with coordinates $\begin{bmatrix}\bar{\mathbf{h}}^{*T} & \bar{\mathbf{u}}^{*T} & h^*\end{bmatrix}^T$ with respect to F_m^*. Consider that the 3D line **L** lies in a 3D reference plane (π) as defined below. Let $\mathbf{X}_1$ and $\mathbf{X}_2$ be two points in the 3D space lying on the line **L**. The central catadioptric projection of the 3D line **L** is fully defined by the normal vector to the interpretation plane $\bar{\mathbf{h}}$. The vector $\bar{\mathbf{h}}$ can be defined by two points in the 3D line as $\bar{\mathbf{h}} = \frac{\mathbf{X}_1 \times \mathbf{X}_2}{\|\mathbf{X}_1 \times \mathbf{X}_2\|}$. Noticing that $[\mathbf{H}\mathbf{X}_1^*]_\times = \det(\mathbf{H})\mathbf{H}^{-T}[\mathbf{X}_1^*]_\times \mathbf{H}^{-1}$ ($[\mathbf{H}\mathbf{X}_1^*]_\times$ being the skew-symmetric matrix associated to the vector $\mathbf{H}\mathbf{X}_1^*$) and according to (3) and (13), $\bar{\mathbf{h}}$ can be written as follow:

$$\bar{\mathbf{h}} \propto \frac{\det(\mathbf{H})\mathbf{H}^{-T}\mathbf{X}_1^* \times \mathbf{X}_1^*}{\|\mathbf{X}_1^* \times \mathbf{X}_1^*\|} \quad (18)$$

Since $\overline{\mathbf{h}}^* = \frac{\mathbf{X}_1^* \times \mathbf{X}_1^*}{\|\mathbf{X}_1^* \times \mathbf{X}_1^*\|}$ is the normal vector to the interpretation plane expressed in the frame F_m^*, the relationship between two views of the 3D line can be written as:

$$\overline{\mathbf{h}} \propto \mathbf{H}^{-T}\overline{\mathbf{h}}^* \tag{15}$$

The expression of the homography matrix in the pixel space can be derived hence using the polar lines. As depicted below, each conic, corresponding to the projection of a 3D line in the omnidirectional image, can be explored through its polar line. Let $\mathbf{l}_i$ and $\mathbf{l}_i^*$ be the polar lines of the image center $\mathbf{O}_i$ with respect to the conics Ω_i and Ω_i^* respectively in the two positions F_m and F_m^* of the catadioptric camera. From equation (6), the relationship given in equation (15) can be rewritten as:

$$\mathbf{l}_i \propto \mathbf{G}^{-T}\mathbf{l}_i^* \tag{16}$$

Where $\mathbf{G} = \mathbf{K}\mathbf{H}\mathbf{K}^{-1} = \mathbf{K}(\mathbf{R} + \frac{\mathbf{t}}{d^*}\mathbf{n}^{*T})\mathbf{K}^{-1}$. As in the case of points the homography matrix related to (π) can be linearly estimated. Equation (16) can be rewritten as: $\mathbf{l}_i \times \mathbf{G}^{-T}\mathbf{l}_i^* = 0$ and $\mathbf{G}$ can thus be estimated using at least four couples of coordinates ($((\mathbf{l}_{ik}, \mathbf{l}_{ik}^*)$, k=1 ... 4). The homography matrix is then computed as $\mathbf{K}^{-1}\mathbf{H}\mathbf{K} = \mathbf{G}$. From **H**, the camera motion parameters (that is the rotation **R** and the scaled translation $\mathbf{t}_{d^*} = \frac{\mathbf{t}}{d^*}$, and the structure of the observed scene (for example the vector **n***) can thus be determined. It can also be shown that the ratio $r = \frac{h}{h^*}$ (ratio of the lines depth) can be computed as follow:

$$r = \frac{h}{h^*} = (1 + \mathbf{t}_{d^*}^T \mathbf{R}^T \mathbf{n}^*) \frac{\|\mathbf{n}^{*T} \times \mathbf{K}^T \mathbf{l}_i^*\|}{\|\mathbf{R}\mathbf{n}^* \times \mathbf{K}^T \mathbf{l}_i\|} \tag{17}$$

These parameters are important since they are used in the design of our control scheme with imaged lines. In the next section, we propose a vision control scheme which allows to fully decouple rotational and translational motions.

4. Control schemes

In order to design an hybrid visual servoing scheme, the features used as input of the control law combine 2D and 3D informations. We propose to derive these informations from imaged points or polar lines and the homography matrix computed and decomposed as depicted in the last section. Let us first define the input of the proposed hybrid control scheme as follow:

$$\mathbf{s} = \begin{bmatrix} \mathbf{s}_v^T & \mathbf{s}_\omega^T \end{bmatrix}^T \tag{18}$$

The vector $\mathbf{s}_v$ depends of the chosen image features. The vector $\mathbf{s}_\omega$ is chosen as $\mathbf{s}_\omega = \mathbf{u}\theta$ where $\mathbf{u}$ and θ are respectively the axis and the rotation angle extracted from $\mathbf{R}$ (*i.e* the rotation matrix between the mirror frame when the camera is in these current and desired positions). The task function $\mathbf{e}$ to regulate to $\mathbf{0}$ is then given by:

$$\mathbf{e} = \left[\mathbf{s} - \mathbf{s}^*\right] = \begin{bmatrix} \mathbf{s}_v - \mathbf{s}_v^* \\ \mathbf{s}_\omega - \mathbf{s}_\omega^* \end{bmatrix} = \begin{bmatrix} \mathbf{s}_v - \mathbf{s}_v^* \\ \mathbf{u}\theta \end{bmatrix} \tag{19}$$

where $\mathbf{s}^*$ is the desired value of $\mathbf{s}$. Note that the rotational part of the task function can be estimated using partial Euclidean reconstruction from the homography matrix derived in Section 3). The exponential convergence of $\mathbf{e}$ can be obtained by imposing $\dot{\mathbf{e}} = -\lambda\mathbf{e}$, the corresponding control law is:

$$\tau = -\lambda \mathbf{L}^{-1}(\mathbf{s} - \mathbf{s}^*) \tag{20}$$

where $\tau = \left[\mathbf{v}^T \quad \boldsymbol{\omega}^T\right]^T$ is the central catadioptric camera velocity ($\mathbf{v}$ and ω denote respectively the linear and angular velocities) , λ tunes the convergence rate and $\mathbf{L}$ is the interaction matrix which links the variation of feature vector $\mathbf{s}$ to the camera velocity $\dot{\mathbf{s}} = \mathbf{L}\tau$.

The time derivative of $\mathbf{s}_\omega = \mathbf{u}\theta$ can be expressed as a function of the camera velocity as:

$$\frac{d(\mathbf{u}\theta)}{dt} = \left[0_3 \quad \mathbf{L}_\omega\right]\tau$$

Where $\mathbf{L}_\omega$ is given in (Malis et al 1999):

$$\mathbf{L}_\omega = \mathbf{I}_3 - \frac{\theta}{2}[\mathbf{u}]_\times + \left(1 - \frac{\sin(\theta)}{\sin\mathbf{c}^2\left(\frac{\theta}{2}\right)}\right)[\mathbf{u}]_\times^2 \tag{21}$$

Where $\sin\mathbf{c}(\theta) = \frac{\sin(\theta)}{\theta}$ and $[\mathbf{u}]_\times$ being the antisymmetric matrix associated to the rotation axis **u.**

4.1 Using points to define $\mathbf{s}_v$

To control the 3 translational degrees of freedom, the visual observations and the ratio σ expressed in (14) are used:

$$\mathbf{s}_v = [x \quad y \quad \delta]^T \tag{22}$$

Where x and y are the current coordinates of a chosen catadioptric image point given by Equation (1), $\delta = \log(\rho)$. The translational part of the task function is thus:

$$\mathbf{e} = \mathbf{s}_v - \mathbf{s}_v^* = \left[\text{x-x}^* \quad \text{y-y}^* \quad \Gamma\right]^T \tag{23}$$

Where $\Gamma = \log\left(\frac{\rho}{\rho^*}\right) = \log(\sigma)$. The first two components of $\mathbf{s}_v - \mathbf{s}_v^*$ are computed from the normalized current and desired catadioptric images, and its last components can be estimated using Equation (14).

Consider a 3-D point **X**, lying on the reference plane π, as the reference point. The time derivative of its coordinates, with respect to the current catadioptric frame F_m, is given by:

$$\dot{\mathbf{X}} = \begin{bmatrix} -\mathbf{I}_3 & [\mathbf{X}]_\times \end{bmatrix} \tau \tag{24}$$

The time derivative of $\mathbf{s}_v$ can be written as:

$$\dot{\mathbf{s}}_v = \frac{\partial \mathbf{s}_v}{\partial \mathbf{X}} \dot{\mathbf{X}} \tag{25}$$

With:

$$\frac{\partial \mathbf{s}_v}{\partial \mathbf{X}} = \frac{1}{\rho(Z+\xi\rho)^2} \begin{bmatrix} \rho Z+\xi(Y^2+Z^2) & \xi XY & -X(\rho+\xi Z) \\ -\xi XY & \rho Z+\xi(X^2+Z^2) & -Y(\rho+\xi Z) \\ \frac{X(Z+\xi\rho)^2}{\rho} & \frac{Y(Z+\xi\rho)^2}{\rho} & \frac{Z(Z+\xi\rho)^2}{\rho} \end{bmatrix}$$

By combining the equations (24), (25) and (14), it can be shown that:

$$\dot{\mathbf{s}}_v = \begin{bmatrix} \mathbf{A} & \mathbf{B} \end{bmatrix} \tau \tag{26}$$

With

$$\mathbf{A} = \frac{1}{\sigma\rho^*} \begin{bmatrix} -\frac{1+x^2(1-\xi(\gamma_x+\xi))+y^2}{\gamma_x+\xi} & \xi xy & x\gamma_x \\ \xi xy & -\frac{1+y^2(1-\xi(\gamma_x+\xi))+x^2}{\gamma_x+\xi} & y\gamma_x \\ \eta_x x & \eta_x y & (\eta_x-1)\xi \end{bmatrix} \quad \text{and} \quad \mathbf{B} = \begin{bmatrix} xy & \frac{(1+x^2)\gamma_x-\xi y^2}{\gamma_x+\xi} & y \\ \frac{(1+y^2)\gamma_x-\xi x^2}{\gamma_x+\xi} & -xy & -x \\ 0 & 0 & 0 \end{bmatrix}$$

Where: $\gamma_x = \sqrt{1+(1-\xi^2)(x^2+y^2)}$ and $\eta_x = \frac{\xi^2+\sqrt{(1-\xi^2)(x^2+y^2)+\xi^2}}{x^2+y^2+\xi^2}$. The task function **e** (see Equation (19)) can thus be regulated to **0** using the control law (Equation (20)) with the following interaction matrix **L**:

$$\mathbf{L} = \begin{bmatrix} \mathbf{A} & \mathbf{B} \\ 0_3 & \mathbf{L}_\omega \end{bmatrix} \tag{27}$$

In practice, an approximated interaction matrix $\hat{\mathbf{L}}$ is used. The parameter ρ^* can be estimated only once during an off-line learning stage.

4.2 Using imaged lines to define $\mathbf{s}_v$

To control the 3 translational degrees of freedom with imaged lines, the chosen visual observation vector is:

$$\mathbf{s}_v = [\log(h_1) \quad \log(h_2) \quad \log(h_3)]^T \tag{28}$$

Where h_1, h_2 and h_3 are the depth of three co-planar lines. From the time derivative of the line depth expressed as a function of the camera velocity (Andreff et al 2002), given by $\dot{h}_k = (\bar{\mathbf{u}}_k \times \bar{\mathbf{h}}_k)^T \mathbf{v}$, it can be shown that:

$$\frac{d(\log(h_k))}{dt} = \begin{bmatrix} \frac{1}{h_k}(\bar{\mathbf{u}}_k \times \bar{\mathbf{h}}_k)^T & 0_3 \end{bmatrix} \mathbf{v} \tag{29}$$

According to (6) and (29), the time derivative of the vector $\mathbf{s}_v$ is thus given by:

$$\dot{\mathbf{s}}_v = [L_v \quad 0_3]^T \tau$$

Where:

$$\mathbf{L}_v = \begin{bmatrix} \|\mathbf{K}^T \mathbf{l}_{i1}\| h_1 & 0 & 0 \\ 0 & \|\mathbf{K}^T \mathbf{l}_{i2}\| h_2 & 0 \\ 0 & 0 & \|\mathbf{K}^T \mathbf{l}_{i3}\| h_3 \end{bmatrix} \begin{bmatrix} (\bar{\mathbf{u}}_1 \times \mathbf{K}^T \mathbf{l}_{i1})^T \\ (\bar{\mathbf{u}}_2 \times \mathbf{K}^T \mathbf{l}_{i2})^T \\ (\bar{\mathbf{u}}_3 \times \mathbf{K}^T \mathbf{l}_{i3})^T \end{bmatrix} \tag{30}$$

Note that the time derivative of $\mathbf{s}_v$ does not depend of the camera angular velocity. It is also clear that $\mathbf{L}_v$ is singular only if the principal point **M** of the mirror frame lies in the 3D reference plane (π). The task function **e** can thus be regulated to zero using the control law (20) with the following square block-diagonal interaction matrix:

$$\mathbf{L} = \begin{bmatrix} \mathbf{L}_v & 0 \\ 0 & \mathbf{L}_\omega \end{bmatrix} \tag{31}$$

As can be seen on equation (30), the unknown depth h_i and the unitary orientations $\mathbf{u}_i$ with respect to the catadioptric camera frame have to be introduced in the interaction matrix. Noticing that $\bar{\mathbf{u}}_i = (\bar{\mathbf{h}}_i \times \mathbf{R}\bar{\mathbf{h}}_i^*) / \|\bar{\mathbf{h}}_i \times \mathbf{R}\bar{\mathbf{h}}_i^*\|$ and using equation (6), the orientation can be estimated as follow:

$$\bar{\mathbf{u}} = \frac{\mathbf{K}^T \mathbf{l}_i \times \mathbf{R}\mathbf{K}^T \mathbf{l}_i^*}{\|\mathbf{K}^T \mathbf{l}_i \times \mathbf{R}\mathbf{K}^T \mathbf{l}_i^*\|}$$

Furthermore, if the camera is calibrated and $\hat{h}_i$ is chosen to approximate h_i, then it is clear that $\hat{\mathbf{L}}_v^{-1}\mathbf{L}_v$ is a diagonal matrix with $\frac{\hat{h}_i}{h_i}$ for i=1, 2, 3 as entries. The only point of equilibrium is thus **s*** and the control law is asymptotically stable in the neighbourhood of **s*** if $\hat{h}_i$ is chosen positive. In practice, an approximated matrix $\hat{\mathbf{L}}^{*-1}$ at the desired position is used to compute the camera velocity vector and the rotational part of the interaction matrix can be set to $\mathbf{L}_\omega^{-1} = \mathbf{I}_3$ (Malis et al 1999). Finally, the control law is thus given by:

$$\tau = -\lambda \begin{bmatrix} \hat{\mathbf{L}}_v^{*-1} & 0 \\ 0 & \mathbf{I}_3 \end{bmatrix} \begin{bmatrix} \mathbf{s}_v - \mathbf{s}_v^* \\ \theta\mathbf{u} \end{bmatrix} \qquad (32)$$

5 Results

5.1 Simulation Results

We present now results concerning a positioning task of a six degrees of freedom robotic arm with a catadioptric camera in eye-in-hand configuration. The catadioptric camera used is an hyperbolic mirror combined with a perspective camera (similar results are obtained with a catadioptric camera combining a parabolic mirror and an orthographic lens, these results are not presented in this paper). From an initial position, the catadioptric camera has to reach the desired position. This means that the task function (refer to equation (19)), computed from the homography matrix between the current and desired images, converges to zero. To be close to a real setup, image noise has been added (additive noise with maximum amplitude of 2 pixels) to the image and the interaction matrix is computed using erroneous internal camera parameters. The first simulation concerns imaged points while the second simulation concerns imaged lines.

5.1.a Imaged points

The initial and desired attitudes of the catadioptric camera are plotted in the Figure 3. This figure also shows the 3-D camera trajectory from its initial position to the desired one. Figure 3 shows the initial (blue *) and desired (red *) images of the observed target. It shows also the trajectory of the point (green trace) in the image plane (the controlled image point has a black trace trajectory). The norm of the error vector is given in Figure 4(b). As can been seen in the Figures 4(c) and 4(d) showing the errors between desired and current observation vectors the task is correctly realized. The translational and rotational camera velocities are given in Figures 4(e) and 4(f) respectively.

5.1.b Imaged lines

Figure 2 shows the spatial configuration of the 3D lines as well as the 3D trajectory of the central catadioptric. The images corresponding to the initial and desired positions are shown by figures 5(c) and 5(d). These figures show the projected 3D lines (conics) and the associated polar lines. The trajectories of the conics and of the corresponding polar lines in the image plane are given in Figures 5(a) and 5(b) respectively. These trajectories confirm that the initial images (conics and polar lines) reach the desired images. Figures 5(e) and 5(f) show respectively the translational and rotational velocities of the catadioptric camera. As shown in Figures 5(g) and 5(h), the error vector **e** between the current and desired observation vectors are well regulated to zeros, and thus the positioning task is correctly realized.

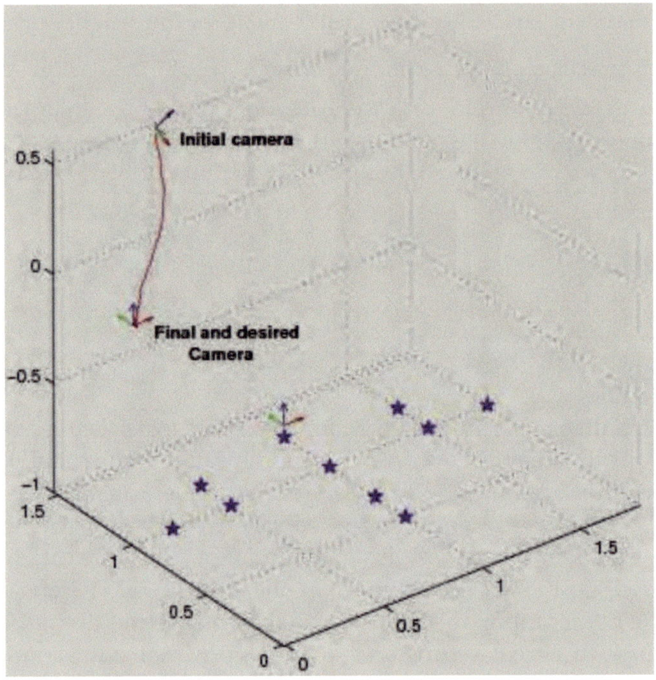

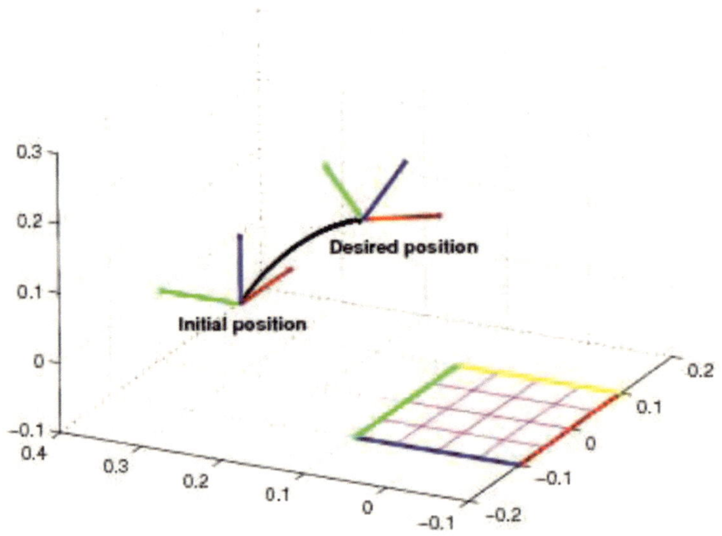

Figure 3. 3D trajectories of the catadioptric camera [meters]: (left) the case of points, (right) the case of lines

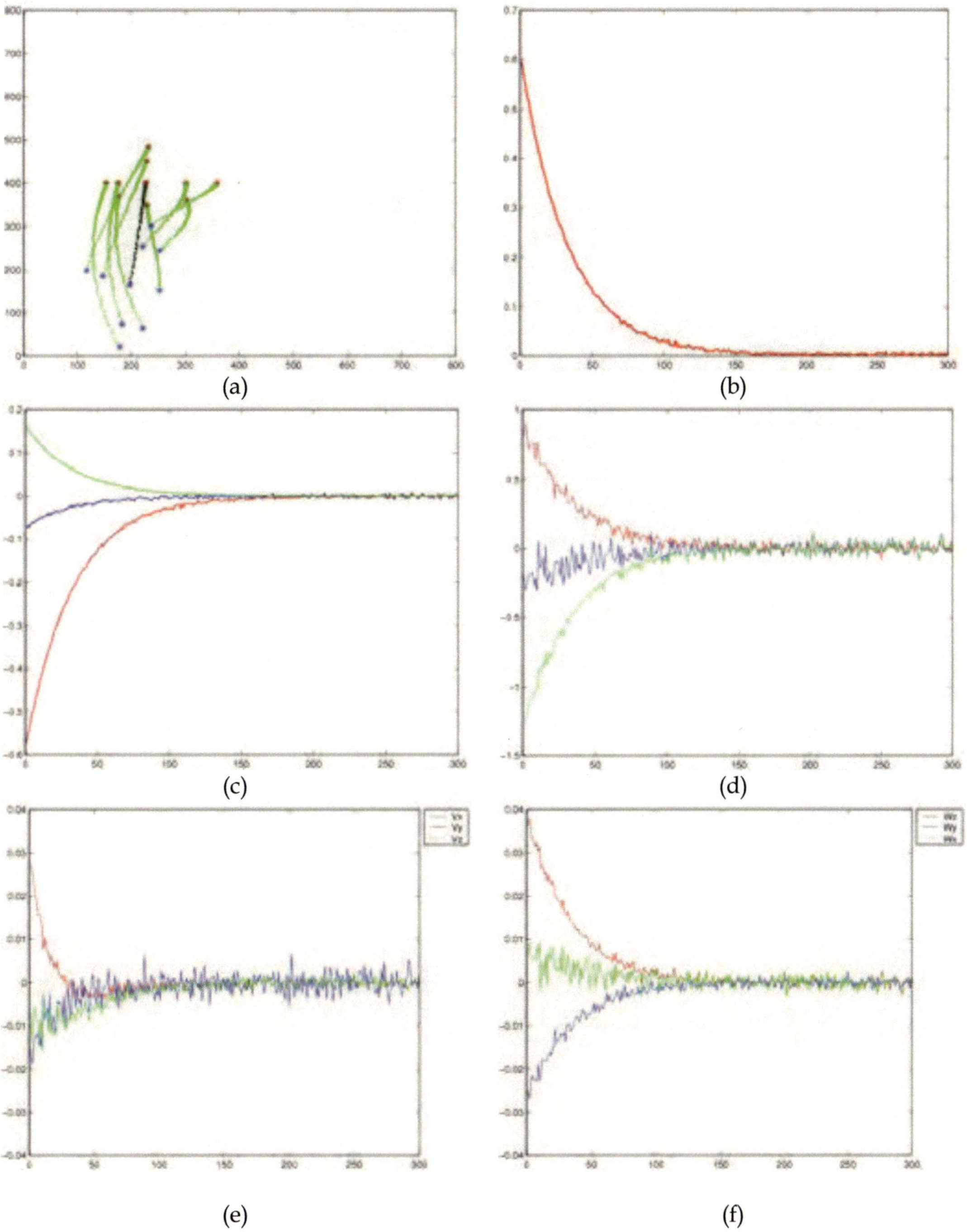

Figure 4. (a) Trajectories in the image of the target points [pixels]. (b) norm of the error vector, (c) error vector: [meters], (d) rotation vector [rad], (e) Translational velocity [m/s], (f) rotational velocity [rad/s]

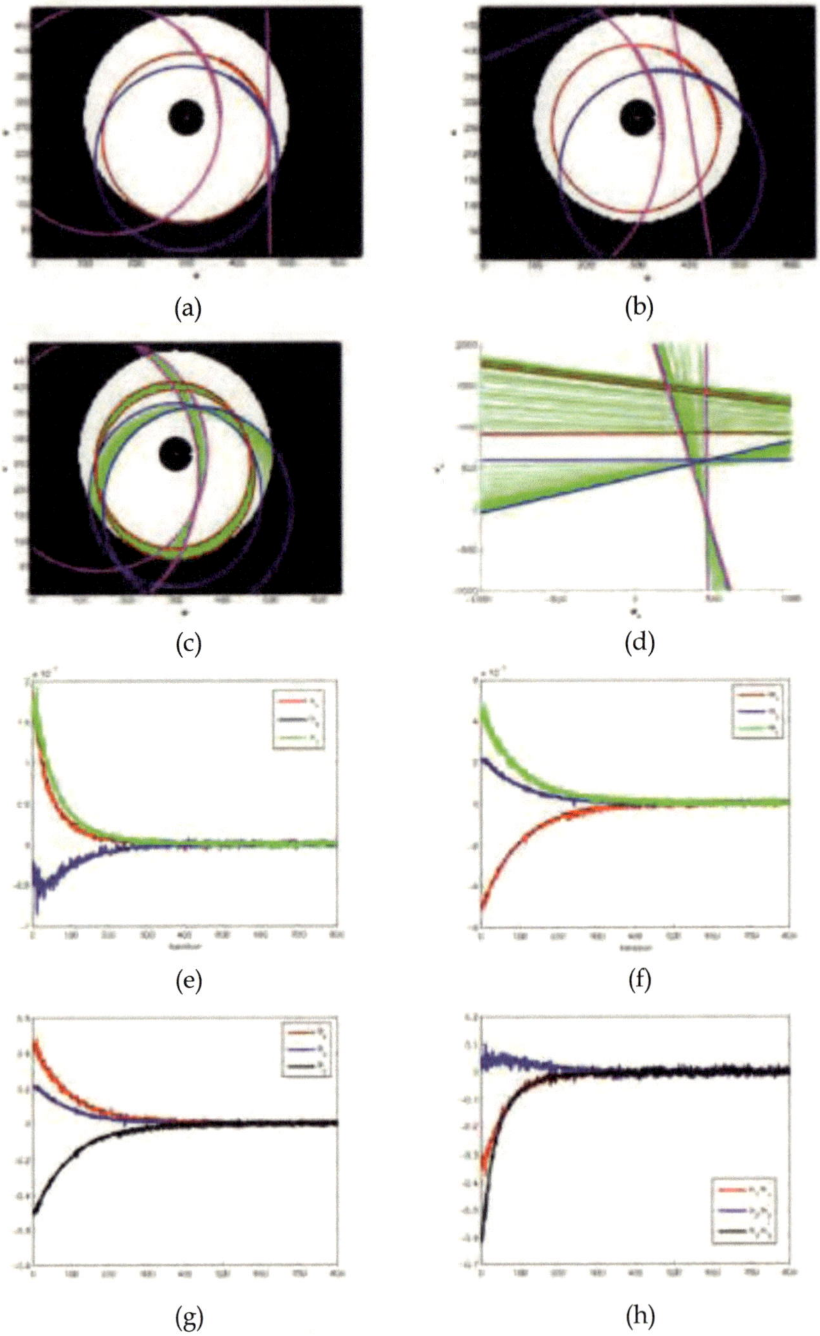

(a) (b)

(c) (d)

(e) (f)

(g) (h)

Figure 5. Visual servoing with para-catadioptric camera: (a) initial image, (b) desired image (c) trajectory of the conics in the image plane, (d) trajectory of the polar line, , (e) translation velocities [m/s], (f) rotational velocities [rad/s], (g) $\mathbf{u}\theta$ errors [rad], (h) $\mathbf{s}_v - \mathbf{s}_v^*$ vector errors

5.1 Experimental Results

The proposed control law has been validated on a six d-o-f eye-to-hand system (refer to Figure 6). Since we were not interested in image processing in this paper, the target is composed of white marks (see Figure 6) from which points or straight lines can be defined. The coordinates of these points (the center of gravity of each mark) are extracted and tracked using the VISP library (Marchand et al 2005). The omnidirectional camera used is a parabolic mirror combined with an orthographic lens ($\xi=1$). Calibration parameters of the camera are: $f.(\varphi-\xi)= 161$ and the coordinates of the principal point are $[300\ 270]^T$. From an initial position the robot has to reach a desired position known as a desired 2D observation vector $\mathbf{s}^*$. Two experiments are presented. In the first one whose results are depicted in Figure 7, the point-based visual servoing has been used. The error on the visual features is plotted on Figure 7(e) while the camera velocities are plotted on Figure 7(c)-(d). These results confirm that the positioning task is correctly achieved. The second experiment has been conducted using the line-based visual servoing. The corresponding results are depicted on Figure 8. We can note that the system still converges.

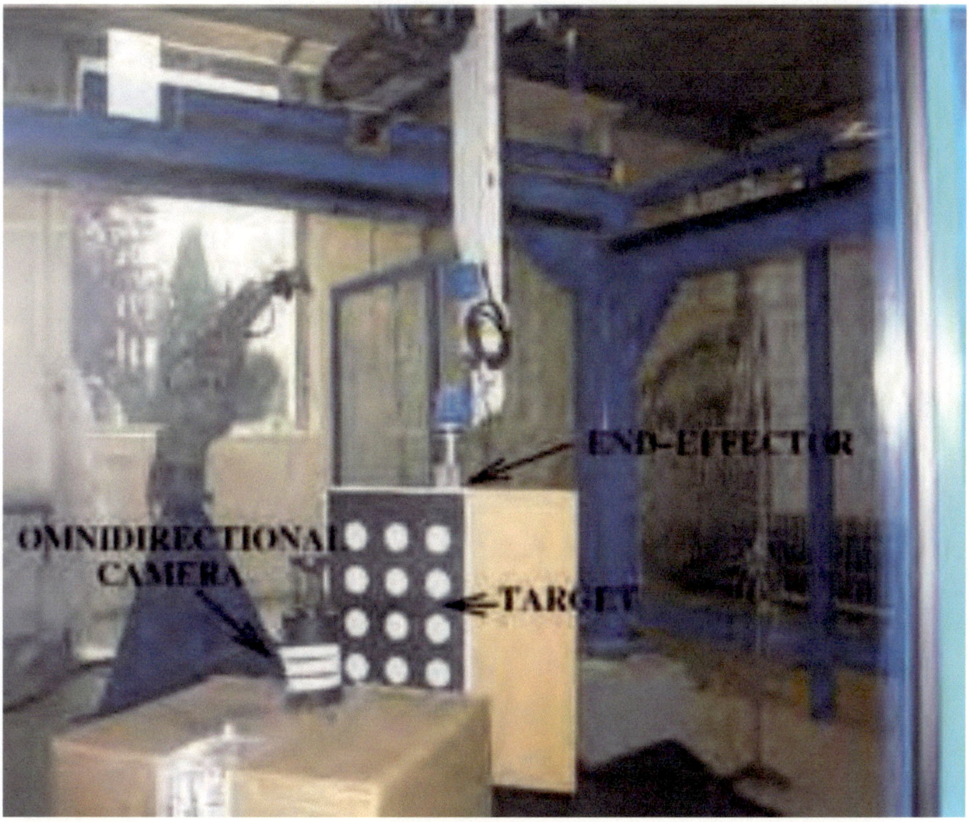

Figure 6. Experimental setup : eye-to-hand configuration

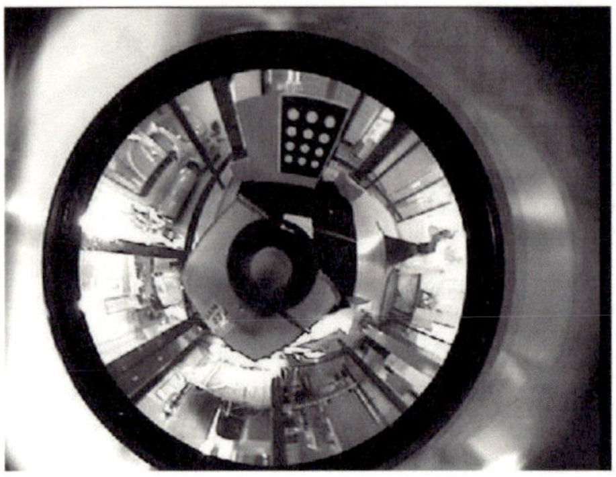

(a)

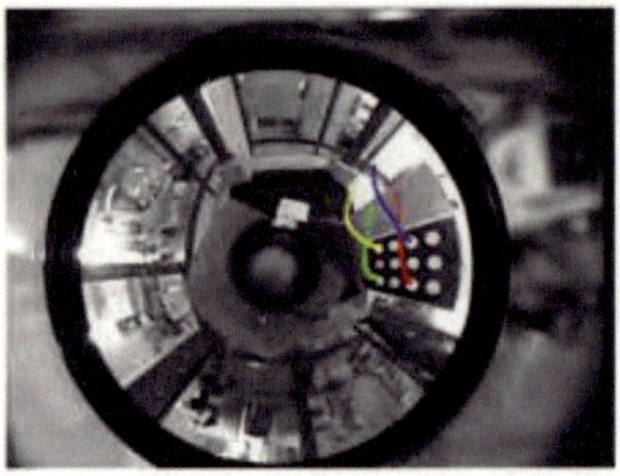

(b)

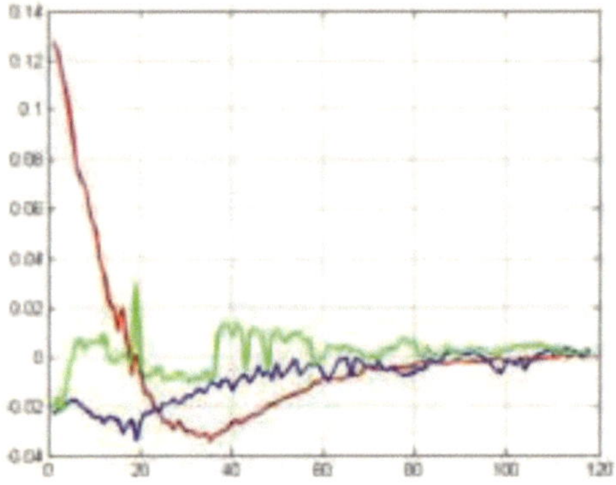

(c)

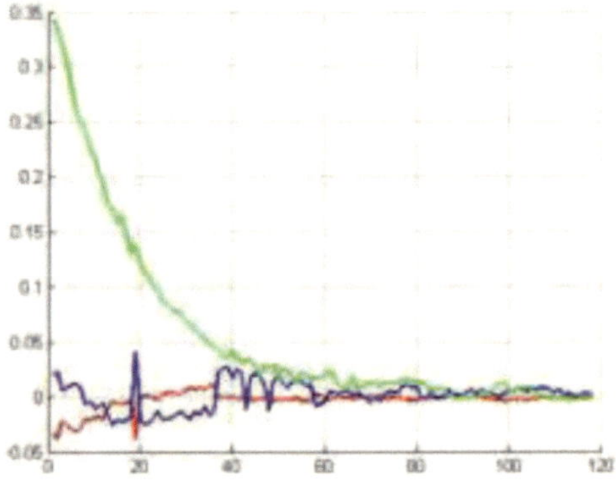

(d)

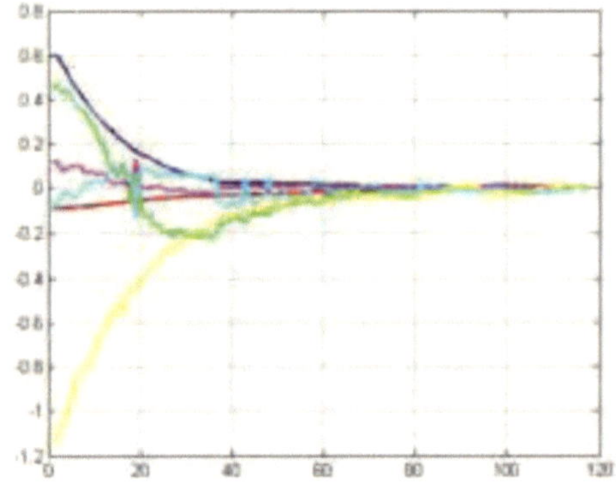

(e)

Figure 7. Visual servoing with lines: (a) initial image, (b) desired image and trajectory of the conics in the image plane (c) translational velocities [m/s], (d) rotational velocities [rad/s], , (c) $\mathbf{s}_v - \mathbf{s}_v^*$ and uθ errors

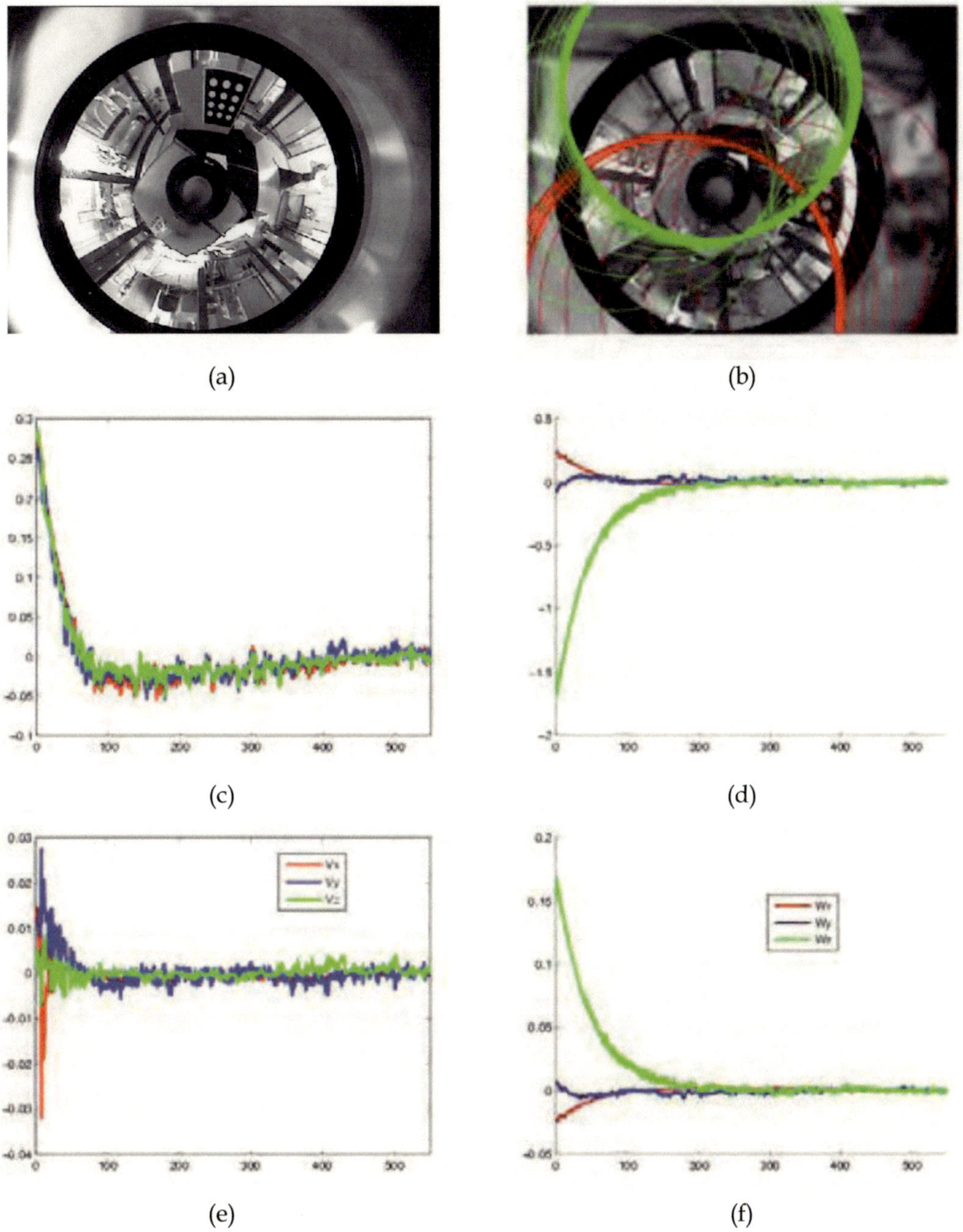

Figure 8. Visual servoing with lines: (a) initial image, (b) desired image and trajectory of the conics in the image plane, (c) $\mathbf{s}_\mathrm{v} - \mathbf{s}_\mathrm{v}^*$, (d) uθ errors [rad] (e) translational velocities [m/s], (f) rotational velocities [rad/s]

6. Conclusion

In this paper hybrid vision-based control schemes valid for the entire class of central cameras was presented. Geometrical relationship between imaged points and lines was exploited to estimate a generic homography matrix from which partial Euclidean reconstruction can be obtained. The information extracted from the homography matrix were then used to design vision-based control laws. Results with simulated data confirmed the relevance. In future work, the robustness and stability analysis with respect to calibration errors must be studied.

7. References

S. Baker & S. K. Nayar (1999). A theory of single-viewpoint catadioptric image formation. *International Journal of Computer Vision*, 35(2):1- 22, November 1999.

J. Barreto and H. Araujo (2002). Geometric properties of central catadioptric line images. *In 7th European Conference on Computer Vision*, ECCV'02, pages 237–251, Copenhagen, Denmark, May 2002.

R. Benosman & S. Kang (2000). Panoramic Vision. Springer Verlag ISBN 0387-95111-3, 2000.

P. Blaer & P.K. Allen (2002). Topological mobile robot localization using fast vision techniques. *In IEEE International Conference on Robotics and Automation*, pages 1031–1036, Washington, USA, May 2002.

G. Chesi, K. Hashimoto, D. Prattichizzo & A. Vicino (2003). A switching control law for keeping features in the field of view in eye-in-hand visual servoing. *In IEEE International Conference on Robotics and Automation*, pages 3929–3934, Taipei, Taiwan, September 2003.

B. Espiau, F. Chaumette & P. Rives (1992). A new approach to visual servoing in robotics. *IEEE Transactions on Robotics and Automation*, 8(3):313–326, June 1992.

S. Hutchinson, G.D. Hager, and P.I. Corke (1996). A tutorial on visual servo control. IEEE Transactions on Robotics and Automation, 12(5):651–670, October 1996.

E. Malis, F. Chaumette, & S. Boudet (1999). 2 1/2 d visual servoing. *IEEE Transactions on Robotics and Automation*, 15(2):238–250, April 1999.

Y. Mezouar & F. Chaumette (2002). Path planning for robust image-based control. *IEEE Transactions on Robotics and Automation*, 18(4):534–549, August 2002.

Y. Mezouar, H. Haj Abdelkader, P. Martinet,& F. Chaumette (2004). Central catadioptric visual servoing from 3d straight lines. *In IEEE/RSJ Int. Conf. on Intelligent Robots and Systems*, IROS'04, volume 1, pages 343–349, Sendai, Japan, September 2004.

E. Malis & S. Benhimane (2003). Vision-based control with respect to planar and non-planar objects using a zooming camera. *In IEEE International Conference on Advanced Robotics*, pages 863–869, July 2003.

R. Vidal, O. Shakernia, & S. Sastry (2003). Formation control of nonholonomic mobile robots with omnidirectional visual servoing and motion segmentation. *In IEEE International Conference on Robotics and Automation*, pages 584–589, Taipei, Taiwan, September 2003.

N. Winter, J. Gaspar, G. Lacey, & J. Santos-Victor (2000). Omnidirectional vision for robotnavigation. *In Proc. IEEE Workshop on Omnidirectional Vision*, OMNIVIS, pages 21–28, South Carolina, USA, June 2000.

22

Industrial Vision Systems, Real Time and Demanding Environment: a Working Case for Quality Control

J.C. Rodríguez-Rodríguez, A. Quesada-Arencibia and R. Moreno-Díaz jr
Institute for Cybernetics (IUCTC), Universidad de Las Palmas de Gran Canaria
Spain

1. Introduction

This chapter exposes an OCR (Optical Character Recognition) procedure able to work with very high speeds.
The architecture of the pattern recognition algorithm we present here includes certain concepts and results which are developed in previous publications [3,4]. We consider a production line of a beverage canning industry where cans with faulty imprinted use date or serial number have immediately to be discharged from the line.
The problem is well-known in the industrial scene. A code or a set of characters is registered on the surfaces (can bottoms) to very high speed. The registration can fail, can take place only partially, or can print wrong something. It is important to know with certainty what has happened. The most general solution is to read what has been printed immediately after print itself.
Surfaces are metallic (tinplate/aluminium) can bottoms for our particular case and the code denotes the limit of the use of the product (beer or similar).

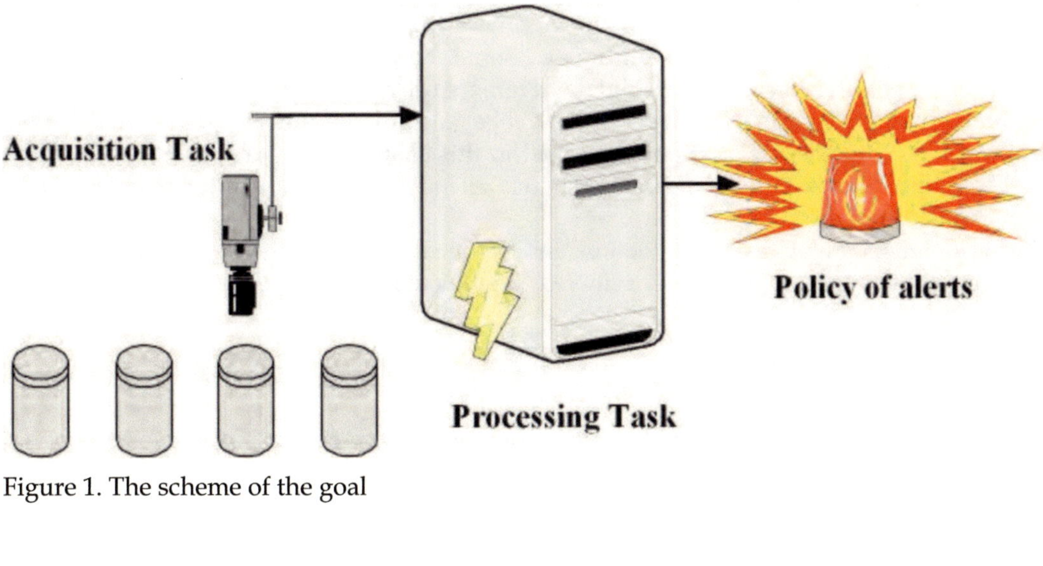

Figure 1. The scheme of the goal

Our goal is to build a capable application to process 120,000 cans per hour (35 cans per second). Nowadays, there is not application on the market which is able to manage this speed.
Therefore, our purpose has to do with an OCR that is confronted to two challenges:

1. Extraction of characters registered on a difficult surface.
2. Processing to very high speed.

Our keys to approach the problem have been:

1. Capable hardware
2. Domain restrictions
3. Intensive calibration
4. Parallel architecture
5. A progressive and aggressive reduction process of the interest area
6. Simple operations in integer arithmetic
7. Two independent tasks: Validation and Traineeship

Here is a brief explanation of these keys.

1. Capable hardware: The critical requirements are that the system is in fact invariant from its position during the text analysis of nearly 30.000 cans per minute in real time. The system has to be reliable and it relies on specific hardware. Thus, a high speed acquisition camera, an efficient acquisition board, a strong multiprocessing system and a considerable bandwidth for main memory load are the basic requirements.
2. Domain restrictions: A specialized environment which is very well known and restricted diminishes the number of contingencies to consider and allows therefore making presumptions easily. View section [1] and section [2].
3. Intensive calibration: There are two types of calibration of the system. The first type is to focus you on guaranteeing an enough quality of image for the treatment. It affects mainly physical parameters of the system. The second type has to do with the training of the system. The system should be trained with expected shapes for comparison.
4. Parallel architecture: Use intensive of multithread at several architecture layers in strong multiprocessing system.
5. A progressive and aggressive reduction process of the interest area: Reducing the input domain contributes to reduce the time of processing.
6. Simple operations in integer arithmetic: Sum, subtraction, multiplication of integers, and integer division are the absolutely dominant operations.
   In computers of general purpose, the integer arithmetic unit is faster than the float arithmetic unit. All procedures described in this chapter disregard float arithmetic for validation computation. The real essential operations are out side of the continuous cycle of validation.
7. Two independent tasks: Validation and Traineeship. Only The Validation Stage is described in this paper. However there is another stage in where the knowledge base is built.

2. Visual Scenario

We will work at an industrially dedicated environment; therefore the scene of events should be restricted. The reality will be mapped to two-dimensional matrixes with values between 0 - 255 representing different levels of grey. The possible states can be anticipated and listed: They are not too numerous neither very complex.

1. There can be nothing but cans and "background" in our field of vision.
2. The "background" has fixed and unchangeable visual characteristics [very dark colour].
3. There is NO background inside the border of a can.
4. Outside the border of a can there can only be background or other cans, but nothing else.

We are only interested in processing a single can within the frame of our camera. Therefore the physical acquisition platform will reinforce the presence of a single clean can in each capture. On the other hand, the hardware/software system will have to guarantee that no can will be lost during acquisition: all can processed by the installation will be processed too by our system.

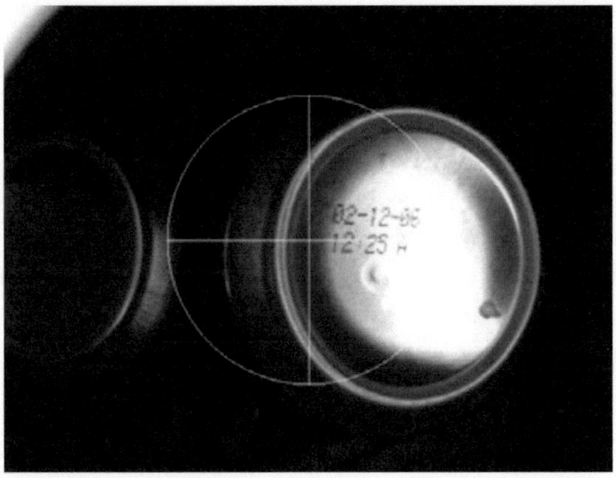

Figure 2. Typical acquisition from camera

3. System Preconditions

The code is associated to a single orientation and processing direction. In order to compare the expected code with the acquired code during validation both codes must have the same orientation and processing direction. The question is: How do we know the orientation and processing direction of the acquired code?

We have the following facts in our favour:

1. Once the print head and the acquisition source camera are fixed, orientation and processing direction are fixed for all cans.
2. The print head and the camera can be freely rotated if it is more convenient to our purposes. There are no other factors to consider except our own satisfaction.
3. Due to the previous fact, we can force to have an orientation and processing direction for the code. Therefore, these are known from the beginning before processing starts. It is not necessary to make a specific computation to get them.

As we will see soon, trying to have the orientation parallel to the natural vertical and horizontal axes will make the computation easier. This is what we are trying to get.

4. Elliptical Histograms Algorithm

The basis of algorithm of the elliptical histograms is analogous to the biological receptive field concept. The computation input field has a specialized shape that maximizes its

perceptiveness to certain stimuli. A purposeful task can be the simple stimulus presence detection.
The stimulus is the can. The task is to determine if a can is in the vision field or not. If so, estimate the position of its centre within the vision field.
The facts which support our procedure are:
1. The cans always are shown up at the vision field like can bottoms.
2. The can bottoms are always brighter than the background.
3. The can bottoms are nearly circular.
4. The can bottoms run a restricted and predictable trajectory inside the vision field.

The idea is to look for any measure that has maximum or minimum values according to fact that the can is present or absent. Arbitrary noise in the image should not provoke false positives or false negative easily. On the other hand, the measure should be computed fast.
The histogram is a classification and count of levels of grey steps. Provide the distribution of colour of a collection of points. It is a very fast operation because only it implies queries, comparisons and sums.
The fact 2) establishes that the presence/absence of a can modifies the distribution of color. Therefore, the fact 2) determines the sensibility to histograms.
We should look for an optimal collection of points that provides very different histograms according to the fact that the can is present or not. The collection of points should be efficient and avoiding unnecessary queries.

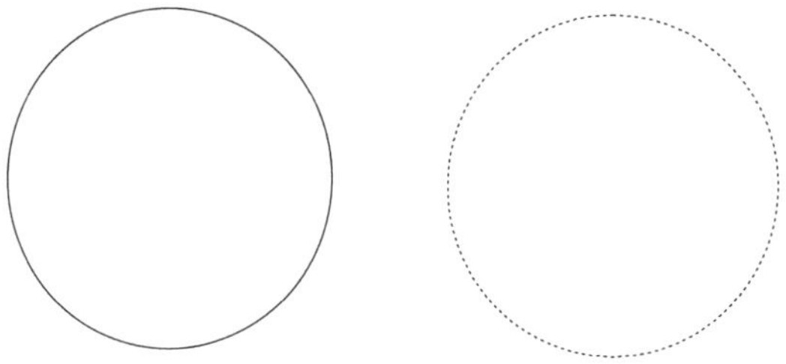

Figure 3. The receptive field shape and queries position

The fact 3) provides us what kind of shape should be looked for inside the image.
The circular shape is suitable like the collection of points of search. The receptive field is defined as a circle (i.e a circular line or circumference).
A sufficiently "bright" histogram for a particular receptive field can give only a hint that there is a can whose centre is also close to the centre of the histogram circle. So, it is an ON/OFF receptive field.
Besides, it is established in the section [2] that the unique objects that would invade the vision field are cans. Only the noise would be able to cause troubles. The shape circular is sufficient complex to distinguish between cans and shapes of luminous noise for the majority of cases.
The procedure would be:
1. A circle which has not been processed yet is chosen. If there is no not-processed circumference then it is declared that there are no cans in the image and we jump to step 5.
2. The histogram for that circular line is computed.
3. If the histogram is enough bright then it is declared that a can has been found and we jump to step 5.

4. Otherwise the circle is marked like processed and we return to step 1.
5. Status of the image declared!

Discussing the general idea, it gives us some hints to optimize making good use of the restrictions of the environment:

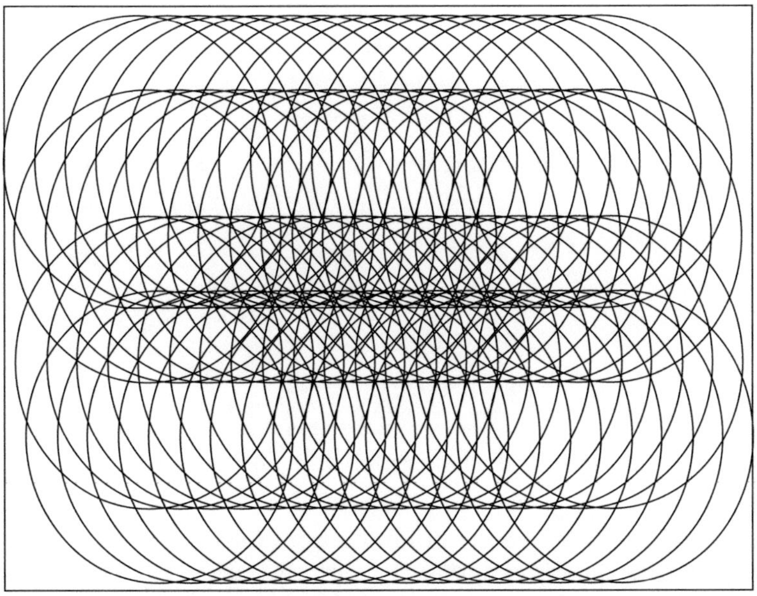

Figure 4. A can could be located at any position sweeping the image with the described receptive fields

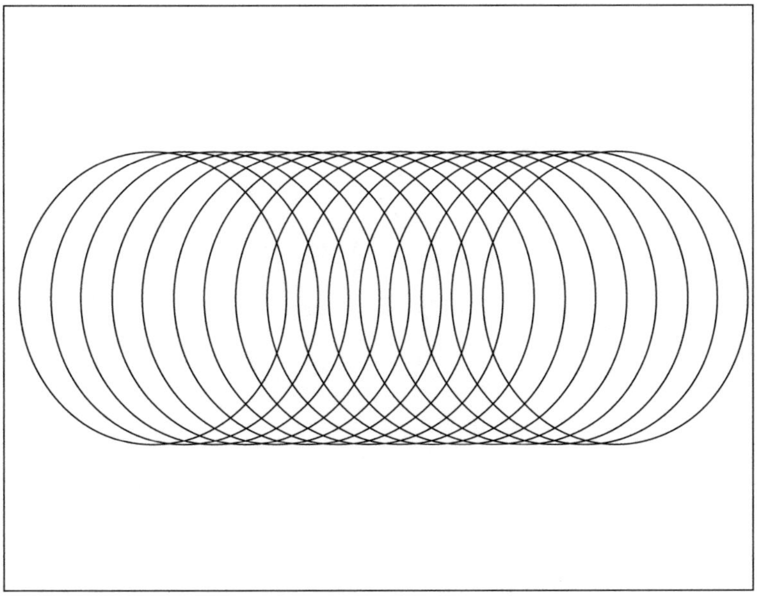

Figure 5. The nature of the chain of can filling imposes that cans move around in a restricted line so the search can be restricted to exploration of that axis of line

A new principle is:
Once the previous location of a circumference in a previous frame is known we can determine which is the next more-probable-position for relocating the can. The search stops immediately when the can is found. Therefore it will be tracked those circumferences that correspond to those positions in decreasing probability order.

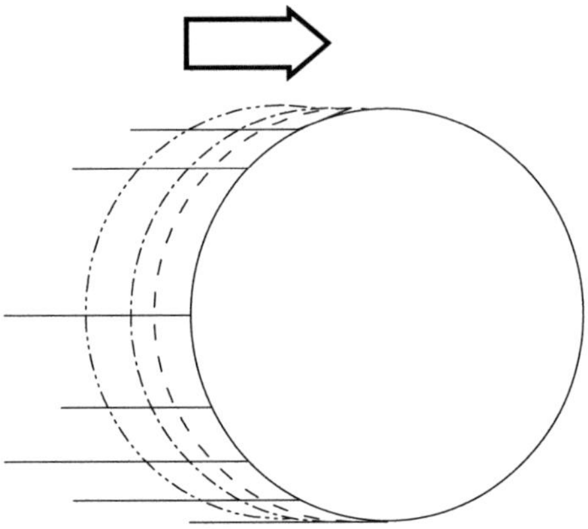

Figure 6. Processing the circles with greater probability of being active first can improve the speed

Why elliptical histograms? The frames produced from the camera are distorted due to the natural limitations of the quality of optics. This distortion does not affect of appreciable way the readability of the code. But the cans leave the circular shape as they get close to the boundaries of the image.

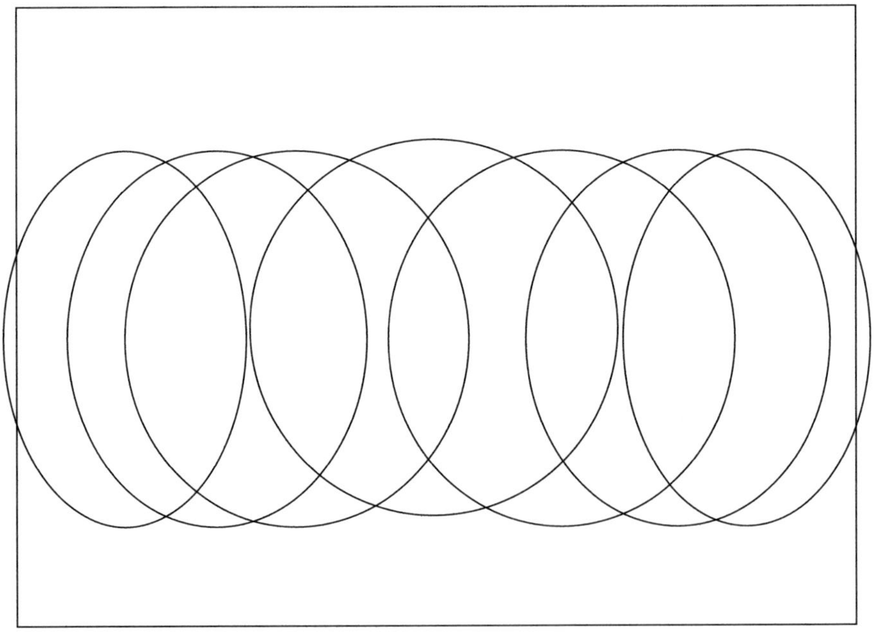

Figure 7. Sweeping with ellipses

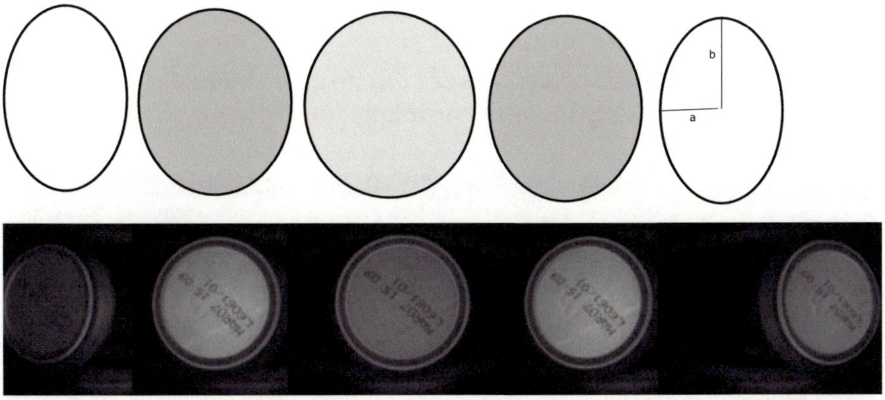

Figure 8. This gradual flattening is contemplated by the procedure turning the circumferences in ellipses. An additional advantage is that fewer points are processed

Can Counter

The can count is made using ellipse activation. There are three important facts:

1. The motion direction of the cans is previously well known (from left to right, or else, from right to left).
2. The ellipse activation order should correspond to that motion direction.
3. When a new can comes into scene, the ellipse activation order breaks the pattern of motion.

   The can counter counts the breakings of fact 3).

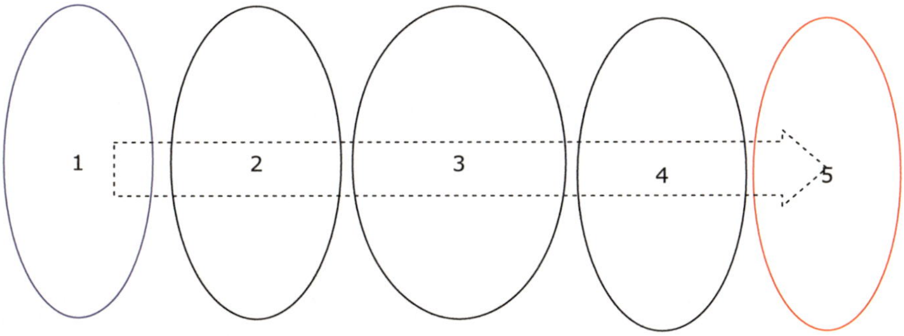

Figure 9. Natural order of ellipse activations

The normal can movement follows the motion sequence [1, 2, 3, 4, 5].
A mistake in the motion sequence (For example, [1, 2, 3, 5, 4]) means that a new can has come in the vision field of the camera completely.

5. Thickening

The pre-process of thickening improves the general quality of the image with a cheaply computer cost. It simplifies superfluous details of the image without harming the readability of the code.

Its main advantage is that it provides a code with less fragmented and more consistent characters.
Its main disadvantage is that characters can stick erroneously among themselves.
The procedure involves applying a limited convolution the winning ellipse of the algorithm of elliptical histograms.

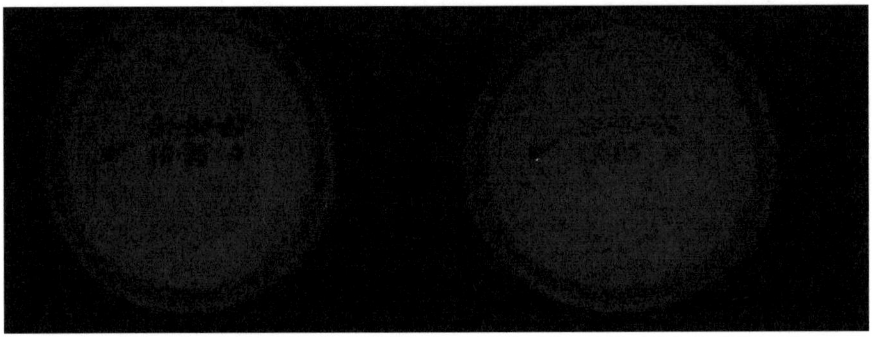

Figure 10. Image after thickening and image before thickening

a	b	c
d	e	f
g	h	i

$$= \mathrm{Min}(a,b,c,d,e,f,g,h,i)$$

Figure 11. This is the convolution mask. Thence there are no complex implicated operations

6. Segmentation by flooding

The reduction of the number of queries is the reason that justifies the application of this technique. A query is the reading/writing of a pixel of the actual image.
It is possible to go through every pixel of the image checking if they are part of the code. A systematic tour will give us the best results. However, it's very important to avoid unnecessary operations/queries. The Flooding Techniques are one of the possible solutions to use.
The mechanism of the flooding technique main goal (also known as Pixel Progressive Addition Method) is to obtain which is result as the systematic tour, but with less operations/queries.
It's use should be success full because it depends on two easily contrastable principles:

1. The majority of queries will give a negative result concerning their belonging to the code.
2. The queries results with positive code are those positions which have only a short-distance from each other positions.

The flooding as well as the segregation of points that are part of the code from those points that are not, groups the located points of code in useful sets. The pixels that form the main semantic object scene (the code) can be grouped in sub-semantic objects (characters). Therefore, this is the decisive step of transforming pixels into abstract entities (characters of code).

Here is the procedure:

1. Select a set of flooding seeds. The flooding seeds are driven queries with a higher probability of finding a code pixel. The selections of seeds are based on some heuristic knowledge.

0	0	0	0	0	0	0	0	0
0	0	0	0	1	0	0	0	0
0	0	0	1	0	1	0	0	0
0	0	0	0	0	1	0	0	0
0	0	0	0	1	0	0	0	0
0	0	0	1	0	0	0	0	0
0	0	0	1	1	1	0	0	0
0	0	0	0	0	0	0	0	0
0	0	0	0	0	0	0	0	0

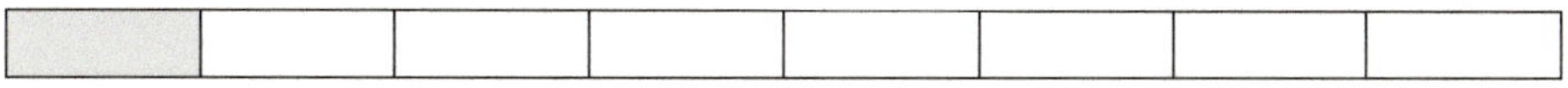

Figure 13. Randomly seeds without ink

2. Choose an not-yet-discarded seed, if there is no one available go to exit. If the seed has not yet been marked as visited, do it and go to step 3. Otherwise discard it and repeat step 2.
3. If there is no ink in the seed, declare it as sterile and discard it .Return to step 2. Otherwise go to step 4.

0	0	0	0	0	0	0	0	0
0	0	0	0	1	0	0	0	0
0	0	0	1	0	1	0	0	0
0	0	0	0	0	1	0	0	0
0	0	0	0	1	0	0	0	0
0	0	0	1	0	0	0	0	0
0	0	0	1	1	1	0	0	0
0	0	0	0	0	0	0	0	0
0	0	0	0	0	0	0	0	0

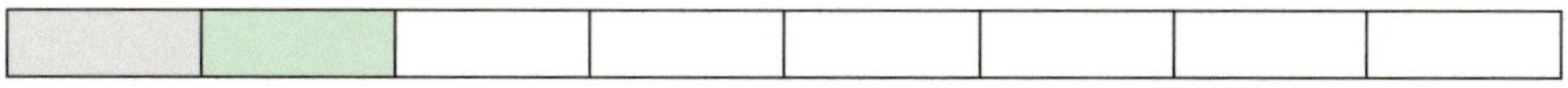

Figure 14. A seed with luck!

4. Open up a flooding point. The seed is declared as the flooding starting point.
5. Look up the immediate proximity neighbours marking all performed queries like visited neighbours. Go to step 6.

0	0	0	0	0	0	0	0	0
0	0	0	0	1	0	0	0	0
0	0	0	1	0	1	0	0	0
0	0	0	0	0	1	0	0	0
0	0	0	0	1	0	0	0	0
0	0	0	1	0	0	0	0	0
0	0	0	1	1	1	0	0	0
0	0	0	0	0	0	0	0	0
0	0	0	0	0	0	0	0	0

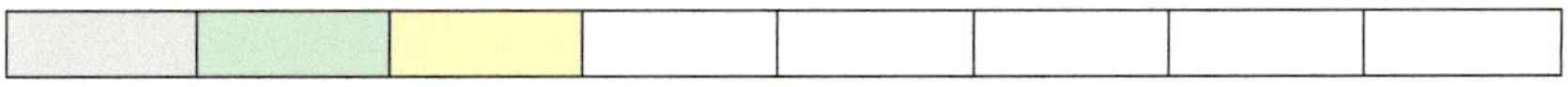

Figure 15. Inspecting neighbours

6. Declare all neighbour marked with ink as a flooding point. Return to step 5. If all neighbours with ink have been processed, go to step 7.

0	0	0	0	0	0	0	0	0
0	0	0	0	1	0	0	0	0
0	0	0	1	0	1	0	0	0
0	0	0	0	0	1	0	0	0
0	0	0	0	1	0	0	0	0
0	0	0	1	0	0	0	0	0
0	0	0	1	1	1	0	0	0
0	0	0	0	0	0	0	0	0
0	0	0	0	0	0	0	0	0

Figure 16. Inspecting neighbours of neighbours

7. Close the current flooding. Discard the current flooding if:
   - It has too many collected points (too big to be a character, so it is just noise).
   - it is too small to be a character (it is noise too) .

   Go to step 2.

0	0	0	0	0	0	0	0	0
0	0	0	0	1	0	0	0	0
0	0	0	1	0	1	0	0	0
0	0	0	0	0	1	0	0	0
0	0	0	0	1	0	0	0	0
0	0	0	1	0	0	0	0	0
0	0	0	1	1	1	0	0	0
0	0	0	0	0	0	0	0	0
0	0	0	0	0	0	0	0	0

Figure 17. The flooding task has concluded

8. Flooding Completed

7. Grouping

The main goal of Grouping is to distribute the flooded zones got in the previous stage between the real characters of the code. It is composed of three steps.

7.1 Division in Bands

This technique tries to separate the lines of printed code. Besides this, you can get additional useful information for noise suppression. The requirement is that the orientation of the expected code has to be known previously. This condition be comes true because it was established in the section [2].

The purpose of this technique is to divide the image in bands. A band is a longitudinal section of an image which is parallel to the code orientation axis. This technique tries to contain each of the different processed code lines in bands. Therefore, a band can be empty (or filled with noise) or contains a code line. Bands are described by their boundaries.

Ideally, the band boundaries are straight lines. However, a band boundary can not cut flooding zones. So it has to surround the flooding zones in an optimal way. Band boundaries have their starting points separated at a certain distance from each other, and should not cross between them.

The speciality of the technique consists of taking advantage of the interlineations code space. It is hope that the interlineations code space could be easily perceived by a band boundary.

The band boundaries are generated by the following procedure:

1. Assume an origin: The beginning of the boundary, and the direction of movement.
2. Check whether the end of the image has been reached or if there has been a cross between boundaries (a band boundary can never cross another boundary). If the check is positive, exit.
3. Apply a collision direction test with a flooded zone.
   3.1. If the test is negative, advance a step in a straight line (direction of movement)

3.2. If the test is positive we surrounded the flooded zone, choosing the direction of movement with less resistance. If there are several options of movement with equal resistance, we choose one randomly.

4. Return to step 2.

7.2 Splitting Flooded Zones

The use of the term "super-zone" is used to designate an oversized flooded zone. The oversize is exposed according to a criteria related the maximal size of the expected character. A super-zone indicates an anomaly. Here is the list of probable anomalies whose symptom causes the final identification of a super-zone:

1. Noise.
2. Two or more characters have merged among themselves in an error.
3. One or more characters have been merged to noise.
4. A severely deformed character.

In those cases the super-zone should be decomposed in sub-zones. Decomposition of super-zone is made by applying the same flooding algorithm described in chapter [5] but the input field is much more restrictive. The new input field will be the same image but with an inferior level of thickening.

The thickening defragment the image hiding their details [4]. Generally this is fine because the excess of details penalizes the general processing. Therefore, ignoring them normally is advantageous. Unfortunately some details that are inadvertently suppressed are critical at times. It is possible to recover the lost details making use of images with inferior levels of thickening.

Here is the procedure:

1. Only the points of coordinates that constitute the located super-zone will be processed. The grey levels will be recovered from a less-thickened image.
2. The segmentation by flooding will be applied like if is described in section [5] (Segmentation by Flooding). As a result, one or more flooded zones will be created.
3. The points of the super-zone which are not yet assigned by the previous step will be associated to the new zones according to some criteria like nearest neighbourhood.
4. If the criterion of step 3 is unable to reassign some points to a new specific flooded zone, these points will not be assigned evermore. The point will be labelled as background.
5. This set of new flooded zones (composed by one or more zones) will finally replace the previous super-zone.
6. If any of these new flooded zones comes out to be a new super-zone, it will be labelled as noise. So the procedure will not be applied recursively.

7.3 Merging flooded zones

In general two flooded zones can be merged if they overlap them self.

Let us define the rules of the overlay algorithm:

1. Our domain will be discrete because the flooded zones that are defined as finite set of point with coordinates in a discrete space. The point coordinates of the flooded zones are expressed like Cartesian pair in the plane.

2. The overlapping dimension of a flooded zone is equal to the greatest distance between the projected points of the flooded zone on the perpendicular axis of the overlapped axis.
3. The traced segment between the borderline points of the overlap dimension is denoted as overlap segment of flooded zone.
4. Two flooded zones are overlapped in relation to a suitable axis of overlay when it is possible to draw at least one parallel line to this axis that cuts its two overlap segments.
5. The overlay property is applied equally to all implicated flooded zones.
6. The overlay among flooded zones from different bands is always zero.
7. A flooded zone can overlap with multiple flooded zones.
8. The number of not-coincidental parallel lines of overlap is the dimensions of the overlay between two flooded zones. Even though the dimension of the overlay is equal for the two flooded zones, the degree of overlay of each flooded zone is the quotient among the fore mentioned dimension and the dimension of its overlapped axis.
9. A flooded zone is included by another one that is overlapped by the first, if all its points are intersected by the overlapped rays. Two or more flooded zones can include themselves mutually.
10. The distance among the overlap segment midpoints should not exceed a certain distance in order that the overlay will be accepted.

Here is the procedure description:

1. A table of overlay with the flooded zones is built.
   The overlay table is a collection of all degree of overlay between the existent flooded zones. It is calculated confronting all the zones among themselves applying the described rules.

The table construction require to establish the overlay axis perpendicular to the code orientation axis.

	Zone I	**Zone II**	**Zone III**	**Zone IV**	**...**
Zone I	0 %				
Zone II		0 %			
Zone III			0%		
Zone IV				0%	
...					

Table 1. Scheme of overlay table

The intersection of row II and column III supply the degree of overlay of the zone II on zone III.

2. The merging couples are recovered from table in strictly decreasing order of degree of overlay.
3. A merging is valid if the maximum size of the merged zone does not exceed the *maximum size for a character.* And the two most distant points of the merged zone do not exceed the limit *of size for a character.*

Once a successful merging was made the overlay table is recalculated for this new zone. On the other hand, the two zones that have been merged are suppressed.
The procedure is iterated. If no new fusions are possible, the procedure stops.

8. Validation

The steps of validation are:

1. Labels of Character
   It is possible to find the coordinates of the flooded codes in terms of the expected codes because it is known that the orientation and processing direction of the printing signs. We will label each flooded zone with the pair: (Line index, position of the character inside the line). In this way (1, 4) means second line (Zero is the first), fourth character.
2. Retrieval of expected character
   It is possible to recover the family of morphologies of the expected character of our base of morphologies of those characters learned by means of the described pair.

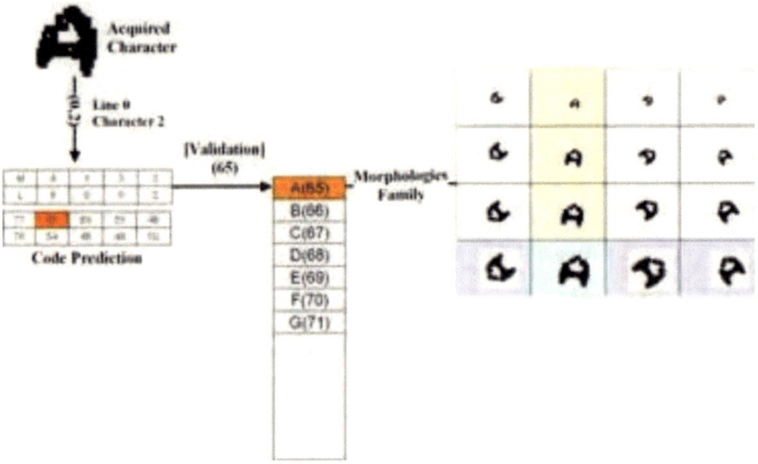

Figure 18. The steps for morphologies recovering

3. Comparison between expected characters and acquired characters
   First calculate the correlations of the acquired character against each one of the recovered morphologies. It is stops when finds a sufficiently seemed morphology.

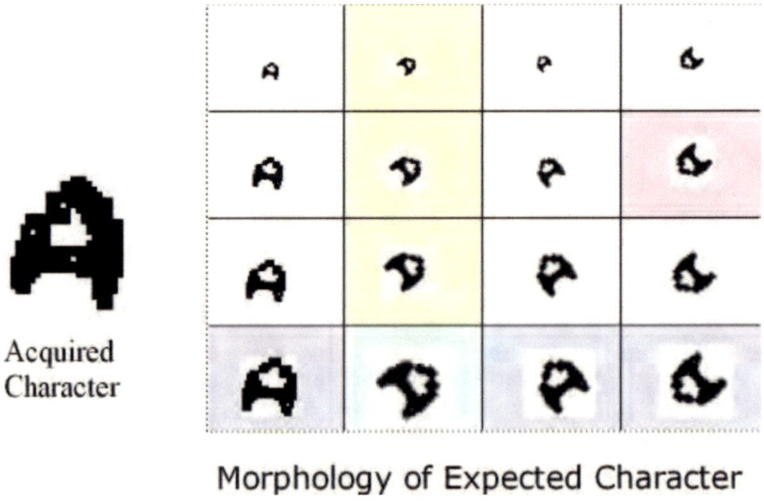

Figure.18. The strongly-hoped inputs for matching

4. Merging with the next character if an error
   If not coincidences/similarities occurs then it is applied a merging among the acquired character with the following should be made. Perhaps code dispersion has happened. Repeat steps 3-4 with the new acquired character. If it is not possible we must go to the next obtained character but we should persist with the expected actual character.
5. Policy of alerts
   If one or more expected characters are NOT found then they are NOT valid and we will declare NOT VALID. The policy of alerts, not described in this document, will make a decision how to act.

You must note: Templates are morphologic representations of the characters. The templates are processed and stored like rectangular bitmaps. The one bit marks presence of ink and the zero bit marks absence ink. A character has a set of associated morphologic templates called morphologies family.

9. Conclusions and future work

In this paper we studied a series of algorithms based on simple operations performed with fast arithmetic. The restriction on the used operations is due to the stress-producing requests of speed. Unfortunately, the obtained results prove that the series of algorithms mentioned IS NOT SUFFICIENT for the requirements.

The problem results in that the processing time for each can is variable and sometimes it is excessive. This is due to the fact that each can can offer different challenges of process complexity. For example cans with a lot of noise generate more flooded zones, and the number of flooded zones enlarges the load of the process. Therefore, some cans are validated more slowly than other cans.

It is not possible to delay the processing of every can. There can be no queues of processes of cans. It is important to manage of that the maximum time of processing per can does not exceed the safety time.[i.e. The time interval between the begin of recording a can and the begin of recording the next can].

The immediate future work will be implement multithreading versions of the series of algorithms. On the other hand, the algorithms could run simultaneously. This is possible if consecutive beers are processed at same time.

In the following scheme, a biologically inspired architecture for this application is presented. The basic ideas of multichanneling in the visual tract are present. On the input image, a multiprocess task is first triggered to extract the area of interest where first text is to be located. Thus, a second multichannel analysis analysis the possible singularities in the text. The final validation consists of determining the coherence and plausibility of text syntactically and semantically. All these processes are independent and are separately operated. Thus, the labels {1}, {2}, {3} and {4} denote different stages within the same visual tract.

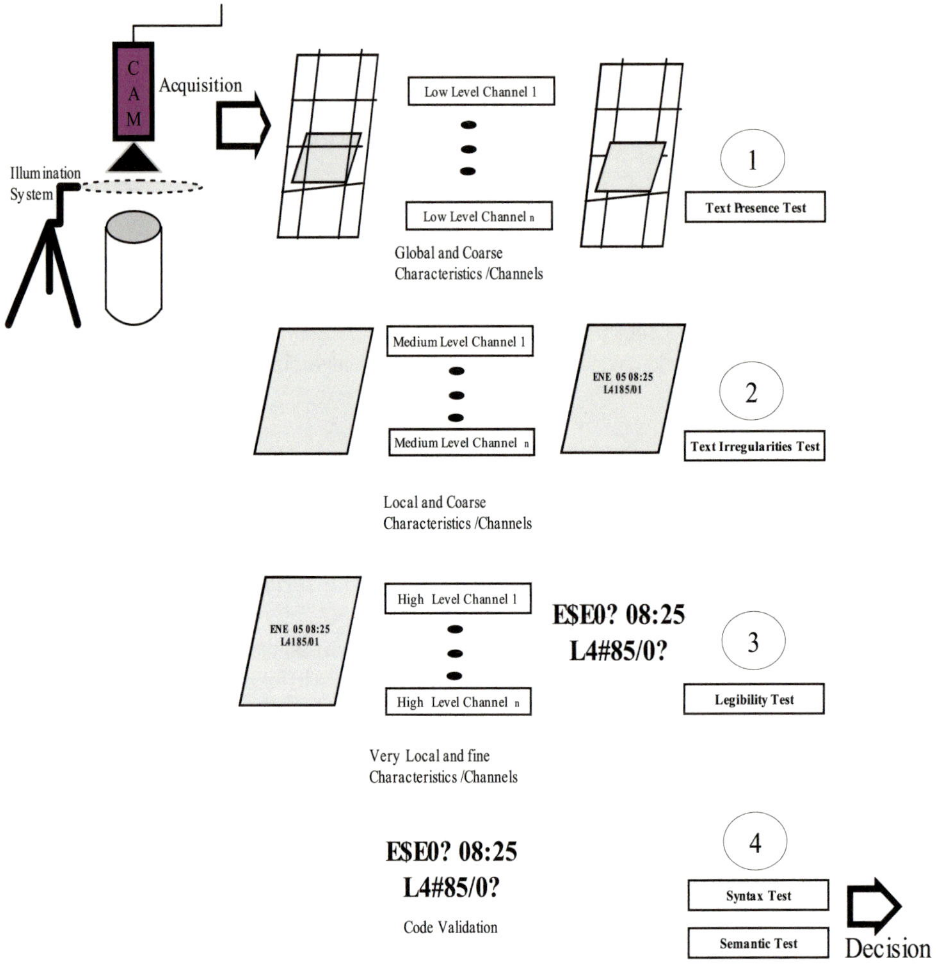

10. References

Alemán-Flores, M., Leibovic, K.N., Moreno Díaz jr, R.: A computacional Model for Visual Size, Location and Movement, Springer Lectura Notes in *Computer Science*, Vol 1333. Springer-Verlag. Berlin Heidelberg New York (1997) 406-419

Quesada-Arencibia, A., Moreno-Díaz jr, R., Alemán-Flores, M., Leibovic, K.N: Two Parallel Channel CAST Vision System for Motion Analysis. Springer Lecture Notes in *Computer Science*, Vol. 2178. Springer-Verlag. Heidelberg New York (2001) 316-327

Quesada-Arencibia, A.: Un Sistema Bioinspirado de Análisis y Seguimiento Visual de Movimiento. *Doctoral Dissertation. PhD Thesys.* Universidad de Las Palmas de Gran Canaria (2001)

J.C. Rodríguez Rodríguez, A.Quesada-Arencibia, R.Moreno-Díaz jr, and K.N. Leibovic: *On Parallel Channel Modelling of Retinal Processes* Vol 2809 Springer-Verlag. Berlin Heidelberg New York (2003) 471-481

Leibovic, K.N., *Science of Vision*, Springer Verlag, New York, 1990.

New Types of Keypoints for Detecting Known Objects in Visual Search Tasks

Andrzej Śluzek[1,2] and Md Saiful Islam[1,3]
[1]*Nanyang Technological University,* [2]*SWPS,* [3]*Dhaka University of Engineering and Technology*
[1]*Singapore,* [2]*Poland,* [3]*Bangladesh*

1. Introduction

Visual exploration of unknown environments is considered a typical and highly important task in intelligent robotics. Although robots with visual capabilities comparable to human skills (e.g. mushroom-picking robots or bird-viewing robots) are apparently unachievable in the near future, but the concept of robots able to search for known objects in unknown surroundings is one of the ultimate goals for machine vision applications. In the scenarios that are currently envisaged, the expectations should be realistically limited. Nevertheless, one can expect that a robot, after a visual presentation of an object of interest, should be able to "learn" it and, subsequently, to detect the same object in complex scenes which may be degraded by typical effects, i.e. partial visibility of the objects (due to occlusions and/or poor illumination) and their unpredictable locations. The purpose of this chapter is to propose a novel mechanism that is potentially useful (it has been confirmed by promising preliminary results) in such applications.

Several theories exist explaining the human perception of objects (e.g. Edelman, 1997). Some researchers promote the importance of multiple model views (e.g. Tarr et al., 1997) others (e.g. Biederman, 1987) postulate viewpoint invariants in the form of shape primitives (geons). From all the theories, however, the practical conclusion is that vision systems detecting objects in a human-like manner should use locally-perceived features as the fundamental tool for matching the scene content to the models of known objects.

The idea of using local features (keypoints, local visual saliencies, interest points, characteristic points, corner points - several almost equivalent names exist) in machine vision can be traced back to the 80's (e.g. Moravec, 1983; Harris & Stephens, 1988). Although stereovision and motion tracking were initially the most typical applications, it was later found that the same approach can be used in more challenging tasks (e.g. matching images in order to detect partially hidden objects). A well-known Harris-Plessey operator (Harris & Stephens, 1988) was combined with local descriptors of detected points to solve object recognition problems in which local features from analysed images are matched against a database of images depicting known objects (e.g. Schmid & Mohr, 1995). The intention was to retrieve images containing arbitrarily rotated and partially occluded objects.

Subsequently developed keypoint detectors address the issues of scale changes (this was the weakest point of the original detectors) and perspective distortions. Generally, to achieve scale invariance of local features, computationally expensive scale-space approaches are used (e.g. Lowe, 2004; Mikolajczyk & Schmid, 2004). So far, no method is known that can scale-invariantly match local features using a one-size window for scanning images captured in arbitrarily changing scales. The perspective distortions are usually approximated by affine transformations (or even ignored altogether). This is acceptable since only relatively minor distortions are typically assumed. Stronger deformations are avoided by using multiple views (differing usually by 15-30 degrees) to model 3D database objects.

Our paper presents how to integrate and expand selected ideas from the abovementioned theories and techniques into an alternative framework that could satisfy the practical requirements of robotic vision systems at lower computational costs than other currently existing solutions. Generally, we follow the fundamental concepts presented in previously published works (e.g. Huttenlocher & Ullman, 1990; Wolfson & Rigoutsos, 1997; Häusler & Ritter, 1999; Ulrich et al., 2003; etc.). In particular:

1. Database objects are represented by 2D images. Multiple images of the same object are used if 3D transformations of the object are expected in the captured scenes, while a single image is needed if only 2D transformations are envisaged.
2. Database objects are modelled as a set of locally computed features (keypoints) characterised by their descriptors. The geometric constraints of the set (i.e. length and orientation of vectors joining the keypoints) are also stored.
3. Keypoints of the same categories are extracted from captured scenes. Subsequently, those keypoints are matched to the models of database objects. If a sufficient number of the keypoints are consistently (i.e. satisfying the geometric constraints of the model) matched to a certain model image, the corresponding database object is considered found in the scene.

What makes our method novel is the definition of local features (keypoints). Therefore, the major sections of this chapter discuss the proposed keypoints and present exemplary results obtained using such keypoints. The actual object detection and/or localisation are only briefly mentioned since the methods used follow the algorithms published in our previous papers or papers of other authors.

Typically used keypoints are based directly (e.g. Harris & Stephens, 1988) or indirectly (e.g. Lowe, 2004; Mikolajczyk & Schmid, 2004) on derivatives of the intensity functions. Such keypoints have many advantages but certain disadvantages as well. For example, the scanning window over which the keypoints are computed should be resized according to the scale of objects present in the image. If the scale is unknown (which is the most typical scenario) additional computations and/or assumptions are necessary. Some authors use computationally intensive search for the optimum scale at which the current keypoint should be processed (e.g. SIFT detector in Lowe, 2004) while others propose a simplifying (but nevertheless justifiable for robotic application) assumption that only a few scales are used and the object would be identified when its distance to the capturing camera corresponds to one of those scales (e.g. Islam et al., 2005). An additional disadvantage of derivation-based keypoints is that some photometric transformations (e.g. excessively high contrasts) may distort the captured image to the point where the original differential properties of the intensities are lost while the visual content of the image is still readable.

We propose keypoints based on the local structural properties of the images, i.e. the contents of scanning windows are approximated by a certain number of structures (parameterised patterns). If the approximation if sufficiently accurate, a keypoint is built and characterised by the parameters describing this approximation. The fundamentals of such keypoints are presented in Section 2.

In Section 3, we discuss how to use such approximation-based keypoints for object detection (including scale-invariance issues). It is shown that, in spite of using uniform scanning windows, objects at arbitrary scales can be matched (within a certain range of scales). Section 4 presents exemplary results of the proposed technique and briefly explains the further steps of object detection. Conclusions and additional remarks are given in Section 5.

2. Approximation-based Keypoints

2.1 Pattern-based Approximations

Recently (in Sluzek, 2005) a method has been proposed for approximating circular images with selected predefined patterns. Although corners and corner-like patterns (e.g. junctions) are particularly popular and important, the method is applicable to any parameter-defined patterns (both grey-level and colour ones, though the latter are not discussed in this chapter).

We assume that a *grey-level circular pattern* is modelled by several configuration parameters and intensity parameters (as shown in exemplary patterns given in Figure 1). Typical patterns are specified by 2-3 configuration parameters and 2-3 intensities. The radius $\boldsymbol{R}$ of a pattern can be arbitrarily selected. Thus, if a configuration parameter is a length (e.g. β_1 in Figure 1B, or β_1 and β_2 in Figure 1C) it should be measured both absolutely and relatively to the radius.

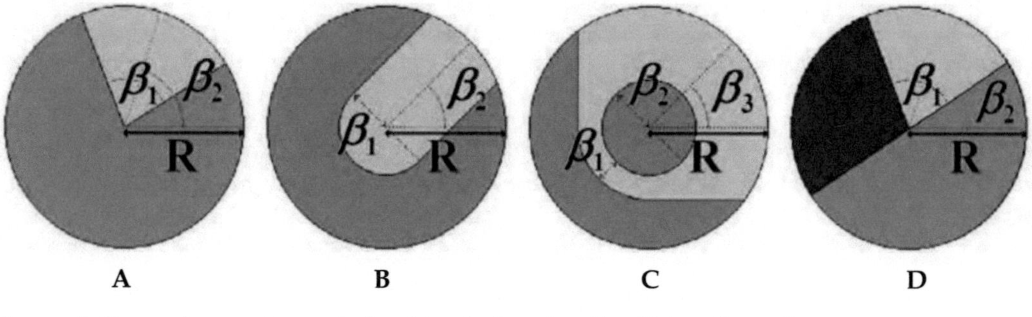

Figure 1. Exemplary patterns defined in circles of radius $\boldsymbol{R}$ (configuration parameters shown)

Circular patterns are considered templates that would be matched to other circular images (or rather to circular windows of a larger image) in order to determine how well that image can be approximated by given patterns. In other words, the optimum values of the parameters should be found to identify the best pattern approximation. This idea (originally applied to edge detection) can be traced back to the 70's (e.g. Hueckel, 1973).

In our previous papers (e.g. Sluzek, 2005) it is explained how to build the optimum approximations for various template patterns (or, alternatively, how to determine that no such approximation exists) using locally computed intensity moments. For several patterns, the explicit solutions are given. For example, the orientation angle β_2 of a corner approximation (see Figure 1A) is obtained from

$$\beta_2 = \arctan 2(\pm m_{01}, \pm m_{10}) \tag{1}$$

while the angular width β_1 is computed as

$$\beta_1 = 2\arcsin\sqrt{1 - \frac{16[(m_{20} - m_{02})^2 + 4m_{11}^2]}{9R^2\left(m_{10}^2 + m_{01}^2\right)}} \tag{2}$$

For T-junctions (Figure 1D) β_1 angular width and β_2 orientation angle can found from

$$\frac{\pi}{2} - \beta_2 - \frac{\beta_1}{2} = \frac{\arctan 2(\pm m_{02} \mp m_{20}, \pm 2m_{11})}{2} \tag{3}$$

and

$$m_{01}\cos\beta_2 - m_{10}\sin\beta_2 = \pm\frac{4}{3R}\sqrt{(m_{20} - m_{02})^2 + 4m_{11}{}^2} \tag{4}$$

where m_{10}, m_{20}, etc. are moments of the corresponding orders computed in the coordinate system attached to the centre of circular windows.
The intensities of such approximations can be estimated using other moment-based expressions (details in Sluzek, 2005).
Exemplary circular windows (containing actual corners, T-junctions and more random contents) are given in the top row of Figure 2. The bottom row shows the optimum corner or T-junction approximations. For some irregular images the approximations do not exist, i.e. the corresponding equations have no solutions.

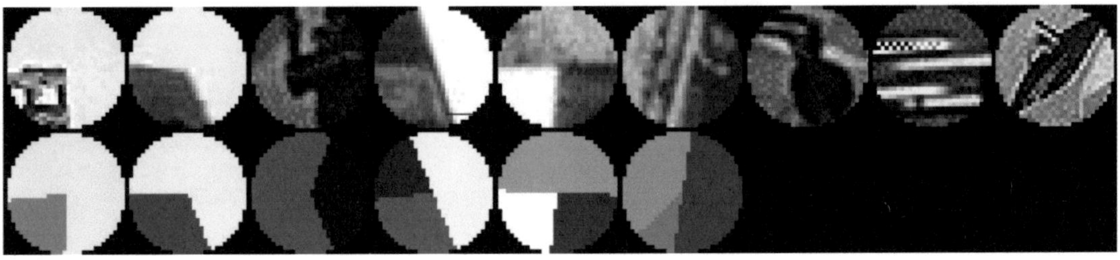

Figure 2. Optimum approximations (using corner or T-junction patterns) for selected circular images of 15-pixel radius

It can be straightforwardly proven that results produced by Eqs (1)-(4) are invariant under linear illumination changes, and that non-orientation configuration parameters (e.g. angular widths β_1 in Figs 1A and 1D) are invariant under any 2D similarity transformation. Extensive tests have also indicated that the results are stable (unlike, for example, the corner approximations discussed by Rosin, 1999) under high- and low-frequency noise, image texturization and partial over- and under-saturation of intensities. The same level of stability has been confirmed for other circular patterns.

2.2 Approximation-based Model Keypoints

Examples in Figure 2 show that even if the approximation exists, there might be a significant visual difference between a circular image and its approximation. Thus, if we can measure the level of similarity between an image and its approximation, the optimum approximation (i.e. the approximation with the highest similarity) indicates how accurately the pattern of interest is actually "seen" in the image.

Alternative methods of quantifying similarity between an image and its pattern approximation have been given in past papers (Sluzek, 2005; Sluzek, 2006). Unfortunately, the complexity of both methods is as high as the complexity of building the approximations. It has been eventually found that highly satisfactory results can be achieved in a simpler way by comparing moments of circular images (these moment have to be computed anyway) and moments of their approximations (those moments can be immediately calculated from the parameters of the approximation). Thus, the similarity between a circular image ***I*** and its approximation ***AI*** can be quantified using one of the following *similarity functions*:

$$sim_1(I,AI) = K - \alpha \frac{abs(m_{20} - ma_{20}) + abs(m_{02} - ma_{02}) + abs(m_{11} - ma_{11})}{m_{20} + m_{02} + abs(m_{11})} \tag{5}$$

$$sim_2(I,AI) = K - \alpha \frac{abs(m_{10} - ma_{10}) + abs(m_{01} - ma_{01})}{abs(m_{10}) + abs(m_{01})} \tag{6}$$

where m_{pq} and ma_{pq} are moments of ***I*** and ***AI*** (respectively) and ***K***, α are arbitrarily selected positive values.

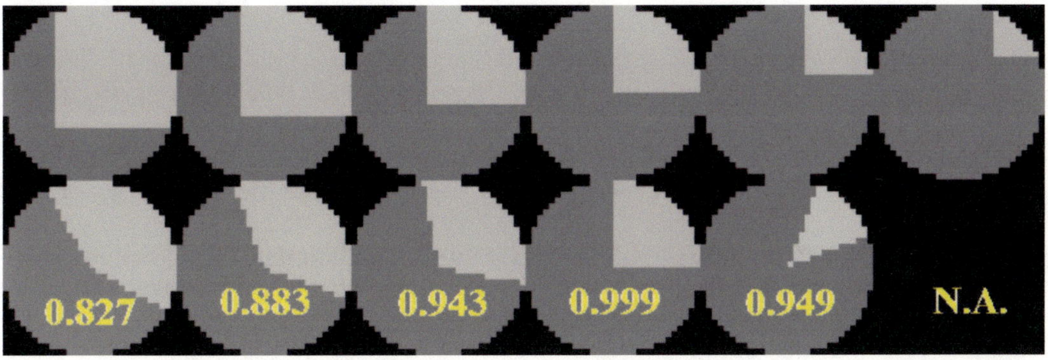

Figure 3. *Top row*: a sequence of windows moving across a high-quality corner image. *Bottom row*: corresponding corner approximations and the similarity levels (for the last window the corner approximation does not exist)

If at certain location an image contains a fragment similar to the pattern of interest, a high level of similarity between the content of a scanning window located there and its approximation is expected. However, a high similarity level would be found not only for the actual location but also for neighbouring locations. The similarity, nevertheless, reaches a local maximum at the location. Figure 3 illustrates this effect.

Moreover, if an image contains a certain pattern, the similarity between the window content and the approximations exists for a certain range of radii of the scanning window and the approximations are consistent over this range of radii (instead, the scanning window may remain the same, but the image is resized correspondingly over the range of scales). An example showing such a consistency both for the configuration and intensity parameters for a selected fragment of a digital image (containing a T-junction) is given in Figure 4.

Thus, our proposal of the novel type of keypoints is based on the above discussion.

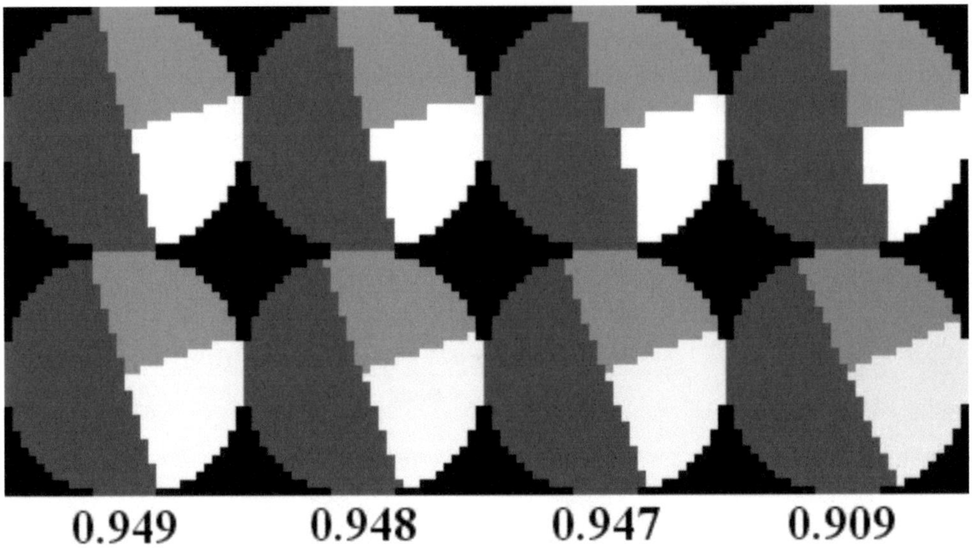

Figure 4. *Top row*: a sequence of 15-pixel windows over a gradually enlarged image of a T-junction. *Bottom row*: corresponding T-junction approximations and the similarity levels

Definition 1

For a given image, pixel (x,y) is (subject to additional requirements explained below) an *approximation-based model keypoint* (shortly *model keypoint*) defined by a circular pattern ***TP*** if for the scanning windows located at (x,y):

1. ***TP*** pattern-based approximation exists for each radius $\boldsymbol{R}$ from a certain range $(\boldsymbol{R_1}, \boldsymbol{R_2})$.
2. The approximations have consistently similar parameters over the whole range of radii $(\boldsymbol{R_1}, \boldsymbol{R_2})$.
3. If several neighbouring pixels satisfying (1) and (2) exist, the model keypoint is located at the pixel where the *similarity* between the scanning windows and their approximations reaches a local maximum.

Typically recommended additional requirements (introduced for practical reasons) are as follows:

- Similarities between the window contents and the approximations should be sufficiently high (keypoints that inaccurately depict the pattern are less useful than the accurate ones).
- Contrasts between intensity parameters of the produced approximation (see Figure 1) should exceed a predefined threshold (keypoints that can be hardly seen usually have no practical importance). For 256-level images, the recommended thresholds are in 15-25 range.
- The similarity functions can by additionally modified proportionally to the contrasts between intensities of the produced approximation (less accurate keypoints with better contrasts might be more important than poorly contrasted keypoints of high accuracy).
- Pattern-specific constraints may exist. For example, the angular width of a corner approximation should not be too close to 180° (it becomes an edge then) or to 0° (it effectively becomes a line tip).

It should be noted that the proposed definition of approximation-based model keypoints is not limited by the proposed method of computing the approximations. In fact, the definition is applicable to any other technique where image fragments similar to selected patterns of interest are searched for.

We propose to use the above-defined *model* keypoints for *model* images of the objects of interest. First of all, such keypoints are stable prominent features that are likely to be preserved in any other image that contains the same fragmnent of the object even if the viewing conditions are changed. Secondly, the number of such high-quality keypoints is usually limited (for a single pattern) even in complex objects. However, if several different patterns are used, the model image can still contain enough keypoints for a reliable detection under partial occlusions. Nevertheless, keypoint candidates from inspected images are matched to a limited number of potential counterparts (those of the same pattern only). Computational complexity of model keypoint detection is quite high because we have to examine each location using scanning windows in numerous scales covering the whole range ($\boldsymbol{R}_1$, $\boldsymbol{R}_2$). Although the moment calculations are reusable, the equations for parameter estimations should be solved separately for each radius. Since model-building operations are usually performed offline, this disadvantage is acceptable. In the next sub-section the issue of online keypoint detection is discussed. This would be important in a real-time search for objects of interest, i.e. in robotic vision applications.

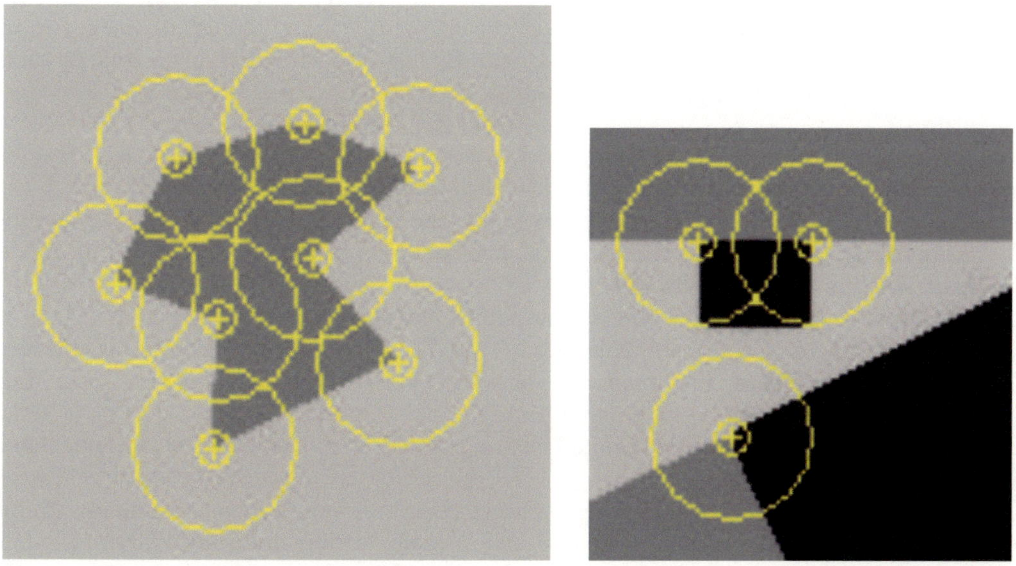

Figure 5. Corner-based model keypoints and 90° T-junction-based model keypoints detected in simple images of good quality. Scanning window radii range from 5 to 20 pixels

Figs 5 and 6 show a few examples of images with model keypoints detected for corner and 90° T-junction patterns. Window radii ranging from 5 to 20 pixels have been used. It should be noticed that in simple images of good quality the model keypoints look prominent to human vision as well. For more complex images, however, many model keypoints look inconspicuously (see Figure 6). Nevertheless, they are also stable features that are consistently present (at least many of them) when the image is distorted.

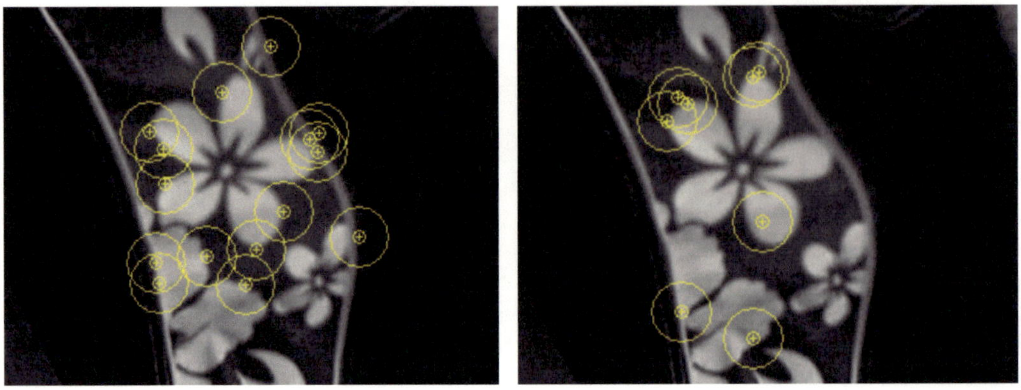

A B

Figure 6. Corner-based model keypoints (A) and 90° T-junction-based model keypoints (B) detected in a more complex image of normal quality. Scanning window radii range from 5 to 20 pixels

2.3 Scene Keypoints for Object Detection

Computational complexity of model keypoints may be too high for real-time applications of machine vision. If, however, similar keypoints can be detected online in inspected images, model keypoints would be very reliable references for matching content of images to the available models. Therefore, we propose a simplified variant of model keypoints, so-called *scene keypoints*. The definition of *scene keypoints* is very similar to Def. 1.

Definition 2

For a given image, pixel (x,y) is an *approximation-based scene keypoint of radius* $\boldsymbol{R}$ (shortly *scene keypoint*) defined by a circular pattern $\boldsymbol{TP}$ if for the scanning windows located at (x,y):

1. The approximations by $\boldsymbol{TP}$ pattern exist for the scanning radius $\boldsymbol{R}$ and for another radius $\boldsymbol{R_{sub}}$, where $\boldsymbol{R_{sub}}$ is a predefined constant percentage of $\boldsymbol{R}$ (the recommended value for $\boldsymbol{R_{sub}}$ is approx. 70% of $\boldsymbol{R}$).
2. The approximations parameters obtained for $\boldsymbol{R}$ and $\boldsymbol{R_{sub}}$ radii are similar.
3. If several neighbouring pixels satisfying (1) and (2) exist, the scene keypoint is located at the pixel where the *similarity* between both scanning windows and their approximations reaches a local maximum.

Usually, the practical constraints defined and explained after Def. 1 are also applicable to the above definition.

Computational complexity of detecting scene keypoints is much lower. Moments of only two windows ($\boldsymbol{R}$ and $\boldsymbol{R_{sub}}$ radius) are computed at each location, and reusability of moment calculations both at the current location and for neighbour pixels can be exploited. The equations for parameter identification are also used only twice.

Figs 7 and 8 contain exemplary images with scene keypoints detected (for corners and 90° T-junctions) using windows of radii 10 and 7 pixels. Obviously, for the same images the number is scene keypoints is larger than the number of model keypoints because the detection algorithm is much less restrictive. Even though for perfect-quality images (compare Figure 5 to Figure 7) we would expect the same keypoints, the presence of additional keypoints can be explained by digital effects and mathematical properties of the moments used. Nevertheless, each model keypoint is also always detected as a scene keypoint

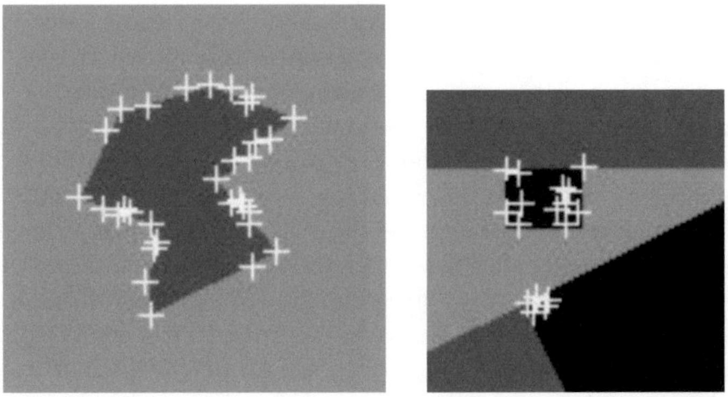

A B

Figure 7. Corner-based 90° scene keypoints (A) and T-junction-based scene keypoints (B) detected in the images from Figure 5. Scanning window radii are 7 and 10 pixels

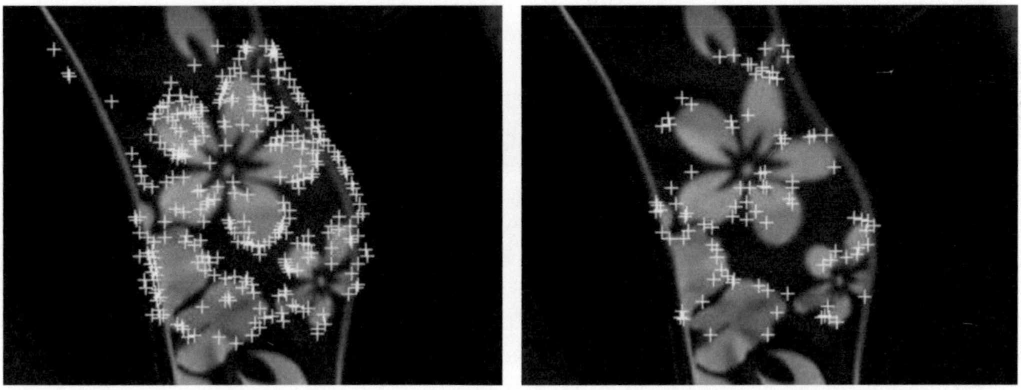

A B

Figure 8. Corner-based scene keypoints (A) and 90° T-junction-based scene keypoints (B) detected in the image from Figure 6. Scanning window radii are 7 and 10 pixels

Matching scene keypoints extracted from analysed images to the database model keypoints is the fundamental operation in the proposed object detection framework. The following section discusses practical aspects of matching. In particular, the adaptability of the method (through selection of thresholds and matching rules) is highlighted.

3. Matching Keypoints for Object Detection

Matching keypoints extracted from images to the database keypoints is used in the majority of works where the goal is to identify objects that might be partially occluded or overlapping (e.g. Lowe, 2004; Mikolajczyk & Schmid, 2004; Islam, 2006; etc.). Unfortunately, the numbers of keypoints are usually very large. Typical scenes used for experiments (e.g. Islam, 2006) contain hundreds of keypoints, while the number of keypoints in databases with just a few objects captured from a reasonable number of viewpoints can easily reach tens of thousands. Thus, the matching procedures become a serious computational problem. In order to optimise the matching and to avoid too many potential matches, researches either propose multidimensional descriptors of the keypoints and/or use carefully designed matching schemes. For example, 128 gradient-based directional descriptors are used in Lowe, 2004, while in Islam, 2006 only five moment descriptors are used but an efficient hashing technique has been developed to speed up keypoint matching.

In the proposed method, the abovemetioned problems are significantly simplified. Even if the overall number of model keypoints is large, they are divided into different categories (defined by different patterns) that can be handled independently. Scene keypoints are similarly divided into the same categories (even though the total number of scene keypoints for typical images may look larger than the numbers seen in other works). Eventually, each scene keypoint is only matched to the model keypoints in the same category which greatly reduced the computational efforts and allows parallelisation of the matching process.

Descriptors of both model and scene keypoints are obviously parameters of the corresponding pattern approximations. Such descriptors can be used more selectively than other descriptors (e.g. Koenderink & van Doorn, 1987; Lowe, 2004; Islam, 2006, etc.) that are based on general properties of image intensities. Generally, the processes of keypoint detection and matching can be adaptively tuned to various applications. Three issues are highlighted below (the problem is scale invariance is separately discussed in Subsection 3.1).

Thresholds

The number of extracted keypoints depends on several threshold values (see Subsections 2.2 and 2.3) defining the acceptable accuracy of pattern approximations and the minimum levels of visual prominence (contrasts) of the scene keypoints. It is possible, for example, to demand high accuracy and to accept very low contrasts. Then the method would be able to identify only those image fragments that are very accurately approximated by the patterns used. However, such fragments may not be even visible to a human eye. Typically, such requirements can be used for search in poorly illuminated scenes (detection of frauds in images may be another application). Alternatively, only highly-contrasted approximations could be accepted as keypoints with less demands regarding the accuracy of the approximations. This would be potentially useful for detecting objects that may be seen differently than in the database images (but the scenes are expected to be well illuminated). Moreover, the level of acceptable differences between the descriptors of model keypoints and scene keypoints determines the overall behaviour of the method (high numbers of keypoints with possibly many false positives *versus* high confidence keypoints only).

Configuration parameters

The configuration parameters of keypoint approximations have a higher priority as they specify geometry of the local structures of the observed scenes. However, the parameters defining rotations of the patterns (e.g. β_2 angle in Figs 1A, 1B and 1D) should be carefully used for matching (unless the search is for objects at certain orientations). Generally, the orientation parameters are used only in later stages (see Section 4). Moreover, parameters indicating distances (e.g. β_1 in Figs 1B and 1C) should be measured both absolutely and relatively to the window radius (for scale invariance, more in Subsection 3.1).

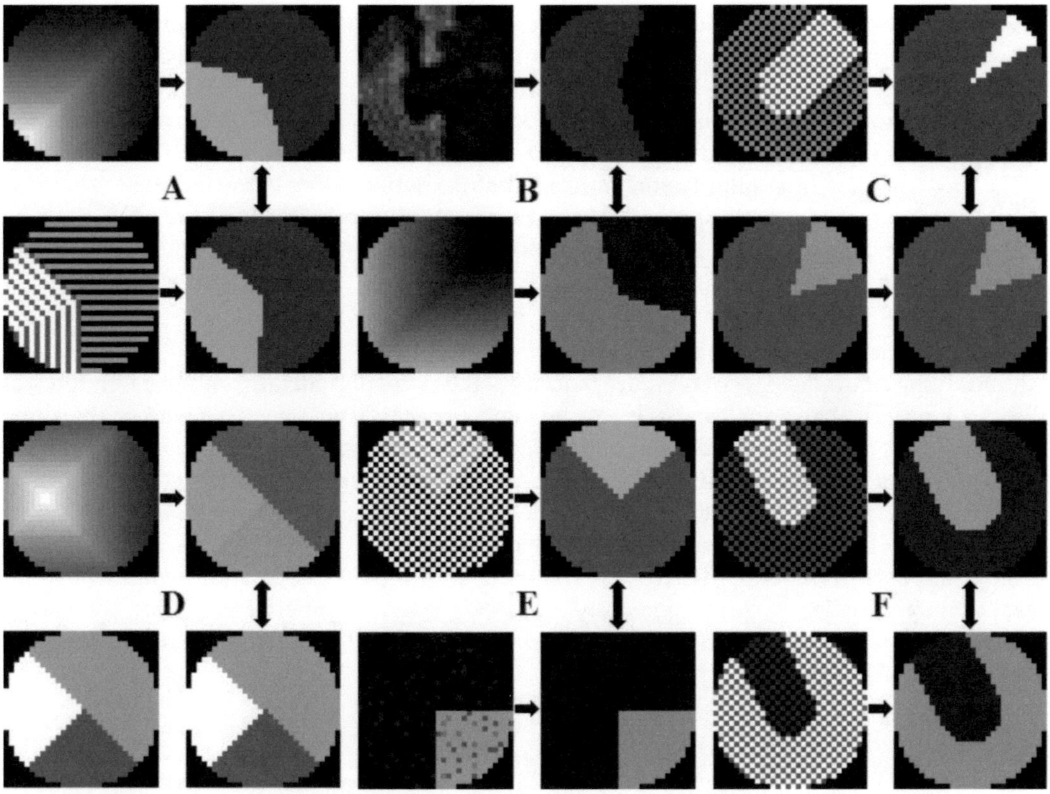

Figure 9. Examples of windows matched using different patterns and for diversified conditions (optimum approximations also shown for references):

(A) Low accuracy of approximations acceptable. High similarity for angular widths and intensities required. Orientation match ignored.

(B) Low accuracy of approximations acceptable. High similarity between angular widths required. Only relational match for intensities. Orientation match ignored.

(C) Low accuracy of approximations acceptable. Similarity between angular widths ignored. Only relational match for intensities. Orientation match required.

(D) No contrast thresholds in approximations. Low accuracy of approximations acceptable. All configuration parameters matched. Intensity matching not used.

(E) High accuracy of approximations required. All configuration parameters matched. Intensities matched proportionally.

(F) Good accuracy of approximations required. High similarity between line widths required. Intensity matching not used

Intensity parameters

The intensity parameters of keypoint approximations can be used more selectively that the configuration parameters (and their significance is usually lower). In the extreme scenarios they are not used in the matching process at all (i.e. only the local structures of the objects are important) although the other extreme is to match them accurately (to detect keypoints viewed in the same illumination conditions). Typically, either only relations between the intensities are verified (e.g. a scene corner keypoint can match a given model corner

keypoint if the acute section is lighter than the obtuse one - see Figure 1A) or the proportions between the intensities of keypoints should match to a certain level.
To illustrate the above issues, Figure 9 presents exemplary pairs of circular windows (they are in the same scale as scale invariance is discussed in Subsection 3.1) that can be matched under various (sometimes not very realistic) assumptions. The windows are already placed at the local maxima of similarity functions so that if keypoints are extracted they would be found at the same locations. The corresponding pattern approximations are also given to highlight that matching is actually performed between the approximations rather than between the original contents of windows.

3.1 Scale Invariance in Keypoint Matching

Although the examples given in Figure 9 address the issue of matching circular windows of the same radius, the same approach can be used for matching *scene keypoints* of the same size. The only difference is that the match should be satisfactorily established both for the outer windows (of radius $\boldsymbol{R}$) and for their sub-windows (of radius $\boldsymbol{R_{sub}}$). However, matching objects shown in arbitrary scales to their models (i.e. matching scene keypoints to the model keypoints) can be done only under additional assumptions.
If a "visual correspondence" between a fragment of a model image and a fragment in an inspected image exists, it can be generally confirmed by a match between the corresponding model keypoint (defined for the radius range ($\boldsymbol{R_1}$, $\boldsymbol{R_2}$) - see Def. 1) and the scene keypoint (defined by radii $\boldsymbol{R}$ and $\boldsymbol{R_{sub}}$) only when:

$$\sigma R_1 \leq R_{sub} \quad \text{and} \quad R \leq \sigma R_2 \tag{7}$$

where $\boldsymbol{\sigma}$ is the *relative scale* between the model image and the processed image.
The relative scale defines how much the size of an object (measured in the image units) has been changed against the size of the same object in the model image. The relative scale is jointly determined by the image resolution, the camera-object distance and the camera focal length. Detailed analysis of relative scale issues in the context of object detection in given in (Saiful, 2006).
In Section 2, we extract exemplary model keypoints using the range of radii ($\boldsymbol{R_1}$, $\boldsymbol{R_2}$) from 5 to 20 pixels, while exemplary scene keypoints are found using 10 and 15 pixels. From Eq. (7) we can immediately calculate that for such conditions images of objects of interest can be prospectively matched to the model images if the relative scale changes from 1.3 to 0.33. It means that the objects can be only insignificantly enlarged, but the up to three times reduced in size. These results correspond to requirements of typical applications (e.g. in mobile robotics) where exemplary objects of interest are available so that their images can be captured from a close proximity. In the actual search operations, however, those objects would be usually seen from a longer distance, i.e. the size reduction in captured images is more likely to happen.
Moreover, the approximation parameters representing distances (e.g. $\boldsymbol{\beta_1}$ and $\boldsymbol{\beta_2}$ in Figure 1C) should be matched is a special way. They are invariant under usage of variable-radius windows in terms of absolute distances, but they are not invariant *relatively* to the radius. Thus, if a scene keypoint is captured in an unknown scale, such parameters cannot be directly matched to the values in model keypoints. However, they can be later used for verifying the validity of the matches (see Sub-section 4.1).

It should be finally remarked that the selection of radius ranges over which the model keypoints are built affects both scale-sensitivity and robustness of object detection. With wider (R_1, R_2) the scale invariance of obviously expanded to more scales. However, the number of model keypoints can be reduced as the pattern approximations must be stable over a wider range of radii. Therefore, the abilities to detect objects (both fully and partially visible ones) deteriorate. For occluded objects, fewer locations corresponding to model keypoints are seen, while for fully visible objects fewer correspondences can be found to verify hypotheses about the presence of objects. Limited (R_1, R_2) results in the opposite effects, i.e. the scale invariance is reduced to a narrower range, but the method is potentially able to detect objects under stronger occlusions and/or in poorer visibility conditions.

4. Framework for Object Detection

4.1 Hypothesis Building and Verification

Generally, keypoint-based object detecting algorithms are voting schemes where an object of interest is considered found if a sufficient number of keypoints are consistently matched to the corresponding model keypoints (e.g. Wolfson & Rigoutsos, 1997). In our method, we propose to use such a method already presented in (Islam, 2006). The method has been applied to different types of keypoints, but it is also naturally applicable (after minor modifications) to the keypoints proposed in this paper.

To detect presence of the objects of interest in processed images, several steps are performed as outlined below. Detailed explanations of the steps are given in (Islam, 2006).

In the first step, clusters of scene keypoints matching the model keypoints are created using Generalised Hough Transform (GHT) similarly to Ulrich et al., 2003. The accumulator of $u \times v$ size is used, where u is the number of objects and v is the number of model images for each object. A scene keypoint falls into an accumulator bin if it matches a model keypoint from the corresponding image. Usually, scene keypoints match several model keypoints (depending on the matching strategy the numbers can be larger or smaller - see Section 3). Each bin that collects a sufficient number of scene keypoints should be considered a hypothesis regarding a presence of the object (seen from a particular viewpoint). All such hypotheses are subsequently verified. It should be noted that eventually several hypotheses can be accepted. If they use different sets of points, such multiple hypotheses indicate the presence of multiple objects in the scene. If two or more accepted hypotheses use similar clusters of scene keypoints and yet produce different results, it means that either partially occluded different objects have similar model keypoints in the visible parts, or different objects accidentally share similar model keypoints.

Simple examples illustrating advantageous and disadvantageous aspects of using such hypotheses are given in Figure 10. The examples are taken from (Islam, 2006) so that different types of keypoints are used, but the same effects can be expected for the proposed keypoints as well.

Hypotheses are verified using the concept of *shape graphs* and *scene graphs*. *Shape graphs* are built for model images while *scene graphs* are built for analysed images; otherwise they are identically defined fully connected graphs. Nodes of the graph for a given cluster of keypoints represent the keypoints (scene keypoints for a scene graph and the matching model keypoints for a shape graph). Each edge of the graph is labelled by the distance between the adjoined nodes (keypoints).

An iterative algorithm is used to find the maximum sub-graphs of a scene-graph and a shape-graph for which all corresponding pairs of edges have approximately proportional label values. This iterative algorithm converges very fast and in most cases only a few iterations are needed. The generated sub-graphs specify the final set of scene and model keypoints used to confirm the validity of the hypothesis. The selected keypoints not only match the model keypoints but also their spatial distributions are similar.

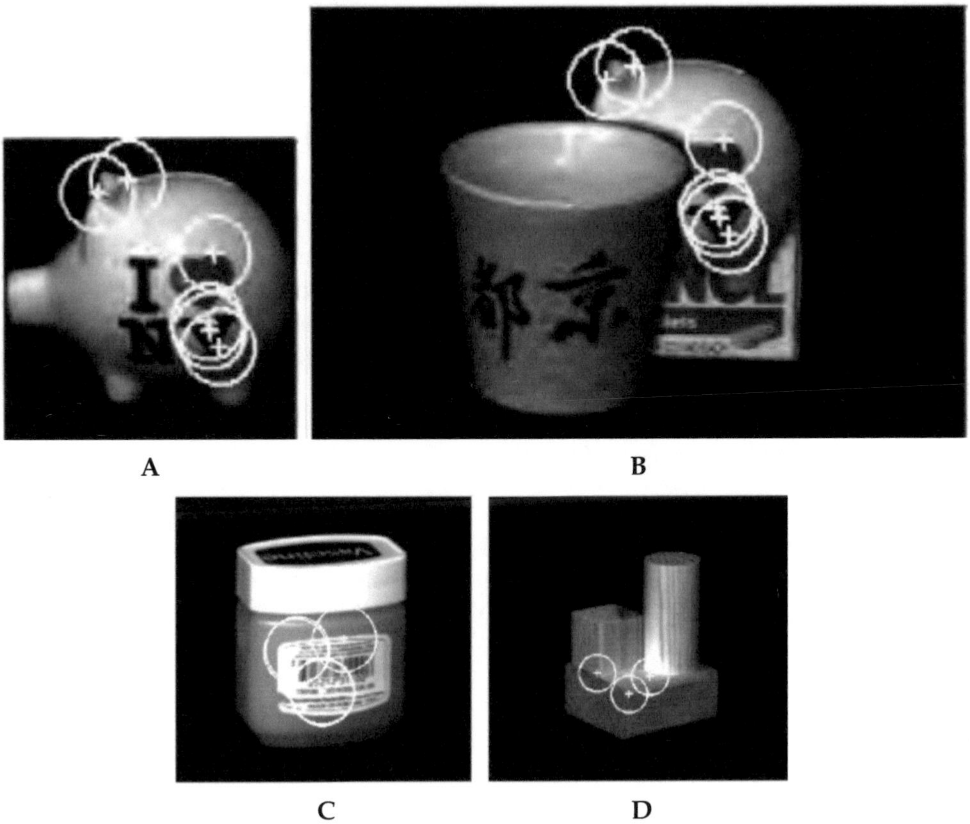

Figure 10. Model images (A and C) successfully matched to test images (B and D, respectively). Clusters of matching keypoints are shown

The minimum number of nodes in the subgraphs (i.e. the number of consistently matched keypoints) required for confirmation of the object's identity may depend on the set of objects under consideration. However, our experiments and statistical analysis show that usually 5 keypoints are enough. It can be noticed, that the incorrect match between Figure 10C and Figure 10D is confirmed only by three keypoints.

The hypotheses verification can be additionally supported by the analysis of configuration parameters of scene keypoints. In particular, only those keypoints from a single cluster would be used for building a scene-graph which are consistently rotated with respect to the corresponding model keypoints (see the last column of Table 2). This is a very powerful constraint that greatly reduces the complexity of the hypothesis verification procedure.

4.2 Exemplary Results

The following example illustrates the process of object detection (i.e. hypothesis verification) briefly explained above. Selected issues regarding keypoint matching are also highlighted.

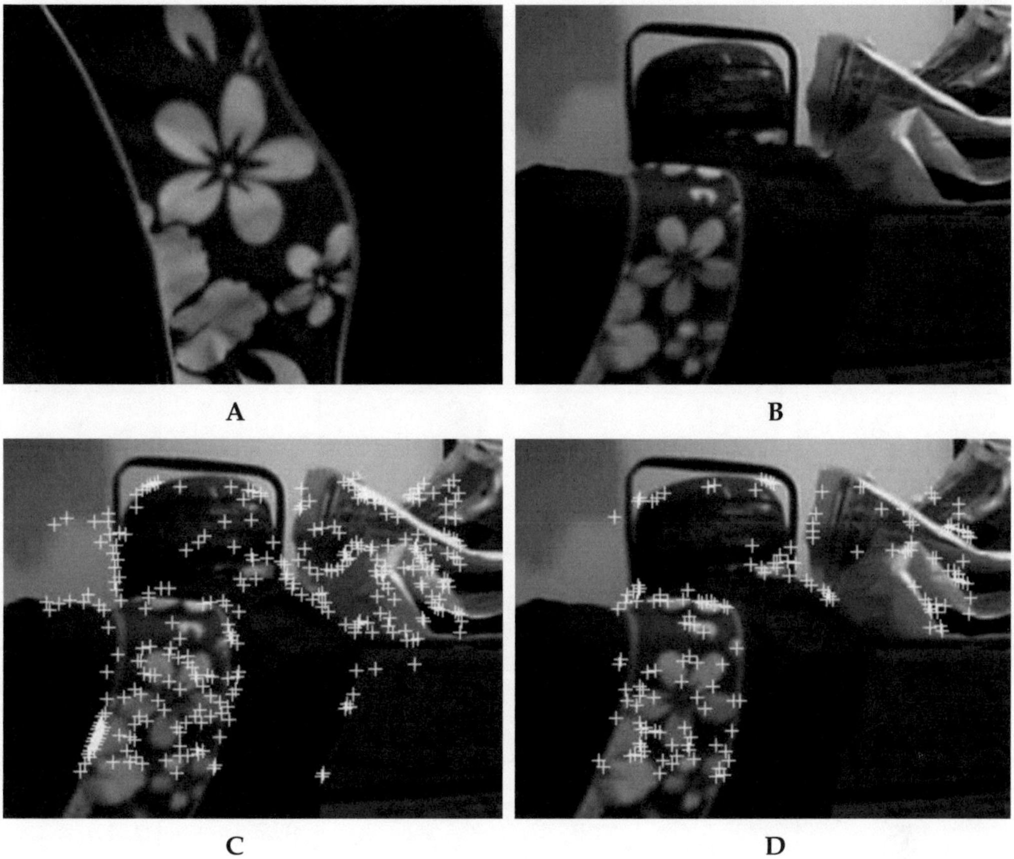

Figure 11. The model image (A) and the test image (B). Corner scene keypoints shown in (C) and 90° T-junction scene keypoints are given in (D)

An exemplary model image and a test image are given in Figure 11. Location of corner scene keypoints and 90° T-junction scene keypoints detected in the test image are also shown.

The selected example deliberately uses a piece of cloth as the object of interest to show that the method has a potential to deal with some non-rigid objects as well. Match results have been obtained using only two types of scene keypoints shown in Figs 11C and 11D. To compensate for non-rigidity of the object, the shape/scene graphs labels have been compared only for the longest edges (so that minor local shape distortions do not affect the hypothesis verification). The additional assumptions are as follows:

- Intensity parameters in scene keypoints and the corresponding model keypoints differ approximately similarly.
- Angular widths in the corner scene keypoints are similar to the angles in the matching model keypoints.
- All scene keypoints should be similarly rotated relatively to the orientations of corresponding model keypoints.

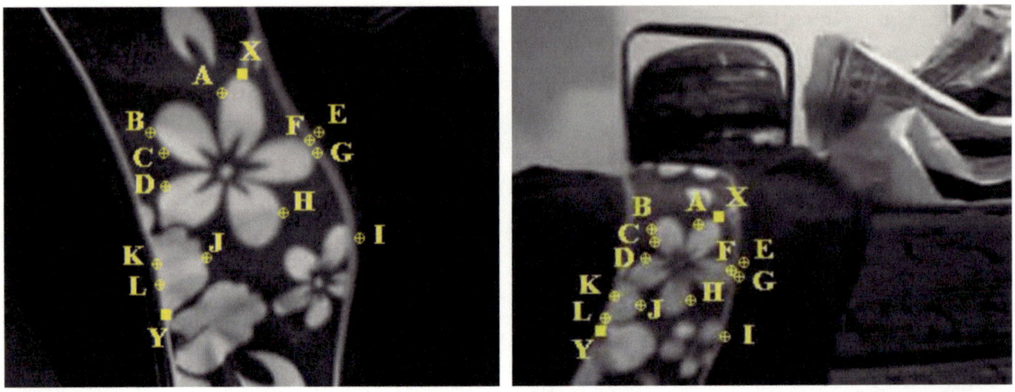

Figure 12. Matched keypoints in the model and test images (⊕ corner keypoints, ■ 90° T-junction keypoints

	A	D	E	I	J	Y
A	×	$\frac{40.0}{69.7}=0.57$	$\frac{37.6}{68.8}=0.55$	$\frac{73.0}{128}=0.57$	$\frac{63.0}{104.5}=0.59$	$\frac{89.8}{145.3}=0.61$
D	$\frac{40.0}{69.7}=0.57$	×	$\frac{60.1}{105.6}=0.57$	$\frac{72.4}{130}=0.56$	$\frac{30.1}{52.5}=0.57$	$\frac{51.9}{81}=0.63$
E	$\frac{37.6}{68.8}=0.55$	$\frac{60.1}{105.6}=0.57$	×	$\frac{46.4}{71.9}=0.63$	$\frac{69.1}{109}=0.63$	$\frac{98.1}{152.4}=0.64$
I	$\frac{73.0}{128}=0.57$	$\frac{72.4}{130}=0.56$	$\frac{46.4}{71.9}=0.63$	×	$\frac{57.4}{99.7}=0.57$	$\frac{79}{134.9}=0.59$
J	$\frac{63.0}{104.5}=0.59$	$\frac{30.1}{52.5}=0.57$	$\frac{69.1}{109}=0.63$	$\frac{57.4}{99.7}=0.57$	×	$\frac{31.4}{53.3}=0.59$
Y	$\frac{89.8}{145.3}=0.61$	$\frac{51.9}{81}=0.63$	$\frac{98.1}{152.4}=0.64$	$\frac{79}{134.9}=0.59$	$\frac{31.4}{53.3}=0.59$	×

Table 1. Distance ratios for the corresponding fragment of the shape graph (denominator values) and the scene graph (numerator values) for Figure 12 images

Figure 12 presents pairs of finally matched keypoints, and Table 1 shows a fragment of the shape/scene graph (only the most distant keypoints are included). Although certain variations of the ratio between the corresponding distances in the shape and scene graphs can be noticed, the average ratio is consistently near **0.6** which can be assumed the approximation of the relative scale between the model image and the test one. This value corresponds to the visual assessment of Figs 11A and 11B.

Corner approximations

	Keypoint type	Intensities	Angular width	Orientation difference
A	model	187 and 57	134°	32°
	scene	160 and 60	149°	
B	model	194 and 46	90°	24°
	scene	165 and 60	104°	
C	model	186 and 45	153°	25°
	scene	151 and 44	157°	
D	model	187 and 48	147°	29°
	scene	135 and 38	146°	
E	model	121 and 18	140°	41°
	scene	91 and 20	154°	
F	model	162 and 35	149°	36°
	scene	136 and 56	152°	
G	model	162 and 38	151°	36°
	scene	117 and 21	154°	
H	model	171 and 53	142°	24°
	scene	137 and 31	153°	
I	model	154 and 10	142°	26°
	scene	123 and 7	151°	
J	model	174 and 48	145°	37°
	scene	143 and 35	156°	
K	model	26 and 172	158°	29°
	scene	19 and 149	158°	
L	model	20 and 169	158°	32°
	scene	14 and 139	160°	

90° T-junction approximations

	Keypoint type	Intensities	Orientation difference
X	model	91, 45 and 179	41°
	scene	95, 61 and 136	
Y	model	142, 4 and 73	32°
	scene	138, 9 and 75	

Table 2. Approximation parameters for the model and scene keypoints used for the match shown in Figure 12

As a further reference, Table 2 compares parameters of corner approximations and T-junction approximations obtained for model and scene keypoints used for the hypothesis confirmation. It shows a relatively high consistency for the orientation differences (ranging from 24° to 42°) for all keypoints and high level of similarity for the angular widths of corner keypoints. The differences between the corresponding intensities are wider (which is unavoidable for images captured in different conditions) but they are consistent as well. In particular, if the intensities differ they change in a similar way for all intensities of a given approximation.

5. Concluding Remarks

We have presented principles and exemplary results of a novel technique for detection of known objects in inspected images. The method is based on new types of keypoints which are the focus of this paper. The proposed keypoints are significantly different from typical gradient-based keypoints used in the alternative techniques. Our keypoints are based on moment-derived pattern approximations of circular patches. Though currently only a few patterns are used (i.e. corners, T-junctions and round tips of thick lines) a wide range of other patterns can be added using the approach presented in our previous works (e.g. Sluzek, 2005). The keypoints are characterised by intensity and configuration descriptors (e.g. angular widths and orientation of the approximations) that are generally robust under illumination changes, noise, texturisation, and other typical real-world effects. More importantly, the keypoints are also scale-invariant within a certain range of scales. This has been obtained by using two different methods for keypoint building in model images and in analysed images.

Model images of database (known) objects are processed in multiple scales in order to identify *model* keypoints that are invariantly characterised within the assumed range of scales. The operation may be computationally expensive, but it is typically performed either offline or in the preliminary phase of deployment when timing constraints are not critical. However, the *scene* keypoints extracted from inspected image are based (unlike keypoints used in other scale-invariant techniques) on a single-scale image scanning and processing. Additionally, the efficiency of keypoint matching is improved by a simultaneous usage of several keypoint types. Even if the overall number of keypoints (both model and scene ones) is comparable to the numbers typically extracted and used by other methods, scene keypoints of a certain category are matched only against the corresponding subset of model keypoints of the same category. Therefore, the computational costs of image analysis are relatively low and the method is suitable for real-time applications (e.g. for exploratory robotics which is considered the primary application area).

Several improvements of the method are currently envisaged First, we propose to enhance the efficiency of keypoint matching by adding (without any significant computational costs) more keypoint descriptors. For that purpose, moment-based expressions invariant under similarity transformations and linear intensity changes are considered. Although generally such invariants (proposed for colour images and areas of arbitrary shapes in Mindru et al., 2004) are rather complex, we intend to apply them to circular images only. For circular images, the following expressions have been found invariant under similarity transformations and linear intensity changes. For other shapes of the processed areas they are not invariant, however.

$$\frac{(m_{20}-m_{02})^2+4m_{11}^2}{R^2\left(m_{10}^2+m_{01}^2\right)} \quad \text{and} \quad \frac{2(m_{20}+m_{02})-R^2 m_{00}}{R\sqrt{m_{10}^2+m_{01}^2}} \tag{8}$$

where $\boldsymbol{R}$ is the circle radius.

Another prospective continuation of the method is to use colour equivalents of the proposed keypoints (with three colour channels processed separately or jointly). We also consider

hardware accelerators for the moment calculations. Selected moment-computing procedures have been already implemented in FPGA as a feasibility study. The results indicate that with a support of an FPGA accelerator a real-time detection of scene keypoints in a TV video stream is feasible.
The primary area of intended applications for the proposed method is intelligent robotics (exploratory robots in particular). The ultimate goal would be a system that can be shown a physical "known object" and subsequently such objects present in complex cluttered scenes can be detected. However, other areas of applications should be highlighted as well. As some recently published results suggest (e.g. Prasad et al., 2004) image retrieval and/or search in visual databases seems to be a potential application area. Using the proposed keypoints, not only the search for known objects or images can be conducted, but also some image-related frauds can be revealed (e.g. detection of almost invisible highly accurate approximations may indicate image doctoring).
Surveillance and/or security systems are another envisaged area for the developed technique. Since such systems are equipped with more and more embedded intelligence, a system that can identify "known intruders" or "particularly dangerous intruders" is a possible scenario. Development of a sensor network with vision capabilities that can eventually incorporate the proposed method has been reported in our recent papers (e.g. Sluzek et al., 2005).

6. References

Biederman, I. (1987). Recognition-by-components: A theory of human image understanding. *Psychological Review*, Vol.94, No.2 (Apr. 1987), pp. 115-147, ISSN: 0033-295X.

Edelman, S. (1997). Computational theories of object recognition. *Trends in Cognitive Sciences*, Vol.1, No.8 (Nov. 1997), pp. 298-309, ISSN: 1364-6613.

Harris, C. & Stephens, M. (1988). A combined corner and edge detector. *Proceedings of 4th Alvey Vision Conference*, pp. 147-151, Manchester, Sep. 1988.

Häusler, G. & Ritter, D. (1999). Feature-based object recognition and localization in 3D-space, using a single video image. *Computer Vision & Iage Understanding*, Vol.73, No.1 (Jan. 1999), pp 64-81, ISSN: 1077-3142.

Hueckel, M.H. (1973). A local visual operator which recognizes edges and lines, *Journal of ACM*, Vol.20, No.2 (Apr. 1973), pp 350, ISSN: 0004-5411.

Huttenlocher, D.P. & Ullman, S. (1990). Recognizing solid objects by alignment with an image. *Int. Journal of Computer Vision*, Vol.5, No.2 (Nov. 1990), pp 195-212, ISSN: 0920-5691.

Islam, M.S.; Sluzek, A. & Zhu, L. (2005). Detecting and matching interest points in relative scale. *Machine Graphics & Vision*, Vol.14, No. 3 (Nov. 2005), pp. 259-283, ISSN: 1230-0535.

Islam, M.S. (2006). Recognition and localization of objects in relative scale for robotic applications. *PhD Thesis*, School of Comp. Engineering, Nanyang Technological University (Dec. 2006), Singapore.

Koenderink, J.J. & van Doorn, A.J. (1987). Representation of local geometry in the visual system. *Biological Cybernetics*, Vol.55, No.6 (March 1987), pp. 367–375, ISSN: 0340-1200.

Lowe, D. (2004). Distinctive image features from scale-invariant keypoints. *Int. Journal of Computer Vision*, Vol.60, No.2 (Nov. 2004) pp. 91-110, ISSN: 0920-5691.

Mikolajczyk, K. & Schmid, C. (2004). Scale & affine invariant interest point detectors. *Int. Journal of Computer Vision*, Vol.60, No.1 (Oct. 2004) pp. 63-86, ISSN: 0920-5691.

Mindru, F.; Tuytelaars, T.; van Gool, L. & Moons, Th. (2004). Moment invariants for recognition under changing viewpoint and illumination. *Computer Vision & Image Understanding*, Vol.94, No.1-3 (April 2004) pp 3-27, ISSN: 1077-3142.

Moravec, H. (1983). Stanford cart and the CMU rover. *Proceeding of the IEEE*, Vol.71, No.7 (July 1983), pp. 872-884, ISSN: 0018-9219.

Prasad, B.G.; Biswas, K.K. & Gupta, S.K. (2004). Region-based image retrieval using integrated color, shape, and location index. *Computer Vision & Image Understanding*, Vol.94, No.1-3 (April 2004) pp 193-233, ISSN: 1077-3142.

Rosin, P.L. (1997). Measuring corner properties. *Computer Vision & Image Understanding*, Vol.73, No.2 (Feb. 1999), pp 291-307, ISSN: 1077-3142.

Schmid, C. & Mohr, R. (1995). Local grayvalue invariants for image retrieval. *IEEE Transactions on Pattern Analysis and Machine Intelligence*, Vol.19, No.5 (May 1997), pp. 530-535, ISSN: 0162-8828.

Sluzek, A. (2005). On moment-based local operators for detecting image patterns. *Image and Vision Computing*, Vol.23, No.3 (March 2005), pp 287-298, ISSN: 0262-8856.

Sluzek, A; Palaniappan, A. & Islam, M.S. (2005). A wireless sensor network for visual detection and classification of intrusions, *WSEAS Transactions on Circuits and Systems*, Vol.4, No.12 (Dec. 2005), pp 1855-1860, ISSN: 1109-2734.

Sluzek, A. (2006). An improved detection algorithm for local features in gray-level images. In: *Computer Vision and Graphics* (*Computational Imaging and Vision*, vol.32), K.Wojciechowski et al. (Eds.), pp 406-412, Springer, ISBN: 1-4020-4178-0, Dordrecht.

Tarr, M.J.; Bülthoff, H.H.; Zabinski, M. & Blanz, V. (1997). To what extent do unique parts influence recognition across changes in viewpoint? *Psychological Science*, Vol.8, No.4 (July 1997), pp. 282-289, ISSN: 0956-7976.

Ulrich, M.; Steger, C. & Baumgartner, A. (2003). Real-time object recognition using a modified generalized Hough transform. *Pattern Recognition*, Vol.36, No.11 (Nov. 2003), pp. 2557-2570, ISSN: 0031-3203.

Wolfson, H.J. & Rigoutsos, I. (1997). Geometric hashing: an overview. *IEEE Computational Science & Engineering*, Vol.4, No.4 (Oct. 1997), pp. 10-21, ISSN: 1070-9924.

24

Biologically Inspired Vision Architectures: a Software/Hardware Perspective

Francesco S. Fabiano, Antonio Gentile, Marco La Cascia and Roberto Pirrone
Dipartimento di Ingegneria Informatica – Università di Palermo
Italy

1. Introduction

Even tough the field of computer vision has seen huge improvement in the last few decades, computer vision systems still lack, in most cases, the efficiency of biological vision systems. In fact biological vision systems routinely accomplish complex visual tasks such as object recognition, obstacle avoidance, and target tracking, which continue to challenge artificial systems. The study of biological vision system remains a strong cue for the design of devices exhibiting intelligent behaviour in visually sensed environments but current artificial systems are vastly different from biological ones for various reasons. First of all, biologically inspired vision architectures, which are continuous-time and parallel in nature, do not map well onto conventional processors, which are discrete-time and serial. Moreover, the neurobiological representations of visual modalities like colour, shape, depth, and motion are quite different from those usually employed by conventional computer vision systems. Despite these inherent difficulties in the last decade several biologically motivated vision techniques have been proposed to accomplish common tasks. For example Siagian & Itti [14] developed an algorithm to compute the gist of a scene as a low-dimensional signature of an image, in the form of an 80-dimensional feature vector that summarizes the entire scene. The same authors also developed a biologically-inspired technique for face detection [13]. Interesting results have also been reported in generic object recognition and classification (see for example [15] [16] [12] [11]). Also on the sensor side the biological vision systems are amazingly efficient in terms of speed, robustness and accuracy. In natural systems visual information processing starts at the retina where the light intensity is converted into electrical signals through cones and rods. In the outer layers of the retina the photoreceptors are connected to the horizontal and bipolar cells. The horizontal cells produce a spatially smoothed version of the incoming signal while the bipolar cells are sensitive to the edges in the image. Signals output from the cells are then used for higher level processing. Several architecture have been proposed to mimic in part the biological system and to extract information ranging from low to high level. For example Higgins [10] proposed a sensor able to perform an elementary visual motion detector. Other researchers proposed sensor to detect mid-level image features like corners or junctions [4] or even to perform higher level tasks such as tracking [6] or texture classification [5]. Robotics represents a typical field of application for hardware implementations of biologically inspired vision architectures.

Robot vision routines such as self localization, or 3D perception via calibrated cameras require large computing capabilities. Autonomous robot platforms have limited space to dedicate to such high level tasks because on board computers are busy most the time with motor control, and sensorial data acquisition. Even more limited embedded hardware is available on small wheeled robots for which almost all sensory computation is delegated to remote machines. Also in the case of robots equipped with onboard computer, most processing focuses on motion control, and low level sensorial data elaboration while heavy computer vision tasks, like image segmentation and object recognition, are performed in background, via fast connections to a host computer. Emerging gigascale integration technologies offer the opportunity to explore alternative approaches to domain specific computing architectures that can deliver a significant boost to on-board computing when implemented in embedded, reconfigurable devices. This paper describes the mapping of low level feature extraction on a reconfigurable platform based on the Georgia Tech SIMD Pixel Processor (SIMPil).
In particular, an adaptation of the Boundary webs Extractor (BWE) has been implemented on SIMPil exploiting the large amount of data parallelism inherently present in this application. The BWE [1] is derived from the original Grossberg's Boundary Contour System (BCS) and extracts a dense map of iso-luminance contours from the input image. This map contains actual edges along with a compact representation of local surface shading, and it is useful for high level vision tasks like Shape-From-Stereo. The Fast Boundary Web Extraction (fBWE) algorithm has been implemented in fixed point as a feed-forward processing pipeline thus avoiding BWE feedback loop, and achieving a considerable speed-up when compared against the standard algorithm. Application components and their mapping details are provided in this contribution along with a detailed analysis of their performance. Results are shown that illustrate the significant gain over a sequential implementation, and most importantly, the execution times in the order of 170 μsec for a 256000 pixel image. These results allow ample room for real-time processing of typical subsequent tasks in a complete robot vision system. The rest of this chapter is organized as follows. Section II introduces the Georgia Tech SIMPil architecture, and implementation efforts on FPGA. Section III provides some remarks on the original Grossberg's BCS, and its derived BWE model. In section IV the fBWE system is described, and its mapping onto SIMPil detailed. Section V reports extensive experiments with the fBWE compared with the BWE results, while in section VI some conclusions are drawn.

2. SIMPil FPGA implementation

The GeorgiaTech SIMD Pixel Processor (SIMPil) architecture consists of a mesh of SIMD processors on top of which an array of image sensors is integrated [8] [7]. A diagram for a 16-bit implementation is illustrated in Figure 1. Each processing element includes a RISC load/store datapath plus an interface to a 4×4 sensor subarray. A 16-bit datapath has been implemented which includes a 32-bit multiply-accumulator unit, a 16 word register file, and 64 words of local memory (the ISA allows for up to 256 words). The SIMD execution model allows the entire image projected on many PEs to be acquired in a single cycle. Large arrays of SIMPil PEs can be simulated using the SIMPil Simulator, an instruction level simulator. Early prototyping efforts have proved the feasibility of direct coupling of a simple processing core with a sensor device [3]. A 16 bit prototype of a SIMPil PE was designed in 0.8 μm CMOS process and fabricated through MOSIS. A 4096 PE target system has been used in the simulations. This system is capable of delivering a peak throughput of about 5 Tops/sec in a monolithic device, enabling image and video processing applications that are currently unapproachable using today's portable DSP technology. The SIMPil architecture is designed for image and video processing applications. In general, this class of applications is very computational intensive and requires high throughput to handle the massive data flow in real-time. However, these applications are also characterized by a large degree of data parallelism, which is maximally exploited by focal plane processing. Image frames are available simultaneously at each PE in the system, while retaining their spatial correlation. Image streams can be therefore processed at frame rate, with only nominal amount of memory required at each PE [8]. The performance and efficiency of the SIMPil have been tested on a large application suite that spans the target workload.

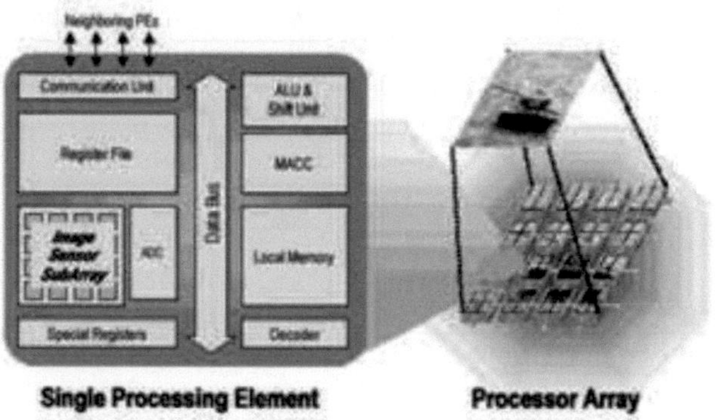

Figure 1. The SIMPiL architecture

For the SIMPil processing element, an application suite is selected from the DARPA Image Understanding suite [17]. These applications, listed in Table 1, are expressed in SIMPil assembly language, and executed using an instruction level simulator, SIMPilSim which provides various execution statistics. This simulator provides execution statistics including dynamic instruction frequency, operand size profiles, PE utilization, and PE memory usage. All applications are executed on a simulated 4096 processing element system with 16 pixels mapped to each PE for an aggregate 256×256 image size. All applications run well within real-time frame-rates and exhibit large system utilization figures (90% or more for most application). Details can be found in [8]. To bring SIMPil performance onto robot platform, a reconfigurable platform based on FPGA devices is being developed. This platform uses a parameterized SIMPil core (SIMPil-K) described in the VHDL hardware description language. The SIMPil-K platform is an array of Processing Elements (PE) and interconnection registers which can be configured to fit any FPGA device at hand. Figure 2 shows the high-level functional schema of a 4×4 SIMPil-K array and its NEWS interconnection network. Each NEWS register supports communication among a particular node (i.e. PE) and its north and west neighbours. By replicating this model, a NEWS (North, East, West, South) network is obtained, with every node connected to its four neighbours. SIMPil-K receives an instructions stream through a dedicated input port. The instruction stream is then broadcast to each PE. To upload and download image data, SIMPil-K uses a boundary I/O mechanism, supported by its boundary nodes (i.e. PEs laid on its East/West edge): every east-edge node uploads a K-bit data word from its boundary-input port to the general purpose register file; every west-edge node downloads a K-bit data word from its register file to the boundary output port. An upload/download operation (one word per node) takes only one clock cycle. Both boundary input and output operations are enabled by a single instruction, XFERB. When a NEWS transfer instruction arrives, it needs only one clock cycle to transfer the data word from each node to a neighbour one, in a specified direction. The SIMPil-K platform can be reconfigured by varying a number of architectural parameters, as detailed in Table 2. This allows for experimentation with a large set of different system configurations, which is instrumental to determine the appropriate system characteristics for each application environment AW and RAW parameters set the address space of register file and memory, respectively. PPE specifies the number of image pixels mapped to each PE. The Influence parameter toggle between a fixed instruction width (24 bit) and a variable one (8+K bits). The interface of a processing element is depicted in Figure 3, below. There are two input ports for clock signals, a reset input port and the instruction stream port. NEWS transfers are carried through the three bidirectional dedicated ports (NEWS ports) which drive three NEWS buses, namely the North/West Bus, East Bus and South Bus.

Image Transforms	**Image Enhancement**
Discrete Fourier Transform	Intensity Level Slicing
Discrete Cosine Transform	Convolution
Discrete Wavelet Transform	Magnification
Image Rotation	Median Filtering
Image/Video Compression	**Image Analysis**
Quantization	Morphological Processing
Vector Quantization	Region Representation
Entropy Coding	Region Autofocus
JPEG Compression	K-means Classification
Motion Estimation	
MPEG Compression	

Table 1. SIMPil Application Suite

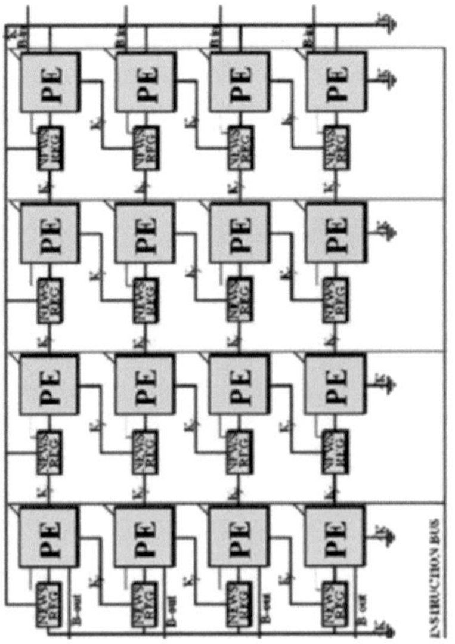

Figure 2. K-bit 4-by-4 SIMPil-K array

Boundary data input and output are carried through the two dedicated boundary ports. The processing element parameterized architecture is described in Figure 4. There are four communication buses shared by the functional units. All functional units can be reconfigured based on the datapath width selected. A single PE can perform integer operations on K-bits. Dedicated barrel shift unit and multiply-accumulate unit are instrumental to speed-up most image processing kernels. The Sleep Unit verifies and updates the node activity state, thus allowing execution flow control based on each PE local data. The SIMPil-K system has been simulated and synthesized on FPGA; synthesis statistics about employed resources has been generated and analyzed. Figure 5 shows resources use percentage achieved by implementing several 16-bit SIMPil-K versions on an eight million gates FPGA: particularly, 2-by-2, 4-by-4 and 8-by-8 16-bit SIMPil-K arrays have a resources use percentage respectively of 3.3%, 13.3%, and 53.3%.

Parameter	Function	Values	Constr.	Def.
K	Word Width	{8, 16, 32, 64}	–	16
X	Array Columns	$X \in N$	$X, Y = 2^j, j \in Z$	4
Y	Array Rows Register	$Y \in N$		4
AW	File Address Width	$AW \in N \cap [1, 16]$	$I = \text{off} \rightarrow AW \leq 4$ $I = \text{on} \rightarrow AW \leq (K/4)$	4
RAW	Local RAM Address Width	$RAW \in N \cap [1, 16\}$	$RAW \leq (K/4)$	4
PPE	Pixel per Processing	$PPE \in N$	$PPE = p^2, p \in N,$ $PPE \leq 2^K$	8
Influence (I)	Instructions Format Change Enable	$I \in$ [on, off]	–	off

Table 2. SIMPil-K Architectural Parameters

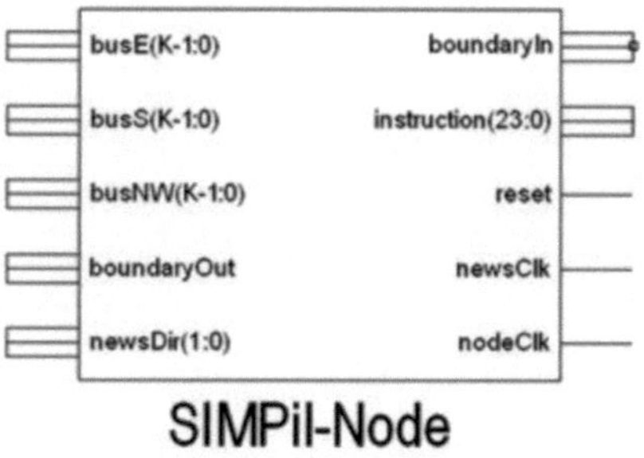

Figure 3. The Processing Element Black Box

3. The Boundary Webs Extractor

The original BCS architecture was proposed by Grossberg and Mingolla [9] as a neural model, aimed to explain some psychological findings about perceptual grouping of contours in vision: it was part of a more complex theory regarding human perception of shapes and colors. In this formulation, the BCS is a multi-layer recurrent network trained using a competitive/cooperative scheme until an equilibrium state is reached. BCS units have dynamic activations that are expressed using differential equations with respect to time. The network takes the input from a gray-level image, with a lattice of receptive fields computing local contrast in small areas. Output is provided as a 2D map of vectors, with the same spatial displacement of the input receptive fields, which are called boundary webs, and describe changes in brightness over the image. A boundary web is locally oriented along a constant brightness line, meaning that image contrast changes along the orthogonal direction. The amplitude of each boundary web is related to the strength of the local contrast. Boundary webs form a piecewise linear approximation of all image contours, while they follow iso-luminance paths inside smoothly shaded surfaces: consequently, they can be regarded as a compact description of image shading. a typical BCS analysis is described in Figure 7(b), while Figure 6 reports an outline of the BCS architecture. The network consists of an input stage used to collect contrast information, the so called OC Filter, and of three layers: *Competition I, Competition II* and *Cooperation*. The OC Filter is used to collect local image contrast along different directions without taking into account contrast orientation.

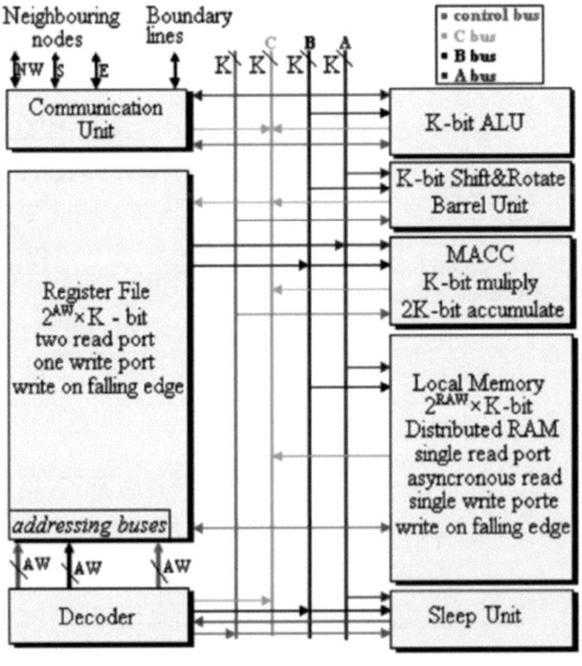

Figure 4. Processing Element K-bit Datapath

All subsequent layers are arranged as a lattice of complex cells, with the same spatial displacement of the receptive fields. Each cell in the lattice has a pool of activation values which are related to the various contrast directions. The first two layers are competitive ones, and their purpose is to refine locally detected contours. The third (output) layer performs long range cooperation between neighboring cells in order to complete extended contours across the image. Finally, the feedback loop is again competitive, and is connected to the first layer in order to enforce winner cells activations. In the OC Filter circular receptive fields at position *(i,j)* sum up input pixels from a squared sub-image $\mathbf{S} = [S_{pq}]$ in two symmetric halves L_{ijk} and R_{ijk} defined for each mask at the k-th orientation. Assuming that $[x]^+ = \max(x, 0)$, the resulting activation at position (i, j) and orientation k is:

$$J_{ijk} = \frac{[U_{ijk} - \alpha V_{ijk}]^+ + [V_{ijk} - \alpha U_{ijk}]^+}{1 + \beta(V_{ijk} + U_{ijk})} \tag{1}$$

where U_{ijk} and V_{ijk} are the summed input in the mask's halves, while α and β are suitable constants. The first competitive layer enforces local winner activations via the feedback signal and the input from the OC Filter, while tends to decrease activation in neighboring cells with the same orientation. In case of strong aligned activations induced by image contours, the aim of the first competitive stage is to reduce the activation diffusion beyond contours endpoints.

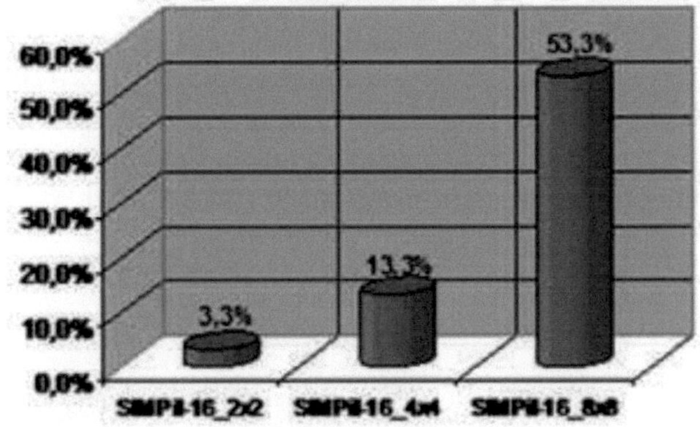

Figure 5. Used resources on eight million gates FPGA

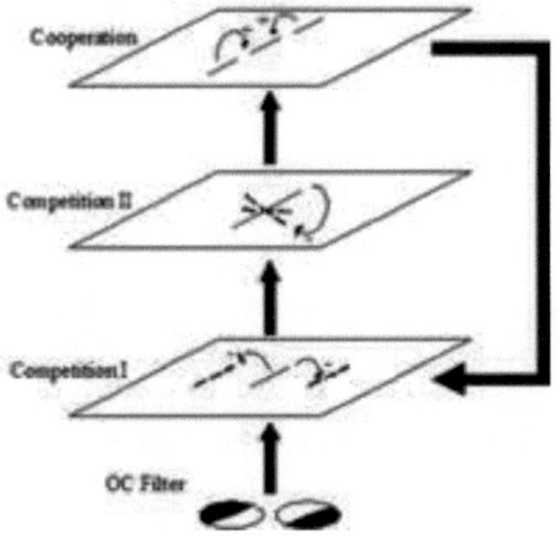

Figure 6. The BCS architecture

This effect results in the illusory contours completion phenomenon which is commonly observed in human perception. Activation laws are, in general, differential equations with respect to time, but in the BCS computational model they are computed at equilibrium (d/dt= 0). In the case of the Competition I layer the dynamic activation rule is:

$$\frac{dw_{ijk}}{dt} = w_{ijk} + I + BJ_{ijk} + v_{ijk} - Bw_{ijk} \sum_{(p,q)} J_{pqk} A_{pqij} \tag{2}$$

and the equilibrium activation w_{ijk} for each cell in this stage is computed as:

$$w_{ijk} = \frac{I + BJ_{ijk} + v_{ijk}}{1 + B\sum_{(p,q)} J_{pqk}A_{pqij}} \tag{3}$$

where v_{ijk} is the feedback signal, A_{pqij} are the coefficient of a small kernel with cylindrical shape, while I and B are suitable constants. In following equations capital letters without indexes are constant values used to tune the model. The second competitive stage performs competition among orientations inside the same cell: this is a local contour refinement mechanism which will be enhanced by the cooperative stage. The activation law has the following form:

$$y_{ijk} = \frac{C[w_{ijk} - w_{ijK}]^+}{D + \sum_{m=1}^{n} [w_{ijm} - w_{ijM}]^+} \tag{4}$$

where capital indexes are referred to orthogonal direction with respect to the current one. The cooperative stage performs long range cooperation between cells with the same orientation that are displaced in a wide neighborhood. In this way long contours completion is enabled. Considering the vector d connecting the position (i, j) with a generic neighbor (p,q), the following quantities can be defined $N_{pqij} = |\mathrm{d}|$ and $Q_{pqij} = \angle \mathrm{d}$, while the cooperative activation law is:

$$\begin{aligned} z_{ijk} = g(\textstyle\sum_{(p,q,r)} (y_{pqr} - y_{pqR})[G_{pqij}^{(r,k)}]^+) \\ + g(\textstyle\sum_{(p,q,r)} (y_{pqr} - y_{pqR})[-G_{pqij}^{(r,k)}]^+) \end{aligned} \tag{5}$$

where:

$$\begin{aligned} g(x) &= \frac{H[x]^+}{K + [x]^+}, \\ G_{pqij}^{(r,k)} &= \exp(-2(N_{pqij}/P - 1)^2) \cdot \\ &\quad |\cos(Q_{pqij} - r)|^R \cos(Q_{pqij} - k)^T \end{aligned}$$

This very complex kernel has the form of two elongated blobs aligned with the orientation k, and exponentially decreasing towards 0. In particular, P represents the optimal distance from the cooperative cell at which maximum input activation is collected. Finally, feedback is provided from the cooperative stage to the first competitive one, in order to enforce those activations that are aligned with emergent contours and decrease spurious ones. The form of the feedback signal is:

$$v_{ijk} = \frac{L[z_{ijk} - M]^+}{1 + L\sum_{p,q} [z_{pqk} - M]^+ W_{pqij}} \tag{6}$$

where W_{pqij} are the coefficient of a small cylinder shaped kernel. BCS provides a compact description of image shading at selectable resolution levels: shading, in turn, can be used to perform shape estimation, while boundary webs can be used as low level features for contour extraction, alignment, or stereo matching. Possible uses of BCS have been explored

by some of the authors resulting in a software implementation of the BCS, called Boundary Web Extractor (BWE) which has been used as a low level feature extraction module in different vision systems. In particular, a neural shape estimation model has been proposed [1] coupling BWE analysis with a backpropagation network trained to classify BWE patterns as belonging to superquadrics surface patches. Input image surfaces are processed by BWE, and the BWE output pertaining to different ROIs is modeled in terms of superquadrics.
Another approach [2] performs BWE analysis on stereo couples. Input images are analyzed both with standard correlation operator over pixels intensities, and with BWE as a supplementary feature. Candidates points are labeled using a measure of the matching probability with respect to both the preprocessing operators. Finally, a relaxation labeling algorithm provides matches for almost all points in the image, and disparities are obtained.
The high resolution achievable by the BWE analysis enables dense depth maps. The main objective of BWE is to perform local brightness gradient estimation, without taking into account the support for perception theories. In this perspective BWE has been slightly modified with respect to BCS, to obtain sharp contrast estimation and emergent contours alignment. In particular, N couples of dually oriented Gabor masks have been used as receptive fields to obtain n activation values discarding, for each couple, the mask providing negative output. The resulting OC Filter is described by the following equation:

$$J_{ijk} = [U_{ijk}]^+ + [V_{ijk}]^+ \tag{7}$$

where U_{ijk} and V_{ijk} are the outputs of two dual Gabor masks. The generic Gabor filter has been selected in our implementation with a width w equal
to 8 pixels, $2N = 24$. The filter equation is:

$$\begin{aligned} M_{ijk} &= \alpha e^{-\beta(\gamma B^2 + C^2)} \sin(\delta C) \\ B &= (w-p)\cos(2k\pi/N) - (q-s)\sin(2k\pi/N) \\ C &= (w-p)\sin(2k\pi/N) + (q-s)\cos(2k\pi/N) \end{aligned} \tag{8}$$

Here s is the application step of the masks; the $\alpha \ldots \delta$ parameters have been heuristically tuned. The kernel in eqs. (3) and (6) have been selected with gaussian shape, and the subtractive term in the exponential part of $G_{pqij}^{(r,k)}$ kernel has been suppressed, and all constant values in the equations have been suitably tuned. To ensure the kernel to be symmetric, its central value has been forced to be 0 in order to avoid the exponential function to give a positive value when $N_{pqij} \equiv 0$. Finally, we can give a formulation of the BWE structure as a 3D matrix containing, at each location (i, j), $2N$ activation values belonging to a star of vectors.

$$\begin{aligned} \mathbf{BW} &= [\mathbf{B}_{ij}] \quad i,j = 1,\ldots,M \\ \mathbf{B}_{ij} &= \{\mathbf{b}_{ijk}\} \quad k = 1,\ldots,2N \end{aligned} \tag{9}$$

Each vector represents the value of the image contrast along the orthogonal direction with respect to its phase. As a consequence of the modified OC Filter behaviour, the location $\mathbf{B}_{ij}$ of the **BW** matrix contains N couples, each of them having a null vector that corresponds to the negative output of the filter with at same orientation.

$$\mathbf{b}_{ijk} = b_{ijk} e^{j\theta_{ijk}}, \quad b_{ijk} = \max\left(|\mathbf{b}_{ijk}|, 0\right), \quad \theta_{ijk} = k\pi/N \tag{10}$$

For computer vision purposes the average boundary webs are noticeable because they provide a single estimation of the local image contrast at each spatial location, both as intensity and direction. The average process is computed using a suitable average function f_{av}:

$$\begin{aligned} \mathbf{A}_{BW} &= [\mathbf{a}_{ij}]\,,\ i,j=1,\ldots,M \\ \forall i,j\ \ \mathbf{a}_{ij} &= a_{ij}e^{j\theta_{ij}} = \mathrm{f}_{av}\left(\mathbf{B}_{ij}\right) \end{aligned} \tag{11}$$

The average function can be selected according to several criteria: the maximum value or the vector sum of all the elements at each location; we selected a form of f_{av} that weights each intensity with the cosine of the angle between the phase value and a mean phase angle, obtained weighting each phase with the respective intensity.

$$\begin{aligned} \mathrm{f}_{av}:\ \theta_{ij} &= k_M\pi/N,\ k_M=\sum_{k=1}^{2N} b_{ijk}k \Big/ \sum_{k=1}^{2N} b_{ijk} \\ a_{ij} &= \frac{\sum\limits_{k=1}^{2N} \mathrm{abs}\left(\cos\left(\theta_{ijk}-\theta_{ij}\right)\right) b_{ijk}}{\sum\limits_{k=1}^{2N} \mathrm{abs}\left(\cos\left(\theta_{ijk}-\theta_{ij}\right)\right)} \end{aligned} \tag{12}$$

Figure 7 makes a comparison between the original BCS and BWE both for the actual output, and for the average one.

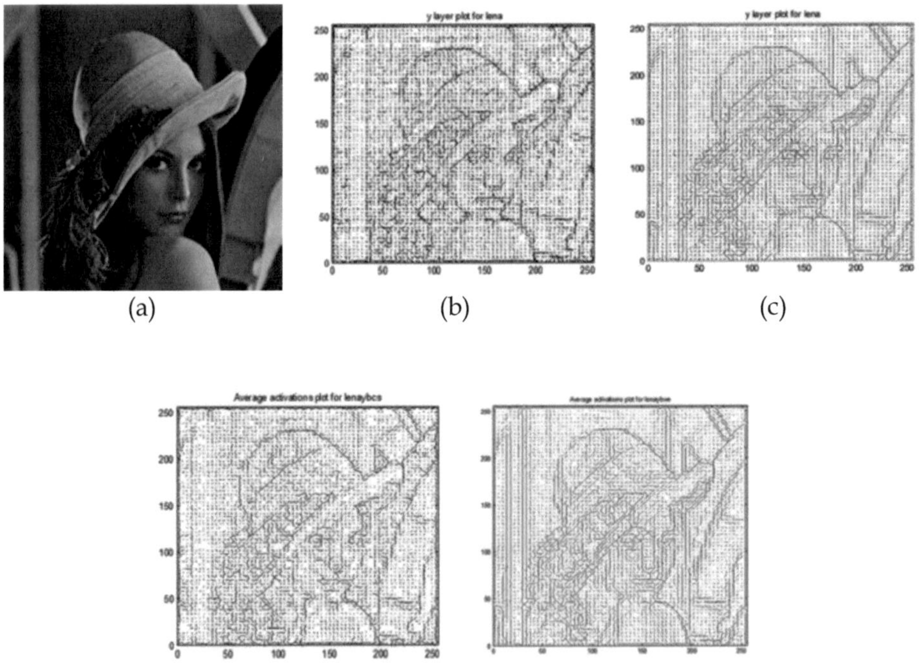

(a) (b) (c)

(d) (e)

Figure 7. Comparison between BCS ((b),(d)) and BWE ((c),(e))

4. The fBWE system

The main idea about the fBWE implementation is to design a massively parallel algorithm that should be robust with respect to noise while producing an output as similar as possible to the true BWE architecture. The main performance drawbacks of the BWE network are the presence of a feedback loop aimed to put the whole system in a steady state, and the use of floating point calculations. The fBWE system is a feed-forward elaboration pipeline that is completely implemented using 16-bit integer maths, according to SIMPil-K requirements. In Figure 8 the fBWE pipeline is shown. The fBWE architecture relies on the cascade of the OC Filter, and a competitive-cooperative pipeline. The SIMPil-K configuration we used, is made of 32×32 PEs with a PPE equal to 64, that is each sub-image is 8×8 pixels wide.

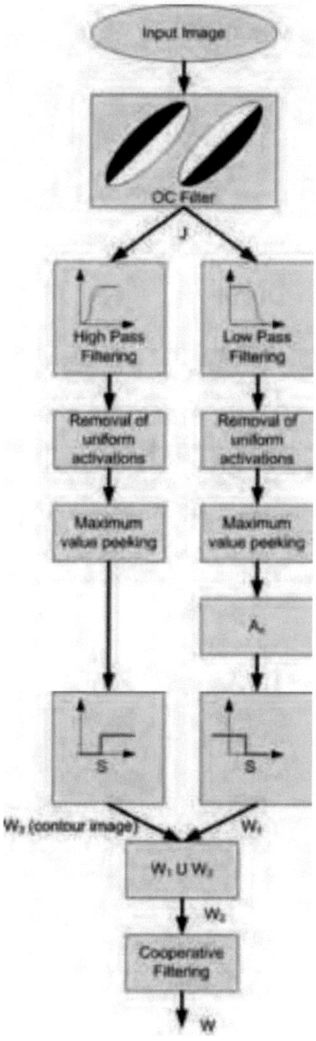

Figure 8. The fBWE pipeline

The whole process has been applied to 256×256 images, and M = 64 so there is a 4 pixels overlapping along each direction between two adjacent neighborhoods. Gabor masks in the

OC Filter have been implemented using equation (8), and have been provided to the PE array as a suitable gray level image. The original floating point values obtained for the weights have been approximated to 8-bit integer values, and the minimum value has been added to each of them to obtain a correct dynamics in the range [0,....,255]. The set of Gabor masks is depicted in Figure 9. The same mask is loaded into all the PEs in one column.

Figure 9. Arrangement of the Gabor masks for the PEs

Each row of the first image contains only 16 different orientations repeated twice, while the second one depicts the last 8 orientations repeated four times. At loading time, the offset is subtracted from each Pixel Register in the PE to correct the weights. After loading the input image the true filtering starts. The R15 register of each PE contains the correct value for the orientation k in order to store the result in the correct position after each filtering step. Due to the overlapping, each mask is used to convolve four neighborhoods shifting only one half of a sub-image between two PEs at each step, according to the scheme West-North-East-South. Finally, the Gabor masks image is shifted in the West direction by 8 pixels starting again the filtering cycle. The same procedure is adopted for the second Gabor masks image, but the filtering cycle is iterated only 8 times. After the filtering phase each PE contains four adjacent locations each containing N non null orientations due to the application of equation (7). The OC Filter output is quit precise in the determination of the orientations, but it suffers from its *locality*. Contours are not perfectly aligned, and they tend to double along a direction due to the activations present in couples of overlapped regions which intersect the same contour line. The competitive-cooperative pipeline tends to eliminate these problems without the use of a feedback scheme. Here the outputs of the OC Filter are grouped as N *orientation* images 64×64 pixels wide. The pipeline is split into two parallel branches: at the first step each orientation image is processed with a 3×3 high pass filter in the left branch, and a median filter of the same size in the right one. The left processing is aimed to enrich details, and to strengthen the contours, while the median filter is a form of blurring intended force close orientations to align thus correcting the OC Filter spurious outputs. The implementation of these filters in SIMPil-K implies that each PE needs a frame of 12 values surrounding the ones stored in its local memory. So a suitable transfer routine has been set up to obtain these values form the 8-neighborhood surrounding the PE. The four filtered values are again stored in the PE's local memory. The next step in both the pipeline branches is the suppression of uniform activation values. When an image region insisting on the location (i, j) exhibits a uniform luminance without perceivable contrast variation along any direction the fBWE activations b_{ijk} are almost of the same magnitude and a sort of little star is visualized in the output. To avoid this behaviour the uniform activations suppression acts according to the following rule:

$$\begin{aligned} \tilde{b}_{ij} - \hat{b}_{ij} \leqslant 0.2\tilde{b}_{ij} &\Rightarrow \forall k\, b_{ijk} \equiv 0 \\ \tilde{b}_{ij} &= \max_k(b_{ijk}) \\ \hat{b}_{ij} &= \min_k(b_{ijk}) \end{aligned} \tag{13}$$

Here the threshold value of 0.8 has been selected on the basis of a trial and error process. After uniform activations suppression the maximum values $\tilde{b}^l_{ij}$ and $\tilde{b}^r_{ij}$ are selected at each location for the left and right branches thus obtaining two average boundary webs images, using *max*(•) in place of the averaging function f_{av}. High pass, and median filters give rise to extremely different dynamics in the two pipeline branches, so a gain element has been placed in the high pass branch to normalize these ranges. The gain factor has been determined as

$$A_s = \frac{\max_{ij}(\tilde{b}^r_{ij})}{\max_{ij}(\tilde{b}^l_{ij})} \tag{14}$$

In all our experiments A_s assumed values between 6 and 7. Before the conjunction of the two branches with the union pixel by pixel of the left (W_L) and right (W_R) image, a sharp threshold S has been applied in order to join exactly W_L and W_R. The value of S has been selected as the 30% of the maximum activation in W_L, and all the values in W_R that are over the value of S are joined with all the values of W_R that are beneath the same threshold. The joined image W_J can be defined as $W_J = [(W_{J,ij}, k_{ij})]$ where for each location (i, j) the amplitude, and the relative orientation value are defined. The last step is the cooperative filtering that generates the fBWE image W, and is aimed to enforce aligned neighboring activations.

An activation is enforced if its orientation is slightly different from the one of the location at the center of the filter mask, otherwise it is decreased. The generic weight M_{pq} of the filter applied to the location (i, j) is defined as:

$$M_{pq} = \begin{cases} 1 - \frac{|k_{pq} - k_{ij}|}{N/2}, & \frac{|k_{pq} - k_{ij}|}{N/2} < N/2 \\ 1 - \frac{||k_{pq} - k_{ij}| - N|}{N/2}, & \text{otherwise} \end{cases} \tag{15}$$

Also in this case it is necessary for each PE to obtain 12 values from its eight neighbors.

5. Experimental Results

Several experiments have been conducted on a set of images with different pictorial features: real images with a lot of shading, highly textured images, high contrast ones, and artificial pictures with both high dynamics (like cartoons) and poor one (Kanizsa figures). In Figure 10 the BWE and fBWE images are reported along with a diagram of the local orientation differences $d_{ij} \triangleq k^{(BWE)}_{ij} - k^{(fBWE)}_{ij}$. It can be noticed that the two implementations are perceptually equivalent, and the major differences are present in the uniform brightness regions. In these parts of the image the BWE exhibits some small residual activations due to the feedback based stabilization process, while the fBWE suppresses them at all. In the case of Kanizsa figures with a few well distinct gray levels (see Figure 11) the OC Filter alone performs better of the fBWE, so it has been selected as the system output. As regards the performance, the BWE execution time in our experiments ranges from 14.94 sec. in the case of Kanizsa figure to 68.54 sec. for the Lena and Tank images, while fBWE has a constant execution time of 0.168 msec. This is an obvious finding because the fBWE is a feed-forward architecture, while the BWE is not, and its convergence to a steady state depends on the input brightness structure.

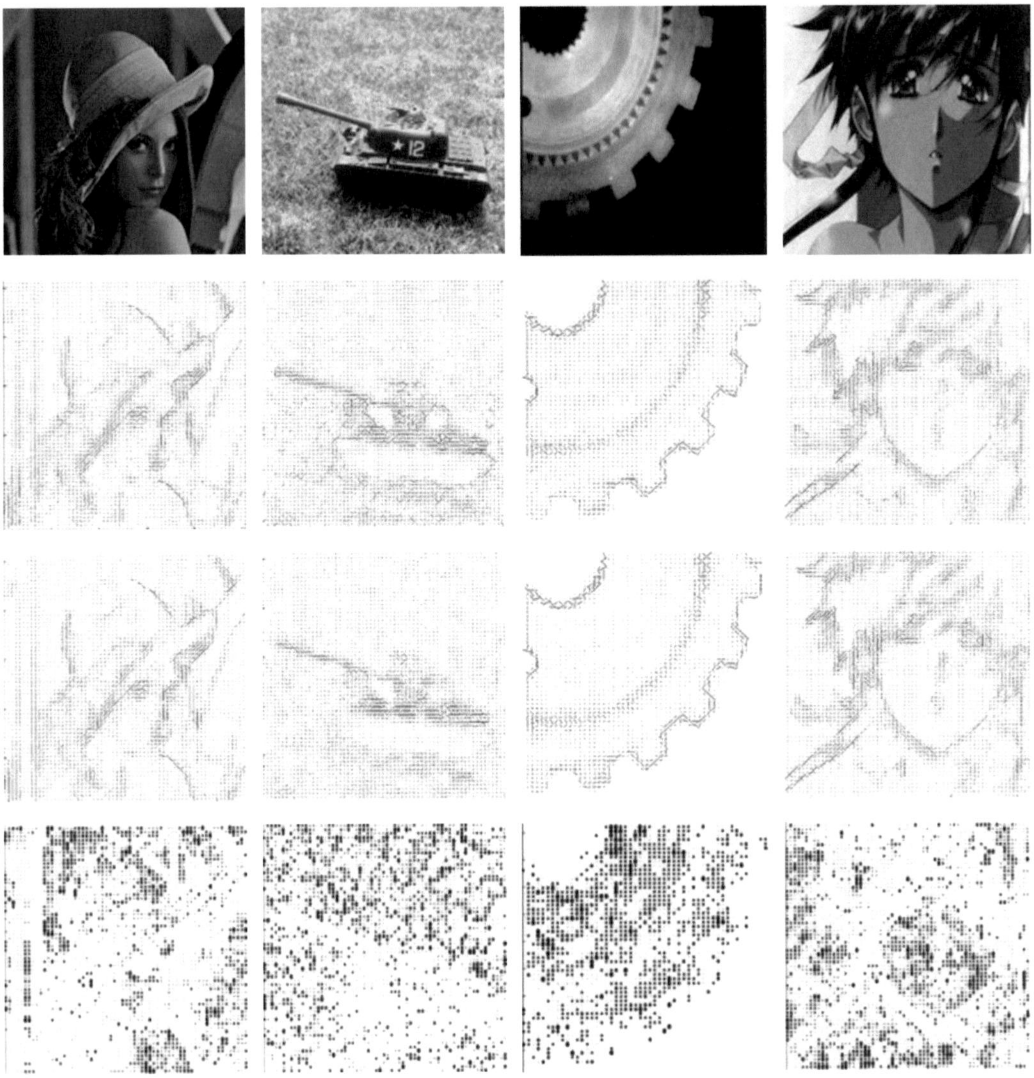

a) Lena ((b) Tank (c) Gear (d) Cartoon

Figure 10. Experimental results, from top to bottom: input image, BWE output, fBWE output, difference

(a) (b) (c)

Figure 11. Experimental results on a Kanizsa figure: (a) input image, (b) fBWE output, (c) OC Filter output

6. Conclusion

A Fast Boundary Web Extraction (fBWE) algorithm was presented in this paper as a fixed-point, data parallel implementation of the BWE. fBWE was mapped on SIMPil-K reconfigurable FPGA based platform.

Application components and their mapping details were provided along with a detailed analysis of their performance. Experimental results illustrate the significant gain achieved over the traditional BWE, with execution times allowing ample room for real-time processing of typical subsequent tasks in a complete robot vision system. Experimental results on an extensive data set illustrate the significant gain achieved over the traditional BWE implementation. Execution times are in the order of 170 μsec for a 256000 pixel image, thus allowing ample room for real-time processing of typical subsequent tasks in a complete robot vision system.

7, Reference

E. Ardizzone, A. Chella, R. Pirrone, and F. Sorbello. Recovering 3-D Form Features by a Connectionist Architecture. *Pattern Recognition Letters*, 15:77–85, 1994. [1]

E. Ardizzone, D. Molinelli, and R. Pirrone. A Fast Robust BCS Application to the Stereo Vision. In M. Marinaro and R. Tagliaferri, editors, *Neural Nets WIRN Vietri-95 Proceedings of the 7th Italian Workshop on Neural Nets*, pages 215–225, Vietri Sul Mare (SA), Italy, 1995. World Scientific Pu., Singapore. [2]

H.H. Cat, A. Gentile, J.C. Eble, M. Lee, O. Vendier, Y.J. Joo, D.S. Wills, M. Brooke, N.M. Jokerst, and A.S. Brown. SIMPil: An OE Integrated SIMD Architecture for Focal Plane Processing Applications. In *Proceedings of the Third IEEE International Conference on Massively Parallel Processing using Optical Interconnection* (MPPOI-96), pages 44–52, Maui Hawaii, USA, 1996. [3]

J. Van der Spiegel and M. Nishimura. Biologically inspired vision sensor for the detection of higher-level image features. In *2003 IEEE Conference on Electron Devices and Solid-State Circuits*, pages 11–16. IEEE Computer Society, Washington DC, USA, December 16-18 2003. [4]

R. Dominguez-Castro, S. Espejo, A. Rodriguez-Vazquez, R.A. Carmona, P. Foldesy, A. Zarandy, P. Szolgay, T. Sziranyi, and T. Roska. A 0.8-μm CMOS two-dimensional programmable mixed-signal focal-plane array processor with on-chip binary imaging and instructions storage. *IEEE Journal of Solid-State Circuits*, 32(7):1013–1026, July 1997. [5]

R. Etienne-Cummings, J. Van der Spiegel, P. Mueller, and Mao-Zhu Zhang. A Foveated Silicon Retina for Two-Dimensional Tracking. *IEEE Transactions on Circuits and Systems Part II: Express Briefs*, 47(6):504–517, June 2000. [6]

A. Gentile, S. Sander, L.M. Wills, and D.S. Wills. The impact of grain size on the eficiency of embedded SIMD image processing architectures. Journal of Parallel and Distributed Computing, 64:1318–1327, September 2004. [7]

A. Gentile and D.S. Wills. Portable Video Supercomputing. *IEEE Trans. on Computers*, 53(8):960–973, August 2004. [8]

S. Grossberg and E. Mingolla. Neural Dynamics of Perceptual Grouping: Textures, Boundaries and Emergent Segmentation. *Perception and Psychophysics*, 38:141–171, 1985. [9]

C.M. Higgins. Sensory architectures for biologically-inspired autonomous robotics. The Biological Bulletin, 200:235–242, April 2001. [10]

F.F. Li, R. Fergus, and P. Perona. Learning Generative Visual Models from Few Training Examples: An Incremental Bayesian Approach Tested on 101 Object Categories. In *2004 Conference on Computer Vision and Pattern Recognition Workshop* (CVPRW'04), volume 12, page 178. IEEE Computer Society, Washington DC, USA, June 27 - July 02 2004. [11]

T. Serre, L. Wolf, S. Bileschi, M. Riesenhuber, and T. Poggio. Robust object recognition with cortex-like mechanisms. *IEEE Transactions on Pattern Analysis and Machine Intelligence*, 29(3):411–426, 2007. [12]

C. Siagian and L. Itti. Biologically-Inspired Face Detection: Non-Brute- Force-Search Approach. *In 2004 Conference on Computer Vision and Pattern Recognition Workshop* (CVPRW'04), volume 5, page 62. IEEE Computer Society, Washington DC, USA, June 27 - July 02 2004. [13]

C. Siagian and L. Itti. Rapid biologically-inspired scene classification using features shared with visual attention. *IEEE Transactions on Pattern Analysis and Machine Intelligence*, 29(2):300–312, 2007. [14]

S. Ullman, E. Sali, and M. Vidal-Naquet. A Fragment-Based Approach to Object Representation and Classification. *In Proceedings of 4th International Workshop on Visual Form IWVF4*, volume LNCS 2059, pages 85–102, Capri, Italy, May 2001. Springer-Verlag, Heidelberg. [15]

P. Viola and M. Jones. Rapid Object Detection Using a Boosted Cascade of Simple Features. In 2001 *IEEE Computer Society Conference on Computer Vision and Pattern Recognition* (CVPR'01), volume 1, pages 511–518. IEEE Computer Society, Washington DC, USA, December 8-14 2001. [16]

C.C. Weems, E.M. Riseman, A.R. Hanson, and A. Rosenfield. The DARPA Image Understanding Benchmark for parallel Computers. *Journal of Parallel and Distributed Computing*, 11:1–24, 1991. [17]

25

Robot Vision in the Language of Geometric Algebra

Gerald Sommer and Christian Gebken
Department of Computer Science, Christian-Albrechts-University, Kiel
Germany

1. Introduction

In recent years, robot vision became an attractive scientific discipline. From a technological point of view, its aim is to endow robots with visual capabilities comparable to those of human beings. Although there is considerable endeavour, the progress is only slowly proceeding, especially in comparison to the level of behavior of human beings in natural environments. This has its reason in lacking insight into the organization principles of cognitive systems. Therefore, from a scientific point of view, robot vision is a test bed for understanding more on cognitive architectures and the mutual support of vision and action in cognitive systems. While in natural systems self-organization of structures and data flow is responsible for their success, in case of technical systems, the designer has to model cognitive systems. Modeling needs a theoretical base which is rooted in the state-of-art knowledge in science, mathematics and engineering.

The most difficult problem to be solved is the design of a useful cognitive architecture. This concerns e.g. the gathering and use of world knowledge, controlling the interplay of perception and action, the representation of equivalence classes, invariants and concepts. Besides, hard real-time requirements have to be considered. The most attractive approach to the design of a cognitive architecture is the framework of behavior-based systems (Sommer, 1997). A behavior is represented by a perception-action cycle. Remarkable features of such architecture are the tight coupling of perception and action, and learning the required competences (Pauli, 2001) from experience.

Another problem to be coped with in designing robot vision systems is the diversity of contributing disciplines. These are signal theory and image processing, pattern recognition including learning theory, robotics, computer vision and computing science. Because these disciplines developed separately, they are using different mathematical languages as modeling frameworks. Besides, their modeling capabilities are limited. These limitations are caused to a large extend by the dominant use of vector algebra. Fortunately, geometric algebras (GA) as the geometrically interpreted version of Clifford algebras (CA) (Hestenes & Sobczyk, 1984) deliver a reasonable alternative to vector algebra.

The aim of this contribution is to promote the use of geometric algebra in robot vision systems based on own successful experience over one decade of research. The application of GA within a behavior based design of cognitive systems is the long-term research topic of the Kiel Cognitive Systems Group (Sommer, 1999). Such a coherent system has to be an embodiment of the geometry and the stochastic nature of the external world. That is, it should enable both internal processes converging at reasonable interpretations of the world and performing useful actions in the environment. We will report on some novel results achieved within the last years which extend the survey papers (Sommer, 2004; Sommer, 2005).

Our main contributions to applications of geometric algebra in robot vision are focussing on the following problems:

- Development of a signal theory for local analysis of multi-dimensional signals (Sommer & Zang, 2005)
- Formulation of computer vision in the framework of conformal geometry (Rosenhahn & Sommer, 2005a and 2005b)
- Knowledge based neural learning by using algebraic constraints (Buchholz & Sommer, 2006)
- Higher-order statistics (Buchholz & Le Bihan, 2006) and estimations (Perwass et al., 2006) in GA.

More details of the results contributed by the Kiel Cognitive Systems Group can be found in the publications and reports on the website http://www.ks.informatik. uni-kiel.de. Here we will report from an engineer's point of view. But the reader should be aware that GA constitutes a framework which has to be adapted to the problem at hand. Therefore, the system designer has to shape this mathematical language in a task related manner. This is both a challenge and a chance at the same time.

In section 2, we will present a bird's eye view on geometric algebra and will also motivate its use in robot vision. Special emphasis will be on the conformal geometric algebra (CGA). A novel approach to local image analysis based on embedding the curvature tensor of differential geometry into a Clifford analysis setting will be presented in section 3. Sections 4 and 5 are dedicated to our recent progress on estimations from uncertain data in CGA. We will handle uncertainty for geometric entities and kinematic operations as well. Parameter estimation methods, based on the principle of least squares adjustment, will be used for evaluating multi-vectors and their respective uncertainties. Also, in section 5 we will focus on the problem of pose estimation in case of uncertain omnidirectional vision. In addition, we will present a novel generalized camera model, the so-called inversion camera model. Again, we will take advantage of the representation power of CGA.

2. A Bird's-eye View on Geometric Algebra

In this section we will sketch the basic features of a geometric algebra representation and compare it with a vector space representation. Special emphasis is laid on the conformal geometric algebra. In addition, we introduce the key ideas of the tensor notation of GA representations and the coupling of the conformal embedding and stochastic concepts.

2.1 Comparison of Vector Algebra and Geometric Algebra

As mentioned in the introduction, the limited modeling capabilities within the disciplines contributing to robot vision are caused to a large extend by the use of vector algebra. That statement has to be justified. First, a vector space is a completely unstructured algebraic framework whose entities, that is the vectors, are directed numbers. This is a richer representation than having only scalars at hand. But the product of vectors, the scalar product, destroys the direction information originally represented in the pair of vectors by mapping them to a scalar. Second, we are mostly interested in vector spaces with Euclidean norm. The basic geometric entities of Euclidean spaces are points. A Euclidean vector space can thus be interpreted as an infinite set of points. There is no possibility of formulating useful subspace concepts in the vector space but set based ones. Third, a cognitive system is reasoning and acting on global geometric entities, like a tea pot. It makes no sense to decompose the world phenomena into point-like entities. Fourth, the most important transformation in robot vision, that is rigid body motion (RBM), has no linear representation in Euclidian space. Instead, if we are interested in describing RBM of points, we have to take advantages of an algebraic trick as extending the dimension of the space for remaining in terms of linear operations. There is no general way for generalizing this trick within the vector space concept to other geometric entities (as a pair of points or a line). Therefore, most of the basic disciplines of robot vision are getting stuck in non-linearities. The resulting iterative solutions are intractable in real-time applications. Finally, besides translation, all other operational entities acting on a vector are not itself elements of the algebra. This makes the description of actions based on certain transformation groups a difficult task.

Geometric algebra enables to overcome most of those problems, at least to a certain extend. In fact, if not specified, the term geometric algebra represents a whole family of geometric algebras. The designer has to select the right one for the problem at hand or has to design a special one with the desired features. Hence, its use enables a knowledge based system design in an algebraic framework which can represent the geometry of interest. Representing geometry in an algebraic framework means thinking in a Kleinian sense (Brannan et al., 1999). Any GA has the following features:

1. It is a linear space, which can be mapped to a vector space again. Its elements are multi-vectors, that is directed numbers of mixed grade. It has a rich subspace structure with each subspace having algebraic properties and interpretations in a geometric or operational sense of representing entities of a certain grade, e.g. of higher order.
2. It represents a geometry of interest. That means, it models geometric spaces equipped with basic geometric entities and a range of higher order geometric entities with useful algebraic properties. Besides, it represents a Clifford group the elements of which are linear operational entities. This makes non-linear operations in vector spaces to linear ones in the chosen GA. That is, both geometric and operational entities are elements of the algebra.
3. A geometric algebra is equipped with a geometric product the action of which on multi-vectors not only enables mappings into certain subspaces but from which also incidence algebraic operations between subspaces can be derived.

This as a whole makes GA a powerful tool for modeling in robot vision and beyond.

2.2 Basic Structure of Geometric Algebra

Here we will only present a sketch of the rich structure represented by a geometric algebra. For more details see (Hestenes & Sobczyk, 1984) or the introduction paper (Hestenes et al., 2001), respectively the tutorial report (Perwass & Hildenbrand, 2003).

A geometric algebra $\mathbb{R}_{p,q,r}$ is a linear space of dimension 2^n constructed from a vector space $\mathbb{R}^{p,q,r}$ with signature (p,q,r), $n = p+q+r$, which we denote $\mathbb{R}_{p,q,r} = \mathbb{G}(\mathbb{R}^{p,q,r})$. The algebra is built by applying the geometric product to the basis vectors $\mathbf{e}_i$ of $\mathbb{R}_{p,q,r}$, $i = 1,\ldots,n$,

$$\mathbf{e}_i\mathbf{e}_j = \begin{cases} 1 & \text{for} \quad i=j \in \{1,\ldots,p\} \\ -1 & \text{for} \quad i=j \in \{p+1,\ldots,p+q\} \\ 0 & \text{for} \quad i=j \in \{p+q+1,\ldots,p+q+r=n\} \\ -\mathbf{e}_j\mathbf{e}_i \equiv \mathbf{e}_{ij} & \text{for} \quad i\neq j \end{cases} \tag{1}$$

The GA $\mathbb{R}_{p,q,r}$ is called Euclidean for $n = p$ and pseudo-Euclidean for $n = p + q$. In the case of $r\neq 0$, its metric is degenerate. The signature (p,q, r) is the key for selecting certain geometric properties of the GA. The geometric product is linear and associative but not commutative. The linear space of a GA is split into a rich subspace structure represented by a set of blades $\boldsymbol{B}_k$ of grade k. Given k independent vectors[1] a_i, $i = 1, \ldots, k$, a k-blade is defined for $k = 1,\ldots,n$ by

$$\boldsymbol{B}_k = \boldsymbol{a}_1\,\boldsymbol{a}_2\ldots\boldsymbol{a}_k = \boldsymbol{a}_1 \wedge \boldsymbol{a}_2 \wedge \ldots \wedge \boldsymbol{a}_k \tag{2}$$

Here $(\wedge)$ indicates the outer product. There are $l_k = \binom{n}{k}$ different k-blades, each having its own direction given by $I_k = \mathbf{e}_{i_1} \wedge \mathbf{e}_{i_2} \wedge \ldots \wedge \mathbf{e}_{i_k}$. Hence, k-blades constitute directed linear subspaces of $\mathbb{R}_{p,q,r}$. In figure 1 we visualize the blade structure of $\mathbb{R}_3$, that is the GA of $\mathbb{R}^3$. By considering next the simple example of the geometric product of two vectors a,b $\in \mathbb{R}_{p,q,r}$ we will get an inductive access to the construction rule of multi-vectors as the algebraic entities of a geometric algebra.

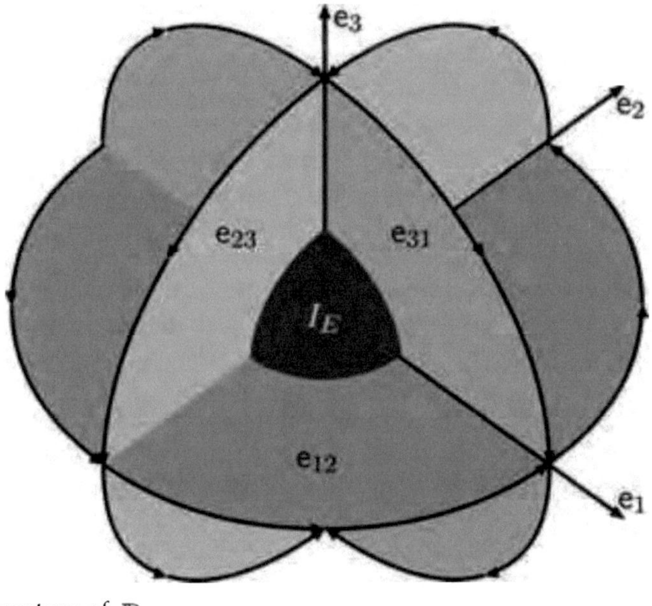

Figure 1. Blade structure of $\mathbb{R}_3$

Here $\langle\cdot\rangle_k$ means the grade-operator which indicates the separation of the linear space $\mathbb{R}_{p,q,r}$ into grade-k entities. Obviously, vectors are of grade one and $\langle\mathbb{R}_{p,q,r}\rangle_1 \equiv \mathbb{R}^{p,q,r}$. Then we get with

$$\boldsymbol{A} = \boldsymbol{a}\,\boldsymbol{b} = \boldsymbol{a}\cdot\boldsymbol{b} + \boldsymbol{a}\wedge\boldsymbol{b} \tag{3}$$

[1]We use lower case letters, as , for algebra vectors or for vector space elements.

a separation of the geometric product into the sum of the inner product

$$a \cdot b = \frac{1}{2}(a\,b + b\,a) = \langle a\,b \rangle_0 \tag{4}$$

and the outer product

$$a \wedge b = \frac{1}{2}(a\,b - b\,a) = \langle a\,b \rangle_2 . \tag{5}$$

The geometric product, $\boldsymbol{a\,b}$, results in the sum of a scalar, $(\boldsymbol{ab})_0$, and a bivector, $(\boldsymbol{ab})_2$.
In contrast to the scalar product of vector algebra, the geometric product of geometric algebra is both grade-decreasing and grade-increasing. In general the multi-vector $\boldsymbol{A}$ is a mixture of k-vectors, $\boldsymbol{A}_k$,

$$A = \sum_{k=0}^{n} A_k \tag{6}$$

with

$$A_k = \langle A \rangle_k = \sum_{j=1}^{l^*} \beta B_{kj}, \tag{7}$$

$l^* \leq l_k$. For the geometric product of homogeneous multi-vectors of grades s and r we get a multi-vector $\mathbf{C}$ with a certain spectrum of different k-vectors,

$$C = A_r B_s = \langle A_r B_s \rangle_{|r-s|} + \langle A_r B_s \rangle_{|r-s|+2} + \ldots + \langle A_r B_s \rangle_{r+s} \tag{8}$$

with the pure inner product $\boldsymbol{A}_r \cdot \boldsymbol{B}_s = (\boldsymbol{A}_r\boldsymbol{B}_s)_{|r-s|}$ and the pure outer product $\boldsymbol{A}_r \wedge \boldsymbol{B}_s = (\boldsymbol{A}_r\boldsymbol{B}_s)_{r+s}$. Hence, the other components result from mixing the inner and outer product.
The blades of grade n are called pseudoscalar, $\boldsymbol{P}$,

$$P = \lambda I \tag{9}$$

with $\boldsymbol{I}$ being the unit pseudoscalar with $\boldsymbol{I}^2 = \pm 1$ if $r = 0$ and λ being a scalar which equals the determinant of matrix algebra. Because $\boldsymbol{I} = \boldsymbol{I}_k \boldsymbol{I}_{n-k}$, a blade $\boldsymbol{B}_k$ is related to its dual one, $\boldsymbol{B}_{n-k}$, by

$$B_k^* = B_{n-k} = B_k I^{-1} \tag{10}$$

This is a useful operation for switching between different representations of a multi-vector. There are several main algebra involutions in GA, like in case of complex numbers the only existing one is conjugation. Let us mention as an example the reversion. If $\boldsymbol{A}_k \in \langle \mathbb{R}_{p,q} \rangle_k$ is a k-vector, then its reverse is defined as

$$\widetilde{A}_k = a_k \wedge a_{k-1} \wedge \ldots \wedge a_1 \tag{11}$$

and the reserve of a multi-vector $\boldsymbol{A} \in \mathbb{R}_{p,q}$ defined as

$$\widetilde{A} = \sum_{k=0}^{n} (-1)^{\frac{k(k-1)}{2}} A_k . \tag{12}$$

The reverse of a k-vector is needed for computing its magnitude,

$$|A_k| = \sqrt{A_k \cdot \widetilde{A}_k} \tag{13}$$

and its inverse,

$$A_k^{-1} = \frac{\widetilde{A}_k}{|A_k|^2} \tag{14}$$

Besides, it should be mentioned that any GA may be decomposed by

$$\mathbb{R}_n = \mathbb{R}_n^- + \mathbb{R}_n^+ \tag{15}$$

into two partial spaces with $\mathbb{R}_n$ representing the odd grade blades and $\mathbb{R}_n^+$ representing the even grade blades and $\mathbb{R}_n^-$ being a GA itself again.
There exist several isomorphisms of algebras. The most important statement is the existence of a certain matrix algebra for every GA (Porteous, 1995). In addition, the following isomorphisms are of practical importance:

$$\mathbb{R}_{p+1,q} \simeq \mathbb{R}_{q+1,p} \tag{16}$$

and

$$\mathbb{R}_{p,q}^+ \simeq \mathbb{R}_{q,p-1}. \tag{17}$$

Examples of the last one are $\mathbb{C} \simeq \mathbb{R}_{0,1} \simeq \mathbb{R}_{2,0}^+$ and $\mathbb{H} \simeq \mathbb{R}_{0,2} \simeq \mathbb{R}_{3,0}^+$ with $\mathbb{C}$ being the algebra of complex numbers and $\mathbb{H}$ being the quaternion algebra.

2.3 Geometric Algebra and its Tensor Notation

We take a look beyond the symbolic level and question how we can realize the structure of geometric algebra numerically. We show a way that makes direct use of the tensor representation inherent in GA.
If $\{E_{1..2^n}\}$ denotes the 2^n -dimensional algebra basis of $\mathbb{R}_n$, then a multi-vector $A \in \mathbb{R}_n$ can be written as $A = \mathsf{a}^i E_i$, where a^i denotes the ith component of a vector[2] $\mathsf{a} \in \mathbb{R}^{2^n}$ and a sum over the repeated index i is implied. We use this Einstein summation convention also in the following. If $B = \mathsf{b}^i E_i$ and $C = \mathsf{c}^i E_i$, then the components of C in the algebra equation $C = A \circ B$ can be evaluated via $\mathsf{c}^k = \mathsf{a}^i \mathsf{b}^j \mathsf{G}^k{}_{ij}$. Here $\circ$ is a placeholder for the algebra product and $\mathsf{G}^k{}_{ij} \in \mathbb{R}^{2^n \times 2^n \times 2^n}$ is a tensor encoding this product (we use sans serif letters as a, g or G to denote vectors, matrices, tensors or generally any regular arrangement of numbers). If we define the matrices $\mathsf{U}, \mathsf{V} \in \mathbb{R}^{2^n \times 2^n}$, as $\mathsf{U}(\mathsf{a}) := \mathsf{a}^i \mathsf{G}^k{}_{ij}$ and $\mathsf{V}(\mathsf{b}) := \mathsf{b}^j \mathsf{G}^k{}_{ij}$, then $\mathsf{c} = \mathsf{U}(\mathsf{a})\,\mathsf{b} = \mathsf{V}(\mathsf{b})\,\mathsf{a}$. This perfectly reveals the bilinearity of algebra products.
We define a mapping Φ and can then write $\Phi(A) = \mathsf{a}$, $\Phi(A\circ) = \mathsf{U}$, $\Phi(A \circ B) = \mathsf{a}^i \mathsf{b}^j \mathsf{G}^k{}_{ij}$ or if $a = \mathsf{a}^i \mathsf{e}_i$ is an element of a Euclidian vector space, $\Phi(a) = \mathsf{a}$ as well. Note that we reduce the complexity of equations considerably by only mapping those components of multi-vectors that are actually needed. As an example, a vector in $\mathbb{R}_n$ can have at least n non-zero components. Also, the outer product of two vectors will not produce 3-vector components, which can thus be disregarded. In the following we assume that Φ maps to the minimum number of components necessary.

2.4 Conformal Geometric Algebra

Recently it has been shown (Rosenhahn & Sommer, 2005a and 2005b) that the conformal geometry (Needham, 1997) is very attractive for most of the problems in robot vision, which

[2] At least numerically, there is no other way than representing multi-vectors as vectors.

are related to shape modeling, projective geometry and kinematic. Conformal geometric algebra (CGA) delivers a non-linear representation of a Euclidean space with remarkable features:
First, CGA constitutes a unique framework for affine, projective and Euclidean geometry. Because the special Euclidean transformation (RBM) is a special affine transformation, we can handle either kinematic, projective or metric aspects of the problem at hand in the same algebraic frame. Second, the basic geometric entities of conformal geometry are spheres of dimension n. Other geometric entities as points, planes, lines, circles,... may be easily constructed. These entities are no longer set concepts of a vector space but elements of CGA. Third, the special Euclidean group is a subgroup of the conformal group, which is in CGA an orthogonal group. Therefore, its action on the above mentioned geometric entities will be a linear operation. Fourth, the inversion operation is another subgroup of the conformal group which can be advantageously used in robot vision. Fifth, CGA generalizes the incidence algebra of projective geometry with respect to the above mentioned geometric entities.
Before we enlighten the structure and features of CGA in more detail, we will have a short look on $\mathbb{R}_3$, the geometric algebra of the Euclidean 3D-space $\mathbb{R}^3$. This will be the starting point for the mentioned non-linear representation in CGA. Additionally, $\mathbb{R}_3$ is the embedding framework for image analysis, which will be described in section 3. The basis of its 8- dimensional space is given by

$$\text{basis}(\mathbb{R}_3) : \{\mathbf{e}_0, \mathbf{e}_1, \mathbf{e}_2, \mathbf{e}_3, \mathbf{e}_{23}, \mathbf{e}_{31}, \mathbf{e}_{12}, \mathbf{e}_{123}\} \tag{18}$$

with $\mathbf{e}_0 \equiv 1$ and $\mathbf{e}_i$ being the basis vectors of $\mathbb{R}^3$ with $\mathbf{e}_0^2 = \mathbf{e}_i^2 = 1$. Here the $\mathbf{e}_i$ constitute the unit 1-blades and the $\mathbf{e}_{ij}$ constitute the unit 2-blades with $\mathbf{e}_{ij}^2 = -1$, see figure 1. The unit pseudoscalar $\mathbf{e}_{123} \equiv I_E$ squares according to $\mathbf{e}_{123}^2 = -1$.
The even subalgebra $\mathbb{R}_3^+$ is isomorphic to the quaternion algebra $\mathbb{H}$ according to equation (17). Its dimension is four and the basis is given by

$$\text{basis}(\mathbb{R}_3^+) : \{\mathbf{e}_0, \mathbf{e}_{23}, \mathbf{e}_{31}, \mathbf{e}_{12}\} \simeq \{1, i, j, -k\}, \tag{19}$$

where i, j, k are the imaginary unit vectors of a quaternion.
The conformal geometric algebra $\mathbb{R}_{4,1}$ of $\mathbb{R}^3$, is built by extending $\mathbb{R}^3$ with a so-called Minkowski plane $\mathbb{R}^{1,1}$, resulting in $\mathbb{R}^{4,1}$. Originally, this construction of the CGA of a pseudo-Euclidean space $\mathbb{R}^{p,q}$ which results in $\mathbb{R}_{p+1,q+1}$, was proposed and analyzed by (Angles, 1980). Only the work of (Li et al., 2001a) has been recognized by the robot vision community as valuable access to the interesting phenomena in a unique framework. The same authors presented also a CGA for spherical geometry (Li et al., 2001b) and a further generalization to cope with Euclidean, spherical and hyperbolic geometry (Li et al., 2001c). But the last two cases have not yet been studied in robot vision.
The basis of the Euclidean CGA $\mathbb{R}_{4,1}$, is of dimension 32. That one of the extended space $\mathbb{R}^{4,1}$ contains as additional basis vectors $\mathbf{e}_+$ and $\mathbf{e}_-$ with $\mathbf{e}_+^2 = 1$, $\mathbf{e}_-^2 = -1$, $\mathbf{e}_+ \cdot \mathbf{e}_- = 0$. Both basis vectors constitute the so-called orthonormal basis of the Minkowski plane. More attractive is to switch to the so-called null-basis $\{\mathbf{e}_o, \mathbf{e}_\infty\}$ with $\mathbf{e}_\infty^2 = \mathbf{e}_o^2 = 0$ and $\mathbf{e}_\infty \cdot \mathbf{e}_o = -1$. This has two reasons. First, both the origin of $\mathbb{R}^3$, represented by $\mathbf{e}_o = \frac{1}{2}(\mathbf{e}_- - \mathbf{e}_+)$, and the point at infinity, represented by $\mathbf{e}_\infty = \mathbf{e}_- + \mathbf{e}_+$, are explicitly accessible. Second, a point x 4,1 of the Euclidian 3D-vector space $\mathbb{R}^3$ is mapped to a

conformal point (null vector) $\boldsymbol{X} \in \mathbb{R}^{4,1}$, with $\boldsymbol{X}^2 = 0$ and $\boldsymbol{X} \cdot \mathbf{e}_\infty = -1$, by the embedding function

$$\mathcal{K} : \boldsymbol{x} \longmapsto \boldsymbol{X} := \boldsymbol{x} + \tfrac{1}{2}\boldsymbol{x}^2\, \mathbf{e}_\infty + \mathbf{e}_o\,. \tag{20}$$

We denote these special vectors by capital letters as well. The mapping $\mathcal{K}$ builds a homogeneous representation of a stereographically projected point (Rosenhahn & Sommer, 2005a). As a grade-1 entity, a point is a special sphere, *S*, (also of grade one) with radius zero. The dual representation of a sphere

$$\boldsymbol{S}^* = \boldsymbol{A} \wedge \boldsymbol{B} \wedge \boldsymbol{C} \wedge \boldsymbol{D} \tag{21}$$

is of grade four and is defined by the outer product of four points. A circle as a 2-dimensional sphere, $\boldsymbol{Z} \in \langle \mathbb{R}_{4,1} \rangle_2$ or $\boldsymbol{Z}^* \in \langle \mathbb{R}_{4,1} \rangle_3$ is defined by

$$\boldsymbol{Z} = \boldsymbol{S}_1 \wedge \boldsymbol{S}_2\,, \quad \boldsymbol{Z}^* = \boldsymbol{A} \wedge \boldsymbol{B} \wedge \boldsymbol{C}\,. \tag{22}$$

By replacing one point in the defining equations (21) or (22) by the point at infinity, $\mathbf{e}_\infty$, a plane, a line or a point pair (a one-dimensional sphere) may be derived. Most interesting for robot vision is the orthogonal representation in $\mathbb{R}_{4,1}$ of the elements of the conformal group C(3). All transformations belonging to the conformal group are linear ones and the null cone, that is the set of all null vectors, is invariant with respect to them. Let $\boldsymbol{G} \in \mathbb{R}_{4,1}$ be an element of the conformal group and $\boldsymbol{U} \in \mathbb{R}_{4,1}$ any entity which has to be transformed by $\boldsymbol{G}$ to $\boldsymbol{U}' \in \mathbb{R}_{4,1}$. Then

$$\boldsymbol{U}' = \boldsymbol{G}\, \boldsymbol{U}\, \widetilde{\boldsymbol{G}} \tag{23}$$

describes this transformation as a (bi-)linear mapping. In general, all algebraic entities with such sandwich product are called versors (Hestens et al., 2001). Given some conditions, certain versors are called spinors (representing rotation and dilation) and normalized spinors are called rotors (representing pure rotation). Interestingly, also translation has a rotor representation (called translator) in CGA. But the most interesting transformation belonging to the conformal group is inversion, see (Needham, 1997), because all other transformations can be derived from it. Let $\boldsymbol{S} = \mathbf{e}_o - \frac{1}{2}\mathbf{e}_\infty = -\mathbf{e}_+$ be a unit sphere located at the origin $\mathbf{e}_o$, then the inversion of any conformal point $\boldsymbol{X} \in \langle \mathbb{R}_{4,1} \rangle_1$ in the unit sphere is written

$$\boldsymbol{X}' = \boldsymbol{S}\, \boldsymbol{X}\, \boldsymbol{S}\,. \tag{24}$$

The elements of the rigid body motion in CGA are called motors, $\boldsymbol{M} \in \mathbb{R}^+_{4,1}$. They connect rotation, represented by a rotor $\boldsymbol{R}$, and translation, represented by a translator $\boldsymbol{T}$, in a multiplicative way,

$$\boldsymbol{M} = \boldsymbol{T}\, \boldsymbol{R}\, \widetilde{\boldsymbol{T}} \tag{25}$$

and can be interpreted as a general rotation (Rosenhahn & Sommer, 2005a). As all versors, they are concatenated multiplicatively. Let $\boldsymbol{M} = \boldsymbol{M}_2\boldsymbol{M}_1$ be a sequence of two motors, then

$$\boldsymbol{U}'' = \boldsymbol{M}\, \boldsymbol{U}\, \widetilde{\boldsymbol{M}} = \boldsymbol{M}_2\, \boldsymbol{U}'\, \widetilde{\boldsymbol{M}}_2 = \boldsymbol{M}_2\, \boldsymbol{M}_1\, \boldsymbol{U}\, \widetilde{\boldsymbol{M}}_1\, \widetilde{\boldsymbol{M}}_2 \tag{26}$$

for all $\boldsymbol{U} \in \mathbb{R}_{4,1}$. Another important feature of linear operations in GA also applies for versors in CGA. It is the preservation of the outer product under linear transformation, which is called outermorphism (Heestens, 1991). Let $\boldsymbol{S}_1, \boldsymbol{S}_2 \in \langle \mathbb{R}_{4,1} \rangle_1$ be two spheres and $\boldsymbol{Z} \in \langle \mathbb{R}_{4,1} \rangle_2$ a circle. Then according to equations (22) and (23) the circle transforms under the action of a motor $\boldsymbol{M} \in \mathbb{R}^+_{4,1}$ as

$$\begin{aligned} \boldsymbol{Z}' &= \boldsymbol{M}\boldsymbol{Z}\widetilde{\boldsymbol{M}} = \boldsymbol{M}(\boldsymbol{S}_1 \wedge \boldsymbol{S}_2)\widetilde{\boldsymbol{M}} = \langle \boldsymbol{M}(\boldsymbol{S}_1\boldsymbol{S}_2)\widetilde{\boldsymbol{M}} \rangle_2 \\ &= \langle \boldsymbol{M}\boldsymbol{S}_1\widetilde{\boldsymbol{M}}\boldsymbol{M}\boldsymbol{S}_2\widetilde{\boldsymbol{M}} \rangle_2 = \boldsymbol{M}\boldsymbol{S}_1\widetilde{\boldsymbol{M}} \wedge \boldsymbol{M}\boldsymbol{S}_2\widetilde{\boldsymbol{M}} = \boldsymbol{S}_1' \wedge \boldsymbol{S}_2' . \end{aligned} \tag{27}$$

These last features of CGA turn out to be very important for robot vision applications as pose estimation, see (Rosenhahn & Sommer, 2005b) and (Gebken et al., 2006). Another important feature of CGA is the stratification of spaces according to (Faugeras, 1995) in one algebraic framework. Because

$$\mathbb{R}_{4,1} \supset \mathbb{R}_{3,1} \supset \mathbb{R}_{3,0} \tag{28}$$

with $\mathbb{R}_{3,1}$ being one possible representation of the projective space in GA, the change of the representations with the respective geometric aspects is a simple task, see (Rosenhahn & Sommer, 2005a).

2.5 Conformal Embedding - the Stochastic Supplement

We have to obey the rules of error propagation when we embed points by means of function $\mathcal{K}$, equation (20). Assume that point x is a random vector with a Gaussian distribution and $\bar{\boldsymbol{x}}$ is its mean value. Furthermore, we denote the 3×3 covariance matrix of x by Σ_x. Let $\mathcal{E}$ denote the expectation value operator, such that $\mathcal{E}[\boldsymbol{x}] = \bar{\boldsymbol{x}}$. The uncertain representative in conformal space, i.e. the stochastic supplement for $\boldsymbol{X} = \mathcal{K}(\bar{\boldsymbol{x}})$, is determined by a sphere with imaginary radius

$$\mathcal{E}\Big[\mathcal{K}(\boldsymbol{x})\Big] = \bar{\boldsymbol{x}} + \tfrac{1}{2}\,\bar{\boldsymbol{x}}^2\,\mathbf{e}_\infty + \mathbf{e}_o + \tfrac{1}{2}\mathrm{trace}\Big(\Sigma_{\boldsymbol{x}}\Big)\mathbf{e}_\infty \tag{29}$$

rather than the pure conformal point $\mathcal{K}\Big(\mathcal{E}[\boldsymbol{x}]\Big)$. However, observing that $\mathcal{K}\Big(\mathcal{E}[\boldsymbol{x}]\Big) \approx \mathcal{E}\Big[\mathcal{K}(\boldsymbol{x})\Big]$ shows why our algorithms do not noticeably differ in the output when using an exact embedding or its approximation. We evaluate the corresponding 5×5 covariance matrix $\Sigma_{\boldsymbol{X}}$ for $\boldsymbol{X} = \mathcal{K}(\bar{\boldsymbol{x}})$ by means of error propagation and find

$$\Sigma_{\boldsymbol{X}} = \mathsf{J}_{\mathcal{K}}(\bar{\boldsymbol{x}})\,\Sigma_{\boldsymbol{x}}\,\mathsf{J}_{\mathcal{K}}^{\mathsf{T}}(\bar{\boldsymbol{x}}), \tag{30}$$

where we used the Jacobian of $\mathcal{K}$.

$$\mathsf{J}_{\mathcal{K}}(\bar{\boldsymbol{x}}) := \frac{\partial \mathcal{K}}{\partial \boldsymbol{X}} = \begin{bmatrix} 1 & 0 & 0 \\ 0 & 1 & 0 \\ 0 & 0 & 1 \\ \bar{x}_1 & \bar{x}_2 & \bar{x}_3 \\ 0 & 0 & 0 \end{bmatrix} . \tag{31}$$

3. Monogenic Curvature Tensor as Image Representation

In this section we will describe how the embedding of local image analysis into a geometric algebra extends the representation in such a way that a rich set of local features will emerge.

3.1 Overview: Local Spectral Representations

Image analysis is a central task of robot vision systems. It is to a main portion local analysis. Image analysis based on local spectral representations (Granlund & Knutsson, 1995), that is amplitude and phase, has been a well-known method of signal processing for years. The aim is to assign a structural or/and geometric interpretation to an image point. That task of computing is called split of identity. In practice, a set of oriented bandpass operators are applied, each consisting of a pair of quadrature filters. The most well-known representative is the complex valued Gabor filter (Gabor, 1946). It delivers a complex valued signal representation, the analytic signal, from which for each chosen orientation at position $\boldsymbol{x} \in \mathbb{R}^2$ a local amplitude and a local phase can be derived. The local amplitude can be considered as a confidence measure of estimates of the local parity symmetry of the signal derived from local phase. Parity symmetry is a measure, which describes the type of structure. The method can be used for detecting lines and edges, analyzing textures, and with some restrictions for detecting corners and junctions.

Regrettably, the analytic signal is neither rotation invariant nor sensitive to discriminate intrinsically 1D and 2D (i1D and i2D) structures. This has its reason in the fact that the analytic signal is indeed only a reasonable complex valued extension of one-dimensional functions. Therefore, with great endeavour the problems of orientation steerability (Freeman & Adelson, 1991) and of generalizing the Hilbert transform (Hahn, 1996) have been attacked.

Only the consequent use of Clifford analysis (Brackx et al., 1982) led us to a multi-dimensional generalization of the analytic signal, called monogenic signal (Felsberg & Sommer, 2001) which overcomes the missing rotation invariance. But also that representation is incomplete with respect to represent intrinsically 2D structures, see the survey paper (Sommer & Zang, 2007).

The monogenic curvature tensor (Zang & Sommer, 2007) further generalizes the monogenic signal. It delivers a local signal representation with the following features:

- It enables classification of intrinsic dimension.
- It delivers two curvature based signal representations which distinctly separate represent intrinsically 1D and 2D structures. One of these is identical to the monogenic signal. Two specific but comparable types of local amplitude and phase can be described.
- In both cases the local phase constitutes a vector that includes also the orientation as a geometric feature.
- In case of i2D structures, an angle of intersection can be derived from the derivations of phase angles.
- Both curvature based signal representations can be embedded in a novel scale-space concept, the monogenic scale-space (Feldsberg & Sommer, 2004), in which local amplitude, phase and orientation become inherent features of a scale-space theory. This enables scale adaptive local image analysis.

All these efforts have been made because of the advantages of phase based image analysis for getting access to geometry and because of the illumination invariance of phase information.

3.2 Monogenic Curvature Tensor

The image representation we want to model should have some invariances:

- Invariance with respect to intrinsic dimension: Both i1D and i2D structures can be modeled. This is possible by the curvature tensor of differential geometry (Koenderink & van Doorn, 1987).
- Invariance with respect to parity symmetry: Both even and odd symmetric structures can be represented. This is possible by designing quadrature phase filters, whose harmonic conjugate component is in quadrature phase relation to the real valued component (Sommer & Zang, 2007). The way to get this is applying a (generalized) holomorphic extension of a real valued multi-dimensional function by a (generalized) Hilbert transform.
- Invariance with respect to rotation: This becomes possible by specifying the generalized holomorphic extension by a monogenic extension (Felsberg & Sommer, 2001), whose operator realization is given by the Riesz transform (Stein & Weiss, 1971).
- Invariance with respect to angle of intersection: Because of the involved differential geometric model, a local structure model for i2D structures is considered for i1D structures intersecting at arbitrary angles.
- Invariance with respect to scale: This requires embedding of the image representation, respective of the operator which derives it into a monogenic scale-space (Felsberg & Sommer, 2004).

Having these invariances in the image representation, in a second step of analysis the corresponding variances can be computed. These are intrinsic dimension, parity symmetry, rotation angle, angle of intersection and intrinsic scale at which these features exist.
We will interpret a 2D-image as a surface in $\mathbb{R}^3$. Let be C the curvature tensor of the second fundamental theorem of differential geometry. Its Monge patch representation is given by

$$\mathsf{C}(\boldsymbol{x}) = \left((1 + f_x{}^2 + f_y{}^2)^{-\frac{1}{2}}\ \mathsf{B}\right)(\boldsymbol{x}) \tag{32}$$

with the Hesse matrix

$$\mathsf{B}(\boldsymbol{x}) = \begin{bmatrix} f_{xx} & f_{xy} \\ f_{xy} & f_{yy} \end{bmatrix} \left(\boldsymbol{x}\right). \tag{33}$$

Then the Gaussian curvature, $\kappa(\boldsymbol{x}) = \det(\mathsf{B})$, and the mean curvature, $\mu(\boldsymbol{x}) = \mathrm{trace}(\mathsf{B})$, are spanning a basis in which the local signal $f(x)$ can be classified according to its intrinsic dimension according to table 1.

Type	μ (Mean Curvature)	κ (Gaussian Curvature)
Elliptic (i2D)		$\kappa > 0$
Hyperbolic (i2D)		$\kappa < 0$
Parabolic (i1D)	$\lvert\mu\rvert \neq 0$	$\kappa = 0$
Planar (i0D)	$\lvert\mu\rvert = 0$	$\kappa = 0$

Table 1. Surface type classification based on Gaussian and mean curvature

The signal representation we want to get is a kind of Hesse matrix in a monogenic representation. This requires two steps. First, according to (Felsberg & Sommer, 2001) we are embedding the originally scalar valued signal $f(x)$ as a vector field $\boldsymbol{f}(x)$ with values directed to the unit vector $\mathbf{e}_3$,

$$\begin{aligned} f(\boldsymbol{x}) : \mathbb{R}^2 \to \mathbb{R} \quad &\longrightarrow \quad \boldsymbol{f}(\boldsymbol{x}) : \mathbb{R}^2 \to \mathbb{R}\,\mathbf{e}_3 \\ \boldsymbol{f}(\boldsymbol{x}) \;=\; \boldsymbol{f}(x\,\mathbf{e}_1 + y\,\mathbf{e}_2) \;&=\; f(x,y)\,\mathbf{e}_3\,. \end{aligned} \tag{34}$$

Second, we are switching from the vector space $\mathbb{R}^3$ to the Euclidean geometric algebra $\mathbb{R}_3 \equiv \mathbb{G}(\mathbb{R}^3)$ and are applying a monogenically extended Hessian operator, $\mathsf{h}_M \in M(2,\mathbb{R}_3)$, which is a 2×2 matrix with monogenic elements. The convolution of the signal f with all elements of the operator matrix results in the monogenic curvature tensor $\mathsf{T}(x) \in M(2,\mathbb{R}_3)$ as signal representation. To be more specific, see (Zang & Sommer, 2007), the monogenic Hessian operator may be splitted into an even operator, $\mathsf{h}_e \in M(2,\mathbb{R}_3^+)$, with spinor valued elements and an odd operator, $\mathsf{h}_o \in M(2,\mathbb{R}_3^-)$ which results from the even operator by applying the Riesz transform $\boldsymbol{h}_R$,

$$\mathsf{h}_M \;=\; \mathsf{h}_e + \mathsf{h}_o \;=\; \mathsf{h}_e \;+\; \boldsymbol{h}_R * \mathsf{h}_e \tag{35}$$

with

$$\mathsf{h}_e(\boldsymbol{x}) \;=\; \begin{bmatrix} \partial_{xx} & -\partial_{xy}\,\mathbf{e}_{12} \\ \partial_{xy}\,\mathbf{e}_{12} & \partial_{yy} \end{bmatrix} (\boldsymbol{x}) \tag{36}$$

and

$$\boldsymbol{h}_R(\boldsymbol{x}) \;=\; \frac{\boldsymbol{x}\,\mathbf{e}_3}{2\pi|\boldsymbol{x}|^3}\,. \tag{37}$$

The monogenic Hessian operator may be interpreted as a rotation invariant and parity symmetry invariant detector of two i1D structures crossing invariant with respect to the angle of intersection. This involved structure model is the most general that could be developed. Nevertheless, it is limited by the model of differential geometry which does not consider derivatives of order higher than two. The structure of the monogenic Hessian operator reveals if we are going to the Fourier domain, take advantage of the derivative theorem of Fourier theory, and are modeling the operator in terms of circular harmonics of order n, $\boldsymbol{C}_n \in \mathbb{R}_3^+$, in polar coordinates $\boldsymbol{u} = (\rho, \alpha)$,

$$\boldsymbol{C}_n(\varrho,\alpha) \;=\; \boldsymbol{C}_n(\varrho)\exp(n\alpha\mathbf{e}_{12})\,. \tag{38}$$

Then we recognize that our model involves circular harmonics of orders $n \in \{0, 1, 2,3\}$,

$$\mathsf{H}_e(\boldsymbol{u}) \;=\; \frac{1}{2}\begin{bmatrix} \boldsymbol{C}_0 + \langle \boldsymbol{C}_2\rangle_0 & -\langle \boldsymbol{C}_2\rangle_2 \\ \langle \boldsymbol{C}_2\rangle_2 & \boldsymbol{C}_0 - \langle \boldsymbol{C}_2\rangle_0 \end{bmatrix} (\boldsymbol{u}) \tag{39}$$

$$\mathsf{H}_o(\boldsymbol{u}) \;=\; \frac{1}{2}\begin{bmatrix} \boldsymbol{C}_1(\boldsymbol{C}_0 + \langle \boldsymbol{C}_2\rangle_0) & \boldsymbol{C}_1(-\langle \boldsymbol{C}_2\rangle_2) \\ \boldsymbol{C}_1(\langle \boldsymbol{C}_2\rangle_2) & \boldsymbol{C}_1(\boldsymbol{C}_0 - \langle \boldsymbol{C}_2\rangle_0) \end{bmatrix} (\boldsymbol{u})\,. \tag{40}$$

As equations (35) and (40) reveal, the Riesz transform is identic to the first order circular harmonic,

$$\boldsymbol{H}_R(\boldsymbol{u}) = \frac{\boldsymbol{u}}{|\boldsymbol{u}|}\mathbf{e}_{12}^{-1} \equiv \boldsymbol{C}_1(\boldsymbol{u})\,. \tag{41}$$

What remains for fulfilling the scale invariance requirement is embedding the monogenic Hessian operator into the monogenic scale-space (Felsberg & Sommer, 2004). This is achieved by replacing the radial component of circular harmonics, $\boldsymbol{C}_n(\rho)$, by a Difference-of-Poisson kernel, $\boldsymbol{H}_{\mathrm{DOP}}$,

$$\boldsymbol{H}_{\mathrm{DOP}}(\varrho; s_1, s_2) = \exp(-2\pi\varrho\, s_1) - \exp(-2\pi\varrho\, s_2) \tag{42}$$

with $s_1 < s_2$ being two different scale parameters. This results in circular harmonic bandpass functions

$$\boldsymbol{C}_n(\varrho, \alpha; s_1, s_2) = \boldsymbol{H}_{\mathrm{DOP}}(\varrho; s_1, s_2)\,\boldsymbol{C}_n(\alpha) \tag{43}$$

Finally, we get the monogenic curvature tensor $\mathsf{T}(\boldsymbol{x})$ as

$$\mathsf{T}(\boldsymbol{x}) = \mathsf{T}_e(\boldsymbol{x}) + \mathsf{T}_o(\boldsymbol{x}) = \Big((\mathsf{h}_e + \mathsf{h}_o) * \boldsymbol{f}\Big)(\boldsymbol{x})\,, \tag{44}$$

respectively its representation in frequency domain.

3.3 Analysis of the Monogenic Curvature Tensor

Having the monogenic curvature tensor (in a scale-space embedding), it will now be analyzed with respect to the represented curvature information (Zang & Sommer, 2007).
By computing the trace of $\mathsf{T}(\boldsymbol{x})$, we get the monogenic mean curvature signal, $f_{\mathrm{i1D}}(x)$: $\mathbb{R}^2 \rightarrow \mathbb{R}_3$, which is specific with respect to i1D structures. It may be written as a vector field

$$\boldsymbol{f}_{\mathrm{i1D}}(\boldsymbol{x}) = \boldsymbol{t}_e(\boldsymbol{x}) + \boldsymbol{t}_o(\boldsymbol{x}) = \mathrm{trace}(\mathsf{T}_e)(\boldsymbol{x}) + \mathrm{trace}(\mathsf{T}_o)\,\mathbf{e}_2(\boldsymbol{x}) \tag{45}$$

$$= \boldsymbol{f}(\boldsymbol{x}) + \Big(\boldsymbol{h}_R * f\Big)(\boldsymbol{x}) \equiv \boldsymbol{f}_M(\boldsymbol{x})\,, \tag{46}$$

which turns out to be identical to the monogenic signal (Felsberg & Sommer, 2001).
By computing the determinant of $\mathsf{T}(\boldsymbol{x})$, we get the generalized monogenic Gaussian curvature signal, $f_{\mathrm{i2D}}(x)$: $\mathbb{R}^2 \rightarrow \mathbb{R}_3$, which is specific with respect to i2D structures. In similar way as f_{i1D}, it may be written as a vector field

$$\boldsymbol{f}_{\mathrm{i2d}}(\boldsymbol{x}) = \boldsymbol{d}_e(\boldsymbol{x}) + \boldsymbol{d}_o(\boldsymbol{x}) = \det{}_R(\mathsf{T}_e)\mathbf{e}_3(\boldsymbol{x}) + \mathbf{e}_1 \det{}_R(\mathsf{T}_o)(\boldsymbol{x}) \tag{47}$$

$$= \boldsymbol{d}_e(\boldsymbol{x}) + \Big(\mathbf{e}_1\mathbf{c}_2\mathbf{e}_3 * \boldsymbol{d}_e\Big)(\boldsymbol{x}) \equiv \boldsymbol{f}_{\mathrm{MC}}(\boldsymbol{x})\,. \tag{48}$$

We call it 'generalized monogenic' because its conjugate harmonic part results from the real part by applying c_2 as generalized Hilbert transform with the result that the relations between $\boldsymbol{d}_e$ and $\boldsymbol{d}_o$ are different to those of $\boldsymbol{t}_e$ and $\boldsymbol{t}_o$. Both signal representations can be interpreted as the result of a spinor valued operator, $\boldsymbol{s}$, which rotates and scales the original vector field $\boldsymbol{f}(\boldsymbol{x}) = f(x, y)\,\mathbf{e}_3$ so that it will be supplemented by a conjugate harmonic component which projects to the plane $\mathbf{e}_1 \wedge \mathbf{e}_2$ and fulfills the conditions $\boldsymbol{t}_e^2 = \boldsymbol{t}_o^2$ and $\boldsymbol{d}_e^2 = \boldsymbol{d}_o^2$. The scaling-rotation is performed in the 'phase plane' $\boldsymbol{f}_s(\boldsymbol{x}) \wedge \mathbf{e}_3 = \langle \mathbf{e}_3 \boldsymbol{f}_s(\boldsymbol{x})\rangle_2$

with $s(x) = e_3 f_s(x)$ being the respective spinor and $f_s \equiv f_{i1D}$ or $f_s \equiv f_{i2D}$. By evaluating the exponential representation of s with respect to the $\mathbb{R}_3^+$-logarithm, see (Felsberg, 2002), the local spectral representations can be computed. These are the local amplitude

$$a(x) = |f_s(x)| = \exp(\langle \log(e_3 f_s(x)) \rangle_0) \tag{49}$$

and the (generalized) monogenic local phase bivector

$$\Phi(x) = \arg(f_s(x)) = \langle \log(e_3 f_s(x)) \rangle_2 . \tag{50}$$

From $\Phi(x)$ follow the local phase $\phi(x)$ as rotation angle within the phase plane,

$$\phi(x) = |(\Phi(x))^*| = \operatorname{atan}\left(\frac{|\langle e_3 f_s(x) \rangle_2|}{|\langle e_3 f_s(x) \rangle_0|} \right) , \tag{51}$$

and the orientation angle $\theta(x)$ of the phase plane within the plane $e_1 \wedge e_2$,

$$\theta(x) = \frac{\langle e_3 f_s(x) \rangle_2}{|\langle e_3 f_s(x) \rangle_2|} . \tag{52}$$

In the case of f_{i1D}, $\theta(x)$ is indicating the orientation of the i1D structure within the image plane and in the case of f_{i2D}, $2\theta(x)$ represents the local main orientation of the i2D structure in a double angle representation which results from the eigenvector decomposition of the structure tensor (Felsberg, 2002). Hence, phase analysis delivers also the orientation information as a consequence of the monogenic representation of the curvature tensor.

In Figure 2, an example signal is analyzed with respect to its local spectral representations. The monogenic curvature tensor is obviously invariant with respect to rotation. In figure 3, two patterns of even and odd symmetric structures are analyzed with respect to local amplitudes and local phases for f_{i1D} and f_{i2D}, respectively. Clearly can be seen the invariances of the monogenic curvature tensor with respect to the intrinsic dimension, parity symmetry and angle of intersection.

We will not discuss in detail the scale-space properties (Zang & Sommer, 2006a). It should only be mentioned that the embedding of the curvature tensor into a monogenic scale-space results in an improved corner detection based on a novel two-dimensional phase congruency method (Zang & Sommer, 2006b) and delivers superior estimates of the optical flow field based on a phase constrained variational approach (Zang et al., 2007).

4. Parameter Estimation from Uncertain Data

Uncertain data occurs almost invariably, especially in computer vision applications. It is hence a necessity to develop and use methods, which account for the errors in observational data. Here, we discuss a parameter estimation from uncertain data in the unified mathematical framework of geometric algebra.

We use conformal geometric algebra (CGA) as introduced in section 2.4. Consequently, the estimation is applicable to (parameterizations of) geometric entities and geometric operators; points, lines, planes, circles or spheres can be treated in very much the same way as rotations or rigid body motions (RBM). In general, our aim is to find multi-vectors that satisfy a particular condition equation, which depends on a set of uncertain measurements. The specific problem and the type of multi-vector, representing a geometric entity or a geometric operator, determine the condition. In the language of CGA we obtain succinct expressions and thanks to the bilinearity of the always involved geometric product, the corresponding equations are linear or at most quadratic in the multi-vector components. In section 2.3 we have introduced a simple way to represent geometric algebra operations in terms of a tensor notation, where the term tensor denotes the classical extension of matrix theory to higher dimensions. This allows us to use well-tried and efficient algorithms without leaving the algebra. Moreover, it paves the way for using the stochastic: standard error propagation, for example, is exact for the geometric product and makes it easily possible to keep track of the uncertainties while doing operations like an intersection.

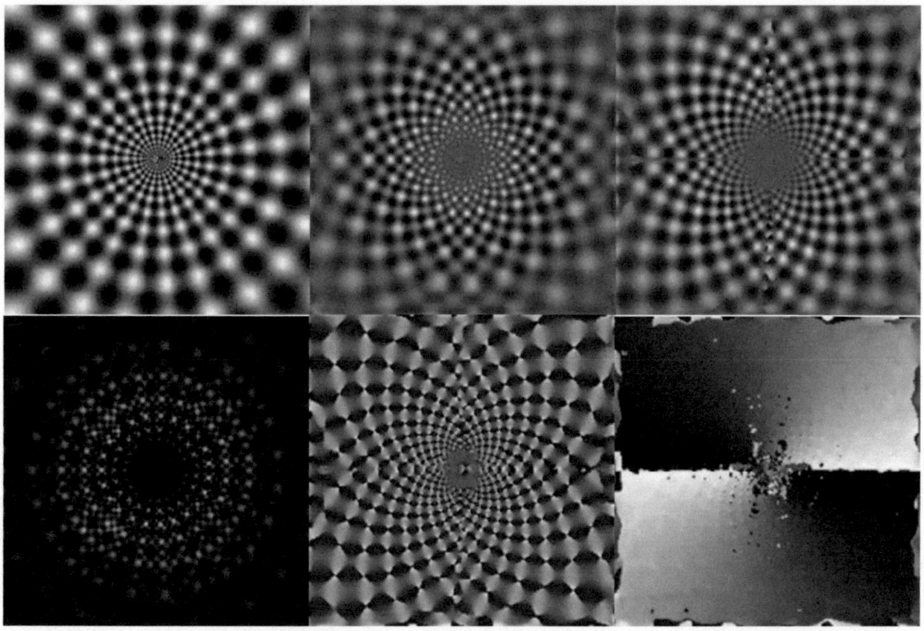

Figure 2. Top: original image (left), even and odd components of f_{i2D} (middle and right). Bottom: local amplitude (left), local phase (middle) and local orientation (right)

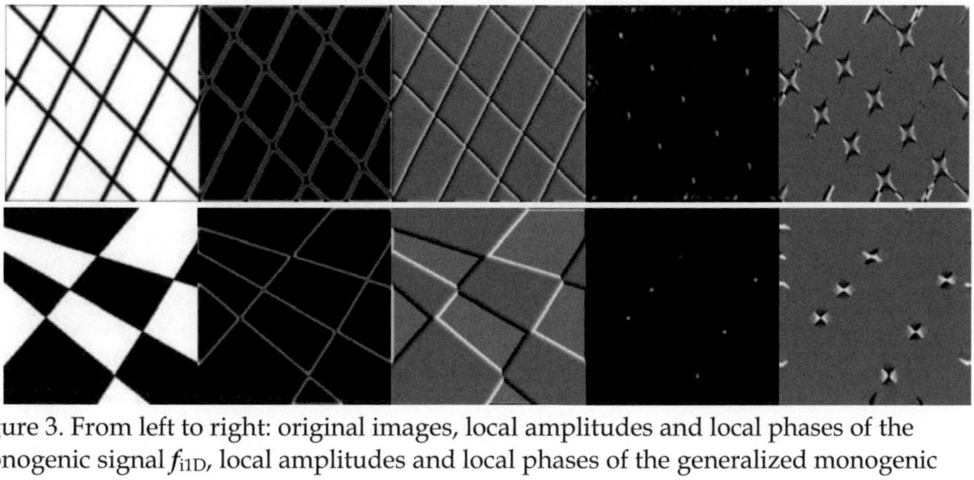

Figure 3. From left to right: original images, local amplitudes and local phases of the monogenic signal f_{i1D}, local amplitudes and local phases of the generalized monogenic Gaussian curvature signal f_{i2D}

The stochastic is one of the fundamental aspects of this section. To account for the uncertainties in observational data we consequently decided on a least squares adjustment parameter estimation. We use the Gauss-Markov and the Gauss-Helmert method. Each of them provides an estimate together with a suitable covariance matrix. Hence, further calculations can be carried out with these uncertain elements, as mentioned above.
This text builds on previous works by (Heuel, 2004) where uncertain points, lines and planes were treated in a unified manner, but not in GA. The linear estimation of rotation operators in GA was previously discussed in (Perwass & Sommer, 2002), albeit without taking account of uncertainty. In (Perwass et al., 2005) the estimation of uncertain general operators was introduced.
The structure of this section is as follows: first, we explain the underlying parameter estimation methods. We then present two applications. For each, we demonstrate in which way we profit from the expressiveness of CGA and we explain how our method can be applied within that framework.

4.1 Stochastic Estimation Method

In the field of parameter estimation one usually parameterizes some physical process $\mathcal{P}$ in terms of a model $\mathcal{M}$ and a suitable parameter vector $\mathbf{p}$. The components of p are then to be estimated from a set of observations originating from $\mathcal{P}$.
Here, we introduce our two parameter estimation methods, the common Gauss-Markov method and the most generalized case of least squares adjustment, the Gauss-Helmert method. Both are founded on the respective homonymic linear models, cf. (Koch, 1997). The word 'adjustment' puts emphasis on the fact that an estimation has to handle redundancy in observational data appropriately, i.e. to weight unreliable data to a lesser extend. In order to overcome the inherent noisiness of measurements one typically introduces a redundancy by taking much more measurements than necessary to describe the process. Each observation must have its own covariance matrix describing the corresponding Gaussian probability density function that is assumed to model the observational error. The determination of which is inferred from the knowledge of the underlying measurement process. The matrices serve as weights and thereby introduce a local error metric.
The principle of least squares adjustment, i.e. to minimize the sum of squared weighted errors $\Delta\mathbf{y}_i$, is often denoted as

$$\sum_i \Delta\mathbf{y}_i^{\mathsf{T}} \Sigma_{\mathbf{y}_i}{}^{-1} \Delta\mathbf{y}_i \longrightarrow \min, \tag{53}$$

where $\Sigma_{\mathbf{y}_i}$ is a covariance matrix assessing the confidence of $\mathbf{y}_i$.
Let $\{\mathbf{b}_1, \mathbf{b}_2, \ldots, \mathbf{b}_N\}$ be a set of N observations, for which we introduce the abbreviation $\{\mathbf{b}_{1..N}\}$. Each observation $\mathbf{b}_i$ is associated with an appropriate covariance matrix $\Sigma_{\mathbf{b}_i}$. An entity, parameterized by a vector $\mathbf{p}$, is to be fitted to the observational data. Consequently, we define a condition function $\mathbf{g}(\mathbf{b}_i, \mathbf{p})$ which is supposed to be zero if the observations and the entity in demand fit algebraically. Besides, it is often inevitable to define constraints $\mathbf{h}(\mathbf{p}) = \mathbf{0}$ on the parameter vector $\mathbf{p}$. This is necessary if there are functional dependencies within the parameters. Consider, for example, the parameterization of a Euclidian normal vector $\mathbf{n}$ using three variables $\mathbf{n} = [n_1, n_2, n_3]^{\mathsf{T}}$. A constraint $\mathbf{n}^{\mathsf{T}}\,\mathbf{n} = 1$ could be avoided using spherical coordinates θ and ϕ, i.e. $\mathbf{n} = [\cos\theta\cos\phi, ,\cos\theta\sin\phi, \sin\theta]$. In the following sections, we refer to the functions $\mathbf{g}$ and $\mathbf{h}$ as G-constraint and H-constraint, respectively.

Note that most of the fitting problems in these sections are not linear but quadratic, i.e. the condition equations require a linearization and estimation becomes an iterative process. An important issue is thus the search for an initial estimate (starting point). If we know an already good estimate $\hat{\mathbf{p}}$, we can make a linearization of the G-constraint yielding $(\partial_{\mathbf{p}}\mathbf{g})(\mathbf{b}_i,\hat{\mathbf{p}})\Delta\mathbf{p} + \mathbf{g}(\mathbf{b}_i, \hat{\mathbf{p}}) \approx \mathbf{0}$. Hence, with $\mathbf{U}_i = (\partial_{\mathbf{p}}\mathbf{g})(\mathbf{b}_i,\hat{\mathbf{p}})$ and $\mathbf{y}_i = -\mathbf{g}(\mathbf{b}_i, \hat{\mathbf{p}})$: $\mathbf{U}_i\Delta\mathbf{p} = \mathbf{y}_i + \Delta\mathbf{y}_i$, which exactly matches the linear Gauss-Markov model. The minimization of equation (53) in conjunction with the Gauss-Markov model leads to the best linear unbiased estimator. Note that we have to leave the weighting out in equation (53), since our covariance matrices $\Sigma_{\mathbf{b}_i}$ do not match the $\Sigma_{\mathbf{y}_i}$. Subsequently, we consider a model which includes the weighting.
If we take our observations as estimates, i.e. $\{\hat{\mathbf{b}}_{1..N}\} = \{\mathbf{b}_{1..N}\}$, we can make a Taylor series expansion of first order at $(\hat{\mathbf{b}}_i, \hat{\mathbf{p}})$ yielding

$$(\partial_{\mathbf{p}}\mathbf{g})(\hat{\mathbf{b}}_i,\hat{\mathbf{p}})\Delta\mathbf{p} + (\partial_{\mathbf{b}}\mathbf{g})(\hat{\mathbf{b}}_i,\hat{\mathbf{p}})\Delta\mathbf{b}_i + \mathbf{g}(\hat{\mathbf{b}}_i, \hat{\mathbf{p}}) \approx \mathbf{0}\,. \tag{54}$$

Similarly, with $\mathbf{V}_i = (\partial_{\mathbf{b}}\mathbf{g})(\hat{\mathbf{b}}_i,\hat{\mathbf{p}})$ we obtain $\mathbf{U}_i\Delta\mathbf{p} + \mathbf{V}_i\Delta\mathbf{b}_i = \mathbf{y}_i$, which exactly matches the linear Gauss-Helmert model. Note that the error term Δy_i has been replaced by the linear combination $\Delta\mathbf{y}_i = -\mathbf{V}_i\Delta\mathbf{b}_i$; the Gauss-Helmert differs from the Gauss-Markov model in that the observations have become random variables and are thus allowed to undergo small changes $\Delta\mathbf{b}_i$ to compensate for errors. But changes have to be kept minimal, as observations represent the best available. This is achieved by replacing equation (53) with

$$\sum_i \Delta\mathbf{b}_i^{\mathsf{T}}\Sigma_{\mathbf{b}_i}{}^{-1}\Delta\mathbf{b}_i \longrightarrow \min\,, \tag{55}$$

where $\Delta\mathbf{b}_i$ is now considered as error vector.
The minimization of (55) subject to the Gauss-Helmert model can be done using Lagrange multipliers. By introducing $\Delta\mathbf{b} = [\Delta\mathbf{b}_1^{\mathsf{T}}, \Delta\mathbf{b}_2^{\mathsf{T}}, \ldots, \Delta\mathbf{b}_N^{\mathsf{T}}]^{\mathsf{T}}$, $\Sigma_{\mathbf{b}} = \mathbf{diag}([\Sigma_{\mathbf{b}_1}, \Sigma_{\mathbf{b}_2}, \ldots, \Sigma_{\mathbf{b}_N}])$, $\mathbf{U} = [\mathbf{U}_1^{\mathsf{T}}, \mathbf{U}_2^{\mathsf{T}}, \ldots, \mathbf{U}_N^{\mathsf{T}}]^{\mathsf{T}}$, $\mathbf{V} = \mathbf{diag}([\mathbf{V}_1, \mathbf{V}_2, \ldots, \mathbf{V}_N])$ and $\mathbf{y} = [\mathbf{y}_1^{\mathsf{T}}, \mathbf{y}_2^{\mathsf{T}}, \ldots, \mathbf{y}_N^{\mathsf{T}}]^{\mathsf{T}}$ the Lagrange function Ψ, which is now to be minimized, becomes

$$\Psi(\Delta\mathbf{p}, \Delta\mathbf{b}, \mathbf{u}, \mathbf{v}) = \frac{1}{2}\Delta\mathbf{b}^{\mathsf{T}}\Sigma_{\mathbf{b}}^{-1}\Delta\mathbf{b} - \left(\mathbf{U}\Delta\mathbf{p} + \mathbf{V}\Delta\mathbf{b} - \mathbf{y}\right)^{\mathsf{T}}\mathbf{u} + \left(\mathbf{H}\Delta\mathbf{p} - \mathbf{z}\right)^{\mathsf{T}}\mathbf{v} \tag{56}$$

The last summand in Ψ corresponds to the linearized H-constraint, where $\mathbf{H} = (\partial_{\mathbf{p}}\mathbf{h})(\hat{\mathbf{p}})$ and $\mathbf{z} = -\mathbf{h}(\hat{\mathbf{p}})$ was used. That term can be omitted, if $\mathbf{P}$ has no functional dependencies. A differentiation of Ψ with respect to all variables gives an extensive matrix equation, which could already be solved. Nevertheless, it can be considerably reduced with the substitutions $\mathbf{N} = \sum_i \mathbf{U}_i^{\mathsf{T}}\left(\mathbf{V}_i\,\Sigma_{\mathbf{b}_i}\,\mathbf{V}_i^{\mathsf{T}}\right)^{-1}\mathbf{U}_i$ and $\mathbf{z}_N = \sum_i \mathbf{U}_i^{\mathsf{T}}\left(\mathbf{V}_i\,\Sigma_{\mathbf{b}_i}\,\mathbf{V}_i^{\mathsf{T}}\right)^{-1}\mathbf{y}$. The resultant matrix equation is free from $\Delta\mathbf{b}$ and can be solved for $\Delta\mathbf{p}$

$$\begin{bmatrix} \mathbf{N} & \mathbf{H}^{\mathsf{T}} \\ \mathbf{H} & 0 \end{bmatrix}\begin{bmatrix} \Delta\mathbf{p} \\ \mathbf{v} \end{bmatrix} = \begin{bmatrix} \mathbf{z}_N \\ \mathbf{z} \end{bmatrix}. \tag{57}$$

For the corrections $\{\Delta\mathbf{b}_{1..N}\}$, which are now minimal with respect to the Mahalanobis distance (55), we compute

$$\Delta \mathsf{b}_i = \Sigma_{\mathsf{b}_i} \mathsf{V}_i^{\mathsf{T}} \left(\mathsf{V}_i \Sigma_{\mathsf{b}_i} \mathsf{V}_i^{\mathsf{T}} \right)^{-1} \left(\mathsf{y}_i - \mathsf{U}_i \, \Delta \mathsf{p} \right). \tag{58}$$

It is an important by-product that the (pseudo-) inverse of the quadratic matrix in equation (57) contains the covariance matrix $\Sigma_{\Delta \mathsf{p}} = \Sigma_{\mathsf{p}}$ belonging to p. The similar solution for the Gauss-Markov model and the corresponding proofs and derivations can be found in (Koch, 1997). Due to outstanding convergence properties we start iterating with the Gauss-Markov method. At the optimum we start the slower Gauss-Helmert method, which ultimately adjusts the estimate according to the uncertainties Σ_{b_i}.

4.2 Fitting a Circle in 3D

Now we show how the estimation method can be used in CGA to fit a circle in 3D-space to a set of N data points $\{b_{1..N}\}$. Each data point is given with its mean b_i and covariance matrix Σ_{b_i}. In order to apply the estimation methods as described, we need a G-constraint and possibly an H-constraint. We therefore give an introduction to circles in CGA.

We represent a circle by the inner product null space $\mathbb{X}$ of a 2-blade C. That space consists of all conformal points $\mathbf{X}$, the inner product of which with the circle C is zero, i.e. $\mathbb{X}$ =.$\{X = \mathcal{K}(x) \,|\, X \cdot C = 0\}$ To understand this relationship, consider the inner product null space of a sphere S_r with radius r and center m. It can be created from a point $S_0 = \mathcal{K}(m) = m + \frac{1}{2} m^2 \mathbf{e}_\infty + \mathbf{e}_o$ by subtracting the term '$\frac{1}{2} r^2 \mathbf{e}_\infty$'. The sphere is thus given by $S_r = m + \frac{1}{2}(m^2 - r^2)\mathbf{e}_\infty + \mathbf{e}_o$. For some vector x it can be verified that $\mathcal{K}(x) \cdot S_r = 0 \in \mathbb{R}$ *iff* $\|x - m\|_2 = r$. Now, consider two intersecting spheres S_1 and S_2. A circle intuitively consists of all points X lying on S_1 and S_2. Intersection can be expressed by the outer product and in fact the circle definition is $C = S_1 \wedge S_2$. For a justification examine the inner product $X \cdot C$

$$X \cdot (S_1 \wedge S_2) = (X \cdot S_1) S_2 \; - \; (X \cdot S_2) S_1 \, . \tag{59}$$

The terms cannot cancel each other if S1 S_1 and S_2 are linearly independent, i.e. if they do not represent the same sphere. The upper equation is therefore zero *iff* X is located on S_1 and S_2 as well.

Remarkably, we have found an appropriate G-constraint right from the definition of the circle's inner product null space itself. It remains to transfer the inner product expression $X \cdot C$ to an equivalent matrix expression. As there are ten basis blades of grade two in $\mathbb{R}_{4,1}$, we have $\Phi(C) = \mathsf{p} \in \mathbb{R}^{10}$. The points $\{b_{1..N}\}$ are embedded and mapped as follows: $\Phi(\mathcal{K}(b_i) = B_i) = \mathsf{b}_i \in \mathbb{R}^5$. Note that our condition equation (59) yields a vector, being defined by five components in $\mathbb{R}_{4,1}$. Consequently, we obtain

$$\Phi(B_i \cdot C) \; = \; \mathsf{U}(\mathsf{b}_i)\,\mathsf{p} \; = \; \mathsf{V}(\mathsf{p})\,\mathsf{b}_i \; = \; \mathsf{g}(\mathsf{b}_i, \mathsf{p}) \; \in \mathbb{R}^5, \tag{60}$$

which can be differentiated easily. Thus, the required Jacobians $\{\mathsf{U}_{1..N}\}$ and V follow from the bilinearity of geometric algebra products in an implicit manner.

Because a circle in 3D-space can be described by a minimum number of six parameters, we face a functional dependency of grade 4 = 10 – 6 within p. As mentioned in section 4.1, we have to introduce constraints on the parameters, namely the H-constraint $\mathsf{h}(\mathsf{p})$. We enforce C to be a circle by requiring that $C \wedge C = \mathbf{0}$, which can be shown to be sufficient. In almost the same way as for the G-constraint, the usage of Φ allows us to derive the H-matrix. Being in

the possession of all necessary matrices, we are able to run the estimation in order to solve for the corrections $\Delta \mathsf{p}$ and $\{\Delta \mathsf{b}_{1..N}\}$.
We remain with this stage and refer the reader to the next estimation example. There, we explicitly derive the constraint functions in terms of the tensor notation.
As mentioned earlier, our method provides the covariance matrix Σ_{p} of the estimated entity p as well. It shows up to which degree the model fits the observations and how advantageously they were initially distributed. It does not reflect to which extend the estimate deviates from a potentially perfect fit, i.e. it is no quality measure for our method. Figure 4 exemplarily shows the uncertainty of an estimated circle. The surrounding tubes, indicated by slices, show the standard deviation of the estimates.

4.3 Fitting two Point Clouds in 3D

In this part, we describe how the proposed methods can be used to estimate an RBM; it extends a rotation, given by a rotor, by a translational component along the axis of rotation. Hence, we can think of it as a screw motion, cf. (Rosenhahn, 2003). In geometric algebra an RBM is represented by an operator called motor. In the scope of pose estimation, the pose is uniquely characterized by an RBM. The estimation of motors is thus a first step towards the perspective pose estimation problem.
Let $\{a_{1..N}\}$ and $\{b_{1..N}\}$ be two sets of N Euclidian points each. The latter represent the observations for which we have the covariance matrices $\{\Sigma_{b_{1..N}}\}$. The set $\{a_{1..N}\}$ is assumed to have no uncertainty. Let $\boldsymbol{A}_i = \mathcal{K}(\boldsymbol{a}_i)$ and $\boldsymbol{B}_i = \mathcal{K}(\boldsymbol{b}_i)$ denote the conformal embedding of $\boldsymbol{a}_i$ and $\boldsymbol{b}_i$, respectively. We search for the motor $\boldsymbol{M}$, which best transforms all points in $\{\boldsymbol{A}_{1..N}\}$ to the respective points in $\{\boldsymbol{B}_{1..N}\}$. The scenario is shown in figure 5.
Using geometric algebra, we can easily write $\boldsymbol{M}\boldsymbol{A}_i\widetilde{\boldsymbol{M}} = \boldsymbol{B}_i$ cf. (Perwass & Sommer, 2002). Note that a motor is a unitary versor, i.e. it has to satisfy $\boldsymbol{M}\widetilde{\boldsymbol{M}} = 1$. Exploiting this fact, we rearrange the previous formula and obtain the G- constraint

$$\begin{array}{ccccccccc} (\boldsymbol{M} & & \boldsymbol{A}_i) & - & (\boldsymbol{B}_i & & \boldsymbol{M}) & = & 0 \\ \downarrow & & \downarrow & & \downarrow & & \downarrow & & \downarrow \\ \mathsf{p}^k & \mathsf{G}^t{}_{kl} & \mathsf{a}_i{}^l & - & \mathsf{b}_i{}^l & \mathsf{G}^t{}_{lk} & \mathsf{p}^k & = & 0^t \end{array}, \tag{61}$$

where we used $\Phi(\boldsymbol{A}_i) = \mathsf{a}_i$, $\Phi(\boldsymbol{B}_i) = \mathsf{b}_i$ and $\Phi(\boldsymbol{M}) = \mathsf{p} \in \mathbb{R}^8$. The tensor G encodes the geometric product. In order to evaluate the matrices U and V, we differentiate equation (61) with respect to p and b, respectively. Hence, we get $\mathsf{U}(\mathsf{b}_i) = \mathsf{G}^t{}_{kl}\mathsf{a}_i{}^l - \mathsf{b}_i{}^l\mathsf{G}^t{}_{lk}$ and $\mathsf{V}(\mathsf{p}) = -\mathsf{p}^k\mathsf{G}^t{}_{lk}$.
Since an RBM is defined by six rather than eight parameters, we need the H-constraint. We again exploit unitarity and choose $\mathsf{h}(\mathsf{p}) = \Phi(\boldsymbol{M}\widetilde{\boldsymbol{M}} - 1) = \mathsf{p}^k\,\mathsf{p}^l\,\mathsf{R}^m{}_l\,\mathsf{G}^t{}_{km} - \delta^{t,1}$. The tensor R encodes the reverse operation and $\delta^{t,1}$ is zero, except for $t = 1$. Differentiation $\partial_{\mathsf{p}}\mathsf{h}$ yields $\mathsf{H}(\mathsf{p}) = \mathsf{p}^l\,(\mathsf{R}^m{}_l\,\mathsf{G}^t{}_{km} + \mathsf{R}^m{}_k\,\mathsf{G}^t{}_{lm})$. The estimate for $\boldsymbol{M}$ can now be computed by simply substituting the matrices $\{\mathsf{U}_{1..N}\}$, V and H into the respective equations given in the theoretical part.

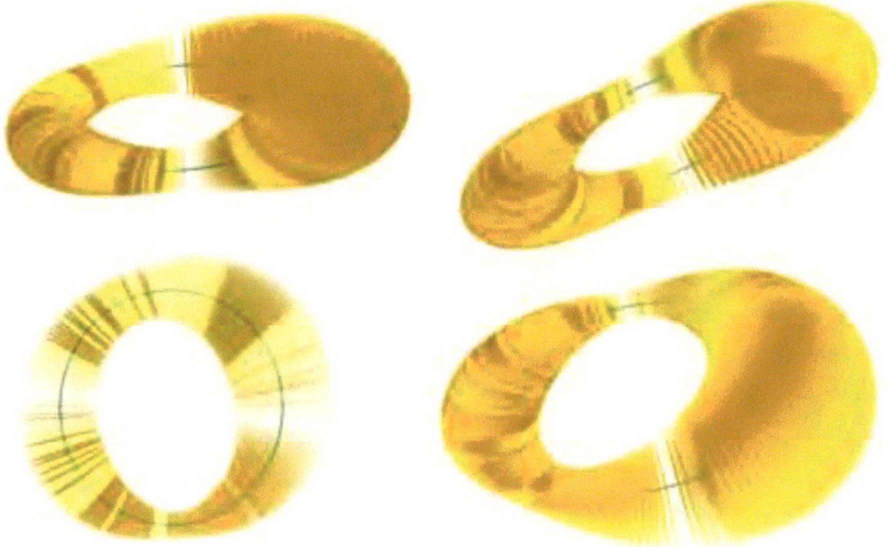

Figure 4. Fitting a circle: four views of a circle's uncertainty (standard deviation)

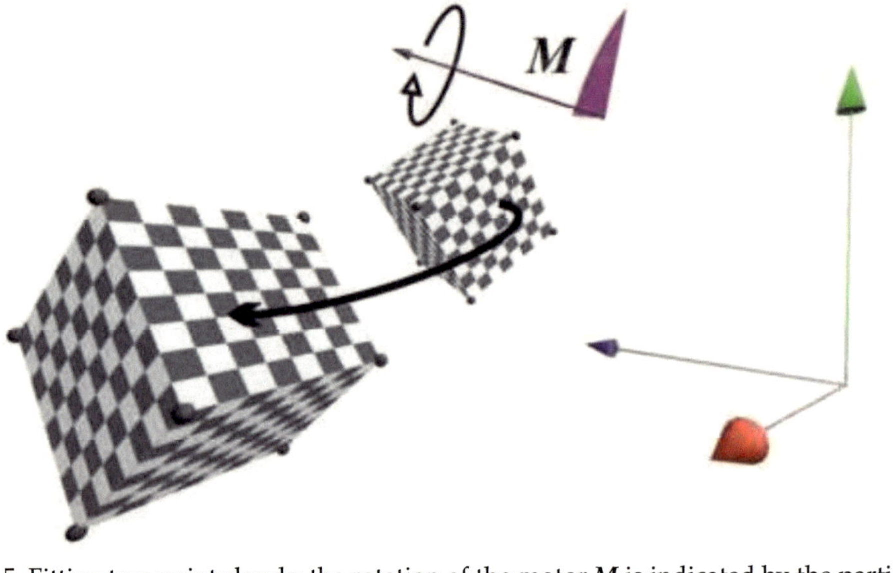

Figure 5. Fitting two point clouds: the rotation of the motor M is indicated by the partial disc. The translational part is specified by the arrow attached to it

5. Pose Estimation from Uncertain Omnidirectional Image Data

We present a sophisticated application of the parameter estimation from uncertain data as depicted in the previous section. It reads 'perspective 2D-3D pose estimation for omnidirectional vision using line-plane correspondences' and has strong geometrical streaks, which is why we spend an extra section. In this context, we introduce the 'inversion camera model', which has the ability to model a variety of distinct camera systems thereby taking image distortions into account.

Pose estimation certainly is a well-studied subject, but not in case of an omnidirectional vision system. Hence, our objective was to develop accurate pose estimation for omnidirectional vision, given imprecise image features, i.e. 2D-sensory data. Note that these features can readily be detected by the method proposed in section 3.

Comparable to triangulation, the accuracy of an estimated pose benefits when landmarks can be seen in clearly different directions. But the most significant advantages of omnidirectional vision are related to navigation, since the objects remain on the image plane under most camera movements. We consider a single viewpoint catadioptric vision sensor. It combines a customary camera with a parabolic mirror and provides a panoramical view of 360°.

We make the assumption to have 3D-models of the interesting objects we observe in the images. Secondly, we assume to know the one-to-one correspondences between the model features and the image features. Note that a model consists of 3D-lines, which mostly represent object edges, which in turn, are likely to generate a line under imaging; consequently, we have lines as image features. We herewith extend our previous work where we had been employing point features and point models.

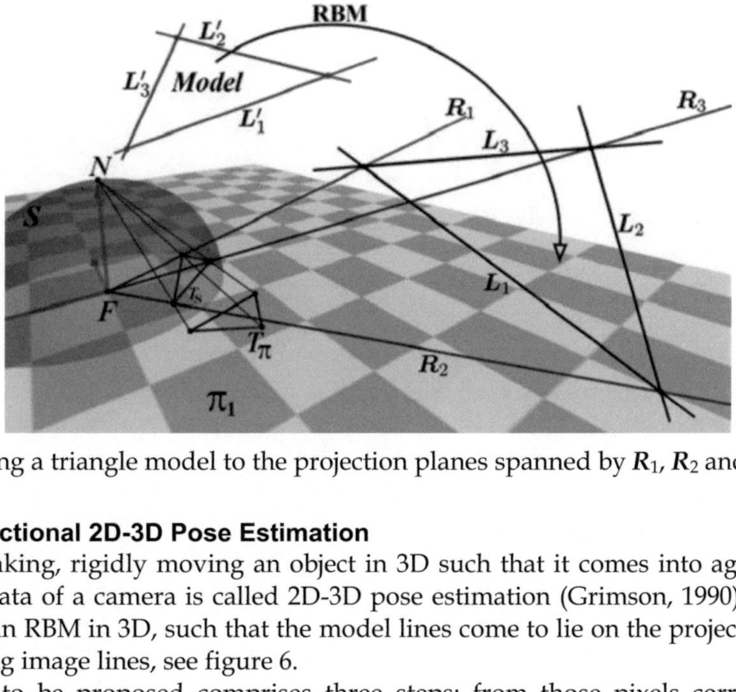

Figure 6. Fitting a triangle model to the projection planes spanned by $\boldsymbol{R}_1$, $\boldsymbol{R}_2$ and $\boldsymbol{R}_3$

5.1 Omnidirectional 2D-3D Pose Estimation

Roughly speaking, rigidly moving an object in 3D such that it comes into agreement with 2D-sensory data of a camera is called 2D-3D pose estimation (Grimson, 1990). Specifically, we estimate an RBM in 3D, such that the model lines come to lie on the projection planes of the underlying image lines, see figure 6.

The method to be proposed comprises three steps: from those pixels corresponding to visible model lines, we estimate projection planes with associated uncertainties. In a second step, a simple algorithm is used to do prior rotation estimation being a first and rough guess at the rotational part of the desired RBM. As a result the model will be aligned such that its lines are nearly parallel to the respective projection planes. We finally estimate the entire pose taking the computed plane uncertainties into account as well.

Before we explain those steps in detail, we give a sketch of catadioptric imaging.

5.2 Omnidirectional Imaging

Consider a camera, focused at infinity, which looks upward at a parabolic mirror centered on its optical axis. This setup is shown in figure 7. A light ray emitted from world point $\boldsymbol{P}_w$ that would pass through the focal point $\boldsymbol{F}$ of the parabolic mirror M, is reflected parallel to the central axis of M, to give point $\boldsymbol{p}_2$ on image plane π_2. Now we use the simplification that a projection to sphere S with a subsequent stereographic projection to π_1 produces an identical image on π_1. Accordingly, point $\boldsymbol{P}_w$ maps to $\boldsymbol{P}_S$ and further to $\boldsymbol{p}_1$, see figure 7. Together with the right side of figure 7 it is intuitively clear that infinitely extended lines form great circles on $\boldsymbol{S}$. Moreover, a subsequent stereographic projection, being a conformal mapping, results in circles on the image plane, which then are no more concentric. For details refer to (Geyer & Daniilidis, 2001).

Our approach exploits that the mapping from a projection ray to an image point is bijective and therefore invertible. Moreover, given an image line, we can compute its projection plane.

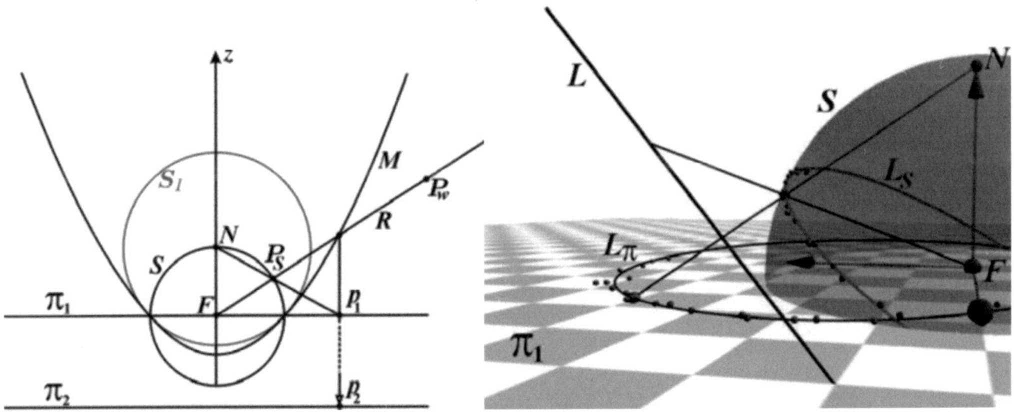

Figure 7. Left: mapping (cross-section) of a world point $\boldsymbol{P}_w$: the image planes π_1 and π_2 are identical. Right: mapping of line $\boldsymbol{L}$ to $\boldsymbol{L}_\pi$ via great circle $\boldsymbol{L}_S$ on $\boldsymbol{S}$. As an example, scattered image data belonging to $\boldsymbol{L}_\pi$ is shown

5.3 Estimating Projection Planes

We must come up with observations in the form of planes for a line-plane fitting; we compute a projection plane for each set of image points that corresponds to a visible model line. To be more specific, we estimate the planes from the stereographically back-projected image points. Hence, the points have to be moved to the projection sphere $\boldsymbol{S}$, see figure 7. This is done by an inversion of the image points in a certain sphere S_I. Note that the (uncertain) image points, initially identically 2D-distributed, thereby obtain distinct 3D-uncertainties, which reflect the imaging geometry. The uncertainties are computed using error propagation, where we profit from the inversion being a linear operation in $\mathbb{R}_{4,1}$. The plane estimation can now be done by restricting the circle estimation, see section 4.2, to the three parameters describing the circle's plane. Recall that we obtain a covariance matrix for each estimated plane.

5.4 Prior Model Alignment

The line-plane pose estimation will prove to be a quadratic problem. In such cases, as mentioned in section 4.1, the linearization requires an initial estimate. The prior model alignment provides such a starting point at very low costs. We like to rotate the model such that the set of unit direction vectors $\{\hat{r}_{1..N}\}$ of its lines lie on the respective planes. Let $\{\hat{n}_{1..N}\}$ denote the set of normal vectors of all planes, which belong to visible model lines. We search for a rotation matrix R such that $\hat{}(\forall i)$: $\hat{n}_i^T R \hat{r}_i = 0 \in \mathbb{R}$.
By Rodrigues's formula (1840) we know that the rotation matrix R regarding a rotation of angle θ around unit vector $\hat{a} = [a_1, a_2, a_3]^T$ can be expressed by an exponential map of $A = [[0, a_3, -a_2]^T[-a_3, 0, a_1]^T[a_2, -a_1, 0]^T]$: $R = \exp(\theta A)$ which is $R = I_3 + \sin\theta\, A + (1 - \cos\theta)A^2$, where I_3 denotes the 3×3 identity matrix. For small angles we obtain $R = I_3 + \theta A$. With this relation and due to the skew symmetric structure of $A' = \theta A$ it is possible to solve for $a' = [\theta a_1, \theta a_2, \theta a_3]^T$, where each line-plane pair gives one line $\hat{n}_i^T A' \hat{r}_i = -\hat{n}_i^T \hat{r}_i$ in an overdetermined system of linear equations. Every run of this procedure yields a rotation matrix, the concatenation of which gives the desired rotation matrix R. Once, the rotated lines are close enough to the planes w.r.t. some threshold the procedure can be stopped.

5.5 Perspective Line-Plane Pose Estimation

Here we derive geometric constraint equations for the stochastic estimation methods presented in the previous section.
Let P be a projection plane, see section 5.3. For any line L lying on P, we have $P \wedge L = 0 \in \mathbb{R}_{4,1}$ A model line L' is transformed by an RBM represented by M, say, via the operation $M\, L'\, \widetilde{M}$. Therefore, if we have estimated the correct M, a model line L' with corresponding projection plane P has to satisfy $P \wedge (M\, L'\, \widetilde{M}) = 0$
Using Φ from section 2.3, we can identify our elements P, L' and M with particular vectors $n \in \mathbb{R}^3$, $l' \in \mathbb{R}^6$ and $p \in \mathbb{R}^8$. For example, n simply denotes the normal vector of the plane represented by P. We contract all constituent product tensors to one tensor Q and obtain condition function g for one line-plane pair

$$g^t(n, p, l') = \sum_{i,j,k,l} p^i\, p^j\, n^k\, l'^l\, Q^t{}_{ijkl} = 0, \tag{62}$$

Algebraically, the constraint $P \wedge L$ may only be non-zero in four of its $2^5 = 32$ components, which is why we have $t \in \{1,...,4\}$. The observations and parameters are n and p, respectively. Hence, differentiating would yield the matrices $\{U_{1..N}\}$ and $\{V_{1..N}\}$ required in section 4.1. The eight components of M are an overparameterization, again, such that we need to include the H-constraint $M\widetilde{M} = 1$ from section 4.3.

5.6 Inversion Camera Model

The inversion camera model can be used for image rectification. Besides, it can readily be incorporated into the previously presented pose estimation methods as inversion embodies the main CGA operation. We briefly discuss both applications.
We go on from section 5.2 in which we dealt with imaging. The considerations were limited to the special case of a parabolic catadioptric imaging system: a stereographic projection had been replaced by an inversion of the projection sphere S in a inversion sphere S_I. This is one case of what the inversion camera model, which was proposed by (Perwass & Sommer,

2006), can handle. It basically expresses a projective mapping in terms of an inversion. It enables a continuous transition between different geometries of imaging, as fisheye optics or the classic pinhole camera, merely by changing two parameters. These determine the constellation of suitable spheres $\boldsymbol{S}$ and $\boldsymbol{S}_I$ in respect to the focal point $\boldsymbol{F}$. In addition to the left side of figure 7, which illustrates a parabolic catadioptric imaging system, figure 8 depicts two further interesting constellations. To demonstrate the versatility of the inversion camera model, recall the imaging principle described in section 5.2. It can equally be applied to the left side of figure 8, where the same operations describe a completely different camera system: 'point $\boldsymbol{P}_w$ maps to $\boldsymbol{P}_S$ and further to $\boldsymbol{p}$'.

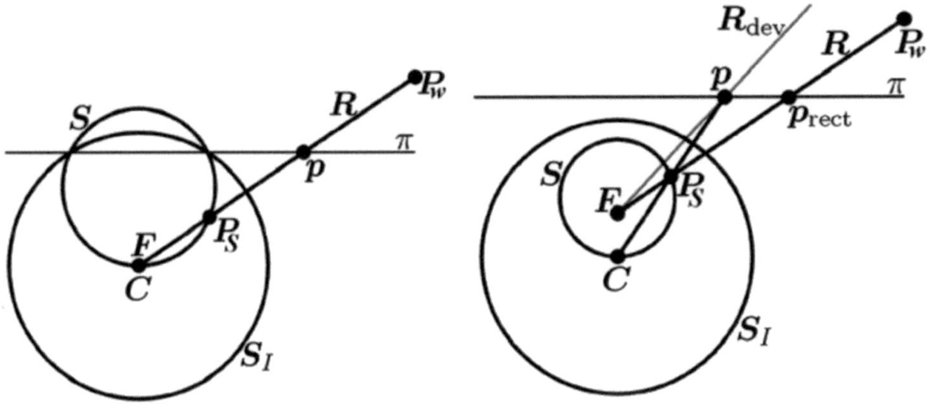

Figure 8. Mapping schemes (cross-section) in terms of the inversion camera model. Left: setup reflecting a pinhole camera. Right: setup modeling a real lens by taking radial distortions into account. Namings are in concordance with figure 7; $\boldsymbol{C}$ denotes the center of S_I

The aim of image rectification is to undo distortions which originate from a variety of optical imperfections. The right side of figure 8 shows the problem. The ray belonging to world point $\boldsymbol{P}_w$ was subjected to distortion which lead to the ray $\boldsymbol{R}_{\text{dev}}$ that eventually produced $\boldsymbol{p}$. However, $\boldsymbol{R}_{\text{dev}}$ deviates from the geometrically true ray $\boldsymbol{R}$ in a non-linear manner depending on the angle to the optical axis. Hence a mapping has to be found that corrects the position of point $\boldsymbol{p}$, within the image plane, such that it comes to lie on its projection ray $\boldsymbol{R}$ again.

We denote the rectified point $\boldsymbol{p}_{\text{rect}}$. In (Perwass & Sommer, 2006), the authors discovered that moving off the inversion sphere $\boldsymbol{S}_I$ from $\boldsymbol{F}$, which distinguishes the mapping schemes in figure 8, results in a mapping suitable to model distortions. It consists of two parts. First a versor $\boldsymbol{K}$, which essentially does the inversion of the image point $\boldsymbol{p}$, is applied. Next, the corresponding ray $\boldsymbol{R}$ is constructed and intersected with image plane π to give $\boldsymbol{p}_{\text{rect}}$.

Our subsequent considerations require a right handed coordinate system. The $\mathbf{e}_3$-axis denotes the optical axis. It points upwards and is incident with $\boldsymbol{F}$. The $\mathbf{e}_1$-axis points to the right and is aligned with the image plane. Hence, all image points lie on the $\mathbf{e}_1$-$\mathbf{e}_2$-plane.

The inversion sphere $\boldsymbol{S}_I$ of radius r is defined by $\boldsymbol{S}_I = s_1\mathbf{e}_3 + \frac{1}{2}s_2\mathbf{e}_\infty + \mathbf{e}_o$, where we used the abbreviation $s_2 = s_1^2 - r^2$. One of the simplest forms $\boldsymbol{K}$ can take on is $\boldsymbol{K} = \mathbf{S}_I\boldsymbol{D}$. In order to handle scaling and for numerically well-balanced equations, the inversion in $\boldsymbol{S}_I$ is preceded by the dilator $\boldsymbol{D}$ (isotropic scaling operator). The dilation operator $\boldsymbol{D}$ for a scaling by a factor d is given by $D = 1 + \gamma E$, where we defined $\gamma = (d - 1)/(d + 1)$. The image point transformation operator K is then given by

$$K = S_I D = k_1 \mathbf{e}_3 + k_2 \mathbf{e}_\infty + k_3 \mathbf{e}_o + k_4 \mathbf{e}_3 E\,, \tag{63}$$

with $k_1 := s_1$, $k_2 := \frac{1}{2}(1-\gamma)\, s_2$, $k_3 := 1 + \gamma$ and $k_4 := -\gamma\, s_1$. Let $P = \mathcal{K}(p)$ be the embedding of an image point p. Similar to figure 8, we denote $P_S = K\,P\,\widetilde{K}$ the point transformed by K. For determining the rectified point p_{rect}, as intended, it remains to intersect the projection ray R, now given by

$$R = P_S \wedge F \wedge \mathbf{e}_\infty = \left(K\,P\,\widetilde{K}\right) \wedge F \wedge \mathbf{e}_\infty\,, \tag{64}$$

with the image plane π. The intersection is an elementary operation in CGA and yields the conformal point $P_{\text{rect}} = \mathcal{K}(p_{\text{rect}})$. Computing $p_{\text{rect}} = \mathcal{K}^{-1}(P_{\text{rect}})$ yields

$$p_{\text{rect}} = \frac{\beta}{1 + \alpha p^2}\, p\,, \tag{65}$$

with the two parameters

$$\alpha := \frac{1 - s_1}{s_1(s_1 - s_2)} \quad \text{and} \quad \beta := \frac{r^2 d}{s_1(s_1 - s_2)}\,. \tag{66}$$

It is noteworthy that p_{rect}/β is the respective expression produced by the so-called division model. It was proposed by (Fitzgibbon, 2001) and can be considered equivalent to the camera inversion model. The division model itself was shown in (Claus & Fitzgibbon, 2005) to have a rectification quality comparable to a fourth order radial polynomial approach. The camera inversion model is thus a sufficiently good approximation of lens distortion for many applications.

In (Perwass & Sommer, 2006), the estimation of lens distortion was successfully combined with pose estimation by means of the estimation methods presented in this text. Specifically, the pose, the focal length and the lens distortion were estimated at the same time. For example, in case of a point-line fitting a model point P' is to be transformed by an RBM M such that it comes to lie on the corresponding rectified projection ray R. In analogy to section 5.5 and with the help of equation (64) it is required for image point $P = \mathcal{K}(p)$ that

$$\left(\left(K\,P\,\widetilde{K}\right) \wedge F \wedge \mathbf{e}_\infty\right) \wedge (M P' M) = \mathbf{0}\,. \tag{67}$$

A respective tensor representation can be derived easily, and the necessary constraints follow from differentiation. With this impressive example of the unifying nature of geometric algebra we conclude this chapter.

6. References

Angles, P. (1980). Construction de revêtements du groupe conforme d'un espace vectoriel muni d'une "métrique" de type (p,q). Ann. Inst. Henri Poincaré, 33(1):33-51.

Brackx, F.; Delanghe, R. & Sommen F. (1982). Clifford Analysis, volume 76 of *Research Notes in Mathematics*. Pitman Advanced Publishing Program, Boston, MA.

Brannan, D.A.; Esplen, M.F. & Gray, J.J. (1999). *Geometry*. Cambridge University Press, Cambridge.

Buchholz, S. & Le Bihan, N. (2006). Optimal separation of polarized signals by quaternionic neural networks. In *14th European Signal Processing Conference, EUSIPCO 2006*, September 4-8, Florence, Italy.

Buchholz, S. & Sommer, G. (2006). On Clifford Neurons and Clifford Multi-layer Perceptrons. *Neural Networks*, accepted for publication.

Claus, D. & Fitzgibbon, A.W. (2005). A rational function lens distortion model for general cameras. In *Conference on Computer Vision and Pattern Recognition (CVPR05)*, volume 1, pages 213-219, Washington, DC, USA, IEEE Computer Society.

Faugeras, O. (1995). Stratification of three-dimensional vision: projective, affine, and metric representations. *Journal of the Optical Society of America*, 12(3):465-484.

Felsberg, M. (2002). Low-level image processing with the structure multivector. *Technical Report* Number 0203, Christian-Albrechts-Universität zu Kiel, Institut für Informatik und Praktische Mathematik, März.

Felsberg, M. & Sommer, G. (2001). The monogenic signal. *IEEE Trans. Signal Process.*, 49(12):3136-3144

Felsberg, M. & Sommer, G. (2004). The monogenic scale-space: A unifying approach to phase-based image processing in scale-space. *Journal of Mathematical Imaging and Vision*, 21:5-26.

Fitzgibbon, A.W. (2001). Simultaneous linear estimation of multiple view geometry and lens distortion. In *Conference on Computer Vision and Pattern Recognition (CVPR01)*, Hawaii, volume 1, pages 125-132.

Freeman, W.T. & Adelson, E.H. (1991). The design and use of steerable filters. *IEEE Trans. Pattern Anal. Mach. Intell.*, 13(9):891-906.

Gabor, D. (1946). Theory of communications. *Journal of the IEEE*, 93(3):429-457.

Gebken, C.; Tolvanen, A. & Sommer, G. (2006). Pose estimation from uncertain omnidirectional image data using line-plane correspondences. In *28. Symposium für Mustererkennung, DAGM 2006*, Berlin, 12.9.-14.9.2006, number 4174 in LNCS, pages 587-596, Springer-Verlag, Heidelberg, Berlin.

Geyer, C. & Daniilidis, K. (2001). Catadioptric projective geometry. *International Journal of Computer Vision*, 45(3):223-243.

Granlund, G.H. & Knutsson, H. (1995). Signal *Processing for Computer Vision*. Kluwer Academic Publishers, Norwell, MA, USA.

Grimson, W.E.L. (1990). *Object Recognition by Computer*. MIT Press, Cambridge, MA.

Hahn, S.L. (1996). Hilbert *Transforms in Signal Processing*. Artech House: Boston, London.

Hestenes, D. (1991). The design of linear algebra and geometry. *Acta Applicandae Mathematicae*, 23:65-93.

Hestenes, D.; Li, H. & Rockwood, A. (2001). New algebraic tools for classical geometry. In G. Sommer, editor, *Geometric Computing with Clifford Algebras*, pages 3-26, Springer-Verlag, Heidelberg, Berlin.

Hestenes, D. & Sobczyk, G. (1984). Clifford Algebra to Geometric Calculus: A Unified Language for Mathematics and Physics. *Fundamental theories of physics*. D. Reidel Publishing Company, Dordrecht, 1987. First publ.

Heuel, S. (2004). *Uncertain Projective Geometry*, volume 3008 of LNCS, Springer-Verlag, Heidelberg, Berlin.

Koch, K.R. (1997). *Parameter Estimation and Hypothesis Testing in Linear Models*. Springer-Verlag, Heidelberg, Berlin.

Koenderink, J.J. & van Doorn, A.J. (1987). *Representation of local geometry in the visual system.* Biol. Cybern., 55(6):367-375.

Li, H.; Hestenes, D. & Rockwood, A. (2001). Generalized homogeneous coordinates for computational geometry. In G. Sommer, editor, *Geometric Computing with Clifford Algebras*, pages 27-59, Springer-Verlag, Heidelberg, Berlin.

Li, H.; Hestenes, D. & Rockwood, A. (2001). Spherical conformal geometry with geometric algebra. In G. Sommer, editor, *Geometric Computing with Clifford Algebras*, pages 61-75, Springer-Verlag, Heidelberg, Berlin.

Li, H.; Hestenes, D. & Rockwood, A. (2001). A universal model for conformal geometries of euclidean, spherical and double-hyperbolic spaces. In G. Sommer, editor, *Geometric Computing with Clifford Algebras*, pages 77-104, Springer-Verlag, Heidelberg, Berlin.

Needham, T. (1997). Visual Complex Analysis. Clarendon Press, Oxford.

Pauli, J. (2001). Learning-Based Robot Vision, volume 2048 of Lecture Notes in *Computer Science*. Springer-Verlag, Heidelberg, Berlin.

Perwass, C.; Gebken, C. & Sommer, G. (2005). Estimation of geometric entities and operators from uncertain data. In *27. Symposium f¨ur Mustererkennung, DAGM 2005*, Wien, 29.8.-2.9.005, number 3663 in LNCS. Springer-Verlag, Heidelberg, Berlin.

Perwass, C.; Gebken, C. & Sommer, G. (2006). Geometry and kinematics with uncertain data. In A. Leonardis, H. Bischof, and A. Pinz, editors, *9th European Conference on Computer Vision, ECCV 2006*, May 2006, Graz, Austria, number 3951 in LNCS, pages 225-237. Springer-Verlag, Heidelberg, Berlin.

Perwass, C. & Hildenbrand, D. (2003). Aspects of geometric algebra in euclidean, projective and conformal space. *Technical Report* Number 0310, Christian-Albrechts-Universität zu Kiel, Institut für Informatik und Praktische Mathematik, September.

Perwass, C. & Sommer, G. (2002). Numerical evaluation of versors with Clifford algebra. In Leo Dorst, Chris Doran, and Joan Lasenby, editors, *Applications of Geometric Algebra in Computer Science and Engineering*, pages 341-349. Birkh¨auser.

Perwass, C. & Sommer, G. (2006). The inversion camera model. In *28. Symposium für Mustererkennung*, DAGM 2006, Berlin, 12.-14.09.2006, number 4174 in LNCS, pages 647-656. Springer-Verlag, Heidelberg, Berlin.

Porteous, I.R. (1995). Clifford Algebras and the Classical Groups. *Cambridge Stud. Adv. Math.*, Cambridge University Press, Cambridge.

Rosenhahn, B. (2003). Pose Estimation Revisited. Technical Report Number 0308, Christian-Albrechts-Universität zu Kiel, Institut für Informatik und Praktische Mathematik, September.

Rosenhahn, B. & Sommer, G. (2005). Pose estimation in conformal geometric algebra, part I: The stratification of mathematical spaces. *Journal of Mathematical Imaging and Vision*, 22:27-48.

Rosenhahn, B. & Sommer, G. (2005). Pose estimation in conformal geometric algebra, part II: Realtime pose estimation using extended feature concepts. *Journal of Mathematical Imaging and Vision*, 22:49-70.

Sommer, G. (1997). Algebraic aspects of designing behavior based systems. In G. Sommer and J.J. Koenderink, editors, *Algebraic Frames for the Perception and Action Cycle*, volume 1315 of Lecture Notes in Computer Science, pages 1-28. Proc. Int.Workshop AFPAC97, Kiel, Springer-Verlag, Heidelberg, Berlin.

Sommer, G. (1999). The global algebraic frame of the perception-action cycle. In B. Jähne, H. Haussecker, and P. Geissler, editors, *Handbook of Computer Vision and Applications*, volume 3, pages 221-264. Academic Press, San Diego.

Sommer, G. (2004). A geometric algebra approach to some problems of robot vision. In J. Byrnes, editor, *Computational Noncommutative Algebra and Applications*, number 136 in NATO Science Series II, pages 309-338. Kluwer Academic Publishers, Dordrecht.

Sommer, G. (2005). Applications of geometric algebra in robot vision. In H. Li, P.J. Olver, and G. Sommer, editors, *Computer Algebra and Geometric Algebra with Applications*, volume 3519 of LNCS, pages 258-277. 6th International Workshop IWMM 2004, Shanghai, China and International Workshop GIAE 2004, Xian, China, Springer-Verlag, Heidelberg, Berlin.

Sommer, G. & Zang, D. (2007). Parity symmetry in multi-dimensional signals. *Communications in Pure and Applied Analysis*, accepted.

Stein, E.M. & Weiss G. (1971). Introduction to Fourier Analysis on Euclidean Spaces, volume 32 of *Princeton Mathematical Series*. Princeton University Press, Princeton, N.J.

Zang, D. & Sommer, G. (2006). The monogenic curvature scale-space. In R. Reulke, U. Eckardt, B. Flach, U. Knauer, and K. Polthier, editors, *11th International Workshop on Combinatorial Image Analysis, IWCIA06*, Berlin, volume 4040 of LNCS, pages 320-332. Springer-Verlag, Heidelberg, Berlin.

Zang, D. & Sommer, G. (2006). Detecting intrinsically two-dimensional image structures using local phase. In K. Franke, K. M¨uller, B. Nickolay, and R. Schäfer, editors, *28. Symposium f¨ur Mustererkennung, DAGM 2006*, Berlin, 12.9.-14.9.2006, number 4174 in LNCS, pages 222- 231. Springer-Verlag, Heidelberg, Berlin.

Zang, D. & Sommer, G. (2007). Signal modeling for two-dimensional image structures. *Journal of Visual Communication and Image Representation*, 18(1):81-99.

Zang, D.; Wietzke, L.; Schmaltz, C. & Sommer, G. (2007). Dense optical flow estimation from the monogenic curvature tensor. In *Int. Conf. on Scale-Space and Variational Methods (SSVM)*, Ischia, Italy.

Algebraic Reconstruction and Post-processing in Incomplete Data Computed Tomography: From X-rays to Laser Beams

Alexander B. Konovalov, Dmitry V. Mogilenskikh, Vitaly V. Vlasov and Andrey N. Kiselev
Russian Federal Nuclear Centre – Zababakhin Institute of Applied Physics
Russia

1. Introduction

Methods of computed tomography are well developed and widely used in medicine and industry. If tomographic data are complete, it is possible to reconstruct the images with sub-millimeter resolution. If the data are incomplete, tomograms may blur, i.e. their resolution degrades, noise increases and artifacts form. The situation is worst if measurement data are so poor that the system of equations which describe the discrete reconstruction problem appears to be strongly underdetermined. In this situation, images of acceptable quality can be obtained with algorithms that regularize the solution and use a priori information about the object, and do post-processing of reconstructed tomograms also with the use of a priori information, as a rule. This chapter provides two examples demonstrating the reconstruction of the internal structure of an object from strongly incomplete measurement data: few-view computed tomography (FVCT) and diffuse optical tomography (DOT) of strongly scattering media. The problem of reconstruction from a small number of views (<10) arises, for example, in experimental plasma research (Pickalov & Melnikova, 1995) or nondestructive testing (Subbarao et al., 1997). DOT is now deemed to hold much promise for cancer detection (Arridge, 1999; Hawrysz & Sevick-Muraca, 2000; Yodh & Chance, 1995). Here the strong incompleteness of data is caused by the fact that the number of source-receiver relations that define the number of measurements is strictly limited. Despite that these types of tomography use different wavelength bands (X-ray and near infrared) and different mathematical models (linear and non-linear), we think it is not only possible, but also interesting to consider them together because in both cases we successfully use similar reconstruction algorithms and similar post-processing methods. The unique possibility to do that comes from the fact that in case of DOT, we use a simplified reconstruction method (Konovalov et al., 2003; 2006b; 2007; Lyubimov et al., 2002; 2003) reducing the inverse problem to a solution of the integral equation with integration along a conditional photon average trajectory (PAT) – an analog of the Radon transform in projection tomography.
In case of FVCT, we use actual data from measurements in a simple experimental radiography setup (Konovalov et al., 2006a). The FVCT procedure is simulated by rotation of the object from exposure to exposure about the centre of the reconstruction region. For

objects, we use a spatial resolution test and an iron sphere with quasi-symmetric cracks resulted from shock compression.

In case of DOT, we use model data from the numerical solution of a time-dependent diffusion equation with an instantaneous point source (time-domain measurement technique). We consider a traditional geometry where sources and receivers are on the boundary of a scattering object in the form of a flat layer (Konovalov et al., 2006b). The object contains periodic structures created by circular absorbing inhomogeneities.

In both cases, the inverse problem is solved using algebraic reconstruction techniques (additive and multiplicative) which we modernized to attain the better convergence of the iterative reconstruction process (Konovalov et al., 2006a; 2006b). Procedures used to calculate the weight matrices are described in detail. Solution correction formulas are modified with respect to distributions of weight sums and solution correction numbers over image elements. Weighted smoothing is performed at each iteration of solution approximation. We use a priori information on whether the solution is non-negative and on the presence of structure-free zones in the reconstruction region.

For post-processing of reconstructed tomograms, we use space-varying restoration (Konovalov et al., 2007), methods for enhancing informativity of images based on its nonlinear color interpretation (Mogilenskikh, 2000) and methods for estimating image informativity based on binary operations and visualization algorithms (Mogilenskikh & Pavlov, 2002; Mogilenskikh, 2003).

Results of investigation help decide how spatial resolution depends on the degree of data incompleteness and draw inferences on whether the modified reconstruction techniques are effective and on the investigated post-processing methods are capable of making tomograms more informative.

The chapter is organized as follows. Section 2 gives a general formulation of the tomography problem. It is shown that the inverse problem of DOT, like the problem of reconstruction from X-ray projections, can be reduced to a solution of an integral equation with integration along the trajectory. The Section describes a discrete model of a 2D reconstruction problem and modernized algebraic techniques. Section 3 gives examples of 2D reconstruction from experimental radiographic data and model diffusion projections from optical inhomegeneities. The Section makes a quantitative analysis of the spatial resolution of tomograms reconstructed from strongly incomplete data. Section 4 describes post-processing methods and gives examples of their use. Section 5 draws inferences and outlines further research in the area.

2. Generality of our approach to reconstruction from strongly incomplete data

2.1 From the Radon transform to the fundamental equation of the PAT method

The problem of reconstruction in computed tomography is known to be formulated as follows: find the best estimation of a function of spatial coordinates $f(\mathbf{r})$, called an object function, from a discrete set of its measured projections. Generally, each projection can be written as a weighting integral

$$g = \int_{\infty} w(\mathbf{r}) f(\mathbf{r}) d^3 r \,, \tag{1}$$

where $w(\mathbf{r})$ is a weighting function which depends on source and receiver positions in space, the type of actual physical measurements and the way of data recording.

In transmission X-ray tomography where the spatial distribution of the extinction coefficient $\mu(\mathbf{r})$ is reconstructed, it is usually assumed that the weighting function is unity along a line L connecting a point source and a point receiver, and zero elsewhere. Then expression (1) turns into the linear integral

$$g = \int_L \mu(\mathbf{r})\, dl \,. \tag{2}$$

In computed tomography, it is known as the Radon transform. Integral (2) is inverted with a linear reconstruction model implemented with the use of both integral algorithms (Kak & Slanay, 1988) and algebraic techniques (Herman, 1980).

Divergence of the probing beam in, for example, proton (Hanson, 1981; 1982) or diffraction (Devaney, 1983) tomography makes it necessary to consider not a line but a narrow 3D strip of a finite length. In this case, it may be needed to change from linear integration (2) to volume one (1) and pose restrictions on the use of the linear reconstruction model.

Diffuse optical tomography (DOT) of strongly scattering media is the most demonstrative example of non-linear tomography. Laser beams used for probing undergo multiple scattering, so photon trajectories are not regular and photons are distributed in the entire volume V under study. As a result, each point in the volume significantly contributes to the detected signal. If, for example, we deal with absorbing inhomogeneities of tissues examined by pulsed probing with the time-domain measurement technique, integral (1), in the approximation of the perturbation theory by Born or Rytov, takes the form (Lyubimov et al., 2002; 2003)

$$g(t) = \int_V \left\{ \int_0^t vP[\mathbf{r},\tau \,|\, (\mathbf{r}_s,0) \rightarrow (\mathbf{r}_d,t)]\, d\tau \right\} \delta\mu_a(\mathbf{r})\, d^3 r \,, \tag{3}$$

where t is the time-gating delay of the receiver recording the signal, v is the light velocity in the media, $P[\mathbf{r},\tau \,|\, (\mathbf{r}_s,0) \rightarrow (\mathbf{r}_d,t)]$ is the density of the conditional probability that a photon migrating from a space-time source point $(\mathbf{r}_s,0)$ to a space-time receiver point $(\mathbf{r}_d,t)$ reaches an intermediate space point $\mathbf{r}$ at time τ, and $\delta\mu_a(\mathbf{r})$ is the distribution function of the absorbing inhomogeneities. Local linearization of the inverse problem of DOT is usually done with multi-step reconstruction algorithms based on the variational formulation of the radiation transport equation (or its diffusion approximation). The Newton-Raphson algorithm with the Levenberg-Marquardt iterative procedure (Arridge, 1999) is a typical example of these algorithms. The multi-step algorithms provide a relatively high spatial resolution (~5 mm) for diffusion tomograms, but they are not as fast as required for real-time diagnostics because we have to solve a forward problem, i.e. the problem of propagation of radiation through matter, many times by adjusting at each linearization step the matrix of coefficients of a system of algebraic equations describing the discrete reconstruction model.

There is a unique opportunity to accelerate the reconstruction procedure: to change in expression (3) from volume integration to integration along a conventional line connecting point source and point receiver. Using a probabilistic interpretation of light transfer by means of the conditional probability density P, Lyubimov et al. (2002; 2003) proved that integral (3) could be presented as

$$g(t) = \int_L \frac{\langle \delta\mu_a(\mathbf{r}) \rangle_P}{v(l)} dl \,, \tag{4}$$

where L is a curve defined by coordinates of the mass centers of the instantaneous distributions P in accordance with

$$\mathbf{R}(\tau) = \int_V \mathbf{r} P[\mathbf{r},\tau | (\mathbf{r}_s,0) \to (\mathbf{r}_d,t)] d^3r \,, \tag{5}$$

which we call a photon average trajectory (PAT). Here l is a distance along the PAT, $v(l)$ is the relative velocity of the mass center of the distribution P along the PAT as a function of l, $\langle \cdot \rangle_P$ is the operator of averaging over the spatial distribution P. Integral equation (4) is a fundamental equation of the photon average trajectories method (PAT method) in case of time-domain measurement technique. It is an analog of Radon transform (2) and can be inverted with the fast algorithms of projection tomography. In other words, converting (3) into (4) offers an opportunity to change from multi-step to one-step reconstruction in the sense that the system of algebraic equations describing the discrete reconstruction model is only inverted once and hence, to achieve significant savings in computational time.

Equation (4) has definitely a number of differences from equation (2), specifically:

(a) Integration is performed along not a straight but curved line;

(b) Under integral (4), there is a weighting distribution $1/v(l)$ which depends on spatial coordinates; and

(c) Trajectory integration is applied not to the object function itself, but to a function averaged over the spatial distribution P.

The latter means that the reconstructed image is degraded by a priori blur which requires additional work, i.e. post-processing of tomogram. With the above differences, it becomes clear that the inversion of equation (4) with the linear reconstruction model requires certain assumptions which may affect the quality of reconstructed images. Nevertheless, our earlier studies (Konovalov et al., 2003; 2006b; 2007; Lyubimov et al., 2002; 2003) and results presented in Sections 3 and 4 show that the PAT method is quite effective in the context of the tomogram quality versus reconstruction speed trade-off.

2.2 Discrete image reconstruction model

In medical applications of X-ray computed tomography, equation (2) is usually inverted by means of integral reconstruction algorithms such as the backprojection algorithm with convolution filtering (Kak & Slanay, 1988). In FVCT where the number of views is small, reconstruction with the integral algorithms gives aliasing artifacts which are present on tomograms as "rays" tangential to reproduced structures (Palamodov, 1990). Different smoothing and regularization methods can be applied to remove these artifacts which strongly restrict the resolution of small details. But the quality of reconstructed images still remains far from satisfactory.

It is also difficult to invert equation (4) with integral algorithms. Here problems arise from not only incomplete data, but also from curved PATs. Our attempts to implement the backprojection algorithm for diffusion tomograms (Konovalov et al., 2003; 2007; Lyubimov et al., 2003) are based on the assumption that the PATs are almost straight lines inside the scattering object. But with this approach it is impossible to reconstruct the spatial distribution of absorbing inhomogeneities near boundaries where photons escape from the object like an avalanche and the PATs strongly bend.

In this case, both in FVCT and in DOT, it is appropriate to use iterative algebraic algorithms implementing a discrete reconstruction model. In this chapter, without loss of generality, we will only consider examples of 2D reconstruction, i.e. reconstructions of 2D images. The generalized discrete model of 2D reconstruction is formulated traditionally (Herman, 1980). Let us establish a Cartesian grid for square image elements so that it covers the object. Assume that the reconstructed object function takes a constant value f_{kl} in an element with indices k and l (hereafter, (k,l)-cell). Let L_{ij} be a straight line or PAT connecting i-source and j-receiver, and g_{ij} be a projection measured by j-receiver from i-source. Then the discrete reconstruction model can be characterized by a system of linear algebraic equations

$$g_{ij} = \sum_{k,l} W_{ijkl} f_{kl}, , \tag{6}$$

where W_{ijkl} is the weight contributed by the (k,l)-cell to the measured value g_{ij}. In the traditional setup of 2D reconstruction, the weight W_{ijkl} is proportional to the length of intersection of the trajectory L_{ij} with the (k,l)-cell (Herman, 1980; Lyubimov et al., 2002).

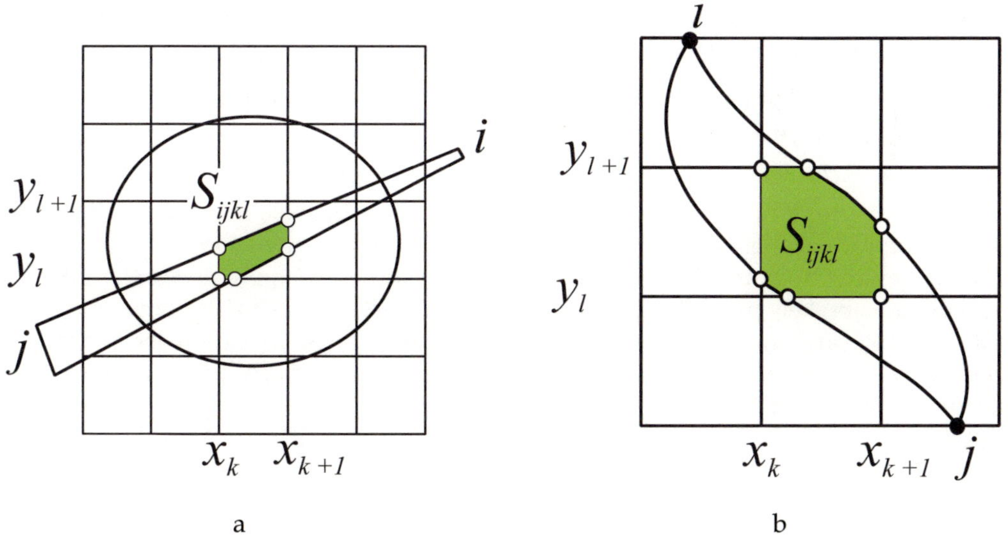

Figure 1. Calculation of weights: (a) X-ray tomography; (b) DOT

In this case, the matrix of coefficients of system (6) (hereafter, weight matrix) appears to be highly sparce because each trajectory intersects very few cells. This fact markedly worsens convergence of algorithms used to solve system (6) that is strongly underdetermined due to incomplete data. To reduce the number of zero elements in the matrix, we modernized the method for calculation of W_{ijkl} having changed the infinite narrow trajectory by a strip of a finite width (Konovalov et al., 2006a; 2006b).

In X-ray tomography, the strip is a long trapeze (Figure 1(a)). Its bases are source aperture (the linear size of the focal spot) and receiver aperture (as a rule, the intrinsic resolution of the recording system). In this case, the weights can be calculated with the formula

$$W_{ijkl} = S_{ijkl} / \delta , \tag{7}$$

where S_{ijkl} is the area of intersection of the strip corresponding to i -source and j -receiver (hereafter, (i,j)-strip) with the (k,l)-cell, and δ is the linear size of the cell. It is obvious that the calculation of S_{ijkl} for trapezoidal strips must not cause difficulty.

The situation is more complicated in DOT. The configuration and size of the appropriate strip must be selected with account for the spatial distribution of the trajectories of photons migrating from the point $(\mathbf{r}_s,0)$ to the point $(\mathbf{r}_d,t)$. According to the above statistical model, the most probable trajectories are distributed in a zone defined by the standard root-mean-square deviation (RMSD) from the PAT in accordance with the formula

$$\Delta(\tau) = \left\{ \int_V |\mathbf{r} - \mathbf{R}(\tau)|^2 P[\mathbf{r},\tau | (\mathbf{r}_s,0) \to (\mathbf{r}_d,t)] d^3r \right\}^{1/2} . \tag{8}$$

This zone is shaped as a banana (Lyubimov et al., 2002; Volkonskii, 1999) with vertices at the points of source and receiver localizations on the boundary of the scattering object. Therefore, for the (i,j)-strip we take a banana-shaped strip (Figure 1(b)) whose width is directly proportional to the RMSD: $\varepsilon(\tau) = \gamma \cdot \Delta(\tau)$. The problem is thus reduced to finding statistical characteristics (5) and (8) of photon trajectories. Note that the exact analytical calculation of $\mathbf{R}(\tau)$ and $\Delta(\tau)$ is difficult for even simple configurations such as a circle or a flat layer. The use of numerical techniques is undesirable because of the necessity to save computational time. Therefore, a number of simplifying assumptions should be done.

Lyubimov et al. (2002) and Volkonskii et al. (1999) propose to approximate the PAT by a three-segment broken line whose end segments are orthogonal to the boundary of the scattering object and the middle segment connects the end ones. This approach is effective if inhomogeneities are located inside the object, but causes distortions if inhomogeneities are near the boundaries where the PATs bend. In this chapter we configure banana-shaped strips in the geometry of a flat layer using a simplified analytical approach based on the analysis of PAT bending near a plane boundary. The approach uses the time-dependent radiation transport equation in the diffusion approximation. Konovalov et al. (2006b) showed that in the case where a instantaneous point source was in a homogeneous half-space (a half-plane in 2D) $y \geq 0$ at a point $(0, y_0)$ and a receiver was at a point $(x_0, 0)$ on the boundary $y = 0$, coordinates of the mass center of the distribution P, moving from the source point to the receiver point could be expressed as

$$\begin{cases} X(\tau) = x_0 \tau / t \\ Y(\tau) = y_0 \left\{ \left[1 + \frac{\tau}{t}\left(\frac{\alpha}{2} - 1\right) \right] \operatorname{erf}\left(\frac{t-\tau}{\alpha\tau}\right)^{1/2} + \left[\frac{\alpha\tau(t-\tau)}{\pi t^2} \right]^{1/2} \exp\left(-\frac{t-\tau}{\alpha\tau}\right) \right\}, \end{cases} \quad (9)$$

where $\alpha = 4Kvt/y_0^2$, K is the diffusion coefficient of the media, $\operatorname{erf}(\xi)$ is the probability integral. If assume that PAT bending near the plane (straight line) of a source S is similar to bending near the plane (straight line) of a receiver D and there is no influence of the opposite boundary, analytical expressions (9) can be easily used to construct the PAT for the flat layer geometry (Figure 2). Indeed, the mass center passes the distance SO and the distance OD during the time $t/2$. If the mass center moved in the half-space $y \geq 0$ from a point S_0 to the point D through the point O, the time $t/2$ would correspond to the distance S_0O. Since component velocity along the X-axis is constant, the point S_0 lies on the perpendicular SS' to the media boundaries. The distance S_0S' can be found through the numerical solution of the equation $Y|_{\tau=t/2} = d/2$, where d is the width of the layer, for y_0 (see expressions (9)). After that the distance OD is calculated with (9) and the distance SO is obtained through its symmetric reflection about the point O.

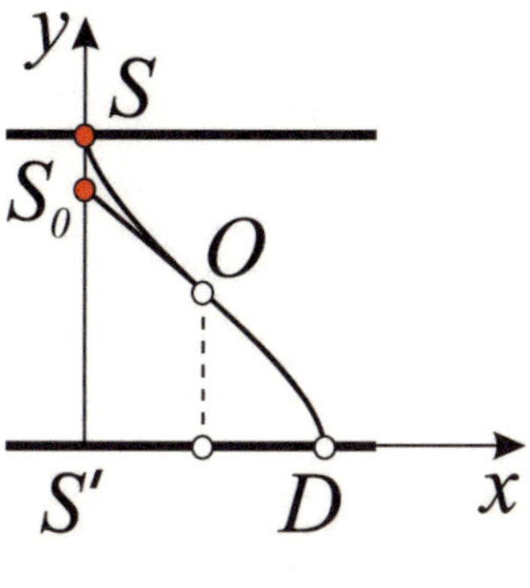

Figure 2. PAT construction for a flat layer

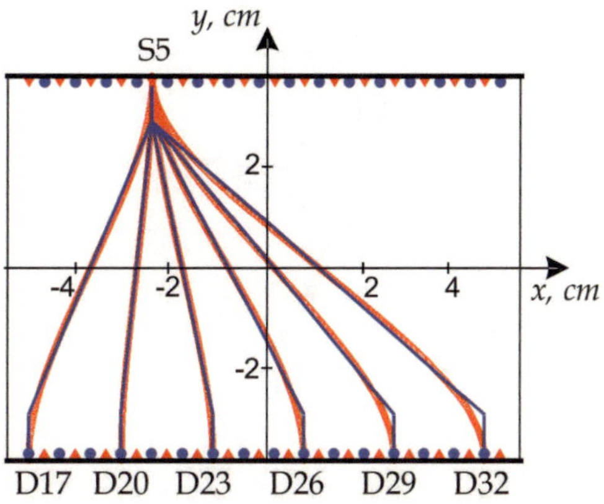

Figure 3. Geometry of data recording for a rectangular object

Figure 3 shows the geometry of data recording we chosen for simulations. Red triangles denote the positions of sources and blue circles do the positions of receivers. It also shows, as examples, six average trajectories reproduced with the above algorithm for $t = 3000$ ps and optical parameters $K = 0.066$ cm and $v = 0.0214$ cm/ps. Blue lines show piecewise-linear approximations of the PATs. Coordinates of the indicated sources and receivers (in centimeters) are as follows: S5 – (-2.52, 4), D17 – (-5, -4), D20 – (-3.06, -4), D23 – (-1.13, -4), D26 – (0.81, -4), D29 – (2.74, -4), D32 – (4.68, -4). In this chapter we study the probing regime in transmission, i.e. only relations between sources and receivers located on the opposite boundaries of the object are considered. The total number of average trajectories therefore

equals to 32×16 (32 sources and 16 receivers). In the reconstruction we will vary the number of sources to study how the spatial resolution depends on the degree of data incompleteness.
High accuracy of RMSD calculation is not crucial for the construction of banana-shaped strips. Therefore, in accordance with the inference of Volkonskii et al. (1999) that RMSD is actually independent of the form of the object, we can use the following simple formula for infinite space:

$$\Delta(\tau) \cong \left[2Kv(t-\tau)\tau / t \right]^{1/2}. \tag{10}$$

Boundaries of banana-shaped strips are defined as follows.
(a) Define a set of discrete times $\{\tau_p\}$.
(b) Construct perpendiculars to tangential lines at PAT points corresponding to times $\{\tau_p\}$ (Figure 4).
(c) Lay off sections of the length $\varepsilon(\tau_p)$ in both directions along each perpendicular.
(d) Construct lines connecting the points which we obtained for different $\{\tau_p\}$.

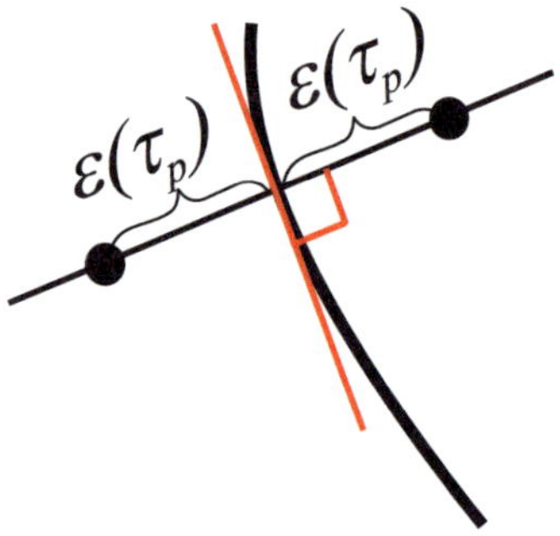

Figure 4. Definition of boundaries for banana-shaped strip

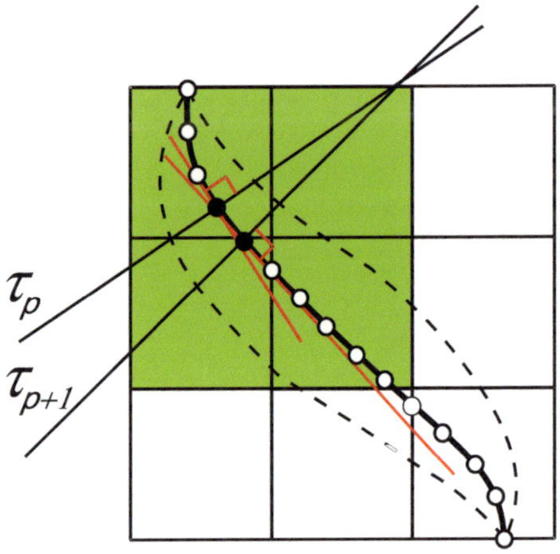

Figure 5. Definition of the discrete relative velocities of mass center of the distribution P

Boundaries of the strips are thus defined by piecewise-linear functions. To calculate the areas S_{ijkl}, we find the points where the strip boundaries intersect the sides of the cell. A polygon with vertices at the obtained points and cell nodes is treated as the intersection of the (i,j)-strip and the (k,l)-cell (Figure 1(b)). Weights are calculated with the formula

$$W_{ijkl} = S_{ijkl} / (v_{ijkl}\,\delta) \tag{11}$$

where v_{ijkl} is the discrete velocity of the mass center of the distribution P for the (i,j)-strip and the (k,l)-cell. Analytically, the velocities $v(\tau_p)$ are determined through differentiation of expressions (9). The array of discrete values $\{v_{ijkl}\}$ is defined with the following algorithm.

(a) Define a set of discrete times $\{\tau_p\}$.

(b) Construct perpendiculars to tangential lines at points of L_{ij} corresponding to the times $\{\tau_p\}$ (Figure 5).

(c) Assign a loop for p, in which the following sequence of steps is performed:

- Find cells where the (i, j)-strip intercepts a strip created by two neighbor perpendiculars corresponding to the times τ_p and τ_{p+1}. In Figure 5, these cells are shown in green.
- To all cells found, assign a value which equals the velocity averaged over two times: $[v(\tau_p) + v(\tau_{p+1})]/2$.
- If some value v_{ijkl}^{old} has already been assigned to a cell, it is updated with the formula

$$v_{ijkl} = \frac{v_{ijkl}^{old} \cdot N + v_{ijkl}^{new}}{N+1}, \tag{12}$$

where v_{ijkl}^{new} is the new value and N is the number of previous updates.

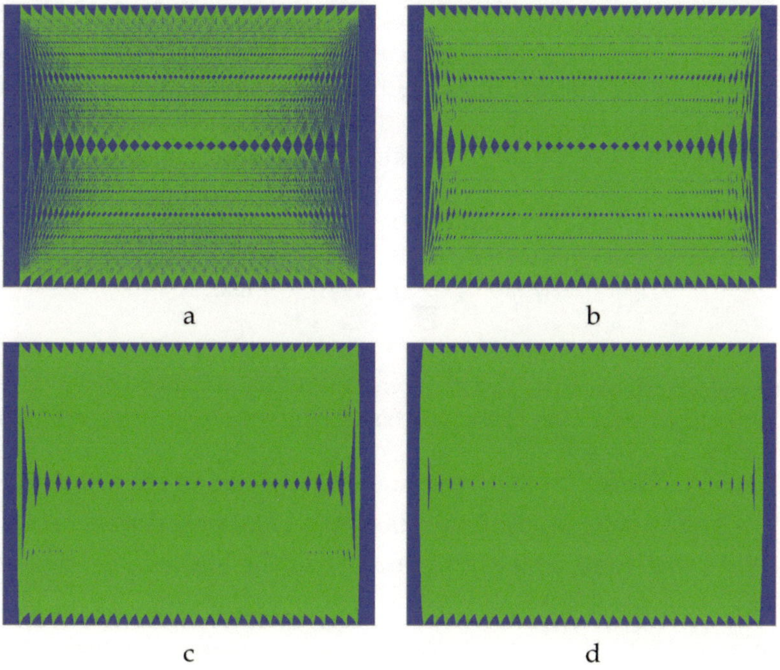

Figure 6. The area of the object filled with banana-shaped strips for different values of coefficient γ: (a) – 0; (b) – 0.05; (c) – 0.15; and (d) – 0.25

(d) All PATs are searched sequentially and, for each of them, the procedure is repeated beginning from step (b).

The proportionality coefficient $\gamma \in (0, 1)$ which defines the width of the banana-shaped strip is selected from a condition dictating that all strips must sufficiently fill the area of the object. Figure 6 shows the filling of the rectangular object presented in Figure 3 for ratio of sources and receivers (hereafter, measurement ratio) 32×16 and γ equal to 0, 0.05, 0.15, and 0.25. In Figure 6(a), (b), and (c), there are extended regions with no strips (shown in blue). This means that, if the grid is of high resolution, there are cells where corrections won't be introduced during the process of reconstruction. In Figure 6(d) these regions are very small in size which minimizes the probability that "dead" cells will appear. That is why we reconstruct the absorbing inhomogeneities embedded in the scattering object shown in Figure 3 using banana-shaped strips whose width is $\varepsilon(\tau) = 0.25\Delta(\tau)$.

It should be noted that the problem of area filling in FVCT is not as decisive as in DOT if even the strips are very narrow. Despite the small number of views, the number of strips corresponding to one view is rather large (> 100).

2.3 Algebraic reconstruction techniques and methods of their modification

When selecting an algorithm to invert system (6), we must remember that in case of very incomplete data, the system appears to be strongly underdetermined. That is why the problem of solution regularization is of great importance in the context of the need to approximate the solution correctly and hence, to obtain tomograms which are free of artifacts. It is well known that the minimum of artifacts corresponds to the minimum of information contained in images. Under these circumstances, it seems appropriate to do reconstruction with an approach based on entropy optimization (Levine & Tribus, 1978). In this chapter we study the multiplicative algebraic reconstruction technique (MART) which implements the entropy maximum method. The problem of solution regularization is formulated as follows. Find the array of values $\{f_{kl}\}$ which satisfies system (6) and the conditions

$$f_{kl} \geq 0, \quad \left(\sum_{k,l} f_{kl} \ln f_{kl} \right) \rightarrow \max . \tag{13}$$

For the purpose of comparison and to demonstrate advantages of the MART, we also consider a well-known additive algebraic reconstruction technique (AART) which does not optimize entropy.

Both MART and AART are based on an iterative procedure of correction of certain initial approximation $\{f_{kl}^{(0)}\}$. At each $(s+1)$-iteration trajectories (strips) from one source only are considered. Thus, the correction is introduced into the elements of the approximation $\{f_{kl}^{(s)}\}$ which correspond to the cells intersected by the given strips. Upon a transition from one iteration to another, the sources are searched cyclically. Original formulas for the correction of the s-th approximation to the solution are written as follows (Herman, 1980)

$$\text{MART}: \quad f_{kl}^{(s+1)} = f_{kl}^{(s)} \cdot \left(g_{ij} \Big/ \sum_{k,l} W_{ijkl} f_{kl}^{(s)} \right)^{\lambda W_{ijkl} / \delta}$$

$$\text{AART}: \quad f_{kl}^{(s+1)} = f_{kl}^{(s)} + \lambda \frac{g_{ij} - \sum_{k,l} W_{ijkl} f_{kl}^{(s)}}{\|\mathbf{W}\|_F^2} W_{ijkl} , \tag{14}$$

where $\lambda \in (0,1)$ is the parmeter which controls the rate of iterative process convergence and $\|\cdot\|_F$ is the Frobenius norm.

Our experience of using the algebraic techniques in FVCT (Konovalov et al., 2006a) and DOT (Konovalov et al., 2006b; Lyubimov et al., 2002) suggests that a number of modifications to formulas (14) are needed to improve convergence in case of strongly incomplete data. So, expressions (14) does not allow for

(a) the non-uniform distributions of weight sums and solution correction numbers over the cells; and

(b) any a priori information on the spatial distribution of reproduced structures.

As a result, both algorithms including the MART with regularization (13) often converge to a wrong solution. Because of the incorrect redistribution of intensity, images exhibit distinct artifacts which are often present in the regions where the structures are actually absent.

To avoid these shortcomings, we here use the following formulas for modified algebraic techniques

Step 1

$$\text{MART}: \quad f_{kl}^{(s+1)} = w_{kl} \cdot f_{kl}^{(s)} \cdot \left(g_{ij} \Big/ \sum_{k,l} W_{ijkl} f_{kl}^{(s)} \right)^{\lambda W_{ijkl} / \widetilde{W}_{kl}}$$

$$\text{AART}: \quad f_{kl}^{(s+1)} = w_{kl} \cdot \left(f_{kl}^{(s)} + \lambda \frac{g_{ij} - \sum_{k,l} W_{ijkl} f_{kl}^{(s)}}{\|\mathbf{W}\|_F^2} \cdot \frac{\delta W_{ijkl}}{\widetilde{W}_{kl}} \right), \tag{15}$$

where $\widetilde{W}_{kl} = \sum_{i,j} W_{ijkl} \big/ N_L$ is the reduced weight sum for the (k,l)-cell, N_L is the total number of strips used in reconstruction, and $\mathbf{w}$ is the matrix of correction factors which allow for a priori information on the object function (see below).

Step 2

$$f_{kl}^{(s+1)} = \frac{1}{(2r+1)^2} \sum_{m=-r}^{r} \sum_{n=-r}^{r} f_{k+m,l+n}^{(s+1)} \,\text{norm}(\widetilde{W}_{k+m,l+n})\,\text{norm}(A_{k+m,l+n}), \tag{16}$$

where the integer r specifies the size $r \times r$ of the smoothing window, A_{kl} is the number of corrections to the solution element corresponding to the (k,l)-cell, and

$$\text{norm}(\xi_{kl}) = \left[\xi_{kl} - \min_{k,l}(\xi_{kl}) \right] \Big/ \left[\max_{k,l}(\xi_{kl}) - \min_{k,l}(\xi_{kl}) \right] \tag{17}$$

is the operator which normalizes the distributions $\{\widetilde{W}_{kl}\}$ and $\{A_{kl}\}$.

Accounting for the distributions of reduced weight sums and correction numbers over the cells is most crucial for DOT where they are markedly non-uniform (Figure 7). Figure 8 shows an example of reconstruction of the scattering object with two circular absorbing inhomogeneities 0.8 cm in diameters (see Section 3.2). Here and after the red triangles represent the localizations of the sources used for reconstruction. The Figure demonstrates advantages of the modified MART. We have bad results without taking into account the distributions $\{\widetilde{W}_{kl}\}$ and $\{A_{kl}\}$ (Figure 8 (b) and (c)).

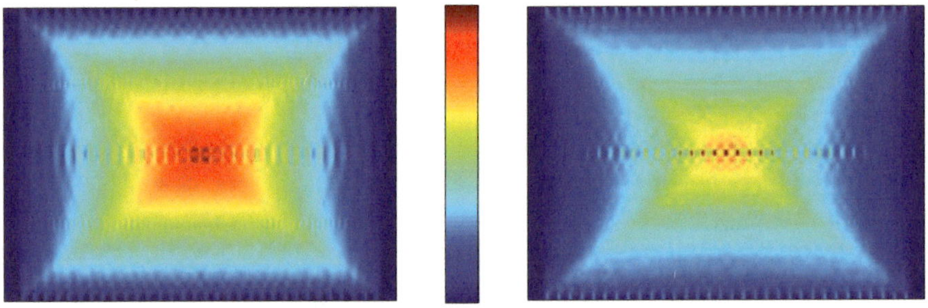

Figure 7. Distributions of reduced weight sums (a) and solution correction numbers (b) over 137×100 grid which cover the object shown in Figure 3

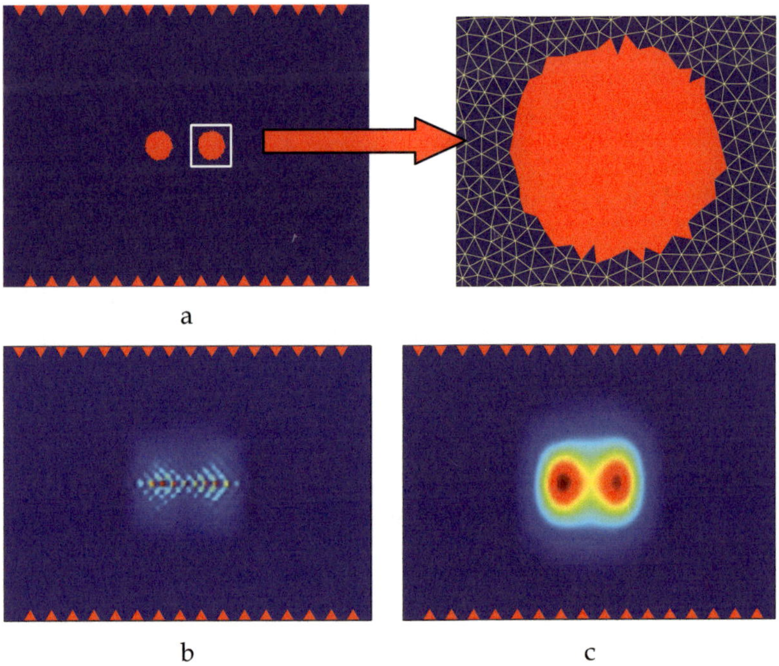

Figure 8. The 0.8-cm-in-diam absorbing inhomogeneities defined on a triangular mesh (a) and results of their reconstruction by the MART: without (b) and with (c) the distributions $\{\widetilde{W}_{kl}\}$ and $\{A_{kl}\}$

To use a priori information on the presence of structure-free zones in the reconstruction region, we developed an algorithm illustrated by Figure 9 which shows the reconstruction of the middle section of the iron sphere compressed by an explosion from radiographic data (see Section 3.1). The algorithm is described by the following sequence of steps:

(a) Reconstruct the image $\{f_{kl}^1\}$ from projections corresponding to the first source only (Figure 9 (a)).

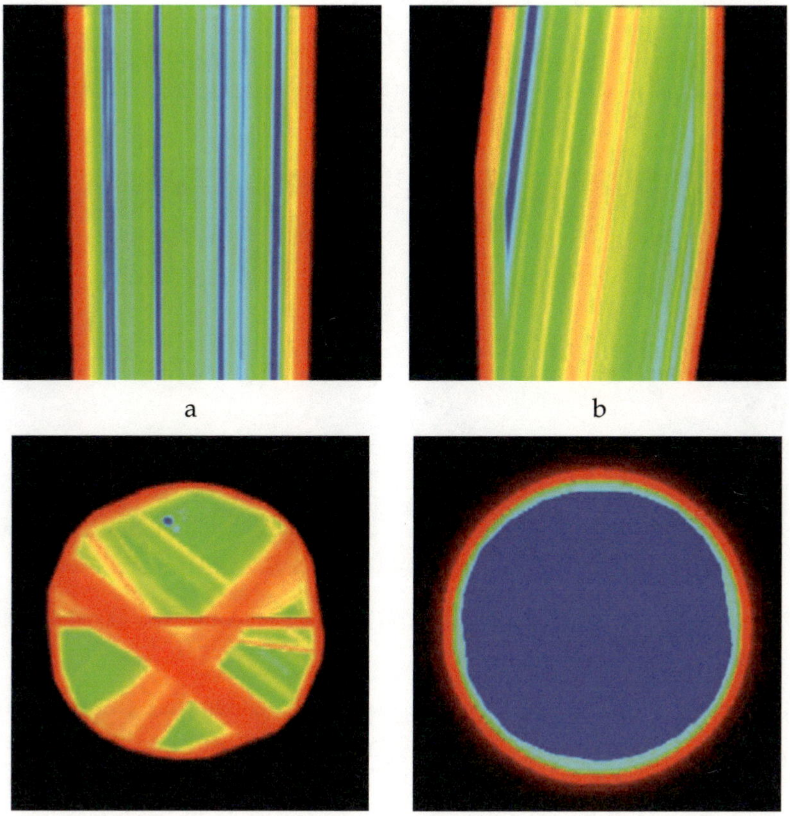

a b

c d

Figure 9. Generation of a useful part of the tomogram: (a) – the image $\{f_{kl}^1\}$; (b) – the image $\{\widetilde{f}_{kl}^2\}$; (c) – the image $\{\widetilde{f}_{kl}^{24}\}$; (d) – the set of multilevel regions

b) Reconstruct the image $\{f_{kl}^2\}$ from projections corresponding to the second source only and compare it with the result obtained at step (a). Following from the result of the comparison, form the image $\{\widetilde{f}_{kl}^2\}$ such that $\widetilde{f}_{kl}^2 = \min(f_{kl}^1, f_{kl}^2)$ for each (k,l)-cell (Figure 9(b)).

(c) Repeat step (b) for each following i-source forming the image $\{\widetilde{f}_{kl}^i\}$ such that $\widetilde{f}_{kl}^i = \min(\widetilde{f}_{kl}^{i-1}, f_{kl}^i)$ (Figure 9(c)). Search all given sources.

(d) For the last image $\{\tilde{f}_{kl}^{last}\}$, define certain ascending sequence of relative thresholds $\{\varepsilon_m\}_1^M$, the largest of which does not exceed, for example, 0.1-0.2 and determine correction factors $\{w_{kl}\}$ using the following relations:

$$\begin{aligned} w_{kl} &= 0, && if \quad \tilde{f}_{kl}^{last} < \varepsilon_1 \cdot \max\{\tilde{f}_{kl}^{last}\}, \\ w_{kl} &= \frac{\varepsilon_m}{\varepsilon_M} && if \quad \varepsilon_m \cdot \max\{\tilde{f}_{kl}^{last}\} \le \tilde{f}_{kl}^{last} < \varepsilon_{m+1} \cdot \max\{\tilde{f}_{kl}^{last}\} \\ w_{kl} &= 1, && if \quad \tilde{f}_{kl}^{last} \ge \varepsilon_M \cdot \max\{\tilde{f}_{kl}^{last}\}. \end{aligned} \tag{18}$$

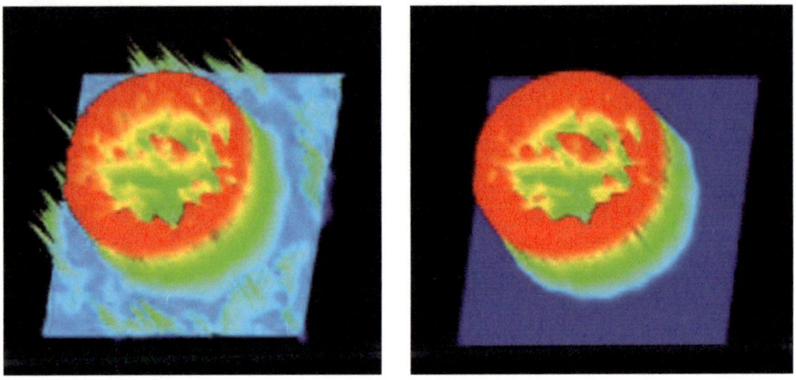

a b

Figure 10. Reconstructions of the sphere section from 24 views by the MART without (a) and with (b) the correction factors $\{w_{kl}\}$

Such a definition of the set of multilevel regions with values that monotonically decrease from unity to zero (Figure 9(d)) allows artifacts to be avoid in the structure-free zones, i.e. where the object function must be zero or close to zero. The effect of accounting for $\{w_{kl}\}$ is demonstrated in Figure 10 which illustrates the reconstruction of the section of a sphere from 24 views by the MART. For visual demonstration, reconstructions are presented as surface plots.

It should be noted that in the case of the AART, it is also appropriate to use a priori information on whether the reconstructed object function is non-negative. For this end, all negative elements in the solution approximation are changed by zeros at each iteration. In the case of the MART, this is not needed because the algorithm works with a priori positive values.

3. Examples of reconstruction of test objects and quantitative analysis of tomograms

3.1 Reconstruction of strongly absorbing structures from few X-ray views

This section gives examples of 2D reconstruction of objects with strongly absorbing structures from experimental radiographic data. The objects include

(a) a foam plastic cylinder 6 cm in diameter with periodical spatial structures in the form of rows of coaxial thin steel rods whose diameters are 1.5, 2.5, 5 and 8 mm, and
(b) an iron sphere 4.8 cm in diameter with lots of internal damages from shock compression.
X-ray projections are detected with a simple experimental setup (Figure 11 (a)). The radiation source is a pocket-size betatron with a small focal spot (about 1 mm) and a relatively small effective energy of the photon spectrum (about 2 MeV). The recording system combines a luminescent amplifying screen and an X-ray film. The object is placed between the source and the recording system so as to ensure that the film fully covers the object's shadow. To determine parameters of the characteristic curve of the recording system (photometric density versus exposure), we register the image of a step lead wedge with the object, as shown in Figure 11. Distances between the source and the object and between the source and the recording system are, respectively, 150 and 220 cm for the cylinder with periodic structures and 120 and 180 cm for the shocked sphere.

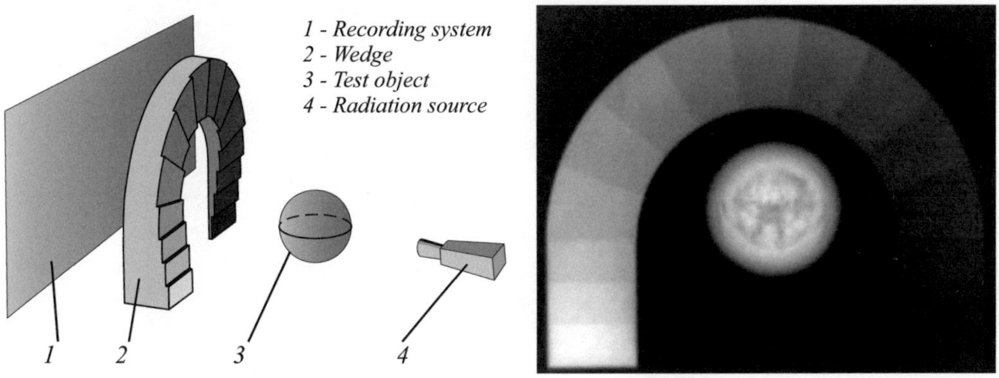

a b

Figure 11. Experimental setup (a) and X-ray photograph of the shocked iron sphere (b)

To collect information, each film with the X-ray image is scanned using a laser scanner with a small focal spot. Digital data collected are converted from scanner counts into film exposures with a technique (Kozlovskii, 2006) developed and experimentally adjusted at Russian Federal Nuclear Center – Zababakhin Institute of Applied Physics. The technique is based on the approximation of the characteristic curve by the relation

$$I = I_0 + I_{\max} \exp(-a \cdot |b - \lg H|^c), \tag{19}$$

where I is the photometric density, H is the exposure, I_0 is a parameter which characterizes the density of film fogging, $I_{\max}$ is a parameter which characterizes the maximum density the film permits, a and c are inclination and shape parameters, and b is a parameter which defines sensitivity of the recording system. The characteristic curve parameters I, $I_{\max}$, a, b and c are found through solving the problem of optimization for the objective function

$$\left[\frac{1}{Z}\sum_{i=1}^{Z}(I_i - I_i^{meas})^2\right]^{1/2} \to \min, \tag{20}$$

where I_i is the photometric density calculated by expression (19) for i-step on the wedge, I_i^{meas} is the experimental density found with the image of the step wedge (Figure 11(b)) and Z is the number of steps on the wedge.

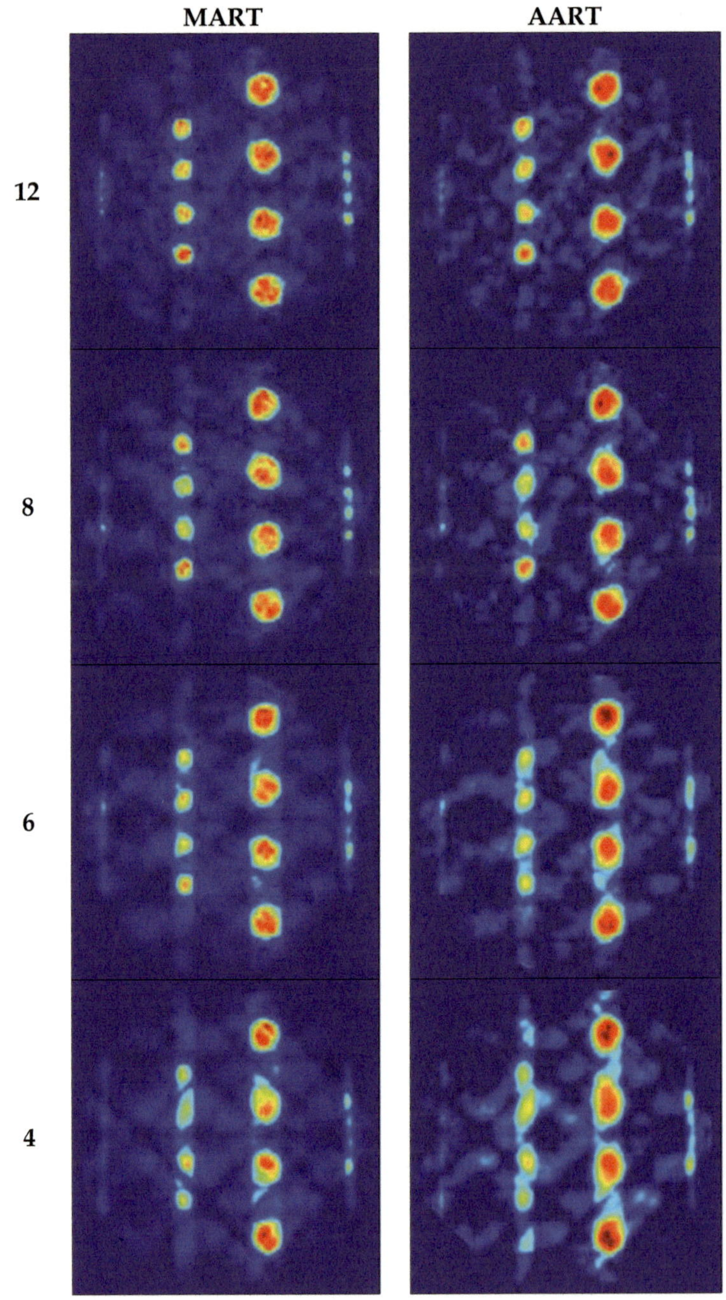

Figure 12. Tomograms of a cross section of the cylinder with periodic structures reconstructed from 12, 8, 6, and 4 views

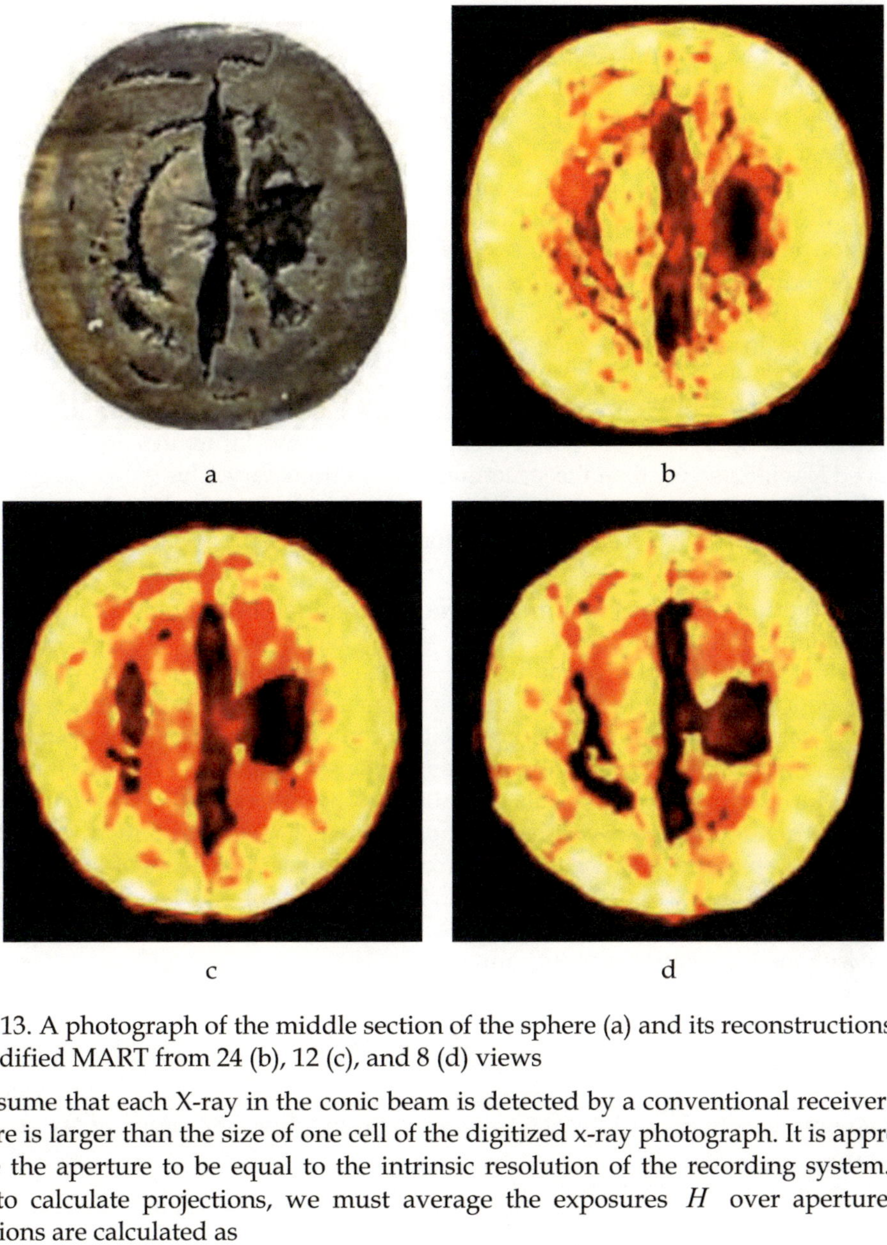

Figure 13. A photograph of the middle section of the sphere (a) and its reconstructions by the modified MART from 24 (b), 12 (c), and 8 (d) views

We assume that each X-ray in the conic beam is detected by a conventional receiver whose aperture is larger than the size of one cell of the digitized x-ray photograph. It is appropriate to take the aperture to be equal to the intrinsic resolution of the recording system. So, in order to calculate projections, we must average the exposures H over aperture areas. Projections are calculated as

$$g = -\log(H/H_0)\,, \tag{21}$$

where H_0 is film exposure without the object (background).

Figure 12 shows the tomograms of a cross section of the cylinder with periodic structures reconstructed from the 1D arrays of projections by the modified MART and AART described in Section 2.3. On the left of the Figure there are the numbers of views used for the reconstruction. It is seen that the quality of reconstructions by the entropy optimizing

MART is a bit better than that of the images reconstructed by the AART. For the images shown in Figure 12, the visual resolution limit seems to be close to 1.5 mm because the row of 1.5-mm-diam rods is clearly seen in the upper images (MART, 12 and 8 views; AART, 12 views) and hardly distinguishable in the others. The quantitative analysis of spatial resolution is given in Section 3.3.

Figure 13 shows the tomograms of a middle section of the shocked sphere reconstructed by the modified MART in comparison with its photo taken after the sphere was cut with an elecroerosion machine. It is seen from Figure 13 (a) and (b) that 24 views allow quite accurate reproduction of a fine fracture pattern (characterizing the reproduction of high-frequency structures) to be obtained. The images in Figure 13 (c) and (d) well reproduce the fracture pattern on whole, but small details are reproduced much worse compared with Figure 13(b).

Tomograms presented in Figure 13 qualitatively differ from those in Figure 12: the spatial structures in the sphere "drop" in reconstruction, i.e. the structures in the center are reproduced less intensively than the structures near its boundary. This is caused by the effect of beam hardening (Kak & Slanay, 1988) which distinctly manifests itself in the reconstruction of strongly absorbing objects. This proves that tomograms need post-processing.

3.2 Reconstruction of optical inhomogeneities embedded in strongly scattering media from model diffusion projections

To demonstrate efficiency of the modified algebraic algorithms for one-step reconstruction of diffuse optical tomograms, we conduct a numerical experiment where we simulate scattering objects with absorbing inhomogeneities and calculate diffusion projections. Four square objects 11×8 cm^2 in size (Figure 3) are considered. Light velocity in the media and diffusion and absorption coefficients are 0.0214 cm/ps and 0.066 cm and 0.05 cm^{-1}, respectively. Each object has two circular inhomogeneities of identical diameters; they are near the center at a distance of one diameter from each other. Diameters of inhomogeneities in different objects are 1.2, 1.0, 0.8 and 0.6 cm. The inhomogeneity absorption coefficient is equal to 0.075 cm^{-1}. To simulate diffusion projections, we solve the time-dependent diffusion equation with the instantaneous point source

$$\frac{1}{v}\frac{\partial\varphi(\mathbf{r},\tau)}{\partial\tau} - K\nabla^2\varphi(\mathbf{r},\tau) + [\mu_a + \delta\mu_a(\mathbf{r})]\varphi(\mathbf{r},\tau) = \delta(\mathbf{r}-\mathbf{r}_s,\tau) \tag{22}$$

for the photon density $\varphi(\mathbf{r},\tau)$ by the finite element method. The signal of the receiver is found with the formula

$$J(\mathbf{r}_d,t) = -K\left.\frac{\partial\varphi(\mathbf{r},\tau)}{\partial\eta}\right|_{\mathbf{r}=\mathbf{r}_d,\tau=t}, \tag{23}$$

where $\partial/\partial\eta$ is the derivative in the direction of the outer normal to the boundary of the object at the receiver point $\mathbf{r}=\mathbf{r}_d$. Accordingly, the diffusion projection $g(t)$ is found as logarithm of the ratio of the non-perturbed signal $J_0(t)$ calculated for the homogeneous medium to the signal $J(t)$ perturbed due to inhomogeneities.

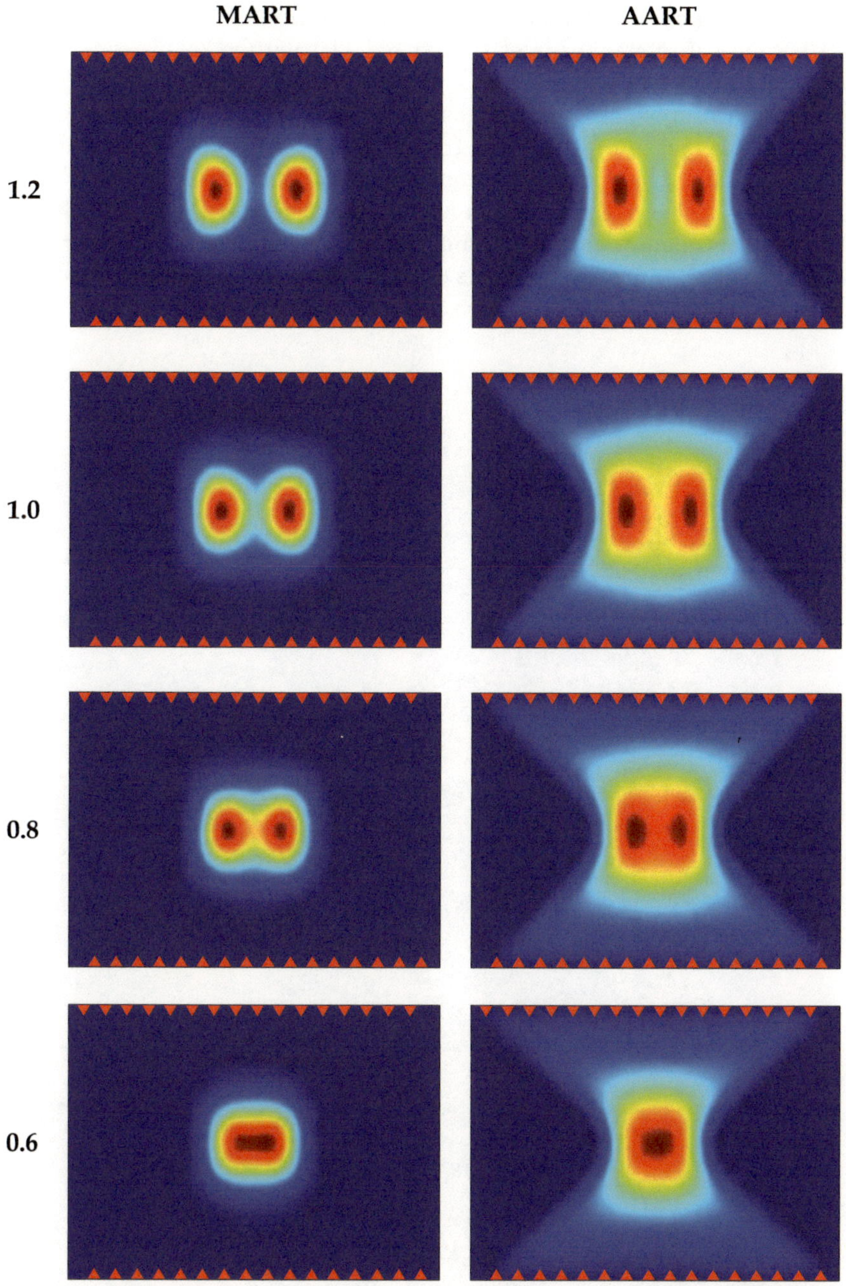

Figure 14. Reconstructions of scattering objects for measurement ratio 32×16

Figure 14 demonstrates the reconstructions of scattering objects by the modified MART and AART for measurement ratio 32×16 from diffusion projections calculated for the time-gating delay $t = 300$ ps. Diameters of inhomogeneities in cm are shown on the left of the Figure. It is seen that the AART that does not optimize entropy is a bit less accurate than the MART in the reproduction of spatial structures. In all tomograms, inhomogeneities are deformed (elongated) because of averaging over the spatial distribution of photons. This makes it necessary to apply post-processing methods to neutralize such blur. To investigate how the degree of data incompleteness influences the quality of tomograms, we reconstruct scattering objects for measurement ratios 16×16, 8×16 and 4×16. As an example, Figure 15 shows a reconstructed object with inhomogeneities 0.8 cm in diameter. The number of sources is given on the left of the Figure. It is seen that in case of 4 sources (the lower row of images), the inhomogeneities are falsely shifted and not resolved relative each other in the case of the AART. The quantitative analysis of spatial resolution is discussed in Section 3.3.

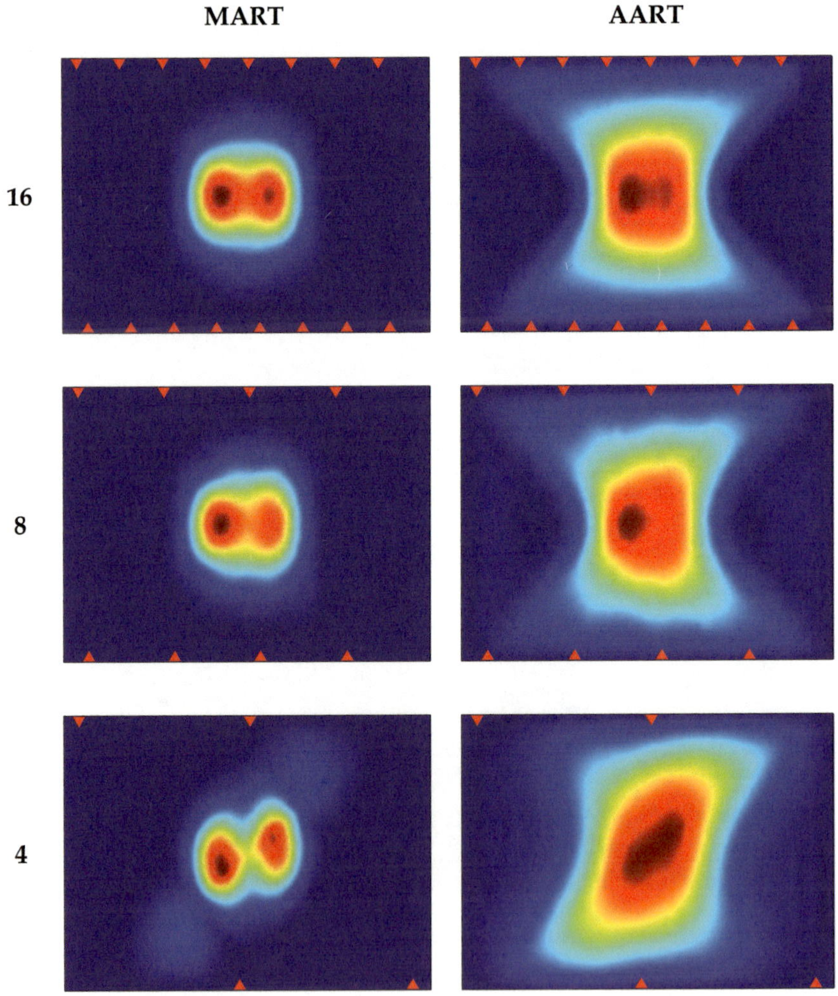

Figure 15. Reconstructions of the object with 0.8-cm-diam inhomogeneities for measurement ratios 16×16, 8×16, and 4×16

3.3 Quantitative analysis of tomogram resolution

In parallel beam projection tomography, the visualization system is usually described with a model of a linear filter invariant to spatial shift (Papoulis, 1968). The model allows the spatial resolution to be evaluated using a modulation transfer function (MTF) defined as the amplitude of system response to the harmonic signal. In the strict sense, the spatially invariant model is not applicable either in FVCT (because of fan beam geometry and strongly incomplete data), or in DOT (no regular straight photon trajectories). That is why, in this Section, we use the MTF only for the rough estimation of the resolution limit. On the contrary, in Section 4.1, blur of diffuse optical tomograms is neutralized with a spatially variant model which accounts for the dependence of spatial resolution on inhomogeneity localization.

To estimate the resolution from images of periodical spatial structures, we use the standard technique described, for example, by Konovalov et al. (2006a) and Lyubimov et al. (2002). From the profile of each reconstructed row of rods (Figure 12) or inhomogeneities (Figure 14 and Figure 15), we define the modulation transfer coefficient (MTC) as the average relative depth of the valley between peaks. The discrete spatial frequencies are assigned to diameters of the rods (inhomogeneities). A dependence of the MTC on spatial frequency is taken as an estimate to the MTF. Figure 16 (FVCT) and Figure 17 (DOT) illustrate the MTFs characterizing accuracy at which spatial structures are reconstructed from incomplete data by the modified MART and AART. It is seen that all curves from MART (red lines) run higher than those from AART (black lines), proving that the multiplicative algorithm that optimizes entropy is less restrictive in the reproduction of high-frequency spatial structures than the additive algorithm. So, for example, in reconstruction from 4 views (Figure 16(d)), 20% contrast (the conventional visual resolution limit (Papoulis, 1968)) corresponds to spatial frequencies 3.4 and 1.9 cycles/cm, if MART and AART are used. That is, if we are limited to 4 views, only spatial structures whose linear sizes are larger than 1.5 and 2.6 mm can be resolved in images reconstructed by the multiplicative and additive algebraic algorithms, respectively. Table 1 contains the estimates of the spatial resolution limit obtained in this manner from Figure 16 and Figure 17. Digits in brackets present similar estimates from the blue curves constructed for MART tomograms after space-varying restoration (see Section 4.1).

Tomography type	Number of views (sources)	Reconstruction technique	
		MART	AART
FVCT	12	1.0	1.5
	8	1.2	1.6
	6	1.4	2.5
	4	1.5	2.6
DOT	32	7.0 (6.0)	8.6
	16	8.1 (6.4)	10.0
	8	8.2 (6.8)	10.1
	4	9.0 (7.0)	12.6

Table 1. Estimated spatial resolution limit (in millimeters) for FVCT and DOT

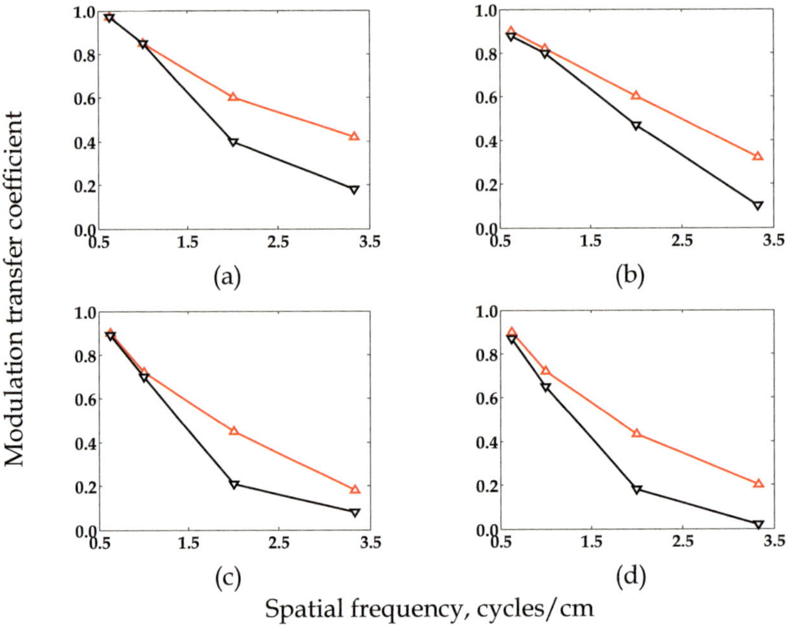

Figure 16. FVCT: MTFs for MART (red lines) and AART (black lines): (a) – 12; (b) – 8; (c) – 6; and (d) - 4 views

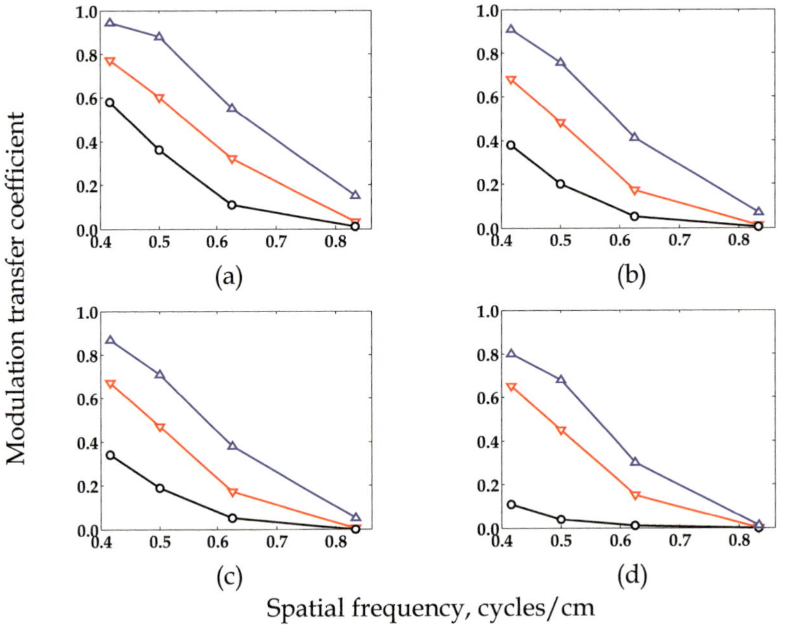

Figure 17. DOT: MTFs for MART (red lines), AART (black lines), and MART after restoration (blue lines): (a) – 32×16; (b) – 16×16; (c) – 8×16; and (d) - 4×16 sources and receivers

Analysis of data presented in the Table suggests that the use of the modified MART in FVCT helps get close to the resolution of medical X-ray tomography which uses the full set of views. As for DOT, the resolution of the PAT method reached again with the modified MART is only slightly worse than the resolution of tomograms reconstructed by the multi-step reconstruction algorithms (Arridge, 1999) and there is still hope to improve it through post-processing.

4. Post-processing of tomograms

4.1 Space-varying restoration

As mentioned in Section 3.3, the strict description of the visualization system both in FVCT and DOT can only be made with a spatially variant blur model. In FVCT, spatial variance at a rough approximation can be neglected because the size of the object is small compared to source-object and object-receiver distances. In DOT, the strong dependence of structure reconstruction accuracy on structure localization directly follows from expressions (8) and (10) which characterize the theoretical limit of spatial resolution. The theoretical resolution tends to zero near boundaries. In the center, the resolution is worst and depends on the degree of data incompleteness (Table 1).

The traditional approach (Fish et al., 1996) to the restoration of images degraded by spatially variant blur is based on the assumption that blur is approximately spatially invariant in small regions of the image. Each such region is restored with its own spatially invariant point spread function (PSF) and results are then sewn together to obtain the full true image. This approach gives blocking artifacts at the region boundaries and they need to be removed by some means or other. In this chapter we restore diffusion tomograms using the blur model of Nagy et al. (2004). In accordance with the model, the image is divided into a number of regions where the PSF is approximately spatially invariant. However, instead of deblurring each region separately and then combining restoration results, the method interpolates individual invariant PSFs and restores the entire image. The discrete restoration problem for a tomogram with blur $\mathbf{f}$ is described by a system of linear algebraic equations

$$\mathbf{f} = \mathbf{Q} \cdot \mathbf{z}, \qquad (24)$$

where $\mathbf{Q}$ is a large, ill-conditioned matrix describing the blurring operator and, $\mathbf{z}$ is a discrete representation of the true image. Matrix $\mathbf{Q}$ contains all non-zero elements of each of the spatially invariant PSF assigned to the individual regions of the tomogram. $\mathbf{Q}$ also accounts for a priori information on the extrapolation of the restored image beyond its boundaries, i.e. boundary conditions. This is necessary to compensate for near-boundary artifacts caused by Gibbs effect. So, for example, in the case of reflexive boundary conditions that we use for restoration, $\mathbf{Q}$ is the sum of the banded block Toeplitz matrix with banded Toeplitz blocks (Kamm & Nagy, 1998) and the banded block Hankel matrix with banded Hankel blocks (Ng et al., 1999).

Each spatially invariant PSF assigned to an individual region of the diffusion tomogram is simulated by performing the following sequence of steps.

(a) On a triangular mesh, we define a point inhomogeneity by three equal values in the nodes of a triangle located at the center of the region. The amplitude of the inhomogeneity is an order of magnitude larger than the amplitude $\delta\mu_a(\mathbf{r})$.

(b) Diffusion projections from the point inhomogeneity are simulated trough the solution of equation (22) with the finite element method.

(c) A tomogram with PSF is reconstructed from obtained model projections by the modified algebraic techniques described above.

For the inversion of system (24), we selected the iterative residual norm steepest descent algorithm (Kaufman, 1993) that converges rather fast and has a semi-convergence with respect to the relative error $\|\mathbf{z}_s - \mathbf{z}\| / \|\mathbf{z}\|$, where $\mathbf{z}_s$ is the approximation to $\mathbf{z}$ on s -iteration. This is of great importance for getting the regularized solution. Here we omit details of the procedure used to restore diffuse optical tomograms reconstructed by the PAT method. They can be found in (Konovalov et al., 2007).

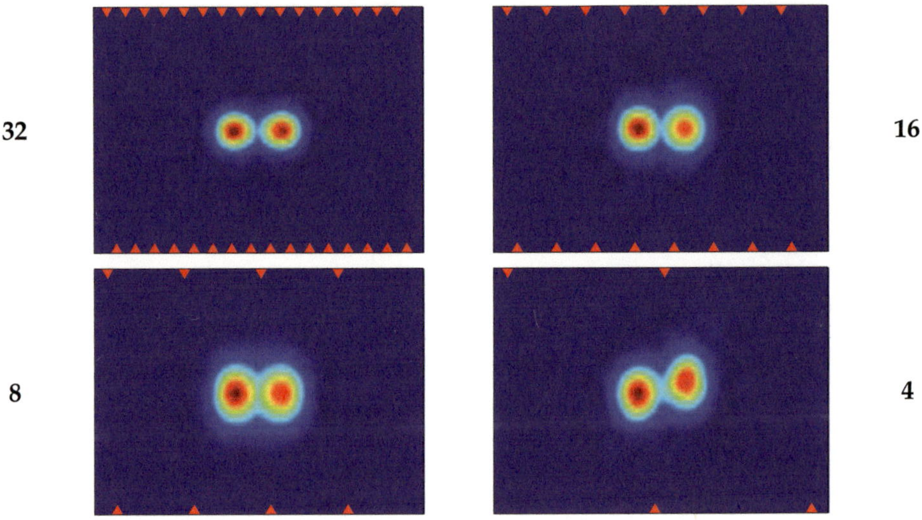

Figure 18. Results of space-varying restoration of MART-tomograms with 0.8-cm-diam inhomogeneities for measurement ratios 32×16, 16×16, 8×16, and 4×16

Figure 18 shows some results of space-varying restoration of diffusion tomograms reconstructed by the MART and presented in Figure 14 and Figure 15. The corresponding number of sources used for reconstruction and simulation of individual PSFs is given on the left and on the right of Figure 18. For restoration, a tomogram is divided into two conditionally spatially invariant regions, each of them containing its own absorbing inhomogeneity. To simulate the PSF, we defined a point inhomogeneity in a triangle located in the center of the inhomogeneity. It is seen from the Figure that we succeeded to not only improve resolution, but also neutralize deformations in the inhomogeneity shape. After restoration, the structures are reproduced much better even through the data are ultimately incomplete (see right image at the bottom of Figure 18). Blue curves in Figure 17 show MTFs constructed from the profiles of restored MART-tomograms. The corresponding estimates of spatial resolution provided in Table 1 in brackets demonstrate a significant gain in resolution (more than 16% for measurement ratio 32×16) due to space-varying restoration.

It should be noted that the problem of restoration of spatially variant blur is also needed in FVCT. However, to get the effect here, the PSF must be defined for each image cell, as the resolution in FVCT is much better than that in DOT (see Table 1). It is extremely difficult to do because of enormous requirements for computing and time resources. Search for an acceptable solution which will help implement a spatially variant model in FVCT is the subject of our short-term interest.

4.2 Post-processing based on nonlinear color interpretation

The effect of gamma-quanta beam hardening (Figure 13) is caused by the polyenergetic spectrum of radiation source and dependence of the object function (extinction coefficient) on the photon energy. Existing methods for eliminating beam hardening artifacts fall into three categories: pre-processing of projection data (Brooks & Chiro, 1976; McDavid et al., 1977), iterative post-processing of reconstructed tomogram (Elbakri & Fessler, 2002; Yan et al., 2000) and dual-energy imaging (Alvarez & Macovski, 1976; Kak & Slanay, 1988; Konovalov et al., 1999; 2000). The pre-processing methods are low efficient when high-contract structures are reconstructed. The most accurate iterative post-processing methods require, as a rule, extensive computation and turn out to be time-consuming. The dual-energy methods presuppose data recording for different spectra of radiation source, as well as additional calibration procedures to measure the effective photon energy (Konovalov et al., 1999; 2000).

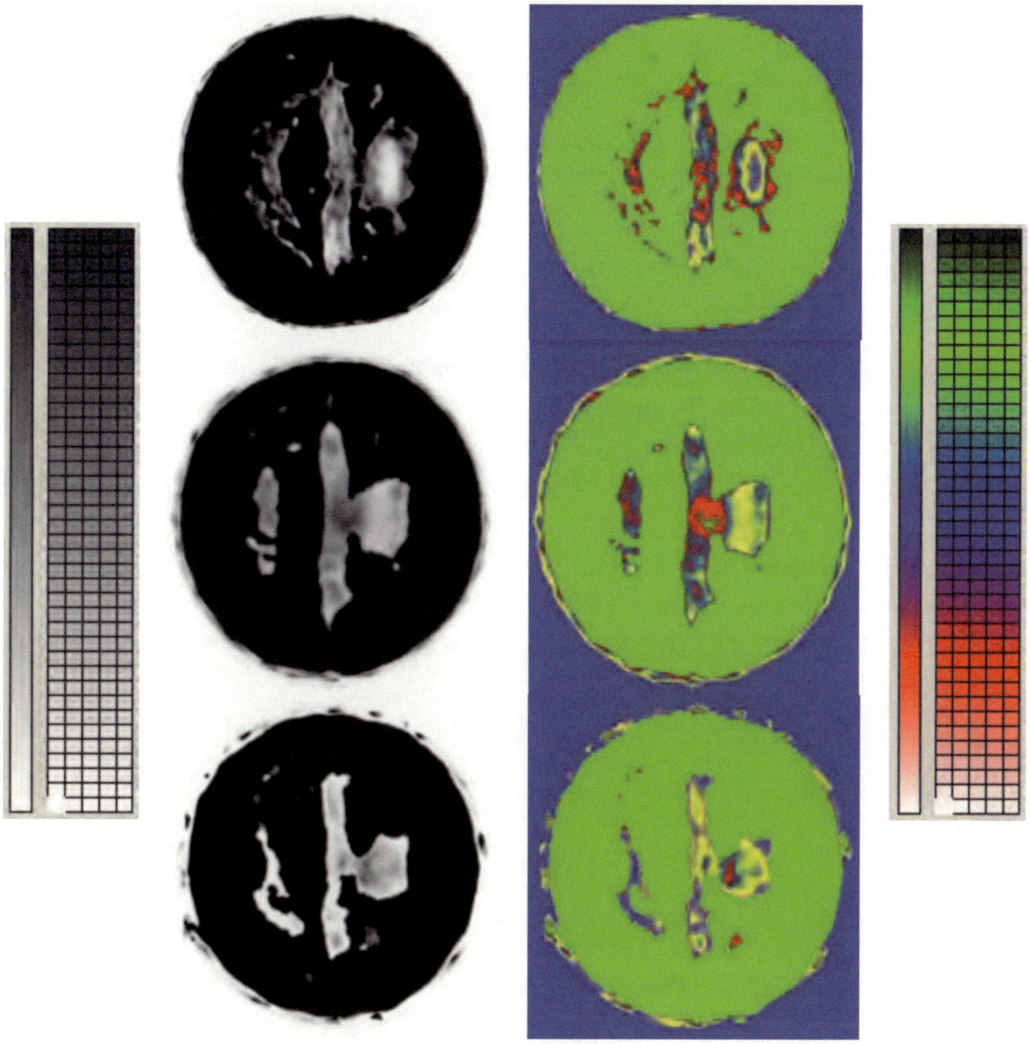

Figure 19. Results of application of linear (left) and nonlinear (right) palette to the images presented in Figure 13(b), (c), and (d)

For "flattening" the image intensity in order to compensate the beam hardening effect, we use simplified approach based on an application of the color interpretation methods. We consider the methods for creation of nonlinear color palettes and nonlinear statistical and analytical functions of correspondence between image intensity and color space. Detailed description of algorithms is given in (Mogilenskikh, 2000). This chapter is mainly focused on illustrative examples of their application.

The color palette is the ordered set of colors from the color space where each color corresponds to its own ordinal number. If the palette is nonlinear, the set of colors form a curvilinear trajectory in the color space. For image visualization with the use of the color palette we should form the law of correspondence between image intensities and colors in the cells (hereafter, correspondence function, CF). The argument value of such function is the image intensity, and the function value is the color or the color index in the palette. The linear CF is usually applied. Figure 19 shows the result of application of the linear black-and-white palette and the linear CF (left), as well as nonlinear palette including four basic colors (blue, yellow, red, and green) and the linear CF (right) to the tomograms given in Figure 13. It is seen that the fracture area is more obviously revealed in the second case.

However, the linear CF does not always allow data interpretation to be informative enough. To enhance the image informativity, we use the nonlinear statistical and analytical CF. The algorithm for creating the nonlinear statistical CF can be briefly described by the following sequence of steps.

(a) Form the linear CF and put color $G(f_{kl})$ in conformity with image intensity f_{kl} in the (k,l)-cell.

(b) Calculate the number of cells $N_G^{cells}(f_{kl})$ corresponding to each color of the palette and define the weights according to the formula

$$W_G(f_{kl}) = N_{col}\,\mathrm{norm}\left[\frac{N_G^{cells}(f_{kl})+1}{N^{cells}}\right], \tag{25}$$

where N_{col} is a number of colors in the palette, N^{cells} is a full number of image cells, and $\mathrm{norm}(\cdot)$ is normalization operator (17).

(c) Calculate the statistical CF in the form of a spline. The following 1st degree spline is used in our case:

$$G^{stat}(f_{kl}) = \left[G(f_{kl}) - N_{col}\mathrm{norm}(f_{kl})\right]\cdot\left[W_G(f_{kl}) - W_{G+1}(f_{kl})\right] + W_G(f_{kl})\,. \tag{26}$$

(d) Form the nonlinear CF through addition of the statistical CF (step(c)) and the linear CF (step (a)).

Left column of images in Figure 20 demonstrates the example of application of such nonlinear CF to tomograms given in Figure 13. Thus, it is possible to automatically distinguish informative contours of factures and simultaneously preserve intensity shades inside the image.

The essence of analytical CF is in applying the nonlinear color coordinate scales to attain the correspondence between the color and the intensity in the cells. Elementary functions and their algebraic combinations are used for that. Right column of images in Figure 20 shows the result of application of exponential CF $G(f) = \exp(60f)$ to images given in Figure 19 on the left. The type of the function is selected on the basis of the a priori information on the homogeneity of high-density structures of the object, which helps to present the internal facture pattern in the palette of two colors: black and white. This allows the informative regions of cracks and their boundaries to be strongly distinguished.

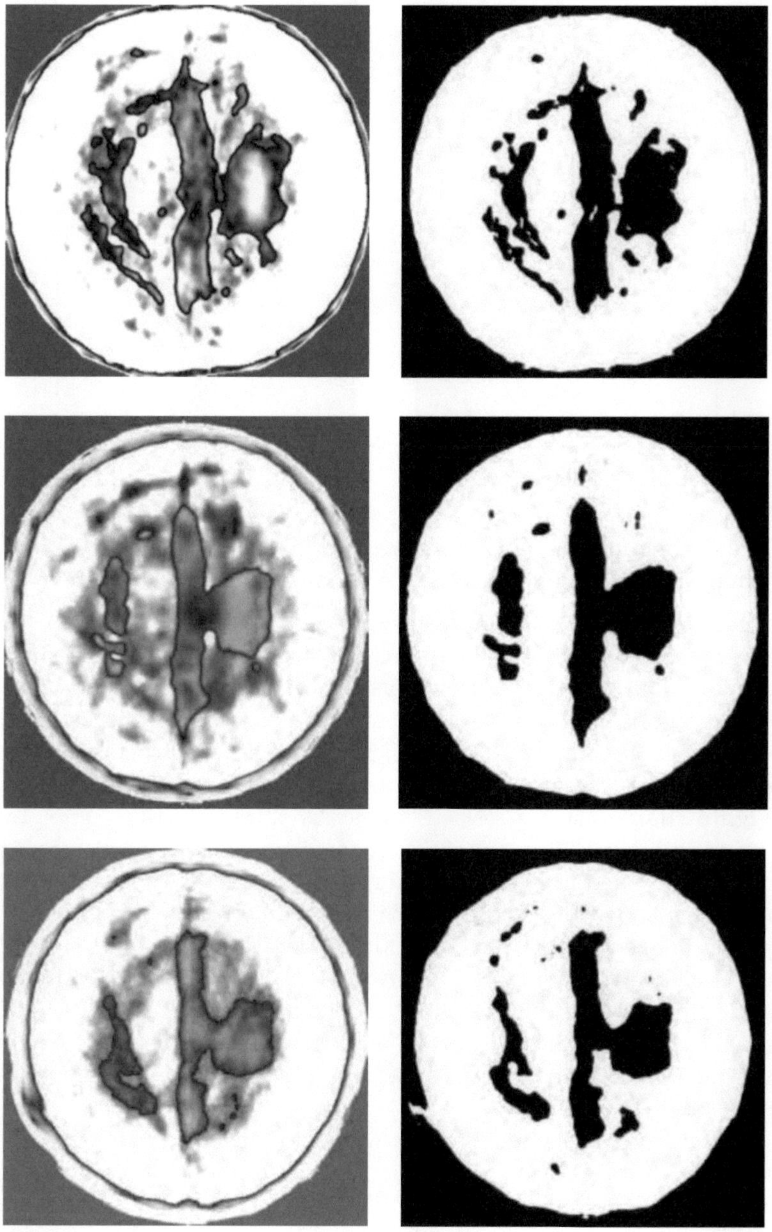

Figure 20. Results of application of statistical (left) and analytical (right) CF to the images presented in Figure 13 and 19 (on the left), respectively

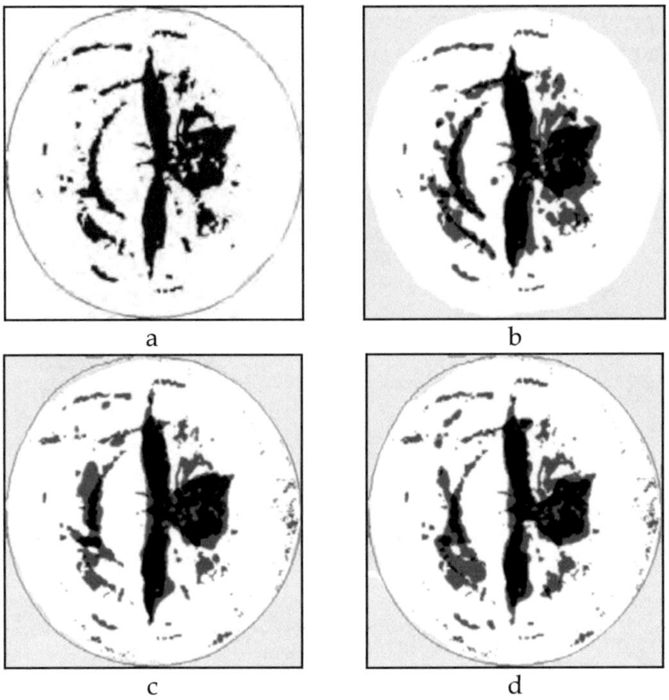

Figure 21. The processed photograph of sphere section (a) and the results of binary operations with processed tomograms reconstructed from 24 (b), 12 (c), and 8 (d) views

To estimate the accuracy of fracture pattern reproduction, we compare the results of tomogram post-processing with the etalon image obtained through processing of the photo presented in Figure 13(a). For comparison, a variety of methods based on binary operations and visualization algorithms (Mogilenskikh & Pavlov, 2002; Mogilenskikh, 2003) can be used. In our case, processing of the photo includes the construction of the same-level isolines, clearing of half-tones between the isolines, and filling of the isolines-bounded areas by black (Figure 21(a)). The processed photo is superimposed onto the processed tomograms given in Figure 20 on the right. As a result of binary operations, one obtains three-tone images presented in Figure 21(b), (c), and (d), where gray color characterizes the difference, and black and white - coincidence. The relations between gray areas and black area of the etalon image are equal to 0.03, 0.19, and 0.28, respectively. These quantitative estimates and visual analysis of Figure 21 show that the accuracy of reproduction of the fine fracture pattern seems to be unsatisfactory for reconstructions by 12 (Figure 21(c)) and 8 views (Figure 21(d)). This conclusion is in agreement with the results of Table 1, which show that the spatial resolution limit is worse than 1.0 mm when the number of views does not exceed 12.

The methods for creating the nonlinear CF are also efficient in the case of the diffusion tomagrams post-processing. The space-varying restoration of tomograms obviously improves but still reproduces incomplete profile of inhomogeneities. And as it follows from Figure 22, nonlinear-CF-based processing of restored tomogram of the scattering object with 0.8-cm-diam inhomogeneities makes it possible to approach a "flat region" of the true profile.

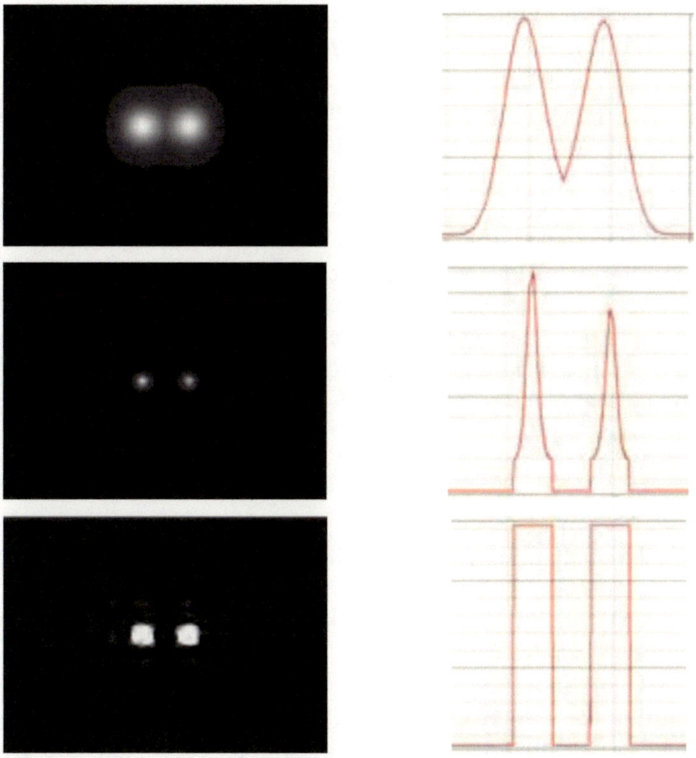

Figure 22. MART-tomogram with 0.8-cm-diam inhomogeneities and its profile after restoration (top), application of exponential CF $G(f) = \exp(14f)$ (center), and application of nonlinear statistical CF

5. Conclusion

In this chapter we consider two examples of algebraic reconstruction in incomplete data computed tomography: few-view X-ray computed tomography and one-step diffuse optical tomography. Multiplicative algebraic reconstruction technique optimizing the entropy allows the better quality of tomograms to be obtained. It is shown that, to enhance the convergence of iterative reconstruction procedure and to minimize the artifact level on tomograms, the conventional formulas of solution correction should be modified. The presented results of reconstruction demonstrate the efficiency of the following our modifications:

(a) To calculate the weight matrix, we use not the lines but the narrow strips which provide the sufficient filling of the reconstruction area.

(b) We take into account the non-uniformity of the distributions of the weight sums and the solution corrections numbers over the image elements.

(c) We calculate the correction factors which account for a priori information on whether the solution is non-negative and on the presence of structure-free zones in the reconstruction area.

For increasing the accuracy of spatial structures reproduction under conditions of the strong incompleteness of data, it is advisable to post-process the reconstructed tomograms with the

use of a priori information about the object. We demonstrate the efficiency of the methods of space-varying restoration and post-processing with nonlinear palette and nonlinear function of correspondence between the palette color and image intensity in the cells. As a result, we obtain the reproduction quality close to that of medical tomograms in the case of few-view tomography and close to quality of diffusion tomograms reconstructed by well-designed multi-step algorithms in the case of diffuse optical tomography.
In conclusion it should be noted that, for calculation, we use a rather slow soft-ware medium like MATLAB and a Windows XP Intel PC with 1.7-GHz Pentium 4 processor and 256-MB RAM. Computational time of the reconstruction-restoration procedure for diffuse optical tomograms is 1.5...2.5 minutes. These digits are better than those for multi-step reconstruction, but they do not satisfy the requirements of real-time medical explorations. In the future, it is interesting to optimize the duration of the diffuse optical image production. The implementation of a spatially variant blur model in few-view computed tomography is also the subject of our short-term interest.

6. Acknowledgements

The authors would like to thank S. P. Antipinskii, E. A. Averyaskin, S. A. Brichikov, V. V. Fedorov, D. M. Gorbachev, S. V. Kolchugin, E. V. Kovalev, E. A. Kozlov, V. M. Kryukov, I. V. Matveenko, A. V. Mikhaylov, L. A. Panchenko, V. N. Povyshev, G. N. Rykovanov, V. V. Smirnov, T. V. Stavrietskaya, V. I. Stavrietskii, T. A. Strizhenok, A. B. Zalozhenkov, and M. N. Zakharov for collaboration in X-ray radiography and few-view computed tomography. The authors also thank A. G. Kalintsev, O. V. Kravtsenyuk, V. V. Lyubimov, A. G. Murzin, and L. N. Soms whose contribution to theory of the photon average trajectories method cannot be overemphasized.

7. References

Alvarez, R. E. & Macovski, A. (1976). Energy-selective reconstruction in X-ray computerized tomography. *Physics in Medicine & Biology,* Vol. 21, No. 5, September 1976, pp. 733-744.

Arridge, S. R. (1999). Optical tomography in medical imaging. *Inverse Problems,* Vol. 15, No. 2, April 1999, pp. R41–R93.

Brooks, R. A. & Di Chiro, G. (1976). Beam hardening in X-ray reconstructive tomography. *Physics in Medicine & Biology,* Vol. 21, No. 3, May 1976, pp. 390-398.

Devaney, A. J. (1983). A computer simulation study of diffraction tomography. *IEEE Transaction on Biomedical Engineering,* Vol. 30, No. 7, July 1983, pp. 377-386.

Elbakri, I. A. & Fessler, J. A. (2002). Statistical image reconstruction for polyenergetic X-ray computed tomography. *IEEE Transactions on Medical Imaging,* Vol. 21, No. 2, February 2002, pp. 89-99.

Fish, D. A.; Grochmalicki, J. E. & Pike, R. (1996). Scanning singular-value-decomposition method for restoration of images with space-variant blur. *Journal of the Optical Society of America A: Optics, Image Science & Vision,* Vol. 13, No. 3, March 1996, pp. 464-469.

Hanson, K. M.; Bradbury, J. N; Cannon, T. M.; Hutson, R. L.; Laubacher, D. B.; Macek, R. J.; Paciotti, M. A. & Taylor, C. A. (1981). Computed tomography using proton energy loss. *Physics in Medicine & Biology,* Vol. 26, No. 6, November 1981, pp. 965-983.

Hanson, K. M.; Bradbury, J. N; Koeppe, R. A.; Macek, R. J.; Machen, D. R.; Morgado, R.; Paciotti, M. A.; Sandford, S. A. & Steward, V. W. (1982). Proton computed tomography of human specimens. *Physics in Medicine & Biology,* Vol. 27, No. 1, January 1982, pp. 25-36.

Hawrysz, D. J. & Sevick-Muraca, E. M. (2000). Developments toward diagnostic breast cancer imaging using near-infrared optical measurements and fluorescent contrast agents. *Neoplasia,* Vol. 2, No. 5, September 2000, pp. 388-417.

Herman, G. T. (1980). *Image Reconstruction from Projections: The Fundamentals of Computerized Tomography,* Academic, New York.

Kak, A. C. & Slaney, M. (1988). *Principles of Computerized Tomographic Imaging,* IEEE Press, New York.

Kamm, J. & Nagy, J. G. (1998). Kronecker product and SVD approximation in image restoration. *Linear Algebra & Its Applications,* Vol. 284, No. 1-3, November 1998, pp. 177-192.

Kaufman, L. (1993). Maximum likelihood, least squares, and penalized least squares for PET. *IEEE Transactions on Medical Imaging,* Vol. 12, No. 2, February 1993, pp. 200–214.

Konovalov, A. B.; Volegov, P. L.; Kochegarova, L. P. & Dmitrakov, Yu. L. (1999). Determination of component concentrations in mixtures of organic liquids using a computer tomograph. *Journal of Analytical Chemistry,* Vol. 54, No. 4, April 1999, pp. 315-319.

Konovalov, A. B.; Volegov, P. L. & Dmitrakov, Yu. L. (2000). A simple method for CT-scanner calibration against evective photon energy. *Instruments & Experimental Techniques,* Vol. 43, No. 3, May 2000, pp. 398-402.

Konovalov, A. B.; Lyubimov, V. V.; Kutuzov, I. I.; Kravtsenyuk, O. V.; Murzin, A. G.; Mordvinov, G. B.; Soms, L. N. & Yavorskaya, L. M. (2003). Application of the transform algorithms to high-resolution image reconstruction in optical diffusion tomography of strongly scattering media. *Journal of Electronic Imaging,* Vol. 12, No. 4, October 2003, pp. 602-612.

Konovalov, A. B.; Kiselev, A. N. & Vlasov, V. V. (2006a). Spatial resolution of few-view computed tomography using algebraic reconstruction techniques. *Pattern Recognition & Image Analysis,* Vol. 16, No. 2, April 2006, pp. 249-255.

Konovalov, A. B.; Vlasov, V. V.; Kalintsev, A. G.; Kravtsenyuk, O. V. & Lyubimov, V. V. (2006b). Time-domain diffuse optical tomography using analytic statistical characteristics of photon trajectories. *Quantum Electronics,* Vol. 36, No. 11, November 2006, pp. 1048-1055.

Konovalov, A. B.; Vlasov, V. V.; Kravtsenyuk, O. V. & Lyubimov, V. V. (2007). Space-varying iterative restoration of diffuse optical tomograms reconstructed by the photon average trajectories method. *EURASIP Journal on Advances in Signal Processing,* Vol. 2007, No. 1, January 2007, ID 34747.

Kozlovskii, V. N. (2006). *Information in Pulsed Radiography,* RFNC–VNIITF publisher, Snezhinsk (in Russian).

Levine, R. D. & Tribus, M. (1978). *The Maximum Entropy Formalism,* MIT, Cambridge, MA.

Lyubimov, V. V.; Kalintsev, A. G.; Konovalov, A. B.; Lyamtsev, O. V.; Kravtsenyuk, O.V.; Murzin, A. G.; Golubkina, O. V.; Mordvinov, G. B.; Soms, L. N. & Yavorskaya, L. M. (2002). Application of photon average trajectories method to real-time reconstruction of tissue inhomogeneities in diffuse optical tomography of strongly scattering media. *Physics in Medicine & Biology*, Vol. 47, No. 12, June 2002, pp. 2109-2128.

Lyubimov, V. V.; Kravtsenyuk, O. V.; Kalintsev, A. G.; Murzin, A. G.; Soms, L. N.; Konovalov, A. B.; Kutuzov, I. I.; Golubkina O. V. & Yavorskaya, L. M. . (2003). The possibility of increasing the spatial resolution in diffusion optical tomography. *Journal of Optical Technology*, Vol. 70, No. 10, October 2003, pp. 715–720.

McDavid, W. D.; Waggener, R. G.; Payne, W. H. & Dennis, M. J. (1977). Correction of spectral artifacts in cross-sectional reconstruction from X-rays. *Medical Physics*, Vol. 4, No. 1, January 1977, pp. 54-57.

Mogilenskikh, D. V. (2000). Nonlinear color interpretation of physical processes, *Proceedings of International Conference on Computer Graphics "Graphicon'2000"*, pp. 201-211, Moscow, August-September 2000, Moscow State University publisher, Moscow.

Mogilenskikh, D. V. & Pavlov, I. V. (2002). Color interpolation algorithms in visualizing results of numerical simulations, In: *Visualization and Imaging in Transport Phenomena*, Sideman, S. & Landesberg, A. (Eds.), *Annals of the New York Academy of Sciences*, Vol. 972, Part. 1, pp. 43-52, New York Academy of Sciences, New York.

Mogilenskikh, D. V. (2003). "CONTOUR" algorithm for finding and visualizing flat sections of 3D-objects, In: *Computer Science and Its Applications*, Kumar, V. et al. (Eds.), *Lecture Notes in Computer Science*, Vol. 2669, pp. 407-417, Springer-Verlag, Berlin/Heidelberg.

Nagy, J. G.; Palmer, K. & Perrone, L. (2004). Iterative methods for image deblurring: a Matlab object oriented approach. *Numerical Algorithms*, Vol. 36, No. 1, May 2004, pp. 73–93.

Ng, M. K.; Chan, R. H. & Tang, W.-C. (1999). A fast algorithm for deblurring models with Neumann boundary conditions. *SIAM Journal on Scientific Computing*, Vol. 21, No. 3, November-December 1999, pp. 851–866.

Palamodov, V. P. (1990). Some singular problems in tomography, In: *Mathematical Problems of Tomography*, Gel'fand, I. M. et al. (Eds.), *Transactions of Mathematical Monographs*, Vol. 81, pp. 123-139, American Mathematical Society, Providence, R. I.

Papoulis, A. (1968). *Systems and Transforms with Applications in Optics*, McGraw-Hill, New York.

Pickalov, V. V. & Melnikova, T. S. (1995). *Plasma Tomography*, Nauka, Novosibirsk (in Russian).

Subbarao, P. M. V.; Munshi, P. & Muralidhar, K. (1997). Performance of iterative tomographic algorithms applied to non-destructive evaluation with limited data. *Nondestructive Testing & Evaluation International*, Vol. 30, No. 6, December 1997, pp. 359-370.

Volkonskii, V. B.; Kravtsenyuk, O. V.; Lyubimov, V. V.; Mironov, E. P. & Murzin, A. G. (1999). The use of the statistical characteristics of the photons trajectories for the tomographic studies of the optical macroheterogeneities in strongly scattering objects. *Optics & Spectroscopy*, Vol. 86, No. 2, February 1999, pp. 253–260.

Yan, C. H.; Whalen, R. T.; Beaupre, G. S.; Yen, S. Y. & Napel, S. (2000). Reconstruction algorithm for polychromatic CT imaging: application to beam hardening correction. *IEEE Transactions on Medical Imaging*, Vol. 19, No. 1, January 2000, pp. 1-11.

Yodh, A. & Chance, B. (1995). Spectroscopy and imaging with diffusing light. *Physics Today*, Vol. 48, No. 3, March 1995, pp. 34–40.

27

AMR Vision System for Perception, Job Detection and Identification in Manufacturing

Sarbari Datta and Ranjit Ray
Robotics and Automation Group, Central Mechanical Engineering Research Institute
India

1. Introduction

Autonomous mobile robots are becoming an integral part of flexible manufacturing system especially for material transport, cleaning and assembly purpose. The advantage of this type of robots is that the existing manufacturing environment need not be altered or modified as in case of conventional AGVs where permanent cable layouts or markers are required for navigation. These robots are also used extensively for survey, inspection, surveillance, bomb and mine disposal, underwater inspection and space robotics. For autonomous navigation, proprioceptive and exteroceptive sensors are mounted on these mobile robots. As proprioceptive sensors measure the kinematic states of the robot, they accrue error over time and they are supplemented by exteroceptive sensors like ultrasonic and laser range finders, camera and global positioning systems that provide knowledge of its local environment which the robot subsequently uses to navigate. Here we describe the vision system of first indigenous autonomous mobile robot, AMR, with manipulator for environment perception during navigation and for job detection and identification required for material handling in a manufacturing environment.

1.1 Autonomous Mobile Robot System (AMR)

The ultimate goal for research on autonomous navigation of mobile robot is to endow these robots with some practical intelligence so that they can relieve or replace the human operators of tedious and repetitive tasks and for this reason manufacturing is one area where mobile robots are becoming a necessity.

Among on-going research on autonomous mobile robots for applications related to manufacturing, University of Massachusetts Amherst is developing a mobile robot with a comprehensive suite of sensors that includes LRF and vision along with a dexterous manipulator, as mobility extends the workspace of the manipulator, posing new challenges by permitting the robot to operate in unstructured environments (Katz et al., 2006). Bundeswehr University Munich is developing vision-guided intelligent robots for automated manufacturing, materials handling and services, where vision guided mobile robots *ATHENE I* and *II* navigates in structured environments based on the recognition of its current situation and a calibration-free manipulator handles various objects using an stereo-vision system (Bischoff & Graefe, 1998).

In this country, mobile robots are being developed in some research institutes in collaboration with academic institutes and private sectors. One such mobile robot is SmartNav built by Zenn Systems, Ahmedabad in collaboration with IIT, Kanpur and BARC (Sen et al., 2004). Our mobile robot with manipulator, AMR, is especially tailored for material handling and transport in a manufacturing environment. The vehicle navigates autonomously and transports jobs and tools from one workstation to another workstation. Figure 1 shows the AMR with all the mounted sensors. Among the sensors, a stereovision camera is mounted in front of AMR for environment perception. Another CMOS camera mounted on the wrist of the manipulator is used for material detection and identification required for pick and place operation. Laser and sonar range finders are used for localization through map building and for obstacle avoidance respectively during navigaiton (Datta et al., 2006). AMR stands on a distributed architecture for performing various tasks without any perceptible delay and for safeguarding the total system against major failure that may occur when the total burden rests on a single point of operation (Datta et al., 2007).

2. AMR Perception

2.1 Prior Art

Color image transmission from the robot while navigating in robot workspace has become very important in the field of mobile robotics, not only for localization by feature identification but also for monitoring of the robot environment through reconstructed images at multiple points in the robot work area. The robot work area can be a huge shop floor or a warehouse encompassing an area of about 200meters, for effective control from a remote host through a single WLAN Access Point.

Figure 1. AMR

Traditional transfer of bitmap images is quite cumbersome. A large image transferred over the Ethernet can take several seconds. To alleviate this problem, progressive image transmission scheme is used where image fidelity, taking advantage of such popular image file formats as JPEG (Joint Photographic Experts Group) and GIF (Graphics Interchange Format), is gradually built up so that the viewer can see an approximated image in its whole without the need to wait for all the data to be received (Tong & Zhang, 1998). But gradual building up of an image in a constantly changing environment becomes a hindrance for mobile robot perception, as high-speed image transmission is absolutely necessary while navigating, to capture the changing scenario.

Similarly, several methods exist for reconstruction of transmitted data. Two approaches that provide robust image transmission through reconstruction are decoder-based adaptive reconstruction and reconstruction-optimized source coding (Hemami, 1995).

Among decoder-based adaptive reconstruction, Smoothing Criterion Reconstruction (SCR), an adaptive algorithm, is designed to exploit the characteristics of the compressed visual information, which reconstructs the lost information of the image using image characteristics such as spatial and temporal correlation (Hemami & Meng, 1995). As such, SCR generally requires extensive computation power, which thwarts the purpose of online viewing of robot environment through fast reconstruction during navigation. Another approach, Vector Quantized Linear Interpolation (VQLI) (Hemami & Gray, 1994) provides reconstruction of equivalent visual quality with less than 10% transmission overhead. Vector Quantization (VQ) is used at the encoder to set appropriate weights for image compression which is decoded for reconstruction. This approach provides reconstruction capabilities without the extensive computational burden as in previous case, but restricts coding of the image for transmission to a proprietary format.

In reconstruction-optimized source coding, a block-based source coding technique Lapped Orthogonal Transform (LOT) is designed to maximize the reconstruction performance (Hemami, 1996). Mean-reconstruction, in which a missing coefficient block is replaced with the average of its available neighobors, is selected and a reconstruction criterion is defined for equal distribution of reconstruction errors across all transform coefficients and a family of LOT is then designed to meet the reconstruction. The overall performance can be gauged by considering both the coding gain and the reconstruction gain. Although the reconstruction-optimized LOT family provides excellent reconstruction capability, but any kind of matrix manipulation required is inconvenient for instant viewing of robot environment through fast reconstruction.

2.2 AMR Image Transmission Network

Reliable transmission and reception of images is imperative for mobile robot perception. Most transmission schemes take advantage of popular JPEG or GIF image format as responsiveness gained from rapid image transmission is more important than perfect image fidelity. Robustness is therefore vital for rapid image transmission and reconstruction in a mobile robot network. Hence, we also take advantage of the most popular and widely supported JPEG image file format (Wallace, 1991) (Schafer, 2001) for transmitting full color images frame by frame from AMR to multiple clients, set at different monitoring points within AMR work area in a manufacturing environment and for reconstructing these images for viewing almost without any perceptible delay.

2.2.1 System Description

A. Server or host

The server or the host computer in AMR's network resides in the mobile robot. For experimental purpose, first a mono-vision camera and then a stereo vision camera is used for grabbing images of the surrounding which are transferred first over Ethernet and then over WLAN, for comparing the transmission characteristics of each medium. In our case, the host computer is a Pentium-4 CPU @ 2.8 GHz with 1 GB RAM loaded with Windows 2000 OS and VC++ 6.0 with an Ethernet interface as well as a WLAN interface. The mono-vision camera is a PULNIX-TMC-6DSP with a Matrox Meteor-II/Standard frame grabber card. Using image control properties of the frame grabber, a color image with a resolution of 768x576 is grabbed and stored in JPEG format. The stereovision camera is a digiclops trinocular camera from PointGrey Research with IEEE-1394 interface. For the stereovision camera, an image with a resolution of 1024x768 is grabbed in raw format and is converted to JPEG format for transmission and display.

B. Multiple clients

Client computers are located at different points within the robot work area. The computers are of various configurations. A typical client computer is a Pentium-4 CPU @ 2.8 GHz with 512 MB RAM loaded with Windows 2000 OS and VC++ 6.0 with Ethernet and WLAN interface. Figure 2 shows AMR architecture.

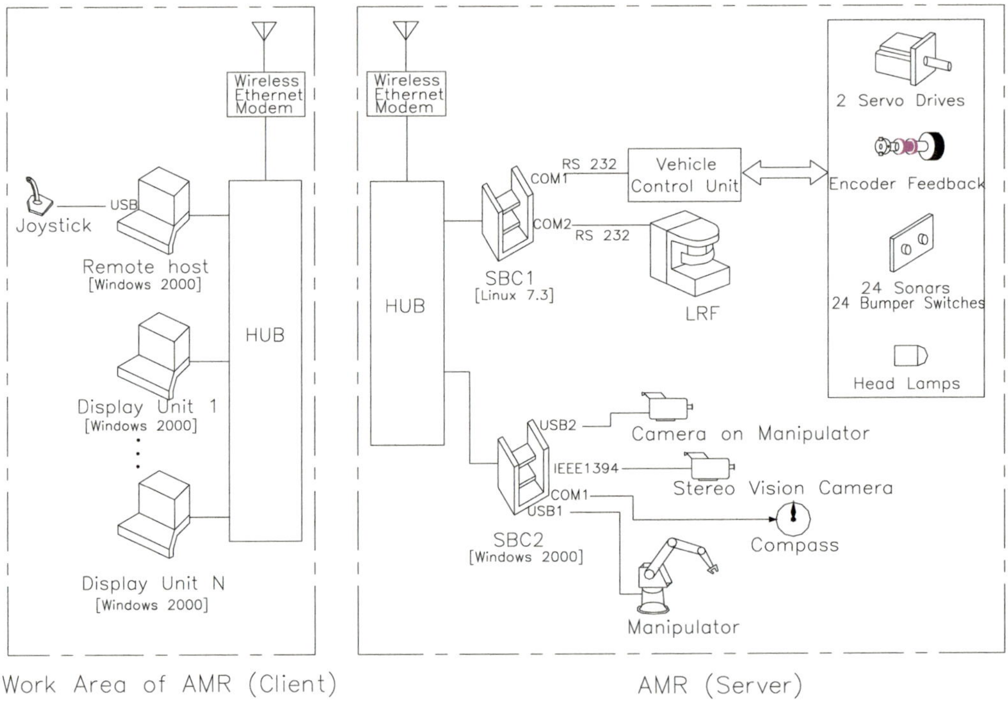

Figure 2. AMR architecture

2.2.2 Methodology for Image Transmission and Reconstruction

A. Image Transmission

High-resolution color images are transmitted over the network using socket communication. Multi-threading is used so that the AMR server can cater to multiple clients. Microsoft Foundation Class (MFC) **CSocket** is used, as this class is highly useful for client/server model communication. **CSocket**, derived from the base class **CObject**, uses serialization protocol to pass data to and from a socket object via a **CArchive** object. An intermediate class **CSocketFile**, also derived from base class **CObject**, is required, as the **CArchive** object attaches to an object of class **CSocketFile** for sending or receiving data.

In our case, for the server side a **CServerSocket** object, inherited from **CSocket,** is created. One **CArchive** object is created for sending data and one for receiving data from the clients, which is associated with **CSocketFile** object in the **CArchive** constructor. The server socket is set in listening mode and on accepting a client, it creates a new object of the class **CListenSocket.**

After an image is grabbed, the image data is assembled which is written to the listening socket for sending to the client through **CArchive** object.

Similarly, for images grabbed from stereovision camera, the images are converted from raster format to JPEG format for ease of transmission using standard technique for image compression. Image data is then serialized using **CArchive** class and written to **CSocket** using **CSocketFile** for transmission to clients.

B. Image Reconstruction

The image data is sent from the host to the clients over WLAN and Ethernet. Data is received on the client side through **CArchive** object, which in turn accesses **CClientSocket** inherited from **CSocket** via **CSocketFile.**

Once the client receives the image data, it reconstructs the image using the COM (Component Object Model) class, **IPicture. IPicture** manages a picture object and its properties. Picture objects provide a language-neutral abstraction for bitmaps, icons, and metafiles. A class **CPicture** is created which holds an ATL (Active Template Library) smart pointer **CComQIPtr** to the **IPicture** interface. Class **CPicture** encapsulates only those methods needed for displaying the images. The image data received by the client is loaded in the memory as a **CMemFile** object using **CArchive** class. **CMemFile** is the **CFile**-derived class that supports memory files.

The image is loaded as a stream using COM class **IStream,** which calls **OleLoadPicture** to load the image in the memory. Finally, **Render** is called at a specified offset which instantiates **IPicture** method for rendering the image onto specified device context. The block diagram in Figure 3 shows the total image transfer scheme described here.

3. Object Detection and Identification for Material Handling

AMR material handling system consists of Intelitek's 5 DOF Scorbot-ER-4u manipulator with a CMOS camera, mounted on the wrist of the manipulator as shown in Figure 4. Once the AMR navigates its way to the target workstation, the manipulator routine is invoked. Figure 5 shows the overall AMR software architecture. SBC2, acting as the server, turns on the manipulator control box, which in turn activates the manipulator. As the manipulator moves over the worktable, the camera scans the worktable and when it detects a job, using template matching identifies the desired job or tool. Adaptive thresholding is used for dynamic image segmentation. Using the gray level distribution of an image, the neighborhood around the highest peak of the histogram is chosen as the threshold region. A novel variation of Otsu's method (Otsu, 1979) is proposed for faster online processing, which chooses the optimal thresholds by maximizing the between-class variance with an heuristic search method for adaptive thresholding. Once the job parameters are calculated, the gripper picks the job and puts it on the platform. In this way, the jobs are stacked on the vehicle and are transported to the next workstation where they are unloaded using reverse operation and AMR continues with its next mission.

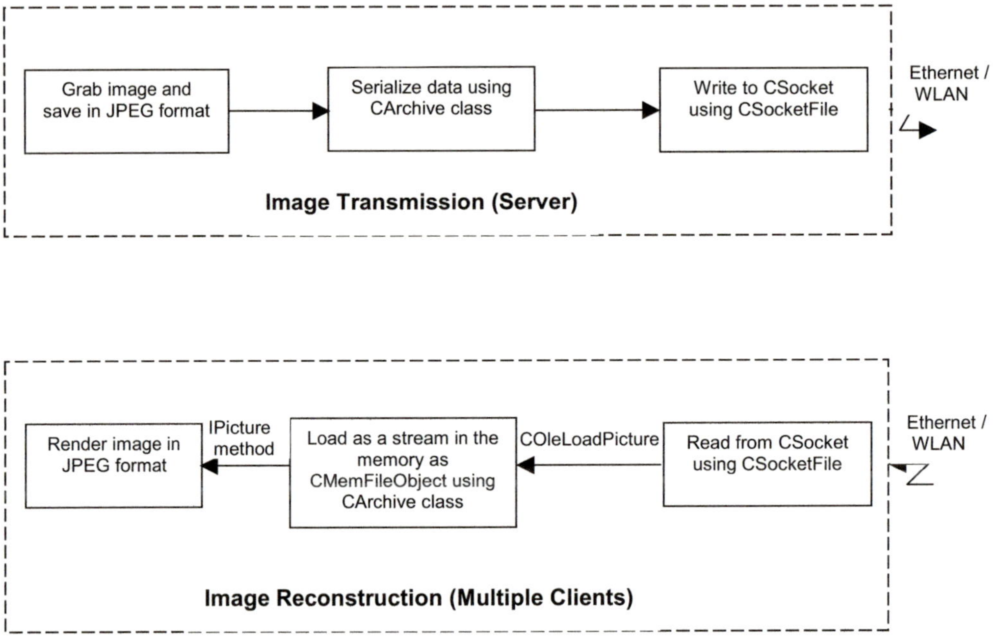

Figure 3. Block diagram of total image transfer scheme

Figure 4. Manipulator setup for material handling using template matching

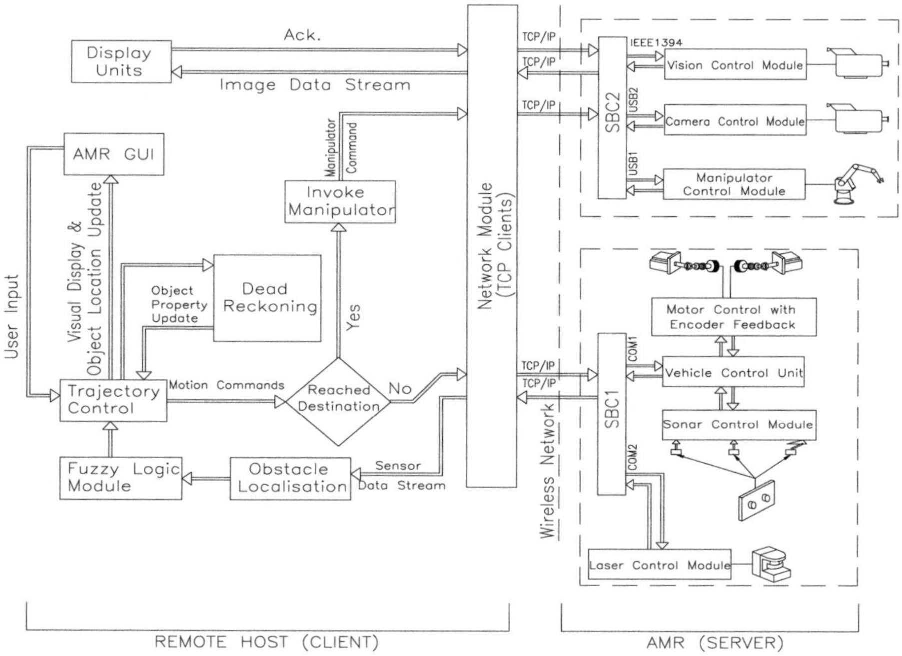

Figure 5. AMR software architecture

3.1 Correlation based Online Template Matching

Template matching is a proven process for classifying unknown samples by comparing them or matching them to known prototypes or templates. The matching process involves (1) moving the template within a search area, the search area may be a sub-image within a larger image or a whole image area (2) at each template location, computing the similarity between the template and the image area over which the template is positioned, and (3) determining the position where a similarity measure is obtained.

The measure of match, *M(f,g)*, represents the degree of similarity between two digital images, $\{f\}$ and $\{g\}$. Correlation measure is one of the few methods to gauge the "measure of match". Other methods include inter-pixel distance measure where measures of match are based on the pixel-by-pixel intensity differences between two images $\{f\}$ and $\{g\}$; sequential similarity detection algorithms (Barnea and Silverman, 1972), which proposes a more efficient alternative to correlation measures for template matching where the measure of match is based indirectly on an error measure for corresponding pixels in $\{f\}$ and $\{g\}$, the images under comparison at any stage during registration process; and sign change criteria (Venot et al., 1984) for registration of dissimilar images where if we take the pixels in the difference image of two images $\{f\}$ and $\{g\}$ which differ only by additive noise with zero mean and a symmetry density function, i.e.

$$d_{ij} = f_{ij} - g_{ij}$$

In row-column order, there will be many sign changes between adjacent d_{ij} and images which have differences significantly greater than the mean of the noise will not produce

many sign changes between adjacent d_{ij}, which is the motivation behind the use of sign change criteria, a basis for measures of similarity between images.
But the most prevalent method for measure of similarity is the correlation measure. The correlation between the template and the image window has been used as a measure of similarity in template matching and image registration since the 1970s (Rosenfeld, 1969).
For digitized images $\{f\}$ and $\{g\}$ of size *A*, the normalized correlation coefficient (*corr*) between $\{f\}$ and $\{g\}$is defined as

$$corr(f,g) = \frac{E[(f - E[f]) \cdot (g - E[g])]}{sd[f] \cdot sd[g]}$$

which is usually simplified to

$$corr(f,g) = \frac{E[f \cdot g] - E[f] \cdot E[g]}{sd[f] \cdot sd[g]}$$

where $E[x]$ is the expected value or mean of a data set $\{x\}$ and $sd[x]$ is the standard deviation of $\{x\}$. The correlation coefficient takes a value in the range of –1.0 to +1.0, providing a quantitative measure of similarity between two data sets.
Though the advantages of the correlation coefficient approach are its reliability and accuracy however, computing the correlation coefficient is extremely expensive. The calculation of correlation coefficients for every possible search point during template matching is extremely time consuming. Thus a search method with both high speed and accuracy is required in making the correlation coefficient method computationally reasonable.
Among fast template matching techniques, bounded partial correlation (BPC), based on the normalized cross-correlation (NCC) is used for finding global distortion minimum or correlation maximum (Stefano & Mattoccia, 2003). It is an extension of successive elimination algorithm (SEA) (Li & Salari, 1995) (Wang & Mersereau, 1999) and partial distortion elimination (PDE) (Bei and Gray, 1985), which allow for notably speeding up the computation required by an exhaustive-search template-matching process. Since BPC is a data dependent optimization technique, the computational benefit depends on the image, the template, the position of the template within the image, the correlation threshold, as well as on whether or not one deploys information concerning the expected matching position.
(Yoshimura & Kanade, 1994) suggest using multi-resolution eigenimages for fast template matching based on normalized correlation. This method allows to accurately detect both location and orientation of the object in a scene at faster rate than applying conventional template matching to the rotated object.
Another existing template matching technique is the use of sum-of-squared-differences (SSD) measure to determine the best match. Unfortunately, this measure is sensitive to outliers and is not robust to variations in the template, such as those that occur at occluding boundaries in the image. To compensate for these drawbacks techniques such as subpixel localization, uncertainty estimation and optimal feature is used for robust measure (Olson, 2000).
Another traditional technique for template matching using cross-correlation and an exhaustive search is Fast Fourier transform (FFT) operations which can be used to calculate the cross-correlation surface (Anuta, 1970). In order to use an FFT, the image dimensions (*N*) must be powers of 2. Therefore it is necessary to pad the template with zeroes in order to make it the same size as the image.

(Vanderbrug & Rosenfeld, 1977) using sum of the absolute valued differences (SAVD) and (Goshtasby et al., 1984) using cross-correlation describe two-stage template matching for reducing the computation required of template matching. This two stage template matching is refined to coarse-fine template matching (Rosenfeld & Vanderbrug, 1977) where a low - resolution template is applied in the first stage, followed by the full resolution template where the match threshold is exceeded. Another class of fast search algorithms is three-step search (Jain, 1981), which is widely used in motion estimation for digital video compression and processing. In the first search step, a search step size of 4 pixels is used. Once an optimal point is found, the step size is reduced to 2 pixels to evaluate the neighborhood of this previously determined optimal point to choose the next search point. In the third step, all the neighboring points of second search point are evaluated to find the final best-matched point. Certainly, this fast search method can speed up the search process, but mismatches or suboptimal matches can occur.

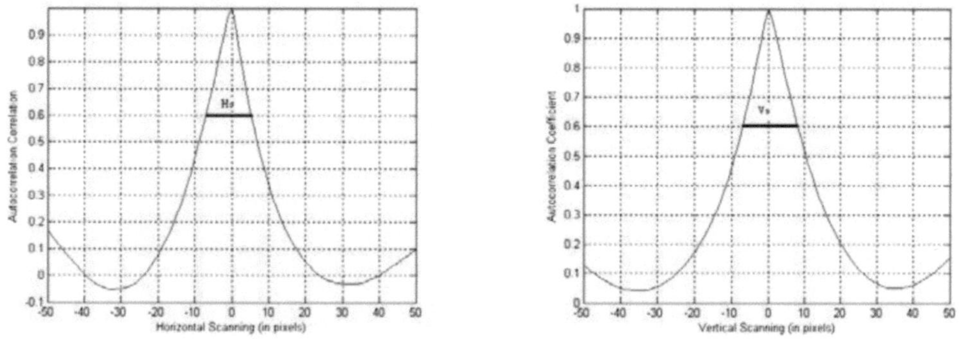

Figure 7. Selection of horizontal and vertical search steps

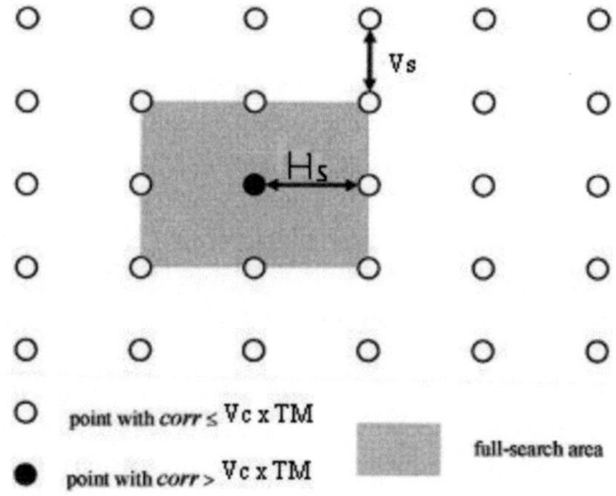

Figure 8. CAPS search lattice

In our AMR vision system application for object detection and identification, after the robot navigates its way to the target workstation, the CMOS camera, mounted on the wrist of a 5 DOF articulated manipulator, identifies pre-defined jobs for pick and place operation using Correlation-based Adaptive Predictive Search (CAPS) method (Shijun et al., 2003), which is based on coarse-fine search method. Using predetermined characteristics computed from its autocorrelation, CAPS method justifiably selects a set of horizontal and vertical search steps rather than consecutive point-to-point search for faster job detection as shown in Figure 7. For a particular cut-off coefficient V_C from the autocorrelation graph in Figure 7, the horizontal and vertical widths, *Hs* and *Vs*, are chosen as step sizes for coarse search. Figure 8 shows the CAPS search lattice with CAPS horizontal and vertical step sizes *Hs* and *Vs*. In our case, *Hs* and *Vs* are determined for $V_C = 0.6$, which yields satisfactory result.

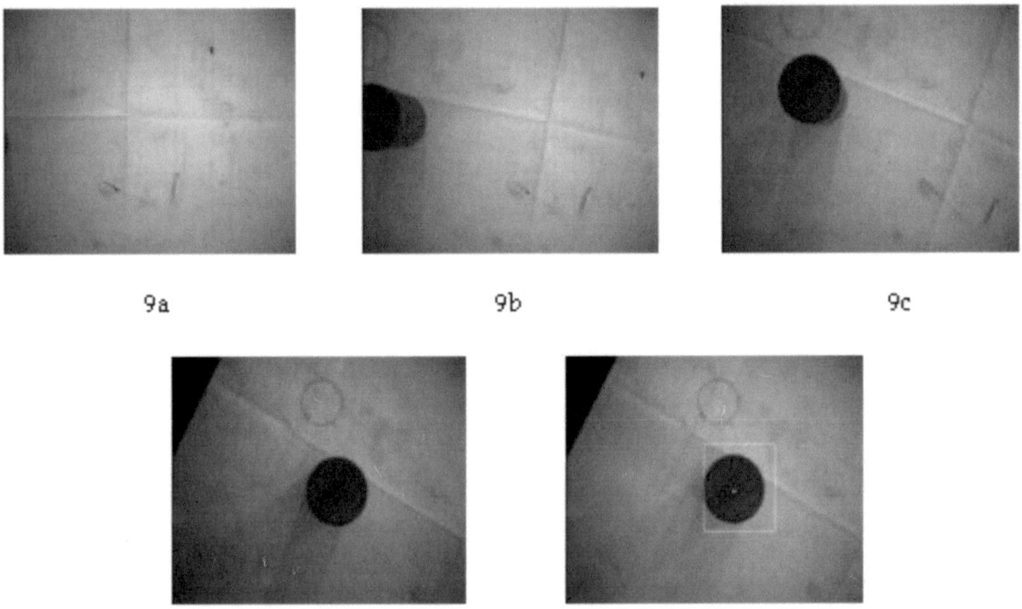

9a 9b 9c

9d 9e

Figure 9. Application of CAPS method on 280x352 image

For our implementation, as the arm moves over the worktable, the camera scans the worktable. As it approaches the job, with each scan, using coarse search technique through pre-calculated vertical and horizontal steps, the correlation coefficient with respect to the stored template is calculated to find out the tentative pose of job and the pose information is then transferred, first with respect to camera and then with respect to manipulator base. Next the camera is moved to this position. Figure 9 shows the sequence of identifying a job based on CAPS method. Figure 9a, 9b and 9c show the result at the end of each coarse search. When the correlation coefficient is greater than matching threshold value T_M, based on the statistics of the template, through fine search technique actual pose of the job is calculated as shown in Figure 9d. In our case, using environment conditions which includes illumination of the work area, the value of $T_M = 0.8$ is found suitable. Figure 9e finally identifies the actual location of the image before thresholding for parametric calculation. Figure 10 gives the block diagram of the CAPS algorithm for template matching.

3.2 Image Thresholding for Proper Gripping

Thresholding is an important and most commonly used technique for image segmentation that tries to identify and extract the image of an object from its background on the basis of the distribution of grey levels in the captured image. Thresholding techniques can be categorised into two classes: global thresholding and local (adaptive) thresholding. In global thresholding, a single threshold value is used to separate the foreground and the background of an image. It is attractive because it is simple and is sufficient in a fixed, structured environment. However, in case of AMR navigating its way from one workstation to another, due to uneven illumination, local thresholding is more appropriate for segregating the image from the background for proper gripping of the object through parametric calculations using Freeman chain coding (Freeman, 1961).

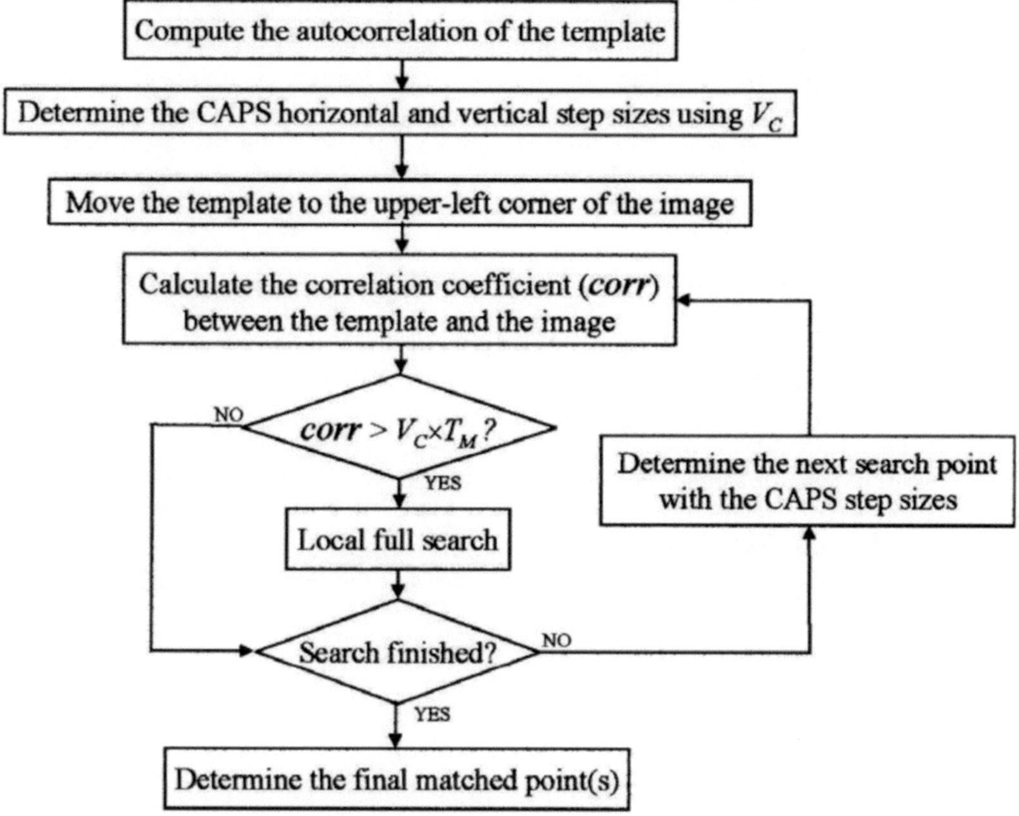

Figure 10. Block diagram of CAPS method

Over the years many image thresholding techniques have been developed and considerable research continues nowadays (Sahoo et al., 1988). The reason for this longterm, ongoing effort is that none of the methods are capable of optimal performance under all conditions.

Thresholding selection techniques can be primarily divided into two groups - bilevel and multilevel thresholding. In an image, if the object is distinct from the background, then the histogram of the grey-level is bimodal. For bilevel thresholding, threshold value is selected that coincides with the valley of the grey-level histogram. Multilevel thresholding is used when the histrogram of the greyscale image is multimodal.

For real time implementation, most thresholding techniques are based on the statistics of the one-dimensional (1D) histogram of grey levels. Many 1D thresholding methods have been investigated. Among frequently used optimal thresholding methods is entropic thresholding. (Pun, 1980; Kapur et al., 1985) proposes an approach, which maximizes *a posteriori* entropy to measure the homogeneity of threshold classes, (Sahoo et al., 1997) proposes a variation to this approach through Renyi entropy. However, these methods are computationally intensive, hence time consuming thus not suitable for real time computation. (Sahoo et al., 1988) in their study on global thresholding concluded that Otsu's method was one of the better threshold selection methods for general real world images with regard to uniformity and shape measures. Otsu's method chooses the optimal thresholds by maximizing the between-class variance with an exhaustive search (Otsu, 1979). The drawback of Otsu's method is as the number of classes of an image increase, Otsu's method exceeds the time limit for multilevel thresholding in real time. To overcome this, (Liao et al.,) proposes a modified approach based on heuristic search method for faster multi-level thresholding.

For our AMR, we have selected one dimension bi-level thresholding using a maximum of eighteen-step on-line heuristic search on a gray-scale image based on Otsu's method for determining the proper image threshold.

3.2.1 Eighteen Step Algorithm for on-line thresholding

Defining Otsu's method for image thresholding, an image is a 2D grayscale intensity function containing N pixels with gray levels from 1 to L. The number of pixels with gray level i is denoted f_i, giving a probability of gray level i in an image of

$$p_i = f_i/N \tag{1}$$

In the case of bi-level thresholding of an image, the pixels are divided into two classes, C1 with gray levels [1, …, t] and C2 with gray levels [t+1, …, L]. Then, the gray level probability distributions for the two classes are

C_1: $p_1/\omega_1(t)$, …. $p_t / \omega_1(t)$ and C_2: $p_{t+1}/ \omega_2(t)$, $p_{t+2}/ \omega_2(t)$,…, $p_L/ \omega_2(t)$ where

$$\omega_1(t)=\sum_{i=1}^{t} p_i \tag{2}$$

and

$$\omega_2(t)=\sum_{i=t+1}^{L} p_i \tag{3}$$

Also, the means for classes C_1 and C_2 are

$$\mu_1=\sum_{i=1}^{t} i.p_i/\omega_1(t) \tag{4}$$

and

$$\mu_2=\sum_{i=t+1}^{L} i.p_i/\omega_2(t) \tag{5}$$

Let μ_T be the mean intensity for the whole image. It is easy to show that

$$\mu_1.\omega_1+\mu_2.\omega_2=\mu_T \tag{6}$$

$$\omega_1+\omega_2=1 \tag{7}$$

Using discriminant analysis, Otsu defined the between-class variance of the thresholded image as

$$\sigma_B^2=\omega_1.(\mu_1-\mu_T)^2+\omega_2.(\mu_2-\mu_T)^2 \tag{8}$$

For bi-level thresholding, Otsu verified that the optimal threshold t* is chosen so that the between-class variance $\sigma_B{}^2$ is maximized; that is,

$$t^*=\underset{1\le t<L}{\operatorname{Arg\,Max}}\left\{\sigma_B^2(t)\right\} \tag{9}$$

As an alternate formulation to Otsu's method, using Eqs. (6) and (7), the between-class variance in Eq. (8) of the thresholded image can be rewritten as

$$\sigma_B^2=\omega_1\mu_1^2+\omega_2\mu_2^2-2\mu_T^2 \tag{10}$$

As the last term of Eq. 10 is independent of the choice of the thresholds, the optimal bi-level threshold is chosen by maximizing a modified between-class variance ($\dot{\sigma}_B^2$), defined as

$$\dot{\sigma}_B^2=\omega_1\mu_1^2+\omega_2\mu_2^2 \tag{11}$$

Hence, Eq. 6 can be written as

$$\mu_T=\sum_{i=1}^{L} i.p_i \tag{12}$$

From Eqs. 6 & 7, modified between-class variance ($\dot{\sigma}_B^2$) can be written as

$$\dot{\sigma}_B^2=\omega_1\mu_1^2+\frac{(\mu_T-\omega_1\mu_1)^2}{(1-\omega_1)} \tag{13}$$

Comparing Eq. 13 with Eq. 8, we find that $\dot{\sigma}_B^2$ value can be directly calculated ignoring the Eq.3, Eq.5 & Eq.6. Again, from the Eq. 9., by OTSU method, optimal bi-level threshold is chosen by maximizing modified between-class variance ($\dot{\sigma}_B^2$) for the gray level from 1 to L. According to the criteria of both Eq. 9 for σ_B^2 and Eq. 13 for $\dot{\sigma}_B^2$ to find the optimal threshold by Otsu method, the search range for the maximal σ_B^2 and the maximal $\dot{\sigma}_B^2$ is $1 \le t^* < L$. This exhaustive search involves (L-1) possible combination, computationally intensive for on-line processing. Using eighteen-step method, we have reduced the computational time by reducing the exhaustive search from (L-1) possible combinations to a maximum of eighteen combinations for detecting the proper threshold. The flowchart in Figure 11 delineates this process.

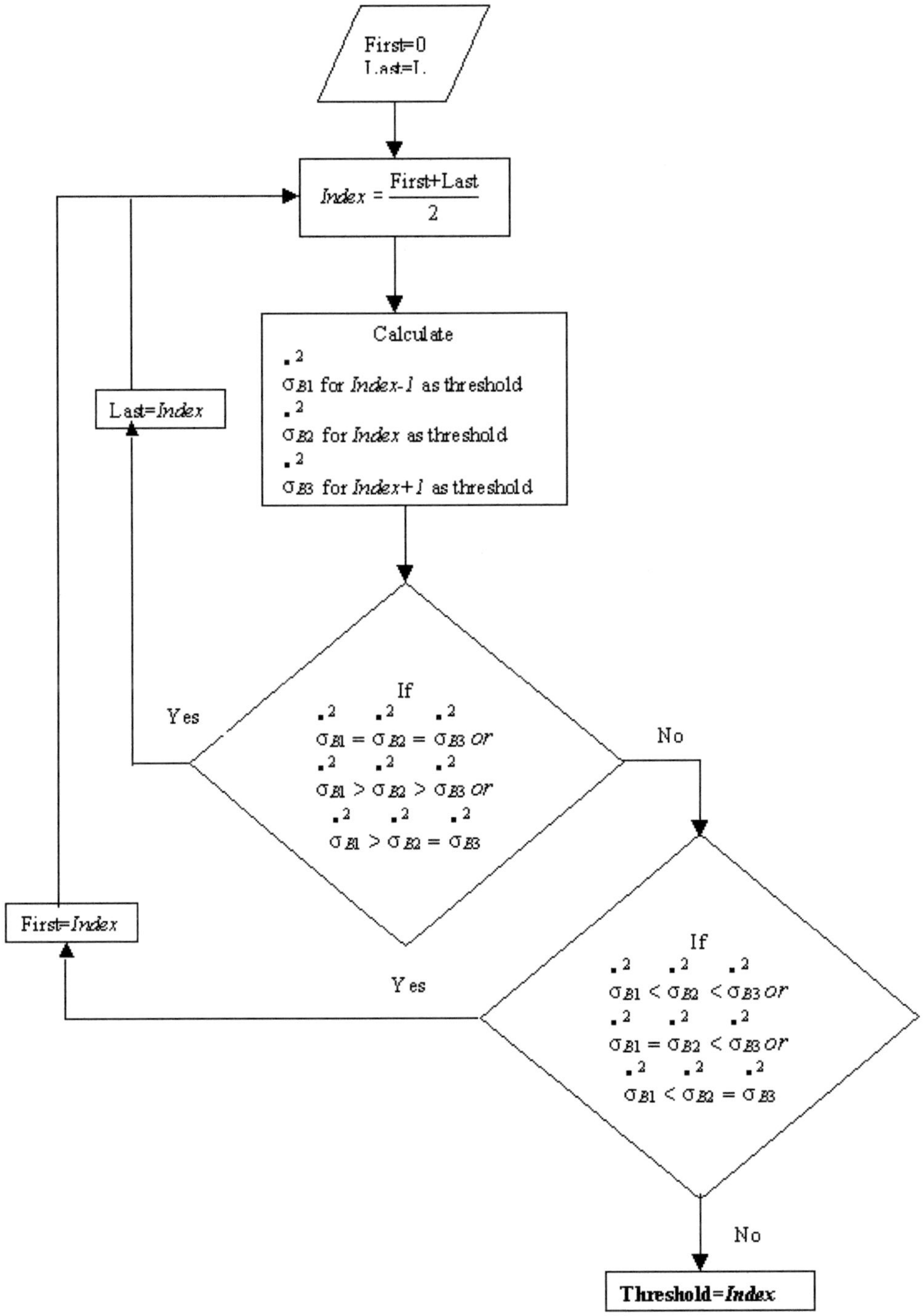

Figure 11. Flowchart of proposed eighteen-step method

4. Results and Discussion

4.1 Analysis of transmission and reconstruction rate for AMR perception

Experimental data of image transmission rate and reconstruction rate is recorded using the 100 Mbps Ethernet and 11Mbps WLAN for mono-vision and stereovision cameras. The data is tabulated, analyzed, graphically illustrated and analyzed in this section.

A. Image transmission and reconstruction using mono-vision camera:

Using the approach discussed above, several processes are tabulated. First, colour images of resolution 768x576 are transmitted frame by frame from a mono-vision camera over 100 Mbps Ethernet and 11 Mbps WLAN and are reconstructed on the client side. The grab rate is around 13 fps, which is hardware dependent, comprising a mono-vision PULNIX-TMC-6DSP camera with a Matrox Meteor-II/Standard frame grabber card. Next the image frame is serialized and is processed as a **CSocket** object. The image data is then written to the **CListenSocket** for transmission. Finally, there is an acknowledgement from the client side as per TCP/IP protocol, before the server is ready for sending the next frame. The process for image transmission is tabulated in Table 1 below:

Approximate time in milliseconds

	Process	Ethernet	WLAN
1.	Assembling an image frame for transmission	110	110
2.	Acknowledgement from client	50	90-120
3.	Total process time	160	200 - 230

Table 1. Time for transmitting a 768x576 JPEG image frame

Next, the process on the client side is recorded. For fast, uninterrupted display, the image data is reconstructed using COM class, **IPicture**. The image data received by the client is loaded as a stream, using COM class **IStream,** in the memory as a **CMemFile** object using **CArchive** class. The breakup of the total process time for receiving the frame-by-frame image data on the client side through Ethernet and over WLAN is given in Table 2. Reading serialized data for reconstruction varies inversely with the throughput rate of the medium and there is no perceptible difference between transmitting image frames over these two media when it comes to viewing the environment through on-line reconstruction of the scene.

Approximate time in milliseconds

	Process	Ethernet	WLAN
1.	Reading serialized image data	280	280-380
2.	Displaying an image frame	50	50
3.	Total process time	330	330-430

Table 2. Time for displaying a 768x576 JPEG image frame

The nature of image transmission over Ethernet and WLAN is graphically illustrated in Figure 12 and Figure 13.

As the throughput rate of Ethernet is higher than that of WLAN, barring few aberrations, total process time for transmitting an image frame over Ethernet is around 160ms while transmitting the same frame over WLAN takes between 200 ms and 230 ms, as given in Table 1. Figure 13 shows that transmission over WLAN is more prone to environmental noise, common in a manufacturing environment. Unlike transmission over Ethernet where a steady rate is maintained, variable transmission rate over WLAN does not hamper the scene-by-scene update of the environment when it comes to viewing through online reconstruction of the scene.

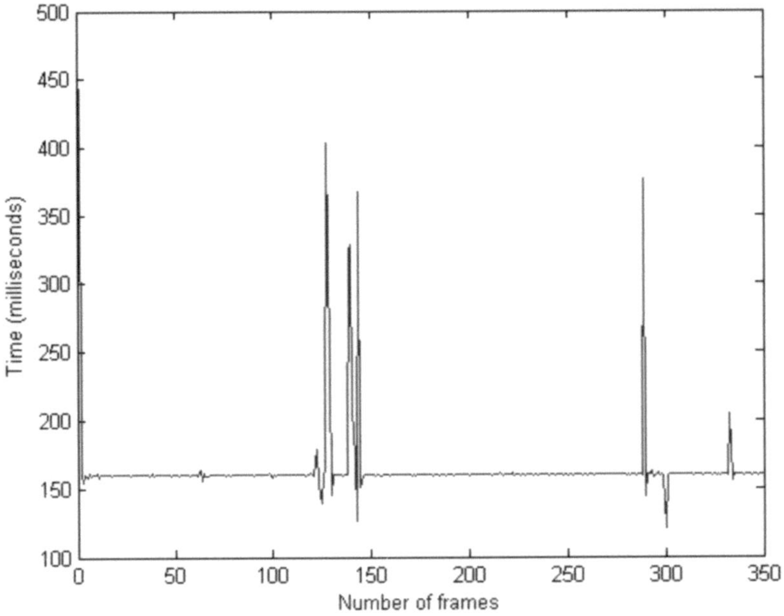

Figure 12. Time for sending a 768x576 image frame over Ethernet

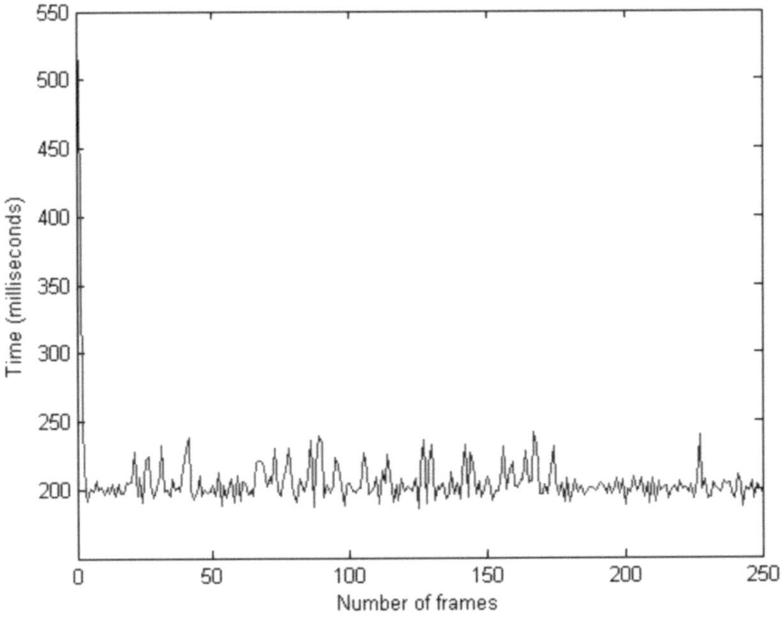

Figure 13. Time for sending a 768x576 image frame over WLAN

B. Image transmission and reconstruction using stereovision camera:
Using the same procedure as mentioned in the above section, stereo images of resolution 1024x768 are converted from raster format i.e. from PPM format to JPEG format. From grabbing the image in PPM format to converting it to JPEG format takes around 1.04 seconds as shown in Figure 14. Hence, with other parameters remaining the same, as described in the above section, total process time for transmitting an image frame over the Ethernet is less than 1.2 seconds and it hovers around 1.3 seconds over WLAN.

4.2 Result of CAPS based template matching

We have implemented CAPS method for online template matching on a 3.6GHz Pentium IV computer running on Microsoft Windows XP platform. For a 76x82 template and the 280x352 image, locating the template using full search took 55.485 seconds whereas using CAPS method with V_C =0.6 and T_M = 0.8 took few milliseconds for coarse search and little more than a second for fine search. Table 3 gives a breakup of search method along with search time for the job shown in Figure 9.

4.3 Result of proposed eighteen-step thresholding

For evaluating our proposed eighteen-step algorithm for thresholding, we have considered four conventional gray images of F16 jet, Baboon, Lena and Peppers of the size 128x128 pixels as shown in Figure 15. Otsu's method, as given in Eq. 8 and Eq. 9, and our proposed algorithm stated in Eq. 13 are implemented in MatLab Version 7.0.1 on a 3.60 GHz Pentium IV computer with Microsoft Windows XP operating system.

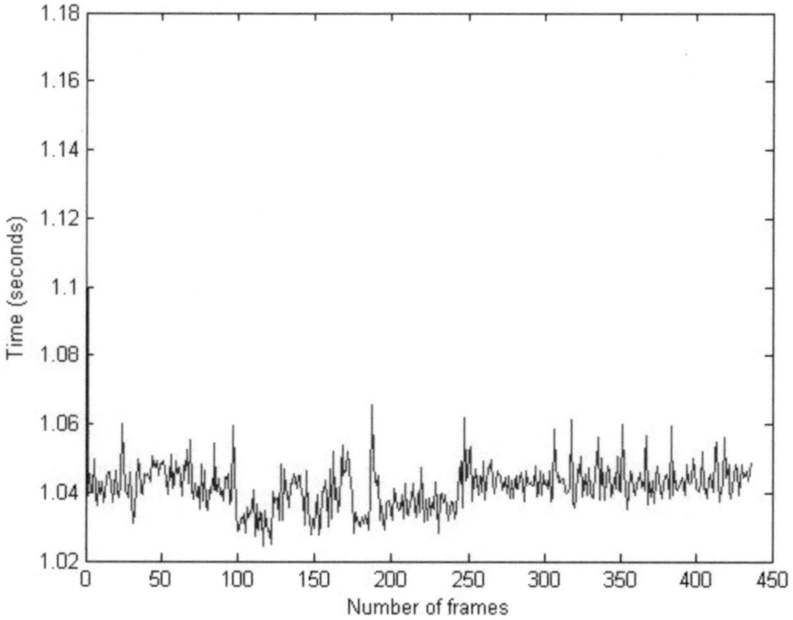

Figure 14. Time for grabbing and converting a 1024 x 768 raster image to JPEG

Coarse Search	
Frame	Time (seconds)
Frame 1 (Fig. 9a)	0.0156
Frame 2 (Fig. 9b)	0.0156
Frame 3 (Fig. 9c)	0.125
Fine Search	
Frame 4 (Fig. 9d)	1.422

Table 3. Computation time for template matching using CAPS method

Table 4 gives the comparative result between Otsu's method and eighteen-step method for bi-level thresholding on these four test images. Figure 16 shows the plot of modified between class variance $\dot{\sigma}_B^2$ against corresponding gray level values required for determining the proper bi-level threshold. The peak for each image sets the threshold for that image. Finally, Figure 17 shows the thresholded test images.

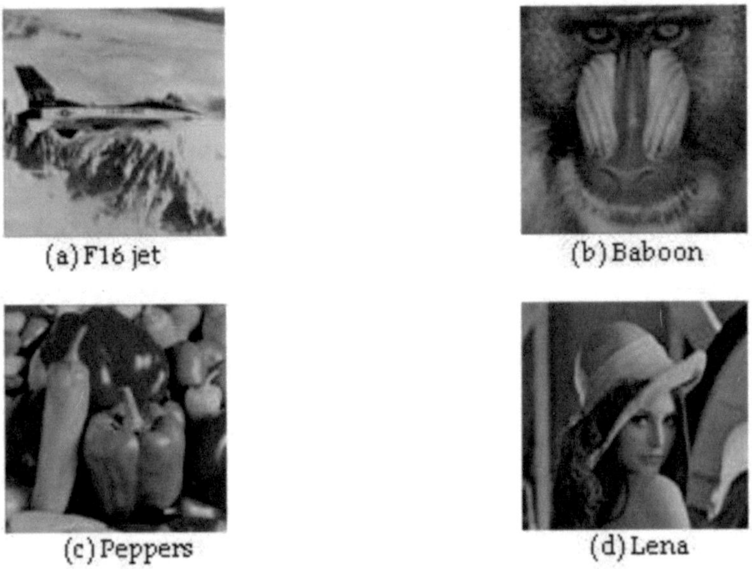

Figure 15. Test images

Images	Computation time (milliseconds)		Bi-Level Threshold
	Otsu's method	Eighteen-Step method	
F16Jet	140	16	155
Baboon	141	16	130
Peppers	141	16	121
Lenna	219	15	118

Table 4. Evaluation of Eighteen-Step method on test images for bi-level thresholding

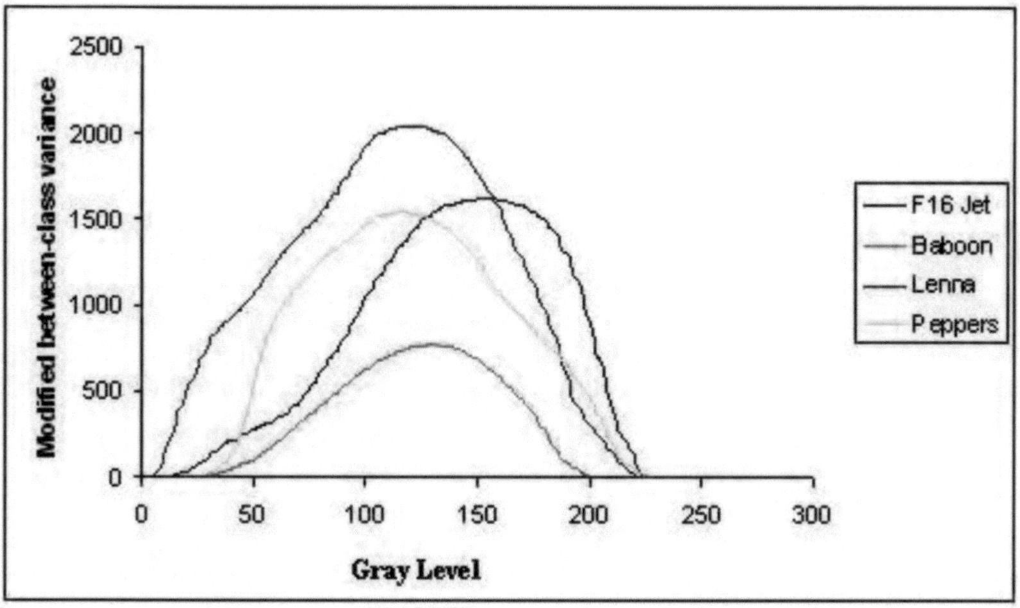

Figure 16. Plot of modified between-class variance against the corresponding gray level value

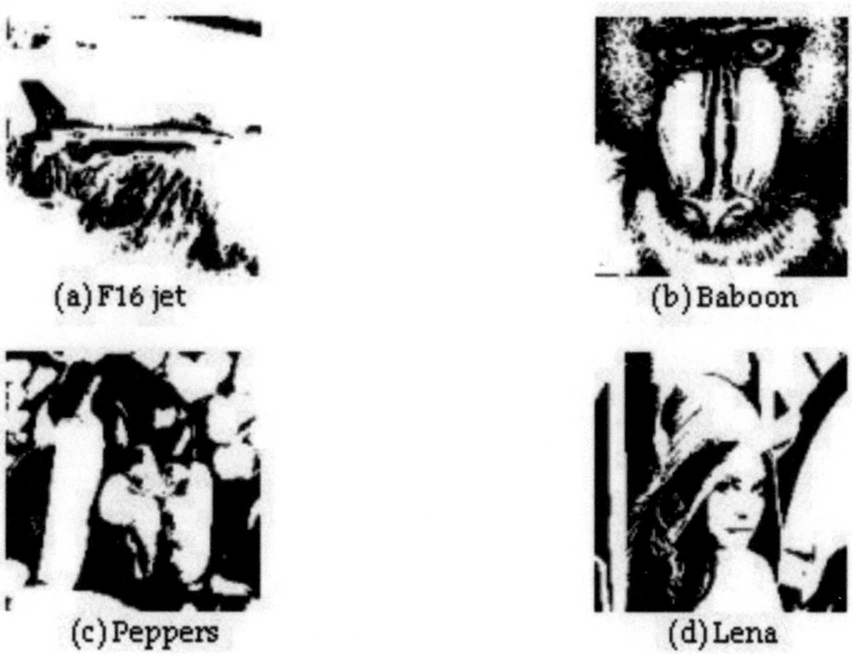

Figure 17. Thresholded images

7. Conclusion

Vision is becoming an integral part of robotic systems not only for navigation but also for job identification for material handling as camera is the only sensor that imparts a feel of spatial sensing through 3-D sensing that is lacking in other sensors like laser or ultrasonic range finders. In AMR, vision plays an integral role in all aspects. It plays a pivotal role for mobile robot perception of environment while navigating, through rapid transmission of images from mobile robot to remote viewers. Moreover, vision also plays a crucial role in online job identification for job handling. Though for all these above tasks, the sheer volume of information to be processed online becomes a hindrance, as it was in the past, but we have shown that by coming up with novel concepts based on existing knowledge and ideas and with continuing advancement in computer architecture, especially with powerful modern processors available today, we can not only overcome these difficulties but use its unique feature to our advantage.

8. Acknowledgement

The authors would like to thank the members of the project team for their help and support in developing an "Autonomous Mobile Robot for Manufacturing Environment" under the aegis of Council of Scientific and Industrial Research (CSIR, India) network project on Advanced Manufacturing Technology. The authors would like to express their sincere gratitude to the Director of the Institute for his assent in publishing this work.

9. References

Anuta, P. E. (1970). Spatial registration of multispectral and multitemporal digital imagery using fast fourier transform techniques, *IEEE Trans. on Pattern Analysis and Machine Intelligence*, Vol. 8, No. 4, October 1970, pp. 353-368, ISSN: 0359-4237

Barnea, D.I. & Silverman, H.F. (1972). A class of algorithms for fast digital image registration, *IEEE Trans. on Computers*, Vol. C-21, February 1972, pp. 179-86

Bei, C.D. & Gray, R.M. (1985). An improvement of the minimum distortion encoding algorithm for vector quantization, *IEEE Trans. on Communications*, Vol. 33, No. 10, October 1985, pp. 1132-33, ISSN: 0096-2244

Bischoff, R. & Volker, G. (1998). Vision-guided intelligent robots for automating manufacturing, material handling and services, *WESIC'98 Workshop on European Scientific and Industrial Collaboration on Promoting Advanced Technologies in Manufacturing*, Girona, June 1998

Datta, S.; Ray, R. & Banerji, D. (2007). Development of autonomous mobile robot with manipulator for manufacturing environment, accepted for publication in *International Journal of Advanced Manufacturing Technology*, Springer Publication

Datta, S.; Banerji, D. & Mukherjee, R. (2006). Mobile robot localization with map building and obstacle avoidance for indoor navigation, *Proc. IEEE International Conference on Industrial Technology*, Vol. 3, pp. 2535-2540, ISBN 1-4244-0726-5, December 15-17 2006, Mumbai, India

Freeman, H. (1961). On the encoding of arbitrary geometric configurations, *IRE Trans. Electronic Computers*, Vol. EC-10, pp. 260-268, June 1961

Goshatby, A.; Gage, S.H. & Batholic, J.F. (1984). A two-stage cross correlation approach to template matching, *IEEE Trans. on Pattern Analysis and Machine Intelligence*, Vol. PAMI-6, pp. 374-78, May 1984

Hemami, S.S. (1996). Reconstruction-optimized lapped orthogonal transforms for robust image transmission, *IEEE Trans. On Circuits and Systems for Video Technology*, Vol. 6, No. 2, April 1996, pp. 168-181, ISSN: 1051-8215

Hemami, S.S. (1995). Digital image coding for robust multimedia transmission, *Symposium on Multimedia Communications & Video Coding*, New York, October, 1995

Hemami, S.S. & Meng, T.H.Y. (1995). Transform-coded image reconstruction exploiting interblock correlation, *IEEE Trans. on Image Processing*, Vol. 4, No. 7, July 1995, pp. 1023-27, ISSN: 1057-7149

Hemami, S.S. & Gray, R.M. (1994). Image reconstruction using using vector quantized linear interpolation, *Proc. ICASSP '94*, Adelaide, Australia, April 1994, Vol. 5, pp. 629-32

Jain, J.R. & Jain, A.K. (1981). Displacement measurement and its application in interframe image coding, *IEEE Trans on Communication*, Vol. 29, No.12, December 1981, pp. 1799-1808, ISSN:0096-2244

Kapur, J.N.; Sahoo, P.K. & Wong, A.K.C. (1985). A new method for gray-level picture thresholding using the entropy of the histogram, *Computer Vision Graphics Image Processing*, Vol. 29, 1985, pp. 273-285

Katz, D. et al. (2006). The Umass Mobile Manipulator UMan: An experimental platform for autonomous mobile manipulator, *Workshop on Manipulator for Human Environment at Robotics: Science and Systems*, Philadelphia, USA, August 2006

Li, W. & Salari, E. (1995). Successive elimination algorithm for motion estimation, *IEEE Trans. on Image Processing*, Vol. 4 No. 1, Jan. 1995, pp. 105-107, ISSN:1057-7149

Liao, P.; Chen, T. & Chung, P. (2001). A fast algorithm for multilevel thresholding, *Journal of Information Science and Engineering*, 17, pp. 713-727, 2001

Olson, C. F. (2000). Maximum-likelihood template matching, *Proc. IEEE Conference on CVPR*, Vol. 2, pp. 52-57, 13-15 June 2000, Hilton Head, South Carolina, USA

Otsu, N. (1979). A threshold selection method from gray-level histogram, *IEEE Trans. System Man Cybernetics*, Vol. 9, March 1979, pp. 62-66

Pun, T. (1980). A new method for gray-level picture thresholding using the entropy of the histogram, *Signal Processing*, Vol.2, 1980, pp. 223-237

Rosenfeld, A. (1969). *Picture processing by computer*, New York: Academic Press, 1969

Rosenfeld, A. & Vanderburg, G. J. (1977). Coarse-fine template matching, *IEEE Trans. on Systems, Man and Cybernetics*, Vol. 7, 1977, pp. 104-107

Sahoo, P.K.; Wilkins, C. & Yeager, J. (1997). Threshold selection using Renyi's entropy, *Pattern Recognition*, Vol. 30, No. 1, pp. 71-84, 1997, Elsevier Science Ltd.

Sahoo, P.K. et al. (1988). A survey of thresholding techniques, *Computer Vision Graphics Image Processing*, Vol. 41, 1988, pp. 223-237

Schaefer, G. (2001). JPEG image retrieval by simple operators, *CBMI '01*, pp. 207-214, Brescia, Italy, September 19-21, 2001

Sen, S; Taktawala, P. K. & Pal, P. K. (2004). Development of a range-sensing, indoor, mobile robot with wireless Ethernet connectivity, *Proceedings of the National Conference on Advanced Manufacturing & Robotics*, pp. 3-10, ISBN 81-7764-671-0, CMERI, January 2004, Allied Publishers Pvt. Ltd., Durgapur

Shijun, S. et al. (2003). Fast template matching using correlation-based adaptive predictive search, *International Journal of Imaging System Technology*, Vol. 13, pp. 169-178, 2003

Stefano. L.D. & Mattoccia, S. (2003). Fast template matching using bounded partial correlation, *Machine Vision and Applications*,Vol. 13, pp. 213-21, ISSN: 0932-8092, Springer-Verlag, 2003

Tong, H.F. & Zhang, D. (1998). A new progressive colour image transmission scheme for the World Wide Web, *Computer Networks and ISDN Systems*, 30 (1998) pp. 2059-2064

Vanderburg, G.J. & Rosenfeld, A. (1977). Two stage template matching, *IEEE Trans. on Computers*, Vol. C-26, pp. 384-93, April 1977

Venot, A.; Lebruchec, J.F. & Roucayrol, J.C. (1984). A new class of similarity measures for robust image registration, *Computer Vision, Graphics and Image Processing*, Vol. 28, pp. 176-84, 1984

Wallace, G.K. (1991). The JPEG Still Picture Compression Standard, *Communications of the ACM*, Vol. 34 No.4, pp. 30-44, 1991

Wang, H. & Mersereau, R. (1999). Fast algorithm for the estimation of motion vectors, IEEE Trans. on Image Processing, Vol. 8, No. 3, March 1999, pp. 435-438, ISSN: 1057-7149

Yoshimura, S. & Kanade, T. (1994). Fast template matching based on the normalized correlation by using multiresolution eigenimages, *Proc. IROS '94*, Vol. 3, pp. 2086-2093, September 12-16 1994, Munich, Germany

28

Symmetry Signatures for Image-Based Applications in Robotics

Kai Huebner[1] and Jianwei Zhang[2]
[1]*Comp. Vision and Active Perception, Royal Institute of Technology, Stockholm*
[2]*Technical Aspects of Multimodal Systems, University of Hamburg, Hamburg*
[1]*Sweden,* [2]*Germany*

1. Introduction

The robots that are to find their way in our future households and everyday lives necessarily have to be mobile and self-dependent. For such autonomous systems it becomes more and more important to efficiently process the incoming data and to thereby eradiate what we might call "intelligent behaviour".
While intelligence in terms of plans and goals are abstract metaphors of each robot's decision process, the perception of the local environment has to be a central issue. Dealing with this demand in the context of intelligent systems shows plainly what sophisticated human visual perception is like. The creators and developers of artificial systems therefore build up a construction kit with construction blocks that try to represent the reproduction of cognitive perception mechanisms by machine algorithms.
In this chapter, we will show how a construction block for symmetry perception can be added to this set. The main issues discuss three layers that describe this block from its origin of biological motivation up to its application for intelligent systems:
1. *Symmetry as a Feature:* The first layer addresses the basic motivation of symmetry as a feature. Therefore, symmetry references to diverse domains are given and new methods developed that provide description and application of symmetry as an image feature. These include two main symmetry measures that offer a variety of symmetry properties for higher-level image processing tasks.
2. *Regional Symmetry Features:* The second layer proceeds to application in relation to modern regional image features. The three steps of detection, description and robust matching of regional symmetry features form the necessary links between the basic motivation and the practical application of symmetry. Symmetry features are evaluated and compared to state-of-the-art features considering their robustness w.r.t. common image transformations.
3. *Integration and Application:* A practical example from the area of mobile robot navigation is proposed in the third layer to demonstrate the capability of the developed symmetry features in applications. For this purpose, the mobile service robot TASeR from the working group of Technical Aspects of Multimodal Systems (University of Hamburg, Germany) is used. The application provides the links to higher-level construction blocks from the set of visual object analysis and robot navigation.

The main issue of this chapter will focus on a conclusion of our work on a fundamental analysis of symmetry as an image feature, followed by a framework on the development of a robust visual symmetry feature detector and on the implementation of symmetry in robot applications. We motivate our work in section 2. In section 3, we show our work on finding symmetry measures valuable for our goal of robotic applications. Section 4 describes the implementation of the developed symmetry measures into a regional feature detector and its evaluation. We propose some preliminary work on exemplary integrating those regional features into robotic image processing for egomotion classification in section 5, before we conclude this chapter in section 6.

2. Motivation

Nowadays, robots are not only meant to sort and stack parcels in unenlivened storage depots. They are supposed to wash dishes, to lead through museum halls or even to play soccer in interaction with humans. For these tasks, a robot must be able to act mobile and self-dependent. It must adapt to its changing environment instead of letting humans adapt a constant environment for the robot. An inflexible model of the world is useless in a world of motion and dynamics. Robots thus have to be equipped with methods that allow them to build their own world model to localize within. They should be able to handle in dynamic or unknown environments by constructing, adapting and expanding their models of the world with a large degree of autonomy. However, the interaction in a world necessarily starts with the perception of things or objects inside. In many applications of our field of research, the human visual system gives a wide inspiration to the solution of common robotic problems and tasks, e.g. distance estimation to objects, object and situation recognition and localisation. We can also observe that a robot's sensor configuration is both depending on the application and on the financial means of constructors, developers and customers. A camera has the advantages of becoming versatile and cheap visual sensor over the last years and of being a system that is very close to our own human visual perception. In the work presented here, we focus on the camera as the only sensor.

If we restrict on visual data only, the problem of selecting special visual features comes up, as images are high-dimensional and thus complex to process. Additionally, images are highly sensitive to unpredictable interferences like rotation, scaling and occlusion of objects, illumination influence, perspective warp and viewpoint change. In (Jepson & Richards, 1993), the meaning of a "good" visual feature that separates the core of information from the clutter basically depends on the application itself. Some other definitions suppose that an image feature is a

- local, meaningful, detectable part of an image (Truco & Verri, 1998),
- a distinguishing primitive characteristic or attribute of an image (Pratt, 2001),
- or a simple environmental measurement serving as a "cue" for inferring complex world properties in structured environments (Taraborelli, 2003).

Each of the definitions shows that image features are something that really point out the compact core of the whole visual data. In our work, we define a good image feature as being robust to the above mentioned transformations in dynamic real-world environments. Additionally, we focus on natural features that can be found in a lot of "untouched" environments, i.e. without artificial landmarks.

Though all imaginable visual features are numerous and manifold in type, they can be divided into one of three main classes belonging to their focus. Common *global features* that describe general properties of an entire image scene are rather inappropriate for the task of visual scene interpretation. While images of single objects can be generalized easily by simple global attributes, e.g. size, colour or texture, it is more difficult to find stable and repeatable features for conglomerate scenes. However, global features give very compact representations of significant image properties.

Many higher-level tasks like scene exploration or object classification and object tracking in complex scenes are therefore grounded on *local features*. Being related to human visual perception, local visual features like edges and corners give clues for efficient scene exploration and allow focusing on well-located interest points. The Scale-Invariant Feature Transform (Lowe, 2004) and the Harris-Laplacian (Mikolajczyk & Schmid, 2004) are popular methods of local feature detection, approaching robustness to rotation and scale. As the exploration of invariant features is an active field of research, well-elaborated comparisons of various local feature detectors and descriptors concerning a set of common transformations have been published (Mikolajczyk & Schmid, 2004; Schmid et al., 2000; Mikolajczyk & Schmid, 2005).

Due to the different characteristics of global and local features, some applications benefit from the combination of both approaches into *regional features*, where a region is defined as an arbitrary subset of the image. The extraction of Maximally Stable Extremal Regions (Matas et al., 2004) highlights the advantage of region-based detectors that produce both sparse and robust features particularly covariant to viewpoint change and affine transformations.

If we consider these issues of different natural visual features, we find local features like edges or corners, regional features like colour or intensity blobs, or global features like colour histograms in the literature. A rather unnoticed type of feature to use in robotic applications is symmetry, though symmetry is present everywhere in our everyday's life. Many objects of our world show a high degree of some symmetric property and humans are usually surrounded with symmetric objects. Plants and animals grow up in a somehow symmetric manner. But even in many other domains like mathematics, art, architecture or manifacturing, symmetry plays a major role.

Let some psychological cites from (Locher & Nodine, 1989) describe the high influence of symmetry on human visual perception:

- Symmetry is a property of a visual stimulus which catches the eye in the earliest stages of vision.
- Most perceptual theories assume that the eye-brain system uses the axis of symmetry as an anchoring point for visual exploration and analysis.

Symmetry comes along with attention and interest, which are supposed to be necessary for a useful natural image feature. We claim that therefore symmetry is worth a view on being used as a feature in the context of robot vision. In the next section, we will start by asking the question on "how can we receive a description of symmetry from the visual data?".

3. Symmetry as a Feature

As mentioned above, symmetry is a fundamental feature that is evaluated throughout several domains, e.g. architecture, art and nature (see Figure 1). Many aspects that concentrate on nature and mathematics are discussed in the book "Fearful Symmetry: Is

God a Geometer?" (Stewart & Golubitsky, 1992). It has been shown in the biological domain that some animals prefer mates that outperform by their symmetric appearance (Enquist & Arak, 1994; Kirkpatrick & Rosenthal, 1994), or that doves are able to distinguish between symmetric and asymmetric patterns (Delius & Nowak, 1982). A very good introduction to several types and appearances of general symmetry can be found in the book "Symmetry – A Unifying Concept" (Hargittai & Hargittai, 1994).

3.1 Definition of Symmetry

Besides this introduction, we also find descriptions of various types of symmetry in that work (Hargittai & Hargittai, 1994). Each type of symmetry can be assigned to a corresponding action that fulfills the basic property of symmetry: keeping the shape after having performed the action. Thus, we can reflect shapes along an axis that are mirror-symmetric, or rotate shapes that are rotationally symmetric, or even shift shapes that are translationally symmetric, without changing their shape. Here, we focus on the first two types of symmetries by giving the following definitions:

- Reflectional symmetry: A shape is symmetric w.r.t. the reflection along an axis. Reflecting the shape along this axis does not result in a change of its appearance. Special cases of reflectional symmetry are horizontal (reflection along a horizontal axis) and vertical mirror-symmetry (reflection along a vertical axis).
- Rotational symmetry: A shape is symmetric w.r.t the rotation about a point and a certain angle α. Rotating the shape at the point about α does not result in a change of its appearance. A shape is n-times rotational symmetric with $n = 2\pi/\alpha$.

These definitions are leaned against more detailed and more general definitions of two-dimensional symmetry types by Zabrodsky et al. (Zabrodsky et al., 1995), which are based on exact invariance. However, almost no object of our world shows invariant symmetry properties from this point of view. For example, faces are highly symmetric, but both halves of one face are never exactly the same. Therefore, we differ our above definitions by using the term "change of appearance". A common face is thus reflectional symmetric, as the reflection does not change perception or appearance for the viewer. Following this definition, we find that or world consists of many symmetric objects.

3.2 Symmetry in Human Perception

How the existence of symmetry influences the human visual system and how this is used for visual scene exploration, was evaluated in psychophysical experiments (Locher & Nodine, 1989). As an important result of those experiments it was shown that especially reflectional symmetries and their orientations are of significant importance for human vision. Eye-tracking experiments show that humans quickly detect and take advantage of horizontal and vertical symmetries. Figure 1 gives two samples of such visual explorations. While the viewer has fully explored the asymmetric shape on the left hand side, the focus clearly concentrates on just one half of the symmetric shape on the right. Hereby, we get a clue that the human eye is able to detect and use symmetry as a visual anchoring point for visual exploration of objects and scenes. Palmer and Hemenway (Palmer & Hemenway, 1978) consider the time of detection of arbitrarily skewed symmetric shapes in similar experiments. They conclude that vertical reflective symmetry is very often and more quickly detected than horizontal reflective symmetries, which is better than arbitrarily skewed reflective symmetries.

Those two references are exemplary for others that also motivate symmetry as a visual feature from the biological and psychophysical point of view (Barlow & Reeves, 1979; Csathó et al., 2003; Ferguson, 2000; Tyler, 1994).

3.3 Symmetry in Computer Vision

Besides its influence on human visual perception, symmetry has also been investigated in computer vision. There are some references that motivate symmetry as a feature in very versatile tasks (Ferguson, 2000; Liu, 2000; Reisfeld et al., 1995; Zabrodsky, 1990). Early work in the area of symmetry axis extraction for object description, like the Symmetry Axis Transform (Blum & Nagel, 1978) and the Smoothed Local Symmetries (SLS) (Brady & Asada, 1984), are very related to the Medial Axis Transform (MAT) offering main axes of a shape. The idea of using symmetry as a feature has been advanced over the last decades. In the following, some recent and related work is referenced.

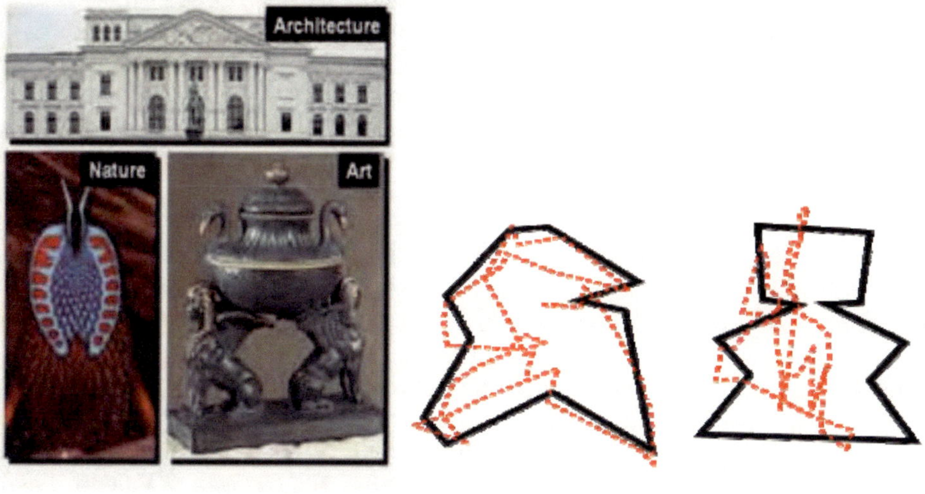

Figure 1. Left: Examples for symmetric structures in architecture, nature and art. Right: Visual explorations both on an asymmetric and a symmetric shape. The path of visual focus covers the whole shape for the asymmetric shape, but only one half of the symmetric shape

Sun (Sun, 1995) and Sun & Si (Sun & Si, 1999) present a fast algorithm to detect the symmetry axis of a shape by gradient histograms. A similar approach analyzing an energy function of the input image is proposed by Scognamillo et al. (Scognamillo et al., 2003). The task of these methods is to detect the main symmetry axis of one shape, thus only images with a single object on a uniform background are useful. An application to symmetry as a feature in an arbitrary scene would therefore need prior segmentation.

Reisfeld et al. (Reisfeld et al., 1995) define a generalized symmetry transform that uses symmetry to extract regions-of-interest in a scene. The two-dimensional operator both includes symmetry as also gradient information. Regions that show a high degree of symmetry, but low contrast, e.g. walls, are therefore not extracted. Di Gesù and Valenti present the Discrete Symmetry Transform (DST) which is speeded up by the selection of non-uniform image regions (Di Gesù & Valenti, 1995). The resulting symmetry image is used for several tasks of face recognition, image segmentation and object classification as also motion analysis (Di Gesù & Valenti, 1996). These approaches suffer from the generality which causes higher effort in calculation time and parametrization. Similar results using symmetry as a detector of interest have been shown by analyzing frequency components of an image (Kovesi, 1997).

Chetverikov (Chetverikov, 1999; Chetverikov, 2003) analyzes the surrounding of each image point with regard to its anisotropy. Based on this result, a symmetry structure is calculated that represents symmetric texture orientation. The extracted feature thereby describes the texture and the image, respectively, as a whole. Liu et al. (Liu et al., 2004) describe patterns considering their symmetry properties, including translational symmetries. Regions that even correspond with regard to their structure of symmetric shape after perspective warp are deeply investigated by Tuytelaars et al. (Tuytelaars et al., 2003). However, these afford a number of pre-processing steps that influence the run-time of each feature detection.

Face recognition based on symmetry description is found in a model-based work by Zabrodsky et al. (Zabrodsky et al., 1993; Zabrodsky et al., 1995). Another model-based approach to segment objects from the visual data by symmetry is proposed by Liu et al. (Liu et al., 1998). Johansson et al. (Johansson et al., 2000) detect rotational symmetries by particularly defined rotational operators, while Loy and Zelinsky (Loy & Zelinsky, 2003) present an efficient and real-time capable feature detector based on radial symmetries.

We find that all these approaches differ both in the methods applied and the results, though all of them handle the problem of detecting symmetries in the visual data. Some describe symmetry properties for a pre-segmented object (Chetverikov, 1999; Liu et al., 2004; Sun, 1995) and are thereby inadequate for the extraction of feature points from cluttered scenes. Some include reflective symmetries of arbitrary orientation (Chetverikov, 1999; Di Gesù & Valenti, 1995; Di Gesù & Valenti, 1996; Kovesi, 1997; Reisfeld et al., 1995; Sun, 1995; Zabrodsky et al., 1995), offer methods to extract rotational symmetries (Johansson et al., 2000; Loy & Zelinsky, 2003; Zabrodsky et al., 1995) or use pre-processing steps (Liu et al., 2004; Tuytelaars et al., 2003) and thereby need additional effort in computing time.

For our scenario, we prefer an approach that extracts symmetric features from the raw visual data without such pre-processing steps, similar to the work by Reisfeld et al. (Reisfeld et al., 1995) and Di Gesù and Valenti (Di Gesù & Valenti, 1995; Di Gesù & Valenti, 1996). A time-line of the mentioned literature is presented in Table 1.

The diagonal line highlights the trend towards detection of very general, different and complex descriptions of symmetry in computer vision. However, a real-time application in robotic systems suffers from this evolution, as more complex algorithms need more processing time.

We found that most image processing operators available for our needs of bilateral symmetry detection in cluttered scenes have the crucial demerit of being large and complex. In our first approach, we therefore proposed a simple, fast and compact operator to extract the regions of interest from images (Huebner, 2003). The psychophysically motivated simple symmetry operator detects horizontal and vertical reflective symmetries only. Resulting symmetry images offer multiple feature extraction methods.

In particular, binary images derived from symmetry axis detection are interesting for further image processing steps. As we show in the next section, the fast operator can be applied to arbitrary images without prior adaptation and without thresholds. The only parameters to specify are the size of the operator mask and the resolution of symmetry data.

Approach key	Method	Reflective	Rotational	Translational	Number of features	Type of features
Blum & Nagel (1978)	SAT	•			b	Object skeleton
Brady & Asada (1984)	SLS	•			b	Object skeleton
Reisfeld et al. (1995)	CF	•			m × n	Symmetry values
Di Gesù et al. (1995)	CF	•			m × n	Symmetry values
Sun (1995)	CF	•			1	Main symmetry axis
Zabrodsky et al. (1995)	MOD	•	•		b	Reconstructions
Kovesi (1997)	FQ	•			m × n	Symmetry values
Liu et al. (1998)	MOD	•			b	Symmetry segments
Chetverikov & Jankó (1999)	CF	•			1	Regularity values
Cross & Hancock (1999)	CF	•			b	Main symmetry axes
Sun & Si (1999)	CFQ	•			b	Symmetry axis points
Johansson et al. (2000)	CF		•		m × n	Symmetry values
Loy & Zelinsky (2003)	CF		•		m × n	Symmetry values
Scognamillo et al. (2003)	CFQ	•			1	Main symmetry axis
Tuytelaars et al. (2003)	MOD	•		•	b	Symmetry groups
Liu et al. (2004)	MOD	•	•	•	b	Classification
Mellor & Brady (2005)	CFQ	•	•		m × n	Symmetry values

Table 1. Time-line of selected approaches on symmetry detection. CF = Convolution Filter. FQ = Frequency analysis (Fourier / Wavelet Transform). CFQ = Hybrid CF/FQ. MOD = model-base

3.4 A Fast One-Dimensional Symmetry Operator

The psychological experiments described in section 3.2 show that vertical and horizontal reflective symmetries are most important for human vision. Based on these results, only these two types were considered for our symmetry approach. This selection proves even more effective if we take into account that it is not necessary to perform any interpolation or to use trigonometric functions, since digital images consist of horizontal and vertical arrays of pixels. Therefore, only pixels in the same image row $R = [p_0, p_{w-1}]$ have to be used for the detection of vertical symmetry for a given pixel $p_i \in R$, where w is is the width of the image. The same holds for horizontal symmetry, considering only one column of the image.

A further requirement of robot vision is the processing of real images. Because of the presence of distortion in real images, an operator that detects exact symmetry will fail and produce erroneous symmetry images. Therefore, we propose the following qualitative symmetry operator based on a normalized mean square error function:

$$S(p_i, m) = 1 - (c \cdot m)^{-1} \sum_{j=1..m} \sigma(j, m) \cdot g(p_{i-j}, p_{i+j})^2, \quad (1)$$

where m>0 is the size of the neighbourhood of p_i along the direction perpendicular to the axis of symmetry. The symmetry value of p_i shall be detected with respect to this axis. The complete number of pixels considered is 2m. c is a normalization constant which depends on the colour space used and on $\sigma(j, m)$, which is a radial weighting function. The difference between two opposing points p_{i-j}, p_{i+j} is determined by a gradient function $g(p_{i-j}, p_{i+j})$, which typically is the Euclidian distance of the corresponding colour vectors. A few example results are presented in Figure 2, demonstrating that the choice of m is important for the performance of the algorithm. Setting m to a low value works out well for the symmetry axes of small objects, while those of bigger objects are enlarged. However, a large value m is better in detecting the symmetry axes of bigger objects. Note that the border regions of the images (left and right for vertical symmetry) are influenced strongly by the effect of fading if the operator reaches out of the image, but symmetry axis points (maxima of the values) are quite stable and independent of m. However, for this operator and for other techniques from the literature, a symmetry value for an image point is detected by a static operator covering a surrounding region around that point. These operators return relative values, i.e. qualities, of symmetry that describe symmetry as low or high inside a pre-determined, fixed region. We call these approaches *qualitative* or *strength-based*, as a quality of symmetry is their output. Results are depending on the operator size chosen and thus not comparable if two different sizes have been used for symmetry feature extraction.

Figure 2. Example image (left). Vertical symmetry image calculated with small operator (m = 10; centre) and with large operator (m = 50; right). Brightness corresponds to symmetry.

3.5 Quantitative Symmetry Extraction using Dynamic Programming

Having uncovered these disadvantages of qualitative operators, we claim that it is more relevant to get *quantitative* or *range-based* information about the size of symmetry instead of its degree. We have therefore proposed a novel approach to symmetry extraction based on Dynamic Programming (Huebner et al., 2005), which we briefly describe in this section.

To keep the motivation of psychophysical work on symmetry perception (Locher & Nodine, 1989; Palmer & Hemenway, 1978), we still restrict our symmetry detection to horizontal and vertical symmetry detection, i.e. reflection with respect to a horizontal or vertical axis. Using this restriction, the problem states to estimate the range around an image point in its row or column in which symmetry is still detectable, i.e. the assignment of opposing points is linear and not erroneous.

The assignment of points is therefore seen as an optimization problem to find the best correspondence between the two opposing patterns. Dynamic Programming offers the global optimum for such problems, including the assumption that the order of pattern elements is kept. See the example in Figure 3.

The example shows two patterns $R = R_0,...,R_4$ and $L = L_0,...,L_4$ for which the best correspondence between their elements shall be found. The solution of this problem is equal to finding the best path in a two-dimensional search space spanned by L and R (Ohta & Kanade, 1985). Each path ranging from (R_0, L_0) to (R_{rmax}, L_{lmax}) inside this search space describes a possible mapping of feature points, as long as the order of elements is kept. This property is only ensured by path elements reaching from one cell to the right, the top-right or the top neighbouring cell in the search space. The optimal path can then be found by Dynamic Programming starting from point (R_0, L_0), using simple error measures (Žganec et al., 1993), as can be seen in Figure 4.

Note that the structure of the path and the overall costs are dependent on the patterns' symmetric correspondence. As the example shows, high symmetry of the patterns results in a diagonal path and low costs. In contrast, the comparison of asymmetric shapes will result in a non-linear path and high costs.

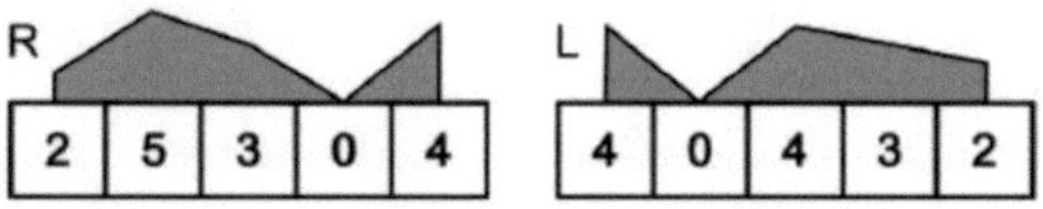

Figure 3. Example patterns to calculate range-based symmetry by Dynamic Programming

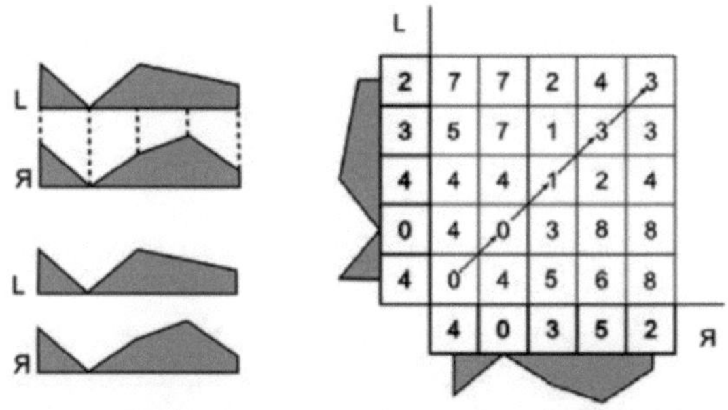

$$C(l,r) = \min(C_1(l,r), C_2(l,r), C_3(l,r)), \quad (2)$$

$$C_1(l,r) = C(l-1, r) + W_1T(l,r),$$
$$C_2(l,r) = C(l, r-1) + W_2T(l,r),$$
$$C_3(l,r) = C(l-1, r-1) + W_3T(l,r),$$

$$T(l,r) = | L_l - R_r |$$

Figure 4. Right: Error measures that are used for Dynamic Programming. Centre: Symmetric patterns' search space including costs and corresponding mapping path ($W_i = 1$). Left: Resulting (linear) correspondences

Practically, it is easier to handle the cost development on the optimal path than to evaluate the path structure. Therefore, our final algorithm efficiently searches optimal paths until a cell (l, r) exceeds a given threshold T. The hereby acquired indices l and r serve as a measure of symmetry. Note that the environment s composed of l and r can be treated intuitively as the size of the symmetric region s = l + r around the considered image point. A search space calculation of an asymmetric pattern is interrupted by exceeding the error T. In this case, l and r are small, as well as the symmetry measure s. On the other hand, a symmetric pattern like the one above results in an optimal path that leads along the search space quite diagonally with small error, which justifies a high symmetric value s.

While this just briefly points out the idea of using a Dynamic Programming approach for symmetry description, we have worked out and optimized this approach as the Dynamic Programming Symmetry (DPS) algorithm in (Huebner et al., 2005). As a main achievement of DPS in contrast to qualitative symmetry operators, the disadvantages of a-priori-sized operators are avoided. In addition, a range-based, comparable description of symmetry is returned instead of a relative measure that describes symmetry as high or low only.

4. Regional Symmetry Features

Based on the symmetry components of qualitative and quantitative symmetry, it is an important task to make symmetry features comparable, stable and repeatable in different images. Robust detection of features is a crucial task for applications that deal with visual information. Image data is high-dimensional, complex and particularly sensitive to a multitude of changes which are mostly unpredictable and may greatly influence the image representation of one and the same object or scene. Therefore, a good feature detection is strongly required in dynamic and unrestricted real world environments. Preferably, this detection is invariant to a number of transformations, namely

- rotation,
- scale change,
- image noise,
- occlusion,
- illumination change and
- image flow.

A visual feature is referred to as "good" if it separates the core of information from the clutter. This basically depends on the application at hand and on the context it is used in (Jepson & Richards, 1993). For our research on vision systems for mobile robots, we define a good feature to be both independent of the transformations above and distinctively repeatable in dynamic environments.

Most features applied in literature are commonly classified either as being global, local or regional. Concerning our definition of a good feature, common global features that describe general properties of an entire image scene are rather inappropriate for our task of robot scene interpretation. While single objects can be generalized easily by simple global features, e.g. size, colour or texture attributes, finding stable and repeatable features is more complex for conglomerate scenes. However, such global features give very compact representations of significant image properties. Therefore, global features are mainly used in image-based applications like image retrieval or image annotation.

Many higher-level tasks like scene exploration or object classification and object tracking in complex scenes are grounded on local features. Being related to human visual perception, local visual features give clues for efficient scene exploration. They allow to focus on well-located interest points. Therefore, a variety of local features have been applied in a range of vision tasks, aiming at high robustness and repeatability. The Scale-Invariant Feature Transform (SIFT) proposed by Lowe (Lowe, 2004) and the Harris-Laplacian by Mikolajczyk and Schmid (Mikolajczyk & Schmid, 2002) are two popular methods of local feature detection. While the SIFT uses local extrema of Difference-of-Gaussian (DoG) filters in scale-space to produce scale-invariant features, the Harris-Laplace operator joins rotational invariant Harris features (Harris & Stephens, 1988) and Laplacian scale-space analysis into an affine invariant interest point detector. As the exploration of invariant features is an active field of research, well elaborated comparisons of various feature detectors and descriptors under a set of common transformations have been published by Schmid et al. (Schmid et al., 2000) and Mikolajczyk and Schmid (Mikolajczyk & Schmid, 2004; Mikolajczyk & Schmid, 2005).

Due to the different characteristics of local and global features, it is beneficial for some applications to combine both approaches. Lisin et al. (Lisin et al., 2005) show two methods where combining local and global features improve the accuracy of a classification task. More than another hybrid-like approach has been found in the detection of regional features, in which regions are defined as arbitrary subsets of the image. The extraction of Maximally Stable Extremal Regions (MSERs) by Matas et al. (Matas et al., 2004) highlights the advantage of a region-based approach: it produces both sparse and robust features that are particularly covariant to viewpoint change and affine transformations. Mikolajczyk et al. compare and evaluate a set of recent affine region detectors in (Mikolajczyk et al., 2005).

Regional features combine the merits of focus point localisation from local features with image-describing methods of global features. As symmetry is a regional feature, it supports the idea of regional features, especially in the context of range-based symmetry description. We reference and compare the regional symmetry features to known state-of-the-art affine region detectors. Therefore, we refer to Harris-affine regions, Hessian-affine regions, intensity-based regions (IBR), entropy-based regions and Maximally Stable Extremal Regions (MSER) that are summarized in (Mikolajczyk & Schmid, 2005). According to those recent state-of-the-art detectors, the symmetry descriptions at hand shall be included in a robust and stable regional feature detector in this section.
A time-line overview on selected work on local, regional and global features, as also on feature evaluation, is presented in Table 2:

Approach key	**Global feature**	**Local feature**	**Regional feature**	**Evaluation**	**Notes**
Harris & Stephens		●			Rotational invariance
Shi & Tomasi (1994)		●			KLT feature tracking
Schmid et al. (1998)		○		●	Evaluation of local detectors (Harris, Improved Harris, Heitger, Horaud, Cottier,Förster)
Milanese et al. (1999)	●				Fourier-Mellin Transform
Lowe (1999)		●			SIFT (DoG) detector
Tuytelaars & van Gool (1999)			●		Edge-based regions (EBR)
Dufournaud et al. (2003)		●			Scale invariance
Tuytelaars & van Gool (2000)			●		Intensity-based regions (IBR)
Mikolajczyk & Schmid (2002)		○	●	○	Harris-affine detector (Harris-affine, Harris-Laplace, Harris-affine regions)
Lowe (2004)		●			Optimized SIFT detector
Matas et al. (2004)			●		MSER detector
Kadir et al. (2004)			●	○	Salient-region detector
Mikolajczyk & Schmid (2004)		○		●	Evaluation of local detectors (Harris, Harris-Laplace, Harris-affine, Harris-affine region, SIFT, Laplace, Hessian, Gradient)
Yavlinsky et al. (2005)	●				Global feature densities
Lisin et al. (2005)	●	●			Combination of global & local
Mikolajczyk & Schmid (2005)		○		●	Evaluation of local descriptors (Div., GLOH, SIFT, PCA-SIFT)
Mikolajczyk et al. (2005)			○	●	Evaluation of regional detectors (Harris-affine, Hessian-affine, EBR, IBR, Salient regions, MSER)

Table 2. Selected approaches on image feature detection, description and evaluation

4.1 Symmetry Feature Description

To extract symmetry features from an image, we first use a small qualitative 1-dimensional operator from section 3.4 to acquire fast symmetry information for each image point. Horizontal and vertical symmetry axis points are detected by a line-independent maxima investigation on the symmetry data. As the pixel-based conjunction of the two resulting binary images can effect loss of feature points in cases where skewed symmetry axes indeed intersect, but do not share a pixel in the horizontal and the vertical binary image, we integrate axis points into straight line segments. Additionally, the segment representation includes useful information about each axis, e.g. length, orientation and variance. Segments with a large maximum variance correspond to curve segments. We iteratively split these at the point of maximum variance until they form straight sub-segments. The feature points are now extracted as intersections of vertical and horizontal symmetry segments. Calculating range-based DPS symmetry measures $s_{v/h}$ at each intersection of a horizontal and a vertical segment reveals an elliptical region feature $\mathbf{f}_i = (\mathbf{y}_i, \theta_i, a_i, b_i)$ parametrized by

$$\begin{aligned} \mathbf{y}_i &= (x(\mathbf{y}_i), y(\mathbf{y}_i)) && \text{(center point)} \\ \theta_i &= (\theta^v + \theta^h) / 2 - \pi/4, && \text{(orientation)} \\ a_i &= s'_v(\mathbf{y}_i), && \text{(1st semi axis)} \\ b_i &= s'_h(\mathbf{y}_i), && \text{(2nd semi axis)} \end{aligned} \qquad (3)$$

where θ^v and θ^h correspond to the orientations of intersecting segments. See Figure 5 for an exemplifying illustration of the main processing steps. Caused by line segmentation, intersections might miss the ideal symmetry maxima point, thus $s'_v(\mathbf{y}_i)$ and $s'_h(\mathbf{y}_i)$ are computed by finding the maximum vertical $s_v(\mathbf{x})$ and horizontal $s_h(\mathbf{x})$ in a small neighbourhood of $\mathbf{y}_i$. As a representation similar to the quadratic equation of central conics, each feature ellipse can also be formulated as

$$F_i = \{ (x,y) \in \mathbf{R}^2 \mid A_iD_i (x-x(\mathbf{y}_i))^2 + 2 B_iD_i (x-x(\mathbf{y}_i))(y-y(\mathbf{y}_i)) + C_iD_i (y-y(\mathbf{y}_i))^2 = 1 \} \qquad (4)$$

where
$$\begin{aligned} A_i &= a_i^2 \sin^2(\theta_i) + b_i^2 \cos^2(\theta_i), \\ B_i &= (a_i^2 - b_i^2) \cos(\theta_i) \sin(\theta_i), \\ C_i &= a_i^2 \cos^2(\theta_i) + b_i^2 \sin^2(\theta_i) \\ D_i &= (a_i b_i)^{-2} \end{aligned}$$

Figure 5. From the left: Vertical and horizontal qualitative symmetry axis points, symmetry segment selection and final regional symmetric features built with range-based symmetry

4.2 Symmetry

For a part of our experiments, we use SIFT descriptor and matching (Lowe, 2004). As another model, we introduced a distribution-based colour descriptor as a very simple form of feature description, as uncertainty of the detector in orientation can better be addressed by the generalization ability of a colour histogram. We adopt the representation of a mean-shift target candidate for robust real-time model tracking from (Comaniciu et al., 2000). The mean-shift model is robust to partial occlusions, clutter, rotation in depth and changes in camera position. The model is weighted according to the shape of the feature ellipse. Let the discrete density $\mathbf{p}'(f_i) = \{ \mathbf{p}'_u(f_i) \}_{u=1..m}$ of a target candidate frame G_i describe the m-bin colour histogram descriptor of a feature $\mathbf{f}_i$. Adopted from (21) in (Comaniciu et al., 2000), this is

$$\mathbf{p}'_u(\mathbf{f}_i) = c_i \cdot \sum_{x \in G_i} K_i(\mathbf{y}_i, \mathbf{x})\, \delta_{uv(\mathbf{x})}, \qquad (5)$$

with the kernel function $K_i(\mathbf{y}_i,\mathbf{x})$ describing a weighting over locations $\mathbf{x}$ with regard to the kernel centre $\mathbf{y}_i$. The Kronecker-δ-function compares the bins u and v($\mathbf{x}$) for equality, where $v(\mathbf{x}) \in \{1..m\}$ maps the colour feature of location $\mathbf{x}$ to its corresponding histogram bin. Finally, c_i is a normalization constant ensuring that all $\mathbf{p}'_u(f_i)$ sum up to 1. We now derive an elliptical target frame G_i and a Gaussian kernel function K_i for each detected image feature $\mathbf{y}_i$ directly from its elliptic feature representation (4). The frame G_i enclosing each $\mathbf{x}$ in F_i can easily be defined by widening the representation to

$$G_i = \{ \mathbf{x} \mid A_iD_i\,(x(\mathbf{x})-x(\mathbf{y}_i))^2 + 2\,B_iD_i\,(x(\mathbf{x})-x(\mathbf{y}_i)) \cdot (y(\mathbf{x})-y(\mathbf{y}_i)) + C_iD_i\,(y(\mathbf{x})-y(\mathbf{y}_i))^2 \leq 1 \}. \qquad (6)$$

Introducing the 2-dimensional Gaussian kernel function $K_i(\mathbf{y}_i, \mathbf{x})$, the correlation matrix M_i that fits the elliptical feature shape in orientation and ratio of the semi axes is given by

$$M_i = l^2 / 2 \begin{bmatrix} C_i & -B_i \\ -B_i & A_i \end{bmatrix}, \qquad (7)$$

where l can be used for scaling both standard deviations of the Gaussian function. Figure 6 shows two kernel shapes of l = 0.5 and l = 1.0 for an exemplary feature $\mathbf{y}_i$.

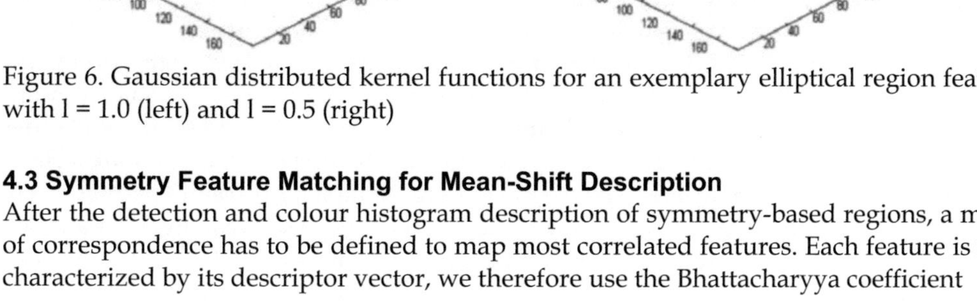

Figure 6. Gaussian distributed kernel functions for an exemplary elliptical region feature $\mathbf{y}_i$ with l = 1.0 (left) and l = 0.5 (right)

4.3 Symmetry Feature Matching for Mean-Shift Description

After the detection and colour histogram description of symmetry-based regions, a measure of correspondence has to be defined to map most correlated features. Each feature is mainly characterized by its descriptor vector, we therefore use the Bhattacharyya coefficient

$$\rho(\mathbf{f}_i, \mathbf{g}_i) = \sum_{u=1..m} (\, \mathbf{p}'_u(f_i) \cdot \mathbf{p}'_u(\mathbf{g}_j)\,)^{1/2} \qquad (8)$$

to compute the similarity of two features $\mathbf{f}_i$ and $\mathbf{g}_j$. The common application of feature matching is given by comparing a feature $\mathbf{f}_i$ from one scene with a set of features $\mathbf{g} = \{\mathbf{g}_k\}_{k=1..n}$ deriving from a second scene. The best match for $\mathbf{f}_i$ is thus given by

$$\mathbf{f}_i \rightarrow \mathbf{g}_i\text{:} \quad \mathbf{g}_i = \text{argmax} \{ \mathbf{g}_k \in \mathbf{g} \} \, \rho(\mathbf{f}_i, \mathbf{g}_k). \tag{9}$$

Feature matching experiments usually describe correspondences between two feature sets **f** and **g**. Depending on the final application, different matching strategies may be reasonable, namely non-injective and injective matching. Non-injective matching allows several $\mathbf{f}_i$ to be assigned to one $\mathbf{g}_j$. This mapping is adequate for applications like classification of multiple features into a number of classes. In applications, where features are meant to be non-ambiguous, one feature from one set should maximally be assigned to one feature of the other set. These assignments describe the symmetric subset of injective feature matches between **f** and **g**. We found that the Mean-Shift descriptor is better for classification tasks between features, while the SIFT descriptor is better for distinctive matches.

4.4 Panoramic Evaluation on Single Images

In this section, we follow the experiments of affine region detectors in (Mikolajczyk et al., 2005) by evaluating the proposed symmetry feature detector in relation to other well-elaborated feature detectors. We compare symmetry features of a set of panoramic images to Harris-Affine and Hessian-Affine Regions (Mikolajczyk & Schmid, 2005), Intensity-Based Regions (IBRs) (Tuytelaars & van Gool, 2000) and Maximally Stable Extremal Regions (MSERs) (Matas et al., 2004). While Hessian-Affine and Harris-Affine offer edge-based regions, IBRs, MSERs and the Symmetry approach are oriented towards area-based regions. We compute these regional feature types for the 1440 × 288 panoramic image in Figure 7 (right). Results are depicted in Figure 8. The histogram in Figure 9 shows a very common distribution of image feature sizes, where the size of an elliptical region is computed as the mean value of its semi axes. Symmetry, MSER and IBR provide few and sparse features with mean feature size, while Harris-Affine and Hessian-Affine detect many small features. For our symmetry detector, the feature count and the run-time do not depend on image size only, but also on symmetric image structure. The main effort is spent on the quantitative symmetry detection, where a growing search space for each image point has to be established. We can conclude that symmetry offers the most sparse set of features with large mean feature size. Additionally, the whole process of feature description and matching is depending on feature count, so symmetry features can be described and matched fastest.

Related approaches emphasize to be covariant under affine transformations like change of scale, rotation and perspective view. Covariance terms that elliptical representations of a feature cover the same region in different images. Range-based symmetry intuitively illustrates the concept of scale robustness, as symmetry is highly proportional to scale. However, as we have only used horizontal and vertical symmetry, the detection of features is not rotational invariant. Symmetry axes of horizontal and vertical operators are able to approximate slightly skewed axes of symmetry, but are rotational invariant for rotations of $n\pi/2$ only. We found that this causes symmetry to be comparatively weak in covariance on affine transformations compared to other approaches (Huebner et al., 2006). Nevertheless, no multiple scale analysis or scale selection is needed, since scale emerges from symmetry.

Figure 7. The first and the last image of a panoramic sequence of 37 images (1440 × 288)

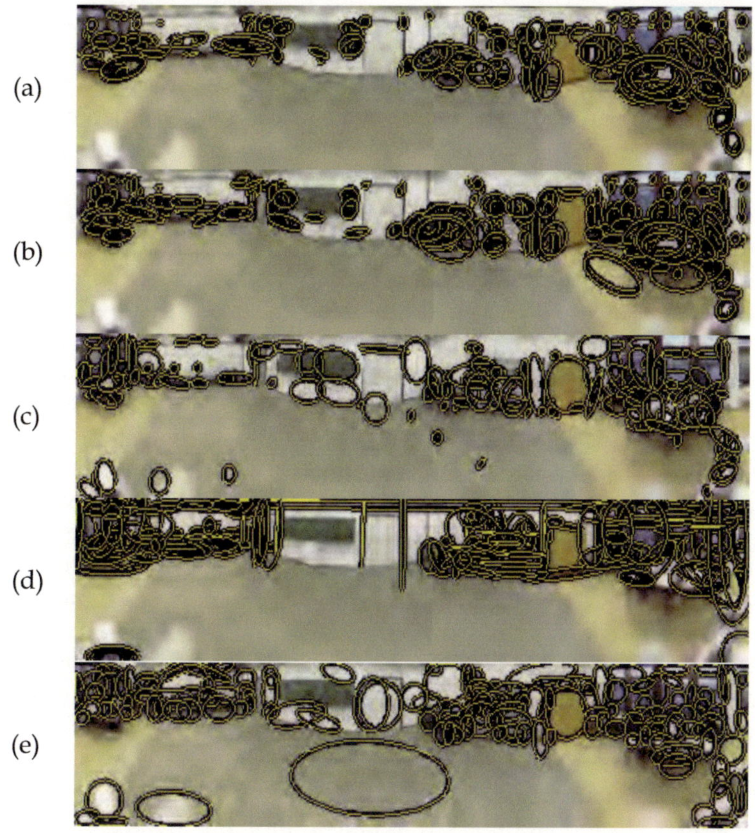

Figure 8. Regional features of the image from Figure 7 (right). (a) Harris-Affine. (b) Hessian-Affine. (c) Intensity-Based. (d) Maximally Stable Extremal Regions. (e) Symmetry Features

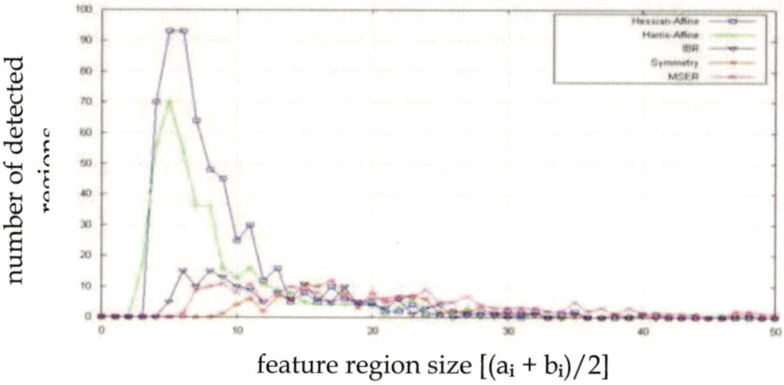

Figure 9. Histogram of feature sizes for the five regional feature detectors

4.5 Panoramic Evaluation on a Sequence of Images

In contrast to the transformations (changes in image blur, scale, rotation, perspective view and JPEG compression) discussed in (Mikolajczyk et al., 2005), panoramic warp is not an affine one. Therefore, we exploit the properties of the detectors in an evaluation experiment on panoramic warp, which naturally includes changes in blur, scale, and panoramic view, as can be seen in the panoramic samples above. We use a sequence of 37 panoramic images that was recorded during a straight movement using a mobile robot platform (see Figure 7). For each of the five detectors, $\mathbf{f_1}$ is computed, being the reference feature set of the first image. We also detect and describe the feature sets $\{\mathbf{g_i}\}_{i=2..37}$ with the SIFT descriptor to compute distinctive matches between $\mathbf{f_1}$ and each $\mathbf{g_i}$. Hereby, we evaluate how sensitive the different detectors are with regard to different levels of panoramic image warp. The number of features and feature matches are shown in Figure 10(a) and 10(b). We find again that symmetry yields very few features and matches. To rate these matches, the repeatabilities $r(\mathbf{f_1}, \mathbf{g_i})$ are computed and plotted in Figure 10(c). The plot presents clearly the repeatability decrease with increasing distance for all approaches, as images differ more from the reference image along the sequence. Additionally, it shows that the matching rates of MSERs and Symmetry are best to find correspondences from the detected features.

However, detected matches are not always correct. There may be false positives, when image regions look the same. To distinguish between false and correct matches, information about the exact image transformation is necessary. In (Mikolajczyk et al., 2005), simple 3×3 homography matrices are used to define the ground truth of where a feature has to be after an affine transformation. On the one hand, panoramic image flow for robot applications is not an affine transformation. There are image regions that do not change (e.g. fixed robot parts in the image, regions along the axis of movement and regions that are far away) or others that warp in a non-linear manner according to their size and their distance to the robot. On the other hand, the environment around the robot is unknown and dynamically changing, which makes panoramic homographies for robot applications impossible to establish. Therefore, we try to approximate each homography H(1,i) between image 1 and image i by a column-based histogram of feature shifts. For each match that results from the feature matchings between $\mathbf{f_1}$ and $\mathbf{g_i}$, we assign its radial shift in x-direction to the column. If there are more shifts assigned to one column, the mean value is assigned. Note that the results of all feature detectors are used to establish these homographies. Empty histogram cells are subsequently filled in by interpolation. To handle outliers, each fifth entry of the histogram is used as a sampling point for a cubic spline that now describes H(1,i). Some resulting homographies $\{H(1,i)\}_{i=2..6}$ are presented in Figure 10(d). The graphs show increasing shift altitude and zero-crossings at the image edges 0 and 2π, respectively, as also at the image centre π. This gives obvious reason that the robot has moved away from a point in the image centre. This is correct, as the robot moved a straight path between image 1 to image 37 (see Figure 7).

After these two steps, we can compare the shifts of the feature matches to the corresponding homography for each image match. Figure 10(e) presents the comparison between the matches of the different detectors and H(1,3). For the cause that homographies are acquired by the complete feature set, they are visibly influenced by these, but outliers are clearly recognizable. The largest outlier in the example in Figure 10(e) can be detected at the left side of the image as a sample of the IBR method. Reviewing the image sequence, we find that this feature is one of those describing one of the monitor screens. It has been matched to one of the other screens in the image and truly is incorrect. In this homography H(1,3) there are few eye-catching outliers for IBR, Harris-Affine, MSER, Symmetry and Hessian-Affine.

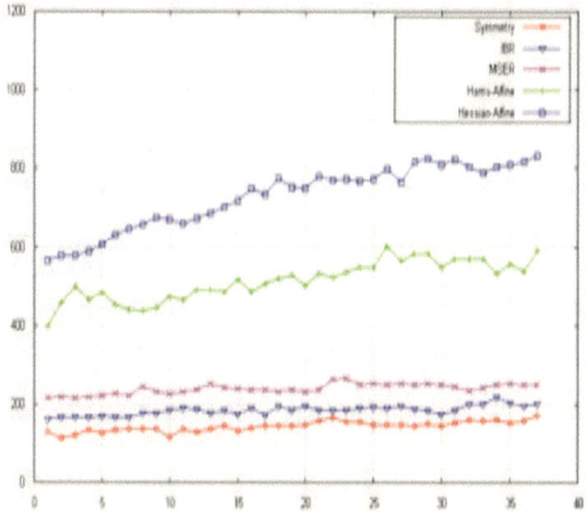

a) Number of features $|\mathbf{g}_i|$ along the sequence

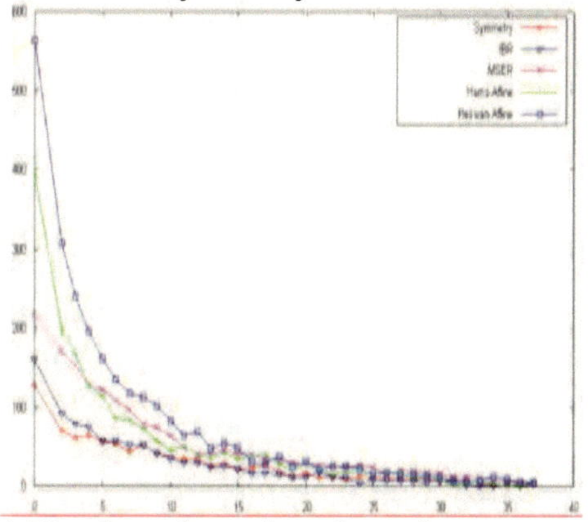

b) Number of matches along the sequence

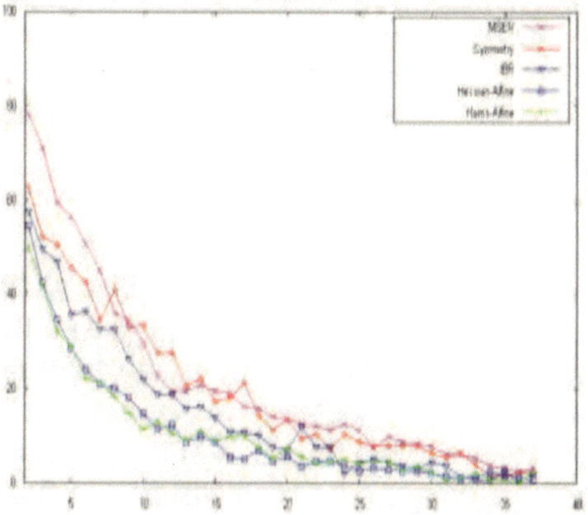

c) Repeatability $r(\mathbf{f}_1, \mathbf{g}_i)$ along the sequence

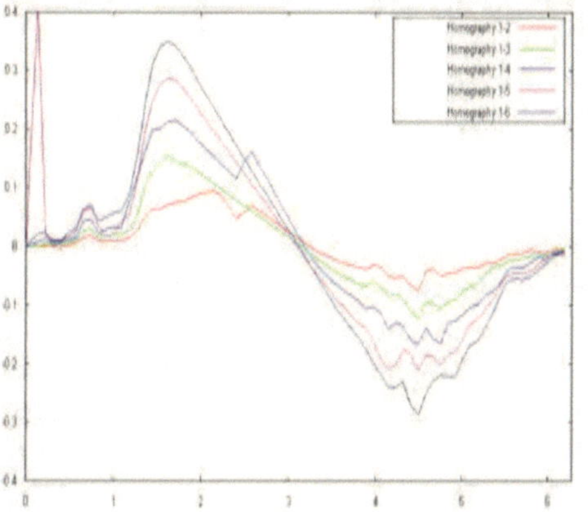

d) Homographies between image 1 and 2-6

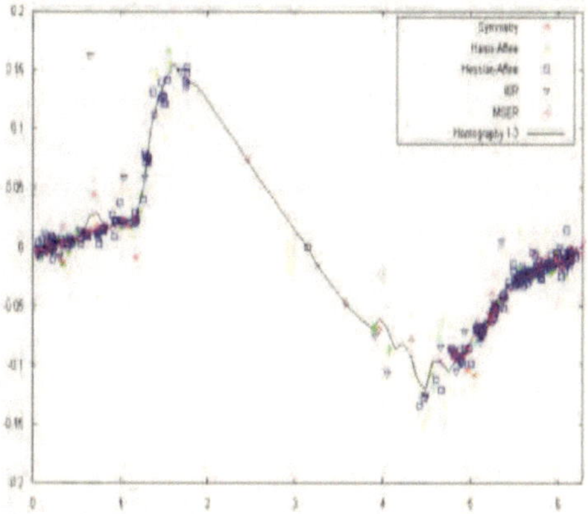

e) Homography errors between images 1 and 3

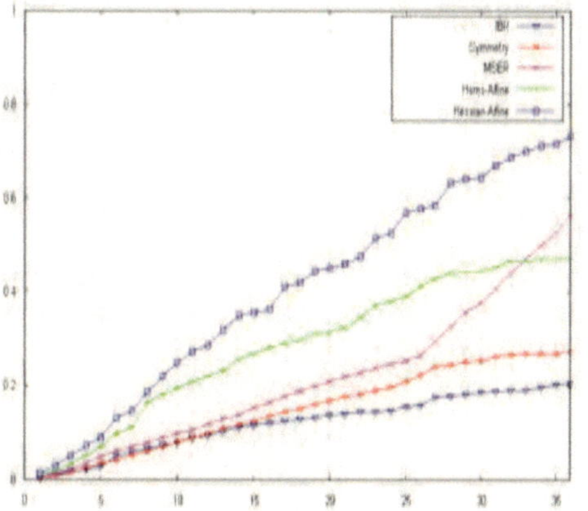

f) Mean homography error H(1,i) along the sequence.

Figure 10. For the comparison of all detectors, features of image 1 are matched to those of images 2-37 of the sequence

The mean deviation of matches about the homographies along the whole sequence is depicted in 10(f). It can be seen that matching correctness decreases for each method the more the image i differs from the reference image 1, but IBR and Symmetry provide best matching correctness for the analysed image sequence.
Concluding, the experiments show that regional symmetry features are successfully applicable for feature detection and matching during panoramic warp. No multiple scale analysis or scale selection is needed, as scale emerges directly from the range-based symmetry component of the detector. The detector offers comparatively few and significant features that support fast description and matching. Matched features are highly stable, distinctive and correct in combination with the SIFT descriptor. Another advantage of the symmetry approach is the strong relationship of extracted features to objects in the scene. Walls, doors, monitors and cabinets are frequently included by one feature.

5. Integration and Application

As we are now able to describe symmetry and apply these descriptions in terms of a regional feature descriptor, we exemplary integrate our method to a robot application based on panoramic vision. In the following application on egomotion classification, we use the Hamburg mobile service robot TASeR (see Figure 13). For further applications based on the symmetry feature approach, we reference to some of our other work on motion detection (Huebner et al., 2005) or object classification (Huebner & Zhang, 2006).

5.1 Egomotion Classification Algorithm

The homographies discussed in the previous section showed that repeatability values strongly decreases yet after few images. Figure 10(c) depicts that repeatability is less than 20% after 15 images (150cm). Thus, a precise and general estimation of depth information is hardly realizable. Another problem is that a feature offset of 0 degree between two images can have multiple causes. Either the featured object lies along the direction of movement, or it is too far so the offset is smaller than a pixel, or it belongs to the robot itself. Because of these difficulties, we do not focus on distance or egomotion estimation. However, the optical flow of feature matchings between images allows reasoning about the robot's movement. By the feature matching technique, extracts of the image flow are detectable in terms of the yet discussed partial homographies. Our goal here is to distinguish between four basic robot movements: no move, move in direction α, turn left and turn right. Figure 11 shows the theoretical image flow and homography graph classes for these movements. The amplitude of a graph is not only dependent on the distance between the two robot positions, but also on the distance to the features, thus we only check for each x the sum of signs of the feature shifts Δx on the image halfs that are defined by x:

$$d_1(x) = \sum_{i=0..w/2} \delta(x+i)\ ,\ d_2(x) = \sum_{i=w/2..w} \delta(x+i) \qquad (10)$$

with ($\delta(j) = 1$, if $\Delta x(j) > \varepsilon$), ($\delta(j) = -1$, if $\Delta x(j) < -\varepsilon$), ($\delta(j) = 0$, otherwise).
The difference $d(x)$ between $d_1(x)$ and $d_2(x)$ is maximal for the x in moving direction, if $d(x)$ is larger than a small threshold t_1, so that movement direction α can be calculated as

$$\alpha = \text{argmax}\{x\}\ d(x) \ \text{ with } d(x) = (\ d_1(x) - d_2(x)\ ). \qquad (11)$$

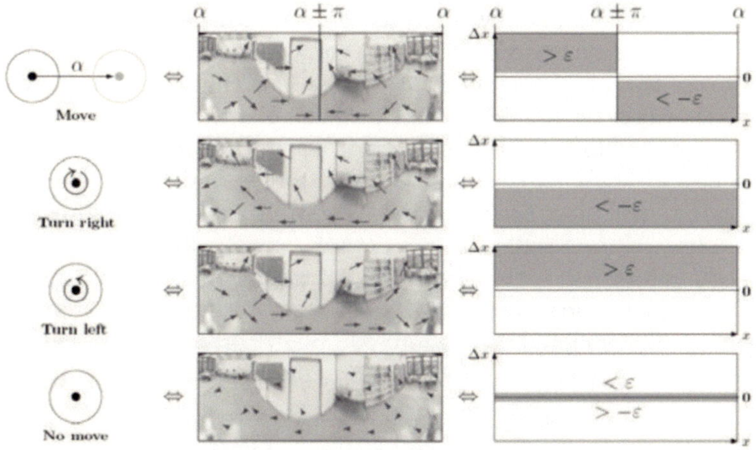

Figure 11. The four basic movements "Move α", "Turn right", "Turn left", and "No move". Typical feature shifts for those movements are shown in the centre column. On the right column, the corresponding homography sectors are depicted, e.g. a "Turn right" action is to result in feature shifts in negative x-direction only

Additionally, the product $d_1(x) \cdot d_2(x)$ is useful, as it may distinguish a sinus-shaped homography graph from a constant one. Therefore, we establish two measures c_1 and c_2 as

$$c_1 = (d_1(x) \cdot d_2(x)) \,/\, w, \; c_2 = -c_1, \text{ if } d_1(x) < 0, \text{ or } c_2 = c_1, \text{ otherwise.} \tag{12}$$

For $c_1<0$, we can assume a movement of the robot in direction α. For $c_1>0$, a turn action or no movement is probable. To distinguish between these two, we use a second threshold t_2. c_2 finally helps distinguishing between "Turn left" and "Turn right" actions.

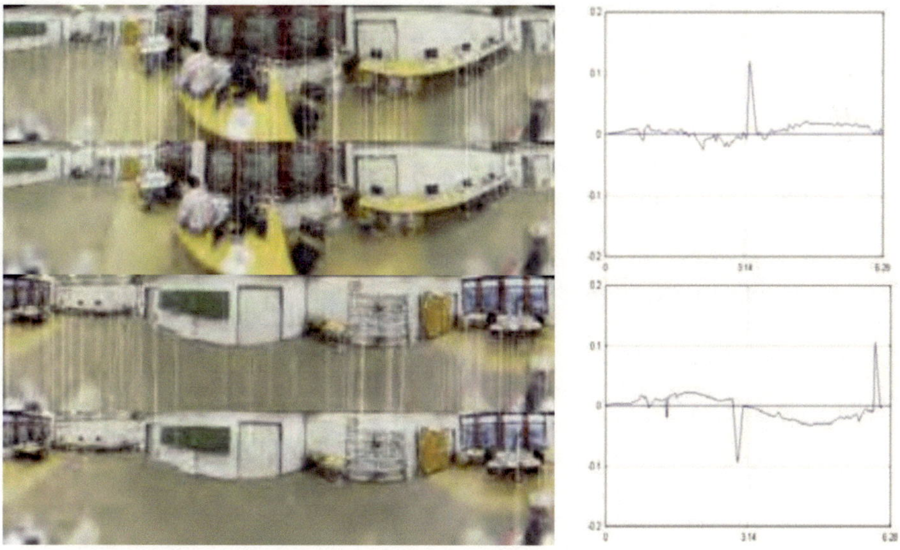

Figure 12. Top: Between images 122 and 123. The algorithm computes $d(\alpha)$=-215, $c_1(\alpha)=c_2(\alpha)$= 0 and correctly returns "No move". Bottom: Between images 24 and 25. The algorithm computes $d(\alpha)$=-428, $c_1(\alpha)$=-95, $c_2(\alpha)$=95 and returns "Move in direction 340°"

The resulting algorithm is applied to a sequence of 200 images that were recorded by the TASeR robot. The odometry sensors allow for a final comparison of the real movements to the estimated ones. For each neighbouring image pair, symmetric regional features are computed and described by the SIFT descriptor for distinctive matching. The symmetry homography is computed like described in section 4.5 and classified by the algorithm.
From this sequence, we show two examples for "No move" and "Move left" in Figure 12. As can be seen from the matching, the homography graphs and the measures d, c_1 and c_2, the algorithm also offers robust results for homography graphs that are influenced by failure matches. The same robustness is also shown by the results on the whole image sequence, as presented in Figure 13. Comparing the real robot route with the estimation, we find a very high correctness of movement classification. Although correctly classified, there is uncertainty in the estimation of the movement direction samples α, which ideally should all be 0.

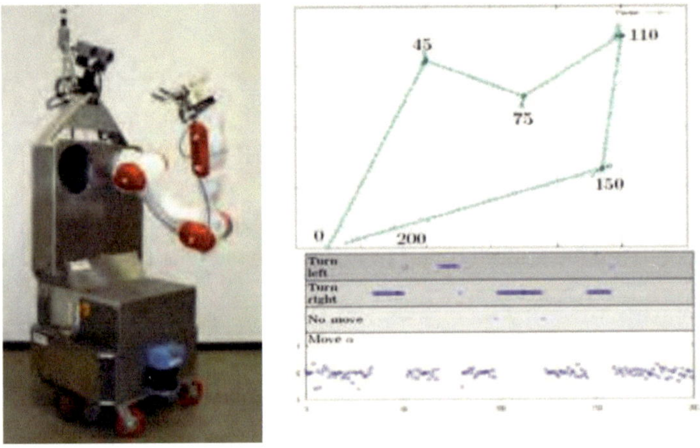

Figure 13. Left: The TASeR robot. Right: The experimental route map delivered from the odometry (top) and the movement classification with our simple algorithm (bottom).

6. Conclusion

In this work, bilateral symmetry has been proposed as a concept for the extraction of features from the visual data and their application to robot navigation tasks. Symmetry in shape and vision is strongly motivated by biological and psychophysical aspects. It is a natural feature that can be found in many scenes, whether they show structured indoor or unstructured outdoor environments. We conclude with a review on the three main topics:
1. *Symmetry as a Feature:* Symmetry has been investigated in several domains like biology, psychophysics, architecture and art. Accordingly, symmetry has also been applied as a valuable attentional feature for the extraction of regions of interest or for object description by symmetric properties in computer vision.
Motivated by psychophysical experiments on symmetry perception, a fast and compact one-dimensional operator was supposed earlier (Huebner, 2003) to handle horizontal and vertical bilateral symmetry measures only. The operator overcomes the problem of symmetry detection methods in literature that use large operators which are mostly unsuitable for robotic real-time tasks. However, each of these strength-based operators returns a relative, commonly normalized value of symmetry for each image element. For

this purpose, a novel method to generate robust range-based symmetry values was proposed that produces symmetry range information for each image point (Huebner et al., 2005). This approach is based on an algorithm computing bilateral quantitative symmetry information using an adopted Dynamic Programming technique. Qualitative and quantitative symmetry measures offer a variety of symmetry representations - especially those of symmetry axes - for higher-level image processing tasks.

It was shown how globally and versatile symmetry can be used as a feature. Even beyond the context of image processing and visual data, symmetry can be used as a general feature of structure. A further task in this topic would be the further workout of the quantitative symmetry approach. The calculation of the Dynamic Programming Symmetry search spaces might be optimized and thereby accelerate computing time. Another open issue is the use of search space path structure for quantitative symmetry computation.

2. *Regional Symmetry Features:* In this part, a new regional symmetry feature matching approach was proposed. It comprises several modular techniques for detection, description and matching of image features based on the symmetry types developed in the previous section. While the qualitative symmetry operator describes symmetry as a relative degree and the quantitative operator describes symmetry as a range, advantages of both were combined in a stable regional feature detector. In combination with descriptors, symmetry features can robustly be matched. The descriptors used were the famous gradient-based SIFT and a Mean-Shift approach that was adopted to the task of feature description. The evaluation including state-of-the-art regional feature detectors shows that the symmetry feature approach is well applicable for robust feature recognition, especially for panoramic image warp. Description and matching of symmetry features is very robust and faster than other approaches that derive larger feature sets. Additionally, symmetry features are strongly related to objects in the scene. Walls, doors, monitors and cabinets are frequently included by one feature.

Besides the advantages of regional symmetry features, their sensibility to rotation is due to this works concentration on horizontal and vertical symmetry measures mainly. This invariance would be an important step to support the task-spanning robustness of the approach. The measures of covariance and overlap might benefit from an additional rotation invariance of the proposed features. Therefore, a further task is to efficiently find a robust orientation measure of symmetry and symmetric features. Along and perpendicular to this orientation, the proposed twofold quantitative symmetry measures could be used.

3. *Integration and Application:* The third topic addressed the applicability of the developed symmetry features for robot navigation by panoramic vision. For this purpose, the mobile service robot TASeR from the Working Group Technical Aspects of Multimodal Systems at the University of Hamburg was used. The capability of symmetry feature matching with regard to simple classification of robot egomotion was presented. The integration of the developed visual symmetry features into high-level object recognition and robot navigation tasks in dynamic environments is thereby motivated.

It is important to state that the step from one or more features to an object has not been made in this work. Features are natural low-level points or regions of attention that are supposed to describe significant visual information and thus might be interesting to be analysed. Objects are understood as higher-level entities filled with semantic descriptions. Those are embedded in higher-level applications like object recognition or autonomous robot navigation of intelligent systems. These tasks are theirselves wide areas of research

such as the detection of robust and natural image features that has been treated in our work. As presented in this work, symmetry can support these tasks.
Returning to the image of a construction set that has been used in the introduction, symmetry is just one of the construction blocks that might help intelligent systems to perceive and act in dynamic environments.

7. References

Barlow, H. B. & Reeves, B. C. (1979). The Versatility and Absolute Efficiency of Detecting Mirror Symmetry in Random Dot Displays. *Vision Research*, 19, pp. 783–793.

Blum, H. & Nagel, R. (1978). Shape Description Using Weighted Symmetric Axis Features. *Pattern Recognition*, 10(3): 167–180.

Brady, M. & Asada, H. (1984). Smoothed Local Symmetries and Their Implementation. *The International Journal of Robotics Research*, 3(3): 36–61.

Chetverikov, D. (1999). Fundamental Structural Features in the Visual World. In *Proc. of the Int. Worksh. on Fundamental Structural Properties in Image and Pattern Analysis*, 47–58.

Chetverikov, D. & Jankó, Z. (2003). Skewed Symmetry of Bidirectional Textures. In *Proc. of the 27th Workshop of the Austrian Association for Pattern Recognition*, pp. 97–102.

Comaniciu, D.; Ramesh, V. & Meer, P. (2000). Real-Time Tracking of Non-Rigid Objects using Mean Shift. In *Proc. of Comp. Vision and Pattern Recognition*, vol. 2, pp. 142–149.

Cross, A. D. J. & Hancock, E. R. (1999). Scale space vector fields for symmetry detection. *Image Vision Computing*, 17(5-6): 337–345.

Csathó, À.; Van der Vloed, G. & Van der Helm, P. A. (2003). Blobs strengthen repetition but weaken symmetry. *Vision Research*, 43, pp. 993–1007.

Delius, J. D. & Nowak, B. (1982). Visual Symmetry Recognition by Pigeons. *Psychological Research*, vol. 44, pp. 199-212.

Di Gesù, V. & Valenti, C. (1995). The Discrete Symmetry Transform in Computer Vision. Technical report, DMA Università di Palermo.

Di Gesù, V. & Valenti, C. (1996). A New Symmetry Operator for the Analysis of Sequences of Images.

Dufournaud, Y.; Schmid, C. & Horaud, R. (2000). Matching Images with Different Resolutions. In *IEEE Conf. on Computer Vision and Pattern Recognition*, pp. 612–618.

Enquist, M. & Arak, A. (1994). Symmetry, beauty and evolution. *Nature*, 372, pp. 169–172.

Ferguson, R. W. (2000). Modeling Orientation Effects in Symmetry Detection: The Role of Visual Structure. *Proceedings of the 22nd Conference of the Cognitive Science Society*.

Hargittai, I. & Hargittai, M. (1994). *Symmetry - A Unifying Concept*. Shelter. ISBN 093607017X.

Harris, C. & Stephens, M. (1988). A Combined Corner and Edge Detector. In *4th ALVEY Vision Conference*, pp. 147–151.

Huebner, K. (2003). A 1-Dimensional Symmetry Operator for Image Feature Extraction in Robot Applications. *The 16th International Conference on Vision Interface*, pp. 286–291.

Huebner, K.; Westhoff, D. & Zhang, J. (2005). Optimized Quantitative Bilateral Symmetry Detection. *International Journal of Information Acquisition*, 2(3): 241–249.

Huebner, K.; Westhoff, D. & Zhang, J. (2006). A Comparison of Regional Feature Detectors in Panoramic Images. In *Proceedings of IEEE Int. Conf. on Information Acquisition*.

Huebner, K. & Zhang, J. (2006). Stable Symmetry Feature Detection and Classification in Panoramic Robot Vision Systems. In *Proceedings of IEEE/RSJ International Conference on Intelligent Robots and Systems*, pp. 3429–3434.

Jepson, A. D. & Richards, W. (1993). What Makes a Good Feature?, *Proceedings of the 1991 York Conference on Spacial Vision in Humans and Robots*, pp. 89–125.

Johansson, B.; Knutsson, H. & Granlund, G. (2000). Detecting Rotational Symmetries using Normalized Convolution. In *Proceedings of the 15th International Conference on Pattern Recognition*, vol. 3, pp. 500–504.

Kadir, T.; Zisserman, A. & Brady, M. (2004). An Affine Invariant Salient Region Detector. In *European Conference on Computer Vision*, pp. 228–241.

Kirkpatrick, M. & Rosenthal, G. G. (1994). Symmetry without fear. *Nature*, 372, pp. 134–135.

Kovesi, P. D. (1997). Symmetry and Asymmetry From Local Phase. In *Proceedings of the 10th Australian Joint Conference on Artificial Intelligence*, pp. 185–190.

Lisin, D.; Mattar, M. A.; Blaschko, M. B.; Benfield, M. C. & Learned-Miller, E. G. (2005). Combining Local and Global Image Features for Object Class Recognition. *Proceedings of IEEE Workshop on Learning in Computer Vision and Pattern Recognition.*

Liu, T.-L.; Geiger, D. & Yuille, A. (1998). Segmenting by Seeking the Symmetry Axis. In *Proceedings of the 14th International Conference on Pattern Recognition*, pp. 994–998.

Liu, Y. (2000). *Computational Symmetry*, chapter 21 of *Symmetry 2000*, pp. 231–245.

Liu, Y.; Collins, R. & Tsin, Y. (2004). A Computational Model for Periodic Pattern Perception Based on Frieze and Wallpaper Groups. *IEEE Transactions on Pattern Analysis and Machine Intelligence*, 26(3): 354–371.

Locher, P. J. & Nodine, C. F. (1989). The Perceptual Value of Symmetry. *Computers and Mathematics with Applications*, 17, pp. 475–484.

Lowe, D. G. (2004). Distinctive Image Features from Scale-Invariant Keypoints. *International Journal of Computer Vision*, 60(2), pp. 91–110.

Loy, G. & Zelinsky, A. (2003). Fast Radial Symmetry for Detecting Points of Interest. *IEEE Transactions on Pattern Analysis and Machine Intelligence*, 25(8): 959–973.

Matas, J.; Chum, O.; Urban, M. & Pajdla, T. (2004). Robust Wide Baseline Stereo from Maximally Stable Extremal Regions. *Image and Vision Computing*, 22(10), pp.761–767.

Mellor, M. & Brady, M. (2005). A New Technique for Local Symmetry Estimation. In *Scale-Space 2005*, pp. 38–49.

Milanese, R.; Cherbuliez, M. & Pun, T. (1998). Invariant Content-Based Image Retrieval Using the Fourier-Mellin Transform. In S. Singh, editor, In *Proceedings of the International Conference on Advances in Pattern Recognition*, pp. 73–82. Springer.

Mikolajczyk, K. & Schmid, C. (2001). Indexing Based on Scale Invariant Interest Points. In *8th International Conference on Computer Vision*, pp. 525–531.

Mikolajczyk, K. & Schmid, C. (2002). An Affine Invariant Interest Point Detector. In *European Conference on Computer Vision*, pp. 128–142. Springer.

Mikolajczyk, K. & Schmid, C. (2004). Scale and Affine Invariant Interest Point Detectors. *International Journal of Computer Vision*, 60(1), pp. 63–86.

Mikolajczyk, K. & Schmid, C. (2005). A performance evaluation of local descriptors. *IEEE Transactions on Pattern Analysis and Machine Intelligence*, 27(10), pp. 1615–1630.

Mikolajczyk, K.; Tuytelaars, T.; Schmid, C.; Zisserman, A.; Matas, J.; Schaffalitzky, F.; Kadir, T. & van Gool, L. (2005). A Comparison of Affine Region Detectors. *International Journal of Computer Vision.*

Ohta, Y. & Kanade, T. (1985). Stereo by Intra- and Inter-Scanline Search Using Dynamic Programming. *IEEE Trans. on Pattern Analysis and Machine Intelligence*, 7(2): 139–154.

Palmer, S. E. & Hemenway, K. (1978). Orientation and Symmetry: Effects of Multiple, Rotational, and Near Symmetries. *Journal of Experimental Psychology: Human Perception and Performance*, 4(4), pp. 691–702.

Pratt, W. K. (2001). *Digital Image Processing*. John Wiley, New York, 3rd edition.

Reisfeld, D.; Wolfson, H. & Yeshurun, Y. (1995). Context Free Attentional Operators: the Generalized Symmetry Transform. *Int. Journal of Computer Vision*, 14: 119–130.

Schmid, C.; Mohr, R. & Bauckhage, C. (2005). Evaluation of Interest Point Detectors. *International Journal of Computer Vision*, 37(2), pp. 151–172.

Scognamillo, R.; Rhodes, G.; Morrone, C. & Burr, D. (2003). A feature based model of symmetry detection. In *Proc. of the Royal Society of London*, vol. 270 *B*, pp. 1727–1733.

Shi, J. & Tomasi, C. (1994). Good Features to Track. In *IEEE Conference on Computer Vision and Pattern Recognition*, pp. 593–600.

Stewart, I. & Golubitsky, M. (1992). *Denkt Gott symmetrisch ?* German translation of the book *Fearful Symmetry: Is God a Geometer?*, ISBN 3-7643-2783-9.

Sun, C. (1995). Symmetry detection using gradient information. *Pattern Recognition Letters*, 16: 987–996.

Sun, C. & Si, D. (1999). Fast Reflectional Symmetry Detection Using Orientation Histograms. *Real-Time Imaging*, 5(1): 63–74.

Taraborelli, D. (2003). What is a Feature? A Fast and Frugal Approach to the Study of Visual Properties. In *Proceedings of the Eighth International Colloquium on Cognitive Science.*

Truco, E. & Verri, A. (1998). *Introductory Techniques for 3-D Computer Vision*. Prentice Hall.

Tuytelaars, T. & van Gool, L. J. (1999). Content-Based Image Retrieval Based on Local Affinely Invariant Regions. In *Visual Information and Information Systems*, pp. 493–500.

Tuytelaars, T. & van Gool, L. J. (2000). Wide Baseline Stereo Matching based on Local, Affinely Invariant Regions. In *British Machine Vision Conference*, pp. 412–422.

Tuytelaars, T.; Turina, A. & Van Gool, L. J. (2003). Noncombinatorial Detection of Regular Repetitions under Perspective Skew. *IEEE Transactions on Pattern Analysis and Machine Intelligence*, 25(4): 418–432.

Tyler, C. W. (editor). (1994) *Spatial Vision*, volume 8(4), Special Issue on The Perception of Symmetry. VNU Science Press..

Yavlinsky, A.; Schofield, E. & Rüger, S. (2005). Automated Image Annotation Using Global Features and Robust Nonparametric Density Estimation. In *Proceedings of the 4th Int. Conference on Image and Video Retrieval*, vol. 3568 of *LNCS*, pp. 507–517. Springer.

Zabrodsky, H. (1990). Symmetry - A Review. *Technical report*, Department of Computer Science, The Hebrew University of Jerusalem, May 1990.

Zabrodsky, H.; Peleg, S. & Avnir, D. (1993). Completion of Occluded Shapes using Symmetry. In *IEEE Computer Society Conference on Computer Vision and Pattern Recognition*, pp. 678–679.

Zabrodsky, H.; Peleg, S. & Avnir, D. (1995). Symmetry as a Continuous Feature. *IEEE Transactions on Pattern Analysis and Machine Intelligence*, 17(12), pp. 1154–1166.

Žganec, M.; Pavešic, N. & Kovacic, S. (1992). Stereo-matching by dynamic programming. *Proceedings of the Slovenian-German workshop "Image processing and stereo analysis"*, 26(1), pp. 37–51.

29

Stereo Vision Based SLAM Issues and Solutions

D.C. Herath, K.R.S. Kodagoda and G. Dissanayake
ARC Centre of Excellence for Autonomous Systems, University of Technology, Sydney Australia

1. Introduction

[1]Simultaneous Localization and Mapping (SLAM) has been one of the active research areas in robotic research community for the past few years. When a robot is placed in an unknown environment a SLAM solution attempts to build a perfect map of the environment while localising the robot with respect to this map simultaneously. Traditionally SLAM utilised endogenous sensor data in the process. Successful SLAM implementations using laser (Guivant and Nebot, 2002), sonar and radar (Clark and Dissanayake, 1999) can be found in the literature, which prove the possibility of using SLAM for extended periods of time in indoor and outdoor environments with well bounded results.

Recent extensions to the general SLAM problem has looked in to the possibility of using 3-dimensional features and the use of alternative sensors to traditionally used lasers and radars. Cameras are competitive alternatives owing to the low cost and rich information content they provide. Despite the recent developments in camera sensors and computing, there are still formidable challenges to be resolved before successful vision based SLAM implementations are realised in realistic scenarios. Monocular camera based SLAM is widely researched (Davison et al., 2004; Kwok et al., 2005), however, binocular camera based SLAM is mostly overlooked. Some of the noted stereo implementations can be found in (Davison and Murray, 2002) and recently in (Jung, 2004). Lack of enthusiasm for research in this direction could possibly be attributed to the misconception that range and bearing information provided by the stereo vision system is directly utilizable providing a simplistic solution to SLAM which is academically less appealing or the apparent success in single camera SLAM implementations.

However, after rigorous analysis and sensor modelling, we found that the standard extended Kalman filter (EKF) based SLAM with small base line stereo vision systems can easily become inconsistent (Herath et al., 2006a) .

This chapter attempts to provide readers with an understanding of the SLAM problem and its solutions in the context of stereo vision. The chapter introduces the Extended Kalman Filter as applied to the generic SLAM Problem. Then, while identifying the prevailing issues inherent in solutions to the SLAM problem in stereo vision context, our solutions are presented with simulated and experimental evaluations. Several components of the stereo

---

1 This work is supported by the ARC Centre of Excellence program, funded by the Australian Research Council (ARC) and the New South Wales State Government.

vision system, including outlier rejection, sensor modelling, inconsistency analysis and alternate formulations of SLAM are discussed.

2. Simultaneous Localisation and Mapping (SLAM)

This section presents an introduction to the Kalman filter in the context of Simultaneous Localization and Mapping beginning with the derivation of the standard Kalman filter equations for a linear discrete system and then extending them to accommodate real world non linear systems, the Extended Kalman Filter (EKF) as implemented in majority of the SLAM solutions.

2.1 Linear Discrete-Time Kalman Filter

In order to derive the Kalman filter for discrete linear system, its process and observation models must be defined. The Kalman Filter consists of three recursive stages. (1) Prediction, (2) observation and, (3) update Stage. For a linear, discrete-time system the state transition equation (process model) can be written as follows

$$\mathbf{x}(k) = \mathbf{F}(k)\mathbf{x}(k-1) + \mathbf{B}(k)\mathbf{u}(k) + \mathbf{G}(k)\mathbf{v}(k) \quad (1)$$

Where $\mathbf{x}(k)$ - state at time k, $\mathbf{u}(k)$ - control input vector at time k, $\mathbf{v}(k)$ - additive process noise, $\mathbf{B}(k)$ - control input transition matrix, $\mathbf{G}(k)$ - noise transition matrix and $\mathbf{F}(k)$ - state transition matrix. The linear observation equation can be written as

$$\mathbf{z}(k) = \mathbf{H}(k)\mathbf{x}(k) + \mathbf{w}(k) \quad (2)$$

where $\mathbf{z}(k)$ - observation made at time k, $\mathbf{x}(k)$ - state at time k, $\mathbf{H}(k)$ - observation model and $\mathbf{w}(k)$ - additive observation noise. Process and observation noise are assumed to be zero-mean and independent. Thus

$$E[v(k)]=E[w(k)]=0, \forall k \text{ and } E[v_i w_j^T]=0, \forall i,j$$

Motion noise and the observation noise will have the following corresponding covariance;

$$E[v_i v_j^{\mathrm{T}}]=\delta_{ij}\mathbf{Q}_i, \quad E[w_i w_j^T]=\delta_{ij}\mathbf{R}_i$$

The estimate of the state at a time k given all information up to time k is written as $\hat{\mathbf{x}}(k/k)$ and the estimate of the state at a time k given information up to time k-1 is written as $\hat{\mathbf{x}}(k/k-1)$ and is called the prediction. Thus given the estimate at (k-1) time step the prediction equation for the state at k^{th} time step can be written as

$$\hat{\mathbf{x}}(k/k-1) = \mathbf{F}(k)\hat{\mathbf{x}}(k-1/k-1) + \mathbf{B}(k)\mathbf{u}(k) \quad (3)$$

And the corresponding covariance prediction;

$$\mathbf{P}(k/k-1) = \mathbf{F}(k)\,\mathbf{P}(k-1/k-1)\mathbf{F}^T(k) + \mathbf{G}(k)\mathbf{Q}(k)\mathbf{G}^T(k) \quad (4)$$

Then the unbiased (the conditional expected error between estimate and true state is zero) linear estimate is

$$\hat{\mathbf{x}}(k/k) = \hat{\mathbf{x}}(k/k-1) - \mathbf{W}(k)[\mathbf{z}(k) - \mathbf{H}(k)\hat{\mathbf{x}}(k/k-1)] \tag{5}$$

Where $\mathbf{W}$(k) is the Kalman Gain at time step k. This is calculated as:

$$\mathbf{W}(k) = \mathbf{P}(k/k-1)\mathbf{H}^T(k)\mathbf{S}^{-1}(k) \tag{6}$$

Where $\mathbf{S}$(k) is called the innovation variance at time step k and given by:

$$\mathbf{S}(k) \ = \ \mathbf{H}(k)\mathbf{P}(k/k-1)\ \mathbf{H}^T(k) + \mathbf{R}(k) \tag{7}$$

and the covariance estimate is

$$\mathbf{P}(k/k) = (\mathbf{I} - \mathbf{W}(k)\mathbf{H}(k)\mathbf{P}(k/k-1)(\mathbf{I} - \mathbf{W}(k)\mathbf{H}(k))^T + \mathbf{W}(k)\mathbf{R}(k)\mathbf{W}^T(k) \tag{8}$$

Essentially the Kalman filter takes a weighted average of the prediction $\hat{\mathbf{x}}(k/k-1)$, based on the previous estimate $\hat{\mathbf{x}}(k-1/k-1)$, and a new observation $\mathbf{z}(k)$ to estimate the state of interest $\hat{\mathbf{x}}(k/k)$. This cycle is repeatable.

2.2 The Extended Kalman Filter

Albeit Kalman filter is the optimal minimum mean squared (MMS) error estimator for a linear system, hardly would one find such a system in reality. In fact the systems considered in this chapter are purely non-linear systems. A solution is found in the Extended Kalman Filter (EKF) which uses a linearised approximation to non-linear models. The extended Kalman filter algorithm is very similar to the linear Kalman filter algorithm with the substitutions;

$\mathbf{F}(k) \rightarrow \mathbf{f}_x(k)$ and $\mathbf{H}(k) \rightarrow \mathbf{h}_x(k)$, where $\nabla\mathbf{f}_x(k)$ and $\nabla\mathbf{h}_x(k)$ are non-linear functions of both state and time step, and $\mathbf{f}_x(k)$, $\mathbf{h}_x(k)$ are the process model and observation model respectively. Therefore the main equations in EKF can be summarized as follows;

1. Prediction equations

$$\hat{\mathbf{x}}(k/k-1) = \mathbf{f}(\hat{\mathbf{x}}(k-1/k-1)\ ,\mathbf{u}(k)) \tag{9}$$

$$\mathbf{P}(k/k-1) = \nabla\mathbf{f}_{\mathbf{x}}(k)\ P(k-1/k-1)\nabla^T\mathbf{f}_{\mathbf{x}}(k) + \mathbf{Q}(k) \tag{10}$$

2. Update equations

$$\hat{\mathbf{x}}(k/k) = \hat{\mathbf{x}}(k/k-1) + \mathbf{W}(k)[\mathbf{z}(k) - \mathbf{h}(k/k-1)] \tag{11}$$

$$\mathbf{P}(k/k) = \mathbf{P}(k/k-1) - \mathbf{W}(k)\mathbf{S}(k)\mathbf{W}^T(k) \tag{12}$$

Where

$$\mathbf{S}(k) = \nabla\mathbf{h}_{\mathbf{x}}(k)\mathbf{P}(k/k-1)\nabla^T\mathbf{h}_{\mathbf{x}}(k) + \mathbf{R}(k) \tag{13}$$

2.3 Filter Consistency

The SLAM formulation presented in the previous section represents the posterior as a unimodal Gaussian. Thus the state estimates are parameterized by what is known as the *moments parameterization*. An important ramification of this representation is that not only it represents the current mean $\hat{\mathbf{x}}(k/k)$ but also gives an estimate of the covariance $\hat{\mathbf{P}}(k/k)$, and when the filter is *consistent,* the estimated covariance should match the Mean Square Error of the true distribution. As will be discussed in the following section this is widely used in interpreting EKF based SLAM results.

However a more appropriate measure of consistency when the true state $\mathbf{x}_k$ is known could be arrived at using the normalized estimation error squared (NEES) as defined by (Bar-Shalom et al., 2001),

$$\varepsilon(k) = (\mathbf{x}(k) - \hat{\mathbf{x}}(k/k))^T \mathbf{P}(k/k)^{-1}(\mathbf{x}(k) - \hat{\mathbf{x}}(k/k)) \tag{14}$$

Under the hypothesis that filter is consistent and is linear Gaussian, ε_k is chi-square distributed with n_x degrees of freedom. Where n_x is the dimension of $\mathbf{x}_k$.

$$E[\varepsilon(k)] = n_x \tag{15}$$

Using multiple Monte Carlo simulations to generate N independent samples, the average NEES can be calculated as

$$\bar{\varepsilon}_k = \frac{1}{N}\sum_{i=1}^{N}\varepsilon_{ik} \tag{16}$$

Then under the previous hypothesis $N\bar{\varepsilon}(k)$ will have a chi-square density with Nn_x degrees of freedom. Then the above hypothesis is accepted if

$$\bar{\varepsilon}(k) \in [r_1, r_2] \tag{17}$$

where the *acceptance interval* is determined on a statistical basis.

2.4 An Example

To illustrate the formulation of the standard EKF, lets consider an example where a simple differential driven robot traversing on a 2D plane. The robot is equipped with a sensor capable of making 3D measurements to point features in the environment (Fig. 1). The robot state is defined by $X_r = [x_r \ \ y_r \ \ \varphi_r]^T$, where x_r and y_r denotes location of the robot's rear axle centre with respect to a global coordinate frame and φ_r is the heading with reference to the x-axis of the same coordinate system. Landmarks are modelled as point features, $\mathbf{p}_i = [x_i \ \ y_i \ \ z_i]^T$, i = 1,...,n. The vehicle motion through the environment is modelled as a conventional discrete time process model as in (9).

$$\begin{bmatrix} x_r(k+1) \\ y_r(k+1) \\ \varphi_r(k+1) \end{bmatrix} = \begin{bmatrix} x_r(k) + \Delta T V(k)\cos(\varphi_r(k)) \\ y_r(k) + \Delta T V(k)\sin(\varphi_r(k)) \\ \varphi_r(k) + \Delta T \omega(k) \end{bmatrix} \tag{18}$$

ΔT is the time step, V(k) is the instantaneous velocity and $\omega(k)$ is the instantaneous turn-rate. The observation model can be represented as,

$$Z\ (k+1) = \begin{bmatrix} z_x(k+1) \\ z_y(k+1) \\ z_z(k+1) \end{bmatrix} = \begin{bmatrix} a \\ b \\ z_{fi}(k+1) \end{bmatrix} \tag{19}$$

where

$$a = (x_{fi}(k+1) - x_r(k+1))\cos(\varphi_r(k)) + (y_{fi}(k+1) - y_r(k+1))\sin(\varphi_r(k))$$
$$b = -(x_{fi}(k+1) - x_r(k+1))\sin(\varphi_r(k)) + (y_{fi}(k+1) - y_r(k+1))\cos(\varphi_r(k))$$

It is to be noted that each feature is defined by a point in 3D space, $\mathbf{x}_{fi}(k) = [x_{fi}(k), y_{fi}(k), z_{fi}(k)]^T$.

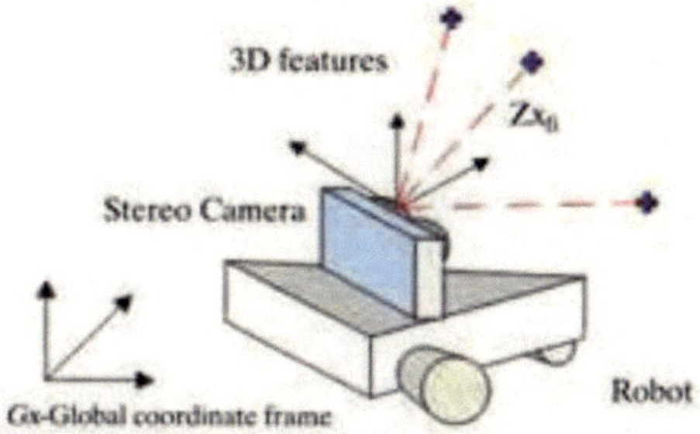

Figure 1. The robot in 3D world coordinates observing a feature in 3D space.

Fig. 2 (a) shows a simulated environment with the path robot has taken amongst the 3D features. Fig. 2 (b) depicts the results of this example implementation on the simulated environment. The three graphs depict the three components of the robot pose. In the top graph of Fig. 2 (b), the middle line represents error between the EKF estimate and the actual value of the x-component of the robot pose against the time. The two outer lines mirroring each other are the 2-standard deviation estimates (2-*sigma*). When the filter is *well tuned* the error lies appropriately bounded within these 2-*sigma* limits. Fig. 2 (c) illustrates a case of filter inconsistency where the filter has become optimistic.

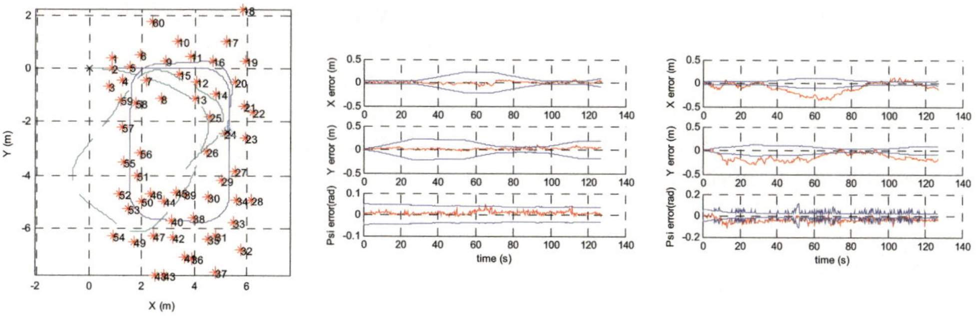

a.) b.) c.)

Figure 2. (a) Simulated environment: solid line – true path, dashed line – odometry path, * - features. (b) State errors with estimated 2-sigma bounds for a well tuned filter (c) An inconsistent filter

3. Stereo Vision

Generally, more precise the sensors used in SLAM more tractable and practical the solution is. Underlying characteristics of the sensor play an important role in determining the scale and practical use of the SLAM algorithm. Sensors such as laser have proven to be very precise in nature and have shown to work well in large environments for extended periods of time (Guivant, 2002; 2003; Wang, 2004). However vision is yet to prove its application in similar environments. In vision, successful implementations to date have used either large baseline stereo cameras (Davison, 1998; Jung, 2004), camera configurations with more than two cameras(Se et al., 2002) providing refined observations or single camera bearing only (Kwok and Dissanayake, 2003; 2004) methods. Principal aim of this section is to asses the performance of a small baseline binocular stereo camera equipped with wide angle lenses in the context of robotic SLAM.

3.1 The Sensor

Stereopsis or Stereoscopic vision is the process of perceiving depth or distances to objects in the environment. As a strand of computer vision research stereo vision algorithms have advanced noticeably in the past few decades to a point where semi-commercial products are available as *off the shelf* devices. However a more augmented approach is needed to realize a sensor useful in SLAM. Following list is an attempt to enumerate the essential components of such a sensor in the context of SLAM.

(1.) Stereo camera-hardware for acquiring stereo images (2.) Calibration information-contains intrinsic and extrinsic information about the camera necessary for correcting image distortion and depth calculation (3.) Interest point (features) selection algorithm-mechanism through witch naturally occurring features in the environment are selected for integration in the state vector (4.) Feature tracking algorithm-Image based mechanism used for data association (5.) Stereo correspondence algorithm-estimates the disparity at corresponding pixels (6.) Filtering-mechanisms used to remove spurious data. A schematic of the components along with interactions amongst each other is outlined in Fig. 3.

3.2 Sensor Error Analysis

As mentioned in the beginning of the chapter characteristics of a sensor dictates the limits of its applications. In the following sections a discussion of an empirical study of the particular sensor of interest is given based on two representative experiments conducted. It was found that even though quantitative error analyses of stereo, based on static cameras are available in the literature they do not necessarily represent the effects of a moving camera. This study fills a void on specific characterisation of noise performance of small baseline large field of view camera in respect to SLAM. In this context several robotic mapping experiments were carried out in order to understand the behaviour of sensor noise.

From previous section on camera modelling the triplet $\mathbf{z} = [u, v, d]^T$ forms the principal observation $\mathbf{z}$ by the sensor. Where (u,v) being the image coordinates of a feature and d is the disparity. Assuming that the errors in the observations to be additive $\mathbf{z}$ can be written as,

$$\mathbf{z} = \mathbf{z}_{true} + \mathbf{v}(\zeta, \mathbf{z}_{true}) \tag{20}$$

Where $\mathbf{z}_{true}$ being the true state of the observation and $\mathbf{v}$ being the additive noise component dependent on the sensor characteristics ξ and on the true state itself as will be shown empirically later. Modelling and understanding the behaviour of $\mathbf{v}$ is the subject of discussion in sections 3.4 and 3.5. In section 3.6 the discussion continues on modelling the error behaviour of the projected form $\mathbf{z}_c$ of this observation in to the 3D coordinate frame.

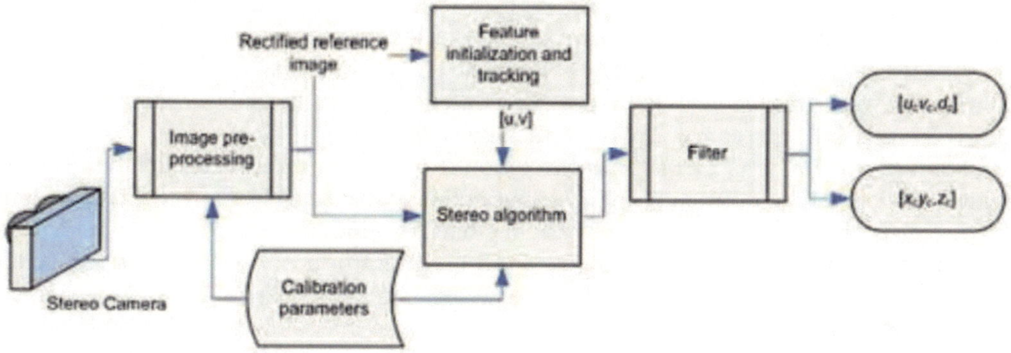

Figure 3. The vision system for a SLAM implementation

3.3 Mapping Experiments

References are made to the two experiments described below in the following sections.
Experiment 1- A pioneer robot mounted with the stereo camera was moved on a controlled path while capturing set of images at each 0.02m interval. The feature selection algorithm was allowed to select 30 features at the beginning of the sequence. The tracking algorithm attempts to track these features between consecutive images.
Experiment 2- Again the robot was moved on a controlled path while observing artificial features laid on a large vertical planar surface. Features were laid out so as to cover the whole field of view of the cameras. A SICK laser was used to maintain parallel alignment between the camera and the surface and to measure the nominal distance between the robot and the surface. Robot was moved in 0.05m increments from a distance of 6m to 1m.
In this experiment 20 features were initialised at each stop and were then tracked for 29 consecutive images. For analysis of this data, at least 9 features were selected manually covering the widest possible area of the planar surface at each stop point. This set of features would then represent the expected sensor behaviour at the given distance.

a.) b.) c.) d.)

Figure 4. Rectified images overlaid with features at (a) 5.4 m (b) 3.9 m (c) 2.4 m (d) 0.9 m

3.4 Uncertainty in Disparity

In order to establish an error model for the disparity an analyses based on the finite data series from experiment 2 was performed. The data presents a unique perspective on the variance in disparity as observations are made at varying distances. In this case an approximate range between 1m and 6m inclusively. This depth range translates to an effective disparity range approximately between 1 and 15 pixels. The stereo correlation algorithm is set to search for a pixel range between 1 and 32.

Following general statistical procedures it is possible to estimate a set of parameters that represent the disparity observation process based on this finite sequence of data. Fig. 5 (a) shows the overall variation in disparity. This is based on the calculated disparity at each individual feature that were manually selected in each initial image combined with all the points that were tracked consecutively are pooled together by subtracting the disparity means corresponding to each individual tracking sequence.

Although by the analysis of the autocorrelation it is easily established that the process is 'white' the general assumption of the distribution being Gaussian is an oversimplification of the true distribution. Especially in the case of small baseline cameras and wide-angle lenses this variation is a complex combination of local biases introduced in the image rectification process and stereo correlation mismatches undetected by the various filtering mechanisms. The distortions introduced by wide-angle lenses induce biases at each pixel in the image. Even though they are constant it is extremely difficult to accurately measure the individual component at pixel level. Also the area correlation algorithm used to estimate the disparities itself is prone to gross errors depending on the construct of the environment in which the images are captured.

In order to understand these subtle variations it is best to analyse the variation in disparity at different depths independently. Fig. 5 (b) shows the variation in observed disparity against the expected disparity. Again the data from experiment 2 are used in the analysis. In this the disparities of the features selected at each distance along with the consecutively tracked points are pooled together and the resulting combined data are subtracted from the population mean.

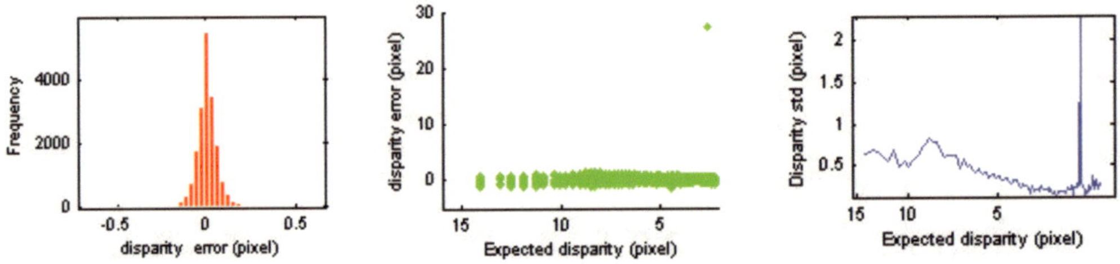

a.) b.) c.)

Figure 5. Disparity error. (a) Distribution (b) Zero mean error distribution with depth (c) Zero mean standard deviation (log scale). The spike in standard deviation is due to a stereo mismatch that was not detected by any of the heuristics applied in stereo correspondence algorithm

Several observations can be made. Firstly, data still contains many visible outliers that are difficult to be eliminated by the various smoothing operations. Secondly a rather intuitive observation is the correlation in the variance of the disparity distribution with the expected disparity. As would be expected variance is smaller for features seen from afar and it increases gradually with nearby features. For faraway features the disparity is small and also the discriminatory information contained within the correlation area is higher compared to a closer observation. This is especially true for environments where lack of texture persists. This gives a higher confidence to the disparity values estimated for features afar as opposed to ones closer. This is a better interpretation for the variance in disparity and based on this interpretation it is better to assume a varying disparity standard deviation correlated with the estimated disparity value as opposed to the general practice of assuming a constant disparity standard deviation. The observation standard deviation is shown in Fig. 5 (c).

It is difficult to estimate an exact relationship between the disparity variation with the estimated disparity. Thus an empirically generated curve based on the results shown in Fig. 5 (b) is used. It was also observed that the variance estimated thus is slightly higher than the one shown above in Fig. 5 (a). This stems from the fact that the local biases are present in the data shown in Fig. 5 (b). This can be illustrated by scrutinising the local distributions present in the disparity data corresponding to each feature location at a given depth. Fig. 8 shows an example local distributions contributing to the overall distribution at a given depth. As can be noticed there are independent local distributions dispersed from the true expected mean. These are a combination of local biases in the image, stereo mismatches and any misalignments of the stereo hardware and the reference system. For practical purposes correcting these errors is difficult and an all encompassing error model is thus adapted.

3.3 Uncertainty in *u* and *v*

In order to model the errors in *u* and *v* for SLAM a dynamic camera error model needs to be studied which would include the behaviour of the tracking algorithm as well as other dynamics involved with the camera motion. From experiment 1 and 2 it is possible to extract a representative set of data for this purpose. Again as discussed for the case of disparity error, u and v also carries components of local bias due to distortion effects and other misalignments. In addition the effects of the feature tracker also contribute when the augmented sensor representation is considered.

For this analysis only a single image is considered at each depth. These images are then assembled from a depth of 1m to 6m. 16 features covering the entire image plane are then initialised in the image corresponding to 1m depth and are then consecutively tracked through to image at 6m depth. This while tracking a set of features at fixed locations in space will map to varying *u,v* coordinates. This essentially captures the overall behaviour of *u,v* in the entire image plane.

Fig. 6 shows the results for both parameters where cumulative data for each point is subtracted by the expected values at each point and then combined together. Qualitatively these results resemble Gaussian distributions. However it is possible to observe various artefacts appearing in the tails of the distributions indicating that a considerable amount of spurious data is present for the reasons discussed earlier. This spuriousness in u,v and d pose considerable challenges to a successful implementation of a SLAM algorithm. Various issues arising from these observations are discussed in the next section

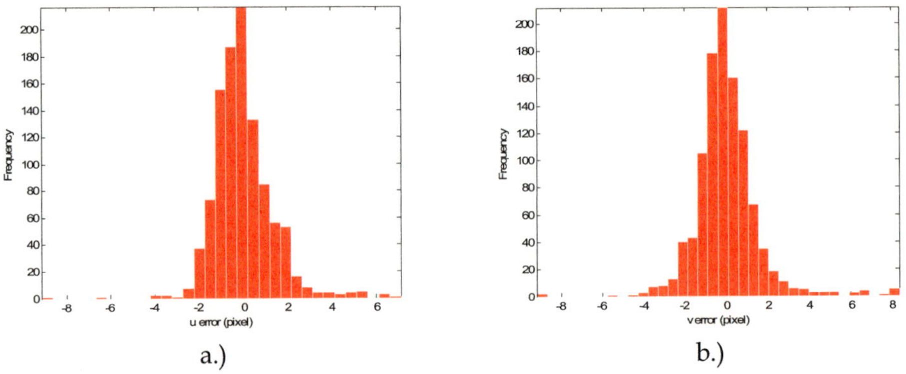

Figure 6. Error distribution (a) in u with standard deviation = 1.34 (b) in v with standard deviation = 1.53

4. Issues and Solutions

Primary goal of this chapter is to elucidate several theoretical and practical issues that have been noted during many implementations of stereo vision based SLAM. In this section a series of such issues that contributes to filter divergence, increase in computational burden and/or complete failure of the filter are illustrated. In each sub-section an issue is presented first with its effects on the algorithm and then possible solutions in averting the consequences are discussed.

4.1 Limited Field of View

One of the most fundamental issues that plague vision based SLAM is the limited field of view (FOV) of the sensor. When compared to traditional sensors like laser and radar the FOV of vision sensors are 20~40% narrower. Even though the 2D structure of the sensor affords more information the narrow FOV limits the ability to observe features for prolonged periods, a desirable requirement to reduce error bounds in the state estimations – a corollary of the results proven in (Dissanayake et al., 2001). As noted in several works(Bailey et al., 2006; Huang and Dissanayake, 2006), notably the increase in heading uncertainty tends to increase the possibility of filter divergence. This has been observed in our implementations, especially in confined office like environments where many of the features observed vanishing from the FOV rapidly and re-observation of them delayed until a large loop is closed.

Slight improvement to this situation is brought through the introduction of wide angle lenses. However, the choice is a compromise between the sensor accuracy and the FOV. Wide angle lenses suffer from noticeable lens distortion (Fig. 7 (a)) and the rectification (Fig. 7 (b)) process introduces errors. One undesirable effect of using such lenses is the local biases in disparity calculation. To illustrate this consider a static camera observing a perfect plane which is parallel to the camera x-y plane. Disparity results of observing several features on this plane are plotted in Fig. 8. As can be seen the biases at various points are noticeable and are high as 2-pixels. This at most violates the fundamental assumption of Gaussian noise model in SLAM.In order to alleviate this issue it is necessary to estimate and apply radial distortion parameters in the rectification process. Also in severe cases, or when higher accuracy is demanded look-up tables are suggested.

Figure 7.An image from a wide angle lens. a.) raw. b.) rectified

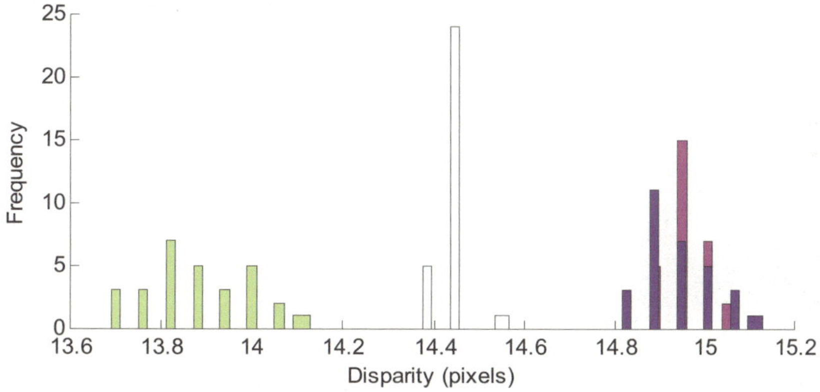

Figure 8. Local biases in disparity (Expected mean disparity is 14.7)

4.2 Number of Features

Each feature added to the filter contributes new information. However with each new feature added to the state vector increases the computational burden. Even with sophisticated algorithms available computational complexity of SLAM still remains high and grows with each added state. Also depending on the data association mechanism used the ambiguity of features could increase leading to false association. This necessitates a reliable ranking mechanism (Shi and Tomasi, 1994) to optimize the number of features processed per image. The ranking criteria should not only look at which are "good features to track" but also its viability as a 3-D observation. Therefore it is possible to integrate other stereo confidence measures like uniqueness in to the ranking mechanism. Such an integrated approach alleviates selecting features that are ineffective as 3D measurements.

Another common issue seen especially in indoors with highly structured built environments is the lapses in suitably textured surfaces needed to generate reliable features and depth measurements. In extreme cases we have observed heavy reliance on other sensors such as odometry in filters. This is a limitation on point feature based implementations and alternative feature forms such as lines and curves would be more appropriate depending on the environment in which the application operates.

The minimum number of features per image is also dictated partially by the environment the application operates as well as the accuracy of the stereo algorithm. As shown earlier the depth accuracy correlates with the depth measured. Thus it is necessary to observe both features that are closer to the camera for short term translational accuracy as well as ones that are further away for long term rotational accuracy. An issue with most feature selectors is that they tend to cluster around small patches of highly textured areas in a scene. This may or may not result in satisfying the condition stated above. In our experience the best value for minimal number of features is thus selected by repeated experimentations in the intended environment.

4.3 Spurious Features

Spurious features occur not only due to structure (e.g. Occlusion) but also due to gross errors in stereo calculations. For instance in Fig. 9 (a) the pole marked with the arrow and the horizontal edge of the partition in the foreground are two distinct disjoint enteritis. However on the image plane the apparent intersection of the two edges is a positive feature location. Such occlusions results in physically non existent features. These features are catastrophic in a SLAM implementation. A possible method was discussed in (Shi and Tomasi, 1994) in identifying such occlusions by a measure of *dissimilarity*.

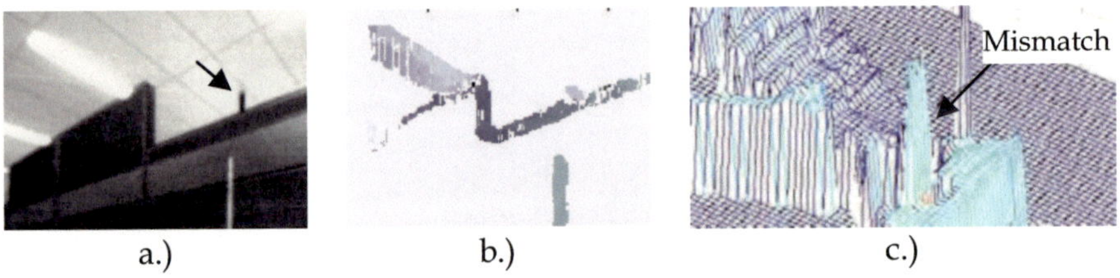

Figure 9. Spurious observations. (a) A rectified image showing several edge profiles. (b) Disparity image (c) Close-up view of the depth profile with a mismatch (see discussion for details)

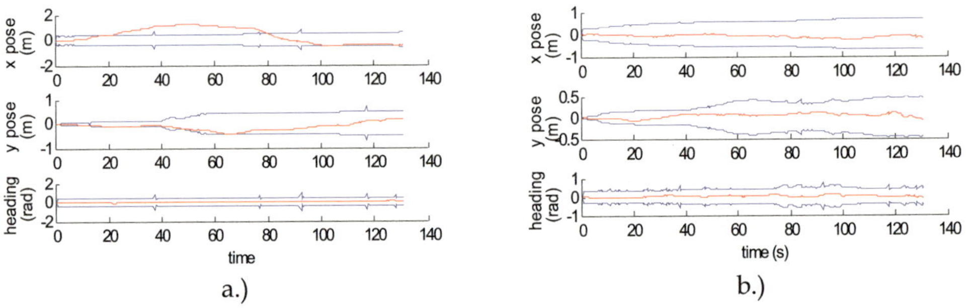

Figure 10. Robot pose error with 2-*sigma* error bounds (a) effects of spurious data (b.) with the RanSaC like filter applied

Depending on the image composition it is possible to generate occasional mismatches (Fig. 9(c)) in stereo correspondence. Most stereo algorithms include multiple heuristics (Konolige, 1997) to alleviate this issue. However it is still advisable to include a statistical validation gate (Cox, 1993) for the occasional mismatch that is not filtered by such heuristics.

A third set of spurious features were observed due to feature tracking mechanisms used. These features tend to drift arbitrarily in the image plane. Such features not only are harder to detect by conventional statistical validation gates but also tend to contribute to filter inconsistencies. A solution to such spurious features based on the RanSaC (Fischler and Bolles, 1981) algorithm was discussed in (Herath et al., 2006b). Fig. 10 shows SLAM results for a real data set with (Fig. 10 (b)) and without (Fig. 10 (a)) the RanSaC like filter while maintaining other filter parameters identical. In this instance the consistency has improved, however, inflated observation noise parameters are used in both cases to accommodate the nonlinearities (see 4.5) in the observation model.

4.4 Static vs. Dynamic Noise Parameters

Most researchers tend to use static noise parameters in their SLAM implementations. These are the noise parameters obtained by observing static features through a static camera. However a more realistic set of values can be obtained by estimating these parameters through data obtained by a moving camera especially in the same application environment. An experiment of this nature was discussed in (Herath et al., 2006a). This encompasses not only the error variation in camera, but also the error variations in the feature tracker and other difficult to quantify dynamic factors. This invariably tends to increase the stereo noise parameters and in some cases is much higher than the theoretical sub-pixel accuracies quoted by stereo algorithms.

Another aspect of noise parameters was illustrated in section 3.2. For a better estimate of the noise parameters it is possible to utilise the empirical knowledge of variation in disparity standard deviation with measured depth. Also in (Jung and Lacroix, 2003) presented another observation, where the variation in disparity standard deviation is correlated with the curvature of the similarity score curve at its peak. This knowledge can enhance the quality of the estimation process.

4.5 Nonlinearity Issues

Realistic SLAM problems are inherently non linear. While EKF implementations are shown to be able to handle this nonlinearity an emerging debate in recent years suggest that the nonlinearity could lead to filter inconsistency(Bailey et al., 2006; Huang and Dissanayake, 2006; Julier and Uhlmann, 2001).

These studies concentrate on eventual failure of the filter in large scale and/or long term SLAM implementations. On the other hand the few stereo vision based EKF solutions present in the literature altogether neglects the filter consistency analysis. It is well known that the standard geometric projection equations used in stereo vision are highly nonlinear and suffers from inherent bias (Sibley et al., 2006; 2005). It is imperative then that an analysis is carried out to estimate the effects of this nonlinearity in the context of EKF SLAM. For this reason a set of Monte Carlo simulations were conducted and were analysed using the NEES criterion presented in section 2.3. The simulated environment presented in section 2.4 (Fig. 2 (a)) was used throughout these Monte Carlo runs. N [=50] runs were carried out for each implementation with [2.36, 3.72] being the 95% *probability concentration region* for $\bar{\varepsilon}(k)$ since the dimensionality of the robot pose is 3.

In Fig. 11 (a) the average NEES for the example in 2.4 is shown to be well bounded. This indicates that for the small loop considered in this example a standard EKF yields consistent results. For this simulation, the observation noise ($\mathbf{R}(k)$) has components

(σ_x=σ_y=σ_z=0.05m) and process noise (**Q**(k)) will remain at (σ_v=0.05m/s,σ_w=5deg/s) for all the simulations.

In the second simulation while adhering to the previous formulation, the observations are now subjected to the geometric transformations of a standard stereo vision sensor.

$$x = \frac{Bf}{d}; y = \frac{-Bu}{d}; z = \frac{-Bv}{d} \tag{21}$$

Where B is the camera baseline and f the focal length. As discussed in the previous section Gaussian noise can be assumed for (u,v,d) and a transformed noise matrix must be used (Herath et al., 2006a) for **R**(k). For all the simulations following noise values (σ_u=1.34,σ_v=1.53,σ_d=0.65) estimated from experimental analysis were used. The average NEES results for this simulation are presented in Fig. 11 (b). The unacceptably large values for the statistics indicate that a straight forward SLAM implementation does not yield consistent results. An important parameter in this experiment is the small baseline (B) used. At a nominal 9cm this corresponds to a commercially available stereo head on which most of our real experiments are based on. It is possible to show through simulation that lager baselines give rise to lower nonlinearity effects. However it remains a key factor for most stereo heads used in indoor and outdoor scenarios.

To further illustrate this phenomenon, consider the Gaussian random variable $[d,u]^T$ (only two components used for clarity) representing the disparity and horizontal image coordinate for a given feature at $x_c = 10m$ and $y_c = 1m$. With B =0.09m and f = 150 pixels, this translates to mean disparity, d of 1.32 pixels and mean u of 15 pixels. A Monte Carlo simulation can be carried out using (21) to transform Gaussian distributed $[d,u]^T$ into $[z_x, z_y]^T$. Fig. 12 (a) and (b) show the resulting distributions with 0.09m and 0.5m as baselines respectively. This clearly indicates the non Gaussian nature of the transformed observations when a small baseline camera is used (Fig. 12 (a)). The smaller the baseline is the shorter the range is at which the nonlinear effect manifest.

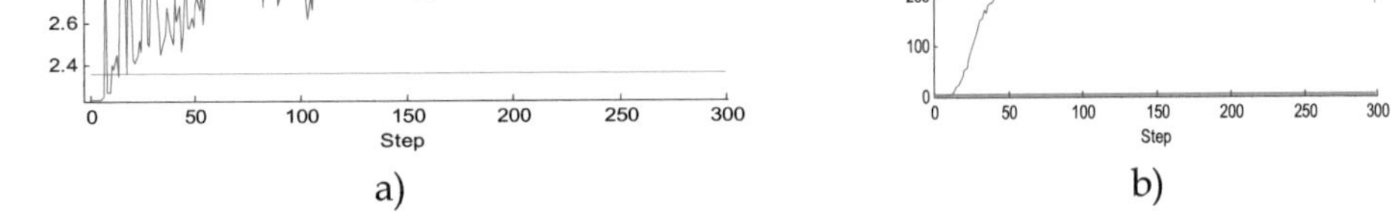

Figure 11. Average NEES of the robot pose (a) Standard EKF (b) Standard EKF with stereo observations

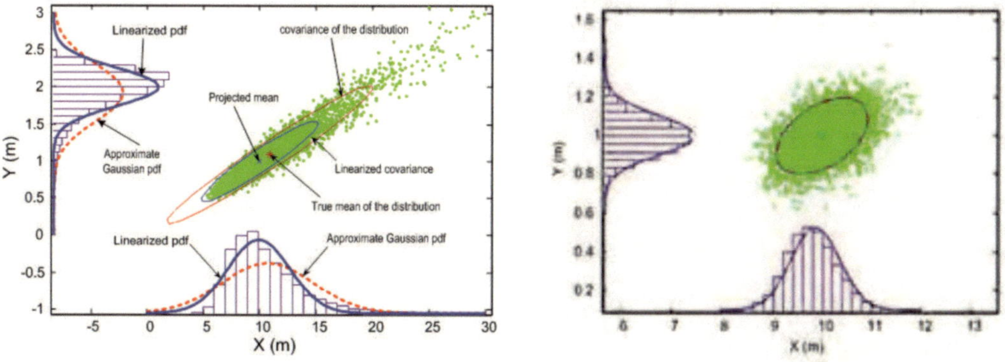

a.) b.)

Figure 12. Errors in projective mapping (a) B=0.09m (b) B=0.5m, linearized and approximated Gaussians are overlapping

A different choice of observation model is tested that yields improved results. As shown above the main cause for the inconsistency is due to the highly nonlinear projective mapping. It is possible to derive a formulation where the principal observation becomes (u,v,d) instead of the widely used (x,y,z) as follows. (Compare this with (19))

$$\hat{\mathbf{z}}(k+1) = \begin{bmatrix} \hat{z}_u(k+1) \\ \hat{z}_v(k+1) \\ \hat{z}_d(k+1) \end{bmatrix} = \frac{f}{x}\begin{bmatrix} -y & -z & B \end{bmatrix}^T \tag{22}$$

where

$$x = (\hat{x}_{fi}(k+1) - \hat{x}_r(k+1))\cos(\phi(k)) + (\hat{y}_{fi}(k+1) - \hat{y}_r(k+1))\sin(\phi(k))$$

$$y = -(\hat{x}_{fi}(k+1) - \hat{x}_r(k+1))\sin(\phi(k)) + (\hat{y}_{fi}(k+1) - \hat{y}_r(k+1))\cos(\phi(k))$$

$$z = \hat{z}_{fi}(k+1)$$

This alleviates necessity of the linearized transformation of the noise matrix ($\mathbf{R}(k)$) as measurements are well represented with Gaussian models. Simulation results with the new observation model for average NEES are presented in Fig. 13 (a). Although the improvement over previous model is apparent, filter still remains optimistic. Finally the unscented Kalman filter (UKF) (Julier and Uhlmann, 2004) is implemented with the previous observation model. The UKF performs a *derivative free* transform of the states resulting in better estimates. UKF is shown to work well with highly non linear systems. However the Monte Carlo simulation results indicate (Fig. 13 (b)) that the improvement against consistency is minimal.

These observations lead us to the belief that standard SLAM implementations could yield inconsistent results even for comparatively smaller loops given small baseline stereo cameras are used. An observation hitherto has not been studied. Current solutions for this issue remains at either in use of wider baseline cameras or in the implementation of small loops with sub map (Williams, 2001) like ideas. Better consistency could also be expected by improving the overall noise performance of the vision system. This includes improving the stereo correspondence, resolution of the images as well as improving the stability of the mobile platform.

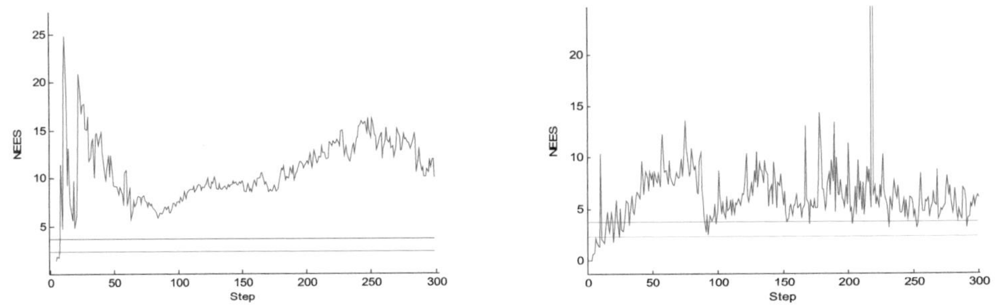

a) b

Figure 13. Average NEES of the robot pose (a) (*uvd*)-observation model (b) UKF

5. Conclusion

In this chapter we have made an attempt to analyse the issues in stereo vision based SLAM and proposed plausible solutions. Correct sensor modelling is vital in any SLAM implementation. Therefore, we have analyzed the stereo vision sensor behaviour experimentally to understand the noise characteristics and statistics. It was verified that the stereo observations in its natural form (i.e. [*u,v,d*]) can safely be assumed to represent Gaussian distributions. Then several SLAM implementation strategies were discussed using stereo vision. Issues related to limited field of view of the sensor, number of features, spurious features, noise parameters and nonlinearity in the observation model were discussed. It was shown that the filter inconsistency is mainly due to inherent nonlinearity presence in the small baseline stereo vision sensor. Since UKF is more capable in handling nonlinearity issues than that of EKF, an UKF SLAM implementation was tested against inconsistency. However, it too leads to inconsistencies. This shows that even with implementations that circumvent the critical linearization mechanism in standard EKF SLAM as in UKF, the nonlinearity issue in the stereo vision based SLAM can not be resolved. In order to address the filter inconsistency a more elegant solution is currently being researched based on smoothing algorithms which shows promising results.

In conclusion this chapter dwelt on some obscure issues pertaining to stereo vision SLAM and work being done in solving such issues.

6. References

Bailey, Tim, Juan Nieto, Jose Guivant, Michael Stevens and Eduardo Nebot. (2006). Consistency of the EKF-SLAM Algorithm. In *International Conference on Intelligent Robots and Systems* (IROS 2006). Beijing, China.

Bar-Shalom, Yaakow, X.-Rong Li and Thiagalingam Kirubarajan. (2001). *Estimation with Applications to Tracking and Navigation*. Somerset, New Jersey: Wiley InterScience.

Clark, S. and G. Dissanayake. (1999). Simultaneous localisation and map building using millimetre wave radar to extract natural features. In *IEEE International Conference on Robotics and Automation*: IEEE.

Cox, Ingemar J. (1993). A review of statistical data association techniques for motion correspondence. *International Journal of Computer Vision* 10(1):53-66.

Davison, A.J. and D.W. Murray. (2002). Simultaneous localization and map-building using active vision. *IEEE Transactions on Pattern Analysis and Machine Intelligence* 24(7):865 - 880

Davison, Andrew J. (1998). Mobile Robot Navigation Using Active Vision. *Thesis*: University of Oxford.

Davison, Andrew J., Yolanda Gonzalez Cid and Nobuyuki Kita. (2004). Real-Time 3D Slam with Wide-Angle Vision. In *IFAC Symposium on Intelligent Autonomous Vehicles.* Lisbon.

Dissanayake, M.W.M.Gamini, Paul Newman, Steven Clark, Hugh F. Durrant-Whyte and M. Csorba. (2001). A Solution to the Simultaneous Localization and Map Building (SLAM) Problem. *IEEE TRANSACTIONS ON ROBOTICS AND AUTOMATION* 17(3):229-241.

Fischler, Martin A. and Robert C. Bolles. (1981). Random Sample Consensus: A paradigm for model fitting with applications to image analysis and automated cartography. *Communications of the ACM* 24(6):381 - 395.

Guivant, Jose E. (2002). Efficient Simultaneous Localization and Mapping in Large Environments. *Thesis.* Sydney: University of Sydney.

Guivant, Jose and Eduardo Nebot. (2002). *Simultaneous Localization and Map Building: Test case for Outdoor Applications.* Sydney: Australian Center for Field Robotics, Mechanical and Mechatronic Engineering, The University of Sydney.

Guivant, Jose, Juan Nieto, Favio Masson and Eduardo Nebot. (2003). Navigation and Mapping in Large Unstructured Environments. *International Journal of Robotics Research* 23(4/5): 449-472.

Herath, D. C., K. R. S. Kodagoda and Gamini Dissanayake. (2006a). Modeling Errors in Small Baseline Stereo for SLAM. In *The 9 th International Conference on Control, Automation, Robotics and Vision* (ICARCV 2006). Singapore.

Herath, D.C., Sarath Kodagoda and G. Dissanayake. (2006b). Simultaneous Localisation and Mapping: A Stereo Vision Based Approach. In *IEEE/RSJ International Conference on Intelligent Robots and Systems* (IROS 2006). Beijing, China: IEEE.

Huang, Shoudong and Gamini Dissanayake. (2006). Convergence Analysis for Extended Kalman Filter based SLAM. In *IEEE International Conference on Robotics and Automation* (ICRA 2006). Orlando, Florida.

Julier, S. J. and J. K. Uhlmann. (2001). A counter example to the theory of simultaneous localization and map building. In *IEEE International Conference on Robotics and Automation,* ICRA 2001.

Julier, S. J. and J. K. Uhlmann. (2004). Unscented filtering and nonlinear estimation. *Proceedings of the IEEE* 92(3):401-422.

Jung, I.K. (2004). Simultaneous localization and mapping in 3D environments with stereovision. *Thesis.* Toulouse: Institut National Polytechnique.

Jung, Il-Kyun and Simon Lacroix. (2003). High resolution terrain mapping using low altitude aerial stereo imagery. In *Ninth IEEE International Conference on Computer Vision* (ICCV'03).

Konolige, Kurt. (1997). Small Vision Systems: Hardware and Implementation. In *Eighth International Symposium on Robotics Research.*

Kwok, N. M. and G. Dissanayake. (2003). Bearing-only SLAM in Indoor Environments Using a Modified Particle Filter. In *Australasian Conference on Robotics & Automation*, eds. Jonathan Roberts and Gordon Wyeth. Brisbane: The Australian Robotics and Automation Association Inc.

Kwok, N. M. and G. Dissanayake. (2004). An efficient multiple hypothesis filter for bearing-only SLAM. In *2004 IEEE/RSJ International Conference on Intelligent Robots and Systems* (IROS 2004)

Kwok, N. M., G. Dissanayake and Q. P. Ha. (2005). Bearing-only SLAM Using a SPRT Based Gaussian Sum Filter. In *IEEE International Conference on Robotics and Automation.* ICRA 2005.

Se, Stephen, David Lowe and Jim Little. (2002). Mobile Robot Localization And Mapping with Uncertainty using Scale-Invariant Visual Landmarks. *International Journal of Robotic Research* 21(8).

Shi, Jianbo and Carlo Tomasi. (1994). Good Features toTrack. In *IEEE Computer Society Conference on Computer Vision and Pattern Recognition* (CVPR '94) Seattle: IEEE.

Sibley, G., G. Sukhatme and L. Matthies. (2006). The Iterated Sigma Point Filter with Applications to Long Range Stereo. In *Robotics: Science and Systems* II. Cambridge, USA.

Sibley, Gabe, Larry Matthies and Gaurav Sukhatme. (2005). Bias Reduction and Filter Convergence for Long Range Stereo. In *12th International Symposium of Robotics Research* (ISRR 2005). San Francisco, CA, USA.

Wang, Chieh-Chih. (2004). Simultaneous Localization, Mapping and Moving Object Tracking. *Thesis*. Pittsburgh, PA 15213: Carnegie Mellon University.

Williams, Stefan Bernard. (2001). Efficient Solutions to Autonomous Mapping and Navigation Problems. *Thesis*. Sydney: The University of Sydney.

30

Shortest Path Homography-Based Visual Control for Differential Drive Robots

G. López-Nicolás, C. Sagüés and J.J. Guerrero [1]
Universidad de Zaragoza
Spain

1 Introduction

It is generally accepted that machine vision is one of the most important sensory modalities for navigation purposes. Visual control, also called visual servoing, is a very extensive and mature field of research where many important contributions have been presented in the last decade [Malis et al.,1999, Corke and Hutchinson, 2001, Conticelli and Allotta, 2001, Tsakiris et al., 1998, Ma et al., 1999]. Two interesting surveys on this topic are [De Souza and Kak, 2002] and [Hutchinson et al., 1996]. In this work we present a new visual servoing approach for mobile robots with a fixed monocular system on board. The idea of visual servoing is used here in the sense of homing, where the desired robot position is defined by a target image taken at that position. Using the images taken during the navigation the robot is led to the target.

A traditional approach is to perform the motion by using the epipolar geometry [Basri et al., 1999, Rives, 2000, Lopez-Nicolas et al., 2006]. These approaches have as drawback that the estimation of the epipolar geometry becomes ill conditioned with short baseline or planar scenes, which are usual in human environments. A natural way to overcome this problem is using the homography model. In [Malis and Chaumette, 2000] it is proposed a method based on the estimation of the homography matrix related to a virtual plane attached to an object. This method provides a more stable estimation when the epipolar geometry degenerates. In [Benhimane et al., 2005] it is presented a visual tracking system for car platooning by estimating the homography between a selected reference template attached to the leading vehicle. A significant issue with monocular camera-based vision systems is the lack of depth information. In [Fang et al., 2005] it is proposed the asymptotic regulation of the position and orientation of a mobile robot by exploiting homography-based visual servo control strategies, where the unknown time-varying depth information is related to a constant depth-related parameter.

These homography-based methods usually require the homography decomposition, which is not a trivial issue. Two examples of approaches which do not use the decomposition of the homography are [Sagues and Guerrero, 2005] which is based on a 2D homography and [Benhimane and Malis, 2006] which presents an uncalibrated approach for manipulators. We present a novel homography-based approach by performing the control directly on the

[1]This work was supported by projects DPI2006-07928, IST-1-045062-URUS-STP.

elements of the homography matrix. This approach, denoted as "*Shortest Path Control*", is based on the design of a specific robot trajectory which consists in following a straight line towards the target. This motion planning allows to define a control law decoupling rotation and translation by using the homography elements. This approach needs neither the homography decomposition nor depth estimation. In this work we have developed three similar methods based on the particular selection of the homography elements. Each method is suitable for different situations.
The chapter is divided as follows, Section 2 presents the homography model developing its elements as a function of the system parameters to be used in the design of the controllers. Section 3 presents the *Shortest Path Control* with three different methods based on the elements of the homography. Sections 4 and 5 present the stability analysis of the controllers and the experimental results respectively. Section 6 gives the conclusions.

2. Homography Based Model

The general pinhole camera model considers a calibration matrix defined as

$$\mathbf{K} = \begin{bmatrix} \alpha_x & s & x_0 \\ 0 & \alpha_y & y_0 \\ 0 & 0 & 1 \end{bmatrix}, \tag{1}$$

where α_x and α_y are the focal length of the camera in pixel units in the x and y directions respectively; s is the skew parameter and (x_0, y_0) are the coordinates of the principal point. We have that $\alpha_x = f\, m_x$ and $\alpha_y = f\, m_y$, where f is the focal length and m_x, m_y are the number of pixels per distance unit. In practice, we assume that the principal point is in the centre of the image ($x_0=0$, $y_0=0$) and that there is no skew ($s=0$).
A 3D point in the world can be represented in the projective plane with homogeneous coordinates as $\mathbf{p}=(x,y,1)^T$. A projective transformation $\mathbf{H}$ exists from matched points belonging to a plane in such a way that $\mathbf{p}_2=\mathbf{H}\,\mathbf{p}_1$. The homography between the current and target image can be computed from the matched points, and a robust method like RANSAC should be used to consider the existence of outliers [Hartley and Zisserman, 2004]. Taking advantage of the planar motion constraint, the homography can be computed from three correspondences instead of four, reducing the processing time.
Let us suppose two images obtained with the same camera whose projection matrixes in a common reference system are $\mathbf{P}_1=\mathbf{K}[\mathbf{I}\,|\,0]$ and $\mathbf{P}_2=\mathbf{K}[\mathbf{R}\,|\,-\mathbf{Rc}]$, being $\mathbf{R}$ the camera rotation and $\mathbf{c}$ the translation between the optical centres of the two cameras. A homography $\mathbf{H}$ can be related to camera motion (Figure 1a) in such a way that

$$\mathbf{H} = \mathbf{K}\left(\mathbf{R} - \mathbf{t}\frac{\mathbf{n}^T}{d}\right)\mathbf{K}^{-1} = \mathbf{K}\left(\mathbf{R} + \mathbf{Rc}\frac{\mathbf{n}^T}{d}\right)\mathbf{K}^{-1} = \mathbf{KR}\left(\mathbf{I} + \mathbf{c}\frac{\mathbf{n}^T}{d}\right)\mathbf{K}^{-1} \tag{2}$$

where $\mathbf{n}=(n_x, n_y, n_z)^T$ is the normal to the plane that generates the homography and d is the distance between the plane and the origin of the global reference.
We consider a mobile robot in planar motion (Figure 1b). In this case the robot position is defined by the state vector (x, z, ϕ) and the planar motion constraint gives:

$$\mathbf{R} = \begin{bmatrix} \cos\phi & 0 & \sin\phi \\ 0 & 1 & 0 \\ -\sin\phi & 0 & \cos\phi \end{bmatrix}, \quad \mathbf{c} = (x,\, 0,\, z)^T. \tag{3}$$

Taking this into account, the homography corresponding to a planar motion scheme can be written as

$$\mathbf{H} = \begin{bmatrix} h_{11} & h_{12} & h_{13} \\ 0 & 1 & 0 \\ h_{31} & h_{32} & h_{33} \end{bmatrix}. \tag{4}$$

The second row of the matrix will be ignored in the design of the control law as it does not give useful information. Developing expression (2) we obtain the homography elements as a function of the parameters involved:

$$\begin{aligned} h_{11} &= \cos\phi + (x\cos\phi + z\sin\phi)\tfrac{n_x}{d} \\ h_{12} &= \tfrac{\alpha_x}{\alpha_y}(x\cos\phi + z\sin\phi)\tfrac{n_y}{d} \\ h_{13} &= \alpha_x\left(\sin\phi + (x\cos\phi + z\sin\phi)\tfrac{n_z}{d}\right) \\ h_{31} &= \tfrac{1}{\alpha_x}\left(-\sin\phi + (-x\sin\phi + z\cos\phi)\tfrac{n_x}{d}\right) \\ h_{32} &= \tfrac{1}{\alpha_y}(-x\sin\phi + z\cos\phi)\tfrac{n_y}{d} \\ h_{33} &= \cos\phi + (-x\sin\phi + z\cos\phi)\tfrac{n_z}{d} \end{aligned} \tag{5}$$

The analysis of these homography elements will lead to the control law design. After computing the homography from the image point matches it has to be normalized. We normalize by dividing $\mathbf{H}/h_{22}$, given that h_{22} is never zero due to the planar motion constraint.

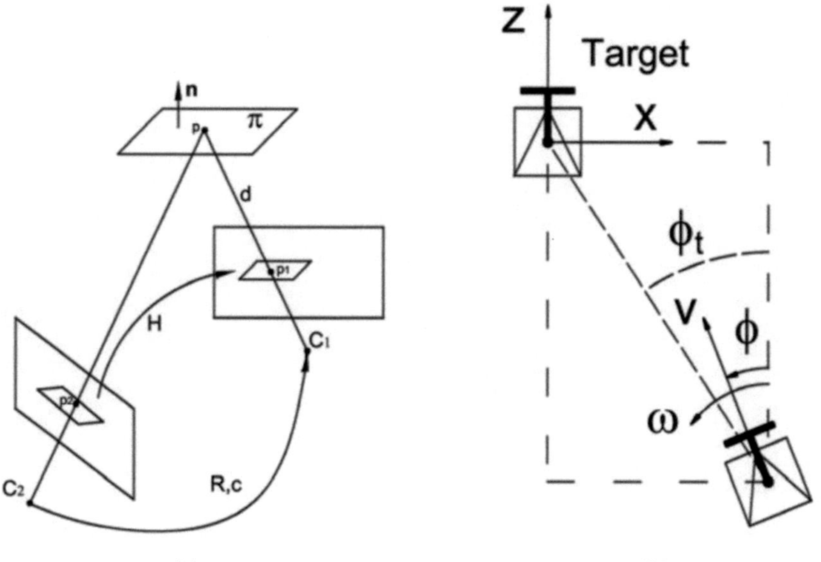

(a) (b)

Figure 1. (a) Homography from a plane between two views. (b) Coordinate system

3. Visual Servoing with *Shortest Path Control*

In this Section the *Shortest Path Control* is presented. The control law design is directly based on the homography elements. Given that our system has two variables to be controlled (the velocities v and ω), we need at least two parameters of the homography to define the control law. Several possibilities appear depending on which homography elements are selected. In our approach we have developed three similar methods which are suitable for different situations. In the experimental results we show the performance of these methods as the calibration or the scene change.

Let us suppose the nonholonomic differential kinematics to be expressed in a general way as

$$\dot{\mathbf{x}} = f(\mathbf{x}, \mathbf{u}) \tag{6}$$

where $\mathbf{x}=(x,z,\phi)^T$ denotes the state vector and $\mathbf{u}=(v, \omega)^T$ the input vector. The particular nonholonomic differential kinematics of the robot expressed in state space form as a function of the translation and rotation robot velocities (v, ω) is:

$$\begin{pmatrix} \dot{x} \\ \dot{z} \\ \dot{\phi} \end{pmatrix} = \begin{pmatrix} -\sin\phi \\ \cos\phi \\ 0 \end{pmatrix} v + \begin{pmatrix} 0 \\ 0 \\ 1 \end{pmatrix} \omega . \tag{7}$$

In the *Shortest Path Control* approach, we propose decoupling the motion, rotation and translation, by following a specific trajectory. Then, we design a navigation scheme in such a way that the robot can correct rotation and translation in a decoupled way. The resulting path of this motion is shown in Figure 2.

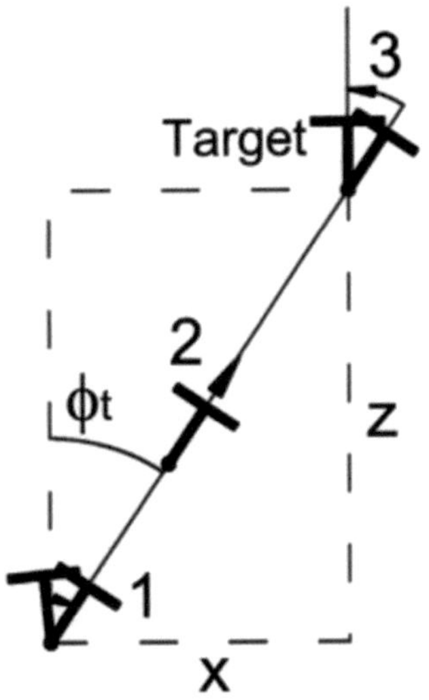

Figure 2. Motion trajectory of the robot consisting in three steps

The motion can be divided in three sequential steps. In the first step the robot rotates until the camera points to the target position. Then, the robot performs a straight translation in the second step until the target position is reached up to a rotation. Finally, the orientation is corrected in the third step. The key point is to establish what conditions have to be held during each phase of the navigation. When the motion starts, the initial homography is the general case (5). It can be seen in Figure 2 that during the second step the robot moves in a straight line with a constant angle respect the global reference ($\phi=\phi_t$). From our reference system we can obtain the geometrical expression $x = -z \tan\phi_t$. Using this expression in (5) we obtain the particular form of the homography that is held during the straight motion of the second step.

$$\mathbf{H}(\phi = \phi_t) = \begin{bmatrix} \cos\phi_t & 0 & \alpha_x \sin\phi_t \\ 0 & 1 & 0 \\ \frac{1}{\alpha_x}\left(-\sin\phi_t + \frac{z}{\cos\phi_t}\frac{n_x}{d}\right) & \frac{1}{\alpha_y}\frac{z}{\cos\phi_t}\frac{n_y}{d} & \cos\phi_t + \frac{z}{\cos\phi_t}\frac{n_z}{d} \end{bmatrix}. \tag{8}$$

At the end of the second step the robot has an orientation error and no translation error (x=0, z=0, $\phi=\phi_t$). Taking this into account, the homography matrix that results at the end of the second step (i.e. in the target position up to orientation error) is

$$\mathbf{H}(x = 0, z = 0, \phi = \phi_t) = \begin{bmatrix} \cos\phi_t & 0 & \alpha_x \sin\phi_t \\ 0 & 1 & 0 \\ \frac{-\sin\phi_t}{\alpha_x} & 0 & \cos\phi_t \end{bmatrix}. \tag{9}$$

This previous expression also implies that $det(\mathbf{H}) = 1$. Finally, at the end of the navigation, when the robot reaches the target pose with the desired orientation the homography will be the identity matrix,

$$\mathbf{H}(x = 0, z = 0, \phi = 0) = \mathbf{I} \tag{10}$$

The particular expressions of the homography just deduced are related graphically with its corresponding positions in Figure 3. It can be seen that the goal of each step is to move the robot having as reference the next desired expression of the homography.

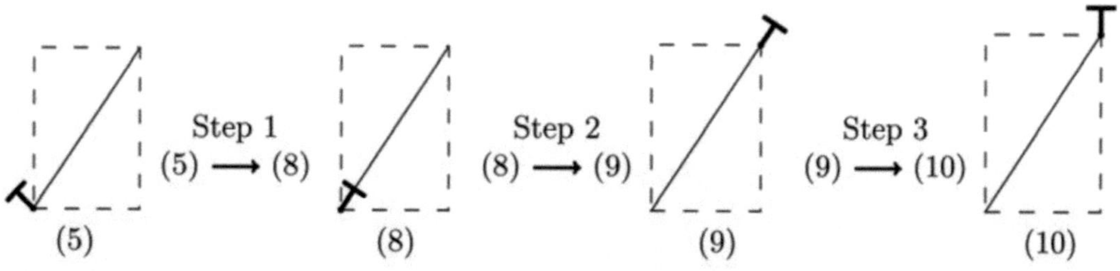

Figure 3. The number below each figure denotes the equation of the homography that holds in that position. In each step, the numbers give the homography equations at the start and at the end of the step

Now we briefly introduce the expressions used to define the controllers of the three different methods of the *Shortest Path Control*. These are detailed in the following subsections. From the previous particular expressions of the homography, we can define the conditions that will be used in each step of the navigation to drive the robot. In the first step we want to reach the orientation $\phi=\phi_t$, where the robot points to the target. The forward velocity is set to zero (v=0) and from (8) we could use h_{11}, h_{12} or h_{13} to set the angular velocity of the robot in a proportional control:

$$\omega = k_\omega(h_{11} - \cos\phi_t) \tag{11}$$

$$\omega = k_\omega h_{12} \tag{12}$$

$$\omega = k_\omega(h_{13} - \alpha_x \sin\phi_t) \tag{13}$$

In this step we have rejected elements h_{31}, h_{32} and h_{33} because they require knowledge about the plane and the robot position, which are unknown. Each one of these expressions (11), (12) or (13) can be used to correct rotation in the first step. The selection of the expressions for each of the three methods depending on the calibration hypothesis is explained below. In method I camera calibration is supposed to be known, while in Method II and III no specific calibration is required.

Once the orientation ϕ_t is gained, the second step aims to get translation to the target equal to zero (x=z=0), keeping the orientation constant during the motion (ϕ=ϕ_t). In this case we could use the parameters h_{31}, h_{32} or h_{33} from (9) to set the robot velocity as

$$v = k_v(h_{31} + \frac{\sin\phi_t}{\alpha_x}) \tag{14}$$

$$v = k_v h_{32} \tag{15}$$

$$v = k_v(h_{33} - \cos\phi_t) \tag{16}$$

In this second step we have rejected elements h_{11}, h_{12} and h_{13} for the correction of v because the value of these elements is constant during this step. Any of the expressions (14), (15) or (16) can be used to compute v during this step. Odometry drift or image noise appear in real situations, so the orientation is corrected to avoid possible errors. Thus, in the three methods the rotation during second step is corrected respectively with the same control of the first step.

In the last step the robot has zero translation error and only needs to perform a rotation in order to reach the target orientation,

$$\omega = k_\omega(h_{ij} - 1)\ with\ (i, j = 1, 3),\ (i = j) \tag{17}$$

$$\omega = k_\omega h_{ij}\ with (j = 1, 2, 3),\ (i \neq j) \tag{18}$$

Then, the velocity is set to zero in this step (v=0) and the rotation can be corrected with expressions of (17) or (18). We have selected ω=$-k_\omega$ h_{13} for the three methods because of the robustness to noise of h_{13} with respect to the rest of the homography elements. Experimental results presented support this decision.

The control loop of the scheme presented is shown in the diagram of Figure 4. An image in the current position is taken at each loop of the control. The homography that links it with the target image is computed from the feature matching. Using the homography, the control performs the three steps. When the homography-based control loop finishes, the robot is in the target position, the current and the target images are the same, and the homography is the identity matrix. Next, the details of the three methods of the *Shortest Path Control* for visual servoing based on homographies for mobile robots are presented in detail.

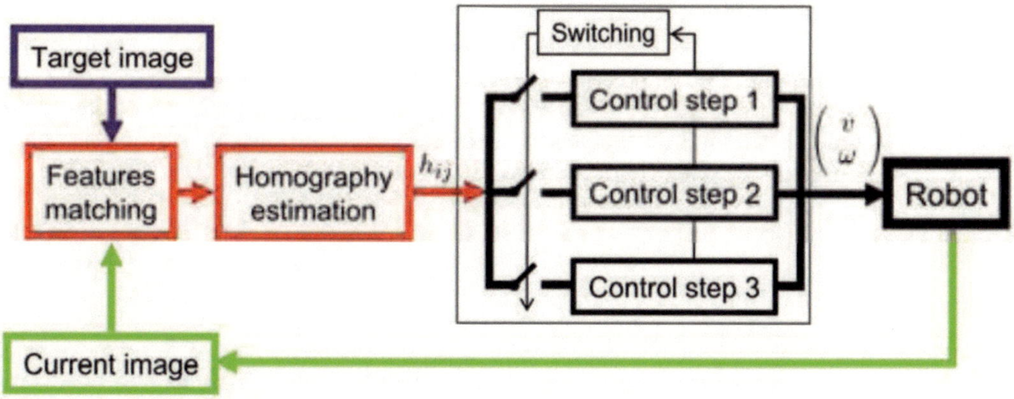

Figure 4. Diagram of the control loop

3.1 Method I: Calibrated Method

In this method we suppose that the calibration matrix of the camera is known, and therefore, the value of the focal length α_x is given. In the first step v is set to zero while the angular velocity could be corrected with (11) or (13), needing the value ϕ_t. This approach is based on the key value ϕ_t, but this value is initially unknown. From (8) we have that $h_{11}=\cos\phi_t$ and $h_{13}=\alpha_x\sin\phi_t$. Taking this into account, we can obtain the next equation, which is true when $\phi=\phi_t$,

$$h_{11}^2 + \frac{h_{13}^2}{\alpha_x^2} = 1. \tag{19}$$

Using this expression we do not need to know the value of ϕ_t to correct the orientation in the first step, and this is corrected until (19) is satisfied. In step two, the orientation is corrected with the same expression to take into account odometry drift or noise. The velocity v in the second step is corrected using (16) which is combined with h_{11} from (9) to remove the unknown parameter ϕ_t from the expression of the control. Third step is based on (17). Then, we define the Method I as

$$Method\ I \begin{cases} Step\ 1: \ v = 0\,,\ \omega = -k_\omega(h_{11}^2 + \frac{h_{13}^2}{\alpha_x^2} - 1)\,. \\ Step\ 2: \ v = -k_v(h_{11} - h_{33})\,,\ \omega = -k_\omega(h_{11}^2 + \frac{h_{13}^2}{\alpha_x^2} - 1)\,. \\ Step\ 3: \ v = 0\,,\ \omega = -k_\omega h_{13}\,. \end{cases} \tag{20}$$

where k_ω and k_v are the control gains.

We avoid the use of the parameter ϕ_t in the velocity v of the second step by using the value of h_{11} from (9) as previously explained. In any case ϕ_t could be computed easily when the first step is finished from (11) or (13). This method needs to know the calibration of the camera (parameter α_x) and this is its main drawback. The next two methods proposed work without knowing this parameter and they have shown to be independent of the focal length.

3.2 Method II: Uncalibrated Method

The previous method is calibrated. In a system, the need of calibration means disadvantages in terms of maintenance cost, robustness and adaptability. In Method II the calibration camera is considered to be unknown, which has many advantages in practice. We can define the control scheme of the Method II selecting expressions where the calibration parameters do not appear explicitly. These expressions are (12), (15) and (17). Then, the control is defined as

$$Method\ II \begin{cases} Step\ 1: \ v = 0\,,\ \omega = -k_\omega h_{12}\,. \\ Step\ 2: \ v = -k_v h_{32}\,,\ \omega = -k_\omega h_{12}\,. \\ Step\ 3: \ v = 0\,,\ \omega = -k_\omega h_{13}\,. \end{cases} \tag{21}$$

where k_ω and k_v are the control gains. With this method the robot is controlled by using a camera without specific calibration; although we assume that the principal point is in the centre of the image, this is a good supposition in practise. Method II requires the plane inducing the homography not to be vertical respect our reference because it is needed $n_y \neq 0$. This is due to the direct dependence of the parameters used from the homography to n_y. This could be a problem since human environments are usually full of vertical planes (walls). In any case the method works if we guarantee that vertical planes are not used, for example constraining to the floor [Liang and Pears, 2002] or the ceiling plane [Blanc et al., 2005].

3.3 Method III: Method with Parallax

The previous method works without specific calibration, but it requires the scene homography plane not to be vertical and this could be a problem in man-made environments, usually full of vertical planes. Method III uses the concept of parallax relative to a plane and overcomes the problem of vertical planes. Using the parallax [Hartley and Zisserman, 2004] the epipole in the current image can be easily obtained from a homography **H** and two points not belonging to its plane. In the first step of Method III the objective is to get orientation $\phi = \phi_t$. In this position the robot points to the target, so the camera centre of the target is projected to (x_0, y_0) in the current image and then $\mathbf{e}_c = (0,0)$. Given that the robot moves in a planar surface we only need the x-coordinate of the epipole (e_{cx}). Then we define the correction of the orientation in step 1 and step 2 with a proportional control to e_{cx}. Once $e_{cx} = 0$ the robot is pointing to the target position. The other expressions of the control are obtained in a similar way to the previous methods using (16) and (17). Then, we define the scheme of Method III as

$$Method\ III \begin{cases} Step\ 1: \ v = 0\,,\ \omega = -k_\omega e_{cx}\,. \\ Step\ 2: \ v = -k_v (h_{11} - h_{33})\,,\ \omega = -k_\omega e_{cx}\,. \\ Step\ 3: \ v = 0\,,\ \omega = -k_\omega h_{13}\,. \end{cases} \tag{22}$$

When the robot is close to the target position and the translation is nearly zero, all the points in the scene can be related by the homography. In this situation the parallax is not useful to correct the orientation. Before this happen we change the orientation control at the end of step 2 to the expression (11). This expression needs the value of ϕ_t, which can be computed previously with the same equation while the rotation is corrected with the parallax procedure. Here, we use neither expression (15) because vertical planes can be easily found

in human environments nor expression (19) because it needs specific calibration. We can detect easily when the parallax is not useful to work with by measuring the parallax of the points not belonging to the plane of the homography. If the result is under a threshold, the parallax procedure is not used any more. In the simulations presented with this approach the threshold is set to 5 pixels.
In the three methods presented the homography is not decomposed, and neither the robot coordinates nor the normal of the plane are computed. This approach requires the selection of the signs of some of the control gains depending on where is the initial robot position and what is the orientation of the plane detected. This can be easily done by taking advantage of the parallax relative to the plane by computing it once at the start. Thus, the sign of the gains is easily determined.

4. Stability Analysis

We define the common Lyapunov function expressing the robot position in polar coordinates ($r(t)$, $\theta(t)$, $\phi(t)$), with the reference origin in the target and θ positive from z-axis anticlockwise, as

$$V = V_r + V_\theta + V_\phi = \frac{(r - r^{G_i})^2}{2} + \frac{(\theta - \theta^{G_i})^2}{2} + \frac{(\phi - \phi^{G_i})^2}{2} \tag{23}$$

This is a positive definite function, where r^{G_i}, θ^{G_i} and ϕ^{G_i} denote the desired value of the parameter in the subgoal position for each step (i=1,2,3). Due to the designed path, the value of θ is constant during the navigation. Although in the case of noisy data the value of θ could vary, it does not affect the control, because the path is defined towards the target independently of the value of θ, thus $V_\theta = 0$. After differentiating we obtain:

$$\dot{V} = \dot{V}_r + \dot{V}_\phi = (r - r^{G_i})\, v \cos(\phi - \theta) + (\phi - \phi^{G_i})\, \omega \,. \tag{24}$$

We analyze the derivative Lyapunov candidate function in each step to show it is strictly negative. This analysis is valid whether if the goal is behind or in front of the initial position.
Step 1. Here the robot performs a rotation with v=0. Thus, we only need to consider $\dot{V} = \dot{V}_\phi$. The desired orientation is $\phi^{G1} = \phi_t$. $\dot{V}_\phi < 0$ is guaranteed if ($\phi - \phi^{G1}$) > 0 and then ω<0; or else, if ($\phi - \phi^{G1}$)<0 and then ω>0. In Method I and II, the sign of ω is guaranteed to be correct, given that the sign of k_ω is selected as previously explained. In Method III, $\omega = -k_\omega e_{cx}$ and, when ($\phi - \phi^{G1}$)>0 then e_{cx}>0 and ω<0, or e_{cx}<0 and ω>0 when ($\phi - \phi^{G1}$) < 0. Therefore $\dot{V}$<0.
Step 2. In this step the robot moves towards the target in a straight line path and we have $\dot{V} = \dot{V}_r + \dot{V}_\phi$. The sign of ($r - r^{G2}$) is always positive. Then, with cos($\phi - \theta$) < 0 we have v>0 and with cos($\phi - \theta$)>0 we have v < 0. In Method II, the sign of v is guaranteed to be correct, given that the sign of k_v is properly selected. In Method I and III, the velocity given by the control and with (8) is $v = k_v\, z\, n_z / (d\cos\phi_t)$, which gives the expected signs. Therefore $\dot{V}_r < 0$.
With $\dot{V}_\phi$ we have the same reasoning of step 1.
Step 3. Similar to the reasoning of step 1, in this case, the sign of ω can be easily checked taking into account that ϕ^{G3}=0 and $h_{13} = \alpha_x \sin\phi_t$. Therefore $\dot{V}$< 0.

So, we have shown that $\dot{V}$<0 for the controllers of the three methods. We have also asymptotic stability given that $\dot{V}$ is negative definite in all the steps.

5. Experimental Results

Several experiments have been carried out with the controllers of the three methods presented by using virtual data. The simulated data is obtained by generating a virtual planar scene consisting of a distribution of random 3D points. The scene is projected to the image plane using a virtual camera, the size of the images is 640×480 pixels. In each loop of the control, the homography between the current and target image is computed from the matched points and the control law send the velocities (v, ω) to the robot. In the experiments, we assume that the camera is centred on the robot pointing forwards. Figure 5 shows the resulting path from different initial positions. The target is placed in (x(m),z(m),ϕ(deg))=(0,0,0°). The different initial positions behind the target are: (−3,−10,−30°), (0,−8,−40°) and (6,−6,0°). The results also show that the method works properly when the target is behind the initial robot position, moving the robot backwards in that case. The different initial positions used in this case are: (−6, 4, 20°), (6, 8, 10°) and (5,2,−50°).

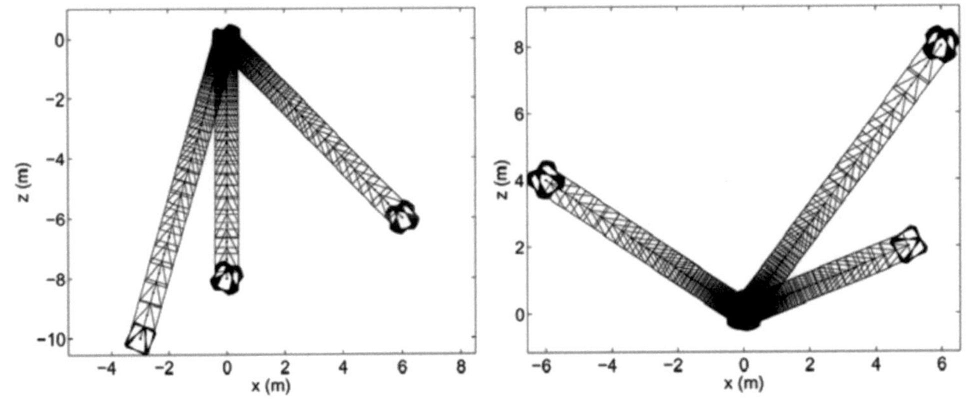

Figure 5. Simulations with target position at (0,0,0°) and different initial positions

The performance of the three methods is exactly the same when using perfect data and quite similar when there is image noise. In Figure 6 two simulations are compared, one without noise, and the other, adding white noise to the image points with a standard deviation of σ=1 pixel using Method III. The evolution along time of the robot position and the homography elements is drawn.

We have tested the controllers with odometry drift and with different values of image noise. The first row of Figure 7 shows the resulting evolution of the robot position when there is odometry drift in rotation of 1 deg/m. As it can be seen the controllers can cope properly with the drift error. Simulations with each method have been carried out using different levels of image noise. The results are shown in the second row of Figure 7 and it can be seen that the methods converge properly in spite of image noise.

The control law of Method I needs the calibration parameter α_x of the camera whereas Method II and III do not use it. In Figure 8 we show the performance of the control to calibration errors. The value of the focal length of the controllers is fixed to f=6 mm while its real value is modified to see the final position error obtained for each Method, (first row of Figure 8). Besides, we have assumed that the principal point is in the centre of the image. In the second row of Figure 8, the value of x_0 used in the controllers is supposed to be zero while its real value is changed. Performance of Method I is sensitive to calibration errors as expected, this is because this control law is related directly with α_x and depends highly on its accuracy. The simulations show that Method II works properly in spite of calibration errors. Finally, results using Method III show that a rough calibration is enough for the convergence, because it is robust to focal length in accuracy and it is only affected by calibration errors in the principal point.

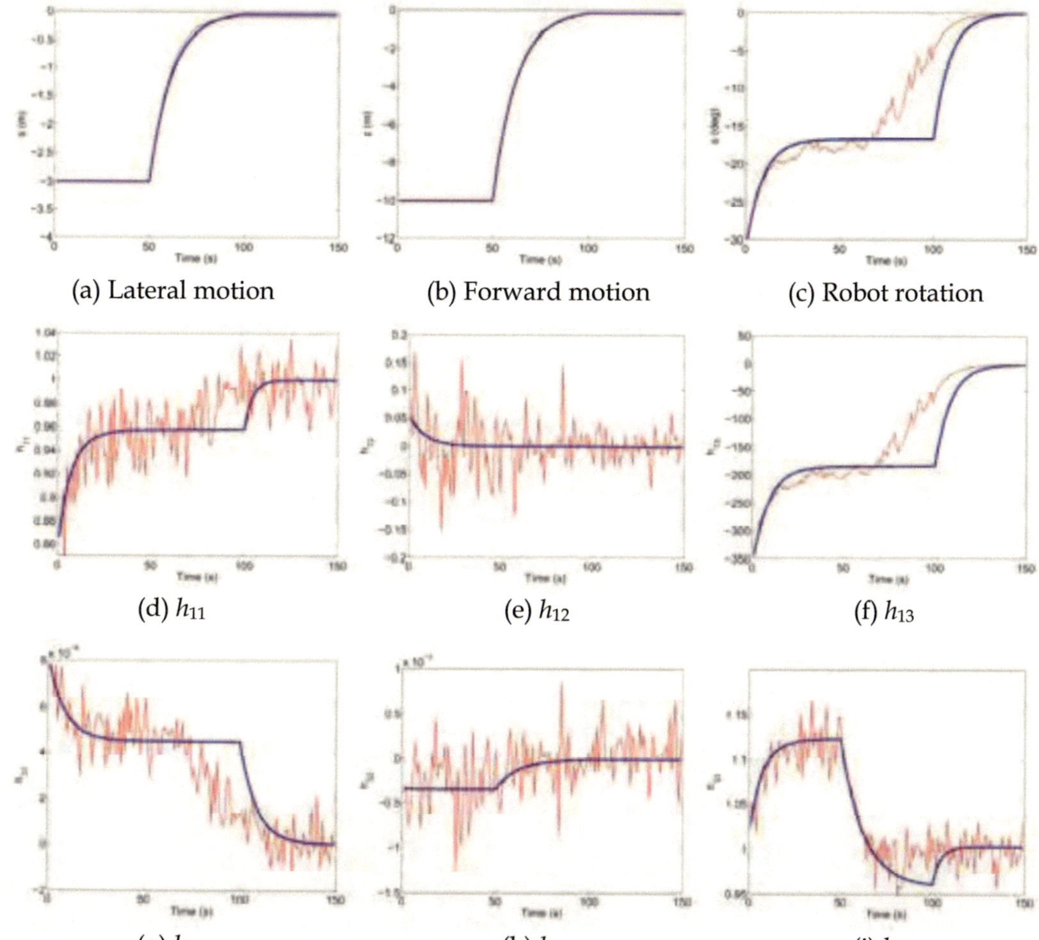

(a) Lateral motion (b) Forward motion (c) Robot rotation

(d) h_{11} (e) h_{12} (f) h_{13}

(g) h_{31} (h) h_{32} (i) h_{33}

Figure 6. Simulation without noise (thick line) and with image white noise of σ=1 pixel (thin line). The initial position is $(x,z,\phi)=(-3, -10, -30°)$ and the target (0,0,0°)

The performance of the methods can be spoiled in some cases by the particular plane that generates the homography. Simulations using different planes are presented in Table 1. The planes are defined by the normal vector $\mathbf{n}=(n_x,n_y,n_z)^T$, and a list of unitary normal vectors is selected to carried out the simulations with $\|n\|=1$. The final error obtained with each method is shown. The initial position is (−3, −10, −30°) and the target is (0, 0, 0°). The results show that Method I and III need $n_z \neq 0$ to work properly. On the other hand, Method II needs $n_y \neq 0$.This is because the Methods are directly related with these parameters of $\mathbf{n}$.

Vertical planes are usually common in human environments; besides, in our monocular system, planes in front of the robot with dominant n_z will be detected more easily. Methods I and III work properly in this case. If we constraint the homography plane detected to be the floor or the ceiling (any plane with $n_y \neq 0$ is enough) the Method II will also work properly.

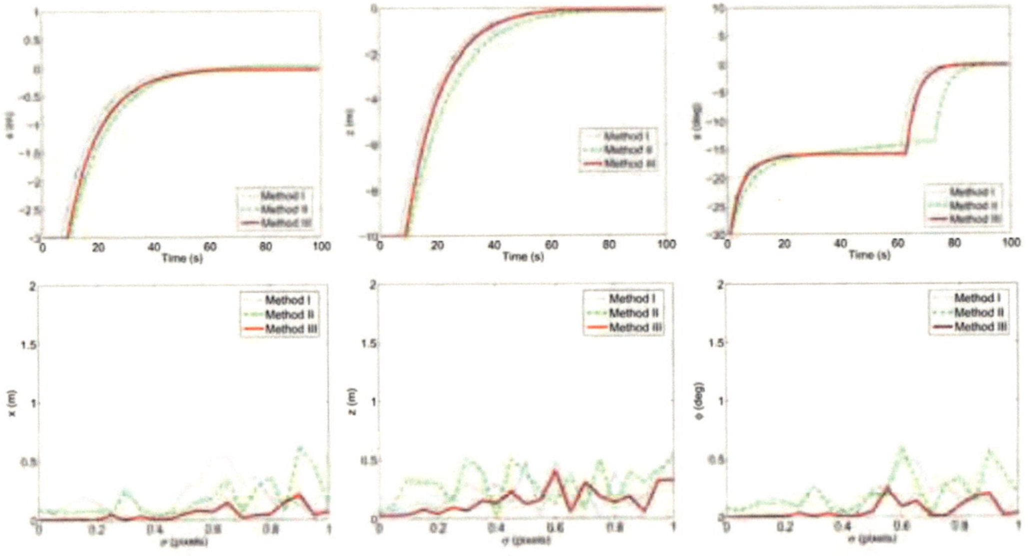

Figure 7. (First row) Simulations with odometry drif of 1 deg/m. The evolution of one simulation in x, z and ϕ is shown for each method. (Second row) Final error of different simulations varying the image noise

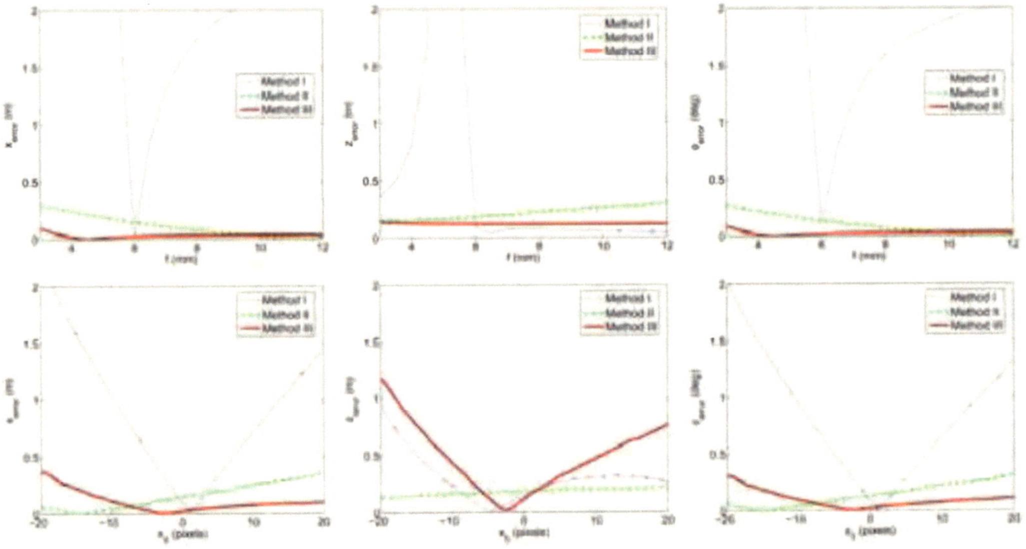

Figure 8. Final error for each method in x,z and ϕ varying the focal length (first row) and varying the principal point coordinates (second row)

n			Method I			Method II			Method III		
n_x	n_y	n_z	x	z	ϕ	x	z	ϕ	x	z	ϕ
0	0	-1.00	0	0	-0.09	-3.00	-10.00	-3.12	0	0	-0.09
-0.20	0.57	-0.80	0.03	-0.00	-0.09	-0.00	-0.00	-0.09	0	0	-0.09
-0.40	0.69	-0.60	-0.00	-0.00	-0.09	-0.00	-0.00	-0.09	-0.00	-0.00	-0.09
-0.60	0.69	-0.40	-0.00	-0.01	-0.09	-0.00	-0.00	-0.09	-0.00	-0.01	-0.09
-0.80	0.57	-0.20	-0.10	-0.34	-0.03	-0.00	-0.00	-0.09	-0.10	-0.34	-0.03
-1.00	0	0	-3.00	-10.00	0	-3.00	-10.00	0	-3.00	-10.00	0
1.00	0	0	-3.00	-10.00	0	-3.00	-10.00	0	-3.00	-10.00	0
0.98	-0.20	0	-3.00	-10.00	0	-0.15	-0.62	0	-3.00	-10.00	0
0.92	-0.40	0	-3.00	-10.00	0	-0.01	-0.04	-0.09	-3.00	-10.00	0
0.80	-0.60	0	-3.00	-10.00	0	-0.00	-0.00	-0.09	-3.00	-10.00	0
0.60	-0.80	0	-3.00	-10.00	0	0	-0.00	-0.09	-3.00	-10.00	0
0	-1.00	0	-3.00	-10.00	0	0	0	-0.09	-3.00	-10.00	0
0	-1.00	0	-3.00	-10.00	0	0	0	-0.09	-3.00	-10.00	0
0.57	-0.80	-0.20	-0.10	-0.34	-0.03	0	-0.00	-0.09	-0.10	-0.34	-0.03
0.69	-0.60	-0.40	-0.00	-0.01	-0.09	-0.00	-0.00	-0.09	-0.00	-0.01	-0.09
0.69	-0.40	-0.60	-0.00	-0.00	-0.09	-0.01	-0.04	-0.10	-0.00	-0.00	-0.09
0.57	-0.20	-0.80	0	0	-0.09	-0.15	-0.62	-0.15	0	0	-0.09
0	0	-1.00	0	0	-0.09	-3.00	-10.00	-3.12	0	0	-0.09

Table 1. Final error for each method in x(m), z(m) and ϕ(deg) varying the normal of the plane that generates the homography: $\mathbf{n}=(n_x, n_y, n_z)^T$

6. Conclusions

We have presented a new homography-based approach for visual control of mobile robots. The control design is directly based on the homography elements and deals with the motion constraints of the differential drive vehicle. In our approach, called *Shortest Path Control*, the motion is designed to follow a straight line path. Taking advantage of this specific trajectory we have proposed a control law decoupling rotation and translation. Three different methods have been designed by choosing different homography elements. Their performance depends on the conditions of the plane or the calibration. The methods use neither the homography decomposition nor any measure of the 3D scene. Simulations shows the performance of the methods with odometry drift, image noise and calibration errors. Also, the influence of the plane that generates the homography is studied.

7. References

Basri, R., Rivlin, E., and Shimshoni, I. (1999). Visual homing: Surfing on the epipoles. International Journal of Computer Vision, 33(2):117–137. [Basri et al., 1999]

Benhimane, S. and Malis, E. (2006). Homography-based 2D visual servoing. *IEEE International Conference on Robotic sand Automation*, pages 2397–2402. [Benhimane and Malis, 2006]

Benhimane, S., Malis, E., Rives, P., and Azinheira, J. R. (2005). Vision-based control for car platooning using homography decomposition. In *IEEE International Conference on Robotics and Automation*, Barcelona, Spain, pages 2173–2178. [Benhimane et al.,2005]

Blanc, G., Mezouar, Y., and Martinet, P. (2005). Indoor navigation of a wheeled mobile robot along visual routes. In *Proceedings of the IEEE International Conference on Robotics and Automation ,ICRA '05*, pages 3365–3370. [Blanc et al.,2005]

Conticelli, F. and Allotta, B. (2001). Nonlinear controllability and stability analysis of adaptive image-based systems. *IEEE Transactionson Robotic sand Automation*, 17 (2): 208–214. [Conticelli and Allotta, 2001]

Corke, P. I. and Hutchinson, S. A. (2001). A new partitioned approach to image-based visual servo control. *IEEE Transactions on Robotics and Automation*, 17 (4) :507–515. [Corke and Hutchinson, 2001]

De Souza, G. N. and Kak, A. C. (2002). Vision for mobile robot navigation: A survey. *IEEE Transactions on Pattern Analysis and Machine Intelligence*, 24 (2): 237–267. [De Souza and Kak, 2002]

Fang,Y., Dixon, W. E., Dawson, D.M., and Chawda, P. (2005). Homography-based visual servo regulation of mobile robots. *IEEE Transactions on Systems, Man, and Cybernetics*, Part B, 35 (5): 1041–1050. [Fang et al., 2005]

Hartley, R. I. and Zisserman, A. (2004). *Multiple View Geometry in Computer Vision*. Cambridge University Press, ISBN: 0521540518. [Hartley and Zisserman, 2004]

Hutchinson, S., Hager, G., and Corke, P. (1996). A tutorial on visual servo control. *IEEE Transactions on Robotics and Automation*, 12 (5):651–670. [Hutchinson et al., 1996]

Liang, B. and Pears, N. (2002). Visual navigation using planar homographies. In *IEEE Conference on Robotics and Automation*, pages 205–210. [Liang and Pears, 2002]

Lopez-Nicolas, G., Sagues, C., Guerrero, J., Kragic, D., and Jensfelt, P. (2006). Nonholonomic epipolar visual servoing. *IEEE International Conference on Robotics and Automation*, pages 2378–2384. [Lopez-Nicolas et al., 2006]

Ma, Y., Kosecka, J., and Sastry, S. (1999). Vision guided navigation for a nonholonomic mobile robot. *IEEE Transactions on Robotics and Automation*, 15(3): 521–537. [Ma et al., 1999]

Malis, E. and Chaumette, F. (2000). 2 ½ D visual servoing with respect to unknown objects through a new estimation scheme of camera displacement. *International Journal of Computer Vision*, 37 (1): 79–97. [Malis and Chaumette, 2000]

Malis, E., Chaumette, F., and Boudet, S. (1999). 2 ½ D visual servoing. *IEEE Transactions on Robotic and Automation*, 15 (2): 234–246. [Malis et al., 1999]

Rives, P. (2000). Visual servoing based on epipolar geometry. In *IEEE/RSJ International Conference on Intelligent Robots and Systems*, volume 1, pages 602–607. [Rives ,2000]

Sagues, C. and Guerrero, J. (2005). Visual correction for mobile robot homing. *Robotics and Autonomous Systems*, 50 (1): 41–49. [Sagues and Guerrero, 2005]

Tsakiris, D., Rives, P., and Samson, C. (1998). Extending visual servoing techniques to nonholonomic mobile robots. In G. Hager, D. K. and Morse, S., editors, *The Confluence of Vision and Control*, Lecture Notes in Control and Information Systems (LNCIS). Springer-Verlag. [Tsakiris et al., 1998]

31

Correlation Error Reduction of Images in Stereo Vision with Fuzzy Method and its Application on Cartesian Robot

Mehdi Ghayoumi and Mohammad Shayganfar
Islamic Azad University Shahr-e-Rey Branch
Iran

1. Introduction

Stereo vision is one of the most active research topics in machine vision. Finding corresponding points in different images of the same scene could be a tough procedure of depth extraction in this field. Correlation is one of the most common approaches that could be applied in this procedure. There are also methods that have been presented to reduce some existing errors associated with this approach. Here, a fuzzy model is demonstrated. Also the experimental results are presented based on a 3p laboratory robot and improvements are illustrated comparing with a neural network method by simulation outcomes.
Vision method at first was used for estimating robot errors more than one decade ago. So far, different companies and research centers have used for robot positioning, calibration, error estimation and error compensation with genetic algorithm, neural networks and fuzzy control algorithms. In general, recognition of 3D objects requires two or more appropriately defined 2D images. With this approximation many methods have been proposed such as structure from motion, (Seitz et al., 1995) (Taylor & Kriegman, 1995) stereo lenses correspondence and shape (Grosso et al., 1996) (Haralick & Shapiro, 1992). Achour and Benkhelif present a new approach for 3D scene reconstruction based on projective geometry without camera calibration. The contribution is to reduce the number of reference points to four points by exploiting some geometrical shapes contained in the scene (Achour & Benkhelif, 2001). In online applications, these methods have some problems. There is a difficulty in finding the correspondence between one image and the others. The most important step in stereo vision is to find two points of two or more images. A general correlation approach including errors is discussed in (Lopez & Plat, 2000). Also, fuzzy logic has applied in some cases such as process control, decision support systems, optimization and a large class of robotic manipulators and other mechanical systems (Hsu et al., 2001).
Here, a fuzzy approach is applied to reduce existent errors to concern with the aspect of improving correlation based stereo vision by reducing errors on a set of points. The experiments are due to a Cartesian robot. So far a neural network approach has been used to get the optimum point in world coordinate for 3p robot(Korayem et al., 2001). Clearly there is no magic panacea for selecting a neural network for the best generalization and also

because of structure and foundation of neural networks, it has some errors. A fuzzy approach can be used to reduce these.

2. Mapping relations in robots

Stereo vision systems determine depth from two or more images which are taken at the same time from slightly different viewpoints. The most important and time consuming task for a stereo vision system is the registration of both images and the identification of corresponding pixels. Two pixels are corresponding when they represent the same point in the real world. A method based on stereo attempts to determine the correspondence for each pixel, which results in a dense depth map. Correlation is the basic method used to find corresponding pixels. Several real time systems have been developed using correlation based stereo(Konolige ,1997)(Matthies et al., 1995) (Volpe et al., 1996) (Guisse et al., 2000) Images of cameras are in two dimensional spaces and for each point with losing the depth in images can obtain one line in real world. The relations in stereo vision demonstrate that measure of depth's points in each image is obtained as shown in(Gonzalez,1998):

$$Z = \lambda - \frac{\lambda B}{x_2 + x_1} \tag{1}$$

Which x_1, x_2 are x coordinate for one point in real world in each image of two cameras. λ and β is focal distance and distance between two focal, respectively. In 3p robot two cameras are not in the same direction. It means each of x and z axis should be rotated and two rotation matrixes can be concatenated into a single matrix:

$$R = R_\alpha R_\theta \tag{2}$$

According to modified relation of camera, commutative matrix is as follows:

$$R = \begin{bmatrix} \cos\theta & \sin\theta & 0 & 0 \\ -\sin\theta\cos\alpha & \cos\theta\cos\alpha & \sin\alpha & 0 \\ \sin\theta\sin\alpha & -\cos\theta\sin\alpha & \cos\alpha & 0 \\ 0 & 0 & 0 & 1 \end{bmatrix} \tag{3}$$

Where θ, α are rotating angles of z and x axis, respectively. Also commutative axis can be obtained with the follow matrix:

$$C = \begin{bmatrix} 1 & 0 & 0 & 0 \\ 0 & 1 & 0 & 0 \\ 0 & 0 & 1 & -z_0 \\ 0 & 0 & 0 & 1 \end{bmatrix} \tag{4}$$

Where z_0 is coordinating of z in world coordinate. According to Eq. 3 and 4, we have:

$$x_1 = \lambda \frac{X\cos\theta + Y\sin\theta}{-X\sin\theta\sin\alpha + Y\cos\theta\sin\alpha - (Z - Z_0)\cos\alpha + \lambda} \tag{5}$$

And:

$$x_2 = \lambda \frac{-X\sin\theta\cos\alpha + Y\cos\theta\cos\alpha + (Z - Z_0)\sin\alpha}{-X\sin\theta\sin\alpha + Y\cos\theta\sin\alpha - (Z - Z_0)\cos\alpha + \lambda} \tag{6}$$

Where x, y and z are coordinates of the image as a point in the real world. It is noted that these equations reduce to Eq. 1 when $X_0 = Y_0 = Z_0 = 0, r_1 = r_2 = r_3 = 0$ and $\alpha = \theta = 0^0$. Fig. 1 shows the method of stereo vision in 3p robot.

Figure 1. Laboratory Cartesian 3p robot

3. Correlation

Correlation is one of the applied methods in stereo vision and it is discussed in this section.

3.1 Correlation method

Although correlation method can be explained with vector but working with a window's form is commonly used. In its simplest form, the correlation between these two real functions $w(x,y)$, $f(x,y)$ is given by(Paulino et al., 2001):

$$c(s,t) = \sum_x \sum_y f(x,y)w(x-s, y-t) \quad t = 0,1,...,N-1, s = 0,1,...,M-1 \tag{7}$$

Where $f(x,y)$ is a digital image with size $M \times N$ and $w(x,y)$ is a similar region with size $J \times K$ ($J \prec M$ and $K \prec N$). The correlation function given in Eq. 7 has drawback, because it is sensitive to scale changes in the amplitude of $f(x,y)$ and $w(x,y)$. A method that frequently used to overcome this difficulty is to perform matching via the correlation coefficient, defined as:

$$\gamma(s,t) = \frac{\sum_x \sum_y [f(x,y) - \bar{f}(x,y)][w(x-s,y-t) - \bar{w}]}{\{\sum_x \sum_y [f(x,y) - \bar{f}(x,y)]^2 [\sum_x \sum_y [w(x-s,y-t) - \bar{w}]^2\}^{1/2}} \tag{8}$$

$$t = 0,1,\ldots, N-1, s = 0,1,\ldots, M-1$$

Where $\bar{w}$ is the average intensity of the mask (this value is computed only once), $\bar{f}(x,y)$ is the average value of $f(x,y)$ in the region coincident with $w(x,y)$, and the summations are taken over the common coordinate to both f and w. It is not difficult to show that $c(s,t)$ is scaled to the range from -1 to 1, independent of scale changes in the amplitude of $f(x,y)$ and $w(x,y)$. If the functions are in the same size, this approach can be more efficient than a direct implementation of correlation in the spatial domain. It is important to note that the dimension of $w(x,y)$ is usually smaller than $f(x,y)$ in implementing Eq. 7.

3.2 Problems of using correlation based stereo vision

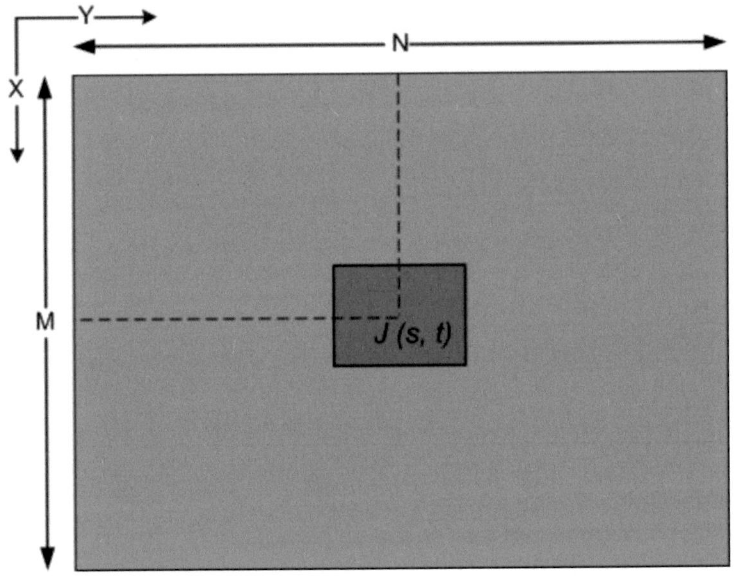

Figure 2. The correlation method

Correlation is used with a fixed rectangular window containing image as shown in Fig.2. The image will be correlated with a second window swiping the area of image. The possible trajectories are defined by the minimal possible existing distance between the camera and object, which suggests the maximum disparity. The position with the highest correlation value determines the pixel that corresponds to the pixel of interest. Larger correlation windows increase the reliability by averaging over a larger area, besides reducing the effects of noise. Generally, the choice of the correlation window size is a trade off between increasing reliability in areas with constant depth and decreasing errors where depth changes. The use of a smaller correlation window reduces the problem, because smaller window does not overlap the depth discontinuity to the same extent(Paulino et al., 2001).

4. Fuzzy System

Fuzzy logic controller utilizes fuzzy to convert the linguistic control strategy based on expert knowledge into an automatic control strategy. This section describes the design of fuzzy system for vision of 3p robot. It also discusses the heuristic approach that has been applied to determine the number of necessary fuzzy input and output set. In the first step, the border points are obtained by exploiting some geometrical relations. Then the fuzzy system is applied to points of correlation area. The best point that is achieved with heuristic method is shown in Fig.3.

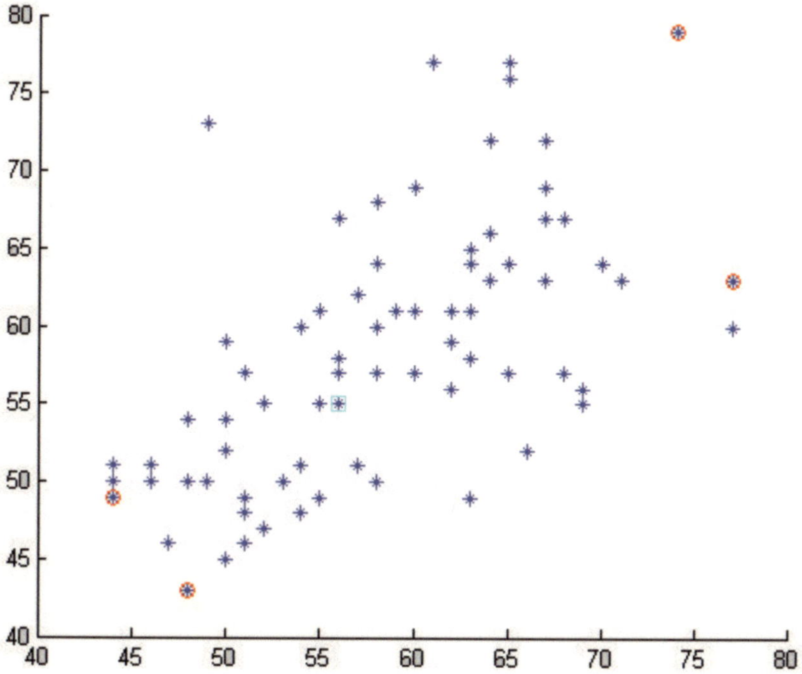

Figure 3. Getting the best point of correlation area

4.1 Getting the border points

The goal is to find the best point of correlation area. In this case, a heuristic method is used to find four points. These points are maximum and minimum coordinates of each axis' correlation area. Then, Eq.9 gives the distance of correlation from these four points as follows:

$$\|\mathbf{X}_1 - \mathbf{X}_2\| = \sqrt{(x_1 - x_2)^2 + (y_1 - y_2)^2 + (z_1 - z_2)^2} \qquad (9)$$

Where $\mathbf{x}_1, \mathbf{x}_2$ are the coordinate of two points(Hirschuller et al., 2001).

4.2 Fuzzy Method

Recently fuzzy system approaches have achieved superior performance. The identification of fuzzy models from input-output data of the process normally lead to representations which are difficult to understand. Fuzzy logic has had great success in running machinery that is computer operated. For instance, fuzzy systems used to formulate the human's knowledge. Fuzzy set theory and fuzzy logic have evolved into powerful tools for managing uncertainties inherent in complex systems(Bender ,1996) (Zhang et al., 1999) (Alexander ,1996). In general, building a fuzzy system consists of three basic steps: structure identification (variable selection, partitioning input and output spaces and choosing membership functions), parameter estimation, and model validation. Fuzzy systems create a systematic process for replacing one knowledge base with a nonlinear mapping. Because of this, we will be able to use systems according to knowledge fuzzy system in engineering applications(Wang ,1997).. The area of correlation points is divided to four parts as shown in Fig. 4.

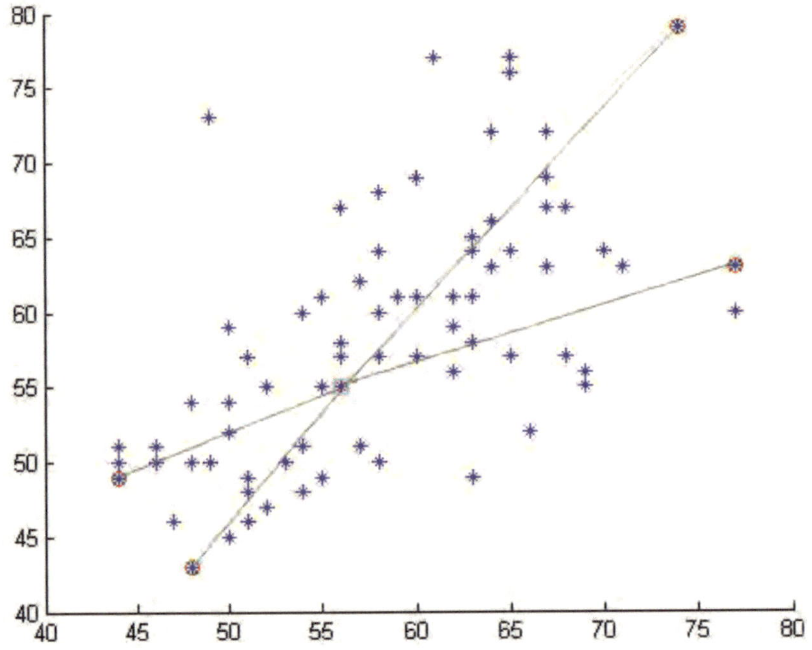

Figure 4. The partions of correlation area

4.2.1 Fuzzification

The computational technique of inputs of fuzzy system is demonstrated in Fig.5. The distances of the centers of images from best point are d_1 and d_2, respectively. The triangular membership functions have been used. Four inputs in the fuzzy system are the distances of center of each area from the images (Fig. 5).
The fuzzy controller employs four inputs by using Euclidian distance, shown in Eq. 9, of each point at each partition of correlation area from the image center. This fuzzy controller has only one control output.

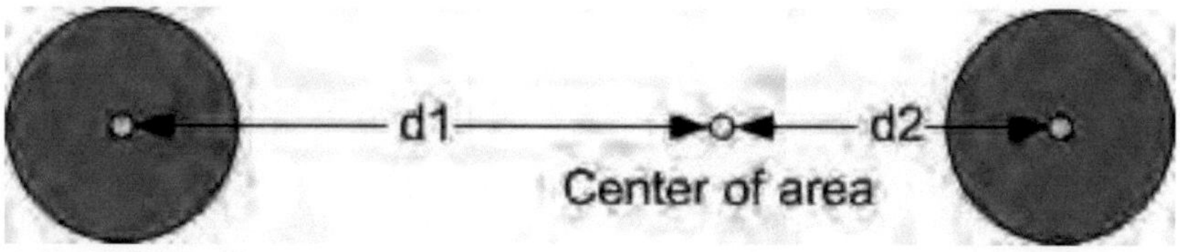

Figure 5. Distances of the centers from best point of images (heuristic method)

4.2.2 Fuzzy Rule Base

The IF part of rule bases include the ratio of the distances of central point in each area from the image center. The THEN part of these rules is suggested for the center of correlation area:

IF input $r = \frac{d_1}{d_2} \succ 1$ THEN output is center of area (1) or center of area (2).

IF input $r = \frac{d_1}{d_2} = 1$ THEN output is center of correlation area.

IF input $r = \frac{d_1}{d_2} \prec 1$ THEN output is center of area (3) or center of area (4).

The above rules can be dedicated for each area. It means the total number of rules is 12.

4.2.3 Defuzzification

The Eq. 10 is applied to defuzzify the fuzzy control rules in the defuzzification step. The defuzzifier which is applied is the center of gravity.

$$y^* = \frac{\sum_{l=1}^{M} \bar{y}^l w_l}{\sum_{l=1}^{M} w_l} \tag{10}$$

5. Algorithm

The diagram belongs to our approach is demonstrated in this section. All the processes described before are shown as an algorithmic approach in Fig. 7.

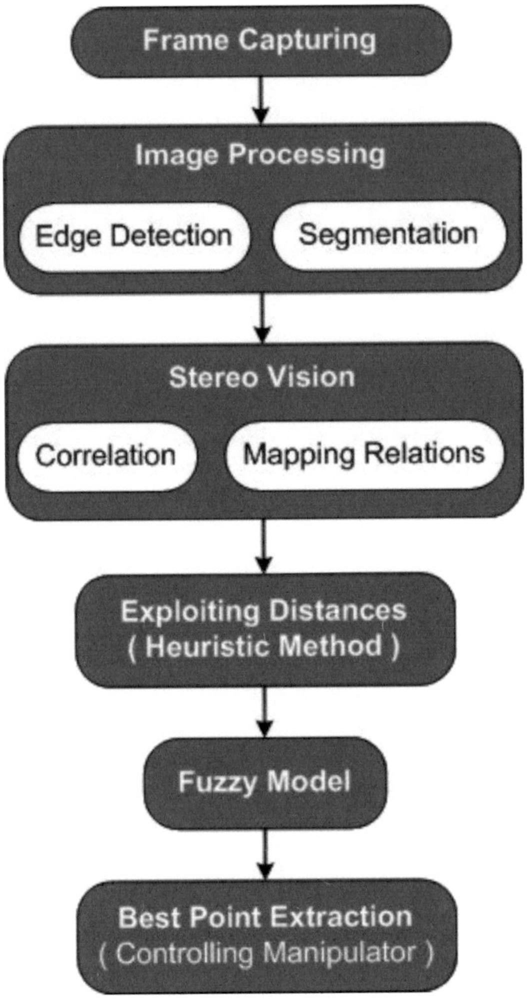

Figure 7. The Processing Diagram

6. Testing Irregular Objects

This method has been used for an unformed object. The edges of images and correlation of images is demonstrated in Fig.8 and 9, respectively.

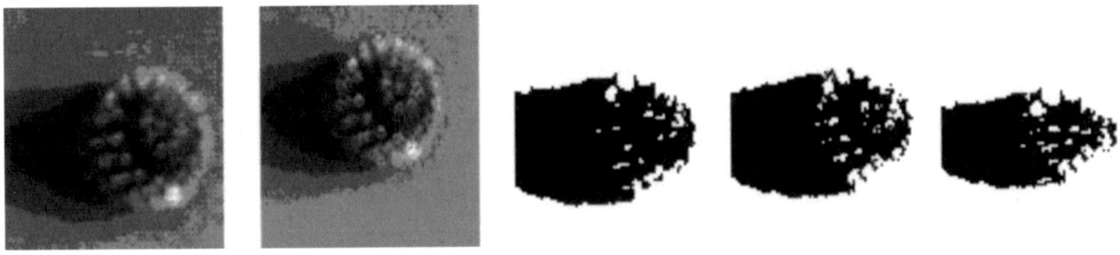

Figure 8. (Left to right) images of: camera 1, camera 2, and binary images: 1, 2, and correlation of images

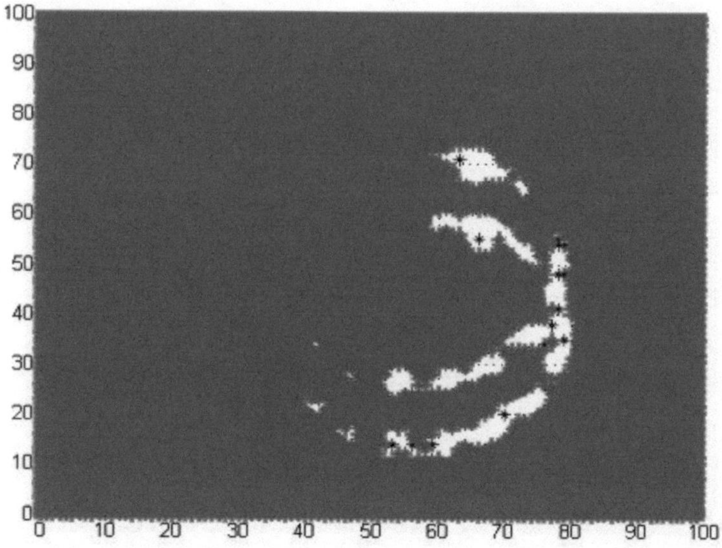

Figure 9. Exploited points of an irregular object

7. Simulation

At first, the implemented software captures two images from two existing cameras belonging to the robot. Then the correlation algorithm gives a set of points to be used in next processing steps. Then, the heuristic method achieves all its necessary data as the correlated points of the correlation process and determines four extreme points to compute available distances. The fuzzy method is also used to find the best point in this case. Fig. 10 demonstrates the steps to get the correlation points. Finally the best coordinates are accessible (Fig. 11).

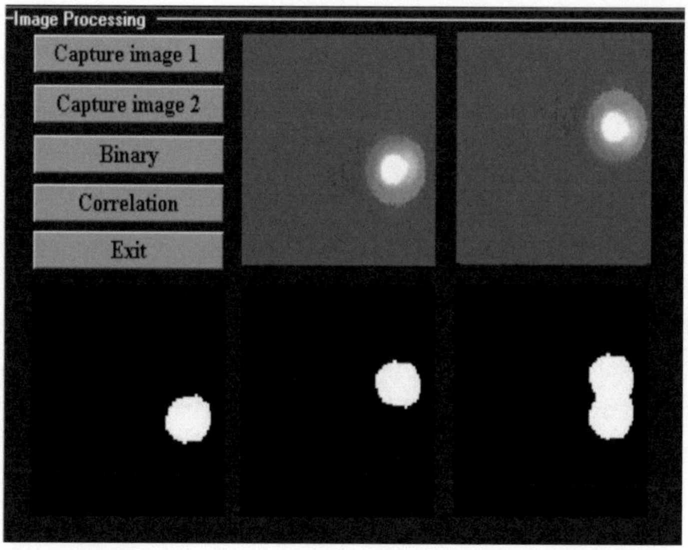

Figure 10. Correlation computin

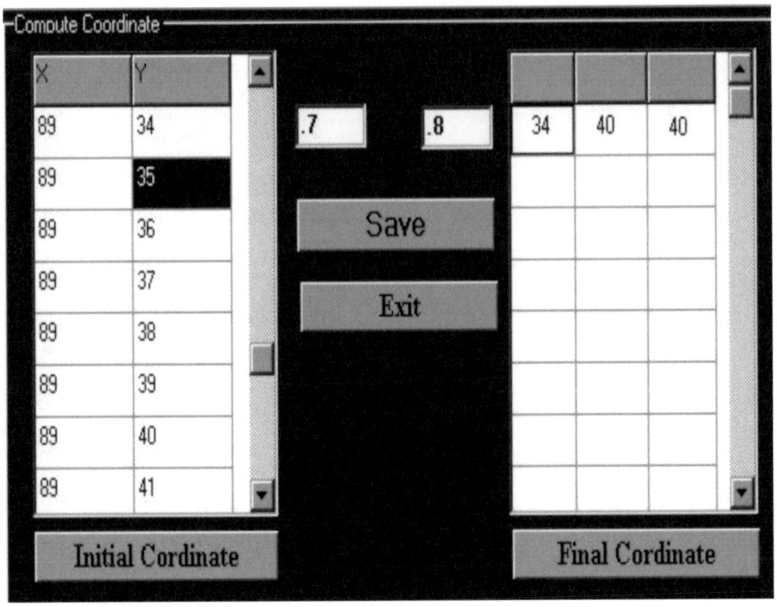

Figure 11. Computation of the best point

8. Experimental Results

In this study, the accuracy of our approach was compared with other approaches based on neural networks on 3P robots (Lopez & Plat, 2000) (Wang, 1992) (Hahnel et al., 2001).which contains some errors according to the structure and foundation of neural networks. Table.1 compares neural network and fuzzy methods on stereo vision for a 3P robot. It demonstrates that the fuzzy method is more reliable.

Type of Object	**Circle**	**Cylinder**	**Cubic Rectangle**	**Cubic Square**
Neural Network	98.3%	98%	97%	97.2%
Fuzzy System	100%	100%	100%	100%

Table 1. Comparison of neural network with fuzzy system in 3p robot

9. Conclusions

Here, applying a fuzzy model in stereo vision of a 3p robot is presented. According to the simulation results, correlation error is reduced where the best result in a 3p robot applying neural networks is about 97% of correctness, but using a fuzzy approach, let us to achieve up to 100%. It is obvious that all these results are achieved by simulated software and different kinds of errors could be occurred in real environment. Some of them are discussed in(Korayem et al., 2001).This fuzzy model can be applied to a large class of robotic manipulators.

10. References

Achour, K., and Benkhelif, M. (2001). A New Approach to 3D Reconstruction without Camera Calibration, *Pattern Recognition*, Vol.34, pp. 2467–2476.

Alexander. (1996). *Distributed Fuzzy Control of Multivariable System*, Kulwer academic publishers.

Bender, E. A. (1996).Mathematical Methods in Artificial Intelligence, *IEEE Computer Society Press*.

Gonzalez, R. C., Woods, R. E.(1998).*Digital Image Processing*, Tennessee university press.

Guisser, L., Payrissat, R., and Castan, S. (2000). PGSD: An Accurate 3D Vision System Using a Projected Grid for Surface Descriptions, *Image and Vision Computing Journal*, Vol.18, pp.463–491.

Grosso, E., Metta, G., Oddera, A., and Sandini, G.: Robust Visual Serving in 3-D Reaching Tasks, *IEEE Trans on Robotics Automation*, Vol.12,(1996) 732–742.

Haralick, R. M., and Shapiro, L. G.(1992). *Computer and Robot Vision*, Addison-Wesley Publisher.

Hahnel, D., Burgard, W., and Thrun, S. (2003). Learning Compact 3D Models of Indoor and Outdoor Environments with a Mobile Robot, *Robotics and Autonomous System*, Vol.44, pp. 15–27.

Hsu, Y., Chen, G., Li, H.(2001). A Fuzzy Adaptive Variable Structure Controller with Applications to Robot Manipulators, *IEEE Transaction Systems man and Cybernetics part*, Vol. 31, pp. 331–340.

Hirschuller, H., Innocent, P. R., and Garibaldi, J.(2000).Real Time Correlation Based Stereo Vision with Reduce Border Errors, *International Journal of Computer Vision*.

Konolige, K. (1997). Small Vision Systems: Hardware and Implementation, *International Symposium on Robotics Research*, London, Springer,pp. 203–212.

Korayem, M. H., Khoshhal, K., Aliakbarpour, H. (2005). Vision Based Robot Simulation and Experiment for Performance Tests of Robot, *International Journal of AMT*, Vol.25,pp. 1218–1231.

Korayem, M. H., Shiehbeiki, N., and Khanali, T. (2005).Design, Manufacturing and Experimental Tests of Prismatic Robot for Assembly Line, *Paper Accepted for Publication in International Journal of AMT*.

Lopez, A., and Plat, F. (2000). Dealing with Segmentation Errors in Region-Based Stereo Matching, *Pattern Recognition* ,Vol.33, pp. 1325–1338.

Matthies, L., Kelly, A., Litwin, T., and Tharp, G. (1995). Obstacle Detection for Unmanned Ground Vehicles: A progress report, *International symposium of Robotics Research*, Munich, Germany.

Paulino, A., Batista, J., and Araujo, H.(2001). Maintaining the Relative Position and Orientation of Multiple Robots Using Vision, *Pattern Recognition Letters*, Vol.22,pp. 1331–1335.

Seitz, S. M., and Dyer, C. R.(1995). Complete Scene Structure from Four Point Correspondences, 5th *Int. Conf on Computer Vision*, pp. 330–337, Cambridge MA.

Taylor, C. J., and Kriegman, D. J. (1995). Structure and Motion from Line Segments in Multiple Images, *IEEE Trans. on Pattern Analysis Machine Intelligence*, Vol.17, pp. 1021–1033

Volpe, R., Balaram, J., Ohm, T., and Ivlev, R. (1996). The Rocky 7 Mars Rover Prototype, *International Conference on Intelligent Robots and Systems*, Vol. 3, pp.1558–1564.

Wang, L.(1997). *A Course in Fuzzy Systems and Control*, Prentice Hall, pp.151–156.
Wang, L., X . (1992). Fuzzy System are Universal Approximate, *Proceedings of the first IEEE Conference on Fuzzy Systems*, pp. 163–1170.
Zhang, J., Knoll, A., and Schwert, V.(1999). Situated Neuro-Fuzzy Control for Vision-Based Robot Localization, *Robotics and Autonomous System*.